THE BEST OF FRANCE

7th Revised Edition

Translation and Adaptation
Emily Emerson, Sheila Mooney

Coordination
Sophie Gayot

Assisted by
Stéphanie Masson

Publisher
Alain Gayot

Paris ■ Los Angeles ■ New York ■ London ■ Munich ■ San Francisco

Published by Gault Millau, Inc.
5900 Wilshire Blvd.
Los Angeles, CA 90036

Advertising Sales:
Pascal Meiers Communication:
5 bis, avenue Foch, 94160 Saint-Mandé, France
tel. (1) 43 28 20 20, fax (1) 43 28 27 27

Please address all comments regarding
The Best of France to:
Gault Millau, Inc.
P.O. Box 361144
Los Angeles, CA 90036

Library of Congress Cataloging-in-Publication Data

Guide de la France. English
    The Best of France / translation and adaptation, Emily Emerson;
coordination, Sophie Gayot, assisted by Stéphanie Masson;
publisher, Alain Gayot. -- 7th ed.
        p.   cm.
    Includes index.
    Cover title: Gayot's The Best of France 95/96.
    ISBN 1-881066-18-5
    1. France--Guidebooks. I. Emerson, Emily. II. Gayot, Sophie.
III. Masson, Stéphanie. IV. Gayot, Alain. V. Title VI. Title:
Gayot's The Best of France 95/96
DC16.G3513 1995
914.404'839--dc20

                                                        95-7606
                                                          CIP

Printed in the United States of America

CONTENTS

FRANCE

Crammed with vivid insights and discerning critiques, this guidebook—the most comprehensive and authoritative available in English—is your passport to the "Best of France." Only Gault Millau can give you the real lowdown on nearly 7,000 French restaurants and hotels, with inside information that will make you a "traveler in the know," always (at least!) one step ahead of the crowd.

For over twenty-five years we at Gault Millau have scoured the French countryside, visiting urban centers and minute hamlets, in search of worthwhile places to eat and stay. Contributors from every region of France participate in our national survey of restaurants and hotels. They work to strict standards, ensuring fairness and continuity of the grading system from Dunkerque to Menton. When, for example, a reviewer spots what appears to be a terrific new place, he or she invariably seeks a second opinion to confirm that the establishment is truly a winner. These thorough, unvarnished appraisals of *grands restaurants*, bistros, brasseries, *auberges*, and hotels are presented in a witty, entertaining style that has earned Gault Millau its international reputation. (And thanks to our ever-expanding family of guidebooks, travelers can now rely on Gault Millau for accurate, up-to-date information on destinations all over the globe).

We're proud to see how Gault Millau has influenced the way people cook, eat, and think about food today. It was Gault Millau who in the early 1970s coined the term *"nouvelle cuisine"* to describe the culinary revolution ignited by chefs like Michel Guérard, Paul Bocuse, and Jean Delaveyne. But like all art forms, cookery evolves with the times. Contemporary "creative cuisine", which bears the stamp of a talented chef's personality, has taken up where "nouvelle cuisine" left off. Today's most inventive cooks—not to be confused with culinary counterfeiters who try to palm off absurd combinations as high gastronomical art—are celebrated in these pages with red chefs' hats, or toques. White toques are awarded to chefs who practice classic cuisine, using time-honored recipes and pluperfect ingredients (we don't mean self-styled "traditionalists" who lazily trot out tired culinary clichés). But whatever their color, when you follow the Gault Millau toques you can be confident that you'll home in on the finest food in France!

Each edition of *The Best of France* salutes budding talents, encourages maturing ones, and pays special homage to those rare chefs who have attained superstar status. This year for example veteran Alain Dutournier of Le Carré des Feuillants in Paris and Philippe Jousse, successor to the late Alain Chapel, joined the elite corps of chefs who boast the stellar rating of 19/20—just one point short of perfection!

The purpose of this guidebook is to help you steer an informed course through all the categories of restaurants and hotels in France. Naturally, the top establishments tend to be quite expensive, but we also take you into cozy bistros and family-style inns where you can indulge your gourmandise without breaking the bank.

So whether you are a first-time visitor or a frequent traveler to France, let Gault Millau help you discover the myriad gastronomic pleasures that France has to offer!

André Gayot

SYMBOL SYSTEMS

RESTAURANTS

G ault Millau ranks restaurants in the same manner that French students are graded: on a scale of zero to twenty, twenty being unattainable perfection. The rankings reflect *only* the quality of the cooking; décor, service, reception, and atmosphere do not influence the rating. They are explicitly commented on within the reviews. Restaurants ranked thirteen and above are distinguished with toques (chef's hats), according to the following table:

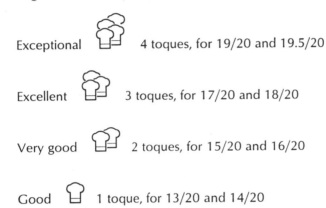

Exceptional   4 toques, for 19/20 and 19.5/20

Excellent   3 toques, for 17/20 and 18/20

Very good   2 toques, for 15/20 and 16/20

Good   1 toque, for 13/20 and 14/20

Toques in red denote restaurants serving creative cuisine; toques in white indicate restaurants serving more traditional food.

Keep in mind that these ranks are *relative*. One toque for 13/20 is not a very good ranking for a highly reputed (and very expensive) temple of fine dining, but it is quite complimentary for a small place without much pretension.

At the end of each restaurant review, prices are given—either *A la carte* (**C**) or *Menus* (**M**) (fixed-price meals) or both. A la carte prices are those of an average meal (a starter, a main course, dessert, and coffee) for one person, including service and a half-bottle of relatively modest wine. Lovers of the great Bordeaux, Burgundies, and Champagnes will, of course, face stiffer tabs. The menu prices quoted are for a complete multicourse meal for one person, including service but excluding wine, unless otherwise noted. These fixed-price menus often give diners on a budget a chance to sample the cuisine of an otherwise expensive restaurant.

A restaurant name in red indicates that its à la carte and/or set menu prices offer particularly good value for money. Look for the prices printed in red at the end of the review.

In France, the service charge is always (by law) included in the price of the food. But it is customary to leave a few extra francs as an additional tip.

5

HOTELS

Our opinion of the comfort level and appeal of each hotel is expressed in a ranking system, as follows:

Very luxurious

Luxurious

Very comfortable

Comfortable

Very quiet

Symbols in red denote charm.

The prices indicated for rooms and half-board range from the cheapest for one person to the most expensive for two.

Sadly, prices continue to creep up, so some places may have become more expensive than our estimates by the time you visit. If you expect to pay a little more—you may end up being pleasantly surprised!

OTHER INFORMATION & ABBREVIATIONS

✪   A laurel wreath indicates restaurants serving outstanding traditional or regional recipes.

Rms: Rooms   **Stes**: Suites
Seas: Season   **Conf**: Conference facilities
Priv rm: Private rooms   **Air cond**: Air conditioning
Pkg: Parking   **No cards**: No credit cards accepted
Half-board: Rate per person for room, breakfast, and one other meal (lunch or dinner)

How to read the locations:

ABBEVILLE 80100	Paris 160 - Amiens 45 - Dieppe 63

The town   The zip code   *Kilometers to Paris and nearby major cities*

Somme

The regional department

A FINAL NOTE

We have made a herculean effort to provide as much practical information as possible: phone numbers, hours, daily and annual closings, fax numbers, specific amenities and special features, prices, credit cards accepted, and more. We've also done our utmost to keep all the information current and correct. But establishments change such things with alarming speed, so please forgive us if you come across incorrect or incomplete information.

TOQUE TALLY

Red toques: Creative cuisine
White toques: Traditional cuisine
The year after the restaurant's name indicates
when its third or fourth toque was awarded.

Four Toques (19.5/20)

L'Aubergade, *Puymirol (see Agen)*, 1987
L'Auberge de l'Ill, *Illhaeusern*, 1990
Jean Bardet, *Tours*, 1985
Georges Blanc, *Vonnas*, 1981
Boyer, *Reims*, 1988
Michel Bras, *Laguiole*, 1986
La Côte d'Or, *Saulieu*, 1990
La Côte Saint-Jacques, *Joigny*, 1986
Pierre Gagnaire, *Saint-Étienne*, 1986
Michel Guérard, *Eugénie-les-Bains*, 1976
Marc Meneau, *Saint-Père-sous-Vézelay*
   (see Vézelay), 1983
Restaurant de Bricourt, *Cancale*, 1990
Robuchon, *Paris 16th*, 1985
Troisgros, *Roanne*, 1987
Marc Veyrat, *Veyrier-du-Lac*
   (see Annecy), 1990

Four Toques (19/20)

L'Ambroisie, *Paris 4th*, 1992
Arpège, *Paris 7th*, 1991
Buerehiesel, *Strasbourg*, 1992
Carré des Feuillants, *Paris 1st*, 1995
Alain Chapel, *Mionnay (see Lyon)*, 1995
Grand Hôtel du Lion d'Or, *Romorantin*, 1988
Le Louis-XV, *Monaco*, 1991
Lucas-Carton, *Paris 8th*, 1978
Georges Paineau, *Questembert*, 1995
Guy Savoy, *Paris 17th*, 1988
Vivarois, *Paris 16th*, 1990

Four Toques (19/20)

Paul Bocuse, *Collonges-au-Mont-d'Or*
   (see Lyon), 1972
Pic, *Valence*, 1990
Taillevent, *Paris 8th*, 1981

Three Toques (18/20)

Amat, *Bouliac (see Bordeaux)*, 1995
Amphyclès, *Paris 17th*, 1990
Apicius, *Paris 17th*, 1988
Arzak, *San Sebastian - Spain*, 1989
Auberge Bretonne, *La Roche-Bernard*, 1990
Auberge des Templiers, *Les Bézards*, 1977
La Barbacane, *Carcassonne*, 1992
Jean-Pierre Billoux, *Dijon*, 1980
Bistrot des Lices, *Saint-Tropez*, 1991
La Bonne Étape, *Château-Arnoux*, 1982
Le Bourdonnais, *Paris 7th*, 1986
La Bourride, *Caen*, 1987
Café de Paris, *Biarritz*, 1995
Jacques Cagna, *Paris 6th*, 1984
Le Centenaire, *Les Eyzies*, 1989
Chabran, *Pont-de-l'Isère (see Valence)*, 1982
Chantecler, *Nice*, 1990
Château de Locguénolé, *Hennebont*, 1994
Le Clos de la Violette, *Aix-en-Provence*, 1992
Faugeron, *Paris 16th*, 1978
La Flamiche, *Roye*, 1993
La Fenière, *Lourmarin*, 1993
Les Jardins de l'Opéra, *Toulouse*, 1990
Lameloise, *Chagny*, 1977
Le Divellec, *Paris 7th*, 1984
Ledoyen, *Paris 8th*, 1990
Léon de Lyon, *Lyon 1st*, 1981
Régis Mahé, *Vannes*, 1991

Le Moulin de Martorey, *Chalon-sur-Saône*, 1989
L'Oasis, *La Napoule*, 1992
La Palme d'Or, *Cannes*, 1986
La Pyramide, *Vienne*, 1991
Les Pyrénées, *Saint-Jean-Pied-de-Port*, 1984
Michel Rostang, *Paris 17th*, 1995
Paul Minchelli, *Paris 7th*, 1995
Bernard Robin, *Bracieux*, 1985
La Tamarissière, *Agde*, 1989
La Terrasse *Juan-les-Pins*, 1986
Thibert, *Dijon*, 1988
Les Trois Marches, *Versailles*, 1977
Le Vieux Moulin, *Bouilland*, 1987

Three Toques (18/20)

Le Crocodile, *Strasbourg*, 1981
Le Grand Véfour, *Paris 1st*, 1995
L'Oustau de Baumanière, *Les Baux-de-Provence*, 1973
La Tour d'Argent, *Paris 5th*, 1972

Three Toques (17/20)

L'Abbaye Saint-Michel, *Tonnerre*, 1988
Albert-Ier, *Chamonix*, 1993
Les Ambassadeurs, *Paris 8th*, 1991
L'Amphitryon, *Lorient*, 1995
Auberge des Cimes, *Saint-Bonnet-le-Froid*, 1991
Balzi Rossi, *Ponte San Ludovico - Italy (see Menton)*, 1992
Les Bas-Rupts, *Gérardmer*, 1995
Le Bateau Ivre, *Le Bourget-du-Lac*, 1991
Le Bateau Ivre, *Courchevel*, 1991
Jean Brouilly, *Tarare*, 1995
Café Royal, *Évian*, 1988
La Cardinale, *Baix*, 1995
Chabichou, *Courchevel*, 1989
La Chancelière, *Montbazon*, 1994
Chantoiseau, *Vialas*, 1993
Le Chapon Fin, *Bordeaux*, 1995
Chiberta, *Paris 8th*, 1992
Clos Longchamp, *Paris 17th*, 1990
La Cognette, *Issoudun*, 1989
Richard Coutanceau, *La Rochelle*, 1991
Le Dauphin, *Toul*, 1992
Domaine de Rochevilaine, *Billiers*, 1993
Christian Étienne, *Avignon*, 1992
Ferme du Letty, *Bénodet*, 1992
La Ferme Saint-Siméon, *Honfleur*, 1994

Jean-Claude Ferrero, *Paris 16th*, 1991
Au Fer Rouge, *Colmar*, 1995
Les Frères Ibarboure, *Bidart*, 1991
Gill, *Rouen*, 1990
Le Golden, *Niort*, 1994
Le Jardin des Sens, *Montpellier*, 1993
Le Jardin du Royal Monceau, *Paris 8th*, 1994
Patrick Jeffroy, *Plounérin*, 1992
Jean-Paul Jeunet, *Arbois*, 1990
Jules-Verne, *Paris 7th*, 1994
Laurent, *Paris 8th*, 1995
Mas du Langoustier, *Ile de Porquerolles*, 1992
Montparnasse 25, *Paris 14th*, 1995
Moulin de l'Abbaye, *Brantôme*, 1991
Le Mungo-Park, *Besançon*, 1994
L'Olivier, *Saint-Tropez*, 1991
Le Palais, *Rennes*, 1993
Passédat, *Marseille*, 1989
Pavillon des Boulevards, *Bordeaux*, 1992
Pavillon Paul Le Quéré, *Angers*, 1992
Au Petit Montmorency, *Paris 8th*, 1991
Les Plaisirs d'Ausone, *Bordeaux*, 1995
Le Pré Catelan, *Paris 16th*, 1988
Résidence de la Pinède, *Saint-Tropez*, 1991
Les Roches, *Aiguebelle (see Le Lavandou)*, 1995
Schillinger, *Colmar*, 1993
Sormani, *Paris 17th*, 1991
La Table d'Anvers, *Paris 9th*, 1994
Laurent Thomas, *Ruy (see Bourgoin-Jallieu)*, 1993
Torigaï, *Nantes*, 1992
La Tour Rose, *Lyon 5th*, 1978
Le Vieux Pont, *Belcastel*, 1995

Three Toques (17/20)

Auberge de la Galupe, *Urt (see Bayonne)*, 1994
Auberge de Noves, *Noves*, 1995
Gérard Besson, *Paris 1st*, 1991
Le Cerf, *Marlenheim*, 1991
Drouant, *Paris 2nd*, 1988
Goumard-Prunier, *Paris 1st*, 1995
Les Gourmets, *Marsannay-la-Côte (see Dijon)*, 1991
Greuze, *Tournus*, 1991
Hiély-Lucullus, *Avignon*, 1994
La Marée, *Paris 8th*, 1994
La Meunerie, *Teteghem (see Dunkerque)*, 1992
Morot-Gaudry, *Paris 15th*, 1992
Jean Ramet, *Bordeaux*, 1983
La Salle à Manger, *Saint-Tropez*, 1994
Zuberoa, *Oyarzun (see San Sebastian - Spain)*, 1995

PARIS

Restaurants

10/20 Joe Allen

30, rue P.-Lescot
42 36 70 13, fax 40 28 06 94
Open daily until 1am. Bar: until 2am. Terrace dining. Air cond. V, AF, MC.
Relaxed and casual: American, in short. Come to Joe's when you feel the urge to sink a few beers or dig into a chef's salad, chili burger, barbecued spare ribs, or apple pie. **C** 170-250 F.

Gérard Besson

5, rue Coq-Héron
42 33 14 74, fax 42 33 85 71
Closed Sun. Open until 10:30pm. Priv rm: 40. Air cond. Garage pkg. V, AE, DC, MC.
Behind an understated exterior, Gérard Besson's restaurant conceals a dining room of well-bred elegance that incorporates rosy-beige fabrics, bleached-wood furnishings, and gleaming *bibelots*. The initial impression of comfort and refined taste is abetted by the menu, a repertoire of noble foodstuffs prepared with polished classicism.
Besson divines with unerring precision the exact time each dish must spend on the fire. His baked John Dory, his pan-roasted sweetbreads, his poached sea bass, and Riesling-braised turbot are all finished to perfection. Seduced by such apparently effortless grace, the dazzled diner falls to with abandon.
Some critics find fault with the occasional superfluous garnish or achingly rich sauce. They should remember that for a classically trained chef, such "virtuoso" touches are second nature. And when it suits him, Besson throws the rule book out the window to produce bold marriages, like his sardine fillets with English mustard and caviar.
Hard choices must be made at dessert time: will it be the confoundedly good iced raspberry biscuit or the novel and delectable lentil confit in vanilla syrup? A competent young sommelière simplifies the task of choosing from the lengthy (costly!) wine list. Martine Besson oversees the relaxed yet efficient service. **C** 450-550 F. **M** 260 F (weekday lunch), 400 F & 650 F (weekdays).

12/20 Brasserie Munichoise

5, rue D.-Casanova - 42 61 47 16
Closed Sat lunch, Sun, Aug. Open until 12:30am. Priv rm: 20. V, MC.
A cozy little brasserie that serves good grilled veal sausages and one of the best choucroutes in Paris. Excellent Hacker-Pschorr beer on tap. **C** 250 F.

11/20 Café Marly

93, rue de Rivoli - 49 26 06 60
Open daily until 1:30am. Priv rm: 300. Air cond. No pets. Garage pkg. V, AE, DC, MC.
Here in the Louvre's new Richelieu wing, you may order the most expensive club sandwich in Paris or a humbler *plat du jour*, served in magnificent surroundings. A very dressy crowd of fashion and literary notables has staked out its turf here—you may find yourself sitting next to Karl Lagerfeld! **C** 200 F.

Carpaccio des Halles

6, rue P.-Lescot
45 08 44 80, fax 40 26 84 73
Open daily until 12:30am. No pets. V, AE, DC, MC.
This engaging little Italian eatery will satisfy your cravings for carpaccio: beef and duck versions are offered, both served with a deliciously tangy sauce. Pasta features prominently on the menu too, in the form of tender ravioli or pappardelle topped with shellfish or bits of prosciutto. Uncomplicated fare at unpretentious prices. **C** 150 F. **M** 71 F, 89 F, 92 F.

Carré des Feuillants ۞

Alain Dutournier, 14, rue de Castiglione
42 86 82 82, fax 42 86 07 71
Closed Sat lunch, Sun, Aug. Open until 10:30pm. Priv rm: 14. Air cond. V, AE, DC, MC.
Alain Dutournier carries off toque number four this year! Mind you, he's made no radical changes in his now-familiar repertoire. But lately his technique has acquired a brillant sheen that compels us to revise our (already high) opinion of his skills. The regularity with which Dutournier produces dishes with layer upon layer of deep, resonant flavors convinces us that he has moved up into the very top rank of French chefs.
His success is based on a firm foundation of authentic ingredients from first-rate producers. He regularly nips down to his birthplace in southwest France, a gastronomic paradise bounded by the Adour River and the countryside of Béarn, to visit his suppliers, sniff the cèpes, and stimu-

late his appetite. Paris? His restaurant's sophisticated setting of stone, blond wood, and hyper-real vegetable paintings might as well be in Gascony! Here Dutournier works with the foods he's loved since childhood, enhancing them with fresh, personal ideas. Crisp-fried eel atop a salad of tarragon and other herbs with a startlingly good nougatine of peppery caramelized garlic; a frothy pheasant consommé dotted with chestnuts; foie gras spread on warm cornbread; savory Pauillac lamb in a tight, sapid jus; a robust garbure (cabbage soup) with duck confit; slow-simmered veal shank that is lacquered on the outside and meltingly tender within—all these dishes brim over with vigorous, exhilarating flavors.

The exciting cellar harbors a mother lode of Southwestern wines, many of them eminently affordable. Indeed, for a table of this caliber Le Carré des Feuillants is surely one of the best values in Paris. C 550-800 F. M 260 F (weekday lunch), 740 F (4 wines incl), 560 F.

Les Cartes Postales

7, rue Gomboust - 42 61 02 93
Closed Sat lunch, Sun. Open until 10:30pm. Air cond. V, MC.
Scores of postcards adorn the beige-and-white walls of this small, pretty, flower-filled restaurant. Yoshimasa Watanabe, disciple of the great Robuchon, creates outstanding cuisine with just the right pinch of the exotic. His dual culinary heritage yields a menu that offers scallops in papaya sauce or mackerel with white radishes and shizo as well as oxtail braised in Médoc wine and a very *grande cuisine* macaronnade of sweetbreads and foie gras. Though varied, the options are relatively few, and desserts are a tone below the rest. Take note of the set lunch: it's a remarkable value. C 350-400 F. M 135 F (weekday lunch), 285 F, 350 F.

12/20 Le Caveau du Palais
17-19, pl. Dauphine
43 26 04 28, fax 43 26 81 84
Closed Sun (& Sat: Oct 1-Apr 30), 10 days at Christmas. Open until 10:30pm. Priv rm: 20. Terrace dining. Air cond. Pkg. V, AE, MC.
The deft, honest cooking (croustillant de chèvre chaud, grilled grouper with basil butter, veal grenadin in a creamy chive sauce) is served in a charming Place Dauphine cellar divided down the center by a wine bar. C 230-360 F. M 160 F.

11/20 Le Comptoir
14, rue Vauvilliers
40 26 26 66, fax 42 21 44 24
Open daily until 1am. Terrace dining. Air cond. V.
Reasonable prices for decent tapas (Spanish-style chicken, cold grilled vegetables, raw tuna) served in a lively bistro atmosphere. C 130-168 F. M 100 F (Sun lunch), 69 F, 89 F.

L'Espadon

Hôtel Ritz, 15, pl. Vendôme
42 60 38 30, fax 42 61 63 08
Closed Aug. Open until 11pm. Garden dining. Air cond. Heated pool. Valet pkg. V, AE, DC, MC.
At lunchtime, business executives join the hotel's elegant clientele to partake of chef Guy

Legay's graceful cuisine. Classic but not conventional, his menu presents a lush charlotte de foie gras aux navets, foie gras once again (this *is* the Ritz) as a filling for ravioli afloat in a truffled chicken bouillon, turbot with fava beans in an admirably light jus, and a colossal, exquisitely tender chop of milk-fed veal. Splendid desserts (don't miss the apricot bergère with chocolate sorbet); sumptuous cellar. The service, need we add, is sheer perfection. C 500-800 F. M 350 F (lunch), 550 F (dinner).

Gaya

17, rue Duphot
42 60 43 03, fax 42 60 04 54
Closed Sun. Open until 10:30pm. Priv rm: 35. Air cond. Garage pkg. AE.
Each day the tide pulls sparkling fresh seafood into this bright and elegant bistro, the lower-priced annex of Goumard-Prunier (see below). The catch of the day sometimes features marinated fresh anchovies, goujonnettes de sole au basilic, or sea bream anointed with virgin olive oil and expertly grilled. C 260-360 F.

Goumard-Prunier

9, rue Duphot
42 60 36 07, fax 42 60 04 54
Closed Sun (summer), Mon. Open until 10:30pm. Priv rm: 25. Air cond. Garage pkg. V, AE, DC.
Jean-Claude Goumard regularly treks out at 3am to the Rungis market to net the very best sole and turbot, the fattest lobsters and prawns, for his chef Georges Lardiot—fish and crustaceans so perfect that no flambé or croûte is ever allowed to mar them. A pinch of turmeric to enliven the shellfish fricassée; a drop of veal juices with soy sauce to accompany the braised sole; precious little butter all around: in short, nothing to interfere with the fresh taste of the sea. Other possibilities include enormous Brittany prawns baked in their shells, crab with Sherry aspic and a delicate parsley sauce, truffled coquilles Saint-Jacques, or a sumptuous and authentic bouillabaisse. Dessert brings excellent chocolate fondant with coffee sauce. Fine cellar; and the service is truly excellent. Little remains, alas, of the restaurant's original décor, designed by Majorelle—the only vestiges, it so happens, are in the restrooms! C 400-700 F.

12/20 Restaurant du Grand Louvre
Museum entrance, under the pyramid
40 20 53 41, fax 42 86 04 63
Closed Tue. Open until 10pm. Priv rm: 80. Air cond. No pets. Garage pkg. V, AE, DC.
Something is cooking under I.M. Pei's glass pyramid. In contrast with the chilly décor, the Louvre's restaurant serves warming, reasonably priced fare: try the meaty headcheese, the grilled salmon with sauce béarnaise, and the fruit gratin laced with Grand Marnier. Non-stop service. C 250-380 F. M 170 F.

Le Grand Véfour

17, rue de Beaujolais
42 96 56 27, fax 42 86 80 71
Closed Sat, Sun, Aug. Open until 10:15pm. Priv rm: 25. Air cond. No pets. Valet pkg. V, AE, DC.
Guy Martin got off to a rough start here. Nearly every food critic in town greeted Martin's arrival

at Le Grand Véfour with a cutting review. Well, we've been following his career for years, and we know that the very worst one could say of Martin's cooking was that some dishes verged on the baroque, with too many discordant flavors vying for attention. Martin's current, more mature style has outgrown these excesses of exuberant youth. The truth is, one dines splendidly at Le Grand Véfour. Surely, the sophisticated gourmands who flock to this exquisite eating house have not been dragged in by force! Martin chooses prime foodstuffs for his classically balanced, robustly flavorful bill of fare. A fanciful touch emerges here and there (there's a delicious braised eel in Port sauce with rutabagas and preserved lemons, for example); yet overall a measured harmony prevails, as in the ravioles de foie gras à la crème truffée, or plump prawns seared in fragrant olive oil, in the baked whole turbot with anchovy purée, or a masterly roast Bresse chicken Miéral, its breast coated with a creamy cèpe sauce and toasted hazelnuts. For our money, this is food worth a solid triple toque.

Of course, much of the magic of the Grand Véfour resides in the sublime surroundings: carved boiserie ceilings, graceful painted allegories under glass, plush carpeting, snowy napery, and fragile Directoire chairs. The service is as elegant as the cosmopolitan clientele. And the bill? Astronomical. **C** 650-1,000 F. **M** 305 F (weekday lunch).

A la Grille Saint-Honoré

15, pl. du Marché-St-Honoré
42 61 00 93, fax 47 03 31 64
Closed Sun, Mon (exc dinner in hunting seas), Aug 1-21. Open until 10:30pm. Priv rm: 30. Terrace dining. Air cond. Pkg. V, AE, DC, MC.

The Place du Marché Saint-Honoré is currently a mess, owing to the construction of a glass gallery designed by Riccardo Bofill. But don't let that discourage you from visiting the glossy pink-and-gray restaurant where Jean Speyer serves tasty, imaginative "market cuisine": sautéed escargots with fennel fondue, lobster fricassée sparked with paprika, roast veal kidneys with anchovies, and wonderful game dishes (partridge with wild mushrooms...) in season. The set meals and affordable wines are Speyer's strongest suit. **C** 310-380 F. **M** 180 F.

11/20 Lescure

7, rue de Mondovi - 42 60 18 91
Closed Sat dinner, Sun, Aug. Open until 10:15pm. Terrace dining. Air cond. V, MC.

Tried-and-trusted French fare served in a feverish bistro atmosphere. Sample the hearty veal sauté or duck confit. Game dishes are highlighted in the autumn and winter hunting season. **C** 150-180 F. **M** 100 F (lunch, wine incl).

Mercure Galant

15, rue des Petits-Champs
42 96 98 89, fax 42 96 08 89
Closed Sat, Sun. Open until 10:30pm. No pets. V, MC.

The service in this grand old restaurant is charming, the décor elegant, and the cuisine better than ever. These days, chef Pierre Ferranti is cooking in a lighter, more imaginative vein, producing such delectable dishes as warm

oysters with perfectly cooked cabbage and Belgian endive, scallops with basmati rice and a generous garnish of fresh morels, and lamb fillet seasoned with spiced olive oil. Interesting cellar with a wide range of Bordeaux. **C** 400-550 F. **M** 210 F (lunch exc Sun), 280 F & 400 F (dinner exc Sun).

Le Meurice

Hôtel Meurice, 228, rue de Rivoli
44 58 10 50, fax 44 58 10 15
Open daily until 11pm. Priv rm: 180. Air cond. No pets. V, AE, DC, MC.

Rosy nymphs cavort across a ceiling further adorned with gilt and crystal chandeliers, in what is surely one of the city's most sumptuous restaurants. Le Meurice is not all show, however: the food served in this royal setting is truly superb. Marc Marchand eschews the pompous cuisine one might expect to find here, for full-bodied dishes with plenty of rustic flavor, like a salad of crisp-cooked cauliflower with langoustines and smoked eel, a delicate crab cake partnered with wee stuffed squid, red mullet accompanied by wild-mushroom risotto, or veal stewed to tenderness with morels and artichokes. Marchand also knows his way around desserts: just taste his nougat soufflé embellished with a scoop of almond ice cream. Faultless service, and a cellar administered by Antoine Zocchetto, an expert sommelier. **C** 450-550 F. **M** 380 F (dinner, wine incl), 300 F (lunch).

La Passion

41, rue des Petits-Champs - 42 97 53 41
Closed Sat lunch, Sun. Open until 10:30pm. Priv rm: 10. Air cond. No pets. V, MC.

Gourmet abandon is what the restaurant's name suggests, but in fact Gilles Zellenwarger's cooking is of the earnest, serious sort. Yet a passionate devotion to culinary craft is evident in his meticulous attention to detail. The classic bill of fare features a rich cassolette of chicken and sweetbreads, skate perfumed with tarragon, and an elegantly herbal sole sautée. Judicious cellar; too bad the setting lacks charm. **C** 320-400 F. **M** 150 F, 200 F, 360 F.

Chez Pauline

5, rue Villedo
42 96 20 70, fax 49 27 99 89
Closed Sat lunch, Sun. Open until 10:30pm. Priv rm: 35. Air cond. V, AE, MC.

By now this wonderful old bistro has earned the rank of institution, for it perfectly represents a certain ideal of French cuisine. Robust and full of frank flavors, the neo-bourgeois dishes are based on uniformly fine ingredients prepared by a veteran chef. Subtlety is not the strong suit here: braises, sautés, and long-simmered stews are André Genin's stock in trade. A recent meal brought a fine calf's-head salad, a rosy escalope of foie gras surrounded by plump grapes, savory baked veal shanks, and a fabulous strawberry soup. The cellar holds memorable Burgundies, and there is an excellent selection of coffees. **C** 350-500 F. **M** 250 F (weekday lunch, wine incl), 220 F, 320 F.

Red toques signify creative cuisine; white toques signify traditional cuisine.

Paolo Petrini
9, rue d'Argenteuil
42 60 56 22, fax 42 36 55 50
Closed Sat lunch, Sun, Aug. Open until 11pm. Air cond. V, AE.
Paolo Petrini hails from Pisa, he's a genuine Italian chef (Paris has so few)! His cooking is as spare and stylized as his small (25 seats) austerely decorated dining room. Yet the full spectrum of Italy's distinctive savors are present in his warm, basil-scented salad of squid, clams, and cannellini beans; a delectable risotto ai porcini; a grilled beef fillet, sliced thin and dressed with balsamic vinegar; pappardelle sauced with a rich, winy hare napped; or tagliarini swathed in melted Fontina. Desserts are well above the ordinary, too, along with a superb selection of Italian wines. **C** 280-340 F.

12/20 Au Pied de Cochon
6, rue Coquillière
42 36 11 75, fax 45 08 48 90
Open daily 24 hours. Priv rm: 40. Terrace dining. Air cond. V, AE, DC, MC.
The atmosphere is at once frantic and euphoric in this Les Halles landmark, renowned for serving thundering herds of pigs' trotters (85,000 annually) and a ton of shellfish every day of the year. **C** 220-350 F.

Restaurant Pierre
10, rue de Richelieu
42 96 09 17, fax 42 96 09 62
Closed Sat, Sun, hols, Aug. Open until 10pm. V, AE, DC, MC.
Country delights from the four corners of France fill the lovely handwritten menu of this traditional bistro. The cuisine is in the reliable hands of Roger Leplu, who uses top-quality ingredients to produce such pillars of French cooking as boudin with onions, mackerel in cider, and bœuf à la ficelle, as well as stuffed cabbage bourguignonne or sheep's tripe and trotters à la marseillaise. Superb desserts. **C** 300-400 F. **M** 210 F.

Le Poquelin 🎭
17, rue Molière
42 96 22 19, fax 42 96 05 72
Closed Sat lunch, Sun, Aug 1-20. Open until 10:30pm. Priv rm: 8. Air cond. Garage pkg. V, AE, DC.
In the red-and-gold dining room where portraits of Molière look down from the walls, chef Michel Guillaumin wins the applause of his regular patrons (many from the Comédie-Française across the street) for his renditions of popular favorites: there's a rustic salad of pig's trotters and white beans, pikeperch poached in Saint-Pourçain wine, spice-coated duck breast, veal kidney in balsamic vinegar sauce, and canard Duchambais. Good notices too for his warm pear tart, and a standing ovation for Maggy Guillaumin's smiling welcome. **C** 330-450 F. **M** 185 F.

Velloni
22, rue des Halles - 42 21 12 50
Closed Sun, hols, Aug 15-25. Open until 11pm. No pets. V, AE, DC, MC.
A bright, comfortable establishment run by a genial Italian host. The chef acquits himself like a born Tuscan in his preparation of tagliarini with fresh crab sauce, beef jowls braised in vino di Montalcino, and ravioli stuffed with spinach and ricotta. Uneven cellar. **C** 230-330 F. **M** 130 F.

12/20 Chez la Vieille
"Adrienne,"
37, rue de l'Arbre-Sec - 42 60 15 78
Lunch only (dinner by reserv for 8 or more). Closed Sat, Sun. Priv rm: 25. Garage pkg. V, MC.
Adrienne Biasin has put away her pots and pans, but her generous homestyle cuisine lives on: the kitchen is now supervised by the excellent Gérard Besson (see above). So the regulars—bankers, press barons, and show-business personalities—still come around for the tasty terrines, quenelles, braised veal, pot-au-feu, and such comforting desserts as baba au rhum and floating island. Comforting is not how we'd describe the prices. **C** 350-380 F.

12/20 Willi's Wine Bar
13, rue des Petits-Champs
42 61 05 09, fax 47 03 36 93
Closed Sun. Open until 11pm. V, MC.
Mark Williamson and Tim Johnston are a witty, wise pair of wine experts. Their cellar holds treasures from all over France and the world, including a peerless collection of Côtes-du-Rhônes. Enjoy them (by the glass, or better, the bottle) along with a good quail salad, tarragon-scented rabbit, or a nice bit of Stilton—a glass of cream Sherry would be good with the latter. If you can't nab a table in the smallish dining room, join the customers sitting elbow-to-elbow at the polished wood bar. **C** 260-320 F. **M** 155 F (wine incl).

Café Runtz
16, rue Favart - 42 96 69 86
Closed Sat, Sun, hols, May 14-23, Aug 7-29. Open until 11:15pm. Priv rm: 40. Air cond. V, AE, MC.
This is an 1880s Alsatian *winstub* whose classic fare ranges from foie gras to excellent choucroute or potato salad with pork knuckle. Good French Rhine wines; cheeky service. **C** 200-300 F.

12/20 Canard'Avril
5, rue Paul-Lelong - 42 36 26 08
Closed Sat, Sun. Open until 10pm. Priv rm: 35. V.
The menu's just ducky: gizzard salad, confit, and magret de canard feature prominently, alongside a handful of similarly hearty Southwestern dishes. The cheap and cheerful prix-fixe meals are sure to quack you up. **C** 200-250 F. **M** 85 F, 125 F.

Le Céladon
Hôtel Westminster, 15, rue Daunou
47 03 40 42, fax 42 60 30 66
Closed Sat, Sun, hols, Aug. Open until 10pm. Priv rm: 60. Air cond. Valet pkg. AE, DC, MC.
Three tastefully lit, flower-filled, and impeccably elegant dining rooms in what is possibly the city's loveliest *restaurant de palace* form the perfect setting for a romantic dinner. Le Céladon's able chef, Emmanuel Hodencq, creates resolutely refined dishes such as a lush timbale of cèpes, macaroni, and tender snails, a

superlative beignet of foie gras sparked with caramel vinegar in a Port sauce hinting of truffles, and an appetizing combination of tender lamb chops and lamb sausage abetted by a savory jus. Only the lobster steamed in a (tough!) cabbage leaf fails to inspire praise. Desserts are divine—try the sautéed pears with licorice ice cream or the lime gratin studded with candied grapefruit peel and laced with rum. Interesting, eclectic cellar. C 350-500 F. M 220-290 F.

12/20 Coup de Cœur
19, rue St-Augustin
47 03 45 70
Closed Sat lunch, Sun. Open until 10:30pm. Priv rm: 60. Air cond. V, AE, MC.
The appealing set meals served in this intimate *salle* (designed by Philippe Starck) win our hearts: the gingery lamb's sweet-breads layered with airy puff pastry, finnan haddie escorted by buttery cabbage, earthy oxtail terrine, red mullet with artichokes, and upside-down mango tart are all delicious and deftly rendered. On the wine list you'll find a wealth of half-bottles. M 170 F (dinner exc Sun, wine incl), 185 F (weekday lunch, wine incl), 160 F (weekday lunch).

Delmonico

Hôtel Édouard-VII,
39, av. de l'Opéra - 42 61 44 26
Closed Sat, Sun, Aug. Open until 9:45pm. Priv rm: 20. Air cond. Pkg. V, AE, DC, MC.
With its lightened décor and livelier atmosphere, this old standby has stepped briskly into the age of the business lunch. Chef Alain Soltys prepares a classic *carte* and laudably generous set meals. We like his curried brill (it deserves better vegetables), roast squab au jus with a wholesome accompaniment of cabbage and wheat berries, and the dainty melon gratin glazed with brown sugar. The service is uniformly charming and there's a fine cellar. C 280-360 F. M 128 F, 168 F.

Drouant
18, rue Gaillon
42 65 15 16, fax 49 24 02 15
Open daily until 10:30pm (midnight at Le Café). Priv rm: 30. Air cond. Valet pkg. AE, DC, MC.
The cream of the city's biz and show-biz sets meet and greet in the Drouant's grand Art Deco staircase. The house repertoire is fairly classic, but Louis Grondard's consummate skill keeps the menu fresh and appealing. First-rate foodstuffs, robust flavors, and perfectly balanced seasonings result in a memorable charlotte de langoustines aux aubergines confites (molded prawns with slow-roasted eggplants), John Dory with tiny squid in a saffron-tinged jus, a succulent fillet of Pauillac lamb in an herbal crust, or roast beef served with rich and mellow bone marrow. Few palates would fail to appreciate desserts like the tarte au café with walnut custard sauce or chestnut croquant and honey-gentian ice cream. The Café Drouant is the haunt of business lunchers (at noon) and theater-goers (at night) in search of reasonably priced bourgeois cooking. C 600-750 F. M 250 F (at Le Café; exc weekday lunch), 290 F (coffee incl), 600 F.

12/20 Gallopin
40, rue N.-D.-des-Victoires
42 36 45 38, fax 42 36 10 32
Closed Sat, Sun. Open until 11pm. Terrace dining. V, AE, DC.
The brassy Victorian décor is a feast for the eyes. The food at Gallopin isn't bad either. Try the house specialties: sole meunière and hot apple tart. Jolly service. C 200-300 F. M 150 F (dinner, wine incl).

12/20 Le Grand Colbert
2, rue Vivienne
42 86 87 88, fax 42 86 82 65
Closed Jul 29-Aug 28. Open until 1am. Air cond. V, AE, MC.
Classic brasserie cuisine (oysters and shellfish, andouillette ficelle, bœuf gros sel, and poached chicken) served in a sprucely restored historic monument complete with frescoes and ornate plasterwork, brass railings and painted glass panels. Expect a warm welcome and swift, smiling service. C 160-250 F. M 155 F (wine incl).

Pierre
"A la Fontaine Gaillon," pl. Gaillon
42 65 87 04, fax 47 42 82 84
Closed Sat lunch, Sun, Aug. Open until 12.30am. Priv rm: 40. Terrace dining. Air cond. Garage pkg. V, AE, DC, MC.
The young chef's personality and well-honed technique shine through the resolutely classic menu, which features an excellent duo of raw salmon and sculpin, duck confit with sautéed potatoes, and praline croustillant. The dining room of this delightful old *hôtel particulier* was recently restored, and the grand terrace's fountain is spectacular when illuminated at night. If only the staff would crack an occasional smile... C 250-400 F. M 165 F (dinner), 210 F.

Le Saint-Amour
8, rue de Port-Mahon - 47 42 63 82
Closed Sat lunch, Sun, hols. Open until 10:30pm. Air cond. V, AE, DC, MC.
Impeccable service and a simple, fresh, generous cuisine distinguish Le Saint-Amour. The new chef offers a 155 F set lunch that delivers a creamy crab and lobster soup brightened with basil, cod pot-au-feu, an ample portion of nicely matured Brie, and decent chocolate cake. Concise but interesting wine list. C 300-400 F. M 155 F.

3RD ARRONDISSEMENT

L'Alisier
26, rue de Montmorency
42 72 31 04, fax 42 72 74 83
Closed Sat, Sun, Aug. Open until 10pm. Priv rm: 35. Air cond. No pets. V, AE, MC.
An inviting, old-fashioned bistro (ask for a table upstairs) where you can enjoy Jean-Luc Dodeman's personalized versions of hearty French favorites. Eggs poached in tarragon-scented veal gravy, beef jowls braised in red wine, and brown-sugar tart with yogurt ice cream are representative of the house style. C 230-300 F. M 149 F.

Ambassade d'Auvergne ⑮ 🟢

22, rue du Grenier-St-Lazare
42 72 31 22, fax 42 78 85 47
Closed Aug 1-16. Open until 10:30pm. Priv rm: 35. Air cond. Garage pkg. V, AE, MC.

Each visit to this embassy brings the same heart-warming experience. The Petrucci tribe's hospitality knows no bounds. The décor, featuring timbers hung with hams, is worn but authentic; the atmosphere is genuinely convivial. Authenticity is equally present in the house specialties: aged country ham, cabbage and Roquefort soup, boudin with chestnuts, cassoulet of lentils from Le Puy, legendary sausages served with slabs of delicious bread, duck daube with fresh pasta and smoky bacon, and so forth. Good desserts (try the aumônière à l'orange, or the mousse-line glacée à la verveine du Velay). The cellar is vast and boasts some little-known Auvergnat wines (Chanturgue, Saint-Pourçain) in a wide range of prices. **C** 215-300 F.

L'Ami Louis

32, rue du Vertbois - 48 87 77 48
Closed Mon, Tue, Jul 15-Aug 25. Open until 11pm. V, AE, MC.

Despite its improbably shabby décor (note the peeling, brownish walls), L'Ami Louis jealously claims the title of "the world's costliest bistro." It is certainly dear to the hearts of the tourists, suicidal overeaters, and skinny fashion models who battle to book a table at this famous *lieu de mémoire*. The heirs of old Père Magnin carry on the house tradition of huge portions, but the ingredients are not so choice as they once were. And nowadays the sauces are sometimes thick or sticky, and the fries a shade too oily. Yet you can still count on gargantuan servings of foie gras fresh from the Landes, giant escargots de Bourgogne, whole roast chicken, or an incomparable gigot of baby Pyrenees lamb. The desserts are ho-hum, the cellar respectable. **C** 600-800 F.

11/20 Le Bar à Huîtres

33, bd Beaumarchais - 48 87 98 92
See *14th arrondissement.*

12/20 Au Bascou

38, rue Réaumur - 42 72 69 25
Closed Sat, Sun, 3 wks in Aug, 1 wk at Christmas. Open until midnight. No pets. V, AE, DC, MC.

Basque-country native Jean-Guy Loustau (formerly the sommelier of Le Carré des Feuillants) runs this smart address. We made a fine meal here of shirred eggs with foie gras, lamb kidney with eggplant caviar, and caramel mousse with crunchy bits of walnut brittle. The wines are top-notch, but why aren't there more half-bottles? **C** 200-240 F. **M** 85 F (lunch).

12/20 Chez Janou 🟢

Corner of 56, rue des Tournelles and 2, rue R.-Verlomme - 42 72 28 41
Closed Sat, Sun, hols. Open until 11pm. Terrace dining. V, AE, DC, MC.

An honest little old-fashioned bistro with turn-of-the-century décor and a pleasant terrace. The neighborhood (Place des Vosges/Bastille) has gone up-market and so have Janou's prices, but the country cooking (poached eggs with

chanterelles, Jerusalem artichokes tossed in hazelnut oil, duck confit) still tastes authentic. Improved wine list. **C** 200-300 F. **M** 180 F (wine incl), 200 F.

11/20 Chez Jenny

39, bd du Temple
42 74 75 75, fax 42 74 38 69
Open daily until 1am. Priv rm: 150. Terrace dining. Pkg. V, AE, DC, MC.

This grand, historic monument of a brasserie, with lovely marquetry upstairs, is still going strong. Many good "world-famous" choucroutes and superb Alsatian charcuteries. **C** 180-300 F. **M** 99 F & 160 F (wine incl).

4TH ARRONDISSEMENT

L'Ambroisie

⑲ 9, pl. des Vosges - 42 78 51 45
Closed Sun, Mon, Feb school hols, 1st 3 wks of Aug. Open until 10:30pm. Priv rm: 14. Air cond. No pets. Valet pkg. V, MC.

Bernard and Danièle Pacaud transformed this former goldsmith's shop under the arcades of the Place des Vosges into the Marais's most gracious and elegant dining room. The setting is worthy of a château, with high ceilings, inlaid stone and parquet floors, book-lined shelves, and a sumptuous seventeenth-century tapestry adorning the honey-hued walls. L'Ambroisie has the lived-in feel of a beautifully maintained private home, of which Danièle is the charming hostess. Don't expect to see much of Bernard, though. He prefers the sizzling sounds of his kitchen to the applause of an appreciative public.

Vivid flavors and masterly technique are the hallmarks of a concise *carte* that comprises seven starters, six fish, and seven meat options, as well as a few *surprises du jour* announced at the table. Creamy lobster soup with scallops and a truffle turnover; red mullet napped with a delicate sauce hinting of orange, honey, and carrot; turbot braised with celery and celery root; saddle of Pauillac lamb in a truffled persillade; a majestic poularde en demi-deuil—all are flawlessly finished: no superfluous detail, no obtrusive spice disturbs their balanced harmony. Come time for dessert, a caramel millefeuille with tart apples, a bitter-cocoa soufflé, or croquant de riz à l'impératrice prolongs the pleasure of a perfect meal. The wines, too, are faultless, selected by Pierre Le Moullac, an exemplary maître d'hôtel–sommelier. **C** 650-1,000 F.

Baracane

⑬ 38, rue des Tournelles - 42 71 43 33
Closed Sat lunch, Sun. Open until midnight. V, MC.

Tables fill quickly in this popular little Southwestern enclave, because the cooking is full-flavored and generous to boot. Lentil salad with slices of dried goose breast or cassoulet with duck confit precede truly delectable desserts (the apple croustillant laced with plum brandy is our favorite). Low-priced regional wines wash it all down. Affable service. **C** 220-300 F. **M** 120 F (wine incl), 75 F.

Benoit

20, rue St-Martin - 42 72 25 76
Closed Sat, Sun, Aug. Open until 10pm. No pets. No cards.
The more things change, the more Benoit's solid, bourgeois cooking stays the same. This is the archetypal Parisian bistro (and surely one of the priciest): velvet banquettes, brass fixtures, lace curtains, and a polished zinc bar compose a seductive décor. Owner Michel Petit (who is anything but!) continues the lusty tradition begun before the Great War by his grandfather. His chef turns out a delicious bœuf à la parisienne, good cassoulet, and a creditable codfish with potatoes and cream. Tasty but unexciting desserts. The excellent cellar is stocked with reasonably priced bottles from Mâcon, Sancerre, Beaujolais, and Saumur. C 450-600 F.

Coconnas

2 bis, pl. des Vosges - 42 78 58 16
Closed Mon (exc summer), Tue (Oct-Mar), Dec 15-Jan 15. Open until 10pm. Priv rm: 65. Air cond. V, AE, DC, MC.
Claude Terrail (La Tour d'Argent) comes around regularly to keep an eye on his little bistro on the lovely Place des Vosges. The menu is short, the atmosphere lively: sample generously served favorites such as poule au pot with a "garden of vegetables" or merlan (whiting) Coconnas. The fixed-price meal offers good value. C 300-450 F. M 160 F.

L'Excuse

14, rue Charles-V - 42 77 98 97
Closed Sun, wk of Aug 15. Open until 11pm. No pets. V, AE, MC.
For an elegant dinner in the Marais, why not reserve a table at this dainty little candybox of a restaurant, decorated with mirrors, engravings, and posters. A new chef has raised the kitchen's standards, witness the well-defined flavors of his vegetable feuilleté with fresh herb sauce, turbot fillet, and white-and-dark chocolate fondant. Long, eclectic wine list; efficient service. C 260-400 F. M 145 F.

10/20 Jo Goldenberg

7, rue des Rosiers - 48 87 20 16
Open daily until midnight. Priv rm: 60. Terrace dining. Air cond. V, AE, DC.
This is the archetypal, and most picturesque, of the Goldenberg restaurants in Paris (see seventeenth arrondissement). The Central European Yiddish cuisine is served in the heart of the Marais's Jewish district. Prepared foods are sold in the take-out shop. C 150-200 F.

11/20 Au Gourmet de l'Isle

42, rue St-Louis-en-l'Ile - 43 26 79 27
Closed Mon, Tue. Open until 10pm. V, MC.
The reception is charming, the crowd young and cheerful, the stone-and-beams décor appealingly rustic. Au Gourmet de l'Isle has enjoyed over 40 years of deserved success for one of the city's surest-value set menus priced at 125 F. Lots of à la carte choices too: artichoke "Saint Louis", beef stewed in Marcillac wine, andouillette with kidney beans. C 190 F. M 130 F.

Le Grizzli

7, rue Saint-Martin - 48 87 77 56
Closed Sun. Open until 11pm. Terrace dining. Garage pkg. V, AE, MC.
At age 95 this Grizzli is still going strong, serving lusty specialties rooted in the Southwest: white-bean salad with duck confit, rabbit with raisins, and veal stewed with dried cèpes. C 200-250 F. M 120 F (lunch), 155 F.

Le Maraîcher

5, rue Beautreillis - 42 71 42 49
Closed Mon lunch, Sun, Aug. Open until 11pm. V, MC.
Lured by the appetizing 120 F set lunch, hungry hordes descend upon this attractive little spot at noon. But even the stiffer à la carte tariffs don't discourage Le Maraîcher's many fans from indulging in the delicate scallop ravioli showered with zucchini curls and sesame seeds, the calf's liver meunière deglazed with Sherry vinegar, and warm orange soup with caramel ice cream. Attentive service. C 250-300 F. M 120 F (lunch, wine incl).

Miravile

72, quai de l'Hôtel-de-Ville
42 74 72 22, fax 42 74 67 55
Closed Sat lunch, Sun. Open until 10:30pm. Priv rm: 45. Terrace dining. Air cond. Pkg. V, AE, MC.
Gilles Épié made a shrewd move when he decided to throw out the Miravile's expensive carte in favor of a 220 F single-price menu. Instead of costly ingredients, Épié relies on his considerable talent to create imaginative dishes packed with robust flavors. Pimientos with codfish and crushed potatoes or rémoulade of duck liver and celeriac are appetizing preludes to skate with sea urchins and spinach, or Provençal-inspired rabbit with olives, or chicken and onion tagine. These, in turn, can be followed by a tarte au café laced with single-malt whisky or bitter-chocolate and caramel ice cream. To drink, there are some 40 wines priced between 115 F and 250 F. Little wonder, then, that customers are flocking back into the Miravile's sunny, Italianate dining room. M 220 F.

Le Monde des Chimères

69, rue Saint-Louis-en-l'Ile - 43 54 45 27
Closed Sun, Mon, Feb school hols. Open until 10:20pm. Pkg. V, MC.
A delightful old "island bistro" run by former TV personality Cécile Ibane. The cuisine is reminiscent of Sunday dinner en famille—if, that is, your family included a French granny who was also a marvelous cook! We recommend the eggs scrambled with fennel, grilled fillet of pollack dressed with olive oil and lemon, oxtail terrine garnished with sweet-and-sour quince and cherries, or chicken sautéed with 40 cloves of garlic. Yummy homemade desserts. C 280-380 F. M 155 F.

Palais de Fès

41, rue du Roi-de-Sicile - 42 72 03 68
Open daily until 11:30pm. No pets. V, AE, DC, MC.
This may be the only Moroccan hotel-restaurant in the city, but a palace it's not. The glittery décor isn't exactly palatial, either, but it's tidy and inviting. Good food is the drawing card here: order the assiette marocaine (spicy sausage, bits of lamb, cold peppers and eg-

15

gplant), followed by one of a half-dozen delicious couscous variations, or a tagine (the lamb with onions would be our choice), or the more-than-decent pigeon pastilla. Excellent value. **C** 150 F. **M** 70 F.

5TH ARRONDISSEMENT

L'Atlas
12, bd Saint-Germain - 46 33 86 98
Open daily until 11pm. Priv rm: 30. Air cond. Pkg. V, AE.
Here's a first toque, which we bet will be followed by more, for Monsieur Eljaziri's surprising, slightly cerebral, determinedly modern version of Moroccan cuisine. The range of options extends well beyond couscous and tagines (though a dozen excellent varieties are offered) to such uncommon dishes as lamb with mallow, monkfish with thyme blossoms, and kidneys with sea-urchin butter. Desserts are more traditional. Decorated with mosaics and ornamental plasterwork, the dining room is perfectly lovely, and so is the service. **C** 190-230 F.

Auberge des Deux Signes
46, rue Galande
43 25 46 56, fax 46 33 20 49
Closed Sun, Sun, May 1, Aug. Open until 10:30pm. Pkg. V, AE, DC, MC.
If there is one restaurant in Paris that must be seen to be believed, it is this medieval hostelry lovingly restored and run by Georges Dhulster. Solid oak beams, Gothic vaults, and windows that frame Notre-Dame: the setting is nothing short of spectacular (despite some heavy-handed neo-Louis XIII touches). The food, consistently generous and well prepared, deserves two solid toques: try the salade périgourdine, boiled-beef ravioli with ginger-scented cabbage, or turbot with buttery leeks. The 140 F set lunch offers relief from the high prices à la carte. Courteous service. **C** 400-650 F. **M** 140 F (weekday lunch), 230 F.

10/20 Le Balzar
49, rue des Écoles - 43 54 13 67
Closed Dec 24-Jan 1, Aug. Open until 1am. Air cond. V, AE.
This Left-Bank/Sorbonne haunt, with its Art Deco woodwork and mirrors, offers decent renditions of traditional brasserie fare (calf's liver, choucroute). **C** 200-300 F.

Le Bistrot d'à Côté
16, bd Saint-Germain - 43 54 59 10
Closed Sat lunch, Sun. Open until 11pm. Terrace dining. Air cond. V, AE, MC.
Michel Rostang has set up another of his popular bistro annexes at this Left-Bank location. He spruced up the 1950s–style interior and put two trusted assistants in charge of the kitchen. Lively house specialties include lentil soup with garlic sausage, codfish fricassée à la lyonnaise, and veal kidney in red-wine sauce. To drink, there are regional wines sold by the half-liter for around 60 F. **C** 135-200 F. **M** 98 F (lunch), 178 F.

Remember to call ahead to reserve your table, and please, if you cannot honor your reservation, be courteous and let the restaurant know.

Le Bistrot du Port
13, quai Montebello
40 51 73 19
Closed Tue lunch, Mon. Open until 10:30pm. Terrace dining. Air cond. No pets. Garage pkg. V.
The comfortable dining room and quayside terrace boast a magnificent view of Notre-Dame. Owner Iza Guyot has decided to take over the cooking duties herself, proposing the likes of profiteroles stuffed with goat cheese in a fresh tomato sauce, lamb noisettes with braised carrots, and old-fashioned coconut custard. Sounds good, but we'll hold back on the rating until Iza gets used to her new post. **C** 240-330 F. **M** 138-168 F.

La Bûcherie
41, rue de la Bûcherie
43 54 78 06, fax 46 34 54 02
Open daily until midnight. Priv rm: 40. Terrace dining. Air cond. Garage pkg. V, AE, DC, MC.
Bernard Bosque is built like a Breton buccaneer and has been running his "Hôtel du Bon Dieu" (the Bûcherie's name at the turn of the century) for over 30 years with great success. Handsome woodwork and contemporary engravings adorn the walls, and there are views of Notre-Dame through the windows of the covered terrace. The cuisine, classic and understated, reflects the seasons. There's game in autumn, a salad of truffled lamb's lettuce, scallops, and foie gras in winter, newly hatched eels from January to March, baby lamb or asparagus and morels in spring. Prices are not of the giveaway variety, but the 230 F lunch menu is quite attractive. The wine list is rich with vintage Bordeaux. **C** 300-470 F. **M** 230 F (wine incl).

Campagne et Provence
25, quai de la Tournelle
43 54 05 17, fax 42 74 67 55
Closed Sun, lunch Sat & Mon. Open until 11pm (w-e 1am). Air cond. V, MC.
Gilles Épié had a bright idea when he turned his ex-Miravile into a Provençal annex. The food is sunny, unhackneyed, and pleasingly priced. We find it hard to resist the mussel soup enriched with fragrant pistou, the meaty grilled peppers with anchovies, a vivid pumpkin risotto studded with bits of bacon, sea whelks accented by spicy chorizo, or rosemary-scented lamb tian. Every wine in the astutely assembled cellar costs under 100 F. A short but sweet 99 F lunch menu is on offer, too. **C** 220-250 F. **M** 99 F (lunch).

12/20 Chieng-Mai
12, rue F.-Sauton
43 25 45 45
Closed Sun, Aug 1-15, Dec 16-31. Open until 11:20pm. No pets. V, AE.
Its cool, stylized atmosphere, efficient service, and interesting Thai menu have won Chieng Mai a growing corps of admirers (it is wise to reserve your table). The repertoire features shrimp soup perfumed with lemongrass, baked crab claws with angel-hair pasta, steamed spicy seafood served in a crab shell, duck breast with basil and young peppercorns, and a remarkable coconut-milk flan. Service is courteous and competent, but the tables are set too close together. **C** 220 F. **M** 122 F, 136 F, 159 & 173 F (exc Sun).

Les Colonies
10, rue St-Julien-le-Pauvre - 43 54 31 33
Dinner only. Closed Sun, Aug. Open until 1am (Mon until 10:30pm). Air cond. V, AE.
The decorator of L'Ambroisie took this old building, which faces the church of Saint-Julien-le-Pauvre, and transformed it with subtle refinements such as painted woodwork, luxurious fabrics, and fine china. A warm breeze from some imaginary Spice Island stirs many of chef Spyros Vakanas's creations, witness his salad of chayote squash dressed with tangy Japanese vinegar, a juicy duck enhanced with the warm flavor of nutmeg, rib steak coated with crushed spices, or the chocolate "shell" with sweet saffron cream sauce. Charming service and a fashionable clientele. Book ahead for late dining. **C** 300-400 F. **M** 170 F, 250 F.

Dodin-Bouffant
25, rue F.-Sauton
43 25 25 14, fax 43 29 52 61
Closed Sat lunch, Sun, Dec 24-26. Open until 11pm. Terrace dining. Air cond. Garage pkg. V, AE, DC, MC.
Economic hard times have hit even this popular spot, where high and not-so-high-society diners once jostled for tables. Franco-American chef Mark Singer prepares the 215 F single-price menu, which we found to be something of a minefield on a recent day. Neither the ho-hum vegetable salad with its stingy garnish of foie gras, nor the overcooked lamb in a gluey tarragon sauce piqued our appetite. Only the delicious hot banana soufflé kept the meal from being a total rout. Just one toque left, and it's looking mighty wobbly... Good-natured service. **M** 215 F.

Inagiku
1, rue de Pontoise - 43 54 70 07
Closed Sun. Open until 11pm. Air cond. V, AE.
Armed with our experience of Japanese restaurants, which we often leave as hungry as we'd come, it seemed a good idea to order a side of sashimi in addition to the Matsu, or big menu. Well, after putting away the assortment of delectably fresh raw fish, the sushi with avocado, the ineffably crisp fried hors d'œuvres, a pile of fat shrimp, some succulently tender beef fillet, and a duo of yummy ginger and chestnut sorbets, we waddled out, happy and absolutely stuffed! **C** 260-360 F. **M** 138 F, 168 F, 188 F, 248 F, 348 F.

12/20 Léna et Mimile
32, rue Tournefort - 47 07 72 47
Closed Sat lunch, Sun. Open until 11pm. Terrace dining.
The terrace of this cozy bistro stretches out onto a charming square. From an appealing single-price menu (apéritif, wine, and coffee are all included) one can choose a basil-scented tourte of fresh sardines, braised pork shanks with lentils, and a satisfying pear feuilleté. **M** 185 F (wine incl), 98 F (lunch).

Mavrommatis
42, rue Daubenton - 43 31 17 17
Closed Sun. Open until 11:30pm. Priv rm: 25. Terrace dining. No pets. Pkg. V.
The Mavrommatis brothers have raised the level of Greek cuisine served in Paris by several notches! Settle down into an Aegean-blue chair and order one—or several—of the 30 delicious

hot and cold starters (octopus salad, tuna carpaccio with sesame seeds, stuffed eggplant, lamb meatballs, etc.). If you can resist making a meal of these mezes, there are worthwhile main dishes too, like red mullet grilled in vine leaves, smothered leg of lamb with herbs, or veal with oaten pasta. The selection of Greek wines is slowly improving. **C** 200-300 F. **M** 120 F ("business" lunch).

Au Pactole
44, bd Saint-Germain
46 33 31 31, fax 46 33 07 60
Closed Sat lunch. Open until 11:45pm. No pets. V, AE, MC.
Roland Magne's lightened traditional dishes offer exceptional value, and his wife, Noëlle, is a perfectly charming hostess. What a shame that the restaurant is not fuller at lunchtime! Dinner is another matter, altogether: even François Mitterrand has been spotted here of an evening (he once brought along his food-loving friend Helmut Kohl). Connoisseurs appreciate Magne's delicious ravioli d'escargots à la crème d'ail, his succulent steak of flash-smoked cod, and one of the best ribs of beef in Paris (it's roasted in a salt crust), which can be followed by a tasty apple tart with sabayon sauce. Sharp-eyed wine buffs can unearth the occasional bargain in Le Pactole's fine cellar. **C** 250-320 F. **M** 149 F, 279 F.

12/20 Le Petit Navire
14, rue des Fossés-St-Bernard
43 54 22 52
Closed Sun, Mon, 2nd wk of Feb, Aug 1-15. Open until 10:15pm. Priv rm: 30. Terrace dining. Pkg. V, AE, DC, MC.
Anchored not far from the Seine for the past twenty-odd years, Le Petit Navire regales its many regular customers with tapenade, garlicky shellfish soup, grilled sardines, and delightful growers' wines. **C** 250-350 F. **M** 150 F.

12/20 Rôtisserie du Beaujolais
19, quai de la Tournelle
43 54 17 47, fax 44 07 12 04
Closed Mon. Open until 11:30pm. Terrace dining. Pkg. V.
Claude Terrail of the Tour d'Argent (across the road) owns a nice little place to spend a lively evening with friends. The spit-roasted Challans duck is a delight, the saucisson pistaché and the salad of boiled beef and lentils are equally delicious. Splendid cheeses, and exemplary Beaujolais (all ten crus) from Dubœuf. **C** 185-230 F.

La Timonerie
35, quai de la Tournelle - 43 25 44 42
Closed Mon lunch, Sun. Open until 10:30pm. Air cond. Pkg. V, MC.
Philippe de Givenchy continues to surprise us with his contemporary, streamlined cuisine. A trifle too trendy in its presentations (lots of clever little heaps and "bushes", now that vertical arrangements are all the rage), his cooking is saved from affectation by its use of simple, unpretentious ingredients: mackerel, pollack, inexpensive cuts of lamb and beef, offal, and pork. Another chef would make bistro chow out of foods like

these, but Givenchy turns them into great modern dishes. Anyone who does what he does with hogs' jowls and a little red wine, or with a mackerel fillet and a handful of herbs, deserves our attention. Not to mention his sea bream roasted with tarragon and chilis in a tight red-wine sauce. Desserts follow the same vein: a homey repertoire glorified by virtuoso technique. The cellar is not vast, but it is perfectly à propos, with a fine selection of growers' wines. C 350-420 F. M 220 F (lunch).

La Tour d'Argent

15-17, quai de la Tournelle
43 54 23 31, fax 44 07 12 04
Closed Mon. Open until 10:30pm. Priv rm: 60. Air cond. No pets. Valet pkg. V, AE, DC.

We hope the sight of those sweet little ducks and drakes bobbing on the Seine between the Ile Saint-Louis and your panoramic table doesn't take away your appetite for the best canard à l'orange you'll ever taste—a pressed duck paddling in a deeply flavorful sauce which has been a house specialty for 100 years. Chef Manuel Martinez, now a Tour d'Argent veteran, knows better than anyone how to work wonders with the web-footed fowl.

Don't expect any audacious novelties or revolutionary changes in the Tour d'Argent tradition. Owner Claude Terrail, eternally charming and diplomatic, has chosen his field of honor once and for all. And what better aide-de-camp than Martinez, battle-tested at the Relais Louis–XIII? Within the limits of a "noble"—but not boring—repertoire, he imbues his creations with such flavor and harmony that you might be too delightedly dazed to notice the astronomical bill. But then, who notices the bill when it's time to buy the Rolls and the diamonds?

You can easily waste 600 F on a ghastly meal elsewhere, and though it might seem galling to spend twice that here, you'll never question the quality of this cuisine: ravioli de foie gras et homard, ragoût de truffes, tantalizing truffled brouillade (scrambled eggs) sauce Périgourdine, crab-stuffed turbot, or a voluptuously tender double veal chop. And what of the *nec plus ultra* of ice creams, the Tour d'Argent's vanilla or pistachio? A year from now you won't have forgotten it! Nor will you forget the sight of dusk's golden light on Notre-Dame or the impressive cityscape spread out before you.

The fabled cellar harbors bottles with prices in four and even five digits—but it also holds unsung marvels costing less than 250 F. And do remember: the lunch menu is only 375 F—put aside a franc and a centime each day for a year and there you are! C 1,200 F and up. M 375 F (lunch).

Restaurant Toutoune

5, rue de Pontoise
43 26 56 81
Closed Mon lunch, Sun. Open until 10:45pm. V, AE.

The arrival of a new chef with a Provençal repertoire has infused fresh life into this popular spot. The 150 F single-price menu features fragrant soups, tasty terrines, snails in a garlicky tomato sauce, sea bream with zucchini, and grapefruit gratin with sabayon sauce. Lively atmosphere. M 150 F

Chez Albert

41, rue Mazarine - 46 33 22 57
Closed Aug. Open until 11pm. No pets. V, MC.

Most of the patrons don't even realize that Albert's is a Portuguese restaurant. The menu, indeed, is largely French but the tasty pork with clams, rabbit à la Ranhado, and half-dozen dishes featuring salt cod (our favorite is the one with eggs and onions) point clearly to the owner's Lusitanian origins. So does the wine list, with its Dãos and Douros. C 180 F. M 95 F.

Allard

41, rue St-André-des-Arts - 43 26 48 23
Closed Sun, Dec 23-Jan 3, Aug. Open until 10pm. Priv rm: 25. Air cond. V, AE, DC, MC.

Prices are starting to cool down a bit, but otherwise little has changed at Allard, from the mellow décor to the handwritten daily menu of saucisson chaud lyonnais, bœuf braisé aux carottes, turbot au beurre blanc, duck with olives, and tarte Tatin. The nostalgic ambience continues to charm the cosmopolitan patrons. C 300-400 F. M 150 F (lunch), 200 F (exc Sat lunch).

11/20 L'Arbuci

25, rue de Buci
44 41 14 14, fax 44 41 14 10
Open daily until dawn. Priv rm: 90. Terrace dining. Air cond. V, AE, MC.

Here's a huge, often crowded brasserie specializing in fresh shell-fish, decent spit-roasted poultry and meats, and banane flambée au Grand Marnier. C 200-270 F. M 72 F & 99 F (lunch, exc Sun).

La Bastide Odéon

7, rue Corneille - 43 26 03 65
Closed 3 wks in Aug. Open until 11pm. No pets. V, MC.

New and noteworthy. Gilles Ajuelos's fresh, clever take on Provençal cooking has us salivating over every dish on the menu. Vigorous flavors distinguish his oven-roasted peppers and tomatoes served forth with crusty country bread, the thick steak of roasted cod with saffron-tinged vegetables and tangy capers, sardine roulade stuffed with herbed chèvre, and snail gnocchi with Swiss chard and garlic confit. For dessert, we like the lemon-berry feuillantine. A warmer touch would improve the rudimentary décor, but the welcome and service are charming. C 230 F.

La Bauta

129, bd du Montparnasse
43 22 52 35
Open daily until 11pm. Priv rm: 45. Terrace dining. Air cond. Garage pkg. V, MC.

A bauta, or carnival mask, is the emblem of this pretty restaurant that proposes a short, appealing list of Venetian specialties. Among the well-executed offerings you'll find marinated sardines, whole-wheat spaghetti topped with tiny squid, gnocchi enriched with sage butter, and crisp-fried seafood tidbits. You can finish up with an authentic tiramisù. While the food is priced within reason, the Italian wines are not. M 105 F & 195 F (lunch, wine incl), 200 F (wine incl).

Le Bélier

L'Hôtel, 13, rue des Beaux-Arts
43 25 27 22, fax 43 25 64 81
Open daily until 1am. Air cond. V, AE, DC, MC.
The theatrical setting, complete with a flower-decked fountain, attracts an elegant, cosmopolitan crowd. Chef Christian Schuliar's classic cuisine is occasionally inconsistent, but his salmon and sculpin in saffron aspic and the succulent sweet-and-sour duck with mushrooms are reliable bets. Prices have been scaled back considerably. **M** 120 F (lunch), 180 F (dinner).

Le Bistrot d'Alex ☺

2, rue Clément - 43 25 77 66
Closed Sun, Dec 24-Jan 2. Open until 10pm. Priv rm: 14. Air cond. V, AE, MC.
Stéphane Guini has stepped up to the stove, to replace Alexandre, his late, lamented father. Lyon and Provence continue to inspire the bistro's zestful menu of pistachio-studded saucisson, fragrant daube de bœuf, and tasty orange flan. You can count on a delightful welcome. **C** 250-350 F. **M** 140 F, 190 F.

Les Bookinistes

53, quai des Grands-Augustins
43 25 45 94, fax 43 25 23 07
Closed Sat lunch, Sun. Open until midnight. Priv rm: 30. Terrace dining. Air cond. Pkg. V, AE, MC.
The latest addition to Guy Savoy's successful string of bistros sports an avant-garde look that obviously suits the young, Left Bank crowd. Crowded is how you might feel in this elbow-to-elbow eatery, but don't let that diminish your enjoyment of the sweet-sour marinated duck breast flanked by yummy fig and onion marmalade, or pan-roasted cod set atop red-cabbage compote, or full-flavored steak of Angus beef. Tasty desserts, too, and brisk, professional service. **C** 220-240 F. **M** 160 F (lunch).

12/20 Brasserie Lutétia

Hôtel Lutétia,
23, rue de Sèvres - 49 54 46 76
Open daily until midnight. Priv rm: 400. Air cond. Valet pkg. V, AE, DC, MC.
The no-nonsense cooking is prepared with considerable finesse in the same kitchens as Le Paris (see below). The superb seafood is attractively priced, and the satisfying bourgeois dishes (veal chop with macaroni gratin, poulet au thym) always hit the spot. **C** 200-250 F. **M** 295 F (wine incl).

Jacques Cagna

14, rue des Grands-Augustins
43 26 49 39, fax 43 54 54 48
Closed Sat lunch, Sun, 3 wks in Aug, 1 wk at Christmas. Open until 10:30pm. Priv rm: 10. Air cond. V, AE, DC, MC.
The roaring success of his bistro annexes has not distracted Jacques Cagna from the business of pleasing the moneyed, cosmopolitan gourmets who prefer to dine at the "old original," with its ancient oak beams and woodwork, Flemish still lifes, and subdued lighting. Elegant? Yes, but this is no museum: food, drink, and—measured—merriment are perfectly at home here.
Lately Cagna has brought his essentially classic *carte* up to date with some rousing, rustic offer-

ings and others that exhale a discreet but seductive Southern perfume. Choosing among them is a delicious dilemma: it's not easy to overlook the lush lobster with beurre blanc sauce, but neither can we resist the daube of suckling pig embellished with tomato ravioli, nor the crisp-crusted sturgeon partnered with herbed pasta in a classic sauce Choron. Dazed by all this deliciousness, we decided to try two exciting, very modern creations that recently appeared on the menu: a divine carpaccio of pearly sea bream with an invigorating garnish of caviar-strewn céleri rémoulade; and superb langoustine fritters served with vegetable "chips" and gazpacho sauce, a dish full of beguiling nuances. Dessert? Of course! No one needs prodding to sample such superlative sweets as a fragile vacherin piled high with candied chestnuts or apple clafoutis with gingerbread ice cream. Jacques Cagna's adorable sister, Anny, who glides among the tables dispensing smiles and good counsel, also oversees a cellar brimming with Hermitages, Côte-Rôties, and vintage Burgundies. **C** 600-900 F. **M** 260 F (lunch), 480 F.

12/20 Casa Bini

36, rue Grégoire-de-Tours
46 34 05 60, fax 43 25 59 62
Closed Sat lunch, Sun. Open until 11pm. V, AE, DC, MC.
Anna Bini is uncompromising when it comes to quality. She travels all the way to Tuscany to seek out the best ingredients. Her little restaurant could easily become one of the top Italian spots in town, but Anna chooses to keep things simple, offering a limited menu of carpaccio, crostoni, and pasta. Her trendy Saint-Germain patrons are perfectly content with this tasty, uncomplicated (and rather too expensive) fare. Anna recently opened two branches of an Italian-style snack bar, Lo Spuntino (94, rue des Saints-Pères, seventh arrondissement; and 17, rue de la Banque, second arrondissement). **C** 220-245 F.

Aux Charpentiers

10, rue Mabillon - 43 26 30 05
Open daily until 11:30pm. Terrace dining. V, AE, DC.
Although he is occupied by his seafood restaurant across the street (L'Écaille de PCB), Pierre Bardèche continues to serve honest home-style cooking in this former carpenters' guild hall. The menu revolves around *plats du jour* such as cod aïoli, stuffed cabbage, and veal sauté, prepared by a capable new chef. Cheerful atmosphere. **C** 180-250 F. **M** 150 F (dinner, wine incl), 100 F (lunch).

12/20 Dominique

19, rue Bréa - 43 27 08 80
Closed Jul 15-Aug 15. Open until 10:30pm. Priv rm: 42. Air cond. V, AE, DC, MC.
This famed Montparnasse Russian troika—takeout shop/bar/restaurant—steadfastly refuses perestroika when it comes to cuisine and décor: purple-and-gold walls, steaming samovars, and goulash Tolstoy. Rostropovitch and Solzhenitsyn have been spotted here, sampling the delicious smoked salmon, borscht, and blinis. And there's vodka, of course, both Russian and Polish. **C** 230-340 F. **M** 80 F (lunch, exc Sun), 155 F.

19

L'Écaille de PCB

"Pierre et Colette Bardèche,"
5, rue Mabillon
43 26 73 70, fax 46 33 07 98
Closed Sat lunch, Sun. Open until 11pm. Priv rm: 8. Terrace dining. Air cond. V, AE.
Pierre and Colette Bardèche welcome the literary lights of this intellectual neighborhood into their warm, mahogany-lined seafood restaurant. Marinated sardines with fennel or a salad of finnan haddie and bacon are lively preludes to the popular osso buco de lotte à l'orientale, John Dory enlivened with coarse-grain mustard, or superb scallops in a creamy garlic sauce. The cellar is of only middling interest, with the exception of a fine, bone-dry Jurançon from Charles Hours. **C** 250-350 F. **M** 125 F, 190 F, 210 F.

12/20 Chez Henri

16, rue Princesse - 46 33 51 12
Closed Sun. Open until 11:30pm. No pets. No cards.
There's no sign outside, since the trendy denizens of the Rue Princesse know just where to find Henri Poulat and his bistro specialties. The cooking can be uneven, but calf's liver with creamed onions, farm chicken in vinegar, roast lamb, and apple clafoutis are usually good bets. Nervous service. **C** 220-250 F. **M** 160 F (dinner).

12/20 Joséphine

"Chez Dumonet,"
117, rue du Cherche-Midi
45 48 52 40, fax 42 84 06 83
Closed Sat, Sun, Jul. Open until 10:30pm. Terrace dining. V, MC.
Joséphine is an early-1900s bistro frequented by prominent jurists, journalists, and an intellectual theater crowd. The food isn't bad, but it used to be better: the current menu lists warm scallop salad, noisettes of lamb with a coffee-flavored sauce, roasted rabbit with sage jus, and pear millefeuille spiced with star anise. Chummy atmosphere, animated by owner Jean Dumonet, a former yachting champ. **C** 300-500 F. **M** 235 F.

Lapérouse

51, quai des Grands-Augustins
43 26 68 04, fax 43 26 99 39
Closed Mon lunch, Sun. Open until 11pm. Priv rm: 50. Air cond. Valet pkg. V, AE, DC, MC.
Lapérouse, a ravishing Belle Époque landmark, has yet another new owner, still another new chef. As for the menu, it's ultraclassic, inspired by the cooking of Escoffier and Dumaine. As soon as we've sampled the timbale Augustin, tournedos Rossini, and omelette soufflée, we'll turn in our rating—stay tuned! **C** 400-800 F. **M** 200 F (lunch), 290 F, 495 F, 680 F.

11/20 Lipp

151, bd St-Germain
45 48 53 91, fax 45 44 33 20
Open daily until 1am. Air cond. V, AE, DC, MC.
Despite the often disappointing food (choucroute, bœuf gros sel) and the cruel whims of fashion, this glossy turn-of-the-century brasserie still manages to serve some 400 to 500 customers a day. And one often catches sight of

a powerful politician or a beauty queen ensconced at a ground-floor table, admiring the gorgeous décor. **C** 270-320 F.

La Marlotte

55, rue du Cherche-Midi - 45 48 86 79
Closed Sat, Sun, Aug. Open until 11pm. Priv rm: 8. Terrace dining. Air cond. Garage pkg. V, AE, DC, MC.
The rustic, timbered setting is softened by madras upholstery and candlelight in the evening. A traditional repertoire is meticulously prepared by chef Patrick Duclos. Try his sprightly vegetable terrine, rabbit with sautéed apples, or braised veal kidney with fresh pasta, then round things off with the delectable chocolate gâteau. Crowded both at lunch and dinner, often with the smart set. **C** 250-330 F.

12/20 La Méditerranée

Place de l'Odéon
43 26 46 75, fax 44 07 00 57
Closed May 1. Open until 11pm. Priv rm: 30. Valet pkg. V, AE, DC, MC.
Thanks to Marc Richard's deft and spirited seafood cuisine, this handsome restaurant on the Place de l'Odéon is once again afloat. The sparkling-fresh fish tartare, grilled sea bass, and bouillabaisse are all absolutely shipshape. Wide-ranging cellar. **C** 300-500 F. **M** 195 F.

Le Muniche

7, rue St-Benoît - 42 61 12 70
Open daily until 1am. Terrace dining. Air cond. V, AE, MC.
In a new location (just around the corner from its former site) the Muniche remains the liveliest, most frenetically crowded of Parisian brasseries. The Layrac brothers and their attentive, smiling staff will regale you with oysters, choucroute, thick-sliced calf's liver, and grilled pigs' ears, washed down with decent *pots* of red, white, and rosé. **C** 250-300 F. **M** 165 F.

Le Paris

Hôtel Lutétia, 45, bd Raspail
49 54 46 90, fax 49 54 46 64
Closed Sat, Sun, Aug. Open until 10pm. Priv rm: 400. Air cond. Valet pkg. V, AE, DC, MC.
Philippe Renard captains the kitchens of Le Paris, a restaurant that looks for all the world like the dining room of a cruise ship. Again this year, Renard confirmed our high opinion of his inventive cuisine. Subtle, well-defined flavors distinguish his bright sorrel soup dotted with Basque country ham and grilled duck liver, his charlotte of crisp-cooked asparagus and plump crayfish, the briny duo of red mullet and lobster with truffled leeks, and braised veal shanks with mushroom-studded pasta. Note the light and luscious desserts, and the excellent 250 F prix-fixe meal. **C** 380-540 F. **M** 250 F (lunch), 495 F (wine incl), 350 F.

10/20 Le Petit Mabillon

6, rue Mabillon - 43 54 08 41
Closed Sun, Mon lunch. Open until 11pm. Terrace dining. V, AE, MC.
The home-style Italian menu features two pasta choices daily (fusilli, lasagne), as well as carpaccio and comforting osso buco. Picturesque décor, leafy garden courtyard. **C** 160-200 F. **M** 75 F.

10/20 Le Petit Saint-Benoît

4, rue Saint-Benoît - 42 60 27 92
Closed Sat, Sun. Open until 10pm. Terrace dining. No pets. No cards.
The crowded sidewalk terrace is a refuge for fashionable fast-food haters in search of cheap eats: hachis parmentier, bacon with lentils, bœuf bourguignon, lamb sauté. C 130 F.

Le Petit Zinc

"Les Frères Layrac," 11, rue Saint-Benoît
42 61 20 60, fax 45 66 47 64
Open daily until 1am. Terrace dining. Air cond. V, AE, DC, MC.
Le Petit Zinc shares the same kitchen and country cooking as the equally popular Le Muniche (see above), but with an emphasis on Southwestern specialties: oysters, shellfish, poule au pot, thick-sliced calf's liver, savory leg of lamb. In summer the terrace spreads its fluttering tablecloths across the pavement. C 250-300 F. M 165 F.

La Petite Cour

8, rue Mabillon
43 26 52 26, fax 44 07 11 53
Open daily until 11:30pm (winter 11pm). Garden dining. V, MC.
Owners and chefs may come and go, but the discreet charm of this comfortable restaurant endures. Patrick Guyader is the man in the kitchen these days, and his repertoire runs to satisfying home-style dishes: sardines gratinées, turnip "choucroute" with smoked fish, and duck tucked under a blanket of mashed potatoes. C 300-350 F.

11/20 Polidor

41, rue Monsieur-le-Prince - 43 26 95 34
Open daily until 12:30am (Sun 11pm). No cards.
Familiar and soothing blanquettes, bourguignons, and rabbit in mustard sauce are served in a dining room that time has barely touched in more than a century. C 130 F. M 55 F (weekday lunch), 100 F.

10/20 Le Procope

13, rue de l'Ancienne-Comédie
43 26 99 20, fax 43 54 16 86
Open daily until 1am. Pkg. V, AE, DC, MC.
The capital's oldest café, restored to its original seventeenth-century splendor, is perhaps not your best bet for a meal. A clientele made up mainly of tourists feeds on unremarkable brasserie fare (shellfish, coq au vin) and uninspired desserts. C 200-350 F. M 99 F (lunch & until 8pm), 119 F (dinner, wine incl, from 11pm), 185 F (summer), 289 F (winter).

Relais Louis–XIII

8, rue des Grands-Augustins
43 26 75 96, fax 44 07 07 80
Closed Mon lunch, Sun, Jul 25-Aug 23. Open until 10:15pm. Priv rm: 22. Air cond. V, AE, DC, MC.
Louis XIII was proclaimed King of France in this luxurious seventeenth-century tavern with its beams and polished paneling. Fresh, scrupulously classic offerings include a warm salad of truffled scallops and mushrooms, a flawless turbot enhanced with sea-urchin roe, and a rich, chocolatey palais d'or with pistachio sauce. In addition to many stupendous and shockingly expensive bottlings (1934 Latour, 1921 Quarts

de Chaume), the cellar boasts a few accessibly priced wines. Note that a (nearly) affordable set meal is offered at lunch. C 420-560 F. M 190 F & 240 F (lunch), 250 F & 350 F (dinner).

La Rôtisserie d'en Face

2, rue Christine
43 26 40 98, fax 43 54 54 48
Closed Sat lunch, Sun. Open until 11pm. Priv rm: 20. Air cond. V, AE, DC, MC.
Jacques Cagna's smart rotisserie with its single-price menu (195 F) continues to attract Parisians hungry for rousing bistro food at reasonable prices. Start off a satisfying meal with crisp, deep-fried smelts or ravioli stuffed with escargots, then follow with thyme-showered lamb chops or spit-roasted farm chicken with mashed potatoes, and finish with an Alsatian apple tart. Whatever you choose, you'll find a frisky, inexpensive wine to accompany it from among the twenty or so on offer. There is another Rôtisserie in the seventeenth arrondissement, at 6, rue Armaillé, tel.: 42 27 19 20. M 195 F.

11/20 Chez Claude Sainlouis

27, rue du Dragon - 45 48 29 68
Closed Sat dinner, Sun, 2 wks at Easter, Aug. Open until 11pm. Air cond. No cards.
Reliable salads and steaks are served here in an amusing, theatrical setting. C 150-200 F.

Yugaraj

14, rue Dauphine
43 26 44 91, fax 46 33 50 77
Closed Mon lunch. Open until 11pm. Priv rm: 18. Air cond. No pets. V, AE, DC, MC.
The best Indian restaurant in the city, hands down. We love the refined surroundings, the smiles of the formally suited waiters, and—especially—the rare delicacies culled from every province of the subcontinent. We unreservedly recommend the herbed chicken sausages redolent of mint, cumin-spiced crab balls, tender lamb that is first roasted in a tandoori oven then sautéed with herbs, or cod suavely spiced with turmeric and fenugreek: the beautifully harmonized flavors bloom subtly on the palate. To finish, try one of the refreshing ices perfumed with cardamom, pistachios, or mango pulp. C 230-330 F. M 130 F (lunch), 180 F, 220 F.

7TH ARRONDISSEMENT

Arpège

"Alain Passard," 84, rue de Varenne
45 51 47 33, fax 44 18 98 39
Closed Sun lunch, Sat. Open until 10:30pm. Priv rm: 12. Air cond. V, AE, DC, MC.
Some call it cold, some say it's stark. But we admire Alain Passard's sleekly elegant dining room from which pictures and *bibelots* have been banished, the better to highlight honey-hued walls of warm wood and etched glass. It is true, though, that the space is small and at certain tables diners may feel hemmed in. But Passard and his *brigade* now have plenty of elbowroom in the spacious kitchens, where they prepare some of the finest food to be had in Paris. Passard cooks in the *grand bourgeois* register, but with a jeweler's precision and the imagination of a poet. Even his more familiar

creations seem new at each tasting: we're thinking of the lobster with sweet-and-sour turnips, a tuna fillet in melted butter fired with chili, rack of lamb enhanced by a truffle fondue, or rosemary-scented sweetbreads flanked by a zingy lemon purée. In season, game dishes like juniper-spiced pheasant or grilled baby boar are not to be missed.

Passard's desserts (chocolate gratin perfumed with star anise, tomate confite with a dozen different spices) are as ingenious as they are seductive. Less seductive, surely, are the prices, which rocketed skyward this year. C 850-1,000 F. M 390 F (lunch), 890 F.

Beato
8, rue Malar - 47 05 94 27
Closed Sun, Mon, 1 wk at Christmas, Aug. Open until 11:30pm. V, AE.
Sure, the setting and service are still starchy, but Beato's menu has visibly loosened up. Alongside the incomparable scampi fritti, shellfish soup, and noble chop of milk-fed veal, you'll now find terrific zuppa di fagioli, warming bollito misto, and tasty gnocchi with hare. It all adds up to a diverse and highly appetizing Italian repertoire. C 230-380 F. M 145 F (lunch, exc Sat).

Le Bellecour
22, rue Surcouf
45 51 46 93, fax 45 50 30 11
Closed Sat lunch, Sun, Aug. Open until 10:30pm. Priv rm: 40. V, AE, DC.
Denis Croset presides over the preparation of gastronomic classics that have made this establishment—a vintage bistro with a vaguely colonial setting—a perennial favorite with the well-heeled locals. We can vouch for the langoustines perfumed with thyme blossoms, plump mushroom-stuffed ravioli, spicy poached skate, lobster risotto, and veal fillet garnished with a lively julienne of pickled lemons. The weekday set lunch is a fine value. Exciting cellar, particularly rich in Burgundies. C 300-400 F. M 160 F (weekday lunch), 250 F (weekdays), 380 F.

11/20 Le Bistrot de Breteuil
3, pl. de Breteuil
45 67 07 27, fax 42 73 11 08
Open daily until 10:30pm. Priv rm: 50. Terrace dining. Air cond. V, AE, DC, MC.
An old corner café converted into an up-to-date bistro, the Breteuil's claim to fame is an all-inclusive menu (your apéritif, coffee, and wine incur no extra charge). On a given day, it might feature salmon tartare, calf's liver in Marsala, or skate in cider-vinegar deglazing sauce. Pleasant terrace. M 172 F (wine incl).

Le Bourdonnais

113, av. de La Bourdonnais
47 05 47 96, fax 45 51 09 29
Open daily until 11pm. Priv rm: 30. Air cond. Garage pkg. V, AE, MC.
Philippe Bardau's inspiration never flags. His current menu is a tour de force, just brimming with flavorful innovations. If you dine à la carte, why not order the creamy lobster soup underscored by a touch of tarragon and finished with a crisp cabbage beignet, then plump for a tender poached squab served with a bouquet of baby vegetables? Or try the juicy grilled salmon made

more interesting still with crisp, smoky bacon. For dessert, the stuffed tangerines en chaud froid are gorgeous, light, and refreshing. At lunchtime, the 240 F menu (it even includes wine) is a paragon of generosity, featuring (for example) curried skate soup, garlicky roast lamb, and a short-crusted bitter-chocolate tart with caramel ice cream. Owner Micheline Coat, a peach of a hostess, greets newcomers as warmly as the politicos and financiers who number among her faithful customers. C 350-600 F. M 240 F (lunch, wine incl), 320 F (dinner), 420 F (tasting menu).

Duquesnoy
6, av. Bosquet
47 05 96 78, fax 44 18 90 57
Closed Sat lunch, Sun, 2 wks in Aug. Open until 10:30pm. Air cond. V, AE, MC.
The top drawer of business and TV flocks to Jean-Paul Duquesnoy's comfortable little restaurant, filling both lunch and dinner sittings year round. The light touch extends from the décor and service (directed with discreet charm by Françoise Duquesnoy) to the cooking. Jean-Paul steers a skillful course between classicism and novelty, pleasing his elegant patrons with crab-stuffed zucchini blossoms, roasted sweetbreads with a peppery caramelized coating and a garnish of sautéed artichokes, and dainty babas au rhum enhanced with candied pineapple and a scoop of coconut ice cream. Exquisite wines from the Loire, Burgundy, and Côtes-du-Rhône swell the rather stiff à la carte prices. C 500-700 F. M 450 F & 550 F (weekdays, Sat dinner), 250 F (weekday lunch).

Écaille et Plume
25, rue Duvivier - 45 55 06 72
Closed Feb school hols, Jul 30-Aug 28. Open until 10:30pm (hunting seas 11:30pm). Priv rm: 10. Air cond. V, MC.
Seasonal game specialties and seafood are Marie Naël's strong points: try the briny salade océane, hake with citrus fruits, foie gras en terrine with potatoes or, in its short season, Scottish grouse flambéed with single-malt whisky. The décor is cozy, the Loire wines well chosen but oh-so-expensive. C 250-330 F.

La Ferme Saint-Simon
6, rue Saint-Simon
45 48 35 74, fax 40 49 07 31
Closed Sat lunch, Sun, Aug 7-16. Open until 10:15pm. Priv rm: 20. Air cond. V, AE, DC, MC.
Parliamentarians, publishing magnates, and food-loving executives savor succulent specialties in the intimate dining rooms of "the farm" (rustic only in name). The cooking is generous and traditional, but with a modern touch: lasagne d'escargots, brill with veal jus, sautéed scallops in puff pastry, fillet of roast spiced duck, and caramelized almond pastry or bitter-chocolate tart. Large and small appetites—and thick and thin wallets—will be equally satisfied. C 300-470 F. M 170 F (lunch).

La Flamberge
12, av. Rapp
47 05 91 37, fax 47 23 60 98
Closed Aug 12-20. Open until 10:30pm. Priv rm: 25. Air cond. No pets. Valet pkg. V, AE, DC, MC.
Roger Lamazère (a professional magician before he bought into the food biz) disappeared

from the Rue de Ponthieu only to pop up—hey, presto!—here on the Left Bank. He brought along the jars of truffles, foie gras en terrine, and handcrafted duck confit that won him renown in his former restaurant. Here too, costly Southwestern dishes account for the best picks on the menu (the cassoulet is memorable). The finishing touches need attention, though: the mediocre garnishes, appetizers, and petits-fours need an extra touch of magic to come level with the rest. **C** 300-500 F. **M** 160 F (weekdays, Sat dinner).

11/20 La Fontaine de Mars
129, rue St-Dominique - 47 05 46 44
Closed Sun. Open until 11pm. Terrace dining. V.
Checked tablecloths, low prices, and hearty country food are the perennial attractions of this modest establishment (duck breast salad, chicken with morels, Southwestern-style apple pie...). To drink, try the good, inexpensive Cahors. **C** 220 F. **M** 85 F (lunch).

Le Florence

22, rue du Champ-de-Mars - 45 51 52 69
Closed Sun, Aug. Open until 10:30pm. Priv rm: 10. Air cond. V, AE, DC, MC.
Charm and elegance combine to make this Italian restaurant an alluring place to dine. Frédéric Giraudeau cooks *con brio*, preparing handcrafted pasta (try the savory duck ravioli), superb sardines marinated in oil and balsamic vinegar, and tender lamb piccata flanked by a gardenful of vegetables (fava beans, artichokes, broccoli, eggplant...). Only the heavy batter coating our scampi fritti marred an excellent repast. Owner Claude Étienne oversees the superb cellar and attentive service. **C** 250-350 F. **M** 89 F (lunch), 180 F (wine incl).

Chez Françoise
Aérogare des Invalides
47 05 49 03, fax 45 51 96 20
Open daily until midnight. Priv rm: 45. Terrace dining. Air cond. Valet pkg. V, AE, DC, MC.
Chez Françoise is an immense subterranean restaurant, a perennial favorite with hungry parliamentarians from the neighboring Assemblée Générale. They blithely ignore the prix-fixe specials and opt instead for the pricier à la carte offerings, like duck terrine with onion compote, roast rack of lamb, poule au pot, and crème brûlée. We, on the other hand, usually choose one of the set meals, which are really a very good deal! **C** 250-400 F. **M** 148 F (exc weekday lunch, Sat dinner, wine incl), 168 F (weekday lunch), 200 F (exc weekday lunch, wine incl), 250 F (weekday dinner, Sat, wine incl).

Gaya Rive Gauche

44, rue du Bac
45 44 73 73, fax 42 60 53 03
Closed Sun. Open until 11pm. No pets. V, AE, MC.
A new branch of the successful Goumard-Prunier seafood empire. Here you'll find the same ultrafresh fish and unfussy preparations: we recommend the bracing tartare of tuna and John Dory, the pan-roast of tiny red mullet, and the suavely spiced tagine à l'orientale. **C** 250-300 F.

Les Glénan

54, rue de Bourgogne - 45 51 61 09
Closed Sat, Sun, 1 wk in winter, Aug. Open until 10pm. Priv rm: 20. Air cond. V, AE, MC.
The fame of Alain Passard's Arpège ought not to obscure the merits of this intimate seafood spot, situated just a few doors away. Christine Guillard manages Les Glénan with energy and charm, while the kitchen is in the capable hands of Thierry Bourbonnais. His sensitive touch brings out all the delicate nuances of his fine ingredients. The 195 F set meal, which includes a half-bottle of Loire Valley wine, features creamy scallop soup, crisp tuna fillet with herbed Belgian endive, and semolina pudding with caramelized pears. **C** 300-350 F. **M** 195 F

Jules-Verne

Tour Eiffel, second floor
45 55 61 44, fax 47 05 29 41
Open daily until 10:30pm. Air cond. No pets. Valet pkg. V, AE, DC, MC.
Chef Alain Reix has succeeded in putting his personal stamp on the repertoire of the high-flying Jules Verne. His is a virile, self-assured style that makes no concessions to prevailing culinary mannerisms or to the current fashion for old-fashioned fare. Each dish has a distinct personality, a "signature" purely its own. His latest menu features a rousing sauté of baby eels with garlicky dandelion greens, as well as fat grilled scallops to which olives and a fennel tart give an extra dose of sunny flavor, and a thick veal chop astutely enhanced with mellow figs and an exotic touch of coriander. The superb ingredients express all their intrinsic savors in a harmony that never falters. For a fitting finale to your feast, you can choose an outstanding apple strudel with spice ice cream, or a warm chocolate-cherry cake. **C** 600-850 F. **M** 300 F (weekday lunch), 660 F (dinner).

Le Divellec
107, rue de l'Université
45 51 91 96, fax 45 51 31 75
Closed Sun. Open until 10pm. Air cond. No pets. Valet pkg. V, AE, DC.
France's Présidents de la République—past and present—honor Jacques Le Divellec with their presence, as do press moguls, TV idols, and other high-toned patrons who fill this "yacht-club" dining room noon and night. But let's be frank: it's not the bigwigs that make this establishment great, it's the fish! The ocean's choicest denizens show up in Jacques Le Divellec's kitchen, where he enhances their pristine flavors with skill and restraint. His scallops steamed to pearly opacity over oyster liquor, and his house-smoked sea bass roasted to moist perfection are both simple and sublime. And nowhere will you find more magnificent raw oysters and sea urchins than at Le Divellec. Of course, if your appetite craves richer fare you could plump for frogs' legs and crayfish in a classic sauce poulette, or braised John Dory with a winy ragoût of sea snails, or the wildly extravagant pressed lobster—the sauces are delicate, the seasonings admirably precise. Desserts, we're pleased to note, have improved of late, and the wine list is better than ever. **C** 700-900 F. **M** 270 F & 370 F (lunch).

Maison de l'Amérique Latine

217, bd St-Germain
45 49 33 23, fax 40 49 03 94
Closed dinner Sat & Sun, Nov 16-Apr 30, Jul 29-Aug 22. Open until 10:30pm. Priv rm: 80. Terrace dining. No pets. V, AE, DC, MC.
This gorgeous town house on the Boulevard Saint-Germain boasts a terrace, a flower-filled garden, and—finally!—a chef worthy of the name. To dine here in summer, amid birdsong and fluttering leaves, on Yasuo Nanaumi's delicate prawn tempura, soy chicken, and tangerine custard soufflé, is a rare treat. To enjoy it, be sure to book your table in advance! True to its cultural vocation, the Maison features a South American wine list. **C** 300-350 F. **M** 215 F (lunch).

Chez Marius

5, rue de Bourgogne
45 51 79 42, fax 47 53 79 56
Closed Aug. Open until 10:30pm. Priv rm: 55. Air cond. Pkg. V, AE, DC, MC.
Dominating the newly refitted décor of this elegant dining room is a scale model of the Palais-Bourbon—that's where the MPs who patronize Marius spend their working hours. We were surprised to find (small) scale models on our plates as well! Though ungenerously apportioned, the seafood à l'américaine, pan-roasted sea bream, and chocolate cake are full of authentic flavor. Costly cellar, heavy on Bordeaux. **C** 300-500 F. **M** 250 F (wine incl), 180 F.

Paul Minchelli

54, bd Latour-Maubourg
47 05 89 86, fax 45 56 03 84
Closed Aug. Open until 10:30pm. Air cond. V, MC.
Everyone knows Paul Minchelli: he's the man who "reinvented seafood" by stripping away meretricious sauces to reveal pure, virginal flavors. Minchelli recently shipped out of Le Duc, the celebrated restaurant he ran with his late brother, and fetched up here, in premises once occupied by Chez Les Anges. Slavik redesigned the space in a spare Art Deco style, featuring Norwegian birch, frosted glass, framed seascapes, and a huge black bar with a dozen stools for casual dining. Minchelli's culinary minimalism requires fish of optimal quality and freshness. He has few equals when it comes to choosing, for example, a sea bass that is perfectly delicious even in its raw state, merely sliced into strips and drizzled with olive oil; or tuna served en tartare with just a bit of crunchy sea fennel for garnish; or sea whelks poached for a brief moment in court-bouillon (they bear no relation to the rubbery mouthfuls encountered elsewhere); or salmon adorned only with a sprinkling of sea salt. Depending on what the tide brings in, Minchelli might choose to pay tribute to a special creature from the deep: lobster, for instance, could be offered in six or seven different guises. In one memorable version, the crustacean is flavored with a touch of honey and chili, and presented with its caramelized juices mixed into al dente bow-tie pasta. Prices here are more moderate than they were at Le Duc, including the tariffs posted on the fine wine list. **C** 350-550 F.

12/20 L'Œillade
10, rue Saint-Simon - 42 22 01 60
Closed Sat lunch, Sun, hols. Open until 11pm. Priv rm: 70. Air cond. Pkg. V, MC.
The single-price menu looks reasonable enough, and the salmon-stuffed crêpes with avocado mousse, spareribs with lentils, and rum-raisin pudding are perfectly decent; but beware of the expensive wine list, which could send your bill right through the roof! **M** 160 F, 195 F.

Le Petit Laurent
38, rue de Varenne
45 48 79 64, fax 42 66 68 59
Closed Sat lunch, Sun, Aug. Open until 10:15pm. V, AE, DC, MC.
Robust cooking is served here in an ultraclassic, comfortable Louis XVI décor. Try the terrine of sweetbreads, the pike-perch with onions in Bourgueil wine, or the roast sea bream with lemon and mango: you'll appreciate, as we do, their precise, clearly defined flavors. Cheerful Sylvain Pommier is making an admirable effort to keep prices down. In fact, his appetizing 175 F menu is one of the best deals on the Left Bank. **C** 300-400 F. **M** 175 F, 240 F.

11/20 La Petite Chaise
36, rue de Grenelle - 42 22 13 35
Open daily until 11pm. Priv rm: 50. Terrace dining. Garage pkg. V.
This charming little restaurant has been serving since the days of Louis XIV (1680). Sit elbow-to-elbow with university students and publishing people and tuck into the fixed-price menu: onion pizza with a flaky crust, steak with Roquefort butter, saumon au beurre blanc are typical offerings. **M** 170 F (wine incl).

Le Récamier
4, rue Récamier
45 48 86 58, fax 42 22 84 76
Closed Sun. Open until 10:30pm. Priv rm: 14. Garden dining. Air cond. Garage pkg. V, AE, DC, MC.
Courtly Martin Cantegrit, owner of this elegant Empire-style establishment, has worked with chef Robert Chassat for more than fifteen years, a most felicitous union. Burgundian classics (game pâtés, jambon persillé, beef bourguignon with fresh tagliatelle) flank subtly lightened dishes (tiny scallops with mushrooms, pan-roasted tuna with pesto sauce), and a top-notch apple tart. Cantegrit's farm supplies the fresh produce. Le Récamier's clientele—politicians, publishers, and media moguls—also enjoy tapping the 100,000-bottle cellar, surely one of the city's best. In summer the restaurant's lovely terrace spills across a sheltered pedestrian zone for fume-free outdoor dining. **C** 400-600 F.

Chez Ribe
15, av. de Suffren
45 66 53 79, fax 47 83 79 63
Closed Sat lunch, Sun. Open until 10:30pm. Priv rm: 30. Terrace dining. Garage pkg. V, AE, DC, MC.
You can still eat here for not much more than 200 F, including a Bordeaux *primeur* or a tasty little white Saumur. Granted, a 168 F prix-fixe meal is not—yet—hard to find, even in Paris, but the frequently changing menu is reliably delicious and well prepared. Recent options have included a tasty terrine de canard, plaice with fresh pasta, and rack of lamb with mild garlic, all

graciously served in turn-of-the-century sur-roundings. **M** 168 F.

Tan Dinh

60, rue de Verneuil
45 44 04 84, fax 45 44 36 93
Closed Sun, Aug. Open until 11pm. No cards.
Tan Dinh's huge wine list has few equals, even among the city's top restaurants—some say it outclasses the food. But Robert and Freddy Vifian are justly proud of their innovative Viet-namese repertoire, which spot-lights light and refined dishes like smoked-goose dumplings, lobster toast, shrimp rolls, chicken with Asian herbs, or veal with betel nuts. If you can resist the cellar's pricier temptations, a dinner here amid the select and stylish Left-Bank crowd need not lead to financial disaster. **C** 300-500 F.

11/20 Thoumieux

79, rue Saint-Dominique - 47 05 49 75
Open daily until midnight. Priv rm: 110. Air cond. No pets. V.
A busy, popular bistro where you can tuck into the hearty classics of Auvergne and the South-west: terrines, cassoulets, duck breast with black-currants, etc. Don't overlook the fine boudin noir, or the cheap-and-cheerful wine list. The dinner crowd is surprisingly glossy. **C** 230 F. **M** 67 F.

Vin sur Vin

20, rue de Monttessuy - 47 05 14 20
Closed Sun, lunch Sat & Mon, Dec 23-Jan 3, Aug 7-21. Open until 10pm. V.
Former sommelier Patrice Vidal has assembled a first-rate cellar made up exclusively of growers' wines, from which he selects a few each week to sell by the glass. They accompany such sturdy bistro standbys as escargots en croûte, veal and vegetable stew, and a tasty pear and chocolate tart. Prices are high and climbing, however, with no prix-fixe relief in sight. **C** 330-430 F.

8TH ARRONDISSEMENT

12/20 Al Ajami

58, rue François-Ier
42 25 38 44, fax 42 56 60 08
Open daily until midnight. Terrace dining. Air cond. V, AE, DC, MC.
Fortunately the menu's perfunctory French of-ferings are outnumbered by authentic dishes from the Lebanese highlands—assorted mezes, chawarma, keftedes, and deliciously sticky pastries. The wines contribute a dash of local color to the refined, gray-and-blue dining room. **M** 99 F (weekday lunch), 119 F (weekdays), 149 F.

12/20 L'Alsace

39, av. des Champs-Élysées
43 59 44 24, fax 42 89 06 62
Open daily 24 hours. Terrace dining. Air cond. Garage pkg. V, AE, DC, MC.
Since this lively brasserie never closes, you can go there any time at all to enjoy perfect oysters, delicious sauerkraut, and the fresh white wines of Alsace. Expect a hospitable welcome, whatever the hour. **C** 200-400 F. **M** 185 F.

Les Ambassadeurs

Hôtel de Crillon, 10, pl. de la Concorde
44 71 16 16, fax 44 71 15 02
Open daily until 10:30pm. Priv rm: 72. Terrace dining. Air cond. No pets. Valet pkg. V, AE, DC, MC.
The magnificent and intimidating dining room, rich with gilt and marble, seems more fitting for an ambassadors' banquet than an intimate din-ner or convivial feast. Diners keep their voices low and their elbows off the table; looks of terror accompany the accidental fall of a fork. Happily, Christian Constant's vivid cuisine goes far to warm up the formal setting. His velouté of Jerusalem artichokes topped with calf's-foot jelly, peppered whiting on polenta with crushed black olives, and sautéed pollack with puréed white beans share an earthy directness that whets the appetite. In a more modern register, he turns out an admirable confit de foie gras with fig purée, a superb sea bream with lemon and fennel, and a truly marvelous double veal chop tenderly simmered in its juices, escorted by braised baby vegetables. The excellent wine list can make an already stiff bill harder to swallow, but sommelier Jean-Claude Maître can usually recommend some more affordable selections. **C** 550-700 F. **M** 340 F (business menu, week-day lunch), 610 F (tasting menu, exc weekday lunch).

L'Avenue

41, av. Montaigne
40 70 14 91, fax 49 52 08 27
Open daily until midnight. Priv rm: 75. Air cond. Pkg. V, AE.
If you book a table in the elegant upstairs dining room, you can mingle with the chic cou-ture and media crowd that flocks into L'Avenue for Christian Hennin's stylish specialties: sea bream with tomato chutney, spicy grilled scam-pi, lamb noisettes with pistou ravioli, and robust *plats du jour*. Desserts are vastly improved, and the cellar holds lots of unpretentious but tasty little wines. Indeed, considering the classy loca-tion at the corner of Avenue Montaigne and Rue François-Ier (the heart of the Golden Triangle), prices are downright reasonable. **C** 220-320 F.

12/20 Bice

Hôtel Balzac, 6, rue Balzac
42 89 86 34, fax 42 25 24 82
Closed Sat lunch, Sun, Dec 22-Jan 2, Aug 4-Sep 1. Open until 11:30pm. Priv rm: 40. Air cond. Pkg. V, AE, DC, MC.
Amiable Italian (or Italian-style) waiters leap and dash among the young, moneyed clientele (Saint-Tropez, *prêt-à-porter*, the Levant) that for-gathers in this refined, blond-wood version of Harry's Bar. If you choose carefully—trofie (house-made pasta), osso buco with risotto alla milanese—you won't be disappointed. Other op-tions tend to be bland and/or overcooked, with the exception of the nicely handled desserts. In any case it's a pricey *pasto*, friends, and the Italian wines are expensive too. **C** 350-450 F.

*The **C** (A la carte) restaurant prices given are for a complete three-course meal for one, including a half-bottle of modest wine and service. **M** (Menus) prices are for a complete fixed-price meal for one, excluding wine (unless otherwise noted).*

Le Bistrot du Sommelier

97, bd Haussmann
42 65 24 85, fax 53 75 23 23
Closed Sat, Sun, Dec 25-Jan 2, Aug. Open until 11pm. Priv rm: 25. Air cond. V, AE, MC.
Crowned "World's Best Sommelier" in 1992, owner Philippe Faure-Brac naturally encourages his chef to cook with wine. Thus, the menu features Bresse chicken au vin du Jura, ris de veau au maury, and rabbit with tiny onions in Chablis. But it's the cellar that captures the true wine buff's interest, with bottles from all over France—and the world. At dinner, a special prix-fixe meal brings six dishes paired with compatible wines. **C** 300-400 F. **M** 370 F (dinner, wine incl).

12/20 Le Bœuf sur le Toit

34, rue du Colisée
43 59 83 80, fax 45 63 45 40
Open daily until 2am. Air cond. V, AE, DC, MC.
From a seat on the mezzanine watch the dazzling swirl of diners and waiters reflected a hundredfold in this mirrored, Art Deco dining room. But don't get so distracted that you can't enjoy the plentiful shellfish platters, the juicy steak with shallots, or the fruity young wines served in *pichets*. **C** 200-300 F. **M** 109 F (lunch, wine incl), 185 F (after 10pm, wine incl).

Le Bristol

Hôtel Bristol, 112, rue du Fg-St-Honoré
42 66 91 45, fax 42 66 68 68
Open daily until 10:30pm. Priv rm: 60. Air cond. No pets. Valet pkg. V, AE, DC, MC.
The atmosphere and prices are about what you'd expect in this heavily guarded hotel near the French President's residence. Seated in the sumptuous wood-paneled dining room or on the garden patio, you'll be served predictably luxurious food (lobster salad, médaillons de Saint-Pierre, tropical fruit laced with Kirsch). The idyll, alas, is sometimes marred by an inattentive waiter or an occasional culinary lapse. The cellar, as you doubtless have guessed, boasts a breathtaking array of expensive vintages. **C** 600-850 F. **M** 330 F, 450 F, 620 F.

12/20 Cap Vernet

82, av. Marceau - 47 20 95 36
Closed Dec 24-25. Open until midnight. Air cond. V, AE, MC.
The 100 F set meal, revised every day, brings such appetizing dishes as a deliciously minty sardine tabbouleh followed by whiting fillet with gnocchi and floating island with green-apple coulis. Fish and shellfish assortments dominate the à la carte offerings. **C** 250-370 F. **M** 158 F (exc Mon lunch, wine incl), 100 F.

Le Carpaccio

Hôtel Royal Monceau, 35-39, av. Hoche
42 99 98 90, fax 42 99 89 94
Closed Aug. Open until 10:30pm. Air cond. No pets. Valet pkg. V, AE, DC, MC.
Executives in expensive suits are the backbone of Le Carpaccio's sleek clientele. Here, in a spectacular winter-garden setting, they feed on scallops wreathed in smoked ham with fava-bean purée, shellfish and assorted fresh vegetables encased in the lightest imaginable tempura batter, dusky cuttlefish tagliatelle

topped with spears of crisp asparagus, and an improbably good raspberry-vinegar gelato. Outrageously priced, these fine dishes (and excellent wines) are served by a rather haughty staff. **C** 450-550 F. **M** 270 F (lunch).

Casa Sansa

45, rue des Mathurins
42 65 81 62, fax 44 94 00 44
Open daily until 1am. Priv rm: 35. Terrace dining. Air cond. Garage pkg. V, AE, MC.
Jean-Marie Pujades is the jovial host of this Catalan outpost, an exuberantly decorated dining room where the fiesta never stops. Suitably vibrant specialties include escalivada (a salad of oven-roasted vegetables), suquet de peix (a lusty seafood stew), squid presented either roasted (a la planxa) or stewed in their ink, escargots à la catalane, and boles de picolat (meatballs in a zesty sauce). The region's heady wines make ideal partners for the food. **C** 170-250 F. **M** 78 F (weekday lunch), 250 F.

12/20 Caviar Kaspia

17, pl. de la Madeleine
42 65 33 32, fax 42 66 60 11
Closed Sun. Open until 12:30am. Priv rm: 25. Air cond. V, AE, DC.
The fine-feathered folk who frequent this dark but charming upper room opposite the Madeleine come to nibble (caviars, salmon roe, smoked sturgeon) rather than feast (smoked fish assortments, borscht, etc.). But all the offerings, large and small, are quite good and are courteously served. Vodka, naturally, is the tipple of choice. **C** 300-500 F.

Chiberta

3, rue A.-Houssaye
45 63 77 90, fax 45 62 85 08
Closed Sat, Sun, Aug. Open until 11pm. Air cond. No pets. V, AE, MC.
Along with Fouquet's, Chiberta is the only haunt of le Tout-Paris left on the Champs Élysées. Nabobs from the worlds of finance and television gather here for lunch, relayed by the *beau monde* in the evening. The dining room is discreet, the modern décor is aging gracefully, the floral displays are as sumptuous as ever, and the food has never been better. Chef Philippe Da Silva executes a menu that highlights sublime sauces and sophisticated herbs and seasonings. Among his recent successes are a salad of red mullet with a coriander jus, pan-seared tuna given a lively touch of chive, turbot braised with bay leaves in a Riesling-based sauce, and stuffed poussin roasted with chanterelles. Along with desserts like the bright grapefruit soup with forest honey and pineapple sorbet, these dishes attest to Da Silva's finesse and polished technique. Proprietor Louis-Noël Richard's passion for red Burgundies is infectious—and fatal for one's bank account! **C** 500-800 F. **M** 290 F.

Clovis

Hôtel Sofitel, 4, av. Bertie-Albrecht
45 61 15 32, fax 42 25 36 81
Closed Sat, Sun, hols, Dec 22-Jan 2, Jul 28-Aug 28. Open until 10:30pm. Priv rm: 70. Air cond. Valet pkg. V, AE, DC, MC.
The understated salmon-pink setting is particularly suited to business lunches, a fact that has not escaped the city's executives. Chef

Dominique Roué has revved up the house repertoire with a perfectly cooked sole fillet abetted by spiced olives and basmati rice, lake char in a sour-cream sauce with Belgian endive, and an array of delicate desserts (try the macaron malaga). Extensive cellar; attentive service. C 350-480 F. M 190 F (dinner), 210 F.

La Couronne

Hôtel Warwick, 5, rue de Berri
45 63 14 11, fax 45 63 75 81
Closed Sat lunch, Sun, hols, Aug. Open until 10:30pm. Priv rm: 100. Air cond. Valet pkg. V, AE, DC, MC.
   Winner of international cooking awards, Paul Van Gessel is in top form these days. A bright Southern touch marked a recent meal here, composed of succulently tender lamb with Niçois vegetables and cracked-wheat salad, a langoustine ragoût with crisp little artichokes and asparagus, and a rich bitter-chocolate cake. The dining room, unfortunately, is stuck into a corner of the Hotel Warwick lobby; that's a shame, because Van Gessel's fine work deserves a larger audience than hotel guests and the business-lunch crowd. C 350-480 F. M 220 F, 270 F.

Diep

55, rue P.-Charron
45 63 52 76, fax 42 56 46 56
Open daily until midnight. Air cond. No pets. Valet pkg. V, AE, DC, MC.
   This is the flagship of the Diep family's restaurant fleet. The décor is Bangkok swank and the food Asian eclectic, but your best bets are the vibrantly spiced and herbed Thai dishes. You'll make a memorable feast if you order the steamed stuffed crab with plum sauce, pork satay dressed with a sweet vinaigrette, giant shrimp sautéed with basil and onions, and the lipsmacking Thai rice dotted with bits of chicken and shellfish. Desserts are not Diep's strong suit: enough said. C 250-310 F. M 420 F (for 2), 780 F (for 4).

11/20 Drugstore des Champs-Élysées

133, av. des Champs-Élysées
47 23 54 34, fax 47 23 00 96
Open daily until 2am. Priv rm: 300. Terrace dining. Air cond. No pets. V, AE, MC.
   Believe it or not, the food at this landmark of 1960s chic is not bad at all. The main-course salads, grills, and crisp pommes frites go very well with the noisy, bustling atmosphere. C 150-300 F.

Chez Edgard

4, rue Marbeuf
47 20 51 15, fax 47 23 94 29
Closed Sun, Aug 1-16. Open until 12:30am. Priv rm: 38. Terrace dining. Valet pkg. V, AE, DC.
   Just because it has often been said that the *gratin* of French politics eats here, don't expect to see Édouard Balladur or Jacques Chirac seated across from you. "Monsieur Paul" serves up to 500 meals here each day, and in any case the Parisian powers-that-be are always whisked off to the quiet private rooms upstairs. Downstairs, amid the typically Gallic brouhaha, the rest of us can choose from a wide range of dishes, from fresh thon à la basquaise to onglet

à l'échalote, all prepared with care and skill. C 250-350 F. M 250 F, 295 F & 355 F (wine incl).

Les Élysées du Vernet

Hôtel Vernet, 25, rue Vernet
44 31 98 00, fax 44 31 85 69
Closed Sat, Sun, hols, Dec 25-31, Jul 31-Aug 31. Open until 10pm. Priv rm: 22. Air cond. No pets. Valet pkg. V, AE, DC, MC.
   Which way to the Riviera please? We'd suggest this elegant address just off the Champs-Élysées. Although you won't have a view of the Mediterranean, chef Alain Solivérès brings the fragrances and flavors of Provence into the glass-roofed dining room. Why not whet your appetite with a dish of brandade-stuffed red peppers before you move on to a magnificent dish of fresh crab with pumpkin gnocchi perfumed by pungent pistou, or a pinkly roasted pigeon flanked by a hachis of its giblets and black olives. To wind things up, try the bitter-chocolate ravioli, a clever and delicious conceit. Competent, attentive service; reasonably priced cellar. C 360-580 F. M 290 F (weekday lunch), 420 F (weekday dinner).

L'Étage Baumann

15, rue Marbeuf
47 20 11 11, fax 47 23 69 65
Closed wk of Aug 15. Open until 12:30am. Priv rm: 22. Air cond. Valet pkg. V, AE, DC.
   The name is new and so is the freshly refurbished décor, but the menu still features glossy fresh shellfish, colossal choucroutes (topped with fish, or ham shanks, or confit de canard...), and expertly aged meats from Scotland and Southwest France. We like the chocolate cake, too, and the thirst-quenching Alsatian wines. C 180-300 F. M 118 F, 150 F

Fakhr el Dine

3, rue Q.-Bauchart
47 23 74 24, fax 47 27 11 39
Open daily until midnight. Air cond. V, AE, DC, MC.
   Delicious Lebanese mezes dazzle the eye as they delight the palate: bone-marrow salad, brains in lemon sauce, spinach fritters, fried lamb's sweetbreads, etc. These tidbits are offered in batches of 8, 10, 15, or 20, depending on the size of the company and your appetite. C 300-400 F. M 250 F (Sun, lunch weekday & Sat, wine incl), 190 F (exc Sat dinner), 335 F & 385 F (wine incl), 150 F (lunch).

La Fermette Marbeuf 1900

5, rue Marbeuf
47 20 63 53, fax 40 70 02 11
Open daily until 11:30pm. Terrace dining. Air cond. V, AE, DC, MC.
   Owner Jean Laurent now pours wines from his personal vineyard in Ramatuelle for his celebrity pals (and the rest of us), who flock to the Fermette for honest, unpretentious fare: andouillette sausage, sole beurre blanc, fillet steak, and so on. Moderate prices, quality foodstuffs, and affable service are the rule in the stunning Salle 1900, an Art Nouveau master-piece. The fine 160 F set menu is now served both noon and night. C 280-320 F. M 160 F

Restaurant names in red draw attention to restaurants that offer particularly good value.

Flora Danica

142, av. des Champs-Élysées - 44 13 86 26
Closed Christmas eve, May 1. Open until 11pm. Priv rm: 60. Terrace dining. Air cond. V, AE, DC, MC.

Salmon—smoked, pickled, marinated, or grilled—and delicious tender herring prepared in every imaginable way are the stars of this limited menu. Upstairs, more elaborate (and costly) dishes are served (there's an interesting terrine of foie gras and reindeer). If the weather is fine, ask to be seated on the patio behind the Flora Danica. **C** 220-400 F. **M** 200 F (beer incl), 270 F.

 Fouquet's

99, av. des Champs-Élysées
47 23 70 60, fax 47 20 08 69
Open daily until 1am. Priv rm: 160. Terrace dining. Valet pkg. V, AE, DC.

After a bout of bad publicity, Fouquet's seems poised for a fresh departure. This listed landmark on the Champs-Élysées (in whose recent revamp Fouquet's played an important part) has acquired the services of Philippe Dorange, one of Jacques Maximin's star pupils. He supervises an attractive menu (roast cod served with white-bean purée, marinated scallops rémoulade...) executed by Laurent Broussier. Fouquet's owners now hope to lure back the fashionable lunchers who have gravitated down the Champs to the Cercle Ledoyen. Here's wishing them luck... **C** 350-450 F. **M** 330 F, 350 F, 400 F, 450 F.

10/20 Chez Francis

7, pl. de l'Alma
47 20 86 83, fax 47 20 43 26
Open daily until 1am. Priv rm: 60. Terrace dining. Air cond. Valet pkg. V, AE, DC, MC.

The smart patrons are reflected and multiplied by rows of engraved mirrors—so much the better for them, since they obviously take more pleasure in whom they're seeing than in what they're eating (though the canard en daube au gratin de macaroni is quite good, as are the shellfish). **C** 200-350 F. **M** 180 F.

11/20 Germain

19, rue J.-Mermoz - 43 59 29 24
Closed Sat, Sun. Open until 9:30pm. No pets.

One of the last bastions of French home cooking anywhere near the Champs-Élysées, this 30-seat restaurant offers beef bourguignon, coq au vin, etc. at popular prices. **C** 180 F.

 Le Grenadin

44-46, rue de Naples
45 63 28 92, fax 45 61 24 76
Closed Sat (exc dinner Sep-Apr), Sun. Open until 10:30pm. Priv rm: 14. Air cond. Pkg. V, AE, DC, MC.

Patrick Cirotte's newly refurbished dining room is more in tune with his intrepid, good-humored cuisine. Pungent herbs and bold harmonies are the hallmarks of his current repertoire. Cirotte's affinity for keen, acidulous flavors is evident in his crab rillettes with leeks in a sprightly vinaigrette, a salad of cabbage and sea urchins, or veal fillet flanked by asparagus and kumquats. But he can also strike a suave note, as in a saddle of rabbit cloaked with a mild, creamy garlic sauce. Desserts don't get short shrift either: his rich chocolate cake with pumpkin coulis, thin sugar tart with tea ice

cream, and flawless millefeuille tempt even flagging appetites. Mireille Cirotte offers reliable advice on wine (note that Sancerres are the pride of her cellar). Just next door is Berry's, Cirotte's successful, value-priced bistro annex. **C** 380-430 F. **M** 188 F, 238 F, 298 F, 320 F.

 Le Jardin des Cygnes

Hôtel Prince de Galles, 33, av. George-V
47 23 55 11, fax 47 20 96 92
Open daily until 10:30pm. Priv rm: 180. Garden dining. Air cond. No pets. Valet pkg. V, AE, DC, MC.

Four months of extensive redecorating have resulted in a newly spacious yet cozy dining room that opens onto a charming patio. It's an alluring stage for Dominique Cécillon's sunny, flavorful cuisine. Recent offerings have included ravioles of foie gras with peppery goat cheese, a subtly spiced pigeon pastilla, pan-roasted red mullet with Provençal vegetables, and white-bean cassoulet enriched with red mullet, lobster, and scallops. All are very nearly as delicious as they are expensive, and are delivered to your table by a high-class staff. If economy is your aim, head over instead to the hotel's Regency Bar, for a good, light little meal. **C** 350-600 F. **M** 260 F (exc Sun lunch), 240 F (Sun lunch).

 Le Jardin du Royal Monceau

Hôtel Royal Monceau, 35, av. Hoche
42 99 98 70, fax 42 99 89 94
Open daily until 10:30pm. Garden dining. Air cond. No pets. Heated pool. Valet pkg. V, AE, DC, MC.

You step into another world when you enter the candy-pink dining room, its french windows opening onto manicured lawns and immaculate flower beds. Surrounded by buildings, this garden seems to have been brought to central Paris by the wave of a magic wand. The same spell operates in the kitchen, where Bruno Cirino, a Southern chef of considerable gifts, conjures up radiantly flavorful Provençal fare.

Cirino is no recent convert to this now familiar repertoire. Provençal cooking is his birthright, and he has a native's knack for finding the foodstuffs that make his cuisine unimpeachably authentic. Like the asparagus (thick as tree trunks!) that compose, along with tiny artichokes and haricots verts, a sumptuous vegetable starter dressed with truffled vinaigrette. Or the chapon de mer and galinette, Mediterranean fishes that he respectively braises in a saffron-stained broth or pan-roasts with squid, green garlic, tomatoes, and picholine olives.

Luscious fruit desserts display the same sunny spirit: braised burlat cherries, verbena-scented baked peaches, pineapple perfumed with lemongrass and swirled with lime sabayon... Service is impeccable, and a youthful sommelier provides sound advice on a wine list studded with such rarities as an amazing late-harvested Sancerre. **C** 490-700 F. **M** 290 F (weekday lunch), 390 F (weekday dinner).

 Lasserre

17, av. F.-Roosevelt
43 59 53 43, fax 45 63 72 23
Closed Mon lunch, Sun, Jul 30-Aug 28. Open until 10:30pm. Priv rm: 56. Air cond. No pets. Valet pkg. V, AE, MC.

One of the few surviving examples of *le grand restaurant à la française*, this grandiose establishment merits your attention for the ethnological interest it presents. Nowhere else is the service so minutely choreographed, the atmosphere so festive yet well-bred (piano music, soft lights, glowing silver, silken carpets...). Don't forget to look up as Lasserre's retractable roof brings you (weather and visibility permitting) the stars. As you look back down you'll notice that the menu is a compendium of costly culinary clichés: duck à l'orange, tournedos béarnaise, and crêpes flambées (too often marred, lately, by heavy sauces and overcooking). But no matter how hard you look at the wine list, you won't find a bottle priced under 300 F! C 700-1,000 F.

Laurent
41, av. Gabriel
42 25 00 39, fax 45 62 45 21
Closed Sat lunch, Sun, hols. Open until 11pm. Priv rm: 84. Terrace dining. No pets. Valet pkg. V, AE, MC.
The economic climate is warming up! At Laurent this welcome change in the weather has brought smiles back to the waiters' faces, and the *carte,* too, reflects the sunnier trend, with lighter dishes and sprightlier sauces. Philippe Braun executes a menu designed by his mentor, Joël Robuchon, which includes fresh anchovies on a bed of fresh-tasting vegetable brunoise, duck liver set atop black beans fired up with hot chilis, and a superb veal chop escorted by tender hearts of lettuce in a savory jus. Now, you may have to sell off a few T-bonds to pay the bill—or else you can do as many of the other high-powered patrons do, and order the excellent 380 F prix-fixe menu. Whatever course you choose, sommelier Patrick Lair will advise you on the appropriate wine. C 800-1,000 F. M 380 F.

Cercle Ledoyen
Carré des Champs-Élysées
47 42 23 23, fax 47 42 55 01
Closed Sat, Sun, Aug. Open until 10:30pm. Air cond. Garage pkg. Valet pkg. V, MC.
Jacques Grange is the man behind the elegantly spare interior of this spacious restaurant, now a favorite haunt of the city's chic and famous. Jean-Paul Arabian oversees the impeccable service, while Ghislaine Arabian does the same for the concise menu. Zesty starters like mackerel in white wine or salmon with horseradish segue into baked bass with roasted apples or rabbit chasseur, and such toothsome sweets as tiramisù or dôme au chocolat. Irrigated by modest but tasty little wines, these offerings add up to perfectly modern meals at a perfectly moderate price. C 250-300 F.

Ledoyen
Carré des Champs-Élysées
47 42 23 23, fax 47 42 55 01
Closed Sat, Sun, Aug. Open until 10:30pm. Priv rm: 150. Air cond. Valet pkg. V, AE, DC, MC.
Lille's Ghislaine Arabian, whom we once dubbed "the best *cuisinière* in the North," has proved her mettle at the luxurious and eminently Parisian Ledoyen. After introducing the locals to Flemish flavors—sauces laced with beer and gin, smoked mussels, gingerbread, and pungent North-country cheeses—she has shown that she can also work wonders outside of her regional

register. Thus, while Ghislaine's signature dishes (crispy hops fritters, crayfish with toasted barley, waffles topped with ice cream redolent of cherry-flavored kriek beer) hold their own on the menu, she balances them with, for example, a tarragon-scented Breton lobster with marinated lettuce, warm calf's head sausage with firm little potatoes, sweet-and-sour duck with rhubarb, and a startlingly good chaud-froid of lightly smoked chicken. Desserts are dazzlingly original. Where else could one find gingerbread and caramelized pears gratinéed with fromage blanc, or a sweet potato simmered to melting tenderness in gueuze beer, or a crème brûlée of incomparable suavity, perfumed with cinnamon and orange? Such marvels have their price, of course, but we say they're worth it! C 550-950 F. M 290 F (weekday lunch), 520 F (weekdays), 590 F, 750 F.

Lucas-Carton
9, pl. de la Madeleine
42 65 22 90, fax 42 65 06 23
Closed Sat lunch, Sun, Dec 22-Jan 4, Jul 29-Aug 25. Open until 10:30pm. Priv rm: 14. Air cond. No pets. Valet pkg. V, MC.
Two camps—one violently pro, the other determinedly con—have turned the Gault Millau office into a battlefield! The bone of contention? The famous half-point that is our highest accolade, our recognition of a chef's supremecy over all but a handful of his peers. One camp avers that Alain Senderens deserves the honor; the adverse camp just as adamantly refuses to bestow it. And since unanimity is our rule for awarding the coveted 19.5, we've arrived at an unprecedented compromise: we're giving Senderens four toques—but no numerical rating. For the record, here's the gist of the opposing arguments.
Not even the naysayers question Senderens's prodigious talent and imagination. Yet, they maintain, nowadays he is more restaurateur than chef. The stoves at Lucas-Carton are manned by the talented Bernard Guéneron, who interprets his mentor's style and ideas. But even the most brilliant disciple (so goes the objectors' argument) cannot replace the master. For proof, they advance Exhibits A, B, and C: breaded turbot à la Kiev; langoustines encased in fried vermicelli and garnished with asparagus and a truffled egg; and croustillant of veal sweetbreads with a novel accompaniment of spiced crayfish and...popcorn! All these dishes are interesting, ingenious, delicious even: but where (they ask) is the heart? The emotion?
In reply, Senderens supporters evoke the thrill of sampling his now classic foie gras de canard steamed in a cabbage leaf—a pure marvel of harmonious flavors. They also point to a fabulous starter based on lobster: first poached, then briefly baked and dressed with cask-aged vinegar, the crustacean is presented with its claw wrapped in paper-thin pastry. Finally, his fans triumphantly cite Senderens's extraordinary saddle of rabbit: stuffed with foie gras, glazed with sugar, cinnamon, and other spices, then enveloped in a crackling phyllo crust—a miraculous dish, made more marvelous still by a glass of vintage Hermitage. You want art? You want emotion? It's all right here!

As you can see, we had reached an impasse. So we'll leave it to you to decide if Alain Senderens merits 19 or 19.5. All you need is a reservation—and sufficient cash to pay one of the world's brawniest tabs! **C** 800-1,500 F and up. **M** 375 F (lunch), 780 F, 880 F, 1,200 F.

 La Luna
69, rue du Rocher
42 93 77 61, fax 40 08 02 44
Closed Sun. Open until 11pm. Air cond. V, AE, MC.
La Luna lost some of its luster when it moved from the Left Bank to its present location near Villiers, but the tides still deposit first-quality seafood right at the door. The retro décor doesn't give a clue to the kitchen's resolutely modern manner of preparing fish: the chef highlights its natural flavors with short cooking times and a light hand. The menu changes from day to day, but you could start out with a trio of tartares (raw salmon, tuna, and sea bream), or a heap of tiny flash-fried squid, then proceed to langoustines baked with rosemary blossoms, sautéed baby soles, or a perfect charcoal-grilled sea bass. Each day, owner Jean-Pierre Durand offers two wine "specials" priced under 100 F. **C** 280-350 F.

 Maison Blanche
15, av. Montaigne
47 23 55 99, fax 47 20 09 56
Closed Sat lunch, Sun. Open until 11pm. Priv rm: 60. Terrace dining. Air cond. Valet pkg. V, AE.
Here in La Maison Blanche atop the Théâtre des Champs-Élysées, diners look out on the glittering dome of the Invalides, the shimmering Seine, and the magnificent buildings that line the quais. In contrast, the dining room sports a spare, avant-garde look that is vaguely Californian. The service, we're pleased to report, is now trouble-free, and the wide-ranging cellar is run by a competent sommelier. So far so good, you say, but what about the food? It's terrific: José Martinez's talent shines brighter every day, in dishes that deftly combine simplicity and sophistication. Don't miss his sun-dried–tomato ravioli, or succulent pan-roasted veal chop with walnuts and chanterelles, or his lush almond cake with apricots. In a word, we've got a winner! **C** 500-600 F.

La Marée
1, rue Daru
43 80 20 00, fax 48 88 04 04
Closed Sat, Sun, Aug. Open until 10:30pm. Priv rm: 36. Air cond. Valet pkg. V, AE, DC.
For the last few years Éric Trompier has worked hard to bring the family's restaurant up to snuff; we're gratified to see him succeed. Forgoing routine, Trompier's chef has composed a menu of seductive, modern dishes that display unerring technique and imaginative flavors. We're thinking of the lobster salad with beet chips, a mile-high millefeuille brimming with fresh vegetables, brill encased in potato "scales" and embellished with a rosemary cream sauce, and la petite marmite tropézienne, a seafood extravaganza that brings all the perfumes of the Riviera to your table. These and other dishes are served, as always, in splendidly comfortable surroundings by a courteous, even benevolent staff. Take your time over the wine list, which features some exceptional bargains. **C** 500-900 F.

Maxim's
3, rue Royale
42 65 27 94, fax 40 17 02 91
Closed Sun. Open until 10:30pm (Sat 11:30pm). Priv rm: 90. Air cond. No pets. Valet pkg. V, AE, DC, MC.
Rumors were rife a few months back that Pierre Cardin was looking to divest himself of Maxim's; the sorry state of the restaurant's façade lent credence to those whispers. Though nothing has occurred to date to confirm—or belie—the gossip, the heart seems to have gone out of this once-glamorous Belle Époque monument. Meanwhile, the stylish staff soldiers on in the half-empty dining room, as if nothing were amiss; and Maxim's most faithful patrons still come in for Michel Menant's coquilles Saint-Jacques à la nage, sole Albert, poularde truffée, and other proficient but vaguely fusty offerings. Perhaps the fun-loving, free-spending Parisians who kept Maxim's legend alive are just waiting for a signal to fill the place with sophisticated chatter and start the Champagne corks popping once again—but who will give that signal? And when? Here's hoping it comes soon! **C** 600-1,000 F.

Daniel Metery
4, rue de l'Arcade
42 65 53 13, fax 42 66 53 82
Closed Sat lunch, Sun, 1st wk of Aug. Open until 10:15pm. Priv rm: 24. Pkg. V, AE.
Daniel Metery has declared war on indigestible prices. He's concocted a trio of judicious single-price menus that let you savor any dish you like from his intelligent, subtle repertoire, with no worries about the cost. We recently composed a commendable meal from such options as artichoke croustillant with plump escargots in a parsley jus, lamb enhanced by a pleasingly sharp vinegar sauce with a faint hint of coconut, and warm madeleines with honey-walnut ice cream. The eclectic wine list has an interesting Bordeaux section. **M** 250 F (dinner), 175 F, 235 F.

11/20 Mollard
Hôtel Garnier,
113, rue St-Lazare - 43 87 50 22
Open daily until 1am. Garage pkg. V, AE, DC, MC.
An extraordinary turn-of-the-century ceramic mural depicts destinations of the trains that depart from the Gare Saint-Lazare across the street. The food is not quite so enchanting. Safe bets include the very good shellfish platter, skate with browned butter, and refreshing crab and salmon tartare. Courteous welcome, discreet service. **C** 220-500 F. **M** 185 F (wine incl).

12/20 L'Obélisque
Hôtel de Crillon,
10, pl. de la Concorde - 44 71 15 15
Closed hols, Aug. Open until 10:30pm. Priv rm: 72. Terrace dining. Air cond. Valet pkg. V, AE, DC, MC.
To eat at the Hôtel de Crillon without breaking the bank, try its other, less formal restaurant. You'll still benefit from top-notch service and a menu supervised by Christian Constant, chef of Les Ambassadeurs (see above). The food is classic bistro fare: pig's trotter sausage with potato purée, pot-au-feu, calf's head, tongue, and brains in sauce gribiche. Sixteen wines are offered by the glass or half-liter jug. **C** 300-420 F. **M** 270 F.

Au Petit Montmorency

5, rue Rabelais
42 25 11 19
Closed Sat, Sun, Aug. Open until 10:30pm. Priv rm: 10. Air cond. No pets. V, MC.

Gun-toting soldiers assigned to the nearby Israeli embassy made Au Petit Montmorency the best-guarded restaurant in Paris! Chef-owner Daniel Bouché, however, found the military presence a trifle overwhelming. So he jumped at the chance to acquire a shop next door to his restaurant, which gave him a new address and an unimpeded entrance. Architect Pierre Parat transformed the space into an elegant, distinctive dining room with red-lacquer walls and midnight-blue seating—a bold scheme that stands out from the all the pink, beige, and gray one sees nowadays.

In short, there's never been a better time to discover Bouché's splendid repertoire, with its soupe aux cèpes, oysters in a fragrant chervil broth, an exquisite rabbit pâté enlivened with chutney, rich duck liver accented by a peppery caramelized sauce, or a sumptuous truffled potato tourte. And by all means save room for the splendid croquem-bouche, a tower of cream puffs with a quartet of different fillings, or for the airy and delicate hazelnut soufflé. Note too that if your fancy runs to game, you should make a point of dining *chez* Bouché in the hunting season. And in every season, Nicole Bouché will help you choose the perfect wine to partner your meal. Lulled by this deliciousness, your shock may be all the greater when the waiter presents the bill. **C** 450-800 F. **M** 250 F (weekdays).

Les Princes

Hôtel George-V, 31, av. George-V
47 23 54 00, fax 47 20 40 00
Open daily until 10:30pm. Priv rm: 460. Terrace dining. Air cond. Valet pkg. V, AE, DC, MC.

In fine weather, book a table on the beautiful flower-covered patio, far more inviting than the cavernous 1930s–style dining room. Wherever you sit, you're sure to savor Jacky Joyeux's attractive menu, filled with piquant, exotic touches. We especially like his cocktail of scallops and lobster with sesame-papaya dressing and the tournedos of sea bream and red mullet in a sauce hinting of coconut. For dessert, try the delectable crêpes soufflées with apple compote. The cellar has improved too, in our estimation, and the service, as always, is impeccable. **C** 450-750 F. **M** 240 F, 450 F.

Le Régence

Hôtel Plaza Athénée, 25, av. Montaigne
47 23 78 33, fax 47 20 20 70
Open daily until 10:15pm. Priv rm: 100. Garden dining. Air cond. Valet pkg. V, AE, DC, MC.

Chef Gérard Sallé's light, spare style has transformed what used to be a pretty stuffy menu. Lobster soufflé and mixed grill have given way to the likes of salmon and bass tartare dressed with fragrant olive oil, braised sea bream with shallots and a zest of coriander, moist charcoal-grilled sea bass, and Bresse chicken simmered en cocotte with tender apples. Flavors are fresh and precisely defined; the ingredients are absolutely prime. The cellar, filled exclusively with mature bottles, is ruinously expensive, but that doesn't seem to bother the wealthy diners who

frequent this opulently luxurious room. Perfect service. **C** 550-700 F. **M** 330 F (w-e).

Régine's Montaigne

14, rue de Marignan
40 76 34 44, fax 40 76 34 34
Closed Aug 1-15. Open until 10:30pm. Priv rm: 70. Air cond. Garage pkg. V, AE, DC, MC.

This pleasantly cozy and intimate restaurant, attached to the Marignan theater, is concealed behind an extremely discreet façade that is easy to miss. Once inside, you'll be warmly welcomed and invited to partake of Antoine Anclin's delicious Provençal cooking: tender baby squid, for example, with a zingy eggplant garnish, or rack of lamb enhanced by a savory jus, and a colorful dessert composed of mandarin oranges and tangy tomato jam. The cellar is small but select. **C** 260-330 F. **M** 180 F, 250 F.

Le Relais Vermeer

Hôtel Golden Tulip,
218, rue du Faubourg-St-Honoré
49 53 03 03, fax 40 75 02 00
Closed Sun, hols, Aug. Open until 10pm. Priv rm: 195. Air cond. Pkg. V, AE, DC, MC.

A luxurious restaurant for a luxurious hotel, owned by the Dutch Golden Tulip chain. In a restful gray-blue-and-pink dining room, sample tasty rabbit terrine with figs, John Dory with Belgian endive, delicate sweetbreads, and gratin de fruits au champagne prepared by the aptly named chef, Frédéric Lecuisinier. **C** 270-430 F. **M** 195 F.

12/20 Sébillon Élysées

66, rue P.-Charron
43 59 28 15, fax 43 59 30 00
Open daily until midnight. Priv rm: 60. Air cond. Valet pkg. V, AE, DC, MC.

As in the sister establishment in Neuilly (see *The Suburbs*), excellent but expensive shellfish platters are followed here by Sébillon's famous leg of lamb, cooked to rosy tenderness and carved before your eyes. Elegant décor, energetic service. **C** 200-400 F.

Shing-Jung

7, rue Clapeyron - 45 22 21 06
Open daily until midnight. No pets. V, AE, DC, MC.

The smiling and cooperative owner of this unprepossessing establishment will try to convince you that Koreans are far more generous than their Japanese neighbors. Indeed, a colossal assortment of raw fish, listed on the menu as "medium", comprised sea bream, salmon, tuna, brill, and mackerel. For the same money (120 F) most Japanese places would serve about one-quarter the quantity. Other unusual and tasty offerings are jellyfish salad, barbecued beef strips, a hotpot of vegetables and beef, and stuffed lentil-flour crêpes. Everything is delicious and incredibly inexpensive. **C** 120 F. **M** 65 F (weekdays).

Stresa

7, rue de Chambiges - 47 23 51 62
Closed Sat dinner, Sun, Dec 20-Jan 3, Aug. Open until 10:30pm. Priv rm: 12. Terrace dining. Air cond. Pkg. V, AE, DC.

This shabby but somehow soothing dining room is always full of press, fashion, and theater people who love the antipasti drizzled with fruity

Tuscan olive oil, the toothsome osso buco, and the smooth tiramisù prepared by Marco Faiola. Claudio and Toni Faiola seat their guests with a sure social sense of who's up, who's down, who's in, who's out. **C** 270-370 F.

Taillevent
15, rue Lamennais
44 95 15 01, fax 42 25 95 18
Closed Sat, Sun, Jul 23-Aug 22. Open until 10:30pm. Priv rm: 32. Air cond. No pets. Valet pkg. V, AE, DC.

Though he keeps one eye on his newest project, the resuscitated Prunier-Traktir restaurant (*see* sixteenth arrondissement), and another on the grandiose Château Français that he opened in Tokyo with his pal, Joël Robuchon, Jean-Claude Vrinat always knows exactly what's cooking at his cherished Taillevent. In the kitchen Philippe Legendre, formerly number two here, is fully in charge and obviously at ease in his job. He delivers a refined, brilliantly realized repertoire that perfectly suits Taillevent's conservative yet sophisticated clientele. So attuned is Legendre to the tastes of his public that he can even risk offering a few rustic *plats*, like pig's foot sausage—though it's truffled, of course—and still garner applause. But most of the menu is more classically inclined: creamy crab soup with panisses (chickpea-flour crêpes), vivid sea-urchin mousse with asparagus tips, red mullet stuffed with black olives, sweetly spiced sea bass with carrots, and a rabbit and spinach pie redolent of wild thyme. Among the wonderful desserts, a luscious caramel and gingerbread "fantasy" stands out in our memory.

Some Taillevent habitués may be startled to observe that the dining room has been—discreetly!—remodeled: the bay window is larger, the decoration has a spruce, youthful look. But one thing that will never change here is the incomparable quality of the cellar, brimful of rare and glorious (occasionally affordable) wines selected by Vrinat and his daughter, Sabine. And as always at Taillevent, the service functions at the highest level of unobtrusive efficiency. **C** 700-900 F.

Le Trente
Fauchon, 30, pl. de la Madeleine
47 42 56 58, fax 42 66 38 95
Closed Sun. Open until 10:30pm. Priv rm: 20. Garden dining. Air cond. Valet pkg. V, AE, DC, MC.

Whoever dreamed up the name (Le Trente—30—is the building's address) of Fauchon's restaurant won't win any prizes for creativity, but the decorator might, for his "Roman fantasy" interior complete with atrium, columns, and *trompe-l'œil* paintings. More patrons show up at lunch than at dinner to feed on Bruno Deligne's attractive offerings: a bracing tartare of salmon and John Dory, grilled sea bass with sauce vierge, and poached Bresse chicken with vegetables. These low-fat options leave plenty of leeway to indulge in the stupendous pastries crafted by Pierre Hermé. **C** 350-500 F. **M** 240 F (dinner).

*Remember to call ahead to **reserve your table**, and please, if you cannot honor your reservation, be courteous and let the restaurant know.*

12/20 Le Val d'Or
28, av. F.-Roosevelt
43 59 95 81
Lunch only. Closed Sat, Sun. V.

Madame Rongier holds firmly to the traditions of French home cooking, pleasing her patrons with beef in bone-marrow sauce and lapin à la moutarde, escorted by well-chosen wines at reasonable "bistro" prices. The ground-floor bar stays open at night, serving wine by the glass, charcuterie, and sandwiches. **C** 250-300 F.

Vancouver
4, rue A.-Houssaye
42 56 77 77, fax 42 56 50 52
Closed Sat, Sun, hols, Aug. Open until 10pm. Air cond. Valet pkg. V, AE.

He shouts, he moans, he never admits he's wrong—but we can't stay mad long at Jean-Louis Decout. Heck, a man who cooks as well as he does can't be all bad! Decout has an instinctive, limpid way of handling fish and shellfish. His style delivers all of the seafood's natural goodness along with a discreet but brilliant touch that puts the briny flavors into even sharper focus. After a plate of perfectly delicious little rock lobsters roasted with the merest hint of herbs and spice, we greedily devoured a smooth red-mullet brandade served with a fillet of the same fish and an anise-scented tomate confite. Nor did we leave a speck of the sweet-and-sour sea bream, its crisp skin "lacquered" with apple cider. Dessert? Of course! How could we re-sist the feather-light fruit tartlets or the lush chocolate éclairs? Chantal Decout welcomes guests with warm hospitality into a lovely bilevel dining room done in tones of ivory with Art Deco stained glass. **C** 320-420 F. **M** 190 F, 380 F.

Chez Vong
27, rue du Colisée
43 59 77 12, fax 43 59 59 27
Closed Sun. Open until midnight. Priv rm: 60. Air cond. Valet pkg. V, AE, DC.

Here's everyone's dream of a Chinese restaurant: embroidered silk, furniture inlaid with mother-of-pearl, lots of little nooks, an air of mystery, and dishes named "quail in a nest of happiness" or "merry shrimps." The cooking is quite well done. Oddly enough, the cellar is rich in fine (and costly) claret. **C** 280-360 F. **M** 250 F (for 10 pers min).

Yvan
1 bis, rue J.-Mermoz
43 59 18 40, fax 45 63 78 69
Closed Sat lunch, Sun. Open until midnight. Air cond. Valet pkg. V, AE, DC.

Yvan Zaplatilek is café society's darling, but he is also a hard-working chef who gives his customers very good food at moderate prices in a most elegant setting. The menu is primarily French, with an occasional Belgian touch here and there (mussels and fries, rabbit ravioli in a beer-based sauce, cod water-zoï). Yvan also has a penchant for exotic seasonings, and turns out an excellent lotte with ginger, foie gras showered with sesame seeds, and veal kidneys spiced with cumin. Note that his newest venture, Le Petit Yvan, just next door, offers an unbeatable all-in menu for 138 F (tel. 42 89 49 65). **C** 250-400 F. **M** 168 F, 188 F, 238 F, 278 F, 298 F.

L'INSTANT
TAITTINGER

UNE HEURE ET DEMIE PASSEE DANS VOTRE ETABLISSEMENT EST LE
PREMIER DES PRIVILEGES. LE SECOND EST D'Y BOIRE DE L'EAU D'EVIAN.

EVIAN. L'EAU MINERALE DES MEILLEURES TABLES DU MONDE.

9TH ARRONDISSEMENT

12/20 L'Alsaco
10, rue Condorcet - 45 26 44 31
Closed Sat lunch, Sun, Dec 24-Jan 4, Aug. Open until 11pm. Priv rm: 40. V.
Look beyond the unremarkable façade and discover an authentic Alsatian *winstub*, decked out in traditional painted wood paneling. Invariably crammed with regulars, L'Alsaco serves a generous rendition of choucroute garnie, a crisp-crusted cream and onion tart (flammekueche), and potatoes blanketed with savory melted Munster cheese and crunchy bits of bacon. To drink, there are Rieslings and Pinot Blancs galore, as well as a huge selection of clear fruit brandies. **C** 150-230 F. **M** 78 F (weekday lunch), 85 F (dinner), 168 F.

Le Bistrot Blanc
52, rue Blanche - 42 85 05 30
Closed Sat, Sun, Aug. Open until 10pm. V, AE, MC.
Bruno Borni, a Marseille native who held the rank of sauce chef at La Tour d'Argent (his sauces are indeed excellent: concentrated, light, and fragrant), cooks with a lilting Provençal accent. Recommended are his fricasséed scallops in tomato coulis, red-mullet fillets with a zingy garnish of tapenade, pigeon baked in a salt crust and, to finish, the citrus fruit "marvel." Charming atmosphere; limited cellar. **C** 250-350 F. **M** 85 F.

La Casa Olympe
48, rue St-Georges
42 85 26 01, fax 45 26 49 33
Closed 1st 3 wks of Aug, Christmas wk. Open until 11pm. No pets. V.
Olympe is back, now occupying the former Casa Miguel, long the city's cheapest deal, with a philanthropically priced 5 F set meal. The wonderful menu reflects Olympe at her best, as though she knew only one way to cook: the right way. Her fans rejoiced to rediscover tried-and-tested favorites like tuna with bacon and onions, guinea-hen ravioli au jus, and spiced roast duckling, as well as such cheeky newcomers as croustillants de boudin au mesclun, chestnut-flour galette topped with spinach and a poached egg, or braised rabbit perfumed with basil on a golden bed of polenta. There is also a marmite brimming with herbed shellfish and tomatoes, whole roast sea bream with rosemary splendidly served on a copper platter, and a magnificent veal chop emboldened with a soupçon of chopped chili and a creamy lemon sauce. Homey desserts include rice pudding and ginger-bread with custard sauce. The wine list is similarly unpretentious and appealing. The premises are small (not to say cramped) though prettily painted in warm tones of yellow and burnt sienna. **C** 220-250 F. **M** 180 F (weekdays).

12/20 La Champagne
10 bis, pl. de Clichy - 48 74 44 78
Open daily until 3am. Priv rm: 30. Air cond. No pets. V, AE, DC.
Until the small hours you can join the carefree, festive crowd that pays high prices for homard flambé, onion soup, oysters, and sauerkraut at this effervescent restaurant. Ask for a table in the attractive upstairs room. **C** 250-500 F. **M** 119 F, 149 F.

Charlot
"Roi des Coquillages," 81, bd de Clichy (pl. de Clichy) - 48 74 49 64
Open daily until 1am. Priv rm: 30. Air cond. Valet pkg. V, AE, DC, MC.
A fine view of the Place de Clichy, a warm welcome, and attentive service will take your mind off the overbearing Art Deco interior. Sparkling fresh oysters, spectacular shellfish assortments, a generous bouillabaisse à la marseillaise, and lobsters prepared every possible way are the staples here. **C** 300-500 F. **M** 185 F (Apr-Sep), 225 F (Oct-Mar).

I Golosi
6, rue de la Grange-Batelière - 48 24 18 63
Closed Aug. Open until 11pm. Air cond. Pkg. V, AE.
Enter this new bistro *a vino* from the Passage Verdeau. You'll discover two levels decorated in a style we can only call "1950s Italian," where you can order cold rabbit herbed with wild thyme, chicken dressed with balsamic vinegar, clove-scented beef stew, and zuppa inglese, all accompanied by irresistible wines (Chardonnay, Barbaresco, Moscato d'Asti) assembled by a passionate oenophile who knows what he's about. **C** 120-140 F.

12/20 Le Grand Café Capucines
4, bd des Capucines - 47 42 19 00
Open daily 24 hours. Terrace dining. Air cond. Garage pkg. V, AE, DC, MC.
The waiter won't pull a face if you order just one course—a shellfish assortment, for example, or salmon tartare, or a grilled pig's trotter. The extravagant décor is a replica of a Roaring Twenties *café boulevardier*. **C** 200-350 F. **M** 119 F (dinner), 185 F.

Les Muses
Hôtel Scribe,
1, rue Scribe - 44 71 24 26
Closed Sat, Sun, hols, Aug. Open until 10:30pm. Priv rm: 80. Air cond. No pets. Valet pkg. V, AE, DC.
The muse of interior design was off duty the day the Hôtel Scribe's basement restaurant was decorated. On the other hand, chef Philippe Pleuen seems privy to a regular fount of inspiration, judging by his inventive, fresh-flavored cuisine. His duck liver with potatoes, succulent beef fillet with artichokes, and chocolate croustillant with mandarin-orange sorbet are well worth the trip down from street level. There's a fine cheese board too, and an array of alluring sweets. The wine list is notable for balance rather than length. **C** 300-400 F. **M** 210 F.

L'Œnothèque
20, rue Saint-Lazare - 48 78 08 76
Closed Sat, Sun, 2nd wk of Feb school hols, May 1-8, Aug 7-28. Open until 10:30pm. Air cond. V, MC.
Daniel Hallée was the sommelier at Jamin before he opened his restaurant-cum-wine shop. Grand vintages at attractive prices and interesting lesser-known growths partner such market-fresh offerings as foie gras en terrine, grilled squid, and prime rib with bone marrow. Superb collection of Cognacs. **C** 200-350 F.

33

Le Saharien
36, rue Rodier
42 85 51 90, fax 45 86 08 35
Closed Sun. Open until 11pm. Air cond. Pkg. V.
Wally has pitched his tent not far from Pigalle, in a bright, cozy setting accented with carved screens, crimson carpets, and Tuareg-style seating. Topping the list of special-ties is his excellent Saharan couscous (no broth, no vegetables), but you can also sample a wonderful dish of mutton with caramelized skin, pigeon pastilla, and honey cake perfumed with orange-flower water. **M** 240 F (wine incl), 150 F (weekday lunch).

 La Table d'Anvers
2, pl. d'Anvers
48 78 35 21, fax 45 26 66 67
Closed Sat lunch, Sun. Open until 10:30pm. Priv rm: 40. Air cond. Garage pkg. V, AE.
While so many chefs fall back on a "safe," reassuring repertoire of neo-bourgeois and bistro dishes to hide their lack of inspiration, Christian Conticini invents and reinvents flavor combinations with a wizardry that is nothing short of staggering. If you're tempted by the prospect of a real gastronomic adventure, we suggest you trek up to his Table at the foot of Montmartre and prepare for a feast! Choose one of the intriguing "theme" menus (featuring novel vegetables, or rare spices, "just desserts"...), or explore an exciting *carte* that is keyed to the seasons. The options are all so enticing that we usually just close our eyes and pick at random! You could start with a tartelette au thon (tuna) surrounded by spring vegetables dressed in a zesty anchovy and green-peppercorn vinaigrette, or lobster gnocchi with divine baby peas (ineffably tender because they've been peeled!) in a rosemary-scented chicken jus, or a brilliantly conceived ravigote that brings together oysters, calf's head, cabbage, and tomato—an amazing harmony of briny and tart flavors, smooth and crisp textures. There follows (for example) grilled red mullet seasoned with artichoke pistou in a saffron-spiced bouillon, or pearly-fleshed sea bass with fava beans and grated fennel, the latter's anise undertones accented by a delicate touch of licorice. Other uncommonly delectable couplings are Conticini's saddle of rabbit with Reblochon cheese atop olive-studded polenta, or his exotically perfumed canard à l'orientale escorted by couscous and spiced chickpeas.
We could go on about these thrilling inventions, but we must leave room to mention the fabulous cheeses, and the astonishing desserts crafted by Christian's brother, Philippe Conticini. Don't be put off by Philippe's imposing waistline: his chocolate-banana-coffee "combo," his macaron au fromage frais, lait d'amande, et griotte, or mango-rhubarb puff pastry with a hint of cinnamon are all light as a summer breeze. An improved cellar now includes some attractive bottles priced under 100 F. **C** 400-600 F. **M** 250 F (lunch, wine incl), 160 F (lunch), 190 F (dinner).

Gault Millau's ratings are based solely on the restaurants' cuisine. We do not take into account the atmosphere, décor, service, and so on; these are commented upon within the review.

12/20 La Taverne Kronenbourg
24, bd des Italiens
47 70 16 64, fax 42 47 13 91
Open daily until 3am. Priv rm: 100. Air cond. Garage pkg. V, AE, DC, MC.
The last of the *cafés-concerts* on the Grands Boulevards (live music nightly) serves robust, unpretentious brasserie fare: shellfish, pork knuckle with cabbage, sauerkraut, and fine Alsatian wines. **C** 190-300 F. **M** 130 F (wine incl).

 Venantius
Hôtel Ambassador,
16, bd Haussmann
48 00 06 38, fax 42 46 19 84
Closed Sat, Sun, Feb 17-27, Jul 28-Aug 28. Open until 10:30pm. Air cond. Valet pkg. V, AE, DC, MC.
Influenced, no doubt, by the dining room's opulent *fin de siècle* décor, chef Gérard Fouché laces his menu with references to the elaborate cuisine of Carême and Escoffier. Still, he's no prisoner of the culinary past, for his more modern, personal creations display plenty of panache. Cases in point: his remarkable duck foie gras flanked by a peppery pineapple marmalade, crab gazpacho zipped up with fresh coriander, a splendid sole stuffed with celery root rémoulade, and breast of Bresse chicken cooked to perfect juiciness in a crust of Breton sea salt. Yet even dishes like these bear occasional traces of lily-gilding.
Sooner or later, Fouché will have to choose between retrospective or forward-looking cuisine. We hope it's the latter, since his flawless technique marks him as a potential three-toque winner. Dining à la carte is an expensive proposition; happily, the 210 F set meal offers an appealing alternative. Ever-so-solemn service. **C** 400-600 F. **M** 210 F (coffee incl).

10TH ARRONDISSEMENT

12/20 Brasserie Flo
7, cour des Petites-Écuries
42 46 15 80
Open daily until 1:30am. Air cond. Pkg. V, AE, DC, MC.
The quintessential Alsatian brasserie, Flo is a jewel: nowhere else will you find the same vivacious atmosphere, superb décor, lively patrons, and delicious sauerkraut, best washed down with carafes of frisky Riesling. **C** 200-300 F. **M** 185 F (from 10pm, wine incl), 109 F (wine incl).

Au Châteaubriant
23, rue Chabrol
48 24 58 94
Closed Sun, Mon, 1 wk in winter, Aug. Open until 10:15pm. Air cond. V, AE.
From the name you'd never guess that this little dining room tucked away near the Gare de l'Est is a noted Italian restaurant. Save for the rotating roster of daily specials, the menu is immutable. Familiar they may be, the sardine lasagne with egg-plant and the millefeuille de filet de veau are still perfectly delicious and courteously served. Tempting desserts; high prices. **C** 250-350 F. **M** 149 F.

12/20 Julien

16, rue du Fg-St-Denis
47 70 12 06, fax 42 42 47 00 65
Open daily until 1:30am. Air cond. Pkg. V, AE, MC.
For the pleasure of dining in these exuberant surroundings (vintage 1880), we are willing to put up with mediocre food; frankly, the kitchen turns out more than its share of botched dishes. But if you stick to the oysters, the cassoulet, or eggs poached in red wine, you'll probably leave with a pleasant memory. C 220-280 F. M 109 F (wine incl).

Le Louis-XIV

8, bd Saint-Denis
42 08 56 56, fax 42 08 23 50
Closed Jul-Aug. Open until 1am. Priv rm: 120. Terrace dining. Valet pkg. V, AE, DC.
The décor is more Louis XV (Pompadour period!) than Louis XIV, but no one seems to mind. The festive, dressy clientele that dines here is too busy tucking into succulent roast duck, roast lamb, roast pigeon, or juicy ribs of beef—preceded, ideally, by a sparkling assortment of fresh shellfish. Jolly ambience, good cellar. C 300-550 F. M 150 F & 170 F (wine incl).

La P'tite Tonkinoise

56, rue du Faubourg-Poissonnière
42 46 85 98
Closed Sun, Mon, Dec 22-Jan 6, Aug 1-Sep 15. Open until 10pm. Garage pkg. V.
Old Indochina hands come regularly for a whiff of the nostalgia that is virtually palpable in this quiet establishment. The chef is a pony-tailed titan, while his wife is indeed a tiny Tonkinoise. Their Vietnamese menu is packed with haunting, exotic flavors: crisp egg rolls, giant grilled shrimp in an extraordinary rice sauce (they're not on the menu—you have to ask for them), a huge dried-noodle cake studded with shrimp and vegetables (my-sao), a juicy duck breast rubbed with five-spice powder, and a savory chicken wing stuffed with onion curry. If they keep it up, they'll soon be topped with two toques! C 200-280 F.

12/20 Terminus Nord

23, rue de Dunkerque
42 85 05 15, fax 40 16 13 98
Open daily until 12:30am. Air cond. V, AE, DC, MC.
Now part of the brasserie group of which Flo (see above) is the flagship, the Terminus serves exactly the same food as the rest of the fleet. Enjoy the lively atmosphere, the gay 1925 décor, and look no farther than the sauerkraut, briny oysters, and grilled meats for a satisfying meal. Nimble service. C 190-300 F. M 95 F (from 10pm, wine incl), 99 F & 141 F (wine incl).

Les Amognes ☺

243, rue du Fg-St-Antoine - 43 72 73 05
Closed Sun, Mon, 1st 3 wks of Aug. Open until 11pm. Terrace dining. V.
Thierry Coué has crossed rich and costly ingredients off his shopping list. The food he serves in his country-style dining room is hearty and full of earthy flavors. Take his creamy split-pea soup: it boasts baby vegetables so fresh you'll be inspired to plant your own! And the succulent roast rack of lamb is ideally accompanied by garlic gnocchi and fragrant white beans. In game season, don't miss the wild-rabbit terrine or the pheasant risotto. The cellar is filled with interesting finds, and the service is gratifyingly attentive. M 160 F.

Astier

44, rue J.-P.-Timbaud - 43 57 16 35
Closed Sat, Sun, Dec 21-Jan 5, end Apr-Aug. Open until 11pm. Air cond. V, AE.
For 130 F, Jean-Luc Clerc will set you up with a slab of savory chicken-liver terrine, followed by rabbit in mustard sauce or a duo of sea whelks and shrimp, nicely aged cheeses, and rich chocolate mousse for dessert. The bistro atmosphere is good-humored and noisy. Intelligent, wide-ranging cellar. M 130 F.

La Belle Époque

Holiday Inn, 10, pl. de la République
43 55 44 34, fax 47 00 32 34
Closed Sat lunch, Sun, Aug. Open until 10:30pm. Terrace dining. Air cond. No pets. V, AE, DC.
Deft technique and focused flavors mark Alain Gruet's foie gras de canard on a bed of crisp greens, spiced veal with sweet peppers, sea bream with sautéed herb-strewn pasta, and delicate tart of saffron-tinged apples and chocolate. Remarkable service in a handsome paneled dining room with an enclosed terrace. Serious cellar. C 250-350 F.

12/20 Chardenoux

1, rue J.-Vallès - 43 71 49 52
Closed Sat, Sun. Open until 10pm. V, AE.
In the heart of the old cabinet-makers' district, this graceful corner bistro (a registered Belle Époque building) flaunts its charms of marble, fanciful moldings, and etched glass. It's a setting peculiarly suited to Bernard Passavant's simple, generous cooking: eggs poached in red wine, daube de bœuf à la provençale, and the like. Connoisseur's cellar. C 200-270 F.

Les Folies

101, rue de St-Maur - 43 38 13 61
Closed Sun lunch, Sun, Aug 10-27. Open until 11pm (Sat dinner 11:30pm). Priv rm: 30. V, AE, DC, MC.
'Twould be folly indeed to overlook this creditable Cambodian spot, where Rosine prepares a fragrant repertoire of Southeast Asian dishes. Before proceeding to the charcoal-grilled marinated meats, try the subtly perfumed soupe machou or the sautéed mussels redolent of basil, garlic, chilis, lemongrass, and peppermint. Advanced students of Cambodian cooking won't want to miss Rosine's natong (catfish), or her blue Mekong shrimp. C 180-230 F. M 98 F, 128 F (wine incl).

Keur Makha

5, rue Guillaume-Bertrand - 43 57 43 95
Closed Mon. Open until 1am. Air cond. V, AE.
Africans in Paris and others in search of exotic tastes favor this address, where Makha himself will guide you through the menu of soyas (skewered veal or fish), womoyo (sea bream with a hot tomato sauce), n'dolé (greens with beef or shrimp), and spicy marinated chicken that is charcoal-grilled to juicy tenderness. The cooking is skillful, the spicing hot but not incendiary. C 250-300 F.

Mansouria
11, rue Faidherbe - 43 71 00 16
Closed Mon lunch, Sun. Open until 11:30pm. Terrace dining. No pets. V.
The trendy Bastille crowd comes here for a taste of Morocco: honeyed pumpkin purée, Moroccan crêpes, a light and flavorful couscous, and mellow, long-simmered tagines. Charming reception and service. **C** 200-300 F. **M** 99 F & 135 F (lunch), 280 F (wine incl), 164 F.

Chez Philippe ✪
106, rue de la Folie-Méricourt
43 57 33 78
Closed Sat, Sun, hols, Aug. Open until 10:30pm. Air cond. Garage pkg. V, AE.
The menu written in purple ink is nothing if not eclectic: herrings Bismarck, grilled lobster, a monumental cassoulet, paella (the best in Paris), York ham with macaroni au gratin, beef bourguignon, turbot Dugléré, rock lobster in Port, and old-fashioned braised hare. Believe it or not, it's all delicious and satisfying. Best of all, these earthy delights are served in the most convivial setting imaginable, complete with a jovial host. Great Burgundies at giveaway prices only add to the gaiety. **C** 300-450 F.

Le Repaire de Cartouche ✪
99, rue Amelot or
8, bd des Filles-du-Calvaire - 47 00 25 86
Closed Sat lunch, Sun, Jul 25-Aug 22. Open until 10:30pm. Priv rm: 25. V, AE, DC, MC.
Emmanuel Salabert, an experienced, skillful chef, presides over this shrine to Southwestern cuisine. Settle down in the wood-paneled dining room and sample the foie gras steamed in a cabbage leaf, steamed mussels in a creamy sauce, pork with prunes and celery, and the flaky Landais apple pie laced with Armagnac. Interesting cellar, manageably priced. **C** 250-350 F. **M** 220 F (Sat), 150 F & 350 F (weekdays).

La Table Richelieu
276, bd Voltaire - 43 72 31 23
Closed Sat lunch. Open until 11pm. Priv rm: 40. Air cond. V, AE, MC.
For fresh seafood, you couldn't do much better than this bright, comfortable restaurant, where Daniel Rousseau treats customers to sparkling shellfish assortments and delicious little red mullet sautéed with Provençal herbs. He's no slouch with meat either, witness his escalopes of foie gras with caramelized endive, or the cunning sausage of veal sweetbreads and fillet flavored with a whisper of lemon and vanilla. Tasty desserts. **C** 300-400 F. **M** 145 F (weekday lunch, wine incl), 200 F, 260 F.

Thaï Éléphant
43-45, rue de la Roquette
47 00 42 00, fax 47 00 45 44
Closed Sat lunch, May 1, Dec 25-28. Open until midnight. Priv rm: 30. Air cond. V, AE, DC, MC.
Filled with flowers, pagodas, and innumerable cheerful waiters, the Thaï Éléphant is not your run-of-the-mill Asian eatery. The menu is miles long, and many of the dishes are fiercely fiery (the hottest are marked with three red elephants). The shrimp curry is quite fine, and so are the Fomyang soup and the garlicky pork. For dessert, try the delicious jasmine tart. **C** 250-370 F. **M** 150 F (weekday lunch), 265 F, 295 F.

11/20 L'Ébauchoir
43, rue des Citeaux - 43 42 49 31
Closed Sun. Open until 10pm. No pets. V.
Here's a big, boisterous neighborhood bistro where the Bastille's trendier denizens regularly tuck into crab soup, calf's liver glazed with honey and coriander, tuna with orange-butter sauce, and old-fashioned molded rice pudding. **C** 150-200 F. **M** 60 F (lunch).

La Flambée
4, rue Taine - 43 43 21 80
Closed Sun, 1 wk at Christmas, Aug 1-21. Open until 10pm. Terrace dining. Air cond. Pkg. V, AE, MC.
The dining room shows some signs of wear, but never mind. Michel Roustan warms things up nicely with his traditional Southwestern charcuteries, tasty confit de canard with sautéed potatoes, and excellent warm apple tart. The good wines are moderately priced. **C** 240-320 F. **M** 80 F (lunch, wine incl), 125 F & 185 F (wine incl).

La Frégate
30, av. Ledru-Rollin - 43 43 90 32
Closed Sat, Sun, Aug 1-22. Open until 10:30pm. Air cond. V, AE.
The huge menu of this friendly haven for bons vivants is dedicated to seafood. Pierre Goueffon turns out a laudable salad of warm scallops set atop truffled lamb's lettuce, a médaillon of monkfish strewn with morsels of fresh crab, and John Dory simmered in aromatic olive oil. Wind up your feast with one of the alluring desserts (lime soufflé and sorbet, strawberry chaud-froid...). Astutely chosen wines. **C** 350-450 F. **M** 150 F (lunch), 200 F, 300 F.

La Gourmandise
271, av. Daumesnil - 43 43 94 41
Closed Sun, Mon dinner, Aug 6-28. Open until 10:30pm. Priv rm: 50. Garage pkg. V, AE.
Gourmand or gourmet, you'll be tempted to indulge in Alain Denoual's cuisine, served in surroundings that some find a trifle pompous. Others question the high prices charged for meager portions. But no one contests the quality of Denoual's warm fish terrine with shellfish fumet or mustardy saddle of tender rabbit, or the dreamy cinnamon ice cream with an apple sablé. It's a shame, though, that Denoual's creative fire is burning so low these days. With just a bit more spark, this food would be worth two toques. **C** 330-450 F. **M** 165 F, 135 F, 220 F, 320 F.

11/20 Les Grandes Marches
6, pl. de la Bastille - 43 42 90 32
Open daily until 1am. Terrace dining. Air cond. Garage pkg. V, AE, DC.
Restored around the same time as the Opéra Bastille was built, this posh brasserie is a fine spot for a post-performance supper. Oysters and other shellfish, steaks, and a splendid turbotin (for two) are all good bets. **C** 250-350 F. **M** 168 F.

Red toques signify creative cuisine; white toques signify traditional cuisine.

12/20 Le Mange-Tout
24, bd de la Bastille - 43 43 95 15
Closed Sun, 1 wk in Aug. Open until 11pm. Priv rm: 18. Terrace dining. Pkg. V, AE, MC.
Uncomplicated cooking, served with a smile and a generous hand. Scrambled eggs with morels, skate with capers, andouillette sausage, and clafoutis are the mainstays of a traditional menu. **M** 98 F (weekdays, Sat lunch), 195 F (wine incl), 130 F, 160 F.

D'Oggi
27, rue de Cotte - 43 41 33 27
Closings not available. Open until 11pm. No pets. V, DC, MC.
Watch your step on the steep stairway that leads down to this tiny vaulted cellar! Once safely seated amid the crowd of happy diners, you'll enjoy delicious pasta, tasty Italian charcuterie, and an admirable tiramisù. The lunch menus are unbeatably priced, but even the à la carte tariffs are easy to take. **C** 180 F. **M** 60 F & 80 F (lunch exc Sun).

L'Oulette
15, pl. Lachambeaudie - 40 02 02 12
Closed Sat lunch, Sun. Open until 10:15pm. Terrace dining. V, AE, MC.
A charmless cohort of office blocks contributes precious little warmth to the surroundings, and the large, dull dining room does nothing to dispel the chill. Happily, Marcel Baudis can be relied upon to kindle a glow with his subtle, spirited South-western cooking. He ignited our enthusiasm recently with a savory chestnut bouillon enriched by tender morsels of guinea hen, an impeccably prepared John Dory in a lively sauce au verjus, and an effiloché de queue de bœuf full of robust, beefy flavor. These earthy yet perfectly modern dishes were followed by pears in flaky pastry (a pleasing variation on tourtière landaise, usually filled with apples) and a luscious sablé aux pommes caramélisées. The cellar is awash in sturdy wines from the Quercy and thereabouts; the service is very attentive. **C** 300-400 F. **M** 230 F (wine incl), 160 F.

La Plantation Paris
5, rue J.-César
43 07 64 15, fax 40 19 92 56
Closed Sun. Open until 11pm. Priv rm: 12. V, AE.
Nouvelle cuisine, Creole-style: blaff de bulots (sea whelks marinated in lime juice and chilis), chicken in pan juices deglazed with pineapple vinegar, and duck with mangoes are expertly handled dishes full of vivid tropical flavors. Watch out for the wines, though: they considerably boost the bill. **C** 220-300 F. **M** 90 F (weekday lunch), 240 F (exc lunch).

Au Pressoir
257, av. Daumesnil
43 44 38 21, fax 43 43 81 77
Closed Sat, Sun, 1 wk at Feb school hols, Aug. Open until 10:30pm. Air cond. Valet pkg. V, MC.
Forgotten by most Parisians since the Colonial Exposition closed 60 years ago, the Porte Dorée district is home to a covey of fine restaurants. Le Pressoir numbers among them: chef Henri Séguin cooks with fine ingredients and a generous spirit, shown to advantage in his roast scallops with pumpkin, braised ox jowl with a suave cèpe coulis, and (in season) a sumptuous

hare à la royale. The wine list offers a wealth of appealing choices, and the service is most accommodating. The décor, which was degenerating from dog-eared to dilapidated, recently received a facelift. **C** 450-580 F. **M** 390 F.

12/20 Le Train Bleu
Gare de Lyon, 12, bd Diderot
43 43 09 06, fax 43 43 97 96
Open daily until 10pm. Priv rm: 100. Garage pkg. V, AE, DC.
The feast is for your eyes only: an extravagant, colossal, delirious, dazzling décor. Food at Le Train Bleu, though on the up-swing, is still of the overpriced "standard French" variety. **C** 300-400 F. **M** 260 F (wine incl).

Au Trou Gascon
40, rue Taine
43 44 34 26, fax 43 07 80 55
Closed Sat, Sun, Christmas wk, Aug. Open until 10pm. Air cond. Pkg. V, AE, DC, MC.
Can it be true, as some readers have said, that sauces are heavy and dishes occasionally botched at the Trou Gascon? You couldn't prove it by us. Our most recent repast found us raving, as usual, over the well-cured Chalosse ham, the warm pâté de cèpes in a bright-green parsley jus, the truffled chop of milk-fed veal with macaroni gratin, and the rich duck and pork cassoulet. To accompany this robust cooking, Nicole Dutournier recommends wonderful Madirans and Jurançons.
True, the bistro décor is faintly frayed; the menu hasn't budged for years; and the prices (save for the lunch-hour set menu) are far from rustic. But as for the cooking, the Trou's two toques are safe! **C** 350-450 F. **M** 180 F (weekday lunch), 380 F (weekdays).

12/20 Les Zygomates
7, rue de Capri - 40 19 93 04
Closed Sat lunch, Sun, Dec 27-Jan 3, Aug 1-24. Open until 10:15pm. No pets. V.
Lots of bright ideas come out of this kitchen: for starters, there's an earthy salad of pork tongue, followed by grenadier (a firm-fleshed fish) with red-wine butter or pig's tail with morels, and ginger-bread ice cream for dessert. Expect a cordial welcome into the incredible dining room—formerly a butcher shop—full of fin de siècle details. **C** 200-250 F. **M** 125 F.

13TH ARRONDISSEMENT

Auberge Etchegorry
Hôtel Vert Galant,
41, rue Croulebarbe - 44 08 83 51
Closed Sun. Open until 10:30pm. Priv rm: 30. Terrace dining. Air cond. V, AE, DC.
Come here for hearty Basque food and wines. A cheerful *patron* plates up excellent regional charcuterie, tasty stuffed squid, and generously served quail paupiettes au foie gras. Lots of charm, and a lively atmosphere. **C** 250-350 F. **M** 155 F & 200 F (wine incl), 135 F.

*The **prices** in this guide reflect what establishments were charging at press time.*

Les Marronniers

53 bis, bd Arago
47 07 58 57, fax 43 36 85 20
Closed Sun, Jul 28-Sep 10. Open until 11pm. Terrace dining. Air cond. Valet pkg. V, AE, DC, MC.
In fine weather one may choose between a table in the pretty pink interior or one on a pleasant patio under the eponymous chestnut trees. The *plats du jour* are usually the best part of chef Lorenzati's reliably appealing menu. Look for a good terrine of duck and wild mushrooms, Auvergne-style turbot, or an exemplary blanquette of baby lamb. Traditional cellar; efficient service. **C** 300-360 F. **M** 200 F (wine incl.).

Le Petit Marguery

9, bd de Port-Royal - 43 31 58 59
Closed Sun, Mon, Dec 23-Jan 2, Aug. Open until 10:15pm. Priv rm: 20. V, AE, DC, MC.
Michel and Jacques Cousin cook in a virile vein (game, offal, fresh fish, regional dishes) for an appreciative and very faithful public. Their bright, old-fashioned bistro is a most convivial spot. Alain Cousin directs the fleet-footed waiters who deliver generous platefuls of braised wild mushrooms, earthy terrine de boudin, cod gratin with oysters and asparagus, or partridge purée with juniper berries, as well as robust bourgeois classics like tuna stewed in Brouilly wine with fresh pasta. The single-price menus help keep costs down. **M** 160 F (lunch), 200 F, 320 F, 450 F.

Tang

44, av. d'Ivry - 45 86 88 79
Open daily until 10pm. No pets. V, AE.
Looks aren't everything. What this huge Asian eatery most closely resembles is a soup kitchen, but the food is authentic, interesting, and incredibly low-priced (the average main dish goes for 40 F). Good bets from the extensive menu are jellyfish with 100-year-old eggs, most of the dim-sum, the spicy Szechuan shrimp, duck with black mushrooms, gingered crab, and fresh, perfectly seasoned four-meat noodles. We should warn you: the language barrier can be daunting—but go ahead and try your luck! **C** 150 F.

Les Vieux Métiers de France

13, bd A.-Blanqui
45 88 90 03, fax 45 80 73 80
Closed Sun, Mon. Open until 10:30pm. Priv rm: 16. Air cond. V, AE, DC, MC.
Onto an austere modern building, chef Michel Moisan (with considerable help from his friends) has grafted the most amazing medieval décor of sculpted wood, stained glass, ancient beams, and antique paintings. What saves all this quaintness from tipping over into kitsch is Moisan's flavorful, personalized cuisine: rabbit with lentils en vinaigrette, séafood minestrone, spiced shoulder of lamb with pearl barley and an array of luscious desserts. The cellar is an oenophile's dream. **C** 350-450 F. **M** 165 F, 300 F.

14TH ARRONDISSEMENT

L'Amuse-Bouche

186, rue du Château - 43 35 31 61
Closed Sat lunch, Sun, Aug 1-15. Open until 10:30pm. V, AE.
Gilles Lambert's alert and graceful cuisine has won him the loyalty of a glossy clientele. Book a table in the elegant apricot-colored dining room and enjoy his marinated scallops and mussels with watercress, pikeperch in a Madiran sauce, or chicken breast stuffed with foie gras, then finish with a superb gâteau mousseux au chocolat amer. Succinct, well-designed wine list. **C** 280-380 F. **M** 160 F.

Les Armes de Bretagne

108, av. du Maine
43 20 29 50, fax 43 27 84 11
Closed Sat lunch, Sun (exc hols), Aug. Open until 11pm. Priv rm: 40. Air cond. Pkg. V, AE, DC, MC.
Here is an establishment that proudly upholds the old-fashioned traditions of hospitality, service, and French culinary showmanship in a luxurious Second Empire dining room. Top-quality seafood from Brittany stars in William Dhenin's best dishes: fresh oysters, sea bass en croûte with beurre blanc, crêpes aux langoustines, and grilled lobster. **C** 300-450 F. **M** 200 F.

Auberge de l'Argoat

27, av. Reille - 45 89 17 05
Closed Sat, Sun, Aug 12-20. Open until 10pm. V, AE, MC.
Here's a welcoming, unpretentious little seafood spot, situated across from the Parc Montsouris. Jeannine Gaulon greets diners warmly, while in the kitchen her chef cooks up soupe de poissons, langoustine and artichoke salad, sole à la bretonne, and grilled sea bream. A few meat dishes round out this agreeable bill of fare. **C** 250-320 F. **M** 100 F (lunch), 180 F.

11/20 Le Bar à Huîtres

112, bd du Montparnasse
43 20 71 01, fax 43 21 35 47
Open daily until 2am. Terrace dining. V, AE, MC.
At this popular oyster bar you can, if you wish, order and eat just one oyster—but that would be a shame. Six or a dozen Belons, fines, or spéciales would surely be more satisfying, as are the gargantuan shellfish platters (190 to 590 F). The cooked fish dishes, however, are skip-pable. Interesting cellar of white wines. **C** 220-300 F. **M** 98 F, 128 F, 198 F.

12/20 Bistrot du Dôme

1, rue Delambre - 43 35 32 00
Open daily until 11pm. V, AE.
Flipping-fresh seafood is presented with becoming simplicity at this fashionable spot: featured are crispy fried smelts, tuna with sauce vierge, and lotte in a garlicky cream sauce. Intelligent wine list; merry ambience. **C** 230-300 F.

La Cagouille

Opposite 23 rue de l'Ouest,
12, pl. C.-Brancusi - 43 22 09 01
Closed Dec 24-Jan 3. Open until 10:30pm. Priv rm: 16. Terrace dining. V, AE.
Gérard Allemandou has a rare talent for drawing hordes of seafood lovers to the most improbable location. A few years ago, not even Parisian taxi drivers had heard of the Place Brancusi. Now the address is noted in every restaurant guide in the city, thanks to La Cagouille. At this *bistro du port*, dishes made from the very freshest fish and shellfish (delivered direct from Atlantic ports) are chalked on a blackboard: depending on the day's catch, they might include exquisite tiny squid in a garlicky sauce of their own ink, baked black scallops from Brest,

fresh fried anchovies, shad in beurre blanc sauce, herbed brill, plump mackerel with mustard sauce, or thick, juicy sole. If you are content to drink a modest Aligoté or Quincy, your bill will hover around 300-350 F. But beware if you succumb to the temptations of the finest Cognac collection in Paris (and maybe the world). C 270-380 F. M 250 F (wine incl), 150 F.

Le Caroubier
122, av. du Maine - 43 20 41 49
Closed Sun dinner, Mon, Aug. Open until 10:30pm. Air cond. V.
Do you like couscous? Here you'll find the genuine article: homemade, hand-rolled, and fragrant with spices. Also on hand are a lively eggplant salad, savory pastillas, and succulent tagines, simmered in the best Moroccan tradition. Heartwarming welcome. C 180-220 F. M 130 F.

La Chaumière des Gourmets
22, pl. Denfert-Rochereau - 43 21 22 59
Closed Sat lunch, Sun, Aug. Open until 10:30pm. Priv rm: 20. Terrace dining. V, AE.
The Chaumière's friendly, provincial dining room still features faded wallpaper, the staff carries on with imperturbable diligence, the wine list remains small, and the house repertoire invariably classic. But in this case, no news really is good news: the delicious salade de ris de veau, the expertly grilled red mullet with ratatouille, and the famously tasty apple tart attest to Jean-Paul Huc's unfailing consistency and flair. C 300-450 F. M 165 F, 240 F.

12/20 La Coupole
102, bd du Montparnasse
43 20 14 20, fax 43 35 46 14
Closed Dec 24. Open until 2am. Air cond. V, AE, MC.
This Montparnasse landmark, respectfully restored and run by the Flo brasserie group, survives with its mystique intact. The menu bears Flo's unmistakable stamp: exemplary shellfish assortments, grilled meats, and carafes of sprightly house Riesling are delivered by swift, efficient waiters. C 250-350 F. M 85 F (lunch exc Sun), 109 F (wine incl).

Le Dôme
108, bd du Montparnasse
43 35 25 81, fax 42 79 01 19
Closed Mon. Open until 12:45am. Priv rm: 10. Air cond. V, AE, DC, MC.
Le Dôme is the capital's top seafood brasserie, with a neo–Art Deco interior, booths that provide cozy comfort and privacy for the high-powered patrons (they include President Mitterrand and Mayor Chirac—who don't, of course, sit together), and a wonderful *carte* prepared by chef Franck Graux. In addition to impeccably fresh oysters and the justly famous lobster salad in a truffled dressing, there is a velvety bouillon de langoustines aux champignons, a hefty turbot hollandaise, sea bass in chive vinaigrette, and bouillabaisse that bears comparison with Marseille's best. Precise, cheerful service, and a cellar filled with bottles that incite you to splurge. C 450-600 F.

Restaurant prices in red draw attention to restaurants that offer particularly good value.

Aux Iles Marquises
15, rue de la Gaîté - 43 20 93 58
Closed Sat lunch, Sun, Aug 1-16. Open until 11:30pm. Priv rm: 15. V, AE, MC.
Once a favorite haunt of Édith Piaf and her friends, the Iles Marquises is decked out with salty nautical décor (shrimp-colored walls with seascape frescoes). Owner-chef Mathias Théry offers a creditable 150 F menu that brings zesty marinated scallops, sea-bream fillet with fresh pasta, then dessert, coffee, and petits-fours. But this good food deserves a better cellar. C 250-400 F. M 130 F, 150 F.

12/20 Justine
Hôtel Méridien, 19, av. du Cdt-Mouchotte
44 36 44 00, fax 44 36 49 03
Open daily until 11pm. Air cond. No pets. Valet pkg. V, AE, DC.
A pretty winter garden in the Méridien Montparnasse is the backdrop to an attractive buffet, one of the best bargains in Paris. For 195 F you can help yourself to any amount of soup, crudités, mixed salads, terrines, and tasty *plats du jour* followed by very good cheeses and desserts. C 250-300 F. M 195 F (buffet).

Lous Landés
157, av. du Maine - 45 43 08 04
Closed Sat lunch, Sun, Aug. Open until 10:30pm. Priv rm: 14. Air cond. V, AE, DC, MC.
Hervé Rumen's South-western specialties range from the frankly robust to more refined versions of country cooking. Taste his truffled escalopes de foie gras au jus de canard, tender Landais squab flavored with three kinds of garlic, or his world-class cassoulet. Desserts are all you would expect from a former colleague of Christian Constant, and the wine list offers some excellent Cahors and Madirans. Marie-Thérèse, a charming hostess, welcomes guests into the pretty green dining room. C 300-400 F. M 190 F, 300 F.

Montparnasse 25
Hôtel Méridien, 19, rue du Cdt-Mouchotte
44 36 44 25, fax 44 36 49 03
Closed Sat, Sun, Dec 23-Feb 2, Jul 29-Aug 29. Open until 10:30pm. Priv rm: 22. Air cond. No pets. Valet pkg. V, AE, DC.
Unlike so many hotel restaurants, which are little more than a convenience for in-house patrons, the Méridien boasts a magnetic menu that draws gourmets from all over Paris. The Art Deco interior opens onto a tiny garden, and the well-spaced tables are just what executives desire for their power lunches. Yet even the most intense negotiations come to a halt when the waiter presents chef Jean-Yves Guého's ingenious, imaginative dishes. This triple-toque winner cooked for years at the Hong Kong Méridien, and it shows in his Cantonese-style sweet-and-sour brill, spiced duck with basil, and rack of lamb in a spiced crust with a jus redolent of Thai herbs. He also entices appetites with his rack of milk-fed veal perfumed with an elusive hint of juniper, scallops encased in a crisp, paper-thin buckwheat crêpe, or tender morsels of pork paired with crayfish in a barley bouillon. The 230 F single-price menu offered at lunch is a steal, and so is the slightly more expensive ver-

sion offered at dinner, which also includes selections from a monumental cheese board. Sommelier Gérard Margeon presides over a cellar awash in remarkable (and affordable) growers' wines. **C** 420-600 F. **M** 230 F (lunch), 290 F & 380 F (dinner).

Pavillon Montsouris ✇
20, rue Gazan
45 88 38 52, fax 45 88 63 40
Open daily until 10:30pm. Priv rm: 40. Terrace dining. No pets. Valet pkg. V, AE, DC, MC.
A walk across the Parc Montsouris at sunset will help you work up an appetite for a fine feast in this turn-of-the-century greenhouse overlooking the park, once a favorite rendezvous of the beautiful spy, Mata Hari. Stéphane Ruel's 255 F menu adds allure to this charming Parisian spot, bringing plenty of custom for his saddle of rabbit with potato salad, sea bass with shallots, veal sweetbreads and kidney in a caramelized garlic cream sauce, and for dessert, a sinful chocolate galette with pistachio ice cream. For even less money (189 F), you can treat yourself to the likes of a keen-flavored salad of skate dressed with lime, lamb's sweetbreads with garlicky cucumbers, and a flaky mango pithiviers. Yvan Courault, who used to manage the Grand Véfour, excels in the gracious art of welcoming guests. **C** 255-280 F. **M** 189 F, 255 F.

Les Petites Sorcières
12, rue Liancourt - 43 21 95 68
Closed Sat lunch, Sun. Open until 10:30pm (by reserv). Terrace dining. V, MC.
Christian Teule, a talented chef of the Robuchon school, fills up his pocket-sized restaurant with an appealing 120 F lunch menu that on a given day might feature house-made jambon persillé followed by duck pot-au-feu with fava beans and pinenuts, with apple tart or baba au rhum for dessert. A la carte choices are more elaborate but no less savory: we especially like the fresh sardine croustillant with anchovy butter, the spiced lamb pie, and the vanilla-scented apricot tart. Good wines are available by the carafe. **C** 180-240 F. **M** 120 F (lunch).

La Régalade
49, av. J.-Moulin
45 45 68 58, fax 45 40 96 74
Closed Sat lunch, Sun, Mon, at Christmas, Easter, Aug. Open until midnight. Air cond. No pets. V.
Don't neglect to book your table in advance, for this antique bistro fills up fast. Here's why: Béarn native Yves Camdeborde (ex-Crillon, no less) serves first-rate cooking that is eminently affordable as well. Regionally rooted but modern in outlook, the menu proposes a sapid terrine of oxtail and leek, calf's liver presented in a thick, rosy-pink slice, succulent wood pigeon barded with bacon, and a comforting assortment of homey desserts. The frisky wines sell for giveaway prices, and the atmosphere at the close-set tables where Claudine Camdeborde seats her guests is merry indeed. **M** 150 F.

*Some establishments change their **closing times** without warning. It is always wise to check in advance.*

Vishnou
13, rue du Cdt-Mouchotte
45 38 92 93, fax 44 07 31 19
Closed Sun. Open until 11:30pm (Fri & Sat midnight). Priv rm: 50. Terrace dining. Air cond. Pkg. V, AE, DC.
Silken saris line the walls of this uncommonly luxurious Indian eating house. A distinguished-looking staff serves forth fragrant dishes that are finely wrought and full of exotic flavors. Savor the subtle Hyderabadi beef, a good vegetable curry, or take advantage of the fine 150 F lunch: shrimp salad, chicken tandoori, basmati rice, and poppadums are followed by a delicious besan barfi for dessert. Amazingly, the wine list is diverse and informative. **C** 250-400 F. **M** 95 F & 150 F (lunch, wine incl), 230 F (dinner, wine incl), 220 F.

15TH ARRONDISSEMENT

L'Agape
281, rue Lecourbe - 45 58 19 29
Closed Aug 6-26. Open until 10:30pm. Terrace dining. V.
The place needs some fixing up, and the staff needs some breaking in, but chef-owner Marc Lamic hit his stride right off the bat. His appealing menu brims with bright ideas and flavors: we gobbled up his delicious confit de canard served with a cold potato terrine, the tasty sculpin fillet encased in a sesame crust, and the savory stuffed saddle of rabbit garnished with ratatouille ravioli. Desserts are more down-to-earth, but then so are the prices. **M** 120 F (exc Sun).

12/20 Le Barrail
17, rue Falguière
43 22 42 61, fax 42 79 93 91
Closed Sat, Sun. Open until 10pm. Priv rm: 12. Air cond. V, AE, MC.
An attractive spot done up in soft pink tones. Alain Magne's cooking is low-key, but the prices are fairly high-tone, owing to a lavish use of truffles, foie gras, langoustines, and other luxuries. Good bets are the salmon and leek lasagne and the savory sautéed beef with carrots. **C** 230-350 F. **M** 110 F (weekdays, wine incl), 140 F (weekday lunch), 160 F.

12/20 Le Bouchut
9, rue Bouchut - 45 67 15 65
Closed Sat lunch (dinner May-Jul), Sun, Aug. Open until 10pm. Terrace dining. Air cond. V, AE, MC.
This intimate little spot, set back from the Avenue de Breteuil, caters to faithful customers who return again and again for Philippe Metais's sea bream seasoned with fennel-flavored oil or parmentier de gésiers de canard confit (duck gizzards topped with fluffy mashed potatoes). For dessert, there's a pretty assortment of strawberry sweets. The fine cellar highlights wines from the Loire Valley. **C** 220-320 F. **M** 120 F (lunch, wine incl), 158 F (wine incl).

12/20 Casa Alcade
117, bd de Grenelle - 47 83 39 71
Open daily until 10:30pm. Priv rm: 40. Air cond. V, MC.
A lively *bodega* offering zesty Basque and Spanish fare. Try the excellent pipérade,

marinated anchovies, generously served paella, or codfish à la luzienne. The wine list features fine bottles from beyond the Pyrenees. **C** 230-330 F. **M** 120 F (weekday lunch, Sat), 160 F.

Les Célébrités

Hôtel Nikko, 61, quai de Grenelle
40 58 20 00, fax 45 75 42 35
Closed Aug 1-31. Open until 10pm. Priv rm: 22. Air cond. Heated pool. Valet pkg. V, AE, DC, MC.
Even for inveterate quibblers like us, it isn't easy to find something to criticize at Les Célébrités. The dining room turned toward the Seine is a paragon of hushed elegance; the menu strikes a studied balance between modernized traditional dishes, updated haute-cuisine classics, and fashionable low-fat fare; no rough edges mar Jacques Sénéchal's virtuoso handling of flawless seasonal foodstuffs. His dishes are characterized by refined yet definite flavors, witness the lobster steamed over Sauternes wine, full-flavored lamb with fava beans, or celestially succulent chop of milk-fed veal. For dessert, there's a sublime chocolate-mocha tartlet. As for the cellar, it's beyond reproach: astutely assembled, appealing and, all in all, affordably priced. Speaking of affordable, the prix-fixe menu still tariffed at 280 F is a very good deal indeed. **C** 380-650 F. **M** 280 F, 370 F.

Le Clos Morillons

50, rue des Morillons - 48 28 04 37
Closed Sat lunch, Sun, 2 wks mid Aug. Open until 10pm. Air cond. V, AE, MC.
The French colonial décor of this charming establishment transports you to the tropics. The feeling lingers as you peruse the menu, for Philippe Delacourcelle's repertoire is redolent of exotic spices. Among the original, expertly rendered dishes are sole with sweet lime leaves, calf's liver scented with cinnamon, suavely spiced snails, and gingered veal with puréed almonds. Delectable desserts and a fine selection of wines priced under 100 F complete the picture. **C** 280-350 F. **M** 160 F, 285 F (weekdays, Sat dinner).

La Dinée
85, rue Leblanc
45 54 20 49, fax 40 60 74 88
Closed Jul 29-Aug 22. Open until 10:30pm. Priv rm: 16. Garage pkg. V, AE, MC.
Christophe Chabanel won his toque at the tender age of 22. Here in his new digs, a pluperfect neighborhood restaurant, he continues to impress us with his finely honed technique and inventive, modern cooking. Among the excellent options on offer, we recommend the delicious terrine of lambs' tongues with Italian parsley, the warm salad of quail and artichokes in a vivid beet jus, and perfectly roasted pikeperch garnished with a zesty anchoïade and skewered squid. **C** 250-300 F. **M** 260 F (weekday dinner, Sun), 160 F (weekday lunch).

12/20 Erawan
76, rue de la Fédération - 47 83 55 67
Closed Sun, Aug. Open until 10:30pm. Air cond. No pets. V, AE, MC.
Lots of regulars crowd into Erawan's little dining rooms to feast on Thai cuisine tailored for Western palates—hot it's not! Recommended are the pork-rind salad with fresh herbs and fried

rice, baked cod strewn with lemon leaves in a spicy sauce, and the delicious Thai fondue. **C** 220-300 F. **M** 75 F (lunch), 106 F, 138 F, 146 F, 172 F.

12/20 La Farigoule
104, rue Balard - 45 54 35 41
Closed Mon dinner, Sun, Aug 12-28. Open until 10pm. Garage pkg. V, AE.
Jean Gras is a colorful sexagenarian who concocts the best, most fragrant bouillabaisse in Paris. His bourride (a garlicky fish soup) isn't half bad either, and he stirs up a rousing rendition of sheep's tripe and trotters à la marseillaise. Every dish is served with a smile and a lilting Provençal accent. **C** 250-350 F.

Fellini
15, rue de la Croix-Nivert - 45 77 40 77
Closed Sat lunch, Sun, Aug. Open until 10:45pm. Air cond. No pets. V, MC.
Giuseppe hails from sunny Napoli, where he learned to cook in a fresh, forthright style that warms our hearts. Pull up a seat in his friendly trattoria, and sample his warm salad of baby squid and white beans drizzled with olive oil, or house-made fettuccine showered with strips of prosciutto, pancetta, olives, and cauliflower. His tiramisù is the lightest we've tried. To wash it all down, uncork a bottle of fine Italian wine from the well-stocked cellar. **C** 250-300 F. **M** 130 F (weekday lunch).

Kim-Anh
15, rue de l'Église
45 79 40 96, fax 40 59 49 78
Dinner only. Open daily until 11:30pm. Air cond. V, AE, MC.
Charming Kim-Anh runs this tidy, flower-filled little Vietnamese restaurant while his wife, Caroline, practices her culinary craft in a lilliputian kitchen made for contortionists. She prepares her dishes with fresh herbs, delectable leaves and shoots, subtle spices, and light sauces. Try the shrimp soup flavored with tamarind, shredded beef fried with peanuts and vinegar, steamed snails Tonkin, a wonderfully piquant stuffed crab, and the best egg rolls in town. Quite a fine wine selection and some surprisingly good desserts. **C** 260-320 F. **M** 220 F.

Morot-Gaudry

8, rue de la Cavalerie
45 67 06 85, fax 45 67 55 72
Closed Sat, Sun. Open until 10pm. Priv rm: 28. Terrace dining. Air cond. V, AE, MC.
It would be hard to find a more ample or appetizing lunch for 220 F (a price unchanged for years) than the one served by Jean-Pierre Morot-Gaudry's rooftop restaurant. It commences with a lusty calf's foot croustillant, then proceeds to rabbit stewed in white wine with wild thyme, and concludes with a selection of cheeses and a tartelette de poires Bourdaloue. Included in the price is one of a dozen delicious wines.
But Morot-Gaudry's à la carte menu also has its charms: we're thinking of his foie gras en terrine laced with sweet wine, the fricassée of snails and salsify with a lively touch of mustard, scallops in a bright, creamy parsley sauce, salmon and

41

smoky bacon with crisp sautéed cabbage, or tender Normandy beef pan-roasted in a richly flavored sauce of vintage Médoc. Some impressive and costly wines are proposed, such as a Montrachet "Marquis de Laguiche" or a Gruaud-Larose '28. But what thrills us chez Morot-Gaudry is the selection of Jurançons, Chinon Vieilles Vignes, Savennières, and Vouvrays which give enormous pleasure without breaking the bank. Danièle Morot-Gaudry's welcome is wonderful, and from the verdant terrace you can glimpse a corner of the Eiffel Tower. C 400-500 F. M 220 F (lunch, wine incl), 390 F.

L'Oie Cendrée 🙂

51, rue Labrouste - 45 31 91 91
Closed Sat, Sun lunch, Dec 24-Jan 5, Aug 1-22. Open until 9:30pm. V, MC.
This family-style dining room is conducive to relaxed, casual dining and the menu provides the wherewithal for a hearty tuck-in. Duck, in every permutation, is the specialty of the house. For top value, choose the 125 F set meal, which brings escargots in crisp pastry with a garlicky cream sauce, magret de canard (duck breast) au gros sel, and warm chocolate-walnut cake. The wine list presents a small selection of regional bottlings. C 250-280 F. M 95 F (Sat), 125 F.

L'Os à Moelle

3, rue Vasco-de-Gama - 45 57 27 27
Closed 2 wks in Aug. Open until 10:30pm. V, MC.
Thierry Faucher gives his customers terrific value for their money, with imaginative, oft-renewed menus inspired by whatever looks fresh and fine at the market. The 140 F set meal, for example, might bring an asparagus feuilleté with coddled eggs or a lively mackerel salad scented with tarragon, with salmon and lentils or guinea fowl and cabbage for a main course, and prune pie for dessert. The 180 F dinner is equally alluring, with the likes of creamy scrambled eggs and meadow mushrooms, tuna-topped pizza showered with basil, squid risotto enriched with lobster cream, and caramelized melon with chocolate quenelles and saffron sauce. With regional wines are uniformly priced (70 F a bottle, 140 F a magnum), this one looks like a real winner! M 180 F (dinner), 140 F (lunch).

Le Père Claude

51, av. de La Motte-Picquet - 47 34 03 05
Open daily until midnight. Terrace dining. Air cond. V, AE, MC.
Claude Perraudin lives like a monk (albeit of the Rabelaisian variety), his existence devoted to feeding his flock of faithful patrons. Working seven days a week (until midnight) in his newly enlarged brasserie, Father Claude oversees a gargantuan rotisserie, where strings of sausages, plump poultry, racks of lamb, and suckling pigs spin slowly on the spit as they roast to crisp, tender perfection. And there are oceans of tasty wine to wash it all down. The prices? Blessedly low, of course. C 220-320 F. M 92 F (weekdays), 115 F (w-e), 250 F, 140 F.

La Petite Bretonnière 🙂

2, rue de Cadix - 48 28 34 39
Closed Sat lunch, Sun, Aug. Open until 9:30pm. Garage pkg. V.
What with the Porte de Versailles exhibition halls just around the corner, we wonder why this bright, charming spot doesn't fill up with visitors

from the trade fairs? They surely couldn't find better food than at La Petite Bretonnière. Alain Lamaison's dishes are lively and daring, particularly in their treatment of vegetables and fruit. He deserves a wider audience for his wonderful white-bean soup enriched with morsels of langoustine and chorizo, pan-roasted scallops swathed in a surprisingly spiced lamb jus and garnished with grape-studded couscous, and his succulent farm pigeon flanked by silken puréed dates. Madirans and Bordeaux are the highlights of a rich cellar. Impeccable welcome and service. C 400-500 F. M 200 F (lunch).

Rascasson

148, rue de Vaugirard
47 34 63 45, fax 47 34 39 45
Closed Sun, Aug. Open until 10pm. Priv rm: 40. Terrace dining. Air cond. V.
Once a pizzeria, now a winsome little seafood spot, the Rascasson is a good place for fresh fish with a Provençal accent. Michel Garbi turns out wonderfully crispy fried rockfish, red mullet enhanced by a zesty marinade, baked rascasse (sculpin), and for dessert, a fine cinnamon-nut cake. The cellar offers a good choice of affordable bottles. M 135 F.

Le Relais de Sèvres

Hôtel Sofitel, 8-12, rue L.-Armand
40 60 30 30, fax 45 57 04 22
Closed Sat, Sun, at Christmas, Aug. Open until 10pm. Priv rm: 15. Air cond. Heated pool. Valet pkg. V, AE, DC, MC.
For its flagship restaurant, the Sofitel chain chose a décor that spells good taste in capital letters: blond woodwork, pale-blue fabric on the walls, Champagne-colored napery, Louis XV chairs... A new chef has just taken over the kitchen (the talented Martial Enguehard has set off to open a place of his own), so we'll wait until he has found his bearings to rate his cuisine. The Relais still boasts a splendid, reasonably priced cellar and an admirably trained staff. C 350-550 F. M 300 F (wine incl).

Restaurant de La Tour

"Roger Conticini,"
6, rue Desaix - 43 06 04 24
Closed Sat lunch, Sun, Aug. Open until 10:30pm. V.
Roger Conticini (his sons run the triple-toque Table d'Anvers in the ninth arrondissement) is at the helm of this engaging little restaurant. The dishes on his trio of single-price menus change often, but all have an earthy, raffish appeal: sardine galette with fresh vegetables, a lusty salad of pig's ear and trotter, mustard-roasted mackerel flanked by potatoes whipped with pungent olive oil, and a famously good blanquette of veal and chicken with basmati rice. Tasty little wines sell for under 100 F. Nice going, Roger! C 210-330 F. M 165 F (dinner), 108 F & 138 F (lunch).

Sawadee

53, av. Émile-Zola - 45 77 68 90
Open daily until 10:30pm. No pets. V, AE, MC.
We think Sawadee is the best Thai restaurant in the city. Spacious, over-decorated, very lively, it offers an immense list of specialties full of unexpected flavors. The salad of pork rinds and fried rice, the skewered shellfish, mussels in a fiery sauce, cod with seaweed and wild lemon,

duck perfumed with Thai basil, and coconut ice cream all come highly recommended. With a bottle of good Thai beer, your tab will hover around 200 F. **C** 260 F. **M** 75 F (lunch exc Sun), 106 F, 138 F, 146 F, 172 F.

Aux Senteurs de Provence ۞
295, rue Lecourbe - 45 57 11 98
Closed Sat lunch, Sun, Aug 7-21. Open until 10pm. Terrace dining. V, AE, DC, MC.
Serge Arce turns out a delicate, freshly fragrant version of Provençal cuisine. Sun-kissed ingredients lend an authentic Southern savor to his tuna in a tarragon marinade (as pretty as it is appetizing), roast galinette (a Mediterranean fish) à la niçoise enhanced by a perfect vegetable brunoise, and generous bouillabaisse. The cellar is modest, but the surroundings are neat and cheerful, with cork-covered walls and jaunty nautical prints. **C** 250-380 F. **M** 152 F.

Pierre Vedel
19, rue Duranton
45 58 43 17, fax 45 58 42 65
Closed Sat lunch (& dinner in summer), Sun, Christmas wk. Open until 10:15pm. No pets. Pkg. V.
Be sure to book your table, because Pierre Vedel's warm Parisian bistro is invariably jam-packed. Little wonder the place is popular, with dishes like shellfish ravioli, chicken-liver terrine with lobster coulis, and sweet-breads en blanquette with wild mushrooms on the menu. True to his Southern roots, Vedel also prepares an admirably authentic bourride de lotte à la sétoise (a garlicky monkfish soup), and a satisfying nougat glacé studded with candied fruit. If you order one of the more modest growers' wines from the interesting list, you can rest assured that the bill won't be too bad. **C** 250-350 F.

16TH ARRONDISSEMENT

Amazigh
2, rue La Pérouse - 47 20 90 38
Closed Sat lunch, Sun. Open until 11pm. Air cond. V, AE, DC, MC.
A Moroccan restaurant with a bill of fare that grazes the two-toque level. Best of show are the savory briouates (deep-fried pastries) filled with shellfish, the eggplant salad sparked with coriander (zalouk), lamb tagine with fried eggplant, and the sumptuous "grand couscous." Also worthy of interest are the tasty stuffed sardines, lamb's brains in tomato sauce, cinnamon-scented oranges, and buttery puff pastry layered with almond cream. Like the setting, the service is pretty posh. **C** 300-400 F.

La Baie d'Ha' Long
164, av. de Versailles
45 24 60 62, fax 42 30 58 98
Closed Sun, Jul 25-Aug 30. Open until 10pm. Priv rm: 20. Terrace dining. Air cond. No pets. V, AE.
Roger, the proprietor of this small Vietnamese spot, is far more interested in his collection of birds and exotic fish than in food. It's his wife, Nathalie, who toils away in the kitchen producing delicious, exotic dishes from her native Vietnam: spicy soups, brochettes perfumed with fresh herbs, duck grilled with ginger. Generous portions. The cellar holds some surprisingly good wines. **C** 180-240 F. **M** 99 F (weekday lunch).

Bellini
28, rue Le Sueur - 45 00 54 20
Closed Sat lunch, Sun, Aug 1-28. Open until 10:30pm. Air cond. V, AE, MC.
Comfy banquettes, smoked mirrors, gray marble, and peach-toned walls create a cozy setting for Bellini's somewhat Frenchified Italian fare. Diaphanous slices of excellent prosciutto di Parma lead into such savory dishes as sautéed squid seasoned with balsamic vinegar, golden tagliatelle topped with your choice of truffles, cèpes, or clams, and red mullet with tangy tapenade. For dessert, we're partial to the incredibly light tiramisù. The cellar harbors appealing wines from Friulia, Tuscany, and the Veneto. **C** 275-330 F. **M** 180 F.

Le Bertie's
Hôtel Baltimore, 1, rue Léo-Delibes
44 34 54 34, fax 44 34 54 44
Open daily until 10:30pm. Priv rm: 14. Air cond. V, AE, DC, MC.
When Le Bertie's opened not long ago, a major London daily ran this tongue-in-cheek headline: "Finally! A good meal in Paris!" The dining room of the Hotel Baltimore cultivates a clubby British look that Parisians adore. And yes, the menu is English—but the potted crab, celery and Stilton soup, fish and chips with tartar sauce, grilled sirloin steak, bread-and-butter pudding, and the rest are prepared by a French chef! The maître d' will astound you with his knowledge of Britain's 400 cheeses; the wine steward will amaze you with his list of twenty prime clarets all priced at just 190 F. And after your meal, you can linger contentedly over a rare whisky or vintage Port. **C** 280-320 F. **M** 160 F, 195 F.

Bistrot de l'Étoile-Lauriston
19, rue Lauriston
40 67 11 16, fax 45 00 99 87
Closed Sat lunch, Sun. Open until midnight. Air cond. V, AE, MC.
This big, bright bistro continues on its successful career. Chef William Ledeuil handles the neo-bourgeois repertoire with admirable ease, offering rabbit persillé or a vibrant vegetable salad showered with Parmesan to start, followed by steak à la bordelaise or stuffed veal shank simmered in a sparky vinegar sauce. For dessert, we warmly recommend the apple-rhubarb crumble. **C** 190-280 F.

La Butte Chaillot
110 bis, av. Kléber
47 27 88 88, fax 47 04 85 70
Open daily until midnight. Priv rm: 20. Air cond. V, AE, MC.
Chef and restaurateur Guy Savoy turned an unpromising site (a former bank) into a fashionable restaurant with a star-studded clientele. The keys to his success are a clever contemporary décor, a swift and stylish staff, and—best of all—an ever-changing roster of irresistible dishes: succulent spit-roasted poultry with perfect whipped potatoes, veal breast perfumed with rosemary and olive oil, and lots of luscious desserts. **C** 250-320 F. **M** 160 F (weekday dinner), 110 F (weekday lunch), 200 F.

Red toques signify creative cuisine; white toques signify traditional cuisine.

Paul Chène

123, rue Lauriston - 47 27 63 17
Closed Sat lunch, Sun, Dec 24-Jan 2, Jul 30-Aug 22. Open until 10:30pm. Priv rm: 30. Air cond. Pkg. V, AE, DC.

Elbowroom is at a premium in Paul Chène's two faded dining rooms, but the owners are unstinting with their hospitality, and the kitchen too has a generous spirit. You're sure to relish mackerel marinated in Muscadet, tasty foie gras, langoustine feuilleté, or beef simmered in red wine. The cellar boasts a varied, judicious selection, yet the house Bordeaux is not to be neglected. C 350-450 F. M 250 F.

Conti

72, rue Lauriston
47 27 74 67, fax 47 27 37 66
Closed Sat, Sun, Dec 30-Jan 8, Aug 5-28. Open until 10:30pm. Air cond. V, AE, DC.

Along with Pascal Fayet of Sormani (see seventeenth arrondissement), Michel Ranvier is the city's leading French exponent of Italian cooking. Perhaps a shade less creative than Fayet, Ranvier nevertheless gives his repertoire a vigorous, vibrant zest. Examples? Here are a few: scallops in a sauce laced with Vin Santo, slivers of wee violet artichokes with bresaola in white-truffle dressing, sea bream with saffron-spiced potatoes, and tender baby lamb sparked with anchovies. Ranvier's pastas are anything but run-of-the-mill: they're filled and sauced with foie gras, or bottarga, or pumpkin and marjoram... The list of fine Italian wines is a wonder to behold, and the staff that moves discreetly about the red-and-black dining room provides exemplary service. C 350-450 F. M 265 F (lunch).

Le Cuisinier François

19, rue Le Marois - 45 27 83 74
Closed Sun dinner, Mon, Aug. Open until 10:30pm. V, MC.

After his stints at La Tour d'Argent, Robuchon, and with Boyer in Reims, Thierry Conte did not, as one might expect, open a place with his name in large letters over the door. Instead, the times being what they are, he settled for an establishment of modest proportions (just 26 seats) and a menu that is most moderately priced. A delicious terrine of lambs' tongues and leeks, braised pollack with fresh herbs, and a papillote of lavender-scented fruit are typical of the modern, uncomplicated dishes on offer. C 220 F. M 140 F.

Duret Mandarin

34, rue Duret - 45 00 09 06
Open daily until 11pm. Priv rm: 60. Air cond. Valet pkg. V, MC.

Just between us, this place really rates closer to two toques, but we don't want the Tang family to get flustered by success. They work hard to deliver (with a smile!) such classic Asian favorites as crispy egg rolls, deep-fried dumplings, and stuffed crab, and such interesting options as steamed scallops with black-bean sauce, "special" roast chicken, and langouste or monkfish spiced with ginger. Here, by the way, we tasted the best Peking duck in town, with optimally crisp skin (order it when you book your table). C 160-260 F. M 79 F & 95 F.

Fakhr el Dine

30, rue de Longchamp
47 27 90 00, fax 47 27 11 39
See 8th arrondissement.

Faugeron

52, rue de Longchamp
47 04 24 53, fax 47 55 62 90
Closed Sat (exc dinner Oct-Apr), Sun, Dec 23-Jan 2, Aug. Open until 10pm. Priv rm: 14. Air cond. No pets. Valet pkg. V, AE, MC.

The dining room's blue-and-saffron color scheme may not be to everyone's taste, but then one doesn't come here to eat the décor! What attracts us is the calm, unruffled ambience and, of course, the subtly inventive cooking of Henri Faugeron. He's a modest, even self-effacing chef, not at all obsessed by novelty. The bases of his repertoire are solidly classic, and he would rather heighten and balance the flavors of superb ingredients than create "surprise" effects. Sterling craftsmanship marks a menu that features scallops poised on a delicate celery cream sauce, escalope of foie gras breaded à la Wiener Schnitzel (a tribute to Austria, Faugeron's second home), lobster tournedos enlivened with Moroccan spices, suprême of guinea fowl in a truffled jus, and a memorable combination of tender dilled rabbit tucked under a fluffy potato blanket. Faugeron's pear millefeuille with honeycream sauce or macaron with caramelized pineapple are final flourishes to be savored along with the last drops of a great Bordeaux, a voluptuous Burgundy, or a more modest Chinon or Sancerre, chosen by world-class sommelier Jean-Claude Jambon.

Under the smiling supervision of hostess Gerlindé Faugeron, a whole squadron of courteous (but never obsequious) waiters tends to the high-class clientele. C 500-900 F. M 340 F (lunch, wine incl), 550 F (dinner, wine incl), 720 F (all-truffle), 290 F (lunch), 320 F (dinner).

Jean-Claude Ferrero

38, rue Vital
45 04 42 42, fax 45 04 67 71
Closed Sat (exc dinner in winter), Sun, May 1-15, Aug 8-Sep 5. Open until 10:30pm. Priv rm: 35. Valet pkg. V, AE.

"All-truffle" or "all-mushroom" menus are now a staple in restaurants throughout France. Jean-Claude Ferrero, who started the vogue, is pleased to see that his idea has caught on. Encouraged by diners' enthusiasm, he's dreamed up still more thematic variations, such as hunt and other seasonal menus, and so keeps his Second Empire hôtel particulier filled with a faithful, very Parisian crowd sprinkled with ambassadors and cabinet ministers.

Ferrero's spirited cooking displays a pronounced Southern tilt, evident in his soupe de poisson à la provençale, mussel gratin, and red mullet escorted by tangy tomato jam. More classically French and full of lusty flavor are his volaille en vessie aux asperges (chicken cooked to ideal juiciness in a pork bladder then garnished with asparagus tips), calf's head rémoulade, and bœuf aux carottes in a deep, winy sauce. Ferrero's inspiration fails, however, when it comes to sweets; crêpes au Grand Marnier or baked Alaska (no less) are oddly banal codas to otherwise remarkable meals. C 400-700 F. M 200 F (weekday lunch), 280 F, 350 F.

Gastronomie Quach
47, av. R.-Poincaré - 47 27 98 40
Open daily until 11pm. Priv rm: 60. Air cond. V, AE, DC, MC.

Aquariums decorate this posh dining room where Monsieur Quach serves Cantonese and Vietnamese dishes that have their good days and their bad: prawns grilled with lemongrass, squid with red peppers, and grilled lamb with five spices can be delicious or bland, depending. But it's the Peking duck that keeps the glossy patrons coming back for more. Served, as it should be, in three separate courses, the duck is indeed a delight. Prices are quite reasonable—for the neighborhood. C 220-300 F. M 92 F (weekday lunch), 109 F.

Le Grand Chinois
6, av. de New-York - 47 23 98 21
Closed Mon, Aug. Open until 11pm. Priv rm: 25. V, AE, DC.

Don't come here for the décor, unless your taste runs to walls plastered with autographed celebrity photos. Come instead for the ginger-spiced hot oysters, the superb dim-sum, sautéed shrimp, and eels with onions. Though the chef isn't perfectly consistent, he also turns out a creditable salmon in sweet-and-sour sauce, hacked pigeon, and crab steamed in bok-choy leaves. What's more, the wine list is amazingly good. Owner Colette Tan welcomes guests and oversees the stylish service. C 300-400 F. M 120 F (weekday lunch, Sat), 354 F (for 2 pers), 1,330 F (for 4 pers).

La Grande Cascade
Bois de Boulogne, near the racetrack
45 27 33 51, fax 42 88 99 06
Closed Dec 20-Jan 20. Open until 10:30pm. Priv rm: 50. Garden dining. Valet pkg. V, AE, DC, MC.

The setting of this former pleasure pavilion is extravagantly Belle Époque. In contrast, the cuisine of Jean Sabine and Frédéric Robert, a couple of enlightened culinary classicists, is reassuring and discreet. You'll be charmed by their crab ravioli in a saffron-stained fumet, sweetbreads in a puff-pastry shell (vol-au-vent) cloaked with a truffled Madeira sauce, and a lovely vanilla-lime mille-feuille. The cellar houses 80,000 bottles, service is formal, and prices are dizzying! C 500-750 F. M 550 F (dinner), 285 F (exc Sun).

Lac Hong
67, rue Lauriston - 47 55 87 17
Closed Aug. Open until 10:45pm. No pets. V, MC.

Vietnam's cuisine may be the most delicately flavorful in all of Southeast Asia. Should you wish to test that proposition, just taste the remarkable dishes served forth by Phan Huu Hau, the voluble owner of this minuscule establishment. Start with a salad of grilled scampi and green papaya, then proceed to escargots perfumed with Chinese basil, crisp rice crêpes stuffed with shrimp, steamed smoked duck with fish sauce, grilled chicken redolent of five-spice powder, or the excellent salt-and-pepper shrimp. Even the Cantonese rice is exquisite: flawlessly cooked

and bursting with flavor. The second toque is not far off... C 260 F. M 89 F (weekday lunch).

Oum el Banine
16 bis, rue Dufrenoy
45 04 91 22, fax 45 03 46 26
Closed Sat lunch, Sun, Aug 10-25. Open until 11pm. Air cond. V, AE, MC.

To enter, knock on the heavy wooden door, just as you would in Morocco. Maria Seguin, a native of Fès, practices authentic Fassi cuisine, whose secrets are handed down from mother to daughter. Five types of couscous are on offer (including the refined Fès version, with caramelized onions and grapes), as well as six kinds of lamb tagine (with olives and pickled lemons, peppers and tomato, zucchini and thyme, etc.). More rarely seen, but typically Moroccan are brains in a piquant tomato sauce, spiced tripe, and calf's foot with chickpeas. C 250-300 F. M 150 F.

Le Pavillon des Princes
69, av. de la Porte-d'Auteuil
47 43 15 15, fax 46 51 16 94
Open daily until 10:30pm. Priv rm: 120. Terrace dining. Pkg. V, AE, DC, MC.

The dining room's high-kitsch décor shouldn't spoil your appetite for Patrick Lenôtre's tasty bourgeois-style cooking. An enticing single-price menu (180 F) shows what this chef can do: among the options are a savory duck-liver terrine, lightly smoked rainbow trout, sea bass perfumed with tarragon, veal shanks au pistou, duck served in two courses, and a spicy tarte feuilletée. Fine cellar, with an emphasis on Bordeaux. You can be sure of a warm welcome when you arrive, and the attentions of a classy staff while you dine. M 180 F, 270 F.

Le Port Alma
10, av. de New-York - 47 23 75 11
Closed Sun, Aug. Open until 10:30pm. Priv rm: 15. Air cond. V, AE, DC, MC.

Paul Canal isn't one to blow his own horn, but Parisian seafood buffs know that he has few peers when it comes to cooking fish and crustaceans. You can count on Canal to pick the best of the day's catch, and prepare his prime specimens with a light, skilled hand. His crab ravioli, prawn croustillant, and fillet of John Dory are fresh as can be, with no superfluous sauces to mask their flavors. Desserts, too, are uniformly delicious, and the superb cellar holds plenty of half-bottles. C 300-500 F. M 200 F (lunch).

Le Pré Catelan
Bois de Boulogne, route de Suresnes
45 24 55 58, fax 45 24 43 25
Closed Sun dinner, Mon, Feb 27-Mar 13. Open until 10pm. Priv rm: 40. Garden dining. Valet pkg. V, AE, DC, MC.

Fine cuisine is the Pré Catelan's main drawing card, of course, but high praise is surely due to decorator Christian Benais, whose transformation of this Second Empire landmark is nothing short of inspired. From on high, splendid reliefs by Caran d'Ache gaze down at plush beige carpet studded with green cabochons, billowing draperies of raw linen and taffeta, and tables skirted in scarlet damask. The effect is pure magic. In winter, a warming blaze crackles in the fireplace; and on balmy days, the scene shifts to the garden, where tables are set beneath flutter-ing parasols.

Chef Roland Durand's spirited cuisine, at once rousingly rustic and urbane, is ideally suited to this setting. Typical of his lively style are mackerel rillettes with green-bean salad, lightly cooked salmon given a jolt of black pepper and a smoky jus of grilled bell peppers, calf's head in a pun-gently herbal ravigote sauce, a startlingly good dish of langoustines in black risotto sparked with Thai basil, or John Dory in a fragrant bouil-labaisse fumet. The sweets here are better than ever; our current favorite is the gingered nougat glacé. The cellar affords a remarkable choice of wines, prudently priced. **C** 500-960 F. **M** 270 F (weekday lunch), 400 F, 690 F.

Prunier-Traktir
16, av. Victor-Hugo - 45 00 89 12
Open daily until 11:30pm. Priv rm: 10. Air cond. Valet pkg. V, AE, DC, MC.

The rebirth of Prunier-Traktir caused great rejoicing among Paris's pearls-and-tweed set, who regarded the demise of this once-brilliant seafood house as a personal loss. The man behind this revival is none other than Jean-Claude Vrinat, of Taillevent. From the moment he opened the doors of a scrubbed and polished Prunier, former habitués took the dining room by storm, thrilled to be back at their old tables amid the beautifully restored Art Deco mosaics. The menu, too, is much as they remember it. Vrinat placed a Taillevent alumnus in the kitchen, and charged him with resuscitating the classic house repertoire. He does an admirable job with the lobster bisque, codfish brandade, sea bass "Émile Prunier," scallops in an aromatic broth, and assortments of bracingly fresh shellfish. There's an excellent cellar, with bottles starting at around 100 F (some wines are available by the glass). And the newly refurbished upstairs dining room now provides space for additional elegant patrons. **C** 300-500 F.

Le Relais d'Auteuil
"Patrick Pignol," 31, bd Murat
46 51 09 54, fax 40 71 05 03
Closed Sat lunch, Sun, 1st wk of Aug. Open until 10:30pm. Air cond. Valet pkg. V, AE, MC.

Food-lovers warmly recommend this res-taurant to their friends, for Patrick Pignol's im-aginative, resolutely modern cuisine is a treat to discover. Uncompromising in his choice of in-gredients, he follows the seasons to obtain the very freshest, finest produce. In summer, he'll feature tiny violet artichokes and other vegetables at the peak of their flavor; in fall, look for sage-scented braised partridge; winter might bring a mammoth sole in a sauce of lightly salted butter and fiery Szechuan pepper, while spring provides the pleasures of baby lamb and new garlic. If Pignol would just keep a tighter rein on his prices, our happiness would be complete! **C** 500-550 F. **M** 230 F (lunch), 390 F, 480 F.

12/20 Le Relais du Bois
Bois de Boulogne, Croix-Catelan,
route de Suresnes - 42 88 08 43,
Closed Sun dinner. Open until 10:30pm. Terrace dining. No pets. V.

This rustic rendezvous—a Second Empire hunt-ing pavilion where naughty ladies and

gentlemen once engaged in rather outrageous behavior—is now the backdrop for tame family parties and corporate banquets. The comfort-able dining room has its charms, but the huge summer garden is truly delightful. Good—if un-exciting—food: fish soup, pot-au-feu, grilled steak, confit de canard. **C** 150-250 F.

Le Relais du Parc
Le Parc Victor-Hugo,
55-57, av. Raymond-Poincaré
44 05 66 10, fax 44 05 66 00
Open daily until 10:30pm. Terrace dining. Air cond. Valet pkg. V, AE, DC, MC.

Le Relais du Parc holds a winning hand: set in the luxurious new Parc Victor-Hugo hotel, it sports a British colonial setting (straight *Out of Africa*) designed by Nina Campbell and boasts a menu conceived and supervised by none other than Joël Robuchon. The cashmere-and-tweed types who live or work hereabouts have made Le Relais their headquarters. They certainly don't mind paying bistro prices for attractive fare like warm mackerel tart, duck parmentier, spit-roasted duck, or a wine-dark civet de lapin ac-cented with smoky bacon. Dessert brings ably executed standards—floating island, cup cus-tards, tarte aux pommes—and there's a fascinat-ing, affordable wine list. **C** 250-350 F.

Robuchon

55, av. R.-Poincaré
47 27 12 27, fax 47 27 31 22
Closed Sat, Sun, Jul 8-Aug 6. Open until 10:15pm. Priv rm: 12. Air cond. Valet pkg. V.

Dining at Joël Robuchon's new restaurant is no simple proposition. No, it's an experience fraught with anxiety, anticipation, excitement, and high emotion! Just consider: after months of waiting, your name finally reaches the top of the interminable reservation list—at last one of the dining room's 45 seats is destined for you! On the appointed day, you arrive at the monumen-tal entrance of Robuchon's Belle Époque town house, where you must ring the bell, identify yourself to the hostess, cross a gallery adorned with precious Daum and Gallé glass, then climb the magnificent (listed!) wrought-iron staircase to the landing, where Madame Robuchon tots up tabs and answers the telephone behind a fabulous Majorelle desk. Dining-room director Jean-Jacques Caimant—or one of his maître d's—will then escort you to the holy of holies.

Now for the bittersweet predicament of com-posing a meal from Robuchon's thrilling menu. Should you begin with a lightly truffled crème de haricots de Vendée (an apotheosis for the humble white bean), or the truffled pig's trotter sliced and served beside a salad of chestnuts dressed with a vinaigrette of Sherry vinegar, truffle oil, truffle jus, and crushed chestnuts? Or would it be wiser to start with the stunning tomato millefeuille layered with a sublime mélange of crabmeat, watercress, and herbs? The dilemmas don't stop there. For you'll have to eliminate either the huge langoustines seared in goose fat then fricasséed with lobster coral and morels, or the fantastic rock lobster roasted with cumin and rosemary, its rare savor heightened further with chopped truffles and aged Parmesan, or the deceptively simple whit-ing fillet, a marvel of delicacy enhanced with tomato confit, asparagus tips, and baby fennel, or else the farm-bred guinea fowl roasted to succulence and set atop a slice of flash-seared foie gras.

Don't even hope that choosing a dessert will be easier (here, we'll help you: order the divine walnut croustillant in a pool of dark-chocolate sauce). Afterward, when you repair downstairs to the spacious new *salon-fumoir*, you can recollect in tranquillity, over coffee and liqueurs, the gastronomic masterworks just sampled, and plan, perhaps, your next dinner *chez* Robuchon—necessarily some months hence, when your name again reaches the top of the waiting list! C 750-1,500 F.

 Le Toit de Passy
94, av. Paul-Doumer
45 24 55 37, fax 45 20 94 57
Closed Sat lunch, Sun. Open until 10:30pm. Priv rm: 25. Terrace dining. Air cond. Pkg. V, AE, MC.
On a fine day, the terrace is unquestionably the place to sit, for the unimpeded view of Passy's rooftops. Yet the dining room, accented with plants and partitions, graced with well-spaced tables and flattering lights, is a comfortable, elegant setting in which to enjoy Yannick Jacquot's subtly imaginative cuisine. Excellent meals can be made of his duck pâté enriched with foie gras and flanked by a complementary céleri rémoulade; ultrafresh langoustines in a suave citrus butter or squab roasted to succulence in a sea-salt crust and escorted by buttery braised cabbage; and the assiette of dainty chocolate sweets. The cellar holds 45,000 bottles, so the wine list will take some perusing. C 420-600 F. M 195 F (weekday lunch), 295 F, 380 F, 495 F.

Vivarois
192, av. V.-Hugo
45 04 04 31, fax 45 03 09 84
Closed Sat, Sun, Aug. Open until 10pm. Air cond. Garage pkg. V, AE, DC, MC.
Claude Peyrot hasn't upped his prices in three years. Merely by holding steady, they are now lower than those posted in many a lesser establishment. Few sophisticated diners-out would bat an eye, nowadays, at paying 245 F for turbot with wild mushrooms, or 215 F for coq au vin stewed in genuine Pommard wine. So when these dishes are prepared by a four-toque chef whose cooking is perhaps the most intelligent and subtle in town, the prices seem—almost—cheap.

Claude Peyrot carries on imperturbably, polishing a concise *carte* which he enriches daily with a half-dozen dishes created on the spur of the moment. The maître d'hôtel might announce the presence of a mousse d'étrilles (a crabmeat concoction that is both ineffably light and rich), potato galettes with foie gras and truffles, or, in hunting season, hare à la royale with a superb quince compote: a regal dish indeed that will forever haunt our gastronomic memory. Even if the aforementioned are not available when you visit Vivarois, Peyrot's feuilleté de truffe and his oxtail braised with mustard—both deserve to go down in culinary history—will surely be on offer, along with a splendid herb-scented roast lobster or poularde au vinaigre. This chef's unrivaled technique, his singular sensitivity and grace, give

every dish he produces a distinctive signature that is uniquely Peyrot's. To add to the pleasure, there are wines, magnificent and modest, of the sort kind that every connoisseur yearns to discover, amassed by sommelier extraordinaire Jean-Claude Vinadier. C 560-800 F. M 345 F (lunch).

 Amphyclès
78, av. des Ternes
40 68 01 01, fax 40 68 91 88
Closed Sat lunch, Sun. Open until 10:30pm. Priv rm: 25. Air cond. Valet pkg. V, AE, DC, MC.
Joël Robuchon initiated Philippe Groult in the art of harmonizing rustic with recherché flavors, to create a rich, diverse palette of tastes. The master is justly proud of his former star pupil, for here at Amphyclès "city" and "country" dishes coexist deliciously in Groult's distinctive, personal repertoire. It successfully embraces both slow-simmered lamb à l'ancienne and a frothy crab soup lavished with caviar; rack of veal ménagère as well as Bresse chicken poached in an elaborate spiced bouillon; and casseroled lamb's trotters alongside smothered lobster and morels with a foie gras–enriched macaroni gratin.
Groult takes special care with vegetable garnishes: his marvelous salads of fresh herbs, a wonderfully smoky split-pea mousseline, or white beans whipped with cream and Parmesan are all delectable enough to make a meal on their own! We should note too that Groult's themed menus—all-truffle, all-mushroom, all-shellfish or game—attract brilliant tables of Parisian gourmets who run up astronomical bills, with the help of costly bottles from the much-improved cellar. C 500-850 F. M 260 F (lunch), 580 F, 780 F.

 Apicius
122, av. de Villiers
43 80 19 66, fax 44 40 09 57
Closed Sat, Sun, Aug. Open until 10pm. Air cond. Valet pkg. V, AE, DC, MC.
We know lots of high-class restaurants where the food is perfectly fine—but the ambience is stuffy and dull. At Jean-Pierre Vigato's Apicius, not only is the food simply fabulous, the atmosphere is as warm as can be. The charm begins to operate from the moment Madeleine Vigato welcomes you into the spectacularly flower-decked dining room, and the urbane sommelier suggests a suitable wine to sip while you peruse the menu.
We've been singing Vigato's praises long enough to feel we needn't repeat ourselves. Though his core repertoire doesn't change much from one year to the next, Vigato keeps himself sharp by offering a half-dozen different starters and entrées each day, (which Madeleine describes at each table in luscious detail). But who would need prodding to reorder such inspiring house classics as Vigato's escalope of foie gras with black-radish confit in a suave sweet-and-sour sauce? Or his unforgettably fragrant truffle risotto? Likewise, plump prawns flash-fried in a diaphanous batter of spices,

Japanese flour, and egg white are well worth eating more than once! As is the cod with crumbled potatoes: Vigato's treatment puts that humble fish into the same noble league as turbot and sole. We can also confidently recommend the spit-roasted sweetbreads with creamy whipped potatoes, the sumptuous tourte de canard, and any of the divine game dishes Vigato prepares during the hunt season. With equal conviction we say that his sweets—an incredible gratin de café moka, crackling licorice custard, an ineffable caramel extravaganza—will provide you with a moment of unalloyed bliss. **C** 550-850 F. **M** 520 F.

 Augusta
98, rue de Tocqueville
47 63 39 97, fax 42 27 21 71
Closed Sat lunch (& dinner May 1-Sep 30), Sun, 2 wks in Aug. Open until 10pm. Air cond. V, MC.
Scrupulously seasonal, rigorously precise, based on the freshest seafood: Lionel Maître's cuisine is all this and more. The clear, direct flavors of his shellfish salad, rockfish soup, fricassée de coquilles Saint-Jacques, sea bass with fava beans in an herbal jus, or langoustines with mellow garlic purée incite us to unashamed gorging! Remarkable wine list; young, eager staff. **C** 410-600 F.

Billy Gourmand
20, rue de Tocqueville
42 27 03 71
Closed Sat lunch (& dinner Jul-Sep), Sun, hols. Open until 10pm. Priv rm: 14. V, AE, MC.
Chef Philippe Billy presents his polished, attractively presented cuisine in a spacious and sprightly dining room decorated with mirrors and plants. Not one to rest on his laurels, he comes up with a new single-price menu each week. On a recent visit it delivered fresh crab ravioli swathed in a mushroom cream sauce, pikeperch in red-wine sauce with a fennel and macaroni gratin, and a frozen prune feuilleté. The engaging *patronne* oversees a fine cellar of Loire Valley wines. **C** 270-410 F. **M** 150 F.

Le Bistrot d'à Côté
10, rue G.-Flaubert
42 67 05 81, fax 47 63 82 75
Open daily until 11pm. Terrace dining. Air cond. Valet pkg. V, AE, MC.
All you want from a bistro: hustle, bustle, and cheeky waiters. Who wouldn't be won over by the simple, savory pleasures of such Lyonnais-style specialties as chicken-liver terrine, pork-and-beef sausage (sabodet), or grilled fresh tuna? The wines, however, are too expensive for this sort of establishment. **C** 250-330 F.

Le Bistrot de l'Étoile-Niel
75, av. Niel
42 27 88 44, fax 42 27 32 12
Closed Sun lunch. Open until midnight. Terrace dining. Air cond. Valet pkg. V, AE.
Here's your typical cheerful neighborhood bistro—except that it's owned and supervised by Guy Savoy. Handily prepared and served with a smile, the fresh sardines showered with basil, comforting blanquette de veau and other *plats du jour*, the chocolate tourte and house Merlot have won a loyal following. **C** 190-280 F. **M** 170 F (Sun dinner).

Le Bistrot de l'Étoile-Troyon
13, rue Troyon - 42 67 25 95
Closed Sat lunch, Sun. Annual closings not available. Open until midnight. Air cond. V, AE, MC.
Guy Savoy can keep a close eye on the firstborn of his bistro annexes, for it stands just across the street from his four-toque restaurant. In the small, convivial dining room you can treat yourself to such heart-warming bourgeois classics as herbed lamb noisettes, duck with red beans, pan-roasted sea trout, and chocolate fondant. Good growers' wines; democratic prices. **C** 250-280 F.

Caves Pétrissans
30 bis, av. Niel
42 27 52 03, fax 40 54 87 56
Closed Sat, Sun, hols, last wk of Feb, 1st 4 wks of Aug. Open until 10:30pm. Priv rm: 12. Terrace dining. V, AE, MC.
Four generations of Pétrissans have overseen this wine shop-cum-restaurant, where patrons linger happily over Jacques Bertrel's tasty cooking. The quality ingredients are simply prepared and generously served; try the tête de veau sauce ravigote, spareribs with buttery braised cabbage, pauté au vinaigre de cidre, and velvety crème brûlée. **C** 250-340 F. **M** 155 F.

Charly de Bab-el-Oued
95, bd Gouvion-St-Cyr
45 74 34 62, fax 45 74 35 36
Open daily until 11:30pm. Air cond. No pets. V, AE, DC, MC.
An inviting place to dream of the *Arabian Nights* amid colorful tiles, cedarwood, and palm trees. Feast on Claude Driguès's excellent couscous, pastillas, and tagines, followed by sweet Eastern pastries made on the premises. Perfect service. **C** 220-270 F. **M** 200 F.

12/20 Les Cigales
127, rue Cardinet - 42 27 83 93
Dinner & groups by reserv. Closed Sat, Sun, Aug. No pets. V.
A quintessential neighborhood bistro, serving a roster of tasty, clever dishes. The décor plays the Provençal card to the hilt (sun-yellow walls, photos of the Riviera...), and so does the bright bill of fare: tomatoes stuffed with creamy goat cheese, grilled sea bream anointed with virgin olive oil, pasta dressed with pistou are all handily turned out by the young *patronne*. All she needs to do now is put together a decent regional cellar. **C** 190-250 F. **M** 60 F, 119 F.

 Clos Longchamp
Hôtel Méridien, 81, bd Gouvion-St-Cyr
40 68 30 40, fax 40 68 30 81
Closed Sat, Sun, last wk of Dec, Jul 29-Aug 30. Open until 10:30pm. Priv rm: 18. Air cond. Valet pkg. V, AE, DC, MC.
We can't figure out why a certain red-jacketed restaurant guide bumped a star from chef Jean-Marie Meulien's rating. After a serious illness he has bounced back, as energetic as ever, with an exciting menu that combines the flavors of the Mediterranean with the spices of Southeast Asia. Meulien is a master craftsman, in the mold of his mentor, Louis Outhier. He recently tempted us with a procession of technically flawless, delightfully sun-kissed dishes: plump pink shrimp atop

an exquisite salad dressed with Champagne vinegar, a deeply flavorful snail and chestnut soup, scallops fired up with Thai spices, sea bass with toasted buckwheat, terrine of duck liver laced with Beaumes-de-Venise wine, and stunning squash blossoms stuffed with cardamom-spiced salmon. A similarly exotic mood inspires the delicate desserts. Award-winning sommelier Didier Bureau administers a cellar of rare and delicious wines, one of which is sure to complement your meal. The Méridien's exuberant central garden has flourished so well you would think you were in a sunnier clime; it almost makes you forget the strange, banana-shaped dining room! C 450-600 F. M 260 F (lunch), 470 F (dinner).

Le Col-Vert
18, rue Bayen - 45 72 02 19
Closed Sat lunch, Sun, Aug 1-28. Open until 10:30pm (Fri & Sat 11pm). Priv rm: 25. Air cond. Garage pkg. V, MC.
Franck Descas is a young chef with impressive credentials and a sprightly, original style. Exotic notes from his native Antilles crop up in dishes like foie gras carpaccio served with a salad of chayote squash, tiny scallops in a dressing brightened with a dash of lime juice, or his novel fish "sausage" with tangy coarse-grain mustard and a garnish of sweet potatoes. His cooking still has a few rough edges, but we applaud his fresh, personal approach—a rarity these days! C 250-370 F. M 150 F.

11/20 Le Congrès
80, av. de la Grande-Armée - 45 74 17 24
Open daily 24 hours. Air cond. V, AE, DC, MC.
A huge barracks-like brasserie, open all day and all night, vigilant about the consistent quality of its classics: shellfish (fresh all year) and large slabs of charcoal-grilled meat. Good tarte Tatin; decent selection of house wines. C 220-270 F. M 179 F (wine incl).

Dessirier
9, pl. du Mal-Juin
42 27 82 14, fax 47 63 98 79
Closed Sun, Aug. Open until 11:30pm. Priv rm: 20. Terrace dining. Valet pkg. V, AE, DC, MC.
A favorable wind has blown this venerable seafood brasserie back into our Guide. The new chef relies on the sound principles of simplicity and accurate timing to produce an unctuous, full-flavored lobster bisque and a particularly tasty cod with tapenade. Desserts, however, still need work. A carafe of house Chablis is a welcome alternative to the costly wine list. Jolly service. C 300-450 F. M 200 F.

L'Étoile d'Or
Hôtel Concorde-La Fayette,
3, pl. du Gal-Kœnig
40 68 51 28, fax 40 68 50 43
Closed Sat, Sun, hols, 1 wk in Feb, Aug. Open until 10:30pm. Priv rm: 35. Air cond. Valet pkg. V, AE, DC, MC.
Jean-Claude Lhonneur, formerly of Le Grand Véfour and La Tour d'Argent, has turned L'Étoile d'Or into one of the best hotel restaurants in town. A bold approach to harmonizing flavors, admirably accurate cooking times, and fragrant, feather-light sauces are the three solid bases of an alluring repertoire. We know: it isn't easy to

find this handsome, wood-paneled dining room, hidden in the labyrinth of the Hôtel Concorde; paying the bill isn't so simple either. But if you make the effort, your reward will be (for example) meltingly savory duck liver in a jus based on Banyuls wine, or a bosky mushroom confit spiked with Calvados, then smothered sea bass perfumed with truffled oil, irresistible stewed ox jowls en ravigote, and a chocolate soufflé that the waiter swears is the best in Paris! These delights are delivered by an exceptionally well trained staff. As for the cellar, it holds few bargains but there are many half-bottles in stock. C 400-700 F. M 270 F.

Faucher
123, av. de Wagram
42 27 61 50, fax 46 22 25 72
Closed Sat lunch, Sun, wk of Aug 15. Open until 10pm. Terrace dining. Valet pkg. V, AE.
Gérard and Nicole Faucher have inaugurated a new price policy at their bright and lovely restaurant. Set meals have been abolished, and à la carte tariffs have come down some 50 percent. Faucher has crossed a few costly items off of his shopping list, but otherwise his cuisine is just as vivid and modern as ever. In fact, he's managed to preserve a few of his signature dishes on the new menu, including the millefeuille of thinly sliced raw beef and spinach leaves and the short ribs en pot-au-feu with a truffled jus. Along-side these veterans, you'll find oxtail ravioli in a savory bouillon and a lusty pairing of veal kidney and andouillette sausage with a potato croustillant. Good desserts and wines from a revised, less expensive cellar complete the picture. Nicole Faucher continues to greet guests with a smile in the cheerful yellow dining room embellished with paintings and elegant table settings. C 220-290 F.

11/20 Chez Fred
190 bis, bd Pereire - 45 74 20 48
Closed Sun, 2 wks mid Aug. Open until 11pm. Terrace dining. V, AE, DC, MC.
An influx of trendies has not spoiled the service, the simplicity of the setting, or the heartwarming sincerity of Fred's cuisine: bacon with lentils, pot-au-feu, and blanquette de veau. No-nonsense wines sold by the *pichet*. C 210-260 F. M 145 F.

La Gazelle
9, rue Rennequin
42 67 64 18, fax 42 67 82 77
Closed Sat lunch, Sun. Open until 11:30pm. V, AE, DC, MC.
With its star-studded ceiling, this is the prettiest African restaurant in Paris. La Gazelle boasts a surprising range of intensely tasty dishes prepared by proprietress-chef Marie Koffi-Nketsin, who comes from Cameroon: try her stuffed crab, fish with seven spices, chicken in peanut sauce, and marinated kid baked en papillote with African corn. Crocodile also features on the menu—connoisseurs, take note! Slow-paced but cheerful service. C 130-220 F. M 130 F & 150 F (weekdays, Sat dinner, wine incl), 95 F (weekday lunch, wine incl).

Restaurant names in red draw attention to restaurants that offer particularly good value.

Goldenberg

69, av. de Wagram
42 27 34 79, fax 42 27 98 85
Open daily until 11:30pm. Terrace dining. Pkg. V.
Patrick Goldenberg creates a typically Yiddish atmosphere of good humor and nostalgia, Jewish jokes and anecdotes in which to enjoy delicious Kosher cooking rooted in the traditions of Russia, Hungary, Romania, Bulgaria... There's smoked and corned beef, wonderful corned goose breast, kneidler in chicken broth, veal sausage, and other Central European classics. For dessert, don't miss the poppyseed strudel. There's also a delicatessen for take-out, and a sunny terrace for fine weather. C 150-250 F. M 98 F.

Graindorge
15, rue de l'Arc-de-Triomphe
47 54 00 28, fax 44 09 84 51
Closed Sun. Open until 11pm. Priv rm: 35. Air cond. Garage pkg. V, AE.
When Bernard Broux (long-time chef at Le Trou Gascon) opened a place of his own, he forsook the Southwest and its earthy tastes in favor of the cuisine of his native Flanders. Broux's menu celebrates hearty Northern savors with a terrine of smoked eel and baby leeks, chicken breast and vegetables in a creamy waterzoï sauce, and strawberries in a sabayon spiked with raspberry-flavored kriek beer. While the wine list merits your attention, beer lovers will be knocked out by the superb selection of rare brews. C 250-350 F. M 130 F & 160 F(weekday lunch), 185 F.

Guyvonne
14, rue de Thann
42 27 25 43, fax 42 27 25 43
Closed Sat, Sun, Dec 25-Jan 1, Jul 31-Aug 28. Open until 9:45pm. Priv rm: 11. Terrace dining. No pets. Pkg. V, AE, MC.
Guy Cros's cooking is as appealing as ever, but his repertoire seems to be shrinking. On our last visit to his intimate, country-style dining room, we were startled to learn that only three of the starters listed were actually available; the choice of desserts seemed awfully brief, too. But as usual, our mood soared as we tucked into the langoustines with fresh artichokes and chanterelles, baby skate in a ginger-spiced sauce, and scrumptious chocolate mousseline layered with mocha spongecake. The cellar is still stocked with first-rate Bordeaux. C 300-380 F. M 180 F.

12/20 Chez Léon
32, rue Legendre - 42 27 06 82
Closed Sat, Sun, Feb 15-24, Aug. Open until 9:45pm. Priv rm: 20. Pkg. V, DC.
A traditional bistro with the usual unvarying roster of robust food—terrines, saucisson chaud, tête de veau vinaigrette, duck confit, and cassoulet. For dessert, look no farther than the homey floating island. Service is pleasant, and so are the Beaujolais wines. C 220-280 F. M 140 F, 170 F.

Le Madigan
22, rue de la Terrasse - 42 27 31 51
Closed Sun lunch, Sun, Aug 8-Sep 5. Open until 9:30pm. Terrace dining. Air cond. V, AE, DC, MC.
After dinner, when it's time for liqueurs, Le Madigan's sober yet sumptuous dining room is

transformed into a concert hall. Hopeful young talents and international prize-winners take their place at the Steinway grand for what are often remarkable recitals. The prelude to these musical soirées is chef Jean-Michel Descloux's fine-tuned cuisine. He turns out a sparkling duet of sole aïoli and potato salad, braised sweetbreads with a Parma-ham jus, and vanilla vacherin. With a selection from the abundantly annotated wine list, you're in for a harmonious evening. C 320-560 F. M 150 F & 250 F (lunch), 180 F & 280 F (dinner).

Le Manoir de Paris
6, rue Pierre-Demours
45 72 25 25, fax 45 74 80 98
Closed Sat lunch, Sun. Open until 10:30pm. Priv rm: 60. Air cond. Valet pkg. V, AE, DC.
Francis Vandenhende and his wife, Denise Fabre (a bred-in-the-bone Niçoise), were among the first in Paris to introduce the sunny savors of the South into their kitchen. Since then, Mediterranean madness has overrun the city's restaurants, and the perusal of a Provençal menu no longer elicits the same thrill of surprise.
Chef Gilles Mery is obviously at ease with the Southern repertoire, though he tends to fuss and complicate his cooking. Some of his dishes merit three toques; others do not. On the debit side are aiguillettes of duck breast encumbered by too many garnishes; a leek and scallop velouté with crayfish and a drizzle of orange oil that—incredibly!—lacks flavor as well as consistency; and a Banyuls sorbet with chocolate chips and walnut sauce—take it back to the drawing board!
To his credit, Mery also delivers sprightly coddled eggs with caper blossoms and pepper confit, risotto enriched with a wonderfully appetizing garnish of chorizo and codfish, sea bream stewed in red wine with a zesty touch of anchovy, and roast squab set atop golden grilled polenta accompanied by tart-sweet green grapes. These lusty creations are staples on the 240 F prix-fixe lunch (surely one of the best deals in the area), which is best partnered by a Côtes-du-Rhône from Remi Aspect's splendid cellar. C 350-500 F. M 240 F & 295 F (lunch), 260 F & 390 F (dinner).

La Niçoise
4, rue Pierre-Demours - 45 74 42 41
Closed Sat lunch, Sun. Open until 11pm. Priv rm: 60. Air cond. V, AE, DC.
Traditional Niçois specialties served in a picture-postcard setting that's reminiscent of Nice at holiday time. Prime ingredients are prepared with touching sincerity, to yield ricotta ravioli in a creamy pistou sauce, old-fashioned simmered tripe redolent of fresh bay leaves, and nougat glacé perfumed with orange-flower water. Perfect Provençal cellar. M 145 F (wine incl), 165 F.

Le Petit Colombier
42, rue des Acacias - 43 80 28 54
Closed Sun lunch, Sat. Open until 10:30pm. Priv rm: 35. Air cond. Garage pkg. V, AE, MC.
Bernard Fournier, official defender of French gastronomy for the EU in Brussels, is first and foremost a model restaurateur. With loving devotion he watches over his *fin de siècle* "provincial" inn, a family heirloom which he runs with the energy of three men. Bernard is Johnny-on-the-spot at market, selecting only prime in-

gredients; at the stoves, executing a *carte* that changes daily; and at tableside, lending an attentive ear to his guests.

The reward for his vigilance is a loyal clientele of contented gourmands who tuck in joyfully to such spirited, full-bodied dishes as hare terrine à l'ancienne enriched with foie gras, pikeperch with shallot-butter sauce, milk-fed veal chops tenderly braised en cocotte, or squab in a tight, truffled jus. Each day also brings a fabulous roast—succulent ribs of beef, for example, or poularde truffée aux petits légumes—carved and served at the table. Nor should we neglect to celebrate Fournier's seasonal game menu, nor the business lunch which is one of the best (and least known) bargains in the city. To toast all these delights, there is a splendiferous cellar with some 50,000 bottles. **C** 400-500 F (dinner). **M** 200 F (lunch), 350 F (dinner).

12/20 Le Petit Salé

99, av. des Ternes - 45 74 10 57
Open daily until 11:30pm. Priv rm: 8. Terrace dining. V, AE, DC, MC.

Petit salé—streaky bacon with lentils—is still the cornerstone of the generous house repertoire. In this vintage 1930s setting, you can also opt for beef-muzzle vinaigrette, sole meunière, pot-au-feu, or brandade de morue (puréed salt cod), to be washed down with a frisky red Anjou sold *au compteur* (you pay only for what you drink). **C** 200-250 F.

Petrus

12, pl. du Maréchal-Juin
43 80 15 95, fax 43 80 06 96
Closed Aug 10-25. Open until 11pm. Priv rm: 22. Air cond. Valet pkg. V, AE, DC, MC.

Young Jacky Louazé is the new skipper aboard the good ship Petrus. At the tender age of 26, he's already learned to handle seafood with discretion and restraint, serving forth a superb carpaccio of sea bream, bass, and salmon, a golden heap of crisp-fried whitebait, gingered tuna cooked as rare as you like, and a sole of pristine freshness caught off the coast of the Ile d'Yeu. To begin, we always choose a dozen or so glossy Marennes oysters, and to finish, we just as invariably order the chocolate soufflé. Fine selection of white wines; attentive service. **C** 350-500 F. **M** 250 F, 350 F.

Il Ristorante

22, rue Fourcroy - 47 63 34 00
Closed Dec 24-Jan 1, Aug 13-29. Open until 10:45pm. Air cond. Garage pkg. V, AE.

We can't resist the charm of the Anfuso clan, who welcome guests into their Venetian-style dining room with heartwarming hospitality. You, too, will succumb when you taste Rocco Anfuso's vibrant, high-spirited *cucina*. Outstanding features of a recent feast were fettuccine with cuttlefish in a dusky sauce of the creatures' ink, rosy lamb under a mantle of tender eggplant, filet mignon with walnut pesto, and cinnamon ice cream with green-apple coulis. The Italian wines are seductive and attractively priced. **C** 210-310 F. **M** 165 F.

---

*Some establishments change their **closing times** without warning. It is always wise to check in advance.*

Michel Rostang

20, rue Rennequin
47 63 40 77, fax 47 63 82 75
Closed Sat lunch, Sun, Aug 1-15. Open until 10:15pm. Priv rm: 25. Air cond. Valet pkg. V, AE, MC.

Michel Rostang is inspired by the culinary heritage of Lyon, Provence, and his native Dauphiné, where powerful flavors and a forthright approach to food are the rule. Yet Rostang is not a "regional" chef. He applies his own standards and measures to the traditional country cooking of France, while reserving plenty of leeway for improvisation. The result is a mostly rousing yet nuanced cuisine, whose flavors usually dovetail with admirable precision. "Mostly"? "usually"? All right, we'll stop hedging. We had a few disappointing meals here this year, particularly the more recent ones. We saw shortcuts and even some unmistakable signs of carelessness: a scorched gratin dauphinois, a soggy tart... What's more, the 298 F set lunch doesn't seem like such a bargain, with dishes that rate only a couple of toques. Given the reputation—and prices—of this establishment, patrons have a right to expect a near-perfect dining experience. So Michel Rostang is back down to three toques from the four he's worn since 1992. Don't misunderstand: there's still plenty to like *chez* Rostang. Flavors, colors, and textures compose an irresistible bouquet in his artichoke galettes lavished with fresh truffles, or in the vivid pumpkin soup dotted with chèvre-stuffed ravioli. Irreproachable too are the pan-roasted lobster en anchoïade, the thick, juicy braised sole with a zesty black-olive compote and Swiss chard in a savory jus, and the beautifully conceived pastorale d'agneau de Provence: the lamb's tongue, noisettes, sweet-breads, and trotters are steeped in a deliciously aromatic jus.

As always, Marie-Claude Rostang welcomes guests graciously into the Rostangs' newly redecorated dining room, and Alain Ronzatti continues to preside over the connoisseur's cellar. **C** 700-900 F. **M** 298 F (lunch), 520 F, 720 F.

Rôtisserie d'Armaillé

6, rue Armaillé - 42 27 19 20
Closed Sat lunch, Sun. Open until 11pm (w-e 11:30pm). Priv rm: 85. Air cond. V, AE, MC.

Jacques Cagna reprises the bistro formula he successfully inaugurated at La Rôtisserie d'en Face (sixth arrondissement). For 195 F you can choose from a wide array of starters and desserts as well as a main course of spit-roasted poultry or meat. Delicious, affordable wines. **C** 300 F. **M** 195 F.

Guy Savoy

18, rue Troyon
43 80 40 61, fax 46 22 43 09
Closed Sat lunch, Sun. Open until 10:30pm. Priv rm: 30. Air cond. Valet pkg. V, AE.

An arsonist set fire to Guy Savoy's restaurant in November 1993. Typically, in less time than it would take most of us to choose new wallpaper, Savoy raised the curtain on a splendid and highly original interior. Beneath a Bedouin-style canvas-swathed ceiling (to replace the elegant *verrière* that melted in the blaze) the room is accented with impressive pieces of African sculpture and fine paintings—it's a smashing success. How on earth, people wonder, does he do it?

Guy Savoy has the uncanniest way of turning an ordeal into opportunity. Even his cooking has gained a fresh, creative edge. Just look at this year's imaginative *carte*: there's a croustillant of calf's foot and peppery black radish on a salad of fresh herbs dressed with a a vibrant parsley jus; a potée of poached fresh vegetables anointed with a powerfully aromatic truffle jus; a hauntingly delicious pheasant and bean soup; roast John Dory accented with crisp, faintly bitter sautéed dandelion greens and sage-scented potatoes. And every day the menu is enriched with a complement of inspired offerings that change according to Savoy's mercurial moods! We've heard some people complain that Savoy's portions are too small; they may have a point. But we applaud the idea of allowing diners to order desserts by the half-helping: thus, for the same money, you can sample both the spiced-cocoa pain perdu and the tingly grapefruit terrine with tea-scented sauce; or else the chocolate fondant with praline feuilleté and the vanilla millefeuille with a bright berry coulis. The wines, delicate or full-bodied (and uniformly expensive), are overseen by Éric Mancio, a sommelier with the soul of a poet. C 700-1,000 F. M 750 F.

🍳 Sormani
4, rue du Général-Lanrezac - 43 80 13 91
Closed Sat, Sun, hols, end Dec, Easter, 1st 3 wks of Aug. Open until 10:30pm. Priv rm: 18. Terrace dining. Air cond. Valet pkg. V, AE.
Scion of an Italo-French family of restaurateurs, Pascal Fayet has culinary talent coursing through his veins! He's taken that innate aptitude and amplified it with a virtuosity and artistic temperament all his own.
Fayet's Italian cuisine is emphatically not the textbook version. His menu fairly crackles with brilliant inventions that will set you to salivating before you've even taken a bite! You could compose a stupendous meal from such offerings as diaphanous ravioli stuffed with sea urchins or truffled goat cheese; pearly raw scallops paired with wee purple artichokes; a "pizza" topped with onion purée, lobster, and arugula; tender tagliatelle enriched with bacon and white beans; a sumptuous white-truffle risotto; veal kidney arranged on a crisply golden polenta galette; or (Fayet's masterpiece) a fat black truffle swathed in a paper-thin slice of veal. An even more exciting alternative is to give Fayet an idea of your tastes and your appetite, then let him improvise a personalized feast just for you. Believe us, it will be a gastronomic memory to treasure! Speaking of treasures, Sormani's cellar holds some fabulous bottles, including a Santa Cristina Chianti and a Venetian Pinot Grigio from Peppoli Antinori. C 400-600 F. M 350 F (lunch, wine incl), 400 F, 450 F, 500 F (wine incl).

🍳 La Soupière
154, av. de Wagram
42 27 00 73, fax 46 22 77 09
Closed Sat lunch, Sun, Aug 8-21. Open until 10:30pm. Priv rm: 6. Terrace dining. Air cond. V, AE, MC.
Christian and Camille Thuillart pamper their guests in a pretty *trompe-l'œil* dining room. There's nothing deceptive about the cooking, however: chef Christian's forthright repertoire

features juicy pikeperch cooked in its skin, calf's liver in a sauce deglazed with balsamic vinegar, and succulent duck with fresh pasta. A passionate connoisseur of rare and expensive mushrooms, he has built special menus around truffles and morels, served when their season is at its height. C 250-350 F. M 185 F (Sat dinner), 130 F, 160 F, 250 F & 270 F (weekdays).

🍳 Le Sud Marocain
10, rue Villebois-Mareuil - 45 72 35 76
Closed Aug. Open until 10:30pm. Priv rm: 10. Air cond. V, AE, DC, MC.
Here's a rare find! This tiny restaurant (it holds just 25), run by a *patron* who looks just like Chico Marx, serves sensational marinated sardines with ratatouille, a light, fragrantly herbal harira soup, several excellent tagines (chicken and olives, lamb with prunes...), and a first-rate couscous royal. C 165-215 F.

🍳 Taïra
10, rue des Acacias - 47 66 74 14
Closed Sat lunch, Sun, Aug 15-22. Open until 10:30pm. Air cond. V, AE, DC, MC.
Taïra Kurihara is endowed with an authoritative technique and a vigorous temperament, qualities that give his cuisine a keen, zestful edge. The best dishes point up his Japanese roots; we recommend the crunchy vegetables drizzled with prawn oil, flash-seared tuna perfumed with icy basil oil, and John Dory finished with a vibrant and unusual caramelized prawn sauce. The salmon "tataki" (served practically raw, just faintly warm, with a piquant vinaigrette) are not everyone's cup of green tea, but we think they're terrific! Fine, affordable cellar; comfortable, pearl-gray décor. C 300-450 F. M 320 F (exc weekday lunch), 150 F, 170 F.

12/20 Le Timgad
21, rue Brunel
45 74 23 70, fax 40 68 76 46
Open daily until 11pm. Priv rm: 10. Air cond. No pets. Garage pkg. V, AE, DC.
Le Timgad could be a palace in Fès, with its extravagant décor of arabesques and enameled tiles. Ahmed Laasri sends forth some very good couscous, but don't neglect his pigeon pastilla, chicken tagine with olives, or succulent spit-roasted lamb. There's a comprehensive cellar of North African wines, and excellent service. It's wise to book in advance at this popular spot. C 260-340 F.

A. Beauvilliers
52, rue Lamarck
42 54 54 42, fax 42 62 70 30
Closed Mon lunch, Sun. Open until 10:45pm. Priv rm: 45. Garden dining. Air cond. No pets. Garage pkg. V, AE, DC, MC.
Édouard Carlier quickly recovered his sang-froid, after an explosion nearly deprived the city of one of its loveliest restaurants. All is back in order now, and Carlier is again surrounded by his collections of nineteenth-century portraits, Carpeaux terracottas, nostalgic bridal garlands, and by his beautifully dressed tables and fanciful floral displays. If ever a restaurant was designed for *fêtes* and celebrations, this is it. Indeed, show-

business personalities, celebrity chefs, and political figures regularly scale the Butte Montmartre to toast their triumphs with Beauvilliers's best Champagne. So why, you're wondering, has the rating been suspended? We'll tell you. After receiving an ominous number of letters that complained of erratic cooking, interminable waits, and sniffy service, we dispatched our investigators to the scene. They returned with mixed impressions. One noted that a famous name or face was indeed a sure ticket to good service and hospitality; another was disappointed by his marinated salmon with caviar cream, a skinny veal chop, and humdrum fruit tart. Even the set lunch, which we've long cited as an example, scored low, owing to a mundane salad of squid and mushrooms, an overcooked tournedos of hake and smoked bacon... Naturally, we'd rather go on praising the brilliant cuisine bourgeoise that Beauvilliers has delivered for years: the superb foie gras in shimmering Sherry aspic, mallard duck in a sauce spiked with single-malt whisky, flanked by exqui-site spätzle and onion marmalade, and the rest of the appetizing roster. But we owe it to Carlier, a perfectionist with the highest standards of refinement, to issue this warning call. **C** 550-900 F. **M** 300 F (lunch, wine incl), 185 F (weekday lunch), 320 F (weekday dinner).

Charlot Ier
"Les Merveilles des Mers," 128 bis, bd de Clichy - 45 22 47 08, fax 44 70 07 50
Open daily until 1am. Air cond. Garage pkg. V, AE, DC, MC.
The traditional house repertoire of seafood classics (bouillabaisse, braised skate, red mullet in aromatic stock) has been beefed up with a few meat dishes, but the best bets here remain the simplest preparations, starting with the extraordinary assortments of briny fresh shellfish. **C** 290-420 F. **M** 190 F.

12/20 Chez Frézet
181, rue Ordener - 46 06 64 20
Closed Sun lunch, Sun. Open until 10:30pm. Priv rm: 90. Garden dining. Pkg. V, AE, MC.
Christian Marie's pocket-sized establishment overlooks a minuscule back garden, which you may admire while enjoying his market-fresh specialties. The 145 F set meal includes an apéritif and a carafe of Côtes-du-Rhône, as well as foie gras de canard en salade, fresh fillet of fish in a deliciously creamy sauce, and an apple-stuffed crêpe. **C** 220-400 F. **M** 145 F (wine incl), 180 F.

Langevin
39, rue Lamarck - 46 06 86 00
Closed Sun dinner (Oct-May). Open until 10:15pm. V.
A glass-enclosed terrace gives patrons a wide-angle view of this picturesque corner of Montmartre. Normandy native Jean-Paul Langevin serves cuisine based on top-notch seasonal ingredients, with a few discreet nods to traditional country cooking. Try his tomatoes stuffed with curried snails, sole paupiettes stuffed with mussels in a lush sauce poulette, and the yummy frozen charlotte aux deux chocolats sauce pistache. Judicious cellar. **C** 270-340 F. **M** 115 F (lunch, wine incl), 198 F (wine incl).

11/20 Chez Marie-Louise
52, rue Championnet - 46 06 86 55
Closed Sun, Mon. Open until 10pm. No pets.
Lobster salad, veal chop grand'mère, lotte with fresh pasta, clafoutis of seasonal fruits—here's honest bistro cooking, unchanged for 30 years, served amid copper saucepans and prints of carousing monks. **C** 200-240 F. **M** 130 F.

Le Restaurant
32, rue Véron
42 23 06 22, fax 42 23 36 16
Closed Sun. Open until 11pm. V, AE, MC.
Yves Peladeau worked his way up from busboy to owner-chef of his Restaurant at the foot of the Butte Montmartre. The dining room is as modern, bright, and à la mode as the imaginative menu: give your taste buds a treat with the marinated sardines, nicely seasoned marinated salmon, and a savory honey-roasted duck spiced with coriander. Small but intelligent wine list (note Charles Joguet's Chinon). The cheapest set meal is a real bargain. **C** 200-280 F. **M** 70 F, 120 F.

12/20 Wepler
14, pl. de Clichy
45 22 53 24, fax 44 70 07 50
Open daily until 1am. Air cond. Garage pkg. V, AE, DC, MC.
A deluxe brasserie providing reliable food and good service. The shellfish is some of the freshest in Paris; other interesting options are the hearty (and truly delicious) headcheese, grilled salmon béarnaise, and a copious choucroute garnie. Fine bouillabaisse, too. **C** 200-400 F. **M** 150 F.

19TH ARRONDISSEMENT

Le Bistrot Roumain
1, rue de Bellevue - 42 41 73 03
Closed Sun, Mon, Aug. Open until 11pm. No pets. V, MC.
Warming, sincere Romanian fare is served here in an adorable farmhouse setting. Try the sturdy stuffed cabbage, the colossal grilled-pepper salad, spicy Transylvanian goulash, Moldavian meat and kidney stew, and baby chicken with garlic sauce. Drink a nice, round Romanian Cabernet, then finish up with the good poppyseed cake. **C** 200 F. **M** 90 F (weekday lunch).

Au Cochon d'Or
192, av. Jean-Jaurès
42 45 46 46, fax 42 40 43 90
Open daily until 10:30pm. Priv rm: 40. Air cond. Valet pkg. V, AE, DC, MC.
Times have changed since the Ayral family set up shop here in 1924. The nearby slaughterhouses are now defunct; butchers and meatpackers have given way to the cultured, worldly crowd disgorged by the Cité des Sciences at La Villette. But the restaurant has evolved along with its clientele. Under René Ayral's management, the kitchen continues to grill, roast, and fry the choicest morsels of beef: filet mignons, prime ribs, and sirloin steaks. Earthier choices include calf's head en salade with a mustardy dressing, pigs' trotters served with sauce Choron, or boudin and apples. An excellent sommelier oversees the wines. **C** 350-500 F. **M** 240 F.

12/20 Dagorno

190, av. Jean-Jaurès
40 40 09 39, fax 48 03 17 23
Open daily until 12:15am (Fri & Sat 1am). Priv rm: 80. Air cond. Valet pkg. V, AE, MC.
Quite a contrast with the futuristic Cité des Sciences, this opulent brasserie actively cultivates its old-fashioned image, offering decent, uncomplicated food. You won't be disappointed by the fresh shellfish assortments, calf's head sauce gribiche, cervelle meunière, or the enormous côte de bœuf sauce bordelaise, but the foie gras en salade is bland, and the wines are too costly. **C** 250-450 F. **M** 158 F (wine incl).

12/20 L'Oriental

58, rue de l'Ourq - 40 34 26 23
Closed Sun. Open until 11pm. Priv rm: 48. Air cond. No pets. V, MC.
In this tiny Lebanese eatery you can gorge on generously served mezes, delicious hummus with minced lamb, spicy sausages, and tasty marinated chicken. Unbeatable prices. And there's a fruity red Kefraya '92 on the wine list that partners the food perfectly. **C** 100-175 F. **M** 75 F (exc Sat dinner), 125 F & 175 F (wine incl), 90 F.

Le Pavillon Puebla

"Christian Vergès,"
Parc des Buttes-Chaumont
42 08 92 62, fax 42 39 83 16
Closed Sun, Mon. Open until 10pm. Priv rm: 90. Garden dining. Pkg. V, AE, MC.
This stylish Napoléon III hunting lodge stands swaddled in greenery at the foot of the Buttes Chaumont park. Owner-chef Christian Vergès remains true to his Catalan roots, producing a menu full of sun-drenched, rousing flavors. The spiced squid in their ink, grilled red mullet with eggplant confit, the lively fricassée of weevers and scampi with fennel and a whiff of anise, and the lush lobster au banyuls will transport you to the Côte Vermeille. One of the city's best crème brûlées is made here and some splendid Banyuls can be found on the extensive wine list. **C** 380-500 F. **M** 180 F, 230 F.

12/20 Le Sancerre

13, av. Corentin-Cariou
40 36 80 44, fax 42 61 19 74
Closed Sat, Sun, Aug. Open until 10:30pm. Pkg. V, AE, DC, MC.
A nostalgic atmosphere reigns at this likeable bistro, a vestige of the old abattoir district of La Villette. The bill of fare features prodigious portions of tasty charcuterie, beef rib sprinkled with coarse sea-salt, and juicy double lamb chops. As for wines, look no further than the wonderful Morgon and Sancerre sold by the centimeter (you pay only for what you drink from the bottle placed on the table). It is wise to book ahead for lunch. **C** 200-320 F. **M** 169 F (weekdays), 110 F.

20TH ARRONDISSEMENT

Aux Allobroges

71, rue des Grands-Champs - 43 73 40 00
Closed Sun, Mon, Aug. Open until 10pm. V.
Olivier and Annette Pateyron have given their little restaurant a spruce new look and a fantastic new menu. It's worth the trip out to the twentieth arrondissement to savor Olivier's plump langoustines poised on a colorful bed of ratatouille, braised lamb with garlic confit, and sautéed yellow plums flambé. The little 83 F set meal also has its charms, what with the tomates confites swirled with green-olive cream, steak with shallots or coriander-spiced skate, followed by cheese *and* dessert. A la carte prices are equally clement, inciting one to splurge on lobster and lotte perfumed with tarragon or Barbary duck enhanced with spices and nuts. Only the wine list needs improvement. **C** 200-250 F. **M** 83 F, 150 F.

Aux Becs Fins

44, bd de Ménilmontant - 47 97 51 52
Closed Sun, Sep 11-20. Open until 9:30pm. Priv rm: 15. Terrace dining. V, AE.
This winsome little bistro runs alongside the Père Lachaise cemetery. The colorful owner (Édith Lefebvre) relies on a faithful clientele of regulars who don't mind the eccentric décor. The cuisine is back on course, and the toque again firmly in place. We recommend the bountiful terrines, juicy grilled meat and fish, the cassoulet "mère Édith," and the tasty (though costly) wines. Adorable service. **C** 230-350 F. **M** 180 F, 240 F.

12/20 A la Courtille

1, rue des Envierges - 46 36 51 59
Open daily until 11pm. Terrace dining. V.
Enjoy a spectacular view of the city from the terrace of this elegant bistro. Even better than the food (which is pretty good: marinated sardines, duck breast with fresh figs, crème brûlée...) is the wine list, compiled with admirable expertise by Bernard Pontonnier and Francis Morel. **C** 200-230 F. **M** 70 F & 100 F (lunch exc Sun).

INDEX OF PARIS RESTAURANTS

PARIS

Hotels

Le Bristol
8th arr. - 112, rue du Fg-Saint-Honoré
42 66 91 45, fax 42 66 34 16
Open year-round. 41 stes 6,500 F. 154 rms 2,500-3,600 F. Restaurant. Air cond. Conf. Heated pool. No pets. Valet pkg. V, AE, DC, MC.
The elegant décor (genuine period furniture, as well as lovely reproductions), the comfortable rooms, the lavish suites, and the prestigious clientele make Le Bristol one of the rare authentic luxury hotels in Paris (as well as one of the most expensive). The Bristol's two distinct wings comprise 35 newer, modern suites housed in a former Carmelite convent, and 150 more traditionally decorated rooms and suites. Among the innumerable amenities are video surveillance, ultramodern conference rooms, a heated swimming pool, a superb laundry service, and a hair salon. An elegant restaurant (Le Bristol) opens onto the lawn and flowers of a formal French garden, see *Restaurants*. The staff is both cordial and impressively trained.

Hôtel de Crillon
8th arr. - 10, pl. de la Concorde
44 71 15 00, fax 44 71 15 02
Open year-round. 45 stes 4,850-26,800 F. 118 rms 2,450-3,950 F. Restaurants. Air cond. Conf. Valet pkg. V, AE, DC.
The Crillon is housed in an honest-to-goodness eighteenth-century palace. Indeed, the accommodations are truly fit for a king, with terraces overlooking the Place de la Concorde, sumptuous public rooms, and an exquisitely trained staff. The guest rooms, though not always immense or well soundproofed, are beautifully decorated; the suites offer all the splendor one could hope for. Everywhere the eye rests on Louis XVI–style furniture, silk draperies, pastel walls, and woodwork ornamented with gold leaf, Aubusson rugs, and polished marble. Relais et Châteaux. Restaurants: Les Ambassadeurs and L'Obélisque, see *Restaurants*.

George-V
8th arr. - 31, av. George-V
47 23 54 00, fax 47 20 40 00
Open year-round. 50 stes 5,700 15,500 F. 248 rms 1,800-3,900 F. Restaurant. Air cond. Conf. Valet pkg. V, AE, DC, MC.
The management has made a Herculean attempt to instill new life and spirit into this landmark. The bar and the restaurant (Les Princes, see *Restaurants*; both open onto a delightful patio) have been redecorated, a Grill has been added, and many of the rooms have been renovated, with as much concern for elegance as for modernity (electronic panels located at the head of the beds allow guests to close the venetian blinds, control both the television and the air conditioning, call room service, and so on). The Galerie de la Paix (now home to a chic tea room), as well as the pictures, rare ornaments, and lovely furniture in the public rooms radiate the legendary George-V charm. But such surroundings cry out for absolutely first-rate service which, alas, is not always provided here.

Le Grand Hôtel
9th arr. - 2, rue Scribe
40 07 32 32, fax 42 66 12 51
Open year-round. 35 stes 3,500-15,000 F. 479 rms 1,550-2,500 F. Rms for disabled. Restaurant. Air cond. Conf. Valet pkg. V, AE, DC, MC.
The renovation of this grand hotel, built in 1862, is now complete. In the past ten years, this monumental Second Empire building has recovered all the splendor it displayed when Empress Eugénie inaugurated it. The huge central lobby, capped by a glittering glass dome, is a wonder to behold. Guest rooms provide everything the international traveler could require in the way of amenities, as well as the most up-to-date business equipment, a health club, and much more. Excellent bar.

Plan to travel? *Look for Gault Millau's other* Best of *guides to Chicago, Florida, Hawaii, Hong Kong, Germany, Italy, London, Los Angeles, New England, New Orleans, New York, Paris, San Francisco, Thailand, Toronto, and Washington, D.C.*

Inter-Continental

1st arr. - 3, rue de Castiglione
44 77 11 11, fax 44 77 14 60
*Open year-round. 58 stes 2,800-20,000 F. 392 rms
1,750-2,500 F. Restaurants. Air cond. Conf. V, AE,
DC, MC.*
Garnier, the architect of the Opéra, designed
this vast hotel; three out of its seven spectacular
salons are listed as historic monuments. With its
remarkably equipped conference rooms, it
responds perfectly to the business world's
needs. As for charm and comfort, you'll find
them both in the lovely patio filled with flowers,
in the décor, and the incomparable loveliness of
many of the rooms (though some are tiny and
dark), as well as in the small singles located in
the attic, from which there is a fine view of the
Tuileries. Bathrooms are often old-fashioned and
on the small side. The suites (with Jacuzzi) are
luxurious. Two restaurants and a bar.

 Meurice

1st arr. - 228, rue de Rivoli
44 58 10 10, fax 44 58 10 15
*Open year-round. 28 stes 5,000-15,000 F. 152 rms
2,200-3,600 F. Restaurant. Air cond. Conf. Valet pkg.
V, AE, DC, MC.*
The Meurice has undergone substantial
renovation in the past few years, to restore its
glamour and prestige. Most recently, the admirable salons on the main floor were refurbished; the guest rooms and suites (which offer
a view of the Tuileries) were equipped with air
conditioning and tastefully redecorated; and the
pink-marble bathrooms are now ultramodern.
The Meurice ranks as one of the best grand
hotels in Paris. An elegant restaurant, Le
Meurice, see *Restaurants*, is lodged in the Salon
des Tuileries, which overlooks the gardens. Tea
and cocktails are served to the sound of quiet
piano music in the Salon Pompadour. A free
secretarial service is available, and guests have
use of the hotel's box at the Longchamp
racetrack during the season.

 Plaza-Athénée

8th arr. - 25, av. Montaigne
47 23 78 33, fax 47 20 20 70
*Open year-round. 42 stes 5,920-10,050 F. 169 rms
2,740-4,750 F. Restaurant. Air cond. Conf. Valet pkg.
V, AE, DC, MC.*
Discretion, efficiency, and friendly courtesy are
the Plaza's trademarks. The rooms and suites are
bright, generous in size, and fitted with every
amenity. The rooms overlooking Avenue Montaigne are perfectly soundproofed. At about
11am, guests gather in the bar (Plaza-Bar
Anglais, where Mata Hari was arrested); and,
from 4pm to 7pm in particular, you'll see them
in the gallery (of which Marlene Dietrich was
particularly fond). The Régence restaurant is
located just across from the wonderful patio,
where tables are set in the summer among
cascades of geraniums and ampelopsis vines,
see *Restaurants*. Dry-cleaning services are
provided, and there is a beauty salon on the
premises.

---

*Remember to call ahead to reserve your room, and
please, if you cannot honor your reservation, be
courteous and let the hotel know.*

 Hôtel Prince de Galles

8th arr. - 33, av. George-V
47 23 55 11, fax 47 20 96 92
*Open year-round. 30 stes 6,500-18,000 F. 140 rms
1,900-3,500 F. Restaurant. Half-board 1,210-1,435 F.
Air cond. Conf. Valet pkg. V, AE, DC, MC.*
Extensive renovations have restored the bril-
liance of this renowned hotel, built in the Roaring Twenties. Marble expanses stretch as far as
the eye can see, walls are accented by handsome prints, and guest rooms have been outfitted with minibars, safes, and a flock of new
facilities. We only wish that the lovely old
mosaics had been preserved. As ever, the hotel's
open-roofed patio is a delightful place to have
lunch on a warm day; the paneled Regency Bar
is another pleasant spot, distinguished by excellent service. Restaurant: Le Jardin des Cygnes,
see *Restaurants*.

 Raphaël

16th arr. - 17, av. Kléber
44 28 00 28, fax 45 01 21 50
*Open year-round. 35 stes 3,000-7,000 F. 52 rms
2,000-2,500 F. Restaurant. Air cond. Conf. Valet pkg.
V, AE, DC, MC.*
Built between the wars, the Raphaël has maintained an atmosphere of refinement and
elegance. The Oriental rugs strewn upon the
marble floors, the fine woodwork, old paintings,
and period furniture make Le Raphaël a
luxurious place to stay, preferred by a wealthy,
well-bred clientele. The spacious rooms are richly furnished in various styles; the wardrobes and
bathrooms are immense. Suite 601 boasts a
huge terrace and a view of the Arc de Triomphe.
Top-drawer reception and service, of course.

 Résidence Maxim's de Paris

8th arr. - 42, av. Gabriel
45 61 96 33, fax 42 89 06 07
*Open year-round. 33 stes 3,500-15,000 F. 4 rms
1,900-2,250 F. Restaurant. Air cond. Conf. Valet pkg.
V, AE, DC, MC.*
Pierre Cardin himself designed the hotel of his
dreams, a small but palatial establishment that
may well be the world's most luxurious. The
landings of each floor are decorated like elegant
salons, with beautiful and unusual antique
pieces and paintings. Polished stone and
sumptuous murals adorn the bathrooms. The
suites must be seen to be believed, particularly
those on the top floor, which are lacquered in
vivid colors and furnished with pieces designed
by Cardin. Obviously, accommodations like
these are well beyond the bank balances of most
mortals.

 Ritz

1st arr. - 15, pl. Vendôme
43 16 30 30, fax 43 16 35 37
*Open year-round. 45 stes 5,600-49,260 F. 142 rms
2,450-4,150 F. Restaurant. Air cond. Conf. Heated
pool. No pets. Valet pkg. V, AE, DC, MC.*
The world's most famous hotel is poised to
enter the 21st century with state-of-the-art
facilities, but without having betrayed the distinctive character that won the Ritz its reputation.
Even if nowadays you can change the video
program or make a phone call without leaving
your bed or marble bath (Charles Ritz was the
first hotel owner to provide private bathrooms
for his clients), nothing has altered the pleasure

of stretching out on a wide brass bed surrounded by authentic antique furniture. Add to that a full view of one of the city's most spectacular squares, in an atmosphere of old-fashioned luxury so enveloping that a new word ("ritzy") had to be coined for it. The liveried staff knows the difference between courtesy and obsequiousness. Recent improvements include an eighteen-meter swimming pool, a squash court, a health club modeled on a thermal spa of antiquity. The restaurant, L'Espadon, see *Restaurants*, has its own garden. Additional entertainment possibilities include a nightclub and several bars.

Royal Monceau
8th arr. - 37, av. Hoche
42 99 88 00, fax 42 56 90 03
Open year-round. 39 stes 3,400-15,000 F. 180 rms 1,950-3,150 F. Rms for disabled. Restaurants. Air cond. Conf. Heated pool & beauty center. Valet pkg. V, AE, DC, MC.

This large, luxurious, and discreet hotel attracts politicians, foreign business people, and entertainers with spacious rooms, magnificent marble bathrooms, and all the usual ingredients of hotel comfort (including excellent room service). Extras include a fashionable piano bar, a spacious health club (with sauna, Jacuzzi, swimming pool, and a massage service), ultramodern conference rooms, and a well-equipped "business club." The rooms overlooking the charming flowered patio are the most sought-after by the hotel's habitués. Restaurants: Le Carpaccio and Le Jardin du Royal Monceau, see *Restaurants*.

Westminster
2nd arr. - 13, rue de la Paix
42 61 57 46, fax 42 60 30 66
Open year-round. 18 stes 2,700-4,300 F. 84 rms 1,600-2,000 F. Restaurant. Air cond. Conf. Valet pkg. V, AE, DC, MC.

Here is a charming mid-size luxury hotel advantageously situated between the Opéra and the Place Vendôme. The pink-and-beige-marble lobby is splendid and luxurious; the bar (with piano) is more than comfortable. Conference rooms are superbly equipped. As for the guest rooms, they are handsomely decorated with attractive fabrics, chandeliers, and Louis XV–style furnishings and are fitted with minibars, safes, and satellite TV. The marble bathrooms and suites have just been renovated. Restaurant: Le Céladon, see *Restaurants*.

FIRST CLASS

Ambassador
9th arr. - 16, bd Haussmann
44 83 40 40, fax 42 46 19 84
Open year-round. 9 stes 2,000-3,500 F. 289 rms 1,200-1,800 F. Restaurant. Air cond. Conf. Valet pkg. V, AE, DC, MC.

A fine traditional hotel, proud of its luxurious fittings. The relatively spacious guest rooms have been modernized in excellent taste with sumptuous fabrics, thick carpeting, and Art Deco furniture. The lobby and public rooms are imposing: pink-marble columns topped with gilded Corinthian capitals, marble floors, and Aubusson tapestries on the walls. The penthouse suites look out over Sacré-Cœur. Restaurant:

Venantius, see *Restaurants*; and a handsome Art Deco bar.

Baltimore
16th arr. - 88 bis, av. Kléber
44 34 54 54, fax 44 34 54 44
Open year-round. 1 ste 3,500 F. 104 rms 1,600-2,500 F. Restaurant. Air cond. Conf. Pkg. V, AE, DC.

Six fully equipped meeting rooms are located on the lower level; the largest and most luxurious is the former vault room of the Banque Nationale de Paris. The comfortable guest rooms are decorated with understated elegance, in keeping with the neighborhood and the tastes of the clientele. Restaurant: Le Bertie's, see *Restaurants*.

Beverly Hills
8th arr. - 35, rue de Berri
53 77 56 01, fax 56 56 52 75
Open year-round. 14 stes 2,500-9,900 F. Air cond. Conf. V, AE, DC, MC.

The extravagant décor of marble, mirrors, and precious woods reeks of money: this apartment-hotel is designed for millionaires, emirs, and merchant princes who want to wallow in luxury. Security is provided for with total electronic surveillance. The huge suites offer every imaginable amenity, from dining rooms to wide-screen TV.

Hôtel Balzac
8th arr. - 6, rue Balzac
45 61 97 22, fax 42 25 24 82
Open year-round. 14 stes 3,000-6,000 F. 56 rms 1,650-2,200 F. Restaurant. Air cond. Garage pkg. V, AE, DC, MC.

A quietly luxurious establishment near the Place de l'Étoile, frequented by celebrities and jet-setters. The huge rooms are decorated in delicate tones, with lovely furniture, beautiful chintzes, and thick carpeting. Most have king-size beds, all have superb modern bathrooms. Unobtrusive yet attentive staff. Restaurant: Bice, see *Restaurants*.

California
8th arr. - 16, rue de Berri
43 59 93 00, fax 45 61 03 62
Open year-round. 13 stes 3,000-6,000 F. 160 rms 1,100-2,200 F. Half-board 1,470-2,480 F. Air cond. Conf. Pkg. Fitness club. V, AE, DC, MC.

A light-filled lobby and a sunny lounge provide a good first impression. The cheerful, adequately sized rooms are decorated with chintzes, paintings, and prints. All boast spacious marble bathrooms. Extremely pleasant service. Accommodations overlooking the courtyard are amazingly quiet, despite the proximity of the Champs-Élysées.

Caron de Beaumarchais
4th arr. - 12, rue Vieille-du-Temple
42 72 34 12, fax 42 72 34 63
Open year-round. 19 rms 620-690 F. Air cond. Pkg. V, AE, DC, MC.

Here's a find: a hotel overflowing with charm, set in the heart of the Marais district. The lobby's eighteenth-century atmosphere is underscored by a stone floor, Louis XVI fireplace, beamed ceilings, and handsome antique furniture. The perfectly comfortable rooms are equipped with air conditioning and double glazing for cool quiet in summer.

Castille

1st arr. - 37, rue Cambon
44 58 44 58, fax 44 58 44 00
Open year-round. 17 stes 2,200-3,000 F. 70 rms 1,300-2,200 F. Rms for disabled. Restaurant. Air cond. Conf. Valet pkg. V, AE, DC, MC.
After a thorough renovation, this hotel next door to· Chanel and just opposite the Ritz provides even more luxurious amenities. Tasteful, elegant décor.

Château Frontenac

8th arr. - 54, rue Pierre-Charron
47 23 55 85, fax 47 23 03 32
Open year-round. 4 stes 1,600-1,650 F. 102 rms 890-1,400 F. Restaurant. Air cond. Conf. No pets. V.
A reasonably priced hotel (given the location), with various sizes of room done in vaguely Louis XV style. Superb marble bathrooms. The soundproofing is effective, but the rooms overlooking the Rue Cérisole are still the quietest. Attentive reception; courteous service. Restaurant: Le Pavillon Frontenac.

Chateaubriand

8th arr. - 6, rue Chateaubriand
40 76 00 50, fax 40 76 09 22
Open year-round. 28 rms 1,000-1,400 F. Restaurant. Air cond. Garage pkg. V, AE, DC, MC.
Built in 1991, this luxury hotel tucked away behind the Champs-Élysées boasts a polychrome-marble lobby and a courteous, professional staff. Classically elegant rooms; beautiful bathrooms.

Claridge-Bellman

8th arr. - 37, rue François-Ier
47 23 54 42, fax 47 23 08 84
Open year-round. 42 rms 950-1,350 F. Restaurant. Air cond. No pets. V, AE, DC, MC.
A small, unpretentious hotel with rooms of reasonable size, each of which boasts a special feature, be it a crystal chandelier, antique furniture, a fine print or painting, or a marble fireplace. Friendly, stylish service.

Concorde-La Fayette

17th arr. - 3, pl. du Général-Kœnig
40 68 50 68, fax 40 68 50 43
Open year-round. 27 stes 3,500-8,000 F. 947 rms 1,400-2,100 F. Restaurants. Air cond. Conf. Valet pkg. V, AE, DC, MC.
The Concorde–La Fayette is immense: a huge oval tower that houses the Palais des Congrès and its 4,500 seats; banquet rooms that can accommodate 2,000; scores of boutiques; four cinemas; nightclubs; and 1,500 parking places. The hotel's 1,000 rooms are neither spacious nor luxurious, but they offer all the modern amenities. Airport shuttles can be relied upon to stop here. Panoramic bar, three restaurants, including L'Étoile d'Or, see *Restaurants.*

Concorde Saint-Lazare

8th arr. - 108, rue St-Lazare
40 08 44 44, fax 42 93 01 20
Open year-round. 23 stes 2,450-5,000 F. 277 rms 1,050-1,650 F. Restaurant. Air cond. Conf. V, AE, MC.
An enormous hotel, built in 1889 by Gustave Eiffel. Sixty of the rooms and suites have just been fully renovated. Streetside rooms offer the most spacious accommodation. Though large, the bathrooms are a bit old-fashioned. The hotel's most arresting feature is the lobby, a

listed architectural landmark, that soars three storeys up to coffered ceilings aglitter with gilt, marble, and crystal chandeliers. A magnificent billiard room on the main floor is open to the public, as are the cocktail lounge and brasserie.

Édouard-VII

2nd arr. - 39, av. de l'Opéra
42 61 56 90, fax 42 61 47 73
Open year-round. 4 stes 2,000 F. 66 rms 950-1,300 F. Restaurant. Air cond. Conf. V, AE, DC, MC.
The years of renovations have finally borne fruit: this hotel is now a luxurious place to stay, with individually styled rooms and beautifully crafted furniture. From the upper storeys, there is a wonderful view of the Opéra. Restaurant: Delmonico, see *Restaurants.*

Élysées Star

8th arr. - 19, rue Vernet
47 20 41 73, fax 47 23 32 15
Open year-round. 4 stes 2,200-3,500 F. 38 rms 1,300-1,900 F. Air cond. Valet pkg. V, AE, DC, MC.
Different decorative styles—from Louis XV to Art Deco—distinguish the various floors of this prestigious hotel near the Champs-Élysées, a para-dise for business people. Superb facilities.

Golden Tulip

8th arr. - 218-220, rue du Fg-Saint-Honoré
49 53 03 03, fax 40 75 02 00
Open year-round. 20 stes 2,300-3,700 F. 52 rms 1,550-1,850 F. Rms for disabled. Restaurant. Air cond. Conf. Heated pool. No pets. Garage pkg. V, AE, DC, MC.
Owned by a Dutch chain, this comfortable hotel is decorated in modern style using traditional materials (marble, wood, quality fabrics, trompe-l'œil paintings). The bright, spacious rooms offer every amenity; all are air conditioned, with splendid marble bathrooms. Restaurant: Le Relais Vermeer, see *Restaurants.*

Hilton

15th arr. - 18, av. de Suffren
44 38 56 00, fax 44 38 56 10
Open year-round. 32 stes 3,500-12,000 F. 424 rms 1,500-2,000 F. Rms for disabled. Restaurants. Air cond. Conf. Pkg. V, AE, DC, MC.
The city's first postwar luxury hotel is still living up to Hilton's high standards. Rooms are airy and spacious, service is courteous and deft, and children—of any age—can share their parents' room at no extra charge. Closed-circuit TV shows recent films. Ten storeys up are the two "Executive Floors," with their particularly fine rooms (spectacular views of the Seine) and special services. The Hilton houses two restaurants and three bars, as well as a hair salon and prestigious boutiques.

Lancaster

8th arr. - 7, rue de Berri
40 76 40 76, fax 40 76 40 00
Open year-round. 9 stes 3,600-7,300 F. 50 rms 1,750-2,550 F. Restaurant. Air cond. Conf. Valet pkg. V, AE, DC, MC.
Inhale the perfume of the immense, breathtaking bouquet of flowers in the lobby, then admire the general setting—furniture, wall hangings, paintings, ornaments—of this refined and luxurious hotel. The ravishing indoor garden, with its flowers, fountains, and statues (meals are served there on sunny days) lends an unex-

pected bucolic touch to this hotel located only a few steps from the Champs-Élysées. The rooms and suites all have period furniture and double windows; their comfort is much appreciated by the aristocrats, statesmen, and business tycoons who frequent the Lancaster. Excellent reception; attentive and punctual service. The small conference rooms have fine equipment.

Littré

6th arr. - 9, rue Littré
45 44 38 68, fax 45 44 88 13
Open year-round. 4 stes 1,325-1,585 F. 93 rms 695-950 F. Conf. No pets. AE, DC, MC.
The style and décor of this four-star hotel are heavy and conservative, but the Littré's many habitués find the old-fashioned comfort and service entirely satisfactory. In the spacious, recently renovated rooms you'll find high, comfortable beds, ponderous furniture, enormous wardrobes, and huge marble bathrooms. English bar.

Lotti

1st arr. - 7, rue de Castiglione
42 60 37 34, fax 40 15 93 56
Open year-round. 6 stes 4,900-6,500 F. 133 rms 1,400-3,300 F. Restaurant. Air cond. Conf. Valet pkg. V, AE, DC, MC.
This elegant hotel is popular with members of the European aristocracy. Each of the spacious rooms, whose comfort is worthy of their clientele, is individually decorated and offers excellent facilities. The restaurant, the lobby, and all the rooms were recently renovated. The charming attic rooms are reserved for non-smokers.

Louvre-Concorde

1st arr. - Pl. André-Malraux
44 58 38 38, fax 44 58 38 01
Open year-round. 22 stes 2,500-5,000 F. 178 rms 1,300-2,000 F. Air cond. Conf. Pkg. V, AE, DC, MC.
From the door of this comfortable, classic hotel, you can see the gardens of the Palais-Royal, the Louvre, and the Tuileries. While most of the guest rooms are spacious and high-ceilinged, offering the décor and all the conveniences we have come to expect from this chain, others are on the small and gloomy side (though they are gradually being renovated). Brasserie, piano bar.

Hôtel Lutétia

6th arr. - 45, bd Raspail
49 54 46 46, fax 49 54 46 00
Open year-round. 27 stes 2,500-6,000 F. 248 rms 950-1,960 F. Restaurants. Air cond. Conf. Valet pkg. V, AE, DC, MC.
A Left Bank landmark, the Lutétia is a noteworthy example of Art Deco style. Marble, gilt, and red velvet grace the stately public areas where government bigwigs, captains of industry, and well-heeled travelers come and go. Leading off the imposing entrance are the lounge, a bar, a brasserie, a restaurant (Brasserie Lutétia and Le Paris, see *Restaurants*), and conference rooms. The large and expensive suites are done up in pink, with understated furniture and elegant bathrooms—the overall look is very 1930s. As for the service, though occasionally impersonal, it is dependably efficient and precise. Renovations are currently underway.

Marignan

8th arr. - 12, rue Marignan
40 76 34 56, fax 40 76 34 34
Open year-round. 16 stes 2,500 F. 57 rms 1,600-2,200 F. Restaurant. Air cond. Conf. Valet pkg. V, AE, DC, MC.
Strategically situated in the heart of the "Golden Triangle," between the Champs-Élysées and Avenue Montaigne, this hotel is a charming establishment, with its listed Art Deco façade and unusual interior decoration (note the Botero sculpture in the lobby). The magnificent rooms are done up in marble and expensive fabrics, with every modern comfort; some even boast a little terrace. There is a restaurant, and an attractive cocktail bar installed beneath a skylight. The high-society prices don't seem to faze the haute-couture crowd that favors the Marignan.

Montalembert

7th arr. - 3, rue de Montalembert
45 48 68 11, fax 42 22 58 19
Open year-round. 5 stes 2,750-3,600 F. 51 rms 1,625-2,080 F. Restaurant. Air cond. V, AE, DC, MC.
The management has been unstinting in its efforts to restore this 1926 hotel to its former splendor with luxurious materials (marble, ebony, sycamore, leather), designer fabrics and linens. Guests love the huge towels, cozy dressing gowns, and premium toiletries they find in the spectacular blue-gray bathrooms. The eighth-floor suites afford a magnificent view of the city. The hotel bar is a favorite rendezvous of writers and publishers.

Pergolèse

16th arr. - 3, rue Pergolèse
40 67 96 77, fax 45 00 12 11
Open year-round. 40 rms 850-1,500 F. Air cond. V, AE, DC, MC.
A new deluxe hotel, the Pergolèse provides a top-class address as well as smiling service and first-rate amenities for what are still (relatively) reasonable prices. Elegant furnishings and décor by Rena Dumas.

Régina

1st arr. - 2, pl. des Pyramides
42 60 31 10, fax 40 15 95 16
Open year-round. 14 stes 2,500-3,500 F. 107 rms 1,000-1,900 F. Restaurant. Air cond. Conf. Valet pkg. V, AE, DC.
Opposite the Tuileries is one of the city's most venerable luxury hotels, with immense rooms, precious furniture (Louis XVI, Directoire, Empire) and—a practical addition—double-glazed windows. The grandiose lobby is graced with handsome old clocks that give the time of all the major European cities. A quiet bar and a little restaurant that opens onto an indoor garden are pleasant places to idle away an hour.

Royal Saint-Honoré

1st arr. - 221, rue Saint-Honoré
42 60 32 79, fax 42 60 47 44
Open year-round. 5 stes 1,600-2,200 F. 75 rms 1,200-1,400 F. Restaurant. Air cond. Conf. No pets. V, AE, DC, MC.
Closed for over a year, the Royal Saint-Honoré is back with a brighter, fresher look. The attentive staff does its utmost to make your stay enjoyable, whether you are in town for business or for pleasure. All of the rooms are spacious; some

boast terraces overlooking the Tuileries. Marble bathrooms.

 ## Saint James et Albany
1st arr. - 202, rue de Rivoli
44 58 43 21, fax 44 58 43 11
Open year-round. 13 stes 1,700-3,200 F. 198 rms 880-1,480 F. Restaurant. Air cond. Conf. Pkg. V, AE, DC, MC.
The hotel's energetic management strives successfully to keep the establishment's standards high. The Saint James et Albany enjoys an exceptional location across from the Tuileries, and provides studios, two-room apartments, suites, and bilevel suites equipped with kitchenettes. The rooms overlook a courtyard or an inner garden and are perfectly quiet. Other amenities include a sauna, a cozy bar with background music, and a restaurant, Le Noailles.

 ## Saint James Paris
16th arr. - 5, pl. du Chancelier-Adenauer
44 05 81 81, fax 44 05 81 82
Open year-round. 31 stes 2,100-3,000 F. 17 rms 1,450-1,900 F. Restaurant. Air cond. Conf. Valet pkg. V, AE, DC, MC.
A staff of 100 looks after the 48 rooms and suites—a luxury level of attention with prices fixed accordingly. The huge rooms are decorated in a low-key 1930s style, with flowers, plants, and a basket of fruit adding warmth. The marble bathrooms are equipped with Jacuzzis. Don't miss the magnificent library, which also houses the hotel's piano bar.

Scribe
9th arr. - 1, rue Scribe
44 71 24 24, fax 42 65 39 97
Open year-round. 11 stes 3,000-5,900 F. 206 rms 1,750-2,200 F. Rms for disabled. Restaurant. Air cond. Conf. Valet pkg. V, AE, DC, MC.
Behind the Scribe's Napoléon III façade stands a prime example of the French hotelier's art. All the rooms, suites, and two-level suites (the latter are composed of a mezzanine bedroom, a living room that doubles as a dining room/office, a bathroom, dressing room, and two entrances) are comfortably furnished in classic style, and offer huge bathrooms. Streetside rooms have double windows and either contemporary or Louis XVI–style furniture; those overlooking the courtyard are furnished with Louis-Philippe–style pieces and are perfectly quiet. A multitude of TV channels is on tap, as well as 24-hour room service. Restaurant: Les Muses, see *Restaurants*; and a bar.

La Trémoille
8th arr. - 14, rue de La Trémoille
47 23 34 20, fax 40 70 01 08
Open year-round. 14 stes 2,780-5,170 F. 94 rms 1,660-2,930 F. Restaurant. Air cond. Conf. Valet pkg. V, AE, DC, MC.
Cozy comfort, antique furniture, balconies with bright flower-filled window-boxes, and service worthy of a grand hotel. Several suites are quite new and remarkably comfortable; all the rooms have lovely bathrooms and modern amenities. The delightful dining room/ salon is warmed by a crackling fire in winter. Restaurant: Le Louis d'Or.

 ## Hôtel Vernet
8th arr. - 25, rue Vernet
44 31 98 00, fax 44 31 85 69
Open year-round. 3 stes 3,200-3,400 F. 54 rms 1,500-2,200 F. Restaurant. Air cond. Conf. Valet pkg. V, AE, DC, MC.
The Vernet is an admirable hotel, combining the best of modern and traditional comforts. The rooms and suites are handsomely decorated with genuine Louis XVI, Directoire, or Empire furniture, and walls are hung with sumptuous blue or green fabric. Jacuzzi in all the bathrooms. Guests have free access to the luxurious Thermes du Royal Monceau health spa. Restaurant: Les Élysées du Vernet, see *Restaurants*.

 ## Vigny
8th arr. - 9, rue Balzac
40 75 04 39, fax 40 75 05 81
Open year-round. 11 stes 2,600-5,000 F. 26 rms 1,900-2,200 F. Restaurant. Air cond. Valet pkg. V, AE, DC, MC.
A handsome and prestigious hotel, the Vigny offers English mahogany furniture, comfortable beds, and fine marble bathrooms: the virtues of another age simplified and brought up to date. The suites provide all-out luxury. Excellent service. Lunch and light suppers are served at the bar (Le Baretto) designed by Adam Tihany. Relais et Châteaux.

Warwick
8th arr. - 5, rue de Berri
45 63 14 11, fax 43 59 00 98
Open year-round. 5 stes 4,000-8,500 F. 142 rms 2,030-2,560 F. Restaurant. Half-board 1,960-2,940 F. Air cond. Conf. V, AE, DC, MC.
Luxurious and modern, just off the Champs-Élysées, this hotel offers bright, spacious, freshly refurbished rooms done in pastel colors and chintz. Efficient soundproofing and air conditioning. There is an attractive bar with piano music in the evening and a pleasant rooftop terrace. Room service available 24 hours a day. Restaurant: La Couronne, see *Restaurants*.

CLASSIC

Agora Saint-Germain
5th arr. - 42, rue des Bernardins
46 34 13 00, fax 46 34 75 05
Open year-round. 39 rms 530-680 F. No pets. V, AE, DC, MC.
A very well kept establishment which was recently redecorated. Bright rooms (a dozen have just been renovated) with comfortable beds, minibar, radio, and television. Bathrooms feature such welcome amenities as hairdryers.

 ## Alexander
16th arr. - 102, av. Victor-Hugo
45 53 64 65, fax 45 53 12 51
Open year-round. 2 stes 1,870 F. 59 rms 830-1,300 F. Air cond. No pets. V, AE, DC, MC.
Stylish comfort and impeccable maintenance distinguish this peaceful establishment, where the rooms are redecorated regularly. There are nice big bathrooms with all modern fixtures. And you can count on a courteous reception.

*The **prices** in this guide reflect what establishments were charging at press time.*

Aramis Saint-Germain
6th arr. - 124, rue de Rennes
45 48 03 75, fax 45 44 99 29
Open year-round. 42 rms 500-800 F. Air cond. Conf. No pets. V, AE, DC, MC.
These new, well-sound-proofed and attractively decorated rooms have soft lighting, modern equipment, and perfect bathrooms. The service is especially attentive. Piano bar; no restaurant, but breakfast is served any time of day.

 ## Bastille Speria
4th arr. - 1, rue de la Bastille
42 72 04 01, fax 42 72 56 38
Open year-round. 42 rms 530-620 F. No pets. V, AE, DC, MC.
The building dates from the nineteenth century, but the rooms are modern and bright, with good equipment. Though not large, they are perfectly quiet thanks to double windows. Very pleasant reception and service.

 ## Bradford
8th arr. - 10, rue St-Philippe-du-Roule
45 63 20 20, fax 45 63 20 07
Open year-round. 2 stes 990-1,200 F. 46 rms 620-990 F. No pets. Garage pkg. V, AE, DC, MC.
A traditional hotel, where elegant simplicity combines with exemplary service to give guests true comfort. Decorated in a predominantly Louis XVI style, the rooms are currently being renovated, but in any case they are spacious and soothing. Good singles; rooms ending with the numbers 6 and 7 are the largest.

 ## Hôtel de la Bretonnerie
4th arr. - 22, rue Ste-Croix-Bretonnerie
48 87 77 63, fax 42 77 26 78
Closed Jul 30-Aug 27. 2 stes 900 F. 28 rms 620-750 F. No pets. V, MC.
A seventeenth-century town house, tastefully renovated and regularly redecorated. The spacious rooms are made cozy with exposed wood beams and antique furniture; the bathrooms are perfectly modern. Look forward to a friendly reception.

 ## Britannique
1st arr. - 20, av. Victoria
42 33 74 59, fax 42 33 82 65
Open year-round. 40 rms 600-830 F. No pets. Garage pkg. V, AE, DC, MC.
A warm welcome and good service characterize this family-run hotel. The rooms are tastefully decorated with pale walls, dark carpeting, minibar, and comfortable modern furniture. Satellite television.

 ## Cayré
7th arr. - 4, bd Raspail
45 44 38 88, fax 45 44 98 13
Open year-round. 126 rms 900-1,200 F. Rms for disabled. Conf. Garage pkg. V, AE, DC, MC.
A pink-and-gray marble floor, glass pillars, and red-leather furniture lend an air of luxury to the lobby. The rooms, modern and thoroughly soundproofed, are impersonal but well equipped (many were just redecorated), and feature marble bathrooms. Good service, too.

Prices for rooms and suites *are per room, not per person. Half-board prices, however, are per person.*

Chambellan Morgane
16th arr. - 6, rue Keppler
47 20 35 72, fax 47 20 95 69
Open year-round. 20 rms 650-900 F. Conf. Pkg. V, AE, DC, MC.
The pink-walled rooms are dainty and fresh, with flowered curtains and functional blond-wood furniture. The tiled bathrooms are equipped with tubs large enough to relax in. Conveniently situated at a point equidistant from L'Étoile, the Champs-Élysées, and the Seine, this hotel offers everything a traveler might wish, except a warm welcome.

Colisée
8th arr. - 6, rue du Colisée
43 59 95 25, fax 45 63 26 54
Open year-round. 45 rms 560-750 F. Air cond. V, AE, DC, MC.
Rooms are on the small side (those with numbers ending in an 8 are more spacious), but quite comfortable, with flowered wallpaper and tiled bathrooms. The four attic rooms have beamed ceilings and considerable charm. There is an inviting red-lacquered bar, but no restaurant.

Commodore
9th arr. - 12, bd Haussmann
42 46 72 82, fax 47 70 23 81
Open year-round. 12 stes 2,300-3,700 F. 150 rms 1,100-2,050 F. Restaurant. Conf. V, AE, DC, MC.
This commendable traditional hotel is located a few steps away from the Drouot auction house. A portion of the rooms were recently renovated in a bright, elegant style (814 has a view of Sacré-Cœur). As for the others, the less said the better. All, however, are spacious; newlyweds should request the honeymoon suite, which must be seen to be believed.

Courcelles
17th arr. - 184, rue de Courcelles
47 63 65 30, fax 46 22 49 44
Open year-round. 42 rms 610-770 F. V, AE, DC, MC.
The corridors of this immaculately kept hotel were recently renovated. All the rooms here are equipped with TV, direct-line telephones, clock-radios, and minibars. Very pleasant reception and service. Note that the bar is reserved for hotel guests only.

Duminy-Vendôme
1st arr. - 3, rue du Mont-Thabor
42 60 32 80, fax 42 96 07 83
Open year-round. 79 rms 648-866 F. Conf. No pets. Pkg. V, AE, DC.
Duminy-Vendôme's rooms have impeccable bathrooms and 1920s–style furnishings. Rooms on the sixth and seventh floors have slightly sloping ceilings, and those with numbers ending in 10 are larger than the rest. A small summer patio is located on the main floor, as is the rather amazing bar, swathed in red velvet.

Élysa
5th arr. - 6, rue Gay-Lussac
43 25 31 74, fax 46 34 56 27
Open year-round. 30 rms 450-720 F. Conf. No pets. V, AE, MC.
In the heart of the Latin Quarter, near the Luxembourg Gardens. The small, inviting rooms have all just been renovated. Marble bathrooms.

Élysées-Maubourg

7th arr. - 35, bd de Latour-Maubourg
45 56 10 78, fax 47 05 65 08
Open year-round. 1 ste 1,200 F. 29 rms 560-730 F. Conf. V, AE, DC.

The 30 rooms of this hotel are decorated in classic good taste, in green, blue, or beige tones. Adequately sized, they are superbly equipped and comfortable. There is a Finnish sauna in the basement, a bar, and a flower-filled patio.

Frantour Suffren

15th arr. - 20, rue Jean-Rey
45 78 50 00, fax 45 78 91 42
Open year-round. 1 ste 3,412 F. 407 rms 856-1,950 F. Rms for disabled. Restaurant. Air cond. Conf. Pkg. V, AE, DC, MC.

The Frantour Suffren is a large, modern hotel located next to the Seine and the Champ-de-Mars. Though somewhat impersonal, the simple rooms are regularly refurbished and offer excellent equipment. There is an attractive, plant-filled restaurant (Le Champ de Mars), and a garden where meals are served in summer.

Holiday Inn République

11th arr. - 10, pl. de la République
43 55 44 34, fax 47 00 32 34
Open year-round. 30 stes 2,295 F. 288 rms 1,460-1,740 F. Rms for disabled. Restaurant. Air cond. Conf. V, AE, DC, MC.

The architect Davioud, who designed the Châtelet, built this former Modern Palace in 1867. Today it belongs to the largest hotel chain in the world, which completely restored and modernized it. The rooms and suites are functional, pleasant, and well soundproofed; the most attractive ones overlook the flower-filled covered courtyard. Restaurant: La Belle Époque, see *Restaurants.*

Le Jardin de Cluny

5th arr. - 9, rue du Sommerard
43 54 22 66, fax 40 51 03 36
Open year-round. 40 rms 520-750 F. Air cond. Conf. No pets. V, AE, DC, MC.

A perfectly functional hotel in the heart of the Latin Quarter, with comfortable rooms and modern bathrooms.

Kléber

16th arr. - 7, rue de Belloy
47 23 80 22, fax 49 52 07 20
Open year-round. 1 ste 950-1,360 F. 21 rms 690-840 F. Conf. Garage pkg. V, AE, DC, MC.

A family-run hotel managed in a thoroughly professional way, this impeccable little establishment has 22 spotless, personalized rooms spread over six floors. All are equipped with double-glazed windows and pretty bathrooms. Bar open 24 hours a day.

Latitudes Saint-Germain

6th arr. - 7-11, rue Saint-Benoît
42 61 53 53, fax 49 27 09 33
Open year-round. 117 rms 640-950 F. Rms for disabled. Air cond. Restaurant. Conf. No pets. V, AE, DC, MC.

This large, modern hotel, formerly a printing works, is located in the heart of Saint-Germain-des-Prés; its gracious turn-of-the-century façade has been preserved. The spacious rooms are well equipped and have just been freshly painted and carpeted. A cellar jazz club provides hot and cool live music every night except Sunday.

Lenox

14th arr. - 15, rue Delambre
43 35 34 50, fax 43 20 46 64
Open year-round. 6 stes 930-960 F. 46 rms 520-640 F. V, AE, DC, MC.

In the heart of Montparnasse, a peaceful hotel with a cozy sort of charm. The penthouse suites have fireplaces, and are most attractive. Rooms vary in size, yet are uniformly comfortable and well maintained. Light meals are served at the bar until 2am (there is no restaurant).

Madison

6th arr. - 143, bd Saint-Germain
40 51 60 00, fax 40 51 60 01
Open year-round. 55 rms 750-1,485 F. Air cond. V, AE, DC.

A comfortable hotel in the heart of Saint-Germain, decorated with a sprinkling of antique pieces; the bathrooms are done up in pretty Provençal tiles. Very well equipped: double glazing, air conditioning, minibar, satellite TV, etc. Smiling service and a generous breakfast buffet.

Méridien Étoile

17th arr. - 81, bd Gouvion-Saint-Cyr
40 68 35 35, fax 40 68 31 31
Open year-round. 18 stes 3,800-7,500 F. 1,007 rms 1,450-2,150 F. Rms for disabled. Restaurants. Air cond. Conf. Valet pkg. V, AE, DC, MC.

This Méridien is the largest hotel in Western Europe, and one of the busiest in Paris. The rooms are small but remarkably well equipped. A variety of boutiques, a nightclub, the Hurlingham Polo Bar, and four restaurants liven things up (for the excellent Clos Longchamp, see *Restaurants*), as does the popular cocktail lounge where top jazz musicians play (Club Lionel Hampton). Other services include spacious conference rooms, a sauna, and travel agencies.

Méridien Montparnasse

14th arr. - 19, rue du Commandant-Mouchotte - 44 36 44 36, fax 44 36 49 00
Open year-round. 35 stes 3,500-4,500 F. 920 rms 1,650 F. Rms for disabled. Restaurants. Air cond. Conf. No pets. V, AE, DC, MC.

Luxurious, soigné, and comfortable—that's the Méridien in a nutshell. Try to reserve one of the newer rooms, which are particularly bright and spacious. Or the Presidential Suite, if your means permit. Certain rooms are for non-smokers only; all afford good views of the city. For fine dining there are two restaurants: Justine and Montparnasse 25, see *Restaurants*; bar; boutiques.

Montana-Tuileries

1st arr. - 12, rue Saint-Roch
42 60 35 10, fax 42 61 12 28
Open year-round. 25 rms 580-1,050 F. V, AE, MC.

This very chic little hotel doesn't actually overlook the Tuileries, but they are only a stone's throw away. All double rooms, well equipped. Numbers 50 and 52 have balconies.

Napoléon

8th arr. - 40, av. de Friedland
47 66 02 02, fax 47 66 82 33
Open year-round. 2 stes 3,750-4,500 F. 100 rms 800-1,650 F. Restaurant. Air cond. Conf. Valet pkg. V, AE, DC, MC.

Admirably situated, this fine hotel provides top-flight service along with excellent equipment and amenities. The spacious rooms have classic décor, and offer good value in this up-market neighborhood. The pleasant banquet rooms (L'Étoile, for example) are much in demand for receptions and conferences.

Hôtel des Nations

5th arr. - "Neotel," 54, rue Monge
43 26 45 24, fax 46 34 00 13
Open year-round. 38 rms 550-600 F. No pets. No cards.

New carpeting and fabric wallcoverings were installed not long ago at this well-kept, functional hotel. Tiled bathrooms, double glazing. Some rooms look out over a garden that in summer is filled with flowers. Courteous service.

Nikko

15th arr. - 61, quai de Grenelle
40 58 20 00, fax 45 75 42 35
Open year-round. 7 stes 3,500-8,700 F. 763 rms 1,430-1,910 F. Air cond. Conf. Heated pool. Valet pkg. V, AE, DC, MC.

Thirty-one floors piled up to resemble an immense beehive. You can opt either for vaguely Japanese-style or modern, ultrafunctional rooms; the large porthole windows overlook the Seine and the Pont Mirabeau. The six upper floors are reserved for luxury rooms with personalized service. Boutiques, conference rooms, a heated swimming pool with sauna, fitness club, and a massage service are just some of the Nikko's attractive features. You'll also find an inviting bar, restaurants (Les Célébrités, see *Restaurants*), and a brasserie within the complex.

Novotel Les Halles

1st arr. - Pl. Marguerite-de-Navarre
42 21 31 31, fax 40 26 05 79
Open year-round. 5 stes 1,520 F. 280 rms 850-930 F. Rms for disabled. Restaurant. Air cond. Conf. Garage pkg. V, AE, DC.

This ultramodern building constructed of stone, glass, and zinc is located in the heart of the former market district, near the Pompidou Center and the Forum des Halles. The huge rooms offer perfect comfort, but their air conditioning prevents you from opening the windows. The restaurant is open from 6am to midnight, and there is a terrace bar. The conference rooms can be tailored to size by means of movable partitions. Other services include a travel agency and a duty-free shop.

Le Parc Victor-Hugo

16th arr. - 55-57, av. R.-Poincaré
44 05 66 66, fax 44 05 66 00
Open year-round. 17 stes 2,650 F. 103 rms 1,690-2,300 F. Restaurants. Air cond. Conf. Valet pkg. V, AE, DC, MC.

Celebrity decorators were called in to refurbish this elegant hotel, which just inaugurated an additional wing. Supremely comfortable, the rooms boast the most refined appointments and every imaginable amenity. The public rooms are furnished with admirable pieces and accented with beautiful sculpture. A large, glorious indoor garden is planted with rare specimens. Restaurant: Le Relais du Parc, see *Restaurants*.

This symbol signifies hotels that are exceptionally quiet.

Paris Saint-Honoré

8th arr. - 15, rue Boissy-d'Anglas
44 94 14 14, fax 44 94 14 28
Open year-round. 7 stes 1,580 F. 112 rms 800-1,055 F. Air cond. V, AE, DC, MC.

Comfortable and functional, favored by business travelers and visitors to the nearby American Embassy, this well-renovated hotel houses seven storeys of pleasant, modern rooms with impeccable bathrooms. The bar, open from 10am to 2am, is decorated with marquetry from the trains of the *Compagnie Internationale des Wagons Lits*. No restaurant, but light meals are available around the clock from room service.

Quality Inn-Rive Gauche

6th arr. - 92, rue de Vaugirard
42 22 00 56, fax 42 22 05 39
Open year-round. 7 stes 760-920 F. 127 rms 650-895 F. Rms for disabled. Air cond. Pkg. V, AE, DC, MC.

Part of an American chain with about 1,000 hotels worldwide, this is a quiet, functional establishment. Well-equipped rooms with minibar and satellite TV, some furnished in cruise-liner style. Piano bar filled with plants. Substantial breakfasts are served until 11am. Impeccable service.

Résidence Bassano

16th arr. - 15, rue de Bassano
47 23 78 23, fax 47 20 41 22
Open year-round. 3 stes 1,600-1,950 F. 27 rms 750-1,150 F. Air cond. V, AE, DC, MC.

Housed in a building of Haussmann vintage, the rooms are not all equally attractive. Yet most are bright and all are thoughtfully designed and equipped, enhanced with Art Deco–style furniture. Among the amenities are a sauna, Jacuzzi, and 24-hour room service.

Résidence Monceau

8th arr. - 85, rue du Rocher
45 22 75 11, fax 45 22 30 88
Open year-round. 1 ste 860 F. 50 rms 675 F. Restaurant. Conf. No pets. V, AE, DC, MC.

Though it lacks atmosphere, the Résidence Monceau is functional and well kept, and employs a helpful, courteous staff. All the rooms have private bathrooms, TVs, minibars, and automatic alarm clocks. Good privacy; breakfast is served on a patio. No restaurant, but snacks are available at the bar.

Résidence Saint-Honoré

8th arr. - 214, rue du Fg-Saint-Honoré
42 25 26 27, fax 45 63 30 67
Open year-round. 91 rms 750-990 F. Air cond. V, AE, DC, MC.

A surprising range of styles has been used in the gradual renovation of the spacious rooms, which are more comfortable than luxurious. Dynamic management, uncommonly courteous staff. The Saint-Honoré auction rooms are situated on the hotel's lower level.

Rond-Point de Longchamp

16th arr. - 86, rue de Longchamp
45 05 13 63, fax 47 55 12 80
Open year-round. 1 ste 900-1,200 F. 56 rms 672-1,000 F. Restaurant. Air cond. Pkg. V, AE, DC, MC.

The sizeable, comfortable rooms are nicely fitted and prettily decorated (gray carpeting, burr-walnut furniture), and have marble bathrooms. There is an elegant restaurant with a fireplace, as well as a billiard room.

Saint-Ferdinand
17th arr. - 36, rue Saint-Ferdinand
45 72 66 66, fax 45 74 12 92
Open year-round. 42 rms 730-880 F. Air cond. V, AE, DC, MC.
This small, functional hotel is of recent vintage. The rooms are tiny (the bathrooms even more so), but they are refurbished regularly and well equipped, with television, minibar, safe, and hairdryer. Soothing décor.

Saxe-Résidence
7th arr. - 9, villa de Saxe
47 83 98 28, fax 47 83 85 47
Open year-round. 3 stes 845 F. 52 rms 623 F. No cards.
Situated between two convents and a bouquet of secret gardens, this hotel is miraculously quiet. The rooms are constantly updated, and there is a 1950s–style bar. Even the singles are of decent size. Courteous reception.

Hôtel de Sévigné
16th arr. - 6, rue de Belloy
47 20 88 90, fax 40 70 98 73
Open year-round. 30 rms 640-760 F. Pkg. V, AE, MC.
A classic hotel. The modern, comfortable rooms are soundproof and with minibars and individual safes. Friendly service and reception.

Sofitel
15th arr. - 8-12, rue Louis-Armand
40 60 30 30, fax 45 57 04 22
Open year-round. 14 stes 1,400-1,600 F. 522 rms 980 F. Restaurants. Air cond. Conf. Heated pool. Valet pkg. Helipad. V, AE, DC.
Thirty-seven meeting and conference rooms (with simultaneous translation available in five languages) are connected to a central administration office. The hotel also features recreational facilities (exercise room, sauna, and a heated swimming pool with sliding roof on the 23rd floor), and a panoramic bar. The rooms, all equipped with magnetic closing systems, are functional (some are on the small side). Restaurant: Le Relais de Sèvres, see *Restaurants*.

Sofitel Paris Saint-Jacques
14th arr. - 17, bd Saint-Jacques
40 78 79 80, fax 45 88 43 93
Open year-round. 14 stes 1,825-2,000 F. 783 rms 930-1,360 F. Rms for disabled. Restaurant. Half-board 1,080-1,515 F. Air cond. Conf. Valet pkg. V, AE, DC, MC.
The Sofitel Saint-Jacques is conveniently close to Orly airport. It offers good-sized rooms with comfortable bathrooms, air conditioning, and blackout blinds that allow long-distance travelers to sleep off their jet lag. For entertainment, there are bars and restaurants; or you could ask one of the staff members to show you the "Deluxe" suite, which has often served as a setting for films.

🌲
This symbol signifies hotels that are exceptionally quiet.

Sofitel Arc-de-Triomphe
8th arr. - 14, rue Beaujon
45 63 04 04, fax 42 25 36 81
Open year-round. 6 stes 1,950-3,200 F. 129 rms 800-1,500 F. Restaurant. Air cond. Conf. Pkg. V, AE, DC.
This solid, austere building, dating from 1925, houses a comfortable hotel that is not, however, long on charm. But the facilities (ultramodern equipment for the business clientele) are first-rate, and are constantly being updated. The largish, bright rooms are decorated with functional furniture (minibars, TVs, and video programming). Room service. Restaurant: Clovis, see *Restaurants*.

Splendid Étoile
17th arr. - 1 bis, av. Carnot
45 72 72 00, fax 45 72 72 01
Open year-round. 7 stes 1,600 F. 50 rms 880-1,158F. Restaurant. Air cond. Conf. No pets. V, AE, DC.
The Splendid Étoile features 57 well-maintained, comfortably furnished, good-sized rooms and suites, all with double glazing (some afford views of the Arc de Triomphe). Attractive English-style bar. Restaurant: Le Pré Carré.

Terrass' Hôtel
18th arr. - 12, rue Joseph-de-Maistre
46 06 72 85, fax 42 52 29 11
Open year-round. 13 stes 1,500 F. 88 rms 900-1,190 F. Restaurant. Half-board 695-910 F. Air cond. Conf. Pkg. V, AE, DC.
A just-completed renovation has spruced up this excellent hotel. Located at the foot of the Butte Montmartre, the Terrass offers a majestic view of almost all of Paris. Rooms are comfortable and nicely fitted, with some attractive furniture and Italian-tile bathrooms. Up on the seventh floor, the panoramic terrace doubles as a bar in summer.

Vert Galant
13th arr. - 41, rue Croulebarbe
44 08 83 50, fax 44 08 83 69
Open year-round. 15 rms 400-500 F. No pets. Pkg. V, AE, DC.
Now for something completely different: this delightful country *auberge* provides adorable rooms (with kitchenette) overlooking an indoor garden where grapes and tomatoes grow! Quiet; good value. Restaurant: Auberge Etchegorry, see *Restaurants*.

Victoria Palace
6th arr. - 6, rue Blaise-Desgoffe
45 44 38 16, fax 45 49 23 75
Open year-round. 110 rms 750-1,300 F. Conf. Garage pkg. V, AE, DC, MC.
A reliable establishment, freshly renovated in 1993. The rooms are sizeable and comfortable, with really spacious closets and good bathrooms. Bar and elevator. The elevator is brand-new.

Vieux Paris   🌲
6th arr. - 9, rue Gît-le-Cœur
43 54 41 66, fax 43 26 00 15
Open year-round. 7 stes 1,270-1,470 F. 13 rms 990-1,170 F. No pets. V, AE.
Here's a hotel that wears its name well, for it was built in the fifteenth century. An overhaul in 1991 turned the Vieux Paris into a luxurious stopover, whose comfort and first-rate amenities

fully justify the high rates. Rooms are handsomely furnished and perfectly quiet, with Jacuzzis in every bathroom. Warm reception.

Yllen

15th arr. - 196, rue de Vaugirard
45 67 67 67, fax 45 67 74 37
Open year-round. 1 ste 910-995 F. 39 rms 490-670 F. Garage pkg. V, AE, DC, MC.
Yllen's modern, functional rooms have understated décor and are well soundproofed—but they are quite small. Corner rooms (those with numbers ending in 4) on the upper floors are the best. Energetic management, friendly reception.

Waldorf Madeleine
8th arr. - 12, bd Malesherbes
42 65 72 06, fax 40 07 10 45
Open year-round. 45 rms 950-1,200 F. Air cond. No pets. Pkg. V, AE, DC, MC.
This handsome freestone building houses an elegant lobby (notice the Art Deco ceiling) and rooms of exemplary comfort, with double glazing and air conditioning. You can count on a smiling reception.

Le Zéphyr
12th arr. - 31 bis, bd Diderot
43 46 12 72, fax 43 41 68 01
Open year-round. 89 rms 530-720 F. Rms for disabled. Restaurant. Air cond. Conf. Garage pkg. V, AE, DC, MC.
Practically next door to the Gare de Lyon, the Zéphyr is a newly renovated hotel with good equipment. Rooms are bright and neat, the welcome is friendly, and service is reliably prompt. Quality breakfasts.

CHARMING

Abbaye Saint-Germain

6th arr. - 10, rue Cassette
45 44 38 11, fax 45 48 07 86
Open year-round. 4 stes 1,750-1,900 F. 42 rms 840-1,450 F. Air cond. No pets. V, AE, MC.
Set back from the street, this serene eighteenth-century residence located between a courtyard and a garden offers well-kept, elegantly decorated rooms which are not, however, particularly spacious; the most delightful are on the same level as the garden (number 4 even has a terrace).

Agora
1st arr. - 7, rue de la Cossonnerie
42 33 46 02, fax 42 33 80 99
Open year-round. 29 rms 370-595 F. No pets. V, AE.
In the heart of the pedestrian district of Les Halles, these rooms are exquisitely decorated and well soundproofed, with newly renovated bath-rooms. Lovely pieces of period furniture and engravings are everywhere; the cleanliness is impressive. Cheerful reception.

Hôtel de l'Alligator

14th arr. - 39, rue Delambre
43 35 18 40, fax 43 35 30 71
Open year-round. 35 rms 430-650 F. Conf. Pkg. V, AE, DC, MC.
Practical, welcoming, and attractive to boot. Rooms are small (balconies on the fifth and sixth floors), but trim and comfortable with good equipment. The breakfast room boasts a skylight and furniture designed by Philippe Starck.

Angleterre

6th arr. - 44, rue Jacob
42 60 34 72, fax 42 60 16 93
Open year-round. 3 stes 1,000-1,100 F. 27 rms 600-1,100 F. Rms for disabled. No pets. V, AE, DC, MC.
Hemingway once lived in this former British Embassy, built around a flower-filled patio. The impeccable rooms are fresh and appealing; some are quite spacious, with high beamed ceilings. Large, comfortable beds; luxurious bathrooms. Downstairs, there is a bar and lounge with a piano.

Atala
8th arr. - 10, rue Chateaubriand
45 62 01 62, fax 42 25 66 38
Open year-round. 1 ste 1,500 F. 48 rms 700-1,300 F. Restaurant. Air cond. Conf. Pkg. V, AE, DC, MC.
In a quiet street near the Champs-Élysées, this hotel provides cheerfully decorated rooms that open onto a verdant garden. Balconies and terraces come with rooms on the sixth and eighth floors. L'Atalante, the hotel's bar and restaurant, offers garden dining in fine weather. Excellent service.

De Banville
17th arr. - 166, bd Berthier
42 67 70 16, fax 44 40 42 77
Open year-round. 39 rms 550-700 F. Restaurant. V, AE, MC.
A fine small hotel that dates from the 1930s. There are flowers at the windows (some of which open to panoramic views of Paris) and all manner of pleasing details in the bright, cheerful rooms. Accommodations are large, and blessedly quiet thanks to thick carpeting. Marble or tile bathrooms. Excellent English breakfasts.

Beau Manoir

8th arr. - 6, rue de l'Arcade
42 66 03 07, fax 42 68 03 00
Open year-round. 3 stes 1,350-1,465 F. 29 rms 995-1,155 F. Air cond. V, AE, DC, MC.
The opulent décor—it features *Grand Siècle* wall hangings—is somehow reminiscent of Versailles. But the Beau Manoir is just steps away from the Madeleine, in the city's fashionable shopping district. Some of the luxurious rooms overlook pretty indoor gardens. Uncommonly delicious breakfasts are served in the hotel's vaulted cellar.

Belle Époque
12th arr. - 66, rue de Charenton
43 44 06 66, fax 43 44 10 25
Open year-round. 4 stes 850-1,250 F. 26 rms 500-670 F. Restaurant. Half-board 410-495 F. Conf. Valet pkg. V, AE, DC.
Not far from the Gare de Lyon, this well-kept hotel is furnished and decorated in 1930s style. Comfortable beds, modern bathrooms, and double glazing throughout. Pretty garden courtyard. The bar is open from noon to 10pm; a restaurant serves breakfast and light meals.

Bersoly's Saint-Germain
7th arr. - 28, rue de Lille
42 60 73 79, fax 49 27 05 55
Closed Aug. 16 rms 580-680 F. V, MC.
Writers, artists, and antique dealers frequent this hotel, whose furniture is largely provided by the nearby "golden triangle" of antique shops. Rooms are named for famous artists, and

reproductions of their paintings adorn the walls. Breakfast is served in the attractive vaulted basement. Faultless reception.

Brighton
1st arr. - 218, rue de Rivoli
42 60 30 03, fax 42 60 41 78
Open year-round. 1 ste 1,420 F. 69 rms 430-900 F. No pets. V, AE, DC, MC.
A dream setting opposite the Tuileries, near the Louvre, is offered at very reasonable prices. The large rooms on the Rue de Rivoli have wonderful views, high molded ceilings, huge brass beds, nineteenth-century furniture, and good-sized bathrooms. The little attic rooms are especially good value.

Centre-Ville Étoile
17th arr. - 6, rue des Acacias
43 80 56 18, fax 47 54 93 43
Open year-round. 20 rms 690-950 F. Restaurant. Air cond. Pkg. V, AE, DC, MC.
A modern hotel with lots of personality and an intimate, comfortable atmosphere. Entirely decorated in black and white with Art Deco touches, the attractive, contemporary rooms boast minitels (electronic telephone directories), satellite TV, and spotless tiled bathrooms.

Crystal Hotel
6th arr. - 24, rue Saint-Benoît
45 48 85 14, fax 45 49 16 45
Open year-round. 1 ste 900-1,140 F. 25 rms 550-840 F. Conf. V, AE, DC.
A charming small hotel with a friendly atmosphere, favored by artists and writers. The rooms are decorated with designer fabrics and wallpaper, and the occasional piece of antique furniture. Thoughtfully equipped bathrooms. Deep, comfy Chesterfield sofas provide a welcoming touch in the lobby.

Danemark
6th arr. - 21, rue Vavin
43 26 93 78, fax 46 34 66 06
Open year-round. 15 rms 590-760 F. V, AE, DC, MC.
This small hotel was carefully renovated in 1930s style. Although the rooms are not very large, they are elegantly furnished, with pleasant lighting, mahogany, ash, or oak furniture and gray-marble bathrooms (number 10 has a Jacuzzi). Charming public rooms.

Les Deux Iles
4th arr. - 59, rue St-Louis-en-l'Ile
43 26 13 35, fax 43 29 60 25
Open year-round. 17 rms 700-810 F. Garage pkg. No cards.
This particularly welcoming hotel, like many buildings on the Ile-Saint-Louis, is a lovely seventeenth-century house. You'll sleep close to the Seine in small, pretty rooms decorated with bright fabrics and painted furniture.

Esméralda
5th arr. - 4, rue Saint-Julien-le-Pauvre
43 54 19 20, fax 40 51 00 68
Open year-round. 18 rms 170 510 F. No cards.
It isn't easy to book a room here, for the Esméralda's reputation for charm and value is known worldwide. The owner, artist Michèle Bruel, has given her hotel a rare personality with paintings, real or *faux* antiques, and curiosities

galore. The rooms are quite small but comfy; the best afford romantic views of Notre-Dame.

L'Hôtel
6th arr. - "Guy-Louis Duboucheron", 13, rue des Beaux-Arts
43 25 27 22, fax 43 25 64 81
Open year-round. 3 stes 2,800-3,800 F. 24 rms 950-2,300 F. Restaurant. Air cond. Conf. V, AE, DC, MC.
"L'Hôtel" provides top-notch amenities and service, of course, but it's the charm of the place that accounts for its enduring popularity. The décor of this delightful Directoire-style building resembles no other—whether it's number 16, the room once occupied by Oscar Wilde, the Imperial room (decorated in a neo-Egyptian style), the Cardinale room (swathed in purple), or number 36, which contains the Art Deco furniture from the home of music-hall star Mistinguett. The seventh floor houses two lovely suites. The atmosphere here reproduces that of a private home and is truly unlike what one usually finds in a hotel. Restaurant: Le Bélier, see *Restaurants*, piano bar on the premises.

Duc de Saint-Simon
7th arr. - 14, rue Saint-Simon
44 39 20 20, fax 45 48 68 25
Open year-round. 5 stes 1,865 F. 29 rms 1,065-1,465 F. Air cond. No pets. No cards.
Set back from the street between two gardens, this quiet, elegant nineteenth-century building houses a most appealing hotel. Fully renovated by its Swedish owners, it provides discreet luxury and comfort, with antiques, fine paintings and objets d'art, good lighting, and enchanting décor. The four rooms on the second floor have terraces that overlook the garden. Room 41, in the annex, boasts an imposing canopied bed. There is a bar, but no restaurant.

Ducs d'Anjou
1st arr. - 1, rue Sainte-Opportune
42 36 92 24, fax 42 36 16 63
Open year-round. 38 rms 390-565 F. V, AE, DC, MC.
Located on the delightful small Place Sainte-Opportune, this ancient building has been restored from top to bottom. The rooms are small (as are the bathrooms) but quiet; rooms 61 and 62 are larger, and can comfortably accommodate three people. Rooms overlooking the courtyard are a bit gloomy.

Éber Monceau
17th arr. - 18, rue Léon-Jost
46 22 60 70, fax 47 63 01 01
Open year-round. 5 stes 1,000-1,300 F. 13 rms 480-630 F. No pets. Garage pkg. V, AE, DC, MC.
This former bordello has been totally renovated, and "adopted," so to speak, by people in fashion, photography, and the movies. Rooms are on the small side, but they are tastefully decorated and furnished, with good bathrooms. A large, two-level suite on the top floor has a lovely terrace. Breakfast is served on the patio in summer.

Élysée
8th arr. - 12, rue des Saussaies
42 65 29 25, fax 42 65 64 28
Open year-round. 2 stes 1,270 F. 30 rms 540-950 F. Air cond. No pets. V, AE, DC, MC.
An intimate, tastefully renovated hotel where you will receive a most pleasant welcome. All

the rooms are different (room 301 is especially elegant); the two suites under the eaves are much in demand. There's an inviting lounge with a fireplace, and an attractive bar.

Ermitage Hôtel
18th arr. - 24, rue Lamarck
42 64 79 22, fax 42 64 10 33
Open year-round. 12 rms 395-440 F. No pets. No cards.
This charming hotel occupies a little white building behind the Basilica of Sacré-Cœur. The personalized décor in each room is punctuated by an antique or *bibelot.* Pretty bathrooms. There is a garden and a terrace for relaxing after a busy day, and you can expect a friendly reception.

Étoile Park Hotel
17th arr. - 10, av. Mac-Mahon
42 67 69 63, fax 43 80 18 99
Closed Jul 20-Aug 20. 28 rms 484-760 F. No pets. Pkg. V, AE, DC, MC.
Modern and decorated in understated good taste, this hotel offers refined guest rooms (ten were just refurnished this year) and comfortable, well-designed bathrooms. Extremely good-humored reception.

Étoile-Pereire

17th arr. - 146, bd Pereire
42 67 60 00, fax 42 67 02 90
Open year-round. 5 stes 956 F. 21 rms 506-706 F. No pets. Garage pkg. V, AE, DC, MC.
Attention to detail is a priority at this welcoming hotel. Located at the back of a quiet courtyard, the spacious, pastel rooms are most attractive, with garden views. Both the atmosphere and service are charming and cheerful.

Ferrandi
6th arr. - 92, rue du Cherche-Midi
42 22 97 40, fax 45 44 89 97
Open year-round. 1 ste 950-1,250 F. 41 rms 440-950 F. V, AE, DC, MC.
In a quiet street near Montparnasse, with a reception area that matches the charm of the rooms. Some of the guest rooms have four-poster beds, others a fireplace. All have good bathrooms (with hairdryers) and double glazing. Delightful welcome.

Garden Élysée
16th arr. - 12, rue Saint-Didier
47 55 01 11, fax 47 27 79 24
Open year-round. 48 rms 900-1,600 F. Rms for disabled. Restaurant. Half-board 1,180-1,730 F. Air cond. Conf. No pets. Valet pkg. V, AE, DC, MC.
All the facilities of a luxury hotel in a bucolic garden setting, between the Trocadéro and the Champs-Élysées. Housed in a new building set back from the street are elegant, unusually spacious rooms with modern marble or tile baths. The 1930s décor is fresh and appealing, and the equipment is particularly fine (satellite television, individual safes, Jacuzzi).

Hameau de Passy

16th arr. - 48, rue de Passy
42 88 47 55, fax 42 30 83 72
Open year-round. 32 rms 485-560 F. V, AE, DC, MC.
Tucked away in a flower-filled cul-de-sac, this exceptionally quiet hotel was modernized in 1990. Roughcast walls and stained-wood furniture decorate the comfortable rooms (some con-

necting) that overlook the garden. Bright, tidy bathrooms; smiling service and reception.

Hôtel du Jeu de Paume
4th arr. - 54, rue St-Louis-en-l'Ile
43 26 14 18, fax 40 46 02 76
Open year-round. 32 rms 795-1,340 F. Conf. V, AE, DC, MC.
This is a seventeenth-century building with a splendid wood-and-stone interior, featuring a glass elevator that ferries guests to their bright, quiet rooms. There is a pleasant little garden, too.

Left Bank Saint-Germain
6th arr. - 9, rue de l'Ancienne-Comédie
43 54 01 70, fax 43 26 17 14
Open year-round. 1 ste 1,400 F. 30 rms 850-990 F. Air cond. V, AE, DC, MC.
An eighteenth-century building, with loads of charm. The tasteful but rather repetitive décor features custom-made walnut furniture in Louis XIII style, lace bedspreads, brass lamps, and marble bathrooms.

Hôtel du Léman
9th arr. - 20, rue de Trévise
42 46 50 66, fax 48 24 27 59
Open year-round. 24 rms 390-730 F. Garage pkg. V, AE, DC, MC.
This charming, out-of-the-ordinary small hotel has been tastefully renovated. Tuscany marble inlays enhance the modern décor in the lobby. The tiny rooms are pleasantly decorated with attractive bedside lamps and original drawings and watercolors. A generous buffet breakfast is served in the vaulted basement.

Lenox
7th arr. - 9, rue de l'Université
42 96 10 95, fax 42 61 52 83
Open year-round. 2 stes 960 F. 32 rms 580-780 F. Restaurant. No pets. V, AE, DC.
These petite but most attractive rooms are decorated with elegant wallpaper and stylish furniture; numbers 22, 32, and 42 are the most enchanting. On the top floor are two split-level suites with exposed beams and flower-filled balconies. The elegant bar stays open until 2am.

Lido
8th arr. - 4, passage de la Madeleine
42 66 27 37, fax 42 66 61 23
Open year-round. 32 rms 800-930 F. Air cond. V, AE, DC, MC.
A laudable establishment, situated between the Madeleine and the Place de la Concorde. The lobby is most elegant, with Oriental rugs on the floor and tapestries on the stone walls. The guest rooms, decorated in pink, blue, or cream, have comfortable beds with white lace covers, modern bathrooms, and double-glazed windows. The staff is thoughtful and courteous.

Lutèce
4th arr. - 65, rue St-Louis-en-l'Ile
43 26 23 52, fax 43 29 60 25
Open year-round. 23 rms 680-830 F. No cards.
A tasteful, small hotel for people who love Paris, this handsome old house has some twenty rooms (there are two charming mansards on the sixth floor), with whitewashed walls and ceiling beams, decorated with bright, cheerful fabrics. The bathrooms are small but modern and impeccably kept. The lobby features lavish bouquets

and a stone fireplace which is often used in winter.

Majestic
16th arr. - 29, rue Dumont-d'Urville
45 00 83 70, fax 45 00 29 48
Open year-round. 3 stes 1,800-2,000 F. 27 rms 1,150-1,450 F. Air cond. V, AE, DC, MC.
Rooms in this exemplary hotel are redecorated by turns, and all boast comfortable beds, fine furniture, and thick carpeting. On the top floor, a lovely penthouse features a small balcony filled with flowers. Old-World atmosphere.

Les Marronniers
6th arr. - 21, rue Jacob
43 25 30 60, fax 40 46 83 56
Open year-round. 37 rms 510-1,020 F. Conf. No pets. Pkg. No cards.
Set back slightly from the Rue Jacob, this delightful hotel is blessed with a small garden shaded by two chestnut trees. Choose a room just above this garden, or one of the rather bizarre but absolutely adorable (and bright) attic rooms on the seventh floor, which have views of the belfry of Saint-Germain-des-Prés. Peace and quiet are assured. Breakfast is served on a bright (weather permitting!) glass-enclosed veranda.

Libertel Moulin
9th arr. - 39, rue Fontaine
42 81 93 25, fax 40 16 09 90
Open year-round. 50 rms 550-950 F. Conf. Pkg. V, AE, DC, MC.
A hotel full of charm and surprises near the Place Pigalle, with an appealing Pompeii-style lobby and rooms of varying sizes (some are extended by a small terrace overlooking the inner courtyards). An excellent buffet-style breakfast is served until 11am.

Le Notre-Dame Hôtel
5th arr. - 1, quai St-Michel
43 54 20 43, fax 43 26 61 75
Open year-round. 3 stes 1,050 F. 26 rms 590-790 F. V, AE, DC, MC.
Situated in a noisy area, but the hotel is protected by effective double glazing. The sixth floor houses three split-level attic rooms with red carpeting, rustic furniture, marble bath, and a mezzanine that affords superb views over Notre-Dame and the Seine.

Panthéon
5th arr. - 19, pl. du Panthéon
43 54 32 95, fax 43 26 64 65
Open year-round. 34 rms 635-750 F. Conf. No pets. Garage pkg. V, AE, DC, MC.
Clever use of mirrors makes the entrance, lounge, and bar seem bigger. The elegant rooms are quite spacious, decorated in Louis XVI or Louis-Philippe style, with pastel wallcoverings. Room 33 has a grand four-poster bed; all rooms are equipped with minibars and cable TV.

Pavillon de la Reine
3rd arr. - 28, pl. des Vosges
42 77 96 40, fax 42 77 63 06
Open year-round. 20 stes 1,950-3,100 F. 35 rms 1,300-1,700 F. Rms for disabled. Air cond. Valet pkg. V, AE, DC, MC.
Part of the hotel dates from the seventeenth century, while the rest is a clever "reconstitution." The rooms and suites, all equipped with marble bathrooms, are tastefully decorated. The furnishings are an artful blend of authentic antiques and lovely reproductions. Accommodations overlook either the Place des Vosges and its garden or a quiet inner patio filled with flowers.

Regent's Garden Hotel
17th arr. - 6, rue Pierre-Demours
45 74 07 30, fax 40 55 01 42
Open year-round. 39 rms 640-930 F. Garage pkg. V, AE, DC, MC.
This handsome Second Empire building, just a stone's throw from the Place de l'Étoile, offers large, nicely proportioned rooms with high, ornate ceilings; some have fire-places. Comfortable and well kept, the hotel also boasts a gorgeous flower garden.

Relais Christine
6th arr. - 3, rue Christine
43 26 71 80, fax 43 26 89 38
Open year-round. 13 stes 2,150-2,700 F. 38 rms 1,520-1,700 F. Air cond. Conf. Pkg. V, AE, DC.
This Renaissance cloister was transformed into a luxury hotel in the early 1980s. While it has retained some of the peace of its earlier vocation, the hotel now possesses all the comfort and elegance of the present age, from double glazing to perfect service. The rooms are all decorated in individual styles, with Provençal prints and pink Portuguese marble baths. The best rooms are the two-level suites and the ground-floor room with private terrace, but all are spacious, comfortable, quiet, and air conditioned. Courteous reception.

Relais Saint-Germain
6th arr. - 9, carrefour de l'Odéon
43 29 12 05, fax 46 33 45 30
Open year-round. 1 ste 1,880 F. 20 rms 1,250-1,580 F. Air cond. V, AE, DC.
A handful of rooms were just added to this tiny hotel; all the accommodations are personalized and decorated in luxurious style, with superb furniture, lovely fabrics, exquisite lighting, and beautiful, perfectly equipped marble bathrooms. The tall, double-glazed windows open onto the lively Carrefour de l'Odéon. You are bound to fall in love with Paris staying at this tiny jewel of an establishment. Exemplary service.

Saint-Grégoire
6th arr. - 43, rue de l'Abbé-Grégoire
45 48 23 23, fax 45 48 33 95
Open year-round. 1 ste 1,290 F. 19 rms 760-890 F. Air cond. Pkg. V, AE, DC, MC.
The cozy lounge is warmed in winter by a fireplace and there's a small garden for fine days. The rooms are painted in subtle shades of yellow and pink, with matching chintz curtains, white damask bedspreads, and some fine antique furniture. Double glazing and modern bathrooms. Perfect breakfasts.

Saint-Louis
4th arr. - 75, rue St-Louis-en-l'Ile
46 34 04 80, fax 46 34 02 13
Open year-round. 21 rms 670-770 F. V, MC.
Elegant simplicity characterizes this appealing hotel, where attention to detail is evident in the gorgeous flower arrangements and polished antiques. Small, perfectly soundproofed rooms offer comfortable beds and thick carpeting un-

derfoot. The modern bathrooms are pretty indeed.

Saint-Louis-Marais

4th arr. - 1, rue Charles-V
48 87 87 04, fax 48 87 33 26
Open year-round. 15 rms 510-710 F. V, MC.
Reasonable prices and a delightful reception at this former convent annex in the heart of historic Paris. Each room is different, but all are charming and comfortable. Numbers 18 and 20 have *trompe-l'œil* décor.

Saint-Merry

4th arr. - 78, rue de la Verrerie
42 78 14 15, fax 40 29 06 82
Open year-round. 11 rms 400-1,000 F. Pkg. No cards.
A former presbytery, this seventeenth-century building is home to an original collection of Gothic furniture, which the owner has been buying at auctions for over 30 years. The telephone booth near the reception desk is a former confessional! Rooms are mostly small, with bathrooms not much bigger than closets, but the charm of the place is such that you have to book well in advance for the summer.

Sainte-Beuve

6th arr. - 9, rue Sainte-Beuve
45 48 20 07, fax 45 48 67 52
Open year-round. 5 stes 1,600-1,650 F. 23 rms 700-1,300 F. No pets. V, AE, MC.
The Sainte-Beuve is a tasteful, harmonious example of the neo-Palladian style of decoration, promoted in particular by David Hicks. In the guest rooms soft colors, chintzes, and the odd antique create a soothing atmosphere. Most attractive too are the marble-and-tile bathrooms, and the elegant lobby with its comfortable sofas arranged around the fireplace.

Hôtel des Saints-Pères

6th arr. - 65, rue des Saints-Pères
45 44 50 00, fax 45 44 90 83
Open year-round. 4 stes 1,500 F. 35 rms 450-1,500 F. Air cond. No pets. V, AE.
Situated in two buildings, with all the quiet, elegantly furnished rooms overlooking a garden. Suite 205 is particularly attractive, and two new rooms with charming beams were just added. Downstairs is a pretty breakfast room, and a bar that opens onto the garden. Professional service.

San Régis
8th arr. - 12, rue Jean-Goujon
44 95 16 16, fax 45 61 05 48
Open year-round. 10 stes 3,050-5,300 F. 34 rms 1,600-2,750 F. Restaurant. Air cond. No pets. Valet pkg. V, AE, DC, MC.
This jewel of a hotel, much appreciated by celebrities from the worlds of show business and *haute couture*, provides a successful mix of traditional comfort and the latest technology. Beautifully kept rooms boast splendid period furniture and paintings, sumptuous bathrooms, and lots of space, light, and character. The staff is irreproachable.

Plan to travel? *Look for Gault Millau's other Best of guides to Chicago, Florida, Hawaii, Hong Kong, Germany, Italy, London, Los Angeles, New England, New Orleans, New York, Paris, San Francisco, Thailand, Toronto, and Washington, D.C.*

Select Hotel

5th arr. - 1, pl. de la Sorbonne
46 34 14 80, fax 46 34 51 79
Open year-round. 1 ste 980-1,300 F. 67 rms 530-890 F. Air cond. V, AE, DC.
A glass-roofed atrium with an abundance of plants has been built at the heart of this attractive hotel next door to the Sorbonne. The pleasant, spacious rooms are functionally furnished. Generous buffet breakfast; bar.

Suède
7th arr. - 31, rue Vaneau
47 05 18 65, fax 47 05 69 27
Open year-round. 1 ste 1,040-1,295 F. 40 rms 510-780 F. Restaurant. No pets. V, AE, DC, MC.
Decorated in tones of gray in a refined but rather austere Empire style, the guest rooms are quiet and nicely equipped. Streetside rooms are a trifle gloomy. Though smaller, those overlooking the indoor garden are much more cheerful, and from the sixth floor, they offer a view of the the Matignon gardens—and, on occasion, the prime minister's garden parties!

Tamise
1st arr. - 4, rue d'Alger
42 60 51 54, fax 42 86 89 97
Open year-round. 18 rms 480-700 F. V, MC.
Designed by the architect Visconti and situated just twenty yards from the Tuileries, this tiny establishment offers authentic luxury at astonishingly low rates (note the pretty English furniture—in keeping with the hotel's name which is French for "Thames").

Trois Collèges

5th arr. - 16, rue Cujas
43 54 67 30, fax 46 34 02 99
Open year-round. 44 rms 360-750 F. Pkg. V, AE, MC.
Benedictine monks once inhabited this hotel; Rimbaud wrote about it, and García Márquez signed the guest list. Situated in the center of the Latin Quarter, the hotel offers elegant rooms decorated with blond-wood furniture and attractive posters. Note the ancient well (over 70 feet deep) in the atrium lobby. Tea room.

Université
7th arr. - 22, rue de l'Université
42 61 09 39, fax 42 60 40 84
Open year-round. 27 rms 550-1,300 F. Air cond. No pets. V, AE, MC.
Comfortable beds and modern bathrooms are featured in an intelligently renovated seventeenth-century residence that is most appealing with its beams, half-timbering, and period furniture. The rooms are provided with comfortable beds and pretty wallcoverings. Rooms on the first floor have unusually high ceilings, while the fifth-floor suites boast flower-decked terraces.

Varenne
7th arr. - 44, rue de Bourgogne
45 51 45 55, fax 45 51 86 63
Open year-round. 24 rms 470-650 F. V, AE, MC.
A cheerful reception is assured at this small hotel whose provincial air is underlined by a courtyard filled with flowers and trees (where breakfast and drinks are served on sunny days). The rooms overlooking the street have double windows.

Villa des Artistes
6th arr. - 9, rue de la Grande-Chaumière
43 26 60 86, fax 43 54 73 70
Open year-round. 59 rms 650-850 F. Air cond. No pets. V, AE, DC, MC.
An oasis of calm amid the noise and bustle of Montparnasse. Luxury, quiet, and comfort are assured in this hotel, built around a garden patio. Excellent value for this district.

La Villa Maillot
16th arr. - 143, av. de Malakoff
45 01 25 22, fax 45 00 60 61
Open year-round. 3 stes 2,300-2,500 F. 39 rms 1,300-1,500 F. Rms for disabled. Half-board 1,547-1,857 F. Air cond. Conf. Valet pkg. V, AE, DC.
Formerly an embassy, this recent conversion is sophisticated and modern: an exemplary establishment. The very comfortable rooms (some equipped with a kitchenette camouflaged in a closet), have a gray-and-beige color scheme that gives them an Art Deco feel. Pink-marble bathrooms; wonderful breakfast buffet served in an indoor garden.

La Villa Saint-Germain
6th arr. - 29, rue Jacob
43 26 60 00, fax 46 34 63 63
Open year-round. 3 stes 1,950 F. 28 rms 800-1,600 F. Air cond. V, AE, DC, MC.
A laser beam projects room numbers onto the doors; the bathroom sinks are crafted of chrome and sanded glass; orange, violet, green, and red leather furniture stands out vividly against the subdued gray walls: Marie-Christine Dorner has created a high-tech environment for this new hotel, which attracts a trendy, moneyed clientele. Jazz club on the lower level (La Villa), with name performers.

Alison
8th arr. - 21, rue de Surène
42 65 54 00, fax 42 65 08 17
Open year-round. 35 rms 440-730 F. V, AE, DC, MC.
The 35 modern, functional rooms are bright and cheerful, with tidy, tiled bathrooms. Bar and lounge on the ground floor. Two mansard rooms on the top floor can be combined to form a suite. Bar.

Ambassade
16th arr. - 79, rue Lauriston
45 53 41 15, fax 45 53 30 80
Open year-round. 38 rms 400-545 F. V, AE, DC, MC.
The rooms behind a lovely façade are decorated with printed wallpaper and lacquered cane furniture. Small gray-marble bathrooms. Ask for a room overlooking the courtyard and you'll think you're in the country.

Aurore Montmartre
9th arr. - 76, rue de Clichy
48 74 85 56, fax 42 81 09 54
Open year-round. 24 rms 350-420 F. Rms for disabled. Conf. V, AE, DC, MC.
A simple hotel offering smallish rooms (those on the sixth floor are larger), all soundproofed and perfectly kept. Minibar. Friendly reception.

Beaugrenelle Saint-Charles
15th arr. - 82, rue St-Charles
45 78 61 63, fax 45 79 04 38
Open year-round. 51 rms 380-450 F. Conf. V, AE, DC, MC.
Near the Beaugrenelle shopping complex, this friendly hotel provides modern, well-equipped rooms decorated in restful colors. Breakfast is served in the rooms upon request. Good value.

Bergère
9th arr. - 34, rue Bergère
47 70 34 34, fax 47 70 36 36
Open year-round. 135 rms 550-990 F. No pets. V, AE, DC.
All the quiet rooms (most of which overlook a courtyard garden) have been freshened up and modernized, including the bathrooms. The setting is modern and simple, with mostly country-style furniture. Fine equipment; inviting public rooms.

Du Bois
16th arr. - 11, rue du Dôme
45 00 31 96, fax 45 00 90 05
Open year-round. 41 rms 410-590 F. Garage pkg. V, AE, MC.
This simple hotel offers excellent value. In addition to a warm welcome, guests find small, well-kept rooms which were attractively redecorated not long ago with Laura Ashley fabrics and wallpaper.

Hôtel des Chevaliers
3rd arr. - 30, rue de Turenne
42 72 73 47, fax 42 72 54 10
Open year-round. 24 rms 560-610 F. V, AE, MC.
In the heart of the Marais, a small hotel frequented by actors and movie folk. The small rooms are bright and pleasantly furnished; some have just been redecorated. Warm reception.

Claret
12th arr. - 44, bd de Bercy
46 28 41 31, fax 49 28 09 29
Open year-round. 52 rms 350-550 F. Restaurant. Half-board 320-650 F. Conf. Garage pkg. V, AE, DC.
This neat, modernized hotel (formerly a gendarmerie) offers a family atmosphere and a wine bar in the basement. Each meticulously maintained room is named for a wine region of France. Brand-new bathrooms.

Hôtel du Collège de France
5th arr. - 7, rue Thénard
43 26 78 36, fax 46 34 58 29
Open year-round. 2 stes 1,030-1,130 F. 25 rms 480-580 F. No pets. Garage pkg. V, AE, MC.
The simple rooms of the Hôtel du Collège de France, located on a quiet little street, are tidy and comfortable. Most charming are the attic rooms, with their wooden beams and a view of the towers of Notre-Dame.

Étoile
17th arr. - 3, rue de l'Étoile
43 80 36 94, fax 44 40 49 19
Open year-round. 25 rms 500-700 F. Conf. V, AE, DC, MC.
L'Étoile is strategically located between the Place de l'Étoile and the Place des Ternes. Rooms are clean, modern, and functional (renovated in 1991). A little pricey, though, for

the level of comfort and service. Buffet breakfast. Courteous reception.

Favart

2nd arr. - 5, rue de Marivaux
42 97 59 83, fax 40 15 95 58
Open year-round. 37 rms 500-620 F. Conf. Pkg. V, AE, DC, MC.
Goya stayed here when he fled to Paris in 1824. Set on a quiet square opposite the Opéra Comique, this hotel exudes a certain faded charm. Reasonable rates.

Flora
10th arr. - 1-3, cour de la Ferme-St-Lazare
48 24 84 84, fax 48 00 91 03
Open year-round. 45 rms 385-550 F. V, AE, DC, MC.
Near the Gare du Nord and the Gare de l'Est, the Flora offers pleasant, well-equipped, modern rooms decorated in pastel shades.

Folkestone

8th arr. - 9, rue Castellane
42 65 73 09, fax 42 65 64 09
Open year-round. 2 stes 1,020 F. 48 rms 700-800 F. No pets. V, AE, DC, MC.
The beamed rooms, decorated with fabric wallcoverings or Japanese grass paper, have Art Deco armchairs and comfortable beds. Generous buffet breakfasts, with sweet rolls and pastries baked on the premises. Gracious reception.

Fondary
15th arr. - 30, rue Fondary
45 75 14 75, fax 45 75 84 42
Open year-round. 20 rms 375-405 F. Pkg. V, AE, MC.
A neat and tidy hotel with polished wood floors. The rooms are decorated in cheerful colors, with bamboo furniture; some have terraces. Service is warm and efficient.

Grands Hommes
5th arr. - 17, pl. du Panthéon
46 34 19 60, fax 43 26 67 32
Open year-round. 1 ste 750-850 F. 31 rms 615-750 F. Conf. V, AE, DC.
Opposite the Panthéon. The fairly spacious rooms are decorated with pink, cream, or floral fabric wallcoverings. Room 22 has a canopied brass bed, 60 and 61 boast balconies and pleasant views. Cable TV, minibar. The staff is friendly and efficient.

Ibis Paris-Jemmapes
10th arr. - 12, rue Louis-Blanc
42 01 21 21, fax 42 08 21 40
Open year-round. 50 rms 440 F. Conf. Garage pkg. V, AE, DC, MC.
Near the Canal Saint-Martin, this well-designed business hotel is perfectly tailored for a busy clientele attending conventions and seminars. The rooms are spacious, modern, and fully equipped. Generous breakfast buffet. The management is friendlier and more attentive than in most chain hotels.

Ibis Paris-Bercy
12th arr. - 77, rue de Bercy
43 42 91 91, fax 43 42 34 79
Open year-round. 368 rms 450 F. Restaurant. Conf. Pkg. V, AE, DC, MC.
This very professional establishment, surely one of the best in the chain, has a superb marble lobby. Guest rooms have blue-and-white décor

and dark carpeting. One room on each floor is reserved for the disabled. Plain, well-kept bathrooms. Elegant bar; pleasant restaurant.

Idéal Hôtel
15th arr. - 96, av. Émile-Zola
45 79 09 79, fax 45 79 73 59
Open year-round. 35 rms 350-430 F. Garage pkg. V, AE, DC, MC.
Here's an establishment that lives up to its name. Fully renovated, it stands at equal distance from the Eiffel Tower and the Porte de Versailles exhibition center. Spruce décor; exceptional comfort. Rates are remarkably reasonable.

Istria
14th arr. - 29, rue Campagne-Première
43 20 91 82, fax 43 22 48 45
Open year-round. 26 rms 460-580 F. V, AE, DC, MC.
Elm furniture and pastel colors grace the rooms and bathrooms of this well-kept hotel, where Mayakovski, Man Ray, and Marcel Duchamp once slept. The building is fully modernized.

Le Jardin des Plantes
5th arr. - 5, rue Linné
47 07 06 20, fax 47 07 62 74
Open year-round. 33 rms 420-640 F. Restaurant. Conf. V, DC, MC.
This hotel, set in a quiet street behind the Botanical Gardens, has appealing, delightfully decorated rooms—flowers and floral motifs abound. On the fifth floor, there is a terrace with a lovely view; in the basement, a sauna and an ironing room. Restaurant–tea room on the ground floor.

Les Jardins d'Eiffel
7th arr. - 8, rue Amélie
47 05 46 21, fax 45 55 28 08
Open year-round. 80 rms 560-860 F. Rms for disabled. Air cond. Conf. Garage pkg. V, AE, DC, MC.
Some rooms are awaiting renovation, but 44 have already been redecorated in attractive colors and re-equipped with double glazing, minibars, hairdryers, and trouser presses. The upper floors overlook the Eiffel Tower. Sauna, many services and amenities, charming reception.

Hôtel Le Laumière

19th arr. - 4, rue Petit
42 06 10 77, fax 42 06 72 50
Open year-round. 54 rms 255-370 F. Pkg. V, MC.
This meticulously kept small hotel is located a few steps away from the Buttes-Chaumont park, in a district where modern hotels are not exactly plentiful. Convenient for the La Villette exhibition center. Rooms are small (those on the courtyard are larger), well soundproofed, and moderately priced.

Longchamp
16th arr. - 68, rue de Longchamp
47 27 13 48, fax 47 55 68 26
Open year-round. 1 ste 900 F. 22 rms 600-750 F. V, AE, DC, MC.
The quiet, comfortable rooms are not large, but they are equipped with minibar, direct-line telephone, and television with two channels in English. Intimate atmosphere, charming reception.

 A red hotel ranking denotes a place with charm.

La Louisiane
6th arr. - 60, rue de Seine
43 29 59 30, fax 46 34 23 87
Open year-round. 80 rms 405-710 F. No pets. V, AE,.
An artistic clientele (writers, dancers, models, musicians) frequents this large Art Deco hotel that stands right in the middle of the Buci street market. Regulars know they will find a warm reception, and rooms that are simple and comfortable, either painted or hung with Japanese grass paper.

Luxembourg
6th arr. - 4, rue de Vaugirard
43 25 35 90, fax 43 26 60 84
Open year-round. 33 rms 600-780 F. V, AE, DC, MC.
Near the Luxembourg Gardens, in the heart of the Latin Quarter. The pleasant rooms, refurbished in 1993, have minibar, hairdryer, and individual safe; small bathrooms. Gracious reception by the charming owner.

Magellan
17th arr. - 17, rue Jean-Baptiste-Dumas
45 72 44 51, fax 40 68 90 36
Open year-round. 75 rms 400-590 F. No pets. Garage pkg. V, AE, DC, MC.
Business people will appreciate the quiet and comfort of the functional rooms (renovated in 1993) offered by this creditable hotel, known for the regularity and quality of its service. Attractive garden. Bar; no restaurant.

Marais
3rd arr. - 2 bis, rue de Commines
48 87 78 27, fax 48 87 09 01
Open year-round. 39 rms 360-480 F. Conf. V, AE, MC.
A simple, neat hotel between Bastille and République offers small, bright, modern rooms. The connecting rooms on the first, second, and fifth floors are ideal for families.

Marsollier Opéra
2nd arr. - 13, rue Marsollier
42 96 68 14, fax 42 60 53 84
Open year-round. 29 rms 480-760 F.
A blessedly peaceful hotel in the heart of Paris. Rooms on the upper floors are the most desirable: number 701 has a rather low ceiling, but it affords a splendid view of the city's rooftops. Rates are reasonable.

Mercure Pont de Bercy
13th arr. - 6, bd V.-Auriol
45 82 48 00, fax 45 82 19 16
Closed 3 wks in Aug, hols. 89 rms 570-670 F. Rms for disabled. Restaurant. Half-board 650-750 F. Air cond. Conf. Pkg. V, AE, DC, MC.
A modern hotel near the Bercy sports complex and the Gare d'Austerlitz, the Mercure offers easy access from the *péripherique* (the Paris ring road). Well suited to the needs of business people, the rooms are soundproofed and have a large desk area. Some rooms have a terrace.

Mercure
14th arr. - 20, rue de la Gaîté
43 35 28 28, fax 43 27 98 64
Open year-round. 6 stes 1,160 F. 179 rms 680-940 F. Rms for disabled. Restaurant. Air cond. Pkg. V, AE, DC.
The comfortable rooms (excellent beds) are just big enough, with double glazing, minibar, direct-line telephone, and ten television channels. Functional bathrooms; generous breakfast buffet.

Mercure-Porte de Versailles
15th arr. - 69, bd Victor
44 19 03 03, fax 48 28 22 11
Open year-round. 91 rms 580-980 F. Restaurant. Air cond. Conf. Pkg. V, AE, DC.
The well-designed, air-conditioned (with individual controls), and soundproofed rooms all offer modern amenities, and are regularly refurbished. The excellent bathrooms are equipped with radios, hairdryers, and magnifying mirrors. Perfect for business people (the exhibition center is close at hand).

Modern Hotel Lyon
12th arr. - 3, rue Parrot
43 43 41 52, fax 43 43 81 16
Open year-round. 1 ste 750-855 F. 47 rms 495-570 F. No pets. V, AE, MC.
The location is most convenient (near the Gare de Lyon). Rooms are comfortable, unpretentious, and equipped with minibars. Thoughtful service.

Neuville
17th arr. - 3, pl. Verniquet
43 80 26 30, fax 43 80 38 55
Open year-round. 28 rms 580-700 F. Conf. Pkg. V, AE, DC, MC.
This pleasing hotel on a quiet square offers simple rooms, tastefully decorated with floral fabrics and equipped with fine bathrooms. Pleasant salon/winter garden and basement wine bar, Les Tartines.

Le Noailles
2nd arr. - 9, rue de la Michodière
47 42 92 90, fax 49 24 92 71
Open year-round. 58 rms 600-850 F. Conf. V, AE, MC.
Metal, glass, and wood compose this hotel's riveting contemporary architecture. Fully renovated in 1990, the Noailles features a restful central patio and comfortable, attractive guest rooms.

Nouvel Hôtel
12th arr. - 24, av. du Bel-Air
43 43 01 81, fax 43 44 64 13
Open year-round. 28 rms 360-520 F. V, AE, DC, MC.
The rooms of the Nouvel Hôtel are peaceful and attractive, and all were just freshly renovated and redecorated (the prettiest is number 9, on the same level as the garden). Good bathrooms; hospitable reception.

Novanox
6th arr. - 155, bd du Montparnasse
46 33 63 60, fax 43 26 61 72
Open year-round. 27 rms 550-680 F. V, AE, DC, MC.
The owner of this hotel, opened in 1989, has used an amusing mixture of 1920s, 1930s, and 1950s styles for the décor. On the ground floor, a large, cheerful room serves as lounge, bar, and breakfast room.

Novotel Bercy
12th arr. - 85, rue de Bercy
43 42 30 00, fax 43 45 30 60
Open year-round. 1 ste 1,250-1,400 F. 128 rms 710-760 F. Rms for disabled. Restaurant. Air cond. Conf. Pkg. V, AE, DC, MC.
An ultramodern steel-and-glass structure, next door to the Bercy sports complex. The rooms are furnished and equipped to the chain's standards, with minibars, direct-line telephones, and

room service from 6am to midnight. In addition to meeting rooms and business facilities, there is a large terrace, used for receptions in fine weather.

Orléans Palace Hôtel
14th arr. - 185, bd Brune
45 39 68 50, fax 45 43 65 64
Open year-round. 92 rms 500-570 F. Restaurant. Conf. V, AE, DC, MC.
A quiet and comfortable traditional hotel that offers good value. The well-equipped and sound-proofed rooms are decorated in an austere style. Indoor garden.

Ouest Hôtel
17th arr. - 165, rue de Rome
42 27 50 29, fax 42 27 27 40
Open year-round. 48 rms 326-406 F. Pkg. V, AE, MC.
This cozy establishment has thick carpeting, efficient double glazing, and modest, modern rooms. Five are fairly spacious, the rest are small and in some cases a trifle dark. The bathrooms are old-fashioned though well maintained.

Parc Montsouris
14th arr. - 4, rue du Parc-Montsouris
45 89 09 72, fax 45 80 92 72
Open year-round. 7 stes 480 F. 28 rms 310-420 F. Pkg. V, AE, MC.
This small, quiet hotel, remodeled in 1992, features plainly furnished white rooms with bright, new bathrooms. The lovely Parc Montsouris is just a short walk away.

Passy Eiffel
16th arr. - 10, rue de Passy
45 25 55 66, fax 42 88 89 88
Open year-round. 50 rms 530-640 F. Air cond. V, AE.
Five storeys of spotless, comfortable rooms (though all are not equally attractive). Four are large enough to suit families. A pleasant break-fast room faces a tiny, glass-enclosed garden.

Perreyve
6th arr. - 63, rue Madame
45 48 35 01, fax 42 84 03 30
Open year-round. 30 rms 430-560 F. AE, DC, MC.
Near the lovely, leafy Luxembourg Gardens, the Perreyve's 30 comfortable rooms have small but faultless bathrooms. There is a little salon on the main floor with mahogany furniture and inviting armchairs.

Hôtel de la Place du Louvre
1st arr. - 21, rue Prêtres-Saint-Germain-Auxerrois - 42 33 78 68, fax 42 33 09 95
Open year-round. 20 rms 496-812 F. V, AE, DC, MC.
Partially renovated in 1993, this hotel is decorated with paintings and sculptures throughout. The fairly large rooms are all comfortably furnished, with good bathrooms. Five charming bilevel rooms are situated under the eaves. Breakfast is served in a vaulted cellar that dates from the sixteenth century. Guests may expect a warm welcome.

Hôtel du Pré
9th arr. - 10, rue P.-Sémard
42 81 37 11, fax 40 23 98 28
Open year-round. 41 rms 395-540 F. Pkg. V, AE MC.
Actually two hotels, comfortable and close to the Gare du Nord and the Gare de l'Est. Downstairs, guests have the use of a bar, a bright lounge, and a pleasant breakfast room. The

guest rooms sport painted wood paneling or Japanese wallpaper, paired with cane and bamboo furniture. Good bathrooms.

Queen's Hôtel
16th arr. - 4, rue Bastien-Lepage
42 88 89 85, fax 40 50 67 52
Open year-round. 22 rms 320-520 F. Air cond. No pets. V, AE, DC, MC.
For an "English" atmosphere and rather petite but delightful modern rooms, try this modest little hotel with a lovely white façade and flower-filled balconies. Excellent reception.

Récamier
6th arr. - 3 bis, pl. Saint-Sulpice
43 26 04 89
Open year-round. 1 ste 800-850 F. 29 rms 360-560 F. No pets. Pkg. V, MC.
Publishers, professors, and physicians jealously guard the address of this, their favorite Parisian hotel. Accommodations are quite simple, gratifyingly quiet, and superbly located next to Saint-Sulpice. To further enhance the peace (and intellectual cachet) of the place, TV has been banned from the rooms. Friendly reception.

Regyn's Montmartre
18th arr. - 18, pl. des Abbesses
42 54 45 21, fax 42 23 76 69
Open year-round. 22 rms 380-455 F. V, AE, MC.
Each of the rooms in this quiet, well-maintained hotel has a direct-line telephone, radio, TV, and bathroom; the décor is simple but pleasant. Charming, warm-hearted reception. Good value.

Le Relais du Louvre
1st arr. - 19, rue Prêtres-Saint-Germain-Auxerrois - 40 41 96 42, fax 40 41 96 44
Open year-round. 2 stes 1,200-1,400 F. 18 rms 580-890 F. Restaurant. Pkg. V, AE, DC, MC.
The original façade of this historic building opposite the Tuileries has been preserved, but the interior is fully modernized. The rooms, decorated by Constance de Castelbajac, overflow with charm. Those with numbers ending in 1 are slightly smaller than the rest. Wonderfully hospitable reception.

Le Relais de Lyon
12th arr. - 64, rue Crozatier
43 44 22 50, fax 43 41 55 12
Open year-round. 34 rms 426-542 F. Pkg. V, AE, MC.
This pleasant hotel provides bright, comfortable, well-equipped rooms which are absolutely quiet (double glazing, blinds). Most overlook a little patch of garden, and those on the fifth floor have a terrace. Friendly reception.

Résidence des Gobelins
13th arr. - 9, rue des Gobelins
47 07 26 90, fax 43 31 44 05
Open year-round. 32 rms 355-445 F. V, AE, DC, MC.
A delightful small hotel in a quiet street not far from the Latin Quarter and Montparnasse. The warm welcome of the young owners merits a detour. Rooms are decorated in blue, green, or orange, a different color for each floor. Terrace.

Résidence Saint-Lambert
15th arr. - 5, rue E.-Gibez
48 28 63 14, fax 45 33 45 50
Open year-round. 48 rms 380-550 F. Pkg. V, AE, MC.
This pleasant, quiet hotel near the exhibition center at Porte de Versailles has tidy, smallish but nicely equipped rooms, some overlooking the garden. A laundry and bar are on the premises.

Riboutté-La Fayette
9th arr. - 5, rue Riboutté
47 70 62 36, fax 48 00 91 50
Open year-round. 24 rms 370-450 F. V, AE, MC.
This small and charming hotel faces Rue La Fayette and is located within walking distance of the Opéra, the Bourse (Stock Exchange), and the *grands boulevards*. Its quiet rooms are small and attractive. The four rooms on the top floor are the most sought-after.

Royal Médoc
9th arr. - 14, rue Geoffroy-Marie
47 70 37 33, fax 47 70 34 88
Open year-round. 41 rms 550-680 F. Restaurant. No pets. V, DC, MC.
Ten minutes away from the Opéra and close to the Bourse and main boulevards, this functional, freshly renovated hotel (with tidy rooms, direct-line telephones, and helpful, multilingual staff) is perfect for international business travelers.

Saint-Dominique
7th arr. - 62, rue St-Dominique
47 05 51 44, fax 47 05 81 28
Open year-round. 34 rms 465-610 F. Pkg. V, AE, MC.
This most modest of the three "Centre Ville" hotels is also the most charming, and the location is excellent. The delightful little rooms are cozy and comfortable.

Hôtel de Saint-Germain
6th arr. - 50, rue du Four
45 48 91 64, fax 45 48 46 22
Open year-round. 30 rms 415-695 F. Conf. Garage pkg. V, DC, MC.
This small hotel with its delightful décor and English furniture offers round-the-clock room service, babysitting, and various tours of Paris (by helicopter, minibus, or on foot).

Saint-Romain
1st arr. - 5-7, rue Saint-Roch
42 60 31 70, fax 42 60 10 69
Open year-round. 34 rms 510-830 F. V, AE, DC, MC.
Recently renovated, this small hotel offers business services that many of its classier cousins do not, such as typing, photocopying, fax, and telex. Simple, comfortable rooms decorated in pretty colors, with marble baths. Breakfast is served in a beautiful vaulted cellar.

Sénateur
6th arr. - 10, rue de Vaugirard
43 26 08 83, fax 46 34 04 66
Open year-round. 42 rms 580-1,500 F. Conf. V, AE.
A comfortable, modern hotel with a huge mural and plenty of greenery brightening up the ground floor. The rooms were freshly redecorated in 1993. Fine views from the top floor.

7e Art
4th arr. - 20, rue Saint-Paul
42 77 04 03, fax 42 77 69 10
Open year-round. 23 rms 295-650 F. Restaurant. Conf. V, AE, DC, MC.
Posters and photographs evoking the movies—known in France as the seventh art—paper the walls. Very small but comfortable rooms with tiny, well-equipped bathrooms. No room service, but light meals are served at the restaurant (City Light).

Solférino
7th arr. - 91, rue de Lille
47 05 85 54, fax 45 55 51 16
Closed Dec 15-Jan 5. 1 ste 750 F. 31 rms 300-650 F. Garage pkg. V, MC.
Almost opposite the Musée d'Orsay, here are simple rooms done in fresh colors, with bath or shower. There is a charming little lounge, a sky-lit breakfast room, and pretty ornaments everywhere. The Solférino is both relaxing and pleasantly old-fashioned. Friendly reception.

La Tour d'Auvergne
9th arr. - 10, rue de La Tour d'Auvergne
48 78 61 60, fax 49 95 99 00
Open year-round. 25 rms 450-650 F. Restaurant. Garage pkg. V, AE, DC, MC.
A competently run, no-nonsense hotel. Each room has décor from a different period; all are furnished with four-poster beds and double-glazed windows. A fine little establishment, ideal for business travelers.

Trocadéro
16th arr. - 21, rue Saint-Didier
45 53 01 82, fax 45 53 59 56
Open year-round. 23 rms 520-620 F.
The smallish rooms are done up in soothing pale tones, and the bathrooms are well equipped. The management and staff are unfailingly cheerful. Note the relatively low prices (considering the neighborhood).

Tim'hôtel Montmartre
18th arr. - 11, rue Ravignan
42 55 74 79, fax 42 55 71 01
Open year-round. 60 rms 440-680 F. V, AE, DC, MC.
On an adorable little square near the Bateau-Lavoir (where Picasso painted the *Demoiselles d'Avignon*), this hotel gives guests a taste of Montmartre's "village" life. Book a room on the upper floors for the best views. Entirely renovated in 1994, the rooms all have full bathrooms and cable TV.

Welcome Hotel
6th arr. - 66, rue de Seine
46 34 24 80, fax 40 46 81 59
Open year-round. 30 rms 340-515 F. No pets. No cards.
You can almost forget the busy intersection of the nearby Boulevard Saint-Germain behind the double windows of these small, cozy, tidy rooms. And if you want a taste of the bohemian life, you'll find it on the sixth floor (though you can take the elevator!) where you will discover a quaint beamed attic. Reasonable rates.

PARIS

Suburbs

Le Van Gogh

2, quai Aulagnier
47 91 05 10, fax 47 93 00 93
Closed Sat, Sun, Feb 24-Mar 14, Aug 6-22. Open until 10pm. Priv rm: 60. Terrace dining. Air cond. No pets. Valet pkg. V, AE, DC, MC.
Robert and Pierrette Daubian have dropped anchor in this ultramodern establishment on Robinson Island. The dining room resembles the interior of a luxury liner, with portholes and bay windows offering views of the Seine. The cuisine looks out to sea, with dishes like lobster and prawn feuilleté, and filet de bar royal cooked with the freshest produce. Desserts are superb (try the delicious berry gratin with Champagne), and there are fine Bordeaux to wash it all down. C 270-450 F.

Novotel Paris-Bagnolet

1, av. de la République
49 93 63 00, fax 43 60 83 95
Open year-round. 8 stes 830 F. 611 rms 540 F. Rms for disabled. Restaurant. Air cond. Conf. Heated pool. Garage pkg. V, AE, DC, MC.
Just outside Paris, this is a good address for seminars and conferences. The rooms are modern, functional, and well sound-proofed. Piano bar.

Adagio
20-22, rue des Abondances
48 25 80 80, fax 48 25 33 13
Open year-round. 75 rms 595-755 F. Rms for disabled. Restaurant. Pkg. V, AE, DC.
This modern, glass-and-concrete hotel has bright, spacious rooms fitted with every convenience and pleasantly furnished. The basement houses a vast complex of conference rooms. Summer terrace.

L'Auberge
86, av. J.-B.-Clément
46 05 22 35, fax 46 05 23 16
Closed Sat lunch, Sun, hols, Jul 28-Aug 21. Open until 9:45pm. Priv rm: 30. Terrace dining. Air cond. Pkg. V, AE, DC.
The bright, tidy little dining room of this mellow provincial dwelling draws a public of well-heeled executive types. We share their enthusiasm for Jean-Pierre Roy's varied, deftly crafted menu featuring a country-style goose terrine studded with grapes, pan-roasted red mullet with a colorful fricassée of peppers and olives, and a curious chocolate dessert served with tarragon cream sauce. The cache of Jura wines in the cellar (which is otherwise strong on Bordeaux) is a relic of the days when the restaurant specialized in food from Franche-Comté. C 320-400 F. M 150 F, 190 F (wine incl).

La Bretonnière
120, av. J.-B.-Clément - 46 05 73 56
Closed Sat, Sun. Open until 9:45pm. V, AE, DC, MC.
A former head waiter, René Rossignol switched to cuisine and brought this restaurant back up to standard. In fact, Rossignol cooks as the nightingale sings: naturally and exquisitely. His new single-price menu lists such fine traditional offerings as wild-duck terrine laced with white rum, lightly cooked salmon with lentils and smoky bacon, and delicate œufs à la neige with pralines. Interesting cellar. M 155 F (base price).

Au Comte de Gascogne
89, av. J.-B.-Clément
46 03 47 27, fax 46 04 55 70
Closed Sat lunch, Sun. Open until 10:30pm. Garden dining. Air cond. Valet pkg. V, AE, DC, MC.
Three palm trees, a fountain, and lots of flowers make it feel like spring all year in the delightful courtyard garden. Business lunches here are actually enjoyable, while dinner in the suburbs becomes an exotic outing. Gérard Vérane, the jovial Gascon who created this tropical greenhouse, recently handed over the kitchen to Henri Charvet, who once served the best meals in Aix-en-Provence. The Gascon flavor lingers on in the half-dozen variations on foie gras, including the wonderful smoked duck foie gras with cucumber and bacon, and in the world-class collection of Armagnacs. But what really captures our attention are the sun-kissed Provençal

dishes: John Dory with fennel-stuffed peppers and tiny artichokes, lobster soup with ravioli filled with green-tomato "jam," red mullet braised in a basil jus flanked by delicious stuffed vegetables, and steamed cod drizzled with Maussane olive oil. Sommelier Patrice Marchand, will help you choose from among the 100,000 wines on offer. **C** 500-700 F. **M** 240 F (lunch).

12/20 La Tonnelle de Bacchus
120, av. J.-B.-Clément - 46 04 43 98
Closed Sat, Sun, Christmas-beg Jan, May. Open until 10pm. Priv rm: 15. Terrace dining. V, AE, DC, MC.
Here's an adorable vintage bistro with a shady summer terrace, where customers divide their interest among a fresh salmon tartare, hearty confit de canard, and cinnamon-scented apple crumble, all washed down with delicious wines, some of which are served by the glass. **M** 120 F.

Paris 28 - Versailles 10 - Orsay 11   *Yvelines*

La Belle Époque
10, pl. de la Mairie
39 56 21 66, fax 39 56 87 96
Closed Sun dinner, Mon. Annual closings not available. Open until 10pm. Terrace dining. Pkg. V, AE, DC, MC.
Alain Rayé made the transition from urban chef to culinary country squire with nary a hitch. His village inn overflows with turn-of-the-century charm, and his menu sparkles with full-flavored enticements. He won us over (and earned an extra point) with an excellent croustillant of foie gras garnished with Port-glazed pears, John Dory paired with zingy pickled lemons, and exquisite Gâtinais rabbit with caramelized eggplant and fabulous olive fritters. Leading the list of luscious desserts was a glorious gâteau de pommes à l'orange. Stupendous, high-priced cellar. The professional service is warmed by the smiling presence of Brigitte Rayé. **C** 400-550 F. **M** 210 F, 250 F, 350 F.

Paris 17 - Lagny 20 - Coulommiers 51   *Val-de-Marne*

L'Écu de France
31, rue de Champigny - 45 76 00 03
Closed Sun dinner, Mon, 1st wk of Sep. Open until 9:30pm. Priv rm: 50. Terrace dining. No pets. Pkg. V.
From the pink dining room you have a grand view of the River Marne, which you can admire along with Alain Desmots's fresh, skillful cooking. Order his dainty "purses" filled with poached oysters in Sherry cream, followed by thyme-rubbed lamb with a Niçois garnish, and Tahitian vanilla ice cream. The list of fine wines and vintage brandies will encourage you to indulge. **C** 300-350 F.

Au Vieux Clodoche
18, rue de Champigny
45 76 09 30, fax 45 94 25 53
Closed Tue dinner, Feb 17-24. Open until 10:30pm (summer 11pm). Priv rm: 200. Terrace dining. Garage pkg. V, AE, DC, MC.
This charming eatery on the banks of the Marne has no difficulty attracting diners from the posh villas and estates nearby, despite the

menu's punishing prices. But the patrons must feel that they get their money's worth, and indeed Brigitte Huerta's good cooking has plenty of appeal: lemon-marinated salmon, rack of spring lamb (in season, of course) with a delectable potato and asparagus tourte, and dark-chocolate tart with coffee ice cream are representative. **C** 380-520 F.

Paris 7 - Saint-Germain-en-Laye 17   *Hauts-de-Seine*

La Barrière de Clichy
1, rue de Paris
47 37 05 18, fax 47 37 77 05
Closed Sat lunch, Sun, 2 wks in Aug. Open until 10pm. Priv rm: 15. Air cond. Pkg. V, AE, DC, MC.
Superchefs Guy Savoy and Bernard Loiseau cut their teeth in the Barrière's kitchen, now manned by Gilles Le Gallès, who trained with Loiseau. By now we're familiar with Gilles's menu—mussel soup, snail fricassée, turbot en papillote, roasted lamb with garlic jus, and so on—but they are fine dishes all, beautifully served in a fresh setting that's full of charm. The two least expensive set meals are deservedly popular (they'd be more so, we bet, if wine were included too). **C** 300-400 F. **M** 150 F (weekday dinner), 220 F (weekdays), 370 F.

La Bonne Table
119, bd J.-Jaurès - 47 37 38 79
Closed Sat lunch, Sun, Aug. Open until 9pm. V, MC.
Gisèle Berger is a true *cordon bleu*, respected for her talent and adherence to tradition. We find her prices a bit high for the suburbs, but the top-quality seafood Gisèle demands for her dishes doesn't come cheap. You'll enjoy her coquilles Saint-Jacques en persillade, superb Breton lobster, brandade en aïoli, bouillabaisse, and apple tart. René, the *patron*, serves his wines a trifle too cold, but his welcome is always nice and warm. **C** 340-460 F.

La Romantica
73, bd J.-Jaurès
47 37 29 71, fax 47 37 76 32
Closed Sat lunch, Sun. Open until 10:30pm. Priv rm: 15. Terrace dining. Valet pkg. V, AE.
Claudio Puglia is a virtually self-taught cook, but his lack of culinary diplomas is more than compensated by his vibrant passion for *la bella cucina*. He tirelessly seeks out the most select olive oils and the finest Italian wines and cheeses to enhance his innovative dishes. Puglia's originality dazzles the palate with a saffron-tinged spinach risotto, a carpaccio like none you've ever tasted (especially those pale French copies so inexplicably popular these days), lasagne without a trace of heavy, overcooked tomato sauce, or sweet-and-savory lotte with raisins, pine nuts, and raspberries. And—of course!—there are a thousand and one different hand-fashioned pastas. The most spectacular is surely the silken-textured fettuccine tossed with sage and prosciutto, then presented in a hollowed-out Parmesan cheese flamed with Cognac! In summer, these *delizie* are served on a romantic garden patio, where you will be

warmly welcomed by your hostess, Laetitia Puglia. **C** 260-360 F. **M** 175 F, 280 F, 350 F.

COURBEVOIE 92400
Paris 11 - St-Germain-en-Laye 13   Hauts-de-Seine

Les Feuillantines
23, pl. de Seine, La Défense 1
47 73 88 80, fax 40 90 96 03
Closed Sat, Sun. Priv rm: 10. Terrace dining. Air cond. Garage pkg. V, AE, DC, MC.
A largely business clientele enjoys a view of the Seine and the Ile de la Jatte from the third-floor terrace of Les Feuillantines. The menu is rather long and expensive, but proposes delicate, handily executed dishes like a crab-stuffed lettuce hearts, caramelized langoustines touched with gentle spices, crisp and airy lamb's brain beignets, and luscious lemon-filled crêpes. **C** 280-400 F. **M** 200 F (wine incl), 220 F.

Mercure
18, rue Baudin
49 04 75 00, fax 47 68 83 32
Open year-round. 6 stes 1,200-1,500 F. 515 rms 680-890 F. Rms for disabled. Restaurant. Air cond. Conf. Garage pkg. V, AE, DC, MC.
This ovoid concrete structure at La Défense dominates an 80-boutique shopping center. The hotel offers every expected comfort, and the management is dedicated to providing even more. Bar; shuttle service to the RER station.

La Safranée sur Mer
12, pl. des Reflets, La Défense 2
47 78 75 50, fax 47 76 46 20
Closed Sat, Sun, Dec 24-Jan 2, Aug. Open until 10:30pm. Priv rm: 30. Terrace dining. Air cond. Valet pkg. V, AE, DC.
With its luxurious wood-paneled décor and fine service, this seafood restaurant is a favorite lunch venue for business people with clients to impress. The chef purchases premium ingredients to prepare his saffron-stained sole with crisp haricots verts, or spiced, smoked swordfish with fresh pasta, or lobster roasted with herbs). Live music is often presented in the evening. **C** 360-500 F. **M** 200 F (dinner, wine incl), 190 F (wine incl), 250 F.

CRÉTEIL 94000
Paris 12 - Evry 20 - Melun 35 - Bobigny 17   Val-de-Marne

Le Cristolien
29, av. P.-Brossolette
48 98 12 01, fax 42 07 24 47
Closed Sat lunch, Sun. Open until 10pm. Priv rm: 25. Terrace dining. Air cond. Garage pkg. V, MC.
The terrace is brand-new, and so is the single-price menu just introduced by chef Alain Donnard. What a pity that these laudable efforts haven't produced more convincing results. Our mussel gratin, dry and stingily served, preceded tender roast lamb flanked by bland scalloped potatoes, and an iced apple tart that was merely inoffensive. On balance, we've decided to take away a point. **M** 195 F.

Novotel Créteil-le-Lac
N 186, rue J. Gabin
42 07 91 02, fax 48 99 03 48
Open year-round. 5 stes 6,100 F. 105 rms 450-480 F. Restaurant. Air cond. Heated pool. Pkg. V, AE, MC.
The rooms in this lakeside hotel were recently modernized. Sports complex with windsurfing nearby.

CROISSY-BEAUBOURG 77183
Paris 29 - Melun 34 - Meaux 30   Seine-et-Marne

L'Aigle d'Or
8, rue de Paris
60 05 31 33, fax 64 62 09 39
Closed Sun dinner, Mon. Open until 9:15pm. Priv rm: 40. Garden dining. Pkg. V, AE, DC.
Last year we sang the Aigle's praises, but this time around it's a different tune. Host Jean-Louis Giliams, brother of owner-chef Hervé Giliams, recently passed away, leaving this establishment at sixes and sevens. After an uneven, mostly disappointing meal, we think it's best to suspend our rating until the kitchen and dining room get their act together again. **C** 450-550 F. **M** 250 F, 450 F.

DISNEYLAND PARIS 77 → Marne-la-Vallée

ENGHIEN 95880
Paris 18 - Argenteuil 16 - Chantilly 32   Val-d'Oise

Le Grand Hôtel d'Enghien
85, rue du Gal-de-Gaulle
34 12 80 00, fax 34 12 73 81
Open year-round. 3 stes 1,400-2,880 F. 48 rms 700-1,200 F. Restaurant. Air cond. Conf. Golf. Valet pkg. V, AE, DC, MC.
The building is undistinguished, but it stands in lovely grounds next to the lake. The spacious, comfortable rooms are decorated with period furniture.

GARENNE-COLOMBES (LA) 92250
Paris 12 - Courbevoie 2 - Pontoise 29   Hauts-de-Seine

Auberge du 14-Juillet
9, bd de la République - 42 42 21 79
Open daily until 9:30pm. V, AE, DC, MC.
An inn's patriotic sign and classic cooking are both quintessentially French. Chef Jean-Pierre Baillon goes beyond the call of duty to prepare admirably fresh, fine-tuned dishes like crab ravioli, pale-pink veal chops ideally partnered with bosky morels, and fresh cod with potatoes and onions. His son turns out the tasty desserts. Charming welcome. **C** 300-450 F. **M** 170 F, 280 F.

Aux Gourmets Landais ✿
Hôtel de Paris,
5, av. Joffre - 42 42 22 86
Closed Sun dinner, Mon, Aug 15-Sep 15. Open until 10:45pm. Terrace dining. Pkg. V, AE, DC, MC.
This comfortable establishment boasts a bit of a garden, and enough greenery to help one forget the surrounding bleakness of downtown Colombes. Alain Velazco cooks with the same charming Southwestern accent that lilts in his conversation. Sample his sturdy cassoulet made with five kinds of meat, his salade landaise en-

riched with superb foie gras, or his homey poulet en fricassée. His occasional forays into seafood are equally successful, witness the salmon ravioli or the prawns with leeks and asparagus. For dessert, we cannot be warm enough in our recommendation for Velazco's apple tourtière spiked with Armagnac. Wide-ranging cellar. C 320-450 F. M 160 F (dinner, wine incl), 120 F (lunch), 200 F.

ISSY-LES-MOULINEAUX 92130
Paris (Pte de Versailles) 1 - Boulogne-B. 1   *Hauts-de-Seine*

12/20 Coquibus
16, av. de la République - 46 38 75 80
Closed Sat lunch, Sun. Open until 10:30pm. Priv rm: 28. Terrace dining. Garage pkg. V, AE, MC.
The sign and the winsome dining room evoke Montmartre, oddly enough, but the hearty, homestyle cooking shows a Southwestern slant, witness the 150 F menu's ox jowls in aspic with a zesty sauce gribiche, pan-roasted squid emboldened with coriander, and suave crème brûlée. C 200-350 F. M 150 F.

Manufacture

20, esplanade de la Manufacture
40 93 08 90
Closed Sat lunch, Sun. Open until 10:30pm. Terrace dining. Air cond. V, AE.
Jean-Pierre Vigato, who also runs the three-toque Apicius in Paris, hasn't opened a second restaurant just to make more money; he sees it as an outlet for another aspect of his personality. La Manufacture is a bright, spacious restaurant converted from an old tobacco factory. Vigato's former number two, David Van Laer, cooks up an appetizing single-price menu that proposes (for example) tomato mousse and gazpacho both vigorously perfumed with basil, and calf's head, tongue, and brains in a piquant sauce ravigote followed by a selection of goat cheeses and iced praline swirled with raspberry fondue—the food is lively, colorful, and most reasonably priced. Short but pertinent wine list; cheerful service. M 180 F.

L'Olivier
22, rue Ernest-Renan
40 93 42 00, fax 40 93 02 19
Closed Sat, Sun. Open until 10pm. V, AE, DC.
After long years of working in other men's kitchens, Marcel Goareguer decided to strike out on his own. His restaurant has already been enthusiastically adopted by local business lunchers, owing to Goareguer's generous, scrupulously handled cuisine. Start with a fine scallop and crab terrine, then try the beef fillet in a peppery sauce accented with nasturtium blossoms. For dessert, there's a delicious pear pudding with cider-spiked custard sauce. The welcome and service, incidentally, couldn't be better. C 290-350 F. M 175 F.

LEVALLOIS-PERRET 92300
Paris (Porte de Champerret) 8 - Neuilly 4   *Hauts-de-Seine*

La Cerisaie
56, rue de Villiers - 47 58 40 61
Open daily until 10pm. Priv rm: 18. Pkg. V, AE.
The handsomely decorated two-level dining room looks out over a pretty square, but we have

eyes only for Gilles Bordereau's appetizing salad of sweetbreads spiced with paprika, rich lobster fricassée, and rosy calf's liver with onion confit. The welcome is warm, but the wine list is confusing. C 350-450 F. M 190 F (exc weekday lunch), 230 F.

Gauvain
11, rue L.-Rouquier - 47 58 51 09
Closed Sat, Sun, Aug. Open until 10pm. Priv rm: 25. Air cond. V, AE, MC.
A commendable establishment, driven by the talent of a creative chef whose personal, regularly renewed repertoire delights his loyal following of executives and locals. From the appetizing dishes on offer, choose a generous salade landaise or tiny scallops in an aromatic broth, then proceed to sea bream with a coarse-grain mustard sauce or saddle of lamb perfumed with cardamom, and round things off with a satisfying walnut crème brûlée. C 180-250 F. M 159 F.

Le Petit Poste
39, rue Rivay - 47 37 34 46
Closed Sat lunch, Sun, 1 wk at Christmas, 3 wks in Aug. Open until 10:30pm. Priv rm: 12. Air cond. Garage pkg. V, AE, DC, MC.
Fifteen tables crowded around the bar—this is exactly the type of bistro Brassens used to write about in his songs. Now it is a favorite with the good people of Levallois, who come to enjoy the cooking of Pierre-Jean Leboucher, formerly of Lucas-Carton and La Marée. His scallops poached in Vouvray, rabbit with bacon and potatoes, and crêpes à la paresseuse display plenty of originality and finesse. Alert service; expensive cellar. C 250-300 F.

La Rôtisserie
24, rue A.-France - 47 48 13 82
Closed Sun. Open until 10pm. Air cond. V, AE, MC.
A former hangar has been converted into a bilevel loft-brasserie with Art Deco fittings, to serve as the scene for Daniel Ballester's remarkably generous cooking. A 150 F single-price menu offers the likes of crab ravioli, foie gras flan with a pungent truffle jus, a puffy omelette stuffed with marrow and napped with sauce bordelaise, or succulent roast chicken and whipped potatoes flavored with olive oil. Excellent desserts conclude these satisfying repasts. Unbeatable value. M 150 F.

LOUVECIENNES 78430
Paris 24 - Versailles 7   *Yvelines*

Aux Chandelles
12, pl. de l'Église - 39 69 08 40
Closed Sat lunch, Wed, Aug 8-22. Open until 10pm. Terrace dining. Pkg. V, AE.
The upstairs dining room offers a view of an enclosed garden. The young owner-chef, Stéphane Dohollon, who studied with Gérard Besson, produces dishes that are so delicate you could almost accuse him of pretension. The set meals are excellent value, particularly the 260 F menu which includes wine. Worth trying this year are rabbit aspic dressed with truffle vinaigrette, turbot baked with citrus fruit, and fresh pineapple poached in tarragon syrup. Perfect, courteous service in an ideal setting for romantic dinners. C 300-400 F. M 260 F (wine incl), 160 F.

MAISONS-LAFFITTE 78600
Paris 21 - Pontoise 18 - St-Germain-en-L. 8   *Yvelines*

Le Laffitte
5, av. de St-Germain - 39 62 01 53
Closed Sun dinner, Mon, Aug. Open until 10pm. Air cond. Garage pkg. V, AE.
Offering good seafood, classic cooking, and an oft-renewed list of carefully prepared dishes, André Laurier's restaurant is an address worth noting and just the place for hearty appetites. Fine raw materials go into his rich saucisson de canard et foie gras, scallops in Champagne, and lamb charlotte with pesto sauce. Desserts are a hair less convincing, however, and the wines are quite expensive. Hospitable welcome. **C** 290-420 F. **M** 195 F (wine incl), 320 F.

Le Tastevin
9, av. Eglé - 39 62 11 67
Closed Feb school hols, Aug 16-Sep 4. Open until 10pm. Priv rm: 25. Garage pkg. V, AE, DC.
Michel Blanchet's patrons are nothing if not faithful (no, that's not quite true: they are also—necessarily—rich). They generously forgive him when he serves the sort of meal for which he cut off his toques last year! Well, this year we too are in a forgiving mood, having dined wonderfully well on a mouthwatering gâteau of foie gras with fresh morels, a lovely and delicious marinière of fresh shellfish, a flawlessly prepared fillet of pikeperch with a tart touch of sorrel, and a first-class cheese board. Blanchet wins back his toques and our esteem. There is a down side, though: prices are incredibly steep, to the point of indecency. Le Tastevin's exceptional wine list, with prime offerings from every region, is simply out of reach for all but the wealthiest connoisseurs. **C** 400-600 F. **M** 230 F (weekday lunch), 520 F (tasting menu).

La Vieille Fontaine
8, av. Grétry - 39 62 01 78
Closed Mon. Open until 10:30pm. Garden dining. V.
Manon Letourneur and François Clerc have renounced *grande cuisine*, its works and pomps (and towering *additions*) to embrace a new faith: the 160 F single-price menu. François Clerc and his team put just as much care into the preparation of their new bourgeois repertoire as they did into the costly, sophisticated dishes of yore. You'll feel no regrets for yesterday when you fork into the lusty millefeuille layered with peppers and house-smoked cuttlefish, tender pork shanks basted with beer, spit-roasted meats, and delicious desserts (there's a yummy baked peach swirled with caramel). The romantic setting hasn't changed an iota, nor has the gracious hospitality of Manon Letourneur. **M** 160 F.

MARNE-LA-VALLÉE 77206
Paris 28 - Meaux 28 - Melun 40   *Seine/Marne*

■ In Disneyland Paris 77206   Access via A4

Auberge de Cendrillon
In the Park, Fantasyland - 64 74 22 02
Open until 10pm. Terrace dining. Air cond. No pets. Pkg. V, AE, DC, MC.
Cinderella presides over this fairytale inn, decorated with portraits of handsome princes,

lovely princesses, splendid carriages, and the rest. One can dine quite honorably here on the 110 F set menu, or choose from the short, simple *carte*. Offerings include a decent foie gras, an impeccable loin of lamb, and tasty Angus beef. It is now possible to enjoy a French or Californian wine with your meal. **C** 230-300 F. **M** 45 F (children), 110 F, 145 F, 175 F.

Blue Lagoon
In the Park, Adventureland
64 74 20 47, fax 64 74 38 13
Closed 2 days a wk mid Sep-mid Jun. Open until 10pm. Air cond. No pets. Pkg. V, AE, DC, MC.
Palm trees and a tropical lagoon are the setting for agreeably spicy dishes: swordfish with pink peppercorns, chicken curry, banana cake with pine-apple sauce. Nearby are the boats that ferry passengers into the *Pirates of the Caribbean*, one of the park's most popular attractions. **C** 200-250 F. **M** 260 F, 145 F, 190 F.

California Grill
Disneyland Hotel
60 45 65 76, fax 60 45 65 33
Open daily until 11pm. Priv rm: 176. Air cond. No pets. Heated pool. Pkg. V, AE, DC, MC.
The "gastronomic" restaurant of the Disneyland Hotel offers American-style dishes based on quality ingredients. In his ultramodern kitchens, the chef and his team prepare warm goat-cheese tart, salmon with a maple-syrup glaze and, for dessert, an ethereal honey-walnut millefeuille. Perfect service. A few inexpensive items are on hand for a quick meal: gourmet sandwiches, shrimp pizza, and the like. **C** 300-450 F. **M** 195 F, 295 F (dinner).

Cheyenne Hotel
Desperado road
60 45 62 00, fax 60 45 62 33
Open year-round. 999 rms 400-675 F. Rms for disabled. Restaurant. Golf. No pets. Pkg. V, AE, DC, MC.
Perhaps the most amusing of all the resort's hotels: fourteen separate structures recall the frontier towns of the Far West. It's not luxurious, but the rooms are tidy and spacious. Adults can enjoy tequila and country music in the saloon-restaurant, while kids have a ball on the playground.

Disneyland Hotel
60 45 65 00, fax 60 45 65 33
Open year-round. 21 stes 3,250-12,500 F. 479 rms 1,650-2,500 F. Rms for disabled. Restaurant. Air cond. Heated pool. No pets. Pkg. V, AE, DC, MC.
This enormous candy-pink Victorian pastiche is the *nec plus ultra* of Disneyland Paris hotels. Sumptuous suites, first-class service; but the pseudo setting and formal atmosphere are surely not everyone's cup of tea. The rates are simply staggering. Restaurants: California Grill (see above) and Inventions.

Key West Seafood
Festival Disney
70 45 70 60, fax 70 45 70 55
Open daily until 11pm. Priv rm: 120. Terrace dining. Air cond. No pets. Pkg. V, AE, DC, MC.
Overlooking the (artificial) lake is a huge space decked out to resemble an unpretentious Florida fish house. The menu features clam chowder, garlic bread, "catch of the day," and Key Lime pie. As in most of the other Disneyland res-

taurants, prices are lower now than when the park first opened. The wine cellar is Californian. C 150-200 F. M 110 F.

12/20 Los Angeles Bar
Festival Disney - 60 45 71 14
Open daily until midnight. Terrace dining. Air cond. No pets. Pkg. V, AE, DC, MC.
Also lakeside is this bright, airy, and modern dining room where you can enjoy pastas, pizzas, and steaks grilled to order (a pity that bottled steak sauce is the only condiment proposed). Warm, friendly "American-style" service. C 120-200 F. M 45 F (children).

11/20 Parkside Diner
New York Hotel
60 45 73 00, fax 60 45 73 33
Open daily until 11pm. Air cond. V, AE, DC, MC.
Good, simple American food. The 145 F single-price menu includes options like hamburgers, pasta, poached salmon, grilled steaks, and caloric desserts (cheesecake, banana cream pie...). C 150-200 F. M 95 F, 145 F.

 ### New York Hotel
(See restaurant above)
Open year-round. 36 stes 3,000-9,000 F. 538 rms 1,025 F. Rms for disabled. Restaurants. Air cond. Conf. Heated pool. Tennis. Golf. No pets. Pkg. V, AE, DC, MC.
Manhattan in the 1930s is the theme, complete with skyscrapers, Wall Street, and Rockefeller Center—there's even an ice-skating rink in winter. The Art Deco guest rooms feature mahogany furniture, king-size beds, and impeccably equipped bathrooms. Among the many amenities are a beauty salon, athletic club, conference center, a restaurant (Parkside Diner, see above), and the Manhattan Jazz Club, which books top-name talent.

Santa Fe Hotel
In the Park, near the Pueblos Indian village
60 45 78 00
Open year-round. 1,000 rms 550 F. Rms for disabled. Restaurant. Air cond. No pets. Pkg. V, AE, DC, MC.
Forty-two "pueblos" make up an ersatz Indian village, dotted with giant cacti; the parking lot is built to look like a drive-in movie theater. Game rooms for the children, and there's an amusing Tex-Mex restaurant, La Cantina.

Sequoia Lodge
In the Park, near lake Buena Vista
60 45 51 00, fax 60 45 51 33
Open year-round. 11 stes 1,500-1,700 F. 1,000 rms 525-775 F. Rms for disabled. Restaurant. Air cond. Pool. Golf. No pets. Pkg. V, AE, MC.
Bare stone and rough-hewn wood evoke a Rocky Mountain lodge. The sequoias have yet to reach their majestic maturity, but guests will find plenty of entertainment at the hotel's restaurants, shops, piano bar, or exercise room.

11/20 Silver Spur Steakhouse
In the Park,
Frontierland - 64 74 24 57
Closed 2 days a wk mid Sep-mid Jun. Open until 10pm. Air cond. No pets. Pkg. V, AE, DC, MC.
Hearty appetites meet their match here, with huge portions of barbecued chicken wings and

prime ribs of beef served in a reconstituted Wild West saloon. C 150-250 F. M 45 F (children), 110 F, 175 F.

11/20 Walt's An American Restaurant
In the Park, Main Street
64 74 12 97, fax 64 74 38 13
Closed 2 days a wk mid Sep-mid Jun. Open until 10pm. Priv rm: 30. Terrace dining. Air cond. No pets. Pkg. V, AE, DC, MC.
A stairway decorated with photographs of Walt Disney leads to a series of charming little dining rooms; the menu lists uncomplicated fare (lobster, main-dish salads, grilled meats) that is elegantly served. Cheerful staff. C 200-250 F. M 45 F (children), 145 F.

12/20 Yacht Club
Newport Bay Club
60 45 55 00, fax 60 45 55 33
Dinner only. Open daily until 11pm. Air cond. No pets. V, AE, DC, MC.
Swordfish steak and grilled Maine lobster are featured in this huge, blue dining room; but in high season, you'll need the patience of a saint to obtain a table, for the queues are beyond belief. M 95 F, 145 F (dinner), 150 F.

Newport Bay Club
(See restaurant above)
Open year-round. 15 stes 1,400-2,000 F. 83 rms 625-875 F. Rms for disabled. Restaurant. Air cond. Conf. Heated pool. Golf. No pets. Pkg. V, AE, DC, MC.
Were it not so enormous, the Newport Bay Club would be an almost-convincing facsimile of a summer resort in New England. The rooms are decorated with pretty white wicker furniture. Good value for the money.

MEUDON	92190
Paris 12 - Versailles 10 - Boulogne 3	Hauts-de-Seine

 ### Relais des Gardes
42, av. du Général-Gallieni
45 34 11 79, fax 45 34 44 32
Closed Sat lunch, Sun dinner. Open until 10pm. V, AE, MC.
Patrick Pierre is the new chef on duty at this handsome brick Relais, where a classical repertoire and style still reign supreme. Yet an occasional—and welcome—creative touch lends extra interest to the oxtail terrine with butter-stewed leeks, langoustines in an agreeably tart little sauce, and crêpes gratinées filled with passionfruit. The service is not flawless, but the cellar (though expensive) is a thing of beauty, with especially fine Bordeaux. The 190 F menu is always worth a look. C 300-450 F. M 190 F.

MONTMORENCY	95160
Paris 18 - Pontoise 20 - Enghien 3	Val-d'Oise

12/20 Au Cœur de la Forêt
Av. du Repos-de-Diane - 39 64 99 19
Closed Thu, dinner Sun & Mon, Feb 17-27, Aug 31. Open until 9:30pm. Terrace dining. Air cond. Pkg. V, MC.
Next time you go walking in the Montmorency forest, ferret around until you find this establishment hidden among the trees. You'll enjoy

the family atmosphere and the nicely crafted, seasonal cuisine, for example a pan-roasted red mullet with parsley and a decent Black Forest cake. Prices, however, are getting out of hand—particularly in view of the small portions! Slow-paced service. C 280-400 F. M 130 F, 190 F.

NEUILLY-SUR-SEINE   92200
Paris (Porte de Neuilly) 8 - Versailles 16   *Hauts-de-Seine*

Le Bistrot d'à Côté
4, rue Boutard
47 45 34 55, fax 47 45 15 08
See *Paris 17th arr.*

12/20 Bistrot Saint-James
2, rue du Général-Henrion-Berthier
46 24 21 06
Closed hols. Open until 10pm. Terrace dining. V, MC.
Sparkling-fresh ingredients go into the appealing dishes featured on this bistro's varied menu. Recent choices have included a lively terrine of goat cheese and red peppers, fish quenelles with fresh tagliatelle, and a creditably crisp millefeuille. There are tasty Bordeaux wines on hand to help these good meals along. C 170-270 F.

12/20 Brasserie des Arts
2, rue des Huissiers - 46 24 56 17
Closed Sun. Open until 10:30pm. Pkg. V, AE, MC.
A simple and unpretentious address often filled with celebrities from this chic suburb. They come for the brioche with bone marrow, chicken-liver terrine, thyme-scented roast rack of lamb, shellfish platters, and crème brûlée. The prices are geared to local incomes. C 200-300 F. M 149 F, 175 F (Sat, weekday dinner, wine incl).

Café de la Jatte
60, bd Vital-Bouhot
47 45 04 20, fax 47 45 19 32
Open daily until midnight. Terrace dining. Air cond. Valet pkg. V, AE, DC.
The décor revolves around the giant skeleton of a pterodactyl surrounded by a jungle of plants. Wicker furniture, gay colors, and lots of space and light provide the rest of the atmosphere. Young waiters zoom around serving plentiful, fresh, and surprisingly well-presented dishes to tables of tanned people "in advertising": raw tuna with sesame seeds, curried chicken with baby spinach, spiced salmon with sorrel salad. The cellar could be a little more inventive. C 250-350 F. M 100 F (weekday lunch).

Carpe Diem
10, rue de l'Église - 46 24 95 01
Closed Sat lunch, Sun, Aug 1-28. Open until 9:30pm. Air cond. V, AE, DC.
This little bistro's faithful customers are obviously drawn to the warm, simple décor, the *patronne*'s gentle attentions, and the diligent service. Serge Coquoin's soigné menu features a crab and asparagus gratin, a grilled veal chop garnished with a quiche of calf's liver and kidneys, and a delicate chocolate raviole with praline sabayon sauce. C 300-400 F. M 180 F (dinner).

A La Coupole
3, rue de Chartres - 46 24 82 90
Closed 2 wks in Aug. Open until 10pm. No pets. V, AE, MC.
Dominique Roudin is the smiling hostess who welcomes guests into this cozy Coupole. Her husband, Pascal, works away in the kitchen, cooking up perfectly seasoned lentil salad enriched with meaty duck gizzards, calf's head with steamed potatoes in a first-class sauce vinaigrette, and satisfying apple marmalade showered with toasted almonds. More good news: the attractive wine list is moderately priced. C 150-250 F.

Jacqueline Fénix
42, av. Charles-de-Gaulle
46 24 42 61, fax 46 40 19 91
Closed Sat, Sun, Aug. Open until 10pm. Priv rm: 40. Air cond. Garage pkg. V, AE, MC.
Headquarters for Neuilly's business-lunch crowd (lots of film and ad executives), Jacqueline Fénix offers a soothing setting, attentive service, and the classic cooking of chef Dominique Dubray. He makes the most of premium ingredients, creating elegant, harmonious meals such as the one we enjoyed recently, which featured oven-roasted sea bream, crisp-skinned red mullet with basil, and poached fruit in a spicy ginger syrup. Exciting cellar. M 265 F, 395 F.

Les Feuilles Libres
34, rue Perronet - 46 24 41 41
Closed Sat lunch, Sun, Aug 1-20. Open until 10pm. Priv rm: 6. Terrace dining. Air cond. V, AE, DC.
Laurent Phelut is the new man in the kitchen, with a program sure to pique your interest. It embraces fricasséed artichokes topped with shavings of Parmesan and curls of foie gras, a winy pork civet, and a delicious chaud-froid of tart cherries with almond-milk ice cream. The wine list is worthy of your perusal. Guests are courteously welcomed and briskly served in this comfy, country-style dining room. C 330-450 F. M 195 F (wine incl).

Focly
79, av. Charles-de-Gaulle - 46 24 43 36
Open daily until 11pm. Air cond. Pkg. V, AE, MC.
No dragons or pagodas in the conservative dining room, no outlandish listings on the menu. Focly serves a classic repertoire of sautéed crab with crispy noodles, rice with shellfish, curried lamb, and ginger ice cream, all skillfully prepared. The salt-and-pepper scampi are easily worth two toques; and the prices are most reasonable. C 180-260 F. M 130 F, 140 F (weekday lunch).

La Guinguette de Neuilly
Ile de la Jatte,
12, bd de Levallois - 46 24 25 04
Closed at Christmas, New Year's day. Open until 11pm. Garden dining. Air cond. V.
Trendy artists are drawn to this old barge and its handful of tables for a cuisine that is forthright and full-flavored: terrine aux trois viandes, streaky bacon with lentils, and veal curry with fiery chilis. In fine weather, ask for a table on the terrace by the Seine. C 200-270 F.

The prices in this guide reflect what establishments were charging at press time.

Hôtel International de Paris
58, bd V.-Hugo
47 59 80 00, fax 47 58 75 52
Open year-round. 3 stes 1,300-2,000 F. 327 rms 600-800 F. Restaurant. Half-board 700-915 F. Air cond. Conf. Garage pkg. V, AE, DC, MC.
A large, rather graceless contemporary hotel surrounded by lawns and gardens. Elegant luxuriously renovated rooms with every amenity. Sumptuous breakfast buffet.

Le Jardin de Neuilly
5, rue P.-Déroulède
46 24 51 62, fax 46 37 14 60
Open year-round. 30 rms 580-1,200 F. Air cond. Conf. Pkg. V, AE, DC, MC.
There is indeed a garden behind the good-looking building that houses this hotel. Rooms are fairly spacious, and furnished with attractive antique pieces. The marble bathrooms are perfectly equipped. Charming reception.

12/20 Chez Livio
6, rue de Longchamp - 46 24 81 32
Closed Sat & Sun (in Aug), at Christmas, New Year's day. Open until 10:45pm. Priv rm: 18. Garden dining. Air cond. V, AE.
A real Italian trattoria in the heart of Neuilly, manned by the Innocenti clan. Here you'll find generous and simple cuisine featuring ravioli al magro, gnocchi with basil, risotto with wild mushrooms, osso buco, and *tutti quanti*. The roof of the dining room rolls back so that you can dine under a canopy of blue sky or stars. Reservations (sometimes hard to come by) are a must. **C** 150-250 F. **M** 110 F (weekday lunch).

Hôtel du Parc
4, bd du Parc
46 24 32 62, fax 46 40 77 31
Open year-round. 71 rms 310-510 F. Rms for disabled. Conf. V, MC.
Between the Porte de Champerret and La Défense, on the Ile de la Jatte facing the Seine, stands this small 1930s hotel with well-equipped, regularly renovated rooms.

San Valero
209 ter, av. Charles-de-Gaulle
46 24 07 87, fax 47 47 83 17
Closed Sat lunch, Sun, Dec 24-Jan 1. Open until 10:30pm. No pets. V, AE, DC, MC.
Come for a fiesta and a feast at Valero's Spanish restaurant: the menu offers paella of course, but also more authentic dishes such as quails in escabeche, scallops in a garlicky sauce with dried tuna, and baby lamb marinated in herbs, a specialty of the Rioja region. The Spanish offerings on the wine list are worthy of your attention. **C** 280-320 F. **M** 150 F (weekdays), 190 F.

Sébillon
"Paris-Bar," 20, av. Ch.-de-Gaulle
46 24 71 31, fax 46 24 43 50
Open daily until midnight. Priv rm: 15. Valet pkg. V, AE, DC, MC.
The chefs come and go, the menu stays the same. The specialties of the house are the famous Sébillon roast lamb and the giant éclair. Add to that the magnificent rib of beef and the tarte Tatin "à l'ancienne," as well as some good, fresh seafood, and a thick salmon steak grilled with fennel. A selection of nice Loire wines at affordable prices. **C** 250-350 F.

12/20 La Tonnelle Saintongeaise
32, bd Vital-Bouhot
46 24 43 15, fax 46 24 36 33
Closed Sat, Sun, Aug 1-22, Dec 24-Jan 2. Open until 10pm. Priv rm: 35. Terrace dining. V, MC.
In summer, crowds tend to gather under the trees and parasols of this Ile de la Jatte terrace. The cuisine is pleasant enough, without being challenging. There are poached eggs bordelaise to start, followed by (for example) confit of canard with garlicky potatoes or five kinds of fish in a buttery sauce. The cellar leans heavily toward Bordeaux. **C** 250-350 F. **M** 160 F, 215 F.

ORLY	94396
Paris 16 - Villeneuve-St-Georges 12	Val-de-Marne

Maxim's
Aérogare d'Orly-Ouest
46 87 16 16, fax 46 87 05 39
Closed Sat, Sun, hols, Aug. Open until 10:30pm. Priv rm: 25. Air cond. Pkg. V, AE, DC, MC.
A complete overhaul has resurrected Maxim's Orly, even giving it some of the cachet of the illustrious mother house. Gil Jouanin, a talented *cuisinier* formerly of the Café de la Paix, is in command of the kitchen. The proximity of the runways seems to have inspired him to reach for new culinary heights, for he makes the most of excellent ingredients in subtle dishes like lobster salad dressed with a snappy orange vinaigrette, artichokes lavished with curls of foie gras, or fillet of Charolais beef with roasted shallots and bone-marrow canapés in a powerfully flavored wine sauce. For dessert, we're partial to the delightful marzipan and pecan parfait. The 30,000-bottle cellar holds wines in every price range, from modest to outrageous. Next door, the Grill serves a quality set menu, including wine, for 260 F. **C** 450-550 F. **M** 290 F (coffee incl).

Mercure Paris-Orly-Aéroport
Orly-Ouest 429
46 87 23 37, fax 46 87 71 92
Open year-round. 1 ste 750-800 F. 193 rms 540-640 F. Rms for disabled. Restaurant. Air cond. Conf. Pkg. V, AE, DC, MC.
The hotel was recently renovated, and provides soundproof rooms decorated in lively, bright colors. The bathrooms are excellent. Rooms can be rented for the day only (10am-6pm) at special rates. Minigolf and airport shuttle bus.

Paris Orly Airport Hilton
Aérogare Orly-Sud 267
45 12 45 12, fax 45 12 45 00
Open year-round. 12 stes 1,300-1,500 F. 347 rms 950-1,300 F. Restaurant. Air cond. Conf. Garage pkg. V, AE, DC, MC.
Functional, comfortable rooms near the airport with a free shuttle service. Excellent facilities for conferences or seminars. Round-the-clock room service. Bar and shops.

---

*Some establishments change their **closing times** without warning. It is always wise to check in advance.*

PERREUX (LE) 94170
Paris 15 - Créteil 11 - Vincennes 6   *Val-de-Marne*

Les Magnolias

48, av. de Bry
48 72 47 43, fax 48 72 22 28
Open daily until 10pm. Priv rm: 20. Air cond. V, AE.
A brilliant and inviting room is concealed behind Les Magnolias' rather graceless façade. Chef Gérard Royant presents an interesting, appetizing single-price menu that features cool crab aspic made cooler still by a ginger-spiced cucumber granita, followed by veal sweetbreads and kidney in a Sherried sauce, and gingerbread cake with a bright apricot coulis. Expensive wine list; warm welcome. **C** 320-400 F. **M** 190 F, 290 F (weekdays, Sat dinner), 350 F (weekday lunch, wine incl).

PONTAULT-COMBAULT 77340
Paris 26 - Melun 29 - Coulommiers 41   *Seine/Marne*

Le Canadel

Aire des Berchères, Saphir Hôtel
64 43 45 47, fax 64 40 52 43
Closed Sat, Sun, Aug. Open until 10pm. Priv rm: 10. Air cond. Heated pool. Pkg. V, AE, DC, MC.
Jean-Pierre Piovan's cooking is rich and admirably traditional: lobster in a satiny sabayon perfumed with basil, roast noisettes of lamb topped with rounds of molten goat cheese, and a delectable banana feuilleté flambé alighted on a pool of coconut velouté sauce. The décor is luscious too: chandeliers, murals, stucco columns, comfortable chairs, and well-spaced tables. Smooth service; top-notch cellar. **C** 310-410 F. **M** 235 F (wine incl), 225 F.

Saphir Hôtel

(See restaurant above)
Open year-round. 21 stes 595-870 F. 158 rms 485-530 F. Rms for disabled. Restaurant. Air cond. Conf. Heated pool. Tennis. Pkg. V, AE, DC, MC.
A brand-new hotel next to Disneyland. Rooms are airy, pleasant, and well equipped. Facilities include conference rooms, sauna, and a superb indoor swimming pool. Grill.

PORT-MARLY (LE) 78560
Paris 21 - Versailles 10 - Louveciennes 3   *Yvelines*

Auberge du Relais Breton

27, rue de Paris
39 58 64 33, fax 39 58 35 75
Closed Sun dinner, Mon, Aug. Open until 9:30pm (Fri & Sat 10pm). Priv rm: 35. Garden dining. V, AE.
Here is an attractive place for a winter meal when a fire is roaring in the immense fireplace, but not to be overlooked in summer when you can sit in the lovely garden and enjoy rather staid, but fresh and carefully executed cuisine. We liked the salad of scallops and lamb's lettuce dressed with delicate hazelnut oil, suprême de turbot aux deux coulis, and the braised sweetbreads with morels. Desserts are so-so, but the cellar is judiciously stocked. **C** 240-320 F. **M** 219 F (wine incl), 159 F.

PUTEAUX 92800
Paris 10 - St-Germain-en-Laye 11   *Hauts-de-Seine*

Les Communautés

Sofitel Paris CNIT, Paris-La-Défense,
in the CNIT, 2, pl. de La Défense
46 92 10 10, fax 46 92 10 50
Closed Sat, Sun, hols, Aug 1-15. Open until 10:30pm. Priv rm: 30. Air cond. Valet pkg. V, AE, MC.
Pierre Miécaze is well into his stride here at the Sofitel, continuing his quest for bold new flavor harmonies. The results of his research are dazzling, even astonishing. If it's still available when you visit (Miécaze constantly revamps his menu) do try the chartreuse of wild mushrooms with foie gras. Or enjoy the tender roast duck breast embellished with a tangy fruit compote and a spicy sauce. This vibrant cuisine is well served by the elegant surroundings of the Sofitel dining room, the superb cellar, and the polished staff. **C** 280-380 F. **M** 150 F, 270 F (dinner).

Sofitel Paris CNIT
(See restaurant above)
Open year-round. 6 stes 2,400-3,000 F. 141 rms 1,280-1,600 F. Rms for disabled. Restaurant. Air cond. Conf. Pkg. V, AE, DC, MC.
The hotel is aimed at business travelers. It provides huge rooms (some boast a view of the Grande Arche), luxurious bathrooms, and 24-hour room service.

Dauphin
45, rue J.-Jaurès
47 73 71 63, fax 46 98 08 82
Open year-round. 30 rms 470 F. Tennis. Valet pkg. V, AE, DC.
The Dauphin stands opposite the Princesse Isabelle, and is run by the same family. Generous buffet breakfasts are set up in the sitting room; guest rooms are comfortable and pretty, with cable television. Some rooms are reserved for non-smokers. Free shuttle to the RER station.

Les Deux Arcs
Sofitel Paris-La Défense,
34, cours Michelet, La Défense 10
47 76 44 43, fax 47 73 72 74
Closed Sat, Sun. Open until 10:30pm. Priv rm: 100. Terrace dining. Air cond. Valet pkg. V, AE, DC.
The elder of the two Sofitel hotels at La Défense is home to a quiet, comfortable restaurant, where wheeler-dealers can talk business in peace while enjoying Éric Corailler's deft and delicious cuisine. He makes a superb persillé de homard—lobster in parsley aspic—perfumed with fresh marjoram, as well as savory ricotta-stuffed rabbit with pasta au pistou, and a sweetly spiced pear gratin enriched with honey butter. The cellar is way too expensive, but a few wines are served by the glass. **C** 300-400 F. **M** 340 F (weekday lunch), 275 F, 290 F.

Sofitel Paris-La Défense
(See restaurant above)
Open year-round. 1 ste 2,500 F. 149 rms 1,280 F. Rms for disabled. Restaurant. Air cond. Conf. Valet pkg. V, AE, DC, MC.
A creditable chain hotel, warmly decorated with gilt mirrors and pale marble. Rooms are quiet, with superb pink-marble bathrooms. Service is top-notch and breakfasts are delicious. Good facilities for conferences.

Fouquet's Europe

In the CNIT, 2, pl. de la Défense, Paris-La Défense - 46 92 28 04, fax 46 92 28 16
Closed Sat, Sun. Open until 10:30pm. Priv rm: 300. Terrace dining. Air cond. No pets. Pkg. V, AE, DC.

The stark and austere CNIT tower at La Défense is the last place you would expect to find modern French cooking that pays homage to its regional roots. But that is just the sort of satisfying food that young Alexandre Faix is regaling his patrons with at Fouquet's Europe. An exceptionally bright pupil of the great Robuchon, Faix cooks with imagination, enthusiasm, and—this is his secret—a rare sense of split-second timing. His dishes are invariably perfectly cooked. You'll see we aren't exaggerating when you taste the rascasse fillet fired up with a jolt of hot chili, tender leg of farm chicken paired with spelt, rosemary-roasted red mullet served with a vivid ratatouille, or rich shortbread topped with apples and rhubarb. Opulent cellar; top-drawer service. **C** 400-550 F. **M** 280 F.

Princesse Isabelle

72, rue J.-Jaurès
47 78 80 06, fax 47 75 25 20
Open year-round. 1 ste 950 F. 30 rms 640 F. Air cond. Tennis. Valet pkg. V, AE, DC.

The rooms of this hotel near La Défense are prettily decorated, and have bathtubs with Jacuzzi or multijet showers. Some rooms open onto the flowered patio. Note that there's a convenient free chauffeur service to the RER and Pont de Neuilly Métro station.

Syjac Hôtel

20, quai de Dion-Bouton
42 04 03 04, fax 45 06 78 69
Open year-round. 2 stes 850-1,500 F. 29 rms 570-850 F. No pets. Pkg. V, AE, DC, MC.

This modern hotel offers a pleasant alternative to concrete high-rises. Rooms are very pleasing, large and well appointed. There are some nice two-level suites (with fireplace) overlooking the Seine, and a pretty flowered patio.

Le Victoria

85, bd R.-Wallace
45 06 55 51, fax 40 99 05 97
Open year-round. 32 rms 395-540 F. Tennis. Garage pkg. V, AE, DC, MC.

Not far from the Arche de La Défense, this recently opened hotel offers comfortable, well-equipped rooms.

ROISSY-EN-FRANCE   **95700**
Paris 26 - Meaux 36 - Senlis 28   *Val-d'Oise*

Holiday Inn

1, allée du Verger
34 29 30 00, fax 34 29 90 52
Open year-round. 1 ste 1,800 F. 243 rms 760-1,080 F. Rms for disabled. Restaurant. Air cond. Conf. Heated pool. Garage pkg. V, AE, DC, MC.

Situated in the old village of Roissy. Rooms are large, bright, and functional. There's a health club for hotel guests (sauna, gym, Jacuzzi, etc.). Free shuttle to the terminals and the exhibition grounds at Villepinte.

Maxim's

Aéroport Charles-de-Gaulle
48 62 16 16, fax 48 62 45 96
Lunch only. Open daily. Air cond. Pkg. V, AE, MC.

It had to happen: what with all those planes boarding for immediate departure, Maxim's talented chef decided one day that he too should take off for new horizons! So a new team is at the controls here now, but we'll wait to judge their efforts until they reach their cruising speed. On the menu, however, you'll find a marinière of prawns flavored with Thai herbs, roast pigeon lacquered with a honey-spice glaze, and peaches wrapped up in a crêpe "purse" and swirled with blackberry coulis. The service is obliging and discreet, and the cellar presents a goodly number of growers' wines in half-bottles. **C** 370-630 F. **M** 280 F.

Sofitel

Aéroport Charles-de-Gaulle
48 62 23 23, fax 48 62 78 49
Open year-round. 8 stes 1,500 F. 344 rms 700-950 F. Rms for disabled. Restaurant. Air cond. Conf. Heated pool. Tennis. Valet pkg. V, AE, DC, MC.

A comfortable airport hotel with a discothèque, sauna, and coffee shop. Round-the-clock room service and a free shuttle to the airport. Entertainment facilities include a disco and piano bar, and there's a coffee shop too.

ROMAINVILLE   **93230**
Paris 10 - Livry-Gargan 9   *Seine-St-Denis*

Chez Henri

72, route de Noisy
48 45 26 65, fax 48 91 16 74
Closed Sat lunch, Mon dinner, Sun, hols, Aug. Open until 9:30pm. rm: 18. Air cond. Pkg. V, AE, MC.

Chef Henri Bourgin is back on track, as our most recent meal amply attested. We could barely restrain ourselves from begging for seconds (or thirds) of his zesty shrimp salad embellished with tomato-basil sorbet, his saddle of rabbit stuffed with snails and escorted by a ragoût of woodland mushrooms, and delicate cream-cheese mousse laced with lime. The second toque sits firmly once again on Henri's head! Connoisseur's cellar; convivial atmosphere in a comfortable, flower-filled dining room. **C** 300-400 F. **M** 150 F.

RUNGIS   **94150**
Paris 13 - Corbeil 26 - Longjumeau 10   *Val-de-Marne*

Holiday Inn

4, av. Ch.-Lindbergh
46 87 26 66, fax 45 60 91 25
Open year-round. 168 rms 795-995 F. Rms for disabled. Restaurant. Air cond. Pkg. V, AE, DC, MC.

Comfortable and well-kept rooms near Orly airport (free shuttle). From your window, you'll look down on the Rungis *halles* (the Paris wholesale food market). Shops.

La Rungisserie

Pullman Paris-Orly, 20, av. Charles-Lindbergh - 46 87 36 36, fax 46 87 08 48
Closed lunch Sat & Sun. Open until 11pm (hols 10pm). Air cond. Pkg. V, AE, DC, MC.

A huge and happy hotel restaurant in a soothing, modern setting. A new chef has just moved into the kitchen, so we'll give him time to get his bearings before we judge his cooking. **C** 300-520 F. **M** 150 F (dinner w-e), 185 F (weekdays).

Pullman Paris-Orly
(See restaurant above)
Open year-round. 2 stes 1,400 F. 188 rms 650 F. Restaurant. Air cond. Conf. Heated pool. Pkg. V, AE, DC, MC.
A reliable, comfortable chain hotel with excellent soundproofing, air conditioning, television, and direct telephone lines. Among the amenities on offer are a non-stop shuttle to and from the airports, a panoramic bar, a restaurant, sauna, shops, and a swimming pool. Deluxe rooms are available ("Privilège") and there are several lounges.

11/20 Quai Ouest
1200, quai Marcel-Dassault
46 02 35 54, fax 46 02 33 02
Open daily until midnight. Terrace dining. Air cond. Valet pkg. V, AE, DC, MC.
Lots of young, perma-tanned faces at this trendy spot, a New York–style eatery with a terrace overlooking the Seine. A squadron of smiling waiters delivers fresh, prettily presented salmon tartare, honey-glazed swordfish, and chicken fricassée. **C** 200-300 F.

Hôtel Quorum
2, bd de la République
47 71 22 33, fax 46 02 75 64
Open year-round. 58 rms 460-570 F. Rms for disabled. Restaurant. Tennis. V, AE, DC.
A bright new hotel with modern, quietly elegant public rooms, and spacious guest rooms with gray-marble baths. The best are on the upper floors with a view over the Parc de Saint-Cloud.

Villa Henri-IV
43, bd de la République
46 02 59 30, fax 49 11 11 02
Open year-round. 36 rms 460-550 F. Restaurant. Conf. Garage pkg. V, AE, DC, MC.
A pleasant address off the boulevard. Rooms are decorated in Louis XVI, Louis-Philippe, or Norman style and are huge, bright, and well equipped.

Melody
15, rue G.-Péri - 48 20 87 73
Closed Sat lunch, Sun, 1 wk at Easter, Aug. Open until 10pm. V, MC.
What a contrast between Melody's restrained beige setting and the unbridled fantasy that comes out of the kitchen! After a longish rough patch, the chef is back in top condition, dreaming up such exciting dishes as a ragoût of langoustines and chicken giblets, or a bold upside-down tart of pears and pigeon gizzards (it's delicious) sprinkled with a touch of caramel vinegar. Traditionalists can always fall back on the savory rack of Causses lamb. The set meals offer top value. **C** 190-250 F. **M** 102 F, 112 F.

12/20 La Table Gourmande
32, rue de la Boulangerie - 48 20 25 89
Closed Sun, Mon dinner, Tue, Wed. Open until 9:30pm. Pkg. V, MC.
Good restaurants are not exactly thick on the ground out here, so we're happy to tell you about this place. The cooking is fresh and skillful, the surroundings are cheerful. Order the sea bream with sorrel or the baked sea bass with asparagus. **C** 200-300 F. **M** 98 F.

Cazaudehore
Hôtel La Forestière
1, av. du Président-Kennedy
34 51 93 80, fax 39 73 73 88
Closed Mon (exc hols). Open until 10pm. Priv rm: 140. Garden dining. Pkg. V, AE, DC, MC.
On the edge of the forest in a wonderful setting of greenery and flowers sits this charming establishment decorated with old prints and English chintzes; for summer dining, there's a huge terrace that looks out over the trees. It is at this point that the superb and unshakeable "Cazau" sometimes goes off track, its luxurious cuisine suffering under the pressure of numbers. Still, when the chef decides to keep things simple, he turns out a reliable salade de tripes en cressonnette, farm chicken with pot-au-feu vegetables, and a lush licorice macaroon. Superb cellar, stylish service. **C** 310-580 F. **M** 360 F (week-end, wine incl), 250 F (weekday lunch).

La Forestière
(See restaurant above)
Open year-round. 5 stes 1,050-1,300 F. 25 rms 680-980 F. Restaurant. Half-board 725 F. Tennis. Pkg. V, AE, MC.
Thirty rooms and suites were recently renovated and pleasantly furnished in an old-fashioned style with fresh, spring-like fabrics. The hotel sits on extensive, flower-filled grounds at the edge of the forest.Relais et Châteaux.

Le Pavillon Henri-IV
21, rue Thiers
39 10 15 15, fax 39 73 93 73
Open daily until 10:30pm. Terrace dining. Air cond. Pkg. V, AE, DC, MC.
Neither the staff nor the patrons appear to be having much fun, but the cuisine fully merits a gourmet's attention. It encompasses dishes so classic as to have nearly disappeared from most modern menus, all deftly prepared. As a result, a meal here resembles nothing so much as a trip to some gastronomic museum; the attractive wine list is a plus. **C** 250-450 F. **M** 240 F (weekday lunch), 640 F.

Le Pavillon Henri-IV
(See restaurant above)
Open year-round. 3 stes 1,900 F. 42 rms 400-1,300 F. Rms for disabled. Restaurant. Half-board 670-870 F. Conf. Pkg. V, AE, DC, MC.
This is where Louis XIV was born, Alexandre Dumas wrote *The Three Musketeers*, and Offenbach composed a number of operettas. Total comfort inhabits the 45 huge rooms and suites. The public rooms are magnificent and there's a splendid view over the extensive grounds.

SAINT-OUEN   93400
Paris 7 - Saint-Denis 4 - Chantilly 34   Seine-St-Denis

Le Coq
de la Maison Blanche
37, bd J.-Jaurès
40 11 01 23, fax 40 11 67 68
Closed Sun. Open until 10pm. Priv rm: 120. Terrace dining. Valet pkg. V, AE.
A covered terrace has been added to extend the 1950s–style dining room, and an oyster bar now provides premium shellfish in season. If the François family would go a step farther and add a bit more zest to the cooking, all would be well. For while we have no complaints about the good asparagus hollandaise or the codfish and vegetables with sauce aïoli, we found the sweetbreads unexciting on a recent visit, and the spit-roasted kid too dry (it badly wanted basting). Still, Alain François is a jovial host who cultivates a convivial atmosphere in this appealing, almost provincial restaurant. C 280-370 F.

SÈVRES   92310
Paris 12 - Boulogne 3 - Versailles 8   Hauts-de-Seine

11/20 Phileas Fogg
5, pl. P.-Brossolette - 46 26 48 80
Closed Sun dinner, Mon. Open until 10:30pm. Terrace dining. V, AE, DC, MC.
Travel no farther than Sèvres railway station to go around the world in 80 dishes. The cooking is nicely handled by the wife of a former scriptwriter for the vintage series *The Avengers*, rerun ad nauseam on late-night French television. Try the tasty bagna cauda, beef braised in Guinness, or murghi sheer (Indian chicken with an almond cream sauce). Simple setting and a smiling welcome. Superb whiskies. C 160-250 F. M 79 F (lunch exc Sun).

SURESNES   92150
Paris (Pte Maillot) 11 - Boulogne 6   Hauts-de-Seine

Les Jardins de Camille
70, av. Franklin-Roosevelt
45 06 22 66, fax 47 72 42 25
Closed Sun dinner. Open until 11pm. Priv rm: 70. Terrace dining. Valet pkg. V, AE.
From the terrace guests can admire a panoramic view of Paris, but the dining room is inviting too, with its bright and cheerful décor. We're handing the chef a toque for the savory, straightforward dishes listed on his terrific 150 F menu. They include excellent jambon persillé (the aspic is made with sprightly Aligoté wine), satisfying bœuf bourguignon, and a scrumptious gingerbread sorbet spiked with rum and raisins. The cellar is splendid and accessibly priced. Attentive service. M 150 F.

Le Pont de Suresnes
58, rue Pasteur
45 06 66 56, fax 45 06 65 09
Closed Sat lunch, Sun, Dec 25. Open until 11:15pm. Terrace dining. Air cond. Valet pkg. V, AE.
The ubiquitous Guy Savoy designed the menu, and Paris-Dakar daredevil Hubert Auriol serves as celebrity host at this hip, glossy restaurant. The loft-like space is further extended by a terrace planted with rosebushes, and a merry ambience

prevails as bright young things tuck happily into such tasty, uncomplicated dishes as duck and artichoke terrine served with onion confit, gurnard in a flavorful shellfish jus, and banane en papillote. C 230-330 F. M 170 F.

VANVES   92170
Paris 8 - Nanterre 12   Hauts-de-Seine

Le Pavillon de la Tourelle
10, rue Larmeroux
46 42 15 59, fax 46 42 06 27
Closed Sun dinner, Mon. Annual closings not available. Open until 10pm. Priv rm: 100. Terrace dining. Pkg. V, AE, DC, MC.
Akio Ikeno, a chef trained by Paul Bocuse, presents a repertoire of delicate dishes like sweetbreads swaddled in a cabbage leaf, steamed sea bass with sauce vierge, and a dainty molded chartreuse à l'orange. The elegant dining room is a perfect setting for this polished cuisine. C 350-550 F. M 195 F (exc hols).

VARENNE-ST-HILAIRE (LA)   94210
Paris 16 - Lagny 22 - St-Maur 3   Val-de-Marne

La Bretèche
171, quai de Bonneuil
48 83 38 73, fax 42 83 63 19
Closed Sun dinner, Mon, Feb school hols. Open until 10pm. Priv rm: 16. Terrace dining. V, AE, MC.
Choose a table on the terrace or in the bright, pink-hued dining room to savor Philippe Regnault's ably prepared tuna in a beurre blanc sauce accented with chives, casseroled lamb's kidneys with glazed shallots, and pear feuilleté swirled with ginger-spiced caramel. Extensive cellar; gracious welcome. C 300-350 F. M 160 F.

Le Pavillon Bleu
66, promenade des Anglais
48 83 10 56, fax 43 97 21 21
Open daily until 11pm.Terrace dining. V, AE, DC.
If the weather is fine, opt for a seat on the elegant covered terrace of this riverside establishment. The cooking here is conservative but capably handled: we like the garlicky salad of peppers and marinated anchovies, the smooth codfish brandade, and the pleasingly tart apple charlotte. Too bad that the cellar is so pricey! C 350-450 F. M 159 F.

Regency 1925
96, av. du Bac
48 83 15 15, fax 48 89 99 74
Closed Dec 24-26. Air cond. Pkg. V, AE, DC.
Michel Croisille does an excellent job of running this engaging brasserie. The atmosphere is warm, the staff swift and smiling. If only the prices were just a wee bit more clement... Fish and game are the main attractions here; don't miss the scallops roasted with cèpes or the simple yet delicious marinière of shellfish. C 350-450 F. M 140 F.

Gault Millau's ratings *are based solely on the restaurants' cuisine. We do not take into account the atmosphere, décor, service, and so on; these are commented upon within the review.*

VÉLIZY 78140
Paris 15 - Versailles 7 - Jouy-en-Josas 4   *Yvelines*

Holiday Inn Paris-Vélizy
22, av. de l'Europe
39 46 96 98, fax 34 65 95 21
Open year-round. 182 rms 725-1,050 F. Rms for disabled. Restaurant. Air cond. Conf. Heated pool. Golf. Garage pkg. V, AE, DC, MC.
Situated near a shopping center, the Holiday Inn offers functional rooms and excellent facilities. Free shuttle to the Pont-de-Sèvres Métro station.

VERSAILLES 78000
Paris 23 - Mantes 44 - Rambouillet 31   *Yvelines*

Bellevue Hôtel
12, av. de Sceaux
39 50 13 41, fax 39 02 05 67
Open year-round. 2 stes 300-500 F. 24 rms 300-450 F. Rms for disabled. Pkg. V, AE, DC, MC.
The Bellevue's Louis XV/XVI–style rooms are soundproofed and well equipped (new beds) but a trifle worn, despite a recent remodeling. Located near the château and conference center.

11/20 Brasserie du Théâtre
15, rue des Réservoirs
39 50 03 21, fax 39 50 74 32
Open daily until midnight (w-e 1am). Terrace dining. V, AE, DC, MC.
Classic brasserie food (fresh shellfish, pepper steak, sauerkraut, steak tartare), served in a supremely Gallic décor of mirrors, glowing woodwork, and leather banquettes. C 160-260 F.

Brasserie La Fontaine
Trianon Palace, 1, bd de la Reine
30 84 38 47, fax 30 21 01 22
Open daily until 10:30pm. Terrace dining. Air cond. Valet pkg. V, AE, DC, MC.
This brasserie annex of the famed Trois Marches (see below) bears the visible stamp of master chef Gérard Vié. He oversees the work of young Emmanuel Laporte, who executes an enticing menu that features a magnificent beef daube served with polenta, a light and lively terrine of skate and baby spinach, rabbit with a snappy garnish of basil-scented artichokes, and a suave pistachio custard with dark-chocolate sauce. The superb old-fashioned décor is accented with a series of amusing animal portraits. C 250 F. M 165 F.

12/20 Au Chapeau Gris
7, rue Hoche - 39 50 10 81
Closed Tue dinner, Wed, Jul. Open until 10pm. Priv rm: 70. Pkg. V, AE, DC, MC.
As the ancient exposed beams attest, this is the oldest restaurant in Versailles, and it attracts an extremely posh crowd. The cuisine is honest enough and reliably fresh, though not always precise. Traditional dishes are the house specialty: sweetbread salad with Sherry dressing, hake with langoustines, and iced Cointreau soufflé. Exceptional wine list. Classic, thoroughly professional service. C 300-400 F. M 155 F.

La Grande Sirène
25, rue du Mal-Foch
39 53 08 08, fax 39 53 37 15
Closed Sun, Mon, Apr 18-27, Aug. Open until 10pm. Air cond. No pets. Garage pkg. V, AE, DC, MC.
On the first floor of this Prussian-blue building, the series of dining rooms done up in eggshell, yellow, salmon, and ivory are the very epitome of *bon goût* as envisioned by the Versaillais. The service is similarly distinguished, the cellar is exciting, and the welcome urbane. How about the food, you say? It's unpretentious and delicious, with an emphasis on fish. But we've suspended the rating because a new chef has just moved into the kitchen. We'll let you know soon how he scores. C 400-500 F. M 148 F (lunch, wine incl), 228 F (dinner), 178 F, 245 F (lunch).

Le Lac Hong
Opposite the Minière ponds, 18, rue des Frères-Caudron, D 91 - 30 44 03 71
Closed Wed, Aug 15-Sep 15. Open until 9:30pm. Pkg. V.
Fine Chinese-Vietnamese cuisine at low prices (caramelized fresh tuna, quail with five-spice powder, grilled crab). Exceptionally affordable wines, charming welcome. C 110-160 F.

La Marée de Versailles
22, rue au Pain
30 21 73 73, fax 39 50 55 87
Closed Mon dinner, Sun, Dec 24-Jan 2, Aug 1-21. Open until 10:30pm. Air cond. V.
Unlike its big sister, La Grande Sirène, who goes in for expensive seafood and high-ticket wines, this shipshape little establishment is far more modest in its aims. But the fish served here is sparkling fresh and perfectly prepared by chef Éric Rogoff. He earns an extra two points and a toque for his turbot baked in veal juices, sweet-and-sour John Dory, the fabulous grilled sole with tarragon butter, and generous "shellfish" set menu. Skilled, stylish service. C 220-280 F. M 240 F.

12/20 Le Pot-au-Feu
22, rue de Satory - 39 50 57 43
Closed Sat lunch, Sun, Aug 15-30, Dec 24-28. Open until 10pm. Priv rm: 10. No pets. V, MC.
Pot-au-feu in its classic or seafood versions get star billing at this rose-colored bistro, but the chef's repertoire also includes mussels à la sétoise, plaice poached in hard cider, and veal confit à l'indienne. Attractive set meals. C 270-370 F. M 115 F, 175 F.

Le Potager du Roy
1, rue du Mal-Joffre - 39 50 35 34
Closed Sun dinner, Mon. Open until 11pm. Priv rm: 15. Air cond. V, AE.
Philippe Letourneur has moved into high gear, presenting a devilishly clever repertoire full of precise, clear-cut flavors. We recently spied the mayor of Versailles, Monsieur Damien (a connoisseur of fine dining), at Le Potager du Roy, taking visible pleasure in a lusty dish of cabbage stuffed with bone marrow, while we enjoyed an exquisite chestnut bouillon accented with morsels of quail meat, ox jowls braised in red wine with cumin-spiced carrots, and a splendid portion of roast lamb escorted by a vegetable tian. All these good things fully deserve a second

toque, which we're pleased to award this year. Note that the second of the two set meals is one of the best deals in Versailles. C 280-380 F. M 120 F (exc Sun), 169 F.

12/20 Le Quai n°1
1, av. de St-Cloud - 39 50 42 26
Closed Sun dinner, Mon. Open until 11pm. Priv rm: 35. Terrace dining. Air cond. V, MC.
A dependable address for fresh shellfish and decent seafood dishes at reasonable prices. Among the better offerings are a spicy fish soup, a refreshing salad of whelks with mayonnaise, and plaice in a sauce enriched with meat jus. Amusing nautical décor; casual service. C 250-400 F. M 115 F, 160 F.

Le Rescatore
27, av. de St-Cloud - 39 50 23 60
Closed Sat lunch, Sun. Open until 10pm. Priv rm: 45. Air cond. Garage pkg. V, AE.
Jacques Bagot is a native of the Norman port of Granville; his speciality is vibrantly fresh fish and seafood prepared in refined, imaginative ways. Try the unusual combination of oysters and duck breast called rôti d'huîtres au magret, a spice-stuffed turbot, or a keen-flavored ballottine of prawns with ratatouille. Fine cellar. C 300-480 F. M 145 F, 200 F, 235 F, 345 F.

Sofitel
2 bis, av. Paris
39 53 30 31, fax 39 53 87 20
Open year-round. 6 stes 1,200 F. 146 rms 850 F. Rms for disabled. Restaurant. Air cond. Pkg. V, AE, DC, MC.
Exceptionally well situated near the Place d'-Armes and the château but set back from the street, this Sofitel offers spacious, modern rooms and prestigious amenities. Excellent reception. Piano bar.

Trianon Palace
1, bd de la Reine
30 84 38 00, fax 39 49 00 77
Open year-round. 22 stes 3,500-7,500 F. 165 rms 890-2,200 F. Restaurant. Half-board 735-1,160 F. Air cond. Conf. Heated pool. Tennis. Valet pkg. Helipad. V, AE, DC, MC.
After sprucing up the place to the tune of $60 million, owner Yusake Miyama has thrown open the gilded gates of his stupendously lavish hotel. From video-conference equipment to a medically supervised spa, it is the last word in luxury. Restaurant: Les Trois Marches, see below.

Les Trois Marches

Trianon Palace, 1, bd de la Reine
39 50 13 21, fax 30 21 01 25
Closed Sun, Mon, Aug. Open until 10pm. Priv rm: 20. Terrace dining. Air cond. Heated pool. Valet pkg. V, AE, DC, MC.
Gérard Vié is as happy as a king in the splendiferous kitchens of the Trianon Palace, where he and his brigade benefit from the most technically sophisticated equipment imaginable. With his every material need thus tended to, Vié can devote his full attention to cooking. This year, he's enriched his repertoire with such regal offerings as boudin blanc à la royale, leg of lamb à la Mailly, and parsleyed capon—dishes that once delighted the kings of France! But don't worry: Vié's cuisine hasn't got lost in a time warp.

He continues to create such modern marvels as plump snails with green lentils redolent of star anise, or spiced lobster with a suave confit of turnips and figs, or Belon oysters and foie gras steamed over seaweed, or spice-glazed pigeon garnished with dried apricots and walnuts. Vié also excels with simpler country-style offerings, full of provincial goodness—beef braised with carrots, cassoulet with Couïza sausages, guinea hen with crisp-tender cabbage. And his desserts are a dream: the green-walnut ice cream with caramelized crème chiboust is just one outstanding example of this pâtissier's art. The brilliant young sommelier will uncork a perfect (and probably pricey) partner to complement Vié's creations, and Robert, the veteran maître d'hôtel, will make certain that that every detail of your meal is memorable. C 600-850 F. M 260 F (weekday lunch), 395 F, 495 F, 595 F, 750 F.

Le Versailles
Petite-Place, 7, rue Ste-Anne
39 50 64 65, fax 39 02 37 85
Open year-round. 48 rms 350-510 F. Rms for disabled. Restaurant. Pkg. V, AE, DC.
Conveniently situated near the entrance to the château and facing the convention center, Le Versailles has modern rooms and recently refitted bathrooms. Garden and patio.

■ In Le Chesnay 78150   NE

12/20 Le Chesnoy
24, rue Pottier - 39 54 01 01
Closed Sun dinner, Mon, Aug 2-22. Open until 10pm. Garden dining. Air cond. V, AE, DC.
Chef Georges Torrès cooks in a fresh, generous vein; his new single-price menu proposes an earthy salad of lamb's sweetbreads and bone marrow, grilled red mullet with tangy eggplant caviar, and apple craquant subtly perfumed with rosemary. Attractive cellar. M 168 F.

Le Connemara
41, route de Rueil - 39 55 63 07
Closed Sun (exc 1st & 2nd Sun of the month), Mon, 2nd wk of Feb school hols, Aug 1-20. Open until 9:30pm. Priv rm: 15. V, MC.
A little sprucing up wouldn't hurt the salmon-hued dining room, and a touch more precision could only help chef Pascal Eynard-Machet's cooking. Classic desserts; the wine list is compiled mostly from shippers' catalogs. C 250-400 F. M 155 F.

L'Étoile de Mer
Pl. du Nouveau-Marché, 17, rue des Deux-Frères - 39 54 62 70
Closed Mon, Sat lunch, Sun dinner, Tue, Wed. Open until 9:30pm. Pkg. V.
L'Étoile de Mer's intimate, modern dining room opens onto the town marketplace. The view features a crowded lobster tank, and beyond it, the fishmonger's shop attached to the restaurant. This is where chef Antoine Vieira takes the freshest, best fish and shellfish, and transforms them into appetizing assortments and cooked dishes. You're sure to like his smooth crab soup, octopus à la portuguaise, and tasty mussels marinière. Charming welcome. Tiny wine cellar. C 190-400 F.

FRANCE A-Z

Restaurants & Hotels

ABBEVILLE   80100
Paris 160 - Amiens 45 - Dieppe 63   *Somme*

Auberge de la Corne
32, chaussée du Bois
22 24 06 34, fax 22 24 03 65
Closed Sun dinner, Mon, Feb 20-Mar 10. Open until 9:30pm. Priv rm: 26. Air cond. V, AE, DC, MC.
Yves Lemalelot is a good chef, indeed he may be the best in the region when it comes to simple dishes based on game and fresh market produce. He gets his fish from the Somme bay, mushrooms from the Crécy forest, and his poultry is always excellent. The dining room, split down the middle by a bar bristling with bottles, is most convivial. This year we enjoyed his flavorful warm oysters in curry sauce, sole with cèpes, and the pear and chocolate charlotte. Service can get a bit ragged on busy Sundays. C 280-370 F. M 98 F, 130 F, 200 F, 280 F.

Hôtel de France
19, pl. Pilori
22 24 00 42, fax 22 24 26 15
Open year-round. 69 rms 246-550 F. Restaurant. Rms for disabled. Half-board 250-370 F. Conf. Pkg. V, AE, DC, MC.
Conveniently located in the center of town, the regularly renovated rooms are spacious (those at the back are quiet). French billiard table.

ABONDANCE   74360
Paris 604 - Annecy 100 - Evian 30 - Thonon 28   *H.-Savoie*

Bel Air   🌲🎿
3 km NE, in Richebourg
50 73 01 71, fax 50 73 08 37
Closed Wed off-seas, Apr 20-May 15, Sep 20-Dec 20. 23 rms 150-280 F. Restaurant. Half-board 180-230 F. Pkg. V, MC.
Located three kilometers from town, this chalet-style hotel offers quiet, pleasant rooms with balconies overlooking the surrounding mountain landscape.

ABREST 03   ➜ Vichy

ADRETS (LES)   83600
Paris 886 - St-Raphaël 21 - Cannes 28 - Draguignan 45   *Var*

12/20 Auberge des Adrets
N 7, towards Mandelieu
94 40 36 24, fax 94 40 34 06
Closed Mon, Oct 31-Mar 1. Open until 10pm. Priv rm: 25. Garden dining. Pkg. V, MC.
The new owner-chef of this charming old inn with a lovely terrace facing the Esterel hills has developed "theme menus", such as one devoted to duck: fresh tasting, earthy hors d'oeuvres, sliced duck breast with apples (slightly over-cooked), a properly cooked duck thigh accompanied by a salad scattered with pine nuts, a nice lemon sherbet, and excellent banana sherbet. Attentive welcome; competent, friendly service. M 120 F (lunch exc Sun), 300 F, 240 F.

Le Chrystalin   🌲🎿
Pl. de l'Église
94 40 97 56, fax 94 40 94 66
Closed Oct-Feb. 15 rms 380-480 F. Restaurant. Half-board 325-400 F. Conf. Pool. Golf. Pkg. V, AE, MC.
A little bit of heaven for travelers. In the heart of the Esterel hills and just a few miles from the Mediterranean, fifteen modern rooms, each with a superb view from its balcony. Rustic furniture, well-equipped bathrooms. Guaranteed relief for the stressed-out.

AGAY   83700
Paris 902 - Cannes 30 - Saint-Raphaël 11 - Nice 63   *Var*

Sol e Mar
2 km SW on N 98, Le Dramont
94 95 25 60, fax 94 83 83 61
Closed Oct 15-Easter. 2 stes 700-1,200 F. 44 rms 420-660 F. Restaurant. Half-board 360-550 F. Conf. Pool. Golf. Garage pkg. V, AE, MC.
Set on the shores of the Mediterranean in relative isolation, this hotel boasts rooms with terraces that afford a sweeping view. Sea-water swimming pools, solarium.

AGDE 34300

Paris 818 - Montpellier 57 - Béziers 22 - Sète 23   *Hérault*

La Tamarissière   {}
4 km SW on D 32 E, at La Tamarissière
67 94 20 87, fax 67 21 38 40
Closed Sun dinner & Mon (Mar 15-Jun 15 & Sep 15-Jan 2). Open until 10:30pm. Priv rm: 20. Garden dining. Pool. Pkg. V, AE, DC, MC.
Although he is already covered with toques and culinary laurels, chef Nicolas Albano chooses not to rest on them. Another sort of Southern chef might laze on the banks of the Hérault in this marvelously unspoilt spot, or play at *boules* in the shade of giant sycamores. But Albano is a restless perfectionist. He's constantly improving and updating his restaurant, or redecorating and refitting the rooms of his hotel with the help of his wife Maïté. They have made what was once a simple family auberge into the best restaurant in the Hérault, while maintaining a friendly, relaxed atmosphere. Try the poached lobster marvelously paired with warm vegetables in coriander honey sauce, fillets of red mullet with tiny squid in pistou, perfectly baked John Dory with new potatoes, onions, and bacon. And for landlubbers, there's a fine farm-raised spiced squab with polenta quenelles. For dessert, sample the fruit soup with Banyuls or the delicate florentine with honey cake ice cream. Who wouldn't want to spend a few sun-drenched hours in the lovely dining room, or on the pool-side patio? All the more so given the seductive prices and the tasty regional wines of Languedoc-Roussillon. The smaller fixed-price menus are a steal. **C** 400-650 F. **M** 145 F (weekdays), 225 F, 345 F.

La Tamarissière
(See restaurant above)
Closed Jan 2-Mar 15. 26 rms 310-600 F. Half-board 410-570 F. Conf. Pool. Golf. Pkg. V, AE, DC, MC.
The decor is refreshing and stylish, although the rooms are on the small side. The surrounding rose garden and pine forest are pure delight, and the Hérault canal passes in front of the hotel. Excellent breakfast and service.

■ In **Le Cap-d'Agde 34300**   *7 km SE on D 32 E*

12/20 Le Brasero
Port-Richelieu II - 67 26 24 75
Closed Nov 7-Feb 28. Open until 11pm. Terrace dining. V, AE, DC, MC.
Delicious fish dishes are earning this restaurant a wide reputation: monkfish bourride, seafood pot-au-feu, and fresh anchovies, all at attractively low prices. Succinct wine list. **C** 190-360 F. **M** 69 F, 110 F, 140 F.

Capaô
Plage Richelieu
67 26 99 44, fax 67 26 55 41
Closed Nov 5-Mar 23. 2 stes 990-1,390 F. 51 rms 370-695 F. Rms for disabled. Restaurant. Half-board 340-840 F. Air cond. Conf. Heated pool. Golf. Pkg. V, AE, DC, MC.
This seafront hotel was recently built, and blends innocuously into a sports and leisure complex. Small but well-designed rooms with terrace-solariums. Sauna; Jacuzzi; bar.

Hôtel Eve
Av. Joliette - 67 26 71 70, fax 67 26 08 65
Closed Oct-Mar. 37 rms 360-595 F. Rms for disabled. Restaurant. Air cond. Pool. Golf. Garage pkg. V, AE, DC, MC.
Even Adam and Eve in their birthday suits would be welcome here. In fact, the hotel is a haven for nudists from Easter to October. Off-season special rates: pay for five nights, stay two nights free. Standard, well-soundproofed rooms.

Saint-Clair
Pl. St-Clair - 67 26 36 44, fax 67 26 31 11
Closed Nov-Apr. 5 stes 330-730 F. 82 rms 240-565 F. Half-board 420-800 F. Air cond. Pool. Golf. V, AE, MC.
Built in the 1970s, this hotel is located just minutes from the harbor. The modern, well-equipped rooms are comfortable; additional amenities include a sauna, Jacuzzi, and games room. Shuttle to the beach.

■ In **Marseillan 34340**   *7 km NE on D 51*

Hôtel du Château du Port
9, quai de la Résistance
67 77 65 65, fax 67 77 67 98
Closed Apr 1-Oct 15. 1 ste 880-1,000 F. 15 rms 240-500 F. Golf. Pkg. V, AE, DC, MC.
An old town house on the quays recently refurbished at great expense in eighteenth-century style. The rooms have genuine charm and are luxuriously appointed. A truly pleasant stop.

See also: Florensac

AGEN 47000

Paris 647 - Bordeaux 142 - Toulouse 108   *Lot/Garonne*

L'Aéroport
3 km SW, in La Garenne
53 96 38 95, fax 53 98 38 55
Closed Sun dinner, Mon, Aug. Open until 9:45pm. Terrace dining. Air cond. Pkg. V, AE, DC, MC.
Patrick Pinard's cuisine seems to be gaining altitude. This year he served us a great game pâté, flavorful sole with cèpes, and a perfect crème brûlée. Good regional cellar. **C** 250-350 F. **M** 95 F (weekdays, Sat lunch), 175 F (Sun lunch), 155 F (exc Sun).

Château Saint-Marcel
Route de Toulouse
53 96 61 30, fax 53 96 94 34
Closed Sun dinner, Mon. Open until 10pm. Terrace dining. Air cond. Valet pkg. V, AE, DC.
Imagine a majestic wide-screen traveling shot of a lovely tree-lined lane leading to a superb château. The plot revolves around the miraculous restorations worked by the château's new owner, Jean Albani. He's put his all into the job. Toiling away in the kitchen is Serge Delanoue, formerly of La Table des Cordeliers in Condom, a chef known for his intrepid exploration of unfamiliar flavor combinations. But this year we were perplexed by what we were served here, and are reserving judgement to see if he can get back to his previous form: cod with bland vegetables, duck breast with overcooked langoustines, very ordinary pear tart. Warm welcome; excellent service. **C** 280-400 F. **M** 160 F, 250 F.

CHAIN HOTELS

During the past decade, chain hotels near major urban centers and road connections have developed enormously in France. This was needed; traditional family-run hotels weren't always making the efforts we would have liked them to make.

Some of these new "ecological" hotels offer minimal comfort and service at rock-bottom prices (they are really just boxes to sleep in), while others offer more comfort as well as the chance to lodge the whole family at low prices and in acceptable conditions. In the latter category, we have tested for you some "products" that are well conceived and appropriately priced, and whose good and bad points we have closely examined. Just to help you decide where to lay your head down at night....

AROUND 300 F

● **Campanile**
This chain offers 350 hotels in Europe, each with around 50 rooms. Near major highway intersections and in city suburbs. Full bathrooms, radio-alarm clock, TV with Canal Plus. A third bed free for children under 12, and, in each hotel, two rooms with two children's beds. Open every day of the year. Pets free. Around 270 F (340 F in Paris and Lyons). Reception from 7am to 11pm, but there's a 24-hour night desk. Buffet breakfasts served from 6:30am. Set menus from 82 F to 102 F, drinks included, oriented around copious buffets. Children's menus at 35 F, a great deal.
Central reservation service: (1) 64 62 46 46. Fax: (1) 64 62 46 61.
For: They are found everywhere, and there's an effort to offer personalized service. **Against**: Often located in industrial zones, in rather depressing surroundings.

● **Climat de France**
163 hotels near industrial zones. Around 30 to 60 rooms with full bathrooms or showers and toilets. Automatic alarm clock, TV with Canal Plus. Third bed free for children under 14. Pets free. Around 270 F. Accessible around the clock (night surveillance or automatic key distributor). Breakfast buffets at 30 F to 40 F. Set menus at 75 F to 140 F.
Central reservation service: (1) 64 46 01 23; free number 05 11 22 11.
For: Open 24 hours. **Against**: Often in industrial zones, and often without personalized welcomes. You can find the same quality at lower prices.

● **Ibis**
400 hotels with 40 to 500 rooms, throughout Europe in the center of cities or at the edge of town, in commercial zones or near airports. Open every day of the year. Full bathrooms or showers and toilets. Automatic radio alarm clock, TV with Canal Plus. Third bed free for children under 12. Pets free. Rooms beginning at 280 F. Receptionist on duty 24 hours a day. Breakfasts served beginning at 6:30am. Set menus from 55 F to 95 F, drinks included.
Central reservation service: (1) 60 77 52 52. Fax: (1) 69 91 05 63,.
For: Dependable formula. **Against**: Some hotels are a bit dated; quality is uneven.

SERVICES FOR CHILDREN

All these hotels are oriented toward families, so children are welcome. Other hotel groups also offer children's services, notably **Novotel**: children under 16 are free if they sleep in their parents' room; breakfast included. 250 Novotel hotels offer gardens and swimming pools.
Information and reservation service: (1) 60 77 27 27.

Château Saint-Marcel

(See restaurant above)

Open year-round. 2 stes 1,500 F. 23 rms 550-950 F. Rms for disabled. Half-board 525-975 F. Air cond. Conf. Pool. Tennis. Golf. Valet pkg. V, AE, DC, MC.

Montesquieu once owned this handsome château, whose majestic suites are done up in a tasteful traditional manner with antiques, ivory satin, and vast bathrooms. The reading room occupies a round tower. View of grounds. One wing, housed in former hangars, has modern, functional rooms.

Hostellerie des Jacobins

1 ter, pl. des Jacobins
53 47 03 31, fax 53 47 02 80

Open year-round. 15 rms 300-550 F. Air cond. Golf. Valet pkg. V, AE, MC.

This imposing early-nineteenth-century town house has had a facelift, and air conditioning has been installed. The rooms are comfortable, cozily decorated and quiet, although the quality is uneven. Supper-trays on request.

12/20 Michel Latrille

66, rue C.-Desmoulins
53 66 24 35, fax 53 66 77 57

Closed Sat lunch, Sun. Open until 10pm. Priv rm: 28. Air cond. Pkg. V, AE, DC, MC.

A pale-colored, elegant dining room made larger by clever use of mirrors is the backdrop for chef Michel Latrille's fresh and simple repertoire: lobster in puff pastry, casserole-roasted young squab, langoustine ravioli, and a warm chocolate dessert. **C** 270-350 F. **M** 99 F (weekdays), 160 F, 200 F, 280 F.

Le Petit Vatel

52, rue R.-Cœur-de-Lion - 53 47 66 00

Closed lunch Sat & Mon, Aug. Open until 10pm. Priv rm: 15. Terrace dining. Air cond. V, AE.

Housed in a centuries-old building on a steep street in the center of town, the decor of the cozy Petit Vatel is a tasteful, rustic grey-on-blue. Christophe Meret's cooking sets confidently to sea with the skill of a practiced but imaginative navigator. The set menu, for example, offers tiny fish stuffed with herbs, slivers of duck breast with grapes, and chocolate mousse with sherbet. If you order à la carte, sample the tasty langoustines sautéed with tomatoes, monkfish with saffron, or brioche bread pudding with caramelized apples. The wine cellar needs fleshing out. Warm welcome; competent, friendly service. **C** 200-280 F. **M** 95 F.

Le Provence

22, cours du 14-Juillet
53 47 39 11, fax 53 68 26 24

Open year-round. 23 rms 275-350 F. Air cond. Conf. Pkg. V, AE, MC.

This little hotel in the center of town has been enlarged and redecorated, and offers soundproof rooms. Meal trays on request. Pub-style bar open every night except Sunday.

---

*Some establishments change their **closing times** without warning. It is always wise to check in advance.*

■ In Bon-Encontre 47240   4 km S on N 113

Mariottat

41, rue de la République
53 96 17 75, fax 53 96 29 05

Closed Sun dinner, Mon, Feb 19-27. Open until 9:30pm. Priv rm: 15. Terrace dining. Air cond. Pkg. Hotel: 10 rms 185-250 F. Half-board 295-350 F. Pkg. V, AE.

Christiane and Éric Mariottat's restaurant is on the way to becoming a site of (gastronomic) pilgrimage like the statue of the Virgin of Bon-Encontre across the street. This is a charming, romantic establishment with modern decor. There's a lovely dining room leading to a terrace; Christiane's welcome is warm; the service is efficient; and Éric's cooking gets better all the time. Fresh market ingredients and regional recipes inspire dishes such as duck giblets stewed with sea scallops, eel à la bordelaise, and prune fritters with Armagnac. Fine wine list, strong on Bordeaux and local selections. **C** 300-400 F. **M** 95 F (weekdays), 150 F, 195 F (Fish), 250 F.

■ In Brax 47310   6 km W on D 656 and D 119

La Renaissance de l'Étoile

Route de Mont-de-Marsan
53 68 69 23, fax 53 68 62 89

Closings not available. Open until 9:30pm. Priv rm: 130. Garden dining. Pkg. V, AE, DC, MC.

Yves Gruel excels in new versions of regional specialties. His restaurant also boasts an admirably well stocked cellar with plenty of half-bottles and wines by the glass. The 164 F menu will satisfy the most robust appetites. Try the sautéed foie gras with marinated grapes, lake fish with fresh girolle mushrooms, and rosemary ice cream with Monbazillac-spiked apple sauce. **C** 300-350 F. **M** 102 F (exc Sun), 164 F, 188 F, 289 F.

La Renaissance de l'Étoile

(See restaurant above)

Closed 1 wk at Feb school hols. 1 ste 325-370 F. 9 rms 225-315 F. Half-board 372-412 F. Conf. Tennis. Pkg. V, DC, MC.

The rooms of this hotel set in a landscape of rare trees are comfortable, largish, and nicely furnished, with attractive bathrooms. Most look out onto the grounds.

■ In Puymirol 47270   17 km E on N 113 and D 16

L'Aubergade

Michel Trama, 52, rue Royale
53 95 31 46, fax 53 95 33 80

19.5   *Closed Mon off-seas (exc hols), Feb 15-Mar 10. Open until 9:30pm. Priv rm: 60. Garden dining. Air cond. Valet pkg. V, AE, DC, MC.*

What's a hyper-talented chef doing in far-flung Puymirol? It's possible Michel Trama wonders the same thing when business is slow and tourists are thin on the ground. But with his wife Maryse by his side, he's managing to hold on in this tiny village perched over the countryside near Agen. And he couldn't be righter, for where else could you find such a marvellous conjunc-

**COLORS
IN
THE
NIGHT**

Marie Brizard

LIQUEURS DE FRANCE DEPUIS 1755

tion of people and place, far from the madding crowd? L'Aubergade has scaled the heights to become a pinnacle of gastronomy, and the steep climb to reach its fastness makes the reward all the more extraordinary. Michel, Maryse and their architect, Yves Boucharlat, transformed their medieval aerie by cleverly mixing the old with the resolutely contemporary. The enclosed garden with its bubbling ornamental pond is enough to make anyone swoon with delight and the galleries, terraces, and wonderful white stone façades have a Florentine feel which perfectly suits this luminous French-Tuscan landscape. As for the pleasures of the table, Trama marries authentic regional cooking deeply rooted in the surrounding countryside with inspired flights of fancy that make the taste buds twitch with pleasure. And his pastries are so good that some people can't resist ordering three or so. Try his sea scallops with truffles and edible seaweed, a delicate anchovy and olive paste tart, creamed baby morel mushrooms cooked in fat from Spanish ham and served with a raw asparagus sauce, or duck breast with juniper berry vinaigrette. One dish should appear in a book on Great Taste Sensations: turbot and shellfish paired with quinoa in a spicy vinaigrette, served with slices of green mango coated with egg white and baked. Out of this world! We also adored the snails with polenta fries, pasta risotto with squid and peppers, potatoes with truffles, and the amusing "hamburger" of warm foie gras with cèpes. As for desserts, they're all superb, and include a chocolate "teardrop" with morello cherries in a vanilla-thyme jelly, craquelin with toasted honey cake ice cream, éclaté of dark chocolate, and the nougatine glacé millefeuille with pralines. Add Maryse's selection of fine Bordeaux and Southwest wines, and Michel's aged Havana cigars, and you have the makings of a magical, unforgettable meal. C 500-800 F. M 160 F, 280 F(weekday lunch), 280 F, 490 F.

Les Loges de l'Aubergade
(See restaurant above)
Closed Feb 15-Mar 10. 10 rms 750-1,410 F. Rms for disabled. Half-board 1,800-2,100 F. Air cond. Conf. Tennis. Golf. Valet pkg. V, AE, DC, MC.
This hotel definitely has an Italian feel to it, both inside and out. For one thing the Tramas had most of the furniture, lighting fixtures, and various accessories made in Italy and they go beautifully with the bare stone walls of this ancient bastide, built for the Counts of Toulouse. The huge, bright rooms and the bathrooms have been very well thought out, with rare care and attention to detail. No wonder newcomers often prolong their stay (though all the rooms are often booked far ahead). From the door handles to the specially woven carpets, everything is pretty, original, and impeccably matched. Dip your feet in the Jacuzzi garden pool while sipping a glass of wine. Tennis and golf nearby. VCRs and babysitting available. Relais et Châteaux.

AHETZE 64 → Bidart

AIGNERVILLE 14 → Bayeux

AIGUEBELETTE (LAC D') **73610**
Paris 551 - Grenoble 53 - Belley 47 - Chambéry 21 *Savoie*

Novalaise-Plage
8 km on D 41, Novalaise-Lac
79 36 02 19, fax 79 36 04 22
Closed Tue off-seas, Jan 1-Apr 9, Oct 1-Dec 31. 10 rms 220-350 F. Restaurant. Half-board 250-340 F. Pkg. V, MC.
This hotel on the edge of a lake has a tiny private beach. The terrace-restaurant faces the mountains.

AIGUEBELLE 83 → Lavandou (Le)

AIGUES-MORTES **30220**
Paris 750 - Arles 48 - Montpellier 32 - Nîmes 39 *Gard*

10/20 Les Arcades
23, bd Gambetta
66 53 81 13, fax 66 53 75 46
Closed Mon (exc Jul-Aug), Feb. Open until 10:15pm (11:15pm in summer). Terrace dining. V, AE, DC, MC.
The arcades belong to a lovely restored sixteenth-century house in a quiet corner of Aigues-Mortes. Old beams and stone walls grace the somewhat somber dining room, which offers a cool respite on a hot summer's day. But the good turbot spoiled by a floury lemon sauce in the guise of hollandaise lost this place its toque this year, in spite of the tasty apple tart. The *patronne* is attentive, the service efficient, the wine list regional, and prices not horrendous (the 115 F menu offers particularly fine value). C 250-350 F. M 115 F, 148 F, 185 F.

Les Arcades
(See restaurant above)
Closed Feb. 6 rms 460-530 F. No pets. V, AE, DC, MC.
A delightful spot within the walls of the old town. There's a magnificent sixteenth-century staircase and just six huge, comfortable rooms.

Hostellerie des Remparts
6, pl. A.-France
66 53 82 77, fax 66 53 73 77
Open year-round. 3 stes 650-830 F. 19 rms 290-455 F. Restaurant. Half-board 405-565 F. Conf. Pkg. V, AE, DC, MC.
An eighteenth-century house in what was once a knight's garrison. The rooms are elegantly furnished and some look out onto the famous ramparts.

AIGUILLON **47190**
Paris 670 - Agen 30 - Marmande 28 - Nérac 25 *Lot/Garonne*

Auberge des Quatre Vents

In Lagarrigue
53 79 62 78, fax 53 88 73 82
Closed Feb school hols. Open until 9:30pm. Priv rm: 18. Terrace dining. Pkg. V, MC.
Regulars flock to the Auberge's delightfully rustic dining room, with its great bow window, full of fresh ideas. Sample his compote of marinated tomatoes and fresh sardines, duck breast with prunes, or the fresh fruit tart with a buttery crust. The lowest priced set menus are great deals. Good wine list. Charming welcome,

courteous and efficient service. **C** 230-330 F.
M 100 F, 150 F, 190 F.

12/20 Le Jardin des Cygnes
Route de Villeneuve
53 79 60 02, fax 53 88 10 22
Closed Dec 17-Jan 10. Open until 9:30pm. Priv rm: 90. Terrace dining. Pool. Pkg. V, AE, MC.
The setting is beautiful—a pond surrounded by foliage, an old willow, and a flower-studded garden. Alain Bénito's cooking remains a model of lightness and generosity, although it could be more imaginative. The menus are moderately priced, and propose the appealing likes of grilled pickerel with shallot vinegar, wild boar in Armagnac sauce, cassoulet, and puff pastry with raspberry sauce. The short wine list offers a good choice of Champagnes and Armagnacs. **C** 200-300 F. **M** 69 F, 96 F, 138 F.

Le Jardin des Cygnes
(See restaurant above)
Closed Dec 15-Jan 15. 24 rms 160-270 F. Half-board 212-277 F. Conf. Pool. Pkg. V, AE, MC.
Well-equipped, comfortable, recently refurbished rooms. There's an inviting pool too, as well as special fishing and golf packages.

Argi-Eder
Route Notre-Dame-de-l'Aubépine
59 29 91 04, fax 59 29 74 33
Closed Sun dinner & Wed off-seas, Nov 15-Apr 8. Open until 9pm. Priv rm: 50. Terrace dining. Air cond. Pool. Pkg. V, AE, DC, MC.
Chef Jean-Pierre Dottax's regional specialties are pulling in gourmets who enjoy dining on the poolside terrace or in the comfortable, terracotta-tiled dining room. We enjoyed our poached eggs with country ham, beef fillet with cèpes cooked in a foil wrapper, and the warm ramuntxo dessert. Magnificent wine list, fine selection of brandies. The *patronne* welcomes guests with a smile, and the service is good indeed. **C** 300-350 F. **M** 100 F, 200 F, 240 F (exc Sun lunch).

Argi-Eder
(See restaurant above)
See restaurant for closings. 4 stes 680-850 F. 36 rms 600-780 F. Half-board 600-660 F. Air cond. Conf. Pool. Tennis. Golf. Pkg. V, AE, DC, MC.
Just outside the village stands this imposing Basque chalet with huge grounds and comfortable (although not well soundproofed) rooms. The terrace by the swimming pool has been enlarged.

Ithurria
59 29 92 11, fax 59 29 81 28
Closed Nov 2-end Mar. Open until 9pm. Priv rm: 25. Air cond. Pool. Pkg. V, AE, DC, MC.
Lovers of Basque country cooking will welcome the return to our guide of this very traditional establishment run by the Isabal family in a pretty village along the pilgrim route to Spain. The cooking offers no surprises (foie gras cooked in a cloth, peppers stuffed with cod, blood sausage with apples), but it's all served in generous portions. **C** 270-360 F. **M** 170 F, 270 F.

Ithurria
(See restaurant above)
Closed Nov 2-Mar. 27 rms 400-600 F. Half-board 550-600 F. Conf. Pool. Pkg. V, AE, DC, MC.
A seventeenth-century inn complete with half timbering, exposed beams, and well polished antiques; the rooms are pleasantly rustic, with pretty views. Lovely pool.

Ohantzea
59 29 90 50
Closed Sun, Mon, Nov 15-Feb 15. 9 rms 210-300 F. Restaurant. Half-board 250-300 F. Pkg. V, AE, MC.
A genuine mountain inn, set in a little village. The bathrooms were recently remodeled. Attractive furnishings, a warm welcome, and children's games in the garden.

12/20 Chez l'Ahumat
2, rue des Écoles - 58 71 82 61
Closed Wed, Mar 20-Apr 2, Aug 31-Sep 13. Open until 9:30pm. Priv rm: 90. Hotel: 13 rms 95-170 F. Half-board 168-185 F. No pets. Pkg. V, MC.
Incredibly low prices—even for the Landes region—explain the surge of tourists into the two tidy dining rooms. Try the regional charcuterie, the terrines, snails, confit of grilled duck, and wood pigeon salmis. Local wines cost less than 40 F. **C** 130-160 F. **M** 51 F, 75 F, 93 F, 135 F.

Le Commerce
3, bd des Pyrénées - 58 71 60 06
Closed Sun dinner, Mon. Open until 9:30pm. Priv rm: 80. Pkg. V, DC, MC.
There's more than a touch of nostalgia in the long dining room with carefully set tables, where you can savor the generous cuisine represented by the first menu: vegetable soup, trout with almonds, grilled steak, and flan. Friendly service. Regional wines are good and there are some magnificent Armagnacs. **C** 150-300 F. **M** 180 F (weekdays, Sat lunch), 66 F, 125 F.

■ **In Ségos 32400**   9 km SW on N 134 and D 260

Domaine de Bassibé
62 09 46 71, fax 62 08 40 15
Closed Jan-Feb. Open until 10pm. Priv rm: 40. Garden dining. Pool. Valet pkg. V, AE, DC, MC.
Chef Ricardo Thomis's domain is regional cooking linked to the land but cleverly landscaped with flavorful ideas. Proof is the tasty lamb tongue with gribiche sauce, stuffed and stewed chicken, warm foie gras, and sautéed red mullet. Fine wine list. Expect a charming welcome into the sunny contemporary dining room fitted out in a former wine cellar. **M** 90 F (weekday lunch), 180 F (wine incl), 240 F.

Domaine de Bassibé
(See restaurant above)
Closed Jan-mid Mar. 7 stes 980-1,080 F. 12 rms 550-825 F. Rms for disabled. Half-board 600-900 F. Conf. Pool. Golf. Valet pkg. Helipad. V, AE, DC, MC.
The atmospheric, comfortable rooms of this former farmhouse, now a beautifully restored hotel, boast exposed beams and mansard roofs. Sunny rooms in the "field house" are pleasant

but less well soundproofed. Courteous welcome. Relais et Châteaux.

See also: Eugénie-les-Bains (Michel Guérard), Villeneuve-de-Marsan

AIRE-SUR-LA-LYS   62120
Paris 236 - Lille 57 - Béthune 25 - Boulogne 60   *P./Calais*

 ### Les Trois Mousquetaires
Château du fort de la Redoute
21 39 01 11, fax 21 39 50 10
Closed Dec 20-Jan 20. Open until 10pm. Priv rm: 92. No pets. Pkg. V, AE, DC, MC.
The Three Musketeers were actually four and so are the Venets—Mom, Dad, Caroline, and Philippe. The latter is our d'Artagnan in the kitchen and thanks to a lot of family advice he has acquired a very sure touch with dishes like sea scallops with brioche and beef marrow, warm oysters with endive, steamed turbot with basil, squab stuffed with vegetables, and a black cherry gratin with sabayon. The pleasant dining room looks out onto wonderful grounds (where it would be so nice to eat...). C 320-450 F. M 108 F (weekdays, Sat lunch), 150 F, 225 F, 330 F.

Les Trois Mousquetaires 🏚️
(See restaurant above)
Closed Dec 20-Jan 20. 2 stes 840-1,010 F. 31 rms 250-540 F. 1 half-board 405-550 F. Conf. No pets. Pkg. V, AE, DC, MC
Lovingly decorated rooms with splendid views, in a large house dating from the last century.

AIX-EN-PROVENCE   13100
Paris 760 - Nîmes 105 - Avignon 75 - Marseille 31   *B./Rhône*

L'Alicate aux Champs
On D 543, between St-Pons & Eguilles, 13290 Les Milles - 42 20 05 85
Closed Sun dinner. Open until 9:30pm. Priv rm: 30. Terrace dining. Valet pkg. V, AE, DC, MC.
A charming little place on a verdant hillside, with a sunny, quietly elegant dining room. Nicole Mercier's bargain-priced set manues feature cuisine as sunny as the surroundings: a flan of asparagus and baby fava beans, cabbage stuffed with duck confit, and a great selection of homey desserts. Friendly welcome. M 180 F, 210 F, 240 F, 280 F.

Hôtel des Augustins
3, rue de la Masse
42 27 28 59, fax 42 26 74 87
Open year-round. 29 rms 500-1,200 F. Air cond. No pets. Valet pkg. V, AE, DC, MC.   D5-15
This beautifully restored twelfth-century convent provides comfortable, quiet rooms with understated furnishings. Two of them have terraces that face a bell-tower. Guests may take their breakfast in the attractive garden.

Les Bacchanales
10, rue de la Couronne
42 27 21 06, fax 42 38 42 23
Open daily until 11pm. Air cond. V, AE.   C5-16
We salute chef Jean-Marc Taillefer, who has added his comfortably decorated establishment to this center-city street given over almost entirely to restaurants. His up-to-date cooking is a

clever blend of flavors: salmon marinated with preserved tomatoes, pot-au-feu and foie gras with marjoram, and for dessert, blancmange with figs and fruit sauce. Professional service. C 280-430 F. M 75 F (lunch exc Sun), 125 F, 174 F, 280 F.

Le Bistro Latin
18, rue de la Couronne
42 38 22 88, fax 42 38 36 15
Closed Sun dinner, Mon lunch. Open until 10:30pm. Priv rm: 20. Air cond. V, AE, DC.   C5-2
Chef Bruno Ungaro knows how to choose his ingredients and has his classic technique down pat. Once he gets a better grip on balancing flavors, his cooking will be above reproach. This year we savored his honey-glazed rabbit with preserved garlic, scampi risotto, and a fine crispy chocolate dessert with apples and crème anglaise. Cheerful, efficient staff. C 250-300 F. M 89 F (lunch exc Sun), 119 F, 184 F, 250 F.

Bleu Marine
Route de Galice
42 95 04 41, fax 42 59 47 29
Open year-round. 87 rms 290-480 F. Rms for disabled. Half-board 395 F. Air cond. Conf. Pool. Tennis. Golf. Pkg. V, AE, DC, MC.   A4-22
A rotunda-shaped building near the center of town, with well equipped, soundproof rooms, mohagany furniture, and generous breakfasts. Very friendly welcome.

Campanile
ZAC du Jas-de-Bouffan, rte de Valcros
42 59 40 73, fax 42 59 03 47
See page 95.   A4-4
A modern and very quiet hotel near the superhighway (and next to the Vasarely Foundation).

La Caravelle
29, bd du Roi-René
42 21 53 05, fax 42 96 55 46
Open year-round. 32 rms 190-420 F. Air cond. Conf. Garage pkg. V, AE, DC, MC.   E5-21
Half of the rooms (the more expensive ones) give onto a lovely succession of indoor gardens. Rooms are renovated regularly.

12/20 La Carraire
Quartier Valcros, chemin de Castel-Blanc
42 24 40 48, fax 42 39 24 57
Closed Sat lunch, Sun. Open until 9:30pm (10pm in summer). Priv rm: 40. Garden dining. Pool. Pkg. V, AE, DC, MC.   A4-6
The kitchen's line is serious, even conservative cookery. But that doesn't mean it's not satisfying: we sampled a fricassée of sea scallops, beef in a pastry crust, chicken with juniper berries, and a caramel and hazelnut cake. Friendly welcome. C 280-380 F. M 125 F, 155 F, 190 F, 250 F.

Le Mas des Écureuils 🏚️
(See restaurant above)
Open year-round. 4 stes 660-760 F. 19 rms 380-760 F. Half-board 545-825 F. Conf. Pool. Golf. Pkg. Helipad. V, AE, DC, MC.
Business meetings are the bread and butter of this small Provençal hostelry, but individual travelers are warmly welcomed too. Guest rooms provide all the usual amenities, including a steam room, and there is an inviting shaded terrace under the trees.

R Restaurant H Hôtel

1 - La Renaissance **H**
2 - Le Bistro Latin **R**
3 - Saint-Christophe **H**
4 - Campanile **H**
5 - Résidence
    Rotonde **H**
6 - Le Carraire
    (Le Mas
    des Ecureuils) **RH**
7 - Mercure
    Paul Cézanne **H**
8 - Pullman Roi René **H**
9 - Le Pigonnet **RH**
10 - Hôtel de France **H**
    et La Vieille
    Auberge **R**
11 - Puyfond **R**
12 - Les Frères Lani **R**
13 - Le Nègre-Coste **H**
14 - Chez Maxime **R**
15 - Hôtel
    des Augustins **H**
16 - Les Bachanales **R**
17 - Le Clos
    de la Violette **R**
18 - Yoji **R**
19 - Le Prieuré **H**
20 - Novotel
    Aix Beaumanoir **H**
21 - La Caravelle **H**
22 - Bleu Marine **H**
    et Holiday Inn **H**
23 - Villa Gallici **H**
24 - Côté Cour **R**
25 - Chez Féraud **R**
26 - A la Cour de Rohan **R**
27 - Château de la Pioline **RH**

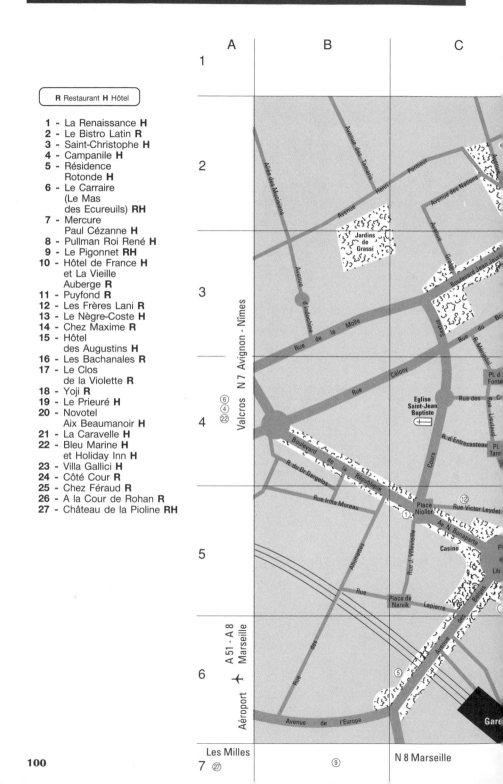

Château de la Pioline
Quartier de la Pioline, 13290 Les Milles
42 20 07 81, fax 42 59 96 12
Open daily until 9:30pm. Priv. rm: 300. Garden dining. Air cond. Pool. V, AE, MC. **A7-27**
Encroaching warehouses don't exactly add to the charm of this beautifully restored *bastide* surrounded by a huge park, but neither do they cancel out its stately dignity. Smoothly professional staff glide about the dining room, delivering distinguished cuisine with pleasing Provençal overtones. Chef Jean-Marie Merly marries flavors exceedingly well in cuisine that this year has been appealingly simplified: a delicious caillette of young rabbit, sea scallops meunière (a bit too much sauce for our taste, though), and a perfectly cooked partridge stuffed with foie gras. Superb wine list, stylish welcome, and efficient service. **C** 370-440 F. **M** 160 F (weekdays), 215 F (exc Sun), 250 F (Sun), 340 F.

Château de la Pioline
(See restaurant above)
Open year-round. 3 stes 1,100-1,600 F. 18 rms 750-1,200 F. Rms for disabled. Half-board 1,030-1,530 F. Air cond. Conf. Pool. Golf. Pkg. Helipad. V, AE, MC.
The luxurious guest rooms are faultlessly appointed and decorated with restrained elegance; all have pleasant views, either of the courtyard and fountain or the formal gardens. Splendid breakfasts.

Le Clos de la Violette
10, av. de la Violette
42 23 30 71, fax 42 21 93 03
Closed Mon lunch, Sun. Open until 9:30pm. Garden dining. Air cond. No pets. V, AE, MC. **C2-17**
Though his restaurant is discreetly tucked away in a residential area, Jean-Marc Banzo, the *patron* of Le Clos de la Violette, is no shrinking violet. His sun-drenched, inventive cooking sings of Provence, with all its barely civilized, sensual flavors. And lately, Banzo's repertoire has attained an exceptional degree of balance and grace, evident in the complex harmony of a green asparagus tart with grilled walnut cream, fresh sardines à la brandade, sea scallops and artichoke hearts in barigoule sauce, black truffle and beef marrow on toast, and fantastic lamb's foot with sage-scented polenta. Dessert brings such subtle pleasures as a warm chocolate tart. The cellar is well stocked along regional lines, with lots of Côtes-du-Rhône and Aix wines. The 195 F menu offers rousing good value (and it changes daily). Brigitte Banzo directs the smooth, professional service. **C** 400-550 F. **M** 195 F (lunch), 330 F, 450 F.

Côté Cour
19, cours Mirabeau
42 26 32 39, fax 42 26 61 07
Closed Sun dinner, Mon, Jun 5-13, Nov 6-14. Open until 11pm. Garden dining. V, AE, DC, MC. **D5-24**
The local smart set has staked out its turf at this chic dining establishment, which occupies an eighteenth-century town house. Happily, though, there is nothing trendy or snobbish about the generous, forthright cuisine, which we awarded an extra point this year. We relished the artichokes with olive oil and coriander, skate with capers and brown butter, and a luscious

chocolate mousse. Limited wine list. **C** 200-270 F.

12/20 A La Cour de Rohan
Pl. de l'Hôtel-de-Ville - 42 96 18 15
Closed dinner off-seas (exc Fri & Sat). Open until 11:30pm (2am during the Festival). Priv rm: 30. Terrace dining. V, MC. **D4-26**
With its subtle Provençal decor, simple but satisfying cuisine, and warm welcome—not to mention "theme" evenings and recitals of classical music—it's no wonder the locals flock here. Try the breakfasts, afternoon teas, and fresh meals with a focus on salads, carpaccios, cold cuts and vegetables, and yummy homestyle desserts. Service is slow, though. **C** 200-300 F.

12/20 Café Féraud
8, rue du Puits-Juif - 42 63 07 27
Closed Sun, Mon lunch, Aug. Open until 10:30pm. Terrace dining. Air cond. Pkg. V, AE, MC. **D4-25**
The locals quickly discovered this recently renovated old house with its simple but refined Provençal decor. The cooking sings of the region: pistou soup and succulent daube in white wine with polenta are good bets, but the desserts are innocuous. Good wine by the carafe. Family-style welcome and fast service. **C** 160-200 F. **M** 98 F, 120 F.

Hôtel de France
63, rue Espariat
42 27 90 15, fax 42 26 11 47
Open year-round. 27 rms 200-350 F. Rms for disabled. Conf. V, AE, MC. **D5-10**
This completely refurbished hotel is just a skip and a jump from the Place des Augustins. Rooms are pleasant and well equipped.

Les Frères Lani
L'Aix-Quis, 22, rue V.-Leydet
42 27 76 16, fax 42 22 68 67
Closed Sun (exc hols lunch), Mon lunch, 1st wk of Jan, Aug 1-15. Open until 10:30pm. Air cond. V, AE, MC. **C5-12**
Behind a plain façade hides a pastel decor set off with wrought-ironwork by a master smith. Joël Lani has constructed a clever menu based on top-notch ingredients. On the 185 F set menu: veal sweetbreads with mushroom jus, sautéed green asparagus, duck breast with curry paired with excellent vegetables, an adequate cheese selection, and a nice crème brûlée with pears. Friendly welcome; rather scattered service. Attractive, accessible cellar. **C** 320-470 F. **M** 95 F, 135 F (lunch exc Sun), 185 F, 245 F, 310 F.

Holiday Inn
5-7, route de Galice
42 59 96 61, fax 42 59 96 61
Open year-round. 4 stes. 90 rms 435 F. Rms for disabled. Restaurant. Air cond. Conf. Pool. Golf. Garage pkg. V, AE, DC, MC. **A4-22**
A functional member of the famous chain, offering well equipped, air-conditioned rooms not far from the city center. Non-smoking rooms available. Pool with a snack bar. Professional service (including room service).

11/20 Chez Maxime
12, pl. Ramus
42 26 28 51, fax 42 26 74 70

Closed Mon lunch, Sun, Jan 15-31. Terrace dining. Air cond. No pets. V. **D4-14**
An extra-warm welcome and excellent meat dishes draw a jostling crowd of locals to the banquettes of this engaging bistrot: fish terrine, rack of lamb with garlic, duck breast in puff pastry, and pears with caramel sauce. Opulent wine list. **C** 200-280 F. **M** 73 F, 90 F (lunch), 120 F, 160 F.

Mercure Paul-Cézanne
40, av. V.-Hugo
42 26 34 73, fax 42 27 20 95
Open year-round. 1 ste 1,000-1,500 F. 54 rms 350-680 F. Air cond. V, AE, DC, MC. **C6-7**
A remarkable little hotel near the famous fountain with pretty rooms (furnished with antiques), all of them bright and airy. Adequate service and breakfasts. A practical stopover.

Le Nègre-Coste
33, cours Mirabeau
42 27 74 22, fax 42 26 80 93
Open year-round. 1 ste 700-770 F. 37 rms 350-650 F. Air cond. Conf. Golf. Garage pkg. V, AE, DC, MC. **D5-13**
The oldest (eighteenth century) of Aix's historic hotels in the town center. All the rooms have been tastefully modernized and soundproofed. Nicely furnished, with a wonderful old-fashioned elavator and a garage service.

Novotel Beaumanoir
Résidence Beaumanoir
42 27 47 50, fax 42 38 46 41
Open year-round. 102 rms 395 F. Restaurant. Air cond. Heated pool. Golf. Pkg. V, AE, DC. **G7-20**
The hotel is near the superhighway, about five kilometers from the city center. It has all the advantages of the chain: modern, airy, and regularly refurbished rooms. Golf practice green. Bar.

Le Pigonnet
5, av. du Pigonnet
42 59 02 90, fax 42 59 47 77
Closed lunch Sat & Sun (exc Jul). Open until 9:30pm. Priv rm: 20. Garden dining. Heated pool. Garage pkg. V, AE, DC, MC. **B7-9**
Chestnut trees surround this stately old dwelling not far from the station. Like the decor, the food here is soothing but never banal. Close attention to cooking times, to vegetable garnishes, and to desserts (some are truly superb) raises the classic cuisine a cut above the ordinary. Note the wealth of reasonably priced half-bottles on the wine list. Solicitous service; high prices. **C** 400-500 F. **M** 250 F, 320 F.

Le Pigonnet
(See restaurant above)
Open year-round. 52 rms 450-1,250 F. Half-board 685-1,035 F. Air cond. Conf. Heated pool. Golf. Garage pkg. V, AE, DC, MC.
A charming Provençal house right in the town center but in an agreeably leafy setting. There's a splendid, shaded terrace and a flower-filled garden. Pleasing, up-to-date rooms.

Looking for a city in a département? Refer to the **index.**

Le Prieuré
Route des Alpes, towards Sisteron
42 21 05 23
Open year-round. 23 rms 185-410 F. No pets. Garage pkg. V, MC. **F1-19**
This exquisitely comfortable, handsomely decorated seventeenth-century hotel was once a priory. Admirably situated opposite Lenfant park, which boasts gardens designed by Le Nôtre. Solarium.

Pullman Roi-René
24, bd du Roi-René
42 37 61 00, fax 42 37 61 11
Open year-round. 3 stes 1,000-1,400 F. 131 rms 640-1,000 F. Restaurant. Half-board 595-1,040 F. Air cond. Conf. Valet pkg. V, AE, DC, MC. **D6-8**
A huge modern hotel with Provençal touches, right in the center of town, offering spacious, comfortable rooms, a garden, and friendly staff. Lovely swimming pool.

12/20 Puyfond
7 km N on N 96 & D 13, Rte de St-Canadet
42 92 13 77, fax 42 92 03 29
Closed Sun dinner, Jan 2-9, Feb 22-Mar 8, Aug 16-Sep 6. Open until 10pm. Priv rm: 50. Garden dining. Pkg. V. **F1-11**
Anne Carbonel's cooking disappointed us on our last visit and lost her her toque: smoked boar in a well seasoned salad that nevertheless lacked finesse, badly cooked mullet with mediocre vegetables, too much Jurançon in the sabayon sauce over apples. **C** 250-320 F. **M** 130 F & 160 F (exc Sun), 190 F (Sun).

La Renaissance
4, bd de la République
42 26 04 22, fax 42 27 28 76
Open year-round. 34 rms 230-330 F. Conf. V, AE, DC, MC. **C5-1**
Well-equipped rooms in an old, recently refurbished house which once belonged to the composer Darius Milhaud.

Résidence Rotonde
15, av. des Belges
42 26 29 88, fax 42 38 66 98
Closed Dec. 42 rms 190-380 F. Pkg. V, AE, MC. **C6-5**
A modern, functional, and central address with excellent bathrooms. The front rooms are efficiently soundproofed.

Saint-Christophe
2, av. V.-Hugo
42 26 01 24, fax 42 38 53 17
Open year-round. 57 rms 310-510 F. Restaurant. Half-board 470-510 F. Air cond. Pkg. V, MC. **C5-3**
The hotel is near the Cours Mirabeau, Aix's main axis, and the imposing Rotonde fountain. Rooms are simply decorated but well appointed. Some have a small terrace.

Villa Gallici
Av. de la Violette.
42 23 29 23, fax 42 96 30 45
Open year-round. 2 stes 1,750-1,950 F. 15 rms 850-1,750 F. Restaurant. Half-board 850-1,350 F. Air cond. Pool. Golf. Valet pkg. V, AE, DC, MC. **C2-23**
Set in a landscaped garden of over two acres dotted with olive trees, oleanders, and cypresses, this exquisite Provençal *bastide* is a highly polished jewel of a hotel. Gilles Dez decorated the interior with verve and style in a manner

inspired by the eighteenth century. The rooms are done up with ravishing fabrics and furniture; the bathrooms are dreamy. In fine weather, a lunch buffet is served poolside.

10/20 Yoji
7, av. Victor-Hugo - 42 38 48 76
Open daily until 11pm. Terrace dining. Air cond. No pets. V, AE, MC. **D5-18**
A good Japanese restaurant complete with tree-shaded terrace. Korean-style fondue and Japanese classics in a Zen decor. The wine list is a total loss. **C** 200-250 F. **M** 56 F, 88 F (exc dinner), 117 F, 167 F, 197 F.

And also...
Our selection of places for inexpensive, quick, or late-night meals.
Le Dernier Bistrot (42 21 13 02 - 19, rue Constantin. Open until 11:30pm.): Honest-to-goodness Provençal family cooking served in a friendly atmosphere (65-125 F).
Les Deux Garçons (42 26 00 51 - 53, cours Mirabeau. Open until midnight.): A brasserie once favored by Camus and Cendrars. Beef with morels, rollmops, smoked salmon and similar uncomplicated fare (120-200 F).
Le Petit Verdot (42 27 30 12 - 7, rue d'Entrecasteaux. Open until 10:30pm.): A welcoming wine bar serving bistrot dishes and meats cooked on the "hot stone" (200-220 F).
Simple Simon (42 96 29 20 - 7, rue Mignet. Open until 7pm, 11pm in summer.): In the center of town, a Very British spot where nice ladies serve fresh salads, seafood pie, and raspberry crumble with vanilla ice cream (150 F).
Trattoria Chez Antoine (42 38 27 10. - 3, rue Clemenceau. Open until 12:30am.): Mediterranean specialties are featured, in a jolly, convivial ambience (90-150 F).

■ In Beaurecueil 13100
10 km E on N 7

Mas de la Bertrande
Chemin de la Plaine
42 66 90 09, fax 42 66 82 01
Closed Feb school hols. 10 rms 350-550 F. Restaurant. Half-board 595-795 F. Conf. Pool. Golf. Pkg. Helipad. V, AE, DC, MC.
Charming hotel with a large garden; the rooms are cool and quiet, and the service is friendly.

Relais Sainte-Victoire
42 66 94 98, fax 42 86 85 96
Closed Sun dinner, Mon, 1st wk of Jan, Feb & Nov school hols. Open until 9pm. Priv rm: 15. Terrace dining. Air cond. Pool. Pkg. V, AE, DC.
René Bergès produces the sort of food that charms the palate and warms the heart. His family's lovely inn in the heart of Cézanne country is constantly filled with happy customers enjoying René's lively repertoire of regional dishes crafted with a generous, personal touch. Try the smoked salmon with scrambled eggs, fillet of beef with tapenade butter, and a crispy grapefruit gratin with fresh fruit mousse. The 250 F menu is a bargain. The large cellar reflects the preferences of a knowledgeable wine lover, the welcome is wonderful, and prices absolutely justified. **C** 280-350 F. **M** 175 F (weekdays), 225 F, 295 F, 420 F.

Relais Sainte-Victoire
(See restaurant above)
See restaurant for closings. 10 rms 400-700 F. Half-board 450-600 F. Air cond. Conf. Pool. Golf. Pkg. V, AE, DC.
At the foot of the Mont Sainte-Victoire—so often painted by Cézanne—the two biggest airy rooms of this hotel are pleasantly decorated and comfortable; the others less so. There's a broad terrace for sun-lit breakfasts.

■ In Bouc-Bel-Air 13320
10 km S on N 8 and D 59

L'Étape Lani
D 6, exit Gardanne on A 51
42 22 61 90, fax 42 22 68 67
Closed Sun dinner, Mon (exc reserv), Aug 15-31, Dec 23-31. Open until 9:30pm. Priv rm: 60. Air cond. Pool. Pkg. V, AE, DC, MC.
The superhighway setting might induce you to pass by, but luckily there's a pastoral flipside of pines and cypress trees to this extremely well maintained little hotel. The entire Lani family lavishes their attentions on you, making this a memorable stopover indeed. Lucien, chef and shining son, offers a "mosaic" of artichokes, asparagus, and salmon; farm-raised squab with spelt tian; and a melon and dark chocolate puff pastry. Excellent wine list. **C** 320-460 F. **M** 135 F, 185 F, 245 F.

■ In Le Canet 13590
8 km SE on N 7

Auberge Provençale
On N 7 - 42 58 68 54, fax 42 58 68 05
Closed Tue dinner & Wed off-seas, Feb school hols. Open until 10pm. Priv rm: 25. Terrace dining. Conf. Pkg. V, AE, DC, MC.
More Provençal than chef Gabriel Astouric you almost could not get. Come here for a taste of the southern sun: foie gras with olives and tapenade, savory monkfish with pistachios cooked in caul fat, delicious caramelized pears in puff pastry. One extra point this year, and kudos for the regional authenticity. Diverse wine list; friendly welcome in a pretty dining room with Provençal decor. **C** 320-360 F. **M** 100 F (weekday lunch), 120 F, 180 F, 230 F.

■ In Châteauneuf-le-Rouge 13790
11 km SE on N 7

La Galinière
On N 7 - 42 53 32 55, fax 42 53 33 80
Open year-round. 4 stes 395-450 F. 13 rms 265-295 F. Restaurant. Half-board 330-450 F. Conf. Heated pool. Golf. Pkg. Helipad. V, AE, DC, MC.
The thick stone walls of this former coach inn keep the clatter and noise of the N7 highway out of your well-appointed room (some of them, however, are definitely on the small side). Modern bathrooms. There is a riding school on the premises.

Gault Millau's ratings *are based solely on the restaurants' cuisine. We do not take into account the atmosphere, decor, service, and so on; these are commented upon within the review.*

■ **In Tholonet 13100**   5 km SE on N 7

12/20 La Petite Auberge
Route de Langesse Campagne Régis
42 66 84 24, fax 42 66 91 19
Closed Sun dinner, Mon. Open until 9:30pm. Priv rm: 100. Terrace dining. Pkg. V, MC.
   An ancient farmhouse on top of a pine-covered hill, where traditional regional treats like smoked salmon bavarian and pieds-et-paquets (a local lamb dish) are offered along with a friendly welcome and a diverse wine list. Good service. **C** 250-400 F. **M** 100 F, 160 F, 250 F.

AIX-LES-BAINS   73100
Paris 536 - Annecy 33 - Chambéry 14 - Lyon 112   *Savoie*

Adelphia
⒔   215, bd Barnier
79 88 72 72, fax 79 88 27 77
Open daily until 10pm. Terrace dining. Air cond. Heated pool. Pkg. V, AE, DC, MC.
   This brand-new hotel facing the lake has a futuristic dining room with a lovely terrace. Excellent products are treated seriously by the kitchen. Try the set menu with a salad bar, trout with almons, and an excellent apple tart. Good wine list with many half bottles at low prices. Courteous welcome, professional service. **C** 200-250 F. **M** 100 F, 150 F, 180 F, 300 F.

Adelphia
(See restaurant above)
Open year-round. 11 stes 450-700 F. Rms 350-550 F. Rms for disabled. Half-board 295-540 F. Air cond. Conf. Golf. Valet pkg. V, AE, DC, MC.
   Near the thermal baths and facing the lake, huge, comfortable, air-conditioned, well maintained rooms. Good breakfasts.

12/20 Le Dauphinois
14, av. de Tresserve
79 61 22 56, fax 79 34 04 62
Closed Dec 15-Feb 15. Open until 9pm. Priv rm: 60. Terrace dining. No pets. Pkg. V, AE, DC, MC.
   This is a large, traditional hotel with a peaceful dining room leading to a pretty garden for summer eating. Prices are reasonable and the repertoire dependable: Savoie hams, lake fish, and fine meat dishes. The 135 F set meal is a treat; to wash it down, order one of the fine, moderately priced local wines. **C** 200-280 F. **M** 105 F (Sun lunch), 95 F, 135 F, 165 F.

Le Grand Café Adélaïde
⒔   Av. de Marlioz
79 88 08 00, fax 79 88 87 46
Open daily until 10pm. Priv rm: 400. Terrace dining. Air cond. Heated pool. Pkg. V, AE, DC, MC.
   The new chef, Bruno Lechêne, regales the chic set with mussels in white wine, breast of roast duck, pickerel cassoulet, chicken fricassée with Beaufort cheese, and a delicate apple tart with apricot sauce. **C** 250-300 F. **M** 85 F, 120 F.

Ariana
(See restaurant above)
Open year-round. 60 rms 380-550 F. Half-board 400 F. Air cond. Conf. Heated pool. Golf. Pkg. Helipad. V, AE, DC, MC.
   Somewhat small, very comfy rooms with individual terraces overlooking the grounds. All

were renovated in 1993. There are remarkable leisure facilities (two indoor pools), and a covered gallery leading to the spa.

12/20 Lille
Le Grand Port
79 63 40 00, fax 79 34 00 30
Closed Wed, Jan 2-Feb 5. Open until 9:30pm. Garden dining. Hotel: 18 rms 250-350 F. Half-board 410 F. Air cond. Conf. Golf. Pkg. V, AE, DC, MC.
   Four generations of the Lille family have given their all to make this lakeside hostelry a plush haven of (rather staid) comfort. The service is precise and the cooking harks back to yesteryear. Expect to spend a tidy sum for your dinner. **C** 250-400 F. **M** 145 F, 255 F, 350 F (exc Sun lunch), 260 F, 360 F (Sun lunch).

12/20 Le Manoir
Behind the spa, 37, rue George-Ier
79 61 44 00, fax 79 35 67 67
Closed Dec 18-Jan 9. Open until 9:30pm. Terrace dining. Heated pool. Pkg. V, AE, DC, MC.
   The outbuildings of two hotels were merged to create this luxurious establishment set amid flower-filled gardens. The decor is warm, the reception and service professional, and the food is of the satisfying, unpretentious variety. Good little cellar, manageably priced. **C** 230-330 F. **M** 138 F, 185 F, 250 F.

Le Manoir
(See restaurant above)
Closed Dec 18-Jan 9. 73 rms 295-495 F. Half-board 325-455 F. Conf. Heated pool. Pkg. V, AE, DC, MC.
   The lovely, recently refurbished rooms are spacious and quiet, with garden views. A friendly, well-run establishment.

Park Hôtel
Av. Charles-de-Gaulle
79 34 19 19, fax 79 88 11 49
Open year-round. 10 stes. 92 rms 420-850 F. Rms for disabled. Restaurant. Half-board 460-755 F. Air cond. Conf. Heated pool. Golf. Pkg. V, AE, DC, MC.
   Brand-new and set in the casino's quiet, green grounds. Spacious, well-equipped rooms. Extremely professional service and very warm welcome. It all adds up to good value for your money. Buffet breakfast. A simple brasserie is on the premises. A fitness center is set to open this year. The new Loges du Parc nearby offers rooms with kitchenettes for long-term stays (tel. 79 35 74 74.).

Pavillon Rivollier
33, bd Wilson
79 88 12 08, fax 79 34 17 22
Closed Oct 15-Easter. 44 rms 160-320 F. Restaurant. Half-board 290-345 F. Air cond. Pkg. V, AE, DC, MC.
   The Pavillon Rivollier moved to this address not long ago: a turn-of-the-century dwelling not far from the casino. All the guest rooms have been refurbished, and the restaurant overlooks the pretty garden. Transport to the spa is free.

AJACCIO 20   → CORSICA

Restaurant names in red draw attention to restaurants that offer particularly good value.

Paris 592 - Chambéry 50 - Annecy 45 - Grenoble 86 *Savoie*

Éric Guillot
Chez Uginet, pont des Adoubes
79 32 00 50, fax 79 31 21 41
Closed Tue dinner, Wed, Jun 25-Jul 5, Nov 12-Dec 5. Open until 9:30pm. Priv rm: 20. Terrace dining. Pkg. V, AE, DC, MC.
Enjoy Éric Guillot's value-packed set meals, which feature (among other good dishes) lamb with mushrooms and Jerusalem artichokes, stuffed farm-raised chicken with Beaufort cheese, lavaret (a salmon-like lake fish) with meat jus and caraway seeds, and a banana and almond gratin. At the same address: the Bouchon des Adoubes, a bistro-style eatery offering 45 F *plats du jour* and a selection of hearty dishes rooted in the region. C 250-360 F. M 115 F (exc Sun), 160 F, 195 F, 295 F, 340 F.

Million
8, pl. de la Liberté
79 32 25 15, fax 79 32 25 36
Closed Sun dinner, Mon, Apr 29-May 10. Open until 9:30pm. Priv rm: 40. Garden dining. Air cond. Pkg. V, AE, DC, MC.
Philippe Million dominates the gastronomic scene of Albertville in his town-center restaurant with its pleasant terrace and pink dining rooms. The chef takes his inspiration from the repertoire of Édouard Hélouis, a cook at the court of Savoie in the nineteenth century, but his personal interpretation is natural, straightforward, and most attractive: saddle of young rabbit with chutney, veal tail and kidneys with spinach and celery root, and a biscuit de Savoie for dessert. C 400-575 F. M 150 F (coffee & wine incl), 180 F, 280 F, 500 F.

Million
(See restaurant above)
Closed Apr 29-May 10. 28 rms 300-550 F. Half-board 400-500 F. Air cond. Conf. Golf. Pkg. V, AE, DC, MC.
A convenient stopover on the way to the area's ski resorts, this hotel, with its comfortable, nicely appointed rooms, is the perfect place to bed down after a feast at the adjoining restaurant.

Le Roma
Chemin du Pont Albertin
79 37 15 56, fax 79 37 01 31
Open year-round. 10 stes 700 F. 136 rms 260-500 F. Rms for disabled. Restaurant. Half-board 300-400 F. Air cond. Heated pool. Tennis. Pkg. V, AE, DC, MC.
On the way to the Tarentaise and Maurienne ski resorts, this hotel has huge, functional, comfortable rooms and excellent facilities. There is a heliport in the grounds.

Paris 677 - Carcassonne 107 - Rodez 79 - Toulouse 76 *Tarn*

Hôtel Chiffre
50, rue Séré-de-Rivières
63 54 04 60, fax 63 47 20 61
Open year-round. 40 rms 280-470 F. Restaurant. Air cond. Conf. Golf. Pkg. V, AE, DC, MC.
Centrally located, this good family-style hotel features recently renovated, well-kept rooms that look out onto a garden-patio.

12/20 Hostellerie du Vigan
16, pl. du Vigan
63 54 01 23, fax 63 47 05 42
Open daily until 9:30pm (10pm in summer). Terrace dining. Pkg. V, AE, DC, MC.
Ensconced on the terrace with a fine view of the square below, sample Francis Combes's carefully crafted cuisine. Choose from hearty bourgeois dishes like crab and zucchini crêpes, sautéed sole fillets, duck confit, and a terrine of tropical fruits. C 200-300 F. M 90 F, 125 F, 170 F, 220 F.

Hostellerie du Vigan
(See restaurant above)
Open year-round. 40 rms 290-350 F. Rms for disabled. Half-board 240-350 F. Conf. Pkg. V, AE.
Rooms here are well maintained and regularly renovated, with fine facilities. The service is exceptionally attentive.

12/20 Hostellerie Saint-Antoine
17, rue St-Antoine
63 54 04 04, fax 63 47 10 47
Closed Sun (exc dinner in seas), Sat lunch. Open until 10pm. Air cond. Pool. Valet pkg. V, AE, DC, MC.
The Rieux family has lived within the walls of this ancient hostelry for 250 years; tradition, for them, is bred in the bone. The culinary know-how handed down from father to son is reflected in the veal terrine with foie gras, fish fillets with olives, and the chocolate and coffee truffier. The local wines of Gaillac get top billing in the limited cellar. You can count on a cordial welcome. C 230-380 F. M 150 F.

Hostellerie Saint-Antoine
(See restaurant above)
Open year-round. 8 stes 750-950 F. 42 rms 360-850 F. Half-board 450-850 F. Air cond. Conf. Pool. Tennis. Valet pkg. V, AE, DC, MC.
This centrally located, quiet, and very comfortable hotel features elegant rooms and a pleasant walled garden. Other noteworthy amenities are the good breakfasts, and (though they are three kilometers away) a swimming pool and tennis courts.

Le Jardin des Quatre Saisons
19, bd de Strasbourg
63 60 77 76, fax 63 60 77 76
Closed Mon (exc hols). Open until 10:15pm. Priv rm: 40. Terrace dining. Air cond. Pkg. V, AE, MC.
Martine Bermond welcomes guests into an attractive decor bright with flowers, arbors, and delicate china, while her husband, Georges, prepares spirited dishes in tune with the seasons. This year we enjoyed his pig's foot with snails, roast pickerel with mushrooms, and a warm chocolate cake with vanilla cream sauce. Their magnificent wine cellar is constantly replenished. C 180-250 F. M 150 F (wine incl), 130 F.

Mercure
41 bis, rue Porta
63 47 66 66, fax 63 46 18 40
Open year-round. 56 rms 320-500 F. Rms for disabled. Restaurant. Air cond. Conf. Golf. Pkg. V, AE, DC, MC.
A converted factory with an attractive brick façade on the edge of the Tarn has been con-

verted into a charming modern hotel. The rooms are adequately comfortable, although the bathrooms could use a facelift. Generous full breakfasts, and, best of all, a superb view of the river and town.

 Moulin de Lamothe ☺
Rue de Lamothe
63 60 38 15, fax 63 47 68 84
Closed Sun dinner off-seas, Wed (exc Jul-Aug), Feb & Nov school hols. Open until 9:30pm. Priv rm: 50. Garden dining. Air cond. Pkg. V, AE, MC.
Set by the River Tarn in lovely green grounds, the Moulin boasts a tastefully furnished dining room and terrace. Chef Michel Pellaprat, a connoisseur of the region's traditional dishes, uses the best local produce to prepare his pumpkin and pig's ear terrine, pickerel à la brandade béarnaise, and a chicory and almond pastry for dessert. Good wines at unbeatable prices; affable reception. **C** 240-340 F. **M** 140 F, 180 F, 250 F.

Pujol
22, av. du Colonel-Teyssier
63 47 97 19, fax 63 47 06 16
Closed Sun dinner, Aug 1-16. Open until 10pm. Priv rm: 50. Air cond. Garage pkg. V, MC.
Chef Jean-Pierre Emonet holds forth here, serving classic cooking in an elegant dining room filled with mirrors and bouquets of fresh flowers. Try his fresh and harmonious nage of langoustines and herbs, John Dory with beurre blanc, and a Saint Martin cake that needs a bit more chocolate. Regional wines; friendly service. But we have just learned that there may be new management in 1995. **C** 180-270 F. **M** 120 F, 170 F, 200 F.

■ **In Fonvialane 81000**   3 km NW

La Réserve
Route de Cordes
63 47 60 22, fax 63 47 63 60
Closed Nov-Apr. Open until 10pm. Priv rm: 200. Terrace dining. Air cond. Pool. Garage pkg. V, AE, DC, MC.
Chef Jean-François Rieux is a master at blending traditional and creative cuisines. In his riverside restaurant which overlooks a pool and a park, guests are treated to foie gras terrine and vegetables à la nage in a Port gelatin (very well prepared), perfectly cooked gigotin of lamb with a tasty goat cheese tourte, and successful fruit eggs rolls with almond cream and vanilla ice cream. The cellar harbors a wealth of fine Bordeaux at reasonable prices. Smiling welcome and service. **C** 300-450 F. **M** 95 F, 125 F (poolside lunch in summer), 160 F, 300 F.

La Réserve
(See restaurant above)
Closed Nov-Apr. 4 stes 850-1,000 F. 20 rms 490-950 F. Half-board 650-900 F. Air cond. Conf. Pool. Tennis. Golf. Garage pkg. Helipad. V, AE, DC, MC.
A haven of tranquility on the banks of the Tarn, La Réserve offers variously decorated, comfortable rooms with river views. Fine service. The bathroom fittings seem a bit dated, and the rooms above the kitchen are imperfectly soundproofed. Guests have use of pedal-boats, canoes, and bicycles. Relais et Châteaux.

ALENÇON   **61000**
Paris 195 - Rouen 145 - Le Mans 49 - Chartres 116   *Orne*

Le Chapeau Rouge
1, bd Duchamp
33 26 20 23, fax 33 26 54 05
Open year-round. 16 rms 160-270 F. Pkg. V, AE, MC.
Located away from the town center, this hotel offers dainty rooms with personalized decor.

Au Petit Vatel
72, pl. du Cdt-Desmeulles
33 26 23 78
Closed Sun dinner, Wed, Feb school hols, Aug 1-23. Open until 9:30pm. Priv rm: 16. Pkg. V, AE, DC, MC.
We know regulars who flock to this Alençon institution just to feast on the fabulous homemade ice creams and sherbets. They would be well advised to try Michel Lerat's fine cooking first, though, such as the 158 F menu: délice of Ecouves cèpes, salmon grilled with sea salt, cheeses, and desserts (a fabulous choice of ice creams and sherbets). Friendly welcome; spacious and sunny dining room. **C** 290-340 F. **M** 118 F, 158 F, 198 F, 238 F.

ALÈS   **30100**
Paris 709 - Albi 230 - Avignon 71 - Nîmes 44   *Gard*

A l'Auberge Cévenole
15 km N on N 106 & D 283, 30110 La Favède - 66 34 12 13, fax 66 34 50 50
Closed Oct 4-Mar. 2 stes 500-600 F. 19 rms 270-550 F. Restaurant. Half-board 320-485 F. Pool. Tennis. Pkg. V.
The hotel offers large, comfortable rooms in a cool, peaceful valley setting. Delightfully designed garden.

■ **In Méjannes-lès-Alès 30340**   8 km SE

Auberge des Voutins
Route d'Uzès - 66 61 38 03
Closed Sun dinner & Mon (exc hols). Annual closings not available. Open until 9:30pm. Priv rm: 20. Garden dining. Pkg. V, AE, DC, MC.
Housed in a pleasant dwelling surrounded by fields and orchards, René Turonnet's cozy little restaurant offers guests vibrant dishes that sometimes fall short in technique. On the first menu this year, we sampled a rather boring melon with duck "ham" and a walnut wine sabayon, a pleasant pan-roasted leg of lamb with sweet curry, poorly aged Cévenol goat cheeses, and an assortment of good and generous desserts. The wine list is mediocre and poor in regional offerings. A point less, in spite of the patronne's smile. The dining room has rustic decor and opens onto a garden terrace. **C** 280-390 F. **M** 150 F, 190 F, 250 F, 320 F.

■ **In Ribaute-les-Tavernes 30720**   10 km S

Château de Ribaute
66 83 01 66
Open year-round. 1 ste 600 F. 5 rms 350-500 F. Half-board 150-200 F. Pool. Tennis. Golf. Pkg. V, MC.
The Chamski's magnificent, listed dwelling features a half-dozen cozy, antique-filled rooms with every modern convenience. Cordial wel-

come; copious breakfasts. A table d'hôte is available for guests.

ALOXE-CORTON 21 → Beaune

ALPE-D'HUEZ (L') 38750

Paris 625 - Grenoble 63 - Briançon 79 - Bourg-d'Oisans 13   Isère

 Au Chamois d'Or
Route de Fontbelle, rond-point des Pistes
76 80 31 32, fax 76 80 34 90
Closed Apr 20-Dec 16. Open until 9:15pm. Terrace dining. Heated pool. Valet pkg. V, MC.
First-quality foodstuffs go into the classic cooking offered at an inn operated by the Seigle family since 1947: try the fricassée of Oisans snails, Loctudy shellfish, and veal fillet in truffle butter with foie gras. Afternoon tea is also served. The best seats in the house are on the fabulous panoramic terrace. **C** 250-400 F. **M** 135 F, 180 F, 220 F (lunch), 210 F, 260 F (dinner).

Au Chamois d'Or
(See restaurant above)
Closed Apr 20-Dec 16. 3 stes 1,930 F. 42 rms 750-1,180 F. Half-board 660-1,230 F. Conf. Heated pool. Tennis. Valet pkg. V, MC.
This hotel offers recently renovated and elegantly styled rooms with loggias, excellent service, and a wealth of amenities (fitness center, heated swimming pool, hotel shuttle-bus), not the least of which is the wonderfully relaxed atmosphere and homemade pastries served at breakfast.

Le Dôme
Pl. du Cognet
76 80 32 11, fax 76 80 66 48
Closed May-Nov. 3 stes 450-800 F. 17 rms 300-700 F. Restaurant. Half-board 375-660 F. Conf. Heated pool. Golf. Pkg. Helipad. V, AE, DC, MC.
A large and modern chalet next to the slopes, with simply decorated, comfortable rooms facing the Oisans Massif. Family-style atmosphere. One of the resort's most pleasant addresses.

Les Grandes Rousses
76 80 33 11, fax 76 80 69 57
Closed May-Jun 15, Sep 15-Nov 30. 6 stes 700-1,000 F. 42 rms 540-780 F. Rms for disabled. Half-board 560-770 F. Conf. Heated pool. Tennis. Golf. Valet pkg. V, AE, MC.
The managers of this immense chalet at the foot of the slopes are constantly upgrading its comfort. Among the many facilities are a winter garden lounge, fitness center, billiard room, heated pool, and tennis courts (summer only).

 Le Lyonnais
Route du Coulet - 76 80 68 92
Closed May, Jun, Sep-Nov. Open until 9:30pm. Terrace dining. Pkg. V.
This elegant eating house carries Lyons bistro-style cooking to its most refined conclusion, with pike quenelles, chicken in vinegar sauce, and cervelle de canut (fresh cheese with herbs), all much appreciated by the skiers who come here. But don't overlook the foie gras cooked in a cloth and the lobster with fresh pasta. There's an extraordinary list of Beaujolais and Côtes-du-Rhônes. Service is deft and discreet. **C** 220-280 F. **M** 120 F, 160 F, 195 F.

 Le Petit Prince
Route de la Poste
76 80 33 51, fax 71 80 41 45
Closed Apr 2-Dec 21. 40 rms 510-750 F. Restaurant. Half-board 470-640 F. Valet pkg. V, AE, DC, MC.
Most of the hotel's very comfortable and modern rooms face south, allowing guests an exceptional view of the Oisans Massif and valley. The public rooms are delightful, and there is a large, sunny terrace as well. Buffet breakfasts.

Royal Ours Blanc
Av. des Jeux
76 80 35 50, fax 76 80 34 50
Closed Apr-Dec 20. 2 stes 1,900-2,300 F. 45 rms 690-1,300 F. Restaurant. Half-board 745-950 F. Conf. Heated pool. Valet pkg. V, AE, DC.
Considered the resort's most distinguished hotel, the Royal Ours Blanc features luxurious rooms and an outstanding fitness center (gym, sauna, Turkish baths, Jacuzzi). Bar. You can expect a polite welcome.

AMBOISE 37400

Paris 206 - Vendôme 50 - Blois 35 - Tours 25   Indre/Loire

Le Belle-Vue
12, quai Ch.-Quinot
47 57 02 26, fax 47 30 51 23
Closed May-Jun. 33 rms 250-320 F. No pets. V, MC.
Set just at the foot of the famed château on the banks of the Loire, Le Belle-Vue offers appealing, comfortable rooms. Charming reception. There is an annex with additional rooms across the river.

Château de Pray
2 km on D 751
47 57 23 67, fax 47 57 32 50
Closed Jan 2-27. 2 stes 820-870 F. 17 rms 520-720 F. Restaurant. Half-board 765-1,210 F. Conf. Garage pkg. V, AE, DC, MC.
Set on a slope overlooking the Loire, this small Louis XIII château is provided with pleasant, quiet rooms.

 Le Choiseul
36, quai Ch.-Guinot
47 30 45 45, fax 47 30 46 10
Closed Nov 26-Jan 15. Open until 9:30pm. Priv rm: 40. Air cond. Heated pool. Pkg. V, AE, MC.
The main dining room, installed between two eighteenth-century houses, is handsome indeed. But ask instead for a table facing the Italian-style terraced garden (the room is smaller but has more charm). Pascal Bouvier has come into his own in the sunny Touraine region and shines with ingeniously prepared dishes like a fricassée of Loire eels and frog's legs, braised and sautéed veal chop with hearts of radicchio and pears, and a delicate semolina cake with rosemary ice cream. Superb wine list. Competent welcome. **C** 300-420 F. **M** 200 F (lunch exc Sun, wine incl), 220 F, 280 F, 390 F.

Le Choiseul
(See restaurant above)
Closed Nov 26-Jan 15. 4 stes 1,100-1,600 F. 28 rms 540-980 F. Rms for disabled. Half-board 950-2,010 F. Conf. Heated pool. Golf. Pkg. Helipad. V, AE, DC, MC.
For those who revel in luxury and peace, this is the place to be. The hotel offers 32 elegantly furnished, air-conditioned rooms with views of

an Italian Renaissance–style garden. Those on the Quai des Violettes have their own garden. Relais et Châteaux.

Le Lion d'Or

17, quai Ch.-Guinot
47 57 00 23, fax 47 23 22 49
Closed Sun & Mon off-seas, Jan-mid Feb. 1 ste 390 F. 22 rms 177-312 F. Restaurant. Half-board 269-338 F. Golf. Pkg. V, MC.
At the foot of the Renaissance château of Amboise stands this neat and well-equipped little hotel, which brims over with traditional charm.

Le Manoir Saint-Thomas
Pl. Richelieu
47 57 22 52, fax 47 30 44 71
Closed Sun dinner, Mon, Jan 15-Mar 15. Open until 9:30pm. Terrace dining. Pkg. V, AE, DC, MC.
The sumptuous, stately decor of beamed ceilings, stained glass, antique chests, velvet curtains, and rich table settings is as heady as the sensational cellar of Chinons and Vouvrays. The serving staff wears theatrical costumes, but the cooking is honest and devoid of theatrics: terrine of young rabbit with hazelnuts and rosemary, roast sea bass with pepper and cumin, pickerel and salmon duo with sorrel sauce, and a strawberry millefeuille. Fine choice of regional wines. **C** 300-350 F. **M** 165 F (weekdays, Sat lunch), 295 F.

Novotel
17, rue des Sablonnières
47 57 42 07, fax 47 30 40 76
Open year-round. 121 rms 400-560 F. Rms for disabled. Restaurant. Conf. Heated pool. Tennis. Pkg. V, AE, DC.
For calm, comfortable rooms with outstanding views of the Loire and the château. Bar.

■ **In St-Ouen-les-Vignes 37530** 7 km NW

L'Aubinière
Rue J.-Gauthier
47 30 15 29, fax 47 30 02 44
Closed Tue dinner, Wed, Feb school hols. Priv rm: 18. Terrace dining. No pets. Pkg. V, AE, MC.
The new young owners started out on a shoestring, but the dining room decor has been improved this year by the addition of a garden terrace, and the cooking is serious and carefully prepared by Jacques Arrayet: snails and mushrooms with an herb coulis, fillet of beef in Chinon wine sauce, chard fondue with garlic cream, and a vanilla rice pudding with a fruit salad. Charming welcome and service. **C** 300-400 F. **M** 98 F (weekdays), 180 F, 260 F, 340 F.

AMBONNAY 51150
Paris 170 - Reims 29 - Epernay 19 - Châlons-sur-Marne 22 *Marne*

Auberge Saint-Vincent
Rue St-Vincent
26 57 01 98, fax 26 57 81 48
Closed Sun dinner, Mon. Open until 9pm. Priv rm: 50. Hotel: 10 rms 300-370 F. Half-board 395-460 F. No pets. Pkg. V, AE, DC, MC.
While Anne-Marie Pelletier ushers guests into a cozy dining room with Louis XIII ceilings and displays of antique china, her husband Jean-Claude keeps busy in the kitchen dreaming up inventive ways to put fine regional ingredients to good use, as in his carp fillet with almonds, guinea fowl salmis, fricandelle à la troyenne (a type of pâté), Maroilles cheese in puff pastry, and a charlotte aux biscuits roses. Fine selection of wines and Champagnes. **C** 280-450 F. **M** 160 F 200 F, 300 F.

AMÉLIE-LES-BAINS 66110
Paris 950 - Prades 60 - Perpignan 37 - Céret 8 *Pyrénées-O.*

Castel Émeraude
La Petite-Provence
68 39 02 83, fax 68 39 03 09
Closed Dec-Jan. 59 rms 240-360 F. Rms for disabled. Restaurant. Half-board 275-325 F. Golf. Pkg. V, AE.
A lovely hotel set in a park alongside the river, with comfortable, quiet rooms. The numerous amenities include terraces, beaches, and a sports center (swimming pool, tennis) all within easy reach.

Grand Hôtel Reine Amélie
Route de la Petite-Provence
68 39 04 38, fax 68 39 13 31
Open year-round. 69 rms 325-420 F. Restaurant. Half-board 367-485 F. Garage pkg. V, AE, DC, MC.
Large, modern, and enveloped in greenery, this hotel is provided with constantly renovated rooms and lounges decorated with rustic Spanish furnishings. Guests enjoy a solarium, and may use the hotel shuttle-bus to the nearby thermal springs.

■ **In Arles-sur-Tech 66150** 4 km SW on D 115

11/20 Les Glycines
Rue du Jeu-de-Paume
68 39 10 09, fax 68 39 83 02
Closed Dec 15-Jan. Open until 9pm. Priv rm: 30. Garden dining. Pkg. V, AE, MC.
In addition to a view of the Canigou Massif from the shady terrace, this reputable restaurant offers diners foie gras terrine, duo of monkfish and salmon with Choron sauce, and Catalan-style crème brûlée. **C** 200-320 F. **M** 75 F, 150 F (weekdays, Sat), 140 F (Sun), 90 F, 200 F.

AMIENS 80000
Paris 135 - Rouen 116 - Lille 115 - St-Quentin 73 *Somme*

Aux As du Don
1-3, pl. du Don
22 92 41 65, fax 22 92 44 64
Closings not available. Open until midnight. Priv rm: 20. Terrace dining. V, AE, DC, MC.
The Aces (Les As) referred to in the name of this, the city's oldest bistro, were champion javelin throwers who celebrated their victories here in the fine eighteenth-century paneled dining room. The simple fare is made from top-quality ingredients: salmon rillettes, mussels à la normande, chicken breast sautéed with Picardy hydromel, and oeufs en neige. **C** 240-300 F. **M** 89 F.

Les Marissons
68, rue des Marissons
22 92 96 66, fax 22 91 50 50
Closed Sat lunch, Sun. Annual closings not available. Open until 10pm. Air cond. Pkg. V, AE, DC, MC.

Les Marissons is housed in a former boat-builder's workshop in the magnificently restored old Saint-Leu quarter, on the site of a fifteenth-century boat-yard by the Somme River. The decor is an elegant blend of yellow and blue tones. But the locals come here to savor Antoine Benoît's cooking, which, when it stays simple, can be very good indeed: slices of chicken breast in tumeric-spiced sauce, fillets of red mullet coated with pistachios, and chaud-froid of pears with almonds. Fine wine list with some wines served by the glass. **C** 300-400 F. **M** 110 F, 135 F, 196 F, 235 F.

Le Postillon
16, pl. au Feurre
22 91 46 17, fax 22 91 86 57
Closed Dec 24-Jan 2. 1 ste 510-660 F. 300-510 F. Rms for disabled. Garage pkg. V, AE, DC.
This small hotel occupies a listed building 300 meters from the cathedral. It offers spacious, nicely fitted rooms at the back, as well as other, more modest accommodation. Pub open until 2am.

10/20 La Soupe à Cailloux
16, rue des Bondes - 22 91 92 70
Closings not available. Open until 10:30pm. Terrace dining. V, AE, DC, MC.
Located in the historic Don quarter of Amiens, this engaging little establishment is simply decorated with a dozen blond-wood tables, and provides decent, wholesome fare. Among the specialties are ficelle picarde (ham and cheese crêpe), pork goulash, monkfish au poivre vert, and a dessert called "Gourmandise de La Soupe". **C** 150-200 F. **M** 65 F (weekday lunch), 90 F.

L'Univers
2, rue de Noyon
22 91 52 51, fax 22 92 81 66
Open year-round. 41 rms 220-435 F. Restaurant. Conf. Golf. V, AE, DC, MC.
This large and comfortable residence, conveniently located between the station and the cathedral, offers attractively furnished rooms and all the usual amenities, including double windows, an elevator, and a minibar.

Le Vivier
593, route de Rouen - 22 89 12 21
Closed Sun, Mon, Jul 25-Aug 23. Open until 10pm. Priv rm: 25. Terrace dining. Pkg. V, AE, MC.
A nautical decor sets the tone for the generous seafood dishes that are the house specialty. Try the raw seafood platter, lobster rillettes, grouper braised with mangoes, and an interesting choice of Alsatian wines. One quibble: the tables are very close together. **C** 270-400 F. **M** 115 F (weekdays), 165 F, 240 F.

And also...
Our selection of places for inexpensive, quick, or late-night meals.
La Dent Creuse (22 80 03 63 - 2, rue Cormont. Open until 11pm.): The superb salads, seafood sauerkraut, and fine pastries served in a relaxed atmosphere attract a young crowd (130-185 F).
Le Saladin (22 92 05 15 - 6, rue des Chaudronniers. Open until 10:30pm.): Various hot and cold salads served in a fantasy-garden decor

(80-120 F).
La Taupinière (22 91 27 83 - 12, rue Cormont. Open 11pm.): Fine grilled foods served in a winsome little spot next to the cathedral (75-160 F).

■ **In Boves 80440**   6 km SE on D 934
Novotel
22 46 22 22, fax 22 53 94 75
Open year-round. 94 rms 395-420 F. Rms for disabled. Restaurant. Conf. Pool. Pkg. V, AE, DC, MC.
A very good hotel enveloped in greenery. Outstanding group facilities; horseback riding; children's playground. Restaurant.

■ **In Dury-lès-Amiens 80480**   5 km S on N 1
L'Aubergade
78, route Nationale
22 89 51 41, fax 22 95 44 05
Closed Sun dinner, Mon, Aug 1-22. Open until 10pm. Priv rm: 20. Pkg. V, AE, MC.
Behind the freshly refurbished façade you'll discover several cozy dining rooms filled with bouquets of fresh flowers, a lovely setting for Régis Grandmougin's professional cooking based on top-quality ingredients. Try his potato charlotte with honey cake and foie gras, smoked brochette with a melon and Port jus paired with bacon-enhanced watercress, and a chocolate croquant with orange ice cream. Fine wine list, competent welcome. **C** 300-450 F. **M** 105 F (exc Sun), 180 F, 230 F, 350 F, 400 F.

La Bonne Auberge
63, route Nationale
22 95 03 33, fax 22 45 37 38
Closed 2 wks in Jun. Open until 10pm. Priv rm: 20. Terrace dining. Air cond. Pkg. V, AE, MC.
Chef Raoul Beaussire's opulent, traditional cuisine (tinged with a regional accent) includes foie gras en brioche, fricassée of young Bresse chicken, and a berry gratin with sherbets. Fine 139 F menu, and a tempting wine list. Charming welcome in a lovely, flower-decked dining room. **C** 300-450 F. **M** 179 F (exc weekday lunch & Sun dinner, wine incl), 139 F, 180 F (exc weekday lunch & Sun dinner), 98 F (weekday dinner, Sat lunch).

Paris 438 - Gérardmer 55 - Saint-Dié 49 - Colmar 8   Haut-Rhin

A l'Arbre Vert
7, rue des Cigognes
89 47 12 23, fax 89 78 27 21
Closed Feb 15-Mar 25, Nov 25-Dec 6. 17 rms 100-350 F. Restaurant. Half-board 260-360 F. Golf. No pets. Pkg. V, AE, DC, MC.
This commodious inn stands before the village fountain; it offers pleasant, unpretentious rooms.

Aux Armes de France
1, Grand-Rue
89 47 10 12, fax 89 47 38 12
Closed Wed, Thu lunch (& dinner Jan-Mar). Open until 9:30pm. Priv rm: 45. Pkg. V, AE, DC, MC.
A new generation of Gaertners is running the show at this eminently traditional Alsatian inn. Philippe and François have kept their father's

far-famed sole fillets with noodles on the menu, but they have added some cleverly retooled versions of regional classics: intensely flavored frog's legs and snails in a lentil cream with parsley jus, a perfectly cooked dish of veal sweetbreads sautéed with truffle sauce and served with a risotto, and succulent raspberry crêpes. Patrons give themselves over to these gastronomic pleasures in a luxurious dining room with wood-panelled ceilings and light-toned wainscotting. Excellent cellar (with many half-bottles); stiff prices. **C** 470-600 F. **M** 360 F, 460 F.

AMOU	40330
Paris 741 - Pau 49 - Dax 31 - Mont-de-Marsan 46	*Landes*

Le Commerce ✿✿
Pl. de la Poste
58 89 02 28, fax 58 89 24 45
Closed Mon off-seas, Feb 15-28, Nov 12-30. Open until 1:30am. Terrace dining. Pkg. V, AE, DC, MC.
Local gourmands flock to this large, convivial restaurant in quest of rigorously prepared regional specialties, like splendid duck breast, fresh liver, dove, and civets. Wash down these earthy delights with sturdy local wines (Tursan and Madiran). Charming and attentive service; bargain prices. **C** 190-270 F. **M** 80 F (exc Sun), 120 F, 160 F, 200 F.

AMPUIS	69420
Paris 495 - Vienne 6 - Condrieu 5 - Lyon 36	*Rhône*

Le Côte-Rôtie
Place de l'Église
74 56 12 05, fax 74 56 00 20
Closed Sep 1-15. Open until 9:30pm. Priv rm: 20. Terrace dining. Pkg. V, MC.
You can't miss this pretty restaurant in the center of the village; behind its blue façade you will find an elegant dining room opening onto a charming garden with a view of the vineyards. And you shouldn't miss Manuel Viron's cuisine. He wowed us this year with inventive dishes like Breton lobster lightly cooked with summer savory and served with coco beans flavored with hazlenut oil, an original rack of lamb cooked rare (a bit too pink) in an herb crust with a black olive "cake", and delicate peaches roasted with thyme, bilberry and verbena jus, served with fruit and ice cream. Friendly welcome by the young patronne. **M** 90 F (weekday lunch), 108 F, 125 F, 160 F, 195 F, 235 F.

ANCENIS	44150
Paris 342 - Angers 53 - Cholet 47 - Nantes 42	*Loire-Atl.*

Terrasses de Bel-Air
Route d'Angers
40 83 02 87, fax 40 83 33 46
Closed Sun dinner, Mon, last wk of Aug. Open until 9:15pm. Priv rm: 30. Garden dining. Pkg. V.
Chef Jean-Paul Gasnier's light, imaginative cuisine and Geneviève Gasnier's graciousness shine as brightly as ever in this attractive restaurant, which boasts a lovely terrace overlooking the Loire. Sample the salmon marinated with melissa, veal sweetbreads in a casserole with orange sauce, and pear puff pastry with maple syrup and quince sherbet. Interesting 150 F menu. And follow Gasnier's excellent advice on which of his fine (and inexpensive) Loire wines

to order with your meal. **C** 220-300 F. **M** 110 F (exc Sun), 150 F, 190 F, 270 F.

Val de Loire
2 km E, Le Jarrier-St-Herblon,
Route d'Angers
40 96 00 03, fax 40 83 17 30
Closed Dec 24-Jan 2. 40 rms 215-300 F. Rms for disabled. Restaurant. Half-board 204-280 F. Conf. Tennis. Pkg. Helipad. C, MC.
A welcoming, recently built hotel surrounded by vineyards and fields. Loire River beaches within easy reach.

ANDELYS (LES)	27700
Paris 92 - Beauvais 63 - Rouen 39 - Evreux 36	*Eure*

La Chaîne d'Or
27, rue Grande
32 54 00 31, fax 32 54 05 68
Closed Sun dinner, Mon, Jan 2-Feb 3, Sep 4-11. Open until 9:30pm. Priv rm: 30. Pkg. V, AE, MC.
This romantic old restaurant overlooking the Seine got a jolt of fresh energy when Francis Chevalliez (ex-Vivarois, ex-Comme Chez Soi) took over the kitchen. Savor the fine first set menu: fresh pasta with tiny squid and shellfish butter, duck jambonnette stuffed with vegetables, well aged cheeses, and a dark and white chocolate cake. **C** 300-400 F. **M** 180 F (weekday lunch, wine incl), 135 F, 220 F, 280 F.

La Chaîne d'Or
(See restaurant above)
Closed Sun & Mon off-seas, Jan. 2 stes 710-740 F. 8 rms 395-540 F. Golf. Pkg. V, AE, MC.
A peaceful, typically Norman inn on the banks of the Seine, with recently renovated soundproof rooms and suites, and thoughtfully appointed bathrooms.

ANDORRA (PRINCIPALITY OF)	
Paris 895 - Toulouse 186 - Perpignan 166 - Foix 103	

■ **In Andorre-la-Vieille**

Andorra Palace
Prat de la Creu
(628) 21 0 72, fax (628) 28 2 45
Open year-round. 20 stes 500-892 F. 96 rms 314-500 F. Restaurant. Half-board 326-370 F. Conf. Heated pool. Tennis. Garage pkg. V, AE, DC, MC.
This is a small luxury hotel that faces the mountains, with comfortable, modern, although rather charmless rooms (minibar/VCR). The outstanding facilities include a sauna and exercise room. Nightclub.

Andorra Park
24, rue Les Canals
(628) 20 9 79, fax (628) 20 9 83
Open daily until 10:45pm. Priv rm: 40. Garden dining. Pkg. Valet pkg. V, AE, DC, MC.
The atmosphere is pleasantly relaxed despite the palatial decor (recently refurbished) and formal service, and there is a delightful garden view. Sample the fresh pasta stuffed with goose liver, red mullet fillets with shallots, beef fillet aux trois saveurs, fritures, and the house flan. The outstanding cellar features wines from Spain and Chile. **C** 300-450 F. **M** 259 F, 340 F.

111

Andorra Park

(See restaurant above)
Open year-round. 40 rms 359-880 F. No pets. Pool.
Tennis. Pkg. V, AE, DC.
This luxurious little hotel tucked into a corner
of a garden in the upper town has been
remodeled from top to bottom; the rooms offer
refined comfort. Slightly cool but thoroughly
professional reception. Marvelous natural swimming pool, tennis, putting and croquet greens.

Eden Roc

1, av. du Dr-Mitjavila
(628) 21 0 00, fax (628) 60 3 19
Open year-round. 1 ste. 56 rms 304-608 F. Conf. No
pets. Pkg. V, AE, DC, MC.
Not only is the location ideal (right in the center
of old Andorra), but the guest rooms of this
commendable hotel are spacious and offer individual balconies with views of the town and
valley. Amenities include a bar, sun room, and
sauna.

Plaza

19, carrer Maria-Pla
(628) 64 4.44, fax (628) 21 7 21
Open year-round. 16 stes 660-1,000 F. 84 rms 470-
770 F. Rms for disabled. Restaurant. Half-board 450-
545 F. Air cond. Conf. Valet pkg. V, AE, DC, MC.
Behind the stern façade of this centrally located hotel hides a spectacular, sun-washed
lobby with a skylight, and magnificent, well-
equipped rooms and suites decorated tastefully
in Empire style. Elegant bathrooms. Courteous
welcome.

■ In Les Escaldes

Les Jardins de Hoste

Route d'Engolasters
(628) 62 7 67, fax (628) 63 3 25
Open daily until 11pm. Priv rm: 25. No pets. Pkg. V,
AE, DC, MC.
Despite the contemporary architecture, the
dining room decor of this restaurant-hotel overlooking the valley is both fuddy-duddy and pompous. The previous chef had made it a
worthwhile dining destination, but he has left,
and we have not yet sampled the new chef's
cooking. Stay tuned for a rating later. M 130 F,
255 F, 310 F, 328 F.

Roc de Caldes

(See restaurant above)
Open year-round. 5 stes 1,600 F. 40 rms 1,000-
1,100 F. Rms for disabled. Half-board 1,100-1,700 F.
Conf. Valet pkg. V, AE, DC, MC.
Built of slate and shale over a series of hillside
terraces, this brand-new hotel boasts an eye-
opening panorama of Andorra roofs cupped by
surrounding mountains. Vast and luxurious, the
rooms obviously aspire to palace-hotel great-
ness while in fact they are cold and impersonal,
functional rather than charming.

Le Rétro

11, carrefour de la Unio - (628) 26 7 16
Closed Mon, Aug 1-31. Open until 11pm. V, AE,
MC.
Chef Alain Despretz follows the seasons with
care, embellishing and refining simple dishes
such as seafood risotto, steamed sea bass (a bit

overcooked), and divine crêpes Suzette.
Regulars know their way blindfolded to this
charming little restaurant tucked away on a quiet
square and decorated in pale-green and rose
hues. Diversified wine list, high prices. C 300-
450 F. M 200 F, 350 F.

Roc Blanc

5, pl. des Coprinceps
(628) 21 4 86, fax (628) 60 2 44
Open year-round. 4 stes 1,365 F. 236 rms 410-775 F.
Restaurant. Half-board 454-565 F. Conf. Heated
pool. Valet pkg. V, AE, DC, MC.
This is one of the resort's better hotels. It is
pleasantly modern with bright, variously sized
rooms. Complete facilities include a hair salon,
boutiques, exercise room, and two restaurants.

■ In La Massana   5 km NW

Rutllan

(628) 35 0 00, fax (628) 35 1 80
Open year-round. 8 stes 700-900 F. 100 rms 270-
450 F. Restaurant. Half-board 325-400 F. Conf.
Heated pool. Tennis. Pkg. V, AE, DC, MC.
A large chalet-style hotel four kilometers from
Andorre-la-Vieille, the Rutllan has good facilities
and pleasant rooms with a view of the valley.
Garden, bar.

ANDUZE   30140
Paris 720 - Montpellier 70 - Nîmes 49 - Alès 13   Gard

Les Demeures du Ranquet

Route de St-Hyppolyte-du-Fort
66 77 51 63, fax 66 77 55 62
Closed Dec-Feb. Open until 9:30pm. Priv rm: 120.
Garden dining. No pets. Pool. Pkg. V, MC.
Anne Majourel has won a loyal following with
her savory, sunny cuisine that is fairly conventional (fine compressé of pleurote mushrooms
and calf's foot, delicate and flavorful cod brandade dariole) until you get to the dessert course,
where you can sample audacious dishes like
sweet eggplant millefeuille and a fig and celery
compote. The pleasant ambience is enlivened
with piano music; the decor features contemporary works of art. Well-chosen wine list.
Though the prix-fixe offerings are reasonably
priced, à la carte choices are expensive. C 350-
450 F. M 150 F, 220 F, 350 F.

Les Demeures du Ranquet

(See restaurant above)
Closed Tue & Wed off-seas, Nov 2-Feb. 10 rms 480-
800 F. Half-board 500-600 F. Air cond. Conf. Heated
pool. Pkg. Helipad. V, MC.
The huge, comfortable rooms blend into an
oak wood at the foot of the Cévennes Mountains. Perfect appointments; dreamy breakfasts.
Helipad.

ANGERS   49000
Paris 305 - Rennes 126 - Tours 106 - Nantes 90   Maine/Loire

Continental Hôtel

12-14, rue L.-de-Romain
41 86 94 94, fax 41 86 96 60
Open year-round. 25 rms 200-300 F. Pkg. V, AE, MC.
A modern and comfortable hotel near the
cathedral, with clean, thoroughly soundproofed,

smallish rooms. Guests can count on a friendly reception, smiling service, and low rates.

Mercure Center
1, pl. P.-Mendès-France
41 60 34 81, fax 41 60 57 84
Open year-round. 83 rms 350-480 F. Rms for disabled. Restaurant. Air cond. Conf. Pool. Golf. Pkg. V, AE, DC, MC.
A large, modern building near the lovely Jardin des Plantes, the Mercure has functional rooms (of which three are equipped for the disabled and sixteen reserved for non-smokers). Good buffet breakfasts. Outstanding service.

Pavillon Paul Le Quéré
3, bd Foch
41 20 00 20, fax 41 20 06 20
Closed Sun dinner. Open until 9:30pm. Priv rm: 52. Garden dining. Air cond. Pkg. V, AE, MC.
What a pleasure it is to cross the threshold of Paul and Martine Le Quéré's elegant nineteenth-century town house! The couple literally spent years planning, working, and remodeling to produce an impressive decor of *trompe-l'œil* woodwork and delicate hues, an ideal setting for Paul's limpid, luminous cuisine. This year, we adored his superb 220 F menu: possibilities include tuna gribiche in a leek and asparagus charlotte with tarragon vinegar, veal shanks in Layon wine with artichoke bottoms and onions cooked in red Anjou wine, farmhouse cheeses, and excellent apricot tart. The 150 F version without cheese or wine is three-toque cooking for bistrot prices! And Mediterranean specialties also appear on the menu, all perfectly prepared and imaginative: red mullet fillets sautéed with thyme; monkfish with aïoli, garlic croquettes, and saffron-scented vegetable butter; croustillant of crab with ginger and preserved lemons. In autumn, a delectable wild duck tourte with a pepper-coated grilled duck fillet should not be missed. And as always, Le Quéré makes unprecedented use of Loire Valley wines in his cooking. Martine Le Quéré, an expert *sommelière*, will guide you in your choice of a superb Loire bottling to complement her husband's subtle dishes. **C** 350-450 F. **M** 220 F (wine incl), 150 F, 360 F.

Pavillon Paul Le Quéré
(See restaurant above)
Closed Sun. 4 stes 1,200 F. 6 rms 450-800 F. Air cond. Conf. Pkg. V, AE.
This handsome town house dates from 1862; the renovation was supervised by the Beaux-Arts commission. Nicely proportioned rooms, charmingly furnished with every imaginable convenience. Excellent breakfasts.

12/20 La Rose d'Or
21, rue Delaâge - 41 88 38 38
Closed Sun dinner, Mon. Open until 9pm. Priv rm: 30. Air cond. No pets. V, MC.
Don't be put off by the look of the place—the street, the façade, the decor—ah! the decor—the dishes, and the rest—for you would miss out on some fine, fresh, straightforward cooking prepared by the owner/chef. We can recommend the tasty (and reasonably priced) duck stuffed with fresh foie gras, skate poached with Roquefort, ragoût of monkfish in Anjou red

wine, and a nice selection of house desserts. **M** 105 F, 145 F, 170 F.

La Salamandre
1, bd du Mal-Foch - 41 88 99 55 (R),
41 88 24 82 (H), fax 41 87 22 21
Closed Sun. Open until 10pm. Pkg. V, AE, DC.
The sculpted woodwork and stained-glass windows impart a certain neo-Renaissance style to La Salamandre's imposing dining room. Daniel Louboutin consistently turns out delicious fare: frog's legs in puff pastry with tarragon cream sauce, squab risotto with truffle jus, and crémet d'Anjou (a dessert made from cream cheese) with wild strawberries. Game in season. Attractive 160 F menu. Excellent selection of local wines. Very pleasant service. **C** 280-380 F. **M** 120 F (weekday lunch, Sat), 160 F, 200 F.

Hôtel d'Anjou
(See restaurant above)
Open year-round. 3 stes 900-1,160 F. 53 rms 350-580 F. Half-board 525-780 F. Golf. Pkg. V, AE, DC.
Fine, spacious rooms may be had at this venerable, flawlessly renovated hotel.

10/20 Tex-Mex
9, rue de Château-Gontier - 41 87 96 00
Closed Sun, lunch Sat & Mon, Aug 1-15. Open until 10:30pm. Terrace dining. V, MC.
The chef, who actually did learn to cook in the U. S. of A., makes laudable efforts to serve authentic Tex-Mex fare here in the French heartland. Chili, enchiladas, onion rings, gambas and the like, all washed down with Mexican beer. **C** 140-210 F.

Le Toussaint
7-9, pl. du Pdt-Kennedy
41 87 46 20, fax 41 87 96 64
Closed Sun dinner, Mon. Open until 9:30pm (10pm in summer). Priv rm: 20. Air cond. V, AE, MC.
With its advantageous location and view of the château, this establishment could survive nicely on the tourist trade, even if it took no trouble with its food and service. But as it happens, the chef is not content merely to go through the motions: he takes pride in his house foie gras with a vanilla infusion, grilled boneless Loire shad with a sorrel purée, and a croustillant of Anjou strawberries. The cellar holds a good selection of Bordeaux and regional wines. **C** 250-350 F. **M** 100 F, 125 F, 190 F, 250 F.

And also...
Our selection of places for inexpensive, quick, or late-night meals.
Brasserie de la Gare (41 88 48 57 - 5, pl. de la Gare. Open until midnight.): The Angers "in" crowd comes here for raw seafood platters, fresh fish dishes, and homestyle fare (130 F).
La Côte de Bœuf (41 66 81 41 - 105, rue de la Madeleine. Open until 10:30pm.): Excellent and copious portions of grilled meats served in a pleasant setting (90-120 F).
Dolce Vita (41 87 23 71 - 9, rue Baudrière. Open until 10:30pm.): Opposite the cathedral, this perfectly decent Italian eatery is a favorite with students (60-70 F).
Le Petit Mâchon (41 86 01 13 - 43, rue Bressigny. Open until 10pm.): A former butcher's shop

transformed into a bistro. Good country-style cooking at low prices (100-120 F).

■ **In Briollay 49125**   14 km N on D 52

 Château de Noirieux
26, route du Moulin
41 42 50 05, fax 41 37 91 00
Closed Sun dinner & Mon (Oct 16-Apr 10), Feb 2-Mar 10. Open until 9:30pm. Priv rm: 80. Garden dining. Heated pool. Valet pkg. V, AE, DC, MC.
  With two red toques firmly in hand, chef Gérard Côme floated downstream from the Château de Marçay in Touraine to his new stronghold at Noirieux. At long last this immense eighteenth-century château with sunny dining rooms on the River Loir has a chef worthy of the magnificent surroundings. Côme has a bent for light, updated contemporary classics, like a luscious warm pavé of Loire pike served with chervil vinaigrette and asparagus tips, a delicious cabbage stuffed with crab and caviar, and crème fumée. He uses only the finest products, but knows the virtue of treating them simply: langoustines perfectly roasted with tarragon accompanied by a tomato and rosemary confit, and tender casserole-roasted squab with a fresh pea jus. Witty desserts, like coquetiers flavored with jasmin tea, and brioche bread pudding with lait de poule. C 320-450 F. M 195 F (weekdays), 230 F, 275 F.

 Château de Noirieux
(See restaurant above)
Closed Feb 2-Mar 10. 19 rms 600-1,250 F. Half-board 560-870 F. Conf. Heated pool. Tennis. Golf. Valet pkg. Helipad. V, AE, DC, MC.
  Set in lovely grounds dotted with hundred-year-old chestnut trees, the eighteenth-century château and fifteenth-century manor house nineteen individually decorated, fully equipped guest rooms. Pretty bathrooms; excellent breakfasts. The quiet grounds boast a must-see chapel, as well as a swimming pool and tennis courts. Delightful welcome.

■ **In Saint-Sylvain-**
   d'Anjou 49480   5 km NE on N 23

Auberge d'Éventard
N 23, route de Paris
41 43 74 25, fax 41 34 89 20
Open daily until 10pm. Priv rm: 25. Terrace dining. Air cond. No pets. Pkg. V, AE, DC, MC.
  The superhighway has siphoned off the traffic that used to thunder by this nineteenth-century inn on the side of the route nationale. Though situated at the gates of Angers it has a decidedly country feel, with its summer terrace, stunning timbered interior, and pretty chintz upholstery. Owner-chef Jean-Pierre Maussion prepares his classic regional repertoire with remarkable precision. Impeccable ingredients and beautiful sauces distinguish his salmon tartare with fresh herbs, osso bucco of farm-raised chicken with tomatoes, and a crisp-crusted bread pudding. The admirable selection of Loire wines includes several magnificent finds straight from the growers. Attractive set meals (but eating à la carte is an expensive proposition). C 300-500 F. M 145 F, 195 F, 345 F (exc Sun dinner).

ANGLES (LES) 30   → Avignon

ANGLET   **64600**
Paris 748 - Biarritz 4 - Bayonne 3   Pyrénées-A.

Atlanthal
153, bd des Plages
59 52 75 75, fax 59 52 75 13
Closed 2 wks in Dec. 4 stes 1,100-1,400 F. 95 rms 610-900 F. Restaurant. Half-board 885-1,090 F. Air cond. Tennis. Golf. Pkg. Helipad. V, AE, DC, MC.
  This is a recent construction overlooking the Plage des Cavaliers, between the sea and the Chiberta woods. On the lower level are rooms equipped for health cures and slimming regimes. The spacious, soberly decorated guest rooms offer all the usual amenities. Good breakfasts.

Château de Brindos
Route de l'Aviation
59 23 17 68, fax 59 23 48 47
Closed Nov. Open until 10pm. Heated pool. Pkg. V, AE, DC, MC.
  The decor of this Basque-style villa is more than a bit overblown, but the dining room offers a splendid view of a lily-dotted lake. Michel Cassouy-Débat combines classic technique and regional ingredients to produce a pipérade of langoustines showered with chives, sautéed veal chops and sweetbreads with an eggplant caviar tian, and a "horn of plenty" dessert with fruits. Sumptuous cellar; impeccable service in a luxurious yet unstuffy atmosphere. C 400-500 F. M 250 F, 300 F, 400 F.

Château de Brindos
(See restaurant above)
Open year-round. 2 stes 1,600-1,950 F. 12 rms 700-1,200 F. Rms for disabled. Half-board 1,150-1,300 F. Conf. Heated pool. Tennis. Pkg. V, AE, DC, MC.
  Exceptionally comfortable rooms and imposing suites await you in a quiet setting of timeless beauty near a forest and lake. Superb swimming pool, private fishing. Relais et Châteaux.

12/20 L'Orangerie
104, bd des Plages
59 63 95 56, fax 59 63 57 84
Open daily until 10pm. Priv rm: 200. Terrace dining. Air cond. Pool. No pets. Pkg. V, AE, DC, MC.
  Business executives and vacationers come here to enjoy serious cuisine in a pretty mauve and blue dining room with a poolside terrace. Try the marinière of clams with lobster essence and fresh trompettes-des-morts mushrooms, veal kidney sautéed in flavorful wild morel mustard, and a delicious chaud-froid of roast pear with bilberries. Complete wine list, competent service. C 240-280 F. M 140 F.

Hôtel
de Chiberta et du Golf
(See restaurant above)
Open year-round. 20 stes 350-1,000 F. 60 rms 270-910 F. Rms for disabled. Restaurant. Half-board 360-1,005 F. Conf. Pool. Tennis. Golf. Pkg. V, AE, DC, MC.
  Nestled between links and lake, not far from the beach, these twin hotel boasts many pretty rooms with salons that open out on the golf greens. Excellent facilities for conferences, health and slimming cures.

12/20 La Soupière
Bd B.A.B. - 59 52 99 00, fax 59 52 29 11
Closed Sun dinner. Open until 10pm. Priv rm: 50. Terrace dining. Hotel: 74 rms 265-305 F. Rms for disabled. Half-board 240-258 F. Conf. Golf. Pkg. V, AE, DC, MC.
Here's a tidy little spot that famished tourists love for its sturdy main courses like duck breast with basil, peppery steak, and monkfish en brochette with garlic cream. Try the pear poached in Beaumes-de-Venise for dessert. Nice little wine list; fast service. **C** 180-230 F. **M** 39 F, 82 F, 88 F, 120 F.

ANGOULÊME   16000
Paris 450 - Périgueux 85 - Bordeaux 116 - Limoges 103 *Charente*

Européen Hôtel
1, pl. Gérard Pérot
45 92 06 42, fax 45 94 88 29
Open year-round. 1 ste 500-750 F. 32 rms 320-480 F. Rms for disabled. Half-board 380 F. Conf. Garage pkg. V, AE, DC.
Behind the pastel façade you'll find spacious, modern, thoroughly equipped rooms (some even have a touch of style). Pleasant reception. Meals are served in the rooms on request.

Mercure Hôtel de France
1, pl. des Halles
45 95 47 95, fax 45 92 02 70
Open year-round. 90 rms 400-650 F. Rms for disabled. Restaurant. Air cond. Golf. Pkg. V, AE, DC, MC.
This thoroughly restored grand hotel in the heart of old Angoulême stands in extensive grounds overlooking the ramparts. The rooms are of various sizes, but all are tastefully furnished and well equipped. Perfect breakfasts, attentive reception and service.

La Ruelle
6, rue des Trois-Notre-Dame - 45 92 94 64
Closed Sat lunch, Sun, Jan 1-10, Feb 21-28, Aug. Open until 10pm. V, AE, DC, MC.
Véronique Dauphin and her husband restored this fine old house with its great timbers, imposing fireplace, and rough-hewn stone walls and turned it into Angoulême's sole gastronomic beacon. Véronique is an inventive chef who recently regaled us with a subtle shellfish bouillon flavored with star anise, a tender and harmonious fresh liver with Jerusalem artichokes, and a perfect version of a regional classic, stuffed cabbage. An extra point this year. Superb, reasonably priced cellar, friendly service, and a relaxed atmosphere. **C** 250-350 F. **M** 150 F (lunch, wine incl), 125 F, 145 F, 210 F.

■ In **La Vigerie 16290**   8 km W on N 141

Le Moulin Gourmand
45 90 83 00, fax 45 96 91 14
Closed Sun dinner & Mon (Jan-Apr), Nov-Dec. Open until 9:30pm. Garden dining. Pkg. V, AE, DC, MC.
Chef Bruno Nicollet relies on superb products prepared in a refined fashion: puff pastry stuffed with young leeks en mouclade, beef fillet sautéed with truffle juice and foie gras, pears and sherbet in a white chocolate crust. The first two set menus will offer your wallet relief from the à la carte prices. The dining room decor is frankly heavy-handed, but some fine antiques and fresh

flowers provide a welcome touch of lightness. The cellar is stocked with lots of vintage Bordeaux. **C** 300-600 F. **M** 150 F (wine incl), 125 F, 280 F, 360 F.

Hostellerie du Maine Brun
(See restaurant above)
Closed Nov-Dec. 2 stes 1,100-1,300 F. 20 rms 325-750 F. Half-board 470-695 F. Pool. Pkg. V, AE, DC, MC.
Picture it: an antique-filled mill set in a pretty park where deer and ducks roam free. The rooms, though large and comfortable, have ageing bath fixtures and worn carpets. Friendly, somewhat careless service; plentiful breakfasts. Relais et Châteaux.

ANNECY   74000
Paris 547 - Lyon 142 - Geneva 43 - Aix-les-Bains 34   *H.-Savoie*

L'Abbaye
15, chemin de l'Abbaye
50 23 61 08, fax 50 27 77 65
Open year-round. 3 stes 800-1,200 F. 15 rms 400-650 F. Restaurant. Half-board 570-820 F. Conf. Golf. Pkg. V, AE, DC, MC.
The seven rooms equipped for *balnéothérapie* (bathing cures) are as pretty, comfortable, spacious, and quiet as the rest. Diligent service. Pleasant bar with a vaulted ceiling; generous breakfasts.

L'Atelier Gourmand
Cour du Pré-Carré, 10, rue Vaugelas
50 51 19 71
Closings not available. Open until 10:30pm. Priv rm: 12. V, AE, DC, MC.
This pretty restaurant above a tea room serves lighter versions of classic dishes in a spacious, light-filled space. The first set menu is a real gift: savory puff pastry stuffed with pleurote mushrooms and flavored with truffles, roast salmon and langoustines cooked to perfection, delicious warm strawberries with sherbet. Small but well chosen wine list. Friendly welcome and efficient service. **C** 270 F. **M** 98 F, 140 F, 190 F.

Le Belvédère
2 km, route du Semnoz, 7, chemin du Belvédère - 50 45 04 90, fax 50 45 67 25
Closed Sun dinner, Mon. Open until 9pm. Terrace dining. Hotel: Closed Oct 16-Mar 31. 9 rms 190-230 F. Half-board 260-280 F. No pets. Pkg. V.
Jean-Louis Aubeneau offers his patrons a spectacular bird's-eye view of Annecy from the leafy terrace and modern dining room of his charming, lively restaurant. The setting perfectly suits the bracing cuisine, based on Atlantic seafood brought in from Aubeneau's native La Rochelle. The prices are ruinous, but some dishes are remarkable: just-cooked langoustines, monkfish osso bucco with a wild mushroom confiture, and hazlenut croustillant with vanilla ice cream. **C** 300-400 F.

Carlton
5, rue des Glières
50 45 47 75, fax 50 51 84 54
Open year-round. 55 rms 405-535 F. Half-board 360-615 F. Conf. Garage pkg. V, AE, DC, MC.
A rosy-pink edifice dating from the 1930s, the Carlton stands just 300 meters from the lake, on a square in central Annecy. The hotel provides very comfortable, commodious, traditional rooms.

La Ciboulette

Cour du Pré-Carré, 10, rue Vaugelas
50 45 74 57, fax 50 45 76 75
Closed Sun dinner, Mon, Jul 1-20. Open until 9:30pm. Priv rm: 15. Garden dining. V.

A chic little restaurant on a pretty courtyard, the recently redecorated La Ciboulette has an inviting air. Accept the invitation! Chef George Paccard's pleasing menu proposes fillets of Lake Geneva perch with a puckery tart coulis, young Bresse chicken in a casserole with fava beans and morels, and a nougatine glacée millefeuille with orange croquants. **C** 290-330 F. **M** 185 F (wine incl), 130 F.

Le Clos des Sens

Annecy-le-Vieux, 13, rue J.-Mermoz
50 23 07 90, fax 50 66 56 54
Closed Mon (exc Jul-Aug), Feb school hols. Open until 10pm. Terrace dining. Pkg. V, AE, DC, MC.

Off to a roaring start in old Annecy, chef Laurent Petit is drawing enthusiastic crowds (and rave reviews) with his bold, imaginative cuisine at moderate prices. This year we savored his langoustines roasted in Vin Jaune with morels, a red mullet tian with tomato confit, sea bass, and a clever chaud-froid of blue-veined Fourme d'-Ambert cheese and wine-poached pears. Warm welcome by Martine Petit, and a fine choice of Savoie wines. **C** 300-350 F. **M** 110 F (lunch exc Sun), 148 F, 188 F, 248 F, 298 F.

12/20 Les Écuries du Pré Carré

Cour du Pré Carré, 10, rue Vaugelas
50 45 59 14
Closed Mon lunch, Sun. Open until 11pm. Terrace dining. MC.

In the center of town behind a varnished wood façade, you will find a spacious, convivial dining room where bistrot cooking is served in generous portions. On the 100 F menu: warm sausage with potato salad, farm-raised chicken with tarragon cream, and crème brûlée. Nice wines by the carafe. **C** 180-260 F. **M** 80 F (weekday lunch), 100 F.

Le Flamboyant

Annecy-le-Vieux, 52, rue des Mouettes
50 23 61 69, fax 50 27 97 23
Open year-round. 32 rms 262-445 F. Golf. Pkg. V, AE, DC, MC.

Pleasant rooms in a quiet hotel not far from the lake. A bar with turn-of-the-century decor is on the premises.

L'Impérial Palace

32, av. d'Albigny
50 09 30 00, fax 50 09 33 33
Open year-round. 7 stes 2,100-3,500 F. 91 rms 850-1,200 F. Rms for disabled. Restaurant. Half-board 665 F. Conf. Heated pool. Golf. Pkg. V, AE, DC, MC.

Huge, deliciously comfortable rooms overlook manicured grounds and the lake. Beauty and fitness institute on the premises; new heated swimming pool.

12/20 Le Pré de la Danse

Annecy-le-Vieux, 16, rue Jean-Mermoz
50 23 70 41, fax 50 09 90 83
Closed Sun dinner, Mon. Open until 9:30pm. Terrace dining. Air cond. Pkg. V, MC.

You might just make a few pirouettes when you spy the 155 F menu: quail parfait with foie gras, chicken breast with Reblochon cheese, country cheeses, desserts. Try a pas de deux with some of the nice little wines on hand. **C** 180-320 F. **M** 98 F (weekdays exc hols), 118 F, 130 F, 155 F, 198 F.

Mercure

RN 201, 3 km S on rte de Chambéry, route d'Aix-les-Bains, 74600 Seynod
50 52 09 66, fax 50 69 29 32
Open year-round. 1 ste 520-580 F. 68 rms 325-480 F. Rms for disabled. Restaurant. Half-board 390-510 F. Conf. Pool. Pkg. V, AE, DC, MC.

An entirely renovated hotel at the edge of Annecy, with comfortable rooms equipped with minibars.

Les Trésoms et la Forêt

3, bd de la Corniche
50 51 43 84, fax 50 45 56 49
Open year-round. 4 stes 550-950 F. 44 rms 270-850 F. Rms for disabled. Restaurant. Half-board 300-650 F. Conf. Heated pool. Golf. Pkg. V, AE, DC, MC.

Halfway between the lake and the forest, this renovated luxury hotel (vintage 1930) provides spacious rooms with bathrooms even a big man can stretch out in. Courteous staff; breakfast buffet.

And also...

Our selection of inexpensive hotels, and places for quick or late-night meals.

Les Artistes (50 45 30 04 - 26, rue Vaugelas. Open until midnight.): A huge, light-filled dining room decorated with reproductions of paintings. Classic bistrot dishes at reasonable prices (duck rillettes, beef cheeks en daube) (150-250 F).

L'Aventure (50 45 45 05 - 33, rue Saint-Claire. Open until 10pm, 10:30pm in seas.): Southwestern cooking under the arcades (cassoulet, duck breast, assiette basquaise, and Buzet wines (85 F, 200 F).

La Bigoudine (50 51 31 22 - 17, fg Sainte-Claire. Open until 10pm, midnight in summer.): Dependable bistrot cooking with a big choice of salads, buckwheat crêpes, and homestyle main dishes (50-180 F).

Brasserie de l'Hôtel de Ville (50 45 00 81 - Pl. de l'Hôtel-de-Ville. Open until 1am.): Classic brasserie cooking and inexpensive menus in a picturesque atmosphere; facing city hall (160-250 F).

Le Croq'en Bouche (50 45 24 06 - 9, fg Sainte-Claire. Open until 10:30pm.): Carefully prepared bistrot cuisine with a very interesting 93 F menu and a large choice of fresh fish dishes (100-160 F).

Le Faucigny (50 45 25 62 - 17, rue Filaterie. Open until 10pm, 11pm in summer.): Try the 79 F menu: rabbit terrine with hazelnuts, roast Bresse chicken à la provençale, nougat glacé. A few specialties à la carte (200 F).

Taverne de Maître Kanter (50 51 02 65 - 2, quai Perrière. Open until 10:30pm.): Seafood, delicious foie gras, choucroute, and sprightly Alsatian wines feature on the menu of this, the best brasserie in town (200 F).

*The **prices** in this guide reflect what establishments were charging at press time.*

■ In Talloires 74290   13 km SE on N 509

L'Abbaye de Talloires
Chemin des Moines
50 60 77 33, fax 50 60 78 81
Closed Sun dinner & Mon lunch off-seas, Dec 15-Mar 15. Open until 9:30pm. Priv rm: 35. Terrace dining. Valet pkg. V, AE, DC, MC.
This engaging yet unassuming restaurant never fails to surprise and please its patrons. Jean Tiffenat offers Savoyard classics, sometimes in new guises: tartifle terrine with bacon and morels, omble chevalier (a lake fish) with fruit butter, roast squab with leek confit. Remarkable lakeside location. Superb wine list. **C** 285-450 F. **M** 98 F, 145 F (lunch), 210 F, 260 F, 290 F, 360 F.

L'Abbaye de Talloires
(See restaurant above)
Closed Dec 15-Mar 15. 3 stes 950-1,580 F. 27 rms 720- 1,180 F. Half-board 660-1,120 F. Conf. Golf. Valet pkg. Helipad. V, AE, DC, MC.
This fief of elegance and good taste sits between lake and mountain, its delightful garden and marvelously appointed rooms flanked by a cloister and large gallery. The Prior's Room (said to be haunted by the prior) is a national historic site. Whirlpool baths, soundproofing. Relais et Châteaux.

Auberge du Père Bise
Route du Port
50 60 72 01, fax 50 60 73 05
Closed Nov 13-Feb 12. Open until 9pm. Priv rm: 40. Terrace dining. Air cond. Valet pkg. V, AE, DC.
Père Bise remains one of the great gastronomical institutions of France, loved by well-to-do foreigners and native foodies alike. So don't be surprised to find the bill as steep as ever. This is the sort of place you go to on a special day. And you won't be disappointed. The welcome and service are flawless, the setting suitably dreamy. Across the handsome garden winks lovely Lake Annecy. Noble, impeccably high-quality ingredients are a specialty: truffles, foie gras, Bresse chickens, flipping-fresh fish. The women of the family are now in charge, Charlyne in the dining room and Sophie, her daughter, in the kitchen. Savor the goose liver parfait with Guérande sea salt; a tatin of potatoes, truffles, and goose liver; and the gratin of crayfish tails. The à la carte choices are much better than the set menus. The wine list is exhaustive, but definitely not cheap! **C** 520-800 F. **M** 450 F, 680 F.

Auberge du Père Bise
(See restaurant above)
Closed Nov 15-Feb 12. 9 stes 2,000-3,800 F. 25 rms 900-1,800 F. Half-board 1,150-2,500 F. Air cond. Conf. Valet pkg. V, AE, DC.
Perched on the edge of the lake, this delightfully romantic hotel provides ideal comfort in an ultraclassic setting. Book a room in the beautiful new Villa des Roses annex. Superb views. Relais et Châteaux.

L'Hermitage
50 60 71 17, fax 50 60 77 85
Closed Nov-Mar 15. Open until 9:30pm. Priv rm: 35. Terrace dining. Heated pool. Pkg. V, AE, DC, MC.
An enchanting lake view lends charm to this otherwise straitlaced restaurant, where local dignitaries are wont to gather. Jean-Jacques Chap-

paz offers féra (a lake fish) braised in Marin wine, rissolet of veal sweetbreads in Malaga, and a bavarois of young rabbit in gelatin. Attractive cellar; diligent service. **C** 240-320 F. **M** 120 F, 140 F, 195 F, 260 F.

L'Hermitage
(See restaurant above)
Closed Nov-Mar 15. 2 stes 700-1,400 F. 37 rms 360-730 F. Rms for disabled. Half-board 520-695 F. Conf. Heated pool. Tennis. Golf. Pkg. V, AE, DC, MC.
This exceptional hotel overlooking Lake Annecy features all newly renovated rooms. Superbly trained staff see to clients' every need. Generous buffet breakfast; brand-new suites and pool. Peace and quiet assured.

Les Prés du Lac
Clos Beau-Site
50 60 76 11, fax 50 60 73 42
Closed Nov 1-Feb 18. 1 ste 1,470-1,800 F. 14 rms 650-1,090 F. Restaurant. Conf. Tennis. Golf. Garage pkg. V, AE, DC, MC.
The beauty of the hotel's lakeside setting and manicured grounds are matched by the lovely guest rooms, decorated with Laura Ashley fabrics and wallpaper. Exceptional fittings; room service.

■ In Veyrier-du-Lac 74290   6 km SE on D 909

L'Amandier
91, route d'Annecy, at Chavoire
50 60 01 22, fax 50 60 03 25
Closed Sun off-seas. Annual closings not available. Open until 10pm. Garden dining. V, AE, DC, MC.
The graceful, inventive cuisine of Alain Cortési continues to please us, and the restaurant is currently being renovated to make it even more comfortable. Choose a table on the terrace in summer to savor Savoyard dishes and fine seafood: monkfish and shellfish bourride with star anise, brandade tian with olive oil and pistou, and more traditional dishes like farcette en ravioles and omble chevalier (a lake fish) with pistou, and génépi sherbet. Very balanced flavors, but we found some dishes a trifle overcooked, perhaps to please contemporary tastes. Jean-François Guillot has stocked the cellar with excellent bottles from his native Bordeaux. **C** 400-500 F. **M** 190 F (weekday lunch, Sat), 330 F (Sun lunch), 250 F (exc Sun), 260 F, 370 F.

La Demeure de Chavoire
71, route d'Annecy
50 60 04 38, fax 50 60 05 36
Closed Jan & Feb (exc w-e). 3 stes 1,000-1,500 F. 10 rms 580-1,000 F. Restaurant. Half-board 500-880 F. Conf. Golf. Garage pkg. V, AE, DC, MC.
This small new hotel sits in a quiet garden some 50 meters from the lake-shore. The old-fashioned, rather precious decor is unique to each room or suite.

Marc Veyrat
13, Vieille Route des Pensières
50 60 24 00, fax 50 60 23 63
19.5   *Closed Jan 10-25. Open until 10:30pm. Priv rm: 30. Terrace dining. Air cond. Valet pkg. V, AE, DC, MC.*
He was written off by those who called him mad, and fretted over by friends who seriously doubted he could survive the recession. Against

117

considerable odds and opposition Marc Veyrat went ahead with his 50-million-franc remodeling of a spectacular 1930s villa on the shores of Lake Annecy, now home to his restaurant and hotel. Not only is the "madman" holding on, he's getting stronger all the time. So don't come to weep about the *crise* (or count pennies—the bill is stiff indeed). Come, instead, to indulge in Veyrat's masterly, mysterious culinary creations that stand convention on its head.
True artists are few and far between in the kitchens of France. Uncompromising Veyrat is the authentic item, a man who never chases after clients with fashionable dishes but instead tries to win them over to his unique style of cooking. And too bad for you if you don't care for it! Happily, most people do. The tables of his decorator's-dream dining room—a lavish, sun-washed affair with coffered ceilings and atrium windows giving onto a flower-filled lakeside terrace—are full. Local Savoyards, Swiss, and even Parisians beat a path to his door.
A naturalist and lover of mountain herbs, Veyrat mixes his palette of flavors with a mastery and originality that astound us. Witness the incredible warm foie gras with ham, chard, Jerusalem artichokes and carrots, or the coco and red beans made sumptuous by their pairing with local truffles, lovingly simmered in celery bouillon. Or sample the sensuous and sublime lightly smoked lobster with an emulsion of summer savory and wild sorrel, or the astonishing red mullet fried in hyssop-scented olive oil. Some of his creations leave us speechless with pleasure: perfectly flavored omble chevalier (a lake fish) in pine honey, a dish not to be found anywhere else; sea bass cooked in a casserole with pink clams on a bed of wild cumin picked on nearby slopes; veal sweetbreads sautéed with melissa and paired with Jerusalem artichoke ravioli; astonishing rack of lamb with pimpiolet; luscious raspberry clafoutis covered with a mousse of mountain saffron pistils; and a warm crêpe scented with angelica. One floats away from the table on wings of joy (uplifted a bit by the fine Chignin-Bergeron and Roussette wines) with but one desire: to start the meal all over again. It's enough to make you forget the size of the bill, and that is saying something. But you can have a marvelous peasant-style feast for only 250 F, wine included, in a chalet annex run by Marc's father. A unique experience, by reservation only. C 650-1,000 F. M 380 F (lunch, wine incl), 300 F (lunch), 495 F, 950 F.

Auberge de l'Éridan
(See restaurant above)
Closed Jan 10-15. 2 stes 4,300-4,800 F. 9 rms 1,500-3,500 F. Air cond. Conf. Valet pkg. V, AE, DC.
Veyrat's magnificent 1930s villa offers guest rooms and suites that overlook a sloping garden and Lake Annecy. The lavender-colored façade is bit of a shock, but turns out to be a traditional local hue. Neither effort nor expense has been spared (*au contraire*). The bathrooms are among the most luxurious in France (some have double Jacuzzis!). Prices are high, but rooms are extraordinarily vast, elegant, and luxurious. After a sumptuous breakfast, wander down to the landing and pick up the Auberge's private boat. Relais et Châteaux.

ANNEMASSE — 74100
Paris 550 - Geneva 7 - Annecy 48 - Evian 39   *H.-Savoie*

Hôtel de Genève
In Ambilly, 38, route de Genève
50 38 70 66, fax 50 38 72 23
Open year-round. 3 stes 750-890 F. 90 rms 300-590 F. Restaurant. Half-board 475-565 F. Conf. Golf. Pkg. V, AE, DC, MC.
Located one kilometer from Geneva, most of this practical, modern, sunny hotel has been remodeled. The rear rooms are less noisy.

Hôtel du Parc
19, rue de Genève
50 38 44 60, fax 50 92 75 71
Closed Dec 23-Jan 12. 30 rms 260-380 F. Golf. Pkg. V, AE, DC, MC.
This classic hotel affords views of the municipal park and Mont Salève and is located only one and a half kilometers from the Swiss border.

■ In Gaillard 74240   2 km SW on D 2

Mercure
Rue des Jardins
50 92 05 25, fax 50 87 14 57
Open year-round. 78 rms 320-495 F. Rms for disabled. Restaurant. Half-board 395 F. Air cond. Conf. Heated pool. Golf. Garage pkg. V, AE, DC, MC.
The Mercure is a modern hotel set in spacious grounds by a river. The rooms are well equipped (two are specially fitted for the disabled), the decor light and clean. One floor is reserved for non-smokers. Bar.

■ In Pas-de-l'Échelle 74620   4 km S on N 206

12/20 Le Baavi
27, rue de la Gare - 50 37 61 53
Closed Tue, Jul, Dec 23-30. Open until 10:30pm. Priv rm: 40. Garden dining. Pkg. V, MC.
Sick of snowy mountain scenery? This Creole kitchen offers a definite change of pace. Try the Antilles specialties, as well as the crab pâté in puff pastry, rabbit with prunes, and fish in broth. Delicious rum-based punches bring a taste of the tropics to these Alpine heights. C 280-370 F. M 145 F, 165 F, 220 F, 250 F (dinner weekdays & Sat, Sun).

ANNONAY — 07100
Paris 546 - Le Puy 86 - Valence 53 - Saint-Etienne 43   *Ardèche*

Marc et Christine
29, av. M.-Seguin
75 33 46 97, fax 75 33 46 97
Closed Sun dinner, Mon, Feb school hols, Aug 16-30. Open until 9:15pm. Garden dining. Pkg. V.
The crumbling façade has been lifted, the gardens enlarged and beautified, and voilà!—this grand old house is sunnier and cheerier than ever. Marc Juilliat's country cooking is firmly rooted in the region. Savor the succulent tomato and basil tart, the snail soup with garden nettles, the halibut roulé with herbs, or the chestnut crème brûlée. The cellar is splendid, the service charming. M 100 F, 140 F, 180 F, 225 F, 280 F.

ANSE 69 → Villefranche-sur-Saône

12/20 Auberge Provençale

61, pl. Nationale
93 34 13 24, fax 93 34 89 88
Closed Tue lunch, Mon, mid Nov-mid Dec, mid Apr-mid May. Open until 10pm (10:30pm in summer). Garden dining. Pkg. V, AE, DC.

Here's a cozy, rather cluttered but adorable old inn, cherished by local seafood lovers. Try the fresh fish, salmon paupiettes, bouillabaisse, and good grilled meats. Charming welcome and service. **C** 230-400 F. **M** 80 F, 145 F, 240 F.

La Bonne Auberge

On N 7, quartier La Brague
93 33 36 65, fax 93 33 48 52
Open daily until 10pm (10:30pm in summer). Priv rm: 35. Air cond. Pkg. V, MC.

Philippe Rostang has made big changes at this renowned old family inn. Instead of aping papa he's opted for a congenial contemporary look and approach: pastel colors, a fixed-price menu, and a nice choice of regional wines. Success! Why not? Try the very tasty eggs in red wine sauce with snails, flavorful lamb croustillant with sorrel, nice cheeses à la provençale with nuts and basil, and an excellent millefeuille. Good choice of regional wines, charming welcome, attentive service. **M** 175 F.

Climat de France

2317, chemin St-Claude
93 74 80 01, fax 93 95 22 48
See page 95.
A classic chain hotel offering functional, decently equipped accommodation.

12/20 Chez Félix

50, bd Aiguillon - 93 34 01 64
Lunch only (Oct-Dec). Closed Jan 3-Mar. No cards.
With its decor straight out of the 1950s, this likeable bistro is ageing gracefully; the unpretentious cooking still has plenty of youthful kick. Try the soupe de poissons, generous bouillabaisse, or one of the homestyle main dishes. For dessert, baked Alaska. **C** 270-350 F.

12/20 La Jarre

14, rue du St-Esprit - 93 34 50 12
Dinner only. Closed Nov-Mar. Open until 10:30pm. Garden dining. V, AE.
Tucked away in the narrow streets of old Antibes, this gracious Provençal dwelling is worth seeking out. Your reward: a pretty garden shaded by a spreading fig tree, smiling staff, and delicious homestyle cooking (oxtail and ox cheeks confit, beef fillet with a crisp pepper craquant, duck breast in sweet-sour sauce). Appealing little cellar. **C** 230-380 F.

12/20 Le Marquis

4, rue de Sade - 93 34 23 00
Closed Mon & Tue lunch. Annual closings not available. Open until 9:30pm. V, AE, MC.
A hard core of habitués regularly fills the Marquis's little dining room. They come for Francis Zany's fine cooking, for example the second set menu: cod brandade quenelles, chopped beef flavored with truffles, cheeses, and dessert.

C 240-350 F. **M** 85 F (weekdays, Sat lunch), 125 F, 185 F.

Mas Djoliba

29, av. de Provence
93 34 02 48, fax 93 34 05 81
Open year-round. 1 ste 700-1,000 F. 13 rms 370-630 F. Restaurant. Half-board 370-500 F. Conf. No pets. Pool. Golf. Pkg. V, AE, MC.

Ideally situated between beach and center, the Mas Djoliba sits in three hectares of idyllic grounds. The rooms have an appealing personal touch.

12/20 Le Romantic

5, rue Rostan - 93 34 59 39
Closed Wed lunch, Tue, Dec 4-27. Open until 9:30pm. Air cond. Pkg. V, AE, DC, MC.
The adorable little dining room of rough-hewn stone and beams is a perfect setting for romantic evenings. The kitchen obliges with suitably seductive creations. The excellent 120 F menu offers tasty taboulé with grilled sardines, sea bream en papillote with baby vegetables and fennel, and dessert. Though small, the cellar offers lots of tempting possibilities. **C** 220-320 F. **M** 120 F, 190 F.

12/20 Le Romarin

28, bd du Mal-Leclerc - 93 61 57 29
Closed Wed, Dec 15-Jan 15. Open until 10pm. Priv rm: 48. Terrace dining. Air cond. Pkg. V, MC.
Prim and proper whitewashed walls, fresh fish, and low prices make this family-style restaurant a winning proposition. Try the 135 F menu: herb-filled fish terrine, duck confit with apples, cheeses, and dessert. **C** 180-250 F. **M** 85 F, 135 F, 155 F.

11/20 Le Transat

17, av. du 11-Novembre - 93 34 20 20
Open daily until 11:30pm. Terrace dining. Air cond. Pkg. V, AE, DC, MC.
Reserve a terrace table at this commendable little seafood spot, and order up a simple shellfish platter or one of the more complicated fish preparations (friture, zucchini blossom fritters, sautéed squid, mixed grill, paella). Freshness guaranteed. **C** 200-300 F. **M** 85 F (lunch exc Sat), 130 F.

Les Vieux Murs

Av. de l'Amiral-de-Grasse
93 34 66 73, fax 93 34 81 08
Open daily until 10:30pm (11pm in summer). Priv rm: 55. Terrace dining. Air cond. No pets. Pkg. V, AE.
While other restaurateurs fret over half-empty dining rooms, Georges and Suzanne Romano are having to turn people away. An astounding success story. Sure, the spacious dining room overlooking Antibes's old city walls has something to do with it. But the biggest attraction is the excellent 200 F menu featuring luscious warm oysters in Champagne sauce, tasty and crisp duck confit, a fresh salad of walnuts and cheeses, and delicious profiteroles with hot chocolate sauce. A fine wine list spotlights regional vintages. Charming welcome. Warm atmosphere. In short, a winner. **C** 300-450 F. **M** 200 F.

A red hotel ranking denotes a place with charm.

And also...

Our selection of places for inexpensive, quick, or late-night meals.

Le Café des Chineurs (93 34 57 58 - 28, rue Aubernon. Open until 10:30pm, 11pm in summer.): A lively Parisian-style brasserie and terrace in the heart of the old city, serving pasta, grills, and *plats du jour* like salmon with wild morels, steak with Roquefort sauce, and a Landes tourtière for dessert. (140-175 F).

L'Eléphant Bleu (93 34 28 80 - 28, bd d'-Aguillon.): A good Thai restaurant that offers a choice of hotness levels, super spicy to not spicy at all; fine vegetarian specialties (200-265 F).

Le Relais du Postillon (93 34 42 36 - 8, rue Championnet. Open until 11pm.): Opposite the post office in old Antibes, a reliable spot with a new chef who offers veal sweetbreads in puff pastry, pot-au-feu of the sea, and other specialties. Good wine list. (75-380 F).

■ **In Cap-d'Antibes 06600**   S

Don César
46, bd de la Garoupe
93 67 15 30, fax 93 67 18 25
Closed Nov 30-Apr 1. 1 ste 1,150-1,600 F. 18 rms 550-1,050 F. Restaurant. Half-board 220 F. Air cond. Conf. Heated pool. Pkg. V, AE, DC, MC.
Functional rooms with south-facing terraces in a well equipped hotel overlooking the sea.

La Gardiole
Chemin de la Garoupe
93 61 35 03, fax 93 67 61 87
Closed Oct 15-Feb. 20 rms 350-650 F. Restaurant. Half-board 520 F. Air cond. V, AE, DC, MC.
Family-style hotel in a pine grove near the beach. Quiet, light-filled, well equipped rooms, some overlooking the beach. Pretty garden and terrace.

Restaurant de Bacon
Bd de Bacon
93 61 50 02, fax 93 61 65 19
Closed Mon, Nov-Jan. Open until 9pm (10:30pm in summer). Terrace dining. Air cond. No pets. Valet pkg. V, AE, DC.
This restaurant facing the ramparts of old Antibes is, in a nutshell, the best seafood restaurant along the Côte d'Azur. The prices are as high as the quality, with the exception of the bargain 250 F menu: fish soup with firey rouille sauce, salade gourmande or sea bass délices; aïoli, fillet of the fish of the day, or seafood marmite; dessert and tiny cakes. As you sit under the bright orange-and-white awning surrounded by plants in pots and contemplate the splendid Baie des Anges, you can savor marvelous seafood specialties: a justly celebrated version of bouillabaisse, and a choice of ten local fish prepared in seven different ways by chef Serge Philippin, who has been pleasing patrons here for more than 16 years. Owners Etienne and Adrien Sordello make sure you receive a charming welcome and tip-top service. Fine although pricey wine list, but there are many local wines for less than 100 F a bottle to relieve your wallet, and many half bottles. Reservations necessary. **C** 370-750 F. **M** 250 F, 400 F (exc dinner Jul-Aug).

ANTRAIGUES   **07530**
Paris 644 - Privas 42 - Aubenas 14 - Vals-les-Bains 9   *Ardèche*

Lo Podello   ✪
75 38 71 48
Closed Thu, Jun, Oct. Open until 11pm. Terrace dining. V, MC.
This delightfully hospitable inn run by chef Hélène Baissade is a sure cure for depression or stress. Her regional repertoire is authentic, fresh, and flavorful: chicken-liver terrine, veal filet mignon with goat cheese, potato fricassée, and a semolina cake with pineapple are sure to cheer you up. But if they don't do the trick, order any of the numerous specialties. **C** 250-300 F. **M** 140 F, 200 F (exc weekdays), 80 F (weekdays).

APT   **84400**
Paris 732 - Avignon 52 - Aix-en-P. 55 - Carpentras 48   *Vaucluse*

Relais de Roquegure
In Saignon - 90 04 88 88, fax 90 74 14 86
Closed Jan 2-Feb 15. 15 rms 190-350 F. Restaurant. Half-board 235-310 F. Conf. Pool. Pkg. V, MC.
In a four-hectare park, a hotel offering a warm welcome.

■ **In Le Chêne 84400**   2.5 km W on N 100

Bernard Mathys
90 04 84 64
Closed Tue, Wed, mid Jan-mid Feb. Open until 9:30pm. Terrace dining. Pkg. V, MC.
Bernard Mathys's freshly revamped decor features a pretty dining room with Directoire chairs and an open-air patio. His cooking is innovative and good-humored, based exclusively on ingredients fresh from the *marché*. Mathys underscores their vigorous Southern flavors in such brilliantly balanced dishes as a confit of young rabbit with shallot vinaigrette, warm oysters in chard leaves, stuffed lamb's foot, and nougat glacé with local candied fruits. Partner these delights with one of the cellar's many fine local bottlings; half bottles available. Warm welcome, sometimes by the chef himself. **C** 300-450 F. **M** 160 F, 250 F, 350 F.

ARBOIS   **39600**
Paris 393 - Lons-le-Saunier 39 - Dole 35 - Pontarlier 56   *Jura*

Jean-Paul Jeunet
9, rue de l'Hôtel-de-Ville
84 66 05 67, fax 84 66 24 20
Closed Wed lunch & Tue (exc Sep, school hols), Dec-Jan. Open until 9:30pm. Pkg. V, DC, MC.
Here we are at the gastronomic summit of the Jura! We think Jean-Paul Jeunet's cuisine is subtle and full of nuance; to our taste, it recalls the style of superchefs Michel Bras and Marc Veyrat, who also love mountain herbs and country flavors. After years of effort, Jeunet has found his stride, creating vibrant combinations that are complex without being precious. This year we were particularly impressed by the originality of dishes like foie gras perfectly paired with Macvin (a local sweet wine) and croustillants of langoustines with heather blossom and anise jus (we

could have skipped the beet chips and vegetable matafan, though, which were unnecessary gilding of the lily). Even the first set menu offers surprises like an assortment of smoked carp fillets with a fresh herb salad and polenta, or a faisselle "de la fruitière" with cream. Elaborate, even recherché desserts include sheep's-milk ice cream flavored with chestnut honey and served with crisp "biscuits" which are actually dried, caramelized Swiss chard leaves! The rich cellar (around 500 wines to choose from) is under the able stewardship of a young sommelier. It showcases Jura wines, many at affordable prices. C 400-600 F. M 175 F, 260 F, 360 F, 480 F.

Jean-Paul Jeunet

(See restaurant above)
Closed Tue (exc Sep, school hols), Dec-Jan. 1 ste 500-580 F. 17 rms 320-520 F. Conf. Pkg. V, DC, MC.
Recently refurbished and intelligently decorated, this small hotel is comfortable, well equipped, and elegantly appointed. Excellent breakfasts.

11/20 Moulin de la Mère Michelle
Les Planches
84 66 08 17, fax 84 37 49 69
Closed for lunch off-seas (exc reserv), Jan. Open until 9pm. Terrace dining. Pkg. V, MC.
Comfortable mock–Louis XIII decor in an eighteenth-century mill house: this is the kind of place you often long to come to for Sunday lunch. The cooking isn't always on par with the surroundings, but order the delicious pochouse (stew) of trout in Savagnin wine and you won't be disappointed. Picturesque but uneven service. C 250-500 F. M 135 F (lunch weekdays & Sat), 165 F (lunch), 220 F, 380 F (dinner), 290 F.

Moulin de la Mère Michelle
(See restaurant above)
Closed Tue. 22 rms 350-650 F. Half-board 450-580 F. Conf. Pool. Tennis. Pkg. V, MC.
Set under the Jura's highest cliff in a beautiful bend of the Planches River, this handsome old mill house has been nicely restored and boasts big country-style rooms with large bathrooms.

ARCACHON	33120

Paris 627 - Biarritz 183 - Bordeaux 60 - Dax 141 — Gironde

Aquamarina
82, bd de la Plage
56 83 63 77, fax 57 52 08 26
Closed Dec 23-Jan 2. 33 rms 195-555 F. Rms for disabled. Pkg. V, AE, DC, MC.
This totally new hotel is located on the seaside grand boulevard; the sunny, low-key rooms are provided with terraces. Room service is available round the clock.

Arc-Hôtel sur Mer
89, bd de la Plage
56 83 06 85, fax 56 83 53 72
Open year-round. 3 stes 1,120-1,885 F. 30 rms 398-898 F. Air cond. Heated pool. Golf. No pets. Valet pkg. V, AE, DC, MC.
Beach-resort charm fills this modern, well-maintained hotel. The rooms are luxurious and soundproofed, with terraces overlooking the sea or gardens. Sauna, Jacuzzi.

L'Écailler Diego Plage

Beach front - 56 83 84 46
Closings not available. Open until 11:30pm. Priv rm: 80. Terrace dining. Air cond. V, AE, DC, MC.
Come here to savor the warm atmosphere with a Spanish flair, the lovely terrace at the edge of the sea, and the sunsets from the upstairs dining room. As for the cooking, opt for simplicity: oysters, raw seafood platters, and the freshest possible grilled fish. C 220-250 F. M 90 F, 140 F.

Grand Hôtel Richelieu
185, bd de la Plage
56 83 16 50, fax 56 83 47 78
Closed Nov 2-Mar 15. 43 rms 300-680 F. Conf. Valet pkg. V, AE, DC, MC.
Set in a pedestrian zone in the center of town, this is a huge, old-fashioned hotel with small, tidy, soundproofed rooms, some with a view of the sea. Direct beach access.

12/20 Le Miramar
37, bd du Gal-Leclerc - 56 83 33 84
Closed Mon off-seas. Open until 11pm. Terrace dining. V, AE, DC, MC.
This brasserie sports a contemporary look, with its comfortable terrace and pretty pink table settings. The fresh, simple dishes available include excellent oysters, brill with beurre blanc sauce (tasty although a bit overcooked), and a yummy homemade lemon tart. The choice of wines is limited but judicious. C 150-200 F. M 75 F (weekdays), 100 F, 130 F, 160 F.

L'Ombrière
Le Gascogne, 79, cours Héricart-de-Thury
56 83 42 52, fax 56 83 15 55
Closed Wed off-seas, school hols. Open until 11pm. Terrace dining. Hotel: 36 rms 147-350 F. Half-board 168-298 F. Conf. V, AE, DC, MC.
The large and lovely dining room has an adjoining flower-bedecked terrace. Eric Lamarque's cuisine features judicious treatments of fine products. On the generous 127 F menu, we enjoyed local oysters, duck breast grilled with black cherries, a cheese assortment with a salad, and a passion fruit mousse cake with orange sauce. Courteous, efficient service. Interesting cellar. C 220-400 F. M 127 F.

Les Ormes

77, bd de la Plage
56 83 09 27, fax 56 54 97 10
Open year-round. 28 rms 250-750 F. Rms for disabled. Restaurant. Half-board 330-620 F. Conf. Tennis. Pkg. V, AE, DC, MC.
Here is a pleasant, unassuming little hotel on the beach (direct access). For preference, reserve one of the seafront rooms, which are spacious and sunny, with individual terraces.

Le Patio
10, bd de la Plage
56 83 02 72, fax 56 54 89 98
Closed Tue (winter), 2 wks in Nov, 2 wks Feb-Mar. Open until 10pm (11pm in summer). Priv rm: 16. Garden dining. Pkg. V, MC.
Good restaurants are hard to come by on the Bassin d'Arcachon and this one—with its cool and pleasant flower-filled garden—enjoys considerable success. Bruno Falgueirettes turns out a salad of veal sweetbreads, monkfish stew, roast

squab, and, for the homesick, a brownie with vanilla ice cream. An otherwise ordinary cellar boasts a fine selection of Champagnes. **C** 220-350 F. **M** 160 F (wine incl).

 Point France
1, rue du Grenier
56 83 46 74, fax 56 22 53 24
Closed Nov 1-Mar 1. 34 rms 295-655 F. Conf. Garage pkg. V, AE, DC, MC.
Point France is a well-designed contemporary hotel facing the beach. Some large rooms open onto a panoramic terrace that overlooks the Bassin d'Arcachon; bathrooms are on the small side. Friendly welcome; efficient service.

 Les Vagues
9, bd de l'Océan
56 83 03 75, fax 56 83 77 16
Open year-round. 30 rms 355-734 F. Restaurant. Half-board 414-604 F. Conf. Pkg. V, AE, DC, MC.
This recently built, many-tiered hotel sits astride the beach with its feet in the water. First-floor rooms boast wide terraces; those on the fourth a superb view of the beach through broad windows. The decor is fresh and modern, done in pastel tones, the welcome charming. Very good breakfasts.

■ In **La Teste 33260**   5 km S

12/20 Chez Diego
Center Captal
56 54 44 32, fax 56 54 28 20
Closed 10 days in Dec. Open until 11pm. Priv rm: 16. Garden dining. Air cond. Pkg. V, AE, DC, MC.
Excellent mussels "Don Diego", good Arcachon oysters, and several Spanish specialties (chipirons, paella) are served here in a colorful setting. Follow up with one of the delectable ice-cream concoctions. Goodish cellar. **C** 250-280 F. **M** 90 F, 140 F, 180 F.

ARCINS   **33460**
Paris 560 - Bordeaux 28 - Margaux 6 - Pauillac 14   *Gironde*

12/20 Le Lion d'Or
Pl. de la République - 56 58 96 79
Closed Sun, Mon, Dec 23-Jan 1, Jul. Open until 9:45pm. Priv rm: 15. Pkg. AE.
Médoc's most picturesque restaurant straddles the *route des châteaux* between Beychevelle and Margaux—Mecca for wine lovers. The food is famously good but straightforward, and much of the charm of the place resides in the jolly wine growers who exchange bottles over the tables. Try the boudin sausage, pheasant terrine, or scrambled eggs with asparagus. **C** 180-250 F. **M** 61 F (weekdays, wine incl).

ARCS (LES)   **73700**
Paris 674 - Bourg-Saint-Maurice 12 - Chambéry 113   *Savoie*

 Les Trois Arcs
Les Arcs 1600
79 07 78 78, fax 79 07 70 07
Open year-round. 6 stes 500-1,000 F. 33 rms 400-900 F. Restaurant. Half-board 350-651 F. V, MC.
This is a modern and well-maintained hotel in the center of the resort, with a sunny terrace and,

from the restaurant, a superb view of Mont Blanc.

ARCS (LES)   **83460**
Paris 854 - Draguignan 10 - St-Raphaël 29   *Var*

 Le Logis du Guetteur
Pl. du Château
94 73 30 82, fax 94 73 39 95
Closed Jan 15-Feb 15. Open until 9:30pm. Priv rm: 20. Garden dining. Pool. Pkg. V, AE, DC, MC.
This old house perches high above a medieval village, affording a lovely view of the Vallée de l'Argens and the Massif des Maures. Chef Max Callegari has learned the virtues of simplicity. Enjoy, as we did, the cock's comb and duck sweetbreads, rack of lamb in a garlic crust with baby vegetables, and an interesting sherbet made from rosemary-scented fresh cheese and served with peaches poached in red wine. This dish alone merits a toque. Friendly welcome, lovely poolside terrace. **C** 300-400 F. **M** 125 F, 179 F, 260 F.

Le Logis du Guetteur
(See restaurant above)
Closed Jan 15-Feb 15. 10 rms. Half-board 390-440 F. Conf. Pool. Golf. Garage pkg. V, AE, DC, MC.
Ten spacious and pleasant rooms with fabulous views, perfect for a romantic weekend break. Horse-riding; kayaks for rent nearby.

La Maison des Vins
N 7 - 94 47 48 47, fax 94 47 50 37
Closed Sun dinner (exc in summer), Mon (exc hols). Open until 10pm. Priv rm: 45. Garden dining. Air cond. Pkg. V, AE, MC.
As the name suggests, this attractive, sunny little restaurant offers a whirlwind tour of fine regional bottlings (at reasonable prices). And the food is good, too: lamb's brain tart with sautéed girolles, roast sea bass with stuffed vegetables, rack of lamb, and a delicate warm peach tart. **M** 120 F (weekday lunch, Sat), 148 F, 260 F.

ARGELÈS-GAZOST   **65400**
Paris 812 - Cauterets 17 - Lourdes 13 - Tarbes 33   *H.-Pyrénées*

12/20 Auberge de l'Arrioutou
15 km SE on D 100,3 km before Route de Hautacan - 62 97 11 32
Open w-e, hols, school hols. Open until 9pm (10pm in summer). Terrace dining. Pkg. No cards.
The view from this marvelous mountain *auberge* is splendid, the cuisine honest and generously served. Your best bets are the local charcuterie, thick cabbage soup, meats grilled over an open fire, pungent Pyrénées cheeses, and delicious homemade desserts. Unbeatable value for money. **M** 70 F, 80 F, 90 F.

 Le Miramont
Av. des Pyrénées
62 97 01 26, fax 62 97 56 67
Closed Nov 1-Dec 20. 2 stes 400-430 F. 25 rms 280-320 F. Rms for disabled. Restaurant. Half-board 230-290 F. No pets. Pkg. V.
Nestled in verdant surroundings, this plush hostelry offers quiet, nicely appointed rooms and attentive service. The entire establishment was freshly renovated in 1993.

12/20 Hostellerie Le Relais
25, rue du Mal-Foch - 62 97 01 27
Closed Nov-Jan. Open until 9pm. Hotel: 23 rms 195-300 F. Half-board 200-250 F. Pkg. V, MC.
Jean Hourtal's cuisine showed some rough edges during our last visit. On the 138 F menu: dryish fish terrine, decent boule de foie gras, overcooked slices of duck breast with wild cranberries, and a good concoction featuring flambéed bilberries for dessert. The recently redone dining room has a view of a majestic mountain landscape. But it can't save the toque.
C 200-250 F. **M** 70 F (exc Sun lunch), 98 F, 138 F, 170 F, 220 F.

Hôtel du Lac d'Estaing
62 97 06 25
Closed Nov 11-Apr. Open until 9:30pm. Terrace dining. Pkg. V, MC.
This grand old hostelry stands in splendid isolation, facing a mountain lake some three kilometers from the nearest village. Christian Houerie is the talented chef, who keeps faith with regional traditions In dishes like grilled tuna with Roquefort sauce and squab with Armagnac and cèpes. But the dishes on the pension meals are much less interesting: good smoked salmon served minus lemon, and bland rabbit in mustard sauce. Family-style welcome. Well equipped cellar. **C** 210-320 F. **M** 85 F (exc Sun lunch), 150 F (Sun lunch), 160 F.

■ **In Saint-Savin 65400**   3 km S on D 101

Le Viscos
62 97 02 28, fax 62 97 04 95
Closed Mon (exc school hols), Dec 1-26. Open until 9:30pm. Terrace dining. Hotel: 16 rms 260-310 F. Half-board 260-340 F. Conf. Pkg. V, AE, MC.
Le Viscos is the name of the region's tallest summit, but it is the Hautacam peak that patrons can spy from the pink-and-prune dining room. Jean-Pierre Saint-Martin feeds this crowd with attractively lightened regional fare: chestnut soup with duck-giblet confit, perfectly seasoned cod with cèpes, and yummy little prune flans. All this merits a second toque. Françoise Saint-Martin presides over a cellar filled with interesting, affordable wines. **C** 200-340 F. **M** 108 F, 156 F, 240 F, 325 F.

12/20 La Renaissance
20, av. de la 2e-D.-B.
33 36 14 20, fax 33 36 65 50
Closed Sun (exc hols), Dec 24-Jan 4. Open until 9:15pm. Priv rm: 100. Pkg. V, AE, DC, MC.
In this version, the Renaissance is set in the suburbs, in a modern building with Louis XIV decor. The menu is classic without falling into tedium: try Emmanuel Brichart's tasty seafood blanquette with fresh herbs, tender cider-marinated beef, and a délice de Normandie for dessert. **C** 230-330 F. **M** 88 F, 138 F, 175 F.

Les Becs Rouges
2 km NE on N 506 & VO 7, in Montroc-le-Planet
50 54 01 00, fax 50 54 00 51
Closed Nov 5-Dec 20. 24 rms 235-555 F. Restaurant. Half-board 337-439 F. Air cond. Conf. Golf. Pkg. V, AE, DC, MC.
The forest runs right up to this hotel, which boasts lovely views of the peaks of Chamonix, and soundproofed rooms with loggia. The clever *pension* system allows guests to take away cold lunches or to dine elsewhere with coupons. A shuttle transports guests from the station to the hotel.

Grands Montets
340, chemin des Arberons
50 54 06 66, fax 50 54 05 42
Closed May 1-Jun 20, Sep 20-Dec 18. 40 rms 526-530 F. Restaurant. Half-board 333-440 F. Golf. Pkg. V, DC, MC.
Located at the foot of the *téléphérique*, this attractive chalet has large rooms, with some duplexes for holidays en famille. Ski lessons, tennis, golf, horse-riding are offered.

Hôtel d'Arlatan
26, rue du Sauvage
90 03 56 66, fax 90 49 68 45
Open year-round. 11 stes 795-1,350 F. 29 rms 385-695 F. Air cond. Conf. Golf. Pkg. V, AE, DC, MC.
Near the Place du Forum, this ancient town house groans with history (parts date from the fourth, twelfth, fifteenth, and seventeenth centuries). The rooms are charming and well appointed, with antique Provençal furniture. Garden. Bar.

L'Atrium
Les Lices, 1, rue E.-Fassin
90 49 92 92, fax 90 03 38 59
Open year-round. 91 rms 450-610 F. Rms for disabled. Restaurant. Half-board 410-560 F. Air cond. Conf. Pool. Pkg. V, AE, DC, MC.
Within walking distance of the center, this recently built hotel with spacious, impersonal, air-conditioned rooms features a rooftop terrace and sun lounge, and an outdoor swimming pool. Fun piano bar. Attentive service. Perfect for conferences or business meetings.

12/20 Côté Cour
65, rue A.-Pichot - 90 49 77 76
Closed Mon dinner, Tue. Air cond. V, AE, DC, MC.
An unassuming place on the face of it, but the dining room is cheerful and elegant, in a rough-hewn way. The well-heeled clientele obviously approves the classic, generous cooking, which includes foie gras sautéed in raspberry vinegar, raw marinated salmon, raw scallops in orange butter, Corsican-style leg of lamb, and a nougat glacé with berries for dessert. Zealous, good-natured service. **C** 200-350 F. **M** 170 F.

*Some establishments change their **closing times** without warning. It is always wise to check in advance.*

Grand Hôtel Nord Pinus

Pl. du Forum
90 03 44 44, fax 90 03 34 00
Closed mid Jan-mid Mar. 5 stes 1,500 F. 23 rms 550-850 F. Restaurant. Half-board 700-1,000 F. Conf. Golf. Pkg. V, AE, DC, MC.
Wrought-iron details and Venetian candelabra flank handsome Provençal antiques in this gorgeous hotel, part of which is a listed historic landmark. As the many bullfight posters suggest, this is a favorite haunt of local matadors and show-biz celebrities.

Lou Marquès

Bd des Lices
90 03 43 20, fax 90 03 33 47
Closed Nov 2-Dec 23. Open until 9:30pm. Priv rm: 18. Terrace dining. Air cond. Heated pool. Valet pkg. V, AE, DC, MC.
This seventeenth-century former Carmelite convent has been turned into a truly elegant, comfortable, and cheery establishment. Chef Pascal Renaud offers sunny dishes like warm foie gras, rack of lamb with summer savory, and rice pudding using rice from the Camargue. The wine list very good, and the choice of whiskies, coffees, and teas is excellent. The cloister annex restaurant offers seductively priced lunches. **C** 330-500 F. **M** 150 F (lunch), 195 F, 300 F, 380 F.

Jules-César

(See restaurant above)
Closed Nov 2-Dec 23. 3 stes 1,700-1,900 F. 52 rms 550-1,000 F. Half-board 535-1,385 F. Air cond. Conf. Heated pool. Valet pkg. V, AE, DC, MC.
Some fine pieces of Provençal furniture grace the huge, comfortable rooms of this former convent, which sits in a garden on the edge of the old town. Charming reception, service, and hospitality are provided in this Relais et Châteaux establishment.

Mas de la Chapelle
Petite route de Tarascon
90 03 23 15, fax 90 06 53 74
Closed Sun & Mon off-seas, Feb. 1 ste 670 F. 14 rms 410-670 F. Restaurant. Half-board 650-710 F. Conf. Pool. Tennis. Pkg. V, AE, DC.
This is a charming old farmhouse hidden in a pretty park. The large, comfortable rooms (renovated in 1993) attest to the generous *tradition camarguaise*, and the service and reception are excellent. The restaurant is housed in a sixteenth-century chapel.

Mireille

Quartier de Trinquetaille, 2, pl. St-Pierre
90 03 70 74, fax 90 03 87 28
Closed Nov 15-beg Mar. 34 rms 299-580 F. Restaurant. Half-board 334-475 F. Air cond. Conf. Pool. Golf. Valet pkg. V, AE, DC, MC.
Fully remodelled, functional rooms (those in the annex near the swimming pool are less grand), and an outstandingly warm welcome make Mireille a pleasant stopover. Dining tables are set up in the patio when the weather is fine. Nearby tennis courts are open to guests.

> *Gault Millau's ratings are based solely on the restaurants' cuisine. We do not take into account the atmosphere, decor, service, and so on; these are commented upon within the review.*

L'Olivier
1 bis, rue Réattu
90 49 64 88
Closed Sun, Mon. Open until 9:15pm. Priv rm: 20. Garden dining. Air cond. No pets. V, MC.
Olive branches abound in the rusticated decor and setting: flying buttresses, rough-hewn stones, and a glassed-in courtyard. Chef Jean-Louis Vidal's cooking has its ups and downs (pretty but bland terrine of young rabbit, sea scallops in sweet-sour sauce likewise) but compensation comes in perfectly prepared foie gras and a nice fruit gratin with crème anglaise. The cheapest set menu is a good deal. Cheerful service. **C** 300-450 F. **M** 138 F, 178 F, 258 F, 350 F.

La Paillote
28, rue du Dr-Fanton
90 06 33 15, fax 90 06 56 14
Closed Thu (exc dinner in seas), Feb-Mar 5. Open until 10pm. Terrace dining. V, AE, DC, MC.
This charming restaurant with gracefully rustic decor has just received a facelift. The fresh cooking shows nary a wrinkle and the prices haven't hit the roof. Chef Jean-Claude Tell is a straight arrow and hits the mark with Provençal flair: fresh mackerel salad with white wine, grilled bull steak with beef marrow, and a croustillant of pears and almonds. The set menus are good deals. Classic wines at reasonable prices. Very warm and courteous welcome. **C** 190-240 F. **M** 60 F (lunch exc Sun), 89 F, 125 F.

Le Vaccarès
Pl. du Forum, entrance rue Favorin
90 06 06 17, fax 90 06 24 52
Closed Sun dinner & Mon (exc hols), Jan 5-Feb 8. Open until 9:30pm (10pm in summer). Priv rm: 25. Terrace dining. Pkg. V, MC.
Chef Bernard Dumas serves sunny regional specialties in a delightful dining room overlooking the picturesque open market of Arles. Try the southern dishes on the excellent 135 franc menu: eggplant à la Provençale, southern-style fresh cod, crème brûlée with orange peel. Very good choice of Rhône Valley and Var wines. Homey welcome. **C** 300-350 F. **M** 135 F, 175 F, 235 F.

And also...
Our selection of places for inexpensive, quick, or late-night meals.
La Gueule du Loup (90 06 96 69 - 39, rue des Arènes. Open until 9:30pm, 10:30pm in seas.): Pass through the amusing doorway, and descend a flight of steps to enjoy adroitly grilled fish and other deft dishes (90 F, 200 F).
Hostellerie des Arènes (90 06 13 05 - 62, rue du Refuge. Open until 10:30pm.): For wonderful pizzas and regional favorites (75 F, 90-130 F).
La Mule Blanche (90 03 98 54 - 9, rue du Pdt-Wilson. Open until midnight.): Grilled meats and fish, and bistro fare prepared by a real chef. Beautiful vaulted dining room, good value (145-210 F).
Poisson Banane (90 06 02 58 - 6, rue du Forum. Open until 12:30am.): Clever, mostly exotic dishes, served in a pretty indoor garden (125 F, 160-210 F).

■ In Raphèle-
lès-Arles 13280   7.5 km SE on N 453

Auberge La Fénière
90 08 47 44, fax 90 08 48 39
*Open year-round. 1 ste 609-640 F. 24 rms 307-
500 F. Restaurant. Half-board 340-503 F. Air cond.
Conf. Pkg. V, MC.*
Situated just outside Arles, this *auberge* is
decorated in a decidedly rustic style, with comfortable rooms that are outstandingly well kept
and equipped.

ARLES-SUR-TECH 66 → Amélie-les-Bains

ARNAGE 72 → Mans (Le)

ARNAY-LE-DUC **21230**
Paris 287 - Autun 28 - Dijon 57 - Beaune 34   Côte-d'Or

Chez Camille
1, pl. Edouard-Herriot
80 90 01 38, fax 80 90 04 64
*Open year-round. 2 stes 600-800 F. 12 rms 395 F.
Restaurant. Half-board 800 F. Air cond. Conf. Golf.
Valet pkg. V, AE, DC, MC.*
Two choices here: pretty rooms in the main
building, or cheaper but still attractive accom-
modation in the nearby annex, Au Clair de Lune.
Sauna.

ARRADON 56 → Vannes

ARRAS **62000**
Paris 179 - St-Quentin 75 - Amiens 65 - Lille 51   P./Calais

11/20 La Coupole d'Arras
26, bd de Strasbourg
21 71 88 44, fax 21 71 52 46
*Closed Sat lunch. Open until 11pm. Pkg. V, AE, DC,
MC.*
Here's a lively, noisy brasserie with a gay 1920s
decor. Locals come here for the fresh seafood,
steak with shallots, fish choucroute, and nougat
glacé with raspberry sauce. Appealing house
wines, served by the pitcherful. The service is
fleet and efficient. C 220-300 F. M 186 F.

La Faisanderie
45, Grand-Place
21 48 20 76, fax 21 50 89 18
*Closed Sun dinner, Mon, Feb school hols, Aug 3-24.
Open until 9pm. V, AE, DC.*
Jean-Pierre Dargent has spent lots of *argent*
making his restaurant on the superb Grand-Place
of Arras one of the most elegant in northern
France. The marvelous vaulted ceiling and impressive stonework make a match for the
smooth service, the costly menu, and rich
cuisine, all of which caters to the affluent. The
ingredients are excellent and the preparation is
often skillful, even daring: try the tasty langoustines with orange "dust" and an asparagus
fricassée, harmonious grilled turbot with a
potato and shellfish crêpe, delicious warm cherries and ice cream encased in pastry. An added
point this year. C 400-500 F. M 175 F, 265 F,
385 F.

Hôtel Moderne
1, bd Faidherbe
21 23 39 57, fax 21 71 55 42
*Closed Dec 24-Jan 2. 53 rms 200-340 F. Rms for
disabled. Restaurant. Half-board 280-370 F. Conf.
Golf. Pkg. V, AE, DC, MC.*
Located in the center of Arras, near the railway
station, this is a pleasantly modern hotel with
comfortable, well-maintained rooms.

Univers
3, pl. de la Croix-Rouge
21 71 34 01, fax 21 71 41 42
*Open year-round. 3 stes 340-380 F. 30 rms 290-
380 F. Half-board 350-650 F. Conf. Golf.
Garage pkg. V, AE, MC.*
In the heart of town, the Univers has risen from
the restored ruins of a magnificent eighteenth-
century monastery with an indoor garden and
cloister. Quiet, well-equipped rooms.

ARTIGUELOUVE 64 → Pau

ARTZENHEIM **68320**
Paris 460 - Sélestat 20 - Colmar 17 - Mulhouse 49   Haut-Rhin

Auberge d'Artzenheim
30, rue du Sponeck
89 71 60 51, fax 89 71 68 21
*Closed dinner Mon & Tue, Feb 15-Mar 15. Open
until 9pm. Garden dining. No pets. Pkg. V, AE, MC.*
Chef Edgar Husser certainly knows his way
around the kitchen, judging by the house terrines, veal kidney in mustard sauce, and Kirsch
mousse. The exceptional cellar is well served by
a veteran sommelier. Swift, professional staff, but
the atmosphere, in spite of the pretty dining
room, somehow lacks warmth. Lovely garden
terrace. C 250-360 F. M 110 F (weekday lunch),
160 F, 225 F, 310 F.

Auberge d'Artzenheim
(See restaurant above)
*Closed Feb 15-Mar 15. 10 rms 245-345 F. Half-
board 265-345 F. Conf. No pets. Pkg. V, AE, MC.*
This is a nice stopover, with a handful of
pleasant rooms decorated with traditional
painted furniture.

ARZON **56640**
Paris 485 - Port-Navalo 2 - Vannes 28 - Sarzeau 11   Morbihan

Miramar
Port du Crouesty
97 67 68 00, fax 97 67 68 99
*Open year-round. 12 stes 1,600-2,400 F. 108 rms
750-1,650 F. Rms for disabled. Restaurant. Half-
board 945-1,700 F. Air cond. Conf. Heated pool.
Golf. Valet pkg. Helipad. V, AE, DC, MC.*
The Miramar's long building resembles an
ocean liner—funnels and all. The rooms are not
cozy, but are very spacious and well equipped,
with views of the sea. The glass-roofed swimming pool is on the "upper bridge"; the Louison-
Bobet *thalassothérapie* treatment institute next
door is connected directly to the hotel. Bar.

ASCO 20 → CORSICA

ASNIÈRES 92 → PARIS Suburbs

ASPREMONT   06790
Paris 940 - Nice 16 - Contes 23 - Levens 15   *Alpes-Mar.*

Le Relais Saint-Jean   ۞
60, route des Castagniers
93 08 00 66, fax 93 08 06 46
Closed Sun dinner & Mon off-seas, Jan 2-31. Open until 9:30pm. Priv rm: 20. Terrace dining. Air cond. Pkg. V, AE, DC, MC.
As authentic as it is delectable, Stéphane Viano's *cuisine niçoise* has conquered the hearts and tummies of local food lovers. We too were won over by his 125 F menu featuring a salad of giblet confit and vegetables à la greque, cod brandade with Niçois olives, warm goat cheese with a salad, and a nougat glacé with dark cherries. Family-style welcome; cozy dining room and a terrace with a spectacular view of mountains and sea. C 160-240 F. M 75 F (weekdays), 98 F, 125 F, 185 F.

AUBAGNE   13400
Paris 791 - Aix-en-P. 36 - Marseille 17 - Toulon 47   *B./Rhône*

Hostellerie de la Source   🌲🍸
St-Pierre-les-Aubagne
42 04 09 92, fax 42 04 58 72
Closed school hols Feb & Nov. 26 rms 300-1,000 F. Rms for disabled. Restaurant. Half-board 540-1,090F. Pool. Tennis. Golf. Pkg. Helipad. V, AE, DC, MC.
This seventeenth-century manor was restored inside and out a few years back. The discreetly modern rooms are extremely well equipped. In addition to a bar and salon, the hotel boasts leafy grounds and a shaded terrace.

10/20 Le Terroir Alsacien
40, av. des Goums - 42 84 90 55
Closed Tue dinner, Sun, Aug. Open until 10pm. Air cond. No pets. Pkg. V, MC.
Snails with watercress in puff pastry, red mullet with pistou, baeckeoffe, and, from September to May, many types of choucroute are served in a chummy Alsatian atmosphere. Extremely democratic prices. C 150-250 F. M 58 F (weekday lunch, wine incl), 165 F (exc weekday lunch), 85 F.

AUBENAS   07200
Paris 633 - Alès 74 - Montélimar 43 - Privas 30   *Ardèche*

Le Fournil
34, rue du 4-Septembre - 75 93 58 68
Closed Sun dinner, Mon, Jan 2-30, Mar 19-27, Jun 5-26, Nov 13-20. Open until 9pm. Priv rm: 18. Terrace dining. Pkg. V, AE, MC.
The vaulted stone dining room, which dates back to the fifteenth century, is a cool, pleasant setting for Michel Leynaud's forthright repertoire. The 150 F set menu is a veritable feast, with appetizers, morel and cream flan, sole with tomato butter, cheeses, and dessert. Small but appealing cellar. C 150-280 F. M 100 F, 150 F, 180 F, 260 F.

Restaurant names in red draw attention to restaurants that offer particularly good value.

AUBIGNY-SUR-NÈRE   18700
Paris 180 - Orléans 74 - Bourges 46 - Vierzon 43 - Cosne 41   *Cher*

Château de la Verrerie   🌲🍸
Oizon - 48 58 06 91, fax 48 58 21 25
Closed Dec 15-Jan 15. 1 ste 1,300 F. 10 rms 880-1,100 F. Restaurant. Half-board 610-820 F. Conf. Pool. Tennis. Pkg. Helipad. V, MC.
Given the choice, we always like to sleep in royal comfort—as one certainly does in this Renaissance château owned by the Count and Countess de Vogüé. The spacious rooms combine the charm of a bygone age with every modern amenity.

AUBRES 26   → Nyons

AUCH   32000
Paris 716 - Toulouse 77 - Tarbes 72 - Agen 71   *Gers*

Daguin
2, pl. de la Libération
62 61 71 71, fax 62 61 71 81
Closed Sun dinner & Mon (exc in summer), 2 wks in Jan. Open until 9:30pm (10pm in summer). Priv rm: 80. Air cond. Valet pkg. V, AE, DC, MC.
You are likely to find American Daguin fans here, and that's no surprise, given the chef's magnetic personality and undeniable talents. But his cooking was more glorious in the past than it is today, we think. It still shines when he treats sublime products with simplicity: foie gras, Gers poultry, cèpes, and lamb from the Pyrénées can be magnificent here. But we were let down by odd combinations like foie gras with honey or with tomatoes, and by the overcooked duck breast, too-brown potato cake, mediocre ratatouille, and awful tiny cakes served with coffee. As ever, Daguin's cellar offers all the vinous treasures of the Southwest, and both service and welcome are as warm as the southern sun. C 400-600 F. M 180 F (weekdays, Sat lunch, wine incl), 300 F, 495 F.

Hôtel de France
(See restaurant above)
Open year-round. 2 stes 970-2,500 F. 28 rms 290-970 F. Half-board 440-950 F. Air cond. Conf. Golf. Valet pkg. V, AE, DC, MC.
This family-run provincial hotel with ultramodern comforts, such as the magnificent suites, one with a sauna and breathtaking view and another with a Jacuzzi. Other facilities include a boutique of regional products, a cookery school, and an eighteen-hole golf course (five kilometers from Auch), as well as chef Daguin's moderately priced bistrot, Côté Jardin, and the Le Neuvième bar where snacks are served. Relais et Châteaux.

Claude Laffitte   ۞
34-38, rue Dessoles
62 05 04 18, fax 62 05 93 83
Closed Sun dinner, Mon. Open until 10:30pm. Priv rm: 30. Terrace dining. V, AE, DC, MC.
Laffitte's picturesque boutique-restaurant is a stronghold of Gascon gastronomy, here based on magnificent local products. The prices, though, force us to turn to the 150 F menu: charcuterie, stuffed chicken, salad with bacon, and dessert. Excellent choice of regional wines.

C 220-500 F. M 75 F, 125 F, 150 F, 250 F, 350 F.

Le Papillon
6 km N on N 21, towards Agen
62 65 51 29
Closed Wed, 1 wk in Feb, 1 wk end Aug-beg Sep. Open until 9:30pm (10pm in summer). Priv rm: 60. Terrace dining. Pkg. V, MC.
The summery contemporary dining room and terrace are a pleasant setting for chef Michel Arsuffi's enticing cuisine. Try the generous and savory terrine of young rabbit with rosemary and prunes, lemongrass-scented seafood pastry, cheeses, and strawberry-filled desserts on the 128 F menu. The wine list, welcome and service could all use some fine-tuning. C 250-350 F. M 69 F (lunch exc Sun, wine incl), 89 F, 128 F, 140 F, 230 F.

AUDIERNE   **29770**
Paris 588 - Quimper 35 - Douarnenez 22   *Finistère*

Le Goyen ۞
1, pl. J.-Simon
98 70 08 88, fax 98 70 18 77
Closed Tue lunch off-seas, Mon, mid Nov-mid Dec. Open until 9pm. Terrace dining. Pkg. V, AE, MC.
The spectacular sea views from the dining room seem straight out of a painting, and the elaborately decorated dining room has the feel of a museum. And that's the problem with some of the dishes here, too: they tend to be overdone and a tad artificial. Are scallops, langoustines, and cherry tomatoes really necessary in a lobster salad? Does the fricassée of scallops need the oddly tasteless addition of truffles? Wouldn't the duck be better without quite so much butter in the sauce? This cooking represents a philosophy that we feel needs some updating. C 400-600 F. M 160 F, 200 F, 260 F, 420 F.

Le Goyen
(See restaurant above)
Closed mid Nov-mid Dec. 3 stes 850-1,300 F. 27 rms 320-680 F. Half-board 420-680 F. Conf. Valet pkg. V, AE, MC.
A solid old establishment above the fishing port, which is attractive without being hugely luxurious. Rooms have been redecorated *à la provençale*, and boast pleasant views. Charming service, perfect breakfasts, gastronomical picnic baskets, and bicycles for rides along the *route des peintres*. Relais et Châteaux.

AUDRIEU   **14250**
Paris 240 - Caen 17 - Bayeux 13 - Deauville 60   *Calvados*

Château d'Audrieu
On D 158 - 31 80 21 52, fax 31 80 24 73
Closed Mon (exc in seas for guests), Dec-Feb. Open until 10pm. Priv rm: 50. Heated pool. No pets. Valet pkg. V, MC.
Set in a vast estate dotted with ancient trees, this is Normandy at its scenic best, and the three dining rooms are surely among the most majestic in France. The cuisine is Norman but with exotic touches: boned Trégorrois squab with a chutney of tropical fruits, warm foie gras with a marmelade of red cabbage, and a delicate pralin cupped in a dark-chocolate shell. Commendable cellar, warm welcome. C 350-450 F. M 150 F (weekday lunch), 295 F, 395 F.

Château d'Audrieu ✿
(See restaurant above)
Closed Dec-Feb. 5 stes 1,900 F. 25 rms 700-1,600 F. Half-board 785-1,415 F. Conf. Heated pool. Valet pkg. V, MC.
Beautiful suites, furnished with fine family heirlooms (the "Joséphine" pavilion is particularly luxurious), and elegantly appointed rooms grace this magnificent dwelling set in manicured grounds. Golf fifteen kilometers away. Excellent breakfasts. Relais et Châteaux.

AUMONT-AUBRAC   **48130**
Paris 535 - Espalion 58 - Mende 42 - Marvejols 23   *Lozère*

Prouhèze
2, route du Languedoc
66 42 80 07, fax 66 42 87 78
Closed Sun dinner & Mon (exc Jul-Aug), Nov-Jan, Mar. Open until 8:45pm. Priv rm: 30. Pkg. V, MC.
Flowers fill the dining room of this cozy place, from the wallpaper pattern to the bouquets on the tables. Chef Guy Prouhèze throws some bouquets of his own; he brings out the best in local ingredients and regional recipes: cassolette of snails with tiny mushrooms, duck breast with honey on a bed of dandelion greens, crème brûlée with candied pineapple. Fine choice of wines and a warm welcome. M 100 F (dinner weekdays & Sat, Sun), 165 F (Sun), 400 F (wine incl), 220 F, 310 F.

Prouhèze
(See restaurant above)
See restaurant for closings. 27 rms 250-520 F. Half-board 400-500 F. Conf. Golf. Pkg. V, MC.
Remodeled and improved from top to bottom, most of the rooms are now spacious, and all are well equipped (some boast huge bathrooms). Nice view of the countryside.

■ In Fau-de-Peyre 48130   8 km W on D 10

12/20 Boucharinc-Tichit
Del Faoû - 66 31 11 00, fax 66 31 30 00
Closed Sun dinner off-seas, Jan. Open until 8:30pm. Terrace dining. Hotel: 21 rms 190-240 F. Half-board 200-220 F. Pkg. V.
This village bistrot's rough-hewn charm is made all the more agreeable by the excellent 100 F menu: lentil salad, charcuterie, frog's legs in garlic and parsley, fresh baby trout, a generous serving of Roquefort, and yummy chocolate mousse. M 55 F, 80 F, 100 F.

AURAY   **56400**
Paris 474 - Lorient 36 - Quimper 97 - Vannes 18   *Morbihan*

La Closerie de Kerdrain
20, rue L.-Billet - 97 56 61 27
Closed Mon dinner & Tue off-seas, Nov 14-30. Open until 9:30pm. Garden dining. Pkg. V, AE, DC.
Fernand Corfmat's bold repertoire is marked by intense flavors, clever combinations, and impressive technique. We were wowed this year by the crab with fennel and onion cream, langoustines and red mullet with artichokes and parmesan, a fricassée of lobster with a jus of lobster coral and sorrel, and a luscious puff pastry of gingery pears and raspberries with caramelized Banyuls. What's more, the setting is

regal, with eighteenth-century woodwork, an enormous marble fireplace, and a pleasant garden vista. A wide choice of wines at reasonable prices. Martine Corfmat is on hand to extend a charming welcome. **C** 300-450 F. **M** 150 F (weekdays, Sat lunch), 100 F (weekday lunch), 200 F, 260 F, 350 F.

La Sterne
La Petite-Forêt
97 56 48 33, fax 97 56 63 55
Closed Sun dinner, Oct 15-Mar 15. Open until 10pm. Garden dining. No pets. Pkg. V, MC.
What the modern motel architecture lacks in charm, the stellar dining room amends with light, comfort, and warmth. Jens Claussen's cooking occasionally misfires, but most of the menu is handily executed, with a focus on seafood. On offer are sea scallops in a jus of baby scallops, tubot with oyster cream sauce, and strawberries à la nage with a touch of mint. Limited wine list. **C** 300-350 F. **M** 98 F (weekdays, Sat lunch), 140 F, 175 F, 250 F.

♠♠ Hôtel du Loch
(See restaurant above)
See restaurant for closings. 30 rms 260-330 F. Halfboard 300-320 F. Conf. No pets. Pkg. V.
The rooms have their drawbacks: narrow bathrooms, poor soundproofing. Excellent breakfasts. Golf course nearby, bicycles for rent.

■ In **Sainte-Anne-d'Auray 56100**   6 km NE

L'Auberge
56, rue de Vannes - 97 57 61 55
Closed Wed (Jul 10-Aug 20), Jan 9-23, Feb 20-27, Nov 6-20. Open until 9:30pm. Priv rm: 20. Garden dining. Pkg. V, AE.
This authentic Breton *auberge* straddles the Saint-Anne pilgrimage route. The inn's newly renovated rooms and Jean-Luc Larvoir's fresh-flavored cooking are deservedly popular with holidaymakers: a pipérade of bar with balsamic vinegar, lamb in bacon cream, baked apples with cinnamon ice cream. Astutely stocked cellar. **C** 210-340 F. **M** 80 F, 130 F (exc Sat dinner & Sun lunch), 178 F, 212 F, 290 F.

Paris 386 - Saint-Léonard 10 - Limoges 12   *H.-Vienne*

Auberge du Bonheur
D 979 - 55 00 28 19
Closed Sun dinner & Mon (exc hols), Sep. Open until 9:30pm. Priv rm: 120. Garden dining. Pkg. V, DC.
As you speed down the route toward Eymoutiers you might easily miss this country inn. That would be a shame, for Vincent Samit's cooking is as pleasing to the eye as to the palate. Pull up a seat on the enchanting terrace (weather permitting), and have a go at the delicious salmon tartare with lime, smoked ham and grilled monkfish, and clafoutis for dessert. Nicely composed cellar. **C** 180-270 F. **M** 80 F, 120 F (weekday lunch, Sat), 155 F, 185 F, 230 F.

Some establishments change their **closing times** *without warning. It is always wise to check in advance.*

AURIBEAU-SUR-SIAGNE   **06810**
Paris 926 - Cannes 16 - Grasse 8 - Nice 45   *Alpes-M.*

Auberge Nossi-Bé
Pl. du Portail - 93 42 20 20
Closed Wed, Nov 15-30, Jan 15-31. Open until 9:30pm. Terrace dining. V, MC.
Set in the last village near Cannes that hasn't been turned into an artists' colony, this simple inn serves refreshingly authentic food. On the 145 F menu we enjoyed a compote of young rabbit, duck confit with stewed cabbage, and a vanilla crème brûlée. Ask for a table on the small terrace overlooking the valley. A real find in this *frou-frou* region! **M** 145 F (weekday lunch, Sat, wine incl), 220 F (dinner).

AURIGNAC   **31420**
Paris 780 - Toulouse 64 - St-Gaudens 35   *H.-Garonne*

Le Cerf Blanc
Rue St-Michel - 61 98 95 76
*Closed Mon. Open until 9:30pm. Priv rm: 80. Terrace dining. Air cond. **Hotel**: 11 rms 150-260 F. Halfboard 280-320 F. Pkg. V, MC.*
Local food-loving regulars and summer tourists on the Cro-Magnon cave circuit crowd the Cerf Blanc, clamoring for chef Dominique Picard's highly personal and seasonal, inventive cuisine. Try the fennel-flavored mussel cake, foie gras with rhubarb, and a great dessert assortment. Fine game in season. The cellar holds some reasonably priced Bordeaux and regional wines. **C** 300-350 F. **M** 85 F (weekdays), 120 F, 170 F, 250 F.

AURILLAC   **15000**
Paris 546 - Brive 98 - Clermont-Ferrand 160   *Cantal*

11/20 Le Bistrot
18, av. Gambetta - 71 48 01 04
Open daily until 2am. Terrace dining. Air cond. Pkg. V, AE, DC, MC.
The census-takers who shake their heads over Cantal's dwindling population ought to drop by Le Bistrot for lunch someday—this is where the crowds are! They're tucking into shellfish assortments, steaks, and the more typically Auvergnat tripoux and pounti (the latter a rustic pork loaf made with Swiss chard and prunes). **C** 100-180 F. **M** 80 F, 100 F, 120 F, 150 F, 200 F.

♠♠ Grand Hôtel de Bordeaux
2, av. de la République
71 48 01 84, fax 71 48 49 93
Closed Dec 22-Jan 7. 23 rms 310-450 F. Restaurant. Conf. Valet pkg. V, AE, DC, MC.
The Grand Hôtel's big white building rises in the city center near the law courts, just opposite the public gardens. Pleasant, well-kept rooms. Bar, evening meal service; the breakfasts (bread and coffee) are awfully stingy.

♠♠ Grand Hôtel Saint-Pierre
Promenade du Gravier
71 48 00 24, fax 71 64 81 83
Open year-round. 29 rms 280-380 F. Restaurant. Half-board 310-435 F. Golf. Pkg. V, AE, DC, MC.
Ideally situated in the center of town, the rooms here are comfortable, decorated with restraint, and very well equipped. Free shuttle to the railway station or airport.

La plus ancienne Maison de Vins de la Champagne : Aÿ - 1584
The oldest Wine House in Champagne : Aÿ - 1584

Hôtel Le Bristol

Paris

112, rue du Faubourg Saint-Honoré - 75008 Paris
Tél. 33 (1) 42 66 91 45 - Fax 33 (1) 42 66 34 16 - Télex : 280 961
A member of
The Leading Hotels of the World

AUTUN   71400

Paris 300 - Dijon 86 - Chalon-sur-Saône 53   Saône/Loire

Saint-Louis

6, rue de l'Arbalète
85 52 21 03, fax 85 86 32 54
Closed Dec 19-Jan 26. 1 ste 370 F. 52 rms 260-
310 F. Restaurant. Conf. Golf. Pkg. V, AE, DC, MC.
This seventeenth-century coaching inn is the
quintessential old-fashioned French hostelry; it is
well maintained and spruced up regularly.
Flower-filled patio.

Les Ursulines

14, rue Rivault
85 52 68 00, fax 85 86 23 07
Open daily until 9:30pm. Pkg. V, AE, DC, MC.
Red velvet upholstery graces the handsome
dining room of this former convent, set in a
courtyard with views of the plain and mountains.
We were a bit disappointed in the quality of the
meats, as bad-tempered as a soon-to-retire post-
al worker, and by the desserts, which need
attention. But we liked the savory lobster à la
nage, a croustillant of red mullet with lemon
sauce, beef pot-au-feu, and duck breast with
ginger, all treated in classic fashion by the unpretentious young chef. C 350-450 F. M 90 F
(lunch exc Sun), 150 F, 200 F, 260 F, 360 F.

Les Ursulines

(See restaurant above)
Open year-round. 5 stes 560-800 F. 32 rms 340-
450 F. Half-board 455-565 F. Conf. Golf. Pkg. V, AE,
DC, MC.
The gaily decorated rooms are all thoughtfully
equipped. The supremely quiet setting of this
former convent affords a fine view of the
countryside and the mountains of the Morvan.

AUVERS-SUR-OISE   95430

Paris 42 - Pontoise 7 - Chantilly 29 - Taverny 6   Val d'Oise

Hostellerie du Nord

6, rue du Gal-de-Gaulle
30 36 70 74, fax 34 48 03 10
Closed 1st wk of Feb school hols, Aug 17-Sep 12.
Open until 10pm. Terrace dining. Pkg. V, AE.
Could one possibly write about a restaurant (or
anything else!) in Auvers-sur-Oise without citing
Van Gogh, who painted the village church and
is buried in the churchyard? Let us turn our
painterly considerations to the Hostellerie du
Nord. Alas, Patrice Galon's competent cooking
needs a bit more focus on the quality of the
ingredients. When he chooses carefully, he
pleases: quail and foie gras salad, sole timbales
with Burgundian snails, and chocolate tart with
almond milk. The cellar is deep and well stocked,
the welcome warm, the service zealous as ever.
C 250-410 F. M 150 F, 230 F, 390 F.

AUXERRE   89000

Paris 174 - Dijon 148 - Nevers 112 - Troyes 79   Yonne

Jean-Luc Barnabet

14, quai de la République
86 51 68 88, fax 86 52 96 85
Closed Sun dinner, Mon. Open until 9:30pm. Priv
rm: 50. Garden dining. Pkg. V, AE, MC.
This year we once again had two contrasting
experiences at Jean-Luc and Marie Barnabet's

charming seventeenth-century post house in the
heart of old Auxerre. The compote of young
chicken in Chablis sauce with a sherbet of
orange sections was artful but not much more
(and priced at a whopping 65 F), but the magnificent sea bass with asparagus was well worth
the 16 rating the restaurant once enjoyed. Let's
see how it goes next year. C 350-450 F. M 320 F
(wine incl), 180 F, 250 F.

Le Jardin Gourmand

56, bd Vauban
86 51 53 52, fax 86 52 33 82
Closed Tue lunch, Mon (exc dinner in seas), Sep 4-
18, Mar 27-Apr 3. Open until 9:30pm. Priv rm: 20.
Terrace dining. Pkg. V, AE, MC.
We're awfully fond of the market-fresh cooking
of Pierre Boussereau, but he is a chef who takes
risks, and this year he stumbled. We could name
a few who never bother to make the effort, but
instead just cheat a bit; we salute risk-taking in
principle. But we thought the sloppy technique
evident in the leek and sardine salad, and the
tuna sautéed with juniper berries, was inadmis-
sable. Given some current upsets in the chef's
personal life, we decided to leave the rating
where it stands. Boussereau is a true chef and a
true creator; may he become so once again.
C 250-350 F. M 98 F, 140 F, 190 F, 220 F,
260 F.

Normandie

41, bd Vauban
86 52 57 80, fax 86 51 54 33
Open year-round. 47 rms 230-360 F. Rms for disabled. Restaurant. Half-board 260 F. Conf. Golf.
Valet pkg. V, AE, DC, MC.
Located on the edge of central Auxerre, the
Normandie is a handsome dwelling with a small
garden-terrace and pleasant, recently renovated
rooms. Sauna.

Parc des Maréchaux

6, av. Foch - 86 51 43 77, fax 86 51 31 77
Open year-round. 25 rms 290-460 F. Rms for disabled. Half-board 360 F. Pkg. V, AE, DC, MC.
Near the center of town, this nineteenth-
century house has elegant, regularly refurbished
rooms, some of which give onto a pretty park.

La Salamandre

84, rue de Paris
86 52 87 87, fax 86 52 05 85
Closed Sun, Dec 20-Jan 5. Open until 10pm. Priv
rm: 70. Air cond. V, AE.
Serge Colas's classic (not hugely original)
cuisine shows great respect for fine ingredients
and a penchant for seafood. Settle down in the
fresh green dining room and taste, for example,
his bracing turbot with hollandaise or the delicious sea bass; the shellfish are fine, too. And
carnivores will appreciate the good veal kidneys
or lamb chops with ratatouille. Attentive, friendly
service. C 330-430 F. M 98 F (weekdays, Sat
lunch), 158 F, 228 F, 268 F.

We're always happy to hear about **your discoveries**
and receive your comments on ours. Please feel free
to write to us stating clearly what you liked or
disliked. Be concise but convincing, and take the
time to argue your point.

■ In **Chevannes 89240** 8 km SW on N 151 and D 1

La Chamaille

In La Barbotière, 4, route de Boiloup
86 41 24 80, fax 86 41 34 80
Closed Mon, Tue, Jan 2-Feb 8, Sep 4-12. Open until 9:15pm. Air cond. Pkg. V, AE, DC, MC.
Picturesque, bucolic, painterly: the lush green setting, complete with babbling brook just outside the dining room, makes for utter relaxation, even though the cooking could use a little renovation, especially in the dessert department. But chef Pierre Siri's cuisine is a celebration of forthright flavors, created with impeccable ingredients: the delicious wild duck with jus, and veal kidneys with a foie gras-embellished choucroute made with Chablis, are still worth two toques. This is a dependable country-lunch spot; classic French quality with no surprises. **C** 320-380 F. **M** 160 F (exc hols), 255 F.

■ In **Venoy 89290** 7 km E on N 65

Le Moulin de la Coudre

86 40 23 79, fax 86 40 23 55
Closed Sun dinner, Mon, Jan 15-Feb 10. Open until 9pm. Priv rm: 30. Garden dining. Pkg. V, MC.
The views of the garden compensate for the rather bland decor, and the 138 F menu offers fresh-tasting, well prepared dishes like smoked duck breast with warm apples, fish fillets with watercress mousse, cheeses, and dessert. Friendly welcome. **C** 250-400 F. **M** 105 F (weekdays), 138 F, 185 F, 265 F, 360 F.

Hostellerie de la Poste

Pl. Vauban - 86 34 06 12, fax 86 34 47 11
Open year-round. 17 stes 1,050-1,350 F. 10 rms 650-900 F. Rms for disabled. Restaurant. Conf. Golf. Valet pkg. V, AE, MC.
A deluxe stopover spot since 1707, La Poste's comfortable, freshly renovated rooms give onto a pretty garden.

Moulin des Ruats

3.5 km on D 427, Vallée du Cousin
86 34 07 14, fax 86 31 65 47
Closed Tue lunch & Mon all-seas, Nov 15-Feb 12. Open until 9:30pm. Priv rm: 90. Terrace dining. Pkg. V, AE, DC, MC.
Set in the spectacular Vallée du Cousin, the Moulin is a rare treat in fine weather. Book a table on the shady terrace, where your ears will be lulled by the chirping birds and gurgling brook. As for the cooking, we'll give newly arrived chef Jean-Pierre Rossi the time to settle in before we assign a rating. **C** 300-350 F. **M** 195 F (weekday lunch, wine incl), 150 F (weekday lunch), 230 F, 280 F, 340 F.

Moulin des Ruats

(See restaurant above)
Closed Nov 15-Feb 12. 1 ste 850 F. 26 rms 300-680 F. Half-board 480-530 F. Pkg. V, AE, DC, MC.
On the banks of the enchanting Cousin River, this former mill house boasts comfortable, rustico-modern rooms, recently redone. Terrific terrace on the river. Good breakfasts.

■ In **Vault-de-Lugny 89200** 6 km NW on D 957 and D 142

Château de Vault-de-Lugny

86 34 07 86, fax 86 34 16 36
Closed Nov 13-Apr 1. 6 stes 1,500-2,200 F. 5 rms 700-1,100 F. Restaurant. Half-board 560-1,310 F. Tennis. Valet pkg. Helipad. V, AE, MC.
This noble, luxurious château sits in fifteen hectares of stream-fed grounds. Rooms and suites are furnished and decorated with refinement, and boast dreamy bathrooms. Horseriding, fishing. Restaurant for guests only.

See also: **Saulieu, Vézelay**

L'Aquarelle

41, rue de la Saraillerie - 90 86 33 79
Closed Tue dinner & Wed (exc Jul-Aug), Aug 23-Sep 6. Open until 10pm (11:30pm in summer). Terrace dining. V, MC.   **D4-15**
A smiling Catherine Oswald welcomes guests into a light, modern dining room dotted with watercolors (there is also a terrace under the trees), where they can comfortably peruse Michel Oswald's attractive menu and a display of his chocolate creations. He deftly turns fine ingredients into such savory offerings as sea scallops with endive cream, foie gras in puff pastry, sea bass with olive oil, and an assortment of chocolate desserts that will make chocoholics swoon. Concise, affordable wine list. **C** 300 F. **M** 150 F, 220 F, 270 F.

Bristol

44, cours J.-Jaurès
90 82 21 21, fax 90 86 22 72
Closed Feb 11-Mar 6. 2 stes 600-800 F. 67 rms 300-600 F. Rms for disabled. Restaurant. Air cond. Conf. Valet pkg. V, AE, DC, MC.   **C5-17**
Recently renovated, this is a fine hotel with comfortable rooms. Sauna.

Brunel

46, rue de la Balance
90 85 24 83, fax 90 86 26 67
Closed Sun, Mon, Jul 15-Aug 15. Open until 9:30pm. Air cond. No pets. V, AE.   **C3-24**
Located under the arcades of a street just steps from the Palais des Papes, this restaurant with its elegantly simple dining room has long been a favorite among local gastronomes attracted by the friendly serice, fine wines, and, most of all, the flavorful cooking redolent of olive oil and the aromas of Provence. Veggie lovers will be in heaven: the "stew" of early vegetables, the pot-au-feu with truffle oil, and the eggplant and zucchini compote bring the freshness of the garden to the table, while the sauté of squid and shellfish with herbs, the excellent John Dory with bay leaves and artichoke cream, the red mullet à la provençale, the braised oxtail, or the lamb fillet with aromatic herbs and spelt will delicately satisfy the appetite. Save room for the artfully crafted warm desserts. Judicious range of prices and a superb all-vegetable menu at 190 F.

C 280-450 F. M 200 F (wine incl), 190 F, 240 F, 400 F.

Cité des Papes
1, rue J.-Vilar
90 86 22 45, fax 90 27 39 21
Closed Dec 3-Jan 16. 2 stes 795 F. 59 rms 300-550 F. Air cond. Garage pkg. V, AE, DC, MC. **D3-19**
Situated near the Palais des Papes, this hotel boasts large, comfortable, air-conditioned rooms in a big modern building.

Cloître Saint-Louis
20, rue du Portail-Boquier
90 27 55 55, fax 90 82 24 01
Closed Jan-Feb. 3 stes 950-1,090 F. 77 rms 450-900 F. Rms for disabled. Restaurant. Half-board 395-620 F. Air cond. Conf. Pool. Golf. Garage pkg. V, AE, DC, MC. **C5-4**
The dignified beauty of this seventeenth-century Jesuit novitiate has been scrupulously respected, in spite of the modern "design" furnishings in the lobby and bar. The rooms are lovely and quiet, with many attractive amenities (cable television, safes, minibar). A sun lounge has been fitted out on the roof. But the breakfast is too expensive.

Danieli
17, rue de la République
90 86 46 82, fax 90 27 09 24
Open year-round. 29 rms 350-490 F. V, AE, DC, MC. **C4-10**
A solid nineteenth-century bourgeois building just a few minutes from the Place de l'Horloge, the Danieli boasts rooms and bathrooms that are quiet, pleasantly decorated, and well equipped.

Les Domaines
28, pl. de l'Horloge
90 82 58 86, fax 90 86 26 31
Open daily until 11pm (midnight in Jul). Priv rm: 80. Terrace dining. Air cond. Garage pkg. V, AE. **D3-6**
No, the food won't leave you rhapsodizing, but this anthracite-and-white eatery in the heart of old Avignon is an intelligent compromise between a wine bar and a family-style restaurant. The menu offerings are simple and generous: Avignon-style stuffed mussels, cassolette of snails with Châteauneuf-du-pape, nougat glacé and the like. The cellar brims with wines from the Côtes-du-Rhône and Côtes-de-Provence, with several available by the glass. Too bad that the service is sometimes as chilly as the modern decor. **C** 200-250 F.

Christian Étienne
10-12, rue de Mons
90 86 16 50, fax 90 86 67 09
Closed Sat lunch, Sun. Open until 9:30pm. Terrace dining. Air cond. Pkg. V, AE, DC, MC. **D3-16**
Christian Étienne, installed in the former residence of the town bailiff, enjoys what is undoubtedly the best location in Avignon, facing the Palais des Papes, with a peerless panorama of the eponymous *place*. An enthusiastic and imaginative chef, he practices a modern, discreetly original brand of French cuisine. This year wasn't his best (all Avignon suffered from the recession), but things picked up in the summer. The chic set, whether local or just passing through, habitually dines here. We still smack our lips at the memory of foie gras with apples, tuna and eggplant in puff pastry, whole lobster with orange butter and star anise, red mullet with black olive coulis, marvelous roast squab with a true jus, Avignon-style lamb daube, and a great dessert selection, such as the yummy pistachio parfait or the licorice-flavored croustillant. The Côtes-du-Rhône's best producers are represented in the cellars. The welcome and service show that spontaneous charm that many great restaurants these days have forgotten. **C** 450-650 F. **M** 160 F (weekday lunch), 280 F, 290 F, 400 F, 480 F.

12/20 La Ferme
Chemin du Bois (Ile de la Barthelasse)
90 82 57 53, fax 90 27 15 47
Closed Mon off-seas, Sat lunch, Jan 2-Feb 7. Open until 9:30pm. Terrace dining. V, AE, MC. **G1-11**
This genuine, old-fashioned Provençal farmhouse with a huge fireplace is an inviting spot for a generous, inexpensive lunch: snail ravioli, marinated anchovies, pickerel fillet, or lamb blanquette with cumin. Small but enticing cellar. Charming service. **M** 100 F, 140 F, 170 F.

La Ferme
(See restaurant above)
Closed Jan 2-Feb 7. 20 rms 310-420 F. Half-board 300-525 F. Air cond. Conf. Heated pool. No pets. Pkg. V, AE, MC.
Set in the verdant heart of the Ile de la Barthelasse, here are a score of adorably decorated, impeccably kept rooms. Swimming pool.

12/20 La Fourchette II
17-17 bis, rue Racine - 90 85 20 93
Closings not available. No pets. **C3-26**
Forks are the focus here, decorating the walls and dipping happily into the likes of onion tart and blood sausage, generous and savory calf's head with a rather watery ravigote, fresh white cheese with honey and almonds, and a classic steamed pudding with orange sauce. Charming welcome and service, good little wines by the carafe. **M** 140 F.

Hôtel de Garlande
20, rue Galante
90 85 08 85, fax 90 27 16 58
Open year-round. 12 rms 200-390 F. V, AE, DC, MC. **D4-7**
This charming little hotel occupies a well-restored, handsome old house in the center of town. All rooms have been carefully redecorated. Good bathrooms.

Le Grangousier
17, rue Galante
90 82 96 60, fax 90 85 31 23
Closed Mon lunch, Sun, Feb school hols, Aug 15-beg Sep. Open until 9:30pm. Priv rm: 6. Air cond. V, AE, MC. **D4-3**
Chef Philippe Buisson plies his polished culinary craft in a singular setting: an old cobbled courtyard under a tall glass roof, not far from the Place de l'Horloge. A bouquet of five set menus showcase the heady perfumes of Provence: house brandade in puff pastry, braised cabbage and duck confit with warm foie gras, warm honey madeleine, and caramel ice cream with warm chocolate sauce. Prodigious regional cellar. **M** 145 F (weekday lunch), 190 F, 250 F, 295 F, 340 F.

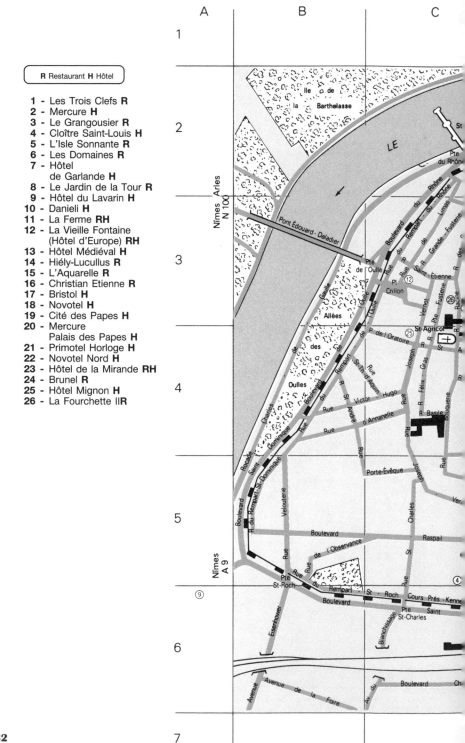

R Restaurant H Hôtel

1 - Les Trois Clefs **R**
2 - Mercure **H**
3 - Le Grangousier **R**
4 - Cloître Saint-Louis **H**
5 - L'Isle Sonnante **R**
6 - Les Domaines **R**
7 - Hôtel
de Garlande **H**
8 - Le Jardin de la Tour **R**
9 - Hôtel du Lavarin **H**
10 - Danieli **H**
11 - La Ferme **RH**
12 - La Vieille Fontaine
(Hôtel d'Europe) **RH**
13 - Hôtel Médiéval **H**
14 - Hiély-Lucullus **R**
15 - L'Aquarelle **R**
16 - Christian Etienne **R**
17 - Bristol **H**
18 - Novotel **H**
19 - Cité des Papes **H**
20 - Mercure
Palais des Papes **H**
21 - Primotel Horloge **H**
22 - Novotel Nord **H**
23 - Hôtel de la Mirande **RH**
24 - Brunel **R**
25 - Hôtel Mignon **H**
26 - La Fourchette II**R**

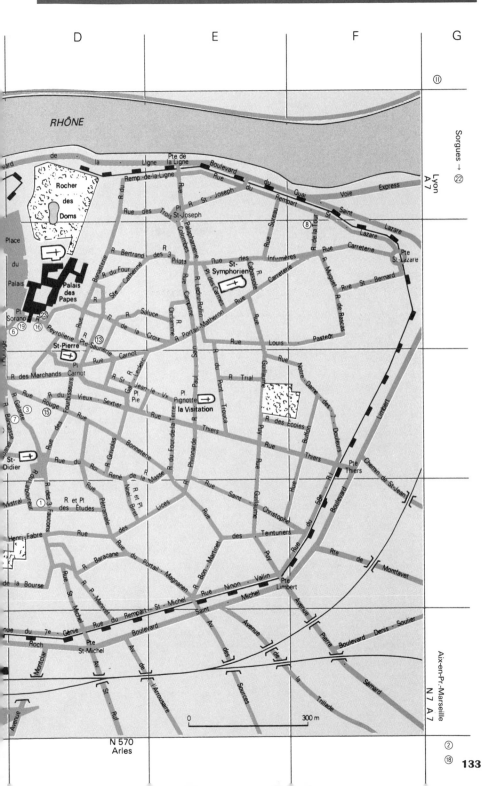

RHÔNE

Rocher
des
Doms

Place
du
Palais

Palais
des
Papes

Pl
Sorano
⑥ ⑲ ⑯ ㉓

Peyrollerie
St-Pierre ⑬

R. des Marchands Carnot

Rue Galante
Bancasse
③ ⑦ ⑮

St-
Didier

Mistral ①
Henri-Fabre

de la Bourse

Roch
Pte
St-Michel

N 570
Arles

Pte de
la Ligne
Remp.de-la-Ligne
Rue des Trois St-Joseph

R Bertrand des 3
Pilats

R du Four
Ste Catherine

R. Saluce
de la Croix
Pte-Saunerie
Pl
Rue Carnot

R St-Jean-le-V.
Pl
Pie
Vieux Sextier
Rue du Fourbisseurs

R et Pl
des Études
des
Rue des
Rue du Portail-Magnanen
R. Bon.-Martinet
Rue Ninon Vallin

Boulevard de-la-Ligne
Rue du Rempart
Quai
Voie Express

Rue St-Joseph
Pl R St-Joseph
Rue des Colonnes
Palaphramerie
R. des
Rue St-
Symphorien
R Ledru-Rollin
R Campane
Oriflamme
R Portail-Matheron

Rue des Infirmières
Rue Carreterie

Rue Louis Pasteur

Pl
Pignotte
la Visitation ⑧

Thiers

Bonneterie
R René
de la Masse
Philonarde

Rue du Roi
R Grivolas
Noel Biret
Lices
Rue
Rue des Teinturiers
Rue Baracane

St-Michel
Rue du Rempart St-Michel
Saint
Michel

Rue Pierre

Pte
Limbert

Avenue
Avenue
des
des
la
Trillade

⑧
R de la Tour
Rue
Carreterie
R. Miguet R de Rascas
R. St-Bernard

Pte
St-Lazare

St-Lazare
Saint
Lazare

Lyon
A 7
Sorgues → ㉒

Pte
Thiers
Chemin de St-Jean

Limbert

Montavet

Boulevard Denis Soulier
Sénard

Aix-en-Pr.-Marseille
N 7 A 7

②
⑱ **133**

0   300 m

Hiély-Lucullus ✿
5, rue de la République
90 86 17 07, fax 90 86 32 38
Closed Tue lunch & Mon off-seas, Jan 16-31, Jun 19-Jul 4. Open until 9:45pm. Air cond. V, MC. **C4-14**
We are ever grateful to retired chef Pierre Hiély, the first of the greats to provide set menus at reasonable prices. He still comes here often to make sure all is well. Hiély's former sous-chef, André Chaussy, now mans the stoves. As ever, the cooking sings of the sun and retains the charm of rusticity without ever seeming contrived. We enjoyed the creamed cauliflower and mussels, rabbit cheeks in puff pastry with prunes, and lamb sausage with sage. And we were equally pleased with the saffron-fragrant seafood stew, turbot fillet with anchovies, and Bresse squab with onion conserve. Enjoy it all in the delightful upstairs dining room whose decor is reminiscent of a turn-of-the-century steamship. The wine list contains some great Côtes-du-Rhône, some at giveaway prices, like the delicious 1993 white Mont-Redon at 98 F. **M** 140 F, 195 F, 310 F.

L'Isle Sonnante
7, rue Racine - 90 82 56 01
Closed Sun, Mon, Aug 7-31. Open until 9:15pm. Terrace dining. Air cond. No pets. V, MC. **C3-5**
Come to this pleasant place near the Place de l'Horloge to sample market-fresh offerings. On the 185 F menu: lamb's brain and spinach in puff pastry, grilled tuna with tomato-basil conserve, well aged cheeses, pastries and sherbets. The 130 F lunch menu includes a main course, cheese or dessert, and a glass of wine. The cellars boast a good choice of moderately priced wines. **M** 185 F.

Le Jardin de la Tour
9, rue de la Tour
90 85 66 50, fax 90 27 90 72
Closed Sun dinner, Mon, Aug 15-31. Open until 10:30pm. Terrace dining. V, AE, DC. **F3-8**
Both the postmodern decor and the trendy cooking cater to the young and fashionable. Jean-Marc Larrue's repertoire includes poached foie gras, fricassée of gambas with spelt, roast squab with garlic mousse, and fritters with acacia-flower honey. Efficient service. **C** 250-350 F. **M** 125 F (weekday lunch, Sat), 175 F, 225 F.

Hôtel du Lavarin
1715, chemin du Lavarin
90 89 50 60, fax 90 89 86 00
Open year-round. 44 rms 360-390 F. Rms for disabled. Restaurant. Half-board 500 F. Pool. Garage pkg. V, AE, DC, MC. **A6-9**
A recently built hotel located outside the city walls, just off the road to Arles, the Lavarin offers well-equipped, modern rooms decorated in soft tones. Pleasant, shaded garden.

Hôtel Médiéval
15, rue de la Petite-Saunerie
90 86 11 06, fax 90 82 08 64
Closed Jan-Feb. 25 rms 190-302 F. V, MC. **D3-13**
Despite the name, this is actually a seventeenth-century town house near the Palais des Papes, with smartly turned-out little salons surrounding a flower-filled patio. Rooms are spacious but rather dark.

Mercure
2, rue M.-de-Médicis
90 88 91 10, fax 90 87 61 88
Open year-round. 105 rms 385-540 F. Rms for disabled. Restaurant. Air cond. Conf. Pool. Golf. Pkg. Helipad. V, AE, DC, MC. **G7-2**
Located at the city's southern end, this hotel offers sunny, roomy accommodation. Half the rooms overlook the garden or pool.

Mercure Palais des Papes
Quartier de la Balance, rue Ferruce
90 85 91 23, fax 90 85 32 40
Open year-round. 87 rms 455-505 F. Air cond. Conf. Valet pkg. V, AE, DC, MC. **C3-20**
Situated within the city walls, the rooms of this hotel are comfortable, functional, modern, and well soundproofed, although not long on charm. The buffet breakfast is a better choice than the one delivered by room service.

Hôtel Mignon
12, rue J.-Vernet
90 82 17 30, fax 90 85 78 46
Open year-round. 16 rms 175-300 F. V, MC. **C4-25**
Tiny and sweet as the name suggests, the Mignon offers small but sunny, soundproofed, and newly refurbished rooms, 200 meters from the Palais des Papes. There is a mini-boutique on the premises.

Hôtel de La Mirande
4, pl. de l'Amirande
90 85 93 93, fax 90 86 26 85
Open daily until 9:45pm. Priv rm: 80. Garden dining. Air cond. Valet pkg. V, AE, DC, MC. **D3-23**
Set in a superb town house restored to life with pride and conviction, La Mirande is one of France's most beautiful hotels. Chef Éric Coisel prepares a menu with an agreeable Provençal accent and a pleasing absence of chic, evident in dishes like fricassée of asparagus with bacon, long-simmered beef cheeks with fresh pasta, squab with sweet garlic butter, and, in a couple of false notes, fatty veal kidney and acidic crème brûlée. **C** 300-450 F. **M** 190 F, 250 F, 350 F.

Hôtel de La Mirande 🏰🌳
(See restaurant above)
Open year-round. 1 ste 2,600 F. 19 rms 1,300-1,900 F. Air cond. Conf. Valet pkg. V, AE, DC, MC.
Nestled in the heart of Avignon, this amazing little "palace", with a delicious secret garden, boasts richly decorated salons and good-sized rooms whose varied decoration and refined details evoke the luxury and comfort of centuries gone by. Views embrace the rooftops of the vieille ville and the Palais des Papes. Royal bathrooms. Rather impersonal reception, however. Concerts of classical music followed by meals guests only are on offer.

Novotel
Route de Marseille
90 87 62 36, fax 90 88 38 47
Open year-round. 79 rms 395-430 F. Rms for disabled. Restaurant. Air cond. Conf. Pool. Golf. Pkg. AE, DC, MC. **G7-18**
Just off the *nationale* 7, these quiet, large, functional rooms are set in verdant surroundings.

> *Some establishments change their* **closing times** *without warning. It is always wise to check in advance.*

Novotel-Nord

Avignon North exit on A 6, 84700 Sorgues
90 31 16 43, fax 90 32 22 21
*Open year-round. 2 stes 840 F. 98 rms 395-450 F.
Restaurant. Air cond. Pool. Tennis. Pkg. V, AE, DC,
MC.* **G2-22**

Situated eight minutes from the center of town
and only yards from the superhighway toll
booth, the Novotel's rooms are quiet, extremely
well equipped, and very comfortable. Excellent
reception. Bar.

Primotel Horloge

3, rue F.-David
90 86 88 61, fax 90 82 17 32
*Open year-round. 70 rms 275-520 F. Rms for dis-
abled. Air cond. Conf. V, AE, DC, MC.* **C4-21**

Strategically located, right on the Place de
l'Horloge. This tastefully decorated, super-
modern hotel tucked among historic buildings
offers perfectly equipped, soundproofed, air-
conditioned rooms with a neo–Louis XVI decor.
It offers one of the best quality-price ratios in
town, in spite of the fact that the garbage collec-
tors bang under your windows hideously early
in the morning.

Les Trois Clefs

26, rue des Trois-Faucons
90 86 51 53, fax 90 85 17 32
*Closed Sun, Nov 15-30. Open until 9:30pm (10pm
during the Festival). Air cond. V, AE, MC.* **D5-1**

As ever, Martine and Laurent Mergnac deftly
wield the *clefs* to success with a warm welcome
and refreshing cuisine. The contemporary decor
is luminous and the prices are a gift. Laurent's
excellent 140 F menu, wine included, offers
vegetable omelets in herb cream encased in puff
pastry, sea bream with a caper-enlivened artichoke confit, and fresh white cheese. Pleasant,
cool garden setting. **M** 140 F (wine incl), 180 F.

La Vieille Fontaine

12, pl. du Crillon
90 82 66 92, fax 90 85 43 66
*Closed Mon lunch, Sun. Open until 10pm. Priv
rm: 60. Terrace dining. Air cond. Valet pkg. V, AE,
DC, MC.* **C3-12**

The cool, shaded courtyard, graced by a mossy
fountain, is the place to dine on a summer's
night; the rose-and-white-dining room, stuffed
with antiques and landscape paintings, is a bit
short on charm for some tastes. Jean-Pierre
Robert's cooking declined a bit this year: lobster
and asparagus salad served without the shellfish
vinaigrette listed on the menu, and overcooked
veal chop with lemon sauce, dropped the rating
by a point, in spite of the superb double chocolate
millefeuille with strawberries and sherbet. Splendid but overpriced wine list; chilly welcome.
M 130 F & 160 F (lunch), 270 F, 370 F.

Hôtel d'Europe

(See restaurant above)
*Open year-round. 3 stes 2,300 F. 44 rms 610-
1,600 F. Restaurant. Air cond. Conf. Golf. Valet pkg.
V, AE, DC, MC.*

This luxurious, seductively splendid hotel is
replete with Aubusson tapestries, precious *objets*, antique paintings, and artwork. The rooms
are gorgeous and grand, with marble
bathrooms. Three elegant, spacious rooftop
suites have private terraces overlooking the
town and the Palais des Papes (which is illuminated by night). Six other rooms have been
thoroughly renovated. Patio-terrace.

And also...

Our selection of places for inexpensive, quick,
or late-night meals.

Au Bain Marie (90 85 21 37 - 5, rue Pétramale.
Open until 11pm.): Good, traditional *cuisine de
femme* served in a charming town house (135-
160 F).
Le Cintra (90 82 29 80 - 44, cours J.-Jaurès.
Open until midnight.): Old-fashioned decor,
smiling service, and a good brasserie menu that
includes grilled meats, duck breast confit,
choucroute (77 F, 160 F).
Entrée des Artistes (90 82 46 90 - 1, pl. des
Carmes. Open until 10:30pm.): Chummy,
Parisian-bistrot atmosphere. Tasty dishes, low
prices (78 F, 115 F).
Les Félibres (90 27 39 05 - 14, rue Limas. Lunch
only.): Bookshop-tea room à la provençale serv-
ing honest traditional fare and delicious homemade pastries (120-150 F).
Le Gourmandin (90 85 88 27 - 18 bis, av.
Moulin-Notre-Dame. Open until 9:30pm.):
Hearty Gascon cuisine served in a pleasantly
rustic setting (95-220 F).
Le Petit Bedon (90 82 33 98 - 70, rue J.-Vernet.
Open until 10:30pm.): Generous, affordable
cooking in a nice setting. Sardines en escabèche,
brandade gratinée, cassolettes, and bargain
wines (100-150 F).
Simple Simon (90 86 62 70 - 27, rue de la Petite-
Fusterie. Open until 1am.): British-style decor,
two daily specials (like "crumbles" or "Indian
meatloaf") (90-120 F).

■ **In Les Angles 30133**   4 km W on N 100

L'Ermitage Meissonnier

Av. de Verdun (route de Nîmes)
90 25 41 68, fax 90 25 11 68
*Open daily until 10pm. Priv rm: 40. Garden dining.
Pkg. V, AE, DC, MC.*

After suffering through the recession, which hit
Avignon particularly hard, chef Michel Meisson-
nier seems to have recovered his momentum,
and diners have rediscovered the route to this
ancient auberge, once one of the region's best
known. The fine old main dining room (which
could use some livening up) and the pretty
garden terrace draw the locals, who savor house
foie gras, young rabbit with artichokes in
barigoule, and croustillant of honey cake. Next
door in the Bouchon bistrot you find an excellent
100 F menu with a choice of five entrées, five
main dishes, and five desserts. **C** 250-400 F.
M 100 F (exc hols), 160 F, 250 F, 350 F, 400 F.

Hostellerie L'Ermitage

(See restaurant above)
*Closed Jan-Feb. 16 rms 250-500 F. Half-board 290-
460 F. Air cond. Pool. Golf. Pkg. V, AE, DC, MC.*

Each of the extremely comfortable,
soundproofed rooms here has a fine bathroom
and minibar. Guests congregate around the
pool, where quick meals and, in the evening,
buffet dinners are served.

A red hotel ranking denotes a place with charm.

■ **In Montfavet 84140**   5 km E on D 53

Auberge de Bonpas
Route de Cavaillon
90 23 07 64, fax 90 23 07 00
*Open daily until 9pm. Priv rm: 23. Terrace dining.
Pkg. V, AE, DC, MC.*
This old roadside inn with a charming terrace and a brand new pool serves authentic, generous fare handily prepared by Richard Genovardo: wild mushroom tourte, salmon steak with tapénade, nougat glacé with Provençal honey. Pleasant welcome. **C** 250-450 F. **M** 120 F (weekdays), 170 F, 210 F, 245 F.

Le Jardin des Frênes
645, av. des Vertes-Rives
90 31 17 93, fax 90 23 95 03
Closed Nov 15-Mar. Open until 9:30pm. Priv rm: 15. Garden dining. Air cond. Pool. Valet pkg. V, AE, DC.
Antoine Biancone has been updating his repertoire of delightful Provençal dishes. Try the tasty, basil-perfumed tomato and aubergine compote, the cabbage stuffed with lamb's brain, veal sweetbreads, and morels, the fresh Montfavet goat cheese with cinnamon, and the prune byzantin for dessert. Irreproachable cellar, warm welcome, and a lovely leafy terrace overlooking lush lawns and rose bushes. **C** 390-500 F. **M** 195 F, 250 F, 350 F, 380 F, 495 F.

Les Frênes
(See restaurant above)
Closed Nov 15-Mar 15. 5 stes 1,600-2,800 F. 15 rms 595-1,600 F. Rms for disabled. Half-board 725-1,225 F. Air cond. Conf. Pool. Golf. Valet pkg. V, AE, DC, MC.
A gorgeous, supremely comfortable hotel, set in a wooded park with flower-filled garden and splashing fountains. The rooms are spread about in various outbuildings set round a superb swimming pool. The decor ranges from Louis XIII to Empire. Most rooms have been redecorated tastefully and equipped with luxurious baths and spa facilities. Capacious parking lot, peerless reception and service. Relais et Châteaux.

■ **In Morières-**
    lès-Avignon 84310   9 km E on N 100

Le Paradou
Av. Léon-Blum
90 33 34 15, fax 90 33 46 93
Closed Jan-Mar 23, Nov-Dec. 1 ste 500 F. 30 rms 270-340 F. Restaurant. Half-board 260-300 F. Air cond. Conf. Pool. Golf. Garage pkg. V, AE, DC, MC.
This modern, Provençal-style building is set in a shady park near Avignon and the airport. Comfortable rooms, good service. Guests have free use of tennis courts three kilometers away.

■ **In Le Pontet 84130**   5 km NE on N 7

Auberge de Cassagne
Avignon North exit on A 6
90 31 04 18, fax 90 32 25 09
Open daily until 9:30pm. Priv rm: 60. Garden dining. Air cond. Heated pool. Valet pkg. V, AE, DC, MC.
This lovely inn surrounded by trees and flower beds is a true oasis in a rather arid environment. Philippe Boucher's handsomely presented, full-

flavored cuisine is ever reliable and inspired. Try the langoustines grilled in their shells with an artichoke and anchovy tart, a tian of squab from the southern Alps with eggplant caviar and fig tart, or the iced pistachio dessert with white chocolate. Exceptional cellar; peerless service by a gracious, disciplined staff. Special children's services include games, high chairs, menus crafted according to their wishes, and baby sitting. Brazilian-style soirées and magic shows are also on hand here. **C** 300-500 F. **M** 220 F, 290 F, 360 F, 450 F.

Auberge de Cassagne
(See restaurant above)
Open year-round. 4 stes 1,180-1,780 F. 26 rms 420-1,180 F. Rms for disabled. Half-board 710-1,055 F. Air cond. Conf. Heated pool. Tennis. Golf. Valet pkg. V, AE, DC, MC.
Hidden in the charmless suburbs of town, this *auberge* is an oasis of luxury and beauty. The rooms are air conditioned but not terribly spacious, housed in a Provençal-style outbuilding opposite the swimming pool. Excellent breakfasts. Access to nearby golf course possible.

Hostellerie des Agassins
Le Pigeonnier
90 32 42 91, fax 90 32 08 29
Closed Sat lunch & Sun off-seas, Jan-Feb. Open until 9:45pm. Priv rm: 25. Garden dining. Air cond. Heated pool. Garage pkg. V, AE, DC, MC.
Young chef Franck Subileau, who trained at La Ferme de Mougins and La Pyramide in Vienne, seems to be well established in this restaurant just outside Avignon. His sunny cooking includes a sauté of squid and ratatouille with oregano, tiny chunks of summer savory-marinated lamb en brochette, and a monkfish and zucchini galette sautéed with basil. But he should strive for more intense flavors, and care as much for essential tastes as for presentation. **C** 190-350 F. **M** 130 F, 190 F, 280 F, 450 F.

Hostellerie des Agassins
(See restaurant above)
Closed Jan-Feb. 28 rms 400-850 F. Half-board 500-700 F. Air cond. Conf. Heated pool. Golf. Garage pkg. V, AE, DC, MC.
The Agassins's pleasant, spacious rooms have a summery feel owing, no doubt, to the wicker furniture. They give onto the garden and swimming pool via a wide terrace. The reception is absolutely charming.

■ **In Villeneuve-lès-Avignon 30400**   3 km NW

L'Atelier
5, rue de la Foire
90 25 01 84, fax 90 25 80 06
Closed mid Nov-mid Dec. 19 rms 240-440 F. Air cond. Golf. V, AE, DC, MC.
Set in the heart of sixteenth-century Villeneuve, L'Atelier boasts a pretty patio, and cozy rooms furnished and decorated à l'ancienne.

Aubertin
1, rue de l'Hôpital
90 25 94 84, fax 90 26 30 71
Closed Sun dinner, Nov 15-30. Open until 9:30pm (10pm in summer). Priv rm: 30. Terrace dining. Air cond. Pkg. V, AE, MC.
The luminous dining room is decorated with lovely photographs, and there are a few tables

on a terrace under the arcades. Chef Jean-Claude Aubertin offers savory, simple cooking that sings of Provence, at very reasonable prices. He has a sure hand, a delicate touch with flavor combinations, and an eye for fine products. Sample the milk-fed lamb from a farm near Gréoux-les-Bains, or the sinfully rich and perfectly prepared lamb sweetbreads with foie gras and morels served with a salad of local greens. Or the red mullet on toast with pistou, the fillet of sea bass coated with spices and nettle butter, or the crispy craquelin glacé made with honey and licorice and served with a tiny chocolate tart. The first two set menus are real winners. C 300-400 F. M 160 F (weekday lunch), 220 F, 295 F.

La Magnaneraie

37, rue Camp-de-Bataille
90 25 11 11, fax 90 25 46 37
Open daily until 9:30pm. Priv rm: 110. Garden dining. Air cond. Pool. Valet pkg. V, AE, DC, MC.
Chef Gérard Prayal's classic, refined cuisine based on superlative ingredients is as flavorful as ever, and the opulent dining room that opens onto a pretty park becomes more charming year by year. Try the roast monkfish in white truffle jus, the stuffed zucchini blossoms with a mushroom cream that might have been ordinary but becomes magical when he prepares it, the marvelous vanilla-scented crème brûléé, and the superb cheeses. But everything he prepares is refined and reliable. Remarkable cellar, particularly in Châteauneuf-du-papes. C 380-500 F. M 170 F, 250 F, 290 F, 330 F.

La Magnaneraie
(See restaurant above)
Open year-round. 25 rms 400-1,000 F. Air cond. Conf. Pool. Tennis. Valet pkg. V, AE, DC, MC.
Where silkworms once munched mulberries, spacious, freshly decorated rooms with nineteenth-century furniture now offer modern comfort and the charm of yore. Magnificent garden.

Le Prieuré
7, pl. du Chapitre - 90 25 18 20
Closed May 1, Nov 2-Mar 18. Open until 9:15pm. Priv rm: 120. Garden dining. Air cond. No pets. Garage pkg. V, AE, DC, MC.
Thriving under the smiling sun of Provence, in what must be one of the most charming spots on earth, chef Serge Chenet's cuisine marries regional flavors in delicate, inventive ways. We fell under the spell of his brandade of fresh cod with langoustines, his delicious cream of fresh peas paired with roasted sea scallops and grated truffle, the John Dory studded with bay leaves on a bed of raw spinach, his breast of squab with spices matched with spelt risotto, and savory grapefruit with lavender honey. An extra point this year. Set in a ravishing Italianate garden, with a cheerful, typically Avignonnais dining room and an excellent wine list strong in Côtes du Rhônes, the Prieuré is a gastronome's godsend. C 350-500 F. M 250 F (wine incl), 195 F, 295 F, 450 F.

Le Prieuré
(See restaurant above)
Closed Nov 2-Mar 18. 10 stes 1,400-1,750 F. 26 rms 550-1,200 F. Half-board 641-1,211 F. Air cond. Conf. Pool. Tennis. Pkg. V, AE, DC, MC.
Whether you book in the old priory, next to the church (smallish rooms), or in the new annex

by the swimming pool (large rooms with a fine view of the park or patios), you'll find the same grand style and luxury, far from prying eyes and the madding crowd. Impeccable reception and service. Relais et Châteaux.

See also: **Baux-de-Provence (Les), Noves**

AVORIAZ 74	→ Morzine

AYTRÉ 17	→ Rochelle (La)

AZAY-LE-RIDEAU	37190
Paris 254 - Tours 26 - Saumur 46 - Châtellerault 60   *Indre/Loire*

L'Aigle d'Or
10, rue A.-Riché
47 45 24 58, fax 47 45 90 18
Closed Tue dinner off-seas, Sun dinner, Wed, Feb school hols, Dec 10-25. Open until 9pm. Priv rm: 40. Garden dining. Pkg. V, MC.
The eagle (aigle) circles not far from the château; his nest is a former store. But the cooking is served with no claws drawn: pleasant salad of sea scallops with strips of smoked salmon, roast saddle of young rabbit with rosemary jus, monkfish with green pea cream, and orange-sauced figs stuffed with prune cream. C 210-270 F. M 88 F (weekday lunch), 140 F, 195 F, 270 F.

Le Grand Monarque
3, pl. de la République
47 45 40 08, fax 47 45 46 25
Closed Jan 1-Mar 25, Nov 15-Dec 31. Open until 10pm. Priv rm: 20. Garden dining. Pkg. V, AE, DC, MC.
Chef Frédéric Arnault's cooking is at its best when it stays traditional, with a few regional influences: fricassée of eels with herb butter, pig's feet in Chinon wine, iced Armagnac soufflé. Rich regional cellar. Courteous welcome, professional service with a smile in this pleasant old house with a walled garden. C 240-360 F. M 95 F (weekday lunch, Sat, wine incl), 160 F, 195 F, 295 F.

Le Grand Monarque
(See restaurant above)
Closed Dec 15-Jan. 1 ste 650-900 F. 25 rms 250-620 F. Half-board 325-500 F. Conf. Pkg. V, AE, DC.
Charming, well-equipped, recently renovated rooms in a tasteful garden setting. Some rooms are soundproofed, most have satellite TV.

BAGES 11	→ Narbonne

BAGNÈRES-DE-BIGORRE	65200
Paris 800 - Lourdes 22 - Tarbes 21 - St-Gaudens 57   *H.-Pyrénées*

La Résidence
Parc thermal de Salut
62 91 19 19, fax 62 95 29 88
Closed Oct 15-Mar. 31 rms 350-370 F. Restaurant. Half-board 325-360 F. Conf. Heated pool. Tennis. No pets. Pkg. V, AE, DC, MC.
Here you'll find quiet, comfortable rooms in a sizeable establishment facing the mountains and the hot-springs spa.

137

■ **In Beaudéan 65710**   5 km S on N 135

12/20 **La Petite Auberge**   ◆
62 91 72 16
Closed Tue, Dec 1-15, Jun 1-15. Open until 9pm. Garden dining. V, AE, MC.
The French countryside sprouts fewer and fewer inns of this type: a rustic—almost primitive—but spotless old farmhouse, where travelers can count on authentic regional cuisine: rib-sticking garbure soup, chicken leg confit (overcooked), good local cheeses served in miniscule portions. Small choice of southwest wines.
C 100-180 F. **M** 76 F, 90 F, 105 F, 150 F.

BAGNOLES-DE-L'ORNE   61140

Paris 234 - Alençon 48 - Argentan 39 - Domfront 19   *Orne*

▲▲ **Lutétia**
Bd P.-Chalvet
33 37 94 77, fax 33 30 09 87
Closed end Oct beg Apr. 33 rms 200-440 F. Restaurant. Half-board 370-530 F. Conf. Garage pkg. V, AE, DC, MC.
A solid establishment set in a peaceful garden, near the center of town, with comfortable, attractively decorated rooms.

Le Manoir du Lys   ◆
Route de Juvigny
33 37 80 69, fax 33 30 05 80
Closed Sun dinner & Mon (Nov-Easter), Jan-Feb. Open until 10pm. Priv rm: 50. Garden dining. Pkg. V, AE, DC, MC.
The ultimate Norman manor, complete with flowered balconies and an apple orchard, offers a fine regional menu. Try the vegetable ravioli in cider, a charlotte of andouille (tripe sausage) from Vire, and teurgoule (thick rice pudding) on the 130 F menu, or order the lamb grazed on salt meadows near Mont-Saint-Michel or the squab from Saint-André-de-Messei à la carte.
C 260-400 F. **M** 130 F, 150 F, 190 F, 210 F, 260 F.

▲▲ **Le Manoir du Lys**   ♣♥
(See restaurant above)
Closed Sun & Mon (Nov-Easter), Jan 8-Feb. 3 stes 680-1,200 F. 20 rms 300-680 F. Half-board 380-600 F. Conf. Tennis. Golf. Pkg. V, AE, DC, MC.
This luxuriously renovated nineteenth-century manor house proposes bright, comfortable rooms recently redecorated in colors that may not please all tastes, but even the birds and deer in the surrounding forest, not to mention the competent staff, welcome you warmly. Should you tire of golf and tennis, you may learn the sylvan art of mushroom-hunting here.

BAGNOLET 93   → **Paris Suburbs**

BAGNOLS   69620

Paris 450 - Lyon 33 - Villefranche 12 - Tarare 20   *Rhône*

Château de Bagnols
74 71 40 00, fax 74 71 40 49
Closed Nov-Mar. Open until 9:30pm. No pets. V, AE, DC, MC.
Set down in the heart of Beaujolais's hilly countryside, this meticulously restored château, complete with moat, keeps, and cobbled courtyard, is the property of Lord and Lady Hamlyn.

They have furnished the place with antiques, rare fabrics, and ornaments. Modern amenities are of course on hand, but cleverly concealed to preserve the illusion of a medieval setting. We must admit that all this lacks soul, but we can't quibble with the pleasure of sitting down to dinner in the former guards' hall with its magnificent fireplace, the biggest sculpted Gothic fireplace left in France. Let's hope the Lyonnais chef has the sense to stick to simple recipes (rabbit confit, steak grilled over the fireplace, and Bresse poultry), which are by far the best choices on the current menu. **C** 350-500 F. **M** 240 F, 330 F, 380 F, 420 F.

▲▲ **Château de Bagnols**   ♣♥
(See restaurant above)
Closed Nov-Mar. 5 stes 3,000-4,000 F. 15 rms 1,900-3,800 F. Air cond. Conf. Golf. Pkg. V, AE, DC, MC.
This hotel is without a doubt the most beautiful château-hotel in France. It's a monument to taste and refinement, from the frescoes dating from the sixteenth and eighteenth centuries, to the quality of the furnishings and the decor of the rooms, all different. But it's a museum you can live in, where it seems natural to sleep in a canopy bed and store your tooth brush in a Charles II goblet. The day when a family of true hoteliers takes up residence here and brings a touch of warmth and friendliness, this palace will become a paradise.

BAGNOLS-SUR-CÈZE   30200

Paris 667 - Pont-Saint-Esprit 11 - Avignon 33 - Nîmes 48   *Gard*

 Les Jardins de Montcaud
Hameau de Combe-Sabran
66 89 60 60, fax 66 89 45 04
Closed Jan-Mar. Open until 10pm. Priv rm: 80. Terrace dining. Air cond. Pool. Pkg. V, AE, DC, MC.
This handsome farmhouse with summery decor and dining terrace stands at the entrance to the lovely, leafy grounds of the château. Jean-Yves Bouvet's light, fresh cuisine is as sunny as Provence: large roast langoustines coated with sesame seeds and served with garden vegetables, delicate and savory calf's head, and, for dessert, a delicate tourtière of pears with honey, pistachios and rosemary. Friendly welcome, competent service. **C** 330-380 F. **M** 130 F (lunch exc Sun), 170 F, 220 F, 260 F, 330 F, 400 F.

▲▲ **Château de Montcaud**   ♣♥
(See restaurant above)
Closed Jan 2-Mar 31. 2 stes 1,450-1,950 F. 30 rms 640-1,680 F. Rms for disabled. Half-board 950-2,200 F. Air cond. Conf. Heated pool. Tennis. Golf. Garage pkg. Helipad. V, AE, DC, MC.
Admirably situated between Avignon and the Cévennes Mountains, this fully restored nineteenth-century château and adjoining farmhouse offer cozy, tastefully decorated rooms. Excellent breakfast. Sauna, steam baths, exercise room. Charming welcome.

▲▲ **Le Mas de Ventadous**   ♣♥
69, route d'Avignon
66 89 61 26, fax 66 79 99 88
Open year-round. 22 rms 500-750 F. Rms for disabled. Restaurant. Half-board 500-600 F. Air cond. Conf. Pool. Tennis. Pkg. V.
These pleasant, sunny, well-equipped rooms are arranged in bungalows surrounded by lawns.

On the grounds is a seventeenth-century pavilion, available for meetings, conferences, etc.

BAIX 07210
Paris 591 - Valence 33 - Montélimar 25 - Privas 16 *Ardèche*

La Cardinale
Quai du Rhône
75 85 80 40, fax 75 85 82 07
Closed Sun dinner & Mon (Jan), Feb 1-Mar 10. Open until 11:30pm. Priv rm: 30. Terrace dining. Pkg. V, AE, DC.
Your attention, please! This establishment, a seventeenth-century Provençal domaine, gave birth to the Relais de Campagne chain, later renamed Relais et Châteaux. The restaurant was all but forgotten for awhile, but last year we awarded it "two toques, in expectation of even better," and now there are three. This will come as no surprise to anyone who has tasted Eric Sapet's intelligent, imaginative cuisine with its focus on natural flavors. Not for nothing did the train with superchefs Joël Robuchon and Jacques Cagna, with a stint at La Tour d'Argent along the way. The refined and sunny tastes of Sapet's dishes have found a perfect setting in the elegantly simple dining room with tile floors and a lovely riverside terrace. Savor the subtle balance of the foie gras with artichokes and a fondant of fresh almonds, the delicious wing of glazed Bresse duck with red onions and roasted figs, a convincing marriage of long-simmered vegetables and summer fruit, the magnificent squab confit with the thigh served in a ballottine of chestnuts and honeyed garlic purée, or the luscious desserts that take you to the heart of nearby Provence, such as a chard and white peach tart, or figs poached in a rhubarb compote with hazlenut croquettes. Add a bottle of Hermitage, Côte-Rotie, or Saint-Joseph, and voluptuousness is guaranteed. A little more discipline in the service department and everything would be perfect. C 450-600 F. M 195 F, 360 F, 450 F.

La Cardinale
(See restaurant above)
Closed Feb 1-Mar 10. 5 stes 1,050-1,650 F. 10 rms 750-1,050 F. Half-board 825-1,175 F. Air cond. Conf. Pool. Tennis. Golf. Pkg. Helipad. V, AE, DC.
Luxury and nature are close companions in this lovely, freshly renovated seventeenth-century mansion with a superb view of the Rhône Valley. Four beautiful rooms in the mansion itself, with the others in La Résidence, an annex three kilometers away surrounded by a large park. Magnificent breakfasts and charming welcome. Relais et Châteaux.

BALDENHEIM 67600
Paris 440 - Marckolsheim 13 - Colmar 28 - Sélestat 9 *Bas-Rhin*

La Couronne
45, rue de Sélestat
88 85 32 22, fax 88 85 36 27
Closed Sun dinner & Mon (exc hols), 1st wk of Jan, last wk of Jul. Open until 9pm. Pkg. V, AE, MC.
The opulence of Alsace is here to taste in this lovely pink house on the edge of the village. From the warm and cozy interior to the first-rate cuisine of Daniel Rubiné, the treasures of the region are on full display. Lightness, a sure sense

of nuance, and prime ingredients are the hallmarks of a menu that features saffrony noodles with foie gras, pickerel matelot, pike and eel in Frankstein wine sauce, and strawberry croustillant. The cellar holds a cache of superb local wines. C 280-430 F. M 150 F (weekdays), 235 F, 300 F, 410 F.

BALEINE (LA) 50450
Paris 325 - Coutances 25 - St-Lô 28 - Villedieu-les-P. 15 *Manche*

Auberge de la Baleine
Le Bourg - 33 90 92 74
Closed Wed off-seas. Open until 8:30pm (10pm w-e). Pkg. V, AE, DC, MC.
Once a village schoolhouse, this rustic inn tucked away in a delightful valley is the showcase for Jean-Charles Vezin's adroit, classic cuisine. Fresh fruit lends a bright accent to offerings like pan-roasted foie gras with raspberries, salmon with beurre à l'orange, and duck confit with grapefruit. Small, affordable cellar. Worthwhile prix-fixe meals. C 190-250 F. M 90 F, 130 F, 175 F.

BANDOL 83150
Paris 842 - Marseille 49 - Toulon 17 - Aix-en-Provence 74 *Var*

Auberge du Port
9, allée J.-Moulin
94 29 42 63, fax 94 29 44 59
Open daily until 9:30pm (11pm in summer). Terrace dining. V, AE, DC, MC.
Jean-Pierre Ghiribelli has let his attention slip, and it shows in the uneven cooking on offer when we last visited this sunny auberge with its pretty garden terrace: savory eggplant cake and fresh Brousse cheese, but a badly cooked red mullet salad, a generous but greasy parrillada, and good profiteroles. We take away a point, especially since the prices are anything but giveaways. Diversified cellar, irreproachble welcome and service. C 330-450 F. M 105 F, 138 F, 148 F, 150 F, 175 F, 188 F, 210 F.

12/20 Chez Babette
1, rue du Dr-Marçon - 94 29 84 17
Open daily until 10pm (11pm in summer). Terrace dining. Air cond. V, AE.
This rustic, friendly bistrot offers down-to-earth carpaccio, fresh pasta with seafood, peppers with anchoïade, and tiramisu. Unbeatable prices. C 120-200. M 68 F, 86 F.

Le Clocher
1, rue de la Paroisse - 94 32 47 65
Closed Wed (Oct-Mar), Sun lunch. Open until 9pm. Priv rm: 22. Terrace dining. No pets. V, AE, DC, MC.
There's no better way to work up an appetite than to walk across one of Provence's best open markets and into the small, sun-drenched dining room of this restaurant at the foot of the town church. Tony Gantel's cuisine is a winning blend of flavors and Provençal perfumes: you'll enjoy his sautéed foie gras with wild cranberries, monkfish with warm aïoli, and a classic but savory nutmeg tart. The lowest priced set menu is a good deal. Excellent choice of regional wines, and Martine Gantel's welcome and service are sunny indeed. C 250-360 F. M 150 F, 190 F.

139

Délos ⚓🍽
Ile de Bendor
94 32 22 23, fax 94 32 41 44
Open year-round. 55 rms 470-1,410 F. Restaurant. Half-board 360-970 F. Conf. Pool. Tennis. No pets. Helipad. V, AE, DC.
Comfortable rooms, decorated in a variety of styles, enjoy an idyllic view of the sea. Numerous sporting activities.

 Ile Rousse
17, bd Louis-Lumière
94 29 46 86, fax 94 29 49 49
Open daily until 10:30pm. No pets. V, AE, DC, MC.
Flying under the flag of new owners, this lovely establishment anchored near the yacht port offers a big dining room with bright, understated Mediterranean decor with a great view of the sea, as well as poolside dining and a terrace overlooking the beach. Chef Laurent Chauviat treats top local ingredients in original ways: delicate shellfish soup, harmonious and perfectly cooked roast capon with sage and honey, subtle lavender blossom crème brûlée. Diversified, fairly priced wine selection. Superb welcome and service. **C** 240-430 F. **M** 150 F, 220 F, 330 F.

Ile Rousse
(See restaurant above)
Open year-round. 2 stes 650-1,100 F. 53 rms 350-1,000 F. Half-board 590-1,200 F. Air cond. Conf. Pool. Golf. Valet pkg. V, AE, DC, MC.
The building designed by Fleury Linossier in Provençal style has huge, sunny, well maintained and modernized rooms, some with views of the sea. Full breakfast. In summer, a buffet is served on the beach. Health center. Excellent welcome and service.

 Moulin de Chaméron
48 61 84 48 (R), 48 61 83 80 (H),
fax 48 61 84 92
Closed Tue off-seas, Nov 15-Feb. Open until 9pm. Garden dining. Heated pool. Pkg. V, AE, MC.
The tranquil beauty of *la France profonde* is embodied in this ancient mill house in the Berry region. Jean Mérilleau's soothing, expertly rendered dishes lend a special charm to the surroundings. The 200 F menu is a case in point: excellent oxtail aûmonière in Menetou wine sauce, delicate pork fillet with garlic sauce, fine cheese assortment, and a delicious chocolate fondant. Superb, fairly priced cellar featuring local wines (Sancerre, Menetou-Salon). **C** 250-330 F. **M** 150 F, 200 F.

 Moulin de Chaméron ⚓🍽
(See restaurant above)
Closed Tue, Nov 15-Feb. 1 ste 650-780 F. 12 rms 330-480 F. Air cond. Conf. Heated pool. Pkg. Helipad. V, AE, MC.
An eighteenth-century mill covered with vines houses adorable guest rooms. Garden; heated pool. All around are heaths and forests to explore.

---

*Some establishments change their **closing times** without warning. It is always wise to check in advance.*

Le Catalan
Route de Cerbère
68 88 02 80, fax 68 88 16 14
Closed Jan 4-Mar 15, Oct-Dec 23. 36 rms 340-520 F. Restaurant. Half-board 480 F. Air cond. Conf. Pool. Pkg. V, AE, DC, MC.
This bit of modern architecture perches on the rocky coast over the Bay of Banyuls. Every room enjoys the view. Bar.

La Littorine ۞
Plage des Elmes - 68 88 09 90 (R),
68 88 03 12 (H), fax 68 88 53 03
Closed Wed off-seas, Nov 15-Dec 15, Jan 5-25. Open until 10pm. Priv rm: 30. Terrace dining. Pkg. V, AE, DC, MC.
A new chef has just taken charge in this pleasant little beach inn, preparing the sunny house specialties: foie gras with apples, grilled sea bass with fennel and basil-scented potatoes, and pears in puff pastry with caramel sauce. Cheerful service. **C** 250-350 F. **M** 210 F (wine incl), 90 F, 150 F, 285 F.

Les Elmes
(See restaurant above)
Closed Nov 15-Dec 15, Jan 3-20. 2 stes 390-460 F. 29 rms 250-460 F. Rms for disabled. Half-board 260-390 F. Air cond. Garage pkg. Helipad. V, AE, DC, MC.
A nice beach hotel, with a carefree, friendly ambience. Ask for one of the new rooms on the top floor: they are well equipped and attractively decorated, although the contemporary decor may leave some people cold.

Le Sardinal
4 bis, pl. P.-Reig - 68 88 30 07
Closed Sun dinner & Mon (exc in summer), Feb 2-7, Nov 15-30. Open until 9:30pm (10:30pm in summer). Priv rm: 45. Terrace dining. Air cond. V, AE.
The 140 F menu is a good sampling of the delicate regional cooking on hand in this friendly establishment with a terrace overlooking the sea: salmon tartare with basil mousse, sea bream sautéed in flavorful seafood butter sauce, beef filet mignon with shellfish and a tender green pepper cream, goat cheeses, and nice house sherbets. Charming reception, and a newly expanded cellar. **C** 180-350 F. **M** 85 F (wine incl), 140 F, 190 F, 290 F.

La Paix
11, av. A.-Guidet
21 07 11 03, fax 21 07 43 66
Closed Sun dinner. Open until 9:30pm. Priv rm: 20. Pkg. V, MC.
Set in a small white house on the village square, this worthy little restaurant aspires to great luxury. In the meantime, Remy Hautecoeur offers nice sautéed gambas in shellfish oil, roast pickerel in beer, squab gallette with chopped eggplant, and a "horn of plenty" with fresh fruit. Good choice of Bordeaux. Service could use some discipline. **C** 300-400 F. **M** 68 F (weekdays, Sat lunch), 95 F, 150 F, 190 F, 250 F.

BARBIZON 77630
Paris 56 - Melun 11 - Fontainebleau 10   *Seine et Marne*

12/20 Les Alouettes
4, rue A.-Barye - 60 66 41 98
*Open daily until 9:30pm. Priv rm: 12. Terrace dining.
Hotel: 22 rms 270-380 F. Tennis. Golf. Pkg. V, AE, DC.*
The soothing green garden reaches right into
the seductive English-style decor. The menu
favors simple cuisine and generous servings:
estouffade of wild boar in Gevrey-Chambertin
sauce will stick to your ribs, and the roast wild duck
has many fans. **C** 300-400 F. **M** 160 F, 190 F.

Le Bas-Bréau
Rue Grande - 60 66 40 05, fax 60 69 22 89
*Open daily until 9:30pm. Priv rm: 40. Garden dining.
Valet pkg. V, AE, MC.*
The likes of Robert Louis Stevenson and
George Sand have tarried in this elegant auberge
on the edge of the Fontainebleau forest, and one
look at the garden will show you why. Jean-
Pierre Tava takes good care of his guests in the
newly redecorated dining room, while chef Alain
Tavernier produces subtle and refined cuisine
based on excellent products: fricassée of frogs'
legs with shallot confit, fillet of bar with sea-
urchin coral and fennel compote, puff pastry
with caramelized mangoes. Excellent house
breads. **C** 500-800 F. **M** 330 F, 390 F (weekday
lunch, wine incl), 380 F.

Le Bas-Bréau
(See restaurant above)
*Open year-round. 8 stes 1,700-2,800 F. 12 rms 950-
1,500 F. Conf. Heated pool. Tennis. Golf. Valet pkg.
Helipad. V, AE, MC.*
Surely the most refined and luxurious inn of
the Paris region, set amid sumptuous rose gardens and extensive grounds. Rooms are
decorated with delightful simplicity; the salon
was redecorated this year. Superb breakfasts.
Relais et Châteaux.

Hostellerie Les Pléiades
Rue Grande - 60 66 40 25, fax 60 66 41 68
Open daily until 9:30pm. Priv rm: 40. Garden dining.
Whether to the sounds of birds singing in the
garden or of a fire crackling in the fireplace, a
dinner here is sure to make you feel cozy, and
the classic cooking is sure to please. Try, on the
first set menu, the fried whiting (a rather stingy
serving), pollack in beurre blanc with excellent
vegetables, Brie (the pasteurized variety), and a
generous serving of warm tart. Charming service. **C** 260-380 F. **M** 145 F, 180 F, 280 F.

Hostellerie Les Pléiades
(See restaurant above)
*Open year-round. 1 ste 650 F. 23 rms 320-550 F.
Half-board 490-520 F. Conf. Pkg. V, AE, DC, MC.*
A charming establishment with inviting, com-
fortable rooms, some of them on the small side.
Professional reception and service.

BARBOTAN-LES-THERMES 32150
Paris 686 - Mont-de-Marsan 43 - Condom 37 - Nérac 44   *Gers*

La Bastide Gasconne ۞
62 08 31 00, fax 62 08 31 99
*Closed Wed (exc Jul-Aug), Oct 30-Mar 26. Open
until 9:30pm. Garden dining. Pool. Pkg. V, AE, MC.*

A new chef and a new pricing strategy have
brought major changes to this pleasant old
domain. Arnaud Lindivat's single set menu at
160 F (there is no à la carte service) offers warm
cheese, well seasoned lentil and potato terrine
with foie gras, blanquette of veal hock and head
(the combination seems a little off balance,
though), and a delicate fresh white peach with a
wine granité. **M** 160 F.

La Bastide Gasconne
(See restaurant above)
*Closed Oct 30-Mar 26. 2 stes 780-1,500 F. 30 rms
650-770 F. Conf. Pool. Tennis. Pkg. V, AE, MC.*
A fine hotel in an eighteenth-century manor
house, where the service is as perfectly gracious
as the appointments are tasteful and comfortable. Guest rooms look over the pool and beautifully tended grounds. Relais et Châteaux.

Cante-Grit
51, av. des Thermes
62 69 52 12, fax 62 69 53 98
*Closed Oct/Apr 15. 23 rms 185-310 F. Restaurant.
Half-board 309-410 F. Conf. Golf. Pkg. V, AE, MC.*
Located near the thermal cure center, this
handsome rustic hotel is clothed in Virginia
creeper. Nicely furnished rooms overlooking the
countryside. Garden.

■ In **Cazaubon 32150**   3 km SW on D 626

12/20 Château Bellevue
Rue J.-Cappin
62 09 51 95, fax 62 09 54 57
*Closed Jan-Feb (exc for groups). Open until 9:30pm.
Priv rm: 50. Terrace dining. Pool. No pets. Garage
pkg. V, AE, DC, MC.*
Choose between the poolside terrace or the
luminous dining room with its polished furniture
and elegant draperies. Either is an appropriate
setting for the chef's terrine of duck confit, zucchini chartreuse, turbot fillet sautéed with herbs,
or saddle of young rabbit. Friendly welcome.
C 270-400 F. **M** 95 F (weekday lunch), 150 F,
210 F.

Château Bellevue
(See restaurant above)
*Closed Jan-Feb (exc for groups). 2 stes 565-575 F.
21 rms 210-500 F. Half-board 310-475 F. Conf. Pool.
Golf. No pets. Garage pkg. V, AE, DC, MC.*
A splendid nineteenth-century residence with
spacious, pleasant rooms, some of which give
onto the pool, while others overlook the courtyard.

BARCELONNETTE 04400
Paris 740 - Nice 209 - Briançon 84   *Alpes/H.-P.*

Azteca
3, rue F.-Arnaud
92 81 46 36, fax 92 81 43 92
*Open year-round. 3 stes 440-500 F. 24 rms 300-
470 F. Rms for disabled. Conf. Garage pkg. V, AE,
DC, MC.*
Mexican motifs dominate the decor of rooms
that look out over the mountains and the Ubaye
Valley. Huge rooms with cheery white wooden
furniture, complete with satellite TV. Very good
breakfasts.

La Mangeoire
Pl. des Quatre-Vents
92 81 01 61, fax 92 81 01 61
Closed Mon, Tue, May 15-31, Nov 12-Dec 5. Open until 9:30pm. Terrace dining. Pkg. V, AE, MC.
   This former stables set in the shadow of the town church boasts pleasantly rustic decor, whether you choose the lovely dining room with a beamed ceiling or a table on the terrace. The new chef, Laurent Dodé, has already won a local following (and two toques) for such refined dishes as a jellied tomato consommé, an excellent lamb and goat cheese gratin, and a delicious espresso-flavored chocolate pot de crème with liqueur de lait. Lengthy, annotated wine list. Unpretentious, smiling service and welcome. **C** 240-340 F. **M** 98 F (dinner), 135 F, 185 F, 240 F.

■ In **Pra-**
Loup 04400   8.5 km SW on D 902 and D 109

Auberge du Clos Sorel
Village de Clos Sorel - 92 84 10 74
Closed Apr-Jul 1, Sep 7-Dec 15. 11 rms 400-800 F. Half-board 400-600 F. Conf. Heated pool. Tennis. Golf. Pkg. V, MC.
   In a handsomely restored, mountainside farm you'll find this lovely inn with a breathtaking view across the valley. Charming, rustic decor; comfortable rooms.

■ In **Sauze 04400**   4 km SE on D 900 and D 209

Alp' Hôtel
92 81 05 04, fax 92 81 45 84
Closed Apr 23-May 28, Oct 15-Dec 21. 8 stes 495-1,200 F. 24 rms 420-470 F. Restaurant. Half-board 360-380 F. Conf. Heated pool. Garage pkg. Helipad. V, AE, DC, MC.
   This modern complex ideally located near the lifts boasts pretty rooms with mountain views, a garden, terrace, and heated pool as well as a bar and a fitness center. Suites have kitchenettes.

Paris 670 - Aubenas 46 - Alès 28 - Pont-St-Esprit 32   *Gard*

Le Mas du Terme
3 km SE on D 901
66 24 56 31, fax 66 24 58 54
Closed Jan-Feb. 6 stes 400-800 F. 20 rms 280-450 F. Restaurant. Half-board 370-420 F. Conf. Pool. Golf. Pkg. V, MC.
   This renovated eighteenth-century Provençal *mas* stands amid vineyards and offers modern, comfortable rooms. For leisure hours, there is a sun room and a billiards room.

Paris 336 - Coutances 48 - Cherbourg 37 - Carentan 43   *Manche*

 La Marine
11, rue de Paris - 33 04 91 71 (R),
33 53 83 31 (H), fax 33 53 39 60
Closed Sun dinner & Mon (Feb-Mar & Oct), Mon lunch (Apr-Jun), Nov-Feb 15. Open until 9:30pm. Terrace dining. Pkg. V, DC, MC.
   The flattering light reflected from the Channel illuminates this dining room, casting a lovely glow on the English period furniture and on chef Laurent Cesne's numerous admirers (many of them are English, too). You are sure to admire his direct, open style which emphasizes fresh ingredients and local traditions. The 190 F menu is remarkable: Normandy foie gras, a delicate cod tart, fresh goat cheese terrine with eggplant confit, and dark chocolate tart with chicory sauce. Excellent choice of Burgundies and Bordeaux, an utterly affable service overseen by Laurent's mom and dad. **C** 300-450 F. **M** 130 F (weekdays, Sat lunch, Sun dinner), 190 F, 380 F.

La Marine
(See restaurant above)
Closed beg Nov-mid Feb. 3 stes 620-790 F. 28 rms 380-520 F. Half-board 380-480 F. Pkg. V, DC, MC.
   One is all but in the drink here at high tide. The comfortable rooms are quiet (double-glazed windows) and well equipped. Lovely sea views, great breakfasts.

Paris 608 - Bordeaux 38 - Libourne 45 - Langon 8   *Gironde*

Château de Rolland
N 113 - 56 27 15 75, fax 56 27 01 69
Closed Wed, Nov 15-Easter. 10 rms 350-650 F. Restaurant. Half-board 500 F. Conf. No pets. Pkg. V, AE, DC, MC.
   Watch the grape vines grow in perfect tranquility, from your spacious and comfortable room in a former monastery.

Paris 463 - Rennes 133 - Vannes 72 - Saint-Nazaire 17   *Loire-Atl.*

Bellevue Plage
27, bd de l'Océan
40 60 28 55, fax 40 60 10 18
Closed Nov 11-Feb 12. 2 stes 650-850 F. 32 rms 350-790 F. Restaurant. Half-board 360-610 F. Conf. Golf. Pkg. V, AE, DC, MC.
   Here are modern, soundproofed rooms near the sea-cure establishments. Sauna; sun room.

Castel Marie-Louise
1, av. d'Andrieu
40 11 48 38, fax 40 11 48 35
Closed Jan 8-Feb 17. Open until 10pm. Priv rm: 60. Garden dining. No pets. Pkg. V, AE, DC, MC.
   Perhaps we have the vaguely stilted atmosphere of the opulent decor in this seaside restaurant to blame for the uneven tone we recently noted in chef Éric Mignard's cooking. Bravo for the lobe of foie gras with hazlenuts, but the langoustines roasted with sage were both contrived and bland, the potato galette with smoked salmon and caviar was off balance in the flavor department, and the half-raw chocolate cake was only half successful. One point less this year. Well stocked cellars, perfect welcome and service. **C** 300-600 F. **M** 150 F (weekday lunch), 430 F (dinner), 195 F, 295 F.

Castel Marie-Louise

(See restaurant above)
*Closed Jan 9-Feb 10. 2 stes 1,300-2,200 F. 29 rms
750-1,850 F. Rms for disabled. Half-board 950-
2,100 F. Conf. Tennis. Golf. Pkg. V, AE, DC, MC.*

The refined, classic decor is regularly spruced
up, the rooms are extremely comfortable, the
service remarkable, and the whole is situated in
a beautiful garden with a sweeping view of the
beach. Sea-cure establishment 100 meters from
the hotel. Relais et Châteaux.

Christina

26, bd. Hennecart
40 60 22 44, fax 40 11 04 31
*Closings not available. 5 stes 750-850 F. 36 rms 380-
550 F. Restaurant. Half-board 375-450 F. Conf. Golf.
No pets. Valet pkg. V, MC.*

Functional, perfectly pleasant, soundproof
rooms benefit from the Christina's beachfront
location. There is a sun room and a little *salon
de thé* with a panoramic view of the bay. Restaurant service available from Easter to October.

12/20 La Ferme du Grand Clos

52, av. de Lattre-de-Tassigny
40 60 03 30
*Closed Wed off-seas. Annual closings not available.
Open until 11pm. Garden dining. Pkg. V.*

Crisp buckwheat galettes and home-style
dishes (coq au vin and cod brandade) are served
with a smile at this simple, tidy little establishment. Appealing cellar. C 160-220 F.

L'Hermitage

5, espl. L.-Barrière
40 11 46 46, fax 40 11 46 45
*Closed Nov 1-Mar 31. Open until 10pm (11:30pm
in summer). Priv rm: 500. Garden dining. Air cond.
Heated pool. No pets. Valet pkg. V, AE, DC, MC.*

This dignified, wood-panelled dining room is
the "gastronomic" showcase of the Hermitage.
Here chef Marc Bayon displays his technical
know-how as applied to the peerless seafood
placed at his disposal. Sample Bayon's langoustines with anchoïade of raw vegetables, cider-
braised sea bream with roast potatoes, and a very
Breton dessert, buttery kouig-aman. The wide-
ranging cellar is expensive, yet is well served by
a knowledgeable sommelier. For less pricey fare,
look into the Eden Beach, a good brasserie also
in the Hermitage. C 400-450 F. M 150 F.

L'Hermitage

(See restaurant above)
*Closed Nov 1-Mar 30. 11 stes 2,000-7,500 F.
210 rms 860-2,360 F. Half-board 1,200-3,020 F. Air
cond. Conf. Heated pool. Tennis. Golf. Valet pkg. V,
AE, DC, MC.*

An imposing (if not exactly charming) luxury
beach hotel, recently renovated. Amenities include a sauna, fitness center, and children's club
in the summer months. Some rooms have great
sea views.

Manoir du Parc

3, allée des Albatros
40 60 24 52, fax 40 60 55 96
*Closed Nov 3-Mar 15. 20 rms 270-520 F. Restaurant.
No pets. Pkg. V, AE, MC.*

A charming turn-of-the-century hotel sheltered
by pines, just 150 meters from the beach. A
recent renovation has made the smallish but
nicely appointed rooms even more attractive.

La Marcanderie

5, av. d'Agen
40 24 03 12, fax 40 11 08 21
*Open daily until 9:30pm (10pm in Jul). Priv rm: 12.
Pkg. V, AE, MC.*

The bright, warm, pastel decor of this converted villa complements chef Jean-Luc Giraud's
personalized cooking based on straight-from-
the-sea ingredients. No special flourishes, but
great satisfaction in the simple, flavorful assortment of tiny clams, mussels, and langoustines,
or the perfect crispy lobster croustillant, followed by a fine chocolate cake. The lowest
priced set menu is a particularly good deal. Wide
choice of Loire Valley wines. Service a is bit
hesitant. C 300-400 F. M 155 F, 190 F, 230 F,
280 F.

La Palmeraie

7, allée des Cormorans
40 60 24 40, fax 40 42 73 71
*Closed Oct-beg Apr. 23 rms 310-440 F. Rms for dis-
abled. Restaurant. Half-board 310-440 F. V, AE, MC.*

Overrun with flowers, this pink-and-white hotel
near the beach offers comfortable rooms, some
with English-style furnishings. Courteous reception.

Le Rossini

13, av. Evens
40 60 25 81, fax 40 42 73 52
*Closed Sun dinner & Mon off-seas, 10 days at Nov
school hols, Jan 10-30. Open until 9:30pm. Priv
rm: 20. Terrace dining. Air cond. Hotel: 14 rms 260-
450 F. Half-board 270-390 F. Golf. Pkg. V, AE, DC.*

Michel Fornaréso's cooking is marked by fresh
ingredients and polished technique. Try the fish
tartare, beef fillet Rossini, and apples and prunes
in Brittany brandy. Charming welcome, comfortable but rather bland decor. C 270-370 F.
M 110 F (weekdays), 160 F, 200 F, 235 F.

Royal

Av. P.-Loti - 40 11 48 48, fax 40 11 48 45
*Closed Nov 15-Dec 15. 8 stes 1,800-3,700 F. 87 rms
700-1,600 F. Rms for disabled. Restaurant. Half-
board 220 F. Conf. Heated pool. Tennis. Golf. Valet
pkg. V, AE, DC, MC.*

A fine seafront hotel that dates from the turn
of the century, set in lovely grounds. In addition
to bright, inviting rooms, there are three restaurants (one for dieters, one on the beach) and
a bar.

Paris 714 - Avignon 31 - Arles 19   B./Rhône

Bautezar

F. Mistral Grande-Rue
90 54 32 09, fax 90 54 49 51
*Closed Jan 5-Mar 15. 10 rms 350-450 F. Restaurant.
V, MC.*

A fine little hotel with character, and views
across the Val d'Enfer.

La Benvengudo

On D 78 F - 90 54 32 54, fax 90 54 42 58
*Closed Nov 15-Feb 15. 3 stes 750-920 F. 17 rms
520-700 F. Restaurant. Half-board 540-630 F. Air
cond. Conf. Pool. Tennis. Golf. Pkg. V, AE, MC.*

A superb Provençal setting and magnificent
furnishings make this vine-covered country
manor a delightful stop. Rooms are well
equipped and offer excellent value for money.

La Cabro d'Or

Val d'Enfer - 90 54 33 21, fax 90 54 45 98
Closed Tue lunch & Mon (Nov 1-Mar). Open until 9:30pm. Garden dining. Pool. Pkg. V, AE, DC, MC.
The little sister of the grand Oustau de Baumanière (see below) is blessed with a colorful garden and a terrace shaded with mulberry trees. It's a luxurious spot in which to enjoy cookery in the Oustau mode, mostly light and full of natural flavors. Enjoy the soup of tiny green peas with mint, leg of young goat cooked on a spit, and nougat glacé with candied fruit. Seductive; expensive wine list. C 300-400 F. M 155 F, 250 F (weekday lunch), 290 F, 360 F.

La Cabro d'Or

(See restaurant above)
Closed Mon (Nov 1-Mar). 8 stes 1,100-1,500 F. 22 rms 605-970 F. Half-board 1,300 F. Air cond. Conf. Pool. Tennis. Pkg. Helipad. V, AE, DC, MC.
In a dramatic setting of rocks and bright flowers, this hotel features good food, a charming welcome, children's activities, and riding. Rooms vary in size and in quality of equipment and furnishings, but were redone this year; the suites are brand new. Relais et Châteaux.

Mas d'Aigret

On D 27 A - 90 54 33 54, fax 90 54 41 37
Closed Wed lunch, Jan 3-Feb 23. Open until 9pm. Terrace dining. Pool. No pets. Pkg. V, AE, DC, MC.
A country jumble of furniture, lace, pictures, and bric-a-brac composes the gay, original decor of this appealing Provençal restaurant. Pascal Johnson's cuisine focuses on excellent products treated with respect: Jerusalem artichoke cream with tiny rissoles of summer savory fresh goat cheese, roast leg of lamb, blanquette of lamb with olives, and a crispy banana tart with orange butter. M 90 F (lunch, wine incl), 190 F (wine incl), 280 F, 350 F.

Mas d'Aigret

(See restaurant above)
Closed Jan 3-Feb 23. 1 ste. 16 rms 350-800 F. Half-board 495-785 F. Conf. Pool. Golf. Pkg. Helipad. V, AE, DC, MC.
The conscientiously renovated rooms are thoughtfully furnished with an eye to detail. Many of the windows face east, making morning the best time to appreciate the views (as you enjoy a delicious breakfast). The pool is ideally situated under a stand of olive trees.

Mas de l'Oulivié

90 54 35 78, fax 90 54 44 31
Closed Nov 1-Mar 20. 20 rms 575-990 F. Restaurant. Air cond. Pool. Tennis. Golf. Pkg. V, AE, DC, MC.
Here is a newly constructed *mas* in the heart of the Vallée des Baux, with bright but smallish rooms, gaily decorated in pure Provençal style. Beautiful landscaped pool site.

L'Oustau de Baumanière

Val d'Enfer
90 54 33 07, fax 90 54 40 46
Closed Thu lunch off-seas, Wed, Nov 15-Dec 7, Jan 16-Mar 3. Open until 10pm. Priv rm: 25. Garden dining. Pkg. V, AE, DC, MC.
When the legendary restaurateur Raymond Thuilier, who founded this world-renowned hostelry and single-handedly revived the village of Les Baux, died two years ago, he was in his late

nineties and as feisty as ever. His grandson and heir-apparent, Jean-André Charial, had been running the place for several years, and he slipped into the breach fully aware of the weight he would have to shoulder.
Patiently, prudently, Charial is reinventing this illustrious bastion of Provençal tradition, set in green gardens at the foot of a cliff, while preserving its Renaissance charm and character. The entrance has been enlarged, and the dining room redecorated in a more cheerful style that becomes truly magical when the candles are lit for dinner. Even the terrace is lovelier, with an expanded perspective on the dramatic countryside. The new menu is in Charial's favorite color, midnight blue. It's the same color that he used on the label of his wine, Château Romanin, produced in spectacular new cellars with the look of a cathedral and well worth a visit. As for the cooking, chef Alain Burnel, closely supervised by Charial, produces dishes that are a model of elegance. The famous roast leg of lamb en croûte is still there, but along with it are new dishes with a focus on superfresh garden vegetables, wild herbs, and fine farm products. The dishes retain natural savors and freshness, in spite of being finely crafted. At the end of April, it's time for just-picked garden fare with sublime tastes; tiny green peas, green beans, carrots, asparagus, tiny fava beans, and minute ratte potatoes, embellished with a bit of truffle butter, make for a matchless celebration. And the bouillabaisse en gelée, truffle ravioli with leeks, red mullet sautéed with pistou, langoustines with spices, rack of lamb roasted with melissa, veal kidney with herbs, duck with olives, pistachio soufflé, or the chocolate millefeuille with chocolate tuiles and cinnamon mousse are all enchanting. Natural, healthful cooking that is getting better and better. Take a table on the rose-bordered terrace facing Les Baux's incomparable cliff crowned by moody medieval ruins that stretch their stones to the sky. The cellar's heady nectars include the best vintages of Condrieu, Côte-Rôtie, and Hermitage, as well as Charial's own Château Romarin reds and rosés. C 450-850 F. M 450 F, 690 F.

L'Oustau de Baumanière

(See restaurant above)
Closed Jan 16-Mar 3. 14 stes 1,700-1,900 F. 6 rms 900-1,100 F. Half-board 2,600-3,100 F. Air cond. Conf. Pool. Tennis. Golf. Valet pkg. V, AE, DC, MC.
The captivating beauty of Provence is on full parade here from the swimming pool (which doesn't look like one) surrounded by flowers to the patrician sixteenth-century *mas* itself, with its rooms of varying sizes, some of which are vast suites. Decor is old-fashioned but charming. For even more peace and quiet, Le Manoir nearby offers just two suites and two rooms in a lovely garden setting. Tennis and riding at the nearby Cabro d'Or; nine-hole golf course two kilometers away. Relais et Châteaux.

La Riboto de Taven

Val d'Enfer - 90 54 34 23, fax 90 54 38 88
*Closed Tue dinner off-seas, Wed, Jan 3-Mar 15. Open until 10pm. Priv rm: 30. Garden dining. **Hotel:** 3 rms 900-1,000 F. Golf. Pkg. V, AE, DC, MC.*
On the edge of the tourists' favorite among Provençal villages, this old country manor stands amid a riot of colorful flowers. In the antique-fur-

nished dining room Jean-Pierre Novi's light, personal cuisine elicits plenty of enthusiasm. Be sure to try his chartreuse of Jerusalem artichoke and asparagus tips, veal sweetbreads with raspberry vinegar (the taste was a bit too strong), and the delicious caramelized fennel tart with vanilla ice cream. Good house bread, charming welcome, excellent choice of Baux wines.C 450- 480 F. M 195 F (lunch, wine incl), 290 F, 420 F.

BAVAY	59570
Paris 230 - Lille 76 - Valenciennes 23 - Maubeuge 14   *Nord*

Le Bagacum
2, rue d'Audignies - 27 66 87 00
Open daily until 9:30pm. Priv rm: 80. Terrace dining. Air cond. Pkg. V, AE, DC, MC.
Pierre Lesne's classic cooking reflects the spirit of the times: foie gras croustade with truffles, stuffed bar fillet in vermouth, perfect orange ice cream. Families come here on weekends; during the week, the pretty dining room in a converted barn is popular for business lunches. The cellar boasts an enticing selection of affordable Champagnes. Zealous service. C 260-360 F. M 90 F (weekdays, Sat lunch), 250 F (wine incl), 180 F.

Hôtel Saint-Maur
1, rue St-Maur
27 66 90 33, fax 27 63 17 22
Closings not available. 8 rms 195-250 F. Restaurant. Half-board 270-420 F. Golf. V, AE, DC, MC.
A small, renovated hotel just a few kilometers from the Gallo-Roman archaeological site at Bavay.

BAVENT 14	→ Cabourg

BAYEUX	14400
Paris 251 - Cherbourg 92 - Caen 27 - St-Lô 36   *Calvados*

Churchill Hotel
14-16, rue St-Jean
31 21 31 80, fax 31 21 41 66
Closed Nov 15-Mar 15. 1 ste 520-680 F. 31 rms 300-460 F. Restaurant. Half-board 360-380 F. No pets. Pkg. V, AE, DC, MC.
This very pretty little hotel in the heart of town offers delightful, well-equipped rooms and satellite television.

Le Lion d'Or
71, av. St-Jean - 31 92 06 90, fax 31 22 15 64
Closed Dec 19-Jan 19. Open until 9:30pm. Priv rm: 30. No pets. Garage pkg. V, AE, DC, MC.
Leaded windows, wood panelling, and a cobbled courtyard create a pleasingly refined setting for Patrick Mouilleau's traditional, regionally rooted cuisine. We enjoyed his andouille (tripe sausage) Bovary, casserole-roasted cockerel with morel stuffing, pickerel braised with ginger, and pear crème brûlée. C 260-380 F. M 150 F (exc weekday lunch), 110 F (weekday lunch), 180 F, 210 F, 320 F.

Le Lion d'Or
(See restaurant above)
Closed Dec 19-Jan 19. 2 stes 800-900 F. 25 rms 240-470 F. Half-board 435-815 F. Conf. Golf. Garage pkg. V, AE, DC, MC.
The rooms of this spacious mansion in the center of Bayeux are arranged around a cobbled courtyard alive with flowers.

■ In **Aignerville 14710**   17 km W on N 13 and D 198

Manoir de l'Hormette
31 22 51 79, fax 31 22 75 99
Closed Jan-Feb. 2 stes 950-975 F. 6 rms 450-550 F. Restaurant. Golf. No pets. Pkg. V, MC.
Superb rustic antiques add the finishing touch to this restored seventeenth-century farm, now a country hideaway. One outbuilding has been converted into an independent residence, for bucolic weekends *en famille*. Simple meals available for guests.

■ In **Crépon 14480**   12 km NE on D 12 and D 112

Ferme de la Rançonnière
Route d'Arromanches
31 22 21 73, fax 31 22 98 39
Open year-round. 35 rms 295-380 F. Restaurant. Half-board 270-310 F. Conf. Pkg. V, AE, DC, MC.
This 500-year-old farm is a listed building, and has been restored with the guidance of the Beaux-Arts commission. The result is a simple, tasteful inn with a family atmosphere near the Normandy Landing beaches. Television in every room; bar-lounge.

■ In **Sully 14400**   3 km NW on D 6

Château de Sully
Route de Port-en-Bessin
31 22 29 48, fax 31 22 64 77
Closed Nov 15-Mar 15. 1 ste 720 F. 23 rms 470-550 F. Restaurant. Half-board 455-495 F. Conf. Heated pool. Tennis. Golf. Garage pkg. Helipad. V, AE, DC, MC.
Superb gentilhommière surrounded by a large park, near Bayeux and the beaches. Recently redone rooms decorate in a rather bland but elegant style, many services and facilities, a restaurant, and fair prices. In short, a good alternative to the coast's hustle and bustle.

BAYONNE	64100
Paris 744 - Bordeaux 176 - Pau 107 - Biarritz 8   *Pyrénées-A.*

11/20 Les Carmes
21, rue Thiers
59 59 14 61, fax 59 25 61 70
Open daily until 10:30pm. Priv rm: 90. Garden dining. Pkg. V, AE, DC, MC.
There have been too many changes of chefs for the quality of the cuisine, already a bit ordinary, to have survived intact: a point less this year. Fish terrine with leeks, duck confit with sautéed cèpes, warm tart of citrus fruits with wild mint. C 200-300 F. M 120 F, 160 F, 190 F.

Le Grand Hôtel
(See restaurant above)
Open year-round. 2 stes 850-1,500 F. 58 rms 340-620 F. Half-board 300-430 F. Air cond. Conf. Golf. Pkg. V, AE, DC, MC.
Spacious, well-kept, but old-fashioned rooms characterie this comfortable hotel in the center of town.

Cheval Blanc 🙂
68, rue Bourgneuf - 59 59 01 33
Closed Sun dinner & Mon (exc Jul-Aug). Open until 10:30pm. Priv rm: 30. Air cond. Pkg. V, AE, DC, MC.
If anyone understands that our Clé d'Or is not the end but the beginning, it's Jean-Claude Tellechea. Five years ago, the Clé gave him the confidence to progress. In his cooking, not his prices, which he miraculously manages to reduce while refining his culinary technique and adding to his customers' pleasure. Both the menus, which begin at 95 F, and the à la carte choices are good deals, with many 100 F main courses that show the chef's inventiveness and precision with local ingredients. Begin with the ultra-fresh langoustines with wild asparagus and ham piperade, sea bream smothered with garlic and served with a piquant "marmikado" sausage (a mixture of tuna, potatoes, tomatoes and peppers, a traditional fisherman's dish), followed by parsley-coated veal sweetbreads with a cèpe-stuffed galette, or plump ravioli stuffed with beef and carrots cooked in Irouléguy wine. Warm welcome in the pure Basque tradition. **C** 260-300 F. **M** 95 F, 158 F, 230 F.

11/20 La Grande Brasserie
3, pl. de la Liberté - 59 59 09 14
Closed Sun. V, AE, DC.
Bayonne's smart set comes in here for the good food served in a warm setting that could use a bit of sprucing up. Everything served is very fresh, but not too exciting: the veal sweetbreads in puff pastry are pleasant but a bit over the top, as is the mixed seafood served in an aluminum foil pouch, and an honest tourtière with apples and prunes. **C** 150-250 F. **M** 89 F (weekday lunch).

Mercure
Av. J.-Rostand
59 63 30 90, fax 59 42 06 64
Open year-round. 1 ste 700 F. 108 rms 230-430 F. Restaurant. Air cond. Pool. Pkg. V, AE, DC, MC.
Practically in the center of town, this modern structure houses renovated rooms overlooking the River Nive and the wooded towpath.

François Miura 🙂
24, rue Marengo - 59 59 49 89
Closed Sun dinner, Wed, Dec 20-30, Jul 10-Aug 10. Open until 10pm. Air cond. V, AE, DC, MC.
We all know that contemporary art requires sacrifice. But would a bouquet of fresh flowers here and there really destroy the rigorous harmonies of the ultra-contemporary decor here? Luckily the hostess's smile warms up the atmosphere, and so do the generous dishes prepared with panache by François Miura: asparagus and tiny sea scallops in parsley cream, rack of lamb with a rosemary infusion and eggplant caviar, and strawberries in puff pastry with orangette sauce. **C** 250-300 F. **M** 107 F, 170 F.

■ **In Urcuit 64990**   12 km E on D 257

12/20 Restaurant du Halage 🙂
On D 261 - 59 42 92 98
Closed Mon. Open until 9pm. Pkg. V.
Over the years this riverside inn has served a dependable menu of good regional fare to a faithful following of locals and tourists. The patronne's best bets are veal sweetbreads in Jurançon, salmon mousse with Champagne sauce, and shad with prunes. Delicious country wines. **C** 170-240 F. **M** 65 F (weekday lunch), 85 F, 148 F, 178 F.

■ **In Urt 64240**   14 km E on D 261

Auberge de la Galupe 🙂
Pl. du Port - 59 56 21 84, fax 59 56 28 66
Closed Sun dinner, Mon, Jan 16-Feb. Open until 9:30pm. Priv rm: 30. Air cond. Pkg. V, AE, MC.
Brilliantly talented chef-owner Christian Parra is a master of regional fare crafted from some of the finest produce in France, served in a lovely old inn on the Adour River. Shad, eel, lamprey, and salmon all swim past the door. From the Chalosse come beef and plump ducks, from the Pyrénées tender milk-fed lamb, sheep's milk cheese, and ibaïona ham, a rival of the famed serrano ham from Spain. And that's not all: the chef procures ultra-fresh seafrood from Saint-Jean-de-Luz, and cèpes for his daubes and civets from the Iraty forest. Winter brings the return of game, from dove to hare. Our poet-chef treats these marvelous products with respect and sensitivity, cheered on by his Provençale wife Anne-Marie. She managed to get him to her native country this year, which is why a gourmande salad with truffles dedicated to "Bruno des collines" appears on the menu, named for Bruno , Parra's alter-ego on the hillside village of Lorgues. At the Parras' place, you'll find simplicity, authenticity, warmth: in short, it's a little corner of paradise. **C** 300-400 F. **M** 240 F.

L'Estanquet 🙂
Pl. du Marché
59 56 24 93, fax 59 56 24 92
*Open until 10pm. Terrace dining. Air cond. **Hotel**: 13 rms 250-300 F. Half-board 210-240 F. Pkg. V, MC.*
Here's a cheerful, tidy little inn where you can feast on robust portions of fine country cooking. Pépette Arbulo's macaronade with sautéed foie gras, savory duck breast poached with stuffed cabbage, fresh and flavorful granité of raspberries and Champagne. Fine wine list, now with many regional offerings. Pleasant service whether you choose the lovely dining room or the plane-tree-shaded terrace. **C** 200-300 F. **M** 65 F (weekday lunch, Sat), 98 F, 145 F, 195 F.

■ **In Ustaritz 64480**   12 km SE on D 932

La Patoula
59 93 00 56, fax 59 93 16 54
*Closed Mon lunch, Sun dinner off-seas, Jan 5-Feb 15. Open until 10pm. Garden dining. **Hotel**: 9 rms 320-460 F. Half-board 250-410 F. Golf. Pkg. V, MC.*
While ducks drift along the Nive River below the terrace and veranda, tourists and business types enjoy the family atmosphere in this pleasant place. Chef Philippe Béraud favors southwestern French dishes with a few excursions into Provence: jellied daube of duck with onion and thyme cream, roast hake en biscaïenne with saffron-scented rice, and puff pastry filled with berries. Attentive service. **C** 250-360 F. **M** 140 F, 240 F.

See also: Biarritz

BAZAS 33430
Paris 625 - Mont-de-Marsan 68 - Bordeaux 62　　Gironde

12/20 Domaine de Fompeyre
Route de Mont-de-Marsan
56 25 98 00, fax 56 25 16 25
Closed Sun dinner off-seas. Open until 9:45pm. Priv rm: 200. Garden dining. **Hotel**: 4 stes 510-700 F. 31 rms 310-420 F. Half-board 370-470 F. Conf. Pool. Tennis. Garage pkg. V, AE, MC.
Nestled in a three-acre estate, this hostelry of recent vintage offers travelers a refined setting and good food. Try the first set menu, with salmon carpaccio marinated in lime juice, shad in Bordelaise sauce, and strawberry tart. Tempting Bordeaux. Friendly and professional welcome and service. C 220-370 F. M 135 F, 220 F.

BAZEILLES 08　　→ Sedan

BAZINCOURT 27140
Paris 70 - Rouen 56 - Gisors 4 - Gournay-en-Bray 20　　Eure

Château de la Rapée
Bazincourt-sur-Epte
32 55 11 61, fax 32 55 95 65
Closed Jan 30-Feb 24. 1 ste 690-790 F. 13 rms 405-505 F. Restaurant. Half-board 610-700 F. Conf. Golf. No pets. Pkg. Helipad. V, AE, DC, MC.
The individually decorated rooms are large and comfortable; the best ones are on the upper floor with views of the countryside. Peace and quiet are guaranteed on this green hilltop.

BEAUCAIRE 30300
Paris 710 - Alès 67 - Arles 20 - Avignon 25　　Gard

Robinson
Route de Remoulins, 2 km N on D 986
66 59 21 32, fax 66 59 00 03
Closed Feb. 30 rms 250-360 F. Restaurant. Half-board 350-450 F. Conf. Pool. Tennis. Pkg. V, MC.
A truly convivial atmosphere and a marvelous setting (in 25 acres of unspoiled grounds) distinguish this Provençal hostelry.

BEAUCET (LE) 84　　→ Carpentras

BEAUDÉAN 65　　→ Bagnères-de-Bigorre

BEAUGENCY 45190
Paris 150 - Blois 31 - Orléans 25 - Vendôme 48　　Loiret

■ In Tavers 45190　　2.5 km SW on N 152

12/20 La Tonnellerie
12, rue des Eaux-Bleues
38 44 68 15, fax 38 44 10 01
Closed Jan 1-Apr 14, Oct 15-Dec 31. Open until 8:45pm. Garden dining. Heated pool. No pets. Pkg. V, AE, MC.
Tourists adore this pretty establishment with its soothing decor and summer terrace. The menu is based on first-rate ingredients: try chef Franck Jourdin's langoustine platter, quail-egg salad, sautéed foie gras, and a mango gratin with a citrus sabayon sauce. C 220-400 F. M 125 F (weekday lunch), 230 F, 310 F.

La Tonnellerie
(See restaurant above)
Closed Jan 1-Apr 14, Oct 15-Dec 31. 8 stes 880-1,435 F. 12 rms 595-880 F. Half-board 608-818 F. Conf. Heated pool. Golf. No pets. Pkg. V, AE, MC.
Bright, fully renovated rooms and suites decorated with quiet good taste. Lovely swimming pool; hiking excursions and river cruises arranged.

BEAULIEU-SUR-DORDOGNE 19120
Paris 520 - Aurillac 64 - Figeac 62 - Limoges 139　　Corrèze

Central Hôtel Fournié
4, pl. du Champs-de-Mars
55 91 01 34, fax 55 91 23 57
Closed mid Nov-mid Mar. Open until 9pm. Priv rm: 20. Garden dining. **Hotel**: 25 rms 170-320 F. Half-board 230-300 F. Garage pkg. V, MC.
This village is a crossroads for Limousin, Quercinois, and Auvergnat culinary customs. Chef Bernard Bessière draws on all of them, and on the fine local foodstuffs, with convincing and very tasty results. Taste his warm salad of foie gras and cèpes, veal sweetbreads with girolle mushrooms, cèpe omelet, and rabbit confit with girolles. The 120 F menu is a bargain. Appealing cellar. C 170-340 F. M 85 F (weekdays, Sat lunch), 120 F, 130 F, 160 F, 250 F.

BEAULIEU-SUR-MER 06310
Paris 943 - Menton 20 - Nice 10 - Cannes 43　　Alpes-Mar.

Carlton
7, av. E.-Cavell
93 01 14 70, fax 93 01 29 62
Closed Sep 30-Apr 10. 32 rms 500-980 F. Restaurant. Air cond. Pool. Golf. Pkg. V, AE, DC, MC.
A discreetly luxurious hotel just 200 meters from the beach, with rooms that are attractive and nicely equipped.

Le Maxilien
43, bd Marinoni - 93 01 47 48
Closings not available. Open until 10:30pm. Priv rm: 16. Terrace dining. Air cond. V, AE, DC, MC.
Make a dive for the charming, shaded terrace of this comfortable establishment, and order the chef's perfectly cooked, market-fresh fish prepared in classic fashion: delicate tarts made from three different fish—John Dory, sea bass, and sea bream—accompanied by a tart sauce, beef fillet in a jus of foie gras and morels (a bit overcooked) and an excellent Tatin tart. The homemade bread is a treat, and the cellar well stocked with some good Provençal wines. Professional welcome and attentive service. C 280-480 F. M 155 F, 265 F, 360 F, 480 F.

Le Métropole
15, bd du Gal-Leclerc
93 01 00 08, fax 93 01 18 51
Closed Oct 20-Dec 20. Open until 10pm. Priv rm: 20. Garden dining. Air cond. Valet pkg. V, AE, MC.
This Italianate villa is a dreamy spot, far from the hordes who invade the Côte d'Azur. Le Métropole provides perfect quiet, soul-stirring beauty, distinguished service, and an elegant ambience. No false note jars the senses, while one's palate is pampered with chef Gilbert Roubaut's classic cuisine based on superb ingredients. Sit yourself down before one of the

Côte d'Azur's most fabulous views and treat yourself to a salad of warm lobster with olive oil, an assortment of steamed local vegetables, turbotin grilled over charcoal, whiting with artichokes à la grecque, crispy John Dory with honey butter, sea bass in a salt crust, or rack of lamb with thyme. All and all, a taste of the good life. **C** 450-700 F. **M** 430 F, 530 F.

Le Métropole

(See restaurant above)
Closed Oct 20-Dec 20. 3 stes 2,260-5,000 F. 50 rms 700-2,720 F. Half-board 880-1,925 F. Air cond. Heated pool. Golf. V, AE, MC.
The air is redolent with the sweet pleasure of good living, in this huge white villa set in over two acres of luxuriant gardens. Rooms are bright and handsomely decorated, and the service is peerless: no detail is too small for attention. Le Métropole draws a moneyed clientele that is anything but flashy. Relais et Châteaux.

La Réserve de Beaulieu

5, bd du Gal-Leclerc
93 01 00 01, fax 93 01 28 99
Closed Nov-Mar. Open until 10:30pm. Priv rm: 120. Terrace dining. Air cond. Pool. Pkg. V, AE, DC, MC.
After a period of turbulence, clear skies have returned to La Réserve. It is one of the few places where guests can sip a cocktail in a room decorated Venetian-style and suspended over the sea, and admire a Riviera sunset while listening to a pianist play Chopin in the background. The cuisine too is in a seriously classical register but the chef manages to hit a few contemporary and personal notes. Chef Jean-Paul Bonin, formerly the Crillon in Paris, succeeds best with simple dishes in a Provençal key: butterfly lasagne with tiny clams, cuttlefish with pancetta, crispy langoustines with ratte potatoes, milk-fed lamp with a fricassée of artichokes and fava beans, or sea bream with Menton lemons in a salt confit. Follow with one of the yummy desserts, like a crispy caramelized lemon tart. **C** 550-850 F. **M** 310 (lunch), 410 F (dinner).

La Réserve de Beaulieu

(See restaurant above)
Closed Nov-Mar. 3 stes 4,400-5,700 F. 30 rms 2,100-4,200 F. Half-board 520 F. Air cond. Conf. Heated pool. Golf. Valet pkg. V, AE, DC.
This lovely, peaceful, turn-of-the-century villa fairly oozes with 1950s–style luxury. The swimming pool looks onto the beach and a small, private harbor.

La Résidence Carlton

9 bis, av. Albert-Ier
93 01 06 02, fax 93 01 29 62
Closed Sep 30-Apr 10. 27 rms 300-650 F. Air cond. Golf. Pkg. V, AE, DC, MC.
This modern hotel with a pleasant garden stands just 200 meters from the beach. Rooms are sunny and prettily decorated. Laundry service.

See also: **Saint-Jean-Cap-Ferrat**

Auberge de la Toison d'Or

4, bd J.-Ferry - 80 22 29 62
Closed Sun dinner, Mon. Open until 9:30pm. Air cond. Pkg. V, AE, MC.
A young couple from the Gers has breathed new life into this *auberge* for tourists near the city's ramparts. The carefully wrought, sensibly priced cooking artfully marries the traditions of Burgundy to those of southwestern France, such as the dishes on the good-value 125 F menu: head cheese and watercress salad, cod fillet with split-pea mousseline, cheese assortment, and dessert. Regional wine list. Friendly, competent welcome. **C** 250-330 F. **M** 87 F, 125 F, 165 F, 235 F.

Le Bénaton

25, rue du Fg-Bretonnière - 80 22 00 26
Closed Thu lunch, Wed. Open until 10pm. Garden dining. V, MC.
Bruno Monnoir's market-fresh cuisine looks deceptively rustic; in fact, the flavor harmonies he devises are complex and pleasing on many levels: a gelée of lentils and cracked wheat with trout and smoked salmon, crispy lamb with a black olive compote, and sinfully rich warm chocolate cake with vanilla ice cream. Friendly welcome, excellent wine list. **C** 260-320 F. **M** 95 F (weekdays, Sat lunch), 130 F (dinner Sat & Sun), 220 F.

Central

2, rue V.-Millot
80 24 77 24, fax 80 22 30 40
Closed Sun dinner (Nov-Mar), Wed (Nov-Jun), Nov 23-Dec 23. Open until 9:30pm. Hotel: 20 rms 340-500 F. V, MC.
Pretty bouquets punctuate the fresh, dainty ground-floor dining room, while the upstairs decor is more quiet and conservative. The tables are beautifully laid, the service is disciplined. Chef Jean Garcin proposes delicious pig's foot in puff pastry with sweet garlic, a tajine of monkfish with saffron, and a fillet of Charolais beef sautéed in an infusion of red wine. Well chosen wine list. **C** 240-360 F. **M** 99 F (weekdays), 130 F, 165 F, 190 F.

Le Cep

27-29, rue Maufoux
80 22 35 48, fax 80 22 76 80
Open year-round. 3 stes 1,200-1,500 F. 49 rms 500-1,000 F. Restaurant. Golf. Pkg. V, AE, DC, MC.
Fifty classy rooms—each one named for a *grand cru* of the Côte d'Or—can be found in this Renaissance mansion located in the heart of Beaune (don't miss the courtyard complete with arcades and a stone stairwell).

12/20 ## La Ciboulette

69, rue de Lorraine - 80 24 70 72
Closed Mon dinner, Tue, last 2 wks of Feb, Aug. Open until 9:30pm. V, MC.
This tasteful, friendly little restaurant offers high ground above the tourist floods. The food is simple, fresh, and adroitly prepared. Try the bargain 87 F menu: house chicken-liver terrine, sautéed steak, fresh white cheese with cream. And don't forget to sample the nice little Burgundies. **C** 185-235 F. **M** 87 F, 119 F.

La Closerie

61, rte de Pommard
80 22 15 07, fax 80 24 16 22
Closed Dec 24-Jan 15. 1 ste 700-750 F. 46 rms 220-540 F. Restaurant. Half-board 300-400 F. Air cond. Heated pool. Golf. Pkg. V, AE, DC, MC.
Set between Beaune and the vineyards is this modern, comfortable, and completely equipped hotel with an attractive swimming pool and garden.

L'Écusson
2, rue du Lt-Dupuis, Pl. Malmédy
80 24 03 82, fax 80 24 74 02
Closed Sun, Wed dinner off-seas, Dec 1-12, Feb 10-28. Open until 9:30pm. Priv rm: 80. Terrace dining. V, AE, DC, MC.
You will never find chef Jean-Pierre Senelet on the front row of any group photo. And his restaurant is just as modest, although it boasts a pretty garden. But this is a chef worthy of attention, one of those who is constantly improving, and does his job with rare simplicity. Sometimes he slips a little: the risotto with chicken skin (he loves skins) could use some work. But more often he creates appealing new savors, always at appealing prices: baby scallops in thyme juice, langoustines with potatoes, lamb fillet in a perfectly simple fat-free jus, and astonishing corn ice cream with banana sauce. C 300-400 F. M 125 F, 175 F, 245 F, 335 F.

Le Jardin des Remparts
10, rue Hôtel-Dieu
80 24 79 41, fax 80 24 92 79
Closed Sun dinner & Mon (exc hols), Feb 6-Mar 6, Aug 1-7. Open until 9:45pm. Priv rm: 50. Garden dining. Pkg. V, MC.
What a pleasure to take a seat in the garden of this 1930s dwelling, set at the foot of Beaune's ramparts, just steps away from the famed Hospices, in the new teak-clad dining room. Roland Chanliaud has won over local food lovers with his accomplished cooking, at bargain prices. On the 130 F menu, try the foie gras terrine with fig compote, gratinéed whiting with goat cheese and caramelized rosemary jus, warm Bresse blue cheese in a salad with grilled colza (rape), and honey cake ice cream with vanilla chiffonade. Friendly welcome, good wine list. C 280-350 F. M 130 F (weekdays, Sat lunch), 170 F, 250 F, 290 F.

Bernard Morillon
31, rue Maufoux
80 24 12 06, fax 80 22 66 22
Closed Tue lunch, Mon, Jan 26-Mar 1. Open until 10pm. V, AE, DC, MC. Terrace dining. Pkg.
In this lovely ancient house near the Hospices, Bernard Morillon serves classic, finely crafted cuisine, always luxuriously on the rich side. Witness the carp pâté with two sauces, generous sea bream, and Bresse chicken in Gevrey wine sauce. Huge wine list that is also supremely classic; professional service. Our pick is the 160 F set menu. C 400-550 F. M 160 F (weekdays), 290 F, 380 F, 420 F.

La Poste
1, bd Clemenceau
80 22 08 11, fax 80 24 19 71
Open year-round. 8 stes 900-1,500 F. 22 rms 400-1,000 F. Restaurant. Air cond. Conf. Golf. Valet pkg. V, AE, DC, MC.

Kind attention is the watchword of this fully renovated traditional hotel with a view of both the city (in the front) and the vineyards (in the back). Some of the rooms are really small, but all are appropriately equipped. Good breakfasts. Billiard room.

■ In Aloxe-Corton 21420
5 km N on N 74

Clarion
80 26 46 70, fax 80 26 47 16
Open year-round. 10 rms 485-790 F. Pkg. V, MC.
Set amid the town's renowned vineyards, this pretty provincial hotel dates from the seventeenth century. Rooms are spacious and tastefully decorated; some have individual terraces. Lots of charm, and excellent breakfasts.

■ In Chorey-
lès-Beaune 21200
4 km NE on N 74

L'Ermitage Corton

N 74 - 80 22 05 28, fax 80 24 64 51
Closed Feb. Open until 9:15pm. Priv rm: 30. Garden dining. Garage pkg. V, AE, DC, MC.
You will not soon forget a stop in this pleasant dining room, renovated this year but still on the demonstrative side. Laurent Parra's cooking also cries out for attention: langoustines grilled with curry and lemon butter, veal sweetbreads and kidneys with baby vegetables, salmon roasted with honey and spices, and a wild strawberry gratin with Grand Marnier. The cellar is magnificent, with bottles in a wide price range. C 200-600 F. M 165 F, 210 F, 350 F, 445 F, 650 F.

L'Ermitage Corton
(See restaurant above)
Closed Feb. 6 stes 1,250-1,800 F. 2 rms 750-1,200 F. Conf. Golf. Pkg. V, AE, DC, MC.
Careful: You could lose your dachshund in the thick-pile carpet of the luxurious suites. But the zealous staff would surely find him for you, while you relax in a warm tub in the pharaonic bathroom. Grandiose fittings and furniture, spectacular breakfasts.

■ In Levernois 21200
5 km SE on D 970 and D 111

Jean Crotet
Route de Combertault
80 24 73 58, fax 80 22 78 00
Closed Tue (exc dinner Apr-Jan), Wed lunch. Open until 9:30pm. Priv rm: 65. Garden dining. Air cond. Valet pkg. V, AE, DC, MC.
Drive five kilometers out of Beaune to reach this handsome establishment set in enchanting wooded grounds. The catch is that this is one of those two-speed restaurants: if you order à la carte, you will have cuisine worth the 16 rating (although the prices are high for the region), but if you choose one of the set menus, which many who come here do, you will be served something that doesn't quite measure up. Many great chefs excel in both areas, moderately priced set menus. Why not here? C 400-850 F. M 200 F (weekday lunch, Sat, wine incl), 380 F, 540 F.

A red hotel ranking denotes a place with charm.

149

Hostellerie de Levernois 🍴

(See restaurant above)
Closed Tue (Dec-Mar). 1 ste 1,550-1,750 F. 15 rms 950-1,300 F. Half-board 1,000-1,400 F. Conf. Tennis. Golf. Valet pkg. Helipad. V, AE, DC, MC.

The formal gardens, the nearby river, and the magnificent trees all add to the pleasure of staying in one of the huge guest rooms of this luxuriously renovated hostelry. Flawless breakfasts; golf course nearby. Relais et Châteaux.

See also: Bouilland, Chagny

BEAUPOUYET 24	→ Mussidan

BEAURECUEIL 13	→ Aix-en-Provence

BEAUSSET (LE)	83330
Paris 822 - Marseille 47 - Aix 64 - Toulon 17	Var

La Cigalière 🍴

At La Daby, N 8, route du Camp
94 98 64 63, fax 94 98 66 04
Closed 1 wk end Feb, 1 wk end Nov. 5 stes 550-660 F. 14 rms 290-350 F. Half-board 315-350 F. Conf. Pool. Tennis. No pets. Pkg. V.

A Provençal farmhouse enveloped in greenery offering a warm welcome, pleasant rooms, excellent coffee at breakfast; restaurant service in season only.

Le Poivre d'Âne

4 km SE on N 8, in Sainte-Anne-d'Évenos
94 90 37 88
Closed Sun dinner (exc Jul-Aug), Mon, Jan 15-Feb 15. Open until 9:30pm. Priv rm: 7. Garden dining. Pkg. V, AE.

It would be hard to find a sunnier, prettier place than this Provençal farmhouse set in a shady garden. Fitted out with perfect taste, the handsome dining room is a showcase for the chef's enticing cuisine, which is based on authentically flavorful local foodstuffs. Savor the stuffed zucchini blossoms, sea bass with green peppers, John Dory with lentils, veal kidney with white beans, and a prune gratin with Armagnac. The service and welcome are as friendly and unaffected as can be. **C** 280-400 F. **M** 130 F (lunch exc Sun), 170 F, 240 F.

BEAUVAIS	60000
Paris 76 - Rouen 80 - Amiens 60 - Pontoise 50	Oise

12/20 La Belle du Coin

67, rue du Gal-Kœnig (route de Rouen)
44 45 07 24, fax 44 45 29 55
Closed Sun dinner, Mon. Annual closings not available. Open until 9:30pm (10pm Fri & Sat). Priv rm: 16. Pkg. V, MC.

Rustic beams, hunting trophies, and the provincial Louis XIII decor are at odds with the traffic that zips by on the highway just outside the door, but the flowers on the table and the fresh, simple cooking are pleasant nonetheless. Lots of customers come in regularly for the oysters and veal sweetbreads in vinaigrette, sole fillet with artichokes, and sautéed fresh figs with honey. Friendly welcome. **C** 230-320 F. **M** 90 F (weekday lunch), 150 F.

A la Côtelette

8, rue des Jacobins - 44 45 04 42
Closed Sun, Jul 14-Aug 15. Open until 10pm. Priv rm: 40. Pkg. V, AE, MC.

This roomy corner house with apricot-colored walls and stained-glass windows is just a stone's throw from the cathedral. The welcome is warm, the service efficient, and the cuisine classic: salmon marinated with herbs, poached young squab, and a chocolate biscuit for dessert. The good-value 155 F menu keeps the bill manageable. **C** 320-400 F. **M** 155 F.

Mercure

Av. Montaigne
44 02 80 80, fax 44 02 12 50
Open year-round. 60 rms for disabled. Restaurant. Conf. Pool. Pkg. V, AE, DC, MC.

Here's a perfectly kept modern hotel, with large, bright rooms. The proximity to the industrial park and the superhighway to Paris are either an advantage or a headache, depending on your point of view.

BELCASTEL	12390
Paris 625 - Rodez 27 - Rignac 11 - Decazeville 27	Aveyron

Le Vieux Pont 🔱

65 64 52 29, fax 65 64 44 32
Closed Sun dinner off-seas, Mon, Jan-Feb. Open until 9pm. V, AE.

Deep in the Rouergue region nestles a picture-perfect medieval village where the occasional tourist supposes that he will be fed a good dose of local charcuterie and a plateful of locally fished, deep-fried whitebait. Well, that was how things used to be, when Fagegaltier *père* ran this venerable village restaurant, but with dizzying speed his two daughters have turned the Vieux Pont into a very fine table indeed. Thirty-year-old Nicole Fagegaltier is a free and solitary spirit, as untamed as her native landscape (she adamantly refuses to appear in the dining room), yet she has already taken her place in the select ranks of France's top young chefs. Her cuisine, firmly rooted in the region, has a dazzling panache which is absolutely her own, and is astoundingly light for this region where sturdy dishes are the norm. Settle in to the simple, cozy dining room and regale yourself with a delicate cod tart with walnut cream as an appetizer, then a vegetable tart with cèpes and foie gras fat, cabbage stuffed with pig's foot and lentils (a masterpiece), fillet of local lamb with extraordinary turnips in clove-scented milk, a platter of local cheeses like Roquefort, Cabecou and Tomme, and finally some desserts your grandmother might have cooked if she had grown up around here, like the luscious cream-cheese tart perfumed with orangeflower water and glazed oranges. Wash this down with a hearty Marcillac, and savor the bill, which is as gentle and friendly as your hostess Michèle's smile. **C** 250-350 F. **M** 130 F, 170 F, 210 F, 300 F.

Le Vieux Pont 🍴

(See restaurant above)
Open year-round. 7 rms 360-420 F. Half-board 400-450 F. Pkg. V, AE, MC.

At the other end of a tiny bridge over the river, the Fagegaltiers have opened seven charming guestrooms in a renovated old house.

BELFORT 90000

Paris 424 - Colmar 70 - Basel 65 - Besançon 90   T./Belfort

 Hostellerie
du Château Servin

9, rue du Gal-Négrier
84 21 41 85, fax 84 57 05 57
Closed Sun dinner, Fri, Aug. Open until 9:30pm. Priv rm: 30. Terrace dining. Air cond. Pkg. V, AE, DC, MC.
It is no easy feat to play in the classical mode with a modern lightness of touch and nary a slip, but that's what Dominique Mathy manages, ever relying on fine ingredients. Try the snail soup with herb butter, lightly smoked salmon with green cabbage, and a hot soufflé of dark cherries flavored with Kirsch. Well chosen wine list. C 300-480 F. M 100 F, 200 F, 250 F, 370 F, 450 F.

 Hostellerie
du Château Servin

(See restaurant above)
Closed Aug. 1 ste 450 F. 9 rms 300-350 F. Conf. Golf. No pets. Garage pkg. V, AE, DC, MC.
The rooms (some are not what we'd call spacious) are decorated in Louis-this and Louis-that—but with an admirable eye to detail.

Le Pot-au-Feu

27 bis, Grande-Rue
84 28 57 84, fax 84 58 17 65
Closed Sun, lunch Sat & Mon, wk of Aug 15. Open until 10pm. V, AE, MC.
Regional cuisine is the star in this cozy place: pastry stuffed with morels and cream, chicken liver "cake", pot-au-feu of young guinea fowl, rack of lamb with thyme, and warm goat cheese with salad. Good cellar of Burgundies; affable service. C 180 F. M 90 F (weekday lunch, wine incl), 150 F (wine incl), 220 F.

BELLEGARDE-SUR-VALSERINE 01200

Paris 508 - Annecy 41 - Geneva 41 - Lyon 121   Ain

La Belle Époque

10, pl. Gambetta
50 48 14 46, fax 50 56 01 71
Closed Jul 4-18, Nov 13-Dec 4. Open until 9pm. Priv rm: 40. Air cond. Garage pkg. V, MC.
This pleasant provincial dining room under a soaring ceiling boasts a glassed-in patio with a view of the Place Gambetta. Michel Sévin presides in the kitchen, cooking up traditional offerings that include lake fish (omble chevalier, féra), crayfish, and spectacular dishes flambéed at your table. The menu changes twice a month. A judicious, far-ranging cellar. C 250-400 F. M 120 F (weekdays), 150 F, 200 F, 260 F.

La Belle Époque

(See restaurant above)
Closed Jul 4-18, Nov 13-Dec 7. 20 rms 250-400 F. Half-board 400 F. Air cond. Conf. Garage pkg. V, MC.
A score of inviting, cozy rooms, fully renovated, are equipped with wall-to-wall carpet, double windows, and pretty accessories.

Some establishments change their closing times without warning. It is always wise to check in advance.

BELLE-ILE-EN-MER 56360

Morbihan

Le Cardinal

In Sauzon
97 31 61 60, fax 97 31 66 87
Closed beg Oct-beg Apr. 76 rms 390-705 F. Restaurant. Half-board 465-610 F. Golf. Pkg. V, MC.
A rather anonymous contemporary hotel, but the surrounding moors and sea views are sublime. Shuttle bus to the nearby Goulphar sea-water spa.

Castel Clara

In Port-Goulphar
97 31 84 21, fax 97 31 51 69
Closed Nov 14-Feb 18. Open until 9pm. Priv rm: 20, Garden dining. Heated pool. No pets. Pkg. V, MC.
Chef Yves Pérou displays a light, restrained touch that respects the simplicity and freshness of his superb ingredients. Taste his warm oysters with fennel and spices, langoustines sautéed in cider with terragon, cotriade (fish soup) of local seafood, local sea bream in a Guérande salt crust, and, for purists, perfectly cooked lobster and langoustes. Appealing selection of affordable wines. The dining room boasts a ravishing view. C 300-450 F. M 390 F (dinner), 170 F, 245 F.

Castel Clara

(See restaurant above)
Closed Nov 14-Feb 18. 10 stes 1,685-1,980 F. 32 rms 760-1,090 F. Rms for disabled. Half-board 610-865 F. Air cond. Conf. Heated pool. Tennis. Golf. Garage pkg. Helipad. V, MC.
Exceptional sea views and tastefully decorated accommodation are what you'll find in this modern hotel-cum-spa. Many amenities; excellent welcome and service. Relais et Châteaux.

10/20 La Chaloupe

97 31 88 27
Closed Nov 15-Dec 15. Open until 11pm. Priv rm: 30. Terrace dining. Air cond. No cards.
An engaging, inexpensive spot for uncomplicated food (chef's salad, crêpes, galettes). C 100-160 F.

Le Contre-Quai

in Sauzon, rue St-Nicolas - 97 31 60 60
Closed Mon (exc school hols), Nov 2-Mar. Open until 10pm. V, MC.
Nestled on a street running parallel to the waterfront, this small establishment aims to charm with its cozy decor of beams and lace lampshades. The cuisine is clever, though a bit uneven, and keeps one coming back for fricassée of shellfish with wild marjoram, creamed lentils with bacon and oysters, fillet of hake with beef marrow, and veal chops with tiny onions. Well-chosen wine list; smiling welcome. Slow-paced service. C 250-350 F. M 135 F (lunch).

La Désirade

Le Petit Cosquet
97 31 70 70, fax 97 31 89 63
Closed beg Jan-mid Mar. 24 rms 390-490 F. Rms for disabled. Restaurant. Heated pool. Golf. Pkg. V, AE, DC.
A new "hotel village" offering plush, intimate rooms that are delightfully decorated with wood panelling, Italian furniture, and English fabrics. Good bathrooms; extraordinary breakfasts.

Manoir de Goulphar
Bangor, in Port-Goulphar
97 31 80 10, fax 97 31 80 05
Closed beg Nov-mid Mar. 60 rms 400-1,015 F. Restaurant. Half-board 480-700 F. Pkg. V, MC.
Some of the small but comfortable rooms in this beautifully situated hotel offer a balcony looking out to sea.

Roz-Avel
In Sauzon, rue du Lt-Riou - 97 31 61 48
Closed Wed, Nov 12-Feb 13. Open until 9:30pm. Garden dining. V, MC.
No question about it, Christophe Didoune deserves a toque for his generous seafood cuisine served in a cozy Breton house with a pretty garden terrace. Worthy of your attention are the flambéed local sea scallops, and fillet of John Dory with artichokes. C 220-350 F. M 95 F.

Paris 503 - St-Brieuc 51 - Morlaix 36 - Lannion 28   Côtes/Armor

Le Relais de l'Argoat
96 43 00 34, fax 94 43 00 76
Closed Sun dinner, Mon, Feb. Open until 9:30pm. Priv rm: 15. **Hotel**: 10 rms 185-230 F. Half-board 260-310 F. Conf. No pets. Pkg. V.
Chef Pierre Marais pleases with classic cooking based on excellent ingredients served generously. The locals love the first set menu: langoustine salad with pleurote mushrooms, filet mignon of pork flambéed with Calvados, cheese assortment, and dessert. C 220-260 F. M 110 F, 140 F, 180 F, 250 F.

Paris 427 - Lyon 46 - Bourg-en-B. 39 - Mâcon 23   Rhône

12/20 Château de Pizay
In St-Jean-d'Ardières
74 66 51 41, fax 74 69 65 63
Closed Dec 23-Jan 2. Open until 9:30pm. Priv rm: 80. Terrace dining. Air cond. Pkg. V, AE, DC, MC.
This dignified château in a wooded park surrounded by vineyards is a splendid sight indeed. The chef applies himself earnestly to the classic repertoire: try his eel terrine with watercress (a tad bland), seafood with spices (perfectly cooked but accompanied by a very bland carp quenelle), good puff pastry filled with Granny Smith apples and vanilla cream sauce. C 300-400 F. M 150 F (lunch), 185 F, 260 F, 345 F.

Château de Pizay
(See restaurant above)
Closed Dec 23-Jan 2. 2 stes 1,650-1,900 F. 60 rms 530-1,150 F. Half-board 495-800 F. Air cond. Conf. Pool. Tennis. Golf. Pkg. Helipad. V, AE, DC, MC.
Overlooking the château's magnificent grounds and swimming pool, these spacious and comfortable guest rooms sport a pleasing contemporary decor.

Paris 556 - Brest 88 - Concarneau 22 - Quimper 16   Finistère

Ferme du Letty
2 km SE, in Letty
98 57 01 27, fax 98 57 25 29
Closed Wed (exc dinner Jul-Aug), Thu lunch, Oct-Feb. Open until 10pm. Priv rm: 30. Garden dining. Pkg. V, AE, DC, MC.
This lovely former farm is Breton to the core, from the blue shutters to the Quimper faïences to the excellent local products dear to the heart of chef Jean-Marie Guilbault. He is committed to developing a modern, yet authentically regional cuisine based on the bounty of Brittany's seas and fields, hauntingly seasoned with the spices that hardy Breton sailors once brought back from exotic lands. You'll find buckwheat, wild thyme from the dunes, and wild garlic, and innovative dishes like sardines with herbs, pig's head with picalilli, and a praliné oatmeal cream that join the rustic and the sophisticated, the humble and the noble. Sometimes this very aromatic cooking goes a bit too far, but the products are always exceptional (especially the duck and veal), as is the quality-price ratio. The wine list, though not strong in half bottles, represents the best of many regions. This restaurant shows that great cuisine, even when it takes risks, does not have to be expensive. A rarity indeed. C 250-450 F. M 98 F, 145 F, 193 F, 295 F, 380 F.

12/20 Gwell Kaër
3, av. de la Plage
98 57 04 38, fax 98 66 22 85
Closed Sun dinner & Mon off-seas, Dec 4-Jan 5. Open until 9pm. Terrace dining. No pets. Pkg. V, MC.
The bay windows command a view of the river mouth and the sea, a superb panorama to admire while trying the 90 F menu: mussel soup with saffron, lieu (an ocean fish) with vegetables, and a coffee mousse glacé. C 250-350 F. M 90 F (weekdays), 130 F, 195 F, 240 F, 380 F (exc Sun).

Gwell Kaër
(See restaurant above)
Closed Dec 11-Jan 9. 23 rms 280-515 F. Rms for disabled. Half-board 300-450 F. Conf. Pkg. V, MC.
Most of these recently renovated blue-and-white rooms have a balcony or a terrace from which to enjoy the ocean view.

Kastel-Moor et Ker-Moor
Av. de la Plage
98 57 04 48, fax 98 57 17 96
Closed Nov-Easter (exc for conf). 82 rms 380-500 F. Restaurant. Half-board 470-520 F. Conf. Heated pool. Tennis. Golf. Pkg. V, AE, DC, MC.
One of these twins is situated on the beach, while the other stands in verdant grounds. They share squash courts and a wooded park. Both offer large, well-equipped rooms that are oddly devoid of charm. Standard breakfasts.

Plan to travel? Look for Gault Millau's other Best of guides to Chicago, Florida, Hawaii, Hong Kong, Germany, Italy, London, Los Angeles, New England, New Orleans, New York, Paris, San Francisco, Thailand, Toronto, and Washington, D.C.

■ In Sainte-Marine 29120   5.5 km W on D 44

 L'Agape
52, rue de la Plage - 98 56 32 70
Closed Tue dinner & Wed (exc hols). Open until 9:30pm. Priv rm: 45. Pkg. V, MC.
Patrick Leguen's succinct but seductive menu showcases his penchant for the fruits of the sea (which is not on display from the rather unattractive raspberry-pink dining room, alas). He offers marvelous gaspacho of red mullet, fabulous Cap Sizun lamb, and an excellent, buttery kouingaman pastry with apples. Give that man a second toque! The cellar is attractive. **C** 350-450 F. **M** 150 F, 200 F, 250 F, 390 F.

BÉNOUVILLE 14	➜ Caen

BERCHÈRES-SUR-VESGRE	28560
Paris 70 - Evreux 43 - Dreux 29 - Ivry-la-Bataille 9	Eure-et-Loir

 Château de Berchères
18, rue du Château
37 82 07 21, fax 37 82 02 08
Closed Sun dinner, 1 wk at Christmas, Aug. Open until 9pm. Priv rm: 30. Garden dining. No pets. Pkg. V, AE, DC, MC.
Sunlight and all the leafy charm of a wooded park flood into the gold-and-white dining room of this nineteenth-century château. The prices are high, but the new chef's cooking shows promise: skate with caper sauce (perfectly cooked but served in a stingy portion) and a luscious crème brûlée with acacia honey. Chic clientele and formal service. **C** 350-650 F. **M** 195 F (dinner).

▲▲ **Château de Berchères**   ▲☂
└┴┘ (See restaurant above)
Closed Sun, 1 wk at Christmas, Aug. 3 stes 1,200-1,400 F. 31 rms 470-985 F. Conf. Tennis. Golf. Pkg. Helipad. V, AE, DC, MC.
The extensive grounds of this pretty eighteenth-century château boast a pond and tennis courts. The rooms vary in size and appointments, but all are attractive and comfortable.

BERGERAC	24100
Paris 522 - Bordeaux 92 - Périgueux 47 - Agen 89	Dordogne

Le Cyrano   ☯
2, bd Montaigne
53 57 02 76, fax 53 57 78 15
Closed at Christmas. Open until 9pm. Priv rm: 50. Air cond. Hotel: 11 rms 210-230 F. Half-board 320-340 F. Conf. Pkg. V, AE, DC, MC.
This roomy, two-story stone house exudes a posh, provincial air that pleases the local bourgeoisie no end. But the main attraction is Jean-Paul Turon's cooking. Sometimes he stumbles (tasteless salad of artichoke bottoms with foie gras) but more often he pleases, with the likes of a flavorful grilled beefsteak, or the delicate but unctuous crêpes soufflées with Grand Marnier. Friendly welcome and service, and a great choice of regional wines. **C** 230-300 F. **M** 90 F, 120 F, 148 F, 200 F.

▲▲ **La Flambée**
└┴┘ 153, av Pasteur
53 57 52 33, fax 53 61 07 57
Closed Jan 2-Apr 2. 1 ste 390-650 F. 20 rms 260-330 F. Restaurant. Half-board 460 F. Conf. Heated pool. Tennis. Golf. Garage pkg. V, AE, DC, MC.
Huge, well equipped although simply decorated rooms (some with terraces) in a group of ancient buildings surrounded by a park. Pool, tennis courts, restaurant. Excellent welcome.

▲▲ **Hôtel de Bordeaux**
└┴┘ 38, pl. Gambetta
53 57 12 83, fax 53 57 72 14
Closed Dec 20-31, Jan 2-15. 2 stes 510-550 F. 38 rms 260-490 F. Rms for disabled. Restaurant. Half-board 340-395 F. Conf. Heated pool. Golf. Valet pkg. V, AE, DC, MC.
The mostly-newly-renovated rooms of this creditable hotel are simple and modern, and there is a swimming pool in the pretty garden.

BERGÈRES-LES-VERTUS 51	➜ Vertus

BERGUES 59	➜ Dunkerque

BERNAY	27300
Paris 150 - Evreux 48 - Lisieux 31 - Rouen 58	Eure

Hostellerie du Moulin Fouret
4 km S, in St-Aubin-le-Vertueux
32 43 19 95, fax 32 45 55 50
Closings not available. Open until 9:30pm. Priv rm: 25. Terrace dining. Pkg. V, AE, MC.
François Deduit's technique is nice and sharp, and so is his eye for detail. His most successful efforts include a tournedos of rabbit, warm foie gras with honey cake, and fine Normandy staples like andouille and Camembert. The first two set meals are remarkable bargains, served with a smile in this handsome Norman mill. **C** 280-380 F. **M** 98 F, 150 F, 270 F.

BERRY-AU-BAC	02190
Paris 149 - Laon 29 - Reims 19 - Soissons 47 - Rethel 44	Aisne

 La Cote 108
N 44 - 23 79 95 04, fax 23 79 83 50
Closed Sun dinner, Mon, Jul 10-25, Dec 26-Jan 18. Open until 9:30pm. Priv rm: 20. Air cond. Pkg. V, AE.
All the "big bubbles" of the Champagne district alight here to partake of Serge Courville's modern, expert cooking. Peerless ingredients and faultless technique produce dishes like the magnificent puff pastry with fresh morels, breast of young squab that literally melts in your mouth, and a luscious dessert assortment. The Courvilles have made a real effort to make the wine list more affordable, and offer some Champagnes for around 220 F a bottle, as well as several half bottles. Madame Courville provides a friendly welcome and excellent attention to guests. **C** 400-450 F. **M** 150 F, 250 F, 320 F, 420 F.

BERRY-BOUY 18	➜ Bourges

BESANÇON   25000

Paris 390 - Nancy 199 - Belfort 90 - Dijon 91   *Doubs*

Mercure
4, av. Carnot
81 80 33 11, fax 81 88 11 14
Open year-round. 67 rms 320-520 F. Restaurant. Conf. Pkg. V, AE, DC.
Surprising link in a hotel chain known for its functional decor; this one is a converted town house with a garden, located close to the center of the city. Not all the accommodation is equally attractive, but the public rooms are very pretty.

Mercure-Parc Micaud
3, av. E.-Droz
81 80 14 44, fax 81 53 29 83
Open year-round. 95 rms 320-510 F. Restaurant. Half-board 400-520 F. Conf. Golf. Pkg. Helipad. V, AE, DC, MC.
Just five minutes from the center, in a verdant setting with a view of the River Doubs, this modern building offers well-maintained rooms and cheerful service.

Le Mungo-Park
11, rue J.-Petit
81 81 28 01, fax 81 83 36 97
Closed Sun, Mon lunch (in seas), Sat lunch off-seas, 1 wk in Feb, Jul 29-Aug 16. Open until 9:30pm. Terrace dining. Pkg. V, MC.
Those who believe that women chefs are more bound to tradition in their cooking than their male counterparts should come here to be proved wrong. Jocelyne Choquart and Benoît Rotschi have given wings to the region's repertoire, and let it soar, shaking up tradition while respecting the innate savors of their homegrown ingredients. Their creations are sometimes simple, sometimes complex, rarely mannered, and never pointless. This is the kind of cooking that gives you ideas to try at home, proof that it's not only original but also adaptable. A galette of morels marries well with clove cream, the curried carp gives a touch of gallantry to a salad of radishes with preserved lemon, smoked trout is jazzed up by an onion and beet salad, and the chicken with morels, foie gras and Vin Jaune might have seemed redundant without the chickpea purée. The service is wonderfully friendly, the wine list not extensive, but astutely conceived by Gérald Lotz; there is now a wide choice of inexpensive Loire wines. Surprising, airy decor at the edge of the Doubs. **C** 400-480 F.

Le Poker d'As
14, square Saint-Amour
81 81 42 49, fax 81 81 05 59
Closed Sun dinner, Mon, Jul 17-Aug 7, Dec 25-Jan 2. Open until 9:45pm. V, AE, DC, MC.
Don't let the eccentric decor throw you off the scent of one of the area's more gifted chefs. Raymond Ferreux thrives on inventing new ways to use fine regional foodstuffs. Sometimes he goes wide of the mark, but often he's right on target: good salmon and herring tartare, veal fillet with Marsala (excellent jus, dry meat), and rhubarb soup. The wine list focuses on the Jura. **C** 250-350 F. **M** 90 F, 125 F, 145 F, 180 F.

And also...
Our selection of places for inexpensive, quick, or late-night meals.
Chez Barthod (81 82 27 14 - 22, rue Bersot. Open until 11pm.): The most fashionable spot in town serves Southwestern specialties on a little garden-terrace. Wines available by the glass (100-200 F).
Les Quatre Saisons (81 82 30 46 - 22, rue Mégevand. Lunch only.) The *patron* prepares succulent traditional dishes served by his cheerful spouse (150 F).

■ **In École-Valentin 25480**   5 km NW on N 57

Le Valentin
ZAC de Valentin, zone Vert-Bois-Vallon
81 80 03 90, fax 81 53 45 49
Closed Sun dinner, Mon, Jul 31-Aug 21. Open until 9:30pm. Priv rm: 35. Garden dining. Pkg. V.
Take a seat in this big, plush manse a short distance outside of Besançon, and turn your appetite over to Jean-François Maire's classic cuisine. Foie gras with lobster tail and claws, ragoût of veal sweetbreads and kidneys with morels, and a pear tart with caramel sauce. Broad (but not always well chosen) cellar. **C** 320-420 F. **M** 112 F, 185 F, 235 F, 335 F.

BESSE-EN-CHANDESSE   63610

Paris 437 - Issoire 35 - Clermont-Ferrand 50   *Puy-de-Dôme*

■ **In Super-Besse 63610**   7 km W

12/20 La Bergerie
Route de Vassivières - 73 79 61 06
Closed Sep 15-Dec 15. Open until 10pm (11pm in summer). Terrace dining. Pkg. V.
Folks flock into this authentic sheepfold for Madame Verny's good local specialties, prepared with a bit more care when it isn't ski season: aligot, croustillant of pig's foot, trout-stuffed cabbage, and lemon verbena bavarian cream. **C** 200-250 F. **M** 88 F (in seas), 115 F, 145 F.

Gergovia
1, rue M.-Gauthier
73 79 60 15, fax 73 79 61 43
Closed Jan 2-13, Mar 26-Jun, Sep 3-Dec 20. 2 stes 380-480 F. 49 rms 150-350 F. Restaurant. Half-board 310-475 F. Conf. Heated pool. Pkg. V, AE.
This huge modern chalet is perhaps the resort's most inviting, with all kinds of sporting equipment and organized activities.

BÉTHUNE   62400

Paris 213 - Arras 33 - Douai 39 - Dunkerque 67   *P./Calais*

La Chartreuse du Val St-Esprit
4 km SW on N 41, 1, rue de Fouquières, 62199 Gosnay
21 62 80 00, fax 21 62 42 50
Open daily until 10pm. Priv rm: 170. Terrace dining. Air cond. Garage pkg. V, AE, MC.
A splendid château hidden in verdant grounds is the scene of generous, deftly prepared meals: this year, the chef proposes crispy chopped

celery with caviar cream, young Bresse chicken with truffles, and desserts to please chocoholics. Interesting cellar. C 300-450 F. M 205 F, 290 F, 380 F.

La Chartreuse du Val St-Esprit
(See restaurant above)
Open year-round. 1 ste 650-1,000 F. 55 rms 320-900 F. Air cond. Conf. Tennis. Golf. Pkg. V, AE, MC.
Perfectly comfortable and spacious rooms look out over a huge green park. The rooms on the upper floor of this imposing château are cozier than the others.

Marc Meurin
15, pl. de la République
21 68 88 88, fax 21 56 37 15
Closed Sun dinner, Mon, Aug. Open until 10pm. Priv rm: 35. V, AE, DC.
Marc Meurin has made this plush, comfortable restaurant one of the finest eating houses in the Pas-de-Calais. The menu confirms his creativity and polished technique: recent additions to the repertoire include an artichoke galette with sautéed foie gras, turbot in a veal jus with caramelized endives, and a chocolate-licorice flan with green tea syrup. Generous menu du marché for 180 F: terrine of young rabbit with thyme, black cod fillet with lemongrass, and a warm chocolate tart. Well chosen wine list.
C 300-450 F. M 180 F (wine incl), 180 F, 280 F.

Le Pavé d'Auge
Pl. du Village
31 79 26 71, fax 31 39 04 45
Closed Mon (exc lunch in seas), Tue, Feb school hols, Nov 20-Dec 13. Open until 9pm. V, MC.
Jérôme Bansard has regained the point he lost two years ago through more precise technique: intensely flavored sole and oysters à la nage, hearty beef à la daube, good teurgoule ice cream. He no longers limits himself to "neo-ter-roir" cooking, and the dining room in an ancient market hall remains charming, right in the middle of one of Normandy's loveliest villages. Good choice of half bottles on the wine list; the service could use some fine-tuning. C 280-360 F. M 130 F (weekdays, Sat lunch, Sun dinner), 170 F, 215 F, 270 F.

Le Cochon d'Or
Le Petit Castel, pl. du Gal-de-Gaulle
32 57 70 46, fax 32 42 25 70
Closed Mon, Dec 15-Jan 15. Open until 9pm. No pets. V, MC.
Charles Folleau is a true Norman chef, with a native's affinity for butter and cream. This place aims to please, and does. Try the 155 F menu: a cake of pleurote mushrooms with shallot butter, duck fillet with poivrade sauce, cheese, and dessert. Nice wine list, pleasant welcome.
C 180-320 F. M 110 F (exc Sat dinner & Sun lunch), 80 F (weekdays), 155 F, 230 F.

10/20 Taverne des Remparts
Pl. du Château - 53 29 57 76
Closed Oct-Mar 15. Open until 9pm. Terrace dining. Pkg. V, MC.
Modest but tasty local fare is on offer here. Order the hearty 95 F menu (soup, chicken with tarragon, salmon-trout with sorrel cream, cabécou, and pastry) and enjoy the pretty setting. In balmy weather, reserve a table on the shaded terrace. C 160-290 F. M 60 F, 95 F, 135 F.

Château du Landel
35 90 16 01, fax 35 90 62 47
Closed Nov 15-Mar 15 (exc for groups). 2 stes 700 F. 15 rms 450-700 F. Restaurant. Half-board 455-575 F. Conf. Heated pool. Pkg. Hellpad. V, MC.
The huge rooms of this seventeenth-century Norman dwelling are decorated in a cozy, attractive style. Guests may relax in the superb public rooms, play billiards, or go for walks on the grounds. Lukewarm welcome.

Auberge des Templiers
N 7 - 38 31 80 01, fax 38 31 84 51
Closed Feb. Open until 9:30pm. Priv rm: 60. Garden dining. Heated pool. Valet pkg. V, AE, DC, MC.
The Sologne region, lovely land of mists and forest pools, is also the setting for this, one of France's great restaurants. An elegant French provincial ambience emanates from the oaken beams overhead, the antique cupboards and tapestries, the tables adorned with candelabra and beautiful china.
More wonderful still, the mystic elements of the landscape must have seeped into the walls of this magical auberge, for every chef who has presided over its kitchen has kept the cooking up to the same superb standard. The rare professionalism of owners Philippe and Françoise Dépée keeps this jewel perfectly burnished no matter who is in charge in the kitchen. But now it looks like Fabrice Vitu, who trained with some of France's top chefs (Senderens, Blanc) and has been here since 1991, might be here to stay. He knows what he does best: no fancy flourishes, no audaciousness, but rather an harmonious mixture of tradition, modernism and country-style savor. His dishes are marked by intense flavors and precise technique: foie gras with black pepper and grapes in a Beaumes-de-Venise jelly; pearl barley risotto with truffles and sea scallops; crab terrine with oysters and sweet peppers; a delicious sauté of frog's legs with chive butter, John Dory in a fumet of green thyme, rosemary and Niçois olives; lobster in Chinon wine sauce; spit-roasted young squab with baby vegetables; or magnificent Sisteron lamb in a parsley and truffle shell. Young rabbit in a papillote with smoked bacon is particularly succulent, and in hunting season, game dishes

are the focus of memorable feasts. François Brochot's dessert creations are outstanding, too: crunchy craquelin topped with pepper-spiked green apples in a chaud-froid sauce, pithiviers with black cherries, and gaufres of candied celery with raspberry sauce are all real winners. Jean-Paul Martin, a most charming sommelier, will help you choose the Burgundy, Bordeaux, or Loire wine that will best suit your meal—and your wallet. **C** 450-750 F. **M** 270 F (lunch), 390 F, 620 F.

Auberge des Templiers
(See restaurant above)

Closed Feb. 8 stes 1,500-3,500 F. 22 rms 600-1,380 F. Half-board 980-1,200 F. Air cond. Conf. Heated pool. Tennis. Pkg. Helipad. V, AE, DC, MC.

The taste and attention to detail lavished on these lodgings—an opulent bungalow on the edge of the park, and a clutch of Sologne-style cottages—know no limits, nor hardly an equal anywhere. One is transported with delight by the ambience and amenities, including the regal breakfasts. Relais et Châteaux.

BÉZIERS 34500
Paris 839 - Montpellier 72 - Narbonne 27 - Perpignan 93 *Hérault*

12/20 L'Ambassade
22, bd de Verdun - 67 76 06 24

Closed Mon dinner, Sun. Open until 10pm. Priv rm: 20. Air cond. V, AE.

Chef Patrick Olry has been focusing his efforts so much on his business-lunch clientele the has lost his culinary way—and his toque. Opt for the 145 F menu instead of the pricey à la carte selection; you will have a rather bland sot-l'y-laisse and frog's leg salad with foie gras, an adequate lamb cutlet with sweet garlic, a good cheese selection, and a very ordinary three-chocolates cake. Good regional cellar; friendly welcome and service. **C** 260-390 F. **M** 110 F (weekdays), 145 F, 195 F, 295 F.

Le Framboisier
12, rue Boieldieu - 67 49 90 00

Closed Sun, Mon, Feb school hols, last 2 wks of Aug. Open until 9pm. Air cond. V, AE, DC, MC.

This elegant, bright restaurant in the center of town is a family affair: Madame Yagues and her daughter offer a friendly welcome in the dining room, Angel Yagues mans the kitchen, and his brother ably serves as wine steward. Yagues' serious, well thought out cooking seemed a little more timid this year than in the past. The basics were good, but there was a lack of intensity in the sautéed sea scallops and pleurote mushrooms in chive cream, a bit of reserve in the chicken breast with tarragon brown sauce and noodles, and a lack of enthusiasm in the cheese assortment, but the nougat glacé with crème anglaise was lively and tasty, the best thing we ate on our last visit. **C** 300-400 F. **M** 150 F, 230 F, 330 F.

Hôtel du Nord
15, pl. J.-Jaurès
67 28 34 09, fax 67 49 00 37

Open year-round. 2 stes 400-450 F. 38 rms 240-400 F. Air cond. Conf. Pkg. V, AE, DC, MC.

The solemn atmosphere will not be to everyone's taste, but the hotel itself is handsome

and centrally located. The old-fashioned rooms offer complete comfort, the public rooms are inviting, and the service impeccable.

12/20 La Potinière
15, rue A.-de-Musset
67 76 35 30, fax 67 76 38 45

Closed Sat lunch, Mon, Sun dinner (exc reserv), May 1-15. Open until 10pm. Priv rm: 30. Air cond. V, AE, MC.

These dining rooms are beflowered and bright despite the lack of windows, and Marc Lavaux's cuisine is inviting and fresh: choose the well-wrought pig's foot salad, breast of young squab, and vanilla-scented crème brûlée, all on the first set menu. Pleasant reception and service. **C** 250-340 F. **M** 140 F, 220 F, 320 F.

BIARRITZ 64200
Paris 747 - Pau 115 - Dax 57 - Bayonne 8 *Pyrénées-A.*

Auberge du Relais
44, av. de la Marne
59 24 85 90, fax 59 22 13 94

Closed Tue off-seas, last 3 wks of Jan. Open until 10pm. Terrace dining. Air cond. V, AE.

The immaculate country decor will put you in the mood to enjoy the *patron*'s fresh, earnest cooking: tasty breaded sea scallops, savory sea bream with ham (the flavors clashed a bit), flavorful and delicate warm apple tart. Warm welcome. **C** 240-300 F. **M** 92 F (exc hols), 152 F, 202 F.

11/20 Brasserie Royale
7, pl. Bellevue - 59 24 19 06

Closed Dec 24. Open until midnight. Priv rm: 60. Terrace dining. Air cond. V, MC.

An attractive brasserie, advantageously (or not, depending on your luck and resources) situated near the casino. Along with the ocean view, enjoy a salad of chipirons (tiny squid), good grilled veal kidney, and a nice apple tourtière, all of which makes for an adequate meal that lacks only finesse. **C** 150-240 F.

Café de Paris
5, pl. Bellevue
59 24 19 53, fax 59 24 18 20

Closed Sun dinner & Mon off-seas. Open until 10:30pm. Priv rm: 40. Garden dining. V, AE, DC, MC.

Didier Oudill was superchef Michel Guérard's faithful right-hand man at Eugenie-les-Bains for more than a decade, then he struck out on his own in Grenade-sur-l'Adour nearby. And now he has begun a new adventure in Biarritz, in the Café de Paris (recently saved from a long decline) on the inaccurately named Place Bellevue. The building was turned into a hotel, and you can choose between a brasserie and the restaurant. The latter has big bay windows, pale walls, and subtle furnishings that will not make you miss the "faux Maxim's" decor of the past. Friendly welcome, attentive service that never feels stiff, and a dedicated young wine steward who will not steer you toward the most expensive bottles (the cheaper ones are not that cheap, however). As for the cuisine, it reflects local Basque traditions, but made new through Oudill's personal discoveries. All dishes are marked by intense flavors that blend harmoniously, such as the spicy layers of lasagne, fresh anchovies and eggplant with an apricot-flavored vinaigrette. Or the combination of fava beans, ham, and hake, a real treat, or the magnificent saddle of young rabbit stuffed with tiny squid on a bed of spinach flavored with clam juice and enlivened with little morsels of red pepper. This is home cooking transcended to the level of culinary art. Other dishes are less brilliant but still clearly worth three toques, like the casserole of monkfish, caramelized onions, green peppers, asparagus, tiny peas and ratte potatoes. One false note: slightly overcooked tiger shrimp in the original salad of shrimp and Basque sheep's milk cheese in a fennel-apple vinaigrette. Fine desserts: peaches roasted with star anise and served with a dollop of vanilla ice cream, and warm dark chocolate tart with aged Banyuls syrup. Intelligent wine list (but with too few half bottles), high but fair prices, chic clientele in the Biarritz tradition: all in all, with Oudill in the kitchen, things are looking up here. C 400-650 F. M 135 F (Bistrot Bellevue), 175 F.

Café de Paris
(See restaurant above)
Open year-round. 1 ste 720-850 F. 19 rms 550-850 F. Half-board 900 F. Golf. V, AE, DC, MC.
Modern and comfortable, decorated in restrained tones of brown and beige, the rooms all boast pleasant fittings such as wicker or faux burred-elm furniture. The marble bathrooms are nice and bright (bathtubs a bit narrow). Some rooms have balconies, all offer a wonderful view over the sea and the Bellevue casino. Ordinary breakfasts, fair prices. No parking lot, no pool.

Château du Clair de Lune
Route d'Arbonne, 48, av. A.-Seeger
59 23 45 96, fax 59 23 39 13
Open year-round. 16 rms 400-650 F. Pkg. V, AE, DC.
This turn-of-the-century manor on splendid grounds a mile or so from the center of Biarritz, offers grand guest rooms where taste and tranquility reign.

Comfort Inn
19, av. de la Reine-Victoria
59 22 04 80, fax 59 24 91 19
Open year-round. 3 stes 485-710 F. 40 rms 335-610 F. Air cond. No pets. Pkg. V, AE, DC, MC.
A fine hotel in the heart of Biarritz, featuring big, well-outfitted rooms. The sea-water spa is just steps away.

Le Croque-en-Bouche
5, rue du Centre - 59 22 06 57
Closed Sun dinner, Mon, last 2 wks of Jun. Open until 10pm. Air cond. V, AE.
Bernard Olasagasti plies his trade with creativity and perfect technique to produce the dishes on the popular, unbeatable set menu that offers as much choice as many a carte: grilled chiperons (tiny squid) sautéed with sweet peppers and croûtons, lamb pastilla with rosemary, brouet (soup) of nuts and eggplant caviar (a model of harmony and finesse), and a yummy puff pastry stuffed with chocolate, walnuts, and hazlenuts with raspberry sauce. Give the man another toque! With a nice bottle of something from the fully stocked cellar, bliss is assured. Elegant dining room; charming welcome. M 120 F, 160 F.

Les Jardins de l'Océan
52, av. de l'Impératrice
59 41 33 00, fax 59 41 33 99
Closings not available. Open until 10pm. Air cond. No pets. Valet pkg. V, AE, DC, MC.
Dine in a huge and delightful winter garden on admirable fresh shellfish assortments, terrific fish, and regional specialties, all prepared with brio by chef Georges Amestoy: tiny red mullet and gambas à la plancha with squid-ink sauce, milk-fed lamb with chorizo jus, sherbet, and chocolate profiteroles with Izarra infusion. The wine list is nicely composed, with a good selection of half-bottles. C 250-350 F. M 195 F, 230 F.

Régina et Golf
(See restaurant above)
Closings not available. 9 stes 1,100-1,500 F. 61 rms 620-1,250 F. Rms for disabled. Half-board 740-1,230 F. Air cond. Conf. Heated pool. Golf. Pkg. V, AE, DC, MC.
We willingly pay the extra fee to enjoy a room with a breathtaking view of the cliffs and the sea. Other rooms look out onto the golf course or pool. A peaceful atmosphere is not the least of the many amenities offered here—others include golf lessons and a sea-water spa.

12/20 Le Petit Doyen
87, av. de la Marne - 59 24 01 61
Closed until 10:30pm (11pm in summer). Priv rm: 20. Air cond. Pkg. V, AE, DC, MC.
In a cozy setting that features fine stonework and a handsome fireplace, the young owners do their utmost to make customers happy and comfortable. They succeed with their 170 F set menu that offers such options as asparagus mousse with sherry-flavored whipped cream, roast sea bream with basil, goat cheese, and Aunt Marie's crème brûlée. Bordeaux dominates the wine list. M 90 F (lunch exc Sun), 170 F.

Les Platanes
32, av. Beausoleil - 59 23 13 68
Closed Tue lunch, Mon, 10 days in winter & in spring. Open until 10pm. Priv rm: 12. V, AE, MC.
Chef-owner Arnaud Daguin is a one-man show. All on his own he travels the length and breadth of the markets from Bayonne to the harbor at Ciboure. Back in his miniscule kitchen, all by himself, he puts together lovely impromptu menus bursting with freshness and an originality that we declare is fully worth two toques. Nothing up his sleeve, not even currently chic herbs, just the freshest products enhanced by carefully reduced jus. Let yourself be seduced by the magical red mullet and artichock soupette, warm fondue of hake and leeks, liver with asparagus, or homey veal sweetbreads and kidneys with mashed potatoes. Pleasant dining room with wicker chairs, and delicious local wines—Madiran, Jurançon, Pacherenc, Colombard—selected by Véronique Daguin. Though the surroundings are modest (the neighborhood is on the "wrong side of the tracks"), this is nonetheless one of the most appealing spots in Biarritz. C 300-350 F. M 150 F (lunch exc Sun), 230 F, 280 F.

The prices in this guide reflect what establishments were charging at press time.

Plaza

Av. Edouard-VII
59 24 74 00, fax 59 22 22 01
Open year-round. 60 rms 298-820 F.
Half-board 400-600 F. Air cond. Conf. Golf. Pkg. V,
AE, DC, MC.
The rooms of this luxury hotel that dates from
the 1930s are decorated in period style. The
beach and the casino are just outside the door.
Friendly, competent service.

 Relais Miramar

13, rue L.-Bobet
59 41 30 00, fax 59 24 77 20
Open daily until 10pm. Priv rm: 30. Terrace dining.
Air cond. No pets. Heated pool. Valet pkg. V, AE,
DC, MC.
The view of the pool and sea helps you forget
the rather charmless dining room. Chef André
Gaüzère, a rising star on the diet circuit, prepares
both diet and gastronomic menus, all with a
touch of local color. Try the huge langoustines,
a delectable green risotto with asparagus, cèpes
with crab fritters, louvine (local ocean fish) in a
sea-salt crust, or casserole-roasted young rabbit
with piperade and meltingly soft carrots. Friendly
service, and an overpriced wine list; wines available by the glass. C 400-450 F. M 290 F, 390 F.

 Miramar

(See restaurant above)
Open year-round. 17 stes 1,580-3,075 F. 109 rms
935-2,575 F. Half-board 820-1,578 F. Air cond. Conf.
Heated pool. Golf. Valet pkg. V, AE, DC, MC.
The style here is all "grand hotel", from the
immaculate rooms to the attentive, stylish service. Amenities include cable TV, sauna, and an
electronic putting green.

 La Rotonde

1, av. de l'Impératrice
59 41 64 00, fax 59 41 67 99
Closed Jan 4-Feb 8. Open until 11pm. Priv rm: 250.
Garden dining. Air cond. Heated pool. No pets. Valet
pkg. V, AE, DC, MC.
Chef Jean-Marie Gautier brings considerable
experience to bear on the menu served in the
monumental ballroom where Empress Eugénie
once entertained. Two different *cartes* and three
set menus, one dedicated to the Empress,
another to dieters: all this gets complicated and
would be better united on a single *carte*. But for
now, savor the lightly smoked shad in a terrine
with leeks, lobster gazpacho with preserved
tomatoes and Espelette peppers, hake with local
ham, Bay of Biscay-style cod ravioli, and lamb
from the Pyrénées with baby vegetables. C 300-
600 F. M 280 F (low-calorie), 280 F, 380 F.

 Le Palais

(See restaurant above)
Closed Jan 4-Feb 8. 21 stes 2,000-6,250 F. 133 rms
1,100-2,650 F. Half-board 1,080-1,705 F. Air cond.
Conf. Heated pool. Golf. Pkg. Helipad. V, AE, DC, MC.
Empress Eugénie had this labyrinthine summer
palace built in just ten months, and here she and
Napoléon III received the nobility of Europe.
Period antiques, huge rooms, poolside cabanas
one may rent for an imperial ransom, and an
eight-hole golf course are calculated to draw a
glittering, international crowd. A "palace" of the
sort one hardly sees anymore; of the sort one
should visit at least once in a lifetime.

 Les Frères Ibarboure

Chemin de Ttalienia
59 54 81 64, fax 59 54 75 65
Closed off-seas, 3 wks mid Nov-beg Dec. Open
until 9:30pm. Priv rm: 35. Garden dining. Air cond.
Pkg. V, AE, DC.
The modern pink hacienda set on a hillside
amid fields and woods doesn't please all tastes,
but the warm family welcome is typically
Basque, and the kitchen is well launched toward
gastronomic stardom. The Ibarboure brothers
play lovely duets in their kitchen, their lovely
sisters Anne-Marie and Marie-Claude manage
the dining room with warmth, and the family's
younger set sneaks in for tastes of this and that.
In the rotunda-shaped dining room or the ancient former chapel, Basque specialties are
celebrated in dishes marked by intense, refined
flavors, some thanks to herbs and spices from
faraway places. Try the surprising but delectable
hake with calf's head and gribiche sauce, warm
Landes asparagus with langoustines enlived with
honey cake and Muscat, tiny squid with a sauce
made from their ink and a ratatouille quenelle,
fillets of Pyrénées lamb with a croustillant of
lamb brains and sweetbreads, and a salad of
alubias, which are plump, meltingly soft beans
straight from Spain. Superb desserts, either variations on the theme of chocolate or whatever
pleases the chef on the day. C 350-400 F.
M 180 F, 230 F, 320 F.

■ In **Ahetze 64210**   5 km S on D 655

12/20 L'Épicerie d'Ahetze

Place du Fronton - 59 41 94 95
Closed Wed off-seas. Open until 11pm. Pkg. V, MC.
Local chef Jacques Bomassi offers seasonal
cuisine based on regional ingredients, served in
an adorable former épicerie. Try the 125 menu:
charcuterie assortment, veal cooked in
Irouléguy wine, and nougat glacé with two
sauces. Good house wine by the carafe. Friendly
welcome and service. C 210-250 F. M 100 F
(lunch exc Sun, wine incl), 125 F.

 Domaine de Rochevilaine

Pointe de Pen-Lan
97 41 61 61, fax 97 41 44 85
Closed Jan 5-Feb 15. Open until 9:30pm. Garden
dining. Heated pool. Pkg. V, AE, DC, MC.
Between Vannes and La Baule, on the sea-
swept Pointe de Pen-Lan, in a dining room overlooking the sea that gives the feel of being on a
great ship, "Captain" Patrick Caillault serves
dishes without a trace of pirating: note the classic
and impeccably prepared croustillant of crab
with shellfish vinaigrette. This year, he's been
experimenting with a whole range of deeply
flavorful dishes like lobster salad with currant
vinaigrette, fennel béarnaise with sea bass, and
a spice infusion with fruits in red wine. And with

surprising but always successful pairings of sweet and sour: tomato confit in a terrine of saffron-scented pasta and anchovy mousse, saffron and citrus enlivening sensational veal sweetbreads, and crispy rhubarb with an unctuous raw milk ice cream. High prices, in spite of some moderately priced wines. Charming, efficient service, and absolutely spectacular sunsets. C 380-500 F. M 120 F (exc Jul-Aug), 250 F, 320 F, 380 F, 400 F.

Domaine de Rochevilaine

(See restaurant above)
Closings not available. 1 ste 1,400-1,800 F. 36 rms 580-1,150 F. Rms for disabled. Half-board 540-825 F. Conf. Heated pool. Golf. Pkg. V, AE, DC, MC.
This manor will accommodate you in huge, mostly renovated rooms, some of which are blessed with a view of flower gardens and the rocky coast. Assiduous service and delicious breakfasts. Sea-water pool and brand-new fitness center.

BIOT	ʋ	06140

Paris 922 - Antibes 8 - Nice 22 - Cagnes 10   Alpes-Mar.

Auberge du Jarrier

30, pass. de la Bourgade
93 65 11 68, fax 93 65 50 03
Closed Wed. Open until 9:30pm. Priv rm: 20. Terrace dining. Air cond. V, AE.
This pretty house with a warm neo-rustic decor has a devoted following among locals and tourists. Christian Métral is a pro at turning out dishes based on excellent local produce: calf's foot in foie gras jelly with baby artichokes, roast John Dory with a risotto of fresh herbs and cuttlefish, and gooey chocolate cake with sesame seeds and almond-milk ice cream. And an incredible wine list that is not kind to your wallet. C 350-500 F. M 250 F, 290 F, 400 F.

Hostellerie du Bois Fleuri

Domaine du Bois-Fleuri
199, bd de la Source
93 65 68 74, fax 92 94 05 85
Open year-round. 1 ste 800 F. 12 rms 350-650 F. Restaurant. Half-board 510-680 F. Conf. Golf. Valet pkg. Helipad. V, AE, DC, MC.
Come to stay at this pink castle in the woods, where you'll find attractive, nicely equipped rooms, a quiet atmosphere, and splendid views from your terrace. Perfect service.

Les Terraillers

11, route du Chemin-Neuf
93 65 01 59, fax 93 65 13 78
Closed Thu lunch, Wed. Open until 10pm. Priv rm: 10. Terrace dining. Pkg. V, AE, MC.
Planted at the foot of the village since the sixteenth century, this elegantly restored pottery is now a restaurant, where Claude Jacques presents his elaborate cuisine with a Mediterranean accent. Who cares if the prices are out of sight and the terrace is noisy? The atmosphere is inviting and the cuisine includes delights like sautéed langoustine tails with a croustillant of vegetables, roast squab with its jus and ravioli, and bitter chocolate charlotte with coffee-whiskey cream sauce. C 380-600 F. M 170 F, 240 F, 300 F, 350 F.

BIRIATOU 64	→ Hendaye

BISCARROSSE	40600

Paris 660 - Dax 97 - Arcachon 39 - Bayonne 132   Landes

Atlantide

Pl. Marsan - 58 78 08 86, fax 58 78 75 98
Closed Dec 18-Jan 3. 33 rms 190-360 F. V, AE, DC.
A recently opened, small hotel in the new Biscarrosse center. Modern, functional, quiet rooms. Courteous welcome.

11/20 Le Mille Pâtes

898, av. de la République
58 78 12 00, fax 58 78 08 77
Closed Oct 15-Dec 6. Open until 10pm. Terrace dining. Pkg. V, AE, DC, MC.
The huge dining room is divided up by Roman "ruins" which underscore the menu's Italian theme: carpaccio of duck breast, Don Patillo macaroni, and a fricassée of duck hearts in Armagnac. Children are kept busy with a film in the games room while their parents eat in peace. C 150-220 F.

BLAGNAC 31	→ Toulouse

BLANQUEFORT 33	→ Bordeaux

BLOIS	41000

Paris 180 - Tours 60 - Orléans 56 - Le Mans 109   Loir/Cher

L'Espérance

189, quai Ulysse-Besnard
54 78 09 01, fax 54 56 17 86
Closed Sun dinner, Mon, Feb school hols, Aug 7-27. Open until 9:30pm. Air cond. No pets. Pkg. V.
Admire the view of the Loire River (and ignore the dining room's drab decor) as you savor Räphael Guillot's good cooking: sea scallop tart with olive purée, lamb chops gratinéed with goat cheese, and crème brûlée made with fresh herbs. C 250-350 F. M 125 F (weekdays, Sat lunch), 170 F, 245 F, 335 F.

L'Horset Blois

26, av. Maunoury
54 74 19 00, fax 54 74 57 97
Open year-round. 78 rms 350-495 F. Rms for disabled. Restaurant. Half-board 585-795 F. Conf. Pkg. V, AE, DC.
This new, attractive hotel is located opposite the conference center and has pleasant rooms.

L'Orangerie du Château

1, av. J.-Laigret
54 78 05 36, fax 54 78 22 78
Closed Sun dinner off-seas (exc hols), Mon. Open until 9:30pm (10pm in summer). Priv rm: 50. Garden dining. Pkg. V, AE, MC.
Renaissance luxury is embodied in this sumptuous dwelling, in spite of the not quite successful pink decor. As we go to press, a new chef, Jean-Marc Molveaux (13 and one black toque at Bérèngere in the Deux-Alpes) has just arrived on the scene. Stay tuned. C 250-300 F. M 100 F (weekdays), 140 F, 195 F, 270 F.

> Restaurant prices in red draw attention to restaurants that offer particularly good value.

159

12/20 La Péniche
Promenade du Mail - 54 74 37 23
Closed Sun (exc hols). Open until 9:30pm. Air cond.
Pkg. V, AE, DC, MC.
This quayside barge with its pretty wood ceiling and sea-water fish tank is a pleasant little spot in which to enjoy tasty dishes like a simple but good shellfish terrine en mousseline with herbs, salmon cooked in a light Vouvray wine sauce, well chosen cheeses, and a good crème brûlée. An extra point this year. Good choice of Bordeaux. C 260-360 F. M 150 F.

Au Rendez-Vous des Pêcheurs

27, rue de Foix
54 74 67 48, fax 54 74 47 67
Closed Mon lunch, Sun, Christmas school hols, 1 wk at Feb school hols, Aug 1-21. Open until 10pm. Priv rm: 10. Air cond. V, AE.
Energetic and enthusiastic, Éric Reithler cultivates an inventive yet fresh and basically simple style of cooking: try the oysters à la nage with chervil and meat jus, omble chevalier (lake fish) roasted in its skin with an olive purée, a gooey chocolate fondant, and Bulgarian cream glacé. You'll be courteously welcomed into a bright, unpretentious dining room, where efficient serving staff see to the patrons' well-being. Attractive cellar, with an emphasis on Loire wines. C 280-320 F. M 140 F.

12/20 Via Vietnam
2, bd Vauban - 54 78 86 99
Closed Wed lunch. Open until 11pm. Priv rm: 70. No pets. V.
Come here for authentic, full-flavored Vietnamese fare: nem (egg rolls), shrimp en brochette, Peking duck, ginger chicken, and other classics. Friendly welcome and fair prices. C 100-160 F. M 55 F (weekdays, Sat lunch), 100 F, 130 F, 150 F (wine incl).

■ In Molineuf 41190   9 km N on N 252

La Poste
9 km W on D 766, 11, av. de Blois
54 70 03 25, fax 54 70 12 46
Closed Sun dinner, Wed, Feb. Open until 9:30pm. Priv rm: 40. Air cond. Pkg. V, AE, DC, MC.
Follow the gourmets into this blue-and-yellow dining room full of flowers and a mural representing the game-rich Sologne region. Thierry Poidras provides well crafted, traditional cuisine. Try the lowest set menu, a real bargain: poultry ballottine with pistachios and onion confit, steak au poivre, salad with walnuts, dessert, and petits fours. The cellar is very good indeed, and like the food, is prudently priced. C 170-300 F. M 85 F, 95 F (exc Sun), 160 F, 210 F.

See also: Bracieux

BOCOGNANO 20   → CORSICA

BOIS-DE-LA-CHAIZE (LE) 85
→ Noirmoutier (Ile de)

BOIS-PLAGE-EN-RÉ (LE) 17 → Ré (Ile de)

BOLLÈNE   84500
Paris 640 - Avignon 50 - Montélimar 34 - Orange 22   Vaucluse

Lou Bergamoutie
Rue de l'Abbé-Prompsault
90 40 10 33, fax 90 40 10 39
Closed Sun dinner, Mon. Open until 10pm. Priv rm: 30. Terrace dining. V.
A brand-new decor provides a perfect setting for the clever and well crafted cuisine of Jean-Luc Kieraga: snail ravioli and oysters with fennel velouté, omble chevalier (lake fish) with hazlenuts and beurre blanc sauce, and a yummy white peach gratin with cider sabayon. Marie-Christine Kieraga provides a warm and hospitable welcome. C 300-400 F. M 150 F, 180 F, 270 F.

Hôtel de Chabrières
7, bd Gambetta
90 40 08 08, fax 90 30 55 22
Open year-round. 10 rms 270-330 F. Half-board 210-320 F. Conf. Golf. Pkg. V, AE, MC.
Unbelievable and right in the center of town: a family pension run by two sisters, just like in the old days. The rooms are impeccable and the atmosphere picturesque.

BOLLEZEELE   59470
Paris 275 - Calais 47 - Dunkerque 24 - St-Omer 19   Nord

Hostellerie Saint-Louis
47, rue de l'Eglise
28 68 81 83, fax 28 68 01 17
Closed Sun dinner, Mon, Jan. Open until 9pm. Priv rm: 60. Pkg. V, AE, MC.
A pleasant stopover for tourists who crave a warm welcome in a cozy setting. Philippe Dubreucq shows a deft touch with his poêlée of langoustines and salmon, a hot-and-cold foie gras duo, sautéed rabbit liver, and a chocolate fondant. Good choice of Bordeaux. C 250-380 F. M 240 F, 310 F (Sun, wine incl), 140 F, 320 F (exc Sun), 140 F (Sun).

Hostellerie Saint-Louis
(See restaurant above)
Closed Sun, Mon, Jan. 2 stes 450 F. 26 rms 250-360 F. Half-board 330-610 F. Conf. Pkg. V, AE, MC.
A hotel with smallish, nicely furnished modern rooms and ten brand-new larger ones, surrounded by a park in a sleepy little village. Friendly welcome and service.

BOLVIR DE CERDANYA (Spain)
→ Bourg-Madame

BON-ENCONTRE 47   → Agen

BONIFACIO 20   → CORSICA

BONNEVAUX-LE-PRIEURÉ   25620
Paris 414 - Pontarlier 45 - Besançon 26 - Ornans 11   Doubs

Le Moulin du Prieuré

81 59 21 47, fax 81 59 28 79
Closed Tue, Wed lunch, Nov 11-Mar 10. Open until 9pm. Priv rm: 35. Terrace dining. Pkg. V, AE, DC, MC.
In the heart of Courbet country nestles a charming thirteenth-century mill, where a young chef with real talent, longtime chef Marc Gatez's

CHAMPAGNE VEUVE CLICQUOT

REIMS - FRANCE

Call home.

AT&T

AT&T Access Numbers

Calling internationally from overseas is fast and easy with AT&T USADirect® and World Connect® Service.
- Available from over 131 countries worldwide.
- Use your AT&T Card or call collect to the U.S.

Dial the number shown below for the country you're in, and AT&T will help you complete your call.

ARMENIA*†	8◊14111	F.Y.R. MACEDONIA*†††	99-800-4288
AUSTRIA*†††	022-903-011		0800-890-110
BELGIUM*	0-800-100-10	MALTA■	19◊-0011
CROATIA†♦	99-38-0011	MONACO*	06-022-9111
CZECH REPUBLIC	00-420-00101	NETHERLANDS*	800-190-11
DENMARK	8001-0010	NORWAY	0◊0010-480-0111
FINLAND	9800-100-10	POLAND†*¹	05017-1-288
FRANCE	19-0011	PORTUGAL†	01-800-4288
GERMANY	0130-0010	ROMANIA	155-5042
GREECE*	00-800-1311	RUSSIA*† (MOSCOW)	00-420-00101
HUNGARY*	00◊-800-01111	SLOVAK REP.	900-99-00-11
ICELAND*	800-9001	SPAIN■	020-795-611
IRELAND	1-800-550-000	SWEDEN	155-00-11
ITALY*	172-1011	SWITZERLAND*	8◊100-11
LIECHTENSTEIN*	155-00-11	UKRAINE†	0500-89-0011
LITHUANIA♦	8◊196	U.K.	

*Public phones require deposit. ¹Dial 010-480-0111 from major Warsaw hotels. †Limited availability. †††Public phones require local coin payment through the call duration. ■ For AT&T **World Connect®** ♦Not available from public phone. ◊Await second dial tone. ● service-terminating calls only.

AT&T lets you dial directly to the States or around the world. For additional information, or to receive a free wallet card, call toll-free in the U.S. 1 800 331-1140, Ext. 722. **TrueWorld℠ Connections** from AT&T.

assistant, has brought a breath of new life with such light versions of classics like lobster salad with Vin Jaune vinegar, exceptional monkfish, and very well chosen Jura wines like the Fruitière d'Arbois Savagnin. If things go on like this, we will have to award a second toque! Lovely setting, handsome furnishings, and high prices. **C** 350-450 F. **M** 220 F (weekday lunch, wine incl), 200 F, 280 F, 350 F.

 Le Moulin du Prieuré
(See restaurant above)
Closed Tue, Nov 11-Mar 10. 8 rms 550-700 F. Pkg. V, AE, DC, MC.
The mill wheel is still in place and the machinery can be admired from the dining room. Guest rooms are decorated in a homespun style, but are nicely equipped.

BONNEVILLE	**74130**
Paris 560 - Chamonix 57 - Annecy 38 - Geneva 28	H.-Savoie

 Le Capucin Gourmand
N 205, in Vougy, route de Genève
50 34 03 50, fax 50 34 57 57
Closed Sun dinner, Mon, Jan 2-6, Aug 17-Sep 8. Open until 9:15pm. Priv rm: 50. Terrace dining. Pkg. V, AE, DC, MC.
The original flavor harmonies the young perfectionist Guy Barbin devises are well served by his precise technique: his sautéed snails with wild nettle sauce has won many fans, but you should also try the duck slices with spices and date purée, or the puff pastry with caramelized apples and green apple sherbet, not to mention the delicate banana tart. Christine Barbin directs the excellent service and manages the splendid cellar; many good wines are available by the carafe. **C** 320-400 F. **M** 210 F (wine incl), 190 F, 230 F, 270 F, 360 F.

Sapeur Hôtel
Pl. de l'Hôtel-de-Ville
50 97 20 68, fax 50 25 73 48
Closed Sun & Mon (exc Aug), 1st 2 wks of Jan. 3 stes 350-400 F. 12 rms 260-350 F. Restaurant. Half-board 300-420 F. Conf. No pets. V, AE, MC.
A pleasant and handy stopover on the ski route from Geneva to Chamonix.

BONSECOURS 76	**→ Rouen**

BORDEAUX	**33000**
Paris 566 - Angoulême 116 - Périgueux 120	Gironde

L'Alhambra
111 bis, rue Judaïque - 56 96 06 91
Closed Sat lunch, Sun. Open until 9:45pm. Priv rm: 20. Air cond. V, MC. **D3-3**
Cuisine at the level of Michel Demazeau's is hard to find at such low prices. This year we savored the harmonious ragoût of cock's comb and kidneys, perfectly roasted, tender squab flavored with basil and served with a delicious potato gratin, and yummy roast pear with caramel sauce and vanilla ice cream. The wine list focuses (naturally) on premium Bordeaux. Friendly welcome and service. **C** 250-350 F. **M** 110 F (lunch), 150 F, 200 F.

L'Arène Catherine
34, rue Ste-Colombe - 56 44 76 08
Open daily until 11:30pm. Terrace dining. Pkg. V, MC. **C5-52**
Alain and Catherine Moretti have created a joyfully celebratory decor here, with striped banquettes and Baroque light fixtures. The young chef's cooking is straightforward and satisfying: parmentier of chicken livers, grilled salmon with fresh parmesan, grilled garlic-breaded chicken, and fine homestyle desserts. The prices are giveaways: all first courses and main courses are priced the same (35 F and 75 F respectively), and there are inexpensive Bordeaux on the wine list. **C** 160-180 F. **M** 85 F (weekday lunch, wine incl), 100 F (dinner).

Hôtel de Bayonne
4, rue de Martignac
56 48 00 88, fax 56 52 03 79
Closed Dec 24, 1st wk of Jan. 36 rms 350-610 F. Air cond. Conf. No pets. V, AE, DC, MC. **D4-12**
After extensive renovations, this eighteenth-century building houses handsome guest and public rooms, decorated in a 1930s style.

12/20 Bistro du Sommelier ✺
163, rue G.-Bonnac
56 96 71 78, fax 56 24 52 36
Closed Sat lunch, Sun. Open until 11pm. Priv rm: 100. Terrace dining. Air cond. Pkg. V, AE, MC. **C3-41**
Nobody beats sommelier Hervé Valverde to the best Bordeaux (served by the glass) at the sweetest prices, with some homestyle dishes to go with them: oxtail terrine, tricandilles (giblets and gizzards) in a salad, calf's head, duck confit, and steaks. Right in the busy center of town, but with a quiet garden courtyard. **M** 95 F (lunch, wine incl), 116 F.

Au Bonheur du Palais
74, rue P.-L.-Lande
56 94 38 63, fax 56 94 38 63
Closings not available. Open until 11pm. Priv rm: 60. Air cond. V, AE, DC, MC. **C4-24**
Come here to enjoy Cantonese and Szechuan cuisine in all its variety, like the crispy trout fillet in sweet-sour sauce, flavorful chicken with star anise, and coconut fritters. Affordable selection of good white wines. Very friendly welcome. **C** 230-300 F. **M** 158 F, 235 F (weekday dinner, Sat).

Le Buhan
28, rue Buhan
56 52 80 86, fax 56 79 02 51
Closed Sun dinner, Mon lunch, 1 wk at Feb school hols, 1 wk beg Sep. Open until 10:30pm. V, AE, MC. **C5-16**
Pascal Michel's cooking is as adroit as appealing as can be: foie gras soufflé with balsamic vinegar sauce, sturgeon with peppery sabayon, and crème brûlée with caramelized milk. The old-rose decor makes an ideal backdrop for glistening glasses filled with vintage Bordeaux. Friendly, dynamic service. **C** 250-340 F. **M** 130 F, 190 F, 250 F.

Looking for a city in a département? Refer to the **index***.*

A   B   C

1

A 63 Arcacho

| R | Restaurant | H | Hôtel |

1 - Le Café du Musée **R**
2 - Normandie **H**
    et Hôtel
    des Quatre Sœurs **H**
3 - L'Alhambra **R**
4 - La Chamade **R**
5 - Château Chartrons **H**
6 - Chez Philippe **R**
7 - Le Vieux Bordeaux **R**
8 - Le Chapon Fin **R**
    et Continental **H**
9 - Les Plaisirs d'Ausone **R**
    et Le Plat dans l'Assiette **R**
10 - Royal Médoc **H**
11 - Mercure
    Pont d'Aquitaine **H**
12 - Hôtel de Bayonne **H**
13 - La Ténarèze **R**
    et Chez Gilles **R**
14 - La Villa Carnot **R**
15 - Hôtel Majestic **H**
16 - Le Buhan **R**
17 - Le Flore (Sofitel
    Aquitania) **RH**
18 - Le Nouveau Saucier **R**
19 - La Petite Sirène **R**
20 - One Star Hotel **H**
21 - Campanile **H**
22 - Didier Gélineau **R**
23 - Le Café Gourmand **R**
24 - Au Bonheur du Palais **R**
25 - Mercure
    Bordeaux-le-Lac **H**
26 - Studio **H**
27 - Le Port de la Lune **R**
28 - La Pelouse **H**
29 - Restaurant
    Le Loup **R**
30 - Au Chipiron **R**
31 - Le Doris **R**
32 - La Coquille d'Œuf **R**
33 - Le Puits Ste-Catherine
    (Hôtel Ste-Catherine) **H**
34 - Gravelier **R**
35 - Claret **H**
36 - Malabar **R**
37 - Ibis Mériadeck **H**
38 -   Pullman **H**
39 - La Cave de Bigoudy **R**
40 - Novotel
    Bordeaux-le-Lac **H**
41 - Bistro du Sommelier **R**
42 - Clemenceau **H**
43 - Royal Saint-Jean **H**
44 - Grand Hôtel Français **H**
45 - Le Chalut **R**
46 - Hôtel Burdigala **H**
47 - La Tupina **R**
48 - Le Clavel Saint-Jean **R**
49 - Jean Ramet **R**
50 - Francs Délices **R**
51 - Pavillon des Boulevards **R**
52 - L'Arène Catherine **R**

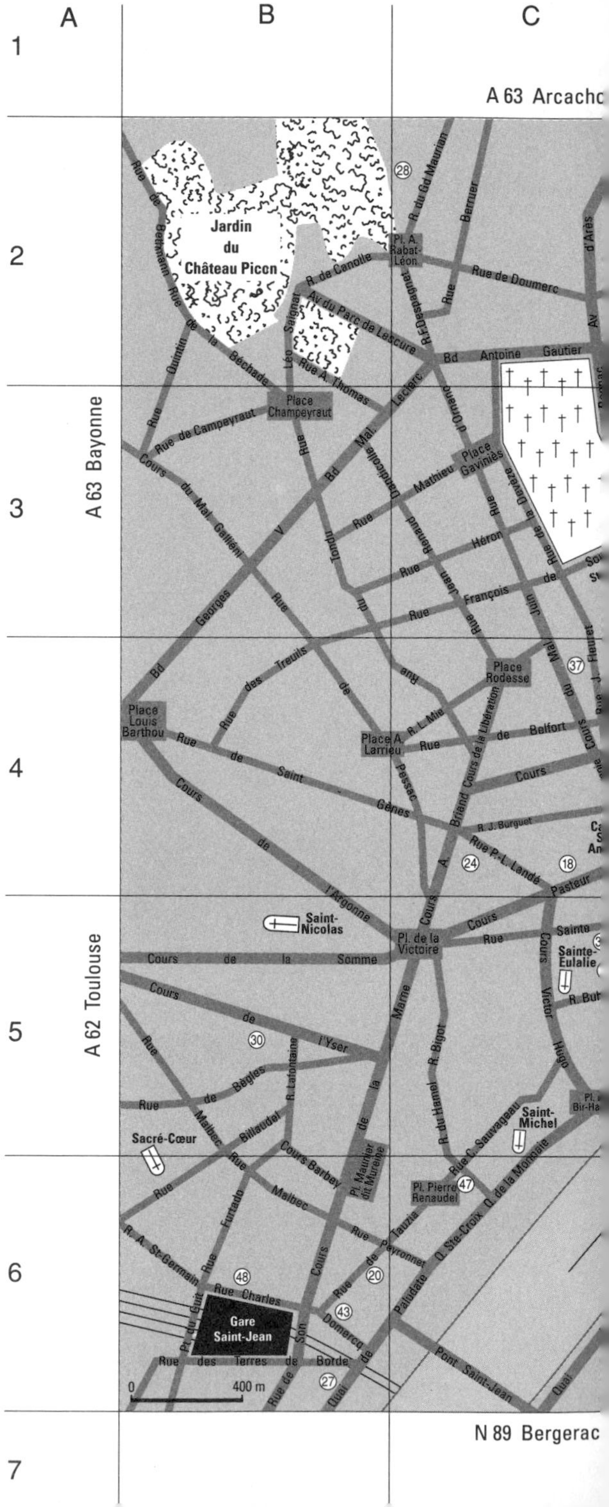

Jardin
du
Château Picon

Place
Champeyraut

A 63 Bayonne

Place
Gaviniès

2

3

Place
Rodesse

Place
Louis
Barthou

Place A.
Larrieu

4

A 62 Toulouse

Saint-
Nicolas

Pl. de la
Victoire

Sainte-
Eulalie

5

Sacré-Cœur

Saint-
Michel

Pl. Pierre
Renaudel

6

Gare
Saint-Jean

0   400 m

N 89 Bergerac

7

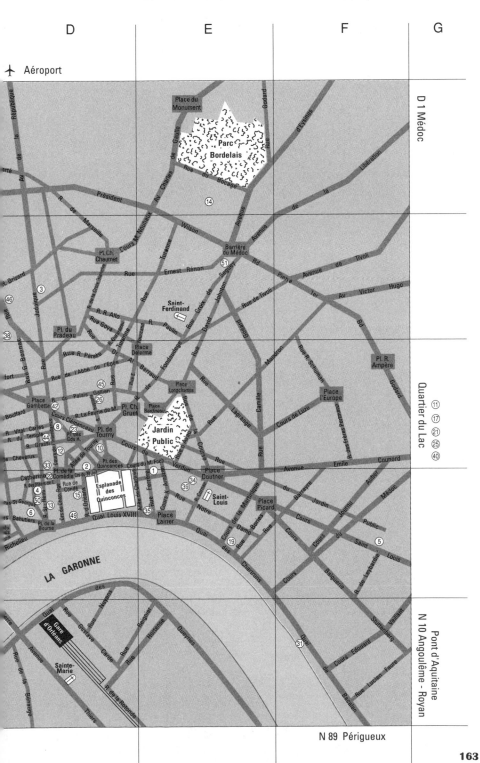

✈ Aéroport

D 1 Médoc

Quartier du Lac

Pont d'Aquitaine
N 10 Angoulême - Royan

N 89 Périgueux

163

Hôtel Burdigala
115, rue G.-Bonnac
56 90 16 16, fax 56 93 15 06
Open year-round. 15 stes 1,180-1,990 F. 68 rms 800-1,400 F. Rms for disabled. Restaurant. Air cond. Conf. Golf. Valet pkg. V, AE, DC, MC. D3-46
A welcome alternative to small, ageing hotels or the big chains, this convenient, modern establishment has good rooms with effective soundproofing. Charming reception and attractive breakfast buffet.

Le Café du Musée
7, rue Ferrère
56 44 70 60, fax 56 44 12 07
Closed Mon. Open until 7pm (Wed 10pm). Terrace dining. Air cond. No pets. V. E5-1
Artistic in the extreme, the café's interior is a splendid, light-flooded contemporary space designed by Andrée Putman, the waiters' garb was designed by Azzedine Alaïa, and the cuisine by able chef Philippe Pelhâte. His bright ideas and sure technique produce dishes like anchoïade with raw vegetables, lamb fillet with caraway, and excellent cinnamon, vanilla, and saffron crème brûlée. **C** 200-300 F.

Le Café Gourmand
3, rue Buffon - 56 79 23 85
Closed Mon dinner, Sun, 1 wk in Feb, 3 wks in Aug. Open until 11pm. Air cond. Pkg. V. D4-23
An inviting spot with panelled interior dotted with film stills and pleasant outdoor terrace. The simplified classic cuisine is inexpensive, and handily prepared by "director" Bruno Oliver: closeup of a calf's head with ravigote sauce, travelling shot of the tricandilles salad (with giblets and gizzards), and a dissolve into honey bread pudding or crème brûlée. Excellent casting of fine Bordeaux by Bruno himself. **C** 150-220 F. **M** 60 F, 75 F (weekday lunch).

Campanile
Quartier du Lac, centre hôtelier
56 39 54 54, fax 56 50 19 58
See page 95. G4-21
This modern, practical hotel overlooks a large garden with a children's play area.

12/20 La Cave de Bigoudy
36, rue Tourat - 56 51 69 43
Closed Aug. Open until 11pm. Terrace dining. Air cond. V, DC, MC. E5-39
An imposing fireplace heats the comfortably rustic dining room while it grills the excellent meats that have earned this spot its reputation. Six very ordinary oysters with excellent sausages, savory fat-free grilled gizzards and giblets, and a generous tourtière pastry flambéed with none other than Calvados. Bring your own bottle or sample the good red Bordeaux on the list. **C** 140-240 F. **M** 95 F, 130 F.

11/20 Le Chalut
59, rue du Palais-Gallien - 56 81 43 51
Closed Sun, Mon, hols, wk of Aug 15. Open until 11pm. Terrace dining. V, AE, MC. D4-45
The sea is the focus in this friendly restaurant. Try the 138 F menu: fish spread with saffron, fish soup with a very spicy rouille sauce, six raw oysters, perfectly cooked but a trifle bland grilled red mullet, and crêpes with sugar that could use a bit more butter. Good choice of regional wines. The Bistrot du Chalut annex offers lower prices. **C** 170-250 F. **M** 75 F (wine incl), 60 F, 138 F, 185 F.

La Chamade
20, rue des Piliers-de-Tutelle
56 48 13 74, fax 56 79 29 67
Closed Sat lunch (& dinner & Sun in Jul-Aug). Open until 10pm. Priv rm: 45. V, AE, MC. D5-4
Everyone approves of Michel Carrère's masterly cooking, rooted in the region yet modern and light, and the new 100 F menu is a real winner: a cassoulette of perfectly cooked savory stuffed peppers, grilled boneless shad fillet with a crispy herb crust and served with vegetables, and an excellent Millas Landais (a cornflour cake). It adds up to fine cooking at mere bistrot prices. Well priced Bordeaux, friendly welcome, professional service. Ignore the 70s decor. **C** 350-450 F. **M** 100 F, 185 F, 260 F.

Le Chapon Fin
5, rue Montesquieu - 56 79 10 10
Closed Sun, Mon, Jul-Aug. Open until 10pm. Priv rm: 20. Garden dining. Air cond. No pets. Pkg. V, AE, DC, MC. D4-8
The turn-of-the-century decor of Bordeaux's most famous restaurant will amaze and delight you, as in no doubt did other well-known patrons such as Sarah Bernhardt, Toulouse-Lautrec, and Winston Churchill. Hostess Géraldine Garcia sets an elegant tone in the dining room, and chef Francis Garcia is now back on track with exuberant but more finely crafted cooking marked by the distinctive flavor of France's Southwest. Try the excellent 150 F menu and see what we mean: perfect salad with a crispy, breaded and sautéed lamb's brain, followed by a thick fillet of hake à l'espagnole paired with perfectly cooked broccoli (a rarity in this country), and a clever banana croustillant à la crêpes Suzette. On the à la carte menu you'll find a delicious saddle of young rabbit with snail pastry, slices of young duck in sweet-sour sauce, classic lamproie bordelaise (lamprey, perhaps the best version of this specialty the city has to offer): cooking that is rich in nuances, artfully prepared, and well balanced. The third toque comes back this year. And the decor is now more spiffy, too. Opulent, fairly priced wine list with many half bottles. **C** 400-500 F. **M** 150 F (lunch), 250 F, 360 F, 400 F.

Château Chartrons
81, cours St-Louis
56 43 15 00, fax 56 69 15 21
Open year-round. 7 stes 1,200 F. 144 rms 690-900 F. Rms for disabled. Half-board 495 F. Air cond. Conf. Valet pkg. V, AE, DC, MC. F5-5
Behind the Victorian façade you'll discover a luxurious and ultramodern hotel complex, with irreproachably appointed rooms, all air conditioned and soundproofed. Facilities include a wine bar, shops, gardens, and an attractive terrace.

12/20 Au Chipiron
56, cours de l'Yser - 56 92 98 59
Closed Sun dinner, Mon, Aug 14-31. Open until 9:30pm. V. B5-30
The chef's gastronomic trophies are the dining room's sole decorations, but the family atmos-

phere, friendly prices, and spirited cuisine make one want to become a regular. The 100 F menu includes tiny crêpes with chiperons (squid), pig's foot crepinette, grilled shad with sorrel, and good classic desserts. **C** 180-280 F. **M** 100 F, 150 F.

Claret
18, parvis des Chartrons
56 01 79 79, fax 56 01 79 00
Open year-round. 97 rms 495-550 F. Rms for disabled. Restaurant. Air cond. Conf. Golf. Pkg. V, AE, DC, MC. **E5-35**
Part of the new "wine city" complex, the Claret is a brand-new hotel with quiet, impersonal rooms. Excellent business services and facilities are offered. Guests may enjoy the buffet breakfast served on a panoramic terrace.

Le Clavel Saint-Jean
44, rue Ch.-Domercq - 56 92 63 07
Closed Sat lunch, Sun. Open until 10:30pm. Priv rm: 60. Air cond. Pkg. V, MC. **B6-48**
Jean-Claude Boudin, who has presided over this classic establishment opposite the Saint-Jean station since August 1992, deserves our notice. Try his Southwestern treats like barigoule of langoustines with preserved tomatoes, tender and delicious duck with a potato crust and woodsy wild mushroom sauce, and a delicious warm apricot tart. Small but well chosen wine list, friendly welcome and service. **C** 250-400 F. **M** 105 F, 195 F, 340 F.

Clemenceau
4, cours G.-Clemenceau
56 52 98 98, fax 56 81 24 91
Open year-round. 45 rms 150-220 F. Air cond. Pkg. V, AE, DC, MC. **D4-42**
This big corner building houses well-equipped rooms, some of them soundproofed. Shopping gallery.

Continental
10, rue Montesquieu
56 52 66 00, fax 56 52 77 97
Open year-round. 50 rms 230-340 F. Air cond. Conf. Pkg. V, AE, DC, MC. **D4-8**
A large and handsome establishment, centrally located in the pedestrian precinct. Wonderful welcome.

12/20 La Coquille d'Œuf
197, rue G.-Bonnac - 56 93 09 86
Closings not available. Open until 10pm (10:30pm in summer). Air cond. V, MC. **C3-32**
The eggshell-colored dining room dotted with decorated eggs provides a pleasant backdrop for uncomplicated dishes based on fine products, like cabécou salad, duck confit with super-tasty wild mushrooms, and a gooey chocolate cake. A charming little spot, where owners and staff all obviously give their best. **C** 180-300 F. **M** 85 F (lunch), 95 F (dinner), 150 F.

12/20 Le Doris
52, quai Bacalan - 56 39 42 30
Closed Sat lunch, Sun, 1st wk of Feb school hols, Aug 15-Sep 1. Open until 10pm. V, MC. **F6-31**
One of Bordeaux's last seamen's bistrots, a noisy, lively place where fish, naturally enough, gets top billing. From the chalkboard menu,

choose some briny Marennes oysters, chiperons in a sauce made from their ink, sea bream in salt crust, and Dieppe-style sautéed sea scallops. **C** 180-240 F. **M** 85 F (weekdays, Sat dinner).

Le Flore
Bd Domergue
56 50 83 80, fax 56 39 73 75
Closed Dec 7-27. Open until 10:30pm. Terrace dining. Air cond. Pkg. V, AE, DC, MC. **G4-17**
Sunshine and reflections from the lake light up this modern, pink-and-green dining room. The cooking is respectable—and predictable: foie gras with a bacon quiche, warm oysters with spinach and foie gras, rack of Pauillac lamb with garlic confit, and a homey cannelé Bordelais cake with prune and Armagnac ice cream. Limited cellar (though some wines are available by the glass). **C** 230-300 F. **M** 100 F, 135 F, 170 F (wine incl).

Sofitel Bordeaux-Le Lac
(See restaurant above)
Open year-round. 8 stes 650-900 F. 202 rms 495-520 F. Air cond. Conf. Heated pool. Pkg. V, AE, DC. Since the renovation of this fully equipped hotel, comfort is the watchword. There are conference rooms, a bar, and a discothèque.

12/20 Francs Délices
54, rue Devise
56 52 28 22, fax 56 44 97 08
Closed 2 wks in Sep. Open until 11pm. Terrace dining. V, AE, DC, MC. **D5-50**
You'll find this long, narrow dining room in the center of town: it's intimate and inviting, bedecked with pretty naïve paintings of Bordeaux. Here hungry hordes can tuck into a pleasing duck foie gras, Mediterranean-style salmon, or duck breast. Nice Bordeaux wines and a smiling welcome. **C** 200-250 F. **M** 64 F (lunch), 89 F, 126 F, 169 F (exc Sun dinner).

Didier Gélineau
26, rue du Pas-St-Georges
56 52 84 25, fax 56 51 93 25
Closed Sun dinner & Mon (Apr 15-Apr 15), Sat lunch & Sun (Apr 16-Oct 14). Open until 10:30pm. Air cond. V, AE, DC, MC. **D5-22**
Customers are quite content at this establishment in the old quarter of Bordeaux, where Marylène Gélineau welcomes them warmly, and where they know they'll find an attractive menu perfectly balanced between tradition and innovation. Didier Gélineau's sauces could be fine-tuned a bit, but all his dishes are full of flavor, and the 100 F menu is a gift. Try the briefly grilled salmon over a rather brusque shellfish oil base, great chicken with onions, and perfectly cooked pickerel served over leek purée: all this merits a second toque. The cellar of lesser-known Bordeaux châteaux is filling out nicely; the Fief de Monjeau at 92 F is a real steal. **C** 300-400 F. **M** 100 F, 170 F, 250 F, 350 F.

12/20 Chez Gilles
6, rue des Lauriers - 56 81 17 38
Closed Sat lunch, Sun. Open until 11:30pm. Terrace dining. Air cond. V, AE, DC, MC. **D5-13**
Interesting food served in an unlikely decor (it puts us in mind of Louisiana...). Gilles Vérin gives his fine regional ingredients a boost with herbs and delicately dosed spices: try the smoked

165

salmon and sorrel tart, grilled beef with spaghetti galette, Brie fritters, dried fruit tart, and almond cream. Attractive 85 F menu, wine-included. **C** 200-300 F. **M** 85 F (wine incl), 130 F, 250 F.

 ### Grand Hôtel Français
12, rue du Temple
56 48 10 35, fax 56 81 76 18
Open year-round. 35 rms 350-610 F. Air cond. Pkg. V, AE, DC, MC. **D4-44**
This traditional hotel in a central, nineteenth-century residence provides comfortable, well-appointed rooms.

 ### Gravelier
114, cours de Verdun
56 48 17 15, fax 56 51 96 07
Closed Sat lunch, Sun, Jan 2-16, Jul 31-Aug 21. Open until 9:45pm. Air cond. V, AE, DC, MC. **E5-34**
Proving that she is indeed her father's daughter, Anne-Marie Troisgros and her young husband, chef Yves Gravelier, offer seductive dishes right in the historic Chartrons district. They handle tip-top foodstuffs with imagination and a discreetly exotic touch to produce dishes as unusual as they are delicious: foie gras in red wine sauce, brill with curry, and squab pot-au-feu with Chinese cabbage. Interesting Burgundy-dominated wine list with many half bottles. **C** 220-300 F. **M** 85 F (lunch), 120 F, 180 F.

Ibis Mériadeck
35, cours du Mal-Juin
56 90 10 33, fax 56 96 33 15
See page 95. **C4-37**
Near the town center, a modern hotel offering comfort at easy prices. Restaurant-brasserie.

Hôtel Majestic
2, rue de Condé
56 52 60 44, fax 56 79 26 70
Open year-round. 1 ste 700-800 F. 49 rms 360-580 F. Rms for disabled. Air cond. Golf. Valet pkg. V, AE, DC, MC. **D5-15**
This comfortable hotel is conveniently situated.

12/20 Malabar
7, rue des Ayres
56 52 18 19
Closed Sun, Mon, 2 wks in Aug. Open until 11pm. V, AE, MC. **C5-36**
Perfectly seasoned Indian cuisine at friendly prices. Try the fine 65 F menu: raïta with potatoes and onions, crisp and savory vegetable samoussas, tender chicken in spicy ginger sauce, and a generous and tasty peach clafoutis. Smiling but slowish service. Pleasant ground-floor dining room and a charming vaulted cellar dining room with a fresh, exotic floral decor. **C** 100-150 F. **M** 45 F, 65 F (lunch, wine incl), 72 F, 92 F, 124 F (dinner).

 ### Mercure Bordeaux-Le Lac
Quartier du Lac, rue du Petit-Barail
56 11 71 11, fax 56 43 07 55
Open year-round. 3 stes. 108 rms 300-350 F. Rms for disabled. Restaurant. Half-board 370 F. Air cond. Conf. Golf. Pkg. Helipad. V, AE, DC, MC. **G4-25**
The functional, comfortable rooms were recently modernized. Near the conference center, and there are special weekend rates for golf lessons and vineyard tours.

 ### Mercure Pont d'Aquitaine
Quartier du Lac, rue du Grand-Barail
56 43 36 72, fax 56 50 23 95
Closings not available. 2 stes 850 F. 98 rms 395-420 F. Restaurant. Air cond. Pool. Tennis. Golf. Pkg. V, AE, DC, MC. **G4-11**
Good business hotel near the convention center and the trade-fair grounds. Pleasant rooms, large bathrooms. Attractive all-in rates are offered on weekends.

 ### Normandie
7-9, cours 30-Juillet
56 52 16 80, fax 56 51 68 91
Open year-round. 100 rms 310-620 F. Conf. V, AE, DC, MC. **D4-2**
This freestone corner building near the port provides comfortable rooms and traditional service. Bar.

12/20 Le Nouveau Saucier
64, rue du Hâ - 56 81 11 22
Closed Sat (exc dinner in winter), Sun, Aug. Open until 10pm. Priv rm: 12. Air cond. V. **C4-18**
The chef's technique doesn't always keep pace with his imagination (maybe the new annex is causing him to spread himself too thin): simple and tasty salad of gizzards and giblets, but the sauce for the veal kidney, sweetbreads, and liver was way too rich, and the île flottante, though its sauce was light and tasty, was sloppily prepared. Nice little wine list, efficient service. **C** 250-350 F. **M** 76 F, 130 F.

 ### Novotel Bordeaux-Le Lac
Quartier du Lac, av. Jean-Gabriel-Domergue - 56 50 99 70, fax 56 43 00 66
Open year-round. 176 rms 395-450 F. Rms for disabled. Restaurant. Air cond. Conf. Pool. Golf. Pkg. V, AE, DC, MC. **G4-40**
Well-equipped hotel near the superhighway and conference center, with a lake to go jogging round.

One Star Hotel
34, rue Tauzia
56 94 59 00, fax 56 94 21 27
Open year-round. 62 rms 235 F. Rms for disabled. Pkg. V, AE, DC, MC. **B6-20**
Ideally located just steps from the Saint-Jean station, in a blessedly quiet street. Heartwarming reception; pleasant atmosphere.

 ### Pavillon des Boulevards
120, rue de la Croix-de-Seguey
56 81 51 02, fax 56 51 14 58
Closed Sat lunch, Sun, Jan 2-9, Aug 14-20. Open until 10pm. Priv rm: 14. Garden dining. Air cond. V, AE, DC, MC. **E3-51**
Don't leave town without a stop at the Pavillon. Outwardly unassuming, this nineteenth-century stone dwelling houses two dining rooms, done up in shades of rosy-beige and teal, which lead out to a lovely veranda and garden. Nelly Franc's charm lends extra warmth to the lively atmosphere.
Chef Régis Franc's cooking reflects a laudable concern for quality, and is characterized by well balanced flavor combinations and intensely flavored jus. But his style, all his own, is a bit too much for Bordeaux, where simple, direct cooking is favored. So it's risky for him to offer dishes

like langoustines with chestnuts, sole fillet with pineapple juice, or the contemporary classic squab chinoiserie, wonderful as all these are. Ditto for the fine wild duck with pear purée or the thick veal chops with shallots and herbs. But he stays true to himself, and is a fanatic about the quality of his products. There's a difference between good and very good, and the Francs are very good indeed. One small suggestion: the dining room's atmosphere could use a bit of warming up. Well chosen wine list, with, rare for this town, some bottles from outside the Bordelais; the young sommelier will not try to drive up your bill. **C** 420-500 F. **M** 200 F (weekday lunch), 250 F, 300 F, 400 F.

 ### La Pelouse
65, rue Pelouse-de-Douet
56 93 17 33, fax 56 24 66 71
Closed Dec 23-Jan 3, Aug 7-23. 36 rms 200-280 F. Pkg. V. **C2-28**
Quiet, practical rooms are available in this recent hotel. Easy parking.

La Petite Sirène
28-29, quai des Chartrons
56 51 22 60, fax 56 51 92 81
Closings not available. Open until 10:30pm. Terrace dining. Air cond. V, AE, DC, MC. **E5-19**
Two Danes have taken over adjoining houses on the Quai des Chartrons, and have named their establishment in honor of Andersen's Little Mermaid. The decor is stripped-down Scandinavian, but the Viking duo's menu is heartwarming indeed: smoked or marinated salmon and herring accompanied by the delicious house breads, and a few less exotic dishes, like oysters poached in Sauvignon, Landes-style chicken breast, and a poppy seed soufflé glacé. **C** 180-220 F. **M** 100 F (weekday lunch, Sat, wine incl), 148 F (exc Sun), 115 F.

Chez Philippe
1, pl. du Parlement
56 81 83 15, fax 56 79 19 36
Closed Sun, Aug. Open until 11:30pm. Terrace dining. Air cond. No pets. V, AE, DC, MC. **D5-6**
The modern paintings that hang in this intimate dining room testify to owner Philippe Techoire's good taste. It soon becomes clear that this same sharp eye has been working hard at the fish market, spotting the best catch of the day. Try the super-fresh and generous raw shellfish platter, turbot with garlic and peppers, and a nice nougat glacé with red fruits. Good selection of white wines, friendly welcome, and sometimes-hesitant service. **C** 300-600 F. **M** 180 F.

Les Plaisirs d'Ausone
10, rue Ausone
56 79 30 30, fax 56 51 38 16
Closed Sun, lunch Sat & Mon, Feb school hols, 2 wks in Aug. Open until 10pm. Priv rm: 50. V, AE. **C5-9**
Here's a living example of today's successful restaurant: a vaulted stone dining room, a fleet and efficient staff, bright, imaginative cuisine colorfully presented and conservatively priced. Hence the well earned third toque. Patrons are visibly charmed with Philippe Gauffre's resolutely modern cooking marked by fearless freedom in his choice of flavors, styles, and products. This culinary daring-do can, as we have seen elsewhere, lead to slip-ups, which is why we have

not awarded the third toque until now. But this year his cooking shows maturity and control, and never lapses into the facile. Examples: the salad of lobster and glazed rabbit (95 F à la carte), served with mixed greens and mellow garlic "tuiles" on a vinaigrette base with just a hint of ginger. And the squab galette with a very pure jus, balanced by a discreet touch of soy sauce. And the thick sole roasted in its skin with a vegetable pistou. And all the other treats on hand here, from the great house breads to the fine baba au rhum, by way of the hot-cold oyster appetizers. In short, Gauffre's cooking has always been lively, but now it's perfectly harmonious, too. Well chosen wine list with many good values, service less jovial than in the past (the price of success!), and lovely decor (ancient stones), in Bordeaux's prettiest district. **C** 320-400 F. **M** 250 F (weekday lunch, wine incl), 150 F, 285 F.

11/20 Le Plat dans l'Assiette
8, rue Ausone - 56 01 05 01
Closed Sun, lunch Sat & Mon, Aug 1-21. Open until 11pm. V, MC. **C5-9**
Here's a *bouchon* in the purest Lyonnais tradition, serving family-style versions of foie gras, quail, duck breast "ham", and the like, and, for dessert, an excellent walnut charlotte. A good address for lunch, in the lower district of old Bordeaux. **C** 140-180 F.

11/20 Le Port de la Lune
59, quai de Paludate
56 49 15 55, fax 56 49 29 12
Open daily until 2am. Terrace dining. V, MC. **B6-27**
Night owls take note: this bistrot swings to jazz bands until late at night, seven days a week. The simple food has no false notes: raw oysters, tender shad fillet, authentic creme brûlée, and lots of nice little wines at friendly little prices. **C** 120-300 F. **M** 100 F.

Pullman
5, rue R.-Lateulade
56 56 43 43, fax 56 96 50 59
Open year-round. 2 stes 800 F. 194 rms 450-550 F. Restaurant. Half-board 605 F. Air cond. Conf. Pkg. V, AE, DC, MC. **D3-38**
Ideal business hotel, where function rules over fancy.

Quality Hôtel Sainte-Catherine
27, rue Parlement-Ste-Catherine
58 81 95 12, fax 56 44 50 51
Open year-round. 1 ste 1,100-1,200 F. 82 rms 530-900 F. Rms for disabled. Air cond. Conf. Pkg. V, AE, DC, MC. **D4-33**
In the heart of the historic district, this beautifully restored eighteenth-century town house provides huge, delightful rooms.

Hôtel des Quatre-Sœurs
6, cours 30-Juillet
57 81 19 20, fax 56 01 04 28
Open year-round. 35 rms 220-390 F. Conf. V, AE, DC, MC. **D4-2**
Wagner slept here once. Nowadays the comfortable rooms have television and minibar, and there's a dry cleaning service.

A red hotel ranking denotes a place with charm.

167

Jean Ramet
7-8, pl. J.-Jaurès
56 44 12 51, fax 56 52 19 80
Closed Sat lunch, Sun, Aug 6-27. Open until 10pm.
Priv rm: 10. Air cond. Valet pkg. V, AE, MC. **D5-49**
The terms one could apply to the striking decor of Jean Ramet's dining room—clean-lined, bold, meticulously crafted—also describe Ramet's distinctive culinary style. He takes his superb ingredients to the limits of their innate possibilities, with a minimum of artifice and no frills at all, such as the very delicately breaded lamb sweetbreads with a virtuoso morel mushroom sauce, or the langoustines with new potatoes. It is a manner that particularly suits the local context: the Bordelais, who like to eat well but shun flashiness, instinctively warm to Ramet's cooking, and demand that certain classics stay on the menu, like the fine terrine of veal sweetbreads, goose fillet in aigrelette sauce, and "Spice Route" desserts. Offerings change with the seasons. This is essential cooking, the kind you always like coming back to, the kind you dream of having. Timeless. Raymonde Ramet orchestrates the vigilant, diligent staff. C 350-450 F. M 150 F (lunch), 280 F dinner, 230 F.

12/20 Restaurant Le Loup
66, rue du Loup - 56 48 20 21
Closed Sun, Mon dinner. Open until 10:30pm (11pm w-e). Priv rm: 35. V, MC. **C4-29**
The slightly somber dining room wants freshening up, but you are given many choices here: generous main courses with garnishes (55 F and 78 F), set menus, or à la carte. The latter offers profiteroles with Port-sauced snails and foie gras, breaded veal sweetbreads in salad, sturgeon in Bordeaux sauce, fillet of beef with foie gras, and gooey chocolate marquise cake with coffee cream. Friendly service. C 240-300 F. M 65 F (weekday lunch, wine incl), 75 F, 105 F.

Royal Médoc

3, rue de Sèze
56 81 72 42, fax 56 51 74 98
Open year-round. 45 rms 200-280 F. Conf. Valet pkg. V, AE, DC, MC. **D4-10**
This centrally located hotel is clean, friendly, and fairly quiet. Bar.

Royal Saint-Jean
15, rue Ch.-Domercq
56 91 72 16, fax 56 94 08 32
Open year-round. 37 rms 330-390 F. Rms for disabled. Restaurant. Half-board 255 F. Air cond. Conf. Pkg. V, AE, DC, MC. **B6-43**
Close to the station, functional yet not impersonal thanks to the high-level service, this hotel offers small, dainty rooms done up in pink and blue, all adequately equipped. Good breakfasts.

Studio

26, rue Huguerie
56 48 00 14, fax 56 81 25 71
Open year-round. 40 rms 98-135 F. Pkg. V, MC. **D4-26**
Right in the heart of town, this hotel has a lovely stone façade, and comfortable, simply decorated rooms. The ones at the back are very quiet. Friendly welcome and very reasonable rates.

La Tupina ✪
6, rue de la Porte-de-la-Monnaie
56 91 56 37, fax 56 31 92 11
Closed Sun, hols. Open until 11pm. Priv rm: 12. V, AE, DC. **C6-47**
The Tupina's two fireplaces cheer up the patrons in winter, and serve as well to spit-roast succulent meat and fowl. Jean-Pierre Xiradakis is devoted to the regional repertoire, and his *carte* is a culinary museum piece listing lusty, well-loved dishes with roots in the Southwest: duck liver pot-au-feu, excellent roast poularde (fatted young chicken) with potatoes fried in duck fat (a trifle greasy). Sublime homestyle desserts, and lots of discoveries on the wine list (even a few Greek wines). C 220-300 F. M 200 F.

Le Vieux Bordeaux
27, rue Buhan
56 52 94 36, fax 56 44 25 11
Closed Sat lunch, Sun, hols, Feb school hols, Aug 1-21. Open until 10:30pm. Priv rm: 20. Garden dining. Air cond. V, AE. **C5-7**
This reliable address for fine food grows better with the years, as a Vieux Bordeaux should; this year it celebrates its twentieth birthday. The two dining rooms opening onto an inner courtyard make a perfect setting in which to enjoy savory, rich dishes like warm oysters with onion mousse, lobster fricasséed vanilla and mango, and true Bresse poularde (fatted young chicken). The desserts (by a young pasty chef) are uneven. Fine and very classic wine list, and a warm welcome. C 250-400 F. M 155 F, 210 F, 260 F.

12/20 La Villa Carnot
2, av. Carnot - 56 08 04 21
Closed Sun, Mon, 1 wk in Feb & in Sep. Garden dining. V, AE, DC. **E2-14**
This villa surrounded by greenery still hasn't undergone the promised renovation of its green and white decor. The cooking is serious and usually delicious (except for an under-marinated fish carpaccio): steamed salmon with a generous serving of perfectly cooked baby vegetables, and a fresh sheep's milk cheese with dark cherries. Good choice of Bordeaux and foreign wines. C 330-450 F. M 95 F, 158 F.

And also...
Our selection of places for inexpensive, quick, or late-night meals.
Casino (56 52 27 58 - 19, cours du Mal-Foch. Lunch only.): The huge terrace is always packed. Good *plats du jour* at around 100 F (100 F).
La Côte de Bœuf (56 51 05 52 - 13, rue des Faussets. Open until midnight.): Lovely charcoal-grilled meats (giant rib steak) for a young, lively clientele (150-200 F).
Le Jour et Nuit (56 91 66 12 - 45, rue Ch.-Domercq.): A nice nest for night owls: steak tartare and fries, oysters, and onion soup (120-200 F).
Le Mably (56 44 30 10 - 12, rue Mably. Open until 11pm.): Classic brasserie with bench seats, big mirrors, and lunchtime crowds (120 F).
Le Rital (56 48 16 69 - 3, rue des Faussets. Open until 11pm.): A rarity in Bordeaux: good fresh pasta in every guise and sauce (75-120 F).

■ **In Blanquefort 33290**   11 km NW on D 210

Hostellerie des Criquets
130, av. du 11-Novembre
56 35 09 24, fax 56 57 13 83
Closed Sun dinner. Open until 10pm. Priv rm: 30. Terrace dining. Heated pool. Pkg. V, AE, DC.
A splendid white dwelling with an elegant dining room, extensive grounds, and a covered pool. As we go to press, a new chef has arrived. We will give him time to settle in before rating the cooking.

Hostellerie des Criquets
(See restaurant above)
Open year-round. 2 stes 620 F. 20 rms 295-310 F. Half-board 350-560 F. Conf. Heated pool. Golf. Valet pkg. V, AE, DC, MC.
The hostelry's charm will lure your attention away from the less attractive surroundings. Rooms here are spacious, thoughtfully decorated, and have impeccable bathrooms. Golf and tennis nearby. Guests can be picked up at the airport or the railway station.

■ **In Bouliac 33270**   9 km SE on D 10

Amat
Saint-James, 3, pl. C.-Hosteins
57 97 06 00, fax 56 20 92 58
Closings not available. Open until 10pm. Priv rm: 150. Garden dining. Pkg. V, AE, DC.
After a particularly bad period of financial worries, Jean-Marie Amat (still here but no longer in financial control of the operation) is proving he is still a great chef. There are a few "classiques du Saint James" on the menu (lobster salad, lamprey à la bordelaise, foie gras with asparagus), but you can tell that his heart is with the perfectly prepared seasonal dishes on the 250 F menu, some of the best cooking ever offered at this price. Eight first courses, nine main courses, and a dessert cart, which could include, for example, sea scallops with ginger, duck foie gras and rabbit liver terrine, or eggplant cream with cumin, followed by shad fillet in red wine sauce, spicy squab with pastilla, or duck civet with cèpes. A fine meal accompanied by a reasonably priced Hauts de Smith (120 F) or a Souley-Ste-Croix (90 F). The remarkably uncomfortable chairs designed by hot architect Jean Nouvel are rarely empty, and the Bordelais continue to brave traffic jams to sample such bargains, even if they do not share Amat's taste for provocative painting. Last time we ate here, Amat himself was dining at a nearby table; he also likes to snack in his well loved "Bistroy" bistrot next door. C 350-500 F. M 180 F, 250 F.

Saint James
(See restaurant above)
Open year-round. 2 stes 1,100-1,350 F. 15 rms 600-850 F. Half-board 850-1,350 F. Conf. Heated pool. No pets. Pkg. V, AE, DC.
Architect Jean Nouvel's design for this hotel was allegedly inspired by the sheds where tobacco leaves are hung to dry. You might like it, or at least be intrigued by it. Or you might spend all your time gazing across the vineyards and valleys of the Garonne to avoid the sight of the (deliberately) rusted ironwork, the polished concrete floors, and the futuristic lighting fixtures.

Le Bistroy ✿
3, pl. C.-Hostein
57 97 06 06, fax 56 20 92 58
Closed Sun. Open until 10:30pm. Terrace dining. Pkg. V, AE, DC.
Jean-Marie Amat's bistrot annex has a decor so cold—with its bare concrete walls, aluminium furniture, and harsh lighting—that it looks nothing like a bistrot. But for a tasty plate of Southwestern food prepared with the market's freshest offerings, you could hardly do better. You'll find the chef's signature in such dishes as pig's foot salad, salmon tartare with olives, beef cheeks with carrots, and roast cod with aromatic herbs. Excellent little wines and jovial atmosphere. C 160-210 F.

■ **In Carbon-Blanc 33560**    1.5 km Pont-d'Aquitaine

Marc Demund
5, av. de la Gardette
56 74 72 28, fax 56 06 55 40
Closed Sun dinner, Mon. Open until 10pm. Priv rm: 16. Garden dining. Pkg. V, AE, DC, MC.
There is ample reward in store for the effort it takes to locate this pretty stone house in the suburbs of Bordeaux. Marc Demund's cooking improves as steadily as the old trees in his garden grow taller and leafier, providing a perfect spot to enjoy the results of fine products treated with superb culinary skill: onions stuffed with rabbit liver, John Dory fillet with coriander, and a banana-chocolate croustillant. Smiling, professional service, a good choice of coffees, and an interminable list of good-value Bordeaux. C 300-400 F. M 100 F, 130 F, 250 F, 350 F.

■ **In Gradignan 33170**   S

Beausoleil ♠♣
Chemin du Plantey
56 89 00 48, fax 56 89 05 74
Open year-round. 32 rms 270-330 F. Restaurant. Half-board 270-385 F. Conf. Pkg. V, AE, DC.
Here is a good place for seminars—or for anyone looking for sunny, spacious rooms which suffer only from a contemporary lack of charm. Verdant surroundings.

■ **In Mérignac 33700**   10 km W on D 106 E

L'Iguane
127, av. Magudas
56 34 07 39, fax 56 34 41 37
Closed Sat lunch, Sun dinner. Open until 10pm. Priv rm: 30. Air cond. Pkg. V, AE, DC, MC.
The chef behind the stoves of this pleasant, modern villa is Didier Lasjuilliarias who once worked with Jean-Marie Amat. He has made a promising start with a menu that highlights sparkling-fresh seafood from the nearby Bassin d'-Arcachon: shad tartare, fillet of bar with grapes and vanilla scented veal, and a chocolate and chestnut dessert. Excellent wines at clement prices. C 260-350 F. M 105 F (weekdays), 140 F, 240 F.

Novotel Bordeaux Aéroport

Av. Kennedy
56 34 10 25, fax 56 55 99 64

Open year-round. 137 rms 450 F. Restaurant. Air cond. Conf. Pool. Golf. Pkg. V, AE, DC, MC.
A shuttle from the airport will convey you to this hotel, set in the middle of wooded grounds with a terrace and games area. The rooms are renovated regularly.

■ **In Pessac 33600**   6 km SW

La Réserve ⚔🌳

By-pass exit 13, 74, av. du Bourgailh
56 07 13 28, fax 56 36 31 02

Closed Dec 15-Feb 15. 2 stes 900-1,200 F. 20 rms 540-890 F. Restaurant. Half-board 840-1,190 F. Air cond. Pool. Tennis. Golf. Pkg. Helipad. V, AE, MC.
The attraction here, besides the nearness of the airport, is the pleasant setting: landscaped grounds with a pond and swans. As for the hotel, the rooms are well appointed, but the decoration is no great shakes. Excellent reception and hospitality.

■ **In Saint-**
Loubès 33450   15 km NE on N 10 and D 13

Au Vieux Logis ❊

57, av. de la République
56 78 91 18 (R), 56 78 92 99 (H),
fax 56 78 91 18

Closed Sun dinner & Sat lunch off-seas, 10 days in Sep. Open until 9:30pm (10pm in summer). Priv rm: 20. Hotel: 7 rms 225-285 F. Half-board 300 F. Conf. Golf. V, AE, DC, MC.
Lots of regulars flock to this welcoming dining room decorated with copper pots and pans and pretty bouquets. Chef Jacques Belot chooses his ingredients well and knows how to turn out appetizing fare inspired by regional traditions. We relish his foie gras with Sauternes, Leyre sturgeon and caviar blinis, and Pauillac lamb. Look for an attractive choice of Bordeaux bottlings, of which a few are served by the glass. **C** 260-360 F. **M** 69 F (for residents only), 85 F, 130 F, 170 F, 260 F.

BORDIGHERA (Italy) → Menton

BORMES-LES-MIMOSAS   83230

Paris 890 - Toulon 40 - Saint-Tropez 35 - Le Lavandou 5   *Var*

L'Escoundudo ❊

2, ruelle du Moulin - 94 71 15 53

Closed Sat & Sun off-seas, Nov 15-Dec 15. Open until 11:30pm. Priv rm: 22. Garden dining. V, MC.
The name means "hidden corner" in Provençal, and tucked away here in this tidy rustic dining room, you'll see the 135 F menu and think "Can they possibly...." Yes, they can! Tomato and goat cheese tart, succulent daube with polenta, and a fresh-tasting dessert. Max Dandine's fresh, inventive interpretations of Provençal dishes include stuffed vegetables, bourride of white fish, young rabbit with shallots and other sunny fare, all with a southern accent. No frozen products are ever used. Resolutely regional wines, and a most pleasant welcome. **C** 200-280 F. **M** 95 F, 135 F, 160 F.

Le Jardin de Perle-Fleurs ❊

100, chemin de l'Orangerie - 94 64 99 23

Closed Mon, Oct-Jun. Open until 11pm. Garden dining. No cards.
On balmy days, Guy Gedda welcomes his faithful patrons into a hanging garden wooded with fig, olive, and apricot trees—this is Provence at its most idyllic. When the sun chooses not to shine, Gedda invites guests (no more than fifteen) to settle into his little dining room, lined with jars of olive oil and homemade preserves. Wherever the feast takes place, you'll be treated to a bouquet of sun-gorged dishes which nobody makes better than Guy. Start out with chickpea-flour panisses fried to irresistible crispness, or zesty totis (croûtons rubbed with herbs, anchovies, and fragrant olive oil), then move on to a salad of earthy local truffles, or marinated raw sardines on herbed toast, or pistou soup or rascasse bourride. And that's not all: Gedda's Mediterranean repertoire also embraces a succulent beef daube, state-of-the-art pieds-et-paquets (lamb's feet and tripe, a Marseillais specialty), and a rich crème brûlée studded with candied chestnuts from local *châtaigniers*. The 230 F single-price menu is indubitably one of the best deals around, and Gedda's cellar harbors a peerless selection of wines from the Var and the Bouches-du-Rhône (no wines from outside Provence allowed, except Champagne). **C** 320-370 F. **M** 230 F.

Le Mas des Iles

38, rue Vue-des-Iles
94 05 32 60, fax 94 64 93 03

Closed Nov 1-Mar 24. 33 stes 590-790 F. 27 rms 390-690 F. Restaurant. Air cond. Conf. Heated pool. Tennis. Golf. Garage pkg. Helipad. V, AE, DC, MC.
The well-equipped rooms have mezzanines and superb views of the bay.

12/20 Les Palmiers

6 km S on D 559, in Cabasson,
240, chemin du Petit-Fort
94 64 81 94, fax 94 64 93 61

Closings not available. Open until 10:30pm. Priv rm: 35. Garden dining. Pkg. V, AE, DC, MC.
Your spirits will revive at the sight of the lovely palms and other Mediterranean trees, visible both from the terrace and from the neo-Provençal dining room. Try the excellent 160 F menu: bouillabaisse soup, sea scallops with fresh pasta, and a jubilé of apples for dessert. Those in the know order various à la carte specialties in advance. **C** 250-300 F. **M** 160 F, 200 F.

Les Palmiers ⚔🌳

(See restaurant above)

Open year-round. 2 stes 1,000-1,280 F. 19 rms 475-575 F. Half-board 445-500 F. Conf. No pets. Pkg. V, AE, DC.
Surrounded by greenery and five minutes' walk from the sea, this hotel has quiet, attractive rooms.

12/20 Chez Sylvia

Restaurant-Pizzéria-Sauveur,
872, av. Lou Mistraou - 94 71 14 10

Closed Wed, Dec-Jan. Open until 10:30pm. Garden dining. Pkg. V, AE, MC.
Sylvia serves Sicilian pizzas, savory brochettes, and sweet cannoli on her shady terrace. **C** 150-240 F.

12/20 La Tonnelle des Délices
Pl. Gambetta - 94 71 34 84
Closed mid Nov-mid Jan. Open until 11pm. Terrace dining. V, MC.
Take a seat on the hanging garden-terrace or in the dining room filled with pretty bric-a-brac to sample Alain Pasetto's fresh Provençal cooking: mussels with garlic and parsley, fish soup, anchoïade, young rabbit with pistou, daube à l'ancienne. The execution of these dishes can get a bit sloppy, though. **C** 230-280 F. **M** 95 F, 130 F, 150 F, 210 F.

BOUC-BEL-AIR 13 ➔ **Aix-en-Provence**

BOUILLAND **21420**
Paris 303 - Autun 55 - Beaune 15 - Dijon 45 *Côte-d'Or*

Le Vieux Moulin
On D 2 - 80 21 51 16, fax 80 21 59 90
Closed Wed (exc dinner Jul-Oct), Thu lunch, Jan 2-25. Open until 9:30pm. Priv rm: 12. Garden dining. Air cond. Heated pool. Pkg. V, MC.
Ah, Le Vieux Moulin: visions of an ancient mill unfold before the mind's eye! In fact, what awaits you here is a rather cold, modern setting better suited to business meetings than to bucolic feasts... But never mind. A glance at the seductive menu will dissipate any lingering disappointment. You should know that most of Jean-Pierre Silva's suppliers live within a 30-kilometer radius of his restaurant, and the products are exceptional. This year we savored the marinated and stewed pickerel (a Burgundian classic), the truite au bleu, and the beef fillet Rossini, all haute cuisine standards transformed by Silva's skillful interpretation. More adventurous delights: croustillant of smoked trout cleverly matched with slices of turnip, fried onion stalks, tomatoes, zucchini, and dried apples. Or the roast pike in herb vinegar with a lentil purée seasoned with a pig's foot, veal kidney cooked in verjus added to a marvelous dried-mushroom risotto, and a fabulous honey cake millefeuille with vanilla ice cream and coffee sauce. Though Silva's soaring imagination wings well beyond the boundaries of the Burgundian *terroir*, the same cannot be said (thank goodness!) of the wine list, which is firmly rooted in the vineyards of Volnay, Vosne-Romanée, and Puligny-Montrachet. Excellent welcome and service overseen by Isabelle Silva. **C** 450-600 F. **M** 190 F, 320 F, 470 F.

Le Vieux Moulin
(See restaurant above)
Closed Wed (off-seas), Jan 2-25. 2 stes 1,200-1,500 F. 24 rms 380-800 F. Rms for disabled. Half-board 625-1,340 F. Conf. Heated pool. Pkg. V, MC.
A bucolic hotel (and new annex) among the apple trees. All your needs are attended to, and only the village rooster is likely to disturb your sleep. If time permits, enjoy a country walk to the romantic ruins of the Abbaye Sainte-Marguerite.

BOULIAC 33 ➔ **Bordeaux**

BOULOGNE-BILLANCOURT 92
➔ **PARIS Suburbs**

BOULOGNE-SUR-MER **62200**
Paris 242 - Lille 115 - Abbeville 80 - Calais 34 *P./Calais*

Ibis

Bd Diderot - 21 30 12 40, fax 21 87 48 98
See page 95.
You can come straight off the ferry to this hotel with well-kept rooms. The bar is open round the clock.

La Liégeoise
10, rue Monsigny
21 31 61 15, fax 21 33 76 30
Closed Sun dinner, Mon. Open until 9:30pm. Priv rm: 50. Terrace dining. V, AE, DC, MC.
Flawless reception and service are backed up by Alain Delpierre's cooking, which displays more finesse and personality every year. And the 155 F menu is a real gift, much appreciated by Her Majesty's subjects who have crossed the Channel: salad with foie gras and slices of smoked duck breast, sole and salmon boudin with delicate vegetables, cheese assortment, and dessert. Splendid cellar. **C** 200-320 Γ. **M** 95 F (weekdays), 155 F, 210 F, 310 F.

La Matelote
80, bd Sainte-Beuve
21 30 17 97, fax 21 83 29 24
Closings not available. Open until 9:30pm. Priv rm: 80. V, MC.
Tony Lestienne's fresh-as-the-sea cooking is back on course this year. We enjoyed the crispy potato crustade, the flavorful John Dory with a cauliflower purée, and the delicious chocolate-chicory cake. The point lost last year comes back to port. Cozy decor. **C** 300-400 F. **M** 160 F, 210 F, 345 F.

■ **In Pont-de-Briques 62360** 5 km S on D 940

Hostellerie de la Rivière
17, rue de la Gare ·
21 32 22 81, fax 21 87 45 48
*Closed Sun dinner, Mon, Feb school hols, Aug 16-Sep 7. Open until 9:30pm. Terrace dining. **Hotel:** 8 rms 260-350 F. Half-board 380-480 F. No pets. Pkg. V, MC.*
Here you'll find cuisine with personality prepared by a father and son duo. Their most recent successes include fricassée of snails in Madiran with a parsley mousse, braised haddock and fresh cod in puff pastry, and peach soup with caramel-nougat ice cream. Well chosen wine list and charming welcome. **C** 280-450 F. **M** 160 F (weekdays, Sat lunch), 200 F, 295 F.

■ **In Wimille 62126** 5 km N on N 1

Le Relais de la Brocante
2, rue de Ledinghem - 21 83 19 31
Closed Sun dinner, Mon. Open until 9:15pm. Priv rm: 25. Air cond. Pkg. V.
Once a school, a presbytery, and a town hall, this old town house was tastefully transformed into a restaurant a few years back. Jean-François Laurent's cooking brims over with imagination and reveals passionate dedication to local ingredients. His virtuoso technique shows to advantage in the crab-stuffed buckwheat crêpe,

fresh sorrel and beef jelly, filet mignon of pork in honey cake sauce, and spice cookies with coffee ice cream. Excellent wine list, and a well priced 160 F set menu. **C** 350-400 F. **M** 130 F (exc Sat dinner), 160 F, 250 F.

BOURBON-LANCY	**71140**
Paris 308 - Autun 62 - Moulins 36 - Nevers 72	Saône/Loire

 Grand Hôtel ⚓
Parc Thermal
85 89 08 87, fax 85 89 25 45
Closed Oct 21-Mar. 1 ste 240-265 F. 29 rms 100-265 F. Half-board 210-350 F. Conf. Pkg. V, MC.
Typically sleepy spa-town hotel. Its rooms are old-fashioned but immaculately kept.

 Raymond
Allée Sornat, route de Moulins
85 89 17 39, fax 85 89 29 47
Closed Sun dinner off-seas, Mon lunch, 2 wks Jan-Feb. Open until 9:30pm. Priv rm: 30. Garden dining. No pets. Pkg. Helipad. V, AE, DC, MC.
This lovely old house lost in the countryside seems to be dozing in its pretty park, and, alas, so is the cooking. The snail crêpe with pig's foot is still savory, the pickerel with cornichons flanked by a zucchini crêpe is still fine, and the vanilla millefeuille pleasant enough, but the asparagus with smoked salmon cream was nothing special and the roast lamb lacked refinement. The third toque is on ice until the chef in this sleeping beauty castle wakes up. The decor is still stunning (don't miss the Art Deco staircase) and the welcome is warm, but the wine list could use some revision. The set menus are kind to your pocketbook. **C** 350-450 F. **M** 160 F (weekdays), 180 F (exc weekdays & hols), 230 F, 290 F, 390 F.

Manoir de Sornat ⚓
(See restaurant above)
Closed Sun off-seas, 2 wks Jan-Feb. 13 rms 300-650 F. Half-board 450-750 F. Conf. Pkg. Helipad. V, AE, DC, MC.
At the end of a lane bordered by plane trees stands this rambling manor house, where you will be lodged in spacious, wonderfully appointed rooms (electric beds, no less), although the decor is very ordinary. Adequate breakfasts and attentive service.

BOURBOULE (LA)	**63150**
Paris 438 - Clermont-Ferrand 53 - Le Mont-Doré 7	Puy-de-Dôme

11/20 Auberge Tournebride
1.5 km N on D 88,
route de Murat-le-Quaire - 73 81 01 91
Closed Mon off-seas (exc hols & school hols), Nov 15-Jan 15. Open until 9pm. Priv rm: 30. Terrace dining. Hotel: 7 rms 150-180 F. Half-board 250-300 F. Conf. No pets. Pkg. V.
The best of the chef's simple, solid repertoire is to be found among the authentic Gascon-style dishes: foie gras, confit, tripe, hot apple tart. The irresistible charm of this converted barn and the plethora of affordably priced menus draw considerable crowds in summer. **C** 230-310 F. **M** 80 F, 150 F, 180 F.

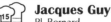
Restaurant prices in red draw attention to restaurants that offer particularly good value.

Les Iles Britanniques ⌂⌂
Quai Gambetta
73 65 52 39, fax 73 81 12 65
Closed Oct 15-Nov. 12 stes 415 F. 24 rms 290-325 F. Restaurant. Half-board 320-360 F. Conf. Golf. Pkg. V, MC.
Spa facilities are available here as well as a sauna, gym, and games room. The pleasant accommodation, currently being renovated, mixes modern and old-fashioned furnishings.

BOURG-CHARENTE	**16200**
Paris 461 - Cognac 9 - Jarnac 4 - Angoulême 34	Charente

La Ribaudière
Pl. du Port - 45 81 30 54, fax 45 81 28 05
Closed Sun dinner & Mon off-seas, Feb. Open until 9:45pm. Priv rm: 80. Terrace dining. Pkg. V, AE, MC.
Thierry Verrat's repertoire includes creative dishes with surprising but always successful flavor combinations: oyster civet and asparagus, corn croustillant and spiced duck confit with creamed morels, blancmange with berries. What's more, the cellar is choice and the welcome warm in the pretty pastel dining room that opens onto a summer terrace and views of the Charente River. **C** 260-360 F. **M** 120 F, 170 F, 200 F, 260 F.

BOURG-EN-BRESSE	**01000**
Paris 425 - Lyon 61 - Mâcon 34 - Geneva 118	Ain

12/20 Auberge Bressane
166, bd de Brou
74 22 22 68, fax 74 23 03 15
Open daily until 10pm. Priv rm: 60. Terrace dining. Garage pkg. V, AE, DC, MC.
'Twas a black day for us last year, and for Jean-Pierre Vullin, whose Auberge we previously considered a paragon, when we had a very disappointing meal here. This year, alas, we had the same experience. The cooking was filled with clashes. Simply roasted Bresse chicken was pleasing, but the marinated salmon was too oily, and the puff pastry with berries was drowned in cream. The restaurant's many fans may not agree with our rating, but we hoped for much better here. **C** 300-450 F. **M** 95 F (exc Sun), 140 F, 175 F, 250 F, 290 F.

Hôtel de France ⌂⌂
19, pl. Bernard
74 23 30 24, fax 74 23 69 90
Open year-round. 1 ste 650 F. 45 rms 160-400 F. Conf. Golf. Garage pkg. V, AE, DC, MC.
A cordial reception awaits you at this old-fashioned hotel, centrally situated on a shady square, and next door to Jacques Guy's restaurant (see below). Breakfasts are quite ordinary, however, and the soundproofing inefficient.

Jacques Guy
Pl. Bernard
74 45 29 11, fax 74 24 73 69
Closed Sun dinner, Mon, Mar 1-15, Oct 8-20. Open until 9:30pm. Priv rm: 30. Terrace dining. Pkg. V, AE, DC, MC.
Jacques Guy's cooking is reliable, regular, and utterly classic. Patrons come back time and again for the delicious poached Bresse chicken in a light tarragon cream sauce and the frog's

legs, but don't miss other treats, like the spicy beef cheeks sausage with a green lentil salad, and the squab with almonds in a flavorful jus. Desserts are Jacques Guy's specialty: heavenly warm fruit tarts, three kinds of chocolate mousse. We'd be happier if the first two set menus offered both cheese *and* dessert). Enticing cellar; attentive service. **C** 300-380 F. **M** 130 F (exc Sun), 170 F, 240 F, 290 F, 340 F.

Le Mail
Route de Villefranche, 46, av. du Mail
74 21 00 26, fax 74 21 29 55
Closed Sun dinner, Mon, Jul 10-25, Dec 23-Jan 13. Open until 9:30pm. Air cond. Pkg. V, AE, DC.
All the provincial virtues are gathered together in this delightful inn, as bright and clean as a new penny: cozy rooms, smiling faces, and Roger Charolles's generous, forthright cooking. Why not order his artichoke and roast langoustine salad, mixed fish with sea urchin cream, roast frog's legs with fines herbes, and a chocolate and chestnut cake. Wide choice of simple wines. **C** 270-400 F. **M** 200 F (wine incl), 120 F, 175 F, 210 F, 300 F.

Terminus
19, rue A.-Baudin
74 21 01 21, fax 74 21 36 47
Open year-round. 50 rms 210-450 F. Rms for disabled. Conf. Golf. Pkg. V, AE, DC, MC.
One of the best hotels in town, the Terminus is set in gardens opposite the station and has well-modernized rooms. Excellent reception.

See also: Thoissey, Vonnas (Georges Blanc)

BOURGES	18000
Paris 226 - Nevers 68 - Dijon 245 - Châteauroux 65   *Cher*

L'Abbaye Saint-Ambroix
Bd de la République
48 70 70 00, fax 48 70 21 22
Closed Sat lunch. Open until 10pm. Priv rm: 50. Air cond. Pkg. V, AE, DC, MC.
After you admire the soaring fifteen-meter vaulted ceiling of this majestic dining room (it was once a Renaissance chapel), settle in to enjoy the elegant service and Christophe Langrée's cooking. The young chef holds credentials from a number of good restaurants, and is constantly progressing. Try the fine first set menu: a tart of fresh sardines and potatoes flavored with liver vinaigrette, roast squab with herbs under the skin, cheeses, and a crispy dark and white chocolate pastry with cherries. Fully stocked cellar, formal service. An added point this year. **C** 260-370 F. **M** 220 F (weekday lunch, wine incl), 180 F (exc weekday lunch), 140 F, 260 F.

Hôtel de Bourbon
(See restaurant above)
Open year-round. 2 stes 820-900 F. 57 rms 410-620 F. Rms for disabled. Air cond. Conf. Golf. Pkg. V, AE, DC, MC.
An ancient abbey in the center of town has been converted into a high-quality hotel. The rooms are impersonal, though well designed and equipped.

Hôtel d'Angleterre
1, pl. des Quatre-Piliers
48 24 68 51, fax 48 65 21 41
Open year-round. 31 rms 382-420 F. Restaurant. Conf. Golf. Pkg. V, AE, DC, MC.
This traditional town residence opposite the theatre provides decent but rather charmless rooms. Some are a trifle noisy. Courteous service, though, and faultless breakfasts.

Le Jardin Gourmand
15 bis, bd E.-Renan
48 21 35 91, fax 48 20 59 75
Closed Sun dinner, Mon, Dec 15-Jan 15, 1 wk in Jul. Open until 9:30pm. Garden dining. V, AE.
This traditional bourgeois residence with a shady pocket garden has a wonderful atmosphere. Here Christian Chauveau turns out perfectly tuned dishes, lacking only a spark of imagination. But the 145 F menu is a real winner: sautéed salmon with fresh sorrel, oven-roasted rabbit with sage and tagliatelle, cheese assortment, and a choice of desserts. Lengthy list of decently priced wines. The service is unusually prompt and the welcome friendly. **C** 250-320 F. **M** 95 F, 145 F, 175 F, 220 F.

Philippe Larmat
62 bis, bd Gambetta - 48 70 79 00
Closed Mon, Sun dinner, Feb 20-27, Aug 21-Sep 4. Open until 9:30pm. Garden dining. V, DC, MC.
Philippe Larmat and his wife Catherine are happily running this pretty establishment composed of three dining rooms and a sunny terrace. Larmat's special knack is for updating classic dishes, thus pleasing both modernists and upholders of culinary tradition. All the region's gourmets flock here for the calf's foot in truffle vinaigrette, couscous of monkfish and lobster, and the chocolate millefeuille with Jamaican pepper. All this is served by a capable staff, and partnered with wines from a small but select and affordably priced cellar. **C** 280-380 F. **M** 95 F (weekdays, Sat lunch), 130 F, 220 F.

■ **In Berry-Bouy 18500**   8 km NW on D 60

La Gueulardière
48 26 81 45, fax 48 26 01 72
Closed Mon dinner, Tue, Jan 20-Feb 12. Open until 10pm. Terrace dining. Garage pkg. V, AE, DC, MC.
On a pretty square in the center of town, this low-slung, all-white restaurant hides behind a thick, green hedge. The excellent 140 F menu offers a pleasing taste of Jean-Claude Poquet's classic yet interesting cooking: melon and ginger cocktail, tuna steaks à la méridionale, spicy lamb sauté, cheeses, and a savarin of fruits. The cellar is well stocked with lots of exciting possibilities. Warm, hospitable welcome and service. **C** 270-350 F. **M** 94 F, 140 F, 185 F, 220 F, 320 F.

BOURGET-DU-LAC (LE)	73370
Paris 527 - Chambéry 11 - Aix-les-Bains 9 - Belley 25   *Savoie*

Le Bateau Ivre
79 25 02 66, fax 79 25 25 03
Closed Nov-beg May. Open until 10pm. Priv rm: 10. Garden dining. Pkg. V, AE, DC, MC.
In late spring and summer, the flower-filled garden and shaded terrace of Le Bateau Ivre are

a must for gourmets traveling through Savoie. Don't miss the chance to savor Jean-Pierre Jacob's creamy risotto of squab, asparagus, and duck confit, the sautéed monkfish, the croustillant of pig's foot with ginger, and the banana roasted with passion fruit, all on the 350 F menu, which we considered the most seductive and not the most expensive. Other fine dishes are the bouillon of mushrooms and oysters, Sisteron lamb with a ragoût of blacks olives and artichokes, and the succulent lake fish that the chef nets from time to time. The cellar boasts a notable stock of rare and interesting finds in a wide range of prices. Members of the Jacob family take care of the service, led by René, the perfectly charming maître d'hôtel. This ship has had its problems (all financial), but the captain shows he still has his craft in hand. C 450-500 F. M 195 F, 350 F, 510 F.

Ombremont
2 km N on N 504
79 25 00 23, fax 79 25 25 77
Closings not available. Open until 10pm. Priv rm: 130. Terrace dining. Pool. Pkg. V, AE, DC, MC.
The lakeside terrace and plush dining room are easy on the eye, while the palate is won over by such polished, proficient dishes as a warm duck liver terrine, a warm Savoyard meat terrine, sea scallops with asparagus tips and lemony parsley cream, and a fresh-fruit dessert with an upside-down cookie crust. Friendly welcome, and tempting wine list. C 320-500 F. M 165 F, 265 F, 365 F.

Ombremont
(See restaurant above)
Closings not available. 4 stes 1,400-1,700 F. 19 rms 590-1,280 F. Half-board 800-1,000 F. Air cond. Conf. Heated pool. Golf. Pkg. Helipad. V, AE, DC, MC.
The spacious rooms and suites are perfectly comfortable, with views of the lake and mountains. Enjoy skiing and boating on the lake. Relais et Châteaux.

L'Orée du Lac
La Croix-Verte
79 25 24 19, fax 79 25 08 51
Closed Nov 15-Jan 15. 3 stes 900-1,250 F. 9 rms 600-920 F. Restaurant. Half-board 545-680 F. Air cond. Conf. Pool. Tennis. Golf. Pkg. V, AE, DC, MC.
A distinguished lakeside hotel set in five acres of grounds close to Le Bateau Ivre (see above). A restaurant service is available to residents.

■ In **Bolvir de Cerdanya**   3 km S, in Spain

Torre del Remei
Cami Real
(34) 72 14 01 82, fax (34) 72 14 04 49
Open daily until 11pm. Priv rm: 40. Garden dining. Air cond. Pool. No pets. Valet pkg. V, AE, DC, MC.
At an arrow's flight from the lovely valley that passes between Bourg-Madame and Puigcerdá, stands this rather amazing baroque "castle" renovated by well-known Spanish hotelier, José Maria Boix. The kitchen takes full advantage of the region's riches: when in season, game, mushroom, and truffles are given star billing on the

menu. But the flavors of the Mediterranean figure prominently as well, in such dishes as a savory fava bean platter, chanterelle mushrooms with jabugo ham, cod sautéed with chickpeas, and a long-simmered oxtail stew. Service is topnotch, and a prize-winning young sommelier will guide you through the cellar's superb stock of Rioja wines. C 300-500 F. M 190 F (wine incl), 230 F.

Torre del Remei
(See restaurant above)
Open year-round. 7 stes 1,500-1,700 F. 4 rms 1,000 F. Air cond. Conf. Pool. Golf. Valet pkg. Helipad. V, AE, DC, MC.
Hard to reach, but paradise once you arrive! Set against the vast, mountainous panorama of the Pyrenees, this baroque brainchild of a Catalan banker was built at the turn of the century. Abandoned during Spain's civil war, it was recently restored with a great deal of taste and refinement. Rooms are huge, bathrooms impressive (Jacuzzis), and breakfasts a delight. A swimming pool and solarium are set in extensive grounds graced with venerable trees. Relais et Châteaux.

■ In **Ruy 38300**   2 km E

Laurent Thomas
Vie-de-Boussieu
74 93 78 00, fax 74 28 60 90
Closed Sun dinner, Wed, Aug 17-Sep 10. Open until 9:30pm. Priv rm: 20. Terrace dining. Air cond. Pool. Pkg. V, AE, DC, MC.
Laurent Thomas's three toques haven't gone to his head; he's keeping prices under control. This modest chef has the magic combination: inventiveness and solid technique. This year we savored the scrambled eggs with tapénade followed by a crunchy fresh fava bean salad with perfect tiny red mullet, Guilvinec sole marinated with asparagus, superb langoustines with a fine meat jus, and a succulent lamb filling in a light but buttery crust. The hare à la royale draws the whole region here in season. Finish up with a light-as-air strawberry millefeuille. The wine list includes many regional Balmes Dauphinoise wines at attractive prices, as well as some excellent Burgundies (like the Maurice Protheau 1990 white Mercurey) chosen by Francis Pierron, who also directs the flawless service. Prices for both the *carte* and the set meals are eminently reasonable for food of this calibre. C 300-350 F. M 140 F (weekday lunch), 200 F, 240 F, 270 F, 340 F.

Les Séquoias
(See restaurant above)
Closed Aug 16-Sep 7. 5 rms 550-750 F. Conf. Pool. Golf. Pkg. V, AE, DC, MC.
A superb stone staircase leads to just five huge, remarkably comfortable rooms. Swimming pool and heliport.

---

*Some establishments change their **closing times** without warning. It is always wise to check in advance.*

BOUSSAC 23600
Paris 335 - Aubusson 47 - Montluçon 34   *Creuse*

 Le Relais Creusois
Route de La Châtre - 55 65 02 20
Closed Tue dinner & Wed (exc Jul-Aug), Feb, 1 wk in Jun. Open until 8:30pm (9pm in summer). V.
Behind this anonymous façade hides a more pleasing dining room with brand-new bay windows overlooking a picturesque valley. We enjoyed the roast lobster with walnut essence, cumin-scented chicken breast with leeks, and breaded veal sweetbreads with new potatoes perked up with lemon zest. Excellent welcome, fine wine list. The set menus are well composed and priced to please. C 250-340 F. M 120 F, 180 F, 250 F, 350 F.

BOUTENAC-TOUVENT 17120
Paris 505 - Royan 29 - Pons 23 - Mortagne-sur-G. 5   *Charente-M.*

Le Relais de Touvent
In Touvent
46 94 13 06, fax 46 94 10 40
Closed Sun dinner & Mon (exc Jul-Aug), Dec 19-28. Open until 9pm. Terrace dining. Pkg. V.
Yannick Mairand's traditional cooking aims to please, and succeeds: witness the many weddings, baptisms, and other festivities held here. We liked his 155 F menu: tasty melon with Pineau de Charentes, six plump Marennes oysters, tender and perfectly cooked steak with good vegetables, a well stocked cheese assortment, and a yummy nougatine glacé. Jacky Mairand, the chef's father, is a cheery host and the small wine list is not too expensive. C 300-390 F. M 90 F (exc Sun), 130 F, 155 F, 165 F, 180 F.

Le Relais de Touvent   🌲
(See restaurant above)
See restaurant for closings. 12 rms 280 F. Half-board 300-340 F. Air cond. Conf. Pkg. V.
Surrounded by weeping willows, this hotel boasts spacious, recently redecorated rooms with sizeable baths.

BOUZIÈS 46 → Cabrerets

BOUZIGUES 34140
Paris 790 - Agde 24 - Montpellier 27 - Béziers 45   *Hérault*

Côte Bleue
Av. L.-Tudesq
67 78 30 87, fax 67 78 35 49
Closed Tue dinner, Wed, Jan 4-Feb 3. Open until 9:30pm. Pkg. V, MC.
The pretty view over the Étang de Thau, the pleasant terrace, bright and modern interior, and handsome tables all conspire to make La Côte Bleue an agreeable stopover. Patrick Marquès's cuisine, based mainly on the freshest local seafood, shows flair and good technique: shellfish ravioli and langoustines in a shellfish consommé, roast turbot with brown fish jus and an eggplant and zucchini tian, and a crispy apple and raisin pastry with caramel sauce. Good choice of regional wines, but the prices are not kind to your pocketbook. C 400-700 F. M 148 F (weekday lunch, Sat), 180 F (Sat dinner, Sun), 250 F, 380 F.

BOVES 80 → Amiens

BOYARDVILLE 17 → Oléron (Ile d')

BOZOULS 12 → Espalion

BRACIEUX 41250
Paris 182 - Romorantin 32 - Blois 18 - Orléans 57   *Loir/Cher*

Hôtel de la Bonnheure
54 46 41 57, fax 54 46 05 90
Closings not available. 2 stes 600-800 F. 11 rms 250-350 F. Conf. Golf. Pkg. V, AE, MC.
A comfortable, modern hotel near the forest, enhanced by lawns and flower beds.

 Bernard Robin
1, av. de Chambord
54 46 41 22, fax 54 46 03 69
Closed Tue dinner & Wed (exc Jul-Aug), Dec 18-Jan 31. Open until 9pm. Terrace dining. Air cond. Pkg. V, MC.
Immaculately run and tended, the Robins' remarkable establishment is a model of successful inn-keeping. Bernard Robin invariably chooses the very finest ingredients, which he handles with the razor-sharp technique of a chef at the height of his powers. Cooking times are unerringly accurate; the light yet concentrated jus he distils lend charm and fragrance to every dish. Every dish has a special something that raises it to gastronomic heights: the terrine of pike and carp is made sublime with pistachios, the large shrimp in shellfish jelly are paired with luscious local asparagus, calf's foot en salade with leek hearts give piquancy to frog's legs, and the sautéed langoustines are enlivened by their match with crunchy gingered apples. And the slices of lobster in olive oil puff pastry with a delicate rouille sauce are a revelation. The cheese board is nothing short of sensational, with its carefully matured specimens purchased from local producers, and desserts are uniformly luscious. A splendid wine list proposes interesting bottles from all over France, with particular emphasis on the Loire (from 100 F). The newly enlarged garden adds to the appeal. C 450 F. M 245 F (exc hols), 295 F, 415 F, 535 F.

BRANTÔME 24310
Paris 480 - Périgueux 27 - Limoges 90 - Nontron 22   *Dordogne*

 Les Frères Charbonnel   ❁
57, rue Gambetta
53 05 70 15, fax 53 05 71 85
Closed Sun dinner & Mon off-seas (exc hols), Feb, Nov 15-Dec 15. Open until 9pm. Priv rm: 20. Terrace dining. Hotel: 19 rms 290-500 F. Half-board 390-450 F. Conf. Golf. Pkg. V, AE, DC, MC.
Be warned: flocks of locals and tourists throng this provincial dining room and terrace at weekends to feast on Jean-Claude Charbonnel's generous portions of Southwestern fare based on the best ingredients: salmon stuffed with oysters, tasty sweetbreads and warm duck foie gras salad, truffle-stuffed pickerel, pig's foot in Périgueux sauce, and homemade ice cream. C 260-500 F. M 160 F, 210 F (Sun lunch), 250 F, 300 F, 400 F.

Moulin de l'Abbaye
1, route de Bourdeilles
53 05 80 22, fax 53 05 75 27
*Closed Mon lunch, Nov 2-Apr 28. Open until 10pm.
Priv rm: 15. Garden dining. Valet pkg. V, AE, DC, MC.*
Here is a rapturously romantic, handsomely restored watermill on the banks of the Dronne: it boasts a lovely garden, elegant dining room, and cellar full of moderately priced Burgundy and Bordeaux. The new chef, Guy Guénégo, has quickly taken the measure of the Périgord. His cooking is often seasoned with Caribbean spices (he spent some time there), but he's never heavy-handed with them. Savor the eel jelly with fennel and sorrel, luscious foie gras, and sublime truffle and potato fritters. Another winner is the squab pot-au-feu chabrot-style (a delicate bouillon), neither too heavy nor too light, served with a stuffed squab thigh. Three toques well in hand, and well deserved. C 380-450 F. M 200 F (weekday lunch), 240 F, 300 F, 450 F.

Moulin de l'Abbaye
(See restaurant above)
Closed Nov 2-Apr 28. 4 stes 1,100-1,400 F. 16 rms 700-1,000 F. Half-board 800-900 F. Air cond. Valet pkg. V, AE, DC, MC.
Ravishingly redecorated with an eye for detail, a score of rooms and suites overlooking the river and the unique sixteenth-century bridge. The town (dubbed "La Venise du Périgord") boasts an abbey founded by Charlemagne. Relais et Châteaux.

BRAX 47	→ Agen

BRÉHAT (ILE DE)	22870
	Côtes/Armor

11/20 Bellevue
Le Port-Clos
96 20 00 05, fax 96 20 06 06
Open daily until 9:30pm. Terrace dining. Hotel: 17 rms 360-430 F. Half-board 365-420 F. V, MC.
The only decent restaurant on the island. Unlike the stupendous views, the food here is not stunning, but it is well prepared, with an emphasis on simple, pleasing fish dishes. Loire Valley wines. C 220-320 F. M 89 F (lunch), 110 F, 170 F.

La Vieille Auberge
96 20 00 24, fax 96 20 05 12
Closed Nov-Easter. 15 rms 330-450 F. Restaurant. Half-board 350-400 F. Conf. No pets. Garage pkg. V.
On the edge of town, this pink stone hotel has welcoming, modern rooms.

BRESSON 38	→ Grenoble

BREST	29200
Paris 590 - Rennes 244 - Saint-Brieuc 145	*Finistère*

 Le Frère Jacques
15 bis, rue de Lyon - 98 44 38 65
Closed Sat lunch, Sun. Open until 9:30pm. V, MC.
Jacques Péron is still showing the other restaurants of Brest how it's done: here the hospitality is warm and genuine, the dining room plush and inviting, the seafood creatively cooked and briny-fresh. Beautiful presentation

enhances the chef's rich fricassée of cockles and pig's feet, black cod fillet in a buckwheat crêpe, and a licorice-scented pear in meringue. Diversified wine list, and a warm welcome by Claudine Péron. C 250-300 F. M 150 F.

Mercure Continental
22, rue de Lyon
98 80 50 40, fax 98 43 17 47
Open year-round. 75 rms 350-480 F. Restaurant. Conf. Golf. Pkg. V, AE, DC, MC.
A big, 1950s–style hotel with an impressive staircase near the railway station. The more recent rooms are the most comfortable. Hearty breakfasts.

Le Nouveau Rossini
22, rue du Commandant-Drogou
98 47 90 00
Closed Sun dinner, Mon, Aug 25-Sep 20. Open until 9:30pm. Priv rm: 30. Terrace dining. Air cond. Gararge pkg. V, AE.
Maurice Mevel's restaurant is in Kérinou, a renovated part of town, in a large stone house surrounded by trees and lawns. The dining room is huge and bright with a veranda set rotunda-like over the garden. On offer: red mullet with a raspberry and green pepper jus, delicious orange and raspberry soup, and two pleasingly delicate dishes marred by slight overcooking: sweetbreads with spinach sauce and cod with an onion-spice compote. Fine cellar at reasonable prices, friendly welcome, competent service. C 200-350 F. M 110 F (weekdays, Sat lunch), 180 F, 340 F.

Novotel
6 km N (ZAC de Kergaradec)
Av. du Baron-Lacrosse, 29239 Gouesnou
98 02 32 83, fax 98 41 69 27
Open year-round. 85 rms 395-445 F. Rms for disabled. Restaurant. Conf. Pool. Golf. Garage pkg. V, AE, DC, MC.
A practical place to stay with free shuttle service to the airport. Plain, comfortable rooms.

Océania
82, rue de Siam
98 80 66 66, fax 98 80 65 50
Open year-round. 1 ste 1,400 F. 80 rms 470-790 F. Rms for disabled. Restaurant. Conf. V, AE, DC, MC.
Guest rooms are large, well equipped, and comfortable but the decor varies from dismal to delightful. Impersonal welcome; decent breakfasts; high prices.

And also...
Our selection of places for inexpensive, quick, or late-night meals.
La Brocherie (98 44 07 69 - 61, rue L.-Pasteur.): This good grill stays open late (80-100 F).
La Chaumine (98 45 10 70 - 16, rue J.-Bart.) Open until 10:30pm.): Breton crêpes, night owls welcome (80 F).
La Choucroutière (98 80 60 03 - 14, rue L.-Blanc.): Choucroute of course, plus hearty fondues and late service (100-130 F).
L'Equinoxe (98 41 97 87 - Rue A.-Colas. By reserv.): In the new "Oceanopolis" museum, this restaurant offers inexpensive salads and smoked-fish assortments (120 F).
La Scala (98 43 11 43 - 30, rue d'Algésiras.) Open until 11pm, w-e until midnight.): Perfect

spot for after-theatre pizzas, pasta, and carpaccio (90-120 F).

BREUIL-EN-AUGE   14130
Paris 204 - Caen 55 - Deauville 20 - Lisieux 9   *Calvados*

Le Dauphin   ☺
 31 65 08 11, fax 31 65 12 08
Closed Sun dinner, Mon. Open until 9pm. Priv rm: 12. No pets. Pkg. V.
Régis Lecomte's creative cooking is gently but surely shaking culinary Normandy out of its rich, creamy torpor, although the setting couldn't be more classic: a simple, flower-filled Normandy auberge. Your taste buds will awaken to the toothsome ravioli of andouille, potatoes, and truffles, the petit salé-style sea scallops, the saddle of rabbit stuffed with blood sausage, and the profiteroles with ice milk and warm chocolate sauce. The cellar is small but discerning; the welcome warm. **C** 320-380 F. **M** 170 F, 220 F (exc Sat dinner).

BREUILLET 17   → Royan

BRIAL 82   → Montauban

BRIANÇON   05100
Paris 693 - Grenoble 116 - Gap 87 - Turin 108   *H.-Alpes*

Parc Hôtel
Central Parc
92 20 37 47, fax 92 20 53 74
Open year-round. 3 stes 430 F. 57 rms 350-380 F. Rms for disabled. Half-board 460-580 F. Conf. Pkg. V, AF, MC
Just 200 yards from the Prorel lift, this large, centrally located hotel boasts modern amenities and a rustic decor. The plumbing, equipment, and service are all one could wish. Bar and common room for socializing.

Le Péché Gourmand
 2, route de Gap - 92 20 11 02
Closings not available. Open until 10pm. Priv rm: 10. Terrace dining. Pkg. V, AE, MC.
This attractive establishment is bright and modern. It appeals to a young, food-loving crowd who appreciates the first-rate local ingredients handled here with well-tempered dexterity by Sandrine Bellet: crisp and tasty craquelin of foie gras and chopped turnips, perfectly cooked local squab paired with rather "off"-tasting olive oil mashed potatoes, original crème brûlée made from sheep's milk. Well chosen wine list with many wines by the glass. Settle down near the fireplace and enjoy. **C** 300-360 F. **M** 120 F (weekdays, Sat lunch), 160 F, 195 F, 210 F, 270 F.

12/20 Vauban
13, av. Gal-de-Gaulle
92 21 12 11, fax 92 20 58 20
Closed Nov 6-Dec 18. Open until 9pm. Priv rm: 30. Pkg. V, MC.
No flights of fancy, but the cooking is reliable and service competent. House terrine, profiteroles stuffed with snails, steamed trout with beurre blanc, and curried veal chop. **C** 140-190 F. **M** 100 F, 115 F, 125 F, 160 F.

Vauban
(See restaurant above)
Closed Nov 6-Dec 19. 44 rms 240-430 F. Half-board 260-345 F. Conf. Pkg. V.
Near the town center and the ski lifts, this large hotel by the Durance River offers spacious accommodation with roomy baths and balconies. Attentive service.

BRIGNOGAN-PLAGE   29890
Paris 538 - Morlaix 53 - Brest 37 - Landemeau 26   *Finistère*

Castel-Régis
Plage du Garo
98 83 40 22, fax 98 83 44 71
Closed Sep 27-Apr 14. 21 rms 240-420 F. Restaurant. Half-board 390-480 F. Conf. Heated pool. Tennis. Pkg. V, MC.
Most of the rooms are in bungalows and all revel in the superb seascape. Some bathrooms boast a Jacuzzi. Smiling reception and service.

BRIOLLAY 49   → Angers

BRIVE-LA-GAILLARDE   19100
Paris 468 - Limoges 96 - Toulouse 212 - Périgueux 73   *Corrèze*

La Crémaillère   ☺
53, av. de Paris
55 74 32 47, fax 55 17 91 83
Closed Sun dinner, Mon. Open until 9:30pm. Garden dining. V, AE, MC.
Charlou Reynal, the most colorful chef in a colorful town, is never so inspired as when he's using lusty local ingredients (goose, cèpes, pork, moutarde de violette...) to produce robust regional dishes. Try his blood sausage with chestnuts, salad of white beans with goose gizzards, lentil terrine with foie gras, scrambled eggs with truffles, steamed baby chicken with parsley, cabécou cheese, and luscious pear flognarde for dessert. Even the 100 F menu deserves the laurel wreath for regional authenticity. And this is more than a restaurant; it has long been a hangout for artists, some of whose works you'll find on the walls. The enclosed garden, shaded by a spreading linden tree, is an ideal spot for whiling away a summer afternoon over a memorable meal and a bottle of local wine. **C** 220-300 F. **M** 100 F, 140 F, 190 F, 220 F.

Chez Francis
61, av. de Paris - 55 74 41 72
Closed Sun, Mar 6-12, Aug 6-20. Open until 10pm. Terrace dining. V.
Chef Francis Tessandier manages to be both inventive and frugal by watching the market carefully for prime, in-season foodstuffs which he handles with flair. And now he has instituted mini-meals at mini-prices, in the style of a tapas bar but with his own inventions: soup of fresh tuna and shellfish with spices (25 F), or frog's legs sautéed with garlic and tomatoes caramelized in meat jus (45 F). In regular-sized portions (but hardly more expensive), you'll discover savory risotto of wild mushrooms and sheep's milk cheese (52 F), sturgeon fillet with bacon-sauced potatoes (90 F), or a thick veal chop with girolles and artichokes (88 F). A real success story. Picturesque turn-of-the-century decor, good choice of Bordeaux, and a warm welcome. **C** 180-240 F. **M** 85 F, 120 F.

■ **In Varetz 19240**   10 km NW on D 901

🏠15 **Château de Castel Novel**
55 85 00 01, fax 55 85 09 03
Closed Oct 17-May 6. Open until 9:15pm. Priv rm: 80. Heated pool. Valet pkg. V, AE, DC, MC.
Once a favorite haunt of the writer Colette, who loved to cook and eat the region's earthy specialties, this imposing red-granite manor house is still a landmark for good food. Pascal Peyramaure, trained at the Crillon in Paris, has given the menu a less stuffy look, a move we approve. We tucked happily into his carpaccio with top-quality olive oil and the perfectly grilled salmon with violet mustard, dishes that leave you feeling light enough to jog around the hills. But we confess we couldn't resist the extremely tender duo of duck and goose foie gras with figs or the succulent veal cutlet with meltingly tender apples. We found the galinette (tub gurnard, a Mediterranean fish) in walnut oil a bit over-cooked, though. Desserts are the house's weak point but progress is being made. The cellar is superb: awash in vintage Bordeaux at most attractive prices. **C** 350-450 F. **M** 180 F (lunch, wine incl), 215 F, 300 F, 370 F.

🏠 **Château de Castel Novel** ▲♥
(See restaurant above)
Closed Oct 17-May 6. 5 stes 1,355-1,490 F. 32 rms 565-1,355 F. Half-board 665-1,130 F. Air cond. Conf. Pool. Tennis. Golf. Pkg. Helipad. V, AE, DC, MC.
The 40-hectare grounds include a three-hole golf course and a barbecue. As for the hotel, it has beautifully decorated rooms, fine service and excellent, varied breakfasts. An annex contains some less luxurious rooms. The grounds are dotted with splendid trees (the magnolias in particular are superb).

Paris 525 - Périgueux 40 - Bergerac 48 - Sarlat 33   *Dordogne*

🍴14 **L'Albuca**
Pl. de l'Hôtel-de-Ville - 53 07 28 73 (R), 53 07 20 01 (H), fax 53 03 51 80
Closed lunch Mon & Tue, Oct 10-Apr 29. Open until 9:30pm. Terrace dining. Pkg. V, AE, DC, MC.
A fine meal awaits you in this delightful establishment overlooking the superb Vézère Valley. Sample the green bean and foie gras salad, the stuffed saddle of young rabbit, the liver ballotine with rosemary jus, and one of several fresh and appealing desserts. The well-stocked cellar is rich in Bordeaux. Distinguished service; charming welcome. **C** 250-350 F. **M** 90 F, 130 F, 170 F, 190 F, 240 F.

🏠 **Royal Vézère**
(See restaurant above)
Closed Oct 11-Apr 29. 4 stes 600-735 F. 49 rms 250-525 F. Half-board 300-650 F. Conf. Heated pool. Golf. Pkg. V, AE, DC, MC.
The rooms look onto the Vézère. Count on classic comfort and obliging service. Relax on the panoramic terrace massed with flowers.

↦ **Siorac-en-Périgord**

↦ **Lagny-sur-Marne**

Paris 225 - Caen 24 - Deauville 19   *Calvados*

12/20 Le Balbec
Promenade M.-Proust
31 91 01 79, fax 31 24 03 20
Open daily until 10pm. Priv rm: 30. Terrace dining. Valet pkg. V, AE, DC.
Tourists flock to this lovely turn-of-the-century establishment overlooking the sea, and the chef is competent in spite of the fact that the truffle juice the menu said would be in the salade folle was not there after all. A professional and smiling welcome and a classic wine list. **C** 200-350 F. **M** 185 F (Sun lunch, wine incl), 190 F (exc weekdays), 140 F (weekdays).

🏠 **Grand Hôtel**
(See restaurant above)
Open year-round. 2 stes 1,500-2,500 F. 68 rms 450-900 F. Half-board 490-920 F. Conf. Golf. Valet pkg. V, AE, DC.
This Belle Époque hotel has undergone a thorough overhaul, to improve the comfort and charm of its spacious rooms and huge bathrooms.

🏠 **Castel Fleuri**
4, av. A.-Piat
31 91 27 57, fax 31 91 31 81
Open year-round. 21 rms 390-440 F. Golf. No pets. V, MC.
Recently modernized, this manor house surrounded by a sweet little garden, offers small, colorful, comfortable rooms and bountiful breakfasts. Sluggish service.

🏠 **Le Cottage**
24, av. du Gal-Leclerc
31 91 65 61, fax 31 28 78 82
Open year-round. 14 rms 250-390 F. Half-board 265-310 F. Conf. Pkg. V, MC.
In a traditional Norman dwelling, simple, well-equipped rooms and a family atmosphere.

🏠 **Hôtel du Golf**
Av. de l'Hippodrome
31 24 12 34, fax 31 24 18 51
Open year-round. 10 stes 550-910 F. 30 rms 340-450 F. Rms for disabled. Restaurant. Half-board 605 F. Air cond. Conf. Heated pool. Tennis. Golf. Valet pkg. Helipad. V, AE, DC, MC.
Between the golf course and the racecourse, this hotel has bright, quiet, modern rooms.

🏠 **Mercure**
Av. M.-D'Ornano
31 24 04 04, fax 31 91 03 99
Open year-round. 1 ste 700-1,000 F. 81 rms 360-680 F. Rms for disabled. Restaurant. Half-board 175-200 F. Conf. Heated pool. Golf. Pkg. V, AE.
A pretty modern hotel with smallish but pleasant rooms and good bathrooms. Smiling service, lovely pool, satellite TV, and first-rate breakfasts.

Restaurant prices in red draw attention to restaurants that offer particularly good value.

In Bavent 14860 — 7 km SW on D 513 and D 95 A

Hostellerie du Moulin du Pré
Route de Gonneville-en-Auge
31 78 83 68, fax 31 78 21 05
Closed Sun dinner & Mon (exc hols & Jul-Aug), Mar 1-16, Sep 27-Oct 27. Open until 9pm. Pkg. V, AE, DC, MC.
The dining room with its blazing fire and lace tablecloths is a winsome setting indeed, and the cooking is of the simple, satisfying variety. Jocelyne Holtz pleases locals and visiting Parisians with the likes of sea-scallop carpaccio with walnut oil, langoustine tails, delicate fish fillets with apples and curry, lamb sweetbreads with morels, and a little tart of fresh sardines with saffron butter. Good little cellar; cheerful, competent service. **C** 280-340 F. **M** 250 F.

In Dives-sur-Mer 14160 S

Chez le Bougnat
27, rue G.-Manneville - 31 91 06 13
Closings not available. Open until 9:30pm (10pm in seas). Garage pkg. No cards.
An old-fashioned bistro that bears a strong resemblance to a Paris métro station with its white-and-green-tiled walls, vintage posters, and banquettes. Ex-butcher Jacky Madeleine certainly knows his way around meats and charcuteries: he buys only the best to turn into appetizing dishes: calf's head, head cheese, and delectable French fries, the real thing. Jovial atmosphere and wines less interesting than they might appear, but at least there's nothing snobbish about the list. **C** 150-200 F. **M** 79 F.

CABRERETS 46330
Paris 566 - St-Céré 66 - Figeac 41 - Cahors 34 *Lot*

In Bouziès 46330 — 6 km SW on D 662

11/20 Les Falaises
65 31 26 83, fax 65 30 23 87
Closed Dec 1-Jan 7. Open until 9pm. Terrace dining. Heated pool. Pkg. V, AE, MC.
The terrace offers a lovely view of the Lot, and the kitchen turns out hearty fare at friendly prices. On the 75 F menu: house terrine, perch fillet in aged Cahors, cabécou cheese and salad, and ice cream. **C** 130-270 F. **M** 46 F, 75 F, 96 F, 127 F, 237 F.

Les Falaises
(See restaurant above)
Closed Dec 5-Jan 7. 39 rms 229-320 F. Rms for disabled. Half-board 246-291 F. Conf. Heated pool. Tennis. Pkg. V, AE, MC.
Guest rooms overlook a garden and swimming pool. Numerous leisure facilities are within easy reach. Cozy lounge with a fireplace.

*We're always happy to hear about **your discoveries** and receive your comments on ours. Please feel free to write to us stating clearly what you liked or disliked. Be concise but convincing, and take the time to argue your point.*

CABRIÈRES-D'AVIGNON 84220
Paris 715 - Avignon 35 - Gordes 7 - Cavaillon 12 *Vaucluse*

Le Bistrot à Michel
Grande-Rue - 90 76 82 08
Closed Jan. Open until 9:30pm. Priv rm: 40. Terrace dining. Pkg. V, MC.
Around about apéritif time, locals line up along the bar of this charming Provençal bistro, or vie for seats on the garden terrace. Monsieur and Madame Bosc cultivate a convivial atmosphere at the tables, while son Yan keeps busy in the kitchen cooking up forthright dishes that focus on regional foodstuffs. Good bets are the snails en croûte with bacon and hazlenuts, John Dory fillet with an anchovy coating, tomatoes and split-pea purée, squab roasted with garlic, and wild rice from the Camargue. Local wines dominate the well-composed cellar. **C** 270-350 F. **M** 100 F (weekday lunch, Sat), 160 F.

CABRIS 06 → Grasse

CADIÈRE D'AZUR (LA) 83740
Paris 821 - Marseille 46 - Toulon 22 - Aix-en-Provence 63 *Var*

René Bérard
Rue G.-Péri
94 90 11 43, fax 94 90 01 94
Closed Sun dinner & Mon off-seas, Jan 10-Feb 22. Open until 9:30pm. Priv rm: 10. Air cond. No pets. Garage pkg. V, AE, MC.
Happy days are here again, as is the toque lost last year, in this restaurant perched high above the Bandol vineyards. Now you will find a friendly welcome, and rejuvenated cuisine concocted from the freshest ingredients by René Bérard and his assistant, Francis Scordel: beef millefeuille with foie gras and truffle juice, roast John Dory, fennel and artichoke confits, and a roast white peach with a verbena-lime granité. Fine wine list. **C** 350-450 F. **M** 115 F (weekday lunch), 180 F (w-e), 235 F, 280 F, 350 F.

Hostellerie Bérard
(See restaurant above)
Closed Jan 10-Feb 22. 4 stes 750-1,200 F. 36 rms 395-750 F. Half-board 470-620 F. Air cond. Conf. Heated pool. Golf. No pets. Garage pkg. Helipad. V, AE, DC, MC.
This Renaissance-era hostelry provides thoughtfully decorated rooms. A recent annex overlooks the garden and swimming pool.

CAEN 14000
Paris 222 - Rouen 124 - Evreux 121 - Cherbourg 119 *Calvados*

La Bourride
15-17, rue du Vaugueux
31 93 50 76, fax 31 93 29 63
Closed Sun dinner, Mon, Jan 2-20, Aug 17-Sep 4. Open until 9:45pm. Priv rm: 20. V, AE, DC, MC.
Michel Bruneau is passionately devoted to the cuisine of Normandy, although that doesn't stop him from trying such tasty flights of fancy as matching vanilla-scented tarbais beans with squab from a nearby farm, or Collioure anchovies with a monkfish fillet. He feels Normandy cuisine should evolve; after all, Normandy itself has always been a cultural crossroads. Just take a seat in his exquisite half-timbered

restaurant (warmed by the charming presence of Françoise Bruneau) and watch through the glass partition as he and his team beaver away in the kitchen, preparing delights like a gaufrette of snails with a delicate nettle stuffing, lobster with tripe essence surrounded by garlic chips, sea scallops exploding with flavor in their intense truffle and pumpkin jus, and sole with an elegant hint of orange-flower water. Bruneau's vivacious personality shines through in every dish. False notes? This year, the orange and licorice soufflé didn't quite live up to the other dishes. The eclectic cellar includes fine ciders (from David), as well as wines from many regions and a cache of ·splendid aged Calvados. C 400-600 F. M 200 F (lunch exc Sun), 320 F, 455 F, 560 F.

Le Dauphin ☺
29, rue Gémare
31 86 22 26, fax 31 86 35 14
Closed Jul 17-Aug 7. Open until 9:30pm. Priv rm: 40. Hotel: 1 ste 460-510 F. 21 rms 320-420 F. Half-board 360-460 F. Conf. Pkg. V, AE, DC, MC.
Robert Chabredier's carte is short and devoted to market-fresh seafood that locals have enjoyed here for close to 30 years. The dining room is decorated in a rather heavy bourgeois style, but it won't detract from your enjoyment of the oysters stuffed with leeks in sabayon sauce, local lamb with garlic jus, berries in puff pastry, and rhubarb sherbet. Good cellar; civil service. C 240-340 F. M 165 F, 235 F, 290 F (exc weekday lunch), 95 F (weekdays).

Mercure
1, rue de Courtonne
31 47 24 24, fax 31 47 43 88
Open year-round. 4 stes 1,100-1,400 F. 110 rms 400-600 F. Rms for disabled. Restaurant. Air cond. Conf. Pkg. V, AE, DC, MC.
Comfortable rooms, but rather dark and not too well soundproofed. Centrally located opposite the harbor.

Moderne
116, bd du Mal-Leclerc
31 86 04 23, fax 31 85 37 93
Open year-round. 40 rms 320-620 F. Rms for disabled. Pkg. V, AE, DC.
A modern hotel with personalized rooms and good bathrooms. Breakfasts are served on the fifth floor with a panoramic view of the town. Sauna.

Le Rabelais
Pl. Foch - 31 27 57 57, fax 31 27 57 58
Closed at Christmas. Open until 10pm. Priv rm: 180. No pets. V, AE, DC.
Simple but fresh and appealing dishes made from impeccable ingredients bring local food lovers and travelers too into this long, bright dining room. Try the salmon and bream tartare with lime, superb fillet of Scottish salmon with basil and fresh tomatoes, and a tasty crème brûlée. Good cellar. The service and reception have a friendly British accent. C 250-370 F. M 80 F (lunch exc Sun), 110 F, 160 F, 250 F.

Holiday Caen City Centre
(See restaurant above)
Open year-round. 92 rms 410-580 F. Rms for disabled. Conf. Golf. V, AE, DC.
Dating from the 1950s, this building opposite the racecourse has been entirely revamped. The

brand-new rooms offer flawless comfort. Cocktail bar.

Le Relais des Gourmets
15, rue Geôle
31 86 06 01, fax 31 39 06 00
Open year-round. 5 stes 770-910 F. 23 rms 300-520 F. Rms for disabled. Restaurant. Half-board 295-600 F. Conf. Golf. Garage pkg. V, AE, DC.
Ideally situated near the château, these well-soundproofed rooms were recently redecorated. Generous breakfasts; faultless service.

Daniel Tubœuf
8, rue Buquet
31 43 64 48
Closed Sun, Mon, Aug 1-21. Open until 9:30pm. Air cond. V.
The theatrical dining room (it was formerly a ballet school) is an ideal setting for Daniel Tubœuf's original cooking based on fine ingredients. We urge you to order his excellent sautéed liver, bar stuffed with oysters, lobster, and breaded sweetbreads. Sometimes he uses a too-free hand with spices, but this is definitely a two-toque restaurant at bargain prices, and the 135 F menu is a steal. Adequate wine list and perfect service. C 280-400 F. M 135 F (weekday dinner), 125 F (lunch), 228 F, 298 F, 368 F.

And also...
Our selection of places for inexpensive, quick, or late-night meals.
Amalfi (31 85 33 34 - 201, rue Saint-Jean. Open until 11pm.): The best pizzas in Caen, and not at all expensive (90-140 F).
L'Assiette (31 85 29 16 - 2, pl. Fontette. Open until 10pm.): Worth trying especially for the 40 different desserts. Friendly and original (120-150 F).
Le Panier à Salades (31 34 22 22 - 24, rue P.-Girard. Open until 11pm.): Good meat dishes, a huge choice of salads, and good desserts in a friendly atmosphere (150-200 F).

■ **In Bénouville 14970**   10 km NE

12/20 Manoir d'Hastings
18, av. de la Côte-de-Nacre
31 44 62 43, fax 31 44 76 18
Closed Sun dinner & Mon (exc Jul-Aug), Nov 15-Dec 5. Open until 9:30pm. Priv rm: 70. Garden dining. Pkg. V, AE, DC.
This elegant old manor house is a reliable source for pleasing, traditional cuisine based on market-fresh ingredients. The regional dishes on offer include lobster in sherry vinegar, squab with foie gras and ginger, John Dory in a pot-au-feu, and warm tarte normande. Courteous welcome; tip-top service. C 230-400 F. M 120 F (weekday lunch), 160 F, 220 F, 260 F, 360 F.

La Pommeraie
(See restaurant above)
Closed Nov 15-Dec 8. 15 rms 400-800 F. Half-board 650-850 F. Conf. Golf. Pkg. V, AE, DC, MC.
This flower-banked building can't match the charm of the manor housing the restaurant, but the rooms are really comfortable. Remarkable breakfasts.

■ **In Fleury-sur-Orne 14000**   4 km S on D 562

L'Ile Enchantée
[14]
1, rue St-André - 31 52 15 52
*Closed Sun dinner, Mon, 1st wk of Feb school hols.
Open until 9:30pm. Priv rm: 15. Pkg. V, MC.*
Owner-chef Alain Jamet's sure-handed technique and fine regional foodstuffs produce such delicious offerings as terrine of foie gras, pig's foot, and andouille, a chartreuse of sole fillets in cider butter, and a croustillant of caramelized apples. Sit upstairs for the best river views. Rich yet reasonably priced cellar, and a friendly welcome. **C** 250-300 F. **M** 125 F, 170 F, 215 F.

■ **In Hérouville-Saint-Clair 14200**   3 km NE

Friendly
2, pl. de Boston
31 44 05 05, fax 31 44 95 94
Open year-round. 2 stes 600 F. 90 rms 390-460 F. Restaurant. Half-board 480-615 F. Conf. Heated pool. Golf. Pkg. V, AE, DC, MC.
This English hotel, complete with mahogany bar and floral-patterned carpet, is equipped with a sauna, gym, and a pool with a wave machine.

CAGNES-SUR-MER   **06800**
Paris 920 - Cannes 22 - Nice 13 - Antibes 11   *Alpes-Mar.*

Le Cagnard
[16]
Haut-de-Cagnes, rue du Pontis-Long
93 20 73 21, fax 93 22 06 39
Closed Thu lunch, beg Nov-mid Dec. Open until 10:30pm. Terrace dining. Air cond. Pkg. V, AE, DC.
This ravishing fourteenth-century dwelling affords a stupendous view of the coast all the way to Antibes. You can enjoy that sweeping panorama from a terrace equipped with a sliding paneled ceiling, which protects you from bad weather or opens to let you admire the stars. Jean-Yves Johany's cooking demonstrates a sure and exacting skill and a genuine respect for the superb ingredients he works with. Try his minestrone of plump langoustines with tomato juice, coco beans, and shell macaroni on the excellent 300 F "menu du soleil", as well as tender chaud-froid of duck with Port, super-fresh and tasty sea scallops roasted with olive oil and shellfish essence, served with julienne vegetables, and a perfect John Dory with Jerusalem artichokes: perfect fish, perfectly cooked. Warm apple tart with tarragon ice cream. All this merits an extra point this year. Superb wine list, courteous welcome, and accomplished service. The prices, naturally, reflect the luxury of the decor. **C** 500-600 F. **M** 250 F (lunch), 300 F, 380 F, 500 F.

Le Cagnard
(See restaurant above)
Open year-round. 10 stes 1,000-1,400 F. 18 rms 350-800 F. Half-board 720-1,200 F. Air cond. Conf. Golf. Valet pkg. V, AE, DC, MC.
Most of these rooms and suites have a private terrace with glorious views. The decor is luxurious and tasteful. Relais et Châteaux.

Les Collettes
Chemin des Collettes - 93 20 80 66
Closed Nov-Dec 27. 13 rms 298-401 F. Pool. Tennis. Pkg. V, MC.

This simple hotel-motel overlooking the sea has plain, pleasantly decorated rooms.

Josy-Jo
[14]
Haut-de-Cagnes, 8, pl. du Planastel
93 20 68 76, fax 93 73 08 69
Closed Sat lunch, Sun, Aug 1-15. Open until 10pm. Terrace dining. V, MC.
For over twenty-five years Jo and Josy Bandecchi have been serving seasonal Provençal food to appreciative customers. There are artichokes à la barigoule, stuffed zucchini blossoms, charcoal-grilled meats and fish, and delectable fresh fruit tarts. Not to mention friendly service and an adorable terrace massed with flowers. **C** 320-400 F.

Picadero
[15]
3, bd de la Plage - 93 22 32 84
Closings not available. Open until 9:45pm. Air cond. Pkg. V, MC.
Gérard Ferri has come back home after a stretch in San Francisco to set himself up in this lovely, light-filled restaurant. He keeps his menu short and changes it weekly, so you are sure of finding the freshest ingredients, skillfully prepared. His set-price Provençal menu is a real winner: delicious warm tart of red mullet, tomatoes, and onion confit, followed by perfectly roasted duck breast with a spicy potato gratin, and an interesting and tasty sweet chard tart with raisins and rum. Short but well chosen wine list, courteous welcome, and competent service. **C** 320 F. **M** 160 F.

Restaurant des Peintres
[16]
Haut-de-Cagnes, 71, montée de la Bourgade - 93 20 83 08, fax 93 20 61 01
Closed Wed, Nov 15-Dec 15. Open until 10pm. Priv rm: 20. Air cond. Valet pkg. V, AE, DC, MC.
The tourists who climb up through the picturesque village to reach this spot probably have no idea that they are approaching one of the best restaurants on the coast. Alain Llorca, trained by Ducasse and Le Stanc, is a remarkable young chef whose repertoire glows with intelligence, generosity, and the sunny savors of Provence. As you feast your eyes on the Mediterranean, tease your palate with such delights as an unctuous chestnut cream with poached truffles, sautéed sea scallops with olive oil and balsamic vinegar, milk-fed spit-roasted lamb with roasted artichokes and fennel, and a remarkable duck foie gras casserole-roasted with fruits and vegetables, followed by a choice of superb cheeses and fine desserts like a delicate crêpe with tangerines and cream, or another with sugar and rum. A sturdy Provençal wine from the affordably priced cellar is the obvious choice to partner a meal like this. The set menus are real bargains. Owners Claudie and Jacques Lorquet greet patrons with genuine warmth. **C** 300-365 F. **M** 200 F, 300 F.

■ **In Cros-de-Cagnes 06800**   2 km SE

La Bourride
[14]
Port de Cros-de-Cagnes
93 31 07 75, fax 93 31 89 11
Closed Wed, Feb school hols. Open until 10:30pm. Priv rm: 30. Garden dining. Air cond. Pkg. V, AE.
A dreamy summer restaurant with a pine-shaded patio (partly covered this year) opposite

181

the port is a perfect setting for a leisurely lunch or dinner. The chef's sun-kissed cuisine is absolutely in tune with the scenery: tender sautéed squid à la provençale, excellent lobster in warm vinaigrette, and lusty versions of the region's traditional seafood soups, bourride and bouillabaisse. Friendly welcome and efficient service. C 270-450 F. M 150 F, 195 F, 290 F.

La Villa du Cros
Bd de la Plage, on the harbor
93 07 57 83
Closed Sun dinner (exc summer), Nov. Open until 10pm (10:30pm in summer). Priv rm: 20. Terrace dining. Air cond. Pkg. V, AE, DC, MC.
Breathe in the invigorating sea air as you peruse Jean Biccherai's enticing menu of seafood specialties. We invariably go for the "catch of the day", whatever it might be, but also worth a try are the warm asparagus with cèpe sauce, sea bass in peppery red wine sauce, or sautéed langoustines with polenta. Good cellar. C 250-300 F. M 120 F, 180 F.

CAHORS	46000
Paris 569 - Rodez 121 - Brive 102 - Montauban 60	*Lot*

Le Balandre
5, av. Ch.-de-Freycinet
65 30 01 97, fax 65 22 06 40
Closed Sun dinner & Mon off-seas, Sat lunch in seas. Open until 9:30pm. Priv rm: 15. Terrace dining. Air cond. No pets. Pkg. V, AE, MC.
Gilles Marre has infused new life into this comfortable and immaculate restaurant done up in turn-of-the-century style. He serves forth finely-crafted cuisine based on suberb local products. His more inventive dishes include salad of lamb sweetbreads with asparagus tips, cardamom egg cream, and sea bass stuffed with mushrooms and dill jus. Traditionalists will opt for hearty fare like eggs "Pierre Marre" with foie gras and truffles, or the fillets of local lamb. Fine desserts. Superb selection of Cahors wines. C 270-400 F. M 170 F (weekday lunch, Sat, wine incl), 120 F (dinner), 220 F, 230 F, 300 F.

Hôtel Terminus
(See restaurant above)
Open year-round. 28 rms 270-460 F. Rms for disabled. Conf. Pkg. V, AE, MC.
This cozy hotel near the train station was completely renovated in late 1994. It boasts large, comfortable, soundproofed rooms and a 1920s-style decor.

France
252, av. J.-Jaurès
65 35 16 76, fax 65 22 01 08
Closings not available. 79 rms 200-350 F. Air cond. Conf. No pets. Pkg. V, AE, DC, MC.
A spotless modern hotel, located between the station and Valentré bridge.

■ In **Lamagdelaine 46090**   7 km NE on D 653

Marco
65 35 30 64, fax 65 30 31 40
Closed Sun dinner & Mon off-seas, Jan 4-Mar 4, last wk of Oct. Open until 9:30pm. Terrace dining. Garage pkg. V, AE, DC, MC.
The nice things we said about this place last year might have gone to Marco's head a bit: the

prices went up as fast as the Virginia creeper on the restaurant's walls. But the dining room, with a garden terrace, is lovely, and the cooking is still generous and intensely flavored. Try Marco's tatin of foie gras with truffle jus, parillada (turbot, monkfish, lobster, and langoustine) with olive oil, and a bowl of berries with Cassis. It's a shame the cheaper set menus lack choices. There are also four guestrooms, all different and very well equipped, around a swimming pool. C 290-430 F. M 120 F (weekdays, Sat lunch), 195 F, 200 F, 295 F.

■ **In Mercuès 46090**   7 km NW on N 20 and D 911

Château de Mercuès
65 20 00 01, fax 65 20 05 72
Closed beg Nov-mid Apr. Open until 9:30pm (10pm in seas). Priv rm: 40. Terrace dining. Pool. No pets. Valet pkg. V, AE, DC, MC.
Owner Georges Vigouroux invested a significant sum in the renovation of this former bishop's residence, and when the work was complete he hired Michel Dussau, a first-rate chef trained in Monte-Carlo by Alain Ducasse. Dussau has put together an enticing menu with an unmistakable Mediterranean accent, although he treats noble Southwestern ingredients equally well. This year we savored the coco beans and shellfish briefly sautéed in warm lobster vinaigrette, and the sole meunière with cod brandade and artichokes with espelette peppers. For a more local flavor, try the fine saddle of lamb, Aquitaine beef, milk-fed veal, farm-produced ham, and gesse soup (made with local beans) with goat cheese ravioli. Not to mention superb foie gras and the local black diamond, the truffle. One point more this year for such a satisfying blend of South and Southwest. As for wines, you would surely not wish to offend the owner by drinking anything other than the superb Cahors that he grows and vinifies himself! C 350-450 F. M 200 F, 295 F, 395 F.

Château de Mercuès
(See restaurant above)
Closed beg Nov-mid Apr. 6 stes 1,400-1,950 F. 25 rms 650-1,500 F. Half-board 940-1,315 F. Conf. Pool. Tennis. Valet pkg. Helipad. V, AE, DC, MC.
The opulent rooms and suites of this impressive château dominate the Lot River valley, a broad and marvelous landscape. Ask for the "bishop's room" or the "tower room" with the sliding glass roof. Relais et Châteaux.

CALAIS	62100
Paris 305 - Amiens 155 - Arras 113 - Dunkerque 39	*P./Calais*

Aquar'Aile
Plage de Calais, 255, rue J.-Moulin
21 34 00 00, fax 21 34 15 00
Closed Sun dinner. Open until 11pm. Priv rm: 180. Air cond. Pkg. V, AE, DC, MC.
Michel and Olivier Taildeman man the stoves of this panoramic restaurant on the second floor of a building overlooking the beach. The dining room is done in silvery sea tones, an ideal setting for their fresh, professional cuisine: turbotin of baby vegetables, braised sweetbreads with spinach, stuffed quail, and crème brûlée with brown sugar. The affable maître d'hotel knows

all the ins and outs of the interesting wine list. Stylish, attentive service. **C** 280-380 F. **M** 160 F, 200 F, 300 F (exc Sun, wine incl), 98 F, 230 F (exc Sun).

12/20 Le Channel
3, bd de la Résistance
21 34 42 30, fax 21 97 42 43
Closed Sun dinner, Tue, Dec 20-Jan 16, Jun 7-16. Open until 9:30pm. Air cond. Pkg. V, AE, DC, MC.
A large harbor-front restaurant offering a generous seafood repertoire and a bargain 90 F menu: smoked halibut, salmon meunière, chicken in wine vinegar, cheeses, and dessert. **C** 230-350 F. **M** 90 F (exc Sun), 340 F (wine incl), 142 F, 205 F.

Côte d'Argent

1, digue G.-Berthe
21 34 68 07, fax 21 96 42 10
Closed Sun dinner, Mon. Open until 10:30pm. Priv rm: 50. Pkg. V, AE, DC, MC.
In this light-flooded dining room that looks out on the waves, what else would one want to eat but seafood? Bertrand Lefebvre's menu comprises saffron-scented mussels, sea bass and red mullet with garden herbs, beef fillet with beef marrow sauce à la bordelaise. Affordable wines and diligent service round out the picture. **C** 240-300 F. **M** 90 F, 130 F, 180 F, 250 F.

12/20 George-V
36, rue Royale
21 97 68 00, fax 21 97 34 73
Closed Sat lunch, dinner Sun & hols, Dec 22-Jan 4. Open until 10pm. Priv rm: 50. Air cond. **Hotel:** *2 stes 460 F. 42 rms 220-370 F. Rms for disabled. Half-board 320 F. Conf. Pkg. V, AE, DC, MC.*
In the neo-colonial dining room of the Grand George (the establishment's "gastronomic" restaurant), you will be served such resolutely classic specialties as marinade of sea scallops, seafood mixed grill, duck breast with herbs, and crème brûlée. Meanwhile, at the Petit George just next door, you'll find a generous 85 F fixed-price meal of bistrot-style fare. **C** 280-380 F. **M** 265 F (wine incl), 150 F (weekday lunch, wine incl), 85 F, 155 F.

Holiday Inn Garden Court
Bd des Alliés
21 34 69 69, fax 21 97 09 15
Open year-round. 3 stes 600-650 F. 62 rms 500-550 F. Rms for disabled. Restaurant. Conf. Pkg. V, AE, DC, MC.
A new hotel, centrally located, with all the comforts of a Holiday Inn: modern and superbly equipped rooms (trouser press; electric kettle). Service is efficient, and there is an exercise room with a sauna. Good breakfasts.

Métropol'Hotel
43, quai du Rhin
21 97 54 00, fax 21 96 69 70
Closed Dec 24-Jan 2. 40 rms 210-390 F. Rms for disabled. Conf. Garage pkg. V, AE, DC, MC.
This quiet, efficiently run hotel in the center of town has small, comfortable, well-appointed rooms. English bar.

CALA-ROSSA 20
→ **CORSICA: Porto-Vecchio**

CALLAS   83830
Paris 870 - Draguignan 15 - Castellane 61   *Var*

12/20 Les Gorges de Pennafort
Route du Mug
94 76 66 51, fax 94 76 67 23
Closed Sun dinner & Mon off-seas, Jan 15-Mar 18. Open until 9pm (10pm in summer). Priv rm: 30. Terrace dining. Air cond. Pool. Pkg. V, AE.
The site is sensational (magnificent gorges just opposite), the restaurant is comfortable (it boasts a broad, shaded terrace), and the cooking is cheerful, though certainly not cheap: red mullet fillet in tomato sauce, lamb crépinette stuffed with red pepper jus, sweetbreads with cabbage and parsley cream, puff pastry stuffed with wood strawberries with an apricot sauce. **C** 300-400 F. **M** 150 F (weekdays), 200 F, 250 F, 340 F.

Les Gorges de Pennafort
(See restaurant above)
See restaurant for closings. 4 stes 850-1,000 F. 12 rms 475-650 F. Half-board 480-580 F. Air cond. Conf. Pool. Tennis. Golf. Pkg. V, AE.
Welcoming, air-conditioned rooms and small, well-appointed marble bathrooms. An annex offers four very attractive larger rooms. Charming welcome.

CALUIRE-ET-CUIRE 69   → Lyon

CALVI 20   → CORSICA

CALVINET   15340
Paris 582 - Aurillac 39 - Rodez 61 - Figeac 39   *Cantal*

Le Beauséjour
Restaurant Puech, route de Maurs
71 49 91 68, fax 71 49 98 63
Closed Sun dinner & Mon (exc hols & Jul-Aug), Jan 15-Feb 15. Open until 9pm (9:30pm in summer). Priv rm: 10. Terrace dining. No pets. Pkg. V, MC.
Extensive renovations have transformed this charming family-style *auberge* into a small hotel with a dozen comfortable new rooms. So feel free to linger over a leisurely dinner in the spacious dining room or on the terrace that overlooks the green countryside of Cantal. Louis-Bertrand Puech is a talented chef who aims to keep quality high and prices low. He makes the most of regional foodstuffs and inexpensive fish for a menu that features the likes of exquisite Salers beef cooked rare, delicious Cantal cheeses, and local chestnuts made into superb ice cream. Try the cabbage stuffed with sweetbreads and girolles and the meaty francandeau (a type of pâté) and you will see why the locals, many of them senior citizens, flock here. **C** 200-280 F. **M** 85 F, 125 F, 180 F, 260 F.

Le Beauséjour
(See restaurant above)
Closed Jan 15-Feb 15. 12 rms 220-300 F. Half-board 240-300 F. Pkg. V, MC.
The spacious guest rooms are equipped with every modern comfort, for a pleasant country sojourn.

CAMBO-LES-BAINS   64250
Paris 760 - Bayonne 20 - St-Jean-de-Luz 31   Pyrénées-A.

Errobia
Av. Chantecler
59 29 71 26, fax 59 29 96 36
Closed Nov-Apr. 1 ste 400-500 F. 13 rms 190-500 F. Heated pool. Pkg. V.
A beautiful, family-style Basque house overlooking a valley, with large, comfortable rooms. Pretty views.

Le Relais de la Poste
Pl. de la Mairie
59 29 73 03, fax 57 29 86 00
Closed Sun & Mon (exc Jul-Aug), Nov-Mar. Open until 8:45pm. Priv rm: 15. Terrace dining.
Hotel: 10 rms 270-320 F. Half-board 400 F. Pkg. V, AE, DC, MC.
The light-filled dining room is a fine setting for Daniel Aube's clever, colorful cuisine. The 160 F menu (a small carafe of Bordeaux included) brings an assortment of Basque charcuterie, grilled steak with béarnaise sauce, and a warm cream-filled puff pastry. What's more, you can count on a delightful welcome from the *patronne*. **C** 280-380 F. **M** 160 F (wine incl), 98 F.

CAMBRAI   59400
Paris 170 - Arras 36 - Saint-Quentin 33 - Lille 63   Nord

12/20 Château de La Motte-Fénelon
All&e Saint-Roch
27 83 61 38, fax 27 83 71 61
Closed dinner Sun & hols. Open until 10pm. Priv rm: 200. Pkg. V, AE, DC, MC.
A big, beautiful castle that hosts numerous conferences and receptions. Travelers on their own are assigned tables in an elegantly decorated cellar dining room with vaulted ceilings, and served fricassée of sea scallops, sole fillet, and praline croustillant napped with caramel. **C** 300-400 F. **M** 120 F (weekday lunch, wine incl), 190 F (Sun lunch, wine incl), 145 F, 195 F, 225 F.

Château de La Motte-Fénelon
(See restaurant above)
Open year-round. 4 stes 950-1,000 F. 36 rms 290-440 F. Half-board 370-640 F. Conf. Tennis. Pkg. V, AE, DC, MC.
The rooms in the château are infinitely more desirable than the ageing, bungalow-style accommodation in the park. The wooded grounds boast two tennis courts.

CAMPOROSSO (Italy)   → Menton

CANALE-DI-VERDE 20   → CORSICA

CANAPVILLE 14   → Deauville

A red hotel ranking denotes a place with charm.

CANCALE   35260
Paris 360 - Saint-Malô 14 - Dinan 34 - Rennes 72   Ille/Vil.

12/20 L'Armada
8, quai A.-Thomas
99 89 60 02, fax 99 89 86 98
Closed Sun dinner (exc hols & Jul-Aug). Open until 9pm. Priv rm: 60. Terrace dining. Pkg. V, AE, MC.
Here is a clean-lined, contemporary restaurant that overlooks the Bay of Mont-Saint-Michel. Seafood, naturally, dominates the bill of fare. Sample the lime-spiked skate terrine, salmon fillet with hollandaise, sole meunière in lemony butter sauce, and thick steaks to please carnivores. Good cellar. **C** 200-350 F. **M** 120 F (Sun lunch), 98 F (exc Sun), 195 F.

Le Bistrot de Cancale
La Houle, 2, quai Gambetta - 99 89 92 42
Closings not available. Open until 10pm. No pets. V, MC.
Jacques Granville, after a stint in Switzerland, has lowered anchor in this sunny bistrot with a pleasant terrace overlooking the sea. His maritime cuisine focuses on freshness, simplicity, and ingenuity: excellent mussels cooked with tomatoes, delicate and savory sardine gratin with grilled eggplant purée, and a delicious strawberry tart with a buttery crust. Good wine list with many wines served by the glass. Friendly welcome, fast service. **C** 180-250 F. **M** 79 F (lunch), 89 F, 149 F, 199 F.

Restaurant de Bricourt
Olivier Rœllinger, 1, rue Du Guesclin
99 89 64 76,
19.5   fax 99 89 88 47
Closed Tue & Wed (exc dinner Jul-Aug), Dec 13-Mar 13. Open until 9:30pm. Priv rm: 30. Valet pkg. V, AE, DC, MC.
Olivier Rœllinger is a great sailor, but even he wasn't prepared for the tempest that broke out when we awarded him a 19.5 rating and named him chef of the year last year. The reservations list just gets longer and longer, and some people are the kind who come just to find fault. In short, stormy weather, and if you're not careful you can capsize. But the Roellingers have kept the barometer pointed to "fair" in their lovely family mansion where even the ducks in the pond look happy. A former chemist, Roellinger converted to cookery when an accident confined him to a wheelchair. Once recovered, he earned his culinary diploma and after stints with master chefs Gérard Vié and Guy Savoy, decided to launch a restaurant in his native Cancale. We are very glad he did. Spontaneous, graceful, revolutionary in its use of spices and herbs, Rœllinger's is the best seafood cuisine we know. There are no gimmicks here. This chef is committed to enhancing—not masking—the pure, authentic flavors of Brittany's bounty. Look into his kitchen, and admire the enormous "pied de cheval" oysters, the shrimps and baby soles caught in the Bay of Mont-Saint-Michel, the briny lobsters, ivory-hued turbots, and firm-fleshed sea bass, the incomparable salt-meadow lamb, milk-fed veal, and miniature potatoes: Rœllinger knows exactly who fished, farmed, or bred each ingredient.
Spices played a crucial role in the history of

Saint-Malo. From these shores sailors departed for exotic lands, to bring back pepper, cinnamon, ginger, mace, and more. Rœllinger employs them with stupefying skill in such extraordinary dishes as John Dory in coconut milk redolent with lemon grass, lily petals, and 14 spices. Sea urchins from the Channel and tiny sea scallops are mingled with edible seaweed, saffron, sumac, cumin, and vetiver in a sauce that is the pure essence of the sea. Tiny skate from Mont-Saint-Michel's bay are enlivened with rum vinegar, ginger, wild sorrel, and peanuts; Breton lobster takes a dip in the Indian Ocean and emerges fragrant with pineapple, vanilla, cinnamon, and pear chutney in a marriage of cultures in which each miraculously retains its identity. But the sea's treasures are not the only ones you find here; Rœllinger also cherishes the herb garden and the farm, whose products are made sublime through divine combinations of flavors. He marries andouille, sea urchin, and fava beans; oysters, chicken broth, reinette apples, and dry cider; tiny potatoes and tiny sea scallops; green asparagus, buckwheat, and haddock; veal chops, cauliflower, and kumquats; and meltingly delicate sweetbreads with licorice. The farm-raised suckling pig with its crispy crust is made unforgettable by its glaze of cinnamon, maple syrup, and elderberry vinegar.
A single meal is not enough to take the measure of Rœllinger's immense talent. And how could one forfeit the chance to sample all of the divine desserts (crisp Breton crêpes with oranges and spiced syrup, apple crumble with cardamom-honey cake ice cream...)? The cellar brims with exciting wines to discover. The service is smooth as silk under Jane Rœllinger's gracious supervision. And when the bill arrives, you'll rub your eyes in wonder—it's light as a sea breeze. **C** 350-480 F. **M** 250 F (lunch).

Les Rimains
(See restaurant above)
Closed Jan 5-Mar 5. 6 rms 650-750 F. Pkg. V, AE, MC.
The Rœllingers have fitted out six lovely rooms in a charming 1930s villa located atop the cliff that overlooks Cancale harbor. Peaceful setting; delectable breakfasts; attentive housekeeper. You have a view of the bay, Mont-Saint-Michel, and La Maison Richeux, the Roellingers' other establishment (see below).

12/20 Le Cancalais
12, quai Gambetta - 99 89 61 93
Closed Sun dinner & Mon (Nov 11-Mar 1) exc at Christmas & school hols. Open until 9:30pm (10pm in seas). Priv rm: 108. Pkg. V, MC.
The covered terrace with a view of the port is the most attractive in town. The seafood on offer is fresh and simply prepared: salmon rillettes, brill with julienned vegetables, and grilled lobster. Small but reliable wine list. **C** 220-320 F. **M** 89 F (lunch), 119 F, 179 F, 250 F.

Le Continental
Sur le port de la Houle, 4, quai A.-Thomas
99 89 60 16, fax 99 89 69 58
Closed Tue lunch, Mon, Nov 12-Mar 17. Open until 9:30pm. Terrace dining. No pets. V, AE, DC, MC.
This mahogany-panelled restaurant opposite Houle harbor has a new chef, Daniel Bry, who as we go to press is in the process of putting

together an attractive menu based on the sea's bounty: langoustines sautéed with gorgonzola, John Dory roasted with veal jus and leek strips, crème brûlée with almonds and candied oranges. Stay tuned. **C** 270-340 F. **M** 130 F, 175 F, 255 F, 375 F.

11/20 L'Émeraude
7, quai A.-Thomas
99 89 61 76, fax 99 89 88 21
Closed Nov 15-Feb 15. Open until 10pm. Terrace dining. Hotel: 16 rms 285-480 F. Half-board 310-420 F. Golf. V, AE, MC.
The *patron* breeds his own oysters and the seafood is always fresh at this cheerful harborfront bistro. Try the sea bass with tomatoes, langoustines with citrus fruits, and the chocolate crêpes. **C** 250-350 F. **M** 95 F (weekdays, Sat lunch), 135 F, 220 F, 285 F, 200 F.

Pointe du Grouin
4 km N on D 201, Pointe-du-Grouin
99 89 60 55, fax 99 89 92 22
Closed Tue, Oct Mar. 17 rms 370-500 F. Restaurant. Half-board 360-435 F. No pets. Pkg. Helipad. V, MC.
A comfortable, tidy hotel located at the tip of the peninsula. TV in the rooms.

■ **In Saint-Méloir-des-Ondes 35350**   7 km SE on D 76

Le Coquillage
Le Point-du-Jour
99 89 25 25, fax 99 89 88 47
Closed Tue lunch, Mon, Nov 14-Dec 15. Open until 9:30pm. Terrace dining. Valet pkg. V, AE, DC, MC.
A seaside bistrot is pretty ordinary fare but a bistrot in a château, that's new! At the Château Richeux, Olivier and Jane Rœllinger have reconverted the ground floor with its stupendous glimpses of the Baie du Mont-Saint-Michel into a simple, clean-lined dining room. There are green wooden chairs, white tablecloths, beach pebbles used as knife rests, and waiters in sailor's blouses to set the tone. The menu is concise, appetizing, and full of bright ideas. The best foodstuffs are treated simply and unpretentiously. We loved the raw seafood platters, duck terrine cooked in a bread oven, tiny stuffed and gratinéed crabs, exquisite andouille with applesauce, John Dory steamed with pepper and edible seaweed, tourte of local lamb with rosemary, and veal kidneys on a spit. The dessert trolley is taller than the excellent little *pâtissier* who crafts the sweets. Exquisite bread; divine salted butter. And the *set* menus are sensational bargains, but so are the à la carte offerings. **C** 200-260 F. **M** 100 F, 158 F.

Maison Richeux
(See restaurant above)
Closed Nov 14-Dec 15. 11 rms 750-1,350 F. Golf. Valet pkg. V, AE, DC, MC.
Chefs who turn their hand to inn-keeping often fall on their faces, but Olivier and Jane Rœllinger have pulled it off brilliantly. This 1925 manor house sits splendidly isolated on a wooded, flower-filled promontory facing the bay. The Rœllingers have, with much taste, managed to give it a family-style atmosphere brimming with warmth and charm. Rooms either look onto the garden or out to sea, all are different yet equally

enchanting, thanks to their cozy comfort and English-style elegance. Jane Rœllinger has succeeded where tried-and-tested decorators have failed. There's a large fruit orchard and a winding path down to the shore. A real London taxi will take you to Cancale. Relais et Châteaux.

Hôtel Tirel-Guérin
3 km S on D 76, La Gouesnière
99 89 10 46, fax 99 89 12 62
Closed Sun dinner off-seas, Dec 15-Jan 15. Open until 9:30pm. Priv rm: 30. Air cond. Heated pool. **Hotel**: *8 stes 570-700 F. 56 rms 270-390 F. Half-board 350-450 F. Conf. Heated pool. Tennis. Golf. Pkg. V, AE, DC, MC.*
A jolly foursome —Roger Tirel and Jean-Luc Guérin married each other's sisters—has been running this establishment for a quarter-century. *Mesdames* greet you warmly in the dining room. The 120 F menu is a good sampling of the traditional cuisine: poultry terrine with foie gras, hake fillet with parsley cream, blue cheese from the Auvergne in a salad with walnuts, and house pastries. Worthwhile wine list. **C** 250-400 F. **M** 120 F (weekdays), 180 F, 210 F, 230 F, 290 F.

CANDÉ-SUR-BEUVRON	41120
Paris 196 - Blois 15 - Tours 50 - Montrichard 23	Loir/Cher

La Caillère
36, route des Montils
54 44 03 08, fax 54 44 00 95
Closed Wed, Jan-Feb. Open until 9:30pm. Priv rm: 20. Garden dining. Pkg. V, AE, MC.
A tranquil, leafy haven in the heart of Touraine, Jacky Guindon's comfortable establishment stands atop a knoll overlooking the Beuvron River. Given a choice, he prefers to cook seafood: sea scallops in a pastry crust with cumin-scented carrots or veal and lamb sweetbreads with langoustines and shrimp jus, for example, and for dessert, grapefruit roasted with orange peel and Grenadine. Fascinating list of Loire Valley wines. **C** 250-300 F. **M** 88 F (weekday lunch), 158 F (wine incl), 228 F, 268 F.

CANET (LE) 13	→ Aix-en-Provence

CANET-PLAGE	66140
Paris 925 - Narbonne 72 - Perpignan 13	Pyrénées-O.

Althea
120, promenade de la Côte-Vermeille
68 80 28 59, fax 68 73 37 27
Closed end Oct-Mar. 48 rms 280-455 F. Restaurant. Half-board 255-342 F. Air cond. Conf. Golf. Pkg. Helipad. V, MC.
Spacious, comfortable, nicely equipped rooms overlooking the sea and Canet pond. Bar; billiard room.

12/20 Le Don Quichotte
22, av. de Catalogne
68 80 35 17, fax 68 73 36 05
Closed Sun dinner & Mon off-seas, Nov 14-Dec 21. Open until 10pm. Terrace dining. Air cond. V, AE, DC, MC.
Simple regional cooking at reasonable prices. Safe bets include vegetable mousse with foie gras, monkfish fillets with vanilla, duck confit with potatoes sautéed with parsley, and an orange douceur with apricot sauce. Try to forget

the decor. **C** 180-280 F. **M** 190 F (wine incl), 95 F, 140 F.

Mar i Cel
Pl. de la Méditerranée
68 80 32 16, fax 68 73 24 52
Closed Nov-Mar. 57 rms 320-500 F. Rms for disabled. Restaurant. Half-board 260-350 F. Air cond. Conf. Heated pool. Golf. Pkg. V, DC, MC.
Located opposite the Espace Méditerranée, this hotel offers comfortable rooms with loggias, as well as an assortment of amenities: exercise room, sauna, terrace swimming pool, solarium, and two bars.

CANNES	06400
Paris 910 - Marseille 165 - Monte-Carlo 52 - Nice 33	Alpes-Mar.

Abrial
24-26, bd de Lorraine
93 38 78 82, fax 92 98 67 41
Open year-round. 51 rms 404-676 F. Restaurant. Half-board 80 F. Air cond. Conf. Golf. Garage pkg. V, AE, DC, MC. **E3-11**
Located next to the superhighway, 400 yards from the beach, this recently built hotel offers bright, comfortable, soundproof rooms with balconies.

Amarante
78, bd Carnot
93 39 22 23, fax 93 39 40 22
Open year-round. 1 ste 590-1,100 F. 70 rms 380-730 F. Rms for disabled. Restaurant. Half-board 480-830 F. Air cond. Conf. Pool. Golf. Garage pkg. V, AE, DC, MC. **D1-16**
A modern hotel decorated in Provençal style, with smallish but very well equipped and soundproofed rooms. Sun room and outdoor pool.

11/20 Athènes
18, rue des Frères-Pradignac - 93 38 96 11
Closed Sun lunch, Tue, Dec 22-28, Jun 8-23. Open until 11pm. Terrace dining. Air cond. Garage pkg. V, AE, MC. **D3-24**
The chef once lived in Istanbul and knows how to mix both Turkish and Greek cuisine. Delicious skewered meats, authentic moussaka and stuffed vegetables. Friendly service. **C** 200-300 F. **M** 98 F (weekday lunch, Sat), 190 F, 150 F.

The Beaches
Lunch only.
Cannes Beach (93 38 14 59 - La Croisette.): Nice and quiet, with fish dishes between 90 and 140 F. Aïoli for 90 F (90 F, 122 F).
Les Dunes (93 94 14 99 - La Croisette.): Family atmosphere, mostly seafood cuisine. Lobster and mango salad, fresh shellfish (68-148 F).
Long Beach (93 38 17 47 - La Croisette.): Family and friends gather for fish soup (85 F), salmon with basil (90 F), and mussel casserole (50 F) (160-210 F).
Martinez (92 98 74 22 - 73, La Croisette.): Not only does the Martinez occupy the largest strip of beach in Cannes, it lays on a lavish Provençal-style buffet in a setting dotted with parasols and a plethora of plants. Dessert buffet open all afternoon (185 F).
Miramar Beach (93 94 24 74 - 67, La Croisette.):

Up-market ambience. The beach mat is free after a meal of fine langoustine salad (110 F) or a whole sea perch (135 F) (200-250 F). **Ondine** (93 94 23 15 - 15, La Croisette.): Facing the sea, near the Carlton, a perfect spot for a lunch with friends. Prices are high, though. (300 F). **Rado Plage** (93 94 20 68 - La Croisette.): Beneath the blue and white parasols, you'll be offered fine seafood and traditional fare: grilled sole (120 F), symphony of the sea (seafood assortment, 119 F), good desserts. Covered terrace in winter. Friendly atmosphere; reasonable prices (200-300 F).

Beau Séjour
5, rue des Fauvettes
93 39 63 00, fax 92 98 64 66
Closed Nov-Dec 15. 46 rms 290-710 F. Restaurant. Half-board 110 F. Air cond. Pool. Pkg. V, AE, DC, MC. **B2-26**
A modern, perfectly equipped residence 300 yards from the beach. All rooms have terraces leading into the garden and swimming pool. Efficient service.

11/20 Au Bec Fin
12, rue 24-Août - 93 38 35 86
Closed Sat dinner, Sun, Dec 20-Jan 20. Open until 10pm. Terrace dining. Air cond. V, AE, DC, MC. **D3-22**
Cheap, cheerful, family-style fare at reasonable prices; too bad there are so many extra-charge items on the menus. Lots of regular customers pile in for the grilled sardines, steak with shallots, and prune tart. **C** 180-250 F. **M** 90 F, 110 F (weekdays, Sat lunch).

La Belle Otéro
Hôtel Carlton, 58, La Croisette
93 39 69 69, fax 93 39 09 06
Closed Sun & Mon off-seas, Jun 11-Jul 3, Nov 1-13. Open until 10:30pm (midnight in Jul-Aug). Terrace dining. Air cond. Valet Pkg. V, AE, DC. **E4-30**
Beneath the low wood-panelled ceiling of a Louis XV dining room that could hardly be less Mediterranean, Francis Chauveau imparts his professional touch to a cuisine that makes the most of premium Provençal produce. The cooking could use a bit more soul, but it's well crafted and opulent. Try the soup of tiny peas with morels, langoustines, and bacon; remarkable Sisteron lamb with stuffed zucchini blossoms and rosemary gnocchi; delicious roast blue lobster with baby fava beans and purple asparagus; Mediterranean skate with aromatic herbs and fried panisses; or the John Dory with baby vegetables and a light jus of sweet peppers and olive oil. Gilles Fallashi is responsible for the superb desserts, like a croustillant of berries with anise. High-class service, of course, and a wonderful wine list. **C** 500-900 F (dinner). **M** 280 F (lunch exc Sun, wine incl), 390 F (dinner), 570 F.

11/20 Le Bouchon d'Objectif
10, rue de Constantine - 93 99 21 76
Closed Nov 15-Dec 10. Open until 10pm (11:30pm in summer). Terrace dining. Pkg. V, AE, MC. **E3-15**
This restaurant-cum-photo gallery provides unpretentious, low-priced dishes like fish soup, beef fillet with morels, monkfish bourride, and tiramisu. **C** 135-200 F. **M** 81 F, 121 F.

12/20 La Brouette de Grand-Mère
Rue d'Oran - 93 39 12 10
Dinner only. Closed Sun, Jul 1-15, Nov 1-Dec 15. Open until 11pm. Terrace dining. Air cond. Pkg. V, MC. **E3-4**
This legendary bistro continues to draw enthusiastic crowds with its single menu: an apéritif with a few pre-dinner tidbits, followed by potatoes à la brouette with a pop of iced vodka, California salad, roast quail with grape sauce, then grilled goat cheese, dessert, and coffee. You may drink as much house wine as you like. **M** 195 F (wine incl).

11/20 Campanile
6 km W on N 7,
Aérodrome de Cannes-Mandelieu, 06150
La Bocca
93 48 69 41, fax 93 90 40 42
Open daily until 10pm. Terrace dining. Air cond. Pool. Pkg. V, AE, DC, MC. **A3-23**
The rotunda-shaped restaurant with a low-key decor, has a big bay window overlooking the pool. Friendly welcome, speedy and dynamic service, a top-flight buffet and careful cooking: charcuteries, fish pot-au-feu, steak with shallots, fettucini with smoked salmon, good cheeses, and tasty desserts. **M** 86 F, 89 F, 112 F (wine incl).

Campanile
(See restaurant above)
See page 95.
Set in lush green grounds, this hotel is located halfway between the airport and the beach. Bountiful buffet breakfasts.

Cannes Palace Hôtel
14, av. de Madrid
93 43 44 45, fax 93 43 41 30
Closed Nov 15-Dec 20. 3 stes 1,200-1,800 F. 99 rms 500-890 F. Half-board 565-620 F. Air cond. Pool. Valet pkg. V, AE, DC, MC. **F5-19**
This modern hotel stands in a quiet residential district 150 yards from the beach. The spacious rooms are perfectly equipped and air conditioned. Numerous facilities; garden.

Carlton
See restaurant La Côte

La Côte

Carlton, 58, La Croisette
93 68 91 68, fax 93 38 20 90 (R);
93 06 40 06, fax 93 06 40 25 (H)
Closed Tue, Wed, Nov. Open until 10:30pm (midnight in summer). Terrace dining. Air cond. No pets. Valet pkg. V, AE, DC, MC. **E4-30**
Chef Sylvain Duparc's lively, fragrant, unpretentious cuisine is responsible for this restaurant's renewed popularity. Try the fresh and vibrant stuffed Provençal vegetables with sage fritters, a delicate and superb first course. Other successes are the perfectly roasted langoustines livened up with just a hint of Espalette peppers, and the casserole of sweetbreads with bacon, baby onions, asparagus tips, chard, and morels, an audacious amalgam of flavors that works. Perfect grilled sea bream, simple and full of flavor. Among the delicious desserts we go for the little tart of wood strawberries, with sublime fruit and a delicious pastry. Magnificent wine list and ideal service: efficient without

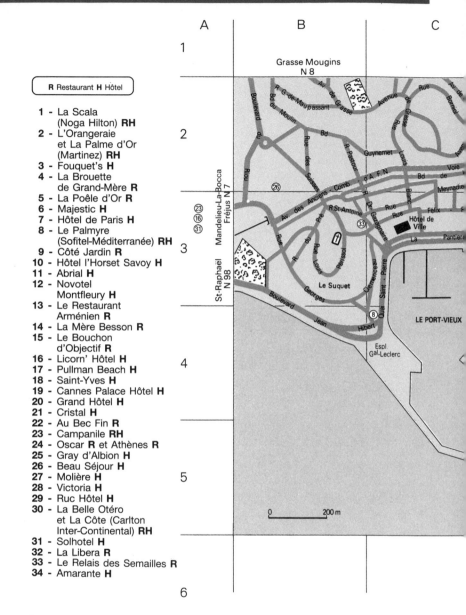

R Restaurant **H** Hôtel

1 - La Scala
 (Noga Hilton) **RH**
2 - L'Orangeraie
 et La Palme d'Or
 (Martinez) **RH**
3 - Fouquet's **H**
4 - La Brouette
 de Grand-Mère **R**
5 - La Poêle d'Or **R**
6 - Majestic **H**
7 - Hôtel de Paris **H**
8 - Le Palmyre
 (Sofitel-Méditerranée) **RH**
9 - Côté Jardin **R**
10 - Hôtel l'Horset Savoy **H**
11 - Abrial **H**
12 - Novotel
 Montfleury **H**
13 - Le Restaurant
 Arménien **R**
14 - La Mère Besson **R**
15 - Le Bouchon
 d'Objectif **R**
16 - Licorn' Hôtel **H**
17 - Pullman Beach **H**
18 - Saint-Yves **H**
19 - Cannes Palace Hôtel **H**
20 - Grand Hôtel **H**
21 - Cristal **H**
22 - Au Bec Fin **R**
23 - Campanile **RH**
24 - Oscar **R** et Athènes **R**
25 - Gray d'Albion **H**
26 - Beau Séjour **H**
27 - Molière **H**
28 - Victoria **H**
29 - Ruc Hôtel **H**
30 - La Belle Otéro
 et La Côte (Carlton
 Inter-Continental) **RH**
31 - Solhotel **H**
32 - La Libera **R**
33 - Le Relais des Semailles **R**
34 - Amarante **H**

being stiff, and children are made to feel welcome. The dining room is an elegant blend of Belle Époque and Art Deco furnishings. **C** 500-600 F. **M** 275 F (weekday lunch, Sat, wine incl), 350 F, 460 F.

Carlton Inter-Continental
(See restaurant above)
Open year-round. 30 stes 3,150-13,200 F. 325 rms 990-3,690 F. Air cond. Conf. Golf. Valet pkg. V, AE, DC, MC.
 The constantly renovated, luxurious rooms are extremely comfortable, and the hotel's thirteen-room penthouse is unquestionably the most "Imperial Suite" on the Côte d'Azur. Superb service; perfectly equipped fitness center.

Côté Jardin
12, av. St-Louis - 93 38 60 28
Closed Mon (exc dinner in seas), Sun, Jan 15-Feb 28. Open until 10pm. Priv rm: 20. Garden dining. Air cond. V, AE.
C1-9
 Come winter, you may feel a bit squeezed in this pretty dining room, but on sunny days head for the garden and Alexandre Walger's cuisine. On the 155 F menu: carrot "cake" with morels,

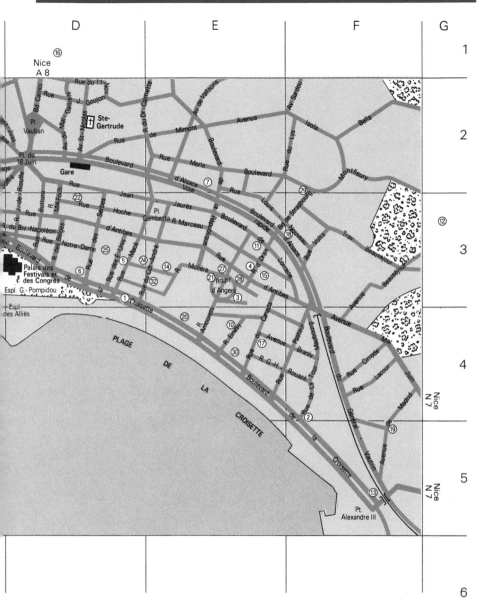

perch fillet with fennel, cheese, and crème brûlée with brown sugar. **C** 180-200 F. **M** 90 F (lunch, wine incl), 155 F.

 Cristal

13, rond-point Duboys-d'Angers
93 39 45 45, fax 93 38 64 66

Open year-round. 7 stes 835-2,000 F. 44 rms 520-975 F. Rms for disabled. Restaurant. Half-board 135-270 F. Air cond. Conf. Heated pool. Golf. Valet pkg. V, AE, DC, MC. **E3-21**
This candy-colored palatial hotel, with its elegantly decorated interiors, provides rather

small, but well-designed rooms with comfortable, modern furniture. The sixth floor boasts a panoramic restaurant and bar, as well as a swimming pool, Jacuzzi, and veranda. Centrally located near the Croisette.

Fouquet's

2, rond-point Duboys-d'Angers
93 38 75 81, fax 92 98 03 39

Closed Oct 28-Dec 28. 10 rms 440-1,400 F. Air cond. Valet pkg. V, AE, DC, MC. **E3-3**
Centrally located, a hundred yards off the Croisette, this uncommonly comfortable hotel

provides daintily decorated rooms with boudoirs and loggias.

Grand Hôtel
45, La Croisette
93 38 15 45, fax 93 68 97 45
Closed Nov 1-Dec 10. 2 stes 2,600 F. 74 rms 550-1,460 F. Restaurant. Half-board 785-1,345 F. Air cond. Conf. Valet pkg. V, AE, DC, MC. **E4-20**
A remarkable little luxury hotel set amid verdant gardens. High-quality reception and service; private beach and park.

Gray d'Albion
38, rue des Serbes
92 99 79 79, fax 93 99 26 10
Open year-round. 14 stes 2,400-5,800 F. 172 rms 590-1,550 F. Rms for disabled. Conf. Golf. Valet pkg. V, AE, DC, MC. **D3-25**
This hotel, though not on the Croisette, offers rather pleasant views of the hills (from the upper floors) or of the sea on the ninth floor where there is a suite with a huge balcony. The rooms are spacious and well equipped, with modern decor; 14 of them were redone this year, as were the meeting rooms and lobby. Direct access to a shopping mall; very chic discothèque ("Jane's") on the premises, piano bar, underground parking. Lovely private beach with a restaurant.

Hôtel l'Horset Savoy
5, rue Fr.-Einesy
92 99 72 00, fax 93 68 25 59
Open year-round. 5 stes 1,370-6,800 F. 101 rms 580-1,420 F. Rms for disabled. Restaurant. Half-board 130-1,250 F. Air cond. Conf. Pool. Golf. Valet pkg. V, AE, DC, MC. **E4-10**
The lobby displays a disconcerting mix of styles, with its colorful antique columns and deep, 1930s–style armchairs. As for the rooms, they are a good deal smaller than one would expect, but thoroughly soundproofed, with marble baths and sea views.

12/20 La Libera
17, rue du Cdt-André - 92 99 00 19
Closed Nov 10-Dec 15. Open until 11pm (midnight in summer). Priv rm: 60. Terrace dining. Air cond. V, AE, MC. **E3-32**
Come here for a relaxed meal of Italian food in a convivial atmosphere: fresh scampi salad with balsamic vinegar, chestnut-flour tagliatelle with tasty and interesting sausages, very well prepared cod à la vicentina. Well chosen selection of wines from the Piedmont. Friendly welcome. **C** 200-300 F. **M** 75 F (weekday lunch, Sat).

Majestic
14, La Croisette
92 98 77 00, fax 93 38 97 90
Closed Nov 13-Dec 27. 25 stes 3,100-11,000 F. 262 rms 750-3,970 F. Restaurant. Half-board 845-3,070 F. Air cond. Conf. Heated pool. Tennis. Golf. Valet pkg. V, AE, DC, MC. **D3-6**
This traditional grand hotel built in the 1920s and lovingly restored and maintained offers an outstanding view of the old harbor. Many rooms and suites have been redone; the top-floor suites, with sublime views, are new. Its new beach restaurant is fitted with a superb landing. Water sports, private beach, golf, exceptional service.

Martinez
See restaurant La Palme d'Or

12/20 La Mère Besson
13, rue des Frères-Pradignac
93 39 59 24, fax 93 99 10 48
Closed Sat lunch, Sun. Open until 10:30pm. Priv rm: 50. Terrace dining. V, AE, DC. **E3-14**
The scent of garlic emanates perpetually from the kitchen of this well-known restaurant. Unvarying *plats du jour* include frog's legs à la provençale, fish soup, Niçois monkfish, veal kidney in aigrelette sauce. Good choice of Provençal wines. The décor is neat and trim, the reception warm. **C** 230-310 F. **M** 130 F (weekdays, Sat dinner).

Molière
5, rue Molière
93 38 16 16, fax 93 68 29 57
Closed Nov 15-Dec 20. 45 rms 360-575 F. Rms for disabled. Air cond. No pets. V, AE, MC. **E3-27**
A conveniently located hotel, not too far from the center of town, offering bright rooms with balconies. Pleasant garden.

Noga Hilton
See restaurant La Scala

Novotel Montfleury
25, av. Beauséjour
93 68 91 50, fax 93 38 37 08
Open year-round. 1 ste 1,500-4,000 F. 180 rms 420-950 F. Restaurant. Half-board 570-1,200 F. Air cond. Conf. Pool. Tennis. Golf. Pkg. V, AE, DC, MC. **A3-12**
Set in the heart of the ten-acre François-André Park, with a view of the bay, this contemporary luxury hotel has unusually spacious rooms, with terraces from the fourth story up. Fitness center on the premises.

L'Orangeraie

Hôtel Martinez, 73, La Croisette
92 98 74 12, fax 93 39 67 82
Closed end Oct-Easter. Open until 10:30pm (1am in summer). Priv rm: 250. Terrace dining. Air cond. Heated pool. Valet pkg. V, AE, DC, MC. **F4-2**
A poolside setting for the more casual of the Martinez's restaurants, which serves the kind of rustic fare that is ever-so-chic these days: skate salad, blood sausage parmentier, "surprise" crêpes. Overpriced wine list. **M** 170 F (lunch).

12/20 Oscar
16, rue des Frères-Pradignac - 93 39 96 00
Open daily until midnight. Priv rm: 80. Terrace dining. V, AE, DC, MC. **D3-24**
In a part of town where restaurants bloom and fade like spring flowers, Oscar has proved a hardy perennial thanks to honest food, affordably priced. The new owner offers sincere cooking like sardines stuffed with basil and veal kidneys sautéed with garlic. Wines by the glass. **C** 150-200 F (wine incl). **M** 100 F.

Plan to travel? Look for Gault Millau's other Best of guides to Chicago, Florida, Hawaii, Hong Kong, Germany, Italy, London, Los Angeles, New England, New Orleans, New York, Paris, San Francisco, Thailand, Toronto, and Washington, D.C.

La Palme d'Or

73, La Croisette
92 98 74 14, fax 93 39 67 82
*Closed Mon & Tue (exc Festival), mid Nov-Dec 20.
Open until 10:30pm. Priv rm: 18. Terrace dining. Air
cond. Heated pool. Pkg. V, AE, DC, MC.* **F4-2**
Chef Christian Willer is Alsatian by birth, but
we suspect that he has the soul of a Southerner.
How else can we explain his profound affinity
for the flavors of Provence? His free yet
authoritative handling of the region's pungent,
sun-kissed bounty makes Willer's cooking the
best Cannes has to offer. With Mediterranean
cuisine now all the rage, chefs everywhere are
tossing olive oil, tomatoes, and basil into their
dishes and calling them "Provençal". Christian
Willer puts such ersatz cooking to shame. The
true spirit of the Midi is palpably present in his
ratatouille with mozzarella puff pastry, John
Dory à la nage with cuttlefish deliciously paired
with grilled artichokes in walnut oil, perfectly
cooked sea perch with a caviar-enhanced potato
crust, red mullet in an infusion of tomatoes and
musserons, and delicious Sisteron lamb roasted
with parsley and green garlic. They lead into a
round of desserts that features a gloriously crisp
waffle topped with berries. But wait, that's not
all: we mustn't forget the impeccable service,
excellent choice of Provençal wines, the truly
sensational all-in set lunch menu, and prices that
are reasonable given the palatial locale. C 500-
850 F. M 295 F (lunch exc Sun, wine incl), 330 F,
550 F.

Martinez

(See restaurant above)
*Closed mid Nov-Dec 20. 12 stes 5,200-13,600 F.
418 rms 720-3,800 F. Air cond. Conf. Heated pool.
Tennis. Valet pkg. V, AE, DC, MC.*
After a period of decline, the world-famous
Martinez, which in the 1930s was a world-
renowned hotel with a glittering guest list, has
undergone a total renovation. Now the equal of
the Carlton and Majestic hotels, it boasts refined
and luxuriously comfortable rooms decorated in
"Roaring Twenties"–style. In the garden is a
sumptuous swimming pool, while on the other
side of the Croisette an elegant private beach is
reserved for hotel guests.

Le Palmyre

2, bd J.-Hibert (plage du Midi)
92 99 73 10 (R), 92 99 73 00 (H),
fax 92 99 73 29
*Closed Nov 25-Dec 26. Open until 10:30pm. Priv
rm: 120. Terrace dining. Air cond. Heated pool. Valet
pkg. V, AE, DC, MC.* **C4-8**
We found the cooking here much more timid
this year than previously, and uneven: bland and
ordinary tomato and eggplant flan, perfectly
cooked skate paired with artichokes, meltingly
tender osso bucco with preserved lemons. One
point less this year. Efficient service, pleasant
blue and ochre decor. **C** 250-300 F. **M** 165 F
(wine incl).

Sofitel le Méditerranée

(See restaurant above)
*Closed Nov 25-Dec 26. 5 stes 1,260-1,950 F.
145 rms 640-1,350 F. Half-board 1,185-1,815 F. Air
cond. Conf. Heated pool. Golf. Pkg. V, AE, DC, MC.*
An attractive hotel, overlooking the old harbor
and bay, with bright and comfortable colonial-

style rooms. Splendid heated swimming pool on
the seventh floor terrace. Warm welcome;
numerous services, including baby-sitting.

Hôtel de Paris

34, bd d'Alsace
93 38 30 89, fax 93 39 04 61
*Closings not available. 5 stes 900-1,800 F. 45 rms
400-700 F. Half-board 85-135 F. Air cond. Conf.
Pool. Golf. No pets. Pkg. V, AE, DC, MC.* **E2-7**
A beautiful, classic dwelling, just 300 yards
from the beach. The nicest rooms look onto the
elegant garden and swimming pool. Effective
soundproofing. Turkish baths, spa, and Jacuzzi.

La Poêle d'Or

23, rue des États-Unis
93 39 77 65, fax 93 40 45 59
*Closed Sun dinner & Mon (winter), Mon & Tue
dinner (summer), last wk of Nov. Open until 10pm.
Air cond. V, AE, DC, MC.* **D3-5**
The Louis XV decor may remind you of a plush
tea room, but the cuisine is serious—in a
strenuously classic mode: poached eggs with
asparagus cream, breast of farm-raised chicken
stuffed with lobster and foie gras, delicate dessert tart. Each month, the cellar features a few
good "special selections". C 350-500 F.
M 115 F (weekdays, Sat), 165 F, 195 F, 220 F.

Pullman Beach

13, rue du Canada
93 94 50 50, fax 93 68 35 38
*Closed Nov 15-Dec 27. 7 stes 870-1,700 F. 94 rms
690-1,230 F. Restaurant. Air cond. Conf. Pool. Valet
pkg. V, AE, DC, MC.* **E4-17**
Just steps from the Croisette, this exemplary
modern hotel features bright and spacious
rooms with all the usual amenities, plus many
extras: video recorders, individual safes, or-
ganised excursions, sauna, bar, room service.

Le Relais des Semailles

9, rue St-Antoine
93 39 22 32, fax 93 39 84 73
*Dinner only. Closed Sun. Open until 11:30pm. Priv
rm: 16. Terrace dining. Air cond. V, MC.* **B3-33**
This intimate, rather posh little spot with a
charming *patronne* features Bertrand Saint-
Vanne's adept cuisine made with splendid
market-fresh ingredients. Try the celery raviolis
flavored with foie gras and truffles, fillets of
Sisteron lamb, and a frozen apricot soufflé with
peaches, nectarines, and almonds. Attractive
wine list. **C** 350-450 F. **M** 150 F, 200 F, 280 F.

12/20 Le Restaurant Arménien

82, La Croisette
93 94 00 58, fax 93 94 56 12
*Closed Mon lunch (Nov 20-Dec 4). Open until
10pm. Terrace dining. Air cond. V, AE, DC.* **F5-13**
Charles Aznavour's favorite restaurant, featuring authentic Armenian specialties. Try the eggplant caviar, cracked-wheat salad, grilled
meatballs with fresh herbs, and mint ravioli.
Good choice of wines from the Var. M 240 F.

Ruc Hôtel

15, bd de Strasbourg
93 38 30 61, fax 93 39 54 18
*Closings not available. 30 rms 290-765 F. Restaurant.
Air cond. Conf. Garage pkg. V, AE, MC.* **F2-29**
Located in a quiet district not far from the
beach, this modern establishment built in an

eighteenth-century style is stylishly decorated with distinguished furniture and fine paintings. Swimming pool; tennis courts.

Saint-Yves
49, bd d'Alsace
93 38 65 29, fax 93 68 50 67
Closed Nov 8-30. 3 stes 500-850 F. 8 rms 250-450 F. Pkg. DC. **F3-18**
An attractive, Côte d'Azur–style villa, with a splendid garden of palm trees. A few suites may be rented by the month or for two weeks.

La Scala
50, La Croisette
92 99 70 00, fax 92 99 70 11
Closed Mon & Tue off-seas. Open until 10:30pm (11pm in summer). Garden dining. Air cond. Heated pool. Garage pkg. V, AE, DC, MC. **D3-1**
You'll find this comfortable, conservatively decorated dining room on the first floor of the luxurious Hilton complex. The Italian-inspired cuisine is generous and full of sunny flavors: vitello tonnato based on good veal (but slightly runny sauce) served with vegetable pasta; penne cooked al dente with pine nuts, olive oil and basil; John Dory sautéed in its juice; berries with ice cream or insipid tiramisu. Excellent pianist in the adjoining piano bar. C 265-320 F.

Noga Hilton
(See restaurant above)
Open year-round. 45 stes 1,600-14,000 F. 180 rms 750-3,190 F. Rms for disabled. Half-board 260-390 F. Air cond. Conf. Heated pool. Golf. Valet pkg. V, AE, DC, MC.
Built on the site of the former Palais des Festivals, the new Hilton offers absolutely comfortable rooms: every conceivable amenity has been provided, including wonderful marble bathrooms. Also on the premises are restaurants, a piano bar, a shopping arcade, and a rooftop swimming pool with a panoramic view. What it lacks in charm it makes up for in comfort. Private beach.

Sofitel le Méditerranée
See restaurant Le Palmyre

Solhotel
In La Bocca, 61, av. du Dr-Picaud
93 47 63 00, fax 93 47 37 33
Closed Nov-Dec. 101 rms 350-740 F. Restaurant. Half-board 110 F. Air cond. Conf. Pool. Tennis. Golf. Garage pkg. V, AE, DC, MC. **A3-31**
A modern building with spacious, agreeable, and well-appointed rooms, most of them with terraces, and a lush park leading to the beach. Stylish, efficient service; bar.

Victoria
Rond-point Duboys-d'Angers
93 99 36 36, fax 93 38 03 91
Closed Nov-Dec, Feb. 25 rms 400-1,200 F. Restaurant. Air cond. Conf. Pool. Golf. No pets. Garage pkg. V, AE, DC, MC. **E3-28**
A modern hotel with quiet, comfortable rooms, located next to the former Palais des Festivals. Pleasant English bar; stylish service.

And also...
Our selection of places for inexpensive, quick, or late-night meals.

Aux Bons Enfants (80, rue Meynadier. Open until 9pm.): Reminiscent of a trattoria, this tiny spot specializes in home-style Provençal food: tomatoes and anchovies, aïoli on Friday, aubergine fritters, and so on. Single 90 F menu.
Caffè Roma (93 38 05 04 - 1, square Mérimée. Open until 10:30pm.): The locals love to meet and greet at this sun-drenched terrace. Try one of the many rum-based punches, and sup on pasta or other Italian specialties at this cheery, crowded spot. Excellent ice cream. Prices a bit high (230-340 F).
L'Éléphant Bleu (93 38 18 70 - 4, rue du Batéguier. Open until 11:30pm.): Thai cuisine is served here in a bright, pretty setting. Authentic fare includes shrimps with Thai basil, fish steamed in coconut milk, beef satay, and a variety of vegetarian dishes (200-280 F).
Le Petit Lardon (93 39 06 28 - 3, rue du Batéguier. Open until 10:30pm.): Bistro-style dishes: a good hors-d'œuvres assortment, daube, red mullet fillets, and authentic pot-au-feu (150-220 F).
Royal Bar (93 39 01 04 - 41, La Croisette.): Don't expect a warm welcome or attentive service, but this is nonetheless a good bet for a drink or a quick meal right on the Croisette (250-280 F).
Le Saint-Benoît(93 39 04 17 - 9, rue du Batéguier. Open until 11:30pm.): A chic little bistrot which works best when the chef keeps things simple: fish tartare, veal kidney meunière. Good regional wines (300-350 F).

■ In **Vallauris 06220**   *6 km NE on D 803*

12/20 La Gousse d'Ail
11, av. de Grasse - 93 64 10 71
Closed Mon dinner (exc in summer), Tue, Nov 13-Dec 12. Open until 10pm. Air cond. V, AE, MC.
A spiffy little Provençal restaurant, where one may enjoy in comfort the owner's generous, skillful cooking: sardines à l'escabèche, rascasse fillet with fisherman's sauce, fresh cream cheese with raspberries. C 190-300 F. M 104 F, 165 F.

Le Manuscrit
224, chemin Lintier - 93 64 56 56
Closed Mon & Tue (exc in summer), Jan 10-31. Open until 9:30pm. Garden dining. Pkg. V.
Once a perfume distillery, Le Manuscrit offers simple, bountiful meals served on the terrace shaded with chestnut trees and parasols, or under the veranda of the spacious winter garden. Try the andouillette sautéed in Muscadet, salmon in Champagne sauce, casserole of veal sweetbreads, etc. It's best to reserve ahead. Short list of reasonably priced wines. Friendly welcome and service. M 95 F (exc Sun), 170 F.

Paris 200 - Dieppe 46 - Rouen 59   *Seine-Mar.*

Le Manoir de Barville
Hameau de Barville
35 97 79 30, fax 35 57 03 55
Open daily until 9pm. Priv rm: 130. Garden dining. **Hotel:** *4 rms 250-380 F. Pkg. Helipad. V, AE, MC.*
Lionel Morin knows how to choose his ingredients—they are always first-rate—and he's already demonstrated that he knows how to handle them with classic skill: snails in garlic

INTERNATIONAL

SINCE 1664

Delicious bonbons made with natural flavours.

In France...

...and all over the world.

cream, monkfish roasted with bacon and cabbage, duck breast with red onion confit. Eclectic cellar at reasonable prices. Charming welcome by the *patronne*. C 250-400 F. M 175 F (weekday lunch), 145 F, 160 F, 200 F, 260 F.

CAP-D'AGDE (LE) 34 → Agde

CAP-D'AIL 06320
Paris 950 - Monte-Carlo 3 - Nice 17 - Menton 12   Alpes-Mar.

 Le Streghe
On the harbor
93 78 39 43, fax 93 41 89 65
Closed Sat lunch, Mon. Open until 11pm. Terrace dining. Pkg. V, AE, MC.
The Riviera's witches (*streghe* in Italian) have formed a new coven here at this lovely harborside restaurant, which boasts a terrace overlooking the waves. The light and interesting Italian cuisine includes wonderful salmon and sea perch carpaccio, fresh salmon with pink peppercorns, veal scallop with sweet Sauris ham, tiramisu. Judicious Italian cellar. The welcome is warm and service attentive. C 300-360 F. M 160 F, 180 F (lunch), 300 F (wine incl), 200 F, 250 F.

CAP-D'ANTIBES 06 → Antibes

CARBON-BLANC 33 → Bordeaux

CARCASSONNE 11000
Paris 905 - Perpignan 107 - Toulouse 92 - Albi 107   Aude

 **Auberge
du Pont-Levis Pautard**
Near Porte Narbonnaise
68 25 55 23, fax 68 47 32 29
Closed Sun lunch, Mon. Annual closings not available. Open until 9:30pm. Priv rm: 30. Terrace dining. Air cond. No pets. Pkg. V, AE, DC.
Olivier Pautard turns out savory, ably prepared regional dishes like duck terrine with grenadine-enhanced onion confit, langoustine ravioli, duck breast with foie gras. Good classic desserts, choice regional wines. Courteous and attentive service. C 270-370 F. M 120 F, 200 F, 250 F.

La Barbacane
Pl. de l'Eglise (La Cité) - 68 25 03 34 (R), 68 71 60 60 (H), fax 68 71 50 15
Closed Sun dinner, Jan 9-Mar 10. Open until 9:45pm. Priv rm: 20. Air cond. Pkg. V, AE, DC, MC.
Chef Michel del Burgo celebrates the sunny, heady flavors of Languedoc and the nearby Mediterranean with the ardent lyricism of a culinary troubador. You too will wax poetic after feasting in La Barbacane's huge dining room, a neo-gothic affair bedecked with fleurs-de-lys and coats of arms. A disciple of Michel Guérard and Alain Ducasse, del Burgo is without a doubt one of the most gifted chefs of his generation. Need convincing? Just try his vegetables simmered with bacon, beef marrow, and daube jus; sautéed foie gras with a liquid polenta containing duck hearts and thigh confit; red mullet with splendid green olives and tomato quenelles; Pauillac lamb with artichokes en barigoule. Anchovies, cuttlefish, tapenade, meat jus, corn:

all combine harmoniously. The cellar holds a fascinating cache of Corbières wines to discover (they are perfect foils for the food), which helps to keep the prices down. A bit. Del Burgo is part of the new generation of French chefs bringing new life to the profession. And the service is above reproach. C 450-580 F. M 250 F (lunch, wine incl), 280 F, 400 F.

 Hôtel de la Cité
(See restaurant above)
Closed Jan 9-Feb 12. 3 stes 1,550-1,750 F. 23 rms 690-1,150 F. Air cond. Conf. Heated pool. Golf. Valet pkg. V, AE, DC, MC.
Extensive restoration accounts for the elegant comfort of the rooms and suites in this gorgeous, thoughtfully equipped little luxury hotel. The grand lounge and library are utterly oustanding. Uncommonly attentive service.

 Château Saint-Martin
Trencavel, 4 km NE, in Montredon
68 71 09 53, fax 68 25 46 55
Closed Wed. Open until 9:30pm. Priv rm: 150. Terrace dining. Pkg. V, AE, DC, MC.
Jean-Claude Rodriguez prides himself on the *soigné* presentations of his flavorful cuisine. Best, in our estimation, are the least complicated dishes: veal kidney with rancio, thyme-scented lamb, duck liver with Sherry sauce. The cellar features regional wines chosen with rare discernment. Beautiful dining room, splendid garden. C 260-350 F. M 160 F, 220 F, 280 F.

Domaine d'Auriac
4 km SW, route de St-Hilaire, in Auriac
68 25 72 22, fax 68 47 35 54
Closed Sun dinner & Mon off-seas (exc hols), Jan 10-31. Open until 9:15pm. Priv rm: 120. Garden dining. Pool. Pkg. V, AE, DC, MC.
A moss-covered manor set in twenty acres of lawns and trees is the distinguished setting for chef Bernard Rigaudis's generous, classic cooking, which you can enjoy in a friendly atmosphere devoid of banquets and conference crowds. His essentially regional repertoire includes salad paysanne with boiled eggs and anchovies, vegetables sautéed in butter, pig's foot in crepinette, rabbit saupiquet with fat French fries cooked in goose fat, veal shanks in mustardy cream sauce, and a hearty cassoulet *maison*. Excellent Languedoc cheeses to savor with a glass of Banyuls, and fine desserts like a classic almond-milk blancmange. Remarkable cellar, featuring uncommon local wines. C 320-400 F. M 250 F (exc hols, wine incl), 450 F (wine incl), 170 F, 250 F, 350 F.

Domaine d'Auriac
(See restaurant above)
Closed Sun & Mon off-seas, Jan 10-31. 23 rms 770-1,300 F. Half-board 770-990 F. Air cond. Conf. Pool. Tennis. Golf. Pkg. Helipad. V, AE, DC.
The comfortable, stylish rooms are gradually being upgraded for added elegance. Delicious breakfasts; charming reception. Relais et Châteaux.

Looking for a city in a département? Refer to the **index**.

Le Donjon
2, rue du Comte-Roger (La Cité)
68 71 08 80, fax 68 25 06 60
Open year-round. 2 stes 650-850 F. 36 rms 290-490 F. Restaurant. Half-board 320-475 F. Air cond. Conf. Valet pkg. V, AE, DC, MC.
A beautiful old building, charmingly restored; the small and very comfortable rooms are decorated with restraint. Delightful walled garden.

12/20 Le Languedoc
32, allée d'Iéna
68 25 22 17, fax 68 47 13 22
Closed Sun dinner off-seas, Mon, Dec 23-Jan 15. Priv rm: 30. Garden dining. Air cond. V, AE, DC.
The Faugeras family take great care in preparing simple, regional dishes (warm salad with quail and foie gras, sea perch roasted with mousserons, stuffed pig's foot, pears in puff pastry), and are constantly improving the restaurant's décor—the flower-banked garden patio is lovely. **C** 240-330 F. **M** 150 F, 270 F.

Montségur
27, allée d'Iéna
68 25 31 41, fax 68 47 13 22
Closed 1 wk in Jan. 21 rms 290-490 F. Half-board 490 F. Air cond. Conf. Pkg. Pkg. V, AE, DC, MC.
A large nineteenth-century manor house updated for comfort with spacious, soundproof rooms. Round-the-clock service. (For restaurant, see Le Languedoc.)

CARDAILLAC 46 → Figeac

CARENNAC 46110
Paris 530 - Cahors 78 - St-Céré 18 - Tulle 58 *Lot*

Auberge du Vieux Quercy ★♥
65 10 96 59, fax 65 10 94 05
Closed Mon off-seas, Nov 15-Mar 15. 22 rms 250-350 F. Restaurant. Half-board 310-330 F. Conf. Pool. Golf. Pkg. V, MC.
Located in the heart of this medieval village, the Auberge provides quiet, prettily decorated, soundproof rooms. Generous breakfasts.

CARNAC 56340
Paris 481 - Quiberon 18 - Auray 13 - Vannes 31 *Morbihan*

Le Bateau Ivre
71, bd de la Plage
97 52 19 55, fax 97 52 84 94
Closed Jan. 1 ste 650-850 F. 18 rms 390-650 F. Restaurant. Half-board 390-590 F. Heated pool. Pkg. V, AE, DC.
A modern seafront hotel with small rooms equipped with kitchenettes, showers, and sunny terraces. Lovely rock garden; decent breakfasts.

Le Diana
21, bd de la Plage
97 52 05 38, fax 97 52 87 91
Closed Sep 30-Easter. 2 stes 1,400-1,500 F. 31 rms 500-1,100 F. Restaurant. Half-board 710-860 F. Conf. Heated pool. Tennis. Valet pkg. V, DC.
This beachfront hotel features comfortable, regularly renovated rooms, some of which have balconies or terraces. Swimming pool and fitness center.

CARPENTRAS 84200
Paris 683 - Cavaillon 26 - Apt 12 - Avignon 23 - Aix 82 *Vaucluse*

Le Coq Hardi
36, pl. de la Marotte - 90 63 00 35
Open year-round. 17 rms 170-310 F. Restaurant. Half-board 270-370 F. Pkg. V, AE, MC.
In the center of town steps from the pedestrians-only section is a former posting inn lovingly remodeled and maintained; excellent quality-price ratio.

Fiacre
153, rue Vigne
90 63 03 15, fax 90 60 51 21
Open year-round. 20 rms 190-450 F. Valet pkg. V, AE, DC, MC.
Quiet, yet centrally located in an eighteenth-century town house, the Fiacre boasts spacious rooms decorated with more than a touch of kitsch. Beautiful garden.

Safari-Hôtel
Av. J.-H.-Fabre
90 63 35 35, fax 90 60 49 99
Open year-round. 14 stes 350-550 F. 42 rms 300-395 F. Rms for disabled. Restaurant. Half-board 340-370 F. Conf. Pool. Tennis. Golf. Pkg. V, AE, DC, MC.
Set in pleasant grounds outside of the town's center, this hotel offers recently remodeled, perfectly equipped rooms. There are also studios to rent with kitchenettes. Fitness center.

15 Le Vert Galant
12, rue de Clapies - 90 67 15 50
Closed Sat lunch, Sun. Annual closings not available. Open until 9:30pm. V.
Some bright watercolors enliven the otherwise plain dining room of this fine old Provençal house. Chef Jacques Mégan's professional touch, respect for fine products, and penchant for straightforward flavors are evident in the generously served 170 F menu that alone earned the chef a second toque: unctuous yet delicate pumpkin soup with tiny bits of bacon and an emusion of hazlenuts, beef cheeks en daube with a perfectly balanced assortment of spices, well aged cheeses, and an amusing cold spelt cream with brown sugar. The menus change weekly to adapt to seasonal market offerings. Good wine list. **M** 170 F, 240 F (exc Sat lunch), 95 F (weekday lunch).

■ In Le Beaucet 84210   10 km SE on D 4 and D 39

14 Auberge du Beaucet
90 66 10 82
Closed Sun dinner, Mon, Jan 17-Feb 7, Oct 10-27. Open until 9pm. Terrace dining. V, MC.
Don't even think about dining (or lunching) here unless you've booked your table in advance. Brigitte Pizzecco can serve only 30 patrons at a time in her exquisite Provençal inn, and her fame is already such that every seat invariably has a taker. Hers is a cuisine full of brawny flavors and heady perfumes. Salad with fresh herbs, rabbit ragoût with tomatoes and basil, good cheeses, and a charming red currant clafoutis are just a few of Brigitte's hearty, heartfelt specialties. Homemade bread and homey, satisfying desserts. **M** 150 F.

■ In Monteux 84170   5 km SW on D 942

Blason de Provence
Route de Carpentras
90 66 31 34, fax 90 66 83 05
Closed mid Dec-mid Jan. 19 rms 250-370 F. Restaurant. Half-board 290-360 F. Conf. Pool. Tennis. Golf. No pets. Pkg. V, AE, DC, MC.
A pleasant family-style Provençal establishment set in extensive grounds, featuring comfortable, personalized rooms. Good fittings.

Le Saule Pleureur   ♦♦
Quartier Beauregard, 145, route d'Avignon - 90 62 01 35, fax 90 62 10 90
Closed Sun dinner, Mon, Mar 1-21, Nov 1-15. Open until 9pm. Garden dining. Pkg. V, AE.
The dining room, though comfortable, is plain; but the flower-filled garden is truly lovely, and now that the terrace is complete, diners may rejoice in the view. Michel Philibert, a young chef of distinction, presents a concise (yet oft-revised) collection of dishes that sing of this sunny land: gratinéed mussels "Suzarella" (on a bed of spinach with aïoli), lamb caillette and chop sautéed with garlic and thyme and served with an unforgettable boulangère (braised potatoes and onions), crispy and succulent oxtail papeton (cooked in a ring mold). Be sure to sample the truffle dishes in season. The 195 F menu is superb. Excellent cellar of Côtes-du-Rhônes. **C** 380-480 F. **M** 195 F, 275 F, 400 F.

■ In Venasque 84210   11 km SE on D 4

Auberge la Fontaine
Pl. de la Fontaine
90 66 02 96, fax 90 66 13 14
Dinner only (exc Sun & hols). Closed Wed, Nov 15-Dec 15. Open until 9:30pm. V, MC.
Housed in a massive eighteenth-century manor in the heart of an old papal village, this charmingly furnished restaurant offers a generous single menu full of hearty, rustic flavors. A recent visit yielded tapenade, mesclun salad with duck liver, fillet of young squab, cheese platter, and choice of desserts. All feature excellent products. Dinner-concerts held monthly. Good wine cellar; affable reception and service. In the Le Bistrot annex, you can sample simpler dishes starting at 25 F. **M** 200 F.

Auberge la Fontaine   ♣♠
(See restaurant above)
Closed Nov 15-Dec 15. 5 stes 700 F. Air cond. Golf. Pkg. V, MC.
Centrally located and pleasantly furnished, with five new perfectly equipped, air-conditioned suites that include kitchens, dining and living rooms, fireplaces, and terraces. Charming atmosphere.

CARRY-LE-ROUET   **13620**
Paris 768 - Salon 51 - Aix 40 - Marseille 27   B./Rhône

La Brise
Quai Vayssière - 42 45 30 55
Closed Sun dinner, Mon. Open until 9:30pm. Priv rm: 80. Terrace dining. Pkg. V, AE, DC.
From the first floor of this nicely decorated restaurant full of plants and polished brass nautical gear you look out over the harbor and bay.

Patrick Barbe's cooking sets to sea and nets all the flavors of the Midi: sea-bass fillets marinated in lime juice, foie gras and langoustine-tail salad, John Dory sautéed with morels, and Belle Hélène for dessert. Short wine list (the prices are fair, though). **C** 300-450 F. **M** 150 F.

L'Escale   ♦♦
Promenade du Port - 42 45 00 47
Closed Nov-Jan. Open until 9:45pm. Priv rm: 90. Terrace dining. V, AE, MC.
Despite the rhetoric from doom-mongers, the sea hereabouts still swims with fabulous fish. Just ask chef Gérard Clor, who likes nothing better than to haggle at the market for flipping-fresh scorpion fish and John Dorys that beckon with their little fins. Carry is also the sea-urchin capital of France, and Clor's cooking navigates these fecund waters like a proud flagship of taste. His loup de velours (boned sea-bass gâteau with a citrus-flavored beurre blanc) is irresistible bait to locals who would mutiny if it were removed from the menu.
Last time we visited we admired the gâteau of boned fish in a citrusy beurre blanc, a treat not to be missed. Ditto for the flavorful snail and garlic ravioli in a light but savory sauce, and the perfectly grilled sea bream or sea bass with fresh vegetables. An assortment of classic desserts is brought around on a cart; note the excellent millefeuille and the chocolate cake. Deep, delightful cellar full of finds, flower-filled seafront setting, seamless service under Dany Clor's baton. In short, true happiness! **C** 450-600 F. **M** 320 F.

CASSIS   **13260**
Paris 803 - Toulon 44 - Marseille 23 - Aubagne 14   B./Rhône

Les Jardins du Campanile
Rue A.-Favier
42 01 84 85, fax 42 01 32 38
Closed Nov-Mar. 2 stes 300-650 F. 36 rms 300-650 F. Rms for disabled. Restaurant. Conf. Golf. No pets. Garage pkg. V, AE, DC, MC.
This hotel, with its garden and swimming pool, evokes a Provençal summer home, complete with bougainvilleas and lemon trees.

La Presqu'île
Quartier de Port-Miou - 42 01 03 77
Closed Sun dinner, Mon (exc Jun-Aug), Nov 5-Mar 1. Open until 10pm. Priv rm: 80. Terrace dining. Air cond. Pkg. V, AE, DC, MC.
Chef Marcel Ricard skillfully perpetuates the updated Provençal cooking for which La Presqu'île, charmingly nestled between sea, pine forest, and cliffs, with a stupendous view of Cap Canaille, has earned its renown. Savor his sea bass braised in Noilly, monkfish in leek cream sauce with red butter, and veal sweetbreads in orange sauce. All very accomplished, even if you might prefer to feast on simpler seafood in a place like this, with such a sublime view of pristine nature. Flawless service. **C** 370-490 F. **M** 240 F, 380 F.

Les Roches Blanches
Route des Calanques
42 01 09 30, fax 42 01 94 23
Open year-round. 5 stes 1,100 F. 26 rms 420-900 F. Rms for disabled. Restaurant. Half-board 670-1,350 F. Pool. Golf. Valet pkg. V, AE, DC, MC.

This agreeable, remarkably well-situated establishment on the Cassis headlands offers small, modern, comfortable rooms. Lovely multi-tiered terraces; sun room; private beach. Note that extensive renovations are in the offing.

CASTÉRA-VERDUZAN 32410

Paris 700 - Toulouse 100 - Auch 23 - Agen 60 - Condom 19   *Gers*

Le Florida

62 68 13 22, fax 62 68 10 44
Closed Sun dinner & Mon off-seas, Wed (in seas), Feb. Open until 9:30pm. Priv rm: 15. Terrace dining. **Hotel:** *24 rms 161-215 F. Half-board 165-222 F. Conf. Pkg. V, AE, DC, MC.*
This is the sort of cozy hostelry where you sit by the fireside, enjoy life, and come away feeling you and the chef-owner are old pals. You'll need a hearty appetite to finish the generous portions of such tasty regional dishes as a foie gras tatin with figs, salmon confit in duck fat with garlic, and a yummy tangerine gratin. Good local wines at bargain prices, superb selection of Armagnacs. **C** 250-350 F. **M** 145 F (Sun, Sat dinner), 70 F (weekdays, Sat lunch), 134 F (exc Sun), 225 F.

CASTILLON-DU-GARD 30210

Paris 690 - Nîmes 25 - Avignon 27 - Pont-du-Gard 4   *Gard*

Le Vieux Castillon

Rue de la Citernasse
66 37 00 77, fax 66 37 28 17
Closed beg Jan-beg Mar. Open until 9pm. Terrace dining. Air cond. Pool. Valet pkg. V, AE, MC.
After the costly restoration of these Huguenot village dwellings with vaulted arches and arcades, diners now enjoy a marvelous setting in which to sample classic cuisine with a muted Provençal accent. Rather ordinary pressed salmon, dryish John Dory in olive oil, but superb squab with foie gras. The chef has ideas, but he does best with classics. Desserts are still a stong point, even though the genius pastry maker who once reigned here has gone elsewhere. The cellar offers a wide range of Côtes-du-Rhônes to complement the cuisine. **C** 400-480 F. **M** 220 F, 280 F, 390 F, 450 F.

Le Vieux Castillon

(See restaurant above)
Closed beg Jan-beg Mar. 2 stes 1,460 F. 33 rms 650-1,360 F. Half-board 1,100-2,260 F. Air cond. Conf. Pool. Tennis. Golf. Valet pkg. V, AE, DC, MC.
Comfortable, charmingly furnished rooms, with a view of either the Rhône Valley or an indoor garden, in a labyrinthine building with walls three feet thick. Relais et Châteaux.

CASTILLONNÈS 47330

Paris 585 - Villeneuve-sur-Lot 33 - Bergerac 27   *Lot/Garonne*

Hôtel des Remparts

Rue de la Paix
53 36 80 97, fax 53 36 93 87
Closed Sun dinner & Wed off-seas, Dec 5-24, Feb 20-Mar 3. Open until 9:30pm. Priv rm: 18. Terrace dining. Pkg. V, AE, MC.
Serge François's original cuisine is on hand in an inventively decorated neo-baroque setting whose dining room gives onto a lovely terrace and plashing fountain. This year we enjoyed his cumin-spiked eggplant millefeuille and langous-

tine tartare with fresh sweet pepper sauce; perfectly cooked fresh cod roasted with pistou and a savory tomato-olive oil emulsion; and slightly oversweet berries in buttery pastry. Eclectic cellar, efficient service, and a friendly welcome. **C** 280-400 F. **M** 95 F (weekday lunch, Sat), 155 F, 195 F, 280 F.

Hôtel des Remparts

(See restaurant above)
Closed Dec 5-24, Feb 20-Mar 3. 10 rms 320-480 F. Half-board 295-340 F. Golf. Pkg. V, AE, DC, MC.
Plumb-line over the ramparts and road, and set in pretty grounds, this nineteenth-century hotel is handsomely furnished and equipped with perfectly functional bathrooms. Reasonable rates.

CAUDEBEC-EN-CAUX 76490

Paris 175 - Rouen 36 - Yvetot 12 - Pont-Audemer 28   *Seine-Mar.*

Manoir de Rétival

2, rue Saint-Clair
35 96 11 22, fax 35 96 29 22
Closed Sun dinner, Mon, Tue (lunch Nov-Apr). Annual closings not available. Open until 10pm. Priv rm: 40. No pets. Pkg. V, AE, DC, MC.
This is an authentic eighteenth-century Norman manor house, with its towers and intricate stone carvings. It was once a hunting lodge, remodeled in neo-gothic style, and has a huge terrace with a spectacular view of the Seine valley and surrounding bucolic countryside. Chef Jean-Luc Tartarin is still winning our admiration. One of Normandy's most gifted chefs, he has great technique that allows him to try all sorts of combinations that inevitably please. This year we enjoyed his papillote of foie gras with truffles and leeks, crispy-skinned bar with balsamic vinegar (the chef has a magic touch with seafood), squab with edible seaweed and a sauce that is an essence of the sea, and truffle fritters with carrots candied in honey. Good cellar, which includes a range of farm-fermented ciders. Youthful, energetic service. Two rooms (handsomely furnished, with delightful views) are reserved for restaurant patrons. **C** 400-550 F. **M** 150 F (lunch exc Sun), 280 F, 340 F, 420 F.

CAVAILLON 84300

Paris 704 - Avignon 27 - Aix-en-Provence 52   *Vaucluse*

Christel

Digue des Grands-Jardins
90 71 07 79, fax 90 78 27 94
Open year-round. 4 stes 600 F. 105 rms 320-480 F. Restaurant. Half-board 320-390 F. Air cond. Conf. Heated pool. Tennis. Golf. Garage pkg. V, MC.
Conveniently situated near the highway, this agreeably modern and functional hotel is fully equipped for conferences. Two billiard rooms; sauna; bar.

Prévot

353, av. de Verdun
90 71 32 43, fax 90 71 97 05
Closings not available. Open until 9:30pm. Priv rm: 25. Garden dining. Air cond. Pkg. V, AE.
Passionately fond of his trade, chef Jacques Prévot is a perfectionist. Every detail of his spruce dining room—the fine china, Louis XVI decor, the attentive service—reflects the same care that goes into the savory Provençal cuisine. Try the

195 F menu: cuttlefish parmentier with a spicy jus, tender and succulent rabbit roasted with artichokes and summer savory, a lovely cheese assortment, and an unctuous licorice-flavored crème brûlée with homemade honey cake. Excellent wine cellar. **M** 130 F (weekday lunch), 195 F, 295 F, 350 F.

■ **In Cheval-Blanc 84460**   5 km SE on D 973

Alain Nicolet
Route de Pertuis
90 78 01 56, fax 90 71 91 28
Closed Sun dinner & Mon (exc Jul-Aug). Open until 9:30pm. Garden dining. Pkg. V, AE, DC, MC.
All the charm of Provence is concentrated in this spot at the foot of the Lubéron, opposite the Alpilles. Nicole Nicolet welcomes patrons warmly into her splendid farmhouse, and watches over their comfort with the assistance of a young, energetic staff.
Alain Nicolet knows how to give a fresh slant to the traditional Provençal repertoire. Seated on the terrace in the shade of olive trees, we gleefully fell upon a salad of curly endive and pig's foot in truffle vinegar, red mullet in pistou sauce with Ventoux spelt, tiny Provençal stuffed vegetables with thyme sauce, fruit fritters, and house sherbets. To drink, the cellar provides delicious Lubéron and Côtes-du-Rhône wines (some served by the glass). **C** 340-400 F. **M** 170 F (weekday lunch), 215 F, 350 F.

CAVALAIRE   83240
Paris 900 - Toulon 61 - St-Tropez 18   *Var*

12/20 Hôtel de la Calanque
Rue de la Calanque
94 64 04 27, fax 94 64 66 20
Closed Jan-Mar 15. Open until 10:30pm. Priv rm: 80. Terrace dining. Pkg. V, AE, DC, MC.
Clinging to one of the most beautiful rocky inlets on the Var coast, this modern restaurant opens onto a stupendous view. The kitchen turns out nicely handled culinary classics which include sea scallops in saffron sauce, squab roasted with sweet garlic (unfortunately the bird was not boned), and chocolate cake. The decor could use a facelift and the prices are rising, but the setting can't be beat. **C** 400-900 F. **M** 150 F, 210 F.

CAVALIÈRE   83980
Paris 890 - Hyères 30 - Le Lavandou 8 - St-Tropez 31   *Var*

Le Club
Plage de Cavalière
94 05 80 14, fax 94 05 73 16
Closed beg Sep 30-May 10. 2 stes. 40 rms. Restaurant. Half-board 700-3,200 F. Air cond. Conf. Heated pool. Tennis. Golf. Valet pkg. V, AE, DC.
A full-dress rehab has restored luster and luxury to this swank seaside residence, which boasts a private beach.

CAZAUBON 32   → Barbotan-les-Thermes

*Some establishments change their **closing times** without warning. It is always wise to check in advance.*

CAZÈRES-SUR-GARONNE   31220
Paris 770 - Toulouse 55 - St-Gaudens 35   *H.-Garonne*

Le Magnolia
6, bd Jean-Jaurès
61 97 02 14, fax 61 90 41 98
Closed Wed dinner, Sun dinner (winter), Mon. Open until 9pm (9:30pm w-e). Garden dining. Pkg. V, MC.
As ever, Bernard Roch combines creativity and absolute precision in his spirited cuisine. Lured by the charm of his little blue dining room set in a corner of a flower-strewn courtyard, we discovered delicious profiteroles of foie gras with balsamic vinegar, duck breast with prunes in red wine sauce, and an apple and Armagnac tourte. Madame Roch is not just an attentive hostess— she's also a knowledgeable *sommelière* who willingly steers guests towards affordable regional bottlings. There's a brand new terrace, too. **C** 200-270 F. **M** 75 F (weekday lunch, Sat), 125 F, 140 F, 170 F, 185 F, 230 F, 270 F.

CENTURI-PORT 20   → CORSICA

CÉRET   66400
Paris 945 - Perpignan 30 - Port-Vendres 36   *Pyrénées-O.*

La Cerisaie
1.5 km on route de Fontfrède
68 87 01 94, fax 68 87 39 24
Closed Jan 4-Feb 3. Open until 9:30pm. Priv rm: 44. Garden dining. Air cond. Heated pool. Pkg. V, MC.
This fine old sun-drenched Catalan dwelling has been upgraded for comfort, and the cherry trees on the terrace reflect the restaurant's new name. Franck Cicognola, just arrived in the kitchen, offers well crafted cooking that is priced high à la carte. Try the 195 F menu: spicy sautéed cuttlefish, tender and tasty young chicken marinated in herbs, cheese assortment that could use some attention, and a delicate pineapple and coconut macaron. The flavors are clear and convincing, and worth the 14 rating. Fine regional wine list. **C** 300-400 F. **M** 150 F (lunch exc Sun), 220 F (dinner), 195 F, 270 F.

La Terrasse au Soleil
(See restaurant above)
Closed Jan 4-Feb 3. 2 stes 1,095-1,195 F. 24 rms 595-795 F. Rms for disabled. Half-board 875-1,075 F. Air cond. Conf. Heated pool. Tennis. Golf. Garage pkg. Helipad. V, MC.
The two modern villas' sunny, pleasant rooms abut a peaceful little park, and offer an outstanding view of the Canigou, the countryside, and the sea. Golf practice green.

Les Feuillants
1, bd La Fayette
68 87 37 88, fax 68 87 44 68
Closed Sun dinner, Mon. Open until 10pm. Priv rm: 40. Terrace dining. Air cond. Pkg. V, AE.
Chef Didier Banyols simply couldn't resist moving into this handsome Belle Époque villa, which was offered to him on a silver platter a few years ago by a food-loving benefactor. His expressive, Catalan-inspired menu is filled with obvious *joie de vivre*, and his motto seems to be "rigor, flavor, lightness". The menu is always full of surprises even for regulars. We recommend that you sample his roast turbot with gentian, chartreuse of celery and purple artichokes,

emincé of duck with cherries, or sautéed cut-tlefish in Punset oil. Or the lipsmacking pig's foot ravioli, or the veal sweetbreads with a ragoût of fava beans and tiny Catalonian peas. Or the red mullet fillets in a Byrrh vinaigrette and fresh white cheese. It's all wonderful. And for dessert, délices de Vallespir, a luscious assortment of delicate, refined, flavorful treats for your sweet tooth. The regional wines are superlative. Friend-ly, family-style atmosphere. C 350-450 F. M 120 F, 330 F, 480 F (wine incl), 230 F, 380 F.

Les Feuillants
(See restaurant above)
Open year-round. 2 stes 700 F. 1 rm 400-700 F. Air cond. Conf. Pkg. V, AE, MC.
A charming little hotel with luxury rooms and suites. Splendid burred-elm furniture and superb breakfasts.

Abbaye des Vaux-de-Cernay
34 85 23 00, fax 34 85 11 60
Open daily until 9:30pm. Priv rm: 400. Heated pool. No pets. Pkg. V, AE, DC.
This beautifully restored Cistercian abbey is a sought-after site for deluxe receptions and con-ferences. Beneath the ribbed vaults of the an-cient refectory, guests dine on Philippe Husser's ambitious, elaborate cooking: sautéed red mul-let fillets with morel-filled puff pastry, breast of roast guinea fowl, fricassée of veal sweetbreads in mustard sauce, a peach poached in wine, and a four-fruit purée. Distinguished cellar; obliging service. C 380-550 F. M 190 F (weekday lunch, wine incl), 200 F (weekdays), 245 F, 285 F, 395 F.

Abbaye des Vaux-de-Cernay
(See restaurant above)
Open year-round. 3 stes 1,580-3,700 F. 120 rms 290-1,050 F. Half-board 490-1,035 F. Conf. Heated pool. Tennis. Golf. Pkg. Helipad. V, AE, DC, MC.
The huge, ostentatiously decorated rooms boast immense bathrooms with copper bath-tubs encased in cane, mosaic, or marble. mar-velous views of the park; impeccable service.

Hostellerie des Clos
Michel Vignaud, rue J.-Rathier
86 42 10 63, fax 86 42 17 11
Closed Thu lunch & Wed (Oct 1-Apr), Dec 21-Jan 7. Open until 9:30pm. Air cond. Valet pkg. V, AE, MC.
As always, the fresh pastel tones of this fashionable country inn, impeccable service, and a warm reception put patrons in a convivial mood to savor Michel Vignaud's creative, seasonal cuisine. Chablis wines find their way into many dishes: the warm pickerel terrine, for example, or the oyster nage, or the chicken jus accompanying the pickerel fillet, or the infusion of spring herbs served with the rack of lamb. The local elixir also makes its mark in the poached grain-fed chicken and the crème renversée. Delectable pastries, superb service, and prices

kept under control (except for the Chablis on the wine list). We're on the way to a third toque here. C 300-500 F. M 168 F, 275 F, 350 F, 420 F.

Hostellerie des Clos
(See restaurant above)
Closed Wed (Oct 1-Apr), Dec 21-Jan 7. 26 rms 250-530 F. Rms for disabled. Half-board 470-670 F. Conf. Valet pkg. V, AE, MC.
Bright, modern, tastefully furnished rooms look out onto flower gardens. Very good breakfasts.

Lameloise

36, pl. des Armes
85 87 08 85, fax 85 87 03 57
Closed Thu lunch, Wed (exc hols), Dec 21-Jan 26. Open until 9:30pm. Air cond. Pkg. V, AE, MC.
This excellent family-owned restaurant, with its ancient walls, antique furnishings, and masses of flowers, is absolutely everything one dreams that a provincial French restaurant should be. It is now in the hands of Jean Lameloise's son, Jac-ques, who is slowly, prudently bringing his father's culinary legacy up to date. Relying al-ways on sublime products, he offers traditional dishes like croustillant of veal sweetbreads with morels, oxtail compote with truffled mashed potatoes, and the best apple tart we tasted anywhere this year. But he has other talents: he knows how to make splendid jus, and can balance textures, colors, and flavors, as in the delightful emulsion of parsley with the snail croustillant or the reduction of carrot jus with the leeks. He creates happy marriages: foie gras with red onion, lobster, and asparagus or, his latest creation, honey cake ice cream. We have to say that we think he should push himself to offer more creative dishes; it's obvious he has a talent for them. But the many fans of this restaurant's traditions can rest assured: the wonderful snail ravioli, young Bresse chicken, and calf's head are still at the peak of perfection. Fabulous cellar of legendary Burgundies. C 360-580 F. M 370 F, 590 F.

Lameloise
(See restaurant above)
Closings not available. 20 rms 650-1,500 F. Air cond. Conf. Valet pkg. V, AE, MC.
Standing proudly on the town square, this fifteenth-century dwelling offers rooms and suites of various sizes, decorated with bright, fresh fabrics, furniture smelling agreeably of beeswax polish, and sumptuous bouquets of white flowers. Incomparable breakfasts. Relais et Châteaux.

Jacky Michel
19, pl. Mgr-Tissier - 26 68 21 51
Closed Sat lunch, Sun, Christmas school hols, Jul 16-Aug 7. Priv rm: 24. Terrace dining. Air cond. No pets. Garage pkg. V, AE, DC.

Every effort has been made to accommodate diners in this beautiful dwelling opposite the church of Notre-Dame-en-Vaux, and they flock here to savor Jacky Michel's stylish, light cuisine. It all works, from the perfect hors d'oeuvres to the tiny pastries served with coffee, by way of dishes that can be rustic or sophisticated, but always rely on top products: a salad of cumin-scented langoustines and potatoes, veal sweetbreads braised with onions and carrots, caramelized strawberries with rhubarb coulis and fromage blanc ice cream. Warm welcome by the *patronne*. The excellent wine list is strong in Burgundies, Bordeaux, and (especially) Champagnes. **C** 350-570 F. **M** 240 F, 320 F, 400 F (weekdays, Sat dinner), 250 F (weekday lunch, wine incl), 150 F (weekdays).

🔼🔼 Hôtel d'Angleterre
🔲 (See restaurant above)
Closed Sun, Christmas school hols. 18 rms 390-550 F. Half-board 490-600 F. Air cond. Conf. Golf. No pets. Garage pkg. V, AE, DC.
A peaceful, modernized hotel, offering large, comfortable "decorator" rooms. Marble bathrooms; excellent breakfasts.

■ **In l'Épine 51460**   10 km E on N 3

🍳 Aux Armes de Champagne
31, av. Luxembourg
26 69 30 30, fax 26 66 92 31
Closed Sun dinner off-seas, Mon, Jan 8-Feb 14. Open until 9:30pm. Priv rm: 200. Pkg. V, MC.
The lovely dining room boasts a wide-angle view of Notre-Dame-de-L'Épine, a superb Flamboyant Gothic basilica—the pride of the village. Chef Patrick Michelon's well-crafted regional cuisine made from first-rate ingredients is good indeed: red tuna tartare with tomatoes and basil, kid roasted with garlic, and a yummy cold strawberry soufflé scented with cardamom. The fine cellar features premium Champagnes (try the one made by Jean-Paul Pérardel) as well as rare bottlings from Alsace, Burgundy, and points farther afield. **C** 350-450 F. **M** 110 F (weekday lunch), 210 F, 290 F, 450 F.

🔼🔼 Aux Armes de Champagne
🔲 (See restaurant above)
Closed Jan 8-Feb 14. 2 stes 1,300 F. 35 rms 380-780 F. Conf. Tennis. Golf. Pkg. V, MC.
Located in the center of town, this hotel provides fully renovated, soundproof rooms with all the amenities, and views of either the village or the garden. Impeccable service.

🍳 Le Moulin de Martorey
Chalon South exit on A 6,
towards Le Creusot, 71100 Saint-Rémy
85 48 12 98, fax 85 48 73 67
Closed Sun dinner, Mon. Open until 9:30pm. Priv rm: 20. Garden dining. Air cond. Pkg. V.
This former mill on the outskirts of Chalon has been extensively remodeled. Some readers find it stark, but we believe its uncluttered spaces are perfectly in tune with owner-chef Jean-Pierre Gillot's cooking. He cleverly selects appropriate

herbs, spices, and vegetables and uses them to transform rather raffish dishes into models of sapidity. Savor, for example, the snails enlivened by their marriage with artichokes en barigoule, the tasty eel and onion matelot in a superb gelatin coating, or the excellent pork cheeks cooked with spices for 10 hours and lightened by a pairing with roast pears. The chef is a master at balancing sweet and sour: lime, wine, and vanilla reduction to sauce a pickerel fillet, and celery with vanilla vinaigrette to embellish warm medallions of lobster. The desserts are to die for: aumônière of prunes and frangipane with a lively verjus crème anglaise, or the fromage blanc sherbet with gratinéed cherries. An added point this year in honor of this intensely flavored cuisine produced with finesse. The serving staff runs as smooth as a Rolls, driven by Pierrette Gillot who also rules the cellar with discernment and proselytic fervor. Sample the Burgundies or Côte Chalonnaise wines with the fine 245 F menu. **C** 300-400 F. **M** 175 F, 245 F, 390 F.

12/20 Restaurant du Marché
7, pl. St-Vincent 85 48 62 00
Closed Sun dinner, Mon, last 2 wks of Aug. Open until 9pm. Priv rm: 30. Terrace dining. Pkg. V, MC.
The kitchen does its best to execute an lengthy, oddly eclectic menu. But the best reasons to visit this narrow little eating house near the cathedral are simple dishes like profiteroles of frogs' legs, sole fillet with haddock, and beef sauced with tangy Époisses cheese. You'll get a very warm reception, and friendly service. In these parts, the "local" wines are Burgundies; and very tasty they are, too. **C** 180-250 F. **M** 80 F (weekdays, Sat lunch), 100 F, 160 F.

🍳 Ripert
31, rue St-Georges
85 48 89 20
Closed Sun, Mon, Jan 2-9, 1 wk at Easter, Aug 1-21. V.
Chef Alain Ripert works in a vigorous, straightforward vein that takes full advantage of the market's seasonal bounty. Each day brings a new trio of appealing set meals that might feature puff pastry stuffed with frogs' legs and watercress sauce, veal sweetbreads with avocado and oranges, and iced nougatine with coriander and honey. Small but interesting cellar of Burgundies. **M** 89 F, 135 F (weekday lunch), 150 F (Sat dinner).

🍳 Saint-Georges
32, av. J.-Jaurès
85 48 27 05, fax 85 93 23 88
Closed Sat lunch. Open until 9:45pm. Priv rm: 95. Air cond. Pkg. V, AE, DC.
Yves and Claude Choux have taken over their parents' well-known establishment, but they haven't altered the charming, cosily decorated dining room cherished by generations of regular customers. Only the freshest ingredients go into Yves's rich, classic cuisine. Tuck into the civet of langoustines and sea scallops, slices of roast duck with poivrade sauce, red wine granité, and apples sautéed with honey and grilled brioche. Or try the friendly bistrot annex, Le Petit Comptoir d'à Côté, for simple dishes at attractive prices. Excellent service; the cellar gets better all the time. **C** 300-400 F. **M** 145 F, 190 F, 230 F, 380 F.

Saint-Georges

(See restaurant above)
Open year-round. 48 rms 270-550 F. Half-board 355-445 F. Air cond. Conf. Garage pkg. V, AE, DC.
This charming, provincial hotel opposite the station offers small but tidy and well-equipped rooms.

Saint-Régis

22, bd de la République
85 48 07 28, fax 85 48 90 88
Open year-round. 38 rms 345-515 F. Restaurant. Half-board 340-550 F. Air cond. Conf. Golf. Garage pkg. V, AE, DC, MC.
A reliable establishment located between the old town and station, with constantly refurbished, nicely equipped rooms decorated in a 1960s style. Lounges; bar.

And also...

Our selection of places for inexpensive, quick, or late-night meals.
Chez Jules (85 48 08 34 - 11, rue de Strasbourg. Open until 10pm.): Fish blanquette, kidneys in morel sauce, and good grilled meats in a rustic atmosphere; low prices (185-275 F).
L'Île Bleue (85 48 39 83 - 3, rue de Strasbourg.): A lively scene come evening, this spot is a good bet for inexpensive seafood (200-250 F).
La Réale (85 48 07 21 - 8, pl. de Gaulle. Open until 10pm.): Traditional, carefully wrought dishes draw a faithful clientele; try the beef fillet with two kinds of pepper or fish mousse with shrimp (85-160 F).

See also: **Chagny, Mercurey**

CHAMALIÈRES 63	→ Clermont-Ferrand

CHAMBÉRY	73000

Paris 560 - Grenoble 57 - Annecy 47 - Lyon 98   Savoie

L'Essentiel

183, pl. de la Gare
79 96 97 27, fax 79 96 17 78
Closed Sat lunch. Open until 10:30pm. Priv rm: 100. Terrace dining. Air cond. **Hotel:** 81 rms 290-450 F. Rms for disabled. Air cond. Golf. Pkg. V, AE, DC, MC.
Opposite the Chambéry station, in a modern dining room with slightly over-the-top decor, Jean-Michel Bouvier offers imaginative, finely crafted dishes based on superb ingredients, like tasty tuna carpaccio, sheep's foot with mushroom fricassée, Alpilles lamb cooked rare and paired with risotto, and luscious warm cherries with bitter almond ice cream. Delicious house breads and extremely fair prices. A few glitches in the service, but all in all, this is an excellent address. C 250-320 F. M 95 F (weekday lunch), 340 F (wine incl), 145 F, 185 F.

Le France

22, fg Reclus
79 33 51 18, fax 79 85 06 30
Open year-round. 48 rms 320-480 F. Air cond. Conf. Valet pkg. V, AE, DC, MC.
A modern and functional establishment, with recently renovated rooms (all air-conditioned and soundproof), some of which boast a mountain view. Bar.

Le Mont-Carmel

In Barberaz, 1, route de l'Église
79 85 77 17, fax 79 85 16 65
Closed Sun dinner, Mon. Open until 10pm. Priv rm: 40. Terrace dining. Pkg. V, AE, MC.
Two minutes out of central Chambéry you come upon this handsome white restaurant whose pleasant, peaceful dining room gives onto a wide terrace overlooking Barberaz. Yves Vincent's cooking is adroit and pleasing: langoustines sautéed with bits of bacon, lamb fillets with coriander and red bean purée, cold strawberry soup with lemon cream. Well-chosen, affordable wines. Friendly welcome and service. C 200-300 F. M 95 F (weekday lunch), 135 F, 180 F, 260 F.

Les Princes

4, rue de Boigne
79 33 45 36, fax 79 70 31 47
Closed Sun dinner, Mon lunch, Jul 15-31. Open until 10pm. Priv rm: 30. Air cond. Pkg. V, AE, DC.
Aided and abetted by a highly professional staff, Alain Zorelle pampers his patrons with a masterly repertoire of updated classics, some of which could use a tad more precision in the execution. This year our preference was the 160 F menu (crab risotto with baby vegetables, Valloire pormonier with a potato galette), the foie gras duos, and the various lobster dishes. Tasty house breads. Admirable cellar. The set menus offer relief from the *carte's* high prices. C 380-460 F. M 100 F (lunch exc Sun), 160 F, 270 F, 320 F.

Les Princes

(See restaurant above)
Open year-round. 45 rms 210-370 F. Rms for disabled. Half-board 370-450 F. Air cond. Conf. Golf. Pkg. V, AE, DC, MC. V, AE, DC, MC.
Situated in downtown Chambéry, this hotel offers 45 mostly renovated, soundproofed rooms, with beamed ceilings and fresh, floral decor.

La Vanoise

44, av. P.-Lanfrey
79 69 02 78, fax 79 62 64 52
Open daily until 10pm. Priv rm: 20. Terrace dining. Air cond. Pkg. V, AE, MC.
Philippe Lenain built himself a handsome outdoor terrace with a view of the park across the way to go along with the comfortable dining room and its Louis XV chairs. As for the cooking, we enjoyed the lamb salad with sweet spices, red mullet with basil, omble chevalier (a lake fish) with melted butter, and whipped pears. Fine cellar. C 300-350 F. M 100 F (exc Sun), 135 F, 170 F, 190 F, 260 F.

And also...

Our selection of places for inexpensive, quick, or late-night meals.
L'Ancolie (79 69 22 98 - 50, av. des Bernardines. Open until 10pm.): Family-style cooking in a friendly atmosphere with fast service: beef with morels, poached eggs vintner's style (100 F).
Le Bistrot (79 75 10 78 - 6, rue du Théâtre. Open until 11pm.): Melon panaché, salmon with basil, and floating island with pralines. Menus between 65 F and 100 F.
La Chaumière (79 33 16 26 - 14, rue Denfert-

Rochereau. Open until 11pm.): A few good seafood dishes are on offer, and a terrace to enjoy them on (130 F).
Le Clap (79 96 27 08 - 4, rue Ste-Barbe. Open until midnight.): Movie posters on the walls, and red mullet fillet with basil and a chocolate timbale with rasberries on your plate. (200-400 F).

■ **In Challes-les-Eaux 73190**   6 km E on N 6

 Hostellerie des Comtes de Challes 🏂🍴
Montée du Château
79 72 86 71, fax 79 72 83 83
Open year-round. 2 stes 720 F. 46 rms 420-600 F. Rms for disabled. Restaurant. Half-board 650 F. Conf. Pool. Tennis. Golf. Pkg. V, AE, DC, MC.
This fifteenth-century castle, set in ten acres, features superb rooms (most have minibars) with views of the valley and the Dent du Chat peak.

■ **In Le Col-de-Plainpalais 73230**   16 km NE on N 512

Le Plainpalais 🏂🍴
79 25 81 79
Closed Apr 15-May 29, Sep 26-Dec 17. 20 rms 200 -340 F. Restaurant. Half-board 225-295 F. Pkg. V, MC.
A chalet at the foot of the ski slopes, with tidy, comfortable rooms and a panoramic lounge. Lovely hiking country all around.

CHAMONIX	74400
Paris 619 - Annecy 96 - Geneva 86 - Albertville 67	H.-Savoie

Les Aiglons
270, av. de Courmayeur
50 55 90 93, fax 50 53 51 08
Closed Oct 15-Dec 15. 4 stes 590-1,070 F. 50 rms 310-720 F. Restaurant. Half-board 445-525 F. Conf. Pkg. V, AE, DC, MC.
For a view of the Bossons glacier and Mont Blanc, for a convenient location next to the lifts, and for amenities like a Jacuzzi, a sauna, sun and fitness rooms, reserve your lodgings at this new four-star hotel.

 Albert-I[er]
119, imp. du Montenvers
50 53 05 09, fax 50 55 95 48
Closed Wed lunch, May 9-18, Oct 23-Dec 5. Open until 10pm. Priv rm: 80. Terrace dining. Heated pool. Valet pkg. V, AE, DC, MC.
Pierre and Martine Carrier have made some desirable changes this year: they replaced the tennis courts with an herb garden (guests have access to the Tennis Club), redecorated the public rooms, and gave the whole place a more contemporary look, while maintaining a local feel. The cuisine remains top-notch: the marvelous "Piedmont, Nice, and Savoie" menu with féra (lake fish) fillet with herbs and wild-cumin-flavored veal jus, duck sausage paired with veal sweetbreads, Bresse squab with goat's milk and lentils, and a cinnamon-spiked apple clafoutis paired with dark chocolate sherbet. Mouth-watering à la carte choices include gazpacho with a gelatin coating made from spingtime vegetables, navarin of Breton lobster and Pied-mont risotto with Fontina cheese, and a luscious

selection of desserts like the dark chocolate "teardrop" in a vivid pool of ethereal gentian cream or a soup of citrus fruits à la bergamote with three kinds of sand tarts. Enjoy this bounty in the bright, panelled dining room whose sweeping panorama takes in jagged alpine peaks. Sommelier Dominique Balson ensures that a corking good time will be had all around, with fabulous finds at affordable prices. C 380-480 F. M 185 F (weekdays, Sat lunch), 300 F, 340 F, 430 F.

 Albert-I[er]
(See restaurant above)
Closed May 9-18, Oct 23-Dec 5. 12 stes 820-1,300 F. 17 rms 570-780 F. Half-board 520-850 F. Conf. Heated pool. Golf. Valet pkg. V, AE, DC.
A friendly, family-style hotel that stands out among Chamonix's finest, with a recently renovated Tyrolean look. The charming rooms are remarkably well equipped, the reception is warm, and the breakfasts (hot rolls, homemade yoghurt, mountain honey) are simply delicious. Relaxation room with sauna and Jacuzzi; driving-range with putting green; lovely flowered grounds.

 Atmosphère
123, pl. Balmat - 50 55 97 97
Closed Oct 31-Dec 15. Open until 11pm. Priv rm: 110. Terrace dining. Air cond. V, AE, DC, MC.
If you can tear your attention away from the splendid view of Mont Blanc framed by the bay window of this warm, intimate dining room (soon to be enlarged, we've been told) you will see that the cuisine is worth your notice: foie gras and duck breast in a salad, escalope Savoyarde, bread pudding and vanilla ice cream. Warm welcome, excellent wine list. C 200-320 F. M 80 F (lunch, wine incl), 99 F, 129 F.

Beausoleil 🏂🍴
5 km NE (N 506), Le Lavancher,
60, allée des Peupliers
50 54 00 78, fax 50 54 17 34
Closed Sep 20-Dec 20. 15 rms 280-540 F. Restaurant. Half-board 280-390 F. Air cond. Tennis. Golf. Pkg. V, AE, MC.
A friendly hotel, set in pastures a few minutes' walk from Chamonix. The owner is a mountain guide.

Eden
2.5 km N, in Les Praz
50 53 06 40, fax 50 53 51 50
Closed Tue off-seas, Nov 3-Dec 3, Jun 1-15. Open until 9:30pm. Priv rm: 16. Garden dining. Hotel: 2 stes 450-500 F. 8 rms 250-450 F. Half-board 280-330 F. Conf. Golf. No pets. Pkg. V, AE, DC, MC.
The chef in this delightfully decorated restaurant offers both elaborate and simple dishes; we prefer the latter. Savor the warm lentil and bacon salad, and slices of rabbit with shallot confit. Appealing regional wine list (good Crépys). C 200-400 F. M 120 F, 150 F, 220 F, 350 F.

Jeu de Paume 🏂🍴
705, route du Chapeau
50 54 03 76, fax 50 54 10 75
Closed Nov 8-Dec 16. 5 stes 1,150-1,250 F. 19 rms 680-970 F. Restaurant. Half-board 575-720 F. Conf. Tennis. Golf. Valet pkg. V, AE, DC, MC.
In the adorable village of Lavancher, Élyane Prache has fitted out a comfortable, intimate chalet with a view of the Vallée d'Argentière.

Handsome furnishings; shuttle-bus for Chamonix.

Le Labrador
In Les Praz, route du Golf
50 55 90 09, fax 50 53 15 85
Closed Oct 15-Dec 8. 1 ste. 32 rms 350-730 F. Restaurant. Half-board 480-720 F. Conf. Golf. Pkg. V, AE, DC, MC.
Situated right on the Chamonix golf course and opposite Mont Blanc, this unusual wooden house features lovely, cozy rooms with comfortable beds and well-designed bathrooms.

Le Matafan   ۞
Allée du Majestic
50 53 05 64, fax 50 55 89 44
Closed Oct 15-Dec 15. Open until 10pm. Priv rm: 120. Garden dining. Heated pool. Valet pkg. V, AE, DC, MC.
His handsome new dining room is spacious and well-lit, the service and reception are perceptibly warmer, and Jean-Michel Morand is more adroit than ever at preparing his regionally inspired dishes, which are more advantageously priced on the set menus. Try the yummy farcement of foie gras with raspberry caramel. Morand's seafood creations are also excellent: a terrine of fresh sardines, a salad of sautéed langoustines with artichokes and fruity ketchup (no kidding), and quick-cooked sea scallops. The cellar offers exciting possibilities from Savoie, Chile, Australia, and beyond! C 300-400 F. M 220 F, 360 F.

Hôtel Mont-Blanc
(See restaurant above)
Closed Oct 15-Dec 15. 19 stes 1,200-1,896 F. 24 rms 548-1,088 F. Half-board 593-739 F. Conf. Heated pool. Tennis. Golf. Valet pkg. V, AE, DC, MC.
A beautiful hotel that is regularly updated, located in the center of Chamonix. In addition to renovated rooms and lovely suites, there is a pretty garden, a swimming pool with a view of Mont Blanc (you can breakfast on the poolside terrace), a sauna, and tennis courts.

Le Prieuré
Allée du Recteur-Payot
50 53 20 72, fax 50 55 87 41
Closed Mar 28-Apr 10, Oct 2-Dec 19. 14 stes 500-700 F. 77 rms 368-776 F. Restaurant. Half-board 368-528 F. Conf. Golf. Pkg. V, AE, DC, MC.
This elegant chalet overlooking Chamonix offers bright, spacious rooms with balconies that face Mont Blanc (for the best view, reserve an upper-floor room). Free shuttle-bus to ski slopes; friendly reception.

La Sapinière
102, rue Mummery
50 53 07 63, fax 50 53 10 14
Closed Apr 18-Jun 12, Sep 25-Dec 21. 30 rms 420-590 F. Restaurant. Half-board 375-440 F. Golf. Garage pkg. V, AE, DC, MC.
A large, quiet house with a garden, this hotel is located a few minutes from the center of town and the Brévent lift. The rooms are comfortable and decorated with restraint, and most have a balcony facing Mont Blanc. Sauna; billiard room.

---

*The **prices** in this guide reflect what establishments were charging at press time.*

And also...
Our selection of places for inexpensive, quick meals.
Le Chaudron (50 53 40 34 - 79, rue des Moulins. Open until 11pm.): In a pleasant little street near the guides' center, a wood-and-stone establishment where you can sample typical local specialties (reblochonnade, tartiflette, fondues) (150-250 F).
L'Impossible (50 53 20 36 - 9, chemin Cry. Open until 11:30pm.): Rustic decor, regional costumes, and, of course, Savoyard cooking: pela, reblochonnade, and steaks cooked on a stone griddle; warm welcome (150-220 F).
Peter Pan (50 54 40 63 - Côte Chavants, in Les Houches. Open until 9pm.): An authentic farmhouse serving equally genuine Savoyard dishes (180 F).
Le Sarpe (50 53 29 31 - 30, passage Mottets. Open until 9:30pm.): Good traditional and Savoyard cooking (Vacherin cheese with potatoes and country ham) (150-230 F).

Paris 464 - Périgueux 33 - Brantôme 6 - Nontron 22   *Dordogne*

Moulin du Roc   ۞
Lieu-dit Moulin du Roc
53 54 80 36, fax 53 54 21 31
Closed Tue, Jan 15-Feb 15, Nov 15-Dec 15. Open until 9:30pm. Priv rm: 20. Garden dining. Heated pool. Pkg. V, AE, DC, MC.
An old ivy-covered mill house set in an exuberantly lush green garden by the River Dronne, the Moulin du Roc is the most eccentrically baroque restaurant imaginable. Past the first shock, one inevitably succumbs to the charm of Lucien Gardillou's welcome, and even more willingly to the charms of the cuisine, the work of Solange Gardillou. She produces some wonderful dishes with a regional accent: homemade breads, fine foie gras, and smoked duck breast with lamb's lettuce salad. But other dishes didn't come up to scratch (and lost the restaurant a point this year): bland périgourdine tourte, overcooked duck breast in salt crust, and inadequate desserts. The cellar is rich in reasonably priced Bordeaux, but no one helps you select them. C 280-420 F. M 150 F (weekday lunch, wine incl), 200 F, 280 F.

Moulin du Roc
(See restaurant above)
Closed Jan 15-Feb 15, Nov 15-Dec 15. 4 stes 680 F. 10 rms 380-600 F. Half-board 550-670 F. Heated pool. Tennis. Golf. Pkg. Helipad. V, AE, DC, MC.
Beneath the beautiful beams and antiquated gears of this converted walnut-oil mill, guests are lodged in dainty and exceptionally comfortable rooms furnished with antiques. Gorgeous breakfasts. Reserve well in advance.

CHAMPAGNE-AU-MONT-D'OR 69 → **Lyon**

CHAMPIGNY 51   → **Reims**

CHAMPILLON 51   → **Épernay**

CHAMPTOCEAUX 49   **Nantes**

CHANCELADE 24 → Périgueux

CHANTEMERLE 05 → Serre-Chevalier

CHANTILLY 60500
Paris 42 - Compiègne 45 - Pontoise 36 - Senlis 10   *Oise*

Le Relais Condé

42, av. du Mal-Joffre - 44 57 05 75
Closed Mon dinner & Tue (exc hols). Open until 10pm. Garden dining. V, AE, MC.
The somber interior of this nineteenth-century former Anglican chapel could use some livening up, but Jacques Legrand's well-crafted cooking is a sure value, although he goes a bit overboard with cream: warm duck sausage with a hazelnut-sprinkled salad, turbot with allspice, and pear tourte. Charming welcome. C 300-370 F. M 155 F, 280 F.

■ In **Coye-la-Forêt 60580**   8 km SE

12/20 Les Étangs
1, rue Clos-des-Vignes
44 58 60 15, fax 44 58 75 95
Closed Mon dinner, Tue, Jan 15-Feb 15. Open until 9:30pm. Priv rm: 65. Garden dining. Pkg. V, AE, DC, MC.
Summer visitors should slip under the bower that leads to an adorable garden to enjoy the slightly conventional but well executed cuisine. This year, try the foie gras sautéed with apples and honey, mushrooms in puff pastry with garlic cream, braised snails, and veal tongue and head with ravigote sauce. C 270-320 F. M 200 F (Sun, wine incl), 150 F, 270 F.

■ In **Gouvieux 60270**   3 km W on D 909

⌂⌂ Château de Montvillargenne ♠♣
Av. F.-Mathet
44 57 05 14, fax 44 57 28 97
Open year-round. 10 stes 240-980 F. 138 rms 240-980 F. Rms for disabled. Restaurant. Heated pool. Tennis. Golf. Garage pkg. V, AE, DC, MC.
Set in extensive grounds, this magnificent nineteenth-century castle boasts warm wood paneling and elegant lounges. Renovated, well-equipped, smallish rooms and various leisure facilities.

■ In **Lamorlaye 60260**   7 km S on N 16

⌂⌂ Hostellerie du Lys ♠♣
In Lys-Chantilly, 63, 7e-Avenue
44 21 26 19, fax 44 21 28 19
Open year-round. 35 rms 195-500 F. Restaurant. Half-board 368-740 F. Golf. Pkg. V, AE, DC, MC.
Situated in a large park, this opulent country inn provides comfortable rooms in a friendly, restful atmosphere. Tennis courts, golf course, and swimming pool are all within easy reach.

> ♠♣
> *This symbol signifies hotels that are exceptionally quiet.*

■ In **Montgrésin 60560**   8 km SE on D 924

12/20 Relais d'Aumale
37, pl. des Fêtes
44 54 61 31, fax 44 54 69 15
Closed Dec 23-30. Open until 10pm. Priv rm: 45. Garden dining. Pkg. V, AE, DC, MC.
Much in favor with the racing set, this bright and comely restaurant features a huge fireplace features satisfying dishes like cèpe and Burgundian snail caviar, fricassée of young Bresse chicken, and pear croustillant. Lovely terrace. C 275-380 F. M 190 F (weekday lunch, Sat, Sun dinner), 210 F (weekday dinner, Sat, Sun lunch).

⌂⌂ Relais d'Aumale ♠♣
(See restaurant above)
Open year-round. 2 stes 700-900 F. 22 rms 450-520 F. Half-board 460-490 F. Conf. Tennis. Golf. Pkg. V, AE, DC, MC.
The Relais's bright rooms look out on the Chantilly forest; restful nights are assured in this comfortable, contemporary setting.

CHAPELLE-SAINT-MESMIN (LA) 45 → Orléans

CHARLEVILLE-MÉZIÈRES 08000
Paris 235 - Metz 160 - Nancy 205 - Reims 82   *Ardennes*

12/20 La Cigogne
40, rue Dubois-Crancé - 24 33 25 39
Closed Sun dinner, Mon, 1 wk in Aug. Open until 10pm. Priv rm: 40. Pkg. V, MC.
This unpretentious but pleasant little restaurant with cozy, provincial decor offers generous dishes like those on the second set menu: skate in hazelnut butter and a sherbet made from Marc de Champagne. The third menu is very good, too. Well chosen wine list. C 200-300 F. M 78 F, 98 F, 140 F.

⌂⌂ Le Clèves
43, rue de l'Arquebuse
24 33 10 75, fax 24 59 01 25
Open year-round. 47 rms 245-380 F. Restaurant. Half-board 270-375 F. Golf. Pkg. V, AE, DC, MC.
Located between the railway station and Place Ducale, this hotel offers fairly quiet, modernized rooms. Groups welcome. Pub on the premises.

La Côte à l'Os

11, cours A.-Briand
24 59 20 16, fax 24 59 48 30
Open daily until 11pm. Priv rm: 70. Terrace dining. Pkg. V, AE, DC, MC.
Richard Soidez looks to sea for his culinary inspiration, but nonetheless knows how to seduce landlubbers. Sample the sea scallops with chicken jus, pickerel fillet with beef marrow, duck foie gras terrine with Sauternes gelatin, and pork shanks with green cabbage. Generous set menus. Detailed, affordable wine list. The long, wood-panelled dining room is filled with of flowers and plants. C 220-350 F. M 160 F (wine incl), 76 F, 89 F, 130 F.

CHARMES-SUR-RHÔNE 07 → Valence

CHAROLLES 71120
Paris 370 - Autun 78 - Mâcon 55 - Roanne 59   Saône/Loire

(13) Moderne
Ex av. de la Gare, 14, av. J.-Furtin
85 24 07 02, fax 85 24 05 21
Closed Sun dinner & Mon off-seas, Dec 27-beg Feb.
Open until 9pm. Priv rm: 25. Pool. Pkg. V, AE, MC.
This quintessential restaurant de province faces
the (more or less defunct) railway station. Everything is where it should be, all is authentic—except the unfortunate artificial flowers! Never
mind. The cooking is generously served but
could use some fine-tuning: good local ham,
overcooked fresh salmon with over-rich sauce,
rather bland steak with marchand de vin sauce
served with good vegetables. A point less this
year. Interesting cellar, warm welcome, inex-
perienced service. C 260-360 F. M 110 F (exc
Sun lunch), 170 F, 210 F, 290 F.

Moderne
(See restaurant above)
See restaurant for closings. 17 rms 250-450 F. Half-
board 310-450 F. Conf. Pool. Golf. Pkg. V, AE, MC.
Most of the rooms have been remodeled to
meet functional Moderne standards, but a few
unrenovated units remain for lovers of the old-
fashioned market-town atmosphere.

CHARTRES 28000
Paris 96 - Orléans 72 - Dreux 35 - Evreux 77   Eure-et-Loir

(13) Le Buisson Ardent
10, rue au Lait - 37 34 04 66
Closed Sun dinner. Open until 9:30pm. V, MC.
To judge by this restaurant's location in the
shadow of the cathedral, one is likely to expect
yet another tourist eatery with stratospheric
prices. Not at all. The menu features nicely
crafted dishes made from fresh market produce:
sautéed langoustines with broccoli, warm foie
gras with raspberries, veal kidney with shallot
cream, and a crispy apple dessert with Calvados-
enhanced butter. Courteous, lively service,
reasonable selection of wines. C 280-320 F.
M 108 F (exc Sat dinner), 158 F, 188 F, 245 F.

11/20 Café Serpente
2, cloître Notre-Dame - 37 21 68 81
Open daily until 11:30pm. Terrace dining. V, MC.
This is the most popular bistro in town, with an
authentic cosmopolitan atmosphere. Good-
humored waitresses serve up amazingly copious
portions of homestyle cooking (grilled veal kidney with mustard sauce, veal birds, etc.). Attractive prices, quick service, open late. Don't miss
it. C 180-260 F.

Mercure
6, av. Jehan-de-Beauce
37 21 78 00, fax 37 36 23 01
Open year-round. 48 rms 380-480 F. Rms for disabled. Conf. Garage pkg. V, AE, DC, MC.
Situated next to the railway station, some 300
meters from the cathedral, this hotel offers comfortable rooms, most of which look onto an
indoor garden.

Novotel
Av. M.-Proust
37 34 80 30, fax 37 30 29 56
Open year-round. 78 rms 390-470 F. Rms for disabled. Restaurant. Pool. Golf. Pkg. V, AE, DC, MC.
This modern, functional hotel is located in a
leafy setting and offers regularly refurbished
rooms. Bar and terrace.

(14) La Truie qui File
Pl. de la Poissonnerie - 37 21 53 90
Closed Sun dinner, Mon, Sep 15-Oct 15. Open until
9:30pm. No pets.
Nicely restored by the town council, this centuries-old hostelry lined with medieval paneling
is looking good these days (though some
touches are rather chilly). No matter. Gilles
Choukroun offers cuisine that is on its way up,
although sometimes a bit hesitant as far as flavor
combinations go, particularly the warm mackerel tart with balsamic vinegar and the fresh cod
steamed with herbs and chicory. But the salmon
roasted in its skin and the oxtail confit simmered
for twelve hours are real winners. Geneviève
Choukroun offers a smiling welcome. Attentive
service, enticing wine list with many fine bottlings from the Loire. C 320-400 F. M 150 F,
240 F, 320 F.

(13) La Vieille Maison
5, rue au Lait - 37 34 10 67
Closed Sun dinner, Mon. Open until 9:30pm. Priv
rm: 15. V, AE, MC.
Bruno Letartre learned his trade at the Grand
Monarque and is trying to turn this venerable
establishment into Chartres's best. Set in the old
town, at the foot of the cathedral, the elegant
decor boasts beamed ceilings and ancient
stones. Letartre's cuisine is good indeed, in spite
of the occasional false step: langoustine gaufrettes and fresh herb salad, sliced farm-raised squab
and fresh pasta with basil, and a delicate apple
tart served with cinnamon ice cream. Costly
wine list. C 380 F. M 145 F, 225 F, 325 F.

And also...
Our selection of places for inexpensive, quick,
or late-night meals.
Le Minou (37 21 10 68 - 4, rue de Lattre-de-Tassigny. Open until 9pm.): A family-run restaurant
frequented by faithful regulars; a lively ambience
assured (150-180 F).
Le Pichet (37 21 08 35 - 19, rue du Cheval-
Blanc. Open until 9:30pm.): Classic cuisine,
country wines in the neighborhood of the
cathedral (110-160 F).
La Taverne (37 34 88 57 - 8, rue Porte-
Cendreuse.): Seafood is the specialty here; sparkling raw shellfish assortments (200 F).
Le Tripot (37 36 60 11 - 11, pl. J.-Moulin.): A
quiet, rustic spot offering good value for money
(100-150 F).

■ In Nogent-le-Phaye 28630   8 km E on D 4

12/20 Relais de la Tour
N 10, Le Bois-Paris - 37 31 69 79
Closed Tue dinner, Wed. Open until 10pm. Air cond.
Garage pkg. V.
The pleasant service helps customers forget
the noisy highway and boring decor, and con-

centrate on the generous portions of duck foie gras, salmon tartare, Alsatian-style snails, and fish choucroute, all well prepared and served by a friendly staff. **C** 200-280 F. **M** 250 F (exc Sun dinner, wine incl), 86 F, 136 F, 188 F, 195 F (exc Sun dinner), 250 F.

■ **In St-Prest 28300**   10 km NE on N 154 and D 6

Le Manoir des Près du Roy ▲♥
37 22 22 27, fax 37 22 24 92
Open year-round. 20 rms 350-550 F. Restaurant. Half-board 400-575 F. Conf. Tennis. Golf. Pkg. Helipad. V, MC.
A fine weekend escape from Paris, for relaxing or for conferences. The 40-acre estate provides golf and tennis facilities, and the spacious, quiet, inviting rooms offer fresh flowers, beams, and fine views of the landscape. Even the older guest rooms have considerable charm.

■ **In Thivars 28630**   7 km S on N 10

La Sellerie
48, rue Nationale - 37 26 41 59
Closed Mon dinner, Tue, Aug 4-24. Open until 9:30pm. Priv rm: 40. Terrace dining. Pkg. V.
Imagination is not Martial Heitz's strong point, but this traditional cuisine is elegant and well prepared. The smiling welcome and excellent Bordeaux add to the enjoyment of rabbit rillettes and carrot confit, sole fillet with asparagus tips, and chocolate soufflé. The decor mixes refinement with rustic charm, and there's a pleasant garden for summer lunches. Good choice of Bordeaux and some wines served by the glass. **C** 280-400 F. **M** 98 F (exc Sun), 135 F, 280 F.

CHASSELAY   69380
Paris 448 - Lyon 22 - Villefranche-sur-S. 15 - L'Arbresle 14   *Rhône*

Guy Lassausaie
Rue Belle-Cize
78 47 62 59, fax 78 47 06 19
Closed Tue dinner, Wed, Aug. Open until 9:15pm. Priv rm: 30. Pkg. V, AE, DC, MC.
When Lyon's food-lovers need a break from their urban routine, they book a table at this pretty, rustic restaurant just twenty kilometers out of town. Guy Lassausaie serves them spirited cuisine with inspired flavor combinations, produced with precise technique. This year we enjoyed the Burgundy snails with pig's foot, chestnut and black caraway seed jus, and foie gras flan with a salad enlivened by walnut oil; roast sea scallops with an intensely flavored seafood butter; squab cooked over fragrant hay and paired with shitake mushrooms; and a luscious chocolate manjari with orange-ginger sauce. Everything Lassausaie prepares is harmonious, never over-the-top. Charming service, and an excellent wine list. The only quibble we have is that the pretty dining room is within a village house that lacks a garden. An extra point this year. **C** 250-350 F. **M** 150 F, 200 F, 290 F, 380 F.

CHASSENEUIL-DU-POITOU 86 → Poitiers

CHÂTEAU-ARNOUX   04160
Paris 717 - Digne 25 - Sisteron 14 - Manosque 38   *Alpes/H.-P.*

La Bonne Étape ♛
Chemin du Lac
92 64 00 09, fax 92 64 37 36
Closed Sun dinner & Mon off-seas, Jan 5-Feb 16. Open until 9:30pm. Priv rm: 25. Air cond. Heated pool. Valet pkg. V, AE, DC, MC.
The Gleize family is altogether too modest. Their charming restaurant is much more than just *bonne*. We think it should be a required stopover on any gastronomic itinerary.
Pierre Gleize and his son Jany, who is gradually taking over here, are passionate about Provence; Pierre knows every local farmer and grower who has provided the kitchen its superb products, and can even point you to must-see attractions in the area (don't miss the Ganagobie priory). Mama Gleize charmingly oversees the front of the house, while Jany is adding a few of his own original dishes to a menu still filled with traitional favorltes. This year we reveled in the exquisite foie gras with potatoes, truffles, and Jerusalem artichokes; the sensational cold fish soup à la brandade with an intense flavor enhanced by almonds; an astonishing sole with a sauce made from Fernet-Branca; a thigh of young rabbit cooked with rosemary, lemon, and green cabbage; and a memorable sautéed lamb fillet redolent of all the herbs of Provence. Superb local goat cheeses, sublime desserts (whatever you do, don't miss the lavender-honey ice cream), and a stupendous cellar holding the likes of a Château Simone blanc de blanc, a 1986 La Migona Bandol from Domaine Tempier, or a little Provençal wine, Clos d'Ière. Amazingly low prices, especially the 190 F menu. **C** 300-500 F. **M** 590 F (wine incl), 190 F, 325 F, 390 F, 490 F.

La Bonne Étape
(See restaurant above)
See restaurant for closings. 7 stes 720-1,400 F. 11 rms 400-900 F. Air cond. Conf. Heated pool. Golf. Valet pkg. Helipad. V, AE, DC, MC.
Pretty, quiet rooms with period Provençal furnishings overlook a swimming pool and garden. Magnificent breakfasts featuring yummy homemade jams. Warm, hospitable service. Relais et Châteaux.

CHÂTEAUBOURG   35220
Paris 330 - Laval 50 - Rennes 20 - Vitré 15   *Ille/Vil.*

Ar Milin'
30, rue de Paris
99 00 30 91, fax 99 00 37 56
Closed Sun dinner off-seas, Dec 23-Jan 2. Open until 9:15pm. Terrace dining. Pkg. V, AE, DC, MC.
A big old mill, an immense park with a river running through it, a bright veranda dining room served by experienced staff: such is the setting for pleasant meals that may, on a given day, feature curried mussels in puff pastry, a galette of salmon and turnip confit, and a meringué with apples. Excellent reception; conference facilities. **C** 200-300 F. **M** 150 F (Sat dinner, Sun lunch), 95 F, 138 F (weekdays, Sat lunch), 190 F.

Ar Milin'
(See restaurant above)
Closed Dec 23-Jan 2. 1 ste 625-665 F. 30 rms 310-540 F. Half-board 380 F. Conf. Tennis. Pkg. Helipad. V, AE, DC, MC.
The more charming among the hotel's well-kept rooms are in the mill and have a view of the river. The others, recently renovated in "modern motel" style, are set in the park.

CHÂTEAUGIRON 35
→ **Rennes**

CHÂTEAUNEUF 71740
Paris 390 - Roanne 30 - Charolles 30   *Saône/Loire*

 La Fontaine
85 26 26 87
Closed Tue dinner, Wed, Jan 23-Feb 17, Nov 15-22. Open until 9pm. Pkg. V, MC.
Behind the banal exterior of this village restaurant lies an extravagant decor of pink-and-pistachio-colored mosaics capped by a pyramidal glass skylight. Therein chef Yves Jury serves an ever-changing array of inventive, full-flavored dishes inspired by his mood and by what looks good at the market, and offered at unbelieveably modest prices. Treat yourself to boned oxtail with vegetables, local veal with braised lettuce scented with rosemary, pike fillet with beurre blanc, or crab-stuffed cannelloni with black olive sauce. Or indulge in foie gras and lobster. Admirable simplicity characterizes the desserts: honey cake with vanilla mousseline, licorice-scented crème brûlée with seasonal fruits, and a grapefruit gratin with a luscious honey-Rivesaltes sabayon. It's all excellent, as is the cellar, which contains many half bottles. Fine service directed by Madame Jury. C 280-350 F. M 115 F (exc Sun), 150 F, 185 F, 270 F, 330 F.

CHÂTEAUNEUF-EN-THYMERAIS 28170
Paris 104 - Chartres 25 - Dreux 21 - Châteaudun 64   *Eure-et-Loir*

Auberge Saint-Jean
4 km N on D 928, St-Jean-de-Rebervilliers
37 51 62 83, fax 37 51 84 52
Closed dinner Sun & Thu, Fri, Mar 15-Apr 7, Sep 14-Oct 6. Open until 9pm. Priv rm: 16. Garden dining. Pkg. V, AE, DC, MC.
This rustico-chic country *auberge* with an enormous open hearth and beamed ceilings is still a soothing setting for Pierre Aubry's traditional, carefully prepared dishes like fresh morels in a casserole, salad of Breton lobster, turbot with a meat jus, and a fruit croustillant for dessert. Prompt service. C 250-320 F. M 140 F (weekday lunch, 165 F, 215 F.

CHÂTEAUNEUF-LE-ROUGE 13
→ **Aix-en-Provence**

Gault Millau's ratings are based solely on the restaurants' cuisine. We do not take into account the atmosphere, décor, service, and so on; these are commented upon within the review.

CHÂTEAUROUX 36000
Paris 250 - Tours 109 - Bourges 65 - Vierzon 57   *Indre*

12/20 La Ciboulette
42, rue Grande - 54 27 66 28
Closed Sun, Mon, hols, Jan 8-31, Jul 30-Aug 23. Open until 10pm. Priv rm: 10. V, MC.
Wine enthusiast Maurice Garnier is a master at unearthing little-known, bargain-priced vintages, but his cellar also boasts some high-class rarities which he magnanimously pours by the glass. To keep them company, he also proposes a few dishes that please us less than the wine does: hearty but ordinary pork terrine with baby vegetables and dull smoked pork with lentils, luckily followed by tender and delicious pear with almonds and orgeat syrup. A point less this year. C 180-280 F. M 135 F, 195 F, 245 F (wine incl).

Le Manoir du Colombier
232, route de Châtellerault
54 29 30 01, fax 54 27 70 90
Closed Sun dinner, Mon. Open until 9:30pm. Priv rm: 50. Garden dining. Pkg. V, AE, DC, MC.
The elegant, outspokenly modern dining room with a broad bay window is something of a surprise in this otherwise old-fashioned country manor. We award chef Gilles Moineau an extra point this year, after savoring his tasty saffron-scented shellfish soup, perfectly cooked calf's liver with sweet-sour sauce, and an unctuous tiramisu. Tempting but pricey choice of Bordeaux. Friendly welcome, slow service. C 290-380 F. M 170 F (weekday lunch, wine incl), 180 F, 230 F, 295 F.

 **Le Manoir du Colombier**
(See restaurant above)
Open year-round. 11 rms 320-500 F. Half-board 490 F. Conf. Golf. Pkg. V, AE, DC, MC.
Châteauroux's best hotel, offering bright, spacious, and well-equipped rooms furnished with wicker and pretty fabrics in a building surrounded by a huge park. Friendly welcome.

12/20 Relais Saint-Jacques
N 20 - 54 22 87 10, fax 54 22 59 28
Closed Sun, Christmas wk. Open until 9:30pm. Priv rm: 100. Air cond. Hotel: 46 rms 310-340 F. Half-board 255-375 F. Conf. Pkg. V, AE, DC.
It's easy enough to forget the charmless surroundings (an awkward building opposite an airfield) when you taste your first forkful of Pierre Jeanrot's traditional cooking: lobster salad with lemony vegetables, foie gras, grilled turbot, and a delicate tart of caramelized apples. We wouldn't mind seeing a few fresh entries on the menu, however, and the wine list needs a revamp too. C 290-330 F. M 100 F (weekdays, Sat lunch), 125 F, 155 F, 210 F, 260 F.

Le Stanislas
Daniel Cotar, 1 rue J.-J.-Rousseau
54 34 82 69, fax 54 07 32 22
Closed Sun dinner, Mon, Jul 31-Aug 21. Open until 10pm. Pkg. V, AE, MC.
Chef Daniel Cotar has already attracted the locals to this new establishment with his extremely traditional cuisine: tasty and delicate squab and duck terrines, tender and flavorful pickerel with sweet-cider vinegar, unctuous

croustillant of pears and caramel with honey cake ice cream. Charming welcome by Joëlle Cotar in a spacious dining room decorated in attractive autumn colors. **C** 350-450 F. **M** 200 F (weekday lunch, coffee & wine incl), 150 F, 280 F, 380 F.

CHÂTELAILLON-PLAGE   17340
Paris 472 - La Rochelle 12 - Niort 60 - Rochefort 21   Charente-M.

12/20   L'Océan
121, bd de la République - 46 56 25 91
Closed Sun dinner & Mon off-seas, Dec 15-Jan 15. Open until 9pm. Priv rm: 16. V, MC.
Though out of sight of this welcoming family-run restaurant, the ocean offers up its piscine bounty in the form of fresh seafood platters and appetizing fish dishes (monkfish à la charentaise and tasty sole). The menu is punctuated here and there by islands of regional specialties. **C** 185-350 F. **M** 72 F, 92 F (exc Sun lunch), 125 F, 215 F.

Les Trois Îles
La Falaise
46 56 14 14, fax 46 56 23 70
Open year-round. 17 stes 450-710 F. 78 rms 350-730 F. Rms for disabled. Restaurant. Half-board 864 F. Conf. Pool. Tennis. Golf. Pkg. V, AE, DC, MC.
Opened in 1987, this sizeable hotel complex is splendidly situated by the sea. In addition to classic hotel rooms, there are studios and duplexes which may be rented by the week. Numerous leisure activities are proposed, including a practice range for golf enthusiasts.

CHÂTELGUYON   63140
Paris 375 - Clermont-Ferrand 21 - Vichy 47   Puy-de-Dôme

11/20   La Grilloute
33, av. Baraduc
73 86 04 17
Closed Tue, beg Oct-beg May. Open until 9:30pm. Terrace dining. V, MC.
In a friendly, relaxed atmosphere, guests are served a singular blend of exotic and traditional fare that runs the gamut from Indian-style grilled chicken to hearty local charcuterie. **C** 150-200 F. **M** 100 F, 115 F.

International 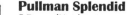
Rue A.-Punett
73 86 06 72, fax 73 86 24 87
Closed Oct 3-Apr 20. 2 stes 560 F. 54 rms 280-410 F. Restaurant. Half-board 380-440 F. Conf. Golf. V, AE, DC, MC.
A traditional hotel decorated in 1930s style. The surroundings are blessedly peaceful (magnificent trees), and the rooms are irreproachably tidy. Free shuttle to town's center.

Pullman Splendid
5-7, rue d'Angleterre
73 86 04 80, fax 73 86 17 56
Closed Nov-Mar. 1 ste 830-1,230 F. 80 rms 290-900 F. Restaurant. Half-board 415-1,270 F. Conf. Heated pool. Golf. Pkg. V, AE, DC, MC.
An immense, very formal hotel set amid lawns and flower gardens providing constantly upgraded rooms. Among the facilities are a spa, a fitness center, sauna, and a nightclub.

CHÂTELLERAULT   86100
Paris 305 - Cholet 128 - Tours 69 - Poitiers 34   *Vienne*

La Charmille
74, bd Blossac
49 21 30 11, fax 49 93 25 19
Closed Wed, 10 days in Oct. Open until 9:30pm. Garden dining. Air cond. Pkg. V, AE, DC, MC.
Cascading plants, beige-marble floors, and walls in tones of peach and salmon impart a posh, peaceful atmosphere to the dining room, a favorite with the well-heeled citizens of Châtellerault and doubtless still among the region's best restaurants. Christian Proust's Charmille is charming as ever, and his cooking, though lacking the audaciousness it once had, is impressive in its wise simplicity and superb technique. This year we enjoyed the fresh morels stuffed with chicken mousse and foie gras, turbot roasted with bay leaves and bacon jus, and golden veal sweetbreads with asparagus tips. The two set-price menus are good deals. The fine wine list showcases the top growths of Bordeaux. Flawless service. **C** 370-420 F. **M** 130 F (weekdays), 190 F.

Grand Hôtel Moderne
(See restaurant above)
Closed 10 days in Oct. 3 stes 700-1,200 F. 21 rms 280-650 F. Pkg. V, AE, DC, MC.
Comfortable rooms, carefully and tastefully decorated. You are assured of a warm welcome from Marie-Jeanne Proust and her staff. Fairly quiet nights, despite the hotel's central location.

CHÂTRE (LA)   36400
Paris 301 - Bourges 71 - Châteauroux 36 - Guéret 53   *Indre*

Château de la Vallée Bleue
Route de Verneuil, in St-Chartier
54 31 01 91, fax 54 31 04 48
Closed Jan-Feb. Open until 9:30pm. Priv rm: 45. Garden dining. Hotel: 1 ste 450-650 F. 12 rms 195-550 F. Half-board 395-495 F. Pool. Pkg. V, AE, MC.
A charming nineteenth-century château, simply and tastefully furnished. Creditable cooking served in liberal portions (smoked sturgeon and grilled country bread, pork fillet à la berrichonne, dark chocolate truffle with coffee sauce), and the cellar is very fine indeed—extensive and astutely chosen. **C** 260-370 F. **M** 125 F, 195 F, 265 F.

■ In Pouligny-Notre-Dame 36160   12 km S

Les Dryades
54 30 28 00, fax 54 30 10 24
Open daily until 9:30pm (10pm in seas). Terrace dining. Air cond. Valet pkg. V, AE, DC, MC.
An astonishing building reminiscent of a Le Corbusier church, or even a specimen of Soviet architecture. The new chef proposes a tasty sea scallop salad enhanced with orange, delicate veal sweetbreads with garlic, a superb cheese assortment (especially the sensational goat cheeses), and a subtle strawberry délice with rhubarb. Good choice of wines, some at high prices. Pleasant service. **C** 330-450 F. **M** 150 F, 230 F, 330 F.

Les Dryades
(See restaurant above)

Open year-round. 5 stes 1,300 F. 80 rms 600-700 F. Restaurant. Half-board 750-775 F. Air cond. Conf. Heated pool. Tennis. Golf. Garage pkg. Helipad. V, AE, DC, MC.

This hotel looks like an ocean liner built of concrete in an ocean of bucolic countryside. But many harassed executives appreciate the understated luxury and huge, admirably equipped rooms decorated in gentle colors. The hotel's strong point is its superb eighteen-hole golf course; there's also a health club. Pleasant, helpful staff.

CHAUDES-AIGUES	15110
Paris 527 - St-Flour 32 - Aurillac 92 - Espalion 56	*Cantal*

 Auberge du Pont de Lanau
4 km N on D 921, 15260 Lanau
71 23 57 76, fax 71 23 53 84

Closed Tue dinner & Wed off-seas, Jan-Feb. Open until 9:30pm. Priv rm: 80. Terrace dining. No pets. Hotel: 8 rms 280-380 F. Half-board 260-320 F. Conf. Pkg. V, MC.

Jean-Michel Cornut seems to prefer classic cooking these days rather than the regional dishes we once enjoyed here: tender foie gras with celery, marbled with duck; well prepared sautéed veal sweetbreads with wild mushrooms; and a delicious nougatine glacé with pistachios and almond sauce. Reserved welcome, competent service; you can dine in front of the fireplace or on a flower-filled terrace. C 250-300 F. M 95 F (weekdays), 170 F, 195 F, 260 F.

10/20 **Aux Bouillons d'Or**
10, quai du Remontalou
71 23 51 42, fax 71 23 53 84

Closed Oct-Easter. Priv rm: 18. Terrace dining. Hotel: 12 rms 240-300 F. Half-board 250-270 F. No pets. Pkg. V, MC.

You are greeted with a smile at this pretty restaurant and treated to good regional dishes: warm goat cheese and bacon in a salad, steak with shallots, and millefeuille. C 170-280 F.

CHAUNY	02300
Paris 123 - Soissons 32 - St-Quentin 30 - Laon 36	*Aisne*

La Toque Blanche
24, av. V.-Hugo
23 39 98 98, fax 23 52 32 79

Closed Sat lunch, Sun dinner, Mon, Jan 2-10, Jul 24-Aug 22. Open until 9:30pm. Priv rm: 60. Pkg. V, MC.

The nineteenth-century grey stone dwelling stands in a wooded park, a haven of peace for gastronomes. Véronique Lequeux makes guests feel at home, and Vincent Lequeux, formerly with Gérard Boyer, regales them with imaginative, personalized culinary creations. You too will smack your lips (quietly, of course) over his harmonious timbale of lobster and frog's legs in a delicate crust, admirable turbot fillet with potatoes and turnips with a light but creamy sauce, or the fine nougat glacé. The second set menu is a bargain. Superb wines at reasonable prices. A second toque this year (a red one, in spite of the restaurant's name). C 420-450 F. M 145 F (weekdays exc Fri dinner, wine incl), 170 F, 275 F, 370 F.

CHÊNE (LE) 84	→ Apt

CHÊNEHUTTE-LES-TUFFEAUX 49
→ Saumur

CHENNEVIÈRES-SUR-MARNE 94
→ PARIS Suburbs

CHENONCEAUX	37150
Paris 213 - Bourges 113 - Tours 35 - Amboise 11	*Indre/Loire*

12/20 **Le Bon Laboureur et Château**
6, rue du Dr-Bretonneau
47 23 90 02, fax 47 23 82 01

Closed Nov 15-Dec 15, Jan 2-Feb 15. Open until 9:30pm. Priv rm: 25. Garden dining. Heated pool. Valet pkg. V, AE, DC, MC.

A million tourists wander through Chenonceaux every year, so the Jeudi family hardly need make an effort to attract customers. And yet they try hard to present a repertoire of polished traditional dishes: langoustines roasted in chive butter, sautéed sea scallops, lamb croustillant with garlic, or a delicate apple tart served warm with sherbet. Charming contemporary decor and a lovely patio. C 280-400 F. M 150 F, 220 F, 300 F.

Le Bon Laboureur et Château
(See restaurant above)

Closed Nov 15-Dec 15, Jan 2-Feb 15. 3 stes 800-1,000 F. 32 rms 300-650 F. Rms for disabled. Half-board 500-700 F. Conf. Heated pool. Valet pkg. V, AE, MC.

Here's a vine-covered *auberge* with pleasant rooms that overlook a flower-filled courtyard. Cocktail bar, herb garden, and all-terrain bicycles for rent.

CHERBOURG	50100
Paris 360 - Caen 119 - Bayeux 92 - Avranches 134	*Manche*

12/20 **Le Faitout**
Rue Tour-Carrée - 33 04 25 04

Closed Mon lunch, Sun. Open until 9:45pm. Terrace dining. V.

It's elbow to elbow here, as the regulars crowd in for the simple home-style cooking (pot-au-feu, calf's head, and less satisfying salads), served in healthy portions. Fine little Bordeaux at a very low price. Relaxed atmosphere. C 110-180 F. M 105 F.

Le Louvre
2, rue H.-Dunant
33 53 02 28, fax 33 53 43 88

Closed Dec 24-Jan 2. 42 rms 170-350 F. Rms for disabled. Golf. Pkg. V, AE, DC, MC.

Near the marina. Spacious rooms with good soundproofing, tiny bathrooms. Pleasant staff.

Mercure
Gare maritime
33 44 01 11, fax 33 44 51 00

Open year-round. 84 rms 350-510 F. Restaurant. Conf. Pkg. V, AE, DC.

The freshly repainted rooms afford extensive views over the harbor. Pleasant service and good breakfasts.

CHESNAY (LE) 78
→ PARIS Suburbs: Versailles

CHEVAL-BLANC 84 → Cavaillon

CHEVANNES 89 → Auxerre

CHEVERNY 41 → Cour-Cheverny

CHEVREUSE 78460
Paris 32 - Rambouillet 19 - Versailles 16 - Etampes 45 *Yvelines*

■ In Saint-Lambert-
des-Bois 78470 5 km NW on D 46

Les Hauts de Port-Royal
2, rue de Vaumurier - 30 44 10 21
Closed Sun dinner, Mon, Aug 15-30. Open until 9:30pm. Priv rm: 18. Terrace dining. Pkg. V, AE, MC.
This charming half-timbered establishment boasts a glorious terrace and a rather attractive honey-and-coral dining room, in which you can sample Francis Poirier's delicate, classic cuisine that has personality: langoustine ravioli and stuffed morels, veal sweetbreads in a "symphony" with lobster, honey-roasted pear with honey cake ice cream. Friendly welcome. C 380-500 F. M 190 F, 250 F, 350 F.

CHINON 37500
Paris 282 - Tours 47 - Poitiers 95 - Angers 80 *Indre/Loire*

Le Chinon
Digue St-Jacques
47 98 46 46, fax 47 98 35 44
Closed Sat & Sun off-seas, Christmas hols. 54 rms 340-380 F. Rms for disabled. Restaurant. Half-board 285-315 F. Conf. Pkg. V, AE, DC, MC.
A modern pyramidal building opposite the Château de Chinon. Bright, comfortable rooms with balconies. Equipped for conferences.

Hostellerie Gargantua
73, rue Haute-St-Maurice - 47 93 04 71
Closed Thu lunch & Wed off-seas, Nov 15-Mar 15. Open until 10pm. Terrace dining. Hotel: 8 rms 160-550 F. Half-board 360-750 F. No pets. Pkg. V, MC.
The setting transports one back to the Middle Ages, an effect intensified on weekend evenings, when the staff don medieval attire. As for the cooking, a new chef is pleasing the many tourist visitors with the likes of grilled blood sausage with sweet-sour apple sauce, slices of duck breast with a pear poached in Chinon, and a fresh fruit gratin with a delicate and delicious sabayon. Competent service by staff who wear medieval costumes at the end of each week. C 280-320 F. M 150 F (exc weekdays), 100 F (weekdays), 220 F.

Au Plaisir Gourmand ☺
2, rue Parmentier
47 93 20 48, fax 47 93 05 66
Closed Sun dinner, Mon, Feb. Open until 9:15pm. Priv rm: 20. Garden dining. Air cond. V, MC.

Jean-Claude Rigollet is no publicity seeker, and his restaurant built of tufa stone at the foot of the Château de Chinon will never attract those who go out to see and be seen. Just as well. His faithful customers and the odd tourist in the know can better appreciate the elegant setting, fine set meals, and the studied simplicity that stands out in both the cooking and the welcome provided by Danielle Rigollet. Jean-Claude works diligently and quietly all year round, producing such toothsome dishes as his young rabbit in a Chinon white wine gelatin, warm goat cheese and walnuts in a salad, salmon with celery in Chinon, and a croquant of iced caramel in chocolate sauce. In season, you can sample lovely fresh morels with a fillet of veal, and as for fish, try the warm salad of monkfish with baby spinach or the pike à languille. For dessert, a raspberry gratin with almonds. Superb choice of Loire wines at reasonable prices, like a Chinon Les Gravières at 90 F or an Anjou white from Papin at 80 F. Fine service, and an excellent quality-price ratio. C 290-380 F. M 175 F, 240 F, 330 F.

■ In Beaumont-en-Véron 37420 5 km on D 749

Château de Danzay 🌲🌲
47 58 46 86, fax 47 58 84 35
Closed beg Nov-end Mar. 2 stes 1,300-1,500 F. 10 rms 650-1,300 F. Restaurant. Half-board 680-1,150 F. Heated pool. Golf. Pkg. V, AE, MC.
This lovely fifteenth-century manor has been completely restored. Spacious rooms sport exposed beams and stone, and everywhere there reigns a warm atmosphere.

■ In Marçay 37500 6 km S on D 749 and D 116

Château de Marçay
47 93 03 47, fax 47 93 45 33
Closed Sun dinner & Mon (exc hols), Nov-Apr. Open until 9:30pm. Priv rm: 80. Terrace dining. Heated pool. Valet pkg. V, AE, MC.
Pascal Bodin seems to have determined to stay mainly in a traditional mode, which is just as well judging by an audaciously put together but bland carpaccio of langoustines with truffle oil and balsamic vinegar that we sampled here. But the rack of Touraine lamb with a garlic compote, the fava bean ragoût, and the gratin of souffléed apples with cinnamon show real freshness and savoir-faire. On other fronts, the service is flawless and the handsome old turreted château surrounded by vineyards and gardens still offers real French hospitality. One of the finest cellars in Touraine. C 370-450 F. M 145 F (weekday lunch, Sat), 240 F, 360 F.

Château de Marçay 🌲🌲
(See restaurant above)
Closed mid Jan-mid Mar. 6 stes 1,350-1,550 F. 32 rms 495-1,295 F. Rms for disabled. Half-board 680 F. Conf. Heated pool. Tennis. Valet pkg. Helipad. V, AE, MC.
Huge, bright rooms with elegant tapestry hangings adjoin spacious bathrooms, some with Jacuzzi. In these peaceful, pampering surroundings, your every need is efficiently attended to. Relais et Châteaux.

CHISSAY-EN-TOURAINE 41
→ **Montrichard**

CHOLET   49300
Paris 350 - Angers 61 - Nantes 61 - Niort 106   *Maine/Loire*

 Le Belvédère
5 km SE on D 20, lac de Ribou
41 62 14 02, fax 41 62 16 54
Closed Sun dinner, Mon lunch, Feb 20-26, Jul 17-Aug 16. Open until 9pm. Terrace dining. No pets.
Hotel: 8 rms 325-370 F. Golf. Pkg. V, AE, DC.
Set in green countryside and overlooking Lake Ribou, this restaurant welcomes patrons with a beamed dining room and a magnificent fireplace, plus a pleasant terrace. Daisuke Inagaki continues to come up with original flavor combinations: try the inventive salad of warm lobster spring rolls, warm foie gras with green asparagus, sole simmered with langoustines, and a "cake" of tiny lamb fillets with eggplant. **C** 270-420 F. **M** 125 F, 225 F (weekdays, Sat), 200 F, 250 F (Sun).

■ **In Maulévrier 49360**   13 km SE on D 20

 Château Colbert   ⚜♣
Pl. du Château
41 55 51 33, fax 41 55 09 02
Closed Feb. 6 stes 600-800 F. 26 rms 300-450 F. Restaurant. Half-board 290-990 F. Conf. Golf. Pkg. V, AE, DC, MC.
Not much happening in this neck of the woods, however the rooms at this prestigious hostelry boast canopied beds and fine fittings. True, the breakfasts are not the stuff of dreams, but the grounds are delightful and amusing events are occasionally scheduled (dog racing, balloon launchings...).

CHONAS-L'AMBALLAN 38   → Vienne

CHOREY-LÈS-BEAUNE 21   → Beaune

CIBOURE 64   → Saint-Jean-de-Luz

CIOTAT (LA)   13600
Paris 805 - Aix 49 - Toulon 37 - Marseille 32   *B./Rhône*

 Miramar
3, bd Beaurivage
42 83 09 54, fax 42 83 33 79
Open year-round. 25 rms 465-765 F. Restaurant. Half-board 635-910 F. Air cond. Conf. Golf. Garage pkg. V, AE, DC, MC.
An old hotel set between the pine forest and the sea. The rooms have been re-equipped and redecorated to suit modern tastes, with attractive wicker furniture.

CLÉCY   14570
Paris 249 - Falaise 31 - Condé-sur-Noireau 10   *Calvados*

12/20 Moulin du Vey
In Le Vey - 31 69 71 08, fax 31 69 14 14
Closed Nov 30-Dec 28. Open until 9:30pm. Priv rm: 280. Terrace dining. Pkg. V, AE, DC, MC.
Both locals and tourists flock to the delightful terrace overlooking the Orne to savor cuisine

that has ideas but whose technique needs polishing: bland rabbit confit; well seasoned salads; interesting and tasty sole with ginger, lime, and wild mushrooms; delicate but overcooked apple tart with vanilla ice cream. **C** 250-330 F. **M** 135 F, 210 F, 280 F, 360 F

Moulin du Vey
(See restaurant above)
Closed Nov 30-Dec 28. 25 rms 380-500 F. Restaurant. Half-board 440-475 F. Conf. Golf. Pkg. V, AE, DC, MC.
Peaceful rooms in the mill itself, which is surrounded by greenery, plus an annex whose accommodation is less elegant and poorly soundproofed.

CLEDEN-CAP-SIZUN   29113
Paris 597 - Quimper 45 - Audierne 10 - Douarnenez 32   *Finistère*

Relais
de la Pointe du Van   ⚜♣
3 km W, baie des Trépassés
98 70 62 79, fax 98 70 35 20
Closed Oct-Mar. 25 rms 250-366 F. Rms for disabled. Restaurant. Half-board 302-360 F. Conf. Pkg. Helipad. V, MC.
Situated next to the beach, this hotel provides small, pleasant rooms with superb sea views. Sauna.

CLEDER   29221
Paris 570 - Plouescat 6 - Brest 49 - St-Pol-de-Léon 9   *Finistère*

Le Baladin
9, rue de l'Armorique - 98 69 42 48
Closed Tue dinner & Mon off-seas. Open until 9:30pm. V.
Pierre Queffelec's seafood dishes are clever and delicate, though not as audacious as they once were. But the 98 F menu is excellent: smoked haddock salad or sea scallops with vegetables, roast fresh cod with thyme or a steak with béarnaise sauce, caramelized puff pastry with strawberries or orange crème brûlée. The wine list needs work. Efficient service. **C** 230-320 F. **M** 79 F, 98 F, 158 F, 195 F.

CLÈRES   76690
Paris 150 - Rouen 23 - Dieppe 44 - Yvetot 34   *Seine/Mar.*

Au Souper Fin
In Frichemesnil,
pl. de l'Église - 35 33 33 88
Closed Wed dinner, Thu, Aug 16-Sep 10. Open until 9pm. Pkg. V.
You may have trouble locating this little inn, for the village is well off the beaten track. Believe us, though, your efforts will be rewarded by Éric Buisset's accomplished, richly flavorful cooking. This year, we enjoyed the salad of huge langoustines, the oven-baked sole with chive cream sauce, the duck breast à la fleur de sel, and the veal sweetbreads sautéed with chervil. For dessert, delicate apple puff pastry tart with chicory, served warm. The cellar is a treasure trove for wine buffs, particularly since the prices are a model of temperance. Special list of wines in half bottles. Charming welcome by Véronique Buisset. **C** 260-400 F. **M** 250 F (wine incl), 160 F, 220 F.

CLERMONT-FERRAND 63000

Paris 389 - Limoges 191 - Lyon 183 - Moulins 96 *Puy-de-Dôme*

Gérard Anglard 🕃
17, rue Lamartine
73 93 52 25, fax 73 93 29 25
Closed Sun, hols, Aug 1-15. Open until 10pm. Priv rm: 18. Garden dining. Air cond. V, AE, MC.

Gérard Anglard offers his many fans (ourselves included) a generous 100 F lunch menu with a hearty potée (stick-to-your-ribs soup) and steak with Charroux mustard sauce, or another featuring whatever is best in the market. But this fine chef who never seems to hit a false note creates more elaborate dishes: snails in brioche with Boudes wine sauce, pickerel with fava beans and bacon, and wild duck with a cabbage compote. Wide choice of wines, including many local ones. Professional service, and a salon that opens onto the terrace. **C** 240-350 F. **M** 100 F (lunch), 160 F, 240 F, 280 F.

🏠🏠 Arverne
16, pl. Delille
73 91 92 06, fax 73 91 60 25
Open year-round. 57 rms 350-440 F. Restaurant. Conf. Golf. Pkg. V, AE, DC, MC.

Modern, functional, and central, with spacious rooms. Bar.

🍴 Jean-Yves Bath 🕃
Pl. du Marché-St-Pierre
73 31 23 23, fax 73 31 08 33
Closed lunch Sat & Mon, hols, Feb school hols, Aug 15-31. Open until 10pm. Priv rm: 35. Terrace dining. Air cond. Pkg. V, MC.

Not everyone admires his ultramodern decor but Jean-Yves Bath, a disciple of Senderens, isn't trying to impress anyone: it's just his personal taste. The same could be said of his surprising, original cuisine based on fine products. This year, he pleased us with his Cantal rissoles and ravioli with meat jus and herbs, sautéed pickerel with veal marrow and cèpe-scented sauce, bits of beef and gausettes rôtis (gratinéed pasta) with Fourme d'Ambert blue cheese, and chocolate cake with "vieux garçon" jam. The chef likes to be involved in everything: greeting customers, taking orders, and cooking; he even gives advice about the wines (not always the best advice, by the way). We just hope he takes time to keep the prices under control. **C** 300-425 F. **M** 260 F, 350 F.

11/20 Brasserie Lyonnaise
12, pl. de la Résistance - 73 93 78 66
Closed Sun. Open until 11pm. Garden dining. Pkg. V.

In the center of Clermont, this attractive brasserie offers appealing Lyonnais specialties at popular prices. The setting has lots of character, and so do the Lyons-style salad, calf's head with ravigote sauce, beef fillet with morels, and a gooey chocolate fondant. **C** 190-300 F. **M** 69 F, 109 F, 165 F.

Clavé
12, rue St-Adjutor
73 36 46 30, fax 73 31 30 74
Closed Sat lunch, Sun, 1 wk in Feb, Aug. Open until 10:30pm. Priv rm: 30. Terrace dining. Pkg. V.

The law courts recently built nearby have altered the atmosphere of this street, which used to be on the seamy side, has drawn a different clientele to discover the cuisine of Jean-Claude Gérard. But since he left the establishment just as we went to press, we will not rate the kitchen now. Owner Alain Clavé will still play his role of hospitable host to perfection. **C** 300-400 F. **M** 100 F (weekday lunch), 150 F, 210 F, 330 F.

🍴 Le Clos Saint-Pierre
Pl. du Marché-St-Pierre
73 31 23 22, fax 73 31 08 33
Closed Sun, hols, Feb & Nov school hols. Open until 10:30pm. Priv rm: 50. Terrace dining. Pkg. V.

Danièle Bath's popular brasserie now houses a wine bar as well as a dining terrace that has Clermont's smart set clamoring for tables when the weather grows warm. The succinct menu of appealing dishes features, for example, a salad of chicken livers and artichokes, a bougnette of pig's foot with lentils, and an ice-cream dessert with walnuts and chestnuts. Côtes-d'auvergne and Frontonnais wines at 9 F per glass. **C** 160-250 F.

🏠🏠 Gallieni
51, rue Bonnabaud
73 93 59 69, fax 73 34 89 29
Open year-round. 80 rms 210-335 F. Restaurant. Half-board 335 F. Conf. Golf. Pkg. V, AE, DC, MC.

Near the town center and with as many parking spaces as modern, comfortable rooms. Hairdresser; bookshop.

🏠🏠 Novotel
32, rue G.-Besse, ZI Le Brezet-Est
73 41 14 14, fax 73 41 14 00
Open year-round. 96 rms 430-490 F. Rms for disabled. Restaurant. Air cond. Conf. Heated pool. Golf. Pkg. V, AE, DC, MC.

A new hotel set in leafy grounds midway between the airport and downtown. All the usual comforts of a good chain hotel. Excellent service.

12/20 La Retirade
82, bd Gergovia
73 34 46 46, fax 73 34 46 36
Closed Sat lunch. Open until 10:30pm. Priv rm: 230. Terrace dining. Air cond. Pkg. V, AE, DC.

The chefs change so often here you can hardly remember their names, let alone their cooking. The latest offers an ambitious range of dishes (sautéed langoustines with Cantal cheese, beef fillet with coriander, and moka crème brûlée). Classic wine list. **C** 280-350 F. **M** 135 F, 150 F, 230 F.

🏠🏠 Mercure-Gergovie
(See restaurant above)
Open year-round. 2 stes 570 F. 122 rms 400-490 F. Half-board 395-425 F. Golf. Pkg. V, AE, DC, MC.

Central and facing the mountains. Pretty fabrics enliven the quiet, spacious, air-conditioned rooms. Conference rooms.

🍴 Le Saint-Émilion
97, av. de la République
73 91 92 92, fax 73 90 21 88
Closed Sun. Open until 10pm. Priv rm: 20. Terrace dining. Pkg. V, AE, DC, MC.

André Joubert's cuisine is reliable and well-crafted, and served in a pleasant modern dining room in a futuristic neighborhood. Try his skate with cider, a favorite among steady customers, and his calf's liver with Sherry sauce, as well as

211

his super-classic but well made desserts (profiteroles, île flottante). The welcome and service are highly professional. **C** 180-250 F. **M** 85 F, 130 F, 170 F.

▲▲ Inter Hôtel République ⚹🌳

(See restaurant above)
Open year-round. 55 rms 270-320 F. Rms for disabled. Half-board 240-350 F. Golf. Pkg. V, AE, MC.
Comfortable beds and perfect soundproofing at this functional hotel in a rather drab industrial area.

12/20 La Table à Poissons
16, rue Claussmann - 73 91 95 69
Closings not available. Open until 10:30pm. Air cond. V, AE, DC, MC.
Seafood fresh from the port at Boulogne is prepared here with a pleasing simplicity: warm salad of cuttlefish and mussels, interesting pot-au-feu of seafood matched with garlic-rich aïoli, and an aumônière glacé for dessert. Small, interesting cellar. **C** 200-250 F. **M** 78 F, 105 F.

Gérard Truchetet
Rond-Point de la Pardieu - 73 27 74 17
Closed Sat lunch, Sun, Aug 15-31. Open until 9:30pm. Priv rm: 50. Air cond. Pkg. V, MC.
Frills are not the forte of veteran chef Gérard Truchetet, who specializes in traditional, regional dishes. Try the warm foie gras in a cinnamon and nutmeg scented bread pudding, an omble chevalier (lake fish) paupiette in sweet vin de paille sauce, and frozen chocolate truffles in honey sauce. Attractive lower-priced set menus. Friendly welcome. **C** 200-300 F. **M** 120 F (weekday lunch), 140 F, 175 F, 200 F.

Gilbert Vacher
69, bd Gergovia (1st floor)
73 93 13 32, fax 73 34 07 13
Closed Sat. Open until 10pm. Priv rm: 60. Terrace dining. V, AE, DC, MC.
Local wheeler-dealers and politicos hang out here to sample Gilbert Vacher's cooking, which includes some reliable dishes: pickerel and salmon with sorrel sauce, slices of duck breast with wild mushrooms, and an exemplary selection of local cheeses. Fairly complete wine list with a few regional offerings. Professional but sometimes bored service. A toque this year. **C** 250-380 F. **M** 100 F, 160 F, 250 F.

And also...
Our selection of places for inexpensive, quick, or late-night meals.
L'Auberge Auvergnate (73 37 82 68 - 37, rue des Vieillards. Open until 10pm.): Bistrot in an area under renovation. Enticing food, wonderful wines (150 F).
L'Auvergnat (73 92 20 91 - 27, av. de l'Union-Soviétique. Open until 9pm.): The Hôtel Saint-André's restaurant. Blue-cheese salad, hearty stews, and other regional dishes (130-160 F).
La Passerelle (73 91 62 12 - 24, rue A.-France.): A mixed clientele of railway workers and politicos appreciates the 75 F menu and the accordion music (75 F).

> *The **prices** in this guide reflect what establishments were charging at press time.*

■ **In Chamalières 63400**   3 km W

Hôtel Radio ✧
43, av. P.-Curie
73 30 87 83, fax 73 36 42 44
Closed Sun, Mon lunch, Jan. Open until 9:30pm. Priv rm: 50. Air cond. Pkg. V, AE, DC.
The next time you drive from Paris to Cannes, why not leave the traffic jams behind and make a detour through the Auvergne countryside to Clermont-Ferrand? Not such a mad idea in fact—not only is it easier on the nerves but it's an ideal opportunity to make the acquaintance of this restaurant we've been telling you about for years.
The rather odd name pays tribute to the early days of the wireless, of which Michel Mioche's father was a fan. Set on a residential hillside, it is a vast, welcoming place with a pre-war charm that belies the Art Deco furnishings. And the entire staff—as well as the dog—share our view that Yvette Mioche is a delightful hostess.
Michel Mioche has left the cooking to Pascal Alonso, and it's a success; it continues to steer a skillful course between rich, regional specialties and the subtler flavors of the sea. Try the Cantal ravioli, veal sweetbreads with lentils and turnip confit, the famous lamb fillet wrapped in bacon, and the magical caramelized pineapple tart with pistachios. If the Mioches ever decide to sell this establishment, we hope it's to Pascal Alonso. **C** 350-400 F. **M** 150 F, 230 F, 380 F.

▲▲ Hôtel Radio ⚹🌳
(See restaurant above)
Closed Jan. 1 ste 750-950 F. 25 rms 250-750 F. Half-board 460-860 F. Air cond. Golf. Pkg. V, AE, DC.
Perched on the heights of Chamalières, this unusual hotel guarantees tranquility. Pretty rooms, decorated in soothing colors, but they could use a bit of freshening up.

■ **In Durtol 63830**   5 km NW on D 941

Bernard Andrieux
Av. du Puy-de-Dôme - 73 37 00 26
Closed Sat lunch, Sun, Aug 1-15. Open until 9:30pm. Priv rm: 16. Air cond. No pets. Pkg. V, AE.
Bernard Andrieux isn't known to be easygoing. He's proud to be a perfectionist, and it shows in his rigorous technique. His cooking is inventive, copiously served, and reasonably priced, for example the 170 F menu: crab and lobster ravioli, a chartreuse of farm-raised chicken with cabbage (a labor of love), and a warm millefeuille with Grand Marnier ice cream. The appetizers and little pastries served with coffee are excellent, too. And this year, the cooking was even better, simplified and refined: roast bar (sea bass) with pepper and vinegar, lobster "steak" with aged bacon, and beef fillet in a salt crust. **C** 360-500 F. **M** 170 F, 250 F, 350 F, 450 F.

L'Aubergade
On D 941 A, route de la Baraque
73 37 84 64, fax 73 30 95 57
Closed Sun dinner, Mon, Mar 1-21, Sep 1-15. Open until 9:30pm. Terrace dining. Pkg. V, DC, MC.
Look carefully to find this attractive building tucked away on a bend in the road. The Zimmermanns will welcome you with a smile to their soothing floral dining room and serve you

generous, proficient regional fare. Try Emile Zimmermann's excellent foie gras, veal kidney with mustard, and a cinnamon and pepper-spiked chocolate cake. **C** 200-350 F. **M** 120 F (weekdays), 175 F, 235 F.

■ **In Pérignat-lès-Sarliève 63170**   4 km SE

Hostellerie Saint-Martin ▲☎

73 79 12 41, fax 73 79 16 53
Open year-round. 35 rms 260-670 F. Restaurant. Half-board 370-520 F. Conf. Heated pool. Tennis. Pkg. V, AE, DC, MC.
The Michelin family used to spend their holidays here, at the foot of the Gergovie plateau, in quiet, wooded grounds. The luxurious rooms are tidily kept and well equipped, but the service is oddly amateurish. The restaurant barely retains a spark of its former glory.

12/20 Le Petit Bonneval

73 79 11 11, fax 73 79 19 98
Closed Sun dinner, Mon, 1 wk at Christmas & at Easter, Jul 20-Aug 10. Open until 9:30pm. Priv rm: 26. Garden dining. Pkg. V.
The large terrace draws customers on sunny days but the charming owners and reliable cooking are attractions whatever the weather. Try the generous 135 F menu: salad with chicken gizzards, haddock fillet, duck thigh confit, cheeses, a choice of desserts. Appealing wine list. **C** 190-240 F. **M** 98 F, 135 F, 165 F, 215 F.

■ **In Royat 63130**   4 km W

La Belle Meunière ۞

25, av. de la Vallée - 73 35 80 17
Closed Sun dinner, Wed, Feb & Nov school hols. Open until 9:30pm. Priv rm: 30. Terrace dining. Pkg. V, AE, DC, MC.
Every year Jean-Claude Bon tries to give a dash more character to his commendable repertoire of regional dishes. This year we enjoyed his slices of chicken with foie gras and asparagus, salmon cooked with sea salt and paired with creamed lentils, squab with mushrooms, and a delicate caramelized apple tart, served warm. Good cellar, with some local wines to offer relief to your wallet. The à la carte prices are rather high. Charming decor, all lace and delicate *bibelots*. **C** 320-350 F. **M** 100 F, 175 F, 210 F.

▲▲ Métropole

2, bd Vaquez
73 35 80 18, fax 73 35 66 67
Closed Oct-Apr. 5 stes 760-930 F. 67 rms 210-580 F. Rms for disabled. Restaurant. Half-board 390-630 F. Conf. Golf. Valet pkg. V, AE, MC.
A few meters from the hot springs, this turn-of-the-century spa hotel was modernied back in the 1950s. Large, comfortable rooms with mis-matched furniture. Some rooms have views over the park.

The **C** *(A la carte) restaurant prices given are for a complete three-course meal for one, including a half-bottle of modest wine and service.* **M** *(Menus) prices are for a complete fixed-price meal for one, excluding wine (unless otherwise noted).*

■ **In Saulzet-le-Chaud 63540**   8 km S on N 89

Le Montrognon

73 61 30 51, fax 73 61 53 11
Closed Sun dinner. Open until 9:45pm. Priv rm: 190. Terrace dining. Air cond. Pkg. V.
Gilles Bettiol's cooking is frank, forthright, and full of flavor, and the first two menus are great deals, expecially the one at 110 F: a feuillantine of scrambled eggs with fresh tomatoes, a chicken roulade with chives, cheese, and dessert. Warm welcome. **C** 250-300 F. **M** 110 F, 160 F, 205 F, 255 F.

CLICHY 92   → PARIS Suburbs

CLISSON   44190
Paris 377 - Nantes 28 - Niort 124 - Poitiers 150   Loire-Atl.

La Bonne Auberge

1, rue O.-de-Clisson
40 54 01 90, fax 40 54 08 48
Closed Sun dinner, Mon, Feb 13-28, Aug 7-31. Open until 9:30pm. Priv rm: 40. Garden dining. Pkg. V, AE, MC.
Old tiles, attractive furniture and tableware grace this elegant restaurant with veranda and flower-filled garden. Serge Poiron ably weds tradition to inspiration in his seasonal menus based on deluxe ingredients. This year, we enjoyed the veal sweetbreads in puff pastry with morels, glazed red mullet fillets with a compote of ginger-spiked vegetables, and a warm chocolate tart with rum ice cream. The clever sommelier guides guests through a fine cellar boasting many regional finds. **C** 370-470 F. **M** 98 F (weekday lunch), 175 F, 280 F, 430 F.

CLOYES-SUR-LE-LOIR   28220
Paris 143 - Chartres 56 - Châteaudun 12   Eure-et-Loir

Hostellerie Saint-Jacques

Pl. du Marché-aux-Œufs
37 98 40 08, fax 37 98 32 63
Closed Nov 15-Mar 15. 21 rms 360-480 F. Rms for disabled. Restaurant. Half-board 420 F. Golf. Pkg.
In the center of town, smallish but very comfortable rooms overlooking the courtyard and terrace of the auberge. Pleasant contemporary decor.

CLUNY   71250
Paris 396 - Autun 83 - Mâcon 24 - Tournus 38   Saône/Loire

Bourgogne

Pl. de l'Abbaye
85 59 00 58, fax 85 59 03 73
Closed Wed lunch, Tue, last 2 wks of Nov-Mar 5. Open until 9pm. Terrace dining. Pkg. V, AE, DC, MC.
We leave the owner to tell you the story of his *auberge* opposite the magnificent abbey. The poet Lamartine was an early visitor, and French and foreign tourists have since followed in his footsteps. The cooking seems to lack imagination, and we can no longer recommend the first set menu as a good deal. The toque is safe for now, but we hope for better things in the future. **C** 250-480 F. **M** 130 F (lunch), 205 F, 330 F.

Bourgogne
(See restaurant above)
Closed Tue, 1st 2 wks of Nov 15-Mar 5. 3 stes 900-1,000 F. 12 rms 400-500 F. Half-board 460-750 F. Conf. Golf. Valet pkg. V, AE, DC, MC.
Quiet, comfortable rooms with attractive furniture. The shutters open onto a view of the abbey and the town's main square.

 Hôtel Saint-Odilon
In Belle-Croix
85 59 25 00, fax 85 59 06 18
Closed Dec 20-Jan 5. 36 rms 270 F. Rms for disabled. Conf. Pkg. V, AE, MC.
A modern hotel, 300 meters from the abbey, with functional rooms overlooking open country.

CLUSAZ (LA)	74220
Paris 579 - Saint-Gervais 40 - Annecy 36 - Mègeve 29	H.-Savoie

 Alpen Roc
50 02 58 96, fax 50 32 67 73
Closed Oct 15-Nov. 103 rms 270-860 F. Rms for disabled. Restaurant. Half-board 290-580 F. Conf. Heated pool. Pkg. V, AE, DC, MC.
A fashionable rendezvous for the smart set on skis. Situated at the heart of the resort, the hotel offers views of the runs, a fitness center, tasteful lounges, and a warm welcome.

12/20 **Chalets de la Serraz**
Route du Col des Aravis
50 02 48 29, fax 50 02 64 12
Closed Apr 15-May, Sep 20-Dec 15. Open until 9:30pm. Priv rm: 40. Terrace dining. Heated pool. Pkg. V, AE, DC, MC.
A high turnover of chefs here, but Marie-Claude Gallay makes sure the cooking stays up to par. In a huge and lovely dining room, sample Provençal stuffed mussels, fondue and pelas with Reblochon cheese, and excellent génépi sherbet. Very warm welcome. **M** 165 F, 210 F (exc weekday lunch), 130, 140 F.

 Chalets de la Serraz
(See restaurant above)
Closed May 2-Jun 11, Sep 19-beg Dec. 1 ste 690-850 F. 10 rms 520-850 F. Restaurant. Half-board 380-550 F. Conf. Heated pool. Garage pkg. Helipad. V, AE, DC, MC.
Little individual cabins are grouped around a larger, traditional Savoyard chalet with a sunny terrace that looks out over the Aravis chain. The warm, wood-panelled rooms are thoughtfully equipped; there are numerous sport and leisure facilities on offer.

L'Ourson
50 02 49 80
Closed Sun dinner & Mon off-seas, Nov 5-Dec 16, May 7-Jun 9. Open until 9:30pm. V, AE, MC.
Vincent Lugrin offers intelligent, extremely well prepared dishes in this establishment right in the heart of the resort. Try the house smoked salmon with caviar cream, cold potato soup with truffles, duck breast with génépi, and génépi mousse with quince sauce. Very reasonable prices. No wonder locals and visitors crowd around the fireplace in winter. **C** 200-300 F. **M** 120 F (wine incl), 78 F, 99 F, 160 F, 230 F.

Le Panorama
50 02 42 12, fax 50 32 67 73
Closed Apr 15-Jun, Sep-Dec 19. 27 rms 230-480 F. Conf. No pets. Pkg. V, AE, MC.
One of the resort's biggest hotels, overlooking the village and the slopes. Each room has its own little balcony and there are apartments to rent by the week. Warm hospitality.

12/20 **Le Saint-Joseph**
Lieu-dit la Croix
50 02 40 06, fax 50 02 60 16
Closed May 10-Jun 10, Nov-Dec 15. Open until 9:30pm. Heated pool. Pkg. V.
For fresh, uncomplicated regional fare in an inviting, wood-panelled setting, this is the place. The usual raclettes, fondues, and tartiflettes are prepared with more than usual care, and may be savored before a roaring log fire. Frogs' legs à la provençale and duck breast are also on hand. Charming welcome; fleet service. **C** 170-250 F. **M** 98 F, 148 F, 185 F.

Alp' Hôtel
(See restaurant above)
Closed May 8-Jun 15, Nov 1-Dec 15. 15 rms 300-450 F. Half-board 320-535 F. Heated pool. Pkg. V.
A tidy, well-run little establishment in the heart of the resort. Sizeable rooms, good bathrooms. Generous breakfasts.

COARAZE	06390
Paris 970 - Nice 28 - Contes 10 - Lucéram 19	Alpes-Mar.

Auberge du Soleil
93 79 08 11, fax 93 79 37 79
Closed Nov 15-Mar 15. 2 stes 495-940 F. 8 rms 320-495 F. Restaurant. Half-board 350-425 F. Conf. Pool. Valet pkg. V, AE, MC.
In the heart of the medieval village far from the noise of traffic, ten elegantly modernized rooms with many thoughtful touches and fairytale mountain views. One of the region's most peaceful and charming hotels.

COCHEREL 27	→ Pacy-sur-Eure

COGNAC	16100
Paris 465 - Angoulême 42 - Niort 80 - Saintes 26	Charente

 **L'Échassier**
2 km S on route de St-Brice, 72, rue de Bellevue - 45 32 29 04, fax 45 32 22 43
Closed Sun dinner. Open until 9:30pm. Priv rm: 20. Pool. Pkg. V, AE, DC, MC.
This white Charentais dwelling set among lawns and tall trees, with its indefinably colonial air, offers accomplished, classic cuisine by the new chef, Jean Locussol: fine foie gras, excellent aumônière of oysters with caviar, perfectly cooked lamb seasoned with thyme and accompanied by a delicate sauce, and a delicious fruit gratin with a Cognac-spiked sabayon. Excellent wine list, especially in Champagnes, and professional, friendly service. The two toques return. **C** 300-450 F. **M** 138 F, 195 F, 320 F.

Looking for a city in a département? Refer to the **index.**

Les Pigeons Blancs

110, rue J.-Brisson
45 82 16 36, fax 45 82 29 29
Closed Sun dinner. Open until 9pm. Priv rm: 12. Garden dining. Pkg. V, AE, DC, MC.
This former post house has been owned by the Tachet family since the seventeenth century. The latest generation has turned it into a restaurant warmly decorated in wood and stone and surrounded by attractive grounds. Jacques Tachet is in the kitchen, producing a menu closely linked to the seasons and the region: tangy puff pastry stuffed with oysters and broccoli, perfectly cooked but a bit bland lamb with garlic, and excellent desserts. Fine wine list with a good choice of Cognacs. **C** 280-370 F. **M** 130 F, 155 F, 200 F, 275 F.

Les Relais Bleus

2 km S, in Châteaubernard, rond-point de la Trache - 45 35 42 00, fax 45 35 45 02
Open year-round. 55 rms 305-345 F. Restaurant. Half-board 275-310 F. Conf. Heated pool. Golf. Pkg. V, AE, DC, MC.
Bright, functional new rooms with ultramodern bathrooms. Good breakfasts; pretty garden.

Le Valois

35, rue 14-Juillet
45 82 76 00, fax 45 82 76 00
Closed Dec 22-Jan 2. 1 ste 500 F. 44 rms 270-390 F. Rms for disabled. Half-board 350-450 F. Air cond. Conf. Golf. Pkg. V, AE, DC, MC.
Recently renovated hotel with pleasant and spacious rooms. Sauna, solarium, bar.

COGOLIN (PLAGE) 83310
Paris 880 - Ste-Maxime 8 - St-Tropez 7 - Cogolin 8 — *Var*

Port-Diffa

Les Trois-Ponts sur la Giscle,
in La Foux (N 98) - 94 56 29 07
Closed Mon off-seas, Nov 13-Dec 21. Open until 10pm (11pm in summer). Terrace dining. Air cond. No pets. Pkg. AE, DC.
Low tables, soft sofas, and Moroccan cooking as tasty as in Marrakesh. Pastilla, little meat pastries, wonderfully light couscous, lemon chicken, lamb tajine, and sticky sweet pastries. Charming service. **C** 250-300 F. **M** 173 F.

COIGNIÈRES 78310
Paris 40 - Versailles 18 - Rambouillet 13 — *Yvelines*

Auberge d'Angèle

296, route Nationale 10
34 61 64 39, fax 34 61 94 30
Closed Sun dinner, Mon. Open until 10pm. Priv rm: 40. Garden dining. Pkg. V, AE.
Inside this half-timbered inn are beams and a rather dark dining room brightened with flowers and Delft-style tiles; outside, there's a leafy paved garden. Encroaching shopping centers and a busy road haven't yet ruined the setting. The skillful cooking swoops from the classic to the inspired: gratinéed smoked salmon crêpes, filet mignon with morels, and a delicate apple tart. **C** 350-450 F. **M** 220 F (weekday dinner, wine incl), 150 F, 246 F, 315 F.

COLLE-SUR-LOUP (LA) 06
→ Saint-Paul-de-Vence

COLLIAS 30 → Uzès

COLLIOURE 66190
Paris 955 - Perpignan 27 - Céret 32 — Pyrénées-O.

La Balette

Route de Port-Vendres
68 82 05 07, fax 68 82 38 08
Closed Nov 13-Dec 15. Open until 10pm (10:30pm in summer). Priv rm: 120. Garden dining. Air cond. Heated pool. Valet pkg. V, MC.
The dining room of this charming restaurant, done up in shades of pink and pale blue, affords picturesque views of the harbor. Local gastronomes flock in for chef Christian Peyre's focused, precise cooking. Sample the zesty Collioure anchovies marinated in Banyuls and the yummy chocolate mousse; the monkfish bourride was a little bland. Friendly service. **C** 300-400 F. **M** 175 F, 255 F, 355 F.

Relais des Trois Mas

(See restaurant above)
Closed Nov 13-Dec 15. 4 stes 995-1,680 F. 19 rms 395-860 F. Half-board 523-755 F. Air cond. Conf. Heated pool. Golf. Garage pkg. V, MC.
The guest rooms sport personalized furnishings, inspired by the painters who have lived and worked in this region. The bathrooms are stupendous. Sea views, fitness center, and a full array of leisure activities complete the picture, but a bit of freshening up wouldn't hurt the decor.

Casa Païral

Impasse des Palmiers
68 82 05 81, fax 68 82 52 10
Closed Nov 2-Apr 2. 2 stes 680-840 F. 26 rms 340-710 F. Air cond. Pool. Golf. Pkg. V, AE, MC.
A delightful Catalan residence in the town center with large, quiet, attractively furnished rooms. Lush garden surroundings.

Nouvelle Vague

7, rue Voltaire - 68 82 23 88
Closed Sun dinner & Mon off-seas, Feb 15-Mar 15. Open until 10pm. Priv rm: 20. Terrace dining. V.
The "New Wave" in the name is a wink not to the nearby sea but to Jean-Luc Godard's famous film (a poster of it enlivens the pleasant pastel interior that opens on a small terrace). The regionally grounded cooking appears on the generous 150 F menu: anchovies, a fricassée of cuttlefish and gambas in zarzuela, lamb fillets with rosemary and garlic cream, and crème catalane, with all the local wine you can drink. Friendly welcome. **C** 170-270 F. **M** 150 F (wine incl), 95 F, 230 F.

COLLOBRIÈRES 83610
Paris 902 - Bormes-les-M. 24 - Grimaud 24 — *Var*

12/20 La Petite Fontaine

1, pl. de la République - 94 48 00 12
Closed Sun dinner, Mon, Feb school hols. Open until 9pm. Terrace dining. Pkg. No cards.
Kid and game in season, and tables on the village square from spring onwards. All year round you'll appreciate the house terrine, anchoïade, lasagne bolognaise, chicken fricassée with a heady dose of garlic, and long-

simmered game dishes. **M** 105 F (weekdays, Sat), 140 F.

COLLONGES-AU-MONT-D'OR 69 → Lyon

COLMAR   **68000**
Paris 445 - Strasbourg 69 - Nancy 141 - Basel 68   Haut-Rhin

Hôtel Amiral
11A, bd du Champ-de-Mars
89 23 26 25, fax 89 23 83 64
Open year-round. 1 ste 710 F. 43 rms 340-710 F. Rms for disabled. Half-board 370-530 F. Conf. Golf. Pkg. V, AE, DC, MC.
A restored maltings on the edge of the old town. Most of the rooms overlook a quiet courtyard. The decoration and furnishings are a shade too functional. Piano bar.

12/20 A l'Échevin
5, pl. des Six-Montagnes-Noires
89 41 60 32, fax 89 24 59 40
Open daily until 10pm. Priv rm: 20. Garden dining. Air cond. Valet pkg. V, AE, MC.
Considerable effort has gone into the restoration of this fifteenth-century dwelling; as for the cuisine, sample the ravioli stuffed with tiny snails and cèpes, duck breast and sautéed langoustines, veal tripe and foot in a potée, and a frozen Grand Marnier soufflé. Attentive staff; good cellar. We'd like this spot better if the prices were more in line with the quality of the food. **C** 275-480 F. **M** 150 F (exc Sun, wine incl), 185 F, 220 F, 320 F.

Le Maréchal
(See restaurant above)
Open year-round. 2 stes 1,300-1,400 F. 28 rms 450-1,200 F. Half-board 550-800 F. Air cond. Conf. Golf. Valet pkg. V, AE.
Lovely spacious rooms with fine furniture in this superb fifteenth-century establishment. Some have views over the Lauch. Appetizing breakfasts.

La Fecht
1, rue Fecht
89 41 34 08, fax 89 23 80 28
Open year-round. 39 rms 290-420 F. Rms for disabled. Restaurant. Half-board 290-340 F. Conf. Garage pkg. V, AE, DC, MC.
Here, close to the scenic parts of old Colmar, are good-sized, comfortable guest rooms, as well as a sauna and an attractive terrace.

Au Fer Rouge
52, Grand-Rue
89 41 37 24, fax 89 23 82 24
Closed Sun dinner & Mon (exc May 1-Oct 31), Jan 8-26. Open until 9:40pm. Priv rm: 35. Terrace dining. Pkg. V, AE, DC, MC.
Patrick Fulgraff has won back the third toque he lost last year, and this fine old family establishment in the heart of historic Colmar is once more a gastronomic mecca. It even has a brand-new terrace with a superb view of Colmar's ancient customs houses. Fulgraff's cooking is classic, but he knows how to produce lighter versions of traditional Alsatian dishes. This year we enjoyed the grilled gambas with tiny julienned squid in an anchovy bouillon, lamb with basil and whole cloves of garlic, and an

array of lush dishes that, while they fail to surprise, certainly satisfy: exquisite raw foie gras with glazed turnips, and squab with a delicious Port jus posed on a bed of succulent polenta. As ever, the cellar overflows with the fragrant, heady wines of the region; the prices are typical of the region, too: high. **C** 450-600 F. **M** 210 F, 295 F (weekday lunch, Sat), 350 F, 470 F.

Mercure Colmar Centre
Rue Golbery
89 41 71 71, fax 89 23 82 71
Open year-round. 4 stes 700 F. 72 rms 360-490 F. Rms for disabled. Restaurant. Conf. Golf. Garage pkg. V, AE, DC, MC.
Near the Unterlinden Museum and the old town. The rooms are decorated in delicate colors, but are on the small side: three are reserved for disabled people and six for non-smokers. Buffet breakfast or room service, as you wish.

12/20 S' Parisser Stewwele   ✲
4, pl. Jeanne-d'Arc
89 41 42 33, fax 89 41 37 99
Closed Tue, Nov 20-28, Jun 19-28, Jan 16-30. Open until 11pm. Priv rm: 40. Terrace dining. Air cond. Pkg. V.
A genuine Alsatian *winstub*, done up in wood and stone, where the hospitable host comes over to see if you really like his raw sauerkraut salad, classic braised oxtail, rabbit civet with cinnamon, and stuffed cabbage (say yes: you'll be telling the truth, and you'll make the man happy). Refreshing local wines are served by the carafe. **C** 160-230 F.

Le Rendez-Vous de Chasse
7, pl. de la Gare
89 41 10 10, fax 88 23 92 26
Closed Sun (exc hols). Open until 10pm. Priv rm: 50. Terrace dining. Pkg. V, AE, DC, MC.
A monumental fireplace is the centerpiece of this luxurious, refined establishment's interior hung with hunting-theme paintings. Michel Burrus's polished cooking rarely has false notes: Munster ravioli with fried parsley, pickerel quenelles with crayfish, and iced Kirsch mousse with cherries. Warm welcome, attentive service. **C** 250-430 F. **M** 395 F (wine incl), 150 F, 250 F.

Terminus Bristol
(See restaurant above)
Closed Sun (exc hols). 10 stes 750-900 F. 70 rms 350-550 F. Rms for disabled. Half-board 450-750 F. Conf. V, AE, DC.
A fine traditional hotel, quiet despite its central location. The rooms are regularly improved and modernized. Facilities include a currency exchange and a car-rental desk.

Schillinger
16, rue Stanislas
89 41 43 17, fax 89 24 28 87
Closed Sun dinner & Mon (exc hols), Jul 3-24. Open until 9:30pm. Priv rm: 25. Air cond. V, AE, DC, MC.
The kitchen has been re-energized since Jean Schillinger's son, Jean-Yves, returned from training under Boyer and Robuchon to take his place at the stoves, and the toques have turned red as a result. Despite his youth, Jean-Yves has already honed his technique to amazing sharpness, and he possesses an acute feel for balancing flavors.

Now, along with the truffle-filled puff pastry and "trianon of squab, veal, and foie gras", the menu contains the likes of a salad of calmars (tiny squid) with herb spaghetti, perfect red mullet with beef marrow and parsnip purée, milk-fed veal in a crust, and monkfish with bacon and garlic. Only the desserts failed to bowl us over this year: too-sweet citrus fruit gratin is too old fashioned for this menu. The cellar is no more chauvinistic than the menu: fine bottlings from all over France are on hand, although we wouldn't mind a touch of imagination; the service, like all the rest, is distinguished and highly professional. Prices are substantial. C 450-600 F. M 280 F (weekdays), 380 F, 520 F.

■ In **Éguisheim 68420**   7 km S on N 83 and D 14

🍳 La Grangelière
15
59, rue du Rempart-Sud
89 23 00 30, fax 89 23 61 62
Closed Thu off-seas, Feb. Open until 10pm. Priv rm: 60. Terrace dining. Pkg. V, MC.
Alain Finkbeiner moved from the Château d'Isenbourg in Rouffach to this medieval wine-growing village, bringing with him a refined and original cooking style. In the half-timbered dining room, roughcast walls and geraniums spilling over window boxes create a rustic atmosphere. Sit yourself down, admire the view of the rampart promenade—and prepare to be seduced. Chartreuse of frog's legs and snails in Riesling, bacon-studded monkfish in Pinot Noir, and a sauté of honey-glazed mangoes and flambéed bananas. Wine list specialized in Alsatian vintages. C 250-350 F. M 120 F, 390 F (wine incl), 180 F.

■ In **Husseren-les-Châteaux 68420**   9 km S

🏠 Husseren-les-Châteaux
Rue du Schlossberg
89 49 22 93, fax 89 49 24 84
Open year-round. 1 ste 810-1,050 F. 35 rms 380-590 F. Rms for disabled. Restaurant. Half-board 512 F. Air cond. Conf. Heated pool. Tennis. Golf. Pkg. V, AE, DC, MC.
A few kilometers south of Colmar, this hillside hotel has views of the Vosges countryside and vineyards. Bright, comfortable rooms, all with mezzanines. Indoor swimming pool, sauna, solarium, table tennis, and children's games room.

See also: **Ammerschwihr, Illhaeusern (Auberge de l'Ill)**

Paris 226 - Chaumont 27 - Bar-sur-Aube 15   Haute-Marne

🏠 Les Dhuits

N 19 - 25 01 50 10, fax 25 01 56 22
Closed Dec 20-Jan 5. 42 rms 250-350 F. Restaurant. Half-board 250-300 F. Conf. Pkg. V, AE, DC.
A large, recently built hotel set back from the main road. Spacious, comfortable, well-

equipped rooms; hunting and fishing holidays can be arranged. The breakfasts and service could be improved.

Paris 402 - Sélestat 30 - Saint-Dié 30 - Obernai 41   Bas-Rhin

🍳 Les Pastoureaux
14
88 97 61 64, fax 88 47 21 73
Open daily until 9pm. Terrace dining. Air cond. Heated pool. Garage pkg. V, AE, DC, MC.
Fans of Jean-Paul Bossée's former Cheneaudière (now Les Princes de Salm, see below) are also flocking to his luxurious bistrot annex with its elegant panelled walls. The single set menu (wine included, and the choice of bottles is wide) is a gift: delicate terrine of foie gras and spiced goose confit, savory fricassée of monkfish with mushrooms, chicken jambonnette stuffed with ultra-fresh leek cream, interesting Munster marinated in Gewurztraminer, and tasty fruit sherbets. Courteous and competent service. M 280 F (wine incl).

🍳 Les Princes de Salm
15
88 97 61 64, fax 88 47 21 73
Open daily until 9pm. Terrace dining. Air cond. Heated pool. Pkg. V, AE, DC, MC.
Luxury is the watchword at this splendid chalet, with its dining room and terrace overlooking the wooded Vosges countryside. The meticulous cooking is equally opulent, a wealth of costly ingredients lavishly combined (a tendency reflected in the memorable *additions*). But Jean-Paul Bossée fully deserves two toques for his personalized dishes: worth ordering are the Munster ravioli with a crisp garnish of fried parsley, juicy and tender breast of duck roasted with spices and accompanied by a pastry stuffed with wild mushrooms, and a delicious puff pastry holding slightly underripe rhubarb served with vanilla ice cream. The cellar fairly bursts with billions of bottles of Alsace's best. Very formal service, warm welcome. M 280 F (wine incl).

🏠 La Cheneaudière   🌲☂
(See restaurant above)
Open year-round. 7 stes 1,490-2,200 F. 25 rms 670-1,160 F. Half-board 855-1,225 F. Conf. Heated pool. Tennis. Pkg. V, AE, DC, MC.
A large, especially quiet hotel. The luxurious, lovingly detailed rooms have terraces overlooking the mountains and forest. Among the many amenities are delicious breakfasts, a covered pool, shops, and a private hunting preserve. Relais et Châteaux.

Paris 610 - Annecy 65 - Chamonix 33 - Megève 5   H.-Savoie

🏠 Aux Ducs de Savoie   🌲☂
Le Bouchet
50 58 61 43, fax 50 58 67 43
Closed Apr 25-Jun 1, Oct 10-Dec 15. 50 rms 445-605 F. Restaurant. Half-board 380-480 F. Conf. Heated pool. Golf. Pkg. V, AE, DC, MC.
A large, modern chalet across from the mountains. Swimming pool in summer and ski tow 100

Gault Millau's ratings are based solely on the restaurants' cuisine. We do not take into account the atmosphere, décor, service, and so on; these are commented upon within the review.

meters away in winter. Sauna, Jacuzzi, billiard room.

 ### Rond-Point des Pistes
Le Haut-Combloux
50 58 68 55, fax 50 93 30 54
Closed Apr 15-Jun 20, Sep 15-Dec 20. 30 rms 280-520 F. Half-board 290-475 F. Conf. Golf. Pkg. V, MC.
Near the ski lifts and cross-country trails, this hotel provides large, intelligently equipped rooms, some with balcony and views of Mont Blanc. Sauna.

COMBREUX	45530

Paris 125 - Orléans 35 - Montargis 36 - Gien 49   *Loiret*

 ### Domaine de Chicamour
5 km SE on N 60
38 55 85 42, fax 38 55 80 43
Closed Dec-Feb. 12 rms 320-355 F. Restaurant. Half-board 380 F. Conf. Tennis. Pkg. V.
A peaceful stopover indeed is this Directoire château hidden in the forest of Orléans. Fresh, bright rooms open onto leafy grounds, with a riding club on the premises.

COMMENTRY	03600

Paris 330 - Moulins 67 - Montluçon 15 - Riom 68   *Allier*

 ### Michel Rubod   🌓
47, rue J.-J.-Rousseau - 70 64 45 31
Closed Sun dinner, Mon, 2 wks at Christmas & beg Aug. Open until 10pm. Priv rm: 25. Pkg. V.
The town itself may not win prizes for charm, but this lovely establishment where you are always greeted with a smile is always a pleasure to visit. Michel Rubod's superbly precise, inventive cooking combines the flavors of his home region with those farther afield. We particularly enjoyed the cod brandade presented in the form of a charlotte with young leeks in truffle oil; the andouillette Dromart (which wins our vote for best andouillette in France) served with cream, celery, truffle juice and mushrooms; the marvelously succulent oven-roasted beef with beef marrow and crushed grapes, served with a Jerusalem artichoke galette; the exquisite Chamberat cheese; the old-fashioned bread pudding with vanilla ice cream and apricot jam; the cakes served with the coffee, and the coffee itself: all this makes for sincere, intelligent, and flavorful cuisine. What's more, Rubod keeps his customers happy with miraculously low prices which we can only applaud. Good choice of Loire and Auvergne wines. C 300-400 F. M 120 F, 190 F, 250 F, 380 F.

COMPIÈGNE	60200

Paris 82 - Amiens 77 - St-Quentin 64 - Senlis 32   *Oise*

 ### Hôtel de France
17, rue E.-Floquet
44 40 02 74, fax 44 40 48 37
Open year-round. 21 rms 125-350 F. Restaurant. Half-board 287-445 F. Conf. Golf. Valet pkg. V, MC.
Conveniently located in a quiet street. Comfortable, reasonably priced rooms.

Hostellerie du Royal-Lieu 🌲🍴
9, rue de Senlis
44 20 10 24, fax 44 86 82 27
Open year-round. 3 stes 590 F. 17 rms 450-520 F. Restaurant. Half-board 650 F. Conf. No pets. Garage pkg. V, AE, DC, MC.
Here is a timbered *auberge* on the quiet outskirts of town, with pleasant rooms decorated in different styles, overlooking wooded parkland.

La Part des Anges
18, rue Bouvines
44 86 00 00, fax 44 86 09 00
Closed 1st wk of Feb hols, Jul 31-Aug 21. Open until 10pm. Priv rm: 30. Terrace dining. Pkg. V, AE, MC.
When Cognac ages in the cask, the vapors that escape are called *la part des anges*. There's nothing vapory or vague about the clean, concentrated flavors of Francis Carpentier's cuisine, crafted from excellent ingredients: cauliflower cream with Chinese artichokes, fine cheeses, and a crispy pineapple turnover. Modest prices for both food and wine, warm welcome, and a sunny setting with a seductive, Latin feel. C 250-350 F. M 130 F, 280 F.

 ### Rive Gauche
13, cours Guynemer
44 40 29 99, fax 44 40 38 00
Closed Mon. Open until 10pm. Priv rm: 20. Pkg. V.
Late of the Vieille Fontaine in Maisons-Lafitte, chef Franck Carpentier-Dervin has already won a following for his highly professional cooking and excellent, affordable fixed-priced menus. The cheapest of these features, for example, a pike and salmon duo with parsley cream, sliced duck breast accompanied by a cabbage and shallot confit with a touch of vanilla, Reblochon cheese croustillant, and a rhubarb and licorice puff pastry. The shortish wine list is growing and contains many half bottles. C 230-300 F. M 120 F, 160 F.

■ In **Élincourt-Sainte-Marguerite 60157**   14 km N on D 142

 ### Château de Bellinglise 🌲🍴
Route de Lassigny
44 96 00 33, fax 44 96 03 00
Open year-round. 2 stes 1,380-1,560 F. 33 rms 715-1,380 F. Restaurant. Half-board 640-1,060 F. Conf. Tennis. Golf. Valet pkg. Helipad. V, AE, DC, MC.
This immense Louis XIII–era castle on a 600-acre estate has been remarkably preserved and restored; guests can stay in one of the attractive rooms in the hunting lodge. Pond, tennis, horseback-riding, rides in a hot-air balloon, skeet shooting, archery, helicopter rides, and conference facilities.

■ In **Rethondes 60153**   8 km E on N 31

 ### Alain Blot
"Auberge du Pont", 21, rue du Mal-Foch
44 85 60 24, fax 44 85 92 35
Closed Sat lunch, Sun dinner, Mon. Open until 9:30pm. Priv rm: 30. Pkg. V.
Alain Blot's cooking merits a pilgrimage to this charming village, famous for its connections with two armistices (1918 and 1940). Harmony reigns in the lovely, light-filled dining room with

a superb terrace. Alain Blot is a master at choosing excellent products and at bringing out their flavors in light, expertly prepared dishes. Savor the lobster with asparagus and basil, lamb from the salt meadows of the Somme with a navarin of Soisson beans, and a puff pastry stuffed with caramelized apples and served with cinnamonvanilla ice cream. Astutely selected wines, remarkably courteous service with a feminine touch. **C** 380-450 F. **M** 190 F (weekdays), 250 F (exc weekdays), 330 F.

CONCARNEAU	29110

Paris 537 - Lorient 52 - Quimper 23 - Saint-Brieuc 130   *Finistère*

Le Galion

15, rue St-Guénolé (ville close)
98 97 30 16, fax 98 50 67 88
Closed Sun dinner & Mon off-seas. Open until 9:30pm. Priv rm: 20. V, AE, DC.
Like us, you'll want to return again and again to this enchanting granite house, which is so obviously the object of loving care and attention. But the cuisine based on the sea's bounty has fallen off a bit: langoustine fricassée with leek cream and a flavorful but overly rich shellfish coulis, dryish and slightly bland monkfish in cider, and adequate vanilla crème brûlée. One point lost this year. Warm welcome, well chosen and fairly priced wine list, and efficient service. **C** 350-400 F. **M** 99 F (weekday lunch), 150 F, 180 F, 245 F, 380 F.

La Résidence des Iles
(See restaurant above)
Open year-round. 5 rms 320-400 F. Half-board 420 F. V, AE, DC.
A friendly, restful atmosphere reigns in the five simply decorated rooms. Very pleasant service.

12/20 Les Sables Blancs
Pl. des Sables-Blancs
98 97 01 39, fax 98 50 65 88
Closed Oct 5-Mar. Open until 9:30pm. Priv rm: 52. Terrace dining. Hotel: 48 rms 190-340 F. Half-board 260-365 F. Conf. Golf. V, DC, MC.
Here you can gaze at the sea as you sample some of its finest, freshest bounty, simply prepared: sea scallops en brochette, steak with green peppercorn sauce, monkfish fillet with langoustine cream, and a Belle-Hélène pear for dessert. **C** 220-350 F. **M** 80 F, 120 F, 140 F, 180 F.

See also: Bénodet, Pont-Aven

CONDÉ-SUR-NOIREAU	14110

Paris 280 - Caen 46 - Falaise 31 - Flers 12   *Calvados*

Le Cerf

18, rue du Chêne
31 69 40 55, fax 31 69 78 29
Closed Sun dinner, Dec 24-31. Open until 9:15pm. Priv rm: 50. Garage pkg. V, AE.
The flower-spangled, ivy-clad façade of this charming inn hides a rustic, typically Norman interior. Chef Patrice Malgrey transforms top-quality ingredients into polished regional dishes full of character: slices of andouille in cider butter, salmon in the same cider butter, veal sautéed with Camembert, and a honey and Pommeau jelly dessert. Wide choice of wines;

genial welcome; efficient service. **C** 200-280 F. **M** 68 F (exc Sun), 90 F, 115 F, 135 F, 160 F, 190F.

CONDEAU 61	→ Nogent-le-Rotrou

CONDOM	32100

Paris 680 - Auch 43 - Agen 38 - Toulouse 110   *Gers*

12/20 Le Moulin du Petit Gascon
Route d'Eauze - 62 28 28 42
Closed Mon (exc Jul-Aug), Dec-Mar 15. Open until 9:30pm (10:30pm in summer). Priv rm: 55. Terrace dining. Pkg. V, MC.
This pleasant little country restaurant's bounteous 140 F menu offers a tasty salade gersoise, followed by a duo of veal kidney and sweetbreads, a salad with warm goat cheese, and house pastry for dessert. **C** 175-260 F. **M** 88 F (weekday lunch), 115 F, 140 F, 180 F.

11/20 L'Origan
4, rue Cadeot - 62 68 24 84
Closed Sun, Mon, Feb 1-15, Sep 13-Oct 4. Open until 11pm. Priv rm: 20. Terrace dining. V, MC.
A convivial setting in shades of Italian red and green, where you can expect a warm welcome and wholesome cooking. We like the seafood salad, the antipasti, the osso buco, and the pizzas cooked in a wood-fired oven, offered at low prices. **C** 100-200 F.

Hôtel des Trois Lys

38, rue Gambetta
62 28 33 33, fax 62 28 41 85
Open year-round. 10 rms 260-550 F. Conf. Pool. Golf. Pkg. V, AE, MC.
Recently and tastefully restored, a superb eighteenth-century residence that now contains ten spacious and comfortable rooms. Friendly service and perfect breakfasts. Unbeatable value.

CONDRIEU	69420

Paris 514 - Lyon 41 - Annonay 34 - Vienne 11   *Rhône*

Beau Rivage

2, rue Beau-Rivage
74 59 52 24, fax 74 59 59 36
Open daily until 9:30pm. Priv rm: 25. Garden dining. Air cond. Garage pkg. V, AE, DC, MC.
Let's make one thing quite clear to the Humanns and their chef Reynald Donet: what we and our readers can't swallow is their prices. As for the cooking, it's interesting and able. This year, we enjoyed the haddock rillettes with pink peppercorns and tomato coulis, veal sweetbreads braised with citrus fruits, and a tiramisu with fruits. The wines are as marvelous as ever, and the setting on the banks of the Rhône has lost none of its charm. **C** 400-550 F. **M** 165 F (weekday lunch, wine incl), 180 F (lunch exc hols), 275 F, 400 F, 600 F.

Beau Rivage
(See restaurant above)
Open year-round. 4 stes 820 F. 20 rms 500-820 F. Air cond. Garage pkg. V, AE, DC, MC.
Quiet, cozy rooms, impeccably kept. Improvements have been made to some of the bathrooms, and air-conditioning has been installed here and there.

CONQUES 12320
Paris 603 - Espalion 50 - Figeac 54 - Rodez 37 *Aveyron*

Hôtel Sainte-Foy
Rue Principale
65 69 84 03, fax 65 72 81 04
Closed Nov 5-Easter. Open until 10:30pm. Air cond. V, AE, MC.
Bernard Lafuente's ably prepared cuisine is served in a comfortable dining room in this seventeenth-century edifice. We enjoyed the interesting foie gras terrine with green lentils, excellent casserole-roasted veal chops with bacon-enhanced potatoes, and a delicious bread pudding with caramelized apples. Imaginative cooking that knows the virtues of simplicity. Good regional wines. **C** 300-400 F. **M** 100 F (lunch Sat & Sun), 140 F, 290 F.

Hôtel Sainte-Foy
(See restaurant above)
Closed Nov 5-Mar. 1 ste 850 F. 18 rms 300-800 F. Restaurant. Half-board 340-590 F. Air cond. Conf. Pkg. V, AE, MC.
A seventeenth-century building next to the abbey in the heart of this lovely village. The adjoining former convent houses an annex.

CONQUET (LE) 29217
Paris 620 - Brest 24 - Brignogan-Plage 57 *Finistère*

Pointe Sainte-Barbe
98 89 00 26, fax 98 89 14 81
Closed Mon off-seas, Nov 12-Dec 16. Open until 9:30pm. Priv rm: 40. No pets. Pkg. V, AE, DC, MC.
Near the tip of a rocky headland with panoramic views, this is the very model of a reliable seashore restaurant. The chef, Alain Floch, knows how to make the most of good, simple things: a pile of scrumptious Prat Ar Coum oysters, the freshest langoustines, and fish caught on the day and prepared without artifice. All perfectly cooked (and the mayonnaise is good, too). **C** 300-400 F. **M** 146 F (Sat), 212 F, 430 F.

Pointe Sainte-Barbe
(See restaurant above)
Closed Nov 12-Dec 16. 49 rms 185-607 F. Rms for disabled. Half-board 299-510 F. Conf. Golf. Pkg. Helipad. V, AE, DC, MC.
Almost all the superb, recently refreshed rooms have sea views, which is what you are paying for if you are lodged in the chilly-looking modern structure that overwhelms the original building. Family atmosphere, cheerful hospitality.

CONTAMINES-MONTJOIE (LES) 74170
Paris 607 - Megève 20 - Annecy 96 - Chamonix 34 *H.-Savoie*

Le Miage

Résidence de Tourisme
50 47 01 63, fax 50 47 14 08
Closed Apr 25-Jun 20, Sep 5-Dec 20. 12 stes 300-800 F. Restaurant. Pkg. V, MC.
Well-equipped rooms and suites with kitchenettes. Catering service available. This recently built hotel is right next to the ski runs.

CONTEVILLE 27210
Paris 184 - Deauville 28 - Le Havre 42 *Eure*

Auberge du Vieux Logis

32 57 60 16, fax 32 57 45 84
Closed Wed dinner, Thu, Jan 20-end Feb. Open until 9:30pm. Priv rm: 30. Pkg. V, AE, DC, MC.
A traditional timbered inn filled with pewter and copperware, a collection of antique pottery, and the smell of polished furniture. Maryse Louet will show you to your table, and her husband Yves offers perfectly prepared, traditional cuisine: warm andouille in the style of Vire with apples and cider, turbot fillet with edible seaweed and clam jus, and a chocolate-and-cherry-filled puff pastry. **C** 300-380 F (weekdays). **M** 130 F, 190 F, 230 F, 290 F, 360 F.

CONTREXÉVILLE 88140
Paris 324 - Epinal 48 - Nancy 76 - Neufchâteau 28 *Vosges*

Cosmos
Rue de Metz
29 07 61 61, fax 29 08 68 67
Closed mid Oct-Apr. 6 stes 716-860 F. 81 rms 358-425 F. Restaurant. Half-board 515-980 F. Conf. Heated pool. Tennis. Garage pkg. V, AE, DC, MC.
Quiet, elegant hotel with its own spa. Attractive period furniture; beautiful grounds. A hairdresser has a salon on the premises.

Établissement et Souveraine
Cour d'honneur et parc thermal
29 08 17 30, fax 29 08 68 67
Open year-round. 31 rms 171-422 F. Restaurant. Conf. Garage pkg. V, AE, DC, MC.
Two superbly renovated luxury hotels that have retained their spa atmosphere. Delightful setting.

COQUILLE (LA) 24450
Paris 421 - Périgueux 53 - Limoges 48 - Nontron 30 *Dordogne*

Les Voyageurs
12, rue de la République
53 52 80 13, fax 53 62 18 29
Closed Mon, Tues lunch, Oct 10-Apr 30. Open until 9pm (9:30pm in summer). Priv rm: 20. Garden dining. Valet pkg. V, DC.
On the long road to Santiago de Compostela, pilgrims may halt at this welcoming inn for generous, sincere dishes prepared by Gilbert Saussot: freshly-bagged grouse, freshly-caught trout, and traditional dishes, such as those on the generous 150 F menu: marinated salmon, duck breast with orange sauce, cheeses, and sherbets made with liqueurs. The wine list features some very attractive bottles of Bordeaux. Friendly service and reception. **C** 200-350 F. **M** 100 F, 150 F, 210 F.

Plan to travel? *Look for Gault Millau's other Best of guides to Chicago, Florida, Hawaii, Hong Kong, Germany, Italy, London, Los Angeles, New England, New Orleans, New York, Paris, San Francisco, Thailand, Toronto, and Washington, D.C.*

CORDES 81170
Paris 681 - Toulouse 78 - Montauban 71 - Albi 25   *Tarn*

 Grand Écuyer
Rue Voltaire
63 56 01 03, fax 63 56 18 83
Closed Mon & Tue lunch (exc Jul-Aug), Oct 16-Apr 15. Open until 9:30pm. Priv rm: 60. Air cond. Pkg. V, AE, DC, MC.
This storied, fifteenth-century hunting lodge built by the Counts of Toulouse sits smack in the center of one of France's loveliest fortified medieval villages. Gothic windows, sculpted columns, and thick stone walls set the tone. The cooking, however, had its ups and downs on our last visit: fine grilled sea bass with baby vegetables, but the langoustine ravioli were bready, and the red mullet salad lacked the coriander the menu said it would have, as well as being served in a parcimonious portion. But it's true that the locale is magical and the cellar splendid. C 370-480 F. M 180 F (exc Sun lunch), 280 F, 320 F, 360 F.

 Grand Écuyer
(See restaurant above)
See restaurant for closings. 1 ste 900-1,400 F. 12 rms 450-850 F. Half-board 590-690 F. Air cond. Conf. Pkg. V, AE, DC, MC.
The enormous fireplaces and period furniture lend plenty of charm, despite the rather overwhelming luxury of the decor. Lavishly equipped new bathrooms and extraordinary breakfasts with lots of rich pastries.

**Hostellerie
du Vieux Cordes**
63 56 00 12, fax 63 56 02 47
Closed Jan. 21 rms 265-420 F. Half-board 295-410 F. Conf. Pkg. V, AE, DC, MC.
A picturesque old house in the ancient heart of Cordes, with simple but comfortable rooms, some with magnificent valley views. Pleasant courtyard.

CORDON 74700
Paris 605 - Annecy 72 - Chamonix 30 - Sallanches 4   *H.-Savoie*

 Le Chamois d'Or
50 58 05 16, fax 50 93 72 96
Closed Apr 15-May, Sep 20-Dec 20. 1 ste 650-800 F. 32 rms 320-620 F. Restaurant. Half-board

360-550 F. Conf. Heated pool. Tennis. Valet pkg. V, AE, DC, MC.
One of Savoie's most pleasant hotels, in an Austrian-style chalet with a wonderful view of Mont Blanc. Sauna.

Les Rhodos
50 58 13 54, fax 50 58 57 23
Closed Apr 10-May 30, Sep 20-Dec 20. 30 rms 200-280 F. Restaurant. Half-board 210-270 F. Pkg. V, MC.
A cozy hotel with fine mountain views from both the terrace and the rooms.

 Les Roches Fleuries
50 58 06 71, fax 50 47 82 30
Closed Apr 15-30, Sep 25-Dec 20. Open until 9pm. Priv rm: 25. Garden dining. Heated pool. No pets. Valet pkg. V, AE, DC, MC.
The calm beauty of Mont Blanc hovers over the pretty terrace and charmingly decorated dining room of this mountain chalet. Chef Dominique Weber has proved his talents with winning dishes the likes of cuttlefish and clam fricassée in olive oil, a plate of truffles and tiny red potatoes, and roast fillet of féra (lake fish) with acha (wild celery). Fine cellar. Delightful welcome. Boîte à Fromages, under the same management, offers fondue, pella and raclettes for 150 F, everything included. C 250-400 F. M 128 F, 175 F, 270 F.

Les Roches Fleuries
(See restaurant above)
See restaurant for closings. 2 stes 650-850 F. 26 rms 370-700 F. Half-board 380-620 F. Conf. Heated pool. Golf. Valet pkg. V, AE, DC, MC.
Oh the views! The Mont Blanc massif is right out your window at this roomy, flower-decked chalet. Small bathrooms, big balconies, and rooms recently redecorated with floral wallpaper and sculpted wood. There is a gym on the premises, as well as a Jacuzzi, steam bath, and tanning room.

Solneige
50 58 04 06
Closed Sep 20-Dec 22. 25 rms 212-284 F. Restaurant. Half-board 245-265 F. Pkg. V.
Well-situated chalet-style hotel with splendid views from the balconies and the terrace full of flowers.

CORENC 38   → Grenoble

CORNILLON-CONFOUX 13
→ Salon-de-Provence

A disclaimer

Readers are advised that prices and conditions change over the course of time. The restaurants, hotels reviewed in this book have been reviewed over a period of time, and the reviews reflect the personal experiences and opinions of the reviewers. The reviewers and publishers cannot be held responsible for the experiences of the reader related to establishments reviewed. Readers are invited to write to the publisher with ideas, comments, and suggestions for future editions.

CORSICA

Bastia 153 - Bonifacio 140 - Calvi 163 - Porto 83   *Corse*

12/20 Auberge de la Terre Sacrée ✪
Route des Sanguinaires - 95 52 00 92
Open daily until 12:30am. Priv rm: 200. Terrace dining. Garage pkg. V, AE, DC, MC.
This unpretentious little wood-paneled restaurant is a stone's throw from the beach. The owner greets you warmly and regales you with a copious and tasty platter of local charcuterie, roast lamb, and a good tarte au broccio (a mild sheep cheese). Nice selection of local wines. Shady, vine-covered terrace. **C** 180-230 F. **M** 80 F.

 ### Campo dell'Oro
Plage Ricanto
95 22 32 41, fax 95 20 60 21
Open year-round. 1 ste 1,500 F. 129 rms 400-850 F. Rms for disabled. Restaurant. Half-board 250 F. Air cond. Conf. Pool. Tennis. Golf. Pkg. V, AE, DC, MC.
Don't miss the new swimming pool (in the shape of the island of Corsica); there's a huge terrace too, as well as rooms that overlook the sea and garden (the view is their best feature).

 ### Costa 🌲🍴
2, rue Colomba
95 21 43 02, fax 95 21 59 82
Open year-round. 53 rms 256-533 F. No pets. V, AE, DC, MC.
Modern and well-kept hotel with a garden, right near the sea (the beach is just 100 yards away). Spacious rooms.

 ### Fesch
7, rue Fesch
95 21 50 52, fax 95 21 83 36
Closed Dec 17-Jan 9. 77 rms 310-375 F. Half-board 490 F. Air cond. Conf. Pkg. V, AE, DC.
Double-glazed windows make for peaceful nights in the small but cozy and comfortable rooms, at this hotel in the heart of the old city.

La Mer
8 km W, route des Iles Sanguinaires
95 52 00 93, fax 95 52 07 15
Closed Nov-Mar 20. Open until 10pm. Terrace dining. Air cond. Pool. Pkg. V, AE, DC, MC.
Go straight through the dining room with its old-fashioned 1950s decor and take a table on the vast seafront terrace to admire the marvelous sunset. The cooking takes inspiration from the boundless sea: the skillfully prepared fresh seafood specialties include a delicate lobster tart with orange-scented onion cream, red mullet fillet in red wine with an artichoke cake, and a luscious strawberry concoction for dessert. Good selection of Corsican wines. An extra point this year. **C** 250-400 F. **M** 200 F.

 ### Dolce Vita 🌲🍴
(See restaurant above)
Closed Nov-Mar 20. 32 rms 420-940 F. Half-board 645-775 F. Air cond. Conf. Pool. Pkg. V, AE, DC, MC.

Rooms are rather small but functional, bright, and well furnished. Some open right onto the pine-shaded lawn facing the beach. Warm welcome, very good service.

 ### Les Mouettes
9, cours L.-Bonaparte
95 21 44 38, fax 95 21 71 80
Closed Oct 15-Apr 15. 1 ste 1,530 F. 19 rms 1,100 F. Restaurant. Half-board 540-860 F. Air cond. Conf. Pool. No pets. Golf. Pkg. V, AE, DC, MC.
The older, nicely renovated building houses old-fashioned but cozy rooms with decent bathrooms. Rooms in the modern building are larger, brighter, and air-conditioned, and some boast sea views as well.

Point U
59 bis, rue Fesch - 95 21 59 92
Closed Sun, Dec 22-28. Open until 11pm. Terrace dining. Air cond. V, MC.
Visit this charming, low-beamed restaurant to savor the cooking of chef Marie-Madeleine Nocéra, who we were delighted to discover has taken over the kitchen again after a few years of managing the dining room. Savor her delicious turbot in cider with tarragon, or Corsican specialties like local veal with olives and rock lobster à l'ancienne. The apples sautéed in Calvados make a yummy dessert. Reasonable prices, convivial atmosphere. **C** 250-380 F. **M** 90 F (lunch exc Sun), 165 F.

 ### La Toque Impériale
Route des Iles Sanguinaires
95 51 56 00, fax 95 52 05 03
Open daily until 11pm. Priv rm: 150. Garden dining. Air cond. No pets. Valet pkg. V, AE, DC, MC.
Chef Serge Lanoix, once rumored to be leaving the kitchens here, is at last report still offering his delicious Corsican and Burgundian cooking (he spent some years in Burgundy) in this lovely restaurant with a luminous dining room and sweeping view of the sea. His inventive, well crafted dishes include raviolis stuffed with kid, rock lobster with tarragon, grilled red mullet, and lobster pâté. The restaurant seems to gear itself to the summer season a bit too much. The wine list is the island's best. **C** 350-500 F. **M** 210 F, 280 F, 480 F.

 ### Eden Roc 🌲🍴
(See restaurant above)
Open year-round. Stes 480-2,420 F. 40 rms 340-1,940 F. Rms for disabled. Half-board 490-1,180 F. Air cond. Conf. Heated pool. Tennis. Valet pkg. Helipad. V, AE, DC, MC.
An imposing building on a hillside overlooking the sea; bright, carefully furnished rooms done in modern style, with pretty geranium-filled balconies facing the golf course. Charming welcome and smiling service. Sea-water spa, all water sports (private beach), and a variety of games equipment.

■ **In Cuttoli-Corticchiato 20167** 18 km NE

12/20 **Chez Pascal**
In Pedi-Morella
95 25 65 73
*Closed Mon, weekday & Sat lunch, Sun dinner, Oct.
Open until 10pm (11pm in summer). Priv rm: 80.
Terrace dining. Pkg. No cards.*
Thick country soup, roast lamb, tender broccio cannelloni, aged sheep's-milk cheese: the island repertoire doesn't change much *chez* Pascal. But since the food is straightforward, generous, and relatively inexpensive, hordes of locals from Ajaccio trek up to this small mountain village to enjoy a country feast. **M** 160 F (wine incl).

ARGENTELLA **20260**
Ajaccio 146 - Calvi 19 - Porto 65 - Galéria 15 *Corse*

Auberge de Ferayola ⚐🌳
95 65 25 25, fax 95 65 20 78
Closed Sep-May. 10 rms 350-410 F. Restaurant. Half-board 320-350 F. Pool. Tennis. No pets. Pkg. V, AE, MC.
Here in the midst of the *maquis*, rest and relaxation are guaranteed. The sea is close at hand.

ASCO **20276**
Ajaccio 125 - Bastia 64 - Corte 42 *Corse*

Le Chalet
12 km SW on D 1, in Haut-Asco
95 47 81 08, fax 95 30 25 59
Closings not available. 22 rms 140-220 F. Restaurant. Half-board 200-220 F. Conf. Pkg. V, AE, DC, MC.
Lovely view over the Cinto Mountains from some of the rooms, which are simple but well kept.

BASTELICA **20119**
Ajaccio 41 - Cauro 19 - Porticcio 34 - Corte 62 *Corse*

U Castagnetu ۞
95 28 70 71, fax 95 28 74 02
Closed Nov 1-Jan 1. Open until 10pm. Terrace dining. Hotel: 15 rms 215-330 F. Half-board 270-305 F. Conf. Pkg. V, AE, DC, MC.
Dine on the little terrace overlooking the village, or in the cool, inviting dining room of this pretty stone house surrounded by chestnut trees. The authentic Corsican cooking includes good house charcuterie, huge ragoûts (pork, lamb) served in earthenware bowls, and unexpectedly refined desserts. Pleasant service, limited cellar. **C** 200-300 F. **M** 85 F (exc Sun), 99 F, 150 F.

11/20 **Chez Paul**
95 28 71 59
Open daily until 11pm. Terrace dining. V, AE, MC.
Overlooking the old village, this mountain bistro serves its own charcuterie (the pigs are raised right here), boar stewed in white wine with cèpes, lamb in a sauce, orange crêpes, and delicious sheep's-milk cheeses, washed down with tasty local wines. **M** 75 F, 95 F, 125 F.

BASTIA **20200**
Ajaccio 153 - Porto 135 - Calvi 93 - Bonifacio 170 *Corse*

⑬ **La Citadelle**
5, rue du Dragon - 95 31 44 70
Closed Sun. Open until 10:30pm. Terrace dining. Air cond. V, AE, MC.
Here in a converted olive-oil mill François Mattei, a former Lenôtre pastry cook, exercises talents that extend well beyond desserts, witness his langoustines in snail butter, veal kidney in herb sauce, and orange-filled puff pastry, as well as many Corsican dishes. **C** 270-350 F. **M** 130 F (weekday lunch), 200 F (dinner).

Piétracap ⚐🌳
Pietranera, route de San Martino
95 31 64 63, fax 95 31 39 00
Closed Dec 15-Feb. 42 rms 300-880 F. Air cond. Conf. Pool. Pkg. V, AE, DC, MC.
In an olive grove overlooking the sea, spacious rooms (some recently added), very well equipped.

⑬ **Le Romantique**
4 bis, rue du Pontetto - 95 32 30 85
Closed lunch Sat & Sun (in seas), Feb. Open until 11pm. Priv rm: 8. Terrace dining. Pkg. V, AE, DC, MC.
Chef Marie-Thérèse Roncaglia excels in seafood dishes, but also offers some terrestrial cooking: puff pastry with salmon, brousse, and fresh mint; casserole-roasted rabbit thigh in red wine; the freshest fish grilled or oven-roasted. There's a lovely terrace overlooking the port. **C** 200-250 F. **M** 120 F.

■ **In Erbalunga 20222** 10 km N on D 80

⚐🏠 **Castel'Brando**
95 33 10 33, fax 95 33 98 18
Closed Oct 15-Mar. 6 stes 500-800 F. 10 rms 350-530 F. Air cond. Pool. Pkg. V, AE.
Set in the heart of a sweet fishing village and just minutes from the sea, this small nineteenth-century manor house boasts handsome rooms with kitchenettes. Ancient palm trees and a Roman bath-style swimming pool add to the charm. Very courteous welcome.

⑬ **Le Pirate**
In Brando - 95 33 24 20
Closed Mon (exc Jul-Aug), Nov-Mar. Open until 9pm (11pm in seas). Terrace dining. Air cond. AE.
Le Pirate stands out in this neck of the woods, not known as a gastronome's paradise. Nothing dazzlingly original here, but ingredients are chosen with discernment and handled with respect for their innate flavors. Good bets are the ravioli stuffed with thyme-scented lamb, shellfish with vegetables, and red mullet à la provençale. The cellar holds some interesting native vintages. **C** 250-320 F. **M** 140 F (weekday lunch), 200 F.

🌳🏠
This symbol signifies hotels that are exceptionally quiet.

In Palagaccio 20200

2.5 km N

L'Alivi
Route du Cap
95 31 61 85, fax 95 31 03 95
Open year-round. 37 rms 450-780 F. Air cond. Conf. Pool. Garage pkg. V, MC.
Here's a comfortable, modern (in the rather chilly cement-oriented style on the outside), well-equipped hotel just above a pebble beach facing the Tuscan islands. Rooms with loggias. Garden with new swimming pool.

BOCOGNANO   20136
Ajaccio 40 - Corte 43   *Corse*

12/20 L'Ustaria
95 27 41 10
Closed Sun dinner off-seas, Feb 25-Mar 25. Open until 9:30pm. Priv rm: 8. Garden dining. No pets. Pkg. No cards.
Mementos abound in this charming family's cozy stone house. The son's adroit cooking features Mediterranean specialties: foie gras with chestnut-flour crêpes, shrimp cake, and wild-fig soup. All are diligently served in the restaurant's two dining rooms, one a bistrot and the other "gourmet". C 250-350 F. M 83 F, 99 F, 135 F, 190 F, 225 F.

BONIFACIO   20169
Ajaccio 140 - Bastia 170 - Porto-Vecchio 27   *Corse*

La Caravelle
On the harbor
95 73 06 47, fax 95 73 02 45
Closed Oct-Mar. Open until 11pm. Priv rm: 270. Terrace dining. Air cond. Garage pkg. V, AE, DC, MC.
Tourists flock to this restaurant, where the seafood-oriented cooking is reliable though with a tendency toward unnecessary elaboration (pink pepper, cherry tomatoes). Focus on the absolutely sensational spaghetti with rock lobster sauce. La Caravelle's façade is the loveliest in this over-built port, where the pavement is being extended to accommodate even more tourists. Good bread, excellent wine list. C 300-500 F. M 250 F (wine incl), 145 F.

La Caravelle
(See restaurant above)
Closed Oct-Mar. 3 stes 1,200-1,500 F. 26 rms 360-1,200 F. Air cond. Conf. Tennis. V, AE, DC.
Across from the marina in the liveliest part of town, here are some 30 attractively decorated, well-appointed rooms in a surprisingly quiet hotel. A three-year renovation has just been completed.

Hôtel Genovese
Haute Ville
95 73 12 34, fax 95 73 09 03
Open year-round. 2 stes 950-1,700 F. 12 rms 700-1,500 F. Air cond. Conf. Golf. No pets. Pkg. V, AE, DC, MC.
The former legionnaires' barracks in the old city overlooking the bay and port is now a deluxe hotel complex. Refined modern decor with opulent rooms and suites. Good breakfasts.

Stella d'Oro
7, rue du Gal-de-Gaulle - 95 73 03 63
Closed Oct 20-Apr 20. Open until 10pm (midnight in Jul-Aug). Air cond. V, AE, DC, MC.
Chef Jeanne-Marie Etori is in charge of the kitchen in this simple, welcoming restaurant. Enjoy her generous servings of well-prepared family-style dishes like pizzas cooked in a wood-fired oven, fresh pasta, and grilled meats and fish. Enticing regional wines. C 150-200 F.

CALA-ROSSA 20   → Porto-Vecchio

CALVI   20260
Ajaccio 163 - Bastia 93 - Porto 80 - Corte 96   *Corse*

L'Abbaye
Route de Santore
95 65 05 56, fax 95 65 30 23
Closed Nov-Mar. 45 rms 300-820 F. Rms for disabled. Restaurant. Half-board 360-880 F. Air cond. Conf. Pkg. V, AE, DC, MC.
In a pastoral setting 100 meters from sea and port, the former Saint François abbey has been artfully converted; it offers tidily kept, comfortable, but overdecorated rooms. Panoramic terrace over the sea. Pleasant welcome.

Hôtel Balanéa
6, rue Clemenceau
95 65 00 45, fax 95 65 29 71
Open year-round. 38 rms 300-1,200 F. Air cond. Conf. Pkg. V, AE, DC, MC.
Attractive, fully renovated old house. The sizeable rooms are air-conditioned and soundproofed; half look out over the port.

Le Magnolia
Pl. du Marché
95 65 19 16, fax 95 65 34 52
Closed Jan-Feb. 12 rms 450-800 F. Restaurant. Half-board 650 F. Air cond. Conf. No pets. V, AE, DC, MC.
An adorable all-white nineteenth-century manor house set in a garden between the church and the marketplace in the old district of Calvi. Rooms are well equipped and decorated with impeccable taste, and there's a magnificent magnolia tree on the premises.

La Signoria
On the airport road
95 65 23 73, fax 95 65 38 77
Closed Nov-Mar. Open until 10:30pm. Priv rm: 12. Terrace dining. Pool. Pkg. V, AE, MC.
Christian Sirurguet's repertoire gleams with Corsican sunshine and bursts with *joie de vivre*. We loved the mouthwatering salmon carpaccio in a sweet-sour sauce with figs and aromatic herbs, young chicken in a chestnut croûte, and a yummy sesame seed and poppy seed croquant. The setting: an intimate dining room in a seventeenth-century residence surrounded by waving palm trees. The cellar focuses on Corsican wines. Competent service. C 380-450 F. M 360 F.

La Signoria
(See restaurant above)
Closed Nov-Mar. 2 stes 1,000-2,000 F. 8 rms 450-1,100 F. Half-board 575-900 F. Pool. Tennis. Golf. Pkg. V, AE, MC.
Absolutely delightful rooms looking out on the mountain beyond the eucalyptus and olive trees

and swimming pool. Rentals of motorboats and sailboats, tennis, and horseback riding.

La Villa
Chemin N.-D.-de-la-Serra
95 65 10 10, fax 95 65 10 50
Closed Jan 2-Mar 31. Open until 10:30pm. Garden dining. Air cond. Heated pool. No pets. Valet pkg. V, AE, DC, MC.
Perched above Calvi in peaceful grounds, La Villa attracts a smart clientele (natives and visitors alike) with its luminous dining room and covered terrace. The food is an additional draw: Jean-Michel Bonnet is an accomplished chef whose elegant dishes continue to merit their toque. Like us, you'll savor his cream of fava beans with croutons, oven-roasted chapon de mer (a local fish) with peppers in olive oil, and an apple and honey puff pastry. The cellar holds a small but choice selection of island wines. Swift, attentive service. C 350-500 F.

La Villa
(See restaurant above)
Closed Jan 2-Mar 31. 7 stes 1,150-2,700 F. 18 rms 800-2,000 F. Half-board 600-1,550 F. Air cond. Conf. Heated pool. Tennis. Golf. No pets. Pkg. Helipad. V, AE, DC, MC.
This is Calvi's most select address, offering spacious, well-equipped, sunny rooms and suites decorated in handsome contemporary style. Each boasts a terrace or balcony with a sweeping view over the grounds and bay. The steep rates are justified.

CANALE-DI-VERDE	20230
Ajaccio 152 - Corte 69 - Aléria 21	Corse

12/20 Le Roc
95 38 83 16
Closings not available. Open by reserv. Priv rm: 30. Terrace dining. Air cond. Pkg. V, AE, MC.
The superb terrace encircled by rocks, close to a meadow overlooking the Alistro Bay, is a well-known beauty spot. The patronne's cooking is conservative but skillfully done: sample her typically Corsican combination of chestnuts and lonzo (a lean pork sausage), duck breast in a raspberry-vinegar reduction, and lime crêpe soufflée. C 250-350 F. M 150 F, 250 F (dinner & Sun, wine incl), 350 F (dinner, wine incl).

CENTURI-PORT	20238
Ajaccio 210 - St-Florent 60 - Bastia 55 - Rogliano 15	Corse

10/20 Le Vieux Moulin
95 35 60 15, fax 95 35 60 24
Closed Nov-Feb. Open until 11pm. Priv rm: 25. Garden dining. Pkg. V, AE, DC, MC.
The setting is wonderful—a small port town at the tip of the Corsican cape. Too bad the quiet, shaded terrace and view are so much better than the overpriced cooking: fish liver salad, macaroni with fresh rock lobster, tiny lasagna with scampi, and a fresh fruit gratin with eau-de-vie. C 320-400 F. M 150 F, 220 F, 270 F.

CORTE	20250
Ajaccio 83 - Bastia 70 - Calvi 96 - Porto 86	Corse

Dominique Colonna
Vallée de la Restonica
95 61 05 45, fax 95 61 03 91
Open year-round. 28 rms 320-540 F. Rms for disabled. Restaurant. Half-board 325-430 F. Conf. Pool. Pkg. V, AE, DC, MC.
Set beside a stream that rushes across Corte's picturesque valley, this hotel of recent vintage offers spacious, tasteful accommodation with good equipment. Generous breakfasts; attentive service.

CUTTOLI-CORTICCHIATO 20	→ Ajaccio

ERBALUNGA 20	→ Bastia

ILE-ROUSSE (L')	20220
Ajaccio 165 - Bastia 68 - Calvi 24 - Corte 72	Corse

La Bergerie
Route de Monticcello
95 60 01 28, fax 95 60 06 36
Closed Mon off-seas (exc hols), Nov 10-Mar 15. Open until 10pm. Priv rm: 60. Garden dining. Pool. Pkg. V, MC.
An eclectic roster of solid, mostly seafood dishes is proposed at this cozily converted old Corsican farmhouse. Seated in the pleasant, shady garden, you can sample the unusual sea-urchin omelette, a Moroccan fish tajine, cous-cous, or paella, and break open a bottle of reasonably priced Corsican wine. Family-style welcome. C 250-300 F.

La Pietra
Route du port
95 60 01 45, fax 95 60 15 92
Closed Oct 20-Mar. 40 rms 280-630 F. Restaurant. Half-board 315-420 F. Air cond. Pkg. V, AE, DC, MC.
This modern hotel stands perched on the rocks of Ile-Rousse. The spare, contemporary, comfortable rooms (a bit of redecoration wouldn't hurt) have loggias that open to a view of the sea. Smiling welcome.

■ **In Pigna 20220**   8 km SE on D 151

11/20 Casa Musicale
95 61 77 31, fax 95 61 77 81
Closed Mon, Jan-Feb 15. Open until 10pm. Priv rm: 70. Terrace dining. Pkg. V, MC.
The harmonious, simple cooking—served on a pleasant terrace suspended between hills and sea—offers variations on the theme of local land-based specialties: tagliatelle with broccio cheese, veal tripe with olives, and a honey parfait. Traditional music is played on Saturdays. C 180-280 F. M 100 F.

The C (A la carte) restaurant prices given are for a complete three-course meal for one, including a half-bottle of modest wine and service. M (Menus) prices are for a complete fixed-price meal for one, excluding wine (unless otherwise noted).

LUCCIANA   20290
Bastia 19 - Poretta Airport 5 - Casamozza 5   *Corse*

Hôtel Poretta
Route de l'aéroport
95 36 09 54, fax 95 36 15 32
Open year-round. 2 stes 680-960 F. 29 rms 340 F. Rms for disabled. Air cond. Conf. Golf. No pets. Pkg. V, AE, DC, MC.
An anonymous modern building practically situated, with the airport just a stone's throw away. Rooms are pleasant, functional, and well equipped.

OLMETO   20113
Ajaccio 65 - Sartène 21   *Corse*

12/20   U Santa Maria
Pl. de l'Église - 95 74 65 59
Open daily until 10pm. Priv rm: 40. Terrace dining. Pkg. V, AE, DC, MC.
Served in a dining room brightened by a collection of earthenware plates, the *patronne*'s copious, fixed-price repertoire sings with pristine regional flavors: herbed tripe, zucchini with broccio cheese, and a broccio cheese tart. **M 130 F, 160 F.**

PALAGACCIO 20   → Bastia

PIGNA 20   → Ile-Rousse (L')

PILA-CANALE   20123
Ajaccio 36 - Propriano 29 - Petreto-Biccisaro 18   *Corse*

Le "20123"
95 24 20 80
Closed Sat & Sun (exc in winter), Wed, Sep 15-Nov 15. Open until 9:30pm. Terrace dining. No cards.
A single—but authentic and delicious—menu has earned a faithful following for this family-run country inn. Book a table on the terrace to taste Marie-Antoinette Habani's home-prepared charcuterie, crêpes stuffed with broccio cheese, wild boar civet with gnocchi, and chestnut flan, washed down with engaging little island wines. Expect a warm welcome. The cellar, however, could stand some improvement. **M 145 F.**

PIOGGIOLA   20259
Calvi 48 - Belgodère 20 - Olmi-Capella 4   *Corse*

12/20   Auberge Aghjola
95 61 90 48, fax 95 61 92 99
Closed Mon lunch, Jan-Mar. Open until 11pm. Terrace dining. Pool. No pets. Pkg. V, AE, DC, MC.
The soul of Corsica in your plate, in this hamlet perched at an altitude of 1,000 meters right in the heart of the island. The owner of this welcoming place concocts some appetizing versions of local dishes: taste one (or several) of his delicious terrines, coppa en croûte, eel, and the local cheeses, and finish up with a refreshing orange and cream-cheese flan (fiadone). These good things are even more delicious when enjoyed on the beautiful shaded terrace. **M 160 F** (only by reserv).

Auberge Aghjola
(See restaurant above)
Closed Nov 15-end Mar. 12 rms 300-375 F. Pool. Pkg. V, AE, DC, MC.
Far, far away from the crowds. Simple but very comfortable rooms.

PORTICCIO   20166
Ajaccio 19 - Sartène 80 - Bastia 153 - Calvi 163   *Corse*

Le Caroubier
Pointe de Porticcio
95 29 40 40, fax 95 25 00 63
Closed Dec. Open until 10:15pm. Terrace dining. No pets. Valet pkg. V, AE, DC, MC.
Chef Gérard Mosiniak has brought his toque-worthy talent to Le Caroubier. This Sofitel hotel-restaurant, encircled by greenery, commands a marvelous setting on a headland in the Gulf of Ajaccio, with a swimming pool that juts out above the rocks and numerous hidden coves below. It's a fine place to savor Mosiniak's ambitious cuisine (warm salad of red mullet with purple artichokes and rice vinegar, veal shanks braised in red Patrimonio wine, and a vanilla yoghurt and rhubarb parfait). Though the selection of wines is rather unoriginal, the prices are reasonable. Streamlined lunch menu available. **C 260-390 F. M 140 F, 280 F.**

Sofitel Porticcio
(See restaurant above)
Closed Dec. 2 stes 1,025-2,220 F. 96 rms 525-1,720 F. Rms for disabled. Half-board 620-1,450 F. Air cond. Conf. Heated pool. Tennis. Valet pkg. Helipad. V, AE, DC, MC.
The 1960s architecture seems to have grown on people, and is now more or less accepted. The comfortable rooms boast terraces for sunbathing, and captivating sea views. Spectacular swimming pool; sea-water therapy treatments. The proximity to Campo dell'Oro airport is convenient; the noise less so.

Le Maquis
On D 55
95 25 05 55, fax 95 25 11 70
Open year-round. 5 stes 1,950-5,550 F. 25 rms 700-1,900 F. Restaurant. Half-board 950-2,950 F. Air cond. Conf. Heated pool. Tennis. Garage pkg. V, AE, DC, MC.
Idyllic bungalows surrounded by flower gardens, a stone's throw from the beach. Fireplace, living rooms, antique furniture: a whole lifestyle. This might just be Corsica's best hotel. There's a restaurant. High prices.

PORTICCIOLO   20228
Ajaccio 178 - Bastia 25 - Barcaggio 32   *Corse*

Caribou
95 35 02 33, fax 95 35 01 13
Closed Sep-Jul. 6 stes 650-800 F. 30 rms 650-800 F. Restaurant. Half-board 600-750 F. Conf. Pool. Tennis. Pkg. V, AE, DC, MC.
A pleasant waterside hotel offering bungalows and comfortable rooms. Superb view over the sea, the cove, the fine sandy beach, and the Isle of Elba.

12/20 Torra Marina
95 35 00 80
Closed Oct-Mar. Open until 10pm. Garden dining. Pkg. V, AE, DC, MC.
Fish fresh from local waters form the basis of this simple, deftly wrought cuisine, served in the cool of the inn's beamed cellar or on the garden terrace. Choose from among the best vintages of upper Corsica to accompany your grilled langoustine, red mullet, and John Dory fillets with shellfish. **C** 240-310 F. **M** 130 F, 150 F (lunch, wine incl).

PORTO 20150
Ajaccio 83 - Bastia 135 - Corte 86 - Calvi 76 - Evisa 23   Corse

 ### Les Flots Bleus
Marine de Porto
95 26 11 26, fax 95 26 12 64
Closed Oct-Mar. 20 rms 290-380 F. Restaurant. Half-board 300-380 F. Pkg. V, MC.
This long building leans up against the mountain, wedged in a cleft in the rock; marvelous views of the coast and the Gulf of Porto. Rooms are comfortable and functional.

■ In Serriera 20147   *3.5 km N on D 81*

 ### Eden Park
Golfe de Porto, plage de Bussaglia
95 26 10 60, fax 95 26 11 57
Closed Oct 15-May 1. 3 stes 600-1,500 F. 30 rms 400-580 F. Restaurant. Half-board 350-740 F. Air cond. Pool. Tennis. Garage pkg. V, AE, DC, MC.
In the mountains but near the sea, bugalows overlooking a pine grove that live up to the hotel's name. Lovely, romantic, air-conditioned rooms, no televisions. Bar with giant-screen TV if you must.

PORTO-POLLO 20140
Ajaccio 133 - Sartène 33 - Propriano 20   Corse

Les Eucalyptus
95 74 01 52, fax 95 74 06 56
Closings not available. 27 rms 260-325 F. Restaurant. Half-board 270-315 F. Tennis. No pets. Pkg. V, AE, DC, MC.
Simple, light rooms in a modern building overlooking the Gulf of Valinco. Panoramic restaurant.

PORTO-VECCHIO 20137
Ajaccio 133 - Sartène 63 - Bonifacio 27 - Bastia 143   Corse

Le Baladin
13, rue du Gal-Leclerc
95 70 08 62, fax 95 70 55 95
Closed Nov 15-Jan 15. Open until 11:30pm. Priv rm: 35. Air cond. Pkg. V, AE, DC, MC.
Decorated in pastel colors, and led by a gifted chef (Pierrick Berthier), Le Baladin has been charming people for twenty years. The current menu features seductive cooking with sometimes over-the-top flavors: sea scallops with frozen leek mousse, meltingly tender lamb in thyme sauce, white chocolate mousse glacé with saffron sauce. Small, adequate wine list. Very gracious welcome and service, overseen by the charming owners. **C** 290-400 F. **M** 160 F (weekdays, Sat dinner).

Belvédère
Route de Palombaggia - 95 70 54 13
Closed Mon (Nov-Jan 5), Jan 5-Mar 31. Open until 10:30pm. Terrace dining. Pool. No pets. Pkg. V, AE, DC, MC.
Set in fragrant pine woods edged by a sandy beach across from Porto-Vecchio, the Belvédère is a refreshing oasis with a patio and panoramic beachfront dining room. As we go to press, Bernard Bach has just taken over here, and is expected to maintain the house tradition for sunny cooking with surprising contrasts: warm anchovy fillets in herb vinaigrette with a preserved tomato tarte tatin and frozen garlic cream, red mullet with tapenade, and a chocolate concoction flavored with tea. **C** 300-500 F. **M** 190 F, 300 F, 380 F.

 ### Belvédère
(See restaurant above)
See restaurant for closings. 3 stes 1,150-4,580 F. 16 rms. Rms for disabled. Half-board 590-2,200 F. Conf. Pool. Golf. No pets. Pkg. V, AE, DC, MC.
The cheerfully decorated rooms are housed in bungalows, to give the hotel a club-like feel. All the freshly refurbished rooms have (not very private) terraces with views of the bay, and are equipped with kitchenettes. Small beach; superb swimming pool.

Le Moby-Dick
95 70 70 00, fax 95 70 70 01
Closed Oct 1-Mar. Open until 9:30pm. Terrace dining. No pets. Garage pkg. V, AE, DC, MC.
The chef here is committed to high-quality ingredients, and it shows: crab salad with preserved tomatoes and chive vinaigrette, a touch of nobility for this shellfish; barigoule of langoustines in delicate olive oil with jullienned carrots and onions; chapon (a Corsican fish) braised Bonifacio style with zucchini, tomatoes, and tarragon; farm-raised, milk-fed lamb enlivened with rosemary; delicate dark chocolate tart with warm orange sauce. Truly fine cooking by a great professional who understands how to balance flavors. You can dine on a terrace just a few yards from the sea. **C** 250-450 F. **M** 170 F (lunch), 200 F (dinner).

Le Moby-Dick
(See restaurant above)
Closed Oct 15-Mar. 44 rms 400-1,520 F. Restaurant. Half-board 470-1,050 F. Conf. Tennis. Pkg. Helipad. V, AE, DC, MC.
The site is stunning (a spit of land between a lake and the sea), though the hotel/leisure complex itself is less pleasing to the eye. Nevertheless, rooms are bright and boast good bathrooms.

Le Régina
Route de Bastia
95 70 14 94, fax 95 70 41 34
Closed Dec 3-Mar 6. Open until 10pm. Priv rm: 80. Terrace dining. Heated pool. Pkg. V, AE, DC, MC.
We came here just as the place opened and only sampled the brand-new menu, but some things can't deceive: the way the sea bream was cooked (perfectly), the reduction of the sauce (daring, the chef used Sangria), and the perfect classicism of the coquelet. The house now has a fine chef; if only the service could be improved. But in general, a good first impression. **C** 300-450 F. **M** 160 F, 230 F.

Hôtel du Roi Théodore

(See restaurant above)

Closed Dec-Feb. 2 stes 600-1,480 F. 37 rms 340-1,000 F. Restaurant. Half-board 200-250 F. Conf. Heated pool. Tennis. Garage pkg. V, AE, DC.

Set back from the road, the hotel offers rooms that are relatively quiet, cool, and well equipped, with views of a garden and a swimming pool surrounded by luxuriant oleanders. The decor is an improbable mix of Corsican and Moroccan styles. Pleasant welcome and very professional service. Boating excursions can be arranged.

■ In Cala-
Rossa 20137   10 km NE on N 198, D 568, D 4

Grand Hôtel de Cala-Rossa 🏵
Route de Cala-Rossa
95 71 61 51, fax 95 71 60 11

Closed Jan 2-Apr 15. Open until 10pm. Garden dining. Air cond. No pets. Valet pkg. V, AE, DC, MC.

This is our pick for Corsica's best restaurant. Chef Georges Billon, a native of Lyon, has had a decade to familiarize himself with Corsica's bounty, starting with local seafood taken straight from the boat to the kitchen: lovely rock lobster sautéed with thyme, served with delicious crêpes filled with fresh herbs. Admirably simple shellfish salad with basil. Fine chapon de mer (a local fish) braised Bonifacio style. Superbly tender roast squab in myrtle wine, perfectly seasoned and cooked, served with olive-studded polenta. Desserts are just as delectable. Such delights seem all the more wonderful when served on the idyllic terrace of this estate hidden behind luxuriant pines, oleanders, and bamboos. Relaxed yet very professional service. The wine list is extensive, but the best bets are Corsican vintages, like the superb Domaine de Torraccia or the Fiumicicli from Sartène. Lower prices at lunch from mid-June to mid-September. **C** 300-400 F. **M** 160 F (lunch exc Sun), 200 F (Sun lunch), 300 F, 400 F (dinner).

Grand Hôtel de Cala-Rossa 🏯 🌲
(See restaurant above)

Closed Jan 2-Apr 14. 3 stes 1,260-2,600 F. 50 rms 450-2,300 F. Half-board 630-1,750 F. Air cond. Conf. Tennis. No pets. Valet pkg. Helipad. V, AE, DC, MC.

The interior architecture and lush gardens of this exceptional establishment are so lovely that one nearly forgets about the beach. Perfect fixtures, furnishings, and soundproofing; yummy breakfasts with croissants, rolls, fresh bread, and homemade jams. Outside, guests may enjoy the private beach with Polynesian straw huts, excursion boats, water-skiing, deep-sea fishing... Try to avoid July and August, though, when crowds and prices increase.

■ In La Trinité-de-Porto-
Vecchio 20137   7 km N on N 18 and D 468

L'Orée du Maquis
RN 198, route de la Lézardière
95 70 22 21

Closed Sun & Mon (exc Jul-Aug), Dec-Apr 15. Open until 9:30pm. Terrace dining. Pool. Pkg. V, AE, MC.

Danielle Carteaud entertains at home in her villa, which she has transformed into a restaurant that serves a maximum of 12 people in winter and 30 in summer. Her guests are encouraged to enjoy the garden and its cork-oak trees, set right in the midst of the *maquis* with a view out to sea. The menu changes daily in tune with what the market offers, but you can be certain that the food will be polished and inventive. A recent meal: lobster ravioli, bar with pistou, pear charlotte. All the best Corsican vintages are on hand, as well as some fine Côtes-du-Rhônes. **M** 125 F, 375 F.

PROPRIANO   20110
Ajaccio 74 - Corte 138 - Sartène 13 - Bonifacio 67   *Corse*

11/20 Le Cabanon
Av. Napoléon - 95 76 07 76

Closed Dec-Mar. Open until 10pm. Priv rm: 120. Terrace dining. Pkg. V, AE, DC, MC.

Seafood prepared with a minimum of fuss is served on a terrace hard by the harbor. The fish is so fresh you feel it has just jumped from the water onto your plate. Try the sea bass in salt crust and you'll see what we mean. **C** 250-400 F. **M** 85 F, 120 F.

Grand Hôtel Miramar 🏵
Route de la Corniche
95 76 06 13, fax 95 76 13 14

Closings not available. Open until 10:30pm. Priv rm: 60. Terrace dining. Air cond. Pool. No pets. Garage pkg. V, AE, MC.

The elegant dining room is quite a sight, but in season everyone prefers the poolside terrace with its view of the sea. Gisèle Louichi, the chef, excels with perfectly prepared dishes favoring the full-bodied flavors of quality Corsican foodstuffs. Try the tasty local ham, terrific zucchini with broccio cheese, mutton with beans, earthy tripettes sartenaise, and bread pudding with pears and vanilla ice cream. Fine selection of Corsican wines. Competent, relaxed service. **C** 300-550 F. **M** 100 F (lunch), 180 F, 260 F (dinner).

Grand Hôtel Miramar 🏯
(See restaurant above)

Closed Oct-Apr. 3 stes 1,100-2,100 F. 25 rms 440-830 F. Half-board 735 F. Air cond. Conf. Heated pool. No pets. Valet pkg. V, AE, DC, MC.

The recently renovated Miramar, situated in two leafy acres high above the Gulf of Valinco, now boasts a sauna as well as huge, bright, and airy rooms with balconies looking out to sea. Affable welcome and service.

QUENZA   20122
Ajaccio 84 - Porto-Vecchio 47 - Sartène 44   *Corse*

12/20 Sole i Monti 🏵
95 78 62 53, fax 95 78 63 88

Closed Oct-Mar 15. Open until 10pm. Terrace dining. No pets. Hotel: 20 rms 275-450 F. Half-board 300-450 F. Conf. Pkg. V, AE, DC, MC.

The owner-chef's simple, solid cooking proves beyond a doubt his love of Corsica: robust charcuteries, old-fashioned grilled suckling pig, and broccio cheese omelettes, washed down with local wines. Enjoy this down-to-earth fare by the fireside in restful surroundings. **C** 230-300 F. **M** 200 F (Sun), 150 F.

SAGONE 20118
Ajaccio 38 - Piana 33 - Porto 45   *Corse*

11/20 L'Ancura
On the harbor - 95 28 04 93
Closed Oct-Mar. Open until 11:30pm. Terrace dining. V.
Refreshing, generous fare is what you'll find at this rustic Corsican inn with a terrace overlooking the sea and another with a view of the mountains: salmon tartare, swordfish rillettes, mixed smoked fish, or fricasséed scampi. **C** 170-300 F. **M** 87 F.

SAINT-FLORENT 20217
Ajaccio 176 - Bastia 23 - Calvi 70 - L'Ile-Rousse 46   *Corse*

Hôtel Dolce Notte
95 37 06 65, fax 95 37 10 70
Closed Oct-Mar. 20 rms 295-580 F. Pkg. V, DC, MC.
Away from the village (and its noise) but right on the sea, this engaging modern hotel offers studio-style rooms with spacious, modern bathrooms and private balconies or loggias from which to admire the view. Genuinely attentive welcome.

12/20 La Rascasse
Esplanade du Port - 95 37 06 99
Closed Mon off-seas, Oct-Mar. Open until 11pm. Terrace dining. Air cond. V, AE, DC, MC.
The terrace overlooks the port, source of the prime ingredients for this restaurant's fresh cooking: the shellfish, sea bream, chapon de mer, etc. are best simply grilled. Try the Grand Marnier soufflé. Charming welcome and service. **C** 210-320 F.

La Table du Roy
95 37 00 06, fax 95 30 14 83
Closed Oct-Mar 10. Open until 10:30pm. Terrace dining. Pool. No pets. Pkg. V, AE, DC.
Flavors of the sea, the *maquis*, and nearby Italy combine in the excellent summery cooking served at this holiday hotel-restaurant with one of the most breathtaking views in northern Corsica—le Cap Corse. François Prudent profers piperade and stuffed macaroni, sea bream in a chestnut-bread crust, scampi fritters, and a soufflé of white peaches flavored with myrtle. Diversified wine list. **C** 300-350 F. **M** 180 F, 250 F.

La Table du Roi
(See restaurant above)
Closed Nov-Apr. 2 stes 900 F. 21 rms 650-1,900 F. Rms for disabled. Half-board 450-950 F. Air cond. Conf. Pool. Tennis. Pkg. Helipad. V, AE, DC.
Small, prettily outfitted rooms (the wrought-iron beds are the work of a local craftsman); some lead directly into the garden, while those on upper floors afford lovely views. Boating excursions arranged.

SERRIERA 20   → Porto

TRINITÉ-DE-PORTO-VECCHIO (LA) 20
→ Porto-Vecchio

CORTE 20   → CORSICA

COTEAU (LE) 42   → Roanne

COTINIÈRE (LA) 17   → Oléron (Ile d')

COUARDE-SUR-MER (LA) 17
→ Ré (Ile de)

COULOMMIERS 77120
Paris 60 - Sens 77 - Meaux 29 - Melun 46   *Seine/Marne*

12/20 Le Clos du Theil
42, rue du Theil - 64 65 11 63
Closed Mon dinner, Tue, Feb 13-28, Aug 16-31. Open until 9:30pm. Priv rm: 35. Air cond. V.
Dig into robust, bountiful cooking in what was once a village grocery store. Try the warm Lyons sausage, beef fillet with shallot confit, and île flottante. You'll be warmly welcomed into a comfortable, pleasant dining room. **C** 270-380 F. **M** 140 F, 195 F.

COURBEVOIE 92   → PARIS Suburbs

COURCELLES-SUR-VESLE 02 → Soissons

COURCHEVEL 73120
Paris 653 - Chambéry 99 - Annecy 96 - Albertville 51   *Savoie*

Les Airelles
Jardin Alpin
79 09 38 38, fax 79 08 38 69
Closed Apr 23-Dec 15. Open until 10:30pm. Priv rm: 60. Terrace dining. Heated pool. No pets. Valet pkg. V, AE, DC, MC.
Chef Michel Renaud is a generous man, and it shows in his simple, carefully prepared, celebratory (to fit the surroundings) and restorative (for the skiers) cuisine. Savor the cabbage stuffed with sliced truffle, the lamb fillet with fat Soissons beans, and the spit-roasted meats. And don't miss the fabulous Savoyard buffet offered for Sunday lunch, with charcuterie, cheeses, gratins, and diots, in itself worth two toques. Theme evenings (gypsy or Russian orchestras, etc.). **C** 460-800 F. **M** 295 F (lunch), 390 F (dinner).

Les Airelles
(See restaurant above)
Closed Apr 23-Dec 15. 4 stes 7,400-13,600 F. 52 rms 2,250-5,700 F. Rms for disabled. Half-board 1,300-2,950 F. Conf. Heated pool. Valet pkg. V, AE, DC, MC.
André and Raymonde Fenestraz have completely remodeled this gorgeous Jardin Alpin hotel in a cheery Austrian style (it reminds us of Sleeping Beauty's Castle). Beautiful rooms, admirably equipped. Sauna, Jacuzzi, and heated garage... Don't miss the spectacular pool! The service could use some fine-tuning.

Alpes Hôtel Pralong 2000
Courchevel 1850, route de l'Altiport
79 08 24 82, fax 79 08 36 41
Closed Apr 17-Dec 16. Open until 10:15pm. Priv rm: 40. Terrace dining. Heated pool. Valet pkg. V, AE, DC, MC.
Truffle and foie gras freaks, this place is for you! Pascal Peyramaure brings his Southwestern flair here in winter, and offers the likes of a potato

stuffed with truffles and foie gras, truffle in a crust, and black-cherry clafoutis. Try them with a Cahors or Bergerac carefully chosen by Gabriel, a peach of a maître d'hôtel. Also worth trying: rack of lamb, roast meats (excellent farm-raised chicken). **C** 400-450 F. **M** 295 F (lunch), 365 F (dinner).

 ## Alpes Hôtel
Pralong 2000

(See restaurant above)

Closed Apr 17-Dec 16. 12 stes 2,690-4,280 F. 68 rms 690-2,200 F. Half-board 690-2,750 F. Conf. Heated pool. V, AE, DC, MC.

A very special hotel set atop Courchevel 1850 opposite the ski lifts. Rooms are huge, comfortable, and attractively decorated. There's a superb buffet breakfast, an indoor swimming pool and golf practice green (to help work off those calories), a leisure center, and a hairdresser. Lots of television channels too! Relais et Châteaux.

 ## Annapurna

Courchevel 1850, route de l'Altiport
79 08 04 60, fax 79 08 15 31

Closed Apr 20-Dec 15. 4 stes 4,700-5,620 F. 57 rms 820-2,820 F. Restaurant. Half-board 1,000-1,660 F. Air cond. Conf. Heated pool. Pkg. V, AE, DC, MC.

This is one of the best hotels of the resort, indeed in all the French Alps. The terraced rooms are spacious, remarkably well appointed, and face full south towards the mountains and the slopes. Amenities and services galore, including a fitness club, masseur, swimming instructor, manicurist, and a piano bar.

 ## Le Bateau Ivre

79 08 36 88, fax 79 08 38 72

Closed mid Apr-mid Dec. Open until 10pm. Terrace dining. Air cond. Valet pkg. V, AE, DC, MC.

This drunken boat has been plagued with stormy financial seas. We don't care who owns the property, so long as they keep Jean-Pierre Jacob in the kitchen, Josie in the dining room, and other family members at their usual places. In spite of the ups and downs, Jacob's cooking is as fine as it ever was, with a return of the imaginativeness we thought was lacking last year. As always, he features exceptional products prepared with fine-honed technique. This year we reveled in the sea scallops sautéed with an anise cream and served over warm oysters, the perfectly roasted John Dory fillet with ravioli bursting with crunchy artichokes and fava beans, and the sublime squab risotto with Parmesan. Desserts like banana roasted with spices and passion fruit, with a sesame cookie and a vanilla bean, show that the chef knows the value of simplicity touched by inspiration. The cellar is wide-ranging, with an understandable bias towards the wines of Savoie, and expensive; this is Courchevel, after all. **C** 450-550 F. **M** 290 F (lunch, wine incl), 350 F, 510 F.

 ## La Pomme de Pin

(See restaurant above)

Closed mid Apr-mid Dec. 49 rms 600-1,500 F. Half-board 715-1,095 F. Conf. Valet pkg. V, AE, DC, MC.

An excellent three-star hotel with rooms that are spacious, bright, and thoughtfully equipped. Comfortable beds and super breakfasts.

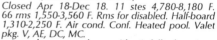 ## Bellecôte

Courchevel 1850
79 08 10 19, fax 79 08 17 16

Closed Apr 20-Dec 17. 2 stes 2,350-3,000 F. 56 rms 1,000-1,750 F. Restaurant. Half-board 900-1,650 F. Conf. Heated pool. Valet pkg. V, AE, DC, MC.

Alongside the Bellecôte run, this luxurious chalet has spacious, pretty wood-paneled rooms looking out onto the mountains. Public rooms are inviting and comfortable, and there are lots of high-quality amenities (hairdresser, sauna, and more).

Byblos des Neiges

L'Écailler, Jardin Alpin
79 08 12 12, fax 79 08 19 38

Closed Apr 17-Dec 18. Open until 10:30pm. Priv rm: 40. Terrace dining. Air cond. Heated pool. No pets. Valet pkg. V, AE, DC, MC.

Two restaurants in this palatial hotel, without a doubt Courchevel's most carefully maintained. in L'Ecailler, a seafood restaurant, sample raw seafood platters and more elaborate fare like a truffled shellfish risotto. In La Clairière, fine buffet lunches are offered, with hot first courses and hearty main dishes (potée stew, for example) in steaming terrines; happiness is the pine-shrouded terrace. **C** 450 F. **M** 380 F (dinner).

Byblos des Neiges

(See restaurant above)

Closed Apr 18-Dec 18. 11 stes 4,780-8,180 F. 66 rms 1,550-3,560 F. Rms for disabled. Half-board 1,310-2,250 F. Air cond. Conf. Heated pool. Valet pkg. V, AE, DC, MC.

A real snow palace with sinfully luxurious rooms, saunas, Jacuzzi, Turkish baths, gym, pool, a piano bar, and lots of restaurants. Sunny terraces and spectacular interiors. Friendly, relaxed ambience.

Caravelle

Jardin Alpin
79 08 02 42, fax 79 08 33 55

Closed Apr 18-Dec 17. 3 stes 880-1,070 F. 57 rms 580-1,000 F. Restaurant. Half-board 580-1,070 F. Conf. Heated pool. No pets. Valet pkg. V.

Here's an attractive and welcoming chalet, recently transformed for the better. Rooms have been cozily decorated and there are loads of extras: sauna, massage, squash courts, gym, and games room.

Carlina

Courchevel 1850
79 08 00 30, fax 79 08 04 03

Closed Apr 18-Dec 17. 7 stes 3,260-4,600 F. 57 rms 910-1,720 F. Restaurant. Half-board 1,275-3,440 F. Conf. Heated pool. Valet pkg. V, AE, DC, MC.

Even more splendid after its recent facelift, this magnificent resort hotel offers untold comfort and every imaginable service: sauna, massage, UVA, and plenty more.

Chabichou

Courchevel 1850, quartier Les Chenus
79 08 00 55, fax 79 08 33 58

Closed May 1-Jun 25, Sep 15-Dec 1. Open until 10:30pm. Terrace dining. Heated pool. Pkg. V, AE, DC, MC.

Michel Rochedy's cooking continues to evolve along the lines that suit him best, and a faithful clientele who knew this place before it became afflicted by the excesses of chic have begun to return. Rochedy's original, inventive cooking includes dishes like those on the not-to-be-missed 160 F menu, served throughout the day, on a lovely terrace: depending on market offerings, you might sample tomato and basil tart, sole and langoustine bourride with aïoli, and tiramisu. The à la carte menu offers an appetizer assortment of roast foie gras, a stuffed clam, scrambled eggs with caviar, a délice of fresh white cheese, a Savoyard crouton, and beef carpaccio. Follow this with a fresh salad of asparagus tips, green beans, and truffles; an excellent consommé served between courses; a wing of farm-raised chicken with girolles; and, for dessert, an apple cristalline with cardamom and sweet cider cream. Rather limited choice of wines, especially at the end of the season, and the bread tends to dry out at this altitude. Jazz and Russian folklore groups some evenings. **C** 375-650 F. **M** 160 F, 260 F, 400 F.

Chabichou

(See restaurant above)
Closed May 1-June 25, Sep 15-Dec 1. 2 stes. 40 rms. Half-board 400-1,900 F. Conf. Heated pool. Valet pkg. V, AE, DC, MC.
The spacious rooms have a bold look which is not to everyone's taste, but they are well equipped; some need a bit more looking after. Well located near the pistes, and reasonably priced. After a generous buffet breakfast, you may repair to the fitness room.

Le Chalet de Pierres

Courchevel 1850, Piste des Verdont, Jardin Alpin - 79 08 18 61, fax 79 08 38 06
Closed Apr 20-Dec 10. Open until 10pm. Terrace dining. Valet pkg. V, AE.
This chalet is jammed with Courchevel's smart set day and night (400 to 600 people served at lunch), but the quality doesn't suffer. The secret? Simple dishes made with top products. Try the warm Beaufort cheese tart, a fresh Biollay salad, tartares, quick-cooked veal scallops, beef fillet, and the famous dessert assortment. It's expensive, but it works! **C** 250-300 F.

Crystal 2000

Route de l'Altiport
79 08 28 22, fax 79 08 28 39
Closed mid Apr-mid Dec. 4 stes 765-1,220 F. 47 rms. Restaurant. Half-board 1,100 F. Conf. Pkg. V, AE, DC, MC.
This huge, attractive modern chalet is perched above Courchevel. There's a large sunny terrace, and all rooms have VCRs. Organized activities; sauna.

Les Ducs de Savoie

Jardin Alpin
79 08 03 00, fax 79 08 16 30
Closed Apr 18-Dec 17. 2 stes 1,240-1,890 F. 68 rms 530-1,530 F. Restaurant. Half-board 700-1,450 F. Conf. Valet pkg. V, AE, DC, MC.
Every room in this large and peaceful chalet of recent vintage has its own terrace. Great service and facilities: saunas, gym, billiard club, and more.

Hôtel du Golf

Courchevel 1650
79 00 92 92, fax 79 08 19 93
Closed Apr 15-Jun 15, Sep 15-Dec 15. 16 stes 820-1,120 F. 41 rms 540-1,800 F. Rms for disabled. Res-

taurant. Half-board 600-960 F. Conf. Pkg. V, AE, DC, MC.
This excellent establishment faces south and boasts several restaurants on the premises, including one specialized in fondues and raclettes. Children may join in a supervised play group between 6 and 9pm. The soundproofing could be better.

Le Lana
Courchevel 1850
79 08 01 10, fax 79 08 36 70
Closed Apr 12-Dec 18. 58 rms 800-1,600 F. Restaurant. Half-board 1,210-2,375 F. Conf. Heated pool. Valet pkg. V, AE, DC.
In the center of Courchevel 1850 with a view of the valley, stands this superb, huge hotel endowed with spacious, pleasant rooms, an inviting terrace, and a full array of services (sauna, massage, gym, Jacuzzi, Turkish bath...).

La Loze
Courchevel 1850, rue Park-City
79 08 28 25, fax 79 08 36 62
Closed Apr 23-Dec 1. 1 ste 1,700-2,300 F. 20 rms 750-1,800 F. V, AE, DC, MC.
Bang in the center of the resort you'll find this Austrian-style chalet, with its cozy (i.e. small), well designed and appointed rooms. Facilities on the premises of Les Airelles (see above) are available to La Loze residents.

Mercure
Jardin Alpin
79 08 11 23, fax 79 08 18 62
Closed Apr 20-Jun, Sep-Nov. 5 stes 800 F. 122 rms 290-800 F. Restaurant. Half-board 540-878 F. Conf. Heated pool. Golf. Valet pkg. V, AE, DC.
A long, low wood-fronted building, pleasantly situated in the Jardin Alpin, Le Mercure has inviting, good-sized rooms with little balconies. The view of the mountain tops is spectacular, and there is a golf course across the way. Friendly welcome and service.

L'Orchidée
Courchevel 1850
79 08 03 77, fax 79 08 18 70
Closed Apr 18-Dec 18. Open until 10pm. Terrace dining. No pets. Valet pkg. V, AE, DC, MC.
The Hôtel des Neiges has come back as one of the resort's top establishments, thanks to the efforts of Martine and Henry Benoist. A new chef, Christophe Turquier (formerly with Girardet and Senderens) has just arrived, but not in time for us to sample his cooking. No rating for now. **C** 350-400 F. **M** 275 F (lunch), 320 F (dinner).

Hôtel des Neiges

(See restaurant above)
Closed Apr 15-Dec 11. 5 stes 1,655-2,280 F. 37 rms 815-2,630 F. Half-board 1,240-1,695 F. Conf. Golf. No pets. Valet pkg. V, AE, DC, MC.
This large and immensely comfortable chalet is situated at the foot of the slopes. Lovely, bright rooms with white walls and floral drapes. You can walk to the heart of the village, but it's very quiet in the hotel. A lively atmosphere is assured thanks to the film-world clientele. Entertainment nightly in the piano bar. Relais et Châteaux.

A red hotel ranking denotes a place with charm.

La Sivolière
Courchevel 1850
79 08 08 33, fax 79 08 15 73
Closed May 2-Nov 15. Open until 11pm. Priv rm: 60. No pets. Valet pkg. V, AE, MC.
Coming to this cozy, informal chalet is like dining at home with friends. Mado Cattelin tells you what's on hand in the kitchen: a salad of Beaufort cheese and Grisons beef, for example, or tartiflette, veal piccata, and chocolate tart. True *cuisine de femme* in a cozy mountain atmosphere. **C** 250-320 F. **M** 180 F, 200 F, 240 F, 260 F, 280 F.

La Sivolière
(See restaurant above)
Closed May 2-Nov 15. 30 rms 750-1,750 F. Half-board 690-1,270 F. Conf. No pets. Pkg. V, AE, MC.
This wonderfully cozy hotel stands among pine trees near the slopes. Rooms are both intimate and functional, and all enjoy a splendid view of the mountains. Lots of fitness equipment and leisure activities. The bar and lounge are now larger and more comfortable than ever.

Les Trois Vallées
Courchevel 1850
79 08 00 12, fax 79 08 17 98
Closed Apr 20-Nov. 5 stes 1,400-2,400 F. 27 rms 700-1,600 F. Rms for disabled. Restaurant. Half-board 880-1,360 F. Conf. Valet pkg. V, AE, MC.
A superb modern chalet that overlooks La Croisette. Rooms are large and very comfy, full of blond wood and pretty fabrics, with furniture painted in the Austrian manner. In addition to marble-clad bathrooms, the hotel offers every conceivable amenity: sauna, Turkish bath, and much, much more. Service is a bit amateurish, but full of enthusiasm. Sumptuous breakfasts can be had in the rooms at any hour.

And also...
Our selection of places for inexpensive, quick, or late-night meals.
Bel Air 1650 (79 08 00 93 - Altitude 2000.): At the top of the Montriond lift you'll find a fresh, family-style set meal featuring tarragon chicken, braised ham and the like, for 110 F.
La Bergerie (79 08 24 70 - Rue Nogenpil. Open until 10:30pm.): Just off the Bellecôte run, fine raclette and Russian soirées (with caviar and live music) (295 F, 550 F).
La Mangeoire (79 08 02 09): Fondue, raclette, and some homestyle dishes in a rustic decor.

COUR-CHEVERNY	41700

Paris 190 - Blois 13 - Romorantin-Lanthenay 28   *Loir/Cher*

■ **In Cheverny 41700**   *1 km S*

Château du Breuil

D 52, route de Fougères-sur-Bièvre
54 44 20 20, fax 54 44 30 40
Closed Sun dinner off-seas (exc hols), Mon lunch, Jan 1-Feb 25. Open until 9:30pm. Priv rm: 20. No pets. Valet pkg. V, AE, DC, MC.
A young chef, Patrick Léonce, has taken over the kitchens of this charming château not far from its noble peers, Chaumont, Chambord, and Cheverny. A nice place to stop, even though the interior decoration could be improved (too

much *faux* furniture). As for the food, it's classic but with modern touches: smoked salmon with eggplant caviar, harmonious lamb in Cheverny wine with baked potatoes, yummy apples with crème caramel and walnuts. Good wine list, reasonably priced, and friendly, efficient service. **C** 380-450 F. **M** 190 F, 370 F.

Château du Breuil

(See restaurant above)
Closed Sun off-seas, Jan 1-Feb 25. 2 stes 1,235-1,500 F. 16 rms 530-895 F. Half-board 605-670 F. Conf. Golf. Pkg. Helipad. V, AE, DC, MC.
The château stands proudly in its wooded grounds, a typical Solognot edifice with fifteenth- and eighteenth-century features, tastefully appointed and furnished. The rooms all have different, personalized decor as well as new bathrooms and fixtures.

COURLANS 39	→ Lons-le-Saunier

COURSEULLES-SUR-MER	14470

Paris 260 - Bayeux 20 - Caen 18 - Arromanches 13   *Calvados*

La Crémaillère et Le Gytan
Bd de la Plage
31 37 95 96, fax 31 37 19 31
Open year-round. 4 stes 400-650 F. 50 rms 145-295 F. Rms for disabled. Restaurant. Half-board 235-295 F. Conf. Golf. Pkg. V, AE, DC, MC.
Pleasant rooms give onto the sea beyond the beach (La Crémaillère) or the garden (Le Gytan).

COURTENAY	45320

Paris 120 - Sens 26 - Montargis 25 - Orléans 96   *Loiret*

La Clé des Champs
Route de Joigny, Les Quatre-Croix
38 97 42 68, fax 38 97 38 10
Closed Tue dinner, Wed, Jan 9-31, Oct 16-30. Open until 9pm. Pkg. V, AE, MC.
This commodious country restaurant features skillful cuisine by Marc Delion. His menu contains some classics as well as some inventive dishes: a snail cromesquis, veal sweetbreads with vanilla and sorrel, and a gooey chocolate dessert with crème anglaise. But the cheese assortment is too expensive (70 F), as is the wine list. **C** 300-460 F. **M** 160 F, 250 F, 320 F.

La Clé des Champs

(See restaurant above)
Closed last 2 wks of Oct & Jan. 1 ste 720-950 F. 6 rms 395-550 F. No pets. Pkg. Helipad. V, AE, MC.
A seventeenth-century farmhouse has been converted into a luxury motel, with a limited number of rooms decorated with real style, rustic chic. It's pleasant, clean, and quiet as can be. Perfect for a romantic weekend. Expensive? Of course, but can you put a price tag on true pleasure?

> *We're always happy to hear about* **your discoveries** *and receive your comments on ours. Please feel free to write to us stating clearly what you liked or disliked. Be concise but convincing, and take the time to argue your point.*

COURTILS 50220
Paris 307 - Rennes 61 - Fougères 37 - Avranches 12   *Manche*

Le Manoir de la Roche-Torin
Route du Mont-St-Michel
33 70 96 55, fax 33 48 35 20
Closed Nov 15-Easter. 1 ste 780 F. 12 rms 400-650 F. Restaurant. Half-board 420-500 F. Conf. Pkg. Helipad. V, AE, DC, MC.
A nineteenth-century edifice with a dozen well-appointed rooms set in five acres of quiet grounds along the shores of Mont-Saint-Michel bay.

COUTAINVILLE 50230
Paris 343 - St-Lô 40 - Coutances 13 - Cherbourg 77   *Manche*

12/20 Hardy
Pl. du 28-Juillet
33 47 04 11, fax 33 47 39 00
Closed Sun dinner & Mon (Oct-Apr) exc hols. Annual closings not available. Open until 9:30pm. Priv rm: 50. Terrace dining. Hotel: 16 rms 260-460 F. Half-board 315-450 F. Golf. Pkg. V, AE, DC, MC.
Two dining rooms, one elegant, the other rustic, where you can sample well-prepared dishes at reasonable prices: ballotine of sea bass with foie gras, brill sautéed with mustard, roast veal sweetbreads with leek compote. Fine cellar. **C** 300-450 F. **M** 102 F, 175 F, 235 F, 320 F.

COUTANCES 50200
Paris 330 - Cherbourg 75 - Avranches 46 - St-Lô 27   *Manche*

Cositel
Route de Coutainville
33 07 51 64, fax 33 07 06 23
Open year-round. 1 ste 390-590 F. 54 rms 275-370 F. Rms for disabled. Restaurant. Half-board 285 F. Conf. Golf. Garage pkg. V, AE, DC, MC.
A modern establishment on the outskirts of town. Rooms are smallish, some with modern decor and others more traditional, but all have modern amenities, along with a view of the cathedral. Nice service. Bar.

COYE-LA-FORÊT 60   → Chantilly

CRÉON 33670
Paris 572 - Bordeaux 24 - Libourne 21 - Langon 30   *Gironde*

Hostellerie Château Camiac
3 km N on D 121
56 23 20 85, fax 56 23 38 84
Closed Wed lunch, Tue, Jan 15-Feb 15. Open until 9:30pm. Priv rm: 100. Terrace dining. Pkg. V, AE, MC.
A new chef has arrived in this elegant establishment with a terrace giving onto a lovely garden. His menu sounds interesting: roast langoustines in a salad with myrtle vinaigrette, a viennoise of veal sweetbreads with thyme and garlic cream, and a warm chocolate tart with coffee sherbet. We will give him a rating when we have had a chance to sample all this. **C** 250-350 F. **M** 130 F (weekday lunch), 165 F, 220 F.

Hostellerie Château Camiac
(See restaurant above)
Open year-round. 2 stes 1,100-1,300 F. 19 rms 390-990 F. Rms for disabled. Half-board 420-685 F. Air cond. Conf. Pool. Tennis. Pkg. Helipad. V, AE, MC.
A fairytale castle set in a quiet estate. In the château itself are brand-new, comfortable rooms and suites; in the carriage house guests find more rustic but very well appointed accommodation.

CRÉPON 14   → Bayeux

CRESSENSAC 46600
Paris 510 - Brive 20 - Gourdon 46 - Sarlat 46   *Lot*

12/20 Chez Gilles
65 37 70 06, fax 65 37 77 15
Open daily until 9:30pm. Pkg. V, AE, DC, MC.
An inviting village inn is the background for Gilles Treille's good country cooking. On the small menu: sea scallops in Noilly-Prat sauce, cèpe omelet, tripe with Madeira, and a honey nougat glacé. **C** 230-340 F. **M** 95 F (exc Sun lunch), 145 F, 235 F, 325 F.

CRÉTEIL 94   → PARIS Suburbs

CRILLON-LE-BRAVE 84410
Paris 690 - Carpentras 14 - Vaison-la-Romaine 19   *Vaucluse*

Hostellerie de Crillon-le-Brave
Pl. de l'Église
90 65 61 61, fax 90 65 62 86
Closed weekday lunch, Jan-Mar. Open until 9:30pm. Garden dining. Valet pkg. V, AE, MC.
Philippe Monti is back on his native turf after gaining credentials in such lofty establishments as Pic and Taillevent, offering dishes that make excellent use of local ingredients: tasty chicken livers in brochette, unctuous pumpkin soup with parsley, a delicious lamb and eggplant "cake", and a yummy walnut tart. Friendly service. **C** 300-400 F. **M** 225 F, 275 F.

Hostellerie de Crillon-le-Brave
(See restaurant above)
Closed Jan-Mar. 4 stes 1,250-1,450 F. 17 rms 750-1,150 F. Half-board 1,010-1,410 F. Conf. Pool. Golf. Valet pkg. V, AE, MC.
Overlooking Mount Ventoux and the Comtat vineyards, these rooms are decorated with charming fabrics and Provençal furniture. Luxurious fittings, beautiful bathrooms, and expensive but exceptionally delicious breakfasts. Personalized welcome and service.

The **C** *(A la carte) restaurant prices given are for a complete three-course meal for one, including a half-bottle of modest wine and service.* **M** *(Menus) prices are for a complete fixed-price meal for one, excluding wine (unless otherwise noted).*

CROISIC (LE)   44490
Paris 460 - Nantes 84 - La Baule 10 - Guérande 10   *Loire-Atl.*

Le Bretagne
11, quai de la Petite-Chambre
40 23 00 51, fax 40 23 18 32
*Closed Sun dinner, Mon (exc Jul-Aug), Nov 15-
Dec 15. Open until 9:30pm (10:30pm in summer).
V, AE, DC, MC.*
This eccentrically decorated restaurant deserves its name: nothing could be more typically
Breton than Michèle Coïc's specialties using
products from the sea and local farms: stuffed
clams, rack of lamb with garlic cream, sole
meunière with mashed potatoes, and île flottante with peaches. Simple but attractive little
menus. Pierre Coïc welcomes customers warmly
into the dining room, which looks out onto the
bustling fish market. **C** 250-350 F. **M** 200 F (Sun,
Sat dinner), 89 F, 119 F (weekdays, Sat lunch),
169 F, 219 F.

12/20   Le Pornic
4, quai Port-Ciguet
40 23 18 56, fax 40 23 18 56
*Closed Thu (Nov 15-Easter), Mon, Tue lunch (Apr-
Jun, Sep-Oct), Feb. Open until 10:30pm (11pm in
summer). Priv rm: 20. V, AE, DC.*
A quayside restaurant with a fresh blue-and-
white decor, serving classic, simple seafood:
fresh shellfish assortments, haddock
choucroute, good scallops with fresh pasta, and
a rich chocolate cake to round it all off. **C** 250-
300 F. **M** 110 F (weekdays), 140 F, 180 F.

CROISSY-BEAUBOURG 77
→ PARIS Suburbs

CROIX-BLANCHE (LA) 71   → Mâcon

CROIX-VALMER (LA)   83420
Paris 879 - Toulon 62 - St-Tropez 12 - Grimaud 12   *Var*

La Brigantine
Bd de la Mer - 94 79 67 16 (R)
94 79 71 11 (H), fax 94 54 37 05
*Closed Oct-Apr. Open until 10pm (10:30pm in sum-
mer). Priv rm: 200. Garden dining.* **Hotel:** *30 rms
530-1,020 F. Half-board 550-820 F. Air cond. Conf.
Heated pool. Tennis. Pkg. V, AE, MC.*
Enjoy a lazy, holiday atmosphere on this shady
seaside patio, with its restful view of beach
umbrellas and Cavalaire Bay. The single set
menu offers vivacious dishes made from fine
products: rock lobster-stuffed ravioli with a
creamy vegetable sauce, fillet of roast veal with
artichoke cream, dessert assortment. **M** 250 F.

Château de Valmer
Route de Gigaro
94 79 60 10, fax 94 54 22 68
*Closed Oct-Mar. 1 ste 1,525-1,600 F. 41 rms 700-
1,200 F. Restaurant. Air cond. Conf. Pool. Tennis.
Golf. Garage pkg. V, AE, DC, MC.*
For a quiet stay, choose this old Provençal
farmhouse situated at the far end of a splendid
palm grove. Direct access to the beach.

---

*Restaurant prices in red draw attention to res-
taurants that offer particularly good value.*

Hôtel de Gigaro
Plage de Gigaro
94 79 60 35, fax 94 54 37 05
*Closed Sep-May 10. 38 rms 540-1,160 F. Restaurant.
Half-board 560-880 F. Air cond. Conf. Pool. Tennis.
Garage pkg. V, AE, DC, MC.*
Airy, comfortable rooms in a pleasant new
hotel swathed in greenery. The leisure center
includes both a bar and a reading room. Just 150
meters away is a private beach.

La Pinède
Plage de Gigaro
94 54 31 23, fax 94 79 71 46
*Closed Nov-Apr. 40 rms 535-1,340 F. Restaurant.
Half-board 720-990 F. Heated pool. Tennis. Golf.
Garage pkg. V, AE, DC, MC.*
A recently built and very pleasant seaside
hotel, set amid eucalyptus trees and umbrella
pines. Rooms are bright, light, and modern;
there's also a lovely terrace from which to gaze
out to sea. Private beach.

Souleias
Plage de Gigaro
94 79 61 91, fax 94 54 36 23
*Closed end Oct-end Mar. Open until 9:30pm. Priv
rm: 14. Garden dining. Heated pool. No pets.
Garage pkg. V, AE, DC, MC.*
What a gorgeous place this is: a splendid *mas*
clinging to a remote hillside, encircled by cottages set amid flowers and olive trees. And what
a success story for the owner, a former chemical
engineer who in record time has turned Souleias
into one of the most sought-after hotels on the
Var coast. On the stunning terrace which juts out
over the Gigaro beach, chef Georges Coquin
serves appealing Provençal dishes like langoustine tails cooked with orange and fennel jus,
roast rack of lamb with Parmesan and a little
vegetable ragoût, honey cake with two kinds of
chocolate. **C** 400-550 F. **M** 180 F (lunch), 240 F,
350 F.

Souleias
(See restaurant above)
*Closed end Oct-end Mar. 5 stes 1,570-2,300 F.
45 rms 620-1,570 F. Half-board 1,135 F. Air cond.
Conf. Heated pool. Tennis. Pkg. V, AE, DC, MC.*
Large, sunny, amazingly comfortable rooms
are housed in little cottages nestled in foliage
and flowers, with heavenly views of the sea and
coastline. The hotel's catamaran takes guests to
the Îles d'Or for outings and picnics.

CROS-DE-CAGNES 06   → Cagnes-sur-Mer

CROUTELLE 86   → Poitiers

CROZANT   23160
Paris 334 - Argenton-sur-Creuse 32 - Guéret 40   *Creuse*

Auberge de la Vallée
55 89 80 03
*Closed Mon dinner off-seas, Jan. Open until 9pm
(10pm in summer). Priv rm: 120. Air cond. V.*
Sample Jean Guilleminot's delicate and accomplished cuisine in a decor replete with
regional folklore imagery: a salad of langoustines
sautéed with tarragon, monkfish in orange
sauce, foie gras millefeuille, and sautéed fruits
with crème brûlée. Inadequate wine list, friendly

service. **C** 200-300 F. **M** 70 F (exc Sun), 100 F, 135 F, 265 F.

CUERS 83 → **Toulon**

CURZAY-SUR-VONNE 86600

Paris 364 - Poitiers 28 - Lusignan 9 - St-Maixent 26   *Vienne*

 Château de Curzay
49 36 17 00, fax 49 53 57 69
Open year-round. 2 stes 1,400 F. 12 rms 650-1,200 F. Restaurant. Air cond. Conf. Heated pool. Golf. Valet pkg. Helipad. V, AE, DC, MC.
Lost in the countryside, an elegant château hotel in a magnificent park with a formal French garden. Huge, tastefully decorated rooms and suites. Dynamic welcome.

CUTTOLI-CORTICCHIATO 20
→ **CORSICA: Ajaccio**

DAMPIERRE-EN-YVELINES 78720

Paris 44 - Versailles 18 - Rambouillet 16   *Yvelines*

 Auberge Saint-Pierre
1, rue de Chevreuse
30 52 53 53, fax 30 52 58 57
Closings not available. Open until 10pm. Priv rm: 120. Terrace dining. Pkg. V, AE.
This old village house opposite the château has added modern wings to accommodate wedding parties and family feasts. Jean-Pierre Cario's cuisine is fresh and professional: twelve different dishes using snails available each day (from among 120 different snail recipes in his repertoire), beef cheeks en daube, lobster navarin, île flottante. Well chosen wine list. **C** 250-350 F. **M** 135 F, 170 F, 250 F, 350 F.

Les Écuries du Château
Château de Dampierre
30 52 52 99, fax 30 52 59 90
Closed Tue. Open until 9pm. Priv rm: 420. Pkg. V, AE, DC.
A charming outbuilding of the seventeenth-century Château de Dampierre has been tastefully transformed into a comfortable, commodious restaurant decorated in tones of beige and pink. Christian Deluchey is a capable chef who treats seasonal produce with care in such classic, technically precise dishes as a delicious mushroom and foie gras galette, veal sweetbreads with langoustines, fruit-filled puff pastry, and exotic sherbets. Appealing cellar with some good, affordable Bordeaux and growers' wines from the Loire. **C** 290-360 F. **M** 200 F, 250 F, 300 F.

DAX 40100

Paris 706 - Biarritz 57 - Mont-de-Marsan 52 - Pau 78   *Landes*

 Grand Hôtel
Rue de la Source
58 90 53 00, fax 58 74 88 31
Open year-round. 8 stes 330-464 F. 130 rms 221-304 F. Restaurant. Half-board 264-347 F. Conf. Garage pkg. V, MC.
Part of the thermal spa. Bright, spacious rooms in a huge, charmless yet well-appointed edifice. Lots of services; conference rooms available. Poor soundproofing and rather chilly welcome.

 Le Moulin de Poustagnacq
40990 Saint-Paul
58 91 31 03, fax 58 91 37 97
Closed Sun dinner, Mon. Open until 10pm. Priv rm: 30. Terrace dining. Pkg. V, AE, DC.
Thierry Berthelier is growing bolder, adding more and more personal touches to his interesting, innovative repertoire. In a handsome all-white dining room that opens out onto a stunning view of forest and lake, sample his langoustine tempura with a walnut salad, roast rack of lamb with tarbais beans, and a chocolate and chicory cake. Attractive wine list. Music (Russian, gypsy, jazz). **C** 300-360 F. **M** 135 F, 180 F, 300 F.

Régina
Bd des Sports
58 90 50 00, fax 58 74 88 31
Closed Nov 27-Feb 25. 21 stes 330-381 F. 109 rms 180-350 F. Restaurant. Half-board 248-320 F. Conf. Heated pool. Pkg. V, AE, DC, MC.
A quiet, modern, comfy hotel linked to the spa by a heated gallery. Most rooms have balconies, and the 25 well-equipped studios have terraces.

 La Renardière
Route de Bayonne, La Pince,
40990 St-Paul, 168, av. de la Résistance
58 91 57 30
Closed Sun dinner, Wed, last 2 wks of Feb, last wk of Nov. Open until 9pm (10pm in summer). Priv rm: 40. Garden dining. Pkg. V, AE, DC, MC.
A nice family atmosphere emanates from this rustic abode which backs onto a pleasant garden. While the *patronne* makes much of her customers, Serge Panzolato prepares an appetizing repertoire which includes sautéed tiny squid with a flavorful Niçoise tian, duck breast unfortunately not accopanied by the cèpes described on the menu and served with bland vegetables, nice raspberry gratin. **C** 240-300 F. **M** 80 F (lunch exc Sun), 120 F, 150 F, 170 F.

Splendid Hotel
2, cours de Verdun
58 56 70 70, fax 58 74 76 33
Closed Nov 27-Feb 26. 6 stes 550-650 F. 159 rms 350-460 F. Restaurant. Half-board 280-510 F. Conf. Heated pool. Pkg. V, AE, DC, MC.
This intelligently modernized old luxury hotel has preserved its enormous rooms, impressive bathrooms, and Art Deco furniture. Spa treatments, fitness classes, and more.

■ **In Pontonx-
sur-l'Adour 40465**   13 km NE on N 124

12/20 **Le Val Fleuri**
58 57 20 75
Closed Mon, Jan 1-15. Open until 10pm. Pkg. V.
The pretty dining room with its beams, big fireplace, and tiled floor has been nicely revamped. José Pozuelo gives a fresh, appealing spin to such traditional dishes as shrimp ravioli with foie gras, salmon in wine sauce, chestnut and orange croustillant, and veal grenadin with mushrooms, accompanied by good regional wines. **C** 200-280 F. **M** 68 F (weekdays), 100 F, 130 F.

DEAUVILLE 14800

Paris 206 - Le Havre 72 - Caen 43 - Lisieux 30 · *Calvados*

10/20 Le Bistrot Gourmet
70, rue Gambetta
31 88 82 52, fax 31 88 44 74
Closed Wed lunch & Tue off-seas. Open until 11pm (midnight in seas). V, AE.
A likeable bistrot in the classic style, serving a mostly down-to-earth repertoire, with the occasional ambitious dish. Try the raw seafood platters, sea bass with tarragon, bouillabaisse, and caramelized apples. C 200-300 F. M 110 F, 148 F, 198 F.

Le Ciro's

Bd de la Mer
31 88 18 10, fax 31 98 66 71
Open daily until 9:30pm (10pm in summer). Terrace dining. Pkg. V, AE, DC.
We've said it before, we'll say it again. This is *the* spot in which to see and be seen in Deauville. Patrick Durant's cuisine deserves better than this "fashionable" reputation. You'll agree when you taste his langoustine croquants with orange butter, the chausson of roasted red mullet with creamy baby carrots, and lovely desserts like the apple fondant with caramel sauce. The cellar houses more than 400 different labels, most from Bordeaux. Exceptional service. C 330-470 F. M 190 F, 320 F.

11/20 Le Drakkar
77, rue E.-Colas
31 88 71 24, fax 31 88 49 27
Closed end Jan-mid Feb. Open until midnight. Terrace dining. Air cond. V, AE, DC, MC.
During the *festival du cinéma*, the film world rubs elbows in this cheerful brasserie. But native Deauvillians also appreciate the curried mussels, sole marinière, salmon tartare with dill, and crème brûlée. Lively, competent service. C 270-320 F. M 89 F (weekday lunch), 120 F, 180 F (weekdays).

L'Étrier
Hôtel Royal, bd E.-Cornuché
31 98 66 33, fax 31 98 66 34
Closed Dec 4-mid Mar. Open until 10:30pm. Priv rm: 120. Terrace dining. Heated pool. Valet pkg. V, AE, DC.
The Hôtel Royal's restaurant has shaken off its staidness with the arrival of Henri Morel, whose cooking reflects diverse inspirations—modern enough to be interesting, yet sufficiently conservative not to offend unadventurous palates. Try the 190 F menu: raw oysters wrapped in a spinach leaf with a sauce redolent of the sea, croustillant of cod with soy sauce, cheese assortment, and a fruit gratin with iced raspberry and verbena. A lobster menu is offered on Tuesdays. Fine cellar. M 320 F (wine incl), 260 F (weekdays), 190 F, 260 F.

Royal

(See restaurant above)
Closed Dec 4-mid Mar. 17 stes 2,800-8,000 F. 270 rms 980-2,200 F. Rms for disabled. Conf. Heated pool. Tennis. Valet pkg. V, AE, DC, MC.
Le Royal is a monumental, old-fashioned luxury hotel on the seafront near the casino. The comfortable and cozy rooms have been renovated

in classic style. Reserve accommodation on the upper floors for a wonderful ocean view. There are facilities for tennis, golf, and swimming, as well as a health club.

Hélios Hôtel
10, rue Fossorier
31 88 28 26, fax 31 88 53 87
Open year-round. 1 ste 700-900 F. 44 rms 300-470 F. Rms for disabled. Air cond. Heated pool. No pets. V, AE, DC, MC.
Between the beach, the casino, and the racetrack, this modern hotel offers pleasant rooms and a little pool in a garden courtyard. Bar.

Le Kraal
Pl. du Marché
31 88 30 58, fax 31 88 47 77
Open daily until 10pm (11pm in summer). Priv rm: 25. Terrace dining. Pkg. V, DC, MC.
Jean Chauvin's fine cuisine with a focus on seafood (salmon and oyster tartare with horseradish cream, lobster sauce vierge) and good homestyle desserts make this one of Deauville's most popular addresses. There is also a brunch at a bargain price: eggs with tripe, lentil salad with bacon, and quail ardéchoise. Warm welcome. C 300-380 F. M 160 F, 320 F.

Mercure Deauville
In Port-Deauville, bd E.-Cornuché
31 88 62 62, fax 31 88 54 93
Open year-round. 68 rms 470-670 F. Half-board 350-550 F. Conf. Pkg. V, AE, DC.
Situated in the center of the Port-Deauville marinas, the hotel offers well-equipped bilevel rooms with balconies facing the port and the beaches. Choose the ones on the Trouville side. Off-season service is inadequate, we find.

La Pommeraie
3 km S on D 278
31 88 19 01, fax 31 88 75 99
Open daily until 10:15pm. Priv rm: 250. Garden dining. Heated pool. Valet pkg. V, AE, DC, MC.
Relax in this airy, recently redecorated dining room, where competent and smiling staff serve forth Patrick Leduc's good cooking. Try his rabbit ballottine with apples and foie gras, red mullet with hazlenut oil, and a chocolate puff pastry with coffee mousse. Intelligent cellar. C 300-380 F. M 195 F.

Hôtel du Golf

(See restaurant above)
Open year-round. 10 stes 1,100-3,000 F. 169 rms 600-1,350 F. Half-board 885 F. Conf. Heated pool. Tennis. Golf. Valet pkg. Helipad. V, AE, DC, MC.
This grand hotel overlooks the sea and offers golf as a major attraction. The wonderfully comfortable rooms have been redone in soothing pastel shades. All sporting activites (swimming, tennis, croquet...) except for golf, may be indulged in free of charge. Newly redone fitness center.

La Potinière
38, rue J.-Mermoz
31 98 66 22, fax 31 98 66 23
Open daily until 10:30pm. Heated pool. No pets. Valet pkg. V, AE, DC, MC.
This luxury hotel, a Deauville institution, carefully cultivates a turn-of-the-century atmosphere. But chef André Plunian refuses to sink into the boring classicism so often encountered in grand

hotel dining rooms. He gives a fresh, assertive touch to his marmite dieppoise, oxtail in Chinon sauce with tagliatelle, and an apple dessert with quince jelly and ginger-spiked caramel sauce. The cellar is of respectable age and size; the staff are young and ultraprofessional. C 350-560 F. M 380 F (wine incl), 290 F (Thu), 250 F.

Hôtel Normandy
(See restaurant above)
Open year-round. 26 stes 1,270-7,500 F. 260 rms 980-1,270 F. Conf. Heated pool. Tennis. Golf. Valet pkg. V, AE, DC, MC.
Despite their modernization, many of the rooms of this *fin-de-siècle* pile hark back nostalgically to Deauville's heyday. Nothing can alter the seductive charm of this supremely comfortable, fashionable, busy hotel, redecorated this year. Sunday brunch is served under the apple trees of the Norman courtyard. Amenities include a gym, a sauna, billiard and video-games rooms.

Le Spinnaker
52, rue Mirabeau
31 88 24 40, fax 31 88 43 58
Closed Tue off-seas & Wed (exc in Aug). Open until 9:30pm. Priv rm: 25. Garage pkg. V, AE, MC.
A cozy, half-timbered eating house between Deauville's port and marketplace, oddly decorated on the outside with blue neon lighting. Pascal Angenard practices fresh, well prepared regional cookery, like a fricassée of Vire andouille with potatoes, sole fillets with a green lentil compote, and dark chocolate tart. Nice cellar and professional service. C 320-400 F. M 160 F (wine incl), 250 F, 320 F.

Le Trophée
81, rue du Gal-Leclerc
31 88 45 86, fax 31 88 07 94
Open year-round. 2 stes 760-1,000 F. 22 rms 330-650 F. Rms for disabled. Restaurant. V, AE, DC, MC.
A new hotel quite near the beach, with recently modernized, bright, and well-soundproofed rooms. Excellent bathrooms (some with whirlpool bath). Terrace-solarium, flower-filled garden. Brasserie on the premises.

■ **In Canapville 14800**   6 km S on N 177

Jarrasse
N 177 - 31 65 21 80
Closed Tue, Wed, Feb school hols, at Christmas. Open until 9pm. Garden dining. Pkg. V, MC.
François Jarrasse threw his *carte* out the window (along with the high prices) and now serves two clever prix-fixe menus. They warrant a stop at this quaint and tidy thatch-roofed inn, where guests are charmingly welcomed. For 160 F you can enjoy a feuilleté de moules à la crème, rabbit in mustard sauce, Norman cheeses, and crêpes soufflées. M 160 F (wine incl), 200 F.

■ **In Saint-Arnoult 14800**   3 km SE on D 218

Campanile Deauville Saint-Arnoult
31 87 54 54, fax 31 87 09 42
See page 95.
This chain offers a high degree of comfort at reasonable prices. The hotel stands between the golf course and the racetrack. Good breakfast buffet.

■ **In Saint-Martin-aux-Chartrains 14130**   8 km SE

Manoir de Roncheville
31 65 14 14, fax 31 65 20 44
Open daily until 10pm. Priv rm: 20. Terrace dining. Pkg. V, AE, MC.
The owner sets down his wheelbarrow to greet you as he stands surrounded by geese and rabbits, and the family dog and cat wander over to say hello. Inside the house full of nooks and crannies you'll savour solid and tasty dishes based on fine ingredients: Normandy foie gras with cider gelatin, veal chops with truffled cream sauce, and calf's liver with an onion compote. C 300-420 F. M 140 F (lunch), 210 F.

Manoir de Roncheville
(See restaurant above)
Open year-round. 2 stes 800-950 F. 6 rms 450-650 F. Half-board 435-685 F. Golf. Pkg. V, AE, MC.
The rooms come in every size, but all are equipped with amenities like hair dryers, safes, and what have you. The view encompasses either a trout stream or the wooded grounds. Service is more friendly than rigorously professional, and the atmosphere is definitely relaxed.

■ **In Touques 14800**   3 km SE on N 834

L'Amirauté
31 81 82 83, fax 31 81 82 93
Open year-round. 6 stes 1,130 F. 115 rms 710-760 F. Restaurant. Half-board 960 F. Conf. Heated pool. Tennis. Golf. Pkg. Helipad. V, AE, DC, MC.
Situated in a rather dreary business district on the edge of the Touques River, this functional, impersonal hotel is best suited for meetings or fitness breaks. Located three kilometers from the sea, it offers helicopter service upon request; guests may swim, play golf or tennis, or work out in the adjacent sports complex. There's a 450 F weekend rate.

12/20 Aux Landiers
90, rue Louvel-et-Brières - 31 88 00 39
Closed Thu lunch, Wed, Feb. Open until 9:30pm. Priv rm: 50. Pkg. V, AE, MC.
Regional ingredients treated with skill and respect by chef Thierry Salmon yield crayfish chartreuse, snails in watercress sauce, duck breast with rosemary, and a chocolate gratin with sherbet. Nice 140 F menu. C 230-350 F. M 100 F (weekday lunch), 140 F, 200 F, 260 F.

Le Relais du Haras
23, rue Louvel-et-Brière
31 81 67 67, fax 31 81 67 68
Open year-round. 1 ste 690-920 F. 7 rms 320-690 F. Restaurant. Half-board 438 F. Air cond. Conf. Golf. Pkg. V, AE, DC, MC.
The brand-new, tastefully furnished rooms of this family-run establishment give onto a pretty orchard. Good breakfasts.

*Some establishments change their **closing times** without warning. It is always wise to check in advance.*

DEUX-ALPES (LES) 38860
Paris 641 - Grenoble 74 - Le Bourg-d'Oisans 25   Isère

Hôtel Ariane
1, promenade des Écrins
76 79 29 29, fax 76 79 25 21
Closed May, Sep-Dec. 101 rms 500-1,100 F. Rms for disabled. Restaurant. Half-board 500-700 F. Conf. Pkg. V, AE, DC, MC.
Along with superb views, the guest rooms have pleasing contemporary furnishings, and most have balconies too. Among the other amenities are a sauna, Turkish bath, and Jacuzzi. Charming welcome.

La Bérangère
76 79 24 11, fax 76 79 55 08
Closed May 1-Jun 20, Sep 4-Dec 15. Open until 9pm. Priv rm: 30. Terrace dining. Heated pool. No pets. Pkg. V, AE, MC.
As they sit here in cozy comfort, diners can watch skiers zoom down snowy slopes and brake at the edge of the hotel's swimming pool. A new chef has just arrived, so no rating for now. Interesting cellar, with many regional treasures. The proprietress welcomes guests warmly.
C 340-450 F. M 200 F, 240 F, 350 F.

La Bérangère
(See restaurant above)
See restaurant for closings. 59 rms 490-850 F. Half-board 520-730 F. Conf. Heated pool. Golf. Pkg. V, AE, MC.
The hotel stands at the foot of the ski runs, and offers all-around comfort and lots of equipment: two swimming pools, tanning salon, hot tubs, and games rooms. Relais et Châteaux.

⑬ Chalet-Hôtel Mounier
P'tit Polyte
76 80 56 90, fax 76 79 56 51
Closed May 2-Jun 20, Sep 10-Dec 17. Open until 9pm. Priv rm: 30. Terrace dining. Heated pool. No pets. Pkg. V, MC.
If a subdued, well-bred but cozy atmosphere is what you seek, book a table at this big stone chalet. The food is unpretentious but ably crafted with fine, fresh ingredients. We were not overjoyed with the omble chevalier roulade with leeks and lentil cream, but were impressed by the grilled pickerel with pig's foot and the rack of lamb with a sweet garlic croquette. Give this place its first toque. C 250-350 F. M 170 F, 125 F, 220 F, 250 F, 280 F.

Chalet-Hôtel Mounier
(See restaurant above)
See restaurant for closings. 48 rms 300-720 F (bkfst incl). Rms for disabled. Half-board 310-580 F. Conf. Heated pool. Tennis. Golf. No pets. Pkg. V, MC.
A handsome chalet, decorated with great attention to detail, and with some terrific extras such as Turkish baths, a sauna, Jacuzzi, solarium, a billiard room, an indoor pool with artificial current, and more. The atmosphere is intimate and welcoming. Guest rooms are good-sized and bright; some have balconies.

La Farandole
18, rue du Cairou
76 80 50 45, fax 76 79 56 12
Closed May 3-Jun 18, Sep 4-Dec 3. 14 stes 800-1,700 F. 46 rms 400-1,000 F. Rms for disabled. Res-

taurant. Half-board 480-820 F. Conf. Golf. Valet pkg. V, AE, DC, MC.
Ideally situated with a view of the glaciers (depending on which side your room is on), this large chalet is splendidly equipped out with satellite television, a fitness center, sauna, Turkish bath, and piano bar. A chauffeured minivan ferries residents to the slopes.

12/20 Les Marmottes
76 79 21 91, fax 76 79 25 79
Closed Apr 17-Jun 26, Sep 5-Dec 20. Open until 9:30pm. Priv rm: 140. Heated pool. No pets. Pkg. V, AE, MC.
The owners aren't nodding over their laurels at Les Marmottes. On the contrary, projects abound to modernize and embellish this attractive family-run hostelry. Meanwhile, the chef busies himself preparing accomplished dishes such as lobster croustillant sautéed in an orange-flavored butter, monkfish médallions, and a chestnut terrine. C 290-375 F. M 130 F, 150 F, 180 F, 200 F, 250 F.

Les Marmottes
(See restaurant above)
See restaurant for closings. 40 rms 400-500 F. Half-board 430-650 F. Conf. Heated pool. Tennis. Golf. Pkg. V, AE, MC.
At the edge of the resort, this large chalet offers roomy, bright accommodation equipped with big bathrooms. Fully equipped fitness room. Shuttle to the ski slopes nearby.

DÉVILLE-LÈS-ROUEN 76   → Rouen

DIEFMATTEN 68780
Paris 521 - Belfort 24 - Mulhouse 23 - Thann 17   Haut-Rhin

⑭ Au Cheval Blanc
17, rue de Hecken
89 26 91 08, fax 89 26 92 28
Closed Tue dinner, Mon, Jul 24-Aug 4. Open until 9pm. Priv rm: 50. Garden dining. Pkg. V, AE, DC.
The flower-decked tables, nicely spaced, laid with pretty china and silverware, are set in an airy, old-fashioned dining room hung with white curtains. In what he terms his "updated, seasonal cuisine" chef Patrick Schlienger blends tradition, authentic regional ingredients, and a healthy dose of imagination. High praise for the quail confit Brillat-Savarin and goose foie gras with dried fruits, a pickerel and frog's legs matelote with tiny noodles, and a meringue-topped rhubarb feuillantine with strawberry sauce. The cellar is particularly rich in wines from Alsace and Burgundy, with lots of half-bottles. C 350-450 F. M 95 F (weekday lunch, wine incl), 160 F 195 F, 260 F, 380 F.

DIEPPE 76200
Paris 185 - Rouen 58 - Abbeville 63 - Le Havre 103   Seine-Mar.

Aguado
30, bd de Verdun
35 84 27 00, fax 35 06 17 61
Open year-round. 56 rms 230-425 F. Conf. No pets. Pkg. V, MC.
A modern, family-run hotel facing the sea. English-style furnishings grace the bedrooms.

La Mélie
2, Grande-Rue du Pollet
35 84 21 19
Closed Sun dinner, Mon. Annual closings not available. Open until 9:30pm. Pkg. V, AE, DC, MC.
From the pink-hued dining room you can watch the boats glide in and out of port under the Colbert Bridge. Exemplary seafood, precisely prepared by Guy Brachais, is what brings people back to this commendable seafood restaurant: we particularly like the langoustines with crisp aubergine fritters, and a delicate but tasty monkfish in cider vinegar. We are less enthusiastic about the crépou normand, which lacked butter and interest. Courteous welcome and service. **C** 230-330 F. **M** 230 F (wine incl), 170 F.

12/20 Le Panoramic
1, bd de Verdun
35 84 31 31, fax 35 84 86 70
Open daily until 1am. Priv rm: 80. Air cond. Garage pkg. V, AE, DC, MC.
You might have to do battle to win a seat in front of the great bay windows facing the coast, but once you do, you'll not be disappointed with the ably prepared, generously served seafood (pot-au-feu of the sea, mussel soup) and landlubber dishes (pleurote mushroom salad, grilled tournedos, and apple aumônière glacé). Good, manageably priced cellar. **C** 220-320 F. **M** 140 F.

La Présidence
(See restaurant above)
Open year-round. 1 ste 820-850 F. 88 rms 330-560 F. Rms for disabled. Conf. Golf. Garage pkg. V, AE, DC, MC.
Only some of the rooms have views out to sea, but they're all comfortably well equipped. English bar and numerous services.

Le Saint-Jacques
12, rue de l'Oranger - 35 84 52 04
Closings not available. Open until 9:30pm. Priv rm: 25. V.
Owner Jean-Pierre Maget, a tireless booster of his beloved Dieppe (he arranges tours of the region on request), has refurbished his eighteenth-century eating house, making an even more seductive setting for chef Benoist Carteret's cuisine. But some of our readers were dissatisfied with their meals here this year, and as for us, we came here twice to find the place closed when it should have been open. We will rate the cooking again when the restaurant makes its closing times clearer. **C** 230-300 F. **M** 65 F (weekday lunch), 99 F (weekdays), 132 F, 166 F, 195 F.

■ **In Martin-Église 76370**   7 km SE on D 1

Auberge du Clos Normand
22, rue Henri-IV
35 04 40 34, fax 35 04 48 49
Closed Mon dinner, Tue, Nov 15-Dec 15, Apr 3-12. Open until 9pm. Priv rm: 35. Garden dining. Pkg. V, AE, MC.
This fifteenth-century Norman inn fairly exudes an air of peaceful charm with its splendid beamed ceiling, pretty *bibelots*, and bright bouquets of fresh flowers. As for the cuisine of Régis Hauchecorne, it is sincere, generous, and well prepared: beautiful lobster salad, perfectly cooked turbot with girolles, and a tasty Grand Marnier soufflé all merit a toque, and here it is. Friendly welcome; the service could be quicker. **C** 170-400 F.

Auberge du Clos Normand
(See restaurant above)
See restaurant for closings. 1 ste 460 F. 7 rms 270-370 F. Restaurant. Half-board 350-400 F. Pkg. V, AE, MC.
The comfortable rooms in a riverside annex of the Clos are all different and pleasantly decorated. Bathrooms are well equipped.

DIEULEFIT	26220

Paris 633 - Montélimar 27 - Valence 72 - Nyons 31   *Drôme*

■ **In Le Poët-Laval 26160**   4 km on D 540

Les Hospitaliers
In Vieux-Village
75 46 22 32, fax 75 46 49 99
Closed Nov 15-Feb. Open until 9:30pm. Terrace dining. Pool. Pkg. V, AE, DC, MC.
From the terrace of Les Hospitaliers there is a magnificent, plunging view of the valley and the medieval village, surely one of the most enchanting sites of the rugged Provençal countryside. While the welcome and service are as courteous (although a bit amateurish) as ever, the classic cooking seems to be bogged down. Too much of a good thing can spoil even an elegant dish like sautéed sturgeon with onion and truffle ravioli. We infinitely prefer the roast farm-raised squab or the rack of lamb with rosemary. The cellar is exemplary, with a good choice of half-bottles. **C** 280-450 F. **M** 160 F, 200 F, 260 F, 395 F.

Les Hospitaliers
(See restaurant above)
Closed Nov 15-Feb. 2 stes 1,010-1,200 F. 22 rms 420-1,150 F. Rms for disabled. Conf. Pool. Half-board 630-1,360 F. Conf. Pool. Pkg. V, AE, DC, MC.
This hotel is a captivating place for a holiday. Beautiful antique furniture graces rooms decorated in perfect taste; most enjoy sweeping views of the valley. Excellent breakfasts.

DIGNE	04000

Paris 760 - Aix-en-Provence 110 - Sisteron 40   *Alpes/H.-P.*

Le Grand Paris
19, bd Thiers
92 31 11 15, fax 92 32 32 82
Closed Sun dinner & Mon off-seas, Dec 20-Feb. Open until 9:30pm. Priv rm: 30. Garden dining. Garage pkg. V, AE, DC, MC.
Jean-Jacques Ricaud's menu proposes such polished classics as pork terrine with lentils and rabbit jambonneau with mustard and tender, tasty spelt. Fine cheeses; pears cooked in wine for dessert. A *volière* of twittering birds enlivens the spacious, flower-decked dining room; their happy chirps can even be heard out on the shaded terrace. Distinguished cellar (wonderful Côtes-du-Rhônes and Bordeaux); impeccable welcome and service **C** 300-450 F. **M** 150 F

(weekday lunch, Sat, wine incl), 195 F, 230 F, 385 F.

Le Grand Paris

(See restaurant above)
Closed Dec 20-Feb. 4 stes 600-725 F. 26 rms 336-480 F. Half-board 400-500 F. Conf. Golf. Garage pkg. V, AE, DC, MC.
The hotel is housed in a seventeenth-century convent, once the home of the Frères de la Trinité. Rooms are spacious, handsomely decorated, and protected from street noise by the terrace's leafy plane trees. The lovely breakfasts are served in antique silver services.

Mistre

63, bd Gassendi - 92 31 00 16
Closed Sat off-seas, hols, Nov 5-20. Open until 9:15pm. Priv rm: 80. Valet pkg. V, AE.
Rolland Comte puts regional and seasonal market-fresh ingredients to good use, and we award him a toque this year for such successful dishes as a meltingly tender and tasty casserole-roasted lamb with black olives and a fine chocolate cake. Competent and friendly welcome and service in the comfortable dining room. Good choice of Provençal wines. C 250-350 F. M 128 F, 180 F, 220 F.

Mistre

(See restaurant above)
Closed Nov 5-20. 19 rms 300-440 F. Half-board 380-460 F. Conf. Valet pkg. V, AE.
In the heart of town, this hotel provides a score of somewhat impersonal rooms with perfectly adequate fittings.

Origan

6, rue Pied-de-Ville - 92 31 62 13
Closed Sun. Open until 9:15pm. Terrace dining. V, AE, MC.
The whole family joins in to run this cheerful establishment. Madame Cochet and her daughter oversee the dining room, while Philippe Cochet mans the kitchen. We wish he could be a bit less timid in his cooking: the rosemary-scented clam soup needed a little something extra, and the venison tian was tasty but lacked finesse, and was served with a too-garlicky pumpkin purée. We liked the fine pear tart, though. Small but well chosen wine list. C 250-300 F. M 98 F, 155 F, 240 F.

See also: **Château-Arnoux**

Diligences et Commerce

14, rue Nationale
85 53 06 31, fax 85 88 92 43
Closed Mon dinner & Tue (exc Jul-Aug), Jun 20-25, Nov 20-Dec 12. Open until 9:30pm. Priv rm: 15. Garden dining. No pets. Pkg. V, AE, DC, MC.
Only the sign and the restaurant's old-fashioned façade recall the glorious era of nineteenth-century coaching inns. The dining room is neat as a pin, the courtyard terrace inviting, and the cooking adroitly done in a classic style: langoustine ravioli, good turbot, young squab in a pastry crust with potatoes. Good wine list, friendly service. An extra point

this year. C 250-350 F. M 95 F, 135 F, 200 F, 320 F.

Jean-Pierre Mathieu

Hôtel de la Gare,
79, av. du Gal-de-Gaulle
85 53 03 04, fax 85 53 14 70
Closed Wed (exc Jul-Aug), mid Jan-mid Feb. Open until 9:30pm. Air cond. Pkg. V, DC, MC.
While Jacqueline Mathieu welcomes guests into a pretty renovated dining room, her husband Jean-Pierre prepares lighter versions of classic dishes. Try the rissolette of sea scallops with an avocado mousse, breast of farm-raised duck and foie gras sautéed with bilberries, and a chocolate bavarian cream. Odd but diverse wine list. C 300-400 F. M 130 F, 185 F, 225 F, 320 F.

Château Bourgogne

22, bd de la Marne
80 72 31 13, fax 80 73 61 45
Open year-round. 7 stes 610-650 F. 113 rms 375-555 F. Rms for disabled. Restaurant. Air cond. Conf. Heated pool. Golf. Pkg. V, AE, DC, MC.   **D2-1**
Here's an excellent, American-style hotel situated in the new, slightly gloomy Palais de la Foire district, ten minutes from the center. Rooms are big and modern, well-ventilated, and recently refurbished. Conference rooms are thoughtfully equipped. Swimming pool.

Jean-Pierre Billoux

14, pl. Darcy
80 30 11 00, fax 80 49 94 89
Closed Sun dinner, Mon, Feb school hols. Open until 9:30pm. Terrace dining. Air cond. Pkg. V, AE.   **B3-4**
Jean-Pierre Billoux is still one of Burgundy's best chefs, imbued with a quiet strength that conceals a very active culinary imagination. The restaurant's traditional decor, reminiscent of an old Burgundian *caveau* where trenchermen could dine heartily (though not very discerningly) and make merry until the drink ran out, is a bit misleading. One can still make merry *chez* Billoux, but the food is no rough-and-ready affair. Modern, subtly savory, Billoux's cooking is informed by rural good sense rather than citified refinements, and he knows how to transform classic dishes with inventive touches. We loved the unexpected but perfect addition of capers, for example, to the fine breast of guinea fowl with foie gras, and the luscious perch gelée enhanced the sautéed frog's legs with turnip confit, as did the tart tomato and lemon compote the veal kidney. And who else would have thought of a banana tarte Tatin? Some dishes are less successful: the duck mousse overwhelmed the excellent salmon it was paired with, and neither the Jura wine nor the caramelized carrots could wake up the bland and slightly overcooked veal sweetbreads. The regional specialties are a delight: snail meurette à l'ancienne and chicken in red wine sauce, for example. In the dining room, Françoise Billoux lavishes attention on her guests, while sommelier Patrice Gillard offers guidance through the intricacies of the enormous wine list. C 450-600 F. M 200 F

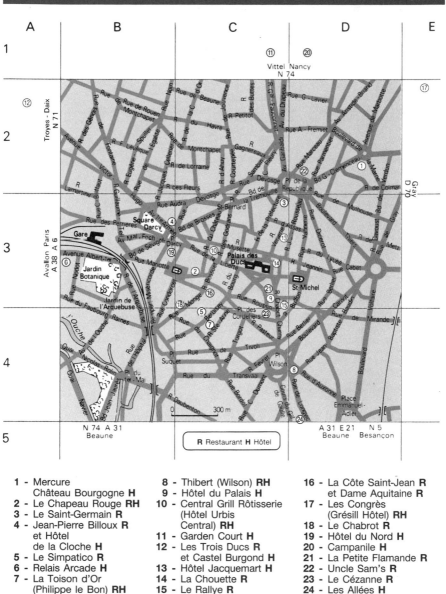

A   B   C   D   E

1

Vittel Nancy
N 74

2

3

4

5

N 74 A 31
Beaune

A 31 E 21   N 5
Beaune Besançon

R Restaurant H Hôtel

1 - Mercure
Château Bourgogne **H**
2 - Le Chapeau Rouge **RH**
3 - Le Saint-Germain **R**
4 - Jean-Pierre Billoux **R**
et Hôtel
de la Cloche **H**
5 - Le Simpatico **R**
6 - Relais Arcade **H**
7 - La Toison d'Or
(Philippe le Bon) **RH**

8 - Thibert (Wilson) **RH**
9 - Hôtel du Palais **H**
10 - Central Grill Rôtisserie
(Hôtel Urbis
Central) **RH**
11 - Garden Court **H**
12 - Les Trois Ducs **R**
et Castel Burgond **H**
13 - Hôtel Jacquemart **H**
14 - La Chouette **R**
15 - Le Rallye **R**

16 - La Côte Saint-Jean **R**
et Dame Aquitaine **R**
17 - Les Congrès
(Grésill Hôtel) **RH**
18 - Le Chabrot **R**
19 - Hôtel du Nord **H**
20 - Campanile **H**
21 - La Petite Flamande **R**
22 - Uncle Sam's **R**
23 - Le Cézanne **R**
24 - Les Allées **H**

(lunch exc Sun, wine incl), 280 F (dinner, Sun lunch, wine incl), 350 F, 480 F.

🏠 **Campanile**
Parc technologique de la Toison-d'Or, allée A.-Nobel
80 74 41 00, fax 80 70 13 44
See page 95.   D1-20
A warm welcome can be expected from the staff. Rooms are comfortable and well kept.

🏠 **Castel Burgond**
2 km NW on N 71, 21121 Daix
3, route de Troyes
80 56 59 72, fax 80 57 69 48
Open year-round. 38 rms 250-270 F. Rms for disabled. Restaurant. Golf. Pkg. V, AE, DC, MC. **A2-12**
An enormous geometric structure in upper Dijon. Rooms are functional, with lots of space and light. Billiard room.

Central Grill Rôtisserie

3, pl. Grangier
80 30 44 00, fax 80 30 77 12
Closed Sun. Open until midnight. Priv rm: 50. Terrace dining. Air cond. Pkg. V, AE, DC.   **C3-10**
A good address, right in the center of Dijon, that stays open till midnight. The food served here is uncomplicated fare made with top-drawer ingredients. In addition to platters of raw seafood, brochettes and spit-roasted meats, there's fine andouillette, perfectly cooked thick fillet of sole, and good desserts. Prices are very reasonable, even for the well chosen wine list, and bargain-priced meals are served until midnight. Diligent, unobtrusive service. **C** 200-300 F. **M** 140 F.

Ibis Central

(See restaurant above)
See page 95.
Definitely superior to its two-star classification, this venerable hotel in the city center has been entirely modernized, and its rooms were recently refurbished.

12/20 Le Cézanne

40, rue de l'Amiral-Roussin - 80 58 92 91
Closed Mon. Open until 9:45pm. Terrace dining. Air cond. V, AE, DC, MC.   **C4-23**
Along this street near the Palais de Justice, restaurants come and go with alarming rapidity. May this one stay around; it deserves to last. Classic, well prepared cooking in a pleasant decor of stone walls with a mezzanine: salmon tian, excellent veal and veal kidneys, and strawberry puff pastry, all at attractive prices. Be sure to reserve at lunch; the word has gotten around. **C** 180-200 F. **M** 69 F, 90 F (lunch exc Sun), 120 F, 180 F.

Le Chabrot

36, rue Monge - 80 30 69 61
Closed Mon lunch, Sun. Open until 10:30pm. Priv rm: 35. Air cond. V.   **C3-18**
Overhead beams coif this appealing bistrot, whose owner's main interest is wine and winemakers. But the young chef is adroit with both elegant and rustic fare. Salmon is a star attraction, but you can also try the tasty mackerel and Jerusalem artichoke tart, calf's head salad, upside down truffle tart, or steak with Epoisses cheese. Prices are reasonable (especially the 69 F lunch menu, a true bargain), and the restaurant has regained the spirit it had lost for awhile. But we would like to see producers' names on the wine list. **C** 150-250 F. **M** 69 F (weekday lunch, Sat), 98 F, 170 F.

Le Chapeau Rouge

5, rue Michelet
80 30 28 10, fax 80 30 33 89
Open daily until 9:45pm. Priv rm: 50. Air cond. No pets. Valet pkg. V, AE, DC.   **C3-2**
Much effort and expense have gone into rejuvenating this renowned provincial hostelry, which had slipped into a slow decline. The proprietor is a keen professional, and has succeeded in giving Le Chapeau Rouge a more youthful, vigorous image. The cooking is classical, but saved from banality by a few special touches. This year's *carte* includes an excellent chicken liver bouillon, a snail chartreuse, and perfectly cooked fish. Only the wine list could

use a bit of rejuvenation. **C** 350-400 F. **M** 220 F (lunch, wine incl), 150 F (wine incl), 200 F (dinner), 390 F.

Le Chapeau Rouge

(See restaurant above)
Open year-round. 2 stes 1,350-1,550 F. 29 rms 460-900 F. Half-board 480-590 F. Air cond. Conf. Valet pkg. V, AE, DC.
Renovations have definitely improved this comfortable family hotel. Half the rooms have been modernized, with Jacuzzis in some of the bathrooms. The good soundproofing is appreciable given the location in the center of town. Service is impeccable.

La Chouette

1, rue de la Chouette
80 30 18 10, fax 80 30 59 93
Closed Mon dinner, Tue, 1st 2 wks of Jul. Open until 10pm. Priv rm: 15. V, AE, DC, MC.   **C3-14**
Lucette and Christian Breuil's cozy establishment is situated in a pretty part of town, also favored by antique dealers. Christian Breuil is an accomplished technician of the old school who knows how to embroider a traditional repertoire based on prime ingredients. But the meal we had this year was disappointing, except for the roast mango with pineapple. Friendly welcome; prices are high given the quality. **C** 400-500 F. **M** 130 F, 150 F, 210 F, 250 F, 320 F.

Hôtel de la Cloche

14, pl. Darcy
80 30 12 32, fax 80 30 04 15
Open year-round. 4 stes 1,200-1,300 F. 76 rms 450-620 F. Restaurant. Air cond. Conf. Golf. Valet pkg. V, AE, DC, MC.   **B3-4**
An indifferent reception, poor service, inferior rooms (apart from a few renovated duplexes), and terribly mundane breakfasts. Time to ring some changes at the Hôtel de la Cloche, once a majestic and flourishing establishment!

10/20 Les Congrès

16, av. R.-Poincaré - 80 72 17 22 (R), 80 71 10 56 (H), fax 80 74 34 89
Open daily until 11pm. Priv rm: 30. Terrace dining. Air cond. Pkg. V, AE, DC, MC.   **E2-17**
A restful, lilac-toned interior lulls one into enjoying this simple, unpretentious cuisine: vegetable terrine, sea scallops with shallot confit, and a dessert assortment. Good local wines. **C** 170-280 F. **M** 88 F, 120 F, 165 F.

Grésill' Hôtel

(See restaurant above)
Open year-round. 47 rms 230-370 F. Conf. Golf. Pkg. V, AE, DC, MC.
A charmless modern construction near the Palais des Congrès et des Sports, with functional, well-kept rooms. Bar and pub.

La Côte Saint-Jean

13, rue Monge
80 50 11 77, fax 80 50 18 75
Closed Sat lunch, Tue, Jul 15-Aug 5, Dec 23-Jan 12. Open until 9:30pm. V, MC.   **C3-16**
A rather chic bistrot decorated with an amusing array of teapots. The cooking is still a bit timid, but the chef turns out worthy, honest dishes like rabbit in parsley gelatin, salmon and saddle of rabbit with girolles in well-reduced jus, and some interesting cheeses (with nuts, cher-

ries, oil, etc.). The cellar needs some work, but we feel this restaurant has earned a toque this year. **C** 300-380 F. **M** 95 F (weekday lunch), 120 F, 145 F, 165 F, 215 F.

La Dame d'Aquitaine
23, pl. Bossuet
80 30 36 23, fax 80 49 90 41
Closings not available. Open until 11pm. No pets. V, AE, DC, MC. **C3-16**
A medieval crypt with ribbed vaulting opens onto an eighteenth-century courtyard right in the heart of Dijon—it's one of the most inviting spots in town. Monique Saléra's Gascon specialties add to the charm: try her duck persillé and duck breast with currants. Judicious cellar, with considerable holdings from the Southwest as well as from Burgundy and Jura; superb choice of Armagnacs. **C** 250-300 F. **M** 120 F, 168 F, 180 F, 225 F, 330 F.

Gresill' Hotel
See restaurant Les Congrès

Holiday Inn Garden Court
1, pl. Marie-de-Bourgogne
80 72 20 72, fax 80 72 32 72
Open year-round. 100 rms 400-430 F. Rms for disabled. Restaurant. Half-board 100-180 F. Air cond. Conf. Golf. Pkg. V, AE, DC, MC. **C1-11**
An attractive hotel of recent vintage in the Toison d'Or commercial complex. Standardized but luxurious comfort in the modern rooms, which are superbly outfitted (video, trouser-press, coffee machine) and soundproofed.

Ibis Central
See restaurant Central Grill Rôtisserie

Hôtel Jacquemart
32, rue de la Verrerie
80 73 39 74, fax 80 73 20 99
Open year-round. 2 stes 290-330 F. 30 rms 150-320 F. V, MC. **A3-13**
This comfortable, family-run hotel stands amid the enticing antique shops of medieval Dijon. You can count on a warm welcome.

Hôtel du Palais
23, rue du Palais
80 67 16 26, fax 80 65 12 16
Open year-round. 16 rms 170-240 F. V, MC. **C3-9**
A scrupulously renovated small hotel, which offers excellent value for money, located a few minutes from the center of Dijon, between the library and the Palais de Justice. Courteous welcome and a cozy atmosphere.

12/20 La Petite Flamande
9, rue des Bons-Enfants
80 67 16 56
Closed Sun. Open until 10pm. Priv rm: 35. V, AE, MC. **C3-21**
Here's a likeable, lively little spot just steps from Dijon's theatre. If simple food with a personal touch is what you prefer, you'll love La Petite Flamande. Pull the cork on a good bottle from northern Burgundy, and enjoy skate, duck carpaccio with hazlenuts, snail and tagliatelle gratin, veal sweetbreads and ravioli, and a soufflé glacé. Speedy service. **C** 180-220 F. **M** 75 F (lunch exc Sun), 65 F, 135 F.

Hôtel Philippe Le Bon
See restaurant La Toison d'Or

Quality Hôtel du Nord
Pl. Darcy
80 30 58 58, fax 80 30 61 26
Closed Dec 23-Jan 9. 1 ste 370-750 F. 27 rms 320-405 F. Restaurant. Half-board 330-445 F. Conf. Golf. Garage pkg. V, AE, DC, MC. **B3-19**
A centrally situated hotel in the best Burgundian tradition, recently renovated. Emphatically rustic decor. The welcome is charming, and there's a wine bar on the lower level.

Le Rallye
39, rue Chabot-Charny
80 67 11 55
Closed Sun, hols, Feb 20-Mar 5, Jul 25-Aug 17. Open until 9:30pm. Priv rm: 15. V. **C3-15**
François Minot is back in the driver's seat at Le Rallye, bringing with him a classic, highly professional repertoire of bourgeois dishes, not always the lightest. Our sole did not set the world on fire. But the leek-filled puff pastry, game terrine, and whiting are textbook examples of how these dishes should be prepared. We applaud Minot's efforts to keep prices reasonable for the food as well as the wine; very personal choices on the wine list. **C** 200-350 F. **M** 90 F, 150 F, 220 F.

Relais Arcade
15, av. Albert-Ier
80 43 01 12, fax 80 41 69 48
Open year-round. 128 rms 300-330 F. Rms for disabled. Restaurant. Conf. Pkg. V, AE, MC. **B3-6**
A stone's throw from the station and the Grévin-Bourgogne complex. Quiet, comfortable little rooms and a decent breakfast buffet. Well-equipped conference rooms.

10/20 Le Saint-Germain
10, rue du Nord
80 73 56 01, fax 80 67 64 51
Closed Sat lunch, Tue, Jul 20-Aug 15. Open until 10pm. V, AE, DC, MC. **C3-3**
This grill room is set in a joyless street, but we come here anyhow for the affordable, down-to-earth cooking: unctuous fish terrine, petit salé with lentils, and wines from local producers at reasonable prices. **C** 190-300 F. **M** 78 F (weekday lunch), 92 F, 135 F, 150 F.

10/20 Le Simpatico
30, rue Berbisey - 80 30 53 33
Closed 1st wk of Jan, 1 wk during the Carnaval, 2 wks mid Aug. Open until 10:30pm. Priv rm: 45. V, AE, MC. **C4-5**
The name fits. An authentic Italian restaurant serving good garlic bread and an assortment of home-style dishes to go with it. Dijon's young crowd flocks here. **C** 180-220 F. **M** 55 F, 70 F (weekday lunch), 89 F, 115 F (dinner exc Sun).

Thibert
10, pl. du Pdt-Wilson - 80 67 74 64 (R)
80 66 82 50 (H), fax 80 63 87 72 (R), 80 36 41 54 (H)
Closed Mon lunch, Sun, 3 wks in Aug. Open until 9:45pm. Air cond. Pkg. V, AE, MC. **D4-8**
Perhaps it is simply a matter of experience and maturity? Whatever the reason, we note with pleasure that Jean-Paul Thibert's talent has at-

tained a new fullness, a serenity that nevertheless leaves plenty of room for his characteristic boldness and verve. Witness the barely cooked langoustines with green coffee beans and fried dill, served with a fantastic brunoise of vegetables flavored with honey and cumin. Thibert's cuisine often marries fatty dishes with welcome touches of acidity. For example, this year's menu presents warm foie gras perked up with a sorrel "milk", and black currant vinegar giving oomph to dried duck paired with orange peel, dried juniper berries, and turnips with prunes. Each dish has incredibly complex flavors, such as the standing rump of veal made sublime by a bit of anchovy jus. Thibert certainly doesn't want for ideas, and produces dishes that are always creative, refined, and balanced. Only the desserts didn't seem to reach the summits this year, though they are excellent. The wines are knowledgeably presented (all the great Burgundies are here), and hostess Maryse Thibert provides a smiling welcome. In short, this restaurant is a pleasure dome, a rare find in these morose times... Thibert's three toques are fully deserved. **C** 400-550 F. **M** 125 F (weekdays, Sat lunch), 195 F, 260 F, 320 F, 410 F.

Wilson

(See restaurant above)
Closed Dec 31. 27 rms 330-450 F. Pkg. V, MC.
Situated on the square of the same name, next to the Restaurant Thibert, this comfortable seventeenth-century coaching inn has been fully, freshly renovated. Rooms are personalized with opulent rustic furnishings.

La Toison d'Or

Cie Bourguignonne des Œnophiles,
18, rue Ste-Anne
80 30 73 52, fax 80 30 95 51
Closed Sun dinner, Aug 8-23. Open until 9:30pm. Priv rm: 120. Pkg. V, AE, DC, MC. **C4-7**
There are several dining rooms and cellars done up in Louis XIII style, an amusing wine museum, a collection of figurines, and a lovely medieval courtyard: such is the Toison d'Or in the heart of old Dijon. The updated classic cooking of Daniel Broyer (croustillant of snails with vegetable butter and soy sauce, fricassée of sole and langoustines with fresh pasta, chocolate cake) is served forth by well-trained staff. The wine list is rich in Burgundies with some interesting bargains on offer. **C** 300-400 F. **M** 130 F (exc weekday lunch), 150 F (weekday lunch, wine incl), 190 F, 240 F.

Philippe Le Bon

(See restaurant above)
Open year-round. 27 rms 320-440 F. Half-board 370-470 F. No pets. No cards.
On a quiet street in the center of town, a former laboratory converted to a comfortable hotel with air-conditioned rooms and a garden; a good base for exploring the ancient heart of Dijon.

10/20 Uncle Sam's

3, rue Claus-Slutter - 80 70 14 15
Open daily until 11pm. Terrace dining. V, AE. **D2-22**
This is our pick of the Tex-Mex restaurants springing up all over town like magic mushrooms. Typical decor (Harley motorcycles, Cadillacs, Hollywood) and well prepared

favorites (meats, chili, fajitas) served in a lively atmosphere. **C** 150-200 F. **M** 49 F (weekday lunch).

Wilson

See restaurant Thibert

And also...

Our selection of places for inexpensive, quick, or late-night meals.
Bistingo (80 30 61 38 - Passage Darcy.): Centrally located, casual little bistro serving fresh market cuisine (140-175 F).
Le Bistrot des Halles (80 49 94 15 - 10, rue Bannelier - Restaurant Billoux. Open until 10:30pm.): Close to the market, a pleasing, inexpensive bistrot that had slipped a bit but should get back on track now that top chef Jean-Pierre Billoux is more closely involved in running it (150-220 F).
La Table Marocaine (80 67 43 81 - 42, rue Pasteur. Open until 10:30pm.): Couscous, tajines, and other Moroccan dishes, meticulously prepared and served.

■ **In Marsannay-la-Côte 21160** 7 km SW on D 122

Les Gourmets

8, rue du Puits-de-Têt
80 51 91 31, fax 80 52 03 01
Closed Sun dinner, Mon, 1st wk of Feb. Open until 9:30pm. Priv rm: 35. Garden dining. V, AE, DC, MC.
Contemporary post-Pompeii is how we would describe Joël Perreaut's new dining room: the turquoise pillars, smoked mirrors, and billowing yellow curtains may conspire to make you feel bilious! Indeed, the shades and nuances of his cooking are far more to our taste. Perreaut's cuisine is punctuated by concise, focused jus and by exciting flavor harmonies, often derived from classic Burgundian recipes made new. The three toques are well earned, but they are white: we find that Perreaut's cooking now contains butter-enriched sauces, fried dishes, and other classic touches that, we feel, are unnecessary embellishments. This year we enjoyed his snail bread pudding, sole with calf's head, squab roasted with spices, mango and morels, and an unforgettable blood sausage with honey cake. The wine list is one of the area's best—it will help you to discover the underrated wines of Marsannay and Fixin—and it is uncommonly rich in half-bottles, as well as containing some wines from outside the region. Nicole Perreaut supervises the professional service. **C** 420-560 F. **M** 165 F, 215 F, 380 F, 480 F.

■ **In Neuilly-lès-Dijon 21800** 7 km SE on N 5

La Flambée

On D905, route de Dôle-Besançon
80 47 35 35, fax 80 47 07 08
Open year-round. 1 ste 630-750 F. 22 rms 300-495 F. Restaurant. Half-board 285-435 F. Air cond. Conf. Heated pool. Golf. Pkg. V, AE, DC, MC.
Quiet, renovated, well-equipped rooms in a luxurious country cottage (the peasants never had it so good!).

■ **In Val-Suzon 21121**   16 km NW on N 71

Hostellerie du Val-Suzon
N 71 - 80 35 60 15, fax 80 35 61 36
Closed Wed lunch & Thu (exc Jul-Sep), Dec 15-Jan 15. Open until 10pm. Priv rm: 20. Terrace dining. No pets. Pkg. V, AE, DC, MC.
Any chef can make an occasional misstep, but Yves Perreau's classic training (enlivened with a contemporary touch) ensures that they are few and far between. In this absolutely charming spot (recently renovated) we partook of an intriguing parmentier millefeuille with Burgundian snails in parsley butter, farm-raised chicken with morels and foie gras, and sautéed strawberries with nougat ice cream. Diversified wine list. Friendly welcome. C 350-450 F. M 160 F (weekday lunch, Sat, wine incl), 128 F (weekday lunch, Sat), 190 F, 260 F, 400 F.

Hostellerie du Val-Suzon
(See restaurant above)
Closed Nov 15-Dec. 1 ste 650-850 F. 16 rms 320-520 F. Restaurant. Half-board 415-500 F. Conf. Golf. Pkg. V, AE, DC, MC.
Comfortable, country-style inn with a chalet-annex. Attractive bathrooms, and a very handsome suite.

See also: **Gevrey-Chambertin**

DINAN	22100
Paris 370 - St-Brieuc 59 - St-Malo 29 - Rennes 51	Côtes/Armor

Avaugour
1, pl. du Champ
96 39 07 49, fax 96 85 43 04
Open year-round. 2 stes 800-1,300 F. 27 rms 300-550 F. V, AE, DC, MC.
Gisèle Quinton lavishes time and effort on this large, attractive establishment. Rooms are comfortable and regularly renovated; some look out onto the ramparts and garden. The bedding is all new this year.

La Caravelle
14, pl. Duclos - 96 39 00 11
Closed Sun dinner & Wed off-seas, Nov 11-Dec 4, Mar 15-25. Open until 9:30pm. Pkg. V, AE, DC.
Chef Jean-Claude Marmion offers well prepared cuisine with a focus on the sea. It may not be the most inventive cooking around, but his first set menu is sure to please: terrine of beef cheeks with ravigote sauce, pollack fillet with a sprinkling of paprika, and a warm cherry dessert. Good wine list, but the Bordeaux are not cheap. Charming welcome by the *patronne* in the pretty pink, orange, and pistachio-hued dining room. C 300-450 F. M 130 F, 180 F, 200 F, 260 F, 350 F.

Chez la Mère Pourcel
3, pl. des Merciers
96 39 03 80, fax 96 87 07 58
Closed Sun dinner & Mon (exc Jul-Aug), Feb 21-Mar 16. Open until 10pm. Terrace dining. V, AE, DC, MC.
The medieval setting is wonderful, with bare stone walls, beams, and wood paneling. Jean-Luc Danjou's lively cuisine is in tip-top form. Premium ingredients go into his fine ormeaux (a type of mollusc) de Saint-Malo with a tasty shallot and beef marrow sauce, capon-style guinea

fowl, and a delicate bittersweet chocolate tart. Diversified cellar, charming welcome. C 300-400 F. M 95 F (weekday lunch), 155 F, 210 F, 280 F, 350 F.

DINARD	35800
Paris 370 - Rennes 72 - Dinan 22 - Lamballe 47	Ille/Vil.

Altaïr
18, bd Féart
99 46 13 58, fax 99 88 20 49
Closed Sun dinner & Mon (exc school hols). Open until 9:30pm. Terrace dining. V, AE, DC, MC.
At a hop and a skip from the beach is this comfy, country-style establishment, made cozy with pitch-pine furnishings. Patrick Leménager's cuisine grows more proficient every day, and succeeds in being both light and full of honest flavor: shellfish and vegetable ragoût, squab crapaudine with sweet garlic, frozen berry mousse. The 120 F menu is excellent. C 230-450 F. M 89 F, 120 F, 160 F, 200 F.

Grand-Hôtel
46, av. George-V
99 88 26 26, fax 99 88 26 27
Closed Nov-Mar. 3 stes 1,150-2,400 F. 63 rms 480-1,200 F. Restaurant. Half board 180 F. Conf. Heated pool. Golf. Valet pkg. V, AE, DC, MC.
A fine example of the last century's grand hotels, facing the Saint-Servan Bay. Rooms are spacious, and some were recently refurbished with period furniture. Great bathrooms.

Novotel Thalassa
Av. Château-Hébert
99 82 78 10, fax 99 82 78 29
Closed Nov 14-Dec 17. 2 stes 1,170-1,500 F. 104 rms 540-800 F. Rms for disabled. Restaurant. Half-board 445-565 F. Conf. Heated pool. Tennis. Golf. Pkg. V, AE, DC, MC.
A spanking-new hotel poised above the waves, with gracious lawns, fountains, and amenities galore. In fact the comfort is several cuts above this chain's usual level. The sizeable guest rooms are prettily fitted out, nicely equipped, and all turned toward the sea. Cordial welcome but alas, ordinary breakfasts.

Reine Hortense
19, rue de la Malouine
99 46 54 31, fax 99 88 15 88
Closed Nov 15-Mar 25. 2 stes 1,600-1,800 F. 10 rms 590-980 F. Golf. Valet pkg. V, AE, DC, MC.
A few souvenirs of Queen Hortense have been preserved along with some highly picturesque furniture. The superb turn-of-the-century salon has a Versailles parquet floor. Direct access to the beach.

■ **In Pleurtuit 35730**   5 km S on D 266

Manoir de la Rance
Château de Jouvente
99 88 53 76, fax 99 88 63 03
Closed Jan 5-Mar 15. 2 stes 800-1,100 F. 8 rms 380-800 F. Golf. Pkg. V, AE, MC.
Ten kilometers from Dinan stands this large, charming hotel perched above the Rance River. Rooms are furnished with period pieces; they are quiet, well equipped, and have lots of character. Breakfasts are delicious, and there is a

pretty terrace, a garden, a bar, and tea room for your pleasure. Smiling service.

DISNEYLAND PARIS 77

→ **PARIS Suburbs: Marne-la-Vallée**

DIVES-SUR-MER 14 → Cabourg

DIVONNE-LES-BAINS 01220
Paris 502 - Geneva 19 - Nyon 13 - Gex 9 - Bourg 120 *Ain*

Le Champagne
Av. de Genève
50 20 13 13
Closed Thu lunch, Wed, Dec 23-Jan 15, 10 days end Jun & beg Oct. Open until 9:30pm. Garden dining. Pkg. V.
We would like to see a few set menus to lighten the bill at Champagne, where you will find honest but rather simplistic cooking: grilled red mullet with béarnaise sauce, warm foie gras with pleurote mushrooms, and a dessert cart. Warm welcome, and there's a lovely garden. C 200-450 F.

Château de Divonne
Route de Gex
50 20 00 32, fax 50 20 03 73
Closed beg Jan-beg Mar. Open until 9:30pm. Priv rm: 80. Terrace dining. Air cond. Pkg. V, AE, MC.
Michel de Matteis, who heads the kitchen at this nineteenth-century manor house overlooking Lake Geneva, has earned the Château de Divonne two toques. He's a capable chef who knows how to give a personal spin to regional ingredients, as well as to the luxurious foodstuffs one expects in a place like this. His cooking is never mannered, even when he tries his hand at updating classic dishes. This year we enjoyed his "marbled" foie gras and smoked squab perfectly paired with a warm fig compote; delicately cooked féra (a lake fish) posed on a ragoût of vegetables and clams; ravioli stuffed with langoustine, green cabbage, and mountain ham; and farcis of petit-gris snails in an herb bouillon. For dessert, savor the lucious pure chocolate fondant paired with candied lemons. An ardent œnophile, Christophe Grémeaux, oversees a wine list as fascinating to read as the most gripping novel; start your meal with a sparkling local wine, Pétillant-de-Bugey-Cerdon, one of the cellar's many finds from Savoie, Jura, and Burgundy. An extra point this year for this gourmand château. C 400-500 F. M 270 F (weekday lunch, Sat, wine incl), 280 F, 380 F, 490 F.

Château de Divonne
(See restaurant above)
Closed beg Jan-beg Mar. 6 stes 1,200-1,700 F. 21 rms 475-1,300 F. Half-board 765-1,230 F. Conf. Tennis. Golf. Garage pkg. Helipad. V, AE, MC.
Enjoy a gorgeous view of Lake Geneva and the Mont Blanc range from an early nineteenth-century manor house situated on 22 wooded hectares. The interior design is nothing special, but you'll love the spacious rooms, modern bathrooms, exquisite breakfasts, and perfect service. There's an eighteen-hole golf course, casino, sailing, and summer music festivals for your entertainment. Relais et Châteaux.

La Terrasse
Av. des Thermes
50 40 34 34, fax 50 40 34 24
Open daily until 9:30pm. Priv rm: 300. Terrace dining. Air cond. Heated pool. No pets. Valet pkg. V, AE, DC, MC.
Jean-Marc Delacourt is a very capable chef. What's more, he's been liberally supplied with the necessary means to compose an intelligent, personalized menu of skillfully revised classic dishes. The mature, mostly foreign patrons simply wallow in the rather pompous atmosphere of this old-fashioned casino restaurant. Try the pastilla of lightly cooked smoked salmon with sweet-sour onion confit, a delicate soup of white coco beans with chicken wings and truffles, or a "paume" of roast veal sweetbreads and morel-stuffed ravioli. Refined and delicate desserts, often fruit-based. The best possible partner is a Jura or Savoie wine from the fine cellar, which contains some superb bottles. C 400-500 F. M 180 F, 320 F.

Domaine de Divonne
(See restaurant above)
Open year-round. 8 stes 1,800-6,500 F. 112 rms 550-1,400 F. Half-board 910-1,720 F. Conf. Heated pool. Tennis. Golf. Valet pkg. V, AE, DC, MC.
Charmingly old-fashioned (not wildly cheerful), this 1930s luxury hotel provides rooms overlooking either the manicured grounds and the Jura Mountains, or Lake Geneva and the Alps. Night club; casino.

DOL-DE-BRETAGNE 35120
Paris 373 - St-Malo 24 - Rennes 54 - Dinan 26 *Ille/Vil.*

La Bresche Arthur
36, bd Deminiac
99 48 01 44, fax 99 48 16 32
Closed Sun dinner & Mon (exc in summer & hols), Feb. Open until 10pm. Priv rm: 50. Pkg. V, MC.
The delightful 125 F menu (eight warm oysters in citrus butter, skate braised in meat jus with a celery mousse, cheeses, and crème brûlée with a vanilla bean) is a good introduction to Philippe Martel's generous, cleverly crafted cooking. Interesting cellar and competent service in the bright, pretty dining room that overlooks a garden. C 230-300 F. M 75 F, 125 F, 180 F, 240 F.

DOLE 39100
Paris 370 - Besançon 57 - Dijon 48 - Lons-le-Saulnier 52 *Jura*

La Chaumière
346, av. du Mal-Juin
84 70 72 40, fax 84 79 25 60
Closed Dec 16-Jan 15, Jun 17-26. 18 rms 295-395 F. Restaurant. Conf. Heated pool. Pkg. V, AE, DC, MC.
On the road to Geneva, a scrupulously renovated hotel with airy, comfortable rooms. Perfect bathrooms.

Les Templiers
35, Grande-Rue
84 82 78 78, fax 84 72 87 62
Closed Sun dinner & Mon lunch (exc school hols). Open until 10pm. Air cond. Pkg. V, DC, MC.
Joël Cesari is flirting with a second toque if he could be a bit more audacious, but for now, he never hits false notes in the dishes served in a pleasant dining room with Gothic architecture.

This year we enjoyed his sautéed snails in a chicken liver tartare, tender milk-fed veal with onions, and roast pickerel with spinach. It was all so good that we were frustrated not to be able to award an extra point. Give it time.... The cellar offers an excellent choice of Arbois wines. **C** 280-380 F. **M** 85 F (weekdays, Sat lunch), 135 F, 200 F, 250 F.

holding the creatures that will be swept almost straight to your plate. Try the salmon and crab tartare topped with strips of smoked salmon, lobster civet with morels and sweet spices, or fisherman's platter with a shellfish fumet. And for die-hard carnivores (too bad for them!), lamb, steak, and duck breast. **C** 280-370 F. **M** 89 F (weekdays), 139 F, 170 F, 250 F.

DOMME   24250
Paris 530 - Gourdon 26 - Sarlat 12 - Cahors 52   *Dordogne*

L'Esplanade ☼
53 28 31 41, fax 53 28 49 92
Closed Mon off-seas, mid Nov-Feb. Open until 9pm (9:30pm in summer). Priv rm: 35. Terrace dining. Air cond. V, AE, MC.
A marvelous panoramic view stretches across the Dordogne River from this huge blue dining room. René Gillard's generous yet delicate cooking makes use of the region's superb ingredients: truffinettes au velours de truffes for truffle fans, sautéed sole with cèpes, and a cold-and-hot strawberry dessert. To avoid high à la carte prices, try the second set menu. You'll also find a well chosen wine list, and a smiling welcome. **C** 350-550 F. **M** 130 F, 150 F, 225 F, 250 F, 350 F.

L'Esplanade 🌲🍃
(See restaurant above)
See restaurant for closings. 2 stes 600-900 F. 23 rms 300-590 F. Half-board 500 F. Golf. V, AE, MC.
Well-renovated, exceptionally quiet rooms. Some offer beautiful views over the Dordogne Valley.

DOUAI   59500
Paris 203 - Lille 37 - Valenciennes 37 - Cambrai 26   *Nord*

La Terrasse
36, terrasse St-Pierre
27 88 70 04, fax 27 88 36 05
Open daily until 10pm. Air cond. Garage pkg. V, MC.
When you visit this comfortable eating house opposite the church of Saint-Pierre, you would do well to close your eyes to the (frightful) decor. But do open them again when Émile Hanique's generous, inventive dishes appear. We enjoyed his trio of fresh fish in a fennel coulis, duck breast glazed with chestnut honey, and pig's foot en crépinette with lentils and truffle essence. Remarkable wine list; warm welcome from Muriel Hanique. **C** 370-500 F. **M** 135 F (wine incl), 176 F, 320 F, 395 F.

La Terrasse
(See restaurant above)
Open year-round. 26 rms 320-640 F. Conf. Golf. Pkg. V, MC.
Just across the way from the collegiate church, this hotel has smallish soundproofed rooms with period furniture and satellite television. Excellent breakfasts with home-baked breads and pastries.

Au Turbotin
9, rue de la Massue - 27 87 04 16
Closed Sun dinner, Sat lunch, Mon, Feb 20-28, Aug. Open until 10pm. Air cond. V, AE, DC, MC.
The repertoire in this newly remodeled and air-conditioned dining room runs to shellfish platters fresh as a sea breeze and handily prepared seafood classics. There's even a tank

---

DOUAINS 27   ➜ Pacy-sur-Eure

DRAGUIGNAN   83300
Paris 876 - Digne 114 - Aix-en-Provence 106 - Toulon 81   *Var*

Les Étoiles de l'Ange
Av. Tuttlingen, col de l'Ange
3 km on D 557, route de Lorgues
94 68 23 01, fax 94 68 13 30
Open year-round. 29 rms 295 F. Restaurant. Half-board 350-500 F. Conf. Pool. Pkg. V, AE, DC, MC.
Set down in an exceptional site between the mountains and the sea, a modern hotel with huge, perfectly appointed, regularly renovated rooms (all have terraces). Poolside grill in summer.

Hostellerie du Moulin de la Foux 🌲🍃
Chemin Saint-Jean
94 68 55 33, fax 94 68 70 10
Open year-round. 30 rms 250-280 F. Rms for disabled. Restaurant. Half-board 245-370 F. Conf. Pool. Golf. Valet pkg. V, AE, MC.
Excellent little inn (a converted mill) with neat, functional rooms overlooking the terrace and trees. Prices are reasonable and service, led by the *patronne*, is cheerful and accommodating.

DREUX   28100
Paris 84 - Chartres 35 - Verneuil 34 - Rouen 97   *Eure-et-Loir*

Le Beffroi
12, pl. Métézeau
37 50 02 03, fax 37 42 07 69
Open year-round. 16 rms 298-327 F. No pets. Pkg. V, AE, DC, MC.
By the river and opposite the thirteenth-century Église de Saint-Pierre, this hotel has comfortable, well-kept rooms, all of them modernized.

■ **In Montreuil 28500** 4.5 km N on D 928 and D 116

Auberge du Gué-des-Grues
Le Gué-des-Grues - 37 43 50 25
Closed Mon dinner, Tue. Priv rm: 25. Terrace dining. Pkg. V, AE, DC.
Don't rush to this cozy establishment expecting adventurous cooking, but Roger Caillault offers fresh, carefully crafted dishes: duck foie gras, salmon in red wine sauce, rabbit with rosemary, and warm apple tart. After lunch, one can walk in the forest just across the way. **C** 280-380 F. **M** 150 F, 250 F.

Plan to travel? *Look for Gault Millau's other* Best of *guides to Chicago, Florida, Hawaii, Hong Kong, Germany, Italy, London, Los Angeles, New England, New Orleans, New York, Paris, San Francisco, Thailand, Toronto, and Washington, D.C.*

12/20   Au Bon Coin

49, av. Kléber, in Malo-les-Bains
28 69 12 63, fax 28 69 64 03
*Closed Dec 23-Jan 5. Open until 10pm. Priv rm: 25.
Air cond. V, AE, DC, MC.*
A collection of photographs forms the backdrop to fresh seafood dishes and a wide choice of shellfish. The day's catch is best served simply grilled; the lobster Thermidor and sole meunière are also reliable. Good selection of white wines. **C** 150-350 F. **M** 70 F (weekdays).

   Borel

6, rue l'Hermitte
28 66 51 80, fax 28 59 33 82
*Open year-round. 48 rms 360-410 F. Conf. Golf. Pkg.
V, AE, DC, MC.*
Some rooms in this excellent little hotel overlook the harbor, and all of them are large, clean, and bright. Extra-pleasant service and reception.

   Hôtel du Reuze

Tour du Reuze, rue J.-Jaurès
28 59 11 11, fax 28 63 09 69
*Open year-round. 2 stes 700 F. 122 rms 350-565 F.
Conf. Garage pkg. V, AE, DC, MC.*
These rooms, located on the twelfth through twentieth floors of a well-situated building, provide fantastic views of the harbor, out to sea, and the Plaine de Flandres. They are comfortable and practical. Fully equipped for business meetings.

   Le Soubise

49 bis, route de Bergues, in Coudekerque
28 64 66 00, fax 28 25 12 19
*Closed Sat lunch, Sun dinner. Open until 10pm. Priv
rm: 40. Pkg. V, AE, DC, MC.*
This former farm and coaching inn, dating from 1761, stands opposite a 30-hectare public garden. Chef Michel Hazebroucq gives his guests a wide array of set meals to choose from. Try the 158 F one: squab pâté, cassoulette of sole fillets, and a warm strawberry-stuffed crêpe. Fine cellar. **M** 95 F, 158 F, 198 F.

■ In **Bergues 59380**   8 km S on D 916

   Au Cornet d'Or

26, rue Espagnole - 28 68 66 27
*Closed Sun dinner, Jun 15-Jul 15. Open until
9:45pm. Priv rm: 20. Pkg. V, AE, MC.*
A lovely, rustic address, dating from the eighteenth century, with a flower-banked façade and a quiet atmosphere; the dining room's Louis XIII decor has recently been renovated. Jean-Claude Tasseri's cooking is deft, delicious, and classic with some Oriental touches: langoustine tails lightly roasted with Indian spices, farm-raised Licques duck grilled with Szechuan peppercorns, and a chicory vacherin with vanilla sauce for dessert. Diligent service. **C** 350-400 F. **M** 150 F (weekdays), 200 F, 380 F.

Gault Millau's ratings *are based solely on the restaurants' cuisine. We do not take into account the atmosphere, décor, service, and so on; these are commented upon within the review.*

■ In **Téteghem 59229**   3 km SE on D 4

   La Meunerie

174, rue des Pierres
28 26 14 30, fax 28 26 17 32
*Closed Sun dinner, Mon, Dec 22-Jan 15. Open until
9:30pm. Priv rm: 70. Air cond. Pkg. V, AE, DC, MC.*
Like many substantial Flemish dwellings, La Meunerie, situated on the outskirts of tiny Teteghem, presents a bland, discreet façade to the world. Inside, however, a plush coziness reigns. This elegantly restored old steam mill—it dates from the early part of the century—was the work of Jean-Pierre Delbé, who passed away in 1992 just as we had awarded him his third toque. Despite their grief, Marie-France Delbé, her daughter Laurence, and young chef Alain Gellé (who worked with Delbé for twelve years), managed to work up enough steam to keep the wheels in motion. The mill is running smoothly once again, and Gellé's cooking, based on fine seafood and local farm products, is very good indeed: langoustines with fresh pasta, turbot fillet with foie gras, roast lobster, and fillet of beef with beef marrow. We also savored the semi-cooked foie gras with girolle mushrooms, the cooked foie gras with an onion compote, and a delicious sea bass fillet with tiny caramelized onions delicately flavored with licorice that has a happy taste remembered from childhood. Fine choice of classic desserts. Superb wine list with 500 references. This is a fine restaurant, but the à la carte prices are getting a bit out of sight. **C** 400-700 F. **M** 250 F, 300 F, 380 F, 450 F.

La Meunerie

(See review above)
*Closed Dec 22-Jan 15. 1 ste 1,350 F. 8 rms 450-
800 F. Restaurant. Golf. Valet pkg. V, DC, MC.*
In the heart of peaceful countryside, this charming hotel has just nine rooms overlooking a courtyard garden—so remember to reserve. Each is decorated in a different style, but all share the same comfort and amenities.

Le Moulin

68 45 81 03, fax 68 45 83 31
*Closed Sun dinner & Mon off-seas, Jan 15-Feb. Open
until 10pm. Priv rm: 25. Air cond. No pets. Pkg. V,
DC, MC.*
Marooned in the middle of vineyards which it dominates from a rocky outcrop, this old windmill built into a rustic stone structure looks amazingly like an ancient ruined castle—the effect is quite surreal. It is an ideal setting for inventive David Moreno, who is in peak form these days. Inspired by the bounty of the sun-blessed Midi, his cooking is creative and wonderfully delicate. You'll be as impressed as we were when you taste his foie gras sautéed with sage and aged Emmenthal, red mullet with macaroni and country ham, squab with spices, and the "very simple" (as the menu puts it) fricassée of truffles and fava beans, a dish with the kind of refined simplicity that characterizes many of Moreno's creations. His cooking is a rare combination of freshness, inventiveness, and precision. The desserts are as interesting as

the other dishes, and include an exceptional souffléed chocolate mousse served with bitter almond ice cream. The cellar holds an exciting array of the region's wines, reasonably priced and presented by a knowledgeable young sommelier. What's more, you can be sure of a friendly welcome and attentive service. The only problem is finding the place; be sure to ask for directions when you reserve your table. C 280-400 F. M 158 F, 229 F, 307 F.

DURTOL 63 → Clermont-Ferrand

DURY-LÈS-AMIENS 80 → Amiens

ÉCOLE-VALENTIN 25 → Besançon

ÉGUISHEIM 68 → Colmar

ÉLINCOURT-STE-MARGUERITE 60
→ Compiègne

ENGHIEN 95 → PARIS Suburbs

ENSISHEIM 68 Mulhouse

ENTRECASTEAUX 83570
Paris 840 - Draguignan 27 - Cotignac 9   Var

Château d'Entrecasteaux
94 04 43 95, fax 94 04 48 92
Closed Dec 24-Jan 2. 2 rms 950-1,250 F. Pool. No pets. Pkg. Helipad. AE.
This magnificent Renaissance château surrounded by vineyards houses just two guest rooms, decorated with unerring taste in a comfortable contemporary style. Concerts and exhibitions are held on the premises.

ENTRECHAUX 84 → Vaison-la-Romaine

ÉPERNAY 51200
Paris 140 - Châlons-sur-Marne 32 - Reims 27   Marne

Au Petit Comptoir
3, rue du Dr-Rousseau
26 51 53 53, fax 26 58 42 68
Closed Sun dinner, Mon, Dec 21-Jan 11, Aug 5-21. Open until 10:30pm. Air cond. Pkg. V, AE.
The great Gérard Boyer of Reims is behind this Petit Comptoir, a charming old-fashioned bistrot with a splendid turn-of-the-century decor (note the magnificent cherrywood bar). Sixty diners at a time can enjoy such satisfying bourgeois dishes as salmon rillettes en robe des champs, roast semi-smoked cod, clafoutis with seasonal fruits, and a frozen chocolate terrine. Many enticing and reasonably priced wines, and name-brand Champagnes at unbeatable prices. C 200-250 F.

■ In Champillon 51160   5 km N

Royal Champagne
RN 2051 - 26 52 87 11, fax 26 52 89 69
Open daily until 9:30pm. Priv rm: 50. Garage pkg. V, AE, DC, MC.
With its lordly view over the vineyards of Épernay, this luxurious Relais et Châteaux offers

just about every amenity its clients could desire—at a price! Last year's affordable set meals have been ousted, although business people (and habitués) can partake of the reasonable "club" lunch for 180 F. Christophe Blot, a pupil of Meneau and Troisgros, proposes classic dishes to which he gives a personal stamp: stuffed morels and local asparagus in chicken jus, fricassée of langoustines and sole with fava beans, warm visitadine and vanilla ice cream with almond milk. Expensive cellar, which includes no fewer than 150 different bubblies. C 400-600 F. M 180 F (weekday lunch, Sat), 400 F (w-e, weekday dinner), 300 F.

Royal Champagne
(See restaurant above)
Open year-round. 3 stes 1,500-1,800 F. 27 rms 800-1,300 F. Half-board 800-1,070 F. Conf. Tennis. Golf. Garage pkg. Helipad. V, AE, DC, MC.
Charming, extra-comfortable bungalows offer a splendid view of the hillside vineyards and the Marne Valley. Relais et Châteaux.

■ In Vinay 51200   7 km S on N 51

La Briqueterie
4, route de Sézanne
26 59 99 99, fax 26 59 92 10
Closed Dec 23-27. Open until 9:30pm. Priv rm: 80. Heated pool. Valet pkg. V, AE, DC, MC.
Christel Trouillard, the owners' daughter, is running this show now and has given the family inn a fresh, youthful outlook. The influx of energy has even affected chef Lieven Vercourteren's cooking, which is better than ever. We recently enjoyed her goose foie gras with Champagne Ratafia, a rosace of lamb with a tarragon-and-rosemary-scented vegetable tian, and blancmange with a warm fruit compote. The Briqueterie's cellar is a treasure trove of premium Champagnes and Bordeaux. Impeccable professional service. C 330-500 F. M 130 F, 170 F, 210 F, 335 F, 380 F.

La Briqueterie
(See restaurant above)
Closed Dec 23-27. 2 stes 1,410-1,620 F. 40 rms 600-880 F. Rms for disabled. Half-board 70 F. Conf. Golf. Valet pkg. Helipad. V, AE, DC, MC.
This handsome stopover in the heart of Champagne's vineyards offers quiet, spacious rooms with deep-pile carpeting and wonderful bathrooms clad in pale marble. Buffet breakfasts are served in a dining room that opens onto the garden. Smiling service.

ÉPINAL 88000
Paris 365 - Nancy 69 - Colmar 92 - Vesoul 82   Vosges

Les Abbesses
Jean-Claude Aiguier, 23, rue de la Louvière
29 82 53 69, fax 29 35 28 97
Closed Sun dinner, Mon, last wk of Aug. Open until 9:30pm. Priv rm: 45. Garden dining. V, AE, MC.
The white and pale-gold dining room with its polished parquet floors has just been redone, and now has softer lighting that adds to the elegance. Jean-Claude Aiguier's cooking is showing more control of his fertile imagination, which sometimes gets the better of his judgement. We enjoyed his lobster hachis Parmentier

249

punctuated with tiny bits of bacon, and seductively fresh sautéed langoustines and delicate sole with baby vegetables that included fritters of tiny carrots with their tops. We also liked the savory "pork assortment", both rustic and refined, presented in two services and in five diffferent ways: civet, head cheese (with slightly too-firm gelatin), blood sausage, andouillette, and pig's foot en crépinette. For dessert, a luscious gratin of mirabelle plums, and a sumptuous crème brûlée with pistachios, incredibly delicate and original. The cellar has some interesting discoveries to offer. The welcome is marred by the fact that the *patronne* obviously gives regulars preferential treatment. **C** 400-500 F. **M** 165 F (weekdays), 280 F, 345 F, 430 F.

Les Ducs de Lorraine

16, quai du Col.-Sérot
29 34 39 87, fax 29 34 27 61
Closed Sun dinner, Mon, Mar 1-8, Aug 16-31. Open until 9:30pm. Air cond. V, AE.
The classic decor of the dining room (silver chandeliers, painted wood) is reflected in Claudy Obriot's cooking, which we would like to see range farther afield than his tried-and-true specialties. Still, you won't be disappointed with his fantaisie of foie gras, fillet of Challans duck, and mirabelle plum soufflé: may they ever remain on the menu. We would like to see more dishes with inventiveness, like his sea scallops in a tartare of amandes de mer (a sweet-tasting shellfish) or the steak of young rabbit with béarnaise sauce and a giblet tourte. Agnès Obriot orchestrates the flawless service in this comfortable dining room with a view of the Moselle River. **C** 320-470 F. **M** 165 F (weekdays), 240 F, 279 F, 360 F, 400 F.

Mercure

13, place E.-Stein
29 35 18 68, fax 29 35 12 11
Open year-round. 2 stes 580-630 F. 44 rms 365-475 F. Rms for disabled. Restaurant. Half-board 332 F. Conf. Golf. Garage pkg. V, AE, DC, MC.
A newly renovated building with spacious, comfortable rooms. The reception is excellent.

ÉPINE (L') 51 → Châlons-sur-Marne

ERBALUNGA 20 → CORSICA: Bastia

ERDEVEN 56410
Paris 490 - Lorient 28 - Carnac 9 - Quiberon 21 *Morbihan*

Château de Kéravéon

1.8 km NE on D 105
97 55 68 55, fax 97 55 67 10
Closings not available. 2 stes 1,510 F. 18 rms 530-790 F. Restaurant. Half-board 590-640 F. Conf. Pool. Golf. Pkg. V, AE, DC, MC.
This huge, handsome residence dating from the sixteenth and eighteenth centuries has a moat, keep, and dovecote. The spacious rooms are thoughtfully decorated. Four kilometers away is the Saint-Laurent golf course.

---

*The **C** (A la carte) restaurant prices given are for a complete three-course meal for one, including a half-bottle of modest wine and service. **M** (Menus) prices are for a complete fixed-price meal for one, excluding wine (unless otherwise noted).*

ERQUY 22430
Paris 450 - Dinan 47 - Dinard 40 - St-Brieuc 35 *Côtes/Armor*

L'Escurial

Bd de la Mer - 96 72 31 56
Closed Sun dinner & Mon (exc Jul-Aug). Open until 9pm. No pets. Pkg. V, MC.
The dining room's best feature is a panoramic sea view framed by a broad bay window. From those waters come Véronique Bernard's raw materials, the sparkling fresh fish and *coquillages* which she handles with respect and intelligence. You'll relish her court-bouillon of mussels, cockles, and langoustines; red mullet with balsamic vinegar; turbot escalopine; and saddle of rabbit with prunes. Good desserts. Small but balanced cellar. **C** 250-320 F. **M** 320 F (wine incl), 98 F, 120 F, 190 F.

ESCALDES (LES) → Andorra (Principality of)

ESCRINET (COL DE L') 07200
Paris 615 - Aubenas 17 - Privas 13 - Montélimar 60 *Ardèche*

12/20 Col de l'Escrinet

Le Panoramic Escrinet
75 87 10 11, fax 75 87 10 34
Closed Sun dinner & Mon lunch off-seas, Nov 16-Mar 15. Open until 9pm. No pets. Hotel: 3 stes 450-480 F. 17 rms 240-340 F. Half-board 300-400 F. Air cond. Conf. Heated pool. Pkg. V, AE, DC, MC.
You can admire magnificent views from this restaurant's spacious dining room. All of Guy Rojon's country dishes are carefully prepared: try the veal sweetbreads with morels and asparagus tips, beef filet mignon with goat cheese, or nougat glacé with strawberry coulis. **C** 260-310 F. **M** 120 F, 180 F, 230 F, 290 F.

ESCURES 14 → Port-en-Bessin

ESPALION 12500
Paris 583 - Figeac 94 - Millau 79 - Aurillac 76 *Aveyron*

L'Eau Vive

Hôtel Moderne, 27, bd Guizard
65 44 05 11, fax 65 48 06 94
Closed Sun dinner & Mon (exc Jul-Aug), Nov 15-Dec 15. Open until 9:30pm. Air cond. Pkg. V, AE.
Jérôme Raulhac is a fan of fishing, and it shows in the excellent treatment he gives to fine river fish, as well as to other local products prepared in traditional fashion. Try the Aveyron-style salad with foie gras and cèpes, the fillets of omble chevalier (a lake fish) with hazelnut cream and "ribbons" of fresh vegetables, and the delicate chocolate tart. The cellar is quirky and wide-ranging, and the welcome warm in a comfortable auberge with recently renovated decor. **C** 230-360 F. **M** 98 F, 160 F, 250 F, 300 F.

Hôtel Moderne

(See restaurant above)
Open year-round. 28 rms 220-350 F. Half-board 240-300 F. Air cond. V, AE.
The name fits, because the whole place has recently been redone, and offers comfortable, sunny rooms with huge bathrooms. Friendly welcome and service.

Le Méjane
Near the old bridge, 8, rue Méjane
65 48 22 37
Closed Sun dinner & Wed (exc Aug), Feb 14-Mar 8, Jun 26-30. Open until 9pm. Air cond. V, AE, DC, MC.
The address of this restaurant in the ancient heart of the city gets passed on by word of mouth. Forget the rather ordinary decor and focus on the vigorous, modern cooking served at moderate prices. We loved the puff pastry stuffed with endive and blue cheese, the sautéed duck, and the fine desserts. The wine list offers a good choice of regional bottlings like Cahors and Marcillac, and the welcome is warm. For all this, we give them two toques. **C** 200-300 F. **M** 83 F (weekday lunch), 155 F (exc Sun), 110 F, 190 F, 240 F.

■ In **Bozouls 12340**　　　　11 km S on D 920

🏠 **Le Belvédère**
Route de St-Julien-de-Rodelle
65 44 92 66, fax 65 48 87 33
Closed Dec. 12 rms 210-280 F. Restaurant. Half-board 215-245 F. Golf. V, MC.
Admire the famous "Trou de Bozouls", a deep gorge, from this pleasant traditional hotel.

ESPELETTE　　　　　　　64250
Paris 761 - Bayonne 22 - St-Jean-de-Luz 25　　Pyrénées-A.

Euzkadi 🔆
Rue Principale - 59 93 91 88
Closed Tue off-seas, Mon, Nov 15-Dec 15, 1 wk in Mar. Open until 8:30pm. Pool. Pkg. V, MC.
Here in the mountains where wild horses roam and chili peppers grow, you can immerse yourself in Basque tradition, food, and song. A wide selection of regional specialties is available in the huge dining room: axoa (veal with chili peppers), ttoro (fish soup), tripoxa (a mutton and veal sausage), elzekaria (vegetable soup), and gâteau basque (a hefty kind of pound cake) for dessert; all but the ttoro is available on the fine 135 F menu. Jocular service and democratic prices. **C** 190-250 F. **M** 95 F, 135 F, 155 F, 175 F.

ÉTAMPES　　　　　　　91150
Paris 49 - Orléans 66 - Melun 47 - Versailles 54　　Essonne

12/20 Auberge de Courpain
Lieu-dit Court-Pain
64 95 67 04, fax 60 80 99 02
Closed Jan 31-Mar 1. Open until 9pm. Priv rm: 130. Terrace dining. Pkg. V, AE, DC, MC.
This ivy-covered former post house stands amid cornfields in the Beauce region. Fine food served in a country-style dining room that opens onto a broad terrace. Among the listings we like are the lobster salad, monkfish blanquette with morels, and nougat glacé with kiwi sauce. Excellent wine list. **C** 350-450 F. **M** 130 F (weekdays, Sat lunch, Sun dinner), 180 F.

🏠 **Auberge de Courpain**
(See restaurant above)
Closed Feb. 4 stes 450-700 F. 18 rms 300-700 F. Rms for disabled. Half-board 450 F. Conf. Golf. Pkg. V, AE, DC, MC.
Pretty, comfortable rooms in a bucolic setting. Small meeting rooms and a billiard room.

■ In **Morigny 91150**　　　　3 km N

🏠 **Hostellerie de Villemartin** 🌲🍴
1, allée des Marronniers
64 94 63 54, fax 64 94 24 68
Closed Sun & Mon (exc hols), Jul 24-Aug 22. 14 rms 310-490 F. Restaurant. Conf. Tennis. Pkg. V, AE, MC.
A truly lovely Directoire-period dwelling, set in wooded grounds by the River Juine. The rooms are immaculate, with classic decor and superb views. Polite, helpful staff.

ÉTAPLES 62　　　　　　→ Touquet (Le)

ÉTRETAT ·　　　　　　　76790
Paris 220 - Le Havre 28 - Rouen 86 - Fécamp 17　　Seine-Mar.

12/20 Le Belvédère
Falaise d'Antifer, 11 km S, 76280 St-Jouin-Bruneval - 35 20 13 76
Closed Sun dinner, Mon, Sep 5-13. Open until 10pm. Garage pkg. V, AE, DC, MC.
You can order excellent langoustines, crabs, and whelks with mayonnaise while watching the supertankers jockey in the bay below. Try the 135 F menu: raw seafood platter, fillet of sea bass Dieppois with rice cooked with edible seaweed, very ordinary cheeses, and an apple tart flambéed with Calvados. An added point this year. Pleasant but scatterbrained service. **C** 200-380 F. **M** 75 F, 135 F, 172 F.

EU　　　　　　　　　　76260
Paris 167 - Dieppe 31 - Abbeville 32 - Le Tréport 5　　Seine-Mar.

🏠 **Domaine du Pavillon de Joinville** 🌲🍴
Route du Tréport
35 86 24 03, fax 35 50 27 37
Open year-round. 2 stes 880 F. 22 rms 395-740 F. Restaurant. Half-board 600-1,120 F. Conf. Heated pool. Tennis. Golf. Pkg. Helipad. V, AE, DC, MC.
This handsome edifice was once King Louis-Philippe's hunting lodge. The perfectly comfortable rooms evoke a grander era, and look out over superb grounds. Pretty public rooms, bar and terrace. Good breakfasts. Fitness center.

12/20 La Gare
20, av. de la Gare
35 86 16 64, fax 35 50 86 25
Closed Aug 16-30. Open until 9:30pm. Priv rm: 15. Terrace dining. Pkg. V, AE, MC.
The elegant dining rooms and the prettily laid tables augur well for the cuisine, but the new chef made a few false steps during our last visit: bland oyster and salmon tartare with dill, fine sole stuffed with langoustines and shellfish butter marred by overly seasoned spinach, and a very ordinary Grand Marnier soufflé. All this at rather high prices. Luckily there are two set menus. Good cellar with a focus on Bordeaux. The staff likes you much better if you are a regular customer. **C** 280-350 F. **M** 80 F (weekdays), 120 F, 190 F.

Looking for a city in a département? Refer to the **index.**

La Gare
(See restaurant above)
Closed Aug 16-30. 22 rms 250-280 F. Half-board 330-550 F. Air cond. Conf. Pkg. V, AE, MC.
A turn-of-the-century hotel with attractive, very comfortable rooms overlooking a quiet square. Attentive welcome and service.

EUGÉNIE-LES-BAINS	40320
Paris 726 - Pau 53 - Mont-de-Marsan 25 - Dax 69	*Landes*

La Ferme aux Grives
Lieu-dit Les Charmilles
58 05 06 07, fax 58 51 13 59
Closed Mon dinner & Tue (exc Jul 12-Sep 11), Jan. Open until 10:30pm. Terrace dining. Pkg. V.
Really, Christine Guérard has surpassed herself, turning this old family *pension* at the edge of the village into an adorable farmhouse. True, the result is a trifle theatrical, but what a magical setting it makes! The first act of *Cyrano de Bergerac* could easily be played out in front of the immense fireplace, where plump Landes chickens and sides of beef sizzle as they turn on a spit. Every detail is a feast for the eye, from the terracotta floor to the beamed ceiling from which succulent hams hang suspended. Try the homestyle regional dishes like bread tourte with herbs, a vinaigrette of grilled leeks with country ham, Castille-style suckling pig, fabulous "Monsieur Parra" blood sausage (a friend gave Guérard the secret recipe...), cassoulet, and a crisp meringue piled with whipped cream to take you down childhood's memory lane. In the adjoining café, a quick lunch can be made of a *plat du jour* and a glass of well-aged wine for about 100 F. **C** 165-230 F. **M** 165 F.

 Michel Guérard
58 05 06 07 (R), 58 05 05 05 (H),
fax 58 51 13 59
19.5 *Closed Thu lunch & Wed (exc hols & Jul 12-Sep 11), Dec-Feb 22. Open until 10:15pm. Priv rm: 16. Garden dining. No pets. Pkg. V, AE, DC.*
In these times when vulgarity and shoddiness are everywhere to be seen, it's a real pleasure to observe Christine and Michel Guérard. Somehow every project they turn their hand to is marked by a natural—almost innocent—grace. They must have a special gift; at any rate, their sense of timing is certainly uncanny. Well before country elegance was all the rage, the Guérards had already created their luxuriously rustic Relais et Châteaux in the Southwest's heartland. Michel invented "cuisine minceur", then everyone else jumped on the bandwagon. Today, he represents the ideal of an authentic lifestyle closely linked to the land. His cooking is an eloquent expression of that ideal.
As one of Guérard's colleagues remarked admiringly, "his technique never smothers the food. The man is simply never wrong". Quite true. In the 25 years we've been following him, never once have we caught him out. On the contrary, it is with barely contained anticipation that we take our place in his lovely dining room. This year's feast featured a fresh soup of chaud-froid stuffed tomatoes, an inspired beef and pork salad with warm potatoes scattered with truffles, grilled duck liver coated with bread crumbs, and sautéed beef with chopped herbs and potato

confit. Or the delightful fried langoustines with marvelous herb puff pastries in a spicy sardine sauce, and a sublime dish of veal shanks stewed for seven hours with a vegetable paysanne. This refined simplicity reminds us of Voltaire's Candide cultivating his garden, aided by the good fairies of culinary expertise. As for dessert, there's the bread pudding with browned sugar à la frangipane, the tender Marquis de Béchamiel cake, the white peach with garden verbena ice cream.... The wine list comprises lordly Bordeaux as well as lusty Jurançons, with a special mention for the white Tursan "Baron de Bachen" from Guérard's own vineyards. Unqualified bliss. **C** 450-650 F. **M** 390 F, 490 F, 650 F.

Les Prés d'Eugénie
(See restaurant above)
Closed Dec 4-Feb 22. 9 stes 1,000-2,000 F. 33 rms 750-1,650 F. Conf. Heated pool. Tennis. No pets. Valet pkg. Helipad. V, AE, DC, MC.
The latest and most breathtaking addition to this fairyland of quiet taste and luxury is the eighteenth-century Couvent des Herbes, restored with exquisite taste. It houses eight enormous rooms that open onto the herb garden. There's a long waiting list... There are also luxurious spa facilities exclusively reserved for guests of Les Prés d'Eugénie. Other amenities include a beauty salon, sauna, and cookery school. Relais et Châteaux.

La Maison Rose
58 05 05 05, fax 58 51 13 59
Closed Jan-Feb 22. 5 stes 550-800 F. 27 rms 400-550 F. Restaurant. Pool. Tennis. Pkg. V, AE, DC.
At the other end of the Prés d'Eugénie's grounds, opposite the Ferme aux Grives, the charming Résidence Maison Rose offers excellent value. Here in an English-style setting, you can rent little suites with kitchenettes at terrifically tempting prices. There is no obligation to take the cure or to eat in the (charming) house restaurant.

EUS	66500
Paris 958 - Prades 5 - Perpignan 39 - Font-Romeu 50	*Pyrénées-O.*

Grangousier
68 96 28 32, fax 68 96 33 69
Closed Tue dinner & Wed off-seas, Oct 15-30. Open until 9pm. Terrace dining. Pool. Pkg. V, AE.
Choose the terrace or one of the cozy wainscotted dining rooms to sample Patrick Fleury's proficient, provocative cuisine. Try his subtle dragées of snails in a verbena-scented infusion, the tasty sea scallops in coconut milk and lime juice, and cherries in well-aged Kirsch with citrus peel. Friendly welcome. Wine buffs will love the cellar. **C** 330-430 F. **M** 195 F, 300 F.

ÉVIAN	74500
Paris 589 - Annecy 81 - Geneva 42 - Montreux 38	*H.-Savoie*

 Café Royal
Domaine du Royal Club Évian
South shore of Lake Geneva
50 26 85 00, fax 50 75 61 00
Closed Dec-Jan. Open until 10pm. Priv rm: 40. Terrace dining. Air cond. No pets. Pkg. V, AE, DC, MC.

Michel Lentz is not only a three-toque chef, he's an organizational whiz. With admirable energy and imagination, he single-handedly manages all the restaurants of the Royal Club Évian. It is at the Café Royal ("his" restaurant, the one obviously closest to his heart) that his skills show to best advantage. In the befrescoed Belle Époque dining room, where memories from another age abound, he serves two types of cooking: everyday fare and more elaborate creations. In the first category, salads, assortments of cold cuts, grilled fish, and simple plats du jour, all well prepared. The latter category is, of course, where Lentz shines: omble chevalier (lake fish) with chanterelle mushrooms, féra (another lake fish) enlivened with a bit of bacon, delicate baby perch, wild mushrooms, lamb rubbed with mountain herbs, incomparable Memmises coriander-spiced bresaola (dried beef), a civet of pork with andouille and juniper, and tender Alpine kid. Many of these creations include mountain herbs and wild plants picked on nearby slopes. For dessert, lovely crèmes de lait browned in the oven, and elegant fruit concoctions. Worth discovering too are the wines of Savoie which sommelier Michel Jobard has selected for your delectation. C 400-550 F. M 340 F.

Hôtel Royal

(See restaurant above)
Closed Dec 4-Feb 12. 29 stes 840-7,000 F. 127 rms 640-2,900 F. Half-board 760-1,690 F. Conf. Heated pool. Tennis. Golf. Valet pkg. Helipad. V, AE, DC, MC.
The owners aim to make this luxury hotel one of the best in Europe. Not a modest ambition, but a realistic one, considering the peerless setting on the wooded mountain slopes above Lake Geneva, the hotel itself, with its gorgeous Art Nouveau frescoes, and the wide-open corporate purse that finances it all. Other advantages include lovely, faultlessly appointed rooms; one of the most effective health and beauty institutes in Europe; indoor and outdoor swimming pools; a world-renowned eighteen-hole golf course; six tennis courts; a heliport; a club for children; the casino of course, and the famous spring chamber-music festival, directed by Russian cellist and composer Mstislav Rostropovich.

Le Gourmandin

Royal Club Évian
South shore of Lake Geneva
50 26 85 00, fax 50 75 61 00
Closed Nov 6-Feb 12. Open until 9:30pm (10pm Fri, Sat, Jul-Aug). Priv rm: 200. Terrace dining. No pets. Valet pkg. V, AE, DC, MC.
Filtered light and flowered curtains embellish the pretty, Directoire-style dining room of the Ermitage hotel. Come here to savor the smoked ham, air-dried beef, lake trout, féra (a lake fish) with bacon, rack of lamb with green thyme, and the sabayon of bilberries. It's all good and reasonably priced. C 300-430 F. M 170 F, 270 F, 310 F, 340 F.

Hôtel Ermitage

(See restaurant above)
Closed Nov 6-Feb 12. 16 stes 740-3,380 F. 75 rms 510-2,260 F. Rms for disabled. Half-board 630-

1,360 F. Conf. Pool. Tennis. Golf. Valet pkg. Helipad. V, AE, DC, MC.
This pleasant Belle Époque hotel recently underwent a thorough overhaul; it offers complete comfort and a relaxed atmosphere in a lovely rural setting. The newly air-conditioned convention center occupies separate premises. Numerous sporting and leisure activities are proposed.

Les Prés Fleuris sur Évian

D 24 - 50 75 29 14 (R), 50 21 08 96 (H), fax 50 70 77 75
Closed Oct-May. Open until 8:30pm. Priv rm: 10. Garden dining. Valet pkg. V, AE, DC, MC.
A fairytale view over Lake Geneva with mountain pastures in the foreground is not the main attraction: that honor falls to Roger Frossard's reassuringly changeless ability to choose only perfect ingredients and prepare them with a pure classicism that never palls. Regulars love his renditions of wild mushrooms, Bresse poultry, and omble chevalier (lake fish). C 450-550 F. M 260 F, 400 F.

Le Triolet

(See restaurant above)
Closed Oct-May. 5 stes 1,400 F. 7 rms 850-1,300 F. Half-board 850-1,150 F. Golf. Valet pkg. V, AE, MC.
A delightfully relaxed atmosphere pervades the quiet, huge, comfortable rooms (with balconies offering spectacular views) of this hotel perched high above Lake Geneva. Relais et Châteaux.

La Toque Royale

Domaine du Royal Club Évian, Casino Royal, south shore of Lake Geneva
50 75 03 78, fax 50 75 48 40
Open daily until 10:30pm. Priv rm: 90. Air cond. No pets. Valet pkg. V, AE, DC, MC.
This lakeside restaurant with its fin-de-siècle interior, attracts gamblers, families, and Swiss gourmets who come for Michel Lentz's well-designed modern yet regionally inspired carte. The cooking is actually carried out by Patrick Frenot: among the offerings are féra (lake fish) with bacon, omble chevalier (another lake fish) à la matouille, veal fillet with morels and polenta negra, or truffled squab. The fine 190 F menu allows you to enjoy the delicious desserts concocted by Eric Hausser, and the 190 F Sunday brunch has many fans. Fine wine list with many Savoie bottlings. C 330-550 F. M 190 F (weekday lunch), 235 F (weekday lunch, wine incl), 550 F (exc weekdays), 280 F, 340 F.

La Verniaz

Neuvecelle-Église
50 75 04 90, fax 50 70 78 92
Closed Nov 20-Feb 11. Open until 9:30pm. Priv rm: 40. Garden dining. Pool. Valet pkg. V, AE, DC, MC.
On the slopes above Évian stands an idyllic dwelling, on grounds dotted with charming guest chalets. When you finally locate the immense dining room, you might well believe that you're still in the garden as you luxuriate in the flood of light and riot of flowers. Chef Christian Métreau does best with simple dishes: chicken on a spit, Charolais beef cooked over charcoal, lake fish, and cherry soufflé with farmhouse Kirsch. C 230-350 F. M 200 F, 260 F, 320 F.

La Verniaz
(See restaurant above)
Closed Nov 20-Feb 11. 6 stes 800-2,000 F. 35 rms
450-900 F. Half-board 550-800 F. Conf. Heated
pool. Tennis. Golf. Pkg. V, AE, DC, MC.
  The pleasant chalet rooms scattered around
the peaceful grounds command a view of Lake
Geneva and an Alp or two. Perfect amenities
and service. Relais et Châteaux.

ÉVREUX	27000

Paris 100 - Rouen 51 - Mantes 44 - Dreux 44   *Eure*

Auberge de Parville
4 km W on N 13, 27180 Parville
32 39 36 63, fax 32 33 22 76
Closed Sun dinner, Mon. Open until 10pm. Priv
rm: 40. Garden dining. Pkg. V, MC.
  Give into temptation and try the langoustine
tempura with fried vegetables, ravioli stuffed
with lobster and black radishes, a salmon-pick-
erel croustillant, and a crépinette of beef cheeks.
For dessert, a tender chicory concoction or
banana mousse. The cellar posts reasonable
prices and offers a good choice of half-bottles.
Charming welcome. C 210-380 F. M 160 F,
265 F, 315 F.

Hôtel de France
29, rue St-Thomas
32 39 09 25, fax 32 38 38 56
Closed Sun dinner, Mon. Open until 10pm. Priv
rm: 20. Hotel: 1 ste 440 F. 15 rms 255-340 F. Half-
board 285-345 F. Conf. Golf. No pets. Pkg. V, AE,
DC, MC.
  Patrons flock faithfully back to this rose-hued
dwelling on a quiet street in the cathedral town
of Évreux to dine in a recently renovated dining
room with a view of a small park. The prices have
gone down here thanks to two set menus that
replaced the à la carte selections, and the new
chef offers traditional cuisine based on fine local
products: terrine of wild boar with a honey-
onion compote, brill cooked in cider with apples, and coffee-flavored desserts. Wide-ranging
cellar; professional service. M 145 F, 185 F.

EYBENS 38	→ Grenoble

EYGALIÈRES	13810

Paris 715 - Avignon 28 - Cavaillon 13 - Marseille 81   *B./Rhône*

Mas de la Brune
90 95 90 77, fax 90 95 99 21
Closed Oct 9-Apr 10. 1 ste. 9 rms. Restaurant. Half-
board 920-1,220 F. Air cond. Heated pool. Golf.
Garage pkg. V, MC.
  Behind their mullioned windows, the ten
rooms of this listed château have real character
and are decorated with care. They boast
sumptuous bathrooms and perfect appointments; service is exceptional too. Outside you'll
find a Roman-style pool and a garden fragrant
with lavender. Take care to confirm your arrival
time if you run late—the management is quite
strict about punctuality. Refined meals available
only to hotel guests in the evening.

A red hotel ranking denotes a place with charm.

12/20 Sous les Micocouliers
90 95 94 53, fax 90 95 94 65
Closed Tue, Nov-Dec 2, Feb 12-28. Open until
11pm (in summer). Priv rm: 40. Terrace dining. V.
  The clued-in customers vie for shady tables
under the lotus trees, or defeated, retreat to the
rustic interior of this cozy bistrot. Wherever they
sit, they can tuck into a warm goat cheese-
stuffed pastry, cool melon with Parma ham,
monkfish bourride, charcoal-grilled sirloin steak,
and a cinnamon-scented apple gratin. Service
and welcome are delightful. C 210-280 F.
M 115 F (weekday lunch, Sat), 168 F (dinner).

EYZIES (LES)	24620

Paris 521 - Périgueux 45 - Sarlat 22 - Bergerac 57   *Dordogne*

Le Centenaire
Le Rocher de la Penne
53 06 97 18, fax 53 06 92 41
Closed Tue lunch, Nov-Mar. Open until 10pm. Garden dining. Air cond. Pool. Valet pkg. V, AE, DC, MC.
  Seasoned travelers will tell you that Le Centenaire is the only world-class table to be found
between Bordeaux and Tours. Why is that
surprising? Because this corner of France—
Périgord—is universally famed as the capital of
good eating. Why, isn't Périgord the home of
foie gras, truffles, duck and goose confit? Well,
if the Mazère tribe had been content to rehash
that ancient litany, their restaurant would not be
the vibrant, spirited, wonderfully unpredictable
place that (we thank heaven!) it is today.
Chef Roland Mazère is a former rugby player
who converted to cuisine after a revelation at
the Troisgros' restaurant in Roanne. He brilliantly
renews his regionally based repertoire with imaginative, intelligent associations of flavors.
Though diners may come here in search of the
robust regional specialties of yore, what they
discover is a tasty cassoulette of goose entrails
(no fun for the kitchen staff who clean them!), a
trio of house foie gras in walnut and prune
gelatin, warm terrine of local cèpes, and an
astonishing rabbit coated with cèpe powder and
served with more cèpes. Mazère's cassoulet is
made with fava beans and contains goose and
duck, summer savory, and golden bacon rind.
But the chef doesn't stop there. He also regales
you with pickerel and artichokes in a marvelously flavorful jus of sage and fresh coriander, a crab
cake, a fat crayfish roasted with garlic and paired
with a bit of squid on toast, and a coconut risotto
with a skewer of fresh fruits. You won't see a dish
like that anywhere else around here! Mazère's
genius lies in his ability to renew local cooking,
even though he often makes use of non-local
ingredients. He has created a French culinary
monument like the other great monuments in
the vicinity. This restaurant is a family affair:
Roland cooks, sister Geneviève manages the
establishment, and brother-in-law Alain Scholly
has assembled a first-rate cellar in collaboration
with the sommelier, Tim Harrison. You'll find
some of the world's greatest wines on the list, as
well as some fine local discoveries at moderate
prices, like the Moulin des Dames white
Bergerac or the 1989 Cahors "Prestige" from
Château du Cèdre, which you can also buy at
the establishment's adjoining wine shop, "Vin

Blanc Rouge". **C** 450-600 F. **M** 180 F (lunch, wine incl), 250 F, 380 F, 500 F.

Le Centenaire
(See restaurant above)
Closed Nov-Mar. 4 stes 900-1,200 F. 20 rms 450-700 F. Half-board 565-820 F. Air cond. Conf. Heated pool. Golf. Valet pkg. V, AE, DC, MC.
The rooms are most comfortable, cheery, and modern though they don't have a particular style. Service, however, is flawless. Relais et Châteaux. Wonderful breakfasts.

Cro-Magnon
53 06 97 06, fax 53 06 95 45
*Closed Wed lunch (exc hols), mid Oct-beg May. Open until 9pm. Priv rm: 20. Garden dining. **Hotel**: 4 stes 650-850 F. 18 rms 360-550 F. Half-board 360-550 F. Heated pool. Golf. Pkg. V, AE, DC, MC.*
Our famed ancestor, Cro-Magnon man, was first discovered at this very site. If he were around to watch, he'd be pleased, we think, to see how far his progeny has evolved when it comes to food, comfort—and manners! (The Leyssalles and their staff are wonderfully courteous and attentive.) Chef Xavier Davoust has composed a menu of forthright, proficiently prepared dishes: raw vegetable assorment with a cool and savory bavarois, interesting salmon with chestnuts and juniper berries, and a perfect banana chaud-froid flavored with vanilla. The cellar lacks many regional offerings but offers lots of top Bordeaux and Burgundies. **C** 290-450 F. **M** 140 F, 180 F, 280 F, 350 F.

Au Vieux Moulin
53 06 93 39, fax 53 06 98 06
Closed Tue lunch, Jan 3-Feb 15. Open until 9:30pm. Terrace dining. Pkg. V, AE, MC.
An adorable low-lying riverside mill on the Beune. The pleasant dining room has a pretty terrace, and Georges Soulie's cooking is characterized by clever flavor combinations. We enjoyed the foie gras ravioli with pressed duck jus, sole sautéed in olive oil and paired with ratatouille-style vegetables, and a walnut soufflé glacé with chicory sauce. **C** 290-430 F. **M** 160 F (wine incl), 85 F, 135 F, 190 F, 320 F.

Au Vieux Moulin
(See restaurant above)
Closed Nov-Mar. 20 rms 260-320 F. Half-board 320-420 F. Pkg. V, AE, MC.
Next to the Museum of Prehistory, along the river. Rooms are large and nicely fitted out.

EZE	**06360**
Paris 959 - Nice 11 - Menton 18 - Monaco 7	Alpes-Mar.

Auberge du Troubadour
Rue du Brec - 93 41 19 03
Closed Mon lunch, Sun, Nov 20-Dec 20, 1 wk at Feb school hols, Jul 1-8. Open until 9:30pm. Priv rm: 8. Pkg. V, MC.
So winsome an inn is naturally clogged with tourists in the high season, but the crush has no adverse effects on the kitchen. Gérard Vuille knows just how to coax the most flavor out of his premium ingredients. Well worth ordering are the sea scallops sautéed with asparagus, tender and flavorful saddle of rabbit with foie gras, light-as-air apple tart, and vanilla ice cream with caramel sauce. The only drawback: the high

prices of the à la carte menu and the wine list. Stick to the 165 F set menu to save your wallet. Cheerful, efficient welcome and service. **C** 300-420 F. **M** 115 F (lunch), 165 F, 245 F.

11/20 La Bergerie
Grande Corniche
93 41 03 67, fax 92 10 81 75
Closed Wed, mid Jan-mid Feb. Open until 10:30pm. Priv rm: 140. Terrace dining. Pkg. V, AE, MC.
The ravioli, mixed grill, pear charlotte, and profiteroles won't win any awards for originality, but the chic customers show no signs of complaining. The secret of La Bergerie's success is good, simple cooking, swiftly served in a charming atmosphere. On balmy days, choose a terrace table with a marvelous view of the sea. **C** 220-300 F. **M** 295 F (wine incl), 190 F.

Richard Borfiga
Pl. du Gal-de-Gaulle
93 41 05 23, fax 93 41 26 79
Closed Mon. Open until 10pm. Priv rm: 80. Air cond. Pkg. V, AE, DC, MC.
Richard Borfiga knows that he needn't search far and wide for choice ingredients: they are ready for the plucking practically on his doorstep! So prepare your palate for a sunny festival of flavors, and after feasting your eyes on the gorgeous view treat your taste buds to Borfiga's basil-scented stuffed courgette blossoms, milk-fed lamb in its jus, or a lemony cookie crust holding fresh fruits. Well stocked cellar. A terrace and a bit more imagination in the cooking would please us. **C** 350-430 F. **M** 180 F, 250 F, 350 F.

Cap Estel
Eze-Bord-de-Mer
93 01 50 44, fax 93 01 55 20
Closed Jan-Apr 6, Oct 23-Dec. 7 stes 1,690-3,040 F. 43 rms 1,040-2,640 F. Restaurant. Half-board 1,100-1,750 F. Air cond. Conf. Heated pool. Valet pkg. V, AE, DC.
Hollywood-style luxury is the rule in this grand hotel set on a rocky promontory overlooking the sea. All the rooms have mesmerizing views and the hotel boasts a private beach and sauna as well as extensive landscaped grounds.

Château de la Chèvre d'Or
Moyenne-Corniche, rue du Barri
92 10 66 66 (R), 93 41 12 12 (H), fax 93 41 06 72
Closed Wed (in Mar & Nov), Dec-Feb. Open until 10:30pm. Priv rm: 35. Terrace dining. Air cond. Pool. Valet pkg. V, AE, DC, MC.
Nature has provided a breathtaking panorama for this eyrie perched 400 meters above the sea, and chef Élie Mazot furnishes additional pleasures, sure to beguile the most jaded palate. Join the (very) rich and famous who dine here on fillet of red mullet in olive oil, a craquante of asparagus with smoked salmon and baby fava bean cream, an assortment of almost forty cheeses, and a pear gratin. The exciting, expensive cellar includes a few bargain bottles, like the Château Ferry-Lacombe Côte de Provence at 130 F or a Château de Tracy 1992 Pouilly-Fumé at 190 F. **C** 480-600 F. **M** 250 F (lunch exc Sun), 360 F (lunch), 560 F.

**Château
de la Chèvre d'Or** 🎋🎋
(See restaurant above)
*Closed Nov 15-Feb. 5 stes 2,600-4,500 F. 16 rms
1,000-2,600 F. Air cond. Conf. Pool. Golf. Valet pkg.
V, AE, DC, MC.*
 A helicopter was needed to transport the building materials, but several new rooms are now ready to receive the jet set who make up the clientele of this neo-Gothic refuge, built in the 1920s. Superb swimming pools, simple meals at the Café du Jardin, and a private parking lot. Relais et Châteaux.

Château Eza ✪
93 41 12 24, fax 93 41 16 64
*Closed Oct 30-Mar 30. Open until 10pm. Priv
rm: 22. Terrace dining. Valet pkg. V, AE, DC, MC.*
 After the culinary pyrotechnics of his predecessor, Bruno Cirino, André Signoret's cuisine strikes one as cool and collected; yet in its own way, his cooking is just as full of flavor, and is equally accomplished. Signoret had no trouble at all adapting to the Provençal repertoire—with the superb ingredients supplied him, and his own precise professionalism, he quickly learned to infuse his dishes with Southern sunshine. Examples? How about a lovely cold langoustine soup, delicate and flavorful? Or a magnificent turbot roasted in its skin with orange-scented beef jus, a dish that in itself is worth three toques? We also reveled in the red mullet fillets served with basil-enhanced baked potatoes and a charming fried zucchini blossom. For dessert, don't miss the effeuillé of pineapple with ice milk in a thyme and lemon gelatin; the wild strawberry tart and macherpone mousse are excellent, too. Fabulous and very expensive wine list (only three bottles under 100 F, and they are all half bottles). You will have a wonderful meal here, if price is no object. **C** 450-600 F. **M** 150 F, 230 F (lunch), 380 F, 530 F.

 Château Eza
(See restaurant above)
*Closed Oct 30-Dec 16. 5 stes 2,500-3,500 F. 5 rms
1,200-3,000 F. Air cond. Golf. Pkg. V, AE, DC, MC.*
 This cluster of medieval dwellings was made into a "château" by Prince William of Sweden. Over-furnished but very luxurious, with mind-boggling views of the sea. Prices are as lofty as the site.

12/20 Le Grill du Château
La Taverne, rue du Barri
92 10 66 65, fax 93 41 06 72
*Closed Mon, Nov 15-Dec 15, Jan 5-Mar 1. Open
until 10:30pm. Priv rm: 30. V, AE, DC, MC.*
 The terrace of this annex to the Château de la Chèvre d'Or affords views of the village, sea, and hills, while the chef supplies simple and delicious marinated salmon, sea bream with fennel, or a warm tarte tatin. **C** 220-300 F. **M** 95 F (lunch), 150 F.

Les Terrasses d'Eze 🎋🎋
Route de La Turbie
93 41 24 64, fax 93 41 13 25
*Closed Dec 21-Jan 31. 6 stes 1,200-2,500 F. 75 rms
550-850 F. Rms for disabled. Restaurant. Half-board*

*555-655 F. Air cond. Conf. Pool. Tennis. Golf. Pkg.
Helipad. V, AE, DC, MC.*
 Ultracomfortable rooms with sunny balconies and wide terraces facing the Med. Splendid breakfasts. Among the facilities are an electronic golf practice range, a fitness center, and a helipad.

■ **In St-Martin-de-Mieux 14700**   3 km SW

 Château du Tertre
31 90 01 04, fax 31 90 33 16
*Closed Sun dinner, Mon, Feb. Open until 9:30pm.
Pkg. V, AE, MC.*
 Determination and a dream: Englishman Roger Vickery had both when he launched this hotel-restaurant in a ravishing château set exactly in the middle of nowhere. The new chef, Jackie Renard, who has trained with some of the top chefs in France, has simplified the menu a bit and offers meticulously prepared dishes based on fine products: pickerel in cider vinegar, artichokes cooked with cébettes (a delicate vegetable resembling a leek), breast of farm-raised chicken with a slice of warm foie gras and a wild-mushroom-stuffed puff pastry, a delicious dish of pressed sardines and trout with aromatic herbs, and an Athis duck with its giblets stewed in bouillon. Rather limited cheese assortment, but the wine list is interesting, and around 80 wines can be sampled by the glass. **C** 300-450 F. **M** 180 F (wine incl), 140 F, 220 F, 290 F, 395 F.

Château du Tertre 🎋🎋
(See restaurant above)
*Closed Feb. 2 stes 750-1,150 F. 9 rms 490-850 F.
Half-board 750-950 F. Golf. Pkg. V, AE, MC.*
 Not vast but loaded with charm, the rooms of this eighteenth-century château look out over green lawns and meadows. Numerous sporting activities offered (riding, croquet, badminton, biking, kiting...).

FAU-DE-PEYRE 48   ➔ **Aumont-Aubrac**

COL DE LA FAUCILLE (LE) 01   ➔ **Gex**

Le Château
10 km E on N 516 & D 145
74 97 42 52, fax 74 88 86 40
*Annual closings not available. Open until 10pm. Priv
rm: 40. Terrace dining. Heated pool. Valet pkg. V,
AE, DC, MC.*
 This establishment facing the Alps and located not far from Lyons offers a pleasant dining room with a vaulted ceiling and a lovely shady terrace where you can sample well prepared dishes like flavorful foie gras, perfectly cooked salmon in spiced red wine, and a brown-sugar enhanced duck breast with a good macaroni gratin. Dedicated welcome and service; high prices. **C** 450-500 F. **M** 300 F, 430 F, 480 F.

Le Château
(See restaurant above)
*Annual closings not available. 39 rms 800-2,000 F.
Half-board 1,740-2,920 F. Air cond. Conf. Pool. Tennis. Golf. Garage pkg. Helipad. V, AE, DC, MC.*
An authentic château flanked by a tall tower, furnished with superb antiques and with lovely rooms decorated with a touch of audaciousness. Relais et Châteaux.

FAYENCE 83440
Paris 910 - Draguignan 34 - Grasse 27 - St-Raphaël 37 *Var*

 Le Castellaras
Route de Seillans
94 76 13 80, fax 94 84 17 50
Closings not available. Pkg.
Uncommon varieties of trees—birch, beech, and weeping cedar—grace the garden of this Provençal villa with a poolside terrace. In the tranquility of the Fayence hills, Alain Carro has found the perfect setting for his finely crafted cuisine: delicious warm green beans with slices of lobster, and a delicious casserole-roasted half squab with meltingly tender baby vegetables and a delicate sauce. This merits an extra point this year, in spite of the too-sweet caramelized croustine of almonds and cherries spiked with Sherry. Fine welcome, service, and cellar. **C** 350-500 F. **M** 165 F, 210 F, 260 F.

 Moulin de la Camandoule
Chemin de Notre-Dame-des-Cyprès
94 76 00 84, fax 94 76 10 40
Closed Tue lunch, Jan 2-Mar 1 (exc for residents), Nov 2-Dec 22 (exc Sat & Sun & residents). Priv rm: 50. Terrace dining. Hotel: 2 stes 635-675 F. 9 rms 295-635 F. Half-board 450-560 F. Air cond. Conf. Pool. Pkg. V, MC.
Young Olivier Rispoli offers interesting and adroit dishes in this pleasant converted mill: warm avocado cream and tomato sherbet, beef fillet in socca (a chickpea flour pancake), saffron-scented ratatouille, and a sabayon glacé with pears and almonds. Fine Provençal cellar, friendly welcome, and candlelit dinners on the terrace in summer. **C** 250-450 F. **M** 175 F, 265 F.

FÉCAMP 76400
Paris 215 - Rouen 71 - Le Havre 40 - Dieppe 64 *Seine-Mar.*

12/20 **Le Viking**
63, bd Albert-Ier
35 29 22 92, fax 35 29 45 24
Closed Sun dinner, Mon. Open until 9:30pm. Priv rm: 120. V, MC.
Set solidly on a hillside, clad in its armor of slate, this bright and comfortable restaurant offers a generous set menu for 195 F: a dozen raw oysters, savory apple sherbet with Calvados, flavorful although slightly overcooked turbot roasted in verjus, nice cheese selection, and a tasty but runny apple and rhubarb gratin spiked with Calvados. **C** 220-340 F. **M** 115 F (weekday lunch, Sat), 90 F (weekdays), 155 F, 195 F, 260 F.

*The **prices** in this guide reflect what establishments were charging at press time.*

FÈRE-EN-TARDENOIS 02130
Paris 110 - Soissons 26 - Reims 46 - Laon 54 *Aisne*

Château de Fère
3 km N on N 967
23 82 21 13, fax 23 82 37 81
Closed Jan 15-Feb 15. Open until 9:30pm. Priv rm: 40. Heated pool. Valet pkg. V, AE, DC, MC.
On the grounds of this country manor stand some wildly romantic medieval ruins—one can watch them decompose (ever so artistically) from the dining-room windows. If, that is, you can tear your attention away from your plate. Chef Éric Briffard employs costly and modest ingredients, rural and exotic flavors, complex and simple techniques in a fascinating culinary counterpoint. And this year some new bargains are offered: a 180 F "business" menu with a choice of 19 wines at lower prices than on the à la carte menu, such as a Château les Hauts-Conseillants Pomerol for 200 F instead of 300 F. We urge you to taste Briffard's salad of fresh pasta, rocket, and octopus with virgin olive oil, his farm-raised duck roasted with peaches and Szechuan peppercorns, and a warm clafoutis of stawberries, rhubarb, and vanilla. Admirable cellar with many well-aged bottles. **C** 420-550 F. **M** 180 F (weekdays), 290 F, 480 F.

Château de Fère
(See restaurant above)
Closed Jan 15-Feb 15. 6 stes 1,150-1,950 F. 19 rms 850-1,200 F. Half-board 805-1,205 F. Conf. Heated pool. Tennis. Golf. Valet pkg. Helipad. V, AE, DC, MC.
There are actually two castles. The one on the hill, half medieval and half Renaissance, is very impressive and totally ruined. The second, of more recent vintage, is where you'll sleep. It was one of the first châteaux to be converted into a hotel, back in 1956. Recently renovated, it offers guests optional tours of Champagne houses, hot-air balloon rides, and trips to nearby Disneyland-Paris.

FERNEY-VOLTAIRE 01210
Paris 510 - Bellegarde 36 - Geneva 7 - Gex 10 *Ain*

Le Chanteclair
13, rue Versoix - 50 40 79 55
Closed Mon dinner off-seas, Sun. Open until 9:30pm. Priv rm: 35. Terrace dining. V.
Laurent Chambon and his team offer intelligent, inspired dishes, some available on a bargain 95 F menu, in the rather faded dining room or on a lovely flower-bedecked terrace. Try the shellfish crème brûlée with oysters on toast, lamb fillet and sweetbreads en barigoule, and squab roasted with spices. **C** 250-300 F. **M** 95 F (lunch), 230 F.

Voltaire Palace
Av. du Jura
50 40 77 90, fax 50 40 83 00
Open year-round. 2 stes 1,300-2,500 F. 118 rms 550-1,350 F. Rms for disabled. Restaurant. Half-board 430-480 F. Conf. Heated pool. Golf. Pkg. V, AE, DC, MC.
A perfect business hotel whose small, soundproofed rooms have views of Mont Blanc or the Jura range. Pleasing buffet breakfasts.

FERTÉ-SAINT-AUBIN (LA)   45240
Paris 152 - Blois 54 - Salbris 35 - Orléans 21   *Loiret*

Ferme de la Lande
Route de Marcilly-en-Villette
38 76 64 37, fax 38 64 68 87
Closed Sun dinner, Mon, Mar 3-13, Aug 21-Sep 5. Garden dining. Pkg. V, MC.
Set down in a bucolic landscape of ferns and pines, this seventeenth-century Sologne farmhouse is a picturesque spot for a fine meal. Laurent Champion prepares a traditional yet refreshing menu that includes a lentil and pickerel terrine, smoked duck breast with a veal glaze, jambonnette of rabbit in a salt crust, and a banana and orange craquant. Opt for the cool covered terrace in summer. Attractive cellar; hospitable welcome. C 250-350 F. M 150 F (weekdays, Sat lunch, wine incl), 135 F, 180 F (weekdays, Sat lunch), 165 F, 220 F (Sun, Sat dinner).

FERTÉ-SOUS-JOUARRE (LA)   77260
Paris 64 - Meaux 20 - Melun 63   *Seine/Marne*

Auberge de Condé
1, av. de Montmirail
60 22 00 07, fax 60 22 30 60
Closed Mon dinner, Tue. Open until 9:30pm. Terrace dining. Air cond. Pkg. V, AE, DC, MC.
An excellent coffee served with delicious little cakes do not make a meal, and, except for them, the first set menu disappointed us: classic salmon tartare, adequate duck and foie gras terrine, bland guinea fowl in Meaux mustard sauce, and a banana délice with an orange sauce spiked with Grand Marnier. Prices are not friendly, nor is the welcome nor the service. The toque stays for now, but it's high time some changes were made! C 550-700 F. M 250 F (weekdays, wine incl), 310 F, 450 F.

Château des Bondons 🌲🍷
47-49, rue des Bondons
60 22 00 98, fax 60 22 97 01
Open year-round. 4 stes 550-850 F. 7 rms 350-500 F. Conf. Pkg. V, AE, DC, MC.
This eighteenth-century château set in lovely wooded grounds was recently restored in impeccable taste. The rooms are huge and quiet, furnished with refinement and perfectly equipped with luxurious bathrooms. Classic breakfasts; smiling welcome.

FIGEAC   46100
Paris 559 - Cahors 71 - Aurillac 67 - Tulle 103   *Lot*

Hôtel des Carmes
Enclos des Carmes
65 34 20 78, fax 65 34 22 39
Closed Sun dinner & Sat off-seas, Dec 24-Jan 3. Open until 9pm. Priv rm: 50. Terrace dining. Pool. Pkg. V, AE, DC, MC.
We've seen more cheerful interiors than this modern, bay-windowed dining room, but the poolside terrace is pretty and bright. Alongside his polished *carte*, Daniel Raynaud presents a generous set meal for just 105 F that it merits an extra point this year: excellent assortment of country ham and pork liver terrine, perfectly cooked fillet of fresh cod paired with luscious olive oil-enhanced mashed potatoes,

and a perfect cabécou goat cheese. Fine choice of Cahors wines. Efficient welcome and service. C 240-380 F. M 105 F, 180 F, 320 F.

Hôtel des Carmes
(See restaurant above)
Closed at Christmas school. 40 rms 290-425 F. Half-board 345-400 F. Conf. Pool. Tennis. Pkg. V, AE, MC.
Modern, functional rooms near the town center but shielded from the noise of traffic.

Château du Viguier du Roy
Rue Droite - 65 50 05 05, fax 65 50 06 06
Open year-round. 3 stes 1,350-3,750 F. 17 rms 570-1,250 F. Restaurant. Air cond. Conf. Heated pool. No pets. Valet pkg. V, AE, DC, MC.
After a meticulous four-year restoration program, a collection of ancient buildings has been converted into a luxury hotel unique in the region. The complex includes a cloister, gardens, a magnificent oak staircase, and gilded eighteenth-century woodwork, as well as contemporary comforts like a heated pool. The huge rooms (some of them bigger than most Parisian apartments) have been fitted out with every possible amenity. A restaurant is set to open in the spring of 1995.

La Puce à l'Oreille 😊
5, rue Saint-Thomas - 65 34 33 08
Open daily until 9:30pm. Terrace dining. V, AE, DC, MC.
Authentic, carefully prepared regional cooking is on hand in this ancient stone house on a tiny alleyway, opening onto a courtyard surrounded by Gothic vaulting. Try the popular 210 F menu: fine semi-cooked foie gras, delicate puff pastry stuffed with snails and cèpes, excellent cabécou goat cheese, and a flavorful quercheois pastis (a flaky prune-filled pastry) with aged plum brandy. Good choice of regional wines; friendly welcome and service. All this deserves a toque! C 180-280 F. M 75 F (exc Sun), 110 F, 135 F, 150 F, 210 F.

■ **In Cardaillac 46100**   9 km N on N 140 and D 15

12/20 Chez Marcel
65 40 11 16
Closed Mon. Open until 8:30pm. No cards.
For 30 years, this commendable inn has done a roaring trade in the ravishing listed village of Cardaillac. Marcel feeds the faithful on stuffed mutton tripe, omelets stuffed with cèpes or truffles, and duck with olives. Hardly refined cuisine, but at these prices who's complaining? C 125-190 F. M 75 F, 105 F (exc Sun lunch), 120 F, 165 F.

FLAVIGNY-SUR-MOSELLE 54   → Nancy

FLÈCHE (LA)   72200
Paris 240 - Le Mans 42 - Tours 72 - Angers 52 - Laval 69   *Sarthe*

12/20 La Fesse d'Ange
Pl. du 8-Mai-1945
43 94 73 60, fax 43 45 97 33
Closed Sun dinner, Mon, 1st wk of Feb school hols, Aug 1-21. Open until 9:30pm. V.
Marble and lacquer compose a sophisticated setting for the chef's alert, forthright menu: foie

gras, Loué duck roasted in maple syrup, blanquette of veal sweetbreads cooked over fragrant hay, and nougat glacé with a raspberry coulis. Charming reception. **C** 220-300 F. **M** 102 F (weekdays, Sat lunch), 150 F, 195 F.

Le Relais Cicéro
18, bd d'Alger
43 94 14 14, fax 43 45 98 96
Closed Dec 24-Jan 3. 2 stes 670-975 F. 19 rms 380-670 F. Conf. Golf. No pets. Pkg. V, AE, DC, MC.
The three wings of this seventeenth-century dwelling surround a garden-courtyard. The decor is different in all the rooms, which are furnished with pretty antique pieces. Meals may be taken in a neighboring restaurant.

FLEURIE	69820

Paris 420 - Lyon 58 - Belleville 12 - Mâcon 21   *Rhône*

Auberge du Cep
Pl. de l'Église
74 04 10 77, fax 74 04 10 28
Closed Sun dinner, Mon, mid Dec-mid Jan. Open until 9pm. Air cond. Pkg. V, AE, MC.
In spite of changes in the running of this establishment brought about by the sudden death of Gérard Cortembert, chef Michel Guérin's fine cooking has not faltered. Sample the frog's legs roasted with garden herbs, a little ragoût of shelled crayfish tails, pistachio-studded cervelas sausage with a lentil ravigote, and farm-raised chicken cooked in Fleurie wine, all served in a lovely dining room filled with lovingly polished furniture. The welcome is remarkably warm, the wine list one of the finest in the Beaujolais, and the service smooth as silk. The prices, though, are out of sight. **C** 400-500 F. **M** 190 F, 240 F, 300 F, 400 F, 550 F.

FLEURINES 60	→ Senlis

FLEURY-SUR-ORNE 14	→ Caen

FLORENSAC	34510

Paris 810 - Montpellier 50 - Béziers 24 - Agde 10   *Hérault*

Léonce
8, pl. de la République
67 77 03 05, fax 67 77 88 89
Closed Sun dinner, Mon, 3 wks from Feb school hols. Open until 9:30pm. Priv rm: 40. Air cond. No pets. Garage pkg. V, AE, DC.
This venerable village café on a square shaded by plane trees was bequeathed to Jean-Claude Fabre by his grandfather, Léonce. But it was his grandmother who gave him a taste for full-flavored dishes, which he brings up to date while preserving their lusty character. Forget the decor and concentrate on your plate. We recommend you try his smoked salmon terrine with red mullet butter, a gigotin of farm-raised chicken with a confit stuffing, and marvelous chocolate desserts. The first set menu is excellent: a crispy warm galette stuffed with poached oysters, a fillet of duck breast cooked on the bone with pepper and curry, a choice of desserts, and little cakes served with the coffee. Eclectic cellar, with some tasty, affordable regional wines. Warm welcome. **C** 250-400 F. **M** 136 F (weekdays, Sat lunch), 230 F, 330 F.

FLOTTE-EN-RÉ (LA) 17	→ Ré (Ile de)

FOIX	09000

Paris 763 - Toulouse 82 - Carcassonne 81   *Ariège*

12/20 Au Camp du Drap d'Or
21, rue N.-Peyrevidal - 61 02 87 87
Closed Sun dinner, Mon, 1st wk of Oct. Open until 9pm. V, MC.
Ignore the stagey decor and concentrate instead on the good cooking, for example the 110 F menu: flavorful and delicate grilled blood sausage, roast leg of lamb (overcooked) served with good vegetables, and a very caramelized and delicious crème brûlée. An extra point this year. Tiny wine list dedicated to the wines of the Southwest. **C** 200-250 F. **M** 75 F, 110 F, 150 F.

Lons-Audoye
6, pl. G.-Duthil
61 65 52 44, fax 61 02 68 18
Closings not available. 1 ste 350-400 F. 39 rms 235-350 F. Restaurant. Half-board 215-285 F. Conf. Golf. V, AE, DC, MC.
Stow your bags in one of the perfectly nice modern rooms, then make a beeline for the pretty garden terrace with a view of the Ariège. This hotel was once a coaching inn, long ago.

FONTAINEBLEAU	77300

Paris 65 - Melun 16 - Nemours 16 - Orléans 88   *Seine/Marne*

Le Beauharnais
27, pl. Napoléon-Bonaparte
64 22 32 65, fax 64 22 17 33
Closed Dec 23-30. Open until 10:15pm. Priv rm: 90. Garden dining. Air cond. Heated pool. Valet pkg. V, AE, DC, MC.
The formerly slapdash service is now friendly and efficient, and the chef, Rémy Bidron, presents well prepared, inventive dishes: original beef jowls parmentière, pleasant marinated tuna fillet grilled with Provençal herbs, and curious sea scallops with avocado and Chinese truffles. Excellent choice of white Bordeaux. Refined yet relaxed dining room. The point lost last year comes back. **C** 300-450 F. **M** 180 F, 290 F.

L'Aigle Noir
(See restaurant above)
Closed Dec 24-30. 6 stes 1,500-2,000 F. 51 rms 950-1,200 F. Rms for disabled. Air cond. Conf. Heated pool. Golf. Valet pkg. V, AE, DC, MC.
Facing the garden or the château, the luxurious rooms are individually decorated in Louis XVI, Empire, or Restoration style. Modern comforts include satellite TV, books in English, a gym, and a sauna; horseback-riding and an indoor driving range, too. Courteous service.

12/20 Le Caveau des Ducs
24, rue Ferrare - 64 22 05 05
Open daily until 10:30pm. Priv rm: 20. Terrace dining. Air cond. Pkg. V, AE, DC, MC.
The dining rooms are fitted out in a series of superbly vaulted cellars in the center of Fontainebleau, near the castle. Simple cuisine is served here, by friendly but very slow staff. Fewer menus would be an improvement. **C** 250-350 F. **M** 95 F (weekdays, Sat lunch), 175 F (lunch, wine incl), 165 F, 230 F.

Legris et Parc
36, rue Paul-Seramy
64 22 24 24, fax 64 22 22 05
*Open year-round. 5 stes 590 F. 26 rms 390-450 F.
Restaurant. Half-board 480-570 F. Conf. V, AE, MC.*
This pleasantly renovated building stands opposite the entrance to the château's grounds. The best of the extremely comfortable rooms (some with canopy beds) look out on the flowers of an indoor garden.

La Table des Maréchaux
9, rue Grande
64 22 20 39, fax 64 22 20 87
*Closed Dec 23-30. Open until 9:30pm. Priv rm: 90.
Garden dining. Valet pkg. V, AE, DC, MC.*
A brand-new chef is expected to maintain the repertoire in this pretty house with a pleasant interior garden. On offer: asparagus-filled puff pastry, rack of lamb in a salt crust, and a pear aumônière. We will give the kitchen time to establish itself before assigning a rating. **C** 250-350 F. **M** 130 F, 180 F.

Napoléon
(See restaurant above)
*Closed Dec 23-30. 1 ste 990 F. 56 rms 650-990 F.
Half-board 770 F. Conf. Golf. Pkg. V, AE, DC, MC.*
This beautiful hotel in the town center provides good service, excellent bathrooms, and a visit to the wine cellar. Friendly management. The rooms facing the courtyard are bigger and quieter.

■ In Thomery 77810
8 km E

Le Vieux Logis
5, rue S.-Carnot
60 96 44 77, fax 60 96 42 71
Open daily until 9:30pm. Priv rm: 100. Garden dining. Heated pool. Pkg. V, AE, MC.
Jean-Luc Daligault has a knack for original seasonings as well as a sound classic technique. Patrons in this refined, glass-roofed dining room are regaled with wonderfully flavorful and original profiteroles stuffed with Burgundy snails and spinach purée, a light and ultrafresh sole with morels perfectly paired with lemony endive and baby vegetables, and a subtle mango and pear gratin spiked with Marsala and served with nougat glacé. Fine Bordeaux and Burgundies at reasonable prices, and a bargain-priced 145 F set menu. No wonder the locals flock here; it's without a doubt the region's best table. A second toque is well deserved. You can expect a warm welcome and vigilant service. **C** 300-450 F. **M** 145 F, 240 F.

Le Vieux Logis
(See restaurant above)
*Open year-round. 14 rms 400 F. Half-board 545 F.
Conf. Heated pool. Pkg. V, AE, MC.*
A perfect stopover with its elegant decor, luxurious bed linen, friendly service, and absolute peace. As a bonus, the breakfasts are out of this world. Tennis courts nearby.

FONTENAY-SUR-LOING 45 → Montargis

> *Restaurant names in red draw attention to restaurants that offer particularly good value.*

Le Manoir
Route de Coulommiers
64 25 91 17, fax 64 25 95 49
*Open daily until 9pm. Priv rm: 150. Garden dining.
Pkg. V, AE, DC, MC.*
This luxurious little Anglo-Norman manor, perfect for weekend breaks, has its own airfield, a marvelous swimming pool, and a brand-new veranda. The classic cuisine of chef Denis Come meets a high standard. Sample his 350 F menu: lobster bisque, excellent smoked salmon with blinis, perfectly grilled sea bream, tender and generously cut châteaubriand steak, and a delicious roast pear with fruit risotto. Sumptuous wine list; friendly service. An extra point this year. **C** 280-450 F. **M** 240 F (weekdays, Sat lunch, wine incl), 350 F.

Le Manoir
(See restaurant above)
*Closed Feb-Mar 6. 4 stes 950-1,150 F. 16 rms 740-790 F. Half-board 755-1,010 F. Conf. Heated pool.
Tennis. Pkg. V, AE, DC.*
These newly renovated rooms are furnished in a variety of styles but there is only one level of creature comforts—high. Rolling lawns and a swimming pool surrounded by trees tempt you outside. Relais et Châteaux.

La Licorne
Allée Sainte-Catherine
41 51 72 49, fax 41 51 70 40
*Closings not available. Open until 9pm. Priv rm: 12.
Garden dining. Pkg. V, AE, DC, MC.*
Step off the well-marked paths leading to the abbey and discover behind this elegant eighteenth-century façade a beautiful, lime-stone-walled dining room with a handful of tables. The generous, full flavors of Michel Lecomte's cooking reflect his training chez Robuchon, Taillevent, Apicius, and L'Ambroisie. This year, try his delicate oyster and leek tart, roast lamb flavored with shellfish and served with potatoes, almond sand tarts, peach tarte tatin, and vanilla ice cream with a berry coulis. The cellar is well stocked with wines from the Anjou and Touraine. The friendly owners plan to open a few guestrooms in the spring of 1995. **C** 250-370 F. **M** 100 F (weekday lunch), 145 F, 185 F, 250 F.

La Peiriero
Av. des Baux
90 54 76 10, fax 90 54 62 60
*Closed Jan 5-Mar, Oct 21-Dec 20. 3 stes 560-660 F.
33 rms 350-460 F. Conf. Pool. Tennis. Garage pkg.
V, AE, DC, MC.*
A traditional Provençal homestead with big rooms that open onto the surrounding hills. An annex houses studios and apartments with kitchen facilities.

La Regalido 🔾
Rue F.-Mistral
90 54 60 22, fax 90 54 64 29
Closed Tue lunch (exc Jul-Sep), Mon (exc dinner in seas), Jan. Open until 9:15pm. Priv rm: 12. Garden dining. Valet pkg. V, AE, DC, MC.
The pleasures for which one pays here—and one does pay—are provided by competently crafted perennial favorites (innovation is not the house style). Enjoy such consistently pleasing fare as sea bass with anise-scented beurre blanc, a thick slice of leg of lamb studded with garlic cloves, and a tender moelleux au chocolate. We are always entranced by the charming vaulted dining room and the garden of this former olive-oil mill, where we know we'll find a warm welcome and a terrific list of the region's best wines.
C 320-420 F. M 160 F (weekday lunch, Sat, wine incl), 200 F (lunch, wine incl), 300 F, 310 F, 390 F.

La Regalido
(See restaurant above)
Closed Jan. 14 rms 640-1,430 F. Half-board 1,085-1,830 F. Air cond. Golf. Valet pkg. V, AE, DC, MC.
The delightful rooms of this turn-of-the-century hostelry look out over the Alpilles. Breakfast may be taken on the charming terraces. Relais et Châteaux.

FONVIALANE 81 → Albi

FORBACH 57600
Paris 385 - Metz 60 - Sarreguemines 19 - St-Avold 23 _Moselle_

 La Bonne Auberge
15, rue Nationale
87 87 52 78, fax 87 87 18 19
Closed Mon, Dec 26-Jan 6, Aug 15-30. Priv rm: 12. Terrace dining. Air cond. No pets. Pkg. V, MC.
It's no mean feat to establish a high-calibre restaurant deep in the mining country of Lorraine, but the Egloff sisters have pulled it off. Lydia (in the kitchen) and Isabelle (in the dining room) have won a loyal following among food lovers from both sides of the border. Lydia's original, highly personal cuisine makes only passing reference to the regional repertoire. Instead, her dishes have a Mediterranean flair and are filled with intense, perfectly balanced flavors: tiny vine-ripened tomatoes stuffed with cod brandade, a delicate dish bursting with the tastes of the sun; a meltingly tender lamb cassoulet made with mogette beans; a lamb tian with a marvelously flavorful ratatouille; and a buttery pastry filled with seasonal fruits. Fine wine list and expert service under Isabelle's direction.
C 380-500 F. M 300 F (exc weekday lunch), 170 F, 240 F (weekday lunch), 380 F.

■ **In Rosbruck 57800** 6 km SW on N 3

Auberge Albert-Marie
1, rue Nationale
87 04 70 76, fax 87 90 52 55
Closed Sun dinner, Mon. Open until 9:30pm. Priv rm: 40. Air cond. Pkg. V, AE, MC.
A bilingual hostess greets the French and German customers who favor this traditional inn, aglitter with elegant table settings. Pierre Sternjacob's cooking seldom fails to please:

fresh and flavorful cèpes, appealingly seasoned monkfish cooked to perfection, a delicious sausage of young rabbit with herbs served with a bland vegetable mousse, and a pleasant vacherin glacé that shouldn't be served quite so cold. Count on expert advice from Patrick, the sommelier (his cellar is truly something!). Pleasant service. C 300-400 F. M 220 F (lunch).

FORCALQUIER 04300
Paris 775 - Aix 66 - Manosque 23 - Apt 42 _Alpes/H.-P._

Charembeau
Route de Niozelles, 3.5 km on N 100
92 75 05 69, fax 92 75 24 37
Closed Dec-Jan. 12 rms 260-336 F. Pool. Tennis. Pkg. V, MC.
Meadows and hills surround this lovely Provençal dwelling, where intelligently designed rooms (some with kitchenettes) look out over the Montagne de Lure. Charming breakfasts.

12/20 **Hostellerie des Deux Lions**
11, pl. Bourguet
92 75 25 30, fax 92 75 06 41
Closed Sun dinner & Mon off-seas. Annual closings not available. Open until 9:15pm. Hotel: 17 rms 280-450 F. Half-board 310-360 F. Pkg. V, AE, MC.
Serious cooking in a sunny neo-Provençal decor: eggs over-easy with tomatoes, basil-scented red mullet, rack of lamb with summer savory, and a gooey fondant au chocolat. Good local wines and a pleasant welcome from the patronne. Obliging service. C 210-330 F. M 140 F, 190 F, 250 F.

FORGES-LES-EAUX 76440
Paris 113 - Dieppe 54 - Beauvais 50 - Rouen 42 _Seine-Mar._

Auberge du Beau Lieu 🔾
Le Fossé - 35 90 50 36, fax 35 90 35 98
Closed Jan 24-Feb 9. Open until 9:30pm. Priv rm: 8. Garden dining. Pkg. V, AE, DC, MC.
Our last meal here was nothing to write home about. We can overlook the beige decor that tries to please all tastes and might be acceptable if the tables weren't so squeezed together that the waiters can't do their jobs properly. But we can't forgive the uneven, facile cooking we sampled: too-vinegary andouille gâteau, very ordinary fillet of sea bream with beurre blanc, tasty croustillant of Neufchâtel and chopped leeks, and a strawberry vacherin served too cold. And all this at very high prices, including the prices of the wines in the excellent cellar. What's happened to Patrick Ramelet, a chef whose praises we've been singing for quite some time? No rating this time around. M 105 F (weekday lunch, Sat, Sun dinner), 144 F, 165 F, 247 F, 304 F, 355 F.

Auberge du Beau Lieu
(See restaurant above)
Closed Jan 24-Feb 9. 3 rms 250-345 F. Garage pkg. V, AE, DC, MC.
It's hard to leave these handsomely decorated and furnished rooms, which open onto manicured lawns and gardens.

Red toques signify creative cuisine; white toques signify traditional cuisine.

FOUESNANT — 29170

Paris 560 - Quimper 15 - Concarneau 13   *Finistère*

12/20 La Pointe du Cap Coz

In Cap-Coz, 81, av. de la Pointe
98 56 01 63, fax 98 56 53 20
*Closed Wed, Jan-Feb school hols. Open until
8:45pm. Priv rm: 15.* **Hotel:** *18 rms 250-380 F. Half-
board 240-320 F. Conf. Golf. No pets. V, AE, MC.*
This Breton establishment sits on a spit of land
surrounded by the sea, giving one the impression of eating aboard a ship. Fresh, forthright
seafood is the thing to order here, but other
dishes merit your attention as well: a fresh nage
of shellfish with a brunoise of vegetables, lamb
flavored with curry and served with ratatouille
(good but a bit overseasoned), and a fine nougat
glacé. Nice little wines at reasonable prices.
C 250-300 F. **M** 98 F, 150 F, 230 F.

FOUGEROLLES — 70220

Paris 363 - Epinal 43 - Vesoul 38 - Luxeuil-les-B. 9   *Haute-Saône*

Au Père Rota

8, Grande-Rue
84 49 12 11, fax 84 49 14 51
*Closed Sun dinner & Mon (exc hols), Jan 2-Feb 24.
Open until 9pm. Pkg. V, AE, DC, MC.*
Jean-Pierre Kuentz fights off the morose influence of his surroundings with a bright, quietly
elegant dining room and a cuisine that is light,
precise, and discreetly inventive. His defense of
la belle cuisine deserves a medal (or maybe two).
Sample the astonishingly good terrine of young
rabbit with cherries, in itself proof of talent in the
kitchen. We also like the pochouse (stew) and
the gandeuillon (a kind of smoked andouille with
potatoes). The desserts are not up to the level of
the rest. Lengthy wine list, efficient service. This
establishment does honor to its region and to
French cuisine! **C** 320-450 F. **M** 200 F (Sat dinner, Sun lunch), 150 F, 155 F, 240 F (weekdays,
Sat lunch), 300 F.

FOUILLADE (LA) 12   → Najac

FRÉJUS — 83600

Paris 890 - Cannes 40 - Ste-Maxime 21 - Hyères 76   *Var*

Aréna

139, rue du Gal-de-Gaulle
94 17 09 40, fax 94 52 01 52
*Closed lunch Sat & Mon. Open until 10pm. Garden
dining. Air cond. Pool. Valet pkg. V, AE, MC.*
The Bluntzer family welcomes you into their
sunny (although not the most joyously
decorated) dining room with open arms and
happily serves you the fresh, classic dishes
prepared by Bruno Masselin: sautéed red mullet
with sea urchin coral, gambas sautéed with
ginger, langoustines in spicy butter sauce, a
lobster navarin, an admirable squab cooked in a
salt crust, and, in season, breast of pheasant with
cabbage chiffonade and a foie gras velouté.
Delicious desserts. Small cellar. Opt for a table
on the garden terrace in summer. A toque this
year. **C** 300-350 F. **M** 115 F, 155 F, 185 F,
290 F.

Aréna

(See restaurant above)
*Open year-round. 1 ste 650-1,200 F. 22 rms 300-
550 F. Half-board 300-420 F. Air cond. Conf. Pool.
Golf. Valet pkg. V, AE, MC.*
What used to be a bank in the center of the
old town is now a tastefully restored hotel. The
rooms are not all large, but they are cozy and
beautifully outfitted, soundproofed and with attractive bathrooms. Good value; delightful service.

Port Royal

In Port-Fréjus
94 53 09 11, fax 94 53 75 24
*Closed Wed, mid Feb-mid Mar. Open until 9:30pm
(10:30pm in summer). Terrace dining. V, AE, MC.*
Fréjus's brand-new yacht port seems to want
to remain a secret; there are no signs directing
you there! But if you manage to find it, your
reward is this friendly restaurant offering the
flavorful, generous cooking of Marcel
Chavanon. His repertoire is traditional, prepared
with sincerity: astonishingly good foie gras
palette, fillets of John Dory with eggplant caviar,
admirable veal sweetbreads paired with
pleurote mushrooms and served with an unctuous sauce. Crisp apple tart with sherbet. Excellent wine list. Prices tend to be on the high side.
C 350-450 F. **M** 145 F (weekday lunch), 195 F.

Les Potiers

135, rue des Potiers - 94 51 33 74
Open daily until 10pm. Air cond. Pkg. V, AE, MC.
It's worth the trek through the charmless old
town to fetch up in this pretty dining room and
tuck into Michel Rouleau's generous cooking
based on market-fresh ingredients: try his crisp
and delicate puff pastry stuffed with snails and
wild mushrooms, saddle of lamb with sweet
onions, superb cheese assortment, and unctuous, flavorful ice cream. Regional wines at
reasonable prices. Nice welcome and prices.
C 220-320 F. **M** 160 F.

La Toque Blanche

In Fréjus-plage,
365, av. V.-Hugo - 94 52 06 14
*Closed Mon, Jun 22-Jul 11. Open until 9:45pm. Ter-
race dining. Air cond. V, AE, DC, MC.*
The classic house repertoire favors costly ingredients: red mullet fillet with tapenade, an
émincé of veal kidneys and sweetbreads, stuffed
zucchini blossoms, caramelized pears. Chef
Jacky Collin's light touch lends style to them all.
The 130 F set meal (sautéed gambas à la
provençale, breast of squab, dessert) is a treat to
enjoy in this blue-toned dining room not far from
the sea. **C** 290-380 F. **M** 130 F, 180 F, 250 F.

FRONTIGNAN — 34110

Paris 774 - Montpellier 22 - Sète 7 - Lodève 62   *Hérault*

Le Jas d'Or

2, bd V.-Hugo - 67 43 07 57
*Closed Tue dinner, Wed. Open until 10pm. Priv
rm: 40. Pkg. V, MC.*
Chef Jean-Jacques Vallon built the bright,
Greco-Roman dining room himself, then went to
work in the kitchen, where he cooks up a number of prize recipes that make this the city's best
restaurant. Seafood reigns supreme: perfectly
cooked red mullet unfortunately drowning a

little in a warm salad with aged Sherry vinaigrette, interesting monkfish in a potato crust with spiced wine sauce, and a flavorful Muscat soufflé glacé. Christine Vallon's smile makes the reasonable bill seem even lighter. C 250-350 F. M 135 F, 180 F.

FUSTE (LA) 04	→ Manosque

GAILLARD 74	→ Annemasse

GANGES	34190
Paris 755 - Montpellier 45 - Alès 48 - Le Vigan 17	Hérault

■ In **Madières 34190**   20 km SE on D 25

Château de Madières
67 73 84 03, fax 67 73 55 71
Closed Nov 2-Apr 7. Open until 9pm (exc reserv). Terrace dining. Heated pool. Pkg. V, AE, MC.
One of the two dining rooms has a vaulted ceiling and a splendid view of the gorges of the Vis river and of the tiny village. Chef Françoise Brucy serves traditional dishes based on the region's best products: tender and tasty duck foie gras, delicious lamb chops grilled with herbs, and a gooey baba liberally spiked with rum. Warm welcome, fine service. C 300-400 F. M 145 F (lunch exc Sun), 190 F, 270 F, 350 F.

Château de Madières
(See restaurant above)
Closed Nov 2-Apr 7. 3 stes 850-1,090 F. 7 rms 560-960 F. Half-board 595-785 F. Air cond. Heated pool. Golf. Pkg. Helipad. V, AE, MC.
An island of charm, protected by the thick walls of a high-perched medieval fortress. Discreetly modern, personalized guest rooms are arranged around a central patio-courtyard; adding to the enchantment are a garden and a lovely terrace.

GAP	05000
Paris 665 - Grenoble 103 - Digne 85 - Avignon 179	H.-Alpes

Le Carré Long
32, rue Pasteur - 92 51 13 10
Closed Sun, Mon, May 1-21. Open until 9:30pm. Priv rm: 30. Air cond. Pkg. V, AE, DC, MC.
What a pleasure to discover this trim little restaurant, situated in one of Gap's less cheerful streets. Monique Fiore-Rappelin's cordial greeting puts one in the right frame of mind to enjoy her husband Bernard's innovative handling of regional ingredients. Order the 220 F menu (apéritif, wine, and service included) that in itself has earned a second toque this year: terrine of pork and duck liver served with pink onion marmalade, superbly prepared lamb en daube with two kinds of thyme, an herb-infused wine granité, an excellent cheese assortment, and a delicious cinnamon-laced apple cake. Well chosen wine list. C 280-350 F. M 220 F (wine incl), 130 F, 270 F.

La Ferme Blanche
Route de Villarobert
92 51 03 41, fax 92 51 35 39
Open year-round. 3 stes 400-450 F. 24 rms 250-450 F. Half-board 375 F. Conf. Pkg. V, AE, MC.
This venerable establishment stands in quiet, open countryside and offers a real respite for the weary. The renovated rooms are all bright, neat, and nicely appointed. The owner himself greets guests with warm cordiality.

Le Patalain
7, av. des Alpes - 92 52 30 83
Closed Sun (exc hols), Sat lunch. Open until 9pm. Air cond. Pkg. V, AE, DC, MC.
Behind a pretty renovated façade you'll find a pleasant dining room brightened by the patronne's smile. Savor Gérard Périnet's delicate, harmonious dishes: millefeuille stuffed with brains and crisp vegetables, lamb fillet en crépinette with a thyme jus, and peach soup enlivened with a fresh mint infusion. Nice little wine list. C 280-330 F. M 115 F, 195 F, 265 F.

GARENNE-COLOMBES (LA) 92
→ PARIS Suburbs

GARIDECH 31	→ Toulouse

GARONS 30	→ Nîmes

GASSIN	83580
Paris 877 - Le Lavandou 33 - St-Tropez 8	Var

La Verdoyante
866, VC de Coste Brigade
94 56 16 23, fax 94 56 43 10
Closed Wed (exc dinner Jul-Aug), Nov-mid Mar. Open until 9:30pm (10pm in summer). Garden dining. Pkg. V.
Soft vineyard breezes and the gentle pace of another era stir this exquisite terrace where yesterday, today, and—we are certain—tomorrow patrons feed on an unvarying menu of Provençal daube, rabbit liver tartinettes, Provençal stuffed capon, rabbit sautéed with garlic, and other perennial favorites. Wash them down with some wines from nearby Minuty, which include a delicious Cuvée Prestige white. C 270-350 F. M 160 F.

GENSAC	33890
Paris 550 - Bordeaux 59 - Bergerac 39	Gironde

Les Remparts
16, rue du Château - 57 47 43 46
Closed Mon dinner, Tue, Jan 2-Feb. Open until 9pm. Priv rm: 12. Pkg. V.
The splendid fireplace which crowns the gracious dining room comes from a nearby château, while the appealing, generous cuisine comes from the inventive and highly capable hands of Éric Povoremo. The excellent 145 F prix-fixe menu includes delicious scorpion fish fillets with basil in a tasty sauce made of cream and fish jus, succulent veal with onion confit, and a yummy crème brûlée. A tip-top wine list with many half bottles. Charming welcome and service by the patronne. C 260-350 F. M 100 F (weekday lunch, wine incl), 145 F, 170 F, 230 F.

Some establishments change their **closing times** without warning. It is always wise to check in advance.

GÉRARDMER 88400
Paris 421 - Colmar 52 - Epinal 40 - Saint-Dié 30   *Vosges*

Les Bas-Rupts et Chalet Fleuri
3 km on D 486
29 63 09 25, fax 29 63 00 40
Open daily until 9:30pm. Priv rm: 40. Garden dining. Heated pool. Pkg. V, AE.
There is no finer place to take in the beauty of the fir-covered Vosges Mountains than in this commodious, perfectly run chalet. Family traditions provide the backbone, constant renovations the pretty face of this comfortable establishment. Chef Michel Philippe, assisted by an alumnus of the Robuchon school, François Lachaud, coaxes every nuance of flavor from his fine regional ingredients. This year, he produced superb raw sea scallops on a bed of celery in truffle vinaigrette, impeccable and generous crab parmentier, and rabbit fillets and crépinettes served with a bayaldi and a delicious girolle mushroom risotto. On the 150 F "terroir" menu you will find such regional favorites as a sauerkraut terrine imaginatively paired with a savory cumin cream sauce, and the house's celebrated tripes au riesling which you can order to take away. Superb cellar of Alsace's finest wines at very reasonable prices. Only the desserts fail to match the high level of the rest (nougat glacé flavored with bergamot, profiteroles, fruit gratin with sabayon). Nevertheless, here is a well earned third toque. May it encourage Michel Philippe in his dream of creating a monument to ecology alligned with the art of living well. C 320-450 F. M 150 F (exc Sat dinner, Sun lunch), 200 F, 290 F, 450 F.

Les Bas-Rupts et Chalet Fleuri ♣️
(See restaurant above)
Open year-round. 2 stes 800 F. 30 rms 350-750 F. Half-board 520-740 F. Conf. Heated pool. Tennis. Pkg. V, AE, MC.
A modern mountain chalet featuring bright, pretty, spacious rooms whose tasteful decor reflects the beauty of the surroundings. New heated swimming pool. Discreet service, terrific breakfasts, and the rerouting of the serpentine route just below will only add to the charm.

Au Grand Cerf
Pl. Tilleul - 29 63 06 31
Open daily until 9:30pm. Priv rm: 40. Garden dining. Heated pool. Pkg. V, AE, DC, MC.
After pursuing the many leisure activities arranged for them by the friendly hosts of this cozy provincial establishment, guests may repair, with a good appetite, to the dining room for fresh, carefully prepared dishes like ham cooked on the bone served with potato fritters, dandelion greens in a salad, and mirabelle plum puff pastry, as well as a changing array of specialties like pikerel fillet with shellfish sauce and dates sautéed in cream. C 250-350 F. M 120 F, 160 F, 195 F, 260 F, 350 F.

Grand Hôtel Bragard ♣️
(See restaurant above)
Open year-round. 6 stes 870-1,010 F. 56 rms 340-600 F. Half-board 350-460 F. Conf. Heated pool. Pkg. V, AE, DC, MC.

These attractive rooms are regularly brought up to date. They feature outstanding appointments and delightful views of the grounds or the mountains, and fitness equipment is on the premises.

GETS (LES) 74260
Paris 595 - Bonneville 37 - Morzine 7 - Geneva 52   *H.-Savoie*

Chalet-Hôtel Crychar
50 75 80 50, fax 50 79 83 12
Closed Apr 15-Jun 18, Sept 15-Dec 15. 12 rms 370-550 F. Restaurant. Heated pool. Golf. No pets. Pkg. V, AE, DC, MC.
Off by itself above the rest of the resort, this small chalet-hotel boasts large rooms and a pretty terrace.

Maroussia ♣️
In La Turche
50 75 80 85, fax 50 75 87 62
Closed Apr 20-Jun 25, Sept 15-Dec 15. 22 rms 250-500 F. Restaurant. Half-board 265-390 F. Golf. Pkg. V, MC.
A pleasant chalet perched high in the mountains, with many fine features. Ski trails start just outside the hotel's door.

GEVREY-CHAMBERTIN 21220
Paris 310 - Beaune 26 - Dijon 13 - Besançon 46   *Côte-d'Or*

11/20 Bonbistrot
Rue du Chambertin
80 34 33 20, fax 80 34 12 30
Closed Sun dinner, Mon, Feb, 1st wk of Aug. Open until 10pm. Priv rm: 130. Terrace dining. Pkg. V, MC.
A short menu of very good dishes served in a down-to-earth setting (country café). We like the snails, the ham in parsley gelatin, and the baba au rhum. C 150-200 F.

Les Grands Crus ♣️
Route des Grands-Crus
80 34 34 15, fax 80 51 89 07
Closed Dec 3-Feb 25. 24 rms 350-430 F. Pkg. V, MC.
A peaceful establishment with neat, renovated rooms situated in the celebrated vineyard opposite a twelfth-century church. There's a pretty flower garden where breakfast is served.

Les Millésimes
25, rue de l'Église
80 51 84 24, fax 80 34 12 73
Closed Wed lunch, Tue, Dec 25-Jan 25. Open until 9:30pm. Priv rm: 20. Garden dining. Air cond. Pkg. V, AE, DC, MC.
This pretty winemaker's house, perched on the village heights, boasts a prodigious cellar, at which no wine buff could turn up his nose: it contains as many bottles of Pétrus and Yquem as it does of Chambertin and Volnay, and its Burgundy collection is the best we know. They accompany a bill of fare that features noble ingredients prepared in rich dishes like creamy chicken soup with green lentils, saddle of young rabbit stuffed with foie gras, a puff pastry stuffed with crab and lobster, and other delights much appreciated by a wealthy, predominantly foreign clientele. C 500-600 F. M 295 F, 560 F.

---

*The **prices** in this guide reflect what establishments were charging at press time.*

Rôtisserie du Chambertin ♻
Rue du Chambertin
80 34 33 20, fax 80 34 12 30
Closed Sun dinner, Mon, Feb, 1 wk in Aug. Open until 9:30pm. Priv rm: 150. Air cond. Pkg. V, MC.
The Rôtisserie remains one of the monuments of Burgundy, an obligatory stop on a pilgrimage through the Côte d'Or. Jean-Pierre Nicolas's cuisine is strictly traditional, a true taste of the region. And there's a charming *caveau* and cooperage museum on the premises. In the dining room with its opulent tapestries and chandeliers, sample the justly celebrated house coq au vin, the fricassée of frog's legs and snails with green cabbage and bits of bacon, and pickerel fillet in Vin Jaune. Costly cellar (true, it's composed mainly of venerable vintages and Gevrey-Chambertin...) with a few lower-priced bottles to offer relief to your wallet (an honorable Aligoté at 75 F). **C** 370-480 F. **M** 260 F, 330 F, 410 F.

■ **In Quemigny-**
Poisot 21220   *9 km W on D 31 and D 35*

12/20 L'Orée du Bois
80 49 78 77
Closed Sun dinner off-seas, Mon, Dec 22-Feb 3. Open until 9pm (9:30pm in summer). Priv rm: 40. Pkg. V, AE, MC.
You won't find many frills here, either in the decor or in the cooking, but the food, prepared by the owner himself, is fresh and forthright. Try the hure (a kind of pâté) of salmon and monkfish, red mullet fillet with pink celery, pickerel roasted with parsley, grilled rack of lamb with garlic cream, and a pear tatin. Good choice of Burgundies from the best producers at reasonable prices (which can't be said of the prices on the *carte*). **C** 200-300 F. **M** 75 F (weekdays), 130 F, 170 F.

GEX	01170

Paris 498 - Lons-le-Saunier 96 - Saint-Claude 44 - Geneva 17   *Ain*

12/20 Auberge des Chasseurs
In Échenevex
50 41 54 07, fax 50 41 90 61
Closed Nov 15-Mar 15. Open until 9:30pm. Priv rm: 35. Garden dining. Heated pool. Pkg. V, AE, MC.
Here's a squeaky-clean inn with a broad terrace and view of the Alps. The menu is a magnet for *bons vivants* in search of good, honest cooking: duck foie gras, marinated salmon, John Dory fillets with green pepper cream sauce, chicken with morels and mushrooms in cream sauce, and a pear-filled puff pastry with a raspberry coulis. **C** 260-390 F. **M** 150 F (dinner exc Sun), 180 F, 200 F, 270 F (exc Sun), 185 F (Sun).

 Auberge des Chasseurs ♨
(See restaurant above)
Closed Nov 15-Mar 10. 15 rms 400-600 F. Half-board 480-700 F. Conf. Heated pool. Tennis. Golf. Pkg. V, AE, MC.
In addition to a full-front view of Mont Blanc, this delightful mountain inn offers comfortable rooms decorated with Laura Ashley fabrics, thoughtful appointments, and exquisite service.

■ **In Le Col-**
de-la-Faucille 01170   *12 km N on N 5*

La Mainaz ♨
N 5 - 50 41 31 10, fax 50 41 31 77
Closed Wed lunch, Nov. 25 rms 305-450 F. Restaurant. Half-board 395-425 F. Conf. Heated pool. Golf. Pkg. V, AE, DC, MC.
A good night's rest is assured in the cozy rooms of this chalet set amid the pines. Superb views of Mont Blanc and Lake Geneva.

GIEN	45500

Paris 154 - Orléans 64 - Bourges 76 - Cosne 41   *Loiret*

Le Rivage
1, quai de Nice
38 37 79 00, fax 38 38 10 21
Closed Sun dinner off-seas, beg Feb-beg Mar. Open until 9:15pm. Air cond. Pkg. V, AE, DC, MC.
The dining room's decor is cozy, the view of the Loire lovely, and the cooking of Thierry Renou blends classicism and modernity: pig's foot crépinettes with langoustine tails, roasted Loire pike with beurre blanc, braised veal sweetbreads with shrimp cream, and a yummy millefeuille gaufré au chocolat. Tempting wine list, professional service. An added point this year. **C** 280-400 F. **M** 135 F (exc Sat dinner, Sun lunch), 230 F, 290 F, 380 F.

Le Rivage
(See restaurant above)
Open year-round. 3 stes 690 F. 16 rms 295-500 F. Air cond. Conf. Pkg. V, AE, DC, MC.
On the quay by the old Anne de Beaujeu bridge. Some of the rooms are simple and well furnished, others definitely more luxurious. Very nice bathrooms, too. First-rate breakfasts; cordial reception.

GIENS	83400

Paris 875 - Toulon 27 - Hyères 12 - Carqueiranne 13   *Var*

11/20 L'Eau Salée
Port Niel - 94 58 92 33, fax 94 58 11 25
Closed Sun dinner & Mon (Jun 15-Sep 15), Jan 7-Feb 15. Open until 10:30pm. Terrace dining. Pkg. V, AE, MC.
Enjoy luminously fresh seafood and other treats like puff pastry filled with cod and aïoli, galinette fillet en bisque, pieds et paquets (lamb's feet and tripe), and a honey marquise with saffron-and-anise sauce, all served on the most wonderful terrace imaginable, overlooking the beach and the harbor. **C** 270-400 F. **M** 120 F (exc Sun lunch), 165 F, 200 F, 220 F.

Le Provençal
Pl. St-Pierre
94 58 20 09, fax 94 58 95 44
Closed Jan-Apr 7, Oct 22-Dec. 41 rms 265-640 F. Restaurant. Half-board 382-600 F. Conf. Pool. Tennis. Golf. Pkg. V, AE, DC, MC.
At the tip of the peninsula you'll find this hotel with simple rooms and sumptuous sea views (that same sea water, by the way, feeds the swimming pool).

GIGONDAS · 84190

Paris 677 - Orange 18 - Avignon 37 - Vaison 15   *Vaucluse*

Les Florets

Route des Dentelles-de-Montmirail
90 65 85 01, fax 90 65 83 80
Closed Tue dinner (exc Nov-Apr), Wed off-seas, Jan, Feb. Open until 9pm. Priv rm: 30. Garden dining. Hotel: 15 rms 345-420 F. Half-board 360-400 F. Golf. Pkg. V, AE, DC, MC.
In a lovely dining room or on a terrace overlooking a ravishing garden, sample fresh and flavorful regional dishes: fresh foie gras and bread pudding, tiny Provençal snails, beef cheeks braised in Gigondas wine, and a half squab on a bed of spelt. The owner, a wine maker himself, has assembled a fine selection of Gigondas. C 250-350 F. M 95 F (lunch exc Sun), 155 F, 210 F.

GILLY-LÈS-CÎTEAUX 21

→ **Nuits-Saint-Georges**

GIMONT · 32200

Paris 699 - Toulouse 51 - Agen 85 - Montauban 70   *Gers*

Château de Larroque 🏵

Route de Toulouse
62 67 77 44, fax 62 67 88 90
Closed Sun dinner & Mon off-seas, Jan 2-18. Open until 9:30pm. Garden dining. Pkg. V, AE, DC, MC.
Built the year Napoléon III was crowned emperor, this majestic château stands in the stillness of the Gascon countryside. From the wide terrace, the landscape seems to stretch into infinity. Over the last twenty years, André Fagedet has perfected a wonderfully rich, inventive cuisine that makes the most of the region's bounty. Be sure to work up an appetite before you sit down to sybaritic portions of a gratin of foie gras-stuffed oysters, savory lobster médaillon with meltingly tender apples, linden-blossom flan, and a fresh and original peach poached with rose petals. The fine cellar presents a wide choice of half-bottles. C 250-450 F. M 180 F (wine incl), 220 F, 285 F.

Château de Larroque ★♣

(See restaurant above)
Closed Jan 2-18. 1 ste 1,350 F. 14 rms 450-1,050 F. Half-board 550-800 F. Conf. Pool. Tennis. Golf. Pkg. Helipad. V, AE, DC, MC.
A delicious Relais et Châteaux in the opulent Gascon countryside. Rooms are first-rate and have all sorts of modern amenities, including big marble bathrooms. Breakfast is served on a pretty terrace. Fishing in a private pond.

GIVERNY 27 · → Vernon

GOLFE-JUAN · 06350

Paris 929 - Nice 27 - Cannes 6 - Antibes 5 - Grasse 21   *Alpes-Mar.*

12/20 Le Bistrot du Port

53, bd des Frères-Roustan - 93 63 70 64
Closed Mon off-seas. Open until 9:30pm. Air cond. No pets. V, MC.
The attractions here are a series of small glassed-in rooms overlooking the port, an enjoyable summer terrace, and simple cuisine based on fresh seafood and fine meats: we liked the beef cheeks en daube, eggplant gratin with pistou, and a vanilla tatin. M 100 F (weekday lunch, Sat), 165 F, 250 F.

Chez Christiane

On the harbor - 93 63 72 44
Closed Mon dinner (in winter), Tue. Open until 10:30pm. Priv rm: 150. Terrace dining. V, AE, MC.
Should rain or wind make the terrace impracticable, Chez Christiane's numerous regulars pile into the bright little dining room to savor chef Marc Berthier's remarkably proficient cuisine. Seafood, naturally enough, dominates the menu: on a given day, you might find a petite marmite du pêcheur, sea bass with mesclun salad, and Provençal bourride (garlicky fish stew). An attractive cellar of white wines perfectly complements this briny fare. C 300-500 F.

GORDES · 84220

Paris 717 - Apt 20 - Avignon 38 - Cavaillon 17   *Vaucluse*

La Bastide de Gordes

Le Village
90 72 12 12, fax 90 72 05 20
Closed Nov 2-Mar 11. 1 ste 1,050-1,400 F. 18 rms 450-1,250 F. Air cond. Heated pool. Tennis. Golf. Garage pkg. V, AE, MC.
Nearly a score of spacious and inviting rooms in a noble Renaissance dwelling, filled with art works and fine furniture. The lodgings are totally comfortable and unostentatious, done up in Provençal style. Gym, sauna, and a little swimming pool on the terrace that faces a splendid view.

Les Bories ★♣

2 km NW on D 177,
route de l'Abbaye de Sénanque
90 72 00 51, fax 90 72 01 22
Closed Dec-mid Feb. 1 ste 1,600-1,900 F. 17 rms 600-1,450 F. Restaurant. Half-board 575-750 F. Air cond. Conf. Heated pool. Tennis. Golf. Pkg. V, AE, DC, MC.
A marvelous spot in a magical corner of Provence. Ten rooms are housed in a little *mas*, the rest are in authentic dry-stone bungalows ("bories"). There's a well-kept garden with a lovely covered pool.

Comptoir du Victuailler

Pl. du Château - 90 72 01 31
Dinner by reserv. Closed Tue & Wed off-seas, Nov 15-Dec 15, Jan 15-Mar 15. Terrace dining. Pkg. V.
In the heart of the village, opposite the Renaissance château which houses the Vasarely Foundation, and in an elegant dining room graced with bouquets of fresh flowers, Joëlle Chaudat serves fine home cooking: compote of young rabbit with fresh herbs, Atlantic turbot with salicornes (edible seaweed), and guinea hen with raspberries. Superb wine list. C 300-400 F. M 100 F (Jul-Aug), 145 F.

Domaine de l'Enclos ★♣

Route de Sénanque
90 72 08 22, fax 90 72 03 03
Closings not available. 3 stes 800-1,800 F. 14 rms 450-950 F. Restaurant. Half-board 400-1,000 F. Air cond. Conf. Pool. Tennis. Golf. Garage pkg. Helipad. V, AE, MC.
Not far from Gordes you'll find this group of bungalows with spacious, comfortable rooms furnished in true Provençal spirit (the bathrooms

are decorated with locally fired tiles). Extras include a fine terrace, a garden, and magnificent views. Courteous welcome, unobtrusive service.

12/20 La Gacholle

Route de Murs
90 72 01 36, fax 90 72 01 81
Closed Nov 15-Mar 15. Open until 9pm. Terrace dining. Heated pool. No pets. Pkg. V, MC.
The grandiose spectacle of the Lubéron lends considerable charm to La Gacholle's attractive dining room and covered terrace. Sample the tender red mullet with garlic ravioli, saddle of young rabbit stuffed with liver and truffles, roasted veal chops en crépinette, and a joconde au muscat for dessert. On hand is a good choice of regional wines. **C** 260-350 F. **M** 155 F (exc Sun lunh), 220 F, 350 F.

La Gacholle

(See restaurant above)
Closed Nov 15-Mar 15. 12 rms 490-750 F. Half-board 450-560 F. Heated pool. Tennis. Pkg. V, MC.
Set in glorious surroundings, this cozily appointed *bastide* houses well-kept, peaceful rooms, as well as a lovely terrace where guests may take their breakfast. Facilities include a very pretty swimming pool and tennis courts. Friendly reception.

Le Mas Tourteron

Chemin de Saint-Blaise, Les Imberts
90 72 00 16, fax 90 72 09 81
Closed Mon, Nov 15-Dec 26, Jan 10-Feb 12. Open until 9:30pm. Garden dining. Pkg. V, AE, MC.
This isolated *mas* nestled at the foot of Gordes is still as attractive as ever with its pretty, Provençal decor and charming walled garden where you can dine under the trees. Elisabeth Bourgeois offers cooking based on regional ingredients: a galette croustillante of lamb sweetbreads in Vin Cuit sauce, a bohémienne of sea bass with aromatic herbs, a parfait fromager en salade, and a dessert cart. Quick light lunches are served at Le Petit Comptoir, in an attractive bistrot setting. **M** 130 F (lunch exc Sun), 280 F, 380 F.

Les Romarins

Route de Sénanque
90 72 12 13, fax 90 72 13 13
Closings not available. 10 rms 400-670 F. Pool. Golf. No pets. Pkg. V, AE.
A fine, traditional *bastide* that overlooks the village of Gordes and its château. Fresh, pleasant rooms are furnished with attractive nineteenth-century antiques. Charming reception.

■ **In Beaumettes 84220**   7 km S on D 2 & D 103

Le Moulin Blanc

Chemin du Moulin
90 72 34 50, fax 90 72 25 41
Open daily until 10pm. Priv rm: 25. Garden dining. Pkg. V, AE, DC, MC.
This old coaching inn with vaulted ceilings, imposing fireplaces, and Louis XIII furniture was a flour mill, once upon a time. On a summer's day book a table on the superb terrace that looks over a leafy park, and enjoy the classic, delicate cooking of chef Anthony Baud: duck foie gras, fillet of John Dory sautéed in its skin, casserole-roasted young guinea fowl in an olive jus, and a

berry gratin topped with brown sugar. **C** 330-400 F. **M** 160 F, 350 F.

Le Moulin Blanc

(See restaurant above)
Open year-round. 1 ste 925-1,180 F. 17 rms 475-935 F. Half-board 450-660 F. Conf. Pool. Tennis. Golf. Pkg. Helipad. V, AE, DC, MC.
A fifteenth-century mill in the heart of the Lubéron. The pretty rooms are comfortably equipped and nicely furnished, some with four-poster beds. Ask for a room on the garden.

■ **In Joucas 84220**   6 km E on D 2 and D 102

11/20 Le Mas des Herbes Blanches

Route de Murs
90 05 79 79, fax 90 05 71 96
Closed Jan 3-Mar 10. Open until 9:30pm. Terrace dining. Heated pool. Pkg. V, AE, DC, MC.
This handsome dry-stone *mas* boasts a tasteful, understated dining room perfectly suited to the luminous and wild beauty of the austere Lubéron landscape. As for the cuisine, it fails to live up to the view: very ordinary lamb sweetbreads with morels, bland farm-raised guinea fowl with truffles under the skin, and a fruit salad offered in place of warm desserts. The prices are much too high, though the welcome is warm. **C** 380-480 F. **M** 270 F (lunch), 375 F.

Le Mas des Herbes Blanches

(See restaurant above)
Closed Jan 3-Mar 10. 6 stes 1,415-2,180 F. 17 rms 685-1,565 F. Half-board 763-1,510 F. Air cond. Conf. Heated pool. Tennis. Pkg. V, AE, DC, MC.
The rooms were ravishingly renovated not long ago. Most of the lodgings give onto the Lubéron and the hotel's extensive grounds, where stipas—the "white grasses" which gave the place its name—grow in profusion. Relais et Châteaux.

Le Phébus

Route de Murs
90 05 78 83, fax 90 05 73 61
Closed Nov-Feb. Open until 10:30pm. Terrace dining. Air cond. Heated pool. Pkg. V, AE, MC.
Reflections from the swimming pool dapple the veranda which runs alongside the pleasant dining room. Here host Olivier Mathieu will ply you with seductive Provençal cuisine crafted by his brother, Xavier. On the 165 F menu, which we award an extra point this year, are tiny endives marinières served with fresh and delicate condiments, perfectly cooked parmentier of lamb shoulder with eggplant, a fine cheese assortment served with the superb house olive bread, and a delicate chocolate tart with honey ice cream. Attractive regional wines. **C** 250-360 F. **M** 140 F, 165 F.

Le Phébus

(See restaurant above)
Closed Nov-Feb. 5 stes 1,345 F. 17 rms 650-910 F. Rms for disabled. Half-board 650-840 F. Air cond. Conf. Heated pool. Tennis. Pkg. Helipad. V, AE, DC, MC.
Five new, hugely comfortable suites (two have private pools) have joined the lovely, large rooms, many with stupendous views. You'll also find period furniture, dainty floral arrangements,

a tempting terrace, good breakfasts, and efficient service.

■ In **Murs 84220**　　　8 km NE on D 15

⌂14 Mas du Loriot
Route de Joucas
90 72 62 62, fax 90 72 62 54
Dinner only. Open by reserv off-seas. Open until 9:30pm. Garden dining. Pool. Pkg. V.
This doll's house stands lost in the garrigue, atop a hill that juts out over the village of Joucas. The Revels reign over a delightful country-style dining room where you can enjoy Madame's light, precise cooking based on first-rate ingredients. Just taste her foie de canard garnished with local asparagus, or her pavé of fresh cod, young rabbit sautéed with sweet garlic and summer savory, and a berry dessert. The Lubéron's best wines are found in the cellar. Reservations essential. **M** 175 F.

⌂⌂ Mas du Loriot　　🌲🍴
(See restaurant above)
Open by reserv off-seas. 5 rms 450 F. Rms for disabled. Half-board 500 F. Pool. Golf. Pkg. V, MC.
Try by all means to book the room with an immense terrace, where you can enjoy the most exquisite breakfast imaginable: warm rolls, local honey, eggs, homemade jams, yoghurt.... There's a pool in the garden.

GOUAREC	22570
Paris 470 - Saint-Brieuc 50 - Carhaix 31	Côtes/Armor

⌂13 Hôtel du Blavet
N 164 bis - 96 24 90 03, fax 96 24 84 85
Closed Sun dinner & Mon (exc Jul-Aug), Jan 31-Feb 27. Open until 9pm. Priv rm: 35. Pkg. V, MC.
This appealing, family-run hotel nestles in a verdant setting right in the middle of Brittany. The peaceful Blavet River, which runs in front of the terrace off the large dining room with its beautiful Breton furniture, inspires Louis Le Loir to produce consistent (if not original) cuisine crafted from excellent raw materials. This year, try the marguerite of sea scallops and marinated salmon, roast empereur with smoked bacon, veal sweetbreads in Port sauce, or a fruit gratin with a Champagne sabayon. On the first set menu, you'll find fish terrine, sirloin steak with shallots, and a Belle Hélène genoise. **C** 280-350 F (weekday lunch). **M** 80 F (exc Sun), 160 F, 220 F, 320 F.

GOUMOIS	25470
Paris 485 - Besançon 93 - Bienne 44 - Maîche 19	Doubs

12/20 Taillard
81 44 20 75, fax 81 44 26 15
Closed Wed off-seas, Nov-Mar. Open until 9pm. Garden dining. Heated pool. Pkg. V, AE, DC, MC.
Swiss travelers know and love this comfortable chalet that overlooks the Doubs Valley, but perhaps it has become too popular for its own good: the cooking is tending toward the facile. Excellent veal sweetbreads, but the morels were bland and the sea scallops rubbery. A point less this year, in spite of the fine wine list. It's time to shape up. **C** 300-450 F. **M** 135 F, 170 F, 260 F, 370 F.

⌂⌂ Taillard　　🌲🍴
(See restaurant above)
Closed Nov-Mar. 4 stes 430 F. 13 rms 275-380 F. Half-board 350-400 F. Air cond. Conf. Heated pool. Pkg. V, AE, DC, MC.
A lovely chalet in a peaceful and charming site, with fully modernized and renovated rooms. Good amenities (there's a billiard room, a library, a swimming pool) and delicious breakfasts.

GOURNAY-EN-BRAY	76220
Paris 96 - Rouen 50 - Beauvais 30 - Gisors 25	Seine-Mar.

Les Trois Maillets
6, rue Barbacane
35 90 82 50, fax 35 09 99 77
Closed Sun lunch, Wed, Jan 10-30. Open until 9:30pm. Terrace dining. Pkg. V, AE, DC, MC.
Philippe Colignon, at the helm of this little bistrot, must have been thinking of other things the last time we dined there: many dishes on the menu were not available, and the 235 F duck menu featured bland foie gras, a tender and fairly savory duck breast with apples and cider, too-salty Neufchâtel cheese, and an original but not quite successful citrus cake. Fine wine list. Placid welcome and service. We prefer to hold back the two toques this place once earned and hope for better things in the future. **C** 220-350 F. **M** 130 F, 195 F, 235 F.

GOUVIEUX 60	→ Chantilly

GRADIGNAN 33	→ Bordeaux

GRAMAT	46500
Paris 524 - Figeac 35 - Cahors 57 - Brive 56	Lot

⌂13 Le Lion d'Or
8, pl. de la République
65 38 73 18, fax 65 38 84 50
Closed Dec 15-Jan 15. Open until 9:15pm. Terrace dining. Air cond. **Hotel:** *15 rms 270-440 F. Half-board 340-380 F. Conf. Pkg. V, AE, DC, MC.*
Spurred on by our criticism last year, René Momméjac has gotten back on track, producing once again the tasty traditional dishes that pleased us here in the past: crayfish fricassée, sole with cèpes, grain-fed squab casserole-roasted with sweet garlic, and a vegetable barigoule. His cooking is never heavy, nor are the prices of the set menus. Good local cabécou (goat cheese) and a choice of Cahors wines. Welcome that toque back! **C** 300-450 F. **M** 100 F (weekdays, Sat lunch), 230 F (Sun), 150 F, 190 F, 300 F

12/20 Le Relais des Gourmands 🎋
2, av. de la Gare
65 38 83 92, fax 65 38 70 99
Closed Sun dinner & Mon lunch (exc Jul-Aug). Open until 9pm. Terrace dining. Pool. Pkg. V, MC.
Traditional country dishes prepared with sincerity and skill. Marinated salmon salad, pork crépinette with cèpes, and salmon-stuffed puff pastry with leek cream sauce. You can be sure of a smiling welcome. Pleasant dining room; shady terrace. **C** 180-330 F. **M** 80 F, 220 F.

Le Relais des Gourmands

(See restaurant above)
Open year-round. 16 rms 270-450 F. Half-board
280-410 F. Air cond. Conf. Heated pool. V, MC.
An authentic Southwestern ambience reigns in
this hotel. Guest rooms are bright, pretty, and
well equipped. There's an attractive swimming
pool in the flower-filled garden.

■ In **Rignac 46500**   5 km NW on N 140

Château de Roumégouse ☻

65 33 63 81, fax 65 33 71 18
Closed Mon lunch (exc Jul-Aug), Oct 29-Apr 10.
Open until 9:30pm. Priv rm: 30. Garden dining.
Pool. Valet pkg. V, AE, DC, MC.
The predominantly English patrons favor Jean-
Louis Lainé's truffled scrambled eggs, foie gras,
confit, and veal kidney in Rocamadour juniper
berry sauce, but we prefer his seasonal menu
which highlights fresh herbs and garden
vegetables: a fine salad of summer truffles,
crayfish galette, and a superb rock of local lamb
with tarragon and white beans. C 300-400 F. M
180 F (lunch, coffee incl), 210 F, 320 F (dinner).

Château de Roumégouse ♣♥

(See restaurant above)
Closed Oct 29-Apr 10. 2 stes 1,100-1,350 F. 14 rms
450-960 F. Half-board 665-890 F. Conf. Pool. Valet
pkg. Helipad. V, AE, DC, MC.
The rooms all have a great deal of charm
(there's even one with a private garden), and
they are elegant, comfortable, and neat as can
be. Wonderful breakfasts. Also a boutique, video
library, and music room. Picnics can be arranged. Relais et Châteaux.

GRANDE-MOTTE (LA)   34280
Paris 747 - Nîmes 44 - Montpellier 20 - Palavas 15   Hérault

Alexandre

Esplanade de la Capitainerie
67 56 63 63, fax 67 29 74 69
Closed Sun dinner & Mon (exc Jul-Aug), Jan 8-Feb 11,
Oct 25-28. Open until 10pm. Priv rm: 40. Terrace
dining. Air cond. No pets. Pkg. V, AE, MC.
The good news is that the dining room with its
view of the sea is to be redecorated in a more
modern, elegant style. But Michel Alexandre's
cooking misfired on our last visit. The cassolette
of oysters in truffle butter had a floury sauce, the
millefeuille of turbot and veal sweetbreads was
bland and drowning in sauce, the fresh cod en
tapenade was agreeably rustic, and the desserts
very ordinary. Once again, we simply can't rank
cooking that's so uneven. The wine list makes
fascinating reading for those interested in discovering the Midi's delicious country wines.
C 350-500 F. M 190 F, 270 F, 360 F.

Hôtel Azur ♣♥

Presqu'île du Port
67 56 56 00, fax 67 29 81 26
Open year-round. 5 stes. 20 rms 395-680 F. Half-
board 395-680 F. Air cond. Pool. Golf. V, AE, DC,
MC.
Away from the madding crowd, but near the
quays, the boats, and the casino. The pretty
rooms (half were recently refurbished) look out
to sea.

Le Quetzal ♣♥

Allée des Jardins
67 56 61 10, fax 67 56 86 34
Open year-round. 52 rms 350-520 F. Restaurant.
Half-board 350-400 F. Air cond. Conf. Pool. Pkg. V,
AE, DC, MC.
The sweet little rooms with large loggias are a
sunbather's dream. The hotel is a modern construction set in a pine forest, though near the
center and port. Charming service.

GRAND-PRESSIGNY (LE)   37350
Paris 293 - Tours 58 - Loches 33 - Châtellerault 29   Indre/Loire

L'Espérance

Pl. du Carroir-des-Robins - 47 94 90 12
Closed Mon, Jan 6-Feb 6. Open until 9:30pm. Priv
rm: 45. Terrace dining. Air cond. Pkg. V, AE, DC.
Market-fresh ingredients and vegetables from
his own garden are the indispensable elements
of chef Bernard Torset's repertoire. He updates
dishes typical of Touraine with lightened sauces
and a vigorous, modern touch. Try his locally
produced foie gras, matelote (a stew) of local
eels, and Touraine squab with spices. The decor
is as rosy as life becomes after a few glasses of
tasty local wine from the well stocked cellar. The
friendly patronne gives excellent advice about
things to see and do in the area. C 280-320 F.
M 100 F (Sun), 150 F, 175 F, 195 F.

■ In **Le Petit-Pressigny 37350**   9 km E on D 103

La Promenade

47 94 93 52, fax 47 91 06 03
Closed Sun dinner, Mon, Jan 2-24, Sep 25-Oct 10.
Open until 9:30pm. Priv rm: 20. Air cond. V, MC.
Jacky Dallais produces generous, bold dishes
at extraordinarily reasonable prices; this is one
of the best quality-price ratios we know. On the
270 F menu, there's a bouillon of carrots, fava
beans, summer savory, and bacon; farm-raised
pork chop with baby cabbage; and a blood
sausage parmentier croustillant, followed by
cheeses and dessert. On the 350 F menu, you
can have the above choices plus fresh morels
sautéed with a poached quail's egg and green
asparagus, Breton lobster with a cauliflower
compote, turbot roasted with girolle mushrooms
and shallots, breast of demi-sel pork caramelized
in Chinon wine, goose liver sautéed with endives
and a lime bigarade, cheeses, and two desserts.
Whew! And the 120 F menu "du marché"
(determined by market offerings) is interesting,
too, and even offered in the evening except on
weekends. It's no wonder the place gets so
packed that sometimes the service and kitchen
can't keep up. C 330-385 F. M 120 F (weekdays, Sat lunch), 190 F, 270 F, 350 F.

GRANE   26400
Paris 598 - Valence 29 - Privas 28 - Montélimar 31   Drôme

Giffon

Pl. de l'Église
75 62 60 64, fax 75 62 70 11
Closed Mon (exc hols lunch), Sun dinner off-seas.
Open until 9:30pm. Terrace dining. Air cond. Pool.
Pkg. V, AE, DC, MC.

Giffon is a moss-covered village inn, a picture of tranquility with its terrace under the plane trees. The owners make every effort to make guests feel at home, and Patrick Giffon's sunny cuisine is seductive: exquisite little stuffed zucchini, snails, lamb tongue and sweetbreads in Rasteau wine, saddle of rabbit with a tapénade made from Nyons olives, tuna tartare with olive oil, médaillon of monkfish and shrimp in an oyster jus, grilled sea scallops in a licorice-scented cream, and picodons (goat cheese). **C** 250-350 F. **M** 130 F (weekdays, Sat lunch), 170 F, 230 F, 280 F, 380 F.

Giffon

(See restaurant above)

Closed Sun off-seas, Mon. 2 stes 750-950 F. 12 rms 220-600 F. Half-board 380-580 F. Air cond. Conf. Pool. Pkg. V, AE, DC, MC.

In spite of the many recent improvements—bigger rooms, suites with balconies, a pool—this hotel has managed to preserve its country auberge charm. So much the better!

GRANGES-LES-BEAUMONT 26

→ **Romans-sur-Isère**

GRANVILLE 50400

Paris 350 - Cherbourg 104 - Coutances 29   *Manche*

12/20 La Citadelle

In La Haute-Ville,
10, rue Cambernon - 33 50 34 10

Closed for lunch exc Sun (Jul-Aug), Sat lunch, Sun dinner, Mon, mid Jan-mid Feb, 10 days end Sep. Open until 9:30pm (10:30pm in seas). V, MC.

A venerable dwelling in the old part of town, with bare stone walls and a relaxed atmosphere, is the setting for classic, forthright cuisine. A typical meal here brings a vegetable and lobster tartare, salmon and sole in a curry-flavored cream sauce, and delicate tuile cookies with Calvados-spiked sabayon. **C** 230-330 F. **M** 90 F (exc Sat), 125 F, 140 F, 190 F, 240 F.

GRANZAY-GRIPT 79 → **Niort**

GRASSE 06130

Paris 938 - Nice 39 - Draguignan 56 - Cannes 17   *Alpes-Mar.*

Pierre Baltus

15, rue de la Fontette - 93 36 32 90

Closed Mon, Feb 14-Mar 9. Open until 10pm. Terrace dining. No cards.

The cozy dining room can hold only fourteen guests—the rest of the space is given over to a large bar and an upright piano. Fish and market offerings are the top-quality ingredients chosen by Pierre Baltus for his feuillantine of sole à la provençale, young Bresse chicken with morels, and a chocolate charlotte for dessert. Competent service. **C** 250-300 F. **M** 95 F, 120 F, 140 F.

11/20 Mas des Géraniums

Quartier San-Peyre, 06650 Opio, 7, route de Nice - 93 77 23 23

Closed Tue dinner, Wed, Oct 22-Nov 30. Open until 9pm. Terrace dining. Pkg. V, MC.

Make a beeline for the lovely, shaded terrace away from the hustle and bustle of the dining room. Nothing particularly memorable on the menu, but everything is prepared with care and offered at prices that are very reasonable for the region. Motherly service by the *patronne.* **C** 250-300 F. **M** 145 F, 180 F.

Panorama

2, pl. du Cours
93 36 80 80, fax 93 36 92 04

Open year-round. 36 rms 265-495 F. Air cond. Golf. V, AE, MC.

A well-appointed, agreeably modern hotel with soundproof rooms and smiling service.

Hôtel des Parfums

Bd E.-Charabot
93 36 10 10, fax 93 36 35 48

Open year-round. 11 stes 725-1,040 F. 60 rms 370-820 F. Rms for disabled. Restaurant. Half-board 420-580 F. Air cond. Conf. Pool. Golf. Pkg. V, AE, DC, MC.

This recently built hotel inspired by traditional Provençal designs, offers bright and cheerful rooms with terraces. Numerous amenities (Turkish bath, spa, gym, tanning salon...).

Hôtel du Patti

Pl. du Patti - 93 36 01 00, fax 93 36 36 40

Open year-round. 50 rms 330-420 F. Rms for disabled. Restaurant. Half-board 310-410 F. Air cond. Conf. Garage pkg. V, AE, DC, MC.

Marvelously situated in the heart of the old town, this hotel is exceptional in its category. The fetching rooms are most comfortable, with individual heating and superb bathrooms. Pleasing service and full breakfasts.

■ In Cabris 06530   5 km SW on D 4

12/20 Le Petit Prince

15, rue F.-Mistral
93 60 51 40, fax 93 60 55 47

Closed Thu, Mon dinner. Open until 10pm (by reserv). Terrace dining. V, AE, DC.

A nice place to stop in the hills behind Cannes. The host's warm welcome is the prelude to tasty, generously served dishes: try the egg galette with foie gras, chicken cutlet with parmesan, and small beef fillets with béarnaise sauce. Or any of the ten or so dishes featuring morels. **C** 200-300 F. **M** 98 F (weekdays), 128 F, 148 F, 188 F.

See also: **Mougins**

GRAU-DU-ROI (LE) 30240

Paris 755 - Nîmes 47 - Arles 53 - Aigues-Mortes 6   *Gard*

■ In Port-Camargue 30240   3 km S on D 62b

Hôtel du Cap

66 73 60 60, fax 66 73 60 50

Closed Nov 15-Feb 15. 60 rms 300-780 F. Restaurant. Half-board 300-545 F. Air cond. Conf. Heated pool. Tennis. Golf. Pkg. V, AE, DC, MC.

This prestigious beach resort boasts comfortable rooms with large terraces where sun-worshippers can cultivate a tan while watching the tide roll in. The hotel is part of a huge residential complex complete with sporting and leisure facilities, as well a sea-water spa.

Relais de l'Oustau Camarguen

3, route des Marines, to Plage sud
66 51 51 65, fax 66 53 06 65
Closed Jan-Mar, Oct 15-Dec. 1 ste 600-850 F. 38 rms 380-495 F. Rms for disabled. Restaurant. Half-board 375-440 F. Air cond. Conf. Heated pool. Golf. Pkg. V, AE, DC, MC.
Set on the edge of the marinas, the comfortable rooms of this authentic Camargue *mas* are all well appointed and give out onto the garden and swimming pool. Fitness center.

Le Spinnaker

Route du Môle
66 53 36 37, fax 66 53 17 47
Closed Sep-beg Apr. Open until 10pm. Garden dining. Air cond. Pool. Pkg. V, MC.
This is an airy, sun-kissed site in the Camargue, where Jean-Pierre Casals presents, with seemingly effortless flair, a vibrant, technically expert cuisine full of *joie de vivre* and bright Southern flavors. On the fine 245 F menu, you'll find voluptuous creamed lentils with Parma ham, a very successful charlotte of Mediterranean tuna marinated à la dijonnaise, rather bland fillets of monkfish roasted in sweet almond oil and served with a delicious fennel purée, and an assortment of rather antiquated desserts. Fine wine list. Maguy Casals's welcome is warm and elegant, and the service is impeccable. **C** 320-420 F. **M** 245 F, 385 F.

Le Spinnaker

(See restaurant above)
Open year-round. 21 rms 430-680 F. Half-board 410-630 F. Conf. Pool. Golf. Pkg. V.
Perfect peace and quiet—the only sounds are the waves and the wind. All the attractive rooms have nice sunny terraces. Great breakfasts.

Paris 342 - Besançon 45 - Dijon 48 - Langres 54   *Haute-Saône*

Château de Nantilly

4 km W on D 2, in Nantilly
84 67 78 00, fax 84 67 78 01
Open daily until 10pm. V, AE, DC, MC.
After many financial ups and downs, this pretty house surrounded by a verdant park seems to have found new life as a prestige stop along the route to southern France. The adroit new chef offers marinated tuna, rather mediocre brill, and delicious veal with vegetables; limited wine list. **C** 300-400 F. **M** 190 F (weekdays), 240 F, 350 F, 420 F.

Château de Nantilly

(See restaurant above)
Open year-round. 3 stes 1,300-1,600 F. 38 rms 700-800 F. Rms for disabled. Half-board 920-1,245 F. Conf. Heated pool. Tennis. Valet pkg. Helipad. V, AE, DC, MC.
A former hunting pavilion set in a huge wooded park complete with a babbling brook. The rooms are comfortable, and each is decorated in an individual style. Some attractive pieces of period furniture help create a cozy atmosphere, and the prevailing peace and quiet make this an ideal address for a weekend break or a low-key business conference.

Château de Rigny

5 km NE on D 2
84 65 25 01, fax 84 65 44 45
Closed Jan 7-31. 24 rms 320-620 F. Restaurant. Half-board 400-550 F. Conf. Heated pool. Tennis. Pkg. Helipad. V, AE, DC, MC.
Here's a gracious château with a lot of atmosphere and character, set in quiet, wooded grounds. Huge rooms and bountiful breakfasts.

11/20 Le Crato

65, Grande-Rue
84 65 11 75, fax 84 64 83 50
Closed Wed lunch in Aug. Open until 9pm. V, MC.
This warm, family-run restaurant filled with regulars who know a good deal when they see one. Try the perfectly honorable (although certainly not exciting) chicken fillet in juniper berry cream sauce, or the andouille brochette with Emmenthal. **M** 85 F, 100 F, 120 F, 145 F.

Paris 720 - Aire-sur-l'Adour 18 - Mont-de-Marsan 15   *Landes*

Hôtel de France

Place des Tilleuls
58 45 19 02, fax 58 45 11 48
Closed Sun dinner & Mon (exc Jul-Aug), Jan 2-18. Open until 9:30pm. Terrace dining. Pkg. V, MC.
A pleasant country dining room is the setting for Jean-Jacques Bernardet's generous, full-flavored cooking. We suggest you savor his cassolette of tiny snails au Colombelle, warm sautéed foie gras with tart apples, and bacon-wrapped wood pigeon. Jovial, professional welcome and service in a resolutely rustic decor. **C** 200-300 F. **M** 70 F (Sat dinner, Sun), 105 F, 160 F, 235 F.

Pain, Adour et Fantaisie

7, pl. des Tilleuls
58 45 18 80, fax 58 45 16 57
Closed Sun dinner & Mon (exc Mon lunch in Jul-Aug). Open until 10:30pm. Priv rm: 30. Terrace dining. Valet Pkg. V, AE, DC, MC.
If Didier Oudill came back to visit his former domaine, he might ask himself why he ever left this charming old house with views of the village arcades on one side and of the green Ardour river on the other. The refined rusticity of the dining room reminds us of superchef Michel Guérard, Oudill's mentor. As for the cooking, Philippe Garret is producing dishes as good as Oudill's were in his early days, before he indulged in more complicated recipes and raised his prices. Not that a meal here is cheap, but the 175 F menu is of such high quality and consistency that we are tempted to award Garret a third toque, if we didn't think it was more prudent to wait a bit. In the meantime, we urge you to sample his perfectly harmonious fondant of house-smoked salmon with an asparagus mousseline and leek jus flavored with coriander seeds, his miraculous grilled turbot in sesame cream with braised fennel and cabbage, his not-quite-as-successful veal sweetbreads sautéed with crisp miques (strips of grilled macaroni), and his luscious warm pear with cherries and an intensely dark, rich chocolate sauce. Grenade came off well in the change of chefs, as you will see. The cellar is rich in wines of the Southwest (though prices are high), the welcome is warm,

271

but the service needs shaping up. **C** 300-500 F.
M 175 F, 400 F.

Pain, Adour et Fantaisie

(See restaurant above)
See restaurant for closings. 1 ste 1,200 F. 9 rms 380-700 F. Air cond. Conf. Golf. Pkg. V, AE, DC, MC.
A handful of guest rooms cleverly fitted into the corners and nooks of two attached houses by the riverside. Modern amenities; decoration that occasionally falls into the coy (viz. the "Egyptian" suite); thoughtfully composed breakfasts.

GRENOBLE	38000
Paris 562 - Lyon 104 - Chambéry 57 - Bourg 142	Isère

Les Alpes

45, av. F.-Viallet
76 87 00 71, fax 76 56 95 45
Open year-round. 67 rms 220-280 F. Rms for disabled. Pkg. V, MC.
Between the railway station and the Isère River, this is one of Grenoble's best two-star establishments.

Alpotel-Mercure

12, bd du Mal-Joffre
76 87 88 41, fax 76 47 58 52
Open year-round. 88 rms 445 F. Rms for disabled. Restaurant. Air cond. Conf. Golf. Pkg. V, AE, DC, MC.
All the advantages of a large international hotel right in the city center. Public rooms; bar.

Angleterre

5, pl. V.-Hugo
76 87 37 21, fax 76 50 94 10
Open year-round. 4 stes 660 F. 66 rms 390-550 F. Air cond. V, AE, DC, MC.
A modern, regularly renovated hotel admirably situated on the edge of Grenoble's largest square (a park), looking out over the Vercors Massif.

12/20 Auberge Napoléon

7, rue Montorge, near parking Philippeville
76 87 53 64
Closed Mon lunch, Sun, May 21-27, Jul 23-Aug 15. Open until 10pm. Air cond. V, AE, DC, MC.
A young Breton chef prepares the house repertoire of culinary classics with a regional accent: sea bream fillet in flavorful oils, Bresse chicken stuffed with morels and foie gras, fillet of Angus beef, and a delicate warm apple tart. Wine buffs will glory in the cellar's offerings. Friendly welcome, attentive service. **C** 250-445 F. **M** 120 F, 178 F, 259 F.

Le Berlioz

4, rue de Strasbourg
76 56 22 39
Closed Sat lunch, Sun, Aug. Open until 10pm. Priv rm: 45. V, AE, DC, MC.
Marc Duriavig's new menu lacks the regional character it once had, except on the 120 F menu, where you'll find mussels in saffron sauce and a cinnamon-scented duck breast. There is now a truffle and foie gras menu. The toque remains, but we wonder whether the new owners of this city-center restaurant will allow the chef to express himself as well as he has done in the past. **C** 250-450 F. **M** 120 F, 160 F, 200 F, 265 F.

Le Grand Hôtel

5, rue de la République
76 44 49 36, fax 76 63 14 06
Open year-round. 6 stes 540-600 F. 66 rms 330-450 F. Air cond. Conf. Golf. V, AE, DC, MC.
A venerable establishment in the city center. A fast-food outlet that opened on the ground floor has cost the hotel considerable prestige. The comfortable rooms are well appointed, and there's a small inner courtyard.

A Ma Table

92, cours J.-Jaurès - 76 96 77 04
Closed Sat lunch, Sun, Mon, Aug. Open until 9:15pm. Priv rm: 12. Pkg. V, MC.
The dining room is so cozy and peaceful it resembles a private home. The cuisine is crafted with loving care by Michel Martin, who works alone in the kitchen (which explains the occasional delays): try the Landes-style salad with house foie gras, fillet of sea bass with herbs, and chicken sausage with ravioli. It's all based on fresh ingredients, carefully prepared. Attentive service. **C** 230-330 F.

Park Hotel

10, pl. P.-Mistral
76 87 29 11, fax 76 46 49 88
Closed Jul 29-Aug 20, Dec 23-Jan 1. 10 stes 1,195-1,695 F. 50 rms 595-995 F. Restaurant. Air cond. Conf. Golf. Valet pkg. V, AE, DC, MC.
Grenoble's top hotel, with highly trained staff and comfortable rooms. Conference facilities and fitness center. Private rooms for business lunches.

Patrick Hôtel

116, cours de la Libération
76 21 26 63, fax 76 48 01 07
Open year-round. 4 stes 595-680 F. 55 rms 223-410 F. Restaurant. Conf. Garage pkg. V, AE, DC, MC.
A modern hotel in which all rooms have bathrooms en suite, satellite television and video, radio-alarms and direct phone lines. Light meals in the rooms round the clock.

Hôtel Président

11, rue du Général-Mangin
76 56 26 56, fax 76 56 26 82
Open year-round. 3 stes 780-900 F. 102 rms 435-600 F. Rms for disabled. Restaurant. Air cond. Conf. Heated pool. Pkg. V, AE, DC, MC.
A modern hotel with well equipped rooms; elegant 1930s style decor. Carefully prepared breakfasts, quiet rooms, professional welcome and service, and a rather austere atmosphere.

Hôtel Rive Droite

20, quai de France
76 87 61 11, fax 76 87 04 04
Closed Christmas-Jan 1. 2 stes 390-500 F. 56 rms 290-360 F. Restaurant. Half-board 355-415 F. Conf. Pkg. V, AE, DC.
This is a large, wood-shuttered house on the quay near the town center. Simple, cozy decor and small but comfortable rooms.

Terminus

10, pl. de la Gare
76 87 24 33, fax 76 50 38 28
Open year-round. 30 rms 250-450 F. No pets. V, AE, DC, MC.
The hotel faces the railway station and is well kept and quiet. Up-to-date facilities.

And also...

Our selection of places for inexpensive, quick, or late-night meals.

L'As de Pique (76 87 32 91 - 14, rue du Lt-Chanaron. Open until 11pm.): Dishes for slimmers, Provençal main dishes, and good little wines. Fashionable (120-140 F).

Bistrot Lyonnais (76 21 95 33 - 168, cours Berriat. Open until 11pm.): Generous and savory fare like frog's legs in a boudin sausage and various dishes based on tripe (entrails) (110-130 F).

Le Brûleur de Loups (76 51 82 18 - 4, rue A.-Chevalier. Open until 10pm.): A good old-fashioned bistro in the historic district (200 F).

La Clairefontaine (76 87 95 30 - 4, rue Beccaria. Open until 10pm.): A friendly bistrot in a dining room with a vaulted ceiling, whose young owners offer market-fresh products with a focus on fish (78-165 F).

Le Couscous (76 47 92 93 - 19, rue de la Poste. Open until midnight.): Your best bet for couscous (70-110 F).

La Différence (76 47 32 56 - 7, rue Génissieu. Open until 10:15pm.): Good cooking at reasonable prices (warm monkfish salad with spinach, John Dory with pink peppercorns) and a wine list that's getting better (181-311 F).

La Girole (76 43 09 70 - 15, rue du Dr-Mazet. Open until 10pm.): Tasty cuisine based on market offerings; try the mushroom dishes (180-300 F).

La Hotte du Père Joël (76 42 04 00 - 8 bis, rue du Vieux-Temple. Open until 10:15pm.): In the historic district near the cathedral, old-fashioned French cooking like stuffed chicken and chicken with morels (100 F).

Le Jardin de Margaux (76 54 83 34 - 10, rue du Pont-Carpin. Open until 10pm.): Excellent quality-price ratio, and fine desserts (150 F).

Le Malassis (76 54 75 93 - 9, rue Bayard. Open until 9:30pm.): One of the oldest restaurants in the historic Notre-Dame district offers fine bourgeois cooking served around a roaring fireplace in winter (150 F).

Les Mouettes (76 50 95 13 - 13, quai C.-Bernard. Open until 9:30pm.): The menu changes almost daily to fit market offerings; fine wine list at reasonable prices (190-300 F).

La Panse (76 54 09 54 - 7, rue de la Paix. Open until 10pm.): You enter by way of the kitchen and dine in a half-Rabelais, half-Brillat-Savarin dining room; friendly atmosphere (100-200 F).

Restaurant La Ripaille (76 87 29 11 - Park Hôtel, 10, pl. P.-Mistral. Open until midnight, 11pm w-e.): Chic brasserie open late; the cooking is mediocre and high-priced (300-400 F).

La Table d'Ernest (76 43 19 56 - 2, rue Doudart-de-Lagrée. Open until 10pm.): Fine cooking cooked to order; good wine list (85-180 F).

■ **In Bresson 38320**   7 km S on D 5 and D 264

Chavant
Rue de la Mairie
76 25 25 38, fax 76 62 06 55
Closed Sat lunch & Mon off-seas, Dec 24-31. Open until 9:30pm (10pm in seas). Terrace dining. Garage pkg. V, AE, DC, MC.
This long-established restaurant offers Jean-Pierre Chavant's tried-and-true dishes like an émincé of artichokes and lamb's tongue en gribiche, salmon with beef marrow, veal sweetbreads with morels, and crêpes Suzette. Pleasant welcome in the handsome, country-house dining room. There's a fine cellar, with a good collection of Armagnacs. C 400-500 F. M 175 F, 385 F.

Chavant
(See restaurant above)
Closed Dec 26-31. 7 rms 480-680 F. Air cond. Conf. Heated pool. Tennis. Golf. Pkg. V, AE, DC, MC.
Seven lovely rooms (some are quite luxurious) for breathing lungfuls of fresh mountain air. Charming countryside nearby.

■ **In Corenc 38700**   3 km

Les Trois Roses
32, av. du Grésivaudan
76 90 35 09, fax 76 90 71 72
Closed Dec 24-31. 1 ste 470-550 F. 50 rms 420-475 F. Air cond. Conf. Golf. Garage pkg. V, AE, DC.
A modern hotel set in spacious grounds not far from the city. Rooms are pristine, soberly decorated, and well fitted. A charming welcome from the owners.

■ **In Eybens 38320**   2 km S on D 5

La Commanderie
76 25 34 58, fax 76 24 07 31
Open year-round. 25 rms 375-630 F. Restaurant. Half-board 315-550 F. Conf. Pool. Golf. Pkg. V, AE, DC, MC.
Hundred-year-old trees stand like sentinels on the grounds of this vintage Dauphiné dwelling. Inside, you'll find pleasant rooms, all individually decorated—some are furnished with fine antiques.

■ **In Meylan 38240**   3 km NE on N 90

Alpha
34, av. de Verdun
76 90 63 09, fax 76 90 28 27
Open year-round. 86 rms 395-485 F. Restaurant. Half-board 425-450 F. Pool. Pkg. V, AE, DC, MC.
This is a recently built hotel on the road to Geneva. Some of the huge rooms have kitchenettes. Good facilities for groups.

■ **In Saint-Martin-le-Vinoux 38950**   2 km NW

Pique-Pierre

Jacques Douvier, 1, rue C.-Kilian
76 46 12 88, fax 76 46 43 90
Closed Sun dinner, Mon, Aug 1-21. Open until 10pm. Garden dining. Air cond. Pkg. V, AE, MC.
Winter or summer, this is where the Grenoblois come when they want great blasts of fresh mountain air and good traditional fare enlivened with chef Jacques Douvier's personal touches. He offers a feuillantine of asparagus and sea scallops with dried tomatoes, salad of suckling pig with pomegranate juice and walnut purée, and a saffron-scented dark chocolate gratin. In fine weather patrons make a beeline for the terrace; otherwise, it's indoors to be

served by an impeccable and smiling staff in a dining room resplendent with wood paneling, fine crystal and silverware. The cellar overflows with good growers' wines, many from the Côtes-du-Rhône. Radiant welcome. **C** 320-350 F. **M** 200 F (weekday lunch, wine incl), 130 F, 155 F, 230 F, 300 F.

■ **In Saint-Paul-de-Varces 38760**   17 km S

12/20 Auberge Messidor
76 72 80 64

Closed Sun dinner & Mon (exc hols). Open until 9:15pm. Priv rm: 18. Terrace dining. Pkg. V, MC.

This old village coaching inn has been in the Perret family for years. André Perret's good cooking has won a loyal following. Try the fresh salmon, fillet of bar (sea bass), médaillons of lobster à l'américaine, and veal sweetbreads with morels. **C** 250-350 F. **M** 127 F, 160 F (exc hols), 190 F, 260 F.

■ **In Le Sappey-en-Chartreuse 38700**   15 km N

Les Skieurs
76 88 80 15, fax 76 88 85 76

Closed Sun dinner & Mon (exc school hols), Apr, Nov-Dec 28. Open until 10pm. Priv rm: 40. Terrace dining. Pkg. V, MC.

This warm and cozy mountain chalet stands at the edge of the village, surrounded by woods. Christophe Jail, trained by Chapel and Verger, turns out traditional dishes prepared with care: leek flamiche, veal filets mignons with morels, and a chocolate-and-cherry dessert. Appealing regional cellar; efficient service. **C** 220-350 F. **M** 108 F (exc Sun), 160 F, 200 F, 250 F.

Les Skieurs
(See restaurant above)

Closed Sun, Mon, Apr, Nov-Dec 28. 18 rms 200-320 F. Half-board 285-330 F. Conf. Pool. Pkg. V, MC.

Pleasant, well-equipped rooms in a peaceful mountain atmosphere. Cordial welcome and good service.

■ **In Uriage 38410**   10 km SE on D 524

Les Terrasses d'Uriage
76 89 10 80, fax 76 89 04 62

Closed Sat lunch off-seas, Sun dinner, Mon, Jan. Open until 9:30pm. Garden dining. Heated pool. Valet pkg. V, AE, DC, MC.

No need to tamper with success. In the Grand Hôtel's restaurant, facing the new casino, Stéphane Cano, with the talented Philippe Bouissou in the kitchen and Martial James overseeing the cellar, have produced what is without a doubt the best restaurant in the Grenoble area. Sample the fresh duck foie gras cooked in wine with a purslane salad, breast of quail roasted in a rosemary "milk", and a fricassée of Bresse chicken with morels and sautéed raw artichokes. This is intelligent cuisine whose audaciousness is backed by solid understanding of how to balance flavors. Leave a little room for the marvelous Trièves cheeses and fine desserts, which include prune terrine, and a honey cake soufflé

with dark-beer sabayon. **C** 330-400 F. **M** 195 F, 180 F (weekday lunch, wine incl), 270 F, 350 F.

Le Grand Hôtel
(See restaurant above)

Closed Jan. 44 rms 385-530 F. Half-board 350-545 F. Heated pool. Tennis. Golf. Valet pkg. V, AE, DC, MC.

Spacious, comfortable accommodation, fine bathrooms, and excellent breakfasts draw patrons to this handsomely renovated Second Empire hotel. On the premises is a hydrotherapy institute, and a heated pool. Excellent quality-price ratio.

■ **In Voreppe 38340**   10 km N on A6

Novotel
76 50 55 55, fax 76 56 76 26

Open year-round. 114 rms 415-425 F. Rms for disabled. Restaurant. Half-board 320-350 F. Air cond. Conf. Pool. Pkg. V, AE, DC, MC.

A fantastic setting at the foot of the Vercors Massif and the Charterhouse. Very comfortable, renovated rooms.

12/20 La Petite Auberge
2.5 km, in Chevalon - 76 50 08 03

Closed Sun dinner, Mon, Jan 4-8, Aug 10-31. Priv rm: 15. Garden dining. Pkg. V, MC.

Stop by in the summer for an alfresco meal and you'd hardly know the sea wasn't just beyond the garden wall! The superlative shellfish and oysters come straight from Marennes, Riec-sur-Belon, and Audierne. Try the raw seafood platters, the salad of red mullet sautéed with vinegar, and a marmite du pêcheur. Good choice of white wines. **C** 300-450 F. **M** 130 F (lunch exc Sun), 160 F, 195 F, 250 F.

Paris 786 - Digne 62 - Aix-en-P. 50 - Manosque 15   Alpes/H.-P.

12/20 La Crémaillère
Route de Riez
92 74 22 29, fax 92 78 19 80

Closed Nov 28-Feb. Open until 9:30pm. Priv rm: 16. Garage pkg. V, AE, DC, MC.

Light floods this pleasant, tidy dining room where you are served cooking that has suffered by many changes of chefs. On the 230 F menu, bland gâteau of artichokes and lamb sweetbreads, bland lamb with garlic cream, and a tasty émincé of warm apples with cinnamon ice cream. The toque goes. Excellent welcome and efficient service. **M** 90 F, 140 F, 230 F.

La Crémaillère
(See restaurant above)

Closed Nov 28-Feb 25. 51 rms 330-370 F. Rms for disabled. Half-board 280-450 F. Conf. Tennis. Garage pkg. Helipad. V, AE, DC, MC.

Comfortable, spacious rooms open onto a patio; the whole place was recently renovated from top to bottom. Good bathrooms. Golf practice green.

Villa Borghèse
Avenue des Thermes
92 78 00 91, fax 92 78 09 55

Closed Dec-Mar 1. 1 ste 900-1,300 F. 69 rms 340-620 F. Restaurant. Half-board 400-500 F. Air cond. Conf. Heated pool. Tennis. Golf. Pkg. V, AE, DC, MC.

A fine modern hotel set against a backdrop of greenery, with tastefully decorated rooms. Special fitness packages are available, and guests may use the neighboring golf course free of charge. Annual spring bridge festival.

GRESSY 77410
Paris 30 - Roissy-Charles-de-Gaulle 9 - Disneyland Paris 25 *Seine/Marne*

Le Cellier du Manoir

Chemin des Carosses
60 26 68 00, fax 60 26 45 46
Open daily until 10pm. Priv rm: 100. Terrace dining. Air cond. Heated pool. Pkg. V, AE, DC, MC.
New and imposing, with a vast yet comfortable and sunny dining room, the Manoir offers Pascal Legrain's astutely prepared cooking: sea scallops à la provençale (very fresh but served in stingy portions), interesting petit-salé of squab with lentils, and a delicious, intensely flavored chocolate tart. Diversified cellar, warm welcome, and good service. **C** 240-350 F. **M** 140 F (weekdays, Sat lunch), 160 F.

Le Manoir de Gressy
(See restaurant above)
Open year-round. 5 stes 1,200 F. 85 rms 750-1,150 F. Air cond. Conf. Heated pool. Tennis. V, AE, DC, MC.
Le Manoir is constructed around a central courtyard on the site of the seventeenth-century manor house of Robert de Frémont. Individually furnished, the rooms abound with style and overlook an interior courtyard with a swimming pool. Choose the rooms on the ground floor, which all have terraces. Good facilities for groups.

GRIGNAN 26230
Paris 630 - Montélimar 28 - Nyons 23 - Valence 71 *Drôme*

12/20 L'Eau à la Bouche
Rue St-Louis - 75 46 57 37
Closed Mon, Jul-Aug. Open until 9pm (10pm in summer). Priv rm: 35. Garden dining. V, MC.
A country restaurant with lace- and flower-decked tables, run by a cheerful *patronne* who serves simple, lively cuisine. The 149 F set menu will get you a Saint-Marcellin cheese in a salad, a fillet of sea bream with smothered leeks, and a "grande-mère" flan. The tiny cellar is resolutely regional. **C** 200-290 F. **M** 99 F, 149 F.

Le Manoir de La Roseraie

Route de Valréas
75 46 58 15, fax 75 46 91 55
Open year-round. 1 ste 1,600 F. 14 rms 630-1,100 F. Restaurant. Half-board 595-805 F. Conf. Heated pool. Tennis. Golf. Pkg. Helipad. V, AE, DC, MC.
Standing at the foot of Grignan's château (where Madame de Sévigné penned her witty letters), this manor house provides guests with bright, gaily decorated rooms in the Provençal style. Lovely bathrooms.

GRIMALDI INFERIORE (Italy)
→ **Menton**

GRIMAUD 83310
Paris 857 - Hyères 45 - Saint-Tropez 10 *Var*

La Boulangerie
Route de Collobrières
94 43 23 16, fax 94 43 38 27
Closed Oct 10-Apr 10. 1 ste 790-1,390 F. 10 rms 580-790 F. Restaurant. Air cond. Conf. Pool. Tennis. Golf. Pkg. V, MC.
An attractive and cozy hotel with a capital view of the Massif des Maures. Video library. In fine weather, lunch is served to guests (many are return visitors) around the superb swimming pool.

10/20 Le Café de France
Pl. Neuve - 94 43 20 05
Closed Tue, Nov-Jan. Open until 10pm. Terrace dining. Pkg. V, MC.
A shaded terrace in a Provençal setting where you can sample uninspired but crowd-pleasing dishes like vegetable terrine, stuffed mussels, and steak with herbs. **C** 230-300 F. **M** 130 F.

Le Coteau Fleuri
Pl. des Pénitents
94 43 20 17, fax 94 43 33 42
Closed Tue (exc Jul-Aug), Nov 28-Dec 19, Jan 3-19. Open until 10pm. Terrace dining. No pets. Hotel: 14 rms 300-475 F. Pkg. V, AE, MC.
Flowers, flowers everywhere engulf this wonderful villa next to the Penitents' Chapel. From the terrace you'll discover a mind-blowing view of the Massif des Maures and the Provençal hill country. Chef Jean-Claude Paillard favors local produce and modernized regional dishes. We prefer the 190 F menu with, for example, baby vegetables with coriander, sea bream in an olive oil emulsion, faisselle (fresh white cheese), and dessert. **C** 350-400 F. **M** 165 F (lunch exc Sun, wine incl), 245 F (Sun lunch, wine incl), 190 F.

Les Santons

Route Nationale
94 43 21 02, fax 94 43 24 92
Closed Wed off-seas, Jan 4-Mar 15, Nov 2-Dec 20. Open until 9:30pm (10:30pm in summer). Priv rm: 40. Air cond. Pkg. V, AE, DC, MC.
Santons—those little painted terracotta Provençal figures which adorn the Christmas crèche—fill this Provençal dining room, the fief of gentle giant Claude Girard, who makes his own wine up north in Chinon. Here's a chef who goes in for classic cuisine with lots of Mediterranean flavor, characterized by fine products, rigorous technique, and delicate sauces. Try his scrambled eggs with truffles, pickerel in beurre blanc, bourride (garlicky fish soup), thyme-scented saddle of lamb, Bresse chicken sauce velours, or thigh of young rabbit stuffed with two kinds of olives. **C** 400-560 F. **M** 180 F (weekday lunch, Sat), 260 F, 410 F.

12/20 Le Verger
Route de Collobrières
94 43 25 93, fax 94 43 33 92
Closed Nov-Mar. Open until 11pm. Garden dining. Pool. Pkg. V, MC.
A charming place to eat, amid flowers and trees. The chef takes few risks, but he offers two good set menus and a classic "carte" containing

the likes of scrambled eggs with truffles, bourride, and lamb brochettes. C 200-300 F. M 100 F (lunch), 150 F.

See also: Port-Grimaud

GROIX (ILE DE) 56590
access via Lorient   *Morbihan*

12/20 Hôtel de la Marine
7, rue du Gal-de-Gaulle
97 86 80 05, fax 97 86 56 37
Closed Sun dinner off-seas, Mon, Jan. Open until 9pm. Terrace dining. Pkg. V, MC.
For a seafood "cure" that will set you right up (but won't set your finances on their ear), try the Huberts' simple, fresh, unassuming cuisine: cotriade (Breton fish soup), shellfish fricassée, bar (sea bass) with wild fennel, and curried fish with two sauces, all served on a pretty terrace in summer or around the fireplace in winter. C 150-250 F. M 68 F (exc Sun dinner), 125 F, 140 F.

GUA (LE) 17600
Paris 488 - Rochefort 26 - Royan 17 - Marennes 18 *Charente-M.*

L'Écluse
On D 733, in Châlons
46 22 82 72, fax 46 22 91 07
Closed Wed lunch, Tue, Sep 20-May 8. Open until 9:30pm (9:45pm in summer). Priv rm: 30. Terrace dining. Pkg. V, AE, DC, MC.
Modern art dots the walls of this pretty dining room which extends out into a shady garden. Linger over Claudine Dupin's bright, wide-awake cooking, marred by the occasional misstep (dry veal scallops, pasta served almost cold), but generally successful, especially when inspired by the briny deep: unctuous mussel soup with saffron, tender squid sautéed à la girondine, cockles and mussels in an olive oil vinaigrette wrapped in two slices of salmon, and a tasty tiramisu. Diversified cellar; cheerful welcome. C 300-400 F. M 145 F, 250 F, 370 F.

Moulin de Châlons
(See restaurant above)
Closed Tue, Sep 20-May 8. 14 rms 350-500 F. Half-board 420-490 F. Conf. Golf. Pkg. V, AE, DC, MC.
This lovely old mill has been restored in fine style. All the rooms are different and well appointed. Big bathrooms; nice views.

GUÉRANDE 44350
Paris 445 - Nantes 77 - La Baule 6 - Vannes 65   *Loire-Atl.*

La Collégiale
63, faubourg Bizienne - 40 24 97 29
Closed Wed lunch, Tue, Dec 20-25, Feb. Open until 11pm (midnight in summer). Priv rm: 25. Garden dining. Pkg. V, AE, DC, MC.
The veranda of this picturesque dwelling looks onto a dreamy garden. But don't let the view distract you from the new chef's 250 F menu: salad of crabmeat and artichoke bottoms, émincé of chicken au saté and zucchini spaghetti, breaded and roasted Camembert with salad, and a buttery tart shell filled with tangerines and warm chocolate. M 130 F, 180 F (exc Jul & Aug), 250 F, 400 F, 450 F.

Manoir Le Cardinal
2.5 km N, near Miroux - 40 24 72 56
Closed Sun dinner & Mon (exc Jul-Aug), end Sep-Easter. Open until 11pm. Garden dining. Pkg. DC.
Massive beams, a beautiful fireplace, and meadow flowers make up the charm of this inviting dining room, housed in a fourteenth-century Breton manor. The *patronne's* cooking is based on seasonal, scrupulously chosen ingredients: chicken liver terrine with onion confiture, duck breast cooked in cider, and a buttery gâteau nantais. C 220-260 F. M 100 F (weekday lunch), 150 F.

Les Remparts
15, bd du Nord - 40 24 90 69
Open year-round. 8 rms 240-280 F. Restaurant. Half-board 280-290 F. V, MC.
A typical little provincial inn with attractive, regularly refurbished rooms.

GUÉRINIÈRE (LA) 85
→ Noirmoutier (Ile de)

GUIDEL 56520
Paris 508 - Lorient 12 - Quimperlé 12 - Concarneau 39 *Morbihan*

Manoir de la Châtaigneraie
Route du Clohars-Carnoët
97 65 99 93, fax 97 21 20 66
Open year-round. 10 rms 500-650 F. Restaurant. Half-board 850 F. Conf. Valet pkg. V, AE, MC.
A fifteen-minute drive from the Lorient airport and three kilometers from the beaches, here is an engaging stone manor house with well-equipped rooms and family-style service. Evening meals are available, but must be ordered a day in advance.

GUINGAMP 22200
Paris 479 - Saint-Brieuc 32 - Brest 114 - Lannion 32 *Côtes/Armor*

Le Relais du Roy
42, pl. du Centre
96 43 76 62, fax 96 44 08 01
Closed Sun off-seas, at Christmas school hols. Open until 9:30pm. Priv rm: 30. No pets. Pkg. V, AE, DC, MC.
The grand, beamed dining room of this venerable mansion is the most select address in town. The experienced chef is a dab hand with fresh seafood and other fine products: taste his warm crab terrine, fillet of Argoat trout with creamy leeks, and veal sweetbreads with foie gras. Well chosen though small wine list. Cordial, professional service. C 250-500 F. M 130 F, 170 F, 195 F (exc Sun).

Le Relais du Roy
(See restaurant above)
See restaurant for closings. 7 rms 450-800 F. Half-board 500 F. Conf. Pkg. V, AE, DC, MC.
Fully renovated this year, this ravishing Renaissance town house provides lovely rooms.

HAGENTHAL 68   → Saint-Louis

HARDELOT-PLAGE   62152
Paris 235 - Arras 110 - Boulogne 15 - Le Touquet 23   *P./Calais*

12/20 L'Orangerie
Av. François-Ier
21 33 22 11, fax 21 83 29 71
Closed Dec 17-Jan. Open until 10:30pm. Priv rm: 180. Garden dining. Air cond. Heated pool. Garage pkg. V, AE, DC, MC.
Light floods in through the windows of this restaurant on the dunes, where the unpretentious cuisine is inspired mostly by the sea. Try the sardine parmentier, sirloin steak pan-fried with shallot confit, and an apple croustillant. **C** 200-330 F. **M** 130 F.

 Hôtel du Parc   ▲✿
(See restaurant above)
Closed Dec 17-Jan. 1 ste 1,000-1,200 F. 80 rms 405-610 F. Rms for disabled. Half-board 405-635 F. Conf. Heated pool. Tennis. Golf. Pkg. V, AE, DC, MC.
Here in the quiet of the dunes and the pines you'll find spacious, gaily decorated rooms that are comfortable and immaculately kept. Attentive service is a hallmark of this fine hotel. Horseback riding facilities nearby.

HAVRE (LE)   76600
Paris 204 - Amiens 179 - Rouen 86   *Seine-Mar.*

 Astoria
13, cours de la République
35 25 00 03, fax 35 26 48 34
Open year-round. 37 rms 150-330 F. Restaurant. Half-board 160-380 F. Golf. Valet pkg. Helipad. V, AE, DC, MC.
Here's a handy hotel with well-equipped rooms opposite the railway station. A smiling and amiable welcome awaits.

Bordeaux
147, rue L.-Brindeau
35 22 69 44, fax 35 42 09 27
Open year-round. 31 rms 370-500 F. Golf. V, AE, DC, MC.
Right in the center of town, facing the winter yacht basin, this hotel offers modern, comfortable, freshly refurbished rooms.

Hôtel Foch   ▲✿
4, rue de Caligny
35 42 50 69, fax 35 43 40 17
Open year-round. 33 rms 285-315 F. Restaurant. Conf. Golf. Pkg. V, AE, DC, MC.
A quiet, centrally located hotel in the shadow of the belfry of Saint-Joseph church and just 300 meters from the marina. All the rooms have been entirely redecorated and are very comfortable.

Le Marly
121, rue de Paris
35 41 72 48, fax 35 21 50 45
Open year-round. 37 rms 265-430 F. V, AE, DC, MC.
A convenient, functional hotel near the car-ferry embarkation point.

11/20 Palissandre
33, rue de Bretagne - 35 21 69 00
Closed Sun, Wed dinner, Sat lunch, 1 wk in Feb, 2 wks in Aug. Open until 9:30pm. V, MC.
Dark wood paneling in the dining room; bright, unpretentious fare from the kitchen: marinade

of salmon flavored with dill, monkfish roasted with green peppers, calf's head with gribiche sauce, and the house crème caramel. **C** 160-220 F. **M** 155 F (wine incl), 78 F, 89 F, 125 F.

 La Petite Auberge
32, rue de Ste-Adresse - 35 46 27 32
Closed Sun dinner, Mon, 1 wk at Feb school hols, Aug 1-21. Open until 9:30pm. Priv rm: 22. Air cond. V, AE, MC.
Lunchtime brings a crowd of regulars who appreciate the appealing set meals that feature Lionel Douillet's classic cooking. Classic, yes, but with a personal touch that takes it out of the ordinary: roast asparagus with diced veal sweetbreads, salmon tartare with bacon cream sauce, and a strawberry feuillantine. The first set menu is generous. Bordeaux dominates the cellar. **C** 280-340 F. **M** 110 F (weekdays), 128 F (Sat, Sun), 150 F, 200 F.

12/20 Le Trois-Mâts
Chaussée d'Angoulême - 35 19 50 50
Open daily until 10:30pm. Priv rm: 200. Terrace dining. Air cond. Pkg. V, AE, DC, MC.
A small open-air terrace protected by glass affords a magnificent view of the port. The welcome is wonderful, the decor nicely refreshed, and the cuisine copious and good: salmon marinated with a touch of dill, sole paupiettes with orange sauce, anise-scented grilled veal chop, and oeufs en neige with crème anglaise. Short, unselective wine list. **C** 200-300 F. **M** 89 F, 91 F, 99 F, 125 F.

Mercure
(See restaurant above)
Open year-round. 96 rms 515-695 F. Half-board 285-310 F. Conf. Pkg. V, AE, DC, MC.
Architecturally light-hearted when compared to the austerity of Auguste Perret's Le Havre (he redesigned it after the war), the hotel has a superb view of the Commerce docks. Rooms have been redone and are large and pleasant (but the windows are small and soundproofing inadequate). Service is simple and breakfasts are satisfying. Renovated facilities for groups.

And also...
Our selection of places for inexpensive, quick, or late-night meals.
Le Bistrot des Halles (35 22 50 52 - 7, pl. des Halles-Centrales.): A charming Lyonnais "bouchon" with beef marrow on toast, quick-cooked cod, Camembert in pastry, and chocolate tart (160 F).
Le Grignot (35 43 62 07 - 53, rue Racine.): A picturesque, lively bistrot with plats du jour, crêpes, and an enormous apple cake (150 F).
Le Petit Bouchon (35 22 80 85 - 44, rue Louis-Philippe.): Fresh products, excellent meats, generous servings, and charming service (160 F).
La Petite Brocante (35 21 42 20 - 75, rue L.-Brindeau.): Homestyle cooking is offered in this little brasserie (pot-au-feu, boeuf bordelaise, fine desserts).
Taverne de Maître Kanter (35 41 31 50 - 22, rue G.-Braque. Open until midnight.): Also known as "Chez Paillette", this is an amusing brasserie serving fresh shellfish and good Alsatian wines (230 F).

In Le Hode 76430
18 km E on D 982

Dubuc
14
On D 982, in Saint-Vigor-d'Ymonville
35 20 06 97
Closed Sun dinner, Mon, Feb 14-28, Aug 8-22. Open until 9pm. Priv rm: 16. Pkg. V, AE, DC, MC.
This restaurant's unpreposessing exterior hides a charming, flower-filled dining room with a wood-paneled fireplace. On our last visit, chef Joël Blondel's *carte* revealed intensely flavored classic cooking with a personal touch: fricassée of snails with wild mushrooms, lemony veal grenadin, and nougat glacé with a currant coulis. Speedy, friendly service. **C** 330-400 F. **M** 200 F (wine incl), 145 F, 325 F.

In Sainte-Adresse 76310
1 km NW

Le Nice Havrais
6, pl. F.-Sauvage
35 46 14 59, fax 35 54 28 52
Closings not available. Open until 11:30pm. Priv rm: 50. V, AE, DC, MC.
A new team has just taken charge of this turn-of-the-century restaurant with a spectacular view of the Seine estuary and the coast. The new menu is strictly traditional: foie gras, sole meunière with fresh pasta, steak au poivre, sherbets. We will rate all this later after they have had a chance to settle in. **M** 125 F, 189 F.

Yves Page
13
7, pl. Clemenceau
35 46 06 09, fax 35 46 85 38
Closed Sun dinner, Mon. Open until 10pm. Priv rm: 15. Terrace dining. V, AE, MC.
The Seine flows into the sea beneath the broad bay windows of Yves Page's comfortable restaurant; opt for the terrace rather than the unexciting dining room. The chef's classic, well prepared cuisine is on display in the 155 F menu: langoustine terrine, scorpion fish fillet and slivered endive, Normandy cheeses, marquise au chocolat, and pears with crème anglaise. **C** 230-310 F. **M** 98 F (exc Sun), 155 F, 248 F.

HENDAYE	64700
Paris 777 - Biarritz 28 - St-Jean-de-Luz 13	Pyrénées-A.

Enbata
14
76, av. des Mimosas
59 48 88 88, fax 59 48 88 89
Open daily until 9:30pm (10pm in summer). Terrace dining. Air cond. Heated pool. Valet pkg. V, AE, DC, MC.
The superb panorama of the ancient village of Fuenterrabia adds to the charm of this modern blue-and-white building with a poolside terrace. The young chef, Scott Serrato, treats regional ingredients judiciously: harmonious and perfectly cooked cassolette of sea scallops with truffles, an assortment of pork "à la tue-cochon du Pays basque" (Basque pig-killing time) that is a triumph of simplicity, and a light-as-air warm chocolate and orange feuillantine with subtle flavors. The cellar is at the very early stages. The welcome and service are as friendly as the prices. **C** 230-250 F. **M** 150 F, 190 F, 250 F.

Ibaïa

(See restaurant above)
Open year-round. 1 ste 1,000-1,500 F. 420 rms 420-795 F. Rms for disabled. Half-board 650-965 F. Air cond. Conf. Heated pool. Golf. Pkg. V, AE, DC, MC.
A modern hotel near the new yacht port offering comfortable rooms with cheery pastel decor and lovely bathrooms, all with vast balconies where you can have breakfast while gazing at the idyllic scenery.

Thalasso Serge Blanco
15
125, bd de la Mer - 59 51 35 00 (R), 59 51 35 35 (H), fax 59 51 36 00
Closed 1 wk in Dec. Open until 10pm. Garden dining. Air cond. Pool. Garage pkg. V, AE, MC.
Picture this: a spacious pink-and-blue dining room that opens onto a terrace, a pool, the Bidassoa estuary, and, in the distance, green mountains. In this idyllic setting, two young chefs, Jean-François Sicallac and Antoine Antunès, serve forth fresh and inventive dishes like txanguro of sea crab with artichokes and mussels in a coriander nage in a happy combination of Basque and Oriental flavors. The macaroni with squid ink and lobster is marvelously subtle, and the berry millefeuille is a winner. Guy Landart oversees the fine service and excellent wine list in a rather too-sober dining room decorated with bullfight posters and with a splendid view of the coast. **C** 300-350 F. **M** 180 F, 250 F.

Thalasso Serge Blanco
(See restaurant above)
Closed 1 wk in Dec. 11 stes 1,720 F. 79 rms 430-760 F. Rms for disabled. Half-board 650-970 F. Conf. Pool. Golf. Garage pkg. V, AE, MC.
You'll find roomy, elegant, well-equipped rooms with balconies (but no air conditioning) in this thalassotherapy (sea-water cure) institute run by rugby star Serge Blanco. Competitive prices, spacious, bright facilities including an outstanding swimming pool. The fitness equipment is modern and complete.

In Biriatou 64700
4 km SE on D 258

Bakéa
14
59 20 76 36, fax 59 20 58 21
Closed Mar 5-16. Open until 9:30pm (10:30pm in summer). Terrace dining. Pkg. V, DC, MC.
The Duvals, Éric and Corine, are the proud owners of this comfortable chalet, which boasts a terrace overlooking the valley. Many elegant Spaniards cross the border to dine here on fine traditional cooking prepared with utmost professionalism and a few touches of fantasy: sea scallops roasted with crispy shallots, veal sweetbreads braised with green asparagus, buttery pastries filled with berries. Friendly welcome and competent service. The cellar holds an interesting collection of vintage Bordeaux. **C** 260-450 F. **M** 160 F, 210 F.

HENNEBONT 56700
Paris 482 - Vannes 56 - Concarneau 55 - Lorient 10 *Morbihan*

Château de Locguénolé
5 km S on D 781, route de Port-Louis
97 76 29 04, fax 97 76 39 47
Closed Mon lunch off-seas, Jan 2-Feb 9. Open until 9:30pm. Priv rm: 230. Garden dining. Heated pool. No pets. Pkg. V, AE, DC, MC.
Without a doubt, three toques sit nicely atop this beautiful château, truly the most enticing establishment in South Brittany! Owner Alyette de la Sablière has luckily acquired a young but very experienced chef, Denis Gros, who won us over again this year with his virtuoso technique and the finesse and touches of fantasy in his cooking. He is one of his early 30s but has a list of credentials as long as your arm (he trained with Bocuse, Robuchon, Guérard, Girardet, then went on to win three toques at Les Templiers). Savor his luscious consommé of pheasant hen with pearl barley, foie gras and red cabbage cooked in beer, oysters from Quiberon that he smokes over seaweed himself, or an exquisite crab charlotte with a jus flavored with crab coral. Or the marvelous langoustine and fruit curry, veal chops with meltingly tender endives, and the perfect marriage of flavors in the lamb rognonnade with coriander. The desserts follow suit: superb date, walnut, and cinnamon fritters; a chocolate dessert with a hint of bergamot; and incredible tangerine "horns" with gentian sherbet. We award all this a well deserved extra point, and long to savor these gastronomic marvels once again in the château's lordly granite-paved, vanilla-and-blue dining room.
C 380-500 F. **M** 190 F, 280 F, 440 F, 480 F, 580 F.

Château de Locguénolé 🌲🎾
(See restaurant above)
Closed Jan 2-Feb 9. 4 stes 1,200-2,100 F. 18 rms 490-1,470 F. Rms for disabled. Half-board 670-1,500 F. Conf. Heated pool. Tennis. Golf. Pkg. Helipad. V, AE, DC, MC.
In this admirable 250-acre domain made for endless strolls, Alyette de La Sablière has patiently created an exceptional hotel complex. A ravishing Renaissance pavilion contains conference rooms, next door to the new relaxation center with large bay windows that frame a view of the open-air swimming pool and bucolic landscapes. The large nineteenth-century residence stands atop a grassy knoll; within are stately drawing rooms, suites, and rooms furnished with antiques as well as with all modern conveniences. A warm welcome from the sea-loving chatelain, Bruno de la Sablière. Relais et Châteaux.

HERBAUDIÈRE (L') 85
→ **Noirmoutier (Ile de)**

HÉROUVILLE-ST-CLAIR 14 → **Caen**

Plan to travel? *Look for Gault Millau's other Best of guides to Chicago, Florida, Hawaii, Hong Kong, Germany, Italy, London, Los Angeles, New England, New Orleans, New York, Paris, San Francisco, Thailand, Toronto, and Washington, D.C.*

HEYRIEUX 38540
Paris 487 - Lyon 24 - Vienne 24 - Bourgoin-Jallieu 20 *Isère*

L'Alouette
3 km SE on D 518, at L'Alouette
78 40 06 08, fax 78 40 54 74
Closed Sun dinner, Mon, Aug 15-Sep 6. Open until 9:30pm. Priv rm: 20. Terrace dining. Air cond. Pkg. V, AE, MC.
The old country bistrot where Jean-Claude Marlhins settled a few years ago is now a spiffy little restaurant, and the fact that the à la carte prices have gotten a little gentler just adds to the charm. Try the asparagus sandwiched in blinis with shellfish sauce, herby lamb in a salt crust with Niçois vegetables, and a strawberry terrine with almond cream and three sauces. Fine and costly wine list; friendly welcome. **C** 250-450 F. **M** 125 F, 155 F (weekday lunch), 180 F, 230 F, 270 F.

HODE (LE) 76 → **Havre (Le)**

HONFLEUR 14600
Paris 192 - Le Havre 57 - Caen 60 - Lisieux 34 *Calvados*

L'Assiette Gourmande
2, quai des Passagers - 31 89 24 88
Closed Mon dinner & Tue (exc Jul-Aug), Jan 23-Feb 6. Open until 10pm. Air cond. V, AE, DC.
Chef Gérard Bonnefoy's restaurant could easily fall into the jaws of this quaint tourist trap. Yet he always manages an elegant sidestep. Classically trained, his are textbook examples of what French sauces should be. And this family-run restaurant with an elegant decor brims over with warmth and charm. Bonnefoy has some interesting—and unorthodox—ideas, always brought to fruition with consummate skill: tiny crab boudins with sweet spices, warm oyster flan with lime-enhanced endives, roast turbot in a tart chicken jus, and casserole-roasted veal sweetbreads. Small wine list with several half bottles. The chef recommends a Château Soransot-Dupré Listrac at 180 F and a Château Rochemorin 1989 Graves at 165 F for their quality-price ratio. Warm welcome and attentive service. **C** 320-440 F. **M** 160 F, 215 F, 295 F, 380 F.

Le Butin de la Mer
Le Manoir, Phare du Butin
31 89 06 06, fax 31 89 54 54
Closed Mon. Open until 9:30pm. Terrace dining. Pkg. V, AE, MC.
This Anglo-Norman manor house is the marine tentacle of the nearby La Ferme Saint-Siméon. Chef Denis Le Cadre oversees the moderately priced seafood dishes, such as those on the fine 130 F menu: six raw oysters, fresh cod with herb taboulé, vinaigrette de poivron, and chocolate mousse with an orange salad. **C** 250-300 F. **M** 130 F.

L'Écrin
19, rue E.-Boudin
31 89 32 39, fax 31 89 24 41
Open year-round. 22 rms 330-850 F. No pets. Garage pkg. V, AE, DC, MC.
Astonishing manor house and park in the town center with idiosyncratic furnishings and a neo-Gothic decor. The huge rooms are very comfortable and boast canopied beds.

La Ferme Saint-Siméon

Rue A.-Marais - 31 89 23 61
Open daily until 9:30pm. Priv rm: 60. Garden dining. Heated pool. Pkg. V, AE.

This historic and truly beautiful Norman house overlooking the Seine estuary, where Monet, Courbet, Sisley, and others came to seek inspiration, is now graced by a suitably high-level kitchen. Thanks to Denis Le Cadre, La Ferme's moneyed patrons can enjoy the likes of lobster with caviar, or witty plays on Normandy classics like "tripes" of sea scallops or Camembert ravioli. Among his dishes are some hits (a salamandre of red mullet in shellfish jus) and a few misses (duck liver terrine with broccoli). Perfectly choreographed service, sumptuous cellar, every detail has been designed to satisfy any guest's whim: in short, for a beautiful establishment, it's a beautiful establishment. Eric Satie, who used to play boules here, could write a symphony to this Ferme (if he were named Mahler). **C** 450-600 F. **M** 240 F (weekday lunch, Sat), 420 F, 550 F.

La Ferme Saint-Siméon

(See restaurant above)
Open year-round. 4 stes 4,400-5,100 F. 39 rms 990-3,510 F. Rms for disabled. Half-board 1,220-2,440 F. Conf. Heated pool. Tennis. Golf. Pkg. V, AE, MC.

Seventeen luxurious rooms with sea view were added not long ago, in a Norman-style manor next to the delightful seventeenth-century farm which houses most of the accommodation. The marble bathrooms boast state-of-the-art equipment; other facilities include a swimming pool, Finnish sauna, Turkish bath, fitness room, solarium, whirlpool, and massages. Opulent decor and irreproachable service. Relais et Châteaux.

Hostellerie Lechat

Pl. Ste-Catherine
31 89 23 85, fax 31 89 28 61
Closed Jan 4-Feb 10. 1 ste 800 F. 22 rms 360-500 F. Restaurant. Half-board 330-400 F. Conf. No pets. V, AE, DC, MC.

Large ivy-covered building facing the handsome church of Saint Catherine. The comfortable beamed rooms have pleasant views and a quiet, provincial atmosphere. Satisfactory service.

La Lieutenance

12, pl. Ste-Catherine - 31 89 07 52
Closed Mon dinner, Tue, Nov 13-Dec 14. Priv rm: 18. Terrace dining. Pkg. No cards.

This traditional old half-timbered eating house with a pleasant terrace and tiny dining room offers excellent fresh seafood platters and grilled fish, as well as sole paupiettes, lamb fillets, and a yummy pear puff pastry with caramel sauce. The first two set menus offer lots of choice and easy-to-digest prices. **C** 230-320 F. **M** 98 F (exc Sat dinner, Sun lunch), 152 F, 216 F.

Beauséjour

Av. de la Tour-du-Lac
58 43 51 07, fax 58 43 70 13
Closed Oct 15-May 6. 1 ste 1,100-1,600 F. 45 rms 350-700 F. Restaurant. Half-board 460-650 F. Conf. Heated pool. Golf. Pkg. V, AE, DC, MC.

Deep in the forest, this beautiful building with a spacious terrace stands next to a saltwater lake. The comfortable, tidy rooms offer views of the lovely swimming pool or lake. Plenty of efficient staff.

Les Huîtrières du Lac

1187, av. du Touring-Club
58 43 51 48, fax 58 41 73 11
Closed Nov 1-Easter. 9 rms 230-280 F. Half-board 320-345 F. Conf. Golf. Pkg. V.

This popular spot is blessed with an impressive lake view from most of the rooms, all of which are well kept and equipped with bathrooms redone this year. Bicycles for rent.

La Poularde de Houdan

24, av. de la République
30 59 60 50, fax 30 59 79 71
Closed 2 wks in Feb. Open until 10pm. Priv rm: 28. Terrace dining. No pets. Garage pkg. V, MC.

The professional, unobtrusive service sets the tone in this sober, almost austere establishment. Sylvain Vandenameele's traditional, well-crafted cooking somehow reflects the environment: truffled chicken aumônière, goujonnade of John Dory with chicken jus, chocolate cake with coffee cream. The small cellar boasts some nice bottlings at reasonable prices. **C** 280-450 F. **M** 150 F (weekday dinner, Sat lunch), 130 F (weekday lunch), 300 F.

La Colombe

La Bayorre - 94 65 02 15
Closed Sun dinner off-seas, Mon (Jul-Aug), Sat lunch. Open until 9:45pm. Pkg. V.

Youthful and bursting with energy, chef Pascal Bonamy purchases market-fresh ingredients, then turns them into delights like crab omelet, young rabbit galette with eggplant caviar, delicious foie gras sautéed with honey cake and a tart jus, cod tournedos with an onion compote, sea bass sauced with a flavorful lemony oil bouillon and paired with artichoke puréé, or a little lamb tart with bits of Parmesan. For dessert, a licorice soufflé glacé. And to wash it all down, the superb white wine from Domaine Sainte-Marguerite. This is where you come to have the best meal the town has to offer. **C** 250-300 F. **M** 130 F.

Les Jardins de Bacchus

32, av. Gambetta - 94 65 77 63
Closed Sun dinner off-seas, Sat lunch (in seas), Mon, 2 wks in Jun. Open until 10pm (10:30pm in summer). Terrace dining. Air cond. Pkg. V, AE, MC.

Jean-Claude Santioni's tasty repertoire is prepared with superb technique, and served in a rather overdone trompe-l'oeil decor. Our quibble: we wish he would try for more simplicity and natural flavors. Caviar doesn't make fine coral butter any better, nor does the roast squab need the brik of young rabbit en vinaigrette and the foie gras-filled puff pastry. Instead of a "braid of red mullet in a truffle crust", why not little whole red mullets in their skins with their livers spread on toast? Whatever, the first set menu is a marvel and Claire Santioni's friendly smile makes everything all right. C 280-380 F. M 140 F, 185 F, 290 F.

Mercure
19, av. A.-Thomas
94 65 03 04, fax 94 35 58 20
Open year-round. 84 rms 340-595 F. Rms for disabled. Restaurant. Half-board 325-375 F. Air cond. Conf. Pool. Pkg. V, AE, DC, MC.
Set in a huge residential and commercial complex along the bypass, this functional new hotel features bright rooms with balconies and perfectly fitted bathrooms. Buffet-style breakfasts and a noisy swimming pool.

La Québécoise
Av. Amiral, 3 km S, in Costebelle
94 57 69 24, fax 94 38 78 27
Open year-round. 11 rms 160-355 F. Half-board 280-370 F. Pool. Golf. V, AE, MC.
A handful of pleasant rooms is housed in this spacious dwelling on the sunny Costebelle hillside.

IGÉ	71960
Paris 394 - Tournus 30 - Mâcon 14 - Cluny 11	Saône/Loire

Château d'Igé
85 33 33 99, fax 85 33 41 41
Closed Dec 1-Mar 1. Open until 9:30pm. Priv rm: 50. Garden dining. Pkg. V, AE, DC, MC.
Laurent Couturier's cooking has brought a welcome personal touch to this handsome little château, once the home of the Counts of Mâcon. Savor it in the elegant Gothic dining rooms decorated with a medieval theme and frequented by a well-heeled clientele: delicious snail soup in a creamy, sorrel-enhanced chicken bouillon; slices of duck breast with orange caramel and ginger; Cointreau soufflé and orange sherbet. Vast, well chosen wine list. Affable welcome. C 300-450 F. M 150 F (weekday lunch), 190 F, 250 F, 295 F, 360 F.

Château d'Igé
(See restaurant above)
Closed Dec 1-Mar 1. 6 stes 875-1,100 F. 7 rms 480-710 F. Half-board 730-945 F. Conf. Golf. Pkg. V, AE, DC, MC.
Charming château and park in a Mâconnais village surrounded by vineyards. Attractive, comfortable rooms are tastefully furnished in authentic country style. Lovely vaulted room for meetings and receptions. Relais et Châteaux.

ILE-ROUSSE (L') 20	➔ CORSICA

ILLHAEUSERN	68150
Paris 448 - Colmar 17 - Sélestat 12 - Strasbourg 60	Haut-Rhin

L'Auberge de l'Ill
Rue de Collonges - 89 71 83 23 (R),
89 71 87 87 (H), fax 89 71 82 83
19.5 *Closed Mon dinner (& lunch off-seas), Tue, Feb 6-Mar 10. Open until 9:30pm. Priv rm: 20. Air cond. Pkg. V, AE, DC, MC.*
If you've decided to take one of the ten delightful guest rooms overlooking the fish-filled River

Ill, you can wet a line right from your window and land your lunch. Better still, leave the question of lunch to the Haeberlins, who will regale you in their legendary restaurant on the river bank. Some great temples of gastronomy inspire more respect than love, and become for many diners merely the object of a once-in-a-lifetime culinary pilgrimage. But in spite of all its laurels, L'Auberge de l'Ill still has the feeling of a welcoming family-run auberge. You are always greeted attentively, whether by the Haeberlins or by their longtime staff: an aperitif by the river, special care taken with children—nothing is neglected. You take a seat in the almond-green dining room whose picture windows frame the garden, while in his spanking-bright kitchen young Marc Haeberlin works magic with the fragrant, flavorful bounty of Alsace.

Marc, ever modest and charming, has found his mark by offering both the rich dishes in the Alsatian culinary tradition (ragoût of frog's legs, admirable assortment of goose dishes, breast of squab with cabbage) and quintessentially modern creations like John Dory cooked in a delicate lemongrass bouillon (and lemongrass is tricky to work with), a sublime lamb fillet with melting potatoes redolent with black olives, and a more rustic thick Aberdeen beefsteak with an oxtail chartreuse. As for the desserts, pastry chef Christophe Fischer has a real talent for flavor combinations (pear, chicory, caramel; apricot and babeurre). This isn't the kind of cooking that alters the culinary landscape, but the spirit of the house, its long experience, and the fluid perfection of each presentation is well worth the 19.5 rating. Of course, all this has its price, but not an extravagant one compared to those of other Alsace establishments. Serge Dubs (voted the world's best sommelier in 1989) will initiate you into the mysteries of Alsatian wines. C 700 F. M 580 F (lunch exc weekdays), 480 F (weekday lunch), 700 F.

Hôtel des Berges
(See restaurant above)
Closed Feb 6-Mar 10. 2 stes 1,800-2,200 F. 9 rms 1,150-1,500 F. Air cond. Conf. Garage pkg. Helipad. V, AE, DC, MC.
Finally, we can spend the night at the Auberge de l'Ill! And so can a handful of other guests, now that nine huge and sumptuous rooms and two suites have been constructed by talented architect Yves Boucharlat out of a converted tobacco-drying barn. Rough-hewn wood, fine fabrics by Pierre Frey, Italian furniture, and traditional porcelain stoves highlight the decor. Farther down the river bank is an adorable fisherman's house on stilts, available for rental complete with a little boat and a fishing pole.

La Clairière
46, route d'Illhaeusern
89 71 80 80, fax 89 71 86 22
Closed Jan-Mar 3. 2 stes 1,200-1,600 F. 25 rms 420-900 F. Heated pool. Tennis. Pkg. V.
On the edge of the Ill forest, comfortable, pleasantly decorated rooms favored by clients of the Auberge de l'Ill. Book well in advance.

*Some establishments change their **closing times** without warning. It is always wise to check in advance.*

ISLE-JOURDAIN (L') 86150

Paris 380 - Poitiers 47 - Confolens 26 - Montmorillon 32 *Vienne*

Auberge de la Grimolée

Port de Salles, Le Vigeant - 49 48 75 22
Closed Tue dinner, Wed, 2 wks in Feb, 3 wks in Oct. Open until 9:30pm. Terrace dining. Pkg. V, MC.
This riverside restaurant's picture windows overlook the spectacular, untamed Vienne. Chef Gérard Alloyeau cruises right along with reliable skill: a lovely warm salad of veal sweetbreads and langoustines, foie gras cooked in Pineau de Charentes, an aumônière of tiny snails with foie gras, and a warm pear millefeuille with caramel sauce. Cordial welcome. **C** 200-270 F. **M** 75 F (lunch exc Sun, wine incl), 100 F, 130 F, 150 F, 180 F, 225 F.

ISLE-SUR-LA-SORGUE (L') 84800

Paris 698 - Avignon 23 - Apt 32 - Carpentras 17 *Vaucluse*

Mas de Cure Bourse ♧

Carrefour de Velorgues
90 38 16 58, fax 90 38 52 31
Closed Sun dinner & Mon off-seas, Jan 2-9, last 2 wks of Oct. Open until 9:30pm. Priv rm: 60. Garden dining. Pkg. V, MC.
Françoise Donzé cooks up the most delicious old-fashioned Provençal dishes in these inspiring surroundings (a former eighteenth-century coaching inn, hidden among the trees). Savor her excellent first set menu: mussel soup, chicken and mushroom ragoût, goat cheese coated with ground hazelnuts, and a warm pear cake with caramel sauce. **C** 250-350 F. **M** 165 F, 195 F, 230 F, 260 F.

Mas de Cure Bourse ▲♥

(See restaurant above)
See restaurant for closings. 2 stes 550-650 F. 11 rms 290-550 F. Half-board 380-495 F. Pool. Pkg. Helipad. V.
Opening onto orchards, these few cozy and elegant rooms are decorated in a spare, fresh, Provençal style. Pleasant service and a sunny swimming pool in a pretty green setting.

La Prévôté

4, rue J.-J.-Rousseau - 90 38 57 29
Closed Nov. Open until 9:30pm. Terrace dining. V, DC, MC.
Set in the back of a gorgeous flower-filled courtyard adjoining the town's majestic church, this handsome restaurant—the best in this adorable little town—is a symphony of hewn stone, exposed beams, and tapestries. Roland Mercier, only 25 years old, is already a polished pro with more than a little imagination. His 180 F menu proves it with salmon and fresh goat cheese cannelloni, duck breast with a lavender-honey glaze, well aged cheeses, and a chestnut soufflé glacé with a hazelnut croquant. Small but well chosen wine list. The *patronne's* welcome is warm. **M** 120 F (weekday lunch), 180 F, 280 F.

---

*Some establishments change their **closing times** without warning. It is always wise to check in advance.*

ISOLA 2000 06420

Paris 830 - Nice 94 - St-Martin-Vésubie 60 *Alpes-Mar.*

11/20 Les Aviateurs

93 23 14 15, fax 93 23 90 59
Closed Sep 10-Nov 15. Open until 10pm. Priv rm: 90. Terrace dining. Pkg. V, AE, DC, MC.
A new chef offers simplified cooking based on grilled meats and brasserie dishes (rustic ravioli gratin topped with Parmesan, fresh and perfectly cooked steak, ordinary apple and caramel feuilleté). Nice little wines to wash it all down. Choose the paneled dining room or a sunny terrace. **C** 160-260 F. **M** 125 F (wine incl), 75 F (lunch).

Le Chastillon

93 23 10 60, fax 93 23 17 66
Closed Apr 24-Dec 18. 3 stes 1,700-4,450 F. 51 rms 470-1,320 F. Restaurant. Half-board 420-790 F. Conf. Golf. Valet pkg. Helipad. V, AE, DC, MC.
Smack in front of the ski runs, this comfortable hotel offers modern rooms with little terraces, good bathrooms. Live entertainment in season.

Le Diva

93 23 17 71, fax 93 23 12 44
Closed May 2-Jun 28, Sep 10-Dec 18. Open until 11pm. Terrace dining. Valet pkg. V, AE, DC.
Philippe Duffourc seems to be attaced to this cozy though opulent chalet with its splendid mountain views. He offered us a choice of classic dishes that seemed a bit too sophisticated for the surroundings: a zucchini papeton and a perfectly seasoned langoustine marinière, sautéed strips of duck breast with tiny white onions in a tart sauce, a cheese assortment that included some great fresh goat cheeses, and desserts that deserve a toque. Good selection of Côtes-de-Provence wines, dynamic and professional service, warm welcome. **C** 360-550 F. **M** 250 F, 430 F.

Le Diva ▲♥

(See restaurant above)
Closed May 1-mid Jun. 5 stes 2,650-3,990 F. 23 rms 745-2,250 F. Half-board 745-1,995 F. Conf. Golf. Valet pkg. V, AE, DC, MC.
A luxurious, chalet-style hotel with a splendid south-facing terrace. The personalized, spacious rooms are decorated with English furniture. Other amenities are twin saunas, a Jacuzzi, and a piano bar.

ISSAMBRES (LES) 83380

Paris 899 - Toulon 83 - Fréjus 11 - Ste-Maxime 10 *Var*

Chante-Mer

Village provençal
94 96 93 23
Closed Sun dinner, Mon (exc dinner Jul-Aug), Dec 15-Jan. Open until 9pm. Terrace dining. Air cond. Pkg. V.
Seated on the sunny terrace, relax and enjoy Mario Battaglia's good, unpretentious cooking: raw salmon in a mustard marinade, sea bass with fennel, and warm apple tart. Friendly welcome, on-target wine list. **C** 230-380 F. **M** 120 F, 170 F, 210 F.

La Réserve

N 98 - 94 96 90 41
Closed Mon lunch, Wed, mid Sep-mid May. Open until 9:30pm. Garden dining. Pkg. V, MC.
There's a beautiful view out to sea from the delightful waterside terrace shaded by parasol pines. What's on your plate is not bad either, for it is simple, fresh, and appetizing: marinated raw tuna, scorpion fish fillet with herbs, bourride, or lamb sautéed with garlic. Sip a cool Provençal vintage, and bask in the sunny, smiling service. C 300-450 F. **M** 180 F, 240 F, 270 F.

Le Saint-Pierre

N 98 - 94 96 89 67
Closed Tue (exc dinner in seas), Jan 2-31. Open until 10pm. Terrace dining. Pkg. V, AE, DC.
Set atop a rocky spur among the coves, this beautiful, luminous restaurant is blessed with a huge terrace that looks out to sea. In these splendid natural surroundings, savor Ernest Loudet's enticing fried sea scallops, gambas roasted with herbs, lobster grilled with basil butter, bouillabaisse. A few regional wines. C 210-590 F. **M** 150 F (weekday lunch), 230 F.

Villa Saint-Elme

N 98, at L'Arpillon - 94 49 52 52
Closed Jan-Feb. Open until 10:30pm. Terrace dining. Air cond. Heated pool. Garage pkg. V, AE, MC.
This white villa from the 1930s, standing between the superhighway and the sea, offers a splendid view of the Golfe de Saint-Tropez though large bay windows overlooking the terrace. Locals flock here (especially in the evening) to sample Thibault Peyroche's maritime cooking. He carefully selects his fish and prepares them simply, pairing them with inventive accompaniments. Try his scorpion fish gâteau with cucumbers and tomatoes, gambas in gazpacho, tuna with a vegetable marmelade, or the croustille of porgy with spices and tender spinach. Fine peach tart, good choice of Provençal wines, an excellent set menu, and three lovely air-conditioned suites (as well as rooms in a more modest annex, unfortunately near the highway and noisy). C 350-600 F. **M** 185 F.

La Cognette   ۞

2, bd Stalingrad
54 21 21 83, fax 54 03 13 03
Closed Sun dinner & Mon off-seas, Jan. Open until 10pm. Terrace dining. Air cond. Pkg. V, AE, DC, MC.
Guests arriving at this quintessential country inn (once described by Balzac, no less) are welcomed warmly by Madame Nonnet into the stately dining room stuffed with lovingly polished antiques. Chef Alain Nonnet and his son-in-law, Jean-Jacques Daumy, man the kitchen. Their repertoire offers old-fashioned specialties of the Berry region, like intensely flavored terrine of calf's head and tongue, or a farm-raised chicken en barbouille. But a few more original dishes are on hand, too, like the delicate mignon of pork cooked in tea with star anise, and an exquisite nougatine glacé. The wine list is remarkable. C 330-500 F. **M** 140 F, 199 F (weekdays, Sat, wine incl), 305 F, 365 F.

La Cognette   🌲🌳

(See restaurant above)
Closed Jan. 3 stes 900 F. 11 rms 300-600 F. Half-board 400-600 F. Air cond. Golf. Pkg. V, AE, DC, MC.
Set in a delightful garden 100 meters from the restaurant via ancient, narrow streets, eleven rooms and three suites await, beautifully maintained and equipped, with romantic decor. The excellent breakfasts feature delicious jams. The Nonnets, who provide a very warm welcome, plan to open a Balzac museum between the restaurant and the hotel sometime this year.

12/20 La Jasse

Chemin du bord de Grau - 42 56 41 86
Closed Sun dinner, Mon, Aug 1-15, Dec 23-27. Open until 9:30pm. Terrace dining. Pkg. V.
On the first warm day, patrons move out of this country inn's rustic dining room onto the terrace. There they tuck enthusiastically into forthright dishes prepared with carefully selected ingredients: head cheese with tomatoes, steamed fillet of sea bass, veal sweetbreads with truffle jus, and a panaché of desserts. Family-style service and atmosphere. C 260-320 F. **M** 150 F, 160 F, 225 F.

Le Saint-Martin

Rond-point Port-Les-Heures-Claires
42 56 07 12, fax 42 56 04 59
Closed Tue dinner, Wed, Nov 2-26. Open until 9:30pm. Terrace dining. Air cond. No pets. Pkg. V, MC.
This sincere and friendly family-run establishment overlooks the Berre pond. Maman welcomes you to a comfortable blue-grey dining room, while Patrick Mencarelli, seconded by his Papa, offers forthright cooking: fresh salmon rillettes in a salad, snail profiteroles, and a braid of salmon and monkfish fillets. For dessert, crème brûlée with brown sugar. C 200-350 F. **M** 160 F, 225 F.

Le Parc de la Grange   🌲🌳

Route de l'Abbaye
51 33 44 88, fax 51 33 40 58
Closed Sat & Sun (Oct 15-Easter), Dec 19-Jan 16. 32 rms 475-850 F. Rms for disabled. Restaurant. Half-board 470-620 F. Conf. Heated pool. Tennis. Golf. Pkg. V, AE, DC, MC.
A nice modern complex placed in a 22-hectare park by the sea, with light, comfortable rooms and good conference facilities. Exercise club, billiards, discothèque, and other amenities.

*We're always happy to hear about **your discoveries** and receive your comments on ours. Please feel free to write to us stating clearly what you liked or disliked. Be concise but convincing, and take the time to argue your point.*

Paris 148 - Sens 30 - Auxerre 27 - Troyes 75 *Yonne*

 La Côte Saint-Jacques
14, faubourg de Paris
86 62 09 70, fax 86 91 49 70
19.5 *Open daily until 9:45pm. Priv rm: 60. Air cond. Heated pool. Valet pkg. V, AE, DC, MC.*

In his mid-30s, Jean-Michel Lorain is an uncommonly intelligent chef, whose cuisine embodies what we like to call "advanced" culinary classicism. Clearly, Lorain is not a "creator" in the manner of Gagnaire, Veyrat, Bras, or Loiseau. But after years of searching and working—with Troisgros, with Girardet, and above all with his father Michel, who continues to keep an eye on him today—Jean-Michel Lorain evolved a distinctive style all his own. And he has brought that style to the brink of perfection: 19.5 out of 20! Lorain's cooking is instinctively rich, but never heavy, and it never fails to amaze with its polish and refinement. Flavors, aromas, proportions, and textures come together in perfect balance. Lorain's dishes are elaborately constructed, thoroughly thought through. This year he regaled us with an intensely flavored dish of sea scallops with endive and chanterelles paired with a lush, foamy froth of jus whipped with butter; a richly scented crab soup into which he slipped beef marrow and cardoons in a felicitous marriage of tastes and textures; royal sea bream matched with truffled flageolets and shallot confit; meltingly tender squab with one foot in Provence (poivrade artichokes) and another in Asia (a tart and spicy apple chutney); and suckling pig with pearl barley and sweet-sour carrots. All this is followed by a splendid collection of cheeses and superb desserts like a pineapple croquant with banana cream, a bergamot parfait with a dried-fruit infusion, a caramelized pear puff pastry, or the ultimate vanilla ice cream, all of which make this restaurant one of France's finest pâtisseries! And don't be surprised this year to see borscht, smoked-eel gelatin with beets, and cabbage stuffed with sturgeon and caviar on the menu; they are the fruits of a culinary exchange Lorain organized last winter, during which he spent a week in Saint Petersburg. One waters Lorain's sublime repasts with fabulous Burgundies, scented out by Jean-Michel's mother, Jacqueline Lorain, one of the most discerning "noses" in France. **C** 600-900 F. **M** 360 F (lunch exc Sun), 680 F.

 La Côte Saint-Jacques
(See restaurant above)
Open year-round. 4 stes 1,900-2,500 F. 25 rms 600-1,750 F. Air cond. Conf. Heated pool. Tennis. Golf. Valet pkg. Helipad. V, AE, DC, MC.

Not satisfied with linking their two buildings on either side of the main road with an elegant underground passage, installing Hollywood-style suites (with luxurious marble bathrooms) over the swimming pool and garden on the banks of the Yonne, the Lorains recently renovated a nearby villa and doubled the size of the garden. For their guests' pleasure, a motorboat is available, as well as a ten-seater launch for "apéritif" cruises and small parties. Rooms in the old building have been enlarged and agreeably remodeled. There's a piano bar. Relais et Châteaux.

La Rive Gauche
Chemin du Port au Bois
86 91 46 66, fax 86 91 46 93
Open year-round. 42 rms 250-650 F. Rms for disabled. Restaurant. Half-board 300-450 F. Air cond. Conf. Tennis. Golf. Pkg. V, AE, DC, MC.

Facing their main establishment on the other side of the Yonne River, the Lorains have built this functional, moderately priced, chain-style hotel with particularly well-kept rooms. The large riverside dining room serves bistrot cooking with fixed-price menus from 92 F to 250 F.

JOUCAS 84 → **Gordes**

JUAN-LES-PINS 06160
Paris 920 - Nice 22 - Cannes 9 - Antibes 2 - Aix 160 *Alpes-Mar.*

Ambassadeur
50-52, chemin des Sables
93 67 82 15, fax 93 67 79 85
Closed Feb 25-Mar 20. 7 stes 1,900 F. 231 rms 700-1,150 F. Rms for disabled. Restaurant. Half-board 170 F. Air cond. Conf. Heated pool. Golf. Valet pkg. V, AE, DC, MC.

Not far from the pine grove you'll find this luxurious modern hotel, whose cozily decorated rooms boast balconies and the very best bathrooms. All the usual amenities are on hand, as well as some delightful extras. Professional service.

Beauséjour
Av. Saramartel
93 61 07 82, fax 93 61 86 78
Closed Oct-Apr 15. 30 rms 500-1,200 F. Air cond. Conf. Pool. Golf. Pkg. V, AE, MC.

A hotel with the atmosphere of a private house, very well situated in a leafy section of Juan-les-Pins. Rooms are light, with shady balconies. Lovely garden and barbecue by the swimming pool.

 Belles Rives
Bd du Littoral
93 61 02 79, fax 93 67 43 51
Closed Oct 10-Mar. Open until 10pm. Garden dining. Air cond. No pets. Valet pkg. V, AE, MC.

Formerly a holiday villa occupied by the likes of Scott and Zelda Fitzgerald, for the last 60 years Belles Rives has been a family-run luxury hotel, with a guest register signed by the Windsors, Édith Piaf, Josephine Baker, Miles Davis, and loads of other celebrities. If they were still around, they would applaud the great progress made by chef Thierry Jeanneret this year. We award him two toques with no reservations for the savory and original "oyster" of veal sweetbreads with sorrel, fresh cod studded with bacon and served with clams and an excellent asparagus-Parmesan risotto, flavorful strips of spiced duck breast (a tad overcooked), and fine desserts. The cellar is improving. Warm welcome and professional service in a dining room with exquisite 1930s decor and views of the sea. **C** 350-600 F. **M** 190 F (lunch), 300 F, 360 F, 430 F (dinner).

Prices for rooms and suites *are per room, not per person. Half-board prices, however, are per person.*

Belles Rives

(See restaurant above)
Closed Oct 10-Mar. 4 stes 1,800-5,300 F. 41 rms
720-2,680 F. Half-board 1,530-2,930 F. Air cond.
Conf. Golf. Valet pkg. V, AE, MC.

With superb views over the bay, these 1930s–
style rooms are all different and extra comfortable, with lovely marble bathrooms. Some rooms
have views of the sea. Business services available,
as well as a private beach and landing dock.

Bijou-Plage

Bd Ch.-Guillaumont - 93 61 39 07
Open daily until 10pm (11pm in summer). Priv
rm: 50. Terrace dining. Air cond. Pkg. V, AE, DC.

Here's a rarity: a real "bijou" of a Riviera beach
restaurant, set just opposite the Lérins Islands,
and open year round to boot. The Japanese chef
deftly selects and prepares utterly fresh fish for
a gilt-edged clientele: biscuit of sardine fillets
with tapenade, a red mullet and ratatouille
galette, poached chapon fillet with Bologna-style
spaghetti, and a "fisherman's plate" with bouillabaisse jus. Appealing Provençal cellar. If you
just want a quick bite, head for the beachside
terrace. C 250-600 F. M 100 F (weekday lunch,
Sat), 165 F, 220 F.

Garden Beach Hotel

La Pinède, 15-17, bd Baudoin
93 67 25 25, fax 93 61 16 65
Closings not available. 16 stes 1,000-3,300 F.
158 rms 600-1,900 F. Restaurant. Half-board 270 F.
Air cond. Conf. Golf. Valet pkg. V, AE, DC, MC.

Housed in a modernist cube constructed on
the site of the former casino, this luxurious hotel
offers every comfort and service. The rather
chilly decor of red and black marble and granite
is warmed by the omnipresent photos of jazz
greats who have graced the local festival, and by
the great sea views from the rooms. Impeccable
service. Lunch buffet and dinner grill service in
summer on the lovely private beach.

Hélios

3, av. du Dr-Dautheville
93 61 55 25, fax 93 61 58 78
Closed Nov 1-Apr 1. 5 stes 1,800-3,000 F. 60 rms
550-1,500 F. Rms for disabled. Restaurant. Half-
board 560-910 F. Air cond. Conf. Golf. Valet pkg. V,
AE, DC, MC.

Another luxurious hotel, this one with its own
private beach (meals are served by the water).
Some of the lovely, large, modern rooms have
splendid balconies, while others are smaller with
characterless furniture and only the merest sliver
of a sea view. Piano bar.

Les Mimosas

Rue Pauline
93 61 04 16, fax 92 93 06 46
Closed Oct-Apr. 34 rms 450-650 F. Pool. No pets.
Pkg. V, MC.

An agreeable white house with a garden in a
residential area 500 meters from the sea. The
bright rooms all have balconies, and are
pleasantly decorated.

Hôtel du Parc

Av. G.-de-Maupassant
93 61 00 00, fax 93 67 92 42
Closed Nov 15-Mar 20. 29 rms 550-1,080 F. Restaurant. Half-board 890-1,190 F. Air cond. Conf.
Pool. Golf. Pkg. V, AE, DC, MC.

Set back from the street, but centrally located,
this hotel stands in leafy grounds opposite the
beach. The lovely guest rooms are large and
provide all you need for a pleasant stay.

Pré Catelan

22, av. des Lauriers (corner av. des Pal-
miers) - 93 61 05 11, fax 93 67 83 11
Open year-round. 18 rms 250-450 F. Restaurant.
Half-board 400-450 F. No pets. Pkg. V, AE, DC, MC.

A little house in a quiet, palm-shaded garden
200 meters from the sea. It has its own private
beach with restaurant.

Restaurant du Casino

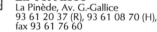

Eden-Casino, bd E.-Baudoin
92 93 71 71, fax 93 61 67 00
Closings not available. Open until 11pm (11:30pm
in summer). Priv rm: 120. Terrace dining. Air cond.
Valet pkg. V, DC, MC.

It's a surprise to find an elegant dining room
with a lovely view of the sea cached in a garish
casino filled with folks playing one-armed ban-
dits. Keep going past the players until you reach
the dining room, and you'll be glad you did. Let's
make one thing perfectly clear, though: this is
not former four-star chef Jacques Maximin's restaurant. However, Maximin has installed one of
his favorite young associates in this deluxe brasserie, and he gave his imprimatur to the quintessentially Provençal repertoire. The 180 F lunch
menu offers a delicious cross-section of dishes
made from consistently top-quality ingredients:
tasty smoked salmon and asparagus en papillote, an intensely flavored chicken viennois with
a ricotta-gnocchi gratin, fine goat cheeses, and
lovely desserts, like the caramel millefeuille with
a crème brûlée mousse and fresh raspberries.
Maximin's spirit is there, even if most of the time
he isn't. Excellent service. C 350-500 F.
M 180 F, 250 F, 320 F, 390 F.

La Terrasse

La Pinède, Av. G.-Gallice
93 61 20 37 (R), 93 61 08 70 (H),
fax 93 61 76 60
Closed Wed off-seas, end Oct-Easter. Open until
10pm (10:30pm in summer). Priv rm: 22. Garden
dining. Valet pkg. V, MC.

Handsome Christian Morisset is a top talent
who has curiously been neglected by the press,
despite his photogenic Salvador Dali–style
moustache. All the better to preserve his unique
character and the magic of this very special spot,
where fortunate guests take their ease on a
terrace surrounded by masses of flowers and
palm trees. The atmosphere of this Art Deco villa
is reminiscent of more gracious days, when Scott
Fitzgerald, Cocteau, and Chanel spent leisurely
holidays at Juan-les-Pins.

Morisset was second chef at Roger Vergé's
Moulin in Mougins and there mastered the
mysteries of sun-gorged Southern cooking
replete with heady perfumes, fresh flavors, and
decisive seasoning. Take the best the market has
to offer, add a pinch of Morisset's imagination,
and you've got an unbeatable combination. Witness the exquisite coriander-scented vegetable
assortment, scampi ravioli in a basil-enhanced
shellfish jus, John Dory cooked in its skin with
rosemary, a plump turbot with truffles in a potato
crust, tender and succulent milk-fed veal with a
girolle ragoût and baby vegetables, or a saddle

of lamb cooked in a clay casserole that seals in its delicious flavor and aroma. Follow this feast with superb cheeses and a mind-boggling array of desserts (including an almond galette with raspberries and rhubarb, and a lipsmacking feuilleté of chocolate and fresh mangoes). Magnificent cellar. Outstanding fixed-price lunch menu featuring a choice among six first courses, six fish or meat dishes, cheese, and dessert; it's one of the Côte d'Azur's best deals. C 550-850 F. M 250 F (lunch), 390 F, 430 F, 480 F, 590 F.

La Terrasse
(See restaurant above)
Closed end Oct-Easter. 5 stes 1,800-3,200 F. 45 rms 500-1,800 F. Rms for disabled. Half-board 250-390 F. Air cond. Conf. Heated pool. Golf. Pkg. V, MC.
On the edge of the lovely pine grove that marks the border between Juan-the-chic and Juan-the-crass, this elegant hotel with a splendid pavillon-swimming pool (but with no direct access to the sea) attracts a cosmopolitan clientele. Cooking classes.

JUILLAC　　　　　　　　　33890
Paris 560 - Bordeaux 56 - Libourne 30 - La Réole 34　　　Gironde

12/20　Le Belvédère
4 km E on D 130, 1, côte de La Tourbeille
57 47 40 33, fax 57 47 48 07
Closed Tue dinner & Wed (exc Jul-Aug), Oct. Open until 9pm. Terrace dining. Pkg. V, AE, DC, MC.
The terrace of the Pestels' chalet dominates the majestic sweep of the Dordogne River from a height of 60 meters. The panorama is also visible from the comfortable country-style dining room, attended by an eager-to-please staff. Chef Michel Pestel sometimes stumbles when he forgets to be simple, witness the 190 F menu with a bland sweet-sour edible algae and shellfish salad, and duck confit with caramelized strawberry vinegar accompanied by two excellent vegetable and potato flans. Good desserts, though portions are stingy. Superb cellar dominated by Bordeaux. C 280-480 F. M 99 F (weekday lunch, wine incl), 130 F, 190 F, 290 F.

JUILLAN 65　　　　　　　→ Tarbes

JULIÉNAS　　　　　　　　69840
Paris 410 - Lyon 65 - Mâcon 17　　　Rhône

Le Coq au Vin
Pl. du Marché
74 04 41 98, fax 74 04 41 44
Open daily until 10pm. Terrace dining. V, AE, DC.
This spruce little country bistrot tastefully redecorated by Claude Clévenot was damaged by an attack that destroyed a fine collection of ceramic roosters (coqs) that were the emblem of the house. The former chef left, and that was an improvement. Come to the charming refurbished dining room to sample frog's legs soup with watercress, chicken liver "gâteau," and roast duck with turnips. Friendly atmosphere. C 190-250 F. M 98 F (exc Sun), 148 F, 198 F.

JUNIES (LES)　　　　　　　46150
Paris 600 - Cahors 24 - Villeneuve-sur-Lot 50 - Toulouse 133　　Lot

La Ribote
On D 660, La Mouline
65 36 25 55, fax 65 36 28 91
Closed Wed off-seas, Jan 5-Feb 12. Open until 9:30pm (10pm in seas). Terrace dining. Pkg. V, AE, DC, MC.
This beautifully restored and appealingly decorated old mill house nestles between the river and surrounding greenery. Gastronomes for miles around flock in for Franck Manenq's imaginative cooking: foie gras with tiny turnips and dried figs, fricassée of veal sweetbreads and lobster with cèpe sauce, chocolate-praline croquant, and a gaufre flavored with orange-flower water. Good wine list. Smiling welcome. C 260-360 F. M 95 F (weekdays), 180 F (Sun, Sat dinner), 130 F, 295 F.

JURANÇON 64　　　　　　　→ Pau

KAYSERSBERG　　　　　　68240
Paris 434 - Colmar 10 - Munster 25 - Sélestat 26　　Haut-Rhin

Chambard
9-11, rue du Gal-de-Gaulle
89 47 10 17, fax 89 47 35 03
Closed Tue lunch, Mon, Mar 1-21. Open until 9:30pm. Pkg. V, AE, MC.
Chambard is a well-known Alsatian restaurant famed for its elegant, understated decor, huge wine cellar, and the remarkably deft and precise cooking of owner-chef Pierre Irrmann. His cooking holds no surprises but is always based on the finest products. Try the red mullet and goose liver in truffle vinaigrette, roast pickerel (excellent but served in a stingy portion), flaky and flavorful apple turnover, and a very ordinary pear sherbet. At these prices, they could at least add some bouquets of fresh flowers to the dining room's decor. Quality service; high prices. C 400-550 F. M 200 F (weekdays), 300 F, 380 F, 450 F.

Chambard
(See restaurant above)
Closed Mar 1-21. 5 stes 850 F. 18 rms 550-850 F. Half-board 850-1,115 F. Conf. Pkg. V, AE, MC.
Pretty little hotel with twenty handsomely decorated, extremely comfortable rooms, some with vineyard views, others overlooking a pretty garden. Excellent breakfast. Cheerful welcome, perfect service.

LACAPELLE-MARIVAL　　　　46120
Paris 565 - Cahors 65 - Figeac 21 - Rocamadour 31　　Lot

La Terrasse
Route de Latronquière
65 40 80 07, fax 65 40 99 45
Closed Sun dinner & Mon off-seas, Jan 2-Mar 15. Open until 9pm (9:30pm in seas). Priv rm: 40. Terrace dining. Hotel: 16 rms 220-280 F. Conf. Pkg. V, AE, MC.
Éric Bizat has taken up the challenge of turning this provincial hostelry into a fine regional restaurant, and we are awarding his efforts an extra point this year. We savored his duck foie gras cooked in a cloth, a baron of rabbit with a fine pain perdu stuffing, and an interesting and deli-

cate green walnut juice soufflé. Excellent first menus, good selection of Cahors wines, charming welcome, and attentive service. The dining room is to be redecorated this year, thank goodness. **C** 290-330 F. **M** 85 F, 125 F, 160 F, 200 F.

LACAVE 46200
Paris 540 - Cahors 65 - Rocamadour 10 - Souillac 10   *Lot*

Château de la Treyne ☺☺
65 32 66 66, fax 65 37 06 57
Closed Wed lunch, Tue, Jan 3-Easter. Open until 10pm. Priv rm: 40. Garden dining. Heated pool. Valet pkg. V, AE, DC, MC.
This aristocratic establishment overlooks the Dordogne River, with a formal garden and vast wooded grounds. Laurent Clément's cuisine has made great progress, leaving behind a rather overcharged classic style to focus on a more modern brand of cooking inspired by fine local products and herbs from the garden. Try his fricassée of tiny snails with quail eggs in a Cahors wine sauce, potato and giblet confit ravioli in a walnut-oil jus, subtle steamed fillet of sea bass with truffle jus, a delicate veal chop cooked over fragrant hay, and a pressé of vegetables with an herb jus. For dessert, the luscious vanilla assiette gourmande. The 180 F Saint-Jacques-de-Compostelle (San Juan de Compostella) set menu is worth a pilgrimage in itself. Fine cellar. Excellent service. **C** 350-500 F. **M** 180 F (lunch, wine incl), 220 F (lunch), 280 F, 370 F.

Château de la Treyne ≜☺
(See restaurant above)
Closed Jan 3-Easter. 14 rms 700-1,600 F. Half-board 1,030-1,950 F. Air cond. Conf. Heated pool. Tennis. Valet pkg. Helipad. V, AE, DC, MC.
The Dordogne rushes by this gracious château. Everywhere one looks one finds beautiful furniture, hangings, and art works. The immense guest rooms are fit for princes or prelates, and breakfast on the terrace overlooking the river is a rare pleasure. Luxurious new bathrooms (with views!) have been added. Pool, tennis courts, walking trails, horseback riding facilities, and canoeing. Note that demi-pension (breakfast and one other meal) are obligatory on weekends. Relais et Châteaux.

Pont de l'Ouysse
65 37 87 04, fax 65 32 77 41
Closed Mon (exc dinner in seas), Jan-Feb. Open until 9:30pm. Priv rm: 30. Garden dining. Heated pool. Pkg. V, AE, DC, MC.
Tucked below the Château de Belcastel, this long, low, handsomely renovated house facing a picturesque ruined bridge, is set in paradisaical surroundings. The murmur of the river soothes guests on the shady terrace in summer, and the fireplace in the apricot-colored dining room warms them in winter. But the main draw is still the fine cooking of Daniel Chambon, who is on his way to becoming the Lot's first three-toque chef. He relies on a network of local farmers, gardeners, goatherds, and gatherers to supply him with the ingredients for his delicious cuisine. Our superb dinner there featured a salad of crayfish and zucchini blossoms, a snail fricassée in a matelote of garden vegetables and summer mushrooms, casserole-roasted brill studded with ginger and sauced with whipped herb butter, and a quarter goose served like a rare steak in a crust of potatoes and garlicky cèpes. Chambon gives a touch of grace to fine local products, like the truffle-stuffed tomato, a model of lightness and flavor and a sure sign of talent in the kitchen. The 150 F menu is a real gift. In winter, savor partridge, wood pigeon or hare à la royale around the fireplace. Fine Cahors and Bergerac wines. **C** 350-450 F. **M** 150 F, 250 F, 350 F, 400 F.

Pont de l'Ouysse ≜☺
(See restaurant above)
Closed Jan-Feb. 1 ste 700 F. 12 rms 350-500 F. Half-board 600-650 F. Heated pool. Pkg. V, AE, DC, MC.
A baker's dozen of ravishing bedrooms, with cozy country decor and white wicker furniture. Breakfast is served in the garden overlooking the placid Ouysse river, with newly installed walking trails along its banks.

LAGNY-SUR-MARNE 77400
Paris 33 - Meaux 21 - Senlis 51 - Melun 42   *Seine/Marne*

Egleny
13, av. du Gal-Leclerc
64 30 52 69, fax 60 07 56 79
Closed Sun dinner, Mon. Open until 9:30pm. Priv rm: 30. Terrace dining. Pkg. V, AE, DC, MC.
The road to Lagny takes one through traffic jams, past suburban towns and sugar-beet fields... But in the old village there stands this lovely old notary's house, with three small adjoining dining rooms that open onto an old-fashioned garden. Here Jean-Yves Gaudet (a chef of disarming modesty) usually creates artful, truly exciting food. But we were disappointed by our meal here this year, and are taking away a point: sole turban with an unsuccessful pastry, tarte dijonnaise with a gooey crust that should have been crisp, and, in contrast, a perfect vol-au-vent. But at these prices, inconsistency is hard to forgive. Even though such missteps are not Gaudet's usual style. Maybe it was the humid weather? Adequate wine list. **C** 400-550 F. **M** 145 F, 250 F, 380 F.

■ In **Bussy-Saint-Georges 77600**   *4 km S*

11/20 Le Clos Saint-Georges
15, av. du Golf
64 66 30 30, fax 64 66 04 36
Open daily until 10pm. Priv rm: 120. Terrace dining. Air cond. Pkg. V, AE, DC, MC.
We were disappointed by our last meal in the bright, modern dining room of this unprepossessing concrete building (happily it has a pleasant garden terrace). The place reminds us of an airport restaurant, but only the prices are flying high; the cooking is very pedestrian. On the 150 F menu: bland salmon chiffonade, fried mussels, and a raspberry charlotte. A point less this year. **C** 260-360 F. **M** 65 F, 75 F, 150 F.

Golf Hotel ≜☺
(See restaurant above)
Open year-round. 96 rms 460-530 F. Rms for disabled. Conf. Tennis. Golf. Pkg. V, AE, DC, MC.
Classic businessman's hotel, not lacking in charm. The smallish rooms are ultramodern and impeccably tidy, with perfect soundproofing; special services include currency changing, pressing, a billiard room....

LAGUIOLE 12210
Paris 552 - Aurillac 82 - Rodez 56 - Espalion 24   *Aveyron*

Auguy ۞
2, allée de l'Amicale
65 44 31 11, fax 65 51 50 81
*Closed Jun 11-18, Nov 15-Jan 5. Open until 9:30pm.
Priv rm: 20. Terrace dining. Pkg. V, MC.*
Madame Auguy has no cause to fear competition from her neighbor, Michel Bras. She cooks in an earthy, rustic register that has everlasting appeal: don't miss her cèpe and foie gras salad, steak of Aubrac beef and aligot (garlicky mashed potatoes with fresh Tomme cheese), spiced bread pudding and honey cake crème glacée. Friendly welcome. C 220-350 F. M 110 F (exc Sun lunch), 150 F, 175 F, 250 F.

Auguy
(See restaurant above)
Closed Jun 10-17, Nov 15-Jan 5. 27 rms 240-300 F. Half-board 230-275 F. Conf. Golf. Pkg. V, DC, MC.
Comfortable, well-equipped but smallish rooms in the center of town. Street-side units are noisy at night and in season. Good, fresh pastries for breakfast.

Michel Bras ۞
Route de l'Aubrac
65 44 32 24, fax 65 48 47 02
19.5 *Closed Mon lunch & Tue, Nov-Mar. Open until 9pm. Air cond. No pets. Valet pkg. V, AE.*
Michel Bras is not just one of France's consummate chefs: he is a genuine artist, a poet, an herbalist, a philosopher, and an uncommonly talented photographer. He is also a happy man, cooking in the glittering kitchens of his extraordinary new restaurant and hotel, designed by architect Éric Raffy. Quite unlike what one would expect to find in such a rugged, mountainous setting, the glass-and-concrete structure is considered by some to be too cerebral, too austere. What is certain is that the panoramic views from the guest rooms—on clear days you can spy the Pyrenees—never fail to take one's breath away. Bras's cooking, in any case, is freshly inspired by these bold surroundings. A chef of this calibre obviously possesses virtuoso technique; what sets Michel Bras apart is his unparalleled knowledge and artful use of mountain herbs, greens, and woodland mushrooms. He combines and contrasts their pristine, vegetal flavors to create a cuisine that is highly personal, utterly original. To see the heights this great chef can reach, sample his sautéed veal tripe, with its crunchy strips of meat mingling with barley and mustard leaves; or the duck foie gras magnificently paired with an apricot and honey vinegar pastry and a glass of local Hydromel (mead), which astonishingly resembles a fine Sauternes. Discover the totally unexpected flavors of tiny green asparagus sautéed raw and adorned with truffle vinaigrette, miniscule turnips stuffed with wild mushrooms and ventrêche, big and crunchy green beans "Helga" in a sublime morel mixture, rabbit kidney and milk skin, sea scallops in a jus that sings of the sea, and a spectacularly tender and juicy breast of squab with fresh coriander and parsley in a delicious giblet jus. Bras's cooking makes use of around 200 varieties of vegetables and herbs, and that's not all: he has just discovered the existence of 180 varieties of potato, the stuff of new culinary dreams. This year Bras is in a dessert phase, having discovered a wonderful cane sugar from the Ile Maurice that is particularly rich in vitamins, minerals, and flavor. With this new delight he has created a dark sugar biscuit with a light sugar milky syrup, nougatine feuilles flavored with cocoa, incomparable oeufs à la neige with a toasty taste accompanied by walnut croquants, astonishing sugar crusts with cocoa and almonds, and candied mandarin oranges with a semolina cake flavored with peppered ratafia. And that's not all: the kitchen also produces such fantastic whimsy as candied flowers, fruits and vegetables perfumed by anise, acacia, dill, or meadowsweet.
Ginette Bras and sommelier Sergio Calderon have put together an enviable cellar of wines, brandies, and other spirits. And you can still sample the delicious Aubrac menu at 200 F, which includes Bras's mother's aligot (garlicky mashed potatoes with Tomme cheese). C 450-750 F. M 200 F (weekdays, Sat lunch), 390 F, 600 F.

Michel Bras
(See restaurant above)
Closed Mon (exc Jul-Aug), Nov-Mar. 15 rms 850-1,500 F. Conf. Golf. No pets. Pkg. Helipad. V, AE.
The fifteen rooms are arranged in tiers so that each can enjoy a spectacular view. Minimal decoration: spacious, white-walled, carpeted, the rooms provide an alternative definition of luxury. Superlative breakfasts. Relais et Châteaux.

LAMAGDELAINE 46 → Cahors

LAMASTRE 07270
Paris 582 - Le Puy 73 - Privas 56 - Valence 40   *Ardèche*

Barattéro

Pl. Seignobos - 75 06 41 50
Closed Mon (exc Jul-Aug), Sun dinner, Dec 15-Feb. Open until 9pm. Priv rm: 45. Pkg. V, AE, DC, MC.
Rigorously crafted cooking based on fine products, served in a cozy dining room: duck foie gras sautéed in Banyuls, fillet of turbot with asparagus tips, plaice aïoli with girolles, local squab roasted with honey and spices, and a chestnut soufflé glacé. The tempting regional cellar drives up your bill, which is much less friendly than the welcome. C 280-420 F. M 160 F, 205 F, 290 F, 360 F, 425 F.

Hôtel du Midi
(See restaurant above)
See restaurant for closings. 13 rms 295-460 F. Half-board 390-450 F. Conf. Pkg. V, AE, DC, MC.
Vast, pleasant rooms with old-fashioned decor, some with views of the garden and countryside. Good and copious breakfasts.

Château d'Urbilhac
2 km, route de Vernoux
75 06 42 11, fax 75 06 52 75
Closed Oct 5-May 1. 13 rms 450-650 F. Half-board 500-575 F. Heated pool. Tennis. Pkg. V, AE, DC.
This Renaissance-style nineteenth-century château is perched at an altitude of 500 meters in a 60-hectare park. A shaded tennis court and panoramic swimming pool are just two of the

many facilities. Rooms are spacious and prettily furnished, with charm and personality.

LAMBERSART 59 → Lille

LAMORLAYE 60 → Chantilly

LANDERNEAU 29220
Paris 571 - Morlaix 39 - Brest 20 - Quimper 70 *Finistère*

Le Clos du Pontic
Rue du Pontic - 98 21 50 91
Closed lunch Sat & Mon (& Sun dinner & Mon off-seas). Open until 9:15pm. Priv rm: 50. **Hotel:** *32 rms 275-360 F. Half-board 275-295 F. Conf. Golf. Pkg. V, MC.*
Patrons are greeted warmly in a newly redecorated dining room that affords a tranquil view of the grounds; come here to sample Jean Saoût's generous cooking: warm oysters gratinéed with a garden vegetable brunoise, veal sweetbreads with langoustines, and an apple feuilleté flambéed with Lambig. Classic cellar. C 290-390 F. M 95 F (weekdays), 165 F, 185 F, 205 Г, 240 F.

LANDERSHEIM 67700
Paris 433 - Strasbourg 24 - Saverne 14 - Haguenau 31 *Bas-Rhin*

Auberge du Kochersberg ۞
Rue de Saessolsheim
88 69 91 58, fax 88 69 91 42
Closings not available. Open until 9:30pm. Priv rm: 50. Air cond. Garage pkg. V, AE, DC, MC.
This huge Alsatian dining room, elegantly rustic, offers Mario Lumann's traditional dishes, such as those on the 350 F menu: tasty and tender foie gras in Gewurztraminer gelatin, interesting and perfectly cooked pickerel with beef marrow quenelles, Marc de Muscat sherbet, slightly bland jambonnette of chicken in a livèche jus, good cheeses, bland strawberries in Kirsch. Superb cellar, perfect service. C 450-700 F. M 210 F (weekday lunch), 700 F (wine incl), 320 F, 410 F.

LANGEAIS 37130
Paris 258 - Angers 83 - Chinon 31 - Tours 25 *Indre/Loire*

■ In Saint-Patrice 37130 9 km SW on N 152

Château de Rochecotte
47 96 16 16, fax 47 96 90 59
Open daily until 9:30pm. Pkg. V, AE, DC, MC.
In this ravishingly beautiful Renaissance château, you can choose the flower-bedecked Italianate terrace or the elegant contemporary dining room, both appropriate settings for Emmanuelle Pasquier's clever, carefully prepared and personalized variations on classics: gâteau of foie gras, smoked bacon, and potatoes in a truffle vinaigrette; delicate sea bass sautéed with spices and accompanied by a black-olive piperade; excellent veal sweetbreads braised in honey and lime juice. Superb desserts. Christelle, number two sister, will skillfully select the region's best wines (at reasonable prices) to match your meal. Friendly, professional welcome and service. C 330-400 F. M 190 F, 280 F.

Château de Rochecotte ♨♥
(See restaurant above)
Open year-round. 2 stes 1,100 F. 26 rms 350-840 F. Half-board 275-620 F. Conf. Pkg. Helipad. V, AE, DC, MC.
Talleyrand gave this breathtaking château to the Duchesse de Dino, his last love. French formal gardens, Italianate terraces, and a rusticated façade form an exquisite jewel case for the hotel's magnificent contemporary rooms. The atmosphere is relaxed, the Pasquier family's welcome heartfelt.

LANGON 33210
Paris 604 - Bordeaux 47 - Marmande 37 - Libourne 54 *Gironde*

Claude Darroze ۞
95, cours du Gal-Leclerc
56 63 00 48, fax 56 63 41 15
Closed Jan 5-20, Oct 15-Nov 5. Open until 9:30pm. Priv rm: 60. Garden dining. Pkg. V, AE, DC, MC.
This gorgeous former coach house boasts classy decor and service staff to match. Chef Claude Darroze, at the height of his powers, has a talent for bringing out the best in his remarkable ingredients. His generous, regional cooking is both simple and intelligent, and we award him an extra point this year for dishes like perfectly cooked langoustines served on a bed of lettuce with snow peas and artichoke bottoms, a real marvel. In season, sample fresh morels stuffed with a fabulous risotto, with a slice of foie gras. And to finish, an ethereal Grand Marnier soufflé. The cellar offers a splendid choice of great bottles from 1920 to 1970. The welcome is friendly, and there's a special room available for small children to nap in, a rare service. Prices are high but justified. C 320-450 F. M 195 F, 320 F, 420 F.

Claude Darroze ♨♥
(See restaurant above)
Closed Jan 5-20, Oct 15-Nov 5. 1 ste 550 F. 14 rms 280-420 F. Half-board 500-600 F. Conf. Golf. Pkg. V, AE, DC, MC.
Spacious, soundproof rooms with lovely, well equipped bathrooms. Sumptuous breakfasts and fine service.

12/20 La Table du Sauternais ۞
7 km W on D 116, in Boutoc
56 63 43 44
Closed Mon. Open until 10pm. Terrace dining. Pkg. V, AE, MC.
This cozy little restaurant favored by holidaymakers sits among vineyards and offers robust regional cooking. On the 170 F menu: langouste salad, fish cassolette, desserts. Excellent cellar. C 210-350 F. M 70 F, 120 F, 170 F.

LANGRES 52200
Paris 294 - Auxerre 155 - Dijon 68 - Vittel 72 *Haute-Marne*

12/20 Grand Hôtel de l'Europe
23-25, rue Diderot
25 87 10 88, fax 25 87 60 65
Closed Mon (exc dinner in seas), Sun dinner, May 8-22, Oct 22-24. Open until 9pm. Priv rm: 16. Garage pkg. V, AE, DC, MC.
Steeped in tradition, this seventeenth-century hostelry is at its most attractive when the kitchen keeps things simple. Stick with the 110 F menu

offering sausage in brioche, roast guinea fowl with morels, cheeses, and dessert. The setting is charming. **C** 150-250 F. **M** 70 F, 100 F, 110 F (weekday lunch, Sat), 190 F, 110 F (Sun).

12/20 Lion d'Or
Route de Vesoul
25 87 03 30, fax 25 87 60 67
Closed Fri dinner (exc Jul-Aug), Sat (exc dinner in seas), end Dec-beg Feb. Open until 9pm. Priv rm: 20. Garden dining. Pkg. V, AE, MC.
If Pierre-Yves Ouary would just lighten up on the cream, we would have no complaints at all about his cooking. On the 95 F menu: fresh mackerel fillet, rabbit à la provençale, dessert. Nice Burgundies on the wine list. Charming welcome. **C** 210-280 F. **M** 78 F (weekdays), 95 F, 145 F, 190 F, 200 F.

LANNION   22300
Paris 515 - Brest 96 - St-Brieuc 63 - Morlaix 38   *Côtes/Armor*

Le Manoir de Crec'h Goulifen
Route de Beg-Leguer, Servel - 96 47 26 17
Open year-round. 7 rms 250-380 F. Tennis. Golf. Pkg. No cards.
Nestled in lush grounds just three kilometers from the sea, this Breton manor promises a quiet night's sleep.

◼ In La Ville-Blanche 22300   4 km E on D 786

La Ville Blanche
96 37 04 28, fax 96 46 57 82
Closed Sun dinner & Mon (exc Jul-Aug), Jan 11-Feb 12. Open until 9pm (10pm in summer). Priv rm: 16. Garage pkg. V, AE, DC, MC.
Four generations of the Jaguin family have operated this pleasant restaurant in a white house. The inventive cuisine is provided by two brothers, Jean-Yves and Daniel: langoustine and leek fricassée, mitonnée of rabbit and pig's cheek with sage, and a millefeuille of caramelized apples. Good choice of Bordeaux. **C** 250-300 F. **M** 90 F (weekday lunch, Sat), 170 F, 230 F, 300 F.

LAON   02000
Paris 139 - Saint-Quentin 46 - Reims 47 - Compiègne 71   *Aisne*

Les Chevaliers
3, rue Sérurier
23 23 43 78, fax 23 23 40 71
Closed Dec 16-Jan 3. 15 rms 150-340 F. Golf. V, MC.
This age-old hotel set in the center of the upper town has been nicely remodeled and boasts simple but comfortable rooms.

La Petite Auberge
45, bd P.-Brossolette
23 23 02 38, fax 23 79 50 38
Closed Sat lunch & Sun (exc hols). Open until 9:30pm. Priv rm: 15. Terrace dining. No pets. V, AE, MC.
Willy-Marc Zorn's refreshing cuisine based on superb products is served in a pleasant, old-fashioned bourgeois setting. This year we enjoyed his rabbit gâteau with onion compote, fillet of fresh cod in thyme-scented meat jus, warm caramelized apples, and crème anglaise

made with white wine. Friendly welcome. **C** 340-430 F. **M** 159 F (wine incl), 125 F, 160 F, 195 F, 260 F.

Le Relais Charlemagne
6 km NE, in Samoussy
23 22 21 50, fax 23 22 18 75
Closed Mon, Sun dinner, Wed, Aug 1-8. Open until 9pm. Priv rm: 60. Garden dining. Pkg. V, AE, MC.
William Gelve and Jean-Pierre Evra offer scrupulous, consistent, classic cuisine: pickerel roasted in a potato crust, foie gras sautéed with cherries, saddle of young rabbit and veal sweetbreads with morels, lobster and sea scallop ragoût with asparagus, and a strawberry palet for dessert. The bright, beflowered dining room is a pleasant place to linger, but the prices are high. Competent service. **C** 350-450 F. **M** 125 F (weekdays), 200 F, 260 F, 330 F.

◼ In Liesse 02350   12 km NE

Château de Barive
23 22 15 15, fax 23 22 08 39
Closed Jan 2-20. Open until 9:30pm. Priv rm: 20. Heated pool. Pkg. V, AE, DC, MC.
This eighteenth-century château has been splendidly restored. Chef Jos Bergman proved his talents at La Truffe in Brussels and Le Florence in Reims. Here he's found the ideal setting (he's in charge of the whole show) and has created a menu featuring the region's best. Try his sumptuous warm sea scallops and oysters with pink caviar, veal sweetbreads and kidneys in sweet-sour sauce, and fresh fruits with a Champagne sabayon. Friendly welcome by Madame Bergman. Short but manageably priced wine list. **C** 300-400 F. **M** 130 F, 150 F, 210 F, 260 F, 330 F.

Château de Barive
(See restaurant above)
Closed Jan 2-20. 2 stes 780 F. 15 rms 380-580 F. Half-board 395-600 F. Conf. Heated pool. Tennis. Pkg. Helipad. V, AE, DC, MC.
Here's a lovely place to stay: a beautifully renovated nineteenth-century hunting lodge set in wooded grounds. The rooms are mid-sized, elegantly decorated, and open onto the surrounding countryside or the garden and duck pond. Amenities include a sauna and a library. Cheerful welcome and service. Full breakfasts on demand.

LATTES 34   → Montpellier

LAVAL   53000
Paris 291 - Tours 140 - Angers 73   *Mayenne*

Le Bistro de Paris
67, rue du Val-de-Mayenne
43 56 98 29, fax 43 56 52 85
Closed Sat lunch, Sun, Aug 15-30. Open until 9:45pm. Priv rm: 20. No pets. V.
Envied by other restaurateurs in the region, award-winning chef Guy Lemercier continues to create flawless meals at unbelievably low prices. His chic little establishment on the banks of the Mayenne, presided over by his smiling wife, is perpetually booked solid. No wonder the competition wishes he would take it elsewhere! We, on the other hand, have been consistently

delighted by Lemercier's oft-renewed repertoire. On a recent visit, we tasted a remoulade of smoked herring served with sautéed sole and salmon, a tartare of sea bass and tiny sea scallops enlivened with coriander, red mullet stuffed with foie gras and flavored with vanilla, and beef fillet paired with roasted andouille doused with wine vinegar. The prices are astonishingly low for such quality: first courses at 85 F, main courses at 95 F, and desserts at 40 F. The cellar is choice and just as democratically priced as the food. Just remember: reserve your table in advance! **C** 260-300 F.   **M** 135 F,   155 F (weekdays), 250 F.

Les Blés d'Or

83, rue V.-Boissel
43 53 14 10, fax 43 49 02 84
Closed Sat lunch, Sun. Open until 10pm. Priv rm: 15. Pkg. V, AE, DC, MC.
A new chef, Mickael Petit, offers fresh, sincere cooking in this elegant country inn. You'll find a warm lentil salad with duck "tidbits", monkfish roasted with rosemary and garlic, and a croquant of pears and apples with cinnamon ice cream. The superb, affordably priced cellar is under the direction of Françoise Portier, daughter of the chef-sommelier who assembled it. **C** 250-350 F. **M** 115 F (lunch).

La Gerbe de Blé

(See restaurant above)
Open year-round. 2 stes 495-585 F. 6 rms 295-495 F. Half-board 395-470 F. Conf. No pets. Valet pkg. V, AE, DC.
The huge, nicely decorated rooms are well equipped and have fine bathrooms; a renovation is in the offing. They are rather noisy, however, as they overlook a busy street. Good Continental or English breakfasts. Friendly owners.

L'Algue Bleue

62, av. du Gal-de-Gaulle
94 71 05 96, fax 94 71 20 12
Closed Thu lunch & Wed off-seas, Oct 15-Mar 14. Open until 10pm. Priv rm: 100. Garden dining. Garage pkg. V, AE, DC.
This seafood restaurant boasts a lovely portside location and view of the Hyères Islands, a leafy terrace, and a pleasant dining room. Chef Bernard Roger nets the best the sea has to offer: langoustine pot-au-feu with basil, pieds-et-paquets (lamb's feet and tripe), fillet of sea bass with a bacon cream and preserved lemons, and a yummy dark chocolate soufflé with orange peel. Nothing suits all this better than a little Château Sainte-Marguerite white. **C** 300 F. **M** 180 F, 250 F, 350 F.

La Calanque

(See restaurant above)
Closed Oct 15-Mar 14. 2 stes 950-1,050 F. 35 rms 500-650 F. Half-board 435-710 F. Conf. Heated pool. Golf. Garage pkg. V, AE, DC.
This handsome, post-war building, set before the moorings, is fully modernized. The guest rooms are decorated in good taste and all have sea views. Boat trips and tuna fishing can be arranged.

Belle Vue

In Saint-Clair
94 71 01 06, fax 94 71 64 72
Closed Oct-Mar. 19 rms 340-750 F. Restaurant. Half-board 400-610 F. Conf. No pets. Pkg. V, AE, DC.
Overlooking the sea and coast, this quiet, charming hotel offers rustic but comfortable rooms.

Les Tamaris

Plage de Saint-Clair - 94 71 07 22
Closed Jan 10-Feb 15, Nov 15-Dec 20. Open until 10:30pm (11pm in summer). Priv rm: 140. Terrace dining. Air cond. Pkg. V, AE, MC.
Raymond, the son of a local fisherman, has run this seaside restaurant for some 30 years. It's a popular spot in summer, and one is invariably obliged to queue for a terrace table. Raymond's recipe for success is fresh seafood, simply but perfectly cooked. His bouillabaisse is monumental. **C** 250-400 F.

■ In Aiguebelle 83980   4.5 km E on D 559

Les Roches

1, av. des Trois-Dauphins - 94 71 05 05 (R)
94 71 05 07 (H), fax 94 71 08 40
Closed Nov 1-Easter. Open until 10pm. Priv rm: 40. Terrace dining. Air cond. Pool. Valet pkg. V, AE, DC.
If the expression weren't so shopworn we'd be tempted to call this seafront restaurant—huddled behind hibiscus hedges and bougainvilleas—a paradise. Well, so be it! Les Roches has become one of the Riviera's most luxurious establishments, and the new chef, Christian Plumail, knows his Provençal ingredients right down to the last olive. And we salute the establishment's effort to keep prices in line, such as with the bargain-priced "menu du marché". On our last visit we savored sunny creations like a delicious soup made from tiny snails and laced with fresh coriander; a creamy crab soup flavored with basil; luscious toasts topped with sardines, peppers, capers and tomatoes; divine pieds et paquets (lamb's feet and tripe) made from Sisteron lamb; grilled John Dory with rosemary and an enlivening touch of orange; pageot (a much-loved local fish) served with a cauliflower and anchovy mousseline; a crisp breast of sweet-sour duck; and hefty chunks of young rabbit sautéed with Niçois olives. For dessert, clafoutis with sautéed bigarreaux and vanilla ice cream, croquant of Carros strawberries, a fresh sablé à la brousse, and dried fruits perfectly matched by sage and honey ice cream. All this, and a sweeping sea view too, in a luminous yellow dining room staffed by supremely skilled waiters. Sommelier Pierre Prat has diligently amassed scores of the best wines of Provence and Corsica. Time slips by like warmed honey when you settle in for a few hours of pure enjoyment, and there's a buffet lunch served by the pool. So if this isn't heaven, please don't tell us! **C** 380-550 F. **M** 280 F, 420 F.

Les Roches

(See restaurant above)
Closed Nov 1-Apr 1. 12 stes 2,200-6,000 F. 33 rms 950-2,300 F. Half-board 1,400-1,650 F. Air cond. Conf. Pool. Golf. Valet pkg. V, AE, DC.
This *petit palace* is unquestionably one of the most refined of recent constructions on this

stretch of coast, unexpected but welcome. The sunny, antique-filled rooms, with terraces overlooking the sea, are furnished with taste, the bathrooms adorned with marble and Salerno tiles. A fire destroyed eight rooms here this year, but the owners have replaced them with even more luxurious accommodation. Shady footpaths wind through a garden studded with cactus and rare trees, leading to the private beach and freshwater swimming pool. Tennis and boating facilities are close at hand, and there's a golf course nearby. Relais et Châteaux.

See also: **Bormes-les-Mimosas, Porquerolles (Ile de), Port-Cros (Ile de)**

LECTOURE	32700

Paris 700 - Agen 36 - Condom 23 - Toulouse 94 - Auch 35   *Gers*

Hôtel de Bastard ☉
Rue Lagrange
62 68 82 44, fax 62 68 76 81
Closed dinner Fri & Sun (Sat lunch off-seas), Jan 2-Feb 14. Open until 9:30pm. Priv rm: 60. Terrace dining. Heated pool. Pkg. V, AE, DC, MC.
Everything about this gorgeous eighteenth-century town house with lovely period decor whispers refinement. Jean-Luc Arnaud's highly personal cooking offers generous portions of regional specialties: gambas sautéed in olive oil and flambéed with Pastis, anise-scented flambéed sea bass, and a tasty apple feuilleté with caramelized crème anglaise. Fine cellar with many Bordeaux, regional bottlings, and excellent Armagnacs. Anne Arnaud's welcome is charming. Discreet service. C 280-350 F. M 80 F (weekdays, Sat), 140 F, 230 F.

Hôtel de Bastard ♠♥
(See restaurant above)
Closed Jan 2-Feb 14. 1 ste 600 F. 28 rms 190-360 F. Half-board 270-460 F. Conf. Heated pool. Golf. Pkg. V, AE, DC, MC.
This superb town house boasts a terrace and garden. Rooms are well kept and equipped. Friendly welcome. Good breakfasts.

LEMBACH	67510

Paris 460 - Strasbourg 56 - Wissembourg 15   *Bas-Rhin*

Auberge du Cheval Blanc ☉
4, rue de Wissembourg
88 94 41 86, fax 88 94 20 74
Closed Mon, Tue, Feb 6-24, Jul 3-21. Open until 9pm. Priv rm: 25. Pkg. V, AE, MC.
Opulence and splendor envelop you as you cross the threshold of this enormous, eighteenth-century coaching inn, operated for untold generations by the Mischler clan. The book-lined, carved-wood dining room, with its stained-glass windows and stone fireplace, is animated by the nightly crush of some 200 eager gastronomes from both banks of the Rhine. Waiters (their bow ties are *never* askew) dash about, serving such luxurious, perfectly executed dishes as a pig's foot crépine with foie gras, rack of lamb in an herb crust, or a monkfish roasted with Szechuan peppercorns and paired with delicious vegetables flavored with sweet garlic, hazelnuts, and meat jus. We also liked the breast of guinea fowl stuffed with foie gras accompanied by a guinea fowl thigh confit with an

elegant garnish of snow peas and tomatoes, and the fine sautéed kidneys in a delicious jus. For dessert, sample the cheesecake garnished with berries (just a bit too sweet). Vast wine list, mainly of shippers' wines. Efficient and attentive service. C 400-600 F. M 170 F, 240 F, 310 F, 395 F.

Gimbelhof ♠♥
9 km N on D 3 and RF
88 94 43 58, fax 88 94 23 30
Closed Nov 15-Dec 26, 1 wk in Feb. 8 rms 78-210 F. Restaurant. Half-board 140-170 F. Pkg. V, MC.
Lost in a magnificent wood, this quiet, modest little hostelry has cozy rooms at unbelievably low prices.

LENS	62300

Paris 203 - Arras 18 - Lille 34 - St-Omer 73   *P./Calais*

Lutétia
29, pl. de la République - 21 28 02 06
Closings not available. 23 rms 180-210 F. Pkg. No cards.
Pleasant and neat as a pin, this family-run hotel is a friendly place to spend the night.

■ **In Bully-les-Mines 62160**   9 km W

12/20 A L'Enfant du Pays
152, rue R.-Salengro
21 29 12 33, fax 21 29 27 55
Closed Sun dinner. Open until 10pm. Pkg. V, AE, DC, MC.
Classic technique applied to first-rate ingredients yields dishes like sea scallop ravioli, puff pastry stuffed with asparagus tips paired with a mousseline sauce, rack of lamb, pig's jowl civet, remarkable cheeses, and a citrus parfait glacé. All accompanied by wines small and great, at reasonable prices. C 160-320 F. M 60 F, 65 F, 80 F (weekdays, Sat lunch), 135 F, 180 F.

LESQUIN (AIRPORT OF) 59	→ Lille

LESTELLE-BÉTHARRAM	64800

Paris 790 - Pau 23 - Lourdes 16 - Laruns 35 - Nay 9   *Pyrénées-A.*

Le Vieux Logis ☉
Route des Grottes
59 71 94 87, fax 59 71 96 75
Closed Sun dinner off-seas, Mon, Jun 12-16. Open until 9pm. Priv rm: 120. Terrace dining. Hotel: 40 rms 210-270 F. Half-board 350-400 F. Conf. Pool. Pkg. Helipad. V, AE, MC.
Between Béarn and Bigorre in an island of greenery, this charming old farmhouse offers a warm, family-style welcome, along with the generous regional cooking of Pierre Gaye and his son Francis: lemon-marinated trout, veal chop with morels, and orange crêpes. Special Béarnaise soirées are organized. C 230-300 F. M 90 F (weekdays, Sat), 140 F, 210 F.

LEVALLOIS-PERRET 92	→ PARIS Suburbs

*Some establishments change their **closing times** without warning. It is always wise to check in advance.*

LEVANT (ILE DU) 83400

Var

 La Brise Marine 🌲
Pl. du Village
94 05 91 15, fax 94 05 93 21
Closed end Sep-Apr. 23 rms 290-445 F. Restaurant. Half-board 445-890 F. Conf. Heated pool. V, MC.
Situated at the high point of the island, overlooking the sea, the Brise boasts handsome, comfortable, well-equipped rooms set round a delightful, flower-filled patio. Superb swimming pool and sun-terrace.

Hôtel Gaétan
94 05 91 78, fax 94 36 77 17
Closed Nov-Mar. 14 rms 220-250 F. Restaurant. Half-board 290-320 F. Conf. V, AE, MC.
Set in a pleasant garden, the Gaétan's rooms are very simple but well kept. Solarium, bar.

Héliotel 🌲
94 05 90 63, fax 94 05 90 20
Closed Sep-Easter. 1 ste 750-1,250 F. 18 rms. Rms for disabled. Restaurant. Half-board 350-475 F. Conf. Heated pool. No pets. V, AE, MC.
Facing the Iles d'Or and hidden in the greenery between the nearby village and Héliopolis, this hotel offers a piano bar and video room (well isolated from the bedrooms).

LEVENS 06670

Paris 955 - Nice 23 - Antibes 44 - St-Martin-Vésubie 37 *Alpes-Mar.*

12/20 Les Santons
3, rue de l'Escalada - 93 79 72 47
Closed Wed, Jan 4-Feb 8, Jun 26-Jul 5, Oct 2-11. Open until 9pm. Garden dining. V, MC.
Join the locals vying for tables on the terrace at this likeable village inn that features tasty, light, and moderately priced cooking. On the 135 F menu: appetizers, old-fashioned chicken terrine, rabbit with tagliatelle, goat cheeses, and a choice of desserts. C 210-310 F. M 100 F (exc Sun), 135 F, 155 F, 238 F.

LEVERNOIS 21 → Beaune

LEZOUX 63190

Paris 390 - Clermont-Ferrand 27 - Vichy 42 *Puy-de-Dôme*

Château de Codignat 🌲
8 km SE on D 223 & D 115 E, in Bort-l'-Etang - 73 68 43 03, fax 73 68 93 54
Closed Nov 5-Mar 20. 4 stes 1,300-2,000 F. 14 rms 600-1,300 F. Restaurant. Half-board 680-1,050 F. Air cond. Conf. Heated pool. Tennis. Valet pkg. Helipad. V, AE, DC, MC.
This fifteenth-century château, complete with weathered wrought iron, armor, and parapets is the centerpiece of a vast country estate. There are four luxurious suites, as well as fourteen spacious rooms, all decorated in the rather heavy Haute Époque style. Some bathrooms are equipped with Jacuzzi. Relais et Châteaux.

12/20 Les Voyageurs
2, pl. de la Mairie
73 73 10 49, fax 73 68 21 60
Closed Sun dinner, Mon, Feb 1-15, Oct 3-20. Open until 9:30pm. Priv rm: 20. Pkg. V, MC.

Travelers gladly halt at this little hotel for the appealing cooking: sole paupiette with crayfish, veal sweetbreads and kidneys with morels, and a marquise au chocolat cake for dessert. C 190-220 F. M 80 F (exc Sun), 240 F (Sun), 120 F, 180 F, 200 F.

LIESSE 02 → Laon

LILLE 59000

Paris 219 - Dunkerque 80 - Bruxelles 116 - Arras 51 *Nord*

Le Baan Thaï 14
22, bd J.-B.-Lebas
20 86 06 01, fax 20 86 03 23
Closed Sat lunch, Sun, last 3 wks of Aug. Open until 10:30pm. No pets. Pkg. V, AE, MC.
This extremely successful (and ever-improving) Thai restaurant serves spicy, sweet-and-sour specialties such as scampi brochettes with saté sauce, caramelized chicken with young ginger, and curried monkfish. Dishes with a wide range of hotness levels are offered. C 250-320 F. M 145 F (lunch), 210 F.

Bellevue 🌲
5, rue J.-Roisin
20 57 45 64, fax 20 40 07 93
Open year-round. 3 stes 760 F. 58 rms 440-560 F. Restaurant. Conf. V, AE, DC, MC.
The wistful charm of a pre-war provincial hotel fills the spacious, comfortable, well-soundproofed rooms of the Bellevue, with their 1930s furniture and excellent bathrooms. The reception is rather solemn. Cocktail bar; room service.

12/20 Le Bistrot Tourangeau
61, bd Louis-XIV
20 52 74 64, fax 20 85 06 39
Closed Sun, Jul 15-Aug 15. Open until 10:30pm. Priv rm: 30. Air cond. Pkg. V, AE, DC, MC.
A white-collar crowd flocks to this wood-paneled restaurant for the copious traditional cooking: pickerel viennoise with sorrel butter, old-fashioned pig's foot galette, sole meunière with steamed potatoes, and a dark chocolate marquise cake. The cellar is magnificent. C 200-300 F. M 100 F (weekdays, Sat lunch), 195 F (dinner), 145 F.

11/20 Brasserie de la Paix
25, pl. Rihour - 20 40 02 27
Closings not available. Open until midnight. Air cond. No pets. V, AE.
A favorite late-night spot, this classic brasserie decorated with painted tiles specializes in raffish, full-flavored dishes: langoustine salad in Sherry vinegar, fish sauerkraut, émincé of duck breast with caramelized fruit, and crème brûlée with walnuts and oranges. C 200-250 F (weekday lunch). M 112 F (lunch exc Sun), 140 F (dinner exc Sun).

Carlton
3, rue de Paris
20 13 33 13, fax 20 51 48 17
Open year-round. 7 stes 980-2,400 F. 53 rms 690-840 F. Rms for disabled. Restaurant. Half-board 1,000 F. Air cond. Conf. Golf. Pkg. V, AE, DC, MC.
Across the road from the opera house and just 200 meters from the railway station. The regular-

ly remodeled rooms are large and comfortable, with well-equipped working areas. The famous Brasserie Jean (good beers and regional stews) is in the same building.

Le Club Clément Marot
16, rue de Pas
20 57 01 10, fax 20 57 39 69
Closed Sun, Christmas-Jan 1, 1 wk in Feb, 3 wks in Aug. Open until 10pm. Priv rm: 50. Terrace dining. Air cond. Garage pkg. V, AE, DC, MC.
Claire and Clément Marot's cozy little establishment is indeed like a club—comfortable and convivial. Prime ingredients go into the meticulous, professional cooking, and the first set menu has many local fans: skate terrine with pike mousseline, lamb navarin, cheeses, and a pear bavarian with raspberry sauce. Nice, well chosen wine list. Friendly welcome and good service. C 270-340 F. M 135 F, 180 F, 220 F.

L'Écume des Mers
10, rue de Pas
20 54 95 40, fax 20 54 96 66
Closed Sun dinner, 3 wks in Aug. Open until midnight. Priv rm: 55. Terrace dining. Air cond. Pkg. V, AE, MC.
Lille's *beau monde* has discovered this reconverted pub, done up by the same family that owns L'Huîtrière (see below) like an elegant schooner. The same suppliers provide flipping-fresh seafood to both. Well-crafted, reasonably priced offerings include salmon tartare, house sardines in oil, aïoli with cod and vegetables, and little vanilla or chocolate pots-de-crème. Attractive set menu served at lunch. C 220-320 F. M 220 F, 230 F, 250 F.

12/20 Le Hochepot 🕄
6, rue du Nouveau-Siècle
20 54 17 59, fax 20 42 92 43
Closed Sat lunch, Sun. Open until 10pm. Terrace dining. Air cond. Pkg. V, MC.
You'll discover lipsmacking, locally brewed beers and the best juniper-flavored Dutch gin in the region, at this absolutely authentic Flemish restaurant with a smart brick decor. Taste the potjevfleisch (three-meat terrine) with a gelatin coating flavored with juniper berries, terrine à l'ail d'Arleux (chicken liver terrine with plump cloves of garlic), and a rather dry brown sugar tart. C 220-320 F. M 95 F (weekday lunch, wine incl), 140 F, 180 F.

Hôtel Alliance
See restaurant Le Jardin du Cloître

L'Huîtrière
3, rue des Chats-Bossus
20 55 43 41, fax 20 55 23 10
Closed dinner Sun & hols, Jul 22-Aug. Open until 9:30pm. Priv rm: 36. Air cond. V, AE, DC, MC.
Wealthy customers continue to flock to this classic, conservative restaurant, whose elegant dining room is upholstered in red, paneled with warm oak, and illuminated by crystal sconces. Before settling in, though, guests must walk through what is doubtless the most impressive fishmonger's in France, its turn-of-the-century decor complete with painted ceramic tiles. It comes as no surprise then that the fish and seafood items on the menu are fabulously fresh, and handled faultlessly: delicately seasoned and

perfectly cooked langoustine ravioli with shellfish jus, and a fine John Dory pan-roasted with potatoes, pepper, olives, and lemon. For dessert, a delicious chicory ice cream with juniper sabayon. The new 280 F menu will bring some relief from the very high prices. The dazzling cellar (40,000 bottles) is administered by three accomplished sommeliers. The service is polished to a high sheen. An extra point this year. C 400-600 F. M 280 F (weekday lunch), 450 F, 550 F.

10/20 Le Jardin du Cloître
17, quai du Wault
20 30 62 62, fax 20 42 94 25
Open daily until 10:30pm. Priv rm: 250. No pets. Garage pkg. V, AE, DC, MC.
Once a convent cloister, now an elegant restaurant, the Jardin du Cloître is a lovely setting, but sadly the cooking fails to match it: paltry sea scallop salad, overcooked fillet of salmon served with too many garnishes, and a croquant made from two kinds of chocolate. C 300-400 F. M 98 F (weekday lunch), 195 F (exc weekdays), 160 F (weekdays).

🏯 Alliance
(See restaurant above)
Open year-round. 8 stes 900-1,500 F. 75 rms 640-750 F. Conf. Pkg. V, AE, DC, MC.
This centrally located luxury hotel, tucked behind seventeenth-century brick-and-stone walls, is built into the former Minimes convent. The rooms are superb, equipped with all the modern conveniences, including magnetized cards instead of keys.

🏯 Novotel-Centre
116, rue de l'Hôpital-Militaire
20 30 65 26, fax 20 30 04 04
Open year-round. 6 stes 600 F. 102 rms 530 F. Restaurant. Air cond. Conf. V, AE, DC, MC.
This modern hotel is strategically located behind the Grand Place, and offers sunny, comfortable, functional and totally soundproofed rooms. Friendly welcome. Bar.

Le Paris
52 bis, rue Esquermoise - 20 55 29 41
Closed Sun (exc hols), beg Aug-beg Sep. Open until 9:45pm. Priv rm: 90. Air cond. Pkg. V, AE, DC, MC.
Proprietor Loïc Martin has skillfully piloted this dignified restaurant through 30-odd years of changing fashions. The classic decor, velvet banquettes, and gleaming silverware make for a peaceful provincial atmosphere. Dedicated to his job, Martin goes to market himself, passing on the perfect produce to his chef Gérard Chamoley, whose cooking pays tribute to tradition. This year taste the salad of veal sweetbreads in hazlenut oil, quick-cooked salmon fillet in Médoc wine sauce, and verbena-enhanced peach soup with vanilla ice cream. Huge choice of game dishes in season. The cellar houses some appealing wines at interesting prices. C 300-420 F. M 150 F (weekday lunch), 196 F, 265 F.

---

*We're always happy to hear about **your discoveries** and receive your comments on ours. Please feel free to write to us stating clearly what you liked or disliked. Be concise but convincing, and take the time to argue your point.*

La Porte de Gand

At La Porte-de-Gand
20 74 28 66, fax 20 31 90 19
Closed Sun dinner, Mon, Dec 25-Jan 4, Aug 6-25, 1 wk at Easter. Open until 9:30pm (10pm by reserv). Priv rm: 80. Terrace dining. Pkg. V, AE, DC, MC.

Robert Bardot gave up the three-toque Flambard and opened this elegant, beautifully decorated restaurant set in a landmark building (a fortified military headquarters built by Louis XIV's architect Vauban). You dine in grand style on fine china with quality cutlery. But to keep prices down, the top-quality ingredients are slightly less "noble" than they were at Le Flambard. Needless to say, the fashionable locals are delighted. Sample the bargain-priced lunch menu: skate brandade with garlic confit and a brunoise of olives, chicken gigotin perfumed with bay leaves and rosemary, cheese, crème brûlée, and little cakes. The 250 F menu is also a fine choice, with the likes of tomato confit with crab meat, sole in a piperade jus, chicken gigotin, and dessert. Top-quality wine list. C 250-550 F. M 190 F (weekday lunch), 290 F, 380 F.

Le Restaurant Sébastopol

1, pl. de Sébastopol
20 57 05 05, fax 20 40 11 31
Closed Sun (exc hols). Open until 10pm. Priv rm: 23. V, AE, MC.

Locals are flocking to sample Jean-Luc Germond's light, original, and flavorful cuisine served in a sober Art Deco setting. Try the delicate, perfectly cooked red mullet tart with pistou butter, delectable calf's foot tournedos and duck confit with rosemary, and impeccable vanilla-scented crème brûlée. Excellent wine list with many Bordeaux. Friendly welcome. C 300-400 F. M 150 F (weekdays, Sat lunch), 260 F.

Le Varbet

2, rue de Pas
20 54 81 40, fax 20 57 55 18
Closed Sun, Mon, hols, Jul 13-Aug 17, Dec 23-Jan 4. Open until 9:30pm. Priv rm: 12. V, AE, DC, MC.

Gilles Vartanian makes sure that his menu changes every two months, so you're sure to find more than just fabulous foie gras and hearty veal kidneys (always listed) to choose from. In response, faithful regulars crowd Le Varbet's cozy dining room, clamoring for Vartanian's modern, generous cuisine: excellent blini with salmon roe, a lemony crab and herb cake, and house vanilla ice cream with strawberries and raspberries. Oddly chosen wine list, dominated by Bordeaux. C 350-400 F. M 350 F (weekday dinner, Sat), 160 F.

And also...

Our selection of places for inexpensive, quick, or late-night meals.
Bar de la Cloche (20 55 35 34 - 13, pl. du Théâtre. Open until 11pm.): At this wine bar you'll find regional dishes and cheery service (130-150 F).
Lakson (20 31 19 96 - 21, rue du Curé-St-Étienne. Open until 10:45pm.): This Scandinavian caterer offers salmon, herring, eels, and sturgeon eggs, to wash down with aquavit and flavored vodkas (180-280 F).
Christian Leclercq (20 74 17 05 - 9, rue Lepelletier. Open until 10pm.): A *maître-fromager* purveys his first-rate dairy wares at three tiny tables (fondue, raclette) (120-200 F).
Lino (20 31 12 17 - 1, rue des Trois-Couronnes.): Sunny Italian specialties are served in this doll's house of a restaurant (carpaccio, fresh lasagna, etc.) (150 F).

■ **In Lambersart 59130**   2 km NW

La Laiterie

138, av. de l'Hippodrome
20 92 79 73, fax 20 22 16 19
Closed Sun dinner. Open until 10:30pm. Priv rm: 40. Garden dining. Garage pkg. V, AE, MC.

When the weather is fine you can dine in the garden of this old café just outside Lille, in a delightful country atmosphere. In winter, the glassed-in dining room is so bright and light that it feels as if you're sitting out of doors! Do not think that the relaxed, family-style manner of the young owners means they are unprofessional. The service is peerless. And chef Ludovic Vantours, seconded by Christophe Thorel, offers inventive cooking: fresh sea flavor and a touch of exoticism in the crab and mango salad with a citrus vinaigrette, and a delicious dodine of young rabbit with a foie gras stuffing that moistens the rabbit meat, flavored with a touch of rosemary and coated with a Beaumes-de-Venise gelatin. Or the savory veal sweetbreads with green asparagus flavored with fresh coriander and served with a fine potato croustillant. Admirable, original choice of wines by Kamel Yeddou. Attentive, un-stiff service. C 300-450 F. M 150 F (weekday lunch), 360 F (wine incl), 240 F, 260 F, 380 F.

■ **In Lesquin (airport of) 59810**   12 km SE

▲▲ Mercure

110, rue J.-Jaurès
20 87 46 46, fax 20 87 46 47
Open year-round. 213 rms 470-520 F. Rms for disabled. Air cond. Conf. Garage pkg. V, AE, DC, MC.

A recent facelift transformed this vast hotel complex into an American-style establishment, with spacious, very comfortable rooms, and a sauna. Shuttle service to the airport.

■ **In Loos 59120**   4 km SW on D 941

L'Enfant Terrible

25, rue du Mal-Foch
20 07 22 11, fax 20 44 80 16
Closed Sun dinner, Mon, Aug 16-31. Open until 9:30pm. Priv rm: 20. Garden dining. Pkg. V, MC.

Owner Jean-Jacques Desplanque's cooking is bold and original. Try the improbably good foie gras marinated in peach wine, harmonious fillet of sea bass with crayfish, and an excellent millefeuille of crêpes flavored with chicory. Classic, affordable cellar; jovial welcome in a large dining room with an ordinary but pleasant decor. C 280-380 F. M 100 F, 150 F, 250 F, 300 F, 400 F.

*Some establishments change their **closing times** without warning. It is always wise to check in advance.*

In Marcq-en-Barœul 59700 5 km NE on N 350

Le Septentrion

Ferme des Marguerites,
Parc du Château du Vert-Bois
20 46 26 98, fax 20 46 38 33
Closed Sun dinner, Mon, Thu dinner, Feb school hols, Aug 1-22. Open until 9:30pm. Priv rm: 80. Garden dining. Pkg. V, AE, DC, MC.
The intimate, old-fashioned decor of the first dining room, and its apricot-colored contemporary counterpart next door, are further brightened by the gorgeous greenery of the surrounding château grounds. Chef Gilbert Lelaurain offers Northern-influenced cooking that occasionally glimmers with warm Southern accents: fricassée of fresh oysters spiced with cinnamon, chicken thigh braised in brown bear with honey cake, and a chicory and juniper berry Délice de Septentrion for dessert. Friendly welcome. C 220-330 F. M 150 F, 180 F, 290 F.

L'Europe

Av. de la Marne
20 72 17 30, fax 20 89 92 34
Open year-round. 1 ste 680-1,300 F. 124 rms 550-680 F. Rms for disabled. Restaurant. Half-board 345-905 F. Air cond. Conf. Golf. Pkg. V, AE, DC, MC.
This mammoth hotel complex provides functional rooms and the biggest conference halls in the region. Sauna; bar; fitness center.

See also: Roubaix, Tourcoing

L'Amphitryon

26, rue de la Boucherie
55 33 36 39, fax 55 32 98 50
Closed Sun, Feb school hols, 1st 2 wks of Aug. Open until 10:30pm. Priv rm: 24. Terrace dining. V, AE, MC.
Pascal Robert's cooking, though resolutely contemporary, draws inspiration from the classic repertoire, reinterpreting and updating it all the while. Try the excellent monkfish fillets roasted with cumin and tomato confit with mint, veal sweetbreads in acacia honey sauce, and a gooey biscuit au chocolat. The setting is gorgeous: bouquets of flowers, fresh linen, and classic tableware fill the comfortable, sunny dining room with exposed half-timbering, set in a pretty street in the town center. Charming, courteous service. Fine, well-balanced wine list. C 240-350 F. M 95 F & 140 F (weekday lunch, Sat), 125 F, 175 F, 280 F.

Le Champlevé

1, pl. du Pdt-Wilson - 55 34 43 34
Closed Sat lunch, Sun. Open until 9:30pm. Air cond. Pkg. V, AE.
Fabrice Amardeilh's cooking offers serious, well prepared dishes in a pleasant blue and white dining room with a new veranda: sea snail ravioli, savory quail gigotin with a corn cake, and an unctuous white chocolate griottin. Fine welcome, rather scattered service; the cellar is intelligently stocked. C 260-320 F. M 98 F (weekday lunch), 150 F (wine incl), 195 F.

Jeanne-d'Arc

17, av. du Gal-de-Gaulle
55 77 67 77, fax 55 79 86 75
Closed Dec 24-Jan 2. 52 rms 240-460 F. Conf. Garage pkg. V, AE, DC, MC.
An excellent stopover, well equipped and just 50 meters from the Bénédictins railway station. The rooms are all different, with decors ranging from contemporary to Louis XV; number 207 is our favorite.

Luk Hôtel

29, pl. Jourdan
55 33 44 00, fax 55 34 33 57
Open year-round. 57 rms 190-360 F. Half-board 220-250 F. V, AE, DC, MC.
Located in the town center, the Luk has luxurious, rather overblown decor, but is an unquestionably comfortable hotel.

Philippe Redon

3, rue d'Aguesseau - 55 34 66 22
Closed Mon lunch, Sun. Annual closings not available. Open until 10pm. Air cond. V, AE, DC, MC.
Philippe Redon offers rigorous, precise, and admirably streamlined cooking. Locals have been flocking to his 1930s–style restaurant since it opened a couple of years ago. And for good reason. Try his sardine tian with lemon and candied ginger, noisettes of milk-fed lamb, and a chocolate-cherry glacé for dessert. Friendly welcome; attractive, reasonably priced wine list. C 270-370 F. M 110 F, 150 F, 200 F, 280 F.

Le Richelieu

40, av. Baudin
55 34 22 82, fax 55 32 48 73
Open year-round. 32 rms 260-340 F. Half-board 380-460 F. Air cond. Golf. Pkg. V, AE, DC, MC.
This quiet hotel in the town center has sunny, well-soundproofed rooms. Warm welcome and a pleasant bar. Meals on trays available.

Royal Limousin

1, pl. de la République
55 34 65 30, fax 55 34 55 21
Open year-round. 11 stes 680-1,200 F. 66 rms 340-580 F. Restaurant. Air cond. Conf. V, AE, DC.
A modern, well situated hotel which offers many facilities and services. The immaculate rooms are spacious and sunny, and some are luxurious. Meals for groups available.

And also...

Our selection of places for inexpensive, quick, or late-night meals.
Le Bœuf à la Mode (55 77 73 95 - 60, rue F.-Chénieux. Open until 10:30pm.): Fine Limousin beef and lamb, simply or elaborately prepared (200-300 F).
Les Petits Ventres (55 33 34 02 - 20, rue de la Boucherie. Open until 10pm.): Robust "pavement" fare (offal, tripe, grilled meats), served at a slow pace in a picturesque, timbered house (150 F).
Le Royalty (55 34 56 65 - 1, pl. de la République.): This elegant eating house is favored by guests from nearby hotels. Brasserie-style food (seafood assortments, *plats du jour*) at reasonable prices (150 F).
Le Versailles (55 34 13 39 - 20, pl. d'Aine. Open until midnight.): Classic French fare in a casual atmosphere (160-180 F).

■ In **Saint-Martin-du-Fault 87510**   11 km NW

Chapelle Saint-Martin
55 75 80 17, fax 55 75 89 50
*Closed Jan-Feb 15. Open until 10pm. Priv rm: 60. No
pets. Valet pkg. V, MC.*
A new chef has just arrived in this lovely former
mansion with an elegant garden and an opulently decorated dining room. We will leave the chef
time to settle in before rating his ravioli of foie
gras and smoked duck, John Dory with garlic
confit and vegetable tempura, and a gooey
chocolate cake with chocolate sherbet, all accompanied by well chosen wines. C 350-450 F.
M 190 F (lunch exc Sun), 250 F, 390 F.

Chapelle Saint-Martin
(See restaurant above)
*Closed Jan-Feb 15. 3 stes 1,350-1,500 F. 8 rms 590-
1,100 F. Rms for disabled. Half-board 750-850 F.
Conf. Heated pool. Tennis. Golf. Valet pkg. Helipad.
V, AE, MC.*
Comfortable, elegant accommodation. The
rooms afford a restful vista over the wooded
grounds. Relais et Châteaux.

■ In **Séreilhac 87620**   18 km SE on N 21

La Meule
N 21 - 55 39 10 08, fax 55 39 19 66
*Closed Tue (in winter, 20 days in Jan. Open until
9pm. Priv rm: 35. Garden dining. **Hotel**: 10 rms
310-500 F. Conf. Pkg. V, AE, DC, MC.*
In 25 years of steady service, chef Nicole
Jouhaud has perfected her peculiar brand of
generous cooking by taking tradition and fitting
it around fresh new ideas. It's a shame the prices
are so high, because we would like to come
more often to this sunny dining room opening
onto a pretty garden. We like the chef's chicken
ambroisie, fillet of sea bass roasted with spices
and verjus sauce, and chocolate tart with almond milk ice cream. C 300-550 F. M 130 F
(weekday lunch), 210 F, 360 F.

LISIEUX	14100

Paris 173 - Evreux 72 - Caen 49 - Deauville 28   *Calvados*

12/20 Aux Acacias
13, rue de la Résistance - 31 62 10 95
*Closed Sun dinner, Mon (exc hols), Jul 16-Aug 2.
Open until 9:30pm. V, MC.*
A springtime breeze swept away the wrinkles
in the façade and decor of this friendly place
where fresh, traditional cooking is on hand. Try
the 125 F menu: a gâteau of smoked salmon
with avocado and lime, filet mignon of pork in a
Port-spiked cream sauce, cheese plate, and
crème brûlée topped with brown sugar. C 210-
280 F. M 85 F (weekdays, Sat lunch), 125 F,
170 F.

Gardens Hotel
Route de Paris
31 61 17 17, fax 31 32 33 43
*Open year-round. 69 rms 260-395 F. Rms for dis-
abled. Restaurant. Half-board 290-335 F. Conf.
Heated pool. Pkg. V, AE, DC, MC.*
A fine modern hotel on the edge of town, with
a swimming pool and manicured lawns. Rooms

are bright and spacious, with perfect appointments. Buffet breakfast. Sports complex nearby.

■ In **Ouilly-
du-Houley 14590**   11 km NE on N 13 and D 137

Auberge de la Paquine
31 63 63 80
*Closed Tue dinner, Wed, Nov 15-Dec 3. Open until
9pm. Garden dining. No pets. Pkg. V, MC.*
This delightful little Norman inn nestles in the
green landscape of the Pays d'Auge. When the
weather is fine, you can eat outside on the banks
of a stream; in winter you're welcomed into a
handsome, rustic dining room. The staff is over-
whelmingly friendly, the cuisine innovative and
based on quality produce. This year, Emmanuel
Champion's winning 150 F menu offers tomato
feuilleté with foie gras, quail pastilla "Lucullus",
cheeses, and profiteroles flavored with mint.
C 300-380 F. M 150 F, 330 F.

LOCRONAN	29136

Paris 565 - Brest 66 - Quimper 17 - Douarnenez 10   *Finistère*

12/20 Manoir de Moëllien
2.5 km NW on C 10, 29220 Plonévez
98 92 50 40, fax 98 92 55 21
*Closed for lunch off-seas (exc hols), Wed, Jan-Mar.
Open until 9:30pm. Priv rm: 45. Pkg. V, AE, DC, MC.*
Your efforts to locate this spruce Breton manor
(it's right on the border of Plonévez-Porzay and
Locronan, if that's any help) will be rewarded by
a satisfying meal. Try the sea scallop aumônière,
veal kidneys braised with mustard, and Grand
Marnier soufflé. Fine cellar. C 230-300 F.
M 124 F, 168 F, 228 F.

Manoir de Moëllien
(See restaurant above)
*Closed Jan-Mar. 10 rms 345 F. Half-board 355 F. Air
cond. Conf. V, AE, DC.*
Rooms are housed in an outbuilding of the fine
seventeenth-century manor; they are soberly
decorated but pleasing nonetheless. All open
directly onto the verdant countryside. Weather
permitting, you can enjoy your breakfast on the
hotel's pretty terrace.

LONS-LE-SAUNIER	39000

Paris 407 - Besançon 88 - Bourg-en-Bresse 61 - Dijon 102   *Jura*

La Comédie
Pl. de la Comédie
84 24 20 66
*Closed Mon dinner, Sun, Apr 17-May 3, Jul 31-
Aug 24. Open until 9:30pm. Air cond. Pkg. V.*
The reception we had here was unpleasant,
and the food not up to par: carpaccio of the fish
of the day was tasty, but the honey-glazed duck
with sesame seeds was less seductive than it
sounded. Well chosen wines. Overall, it's no
longer worth a 14 rating. C 250-410 F. M 95 F,
140 F.

*Red toques signify creative cuisine; white toques
signify traditional cuisine.*

297

■ **In Courlans 39000**   6 km W on N 78

Auberge de Chavannes
84 47 05 52

Closed Sun dinner, Mon, Feb 7-Mar 7, Jun 27-Jul 4. Open until 9pm. Garden dining. Air cond. Pkg. V, DC, MC.

Perhaps the least well known of our three-toque chefs, but surely one of the most patient, Pierre Carpentier has been waiting 23 years for his day to come. He reckons it should arrive sometime in 1997, when a new trans-European superhighway will bring droves of potential customers to within three kilometers of his roadside inn!

We're glad that we've already recognized the talent and integrity, the precision and sensitivity of Carpentier's cuisine. Local farmer friends supply him with the raw materials for such dishes as foie gras in a salt crust, rustic grillons of veal sweetbreads on a bed of wild mushrooms accompanied by a delicate grilled corn galette, and an ethereal crispy strawberry millefeuille. But the chicken neck stuffed with calf's foot was too fatty and needed a sauce with more verve. The dessert cart holds no surprises. Monique Charpentier extends a charming welcome, and tirelessly promotes the region's wines, from growers' Côtes-du-Jura to the famous Château-Chalon. C 350-400 F. M 160 F, 250 F, 320 F.

LOOS 59   ➺ Lille

LORGUES   83510
Paris 850 - Draguignan 13 - Brignoles 33 - St-Raphaël 43   *Var*

Chez Bruno
Route de Vidauban
94 73 92 19, fax 94 73 78 11

Open daily until 9pm. Priv rm: 14. Garden dining. Pkg. V, AE.

At six-foot-five, weighing in at over 300 pounds, Clément Bruno is literally a giant of a man. After various adventures, he turned to cooking, remodeling the family house in a lovely corner of Provence, and using as his base his mother's own cooking. Now the friend of chefs and supported by a fine team, he offers generous cuisine that sings of the spirit of Provence. He's built part of his reputation on the truffle, not the great black one of France's Southwest but the "summer truffle" of the Haut Var, which he liberally scatters over numerous dishes. Sample his grilled truffle toasts doused with superb olive oil from the Moulin de Gervasonie in Aups, a fine warm salad of local vegetables, morel-stuffed ravioli in a truffle and walnut sauce, a savory lamb shoulder cooked for hours with boulangère potatoes and paired with a fricassée of tiny chestnuts, and, to top it all off, a chocolate cake glacé that's worth a round of applause. The menu changes almost daily, and the Provençal wines are among the best around; sometimes he offers a bottle as a gift. Don't miss the fresco Bruno put on the wall of a little farmhouse nearby, representing some of France's great chefs as the twelve apostles. A little joke on Paul Bocuse, and the press loves it. M 270 F.

LORIENT   56100
Paris 491 - Quimper 68 - Vannes 56 - Rennes 145   *Morbihan*

L'Amphitryon
Quartier Keryado, 127, rue du Col.-Müller
97 83 34 04, fax 97 37 25 02

Closed Sat lunch & Sun (exc hols), Apr 24-30, Aug 28-Sept 6. Open until 10:30pm. Air cond. No pets. V, MC.

A third toque this year for Jean-Paul Abadie's sure-handed, full-bodied cooking, which cleverly joins the traditions of his native Gers and those of his wife Véronique's Brittany. Every flavor is fully focused, each dish is balanced to perfection. Witness the iced tapenade, peppers and pimentoes with tiny sardines, or the touch of garlic in the sautéed apples pairing Pyrenees lamb. And Abadie's use of spices is a reminder that Lorient was once a major port in the spice trade: cardamom enlivens a consommé with crab and asparagus, and a sautéed lobster is seasoned with karigosse, a mixture of three Indian curries first concocted by a pharmacist in nearby Auray. All Abadie's dishes offer the best of Brittany's sea and farmland. Véronique helps customers choose among the dozen or so desserts (this year we swooned over the date fritters) and the well chosen wines; the list is strong on Bordeaux, Burgundies, Côtes-du-Rhônes, and includes some good foreign bottles. The restaurant's name—it means "he who knows how to receive"—certainly fits. C 300-400 F. M 100 F (weekday lunch), 150 F (weekdays), 230 F, 310 F, 360 F.

12/20 Le Bistrot du Yachtman
14, rue Poissonnière - 97 21 31 91

Closed Mon dinner, Sun, last 2 wks of Aug. Open until 10pm. Priv rm: 40. Air cond. V.

In a pink and black dining room, sample the 135 F menu: sautéed sea scallops with cèpes, médallions of veal kidneys and sweetbreads with ginger, cheeses, fruit gratin. Small wine list. C 210-260 F. M 75 F, 110 F, 135 F, 180 F.

Mercure
31, pl. J.-Ferry
97 21 35 73, fax 97 64 48 62

Open year-round. 58 rms 295-495 F. Rms for disabled. Conf. Golf. V, AE, DC, MC.

This hotel offers large, constantly updated, and well-equipped rooms, all within easy reach of the conference center and wet dock. Conference facilities, bar.

Novotel
5 km NE on N 24, Kerpont-Bellevue,
56850 Caudan
97 76 02 16, fax 97 76 00 24

Open year-round. 88 rms 395-450 F. Rms for disabled. Restaurant. Conf. Heated pool. Golf. Pkg. V, AE, DC, MC.

A pleasant hotel set in five acres of wooded grounds, with simply decorated, comfortable rooms. Beaches and golf courses close by.

Le Pic
2, bd Franchet-d'Esperey
97 21 18 29, fax 97 21 92 64

Closed Sat lunch & Sun (exc Feb), Jan 2-15, Aug 28-Sep 3. Open until midnight. Priv rm: 28. V, MC.

Here's a friendly, generous, and unaffected restaurant that ranks among Lorient's best. The young chef continues to delight customers with lively dishes like tiny mackerel en escabèche with warm sweet potatoes, roast veal filet mignon with a rosemary jus, and baba au rhum with whipped cream. The wines are superb. **C** 220-320 F. **M** 65 F, 90 F, 140 F, 175 F, 260 F.

12/20 La Sardegna
28-30, rue P.-Guieysse - 97 64 13 05
Open daily until 11:30pm. Priv rm: 20. Terrace dining. V, AE, DC, MC.
Delicate Italian aromas permeate the rustic dining room of this likeable late-night restaurant next to the station. Specialties include a large selection of pizzas, carpaccio of Parma ham, saltimboccas, and Italian charcuterie. Amiable service; appealing wines. **C** 130-180 F.

■ In **Ploemeur 56270**   6 km W on D 162

12/20 Le Vivier
Lomener - 97 82 99 60, fax 97 82 88 89
Closed Jan 2-22. Open until 11pm. Priv rm: 18. Pkg. V, AE, DC, MC.
Poised on the rocks opposite the Ile de Groix, Le Vivier is a reliable source of fresh shellfish assortments, or more elaborate preparations like rillettes made with two kinds of salmon and grilled turbot. **C** 220-380 F. **M** 98 F (weekdays), 165 F, 240 F.

See also: **Hennebont**

LORRIS	45260

Paris 125 - Orléans 49 - Gien 26 - Montargis 22   *Loiret*

Guillaume de Lorris
8, Grande-Rue - 38 94 83 55
Closed Tue dinner, Wed, Feb 15-Mar 12, Jul 17-29. Open until 9pm (9:30pm in summer). V, MC.
Jean-Pierre de Boissière wandered the countryside for a while (the Auberge des Templiers in Les Bézards and Château d'Artigny in Montbazon, among others) before undertaking the resuscitation of this formerly down-at-heel inn. His smiling wife learned all there is to know about welcome and service from her Relais et Châteaux experience. Slowly but surely they've used their talents and the limited means at their disposal to transform the dining room into something truly cheery. Settle in and enjoy the reasonably priced, professional cooking: langoustine gratin with asparagus, farm-raised squab with a Gatinais honey glaze, and a caramelized peach millefeuille. The generous first set menu includes a pike parfait with aigrelette sauce, jambonette of chicken with Orléans vinegar, and a gooey chocolate fondant. **C** 270-350 F. **M** 115 F, 175 F.

This symbol signifies hotels that are exceptionally quiet.

LOUARGAT	22540

Paris 500 - Guingamp 14 - Morlaix 41 - St-Brieuc 45   *Côtes/Armor*

12/20 Manoir du Cleuziou
4 km NW on D 33 A
96 43 14 90, fax 96 43 52 59
Closed Dec 22-27, Feb. Open until 10pm. Terrace dining. Heated pool. Pkg. V, AE, MC.
The rough-hewn setting of bare stone and beams is a favorite with locals and British travelers, who come here to savor salmon carpaccio, monkfish navarin in cider, and crème brûlée flavored with Ceylon tea. **C** 180-280 F. **M** 150 F (weekday lunch, wine incl), 90 F (weekday lunch), 170 F (Sun), 125 F, 195 F.

Manoir du Cleuziou
(See restaurant above)
Closed Feb. 28 rms 320-420 F. Rms for disabled. Half-board 325 F. Heated pool. Tennis. Pkg. V, AE.
The pretty rooms, housed in a splendid Renaissance manor, are simple, comfortable, but poorly soundproofed.

LOURDES	65100

Paris 797 - Pau 40 - Tarbes 20 - Argelès-G. 13   *Hautes-Pyrénées*

L'Ermitage
Bd Sempé - 62 94 08 42, fax 62 42 19 88
Closed Oct 20-May 1. Open until 9pm. Air cond. V, AE, DC.
L'Ermitage is a gastronomic miracle in a city where good tables are few. Blessed be Daniel Chaubon, a disciplined, inventive chef who takes fine regional ingredients and converts them into virtuously light dishes. Try the delicate, subtly flavored artichoke charlotte, fresh salmon in Madiran wine sauce with a delicious vegetable mousse, and a too-sugary two-chocolate croquant. Fine wine list, perfect welcome and service. **C** 190-260 F. **M** 78 F, 138 F, 198 F.

Gallia-Londres
26, av. B.-Soubirous
62 94 35 44, fax 62 42 24 64
Closed Jan-Mar, Oct 20-Dec. 90 rms 550-750 F. Rms for disabled. Half-board 450-600 F. Golf. V, AE, MC.
A classic grand hotel offering period rooms with balconies above the pilgrimage route. Lovely garden; bar and pub.

Hôtel de la Grotte
66, rue de la Grotte
62 94 58 87, fax 62 94 20 50
Open year-round. 4 stes 1,200 F. 82 rms 310-510 F. Rms for disabled. Restaurant. Half-board 310-635 F. Conf. Golf. Pkg. V, AE, DC, MC.
From the upper floors, one of the best views in Lourdes takes in the river, sanctuaries, and the Pyrenees. Attractive garden by the Adour.

Paradis
15, av. du Paradis
62 42 14 14, fax 62 94 64 04
Closed Nov 1-Apr 1. 2 stes 1,000 F. 300 rms 370-480 F. Rms for disabled. Restaurant. Half-board 360-480 F. Air cond. Conf. Golf. Garage pkg. V, AE.
A brand-new hotel near the sanctuaries. Five meeting rooms, and thirty rooms for the handicapped.

LOURMARIN   **84160**
Paris 736 - Salon 36 - Apt 18 - Avignon 56   *Vaucluse*

 L'Agneau Gourmand
Route de Vaugines
90 68 21 04, fax 90 68 11 97
Closed Thu lunch, Wed, Jan 2-Feb 17, Nov 6-Dec 15. Open until 9:30pm. Priv rm: 20. Terrace dining. No pets. Pkg. V, AE, MC.
Housed in a delightful old *bastide*, this attractive restaurant with a vaulted dining room features the refined, nicely presented cooking of Jean-Pierre Vollaire. Among his dishes, all using the best products, you'll find a salmon fivolité with a fresh herb coulis, saddle of Sisteron lamb with stuffed Provençal vegetables, and a delicate soufflé flavored with lavender. Fine though short wine list. **C** 290-390 F. **M** 140 F (weekday lunch Jun-Sep), 175 F, 235 F.

 Hôtel de Guilles   ♣♥
(See restaurant above)
Closed Jan 2-Feb 17, Nov 6-Dec 15. 28 rms 390-590 F. Half-board 425-525 F. Conf. Pool. Tennis. Golf. Pkg. V, AE, DC, MC.
Tuscan-like atmosphere and *art de vivre*, complete with crickets to underscore the total silence. Sports activities available. There's a garden of aromatic herbs and flowers.

La Fenière   ۞
9, rue du Grand-Pré
90 68 11 79, fax 90 68 18 60
Closed Tue lunch (in summer), Sun dinner off-seas, Jan 3-19, Feb 27-Mar 5, Jun 26-Jul 2, Oct 2-8. Open until 9:30pm. Air cond. Pkg. V, AE, DC, MC.
The interior of Reine Sammut's reconverted hayloft restaurant in a back lane of this sunny village is a bit overdecorated for our taste, but this is the only false note in an otherwise authentic dining experience.
Reine is undoubtedly one of France's finest *cuisinières*, blessed with an unerring sense of flavor and proportion, as well as a fertile imagination. And with her husband Guy she has created more than a restaurant here: it's a place where friendship combines with fine cooking based on the best local products Provence has to offer. But Reine's attachment to culinary traditions doesn't preclude a modern approach to cooking. Her light and limpid jus, her unconventional flavor combinations are utterly contemporary. Sure to make your taste buds revel are her delicate potato, foie gras, and truffle tart; her irresistible pumpkin risotto enhanced with saffron, cuttlefish, and lemongrass; a papillote croustillante of whiting stuffed with garlic purée; beef marrow sherbet with stuffed ratte potatoes; a signature version of pieds et paquets Marseillais; breast of squab with preserved garlic; a creamy nut and grape cake; warm chocolate tarts; or the galette de Reine with Provençal almonds. If only there were a garden! But console yourself for the lack of an olive tree with the exceptional wines, like the 1982 Cuvée Velours from Chapoutier, the Fonsalette 1990 white, or the Mas Jullien from the Languedoc, among many others. **C** 400-550 F. **M** 180 F, 280 F, 460 F.

 Le Moulin de Lourmarin
Rue du Temple
90 68 06 69, fax 90 68 31 76
Closed Tue off-seas, beg Jan-mid Feb. Open until 10:30pm (11pm in summer). Priv rm: 20. Terrace dining. Air cond. Pool. Valet pkg. V, AE, DC, MC.
Édouard Loubet-Lacroix presides over the kitchens of this beautifully restored oil mill, turning out light, surprising, superbly aromatic cooking that could use a bit of simplifying and personalization at times. Nevertheless it's getting better and better, and we herewith award it two extra points and two toques. We were especially impressed by the frog's legs au mouron (in an infusion) and the fantastic roast lamb. Excessively formal service. Sumptuous, high-priced wine list. Gorgeous terrace. **C** 400-500 F. **M** 180 F (exc Sun lunch), 250 F, 320 F.

Le Moulin de Lourmarin
(See restaurant above)
See restaurant for closings. 2 stes 1,600-2,600 F. 20 rms 600-1,500 F. Half-board 700-950 F. Air cond. Conf. Pool. Golf. Valet pkg. V, AE, DC, MC.
A covered footbridge leads from the mill to this restored house offering fully equipped rooms (one with terrace) and attractive bathrooms. Sauna.

LOUVECIENNES 78   → **PARIS Suburbs**

LOYETTES   **01800**
Paris 468 - Bourg 51 - Lyon 33 - Vienne 48   *Ain*

La Terrasse
10, pl. des Mariniers
78 32 70 13, fax 78 32 73 32
Closed Sun dinner, Mon, 2 wks in Feb. Open until 10pm. Priv rm: 12. Terrace dining. Pkg. V, AE.
You'll like this riverside restaurant for its charming terrace on the Rhône and for Gérard Antonin's regional dishes, prepared with the help of his son Philippe: veal sweetbreads in truffle butter, a salmon assortment, and astonishing casserole-roasted lobster with macaroni. Antonin's pride and joy is his game menu served in season; he's a hunter himself. Superb but costly wines. **C** 300-450 F. **M** 180 F, 250 F, 320 F, 400 F.

LUC (LE)   **83340**
Paris 840 - Toulon 53 - Brignoles 22 - St-Raphaël 43   *Var*

Le Gourmandin
8, pl. Brunet
94 60 85 92, fax 94 47 91 10
Closed Sun dinner & Mon (exc hols), Mar 1-7, Sep 1-10. Open until 10pm. Priv rm: 40. Pkg. V, MC.
This handsome little restaurant on the village square is surprisingly difficult to find. It's worth the trouble, though, for Uta Schwartz's warm welcome and her husband Patrick's polished, plentiful dishes served at very reasonable prices: zucchini blossoms stuffed with scorpion fish mousse with an étrille (tiny crab) coulis, rack of lamb in a tapenade crust, and a lemony strawberry gratin with apricot sauce. The first two set menus are real bargains. Charming welcome; attentive service. **C** 200-300 F. **M** 135 F (weekday dinner, Sat, Sun lunch), 98 F (weekday lunch, Sat), 220 F.

LUCCIANA 20 → CORSICA

LUMBRES 62380

Paris 266 - Arras 86 - Boulogne 40 - St-Omer 13   P./Calais

Moulin de Mombreux
Route de Bayenghem
21 39 62 44, fax 21 93 61 34
Closed Dec 20-29. Open until 9:30pm. Priv rm: 30.
Pkg. V, AE, DC, MC.

Admire this former watermill's impressive wooden works over an apéritif in the lounge, before you go up to the dining room to try the direct, delicate cooking of Jean-Marc Gaudry: escalope of foie gras with honey cake, chicken breast with vegetable and girolle mushroom ravioli, grilled red mullet with a pepper coulis, and apple tart. C 300-450 F. M 210 F, 330 F, 510 F.

Moulin de Mombreux
(See restaurant above)
Closed Dec 19-28. 24 rms 500-700 F. Conf. Golf. Pkg. V, AE, DC, MC.

This peaceful hotel offers several small, neat rooms with views of the river and paddling ducks.

LUNÉVILLE 54300

Paris 340 - Strasbourg 124 - Metz 92 - Nancy 35   Meurthe/M.

Château d'Adoménil
In Réhainviller-Adoménil
83 74 04 81, fax 83 74 21 78
Closed Mon & Tue lunch (Apr 15-Oct), Mon, Tue lunch, Sun dinner, Feb 20-Mar 8. Open until 9:30pm. Priv rm: 35. Terrace dining. Air cond. Pkg. V, AE, DC, MC.

Set in splendid grounds, this graceful nineteenth-century mansion boasts ornate, theatrically decorated dining rooms, where hostess Bernadette Million and her staff will make you glad you traveled to this remote corner of Lorraine. Michel Million's sparkling, lively cuisine is above reproach: you'll relish his sea bass in verjus, croustillant of squab in wine lees with a delicate crust enveloping tender meat and accompanied by excellent baby vegetables, superbly cooked langoustines coated with poppyseeds, and, for dessert, an "assiette lorraine" featuring the golden mirabelle plum (warm tart, soufflé, croustillant, mousse glacée, and sherbet). Fine wine list rich in white Burgundies, and service much warmer and more dynamic than last year. C 400-520 F. M 220 F, 330 F, 380 F, 430 F.

Château d'Adoménil
(See restaurant above)
Closed Sun & Mon (Nov 1-Apr 15), Feb 20-Mar 8. 1 ste 1,200 F. 7 rms 450-850 F. Half-board 680-1,080 F. Pkg. Helipad. V, AE, DC, MC.

Seven comfortable, very luxurious rooms in a quiet setting. Superb breakfasts. A railway passes nearby and a peacock screeches on the roof, but overall the atmosphere is restful and the prices almost reasonable. Relais et Châteaux.

> Gault Millau's ratings are based solely on the restaurants' cuisine. We do not take into account the atmosphere, décor, service, and so on; these are commented upon within the review.

LURBE-SAINT-CHRISTAU 64660

Paris 795 - Lourdes 60 - Oloron-Ste-Marie 9   Pyrénées-A.

Au Bon Coin
59 34 40 12, fax 59 34 46 40
Closed Tue, Feb 1-21, Oct 13-Mar 30. Open until 9pm. Priv rm: 12. Garden dining. Hotel: 18 rms 280-330 F. Rms for disabled. Half-board 300 F. Conf. Pool. Pkg. V, MC.

Flickers of reflected firelight gleam in the copper and pewter pots that decorate this cozy mountain inn, recently remodeled and now with a lovely covered terrace. The owner-chef, Thierry Lassala, is determined to keep quality high, and his efforts are evident in the three savory salads with salmon confit, grilled quail, and dried duck breast; the generous assortment of thyme-scented Pyrenees lamb dishes (sautéed sweetbreads, grilled fillet, and in a charlotte with eggplant), and excellent chocolate desserts. Lots of Bordeaux and regional wines in the cellar; charming welcome. C 270-350 F. M 100 F (weekdays), 85 F, 140 F, 200 F.

Relais
de la Poste et du Parc
In St-Christau
59 34 40 04, fax 59 34 46 55
Closed end Oct-end Mar. 3 stes 470-570 F. 43 rms 340-390 F. Restaurant. Half-board 320-425 F. Conf. Pool. Tennis. Golf. Pkg. V, MC.

Two rambling, white, green-shuttered houses stand in the spa's immense grounds. Inside, the quiet and restful rooms ensure a relaxing stay; all have been recently renovated and are very well equipped. Nearby is a small lake for boating, and there's a gym for the more active.

LUYNES 37230

Paris 248 - Tours 13 - Langeais 14 - Chinon 45   Indre/Loire

Domaine de Beauvois
2 km NW on D 49
47 55 50 11, fax 47 55 59 62
Closed Jan 8-Mar 11. Open until 9:15pm. Priv rm: 25. Terrace dining. Heated pool. No pets. Valet pkg. V, AE, DC, MC.

This country manor set in 150 hectares of wooded grounds ranks among the most luxurious establishments in Touraine. Stéphane Pineau is now the chef here, offering classic dishes like a warm salad of artichoke bottoms and langoustines, rabbit thigh with bacon accompanied by interesting carrot and prune rouleaux (a bit dry, this dish), and a perfect chicory mousse. Fine wine list at reasonable prices, with many grands crus available by the glass. Irreproachable service. C 300-400 F. M 200 F (weekday lunch, wine incl), 210 F, 260 F, 360 F.

Domaine de Beauvois
(See restaurant above)
Closed Jan 8-Mar 11. 4 stes 1,460-2,100 F. 32 rms 700-1,360 F. Half-board 1,095-1,755 F. Air cond. Conf. Heated pool. Tennis. Valet pkg. Helipad. V, AE, DC, MC.

Ideally situated for a holiday touring the nearby Châteaux de la Loire, this fine hotel has huge, frequently updated and delightfully furnished rooms with marble bathrooms. Fishing, riding, and other sporting activities are proposed, and visits to local wine growers are organized after the autumn harvest. Relais et Châteaux.

LYON	69000
Paris 462 - Grenoble 106 - Valence 100 - Geneva 190	Rhône

Lyon's restaurants and hotels are classified by arrondissement. An alphabetical index on page 317 enables you to find the correct arrondissement (or nearby town or village) for all the establishments mentioned here.

LYON	1ST

Anticipation

7, rue Chavanne - 78 30 91 92
Closed Mon (exc hols), Aug 1-22. Open until 11:15pm. Air cond. Garage pkg. V, AE, MC. Y2-48
Come to this little restaurant between the Saône and Saint Nizier church to sample the cooking of a former assistant to Georges Blanc, John Rosiak. The 82 F lunch menu draws the locals in droves, and the à la carte menu offers original, carefully prepared dishes like red mullet fillets en escabèche, a tian of Lyonnais sausage, and a rum and grape soufflé glacé. C 200-250 F. M 82 F (weekdays, Sat lunch), 127 F, 165 F, 210 F, 290 F.

12/20 L'Assiette Lyonnaise

19, pl. Tolozan - 78 28 35 77
Closed Sat lunch, Sun. Open until 11:30pm. Priv rm: 12. Terrace dining. Air cond. Pkg. V, AE. Z1-24
L'Assiette is a chic brasserie with 1930s–style decor, air conditioning, and a man to park your car (quite a novelty in Lyon). Come here for classic Lyonnais specialties washed down with carafes of delicious wines. C 210-250 F. M 98 F, 135 F (weekdays, Sat dinner).

Bar du Passage

8, rue du Plâtre
78 28 12 61, fax 72 00 84 34
Closed Sat lunch, Sun. Open until 11pm. Priv rm: 45. Air cond. V, AE, MC. Y2-65
This is the popular bistrot annexe of the Passage restaurant (next door), often preferred by trendy locals to the mothership. Atmosphere, atmosphere: the walls are decorated with *trompe-l'œil* paintings, and the curtains and seats of heavy velvet were recovered from a theatre. The short but sweet menu offers Parma ham, tuna steak, and Angus beef. C 180-200 F.

12/20 La Gousse d'Ail

20, rue du Sgt-Blandan - 78 30 40 44
Closed Jul 31-Aug 24. Open until 10:30pm. No pets. V. X1-42
Tucked away in the Terreaux district, this tidy and tasteful little bistrot features modern dishes like a millefeuille of veal with chanterelle mushrooms, a warm salad of langoustine tails, and a sea scallop and lobster chartreuse. C 170-210 F. M 98 F, 148 F, 190 F.

Léon de Lyon

1, rue Pléney
78 28 11 33, fax 78 39 89 05
Closed Sun (& Mon lunch Jul-Aug). Open until 10pm. Priv rm: 30. Air cond. Valet pkg. V, AE, MC. Y2-22

Owner of several establishments in the same quiet street, Léon seems to lord it over a miniature Lyon, a small gastronomic universe all its own. The freshly redecorated main restaurant is a cozy nest of warm wood paneling, leather-covered chairs, and stained-glass windows, with atmosphere suspended somewhere between that of a good old English club and an elegant French brasserie.
Lacombe's cooking brashly takes tradition in hand, then turns it on its head. Our experience here this year amply confirmed the three toques: boudin sausage tartelette, pig's ear "cake", and a pain rissolé of rillettes and potatoes, something you won't find anywhere else in this ancient capital of the Gauls. The pig's jowl salad, with meat cooked for seven hours, is another curiosity but not one of our favorites. But the Bresse chicken au vinaigre with a delicious tart sauce, cock's comb and a melt-in-your-mouth chicken liver gâteau, three versions on the theme of suckling pig (braised, sautéed, and confit, all much lighter than you would expect) with an exquisite sage jus, and to top it off the fine cheeses from Mère Richard. For dessert, try the raisin parfait delicately flavored with Grand Marnier (or any dessert; Lacombe is a dessert specialist). Nary a false note from beginning to end. See *Le Petit Léon* listed under the "And also..." heading. C 450-600 F. M 250 F (lunch), 490 F.

12/20 La Mandarine

10, rue Rivet - 78 28 01 74
Closed Sat lunch, Sun, Aug. Open until 10:30pm. Priv rm: 40. V, AE. X1-44
Daniel Perrier's cooking has won many local fans with the likes of raw salmon and red mullet tartare, fillet of salmon with frog's legs, veal kidney à l'ancienne, and a chestnut soufflé glacé. The cellar should tone down the prices and show some ambition. Bistrot decor, friendly welcome and service. C 250-350 F. M 132 F, 182 F.

La Mère Brazier ♣

12, rue Royale
78 28 15 49, fax 78 28 63 63
Closed Sat lunch (& dinner Jun 18-Jul), Sun, Jul 31-Aug 29. Open until 10pm. Priv rm: 20. Pkg. V, AE, DC, MC. D2-8
In the wood-paneled dining room of this repository of Lyonnais tradition (or in the pleasant bar with its blue hand-painted tiles and hunting prints), Carmen and Jacotte Brazier greet patrons (even those they've never seen before) as warmly as if they were life-long pals (too bad the prices are unfriendly). The food, too, is as familiar as an old family friend, from the artichoke bottoms stuffed with foie gras to the galette Bressane, the Bresse chicken demi-deuil to the vanilla ice cream drizzled with hot chocolate sauce. C 350-400 F. M 170 F (weekday lunch), 290 F, 370 F.

La Meunière

11, rue Neuve - 78 28 62 91
Closed Sun, Mon, Jul 14-Aug 15. Open until 9:45pm. V, AE, DC. Y2-50
Here's a genuine Lyonnais *bouchon* featuring a large central table laden with bounteous hors d'œuvres, desserts, and jugs of house wine (Beaujolais, naturally). For 140 F, you can have a buffet Lyonnais, calf's head gribiche, cervelle

de canut (fresh cheese with herbs), and a choice of desserts. The atmosphere is warm and convivial, the prices angelic. **C** 175-250 F. **M** 90 F, 105 F, 140 F.

Les Muses

Opéra de Lyon, pl. de la Comédie
72 00 45 58, fax 78 29 34 01
Closings not available. Open until midnight. Terrace dining. Air cond. V, MC. **Z1-6**
A chic clientele has already discovered this contemporary dining room near Lyons' opera house. Simple, perfectly prepared dishes include a delicate herring and potato terrine, nicely cooked and flavorful salmon fillet sautéed with bacon, and a delicious cherry compote with honey ice cream. Well chosen small wine list. Relaxed welcome and service. **C** 200-270 F.

Le Passage

8, rue du Plâtre
78 28 11 16, fax 72 00 84 34
Closed Sat lunch, Sun. Open until 10pm. Priv rm: 40. Air cond. V, AE, DC, MC. **Y2-46**
Actors, dancers and writers—Lyon's little *beau monde*—flock to Le Passage to bask in the theatrically lit decor (rather good copies of contemporary masterpieces, in the windowless downstairs dining room; overstuffed leather armchairs, rescued from the Majestic theatre, and elaborate Second Empire woodwork, upstairs). But decoration is only half the equation: the sophisticated-yet-rustic cooking—urbane interpretations of hearty Lyonnais dishes—keeps the *artistes* coming back for more. New chef Christian Bacque offers salmon fillets delicately flavored with marjoram, perfectly cooked duck breast, sautéed fillets of red mullet with an artichoke salad, and rabbit liver with calf's tail. Snappy wine list featuring both big guns and quiet little finds. Efficient service. **M** 175 F (lunch), 220 F, 290 F.

La Romanée

19, rue Rivet
72 00 80 87, fax 72 07 88 44
Closed Sat lunch, Sun dinner, Mon, Aug. Open until 9:30pm. Air cond. V, MC. **B2-37**
Élisabeth and Daniel Denis are happy as can be in their cozy little restaurant decorated with a modern touch. Élisabeth wields the pots and pans, producing tasty parsleyed crab with sea urchin coulis, house foie gras, monkfish bourride with mussel jus, and pear with almonds for dessert. Daniel has put together an astonishing list of Côtes-du-Rhône (120 bottlings, priced from 60-100 F). Be sure to reserve ahead, especially for dinner: the place is always fully packed. **C** 230-300 F. **M** 98 F, 145 F, 185 F.

Le Saint-Alban

2, quai J.-Moulin
78 30 14 89, fax 72 00 88 82
Closed Sat lunch, Sun, Aug 1-22, Mar 1-7. Open until 10pm. Air cond. V, AE. **Z1-15**
Jean-Paul Lechevalier's small, elegant restaurant on the banks of the Rhône is invariably full of jovial Lyonnais food lovers, even though the prices have shot up lately. Sample the warm rabbit sausage with prunes, whole sole with braised fennel and squid, and a squab with roseval potatoes redolent of garlic and parsley. The wine list concentrates on northern Côtes-du-Rhône, and the service is faultless in a pleasant

dining room with exposed stone walls and Provençal fabrics, near the banks of the Rhône. But the welcome can be chilly if you are not known here. **C** 300-380 F. **M** 148 F, 195 F, 245 F, 290 F.

12/20 Au Temps Perdu

2, rue des Fantasques - 78 39 23 04
Closed Sat lunch, Sun. Open until 11pm. V. **C2-78**
Time has stood still since circa 1920 in this genially decorated bistrot boasting a fine view of the valley. Kamel Bellouere is evolving, and this year offered puff pastry stuffed with saffron-scented mussels and haddock, lamb and eggplant charlotte, and a macaroni gratin with basil. The toque is not far away. **C** 180-280 F. **M** 68 F (lunch), 95 F, 119 F, 159 F.

And also...

Our selection of places for inexpensive, quick, or late-night meals.
Le Boulevardier (78 28 48 22 - 5, rue de la Fromagerie. Open until midnight.): Pleasant ambience, Lyonnais specialties, and a 45 F lunch menu (65 F, 89 F).
Hugon (78 28 10 94 - Le Bouchon Lyonnais, 12, rue Pizay. Open until 10pm.): A dozen first courses, *plats du jour*, and typical Lyonnais desserts, prepared practically before your eyes by Arlette Hugon (120-150 F).
Le Petit Léon (72 00 08 10 - 3, rue Pléney. Lunch only & dinner by reserv for groups.): Well-prepared set meals and inexpensive local wines (95 F).

Assiette et Marée

49, rue de la Bourse
78 37 36 58, fax 78 37 98 52
Closed Sun, Mon, Aug 14-Sep 13, Jan 1-10. Open until 11pm. Priv rm: 120. Terrace dining. Air cond. V, MC. **Z2-41**
The formula—offering fresh seafood and shellfish in a cheerful setting—has worked so well that the owners have opened a second establishment in the third district. Try the marinated fish (sardines à l'escabèche, tiny mackerel in white wine) and excellent grilled fish like turbot, sea bass, and John Dory, served with sauce vierge and sautéed potatoes. Bouillabaisse is on hand in the evening. Fine though limited choice of white wines. Cute little terrace. **C** 150-200 F. **M** 100 F (lunch).

Bellecordière

18, rue Bellecordière
78 42 27 78, fax 72 40 92 27
Open year-round. 45 rms 280-350 F. V, AE. **Z4-49**
Conveniently set by the Place Bellecour, an appealing little establishment with bright, smallish rooms decorated in soothing tones of blue and white. Warm welcome.

12/20 Les Belles Saisons

Esplanade de la Gare, 12, cours de Verdun-Rambaud - 78 37 58 11, fax 78 37 06 56
Open daily until 10:30pm. Priv rm: 300. Air cond. Valet pkg. V, AE, DC, MC. **B6-60**
At this hotel-restaurant you can expect to find a comfortable wood-paneled interior, lovely

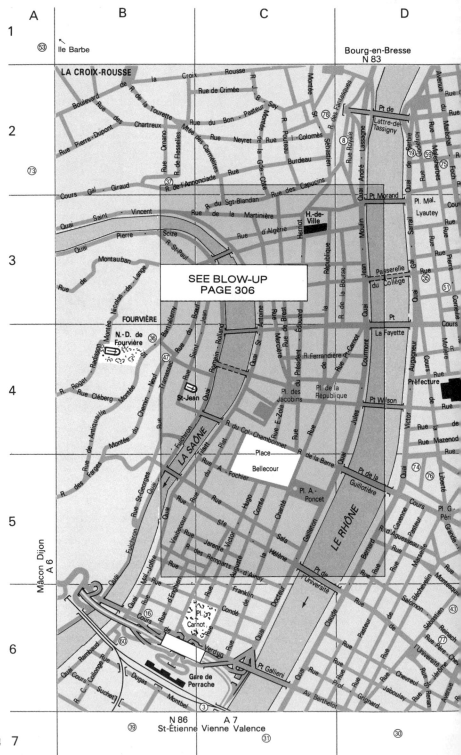

A B C D

1

⑤³ Ile Barbe

Bourg-en-Bresse
N 83

LA CROIX-ROUSSE

2

⑦³

Cours Gal - Giraud

FOURVIÈRE

3

**SEE BLOW-UP
PAGE 306**

N.-D. de
Fourvière ㊱

St-Jean

4

LA SAÔNE

Place
Bellecour

LE RHÔNE

5

Mâcon Dijon
A 6

Pl.
Carnot

6

Gare de
Perrache

N 86   A 7
St-Étienne Vienne Valence
㊴   ③

㉛   ㉚

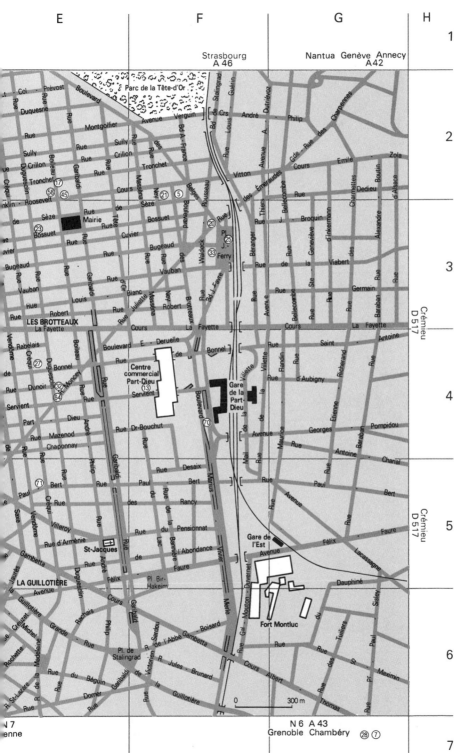

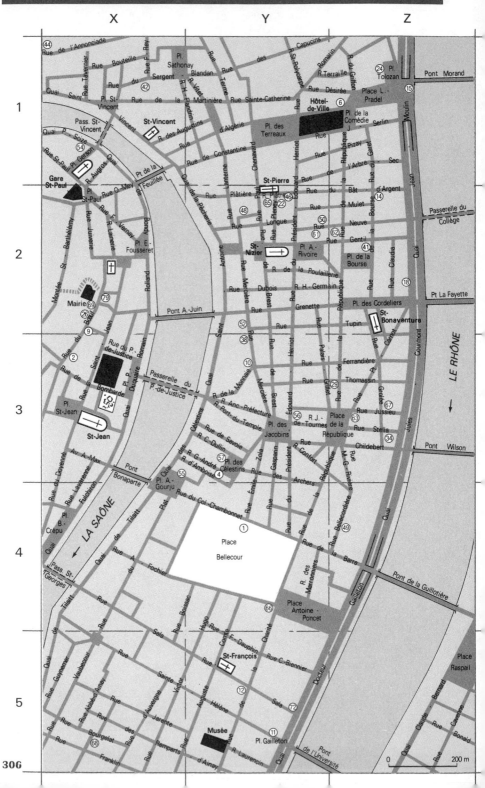

1 - Le Neuf (2e) **R**
2 - Les Adrets (5e) **R**
3 - Le Moulin à Poivre (2e) **R**
4 - Christian Bourillot (2e) **R**
5 - L'Helvétie (6e) **R**
6 - Les Muses (1er) **R**
7 - Mercure Park Hôtel (8e) **H**
  et Laennec **H**
8 - La Mère Brazier (1er) **R**
9 - Comptoir du Bœuf (5e) **R**
10 - Le Bistrot de Lyon (2e) **R**
11 - Le Vivarais (2e) **R**
12 - La Tassée (2e) **R**
13 - Pullman
  Part-Dieu (3e) **H**
14 - L'Italien de Lyon (2e) **R**
15 - Le Saint-Alban (1er) **R**
16 - Le Bistrot de la Mère (2e) **R**
  Brasserie Georges (2e) **R**
  Bristol (2e) **H**
  et La Mère Vittet (2e) **R**
17 - Cazenove (6e) **R**
18 - Nandron (2e) **R**
19 - Le Restaurant
  des Gourmets (6e) **R**
20 - Lutétia (6e) **H**
21 - Le Gourmet de Sèze (6e) **R**
22 - Léon de Lyon (1er) **R**
23 - Le Roosevelt (6e) **H**
24 - L'Assiette
  Lyonnaise (1er) **R**
25 - Le Gourmandin (6e) **R**
26 - La Tour Rose (La Maison
  de la Tour) (5e) **RH**
27 - Holiday Inn
  Crowne Plaza (3e) **H**
28 - Auberge
  Savoyarde (8e) **R**
29 - Le Rive Droite (2e) **R**
30 - Le Fédora (7e) **R**
31 - Mercure
  Lyon-Gerland (7e) **H**
32 - L'Alexandrin (3e) **R**
33 - Brasserie
  des Brotteaux (6e) **R**
34 - Plaza République (2e) **H**
35 - L'Épicurien (6e) **R**
36 - Les Terrasses de Lyon
  (Villa Florentine) (5e) **RH**
37 - La Romanée (1er) **R**
38 - Le Mercière (2e) **R**
39 - Charlemagne (2e) **H**
40 - Assiette et Marée (3e) **R**
41 - Assiette et Marée (2e) **R**
42 - La Gousse d'Ail (1er) **R**
43 - Thierry Gache (7e) **R**
44 - La Mandarine (1er) **R**
45 - Pierre Orsi (6e) **R**
46 - Le Passage (1er) **R**
47 - Les Lyonnais (5e) **R**
48 - Anticipation (1er) **R**
49 - Bellecordière (2e) **H**
50 - La Meunière (1er) **R**
51 - Gervais (6e) **R**
52 - Le Layon (2e) **R**
53 - Auberge de l'Ile (9e) **R**

54 - Têtedoie (2e) **R**
55 - La Voûte (2e) **R**
56 - Grand Hôtel
  des Beaux-Arts (2e) **H**
57 - Chez
  Jean-François (2e) **H**
58 - Le Rive Gauche (6e) **R**
59 - Le Quatre
  Saison (6e) **R**
60 - Les Belles Saisons
  (Pullman Perrache)
  (2e) **RH**
61 - Le Nord (2e) **R**
62 - Kun Yang (2e) **R**
63 - Carlton (2e) **H**
64 - Bistrot d'en Face (3e) **R**
65 - Bar du Passage (1er) **R**
66 - Royal (2e) **H**
67 - Grand Hôtel
  Concorde (2e) **H**
68 - Fleur de Sel (5e) **R**
69 - Cour des Loges (5e) **H**
70 - Mercure (3e) **H**

71 - J.-C. Péquet (3e) **R**
72 - Les Trois Dômes
  (Sofitel) (2e) **RH**
73 - Les Eaux Vives
  (Hôtel de Lyon
  Métropole) **RH**
74 - A Ma Vigne (3e) **R**
75 - Jean-Pierre Bergier (6e) **R**
76 - Hôtel Bleu Marine (3e) **H**
77 - Le Dôme des Saveurs (7e) **R**
78 - Au Temps Perdu (1er) **R**
79 - Restaurant des Arts (5e) **R**

china, and perfect service. The well-crafted cuisine includes warm foie gras with caramelized apples, roast salmon with delicate bits of bacon, émincé of veal in a chestnut crust, and a pineapple croquant successfully seasoned with dill. **C** 230-300 F. **M** 135 F (wine incl), 120 F, 175 F, 250 F.

Pullman Perrache

(See restaurant above)
Open year-round. 2 stes 1,300 F. 122 rms 490-820 F. Rms for disabled. Air cond. Conf. Valet pkg. V, AE, DC, MC.
Next to Lyon-Perrache railway station, this splendidly renovated nineteenth-century hotel features large, air-conditioned, soundproofed rooms with all the usual amenities. Shops; piano bar; winter garden.

11/20 Le Bistrot de la Mère

26, cours de Verdun
78 42 16 91, fax 78 42 40 70
Closed Mon. Open until 1:30am Terrace dining. Pkg. V, AE, DC, MC. **B6-16**
This sparkling, white-lacquered bistrot (an annex of the famed La Mère Vittet) offers appetizing Lyonnais specialties and delicious fresh oysters in season. Choose from snail fricassée, lamb chops with a potato gratin, sea bream with basil, and trout with almonds. Fine regional wines, many available by the carafe. **C** 150-200 F. **M** 68 F, 75 F, 120 F.

12/20 Le Bistrot de Lyon

64, rue Mercière
78 37 00 62, fax 72 41 76 56
Closed May 1, at Christmas. Open until 1:30am Priv rm: 40. Terrace dining. Air cond. V, AE. **Y3-10**
We had two meals here this year, one acceptable (excellent warm asparagus), and the other a total washout (hard Lyonnais salad, dry andouillette, undercooked steamed potatoes). The toque has to go. **C** 200-250 F. **M** 130 F (lunch), 150 F (dinner).

Christian Bourillot

8, pl. des Célestins
78 37 38 64, fax 78 38 20 35
Closed Mon lunch, Sun, Dec 23-Jan 2, Jul 5-Aug 5. Open until 10pm. Priv rm: 20. Air cond. Pkg. V, AE, DC, MC. **Y3-4**
The imposing decor with mahogany paneling, white damask tablecloths, and silver chandeliers has changed little over the years, and the traditional regional specialties still please: quenelles with lobster sauce, Bresse chicken, and fine desserts. There's a magnificent selection of Burgundies, and Anne-Marie Bourillot and her staff treat guests like old friends. It's too bad the prices are a bit too high. **C** 450-600 F. **M** 160 F, 250 F, 350 F, 450 F.

12/20 Brasserie Georges

30, cours de Verdun
72 56 54 54, fax 78 42 51 65
Closed May 1. Open until 11:15pm. Priv rm: 100. Terrace dining. Air cond. V, AE, DC, MC. **B6-16**
Founded in 1836, this bustling, noisy restaurant has welcomed many famous visitors over the years. Like them, we cast our eyes upward at every visit to admire the 600 square meters of grandiloquent ceiling frescoes. Then

we turn our attention to the pike quenelles, calf's liver sautéed in beer, and the house baba au rhum. An orchestra performs on Saturday nights. **C** 170-230 F. **M** 85 F, 110 F (exc Sun lunch), 160 F (Sun lunch), 120 F.

Bristol

28, cours de Verdun
78 37 56 55, fax 78 37 02 58
Open year-round. 3 stes 650-690 F. 110 rms 300-523 F. Rms for disabled. Restaurant. Air cond. Conf. Pkg. V, AE, DC, MC. **B6-16**
Centrally located next to Lyon-Perrache station, this hotel has neat, soundproofed rooms as well as a fitness center and sauna.

Carlton

4, rue Jussieu
78 42 56 51, fax 78 42 10 71
Open year-round. 83 rms 410-650 F. Air cond. V, AE, DC. **Z3-63**
A distinguished hotel offering soundproofed rooms, some redecorated in 1930s style. Friendly welcome, and the bar has a billiard table.

Charlemagne

23, cours Charlemagne
78 92 81 61, fax 78 42 94 84
Open year-round. 116 rms 395-545 F. Restaurant. Conf. Pkg. V, AE, DC, MC. **B7-39**
Two hotels (Charlemagne and Résidence) in one, with contemporary or period rooms, recently renovated and well equipped. Lyon-Perrache station and the pedestrian precinct are within easy reach. Gift shop and bar.

Fleur de Sel

7, rue Adélaïde-Perrin
78 37 40 37, fax 78 37 26 37
Closed Sun, Mon, hols, Aug. Open until 9:30pm. Priv rm: 34. V, MC. **X5-68**
Chef Cyril Nitard, who has trained with some of France's best, offers fine cuisine at low prices, and the locals have been quick to flock here. The façade may not be much, but the dining room decor is pleasant and refined, and the cooking top-notch: mushroom ravioli in fine olive oil from Mausanne, a tatin of tomato confit with squab and tiny fava beans, and red mullet with a chicken jus and beef marrow cromesquis. Excellent house breads and fine wines like an Alain Graillot Crozes-Hermitage. Who said grande cuisine had vanished from Lyons? We wish there were some set menus, though. **C** 150-300 F.

Grand Hôtel Concorde

11, rue Grôlée
72 40 45 45, fax 78 37 52 55
Open year-round. 3 stes 1,850-2,450 F. 140 rms 595-890 F. Restaurant. Air cond. Conf. Valet pkg. V, AE, DC, MC. **Z3-67**
This huge structure on the banks of the Rhône offers large and remarkably well soundproofed rooms. Traditional reception and service, numerous conference facilities.

Grand Hôtel des Beaux-Arts

73, rue du Président-Herriot
78 38 09 50, fax 78 42 19 19
Open year-round. 79 rms 340-585 F. Air cond. Conf. V, AE, DC, MC. **Y3-56**
Right next to Place des Jacobins, this large hotel combines modern comfort with tradition, and features recently renovated 1930s–style rooms (those at the back are quietest).

L'Italien de Lyon
25, rue du Bât-d'Argent
78 39 58 58, fax 72 07 98 96
Closed Sun. Open until midnight. Priv rm: 40. Garden dining. Air cond. V, AE. **Z2-14**
On duty in the kitchen of this elegant trattoria (note the Murano chandeliers) is an authentic Italian chef, who performs as patrons look on appreciatively. Among the offerings are mushroom risotto, pasta "cushions" enveloping a fish filling, and a well made tiramisu. Less convincing are the pizzas and appetizer buffet. **C** 180-200 F. **M** 105 F.

12/20 Chez Jean-François
2, pl. des Célestins - 78 42 08 26
Closed Sun, hols, Jul 25-Aug 25. Open until 10:30pm (later by reserv). Air cond. V, MC. **Y3-57**
The more popular the play at the theatre next door, the larger the crowd at Jean-François Courtois's restaurant. Specialties include artichoke terrine, skate with shallots, and slices of duck breast with lime sauce. Small, inexpensive cellar with lots of local wines. **C** 185-290 F. **M** 85 F, 120 F, 160 F.

12/20 Kun Yang
12, rue Neuve - 78 39 98 12
Open daily until 10:15pm. Priv rm: 30. Air cond. V, AE, DC, MC. **Y2-61**
Kun Yang offers Oriental specialties like Peking duck, gambas tails and sea scallops, Chinese fondue, and sole sautéed with soybeans. There's an aquariam serving as a wall mural. **C** 200-250 F. **M** 114 F, 150 F, 170 F.

12/20 Le Layon
52, rue Mercière
78 42 94 08, fax 78 21 05 72
Open daily until 11:30pm. Priv rm: 45. Terrace dining. Air cond. V, AE, MC. **Y2-52**
Set in a handsome seventeenth-century building, with two pleasant, sunny rooms, Le Layon offers fresh, straightforward food: smoked-salmon rillettes with dill, fricassée of pleurote mushrooms with persillade, fish assortment with langoustine fumet, and squab stuffed with cabbage. Good wines sold by the carafe. **C** 200-260 F. **M** 85 F, 105 F, 148 F.

Le Mercière
56, rue Mercière
78 37 67 35, fax 72 56 06 48
Open daily until 11:30pm. Priv rm: 30. Terrace dining. Garage pkg. V, AE, MC. **Y3-38**
Jean-Louis Manoa runs one of the best bistrots in town, where you can dine delightedly on traditional Lyonnais dishes, as well as on some more elaborate fare. Try his excellent andouillette de Fleurie poached in Mâcon wine (huge and full-flavored, with nary a trace of fat) and poached eggs in red wine sauce, both offered on the set menus. More elaborate dishes are offered à la carte, like lamb sweetbreads with morels and duck foie gras cooked in a cloth. Brisk service. **C** 120-180 F. **M** 68 F (lunch exc Sun), 89 F, 130 F.

11/20 La Mère Vittet
26, cours de Verdun
78 37 20 17, fax 78 42 40 70
Closed May 1. Open 24 hours. Priv rm: 50. Terrace dining. Air cond. Pkg. V, AE, DC, MC. **B6-16**
The atmosphere of this huge 24-hour brasserie, the displays of glossy fresh oysters, the charming service, and time-honored reputation all contribute to its lasting success. We suggest you sample veal sweetbreads in a parsley emulsion, chicken leg with tarragon sauce, salmon tartare, and grilled red mullet with beurre nantais. **C** 200-380 F. **M** 100 F, 148 F, 160 F, 245 F.

12/20 Le Moulin à Poivre
11, quai de Perrache - 78 37 36 86
Closed Sat, Sun, Aug. Open until 9pm. V. **C6-3**
The owners raise their own ducks and geese, which explains the number of Southwestern specialites featuring these birds. Try the duck foie gras sautéed with reinette apples, veal sweetbreads in a truffle vinaigrette, médallion of veal with watercress coulis, beef fillet cooked in white Burgundy, and delicate orange crêpes, all paired with good wines from Cahors. The stonewalled dining room is not our favorite feature. **C** 280-380 F. **M** 170 F, 230 F.

Nandron
26, quai J.-Moulin
78 42 10 26, fax 78 37 69 88
Closed Sat, Jul 29-Aug 27. Open until 10pm. Priv rm: 60. Air cond. Valet pkg. V, AE, DC, MC. **Z2-18**
This culinary institution perched above the Rhône doesn't pack in the crowds as much as it once did in these bargain-hunting days, and the kitchen seems to have let that affect the cooking. But the rating stays the same this year thanks to the superb pike quenelles (you won't find any better elsewhere), Bresse chicken au vinaigre with potato crêpes, casserole-roasted veal kidney, and a splendid wine list for those with bottomless wallets. Warm welcome by Odette Nandron. **C** 350-600 F. **M** 200 F, 350 F, 450 F.

12/20 Le Neuf
7, pl. Bellecour - 78 42 07 59
Closed Sun, 1 wk in Jul & in Aug. Open until 9:30pm. Air cond. V, MC. **Y4-1**
In spite of the generous cooking and reasonable prices, we were disappointed by the meals we had here this year, which seemed faulty in both conception and realization: undercooked seafood tagliatele, strips of duck breast that had a slightly over-the-top taste, and a bland strawberry gratin. Even the service stumbled a bit, in the pleasant dining room with its simple brasserie decor. The toque goes. **C** 180-220 F.

Le Nord
18, rue Neuve
78 28 24 54, fax 78 28 76 58
Open daily until 11:30pm. Priv rm: 64. Terrace dining. Air cond. V, AE, MC. **Y2-61**
This brightly decorated, 90-year-old brasserie is the first run by Paul Bocuse, and offers reliable fare at very reasonable prices: sauerkraut, chicken cooked in beer, and meats roasted in front of your eyes. Fine Beaujolais are the perfect match. The only catch: the tables are crowded together. You can't have everything. **C** 160-200 F. **M** 150 F (Sun), 95 F, 110 F (wine incl).

Plaza République
5, rue Stella
78 37 50 50, fax 78 42 33 34

Open year-round. 4 stes 710 F. 79 rms 400-610 F. Rms for disabled. Air cond. V, AE, DC, MC. **Z3-34**
The former Grand Hôtel des Étrangers has been reborn with a new, elegant interior. Well-equipped, well-soundproofed and nicely furnished rooms. Convenient location. Buffet breakfast; tea room.

Pullman Perrache
See restaurant Les Belles Saisons

 Le Rive Droite
6, rue Thomassin - 78 37 63 04
Closed Mon dinner, Sun, Aug. Open until 10pm. Priv rm: 20. Air cond. V, MC. **Z3-29**
It's hard to book a table in Roger Douillé's resolutely modern bistrot, packed lunch and dinner with regulars who come for the simple yet highly professional fare offered in one of Lyons's most chic districts: seafood salad, house-smoked salmon, Lyonnais-style gras double (tripe), and a marmite du pêcheur. There are several set menus. **C** 190-250 F. **M** 75 F (lunch, wine incl), 85 F (dinner), 120 F.

 Royal
20, pl. Bellecour
78 37 57 31, fax 78 37 01 36
Open year-round. 1 ste 1,500 F. 79 rms 590-890 F. Restaurant. Air cond. Conf. Pkg. V, AE, DC. **Y4-66**
A traditional hotel on the Place Bellecour with well-equipped period rooms. Good service; quiet bar; conference rooms.

Sofitel-Bellecour
See restaurant Les Trois Dômes

 La Tassée
20, rue de la Charité
78 37 02 35, fax 72 40 05 91
Closings not available. Open until 10:30pm. Priv rm: 100. Air cond. V, AE, DC. **Y5-12**
Life for many a well-heeled, food-loving Lyonnais revolves around this gastronomic institution. The atmosphere is relaxed and cheerful, the interior brightened by colorful vineyard frescoes. But we were disappointed this year by the salade lyonnaise (hard) and the chicken with vinegar (very ordinary). The toque is just barely in place. **C** 250-350 F. **M** 120 F, 165 F, 230 F, 300 F.

Les Trois Dômes
20, quai du Dr-Gailleton
72 41 20 20, fax 72 40 05 50
Closed Aug. Open until 10pm. Priv rm: 250. Air cond. Valet pkg. V, AE, DC, MC. **Y5-72**
Alain Desvilles presides over the kitchens of this eighth-floor, panoramic restaurant. The magnificent view of the Rhône below is one of the Trois Dôme's major attractions. Too bad the prices aren't more down-to-earth, like Desvilles's deft cooking: a lobster mesclun with almonds, salmon tartare with quail's eggs, grilled sea bass with a simple sauce vierge (on request), fine cheeses, and a caramelized pineapple and lime chiboust. For wallet relief, try the 150 F option (one main dish). The extensive wine list has skyscraper prices. Cordial welcome and tip-top service. **C** 300-400 F.

A red hotel ranking denotes a place with charm.

Sofitel-Bellecour
(See restaurant above)
Open year-round. 29 stes 1,050-1,800 F. 138 rms 870 F. Air cond. Conf. Valet pkg. V, AE, DC, MC.
Conveniently located in the center of town, this hotel is now totally renovated. Good breakfasts. Shopping arcade with many boutiques.

Le Vivarais
1, pl. du Dr-Gailleton
78 37 85 15, fax 78 37 59 49
Closed Sun, Dec 25-Jan 1, Jul 16-Aug 16. Open until 10:15pm. Air cond. Pkg. V, AE, DC. **Y5-11**
Robert Duffaud, a former pupil of the lamented Alain Chapel, runs one of the most popular *bouchons* in town. We're partial to his duck foie gras cooked in a cloth, guinea fowl fricassée, tripière du Vivarais, and the choice of desserts. On the first set menu you'll find sausage with steamed potatoes, salmon mousse with mushrooms, and cervelle de canut (fresh cheese with herbs). Good wines from Mâcon and Beaujolais. **C** 180-280 F. **M** 100 F, 130 F.

12/20 La Voûte
Chez Léa, 11, pl. A.-Gourju
78 42 01 33, fax 78 37 36 41
Closed Sun. Open until 9:45pm. Priv rm: 60. Terrace dining. Air cond. No pets. V, AE, DC, MC. **X3-55**
Popular with tourists, this timeless bistrot offers honest, typically Lyonnais dishes at reasonable prices: crayfish quenelles, pickerel à la farigoulette, tripe, and game dishes in season. **C** 200-250 F. **M** 118 F, 133 F.

And also...
Our selection of places for inexpensive, quick, or late-night meals.
Le Pasteur (78 37 01 04 - 83, quai Perrache. Open until 10pm.): The menu of this Perrache neighborhood *bouchon* changes daily. Guignol puppet shows on Friday nights (120 F).
Chez Rabatel (78 37 14 98 - 11, pl. A.-Gourju. Open until 9:30pm.): Chez Lea's annex serves pig's feet with lentils and sirloin steak with shallots (105 F).
Le Shalimar (78 42 18 20 - 39, quai Gailleton. Open until 10:30pm.): A pleasing Indian restaurant with a *menu-dégustation* and fine fresh chapatis (95-130 F).

L'Alexandrin
83, rue Moncey
72 61 15 69, fax 78 62 75 57
Closed Sun, Mon, Dec 24-Jan 1, May 25-29, Jul 14-17, Aug 6-27. Open until 9:30pm. Terrace dining. Air cond. Pkg. V, AE, MC. **E4-32**
Alain Alexanian's highly personal, professional cooking is as modern and inspired as ever. What's more, he manages to hold the line on prices in his relaxed restaurant set in Les Halles. Try his "winter salad" with beet chips, red mullet with an artichoke and sunflower purée, fillet of young rabbit grilled with Armagnac-soaked prunes, and curly cabbage soup with smoked bacon and sabodet sausage. For dessert, there's a superbly simple baked apple with caramel butter paired with dried-fruit ice cream. Véronique Alexanian supervises the prompt, af-

fable service, as well as the cellar, rich in fine Côtes-du-Rhônes. An extra point this year. **C** 280-380 F. **M** 160 F, 155 F, 195 F.

Assiette et Marée
26, rue Servient
78 62 89 94, fax 78 60 39 27
Closed Sun, Mon, Jan 1-10, Aug 14-Sep 15. Open until 10pm. Priv rm: 60. Air cond. V. **E4-40**
This cheery seafood restaurant sports a bright yellow awning and contemporary decor. The owners trained under the legendary Bocuse and are enjoying a tidal wave of success with their glistening fresh fish simply cooked and vivaciously served in a jolly, relaxed ambience. Soup of grilled fish, sea snails with mayonnaise, grilled sea bream and sole, fine Saint Marcellin cheese, and well chosen wines. The desserts are much improved this year. **C** 150-200 F.

Bistrot d'en Face
220, rue Du Guesclin
72 61 96 16, fax 78 60 59 97
Closed Sun, Aug. 8-29. Open until 9:30pm. V, AE, MC. **E4-64**
Maître d' Jérôme André and chef Olivier Belval have come up with a winning anti-recession cure. Together with Jean-Paul Lacombe (of Léon de Lyon fame), the dynamic duo opened this bistrot in the Halles neighborhood near the Part-Dieu train station, and their success is justified. The 105 F single menu changes weekly, and might include a leek and fresh goat cheese terrine, rabbit thigh in mustard sauce with polenta, chicken liver "cake", and rice pudding with crème anglaise. Outstanding welcome. **M** 105 F.

Hôtel Bleu Marine
4-6, rue Mortier
78 60 03 09, fax 78 60 01 95
Open year-round. 8 stes 480 F. 131 rms 290-480 F. Rms for disabled. Pkg. V, AE, DC, MC. **D5-76**
A well equipped hotel in the center of town, with soundproofed (although not air-conditioned) rooms. Good quality-price ratio.

Holiday Inn Crowne Plaza
29, rue de Bonnel
72 61 90 90, fax 72 61 17 54
Open year-round. 2 stes 2,100-2,600 F. 156 rms 795-1,200 F. Rms for disabled. Restaurant. Air cond. Conf. Valet pkg. V, AE, DC, MC. **E4-27**
A new chain hotel with an American-style decor that boasts a full complement of amenities: a boardroom for business meetings, sauna, Turkish baths, rooms reserved for non-smokers, and others adapted for the disabled, piano bar, American restaurant. Free shuttle service to Lyon Part-Dieu station.

Mercure
Lyon Part-Dieu, 47, bd Vivier-Merle
72 34 18 12, fax 78 53 40 69
Open year-round. 124 rms 395-575 F. Rms for disabled. Restaurant. Air cond. Conf. Golf. Pkg. V, AE, DC, MC. **F4-70**
Convenient to the TGV and to the métro, the Mercure features comfortable, soundproofed rooms with air conditioning.

Restaurant prices in red draw attention to restaurants that offer particularly good value.

J.-C. Péquet
59, pl. Voltaire - 78 95 49 70
Closed Sat, Sun, Aug. Open until 9:30pm. Air cond. V, AE, DC, MC. **E3-71**
Jean-Claude Péquet's charming restaurant, recently enlarged, offers earnest, professionally prepared but mundane dishes like spinach salad with creamed chicken livers, rabbit thigh with summer savory, and a salad of dandelion greens with bacon. Extra-charming welcome. **C** 230-280 F. **M** 150 F, 190 F, 260 F.

Pullman Part-Dieu
129, rue Servient
78 63 55 00, fax 78 63 55 20
Open year-round. 245 rms 560-660 F. Restaurant. Air cond. Conf. Valet pkg. V, AE, DC, MC. **F4-13**
Europe's tallest hotel, the Pullman Part-Dieu provides functional, well-furnished rooms with awe-inspiring views of the city and the Rhône.

12/20 A Ma Vigne
23, rue J.-Larrivé - 78 60 46 31
Open daily until 9pm. V. **D5-74**
Madame Giraud's tiny, bustling restaurant serves cold roast ham, thick steaks accompanied by the best fries in town, and delicious house tarts, all washed down by nice wines served by the carafe. **C** 150-240 F.

And also...
Our selection of places for inexpensive, quick, or late-night meals.
Merle (78 62 30 29 - Halles de la Part-Dieu, 102, cours Lafayette. Open until 10pm.): This is arguably the best seafood specialist in Les Halles. Oysters, shellfish, snails, moules marinière are served at the old-fashioned bar or in the comfortable dining room (160-200 F).
Le Val d'Isère (78 71 09 39 - 64, rue de Bonnel. Lunch only.): Come here at the crack of dawn and watch the chefs tuck in to skate with beurre noir sauce and stuffed pig's foot as they return from market (100-150 F).

Les Eaux Vives
85, quai Joseph-Gillet
78 29 20 20, fax 78 39 99 20
Open daily until 10pm. Priv rm: 250. Terrace dining. Air cond. Pool. Valet pkg. V, AE, DC, MC. **A2-73**
Stéphane Gaborieau has trained with some of France's best chefs, and provides delicate, subtle cooking based on superb products, presented in a menu that changes often to fit market offerings. His technique is exemplary, and this year produced such delicious fare as a terrine of braised veal sweetbreads with fresh girolle mushrooms, tender spiced Collioure anchovies paired with a marvelous Basque vegetable confit, roast grénadin of milk-fed veal, fricassée of artichokes and girolles with light-as-air potato chips, and a red-plum vol-au-vent. The 150 F menu is a great bargain, and there's a fine children's menu at 100 F with several choices. The wine list is limited but carefully chosen; the service still a bit stiff. Everything takes time. But two toques make a great start. **C** 280-420 F. **M** 150 F, 210 F, 290 F.

Hôtel de Lyon Métropole
(See restaurant above)
Open year-round. 1 ste 455-690 F. 118 rms 495-595 F. Restaurant. Half-board 260 F. Air cond. Conf. Heated pool. Tennis. Golf. Valet pkg. Helipad. V, AE, DC, MC.
Large new building in a sports complex next to the Saône. The rooms are large, modern, and tastefully furnished. Delicious breakfasts.

And also...
Our selection of places for inexpensive, quick, or late-night meals.
La Marmite en Bois (78 28 13 56 - 1, rue Dumont. Open until 10pm.): Fresh, appealing Mediterranean cooking on a fine set menu (170-280 F).
Sorey (78 27 95 56 - 10, pl. F.-Rey. Open until 11:30pm.): Featuring fresh cooking and Provençal decor, this restaurant is popular with the theatre crowd (98-140 F).

LYON **5TH**

 Les Adrets
30, rue du Bœuf
78 38 24 30, fax 78 42 79 52
Closed Sat, Sun, Jan 2-9, Aug 1-29. Open until 10pm. Priv rm: 40. V, MC. **X3-2**
For the modest sum of 135 F, you get a superb Renaissance setting, dedicated service, and tiny snails sautéed with figs, sweet-sour duck breast with a confit of girolle mushrooms, cheese, and dessert. C 190-250 F. M 75 F (lunch, wine incl), 95 F, 135 F, 165 F.

12/20 **Comptoir du Bœuf**
2, pl. Neuve-Saint-Jean
78 92 82 35, fax 78 42 26 02
Closed Sun. Open until midnight. Terrace dining. V. **X2-9**
Wines sold by the glass and a delightful terrace draw the crowds to this friendly annex of La Tour Rose. The short list of zesty dishes includes Serrano ham, cuttlefish ragoût with basmati rice, chicken in vinegar sauce, and oeufs en neige. C 200-250 F.

 Cour des Loges
6, rue du Bœuf
78 42 75 75, fax 72 40 93 61
Open year-round. 10 stes 2,000-3,000 F. 53 rms 880-1,700 F. Rms for disabled. Restaurant. Air cond. Conf. Pool. Golf. Pkg. V, AE, DC, MC. **X2-69**
In the heart of the old town, a sumptuous hotel made up of four buildings from the fourteenth, seventeenth, and eighteenth centuries. The unique interior courtyard with its Florentine arcades and hanging gardens, the lounges, basement wine and tapas bars, the covered pool, the contemporary paintings and lithographs, all contribute to a tasteful, harmonious whole unequaled anywhere else in Lyon. On the down side, rooms are darker than one could wish, since a few surrounding streets are so narrow; and in a few instances, comfort has been sacrificed to aesthetic considerations. Additional amenities include a sauna, Jacuzzi, and a fitness center.

A red hotel ranking denotes a place with charm.

12/20 **Les Lyonnais**
1, rue Tramassac
78 37 64 82, fax 72 56 06 48
Open daily until 11:30pm (midnight w-e). Priv rm: 35. V, MC. **B4-47**
This chic bistrot operated by Le Mercière's Jean-Louis Manoa has one of the best quality-price ratios around. For only 89 F, you can have young rabbit in tarragon gelatin, blood sausage with two kinds of apples, and a delicate apple tart. And that's just a sample; the menu changes often. The dining room features portraits of 150 well known Lyonnais residents. M 89 F.

La Maison de la Tour
See restaurant La Tour Rose

 Restaurant des Arts
14, rue du Bœuf - 78 37 01 87
Closed Sun & Mon lunch (exc hols). Open until 11:30pm. Priv rm: 50. V. **X2-79**
Set in the heart of historic old Lyons' pleasant pedestrian precinct, this appealing, old-fashioned restaurant offers traditional dishes made by skilled chef Vincent Verneveaux. The set menus are an excellent value. For 100 F you get salade lyonnaise, leek terrine, and a good gibelotte (rabbit fricassée), along with an aperitif, a glass of wine, and coffee. And the à la carte menu is well worth a try, too. The *patronne*'s welcome and service are charming. C 200-250 F. M 96 F, 149 F (wine incl).

 Les Terrasses de Lyon
25, montée Saint-Barthélemy
72 56 56 56, fax 72 40 90 56
Open daily until 9:45pm. Priv rm: 20. Terrace dining. Air cond. Heated pool. Pkg. V, AE, DC, MC. **B4-36**
An ancient convent has been converted into an elegant restaurant with sunny contemporary decor and stunning city views. Chef Fabrice Bugaud offers classic cuisine with finesse, such as the first set menu (a bit expensive): cod brandade, a fresh salad of sliced veal scented with tarragon, a generous and perfectly cooked fillet of scorpion fish with potatoes, good cheese assortment, and a pleasant fruit soup. Fine wine list; highly professional welcome and service. C 300-400 F. M 160 F (weekday lunch, Sat), 190 F, 270 F, 350 F.

 Villa Florentine
(See restaurant above)
Information not available. No pets.
An ancient convent on the Fourvière hill has become a luxurious hotel with a superb panorama of the city from the terrace and the sunny, spacious rooms with modern decor. Everything is of the highest possible quality (right at the limit of being over-the-top, in fact), and the whole is classified a national historic monument. A palatial establishment well suited to a metropolis the like Lyons.

Têtedoie
54, quai Pierre-Scize
78 29 40 10, fax 72 07 05 65
Closed Sat lunch & Sun (exc hols), Aug 10-24. Open until 11pm. Air cond. Valet pkg. V, AE. **X1-54**
A lovely establishment on the banks of the Saône with its supporters and critics. We feel the prices are too high, not in step with the times. The cooking is sincere and usually although not

always well prepared: excellent fish assiette, overcooked skate with aromatic herbs drowned in sauce, and crème brûlée that would be better without the Grand Marnier. The wine list is pricey, too, though well chosen. Excellent welcome. C 260-360 F. M 145 F, 180 F, 220 F, 260 F.

La Tour Rose

22, rue du Bœuf
78 37 25 90, fax 78 42 26 02
Closed Sun. Open until 10:30pm. Priv rm: 200. Garden dining. Air cond. Valet pkg. V, AE, DC. **X2-26**
Philippe Chavent's La Tour Rose occupies a magnificent Renaissance convent, with monumental staircases and inner courtyards and views of old Lyon's red-tiled roofs. The dining room in the former chapel—alone worth the trip—is a showcase for the city's silk-weaving industry.
Chavent has said that in these straightened times, people are looking for affordable prices when they go out to eat, but he doesn't apply that principle here, especially following the recent costly refurbishing of the superb premises. (For Chavent cooking at lower prices, try his Comptoir du Bœuf or the Les Muses restaurant in the new Lyons opera.) And what's more, we feel the quality has slipped a bit. On our last visit, the service was both snobbish and awkward, and the cooking seemed to have lost its former inventiveness. That said, there are still some magnificent dishes here, those that sparked Chavent's meteoric success: barely cooked smoked salmon, potato salad with caviar, roast skate with a saffrony potato purée, and a marvelous warm madeleine with honey ice cream. New dishes we enjoyed include poached eggs with sea urchin purée accompanied by fried beets, slices of roast duck breast with fruit chutney (a few vegetables on the side would have been welcome, though), and well made desserts like bergamot-perfumed crème brûlée and crisp, lemony egg whites. C 550-700 F. M 295 F, 500 F, 595 F (20% discount on weekday lunch).

La Maison de la Tour

(See restaurant above)
Open year-round. 6 stes 1,500-2,800 F. 6 rms 950-1,650 F. Air cond. Conf. Valet pkg. V, AE, DC.
In the heart of the old town, this hotel's delightful rooms and suites (some with two levels, all with terraces), are named after Lyonnais silk firms whose opulent fabrics were used for the furnishings. Three hanging gardens contribute to the restful atmosphere.

Villa Florentine

See restaurant Les Terrasses de Lyon

And also...

Our selection of places for inexpensive, quick, or late-night meals.
Brasserie de Bondy (78 28 37 34 - 16, quai de Bondy. Open until 12:30am.): Lyons' best sauerkraut, as well as many Alsatian specialties, with beers and wines that go with them (150 F). La Conciergerie (78 83 23 39 - 12, quai P.-Scize. Open until 11pm.): Trendy atmosphere, jovial service, and modern cuisine at reasonable prices (100-200 F).

Le Coquemar (78 25 83 32 - 23, montée de Fourvière. Lunch only.): These well-prepared family-style dishes won't break the bank (75-80 F).

Jean-Pierre Bergier

20, rue Sully
78 89 07 09, fax 78 89 89 94
Closed Sat lunch, Sun, Aug 1-25. Open until 9:30pm. Priv rm: 25. Air cond. V. **D2-75**
The delicious cooking with a pleasing personal touch and a menu that changes every 10 days have won a devoted local following. Jean-Pierre Bergier turns out sautéed red mullet with tomato confit, croustillant of boned rabbit, and delicious desserts like fresh fruits in Muscat wine. C 270-310 F. M 110 F (weekday lunch, wine incl), 120 F, 165 F, 265 F.

11/20 Brasserie des Brotteaux

1, pl. Jules-Ferry - 72 74 03 98
Closed Sat dinner, Sun. Open until 11:30pm. Priv rm: 40. Terrace dining. Pkg. V, AE, MC. **F3-33**
This charming brasserie with authentic turn-of-the-century decor is the place to go for raw vegetable plates, delicious chicken-liver gâteau, andouillette with mustard sauce, and nice apple tart, all served with a smile and washed down with a carafe of the house Mâcon. C 150-250 F. M 75 F, 100 F, 155 F.

Cazenove

75, rue Boileau
78 89 82 92, fax 72 44 93 34
Closed Sat, Sun, Aug. Open until 10pm. Air cond. V, AE, MC. **E2-17**
Pierre Orsi's 1900-style bistrot annex is as chic as ever, though the prices aren't that much lower than in his main restaurant next door, and the decor is not what you'd call relaxed. On the good side, the welcome is warm and the cuisine honest and well prepared. Try the 180 F menu (not really what we'd call bistrot style, but never mind): appetizers, house-smoked salmon, aïoli with black olives, golden cod with spices, superb Saint Marcellin from top supplier Richard, and a fine choice of desserts (such as crêpes Suzette). It's all just right; Orsi can't be otherwise. C 250-300 F. M 180 F (weekday lunch), 260 F, 450 F.

12/20 L'Épicurien

3, rue Bugeaud - 78 24 49 51
Closed 1st 3 wks of Aug. Open until 9:30pm. V, AE, MC. **D3-35**
Unpretentious cooking is offered in the spacious, restful dining room done up in pale shades of green. On the 98 F menu: a plate of cucumbers and radishes, seasonal salad with Gruyère cheese and walnuts, poached hake, and fresh fromage blanc. Pricey cellar rich in Bordeaux and Burgundies. C 190-260 F. M 98 F, 150 F.

Gervais

42, rue P.-Corneille
78 52 19 13, fax 72 74 99 14
Closed Sat lunch (& dinner in seas), Sun, Jul 3-Aug 3. Open until 10pm. Priv rm: 18. Air cond. V, AE, DC, MC. **D3-51**
Gervais Lescuyer's customers are as faithful as his flavorful, nicely presented cooking is consis-

tent. Savor the scallop salad, chicken fricasséed in raspberry vinegar, and nougat glacé. Devoted service; fine wine list. Try the Saint Joseph from Saint Désirat. **C** 300-400 F. **M** 150 F (weekdays, Sat), 185 F.

Le Gourmandin
14, pl. Jules-Ferry
78 52 02 52, fax 78 52 33 05
Closed Sat lunch, Sun. Open until 9:45pm (10pm in summer). Priv rm: 42. Terrace dining. Air cond. Valet pkg. V, AE, DC, MC. **F3-25**
Restaurateur Daniel Abattu is struggling valiantly against the recession by offering a fine 135 F lunch menu. The superb terrace remains Lyons' loveliest. Try the leeks in vinaigrette (we could do without the onions that smother them, though), duck thigh confit, navarin of lamb, and simple desserts based on fresh fruit. To drink, a Duboeuf Beaujolais or a Morgon from Lapierre. Efficient service. **C** 250-350 F. **M** 135 F, 198 F, 269 F.

Le Gourmet de Sèze
129, rue de Sèze
78 24 23 42, fax 78 24 23 42
Closed Sat lunch, Sun, Feb school hols, Aug. Open until 9:30pm. Air cond. V, AE, MC. **F2-21**
Bernard Mariller's culinary passport is stamped with some pretty impressive visas: Lameloise, Troisgros, Robuchon... He's in his own place now, a rather solemn pink and grey dining room where he offers lamb's foot barigoule, sautéed monkfish with garlic croquettes and tomato confit, rabbit with basil cream sauce, rack of Sisteron lamb with Provençal canneloni, and very pleasing desserts. Eclectic cellar, courteous welcome, and efficient service. **C** 250-350 F. **M** 120 F (weekdays), 165 F, 240 F.

L'Helvétie
4, bd des Brotteaux
78 24 38 18, fax 78 52 25 44
Closed Sun. Open until 1am. Priv rm: 100. Terrace dining. Air cond. V, AE, DC. **F2-5**
Through the popular ground-floor brasserie and up the stairs you'll find a plush, modern restaurant decorated with mirrors and potted plants. Come here for a first course of a fine soup (of mussels, or langoustine minestrone), followed by flambéed veal kidneys, various sauerkraut dishes, and a platter of fresh raw fish direct from the brasserie. **C** 280-380 F. **M** 100 F, 150 F, 215 F.

Lutétia
112-114, bd des Belges
78 24 44 68, fax 78 24 44 68
Open year-round. 55 rms 420-520 F. Air cond. Pkg. V, AE, DC, MC. **F3-20**
A simple hotel facing the former Brotteaux train station, with light, pleasantly modern and properly equipped rooms, most with double-glazed windows (it's noisier on the boulevard side).

Pierre Orsi
3, pl. Kléber
78 89 57 68, fax 72 44 93 34
Closed Sun dinner, Aug 10-20. Open until 9:30pm. Priv rm: 50. Air cond. V, AE, MC. **E2-45**
Pierre Orsi's luxurious restaurant is a sumptuous showcase of marble, silverware, and crystal. But the menu is tricked out with so many

délices, farandoles, and *méli-mélos* that it reads like a throwback to the frivolous Belle Époque, and the service is so attentive it can feel smothering. No matter, Orsi's cooking is still based on superb products prepared in marvelous ways: his foie gras is one of the best we know, his smoked salmon is incomparable, his roast veal sweetbreads à l'ancienne impeccable, and his wine list up to the calibre of the cooking. Orsi is a perfectionist, sometimes so much so that it borders on the ludicrous. But why fault him for this? **C** 400-700 F. **M** 180 F (lunch exc Sun), 320 F, 400 F, 500 F, 600 F.

Le Quatre Saisons
15, rue Sully - 78 93 76 07
Closed Sat lunch, Sun, Aug 8-30. Open until 9:30pm. Priv rm: 20. Air cond. V, AE, DC, MC. **D2-59**
The neighborhood crowd flocks to this cozy bourgeois restaurant where a bargain 120 F menu is on offer. The à la carte dishes are conventional as can be, like the steak with béarnaise sauce or the pear Belle Hélène. The fish dishes are more creative: medallions of monkfish in green apple jus, and roast pickerel in veal jus. Claude Auberger cooks with a steady hand. **C** 300-380 F. **M** 120 F (weekdays), 180 F, 240 F, 310 F.

Le Restaurant des Gourmets
Chez Luigi, 14, rue de Godefroy
78 89 37 13, fax 78 94 27 84
Closed Sat lunch, Sun, Aug. Open until 10pm. Air cond. V, AE, DC, MC. **D2-19**
Classic dishes, attentive service, and an intimate decor help to make this restaurant popular, and owner Luigi Ricci's personality does the rest. And he's even lowered the prices. He prepares foie gras and sea bass en croûte as well as the osso-buco and tiramisu from his native Italy. With them, drink a Saint Véran or, what else, a Chianti. **C** 200-300 F. **M** 80 F, 125 F, 149 F, 200 F.

12/20 Le Rive Gauche
31, cours F.-D.-Roosevelt - 78 89 51 21
Closed Sat, Sun. Open until 11pm. Terrace dining. V, AE. **E2-58**
The whole neighborhood flocks to this cozy bistrot with antique engravings on the walls, where you can sample the 79 F daily special, seafood, or the 135 F menu. We liked the properly cooked roast lamb with thyme, veal chops sautéed with morels, a strawberry dessert, and local wines by the carafe. Lively and friendly welcome and service. **C** 150-200 F. **M** 79 F (weekday lunch), 99 F, 135 F, 149 F.

Le Roosevelt
25, rue Bossuet
78 52 35 67, fax 78 52 39 82
Open year-round. 4 stes 630-680 F. 83 rms 400-500 F. Air cond. Conf. Pkg. V, AE, DC, MC. **E3-23**
A modern, neat hotel offering many amenities for business travelers. Efficient room service, rooms renovated this year, and good conference facilities (you can even hook up a telex in your room).

And also...
Our selection of places for inexpensive, quick, or late-night meals.

Le Théodore (78 24 08 52 - 34, cours F.-D.-Roosevelt. Open until 10pm, 11pm w-e.): Savor reliable bistrot cooking in this reliable spot that's so popular it's best to reserve (180-240 F).

LYON   7TH

12/20 Le Dôme des Saveurs
45, rue Anvers - 78 72 32 53
Closed Sat lunch, Sun, 3 wks in Aug. Open until 10:30pm. V, AE.   **D6-77**
Don't let the unprepossessing exterior deter you. Inside is a gracious dining room where the solid cooking is a steal: mellow smoked salmon and duck breast, a foie gras pavé, squid ragoût, pink trout with star anise, gooey chocolate fondant, and more. C 180-220 F. M 95 F, 130 F, 170 F.

Le Fédora
249, rue M.-Mérieux
78 69 46 26, fax 72 73 38 80
Closed Sat lunch, Sun, Dec 22-Jan 4. Open until 10pm. Priv rm: 45. Garden dining. Air cond. V, AE, DC.   **D7-30**
The Judéaux family provide superior seafood in their newly refurbished restaurant, and very reasonable prices. Weather permitting, book your table on the garden patio to sample Daniel Judéaux's 169 F menu: squid salad with mustard and beans, and mixed fish assortment flavored with star anise accompanied by parsleyed rice. On the à la carte menu, savor delicious treats like sea bream braised in anchovy jus with a leek gratin, or roast tuna with olive purée, red mullet with foie gras and a warm sweet pepper salad. All the chef's dishes are prepared with a sure hand, perfectly cooked, and flavorful. Very well chosen wines, pleasant dining room, and a warm welcome. C 360-450 F. M 135 F, 169 F, 280 F.

Thierry Gache
37, rue Thibaudière
78 72 81 77, fax 78 72 01 75
Closed Sun dinner. Open until 10:30pm. Priv rm: 45. Air cond. V, AE.   **D6-43**
Thierry Gache's toque is red because he is a highly creative chef. Though he tends to over topple on occasion, he is skilled enough to right the keel in time. His 112 F set menu offers a lamb confit, tapenade and a bitter orange coulis, a pôtée (stew) of red mullet filets en chartreuse, and cheese or dessert. The à la carte prices are not as friendly. Service is very slow. C 350-400 F. M 112 F, 168 F, 208 F, 258 F, 390 F.

Mercure-Gerland
70, av. Leclerc
72 71 11 11, fax 72 71 11 00
Open year-round. 12 stes 670 F. 182 rms 350-490 F. Rms for disabled. Restaurant. Air cond. Conf. Heated pool. Golf. Garage pkg. V, AE, DC, MC.   **C7-31**
Near the confluence of the Rhône and the Saône, this modern hotel offers comfortable rooms with double glazing. Good conference facilities; river excursions.

And also...
Our selection of places for inexpensive, quick, or late-night meals.
Carnegie Hall (78 58 85 79 - 253, rue M.-Mérieux. Open until 12:30am.): Sink your teeth

into a juicy steak or chops at this red-brick grill in the old slaughterhouse district (150-200 F).

LYON   8TH

12/20 Auberge Savoyarde
72, av. des Frères-Lumière - 78 00 77 64,
Closed Sun, hols, Aug. Open until 9:30pm. Air cond. Garage pkg. V, AE, DC, MC.   **G7-28**
Copious, uncontrived dishes served in a simple, country-style dining room overlooking a tiny garden. Salmon with dill, sole meunière, steak with shallots, and Baked Alaska. C 150-280 F. M 82 F, 120 F.

Laennec
36, rue Seignemartin
78 74 55 22, fax 78 01 00 24
Open year-round. 14 rms 275-355 F. Pkg. V.   **G7-13**
A new little hotel in a quiet district. Meals on trays.

Mercure Park Hotel
4, rue du Pr-Calmette
78 74 11 20, fax 78 01 43 38
Open year-round. 72 rms 330-390 F. Restaurant. Half board 420 F. Conf. Pkg. V, AE, DC, MC.   **G7-7**
This huge hotel has newly renovated rooms and pleasant lounges. Meals served on the terrace in summer.

LYON   9TH

12/20 Auberge de l'Ile
Ile Barbe, pl. Notre-Dame
78 83 99 49, fax 78 47 80 46
Closed Sun dinner, Mon, Feb school hols, Aug 7-21. Open until 10pm. Priv rm: 30. No pets. Pkg. V, AE, DC, MC.   **A1-53**
A few years ago, the owners of this venerable institution on the enchanting isle of Sainte-Barbe put their son, Jean-Christophe Ansanay-Alex, in charge of the kitchen. Although his cooking is sometimes a bit unsure, it's interesting: tempura of plump langoustines, frog's legs with garlic chips, baby fava beans and mousseron mushrooms, calf's liver in vinegar butter, almond milk ice cream flavored with licorice and honey cake. A quest for more natural flavors would please us. The welcome and service could be more natural, too. C 330-400 F. M 150 F (weekdays), 175 F, 250 F, 320 F.

■ In Caluire-et-Cuire 69300   3 km N

Auberge de Fond Rose
23, quai Clemenceau
78 29 34 61, fax 72 00 28 67
Closed Sun dinner off-seas. Open until 9:30pm. Priv rm: 80. Terrace dining. Pkg. V, AE, DC, MC.
Michel Brunet, a fervent disciple of Paul Bocuse, offers solid, well prepared dishes in his restaurant nestled in a pleasant garden alongside the Saône. On hand are foie gras salad, casserole-roasted squab, and grenadin of lamb en croûte. He grows many of his own vegetables and herbs, and makes a laudatory effort to keep prices down. C 450-500 F. M 185 F, 250 F, 350 F, 425 F, 450 F.

In Champagne-au-Mont-d'Or 69410
9 km N

Les Grillons
18, rue D.-Vincent
78 35 04 78, fax 78 35 59 58
Closed Sun dinner, Mon, Aug 21-Sep 10. Open until 8:30pm. Priv rm: 54. Terrace dining. Pkg. V, MC.
Set in handsome grounds, this turn-of-the-century *hôtel particulier* boasts a splendid summer terrace with leafy chestnut trees and a 200-year-old sequoia. The dining room is weighted down by thick burgundy curtains. On the 145 F menu: snail-stuffed puff pastry with red butter sauce, saddle of lamb sautéed with coriander, aged cheeses, and a dessert assortment. On the 195 F menu you'll find émincé of pickerel in truffle oil or a duck breast spiced with juniper berries. Small wine list of Bordeaux and Burgundies, with too few half bottles. C 320-400 F. M 110 F (exc weekday dinner & Sun), 145 F, 195 F, 280 F, 345 F.

In Collonges-au-Mont-d'Or 69660
9 km N on N 51

Paul Bocuse
50, quai de la Plage
72 27 85 85, fax 72 27 85 87
Open daily until 9:30pm. Priv rm: 50. Air cond. V, AE, DC, MC.
Paul Bocuse continues his travels and business ventures, leaving his kitchen in the capable hands of chefs Roger Jaloux and Christian Bouvarel. Getting a glimpse of Bocuse himself (in the flesh) is a rare occasion much appreciated by the many foreign tourists who make pilgrimages here (his portraits, on the other hand, are all over the place). His team's mission is to perpetuate the Bocuse legend without too many excursions into individual creativity. In any case, Bocuse, for all his high-profile media attention, was never a creative chef, but rather a perpetuator of tradition. Still, since we liked them once, we can still enjoy the fixtures of his menu, like foie gras terrine, turbot in hollandaise, veal kidney à la dijonnaise, and volaille en vessie sauce fleurette. But, Monsieur Paul (as he is known here), we must ask why the famous sea bass en croûte à la Fernand Point provoked nothing but dismay at the table next to us on our last visit? Perhaps the fish had passed its prime, a rare accident here where the products are habitually of the finest quality, including the great Richard cheeses. Apart from this, we have no criticism; the Bernachon chocolate cake is a monument, the wine list outstanding (and the sommelier steers you toward affordable bottles), the service smooth as silk, the coffee and chocolate truffles that come with it top-class. You just have to keep in mind that you do not come here to taste the cooking of "France's best chef," nor will you taste the best meal in the world, but instead you will sample good, savory, authentic dishes in a temple to bourgeois cooking the way they like it best in this region. C 600-1,100 F. M 340 F (lunch exc Sun), 440 F, 550 F, 610 F, 710 F, 740 F.

In Mionnay 01390
19 km N on N 83

Alain Chapel
N 83 - 78 91 82 02, fax 78 91 82 37
Closed Tue lunch, Mon, Jan. Open until 9pm. Priv rm: 45. Garden dining. Valet pkg. V, AE, DC, MC.
The new superhighway that loops east of central Lyons now has a Mionnay exit. It might as well be called the "Alain Chapel" exit, so inseparable are the two names. Great chefs never die, the saying goes. Both their name and recipes—even their cooking style—live on. But carrying forward the flame can be hazardous indeed. Whoever takes over the kitchen is open to double-edged criticism: either he imitates and falls short, or innovates and betrays.
Luckily, gifted chef Philippe Jousse was trained by the master himself and is perfectly at ease with Chapel's technique and the house repertoire. He works with the same phenomenal ingredients for which the restaurant has always been famed: the bread tastes of fresh-milled flour, the butter of spring meadows; even the frogs' legs evoke pure country streams. And slowly but surely the skillful Jousse is making his own mark. He has even managed to develop several delicious new dishes and compose stunning variations on Chapel themes; the master's Ile de Sein lobster in a casserole with potatoes, for example, has been transformed into a lobster ragoût with tiny, succulent ratte potatoes from the Ardèche. The lièvre à la royale served in two courses has become a saddle of roast hare with a coating of chestnuts stewed in milk and vegetables, with the thighs en civet with pepper-spiked quinces and a squash confiture. Jousse has perfected the art of preserving the Chapel spirit while breathing new life into it and producing deceptively simple, almost rustic dishes that are in reality very complex. His technique is sure, his matches of flavors full and surprising. The small dining room was not full the last time we visited; the world needs to know that there is once again a great table at Mionnay, one that we award this year with four toques. A celebration of flavors awaits you here: an astonishing ragoût of cock's comb and kidneys with crayfish and mushrooms whose well balanced tastes explode in the mouth, a flan of crab and spider-crab with hearts of purple artichokes, sea scallops with shallots and oysters with leeks in a mélange of earth and sea, leg of lamb braised with leek tops on a bed of creamy macaroni, and the sublime langoustines paired with plump ravioli stuffed with fresh cheese and bathed in a coriander infusion. The desserts, which Chapel would have been proud to claim as his own, include an apple millefeuille with Calvados-spiked "mordante" sauce, and an almond and roast fig strudel with a caramelized milk ice cream. The service is superb: friendly, efficient, and joyful. C 550-1,000 F. M 280 F (weekday lunch), 560 F, 680 F, 780 F.

Alain Chapel
(See restaurant above)
Closed Jan. 14 rms 650-800 F. Conf. Golf. Valet pkg. V, AE, DC, MC.
Even if you arrive here on horseback, make a point of visiting the incredible garage. And getting here by car is easier now that there's a

INDEX OF LYON RESTAURANTS AND HOTELS

Mionnay exit off the superhighway. As for the accommodation: guest rooms are bright and cheerful (but small) and the bathrooms sport beautiful faïence tiles. The breakfasts are superb. Overall, the quality of the hotel fails to match that of the restaurant. Relais et Châteaux.

■ In Rillieux-
la-Pape 69140   7 km N on N 83 and N 84

Larivoire
On the Rhône shore, chemin des Iles
78 88 50 92, fax 78 88 35 22
Closed Mon dinner, Tue, Feb 17-24. Open until 10pm. Priv rm: 60. Garden dining. Pkg. V.
Fine weather fills Larivoire's lovely riverside terrace with happy diners. But in a storm, the elegant, rose-colored dining room is also a welcome haven. Food lovers have been flocking here for decades—generations even. Chef Bernard Constantin (the third to bear that proud name since 1904) prepares a short but imaginative and skillful menu that features the delightful likes of crab millefeuille, half-smoked salmon and oysters with potatoes, and a fricassée of lobster and mango flavored with vanilla. This is a restaurant you can count on. Chantal Constantin's welcome is manifestly heartfelt. **C** 350-400 F. **M** 150 F (weekday lunch), 190 F, 300 F, 380 F.

■ In La Tour-
de-Salvagny 69890   10 km NW on N 7

La Rotonde
200, av. du Casino - 78 87 02 70
Closed Sun dinner, Mon, Jul 20-Aug 31. Open until 10:15pm. Priv rm: 350. Air cond. Pkg. V, AE, DC, MC.
Maximin is at it again! Financed by the Partouche casino group, this elegant restaurant draws a *belle clientèle* glad to savor the master chef's creations as interpreted by capable Philippe Gauvreau. Maximin himself steps in now and again to stir the sauce and make sure all is well. And all is well indeed! Witness the succulent couennée made with veal sweetbreads, calf's feet, rind, and country bread dipped in bouillon, a gutsy tip of the hat to Lyonnais cooking. Other dishes we savored are the bouillon of young guinea fowl with ravioli and Drôme olives, the fresh foie gras terrine in a white Port gelatin with a vermicelle cake, or the délices de Savoie (chestnut ice cream and a crique bread pudding). The welcome and service are tip-top, the dining room an elegant affair with picture windows, billowy curtains, and polished parquet floors. The young sommelier has put together a very fine wine list. The prices are starting to get a bit out of hand, though. **C** 350-500 F. **M** 190 F, 210 F, 310 F, 400 F, 500 F.

■ In Villeurbanne 69100   NE

Le Congrès
Pl. du Cdt-Rivière - 78 89 81 10
Closed Dec 23-Jan 2. Open until 10:30pm. Priv rm: 40. Air cond. Garage pkg. V, AE, DC, MC.
Business lunches don't feel like a chore in this comfortable modern restaurant. The bill of fare

runs to adroitly prepared, full-flavored dishes like spiced lamb tartare, monkfish flavored with cloves and a lentil étuvée, and a warm salad of squab enhanced by spices and honey. The desserts are limited. Interesting cellar; cheerful reception. **C** 250-400 F. **M** 95 F, 130 F, 160 F, 210 F, 260 F.

Le Congrès
(See restaurant above)
Open year-round. 2 stes 550-750 F. 134 rms 250-375 F. Half-board 425-520 F. Air cond. Conf. Garage pkg. V, AE, DC, MC.
Near Lyon Part-Dieu railway station and the Tête d'Or park, this freshly renovated modern hotel has well-equipped meeting rooms and an American bar.

MÂCON	71000

Paris 395 - Lyon 68 - Bourg 34 - Chalon-sur-S. 58   *Saône/Loire*

Mercure Saint-Albain
Aire de St-Albain, 71260 St-Albain
85 33 19 00, fax 85 33 19 00
Open year-round. 3 stes 900 F. 95 rms 270-495 F. Restaurant. Air cond. Conf. Heated pool. Golf. Garage pkg. V, AE, DC, MC.
Just off a superhighway rest area, the Mercure is hidden by greenery. The hotel is modern and graceless, but the rooms are handsome, spacious, and functional. Good conference facilities.

■ In La Croix-
Blanche 71960   14 km W on N 79

Le Relais du Mâconnais
85 36 60 72, fax 85 36 65 47
Closed Sun dinner & Mon off-seas, Jan. Open until 9:30pm. Priv rm: 12. Terrace dining. Hotel: 2 stes 440-500 F. 18 rms 270-360 F. Half-board 400-490 F. Conf. Pkg. V, AE, DC.
Don't be put off by the outside of this reconverted filling station. The dining room is cheery and full of flowers, the welcome warm, and guests can dine on a lovely terrace. Christian Lannuel demonstrates his great skill, and a flair for flavorful marriages with parsleyed rabbit in Pouilly-Fuissé sauce, red mullet with a vanilla-flavored beurre blanc, casserole-roasted rack of lamb with rosemary and garlic, and excellent classic desserts. Fine, reasonably priced cellar. Zealous welcome. **C** 280-370 F. **M** 130 F, 195 F, 220 F, 270 F.

■ In Replonges 01750   4 km E

La Huchette
On N 79 - 85 31 03 55, fax 85 31 10 24
Closed Tue lunch & Mon off-seas, Nov 6-Dec 12. Open until 9:30pm. Priv rm: 15. Garden dining. Pkg. V, AE, DC, MC.
We'll give the new chef time to settle in before rating his quail salad with green cabbage confit, saffroned langoustine paupiette, and a light mousse of pears and caramel. **C** 280-350 F. **M** 150 F, 210 F.

Red toques signify creative cuisine; white toques signify traditional cuisine.

La Huchette

(See restaurant above)
Closed Mon off-seas, Nov 6-Dec 12. 1 ste 850 F. 11 rms 350-600 F. Rms for disabled. Half-board 450-550 F. Heated pool. Golf. Helipad. V, AE, DC, MC.
The spacious, well-equipped, rustic rooms are very attractive. Excellent service; pool.

■ In Saint-Laurent-sur-Saône 01620

3 km W on N 79

Le Saint-Laurent

Left bank, 1, quai Bouchacourt
85 39 29 19, fax 85 38 29 17
Closed Jan 2-Feb 10. Open until 10pm. Priv rm: 20. Terrace dining. V, AE, DC, MC.
The Saint-Laurent met with rousing success from the second it opened. Set opposite Mâcon's historic district, the restaurant boasts a broad quayside terrace for summer dining as well as a dining room overlooking the swimming pool. Try the iced sweet peppers with avocado, fish tartare, grilled beef fillet, and crème brûlée. **C** 220-280 F. **M** 98 F (weekdays), 150 F, 200 F.

MADIÈRES 34 → Ganges

MADIRAN 65700

Paris 700 - Tarbes 39 - Maubourguet 13 *H.-Pyrénées*

Le Prieuré 🔇

62 31 92 50, fax 62 31 90 66
Closed Sun dinner & Mon off-seas, Jan 15-30. Open until 9pm. Terrace dining. Pkg. V, AE, MC.
This remodeled old priory marries white-and-grey contemporary decor with exposed beams and stone walls—a chic backdrop for Michel Cuénot's capable cooking, which is firmly rooted to the region's soil and seasons. Try the excellent 90 F menu: beef cheeks terrine with gribiche sauce, fillet of salmon-trout with sweet peppers, and a mint soufflé glacé with hot chocolate sauce. Fine choice of regional wines. Warm welcome and attentive service. **C** 250-350 F. **M** 230 F (exc Sun), 90 F, 159 F.

Le Prieuré

(See restaurant above)
See restaurant for closings. 10 rms 230-310 F. Half-board 240-335 F. Conf. Pkg. V, AE.
The priory's carefully restored rooms are comfortable, well equipped, and perfectly kept. Tasteful contemporary decor. Ideal for rest and relaxation. Copious breakfasts.

MAGESCQ 40140

Paris 698 - Soustons 10 - Bayonne 42 - Castets 12 *Landes*

Relais de la Poste 🔇

58 47 70 25, fax 58 47 76 17
*Closed Mon dinner (lunch Jul-Aug), Tue (exc in summer), Nov 20-Dec 20. Open until 9:30pm. Priv rm: 30. Air cond. Heated pool. Pkg. **Hotel:** 2 stes 850-920 F. 10 rms 480-650 F. Half-board 650-850 F. Conf. Tennis. Golf. No pets.V, AE, DC, MC.*
The festival of regional favorites continues year-round at the Coussaus' old coaching inn, now a chic restaurant-hotel with modernized rooms and decor. The foie gras is still superb, as are the duck dishes (fillets, confit, or breast). But

two creations are clearly at the two-toque level: the fork-tender breast of squab cooked rare and paired with girolle mushrooms, and the magnificent fresh lamprey eel from the Ardour river, served with a rich and powerful sauce. The fine fries are cooked in goose fat, there's a new bread oven providing superb warm bread, the cellar is stupendous and the desserts excellent. The only flaws: a bland consommé, a boring house pâté, and an overly acidic tomato sauce that spoiled the fine fresh morels served with a delicious sauté of veal sweetbreads. With these prices, high in particular for this region, everything should be flawless. Another quibble: you have to insist on tap water if you don't want to pay for the mineral water that's served automatically. **C** 350-450 F. **M** 280 F, 390 F.

MAGNY-COURS 58470

Paris 251 - Moulins 42 - Nevers 12 - Bourges 80 *Nièvre*

La Renaissance

Le Bourg
86 58 10 40, fax 86 21 22 60
Closed Sun dinner, Mon, 3 wks Feb-Mar, 2 wks in Aug. Open until 9:30pm. Priv rm: 35. Terrace dining. Air cond. Pkg. V, AE.
Jean-Claude Dray's opulent repertoire is composed of old favorites so well prepared with such top-quality ingredients, that we wouldn't dream of criticizing them. Savor his ham cooked on the bone and served with a spicy sauce, roast salmon in a tart orange sauce, veal kidney cooked rare with shallot confit, and a lamb blanquette à l'anglaise. Nice choice of cheeses and desserts. The cellar is as rich as the cooking, but includes some good buys, such as a Dagueneau Pouilly-Fumé at 160 F, and a Domaine Balland-Chapuis Coteaux-du-Giennois (white or red) at 82 F. Courteous service. **C** 450-600 F. **M** 120 F (weekday lunch), 150 F, 200 F, 300 F.

La Renaissance

(See restaurant above)
See restaurant for closings. 3 stes 500-700 F. 6 rms 350-500 F. Air cond. Conf. Golf. Pkg. Helipad. V, AE.
The country inn *par excellence*, La Renaissance offers quiet, stylishly decorated rooms that have just been renovated, and some new luxury suites. Exceptionally good breakfasts, served on the terrace in summer.

MAISONS-LAFFITTE 78 → PARIS Suburbs

MALBUISSON 25160

Paris 467 - Besançon 75 - Pontarlier 15 - Salins 49 *Doubs*

Le Bon Accueil

81 69 30 58, fax 81 69 37 60
Closed Sun dinner (exc hols), Tue lunch, Mon, 1 wk in Apr, Dec 20-Jan 20. Open until 9pm. Pkg. V, AE, MC.
When Marc Faivre follows his inclinations and gives his creative spirit free rein, he never fails to please, witness his foie gras with Jerusalem artichokes and ginger, unequaled elsewhere. When he prepares more mundane dishes, like a pickerel with sea urchin sauce, he is less captivating. It's easy to see, but he should stick to the things that inspire him most. The second toque departs, we hope not for long. **C** 320-400 F. **M** 90 F, 150 F, 205 F, 255 F.

Le Bon Accueil

(See restaurant above)
Closed Sun off-seas (exc hols), Mon, 1 wk in Apr,
Dec 20-Jan 20. 2 stes 360-380 F. 10 rms 210-300 F.
Half-board 250-330 F. Golf. Pkg. V, MC.
Two rooms were remodeled in 1992, three
more in 1993, all in good taste. Comfortable and
restful; good value, too.

Jean-Michel Tannières

Grande-Rue
81 69 30 89, fax 81 69 39 16
Closed Mon, Tue lunch, Sun dinner (Nov-Apr),
Apr 15-30. Open until 9pm. Priv rm: 30. Terrace
dining. Pkg. V, AE, DC, MC.
The sunny dining room has a cozy feel and
overlooks a pretty garden with a burbling brook.
In these charming surroundings, sample Jean-
Michel Tannières' harmonious cooking with
forthright, intense flavor: green asparagus soup
with morels, beef fillet in a salt crust, and a
bilberry tart. Intelligent choice of wines, especially from Burgundy, Jura, and Chablis. **C** 300-
400 F. **M** 130 F, 190 F, 290 F, 370 F.

Jean-Michel Tannières

(See restaurant above)
Closed Mon (exc Jul-Aug), Apr 15-30. 1 ste 300-
390 F. 6 rms 230-350 F. Half-board 320-390 F. Conf.
Pkg. V, AE, DC, MC.
Rooms and a single suite near the shores of
Saint-Point lake and the forest.

MALÈNE (LA) 48210
Paris 619 - Mende 42 - Florac 41 - Millau 42 Lozère

Manoir de Montesquiou

66 48 51 12, fax 66 48 50 47
Closed end Oct-end Mar. Open until 9:15pm
(9:30pm in summer). Terrace dining. No pets. Pkg.
V, DC, MC.
What could be more enchanting than this
Renaissance manor house, with its wide-angle
view of the Gorges du Tarn? The dining room is
decorated with armloads of flowers—a fresh,
feminine setting for Évelyne Gullenet's cuisine.
The bill of fare is original and neatly executed.
We're partial to the pear accompanied by
smoked slab bacon and Causses blue cheese on
toast, a warm trout salad with an onion compote
enlivened with fresh coriander, an excellent
cheese assortment, and an "assiette exotique au
rhum" (pleasant but a bit over the top). Fine
cellar. **C** 260-350 F. **M** 165 F, 250 F.

Manoir de Montesquiou

(See restaurant above)
Closed end Oct-end Mar. 2 stes 760 F. 10 rms 420-
570 F. Half-board 515-610 F. Golf. Pkg. Helipad. V,
DC, MC.
Eye-popping views of the gorges and the steep,
wild Causses are what you'll find in addition to
the rooms' majestic period furnishings
(canopied beds, no less). But the mediocre
breakfasts are too expensive. Friendly welcome.

Some establishments change their **closing times**
without warning. It is always wise to check in ad-
vance.

MANCIET 32370
Paris 750 - Aire-sur-l'Adour 30 Gers

La Bonne Auberge ☺

Place Pesquerot
62 08 50 04, fax 62 08 58 84
Closed Sun dinner. Open until 9:30pm. Terrace
dining. No pets. V, AE, DC.
Full-bodied terroir cooking is served in a cozy
dining room stuffed with pretty country antiques. Try the foie gras and mushroom ravioli,
sautéed sea scallops and cèpes, goose tripe
"grand-mère", and a croquant of caramelized
apples. Well stocked cellar with a superb choice
of Armagnacs. The patronne's welcome is as
warm as the surrounding Gers countryside.
C 250-320 F. **M** 80 F, 160 F, 250 F.

MANDELIEU 06210
Paris 850 - Cannes 8 - Nice 38 - La Napoule 2 Alpes-Mar.

Hostellerie du Golf

780, bd de la Mer
93 49 11 66, fax 92 97 04 01
Open year-round. 16 stes 580-860 F. 39 rms 330-
640 F. Rms for disabled. Restaurant. Half-board 370-
670 F. Conf. Pool. Tennis. Golf. Garage pkg. Helipad.
V, AE, DC, MC.
The golfing greens spread beyond the trees
that surround this large, single-story hotel built
in the neo-Provençal style. The spacious rooms
are decorated with pretty fabrics and modern
furnishings.

See also: Cannes, La Napoule

MANOSQUE 04100
Paris 767 - Aix-en-P. 53 - Digne 57 - Sisteron 52 Alpes/H.-P.

■ In **La Fuste 04210** 6.5 km SE on D 907 and D 4

Hostellerie de la Fuste ☺

92 72 05 95, fax 92 72 92 93
Closed Sun dinner & Mon off-seas (exc hols), Jan 10-
Feb. Open until 9:30pm. Priv rm: 60. Garden dining.
Pool. Pkg. V, AE, DC, MC.
Set in a luminous Provençal landscape, this
inviting auberge de charme is redolent with the
fragrance of the fertile countryside. The decor is
a mite overloaded but cozy all the same, a
veritable cocoon lovingly spun by Daniel Jourdan and his family. Son-in-law Dominique's
supremely authentic Southern cuisine takes the
region's best ingredients and transforms them
into palate-pleasing dishes like sliced truffles
over olive oil-sauced mashed potatoes, tender
veal shanks braised with potatoes, admirable
anise-flavored bread pudding, and nougat glacé
with almonds. The young squab with risotto,
though, had a too-strong taste. The welcome is
as sunny as the cellar's nice little Lubéron wines,
as well as Burgundies and Côtes-du-Rhône. It's
too bad the prices at this lovely place are so
unfriendly! **C** 600-700 F. **M** 270 F, 360 F, 450 F.

Hostellerie de la Fuste 🌲

(See restaurant above)
See restaurant for closings. 3 stes 1,000-1,400 F.
11 rms 600-1,000 F. Half-board 700-1,000 F. Air

cond. Conf. Heated pool. Golf. Pkg. Helipad. V, AE, DC, MC.
This attractive *bastide* has comfortable, spacious rooms. The reception is excellent. Fine covered swimming pool. Outstanding breakfasts.

MANS (LE) 72000
Paris 216 - Rennes 145 - Tours 81 - Angers 88　　　*Sarthe*

Arcade
40, rue du Vert-Galant
43 24 47 24, fax 43 24 58 41
Open year-round. 91 rms 270 F. Rms for disabled. Restaurant. Half-board 340 F. Pkg. V, AE, MC.
This five-story modern hotel sits on the banks of the Sarthe, five minutes from the town center. The smallish rooms (those on the upper floors are larger) overlook the embankment or a courtyard. Bar.

Patrick Bonneville
14, rue Bourg-Belé - 43 23 75 00
Closed Wed, dinner Tue & Sun, 1 wk at Feb school hols, Aug. Open until 10pm. Priv rm: 35. Pkg. V, AE.
Patrick and Chantal Bonneville's restaurant is located in a rather lifeless neighborhood, but the dining room is welcoming, with sunny yellow and blue decor and a romantic fresco. As for the cooking, it's fresh and prepared with refined technique: perfectly cooked and tasty John Dory galette with tarragon butter, lightly roasted pickerel paired with delicious slices of marinated turnips, and a fine mascarpone cheese mousse with raspberry sauce. Wide-ranging cellar. Courteous, eager service. **C** 250-360 F. **M** 170 F (wine incl), 130 F, 135 F, 180 F, 240 F.

Chantecler
50, rue de la Pelouse
43 24 58 53, fax 43 77 16 28
Open year-round. 3 stes 440-515 F. 32 rms 220-340 F. Restaurant. Golf. Garage pkg. V, MC.
Centrally located near the station, this recently redecorated hotel has double glazing. A veranda has been added. Zealous service. Restaurant: La Feuillantine, see below.

La Ciboulette
14, rue de la Vieille-Porte
43 24 65 67, fax 43 87 51 18
Closed Sat lunch, Sun, Aug 1-20. Open until 10pm. V, AE.
Near the Place de l'Éperon, the Ciboulette's charming, bistrot-style dining room is a late-night favorite. This year, a "menu-carte" and a special bistrot menu offer relief to your wallet and even more reason to come here to sample Jack Desmat's savory dishes: clam-stuffed puff pastry enhanced with saffron, salmon fillet with grapefruit butter, and a Chartreuse parfait with orgeat-flavored whipped cream. **M** 115 F, 150 F.

Concorde
16, av. du Gal-Leclerc
43 24 12 30, fax 43 24 85 74
Open year-round. 55 rms 380-700 F. Restaurant. Half-board 500 F. Conf. Golf. Pkg. V, AE, DC, MC.
Set in the historic center of town, the Concorde is a nicely remodeled, attractive old hotel with rather threadbare beige-toned decor. Good but pricey traditional breakfast. Minimal service.

La Feuillantine
19 bis, rue Foisy
43 28 00 38, fax 43 23 22 31
Closed Sat lunch, Sun, Apr 16-23, Aug 13-20, Dec 22-Jan 3. Open until 10pm. V, AE, MC.
Jean-Claude Adam's cooking is full of good intentions that work thanks to this veteran chef's skill and winning personal touch. Try the tasty langoustines with an asparagus tips salad, turbot in a tasty infusion, and apple tart. Huge mirrors, mosaics, and potted plants give this restaurant a 1930s feel. **C** 200-300 F. **M** 300 F (wine incl), 70 F, 90 F (weekdays), 135 F.

Green 7
Route de Tours, 447, av. G.-Durand
43 85 05 73, fax 43 86 62 78
Open year-round. 40 rms 245 F. Rms for disabled. Restaurant. Half-board 285 F. Golf. Pkg. V, AE, MC.
A former hunting lodge, this American-style, modernized hotel is near the route of Le Mans' famous auto race. Well-equipped rooms painted in bold colors. English breakfasts.

Le Grenier à Sel
26, pl. de l'Éperon
43 23 26 30, fax 43 77 00 80
Closed Sun dinner, Mon, 1 wk at Feb school hols, Aug 1-20. Open until 10:15pm. Air cond. Pkg. V.
This former salt storehouse makes a handsome restaurant with an elegant, flower-filled dining room, and widely spaced tables set under a mirrored ceiling; contemporary paintings hang on the walls. Bruno Godefroy's cooking is a medley of chic and rustic, with a marked preference for fish and seafood: sea scallops in a salad, turbot fillet with langoustines, ostrich fillet, and a delicate apple tart spiked with cinnamon. Fine wine list. **C** 190-260 F. **M** 95 F (exc Sun, wine incl), 120 F, 230 F, 270 F.

Hippolyte
12, rue H.-Lecornué
43 87 51 00, fax 43 87 51 01
Open daily until 11:30pm. Terrace dining. Air cond. V.
The competition hereabouts have envy in their hearts whenever they walk by this new establishment's fully booked 1900–style dining room; the reasonable prices have won fans. As for Franck Morillon's cooking, though, it's simple brasserie fare with just a few special touches: slightly overcooked turbot en meurette, pleasant duck breast with turnips, and a fine puff pastry holding caramelized apples. Interesting 94 F option with a main dish, dessert, a glass of wine and coffee. Friendly welcome; professional service. **C** 180-250 F. **M** 100 F.

Novotel
Bd R.-Schumann
43 85 26 80, fax 43 75 31 76
Open year-round. 94 rms 395-460 F. Rms for disabled. Restaurant. Half-board 550-650 F. Conf. Pool. Golf. Pkg. V, AE, DC, MC.
Here is a modern hotel with large rooms and good conference facilities. Ask for a room overlooking the river, rather than the street. We've seen better breakfasts.

Looking for a city in a département? Refer to the index.

321

■ In **Arnage 72230** 9 km S on D 147 or A 11 exit 9

 Auberge des Matfeux
500 m beyond the village, via D 147, N 23
43 21 10 71, fax 43 21 25 23
Closed Mon, dinner Sun & hols, Feb 5-27, Jul 24-Aug 11. Open until 9pm. Pkg. V, AE, DC, MC.
The Le Mans auto race seems a million miles away from this grand old restaurant surrounded by pine trees, embellished this year by an enclosed terrace. Chef Alain Souffront, assisted more and more by his son Xavier, presides over the modern interpretation of classic dishes made from quality ingredients (including some grown in the restaurant's own garden). Try inventive dishes like gourmandine of lobster in sweet-sour sauce, delicious warm foie gras with girolle mushrooms, an intensely flavored warm "ribbon" of smoked salmon with potatoes, an interesting fillet of ostrich with shallot confit, an exquisite chicken breast in Vouvray sauce, and desserts that are getting better all the time (banana spring rolls, pear roasted with honey and spices, or a simple but very tasty nage of berries). Xavier's influence leaves us confident the restaurant will be in good hands when his father retires. Fine cellar with bargain bottles listed in red. **C** 300-430 F. **M** 258 F, 335 F (wine incl), 108 F, 168 F, 208 F, 235 F, 285 F.

MANTES-LA-JOLIE . **78200**
Paris 60 - Evreux 44 - Rouen 81 - Versailles 44 *Yvelines*

 Moulin de la Reillère
171, route de Houdan - 30 92 22 00
Closed Sun dinner, Wed. Annual closings not available. Open until 10pm. Priv rm: 15. Terrace dining. Pkg. V, AE.
In fine weather take a table on the terrace of this gorgeous mill house next to a babbling mill run and dig into Rolland Ménard's fresh, full-flavored specialties. Try the first set menu: a salad of giblets confit and smoked duck breast, a "braid" of salmon and scorpion fish with two cream sauces, cheeses, and dessert. The wine list is full of finds. The *patronne's* welcome is friendly, the service both competent and discreet. **C** 280-480 F. **M** 150 F, 240 F.

MARÇAY 37 → **Chinon**

MARCQ-EN-BARŒUL 59 → **Lille**

MARGAUX **33460**
Paris 598 - Bordeaux 22 - Lesparre-Médoc 20 *Gironde*

 Le Relais de Margaux
Chemin de l'Ile-Vincent
56 88 38 30, fax 57 88 31 73
Closed Mon, Jan 5-Mar 5. Open until 10pm. Priv rm: 150. Garden dining. Air cond. Heated pool. No pets. Pkg. V, AE, DC, MC.
Quiet luxury and refinement give this former wine cellar a special cachet. The tables are laid before a grand terrace, and the service is equally grand. And what a bedazzling array of bottles and half-bottles! Under the new chef, Jean-Marie Visilit, the cuisine has taken a turn for the better, offering traditional dishes and ones with exotic touches (the chef spent some time in Polynesia). Taste his frog's legs gratin with sautéed mush-

rooms, Leyre river sturgeon with green lentils and bacon, turbot poached in milk and served with little zucchini slices, and delicious desserts with an emphasis on chocolate. **C** 300-450 F. **M** 190 F (weekdays, Sat lunch, wine incl), 160 F.

Le Relais de Margaux ≜♣
(See restaurant above)
Closed Jan-Feb. 3 stes 1,350-1,620 F. 28 rms 875-1,415 F. Half-board 955-1,105 F. Air cond. Pool. Tennis. Golf. No pets. Pkg. Helipad. V, AE, DC, MC.
This sumptuous hotel set in the heart of the wine-growing region is surrounded by 55 hectares of grounds, with swimming pool, tennis courts, and heliport. The elegantly decorated rooms have admirably equipped bathrooms. Generous breakfasts.

MARGUERITTES 30 → **Nîmes**

MARLENHEIM **67520**
Paris 437 - Strasbourg 20 - Saverne 19 - Molsheim 12 *Bas-Rhin*

Le Cerf ✿
30, rue du Gal-de-Gaulle
88 87 73 73, fax 88 87 68 08
Closed Tue, Wed. Open until 9:30pm. Priv rm: 25. Terrace dining. Air cond. Hotel: 2 stes 600-650 F. 13 rms 450-600 F. Conf. Pkg. V, AE, DC, MC.
If you arrive from the north, this marvelous hostelry marks the start of the wine route. You won't be disappointed: everything about this old coaching inn is absolutely authentic, from the half-timbered house, to the cobbled courtyard, and the window sills massed with red and white flowers. The hospitality is genuine too, proffered by the Husser family, who have run Le Cerf for over six decades. Robert Husser recently traded in his chef's whites for a gardener's apron; he now cultivates the herbs and flowers that his son, Michel, uses in his state-of-the-art kitchens. Michel trained with Senderens and Haeberlin, then came home to don his own toques. His special gift is an ability to lend spirit, lightness, and fantasy to his region's culinary traditions, but this year his cooking failed to live up to our past experiences. His presskopf of calf's head was evidence of superb technique, but the overcooked vol-au-vent with a textbook cream sauce that lacked soul lost the restaurant a point this year. The cellar is matchless. Perhaps routine has been creeping into the kitchen. **C** 450-550 F. **M** 295 F (lunch exc Sun, wine incl), 335 F, 395 F, 485 F.

MARMANDE **47200**
Paris 684 - Agen 58 - Bordeaux 89 - Bergerac 58 *Lot/Garonne*

12/20 Auberge du Moulin d'Ané
4 km E on D 933 and D 267, in Virazei
53 20 18 25, fax 53 89 67 99
Closed Sun dinner & Mon (exc hols), Feb school hols, Aug 16-Sep 6. Open until 9:30pm. Terrace dining. Air cond. Pkg. V, AE, DC, MC.
It's too bad that the cooking in this lovely restaurant with a crackling fireplace and garden terrace has fallen off a bit: boring duck breast carpaccio with foie gras, a perfectly cooked roulé of sole with sea scallops unfortunately drowning in sauce, and dull cakes served with the coffee have lost the restaurant its toque.

C 210-320 F. M 90 F, 98 F, 160 F (weekday lunch, wine incl), 140 F, 150 F, 230 F.

Le Trianon 🕄
Route d'Agen, N 113 - 53 20 80 94 (R), 53 64 16 14 (H), fax 53 20 80 18
Open daily until 10pm. Priv rm: 30. Terrace dining. Pkg. V, AE, DC, MC.
Don't be put off by the drab modern neighborhood or the charmless building next to the highway. Inside, the pleasant dining room has been elegantly decorated in pastel colors, the welcome is warm, and Thierry Arbeau, whose cooking we have enjoyed elsewhere, seems at the top of his form since moving here. He treats local products with great personality and address: harmonious and perfectly cooked nage of monkfish, sea bream, and salmon; superb fantaisie of beef with veal sweetbreads; delightful salmon fillet on a bed of fava beans; and a delicious chocolate fondant with crème anglaise. Servings are very generous, and many dishes are available in half portions (enough for many diners) at half price. Fine set menus and a tempting wine list at reasonable prices. C 250-380 F. M 75 F (weekdays), 120 F, 165 F, 200 F, 250 F.

Le Capricorne
(See restaurant above)
Closed Jan 1-8. 34 rms 260-280 F. Rms for disabled. Restaurant. Half-board 230-330 F. Conf. Pool. Pkg. V, AE, DC, MC.
A modern, comfortable stopover on the outskirts of town. The rooms at the back, overlooking the swimming pool, are especially quiet.

MARSANNAY-LA-CÔTE 21	→ Dijon

MARSEILLAN 34	→ Agde

MARSEILLE	13000
Paris 771 - Lyon 315 - Nice 188 - Toulouse 400	B./Rhône

René Alloin
8, pl. de l'Amiral-Muselier (8th)
91 77 88 25, fax 91 77 76 84
Closed Sat lunch, Sun, dinner, Mon. Open until 10:30pm. Priv rm: 300. Terrace dining. Air cond. V.
Top local chef René Alloin finally has a restaurant all his own. The loud Mediterranean decor needs to mellow to subtler tones, but the food is already a Lucullan treat: puff pastry with sheep's feet, red mullet fillets en barigoule, and apricot profiteroles with rosemary and almond milk. The cellar is a bit shallow, but the price is right. Charming welcome. C 280-350 F. M 185 F, 230 F.

L'Ambassade des Vignobles
42, pl. aux Huiles (1st)
91 33 00 25, fax 91 54 25 60
Closed Sat lunch, Sun, Aug. Open until 10:30pm. Priv rm: 40. Air cond. Garage pkg. V, AE.
In a setting of rough stones and beams in Marseille's dockyards, this wine-growers' embassy presents the rare opportunity to taste perfectly partnered food and wine. The 280 F menu changes every two or three months, to showcase the specialties of a particular region with the wines that best match them. Specialties include purple artichokes and tiny snails en barigoule, young rabbit grilled in rosemary wine and paired with a spelt risotto, and a sablé mousseline flavored with orange-flower water. The wines are superb, at a wide range of prices. C 310 F. M 140 F, 180 F, 240 F, 280 F (wine incl).

Les Arcenaulx 🕄
25, cours d'Estienne-d'Orves (1st)
91 54 77 06, fax 91 54 76 33
Closed Sun. Open until 11:30pm. Priv rm: 150. Terrace dining. Air cond. Garage pkg. V, AE, DC, MC.
Raymond Rosso presides over the kitchens of this famous restaurant-cum-bookshop run by the Laffite sisters. Try his revisited regional specialities prepared with a skillful hand: a panisses and cumin-marinated sardine millefeuille, veal kidney and sweetbreads scented with licorice and served over sautéed endives, and a délice de Chine made with Earl Grey tea and peaches. Well chosen wines; charming welcome by Simone Laffite. C 210-300 F. M 180 F, 225 F.

L'Assiette Marine
148, av. P.-Mendès-France (8th)
91 71 04 04
Open daily until 10:30pm. Priv rm: 50. Terrace dining. Air cond. Garage pkg. V, MC.
Jean Luc Sellam abandoned his former quarters (too shabby and outdated for his bright, modern cuisine) in favor of this beachfront restaurant in a shiny new commercial district. It's hard to find a quiet spot on the terrace, amidst the noisy merchants whose businesses are nearby, but the blue and yellow dining room is cozy, and the cooking light and inventive: red mullet fillets sautéed in a saffron vinaigrette, a "cake" of eggplant and lamb with truffles, and berry soup for dessert. Small, eclectic wine list; courteous welcome. C 300-350 F. M 135 F, 220 F, 300 F.

Capitainerie des Galères
46, rue Sainte (1st)
91 54 73 73, fax 91 54 77 77
Open year-round. 141 rms 205-250 F. Rms for disabled. Restaurant. Half-board 385 F. Air cond. Conf. Pkg. V, AE, MC.
Just steps from the Old Port, this hotel provides functional rooms (some are on the small side), perfectly suited to an overnight stop. Cheerful reception.

Le Carré d'Honoré
34, pl. aux Huiles (1st) - 91 33 16 80
Closed Sat lunch, Sun, Aug 15-31. Open until 10:30pm. Priv rm: 60. Terrace dining. Garage pkg. V, AE, DC, MC.
Chef Jean-Marc Rutano offers fresh, nicely crafted cooking in the pleasant, Provençal decor of his bilevel dining room: a sauté of scampi and langoustine tails, spiced swordfish with a vegetable risotto, and duck breast with olives. Well chosen wines; friendly service. C 270-360 F. M 85 F (weekday lunch), 130 F, 260 F.

Concorde Palm Beach
2, promenade de la Plage (8th)
91 16 19 00, fax 91 16 19 39
Open year-round. 1 ste 1,680 F. 144 rms 655 F. Restaurant. Air cond. Conf. Pool. Pkg. V, AE, DC, MC.
This huge, modern hotel complex offers spacious, recently redecorated rooms looking out to sea. Auditorium for business meetings.

Concorde Prado
11, av. de Mazargues (8th)
91 76 51 11, fax 91 77 95 10
Open year-round. 1 ste 900 F. 80 rms 595 F. Restaurant. Air cond. Pkg. V, AE, DC, MC.
Here is a modern luxury hotel near the conference center. Pleasant rooms with air-conditioning, TV, and minibars. Shops; meeting rooms. Pleasant welcome.

Le Corbusier
280, bd Michelet (9th)
91 77 18 15, fax 91 71 09 93
Open year-round. 23 rms 175-295 F. Rms for disabled. Restaurant. Half-board 260-350 F. Conf. Golf. Pkg. V, AE, DC, MC.
This 1952 concrete building, the *maison du fada*, was designed by Le Corbusier as part of a housing project, and offers simple, inexpensive third-floor rooms that overlook the city and a shopping gallery. Affable welcome.

Les Échevins ⑬
44, rue Sainte (1st)
91 33 08 08, fax 91 54 08 21
Closed Sat lunch, Sun, Aug 1-16. Open until 10:30pm. Priv rm: 40. Air cond. V, AE, DC, MC.
Take a table under the 1637 cathedral ceiling of the Moréni's lovingly embellished restaurant, full of fine regional antiques. Jeanne Moréni's ever more polished repertoire is a happy blend of her native Southwest and sunny Provence: red mullet salad with tapenade, duck breast with morels, and blancmange with apricot sauce. Nicely balanced cellar with some fine Armagnacs. Warm reception and service. C 230-360 F. M 150 F (weekday lunch), 220 F, 330 F.

11/20 L'Épuisette
Vallon des Auffes (7th)
91 52 17 82, fax 91 59 18 80
Closed Sun dinner, Jan 2-31. Open until 10pm. Priv rm: 18. Pkg. V, AE, DC.
The view from L'Épuisette's broad veranda takes in the Planier lighthouse, while the dining room is decorated with elegant and original touches (chandeliers and parquet floor). Fresh fisherman's salad, dryish sautéed monkfish fillet, and hearty classic desserts. Well chosen wines. Ridiculous prices. C 400-450 F. M 200 F, 270 F, 350 F.

La Ferme ⑭
23, rue Sainte (1st)
91 33 21 12, fax 91 33 81 21
Closed Sat lunch, Sun, Aug. Open until 10:30pm. Air cond. V, AE, DC, MC.
The elegant Italianate decor is unlike anything we've ever viewed in a farmhouse, on either side of the Alps. Seated amid columns and frescoes in this, one of the city's finer restaurants, patrons delight in Pascal Maufroy's generous new 200 F menu: warm galette of swordfish and cuttlefish, daube de boeuf with pasta, cheese assortment, and a choice of desserts. Well chosen wine list. Very attentive service. C 330-390 F. M 130 F (lunch), 200 F.

12/20 Chez Fonfon
140, rue du Vallon des Auffes (7th)
91 52 14 38, fax 91 59 27 32
Closed Sun, Mon, Oct, Dec 24-Jan 2. Open until 10pm. Priv rm: 60. Air cond. V, AE, DC, MC.

Do people come to this homey restaurant tucked away in a rocky inlet for the food, or to pay homage to the patriarch of Marseille's chefs? Both, decidedly. For the bouillabaisse and bourrides are generous and authentic, the fish luminously fresh (rosace of monkfish with julienned vegetables, lobster and sea scallop ravioli). C 300-400 F.

La Garbure ⑬
9, cours Julien (6th)
91 47 18 01, fax 91 42 58 35
Closed Sat lunch, Sun, Jul 14-Aug 18. Open until 11pm. Priv rm: 18. Terrace dining. Air cond. Pkg. V, DC, MC.
Arnaud Lafargue simmers and serves his Gascon-Béarnaise specialties in this charming cellar restaurant, lit by chandeliers and the smiles of satisfied customers. Try his salad of smoked goose with fennel, duck duo with caramelized onions, duck breast croustillant with foie gras, and an apple tourtière (pastry) with prune ice cream. Dieters should dine elsewhere. Well chosen wine list with fine Bordeaux and a great choice of Armagnacs. C 200-300 F. M 140 F.

Holiday Inn
Marseille City Center, 103, av. du Prado (6th) - 91 83 10 10, fax 91 79 84 12
Open year-round. 4 stes 950 F. 115 rms 580-680 F. Rms for disabled. Restaurant. Air cond. Conf. Valet pkg. V, AE, DC, MC.
This brand-new member of the famous chain is right in the heart of the city; you'll spot it by its smoked-glass façade. Perfectly equipped, air-conditioned rooms with neo-Hellenic decor.

12/20 Au Jambon de Parme
67, rue de la Palud (6th) - 91 54 37 98
Closed Sun dinner, Mon, Jul 12-Aug. Open until 10:15pm. Priv rm: 20. Air cond. Pkg. V, AE, DC, MC.
Favored by businessmen and a society crowd, this classic, comfortable restaurant serves Italian and French specialties (fried cuttlefish, émincé of sea bass, veal piccata, Modena-style tortellini, and oven-baked lamb). Plush atmosphere, with prices to match. C 260-350 F. M 180 F.

Chez Loury ⑬
Le Mistral, 3, rue Fortia (1st)
91 33 09 73, fax 91 33 73 21
Closed Sun, May 15-31. Open until 11pm. Priv rm: 26. Terrace dining. Air cond. Pkg. V, AE, DC.
The Loury husband-and-wife team presides over one of the best restaurants in town, and the dining room is now air-conditioned. Bernard Loury's bouillabaisse is a terrific (and inexpensive) way to savor the very spirit of Marseille. Other options are equally authentic: seafood fricassée, pieds et paquets (a local veal dish), extraordinary herb sherbets, and skate salad with capers. C 200-250 F. M 240 F (wine incl), 120 F, 150 F.

Lutétia
38, allées L.-Gambetta (1st)
91 50 81 78, fax 91 50 23 52
Open year-round. 29 rms 235-310 F. V, AE, DC, MC.
Set in a quiet street near the Canebière and the station, this hotel has bright, modern, recently renovated rooms.

Mercure
See restaurant L'Oursinade

Miramar

12, quai du Port (2nd)
91 91 10 40, fax 91 56 64 31
Closed Sun, Dec 23-Jan 6, Aug 1-22. Open until 10pm. Terrace dining. Air cond. Pkg. V, AE, DC, MC.
Hooray! The decor of this Marseille institution run by the Minguella brothers has been refreshed and improved. Too bad efforts to keep down prices are still unsuccessful. But customers are prepared to pay for the fabulously fresh fish dishes, deftly prepared by Jean-Michel Minguella. He's at his best with simple, direct dishes like raw sea scallops marinated with capers and chives and delicious sea bream with gros sel. The sea urchins with ginger were imperfectly cooked and rather bland, though. Remarkable cellar; professional welcome and service. C 320-500 F.

New Hotel Astoria

10, bd Garibaldi (1st)
91 33 33 50, fax 91 54 80 75
Open year-round. 58 rms 290 F. Air cond. No pets. Pkg. V, AE, DC, MC.
Near the Canebière, this turn-of-the-century hotel has been thoroughly and pleasantly modernized. It has huge, sunny, well-equipped rooms, and an attractive entrance hall.

New Hotel Bompard

2, rue des Flots-Bleus (7th)
91 52 10 93, fax 91 31 02 14
Open year-round. 46 rms 350 F. Rms for disabled. Air cond. Conf. Pool. Golf. Pkg. V, AE, DC, MC.
Set in quiet grounds just minutes from the Old Port and the town center, the Bompard houses bright, large rooms that are both functional and comfortable (just avoid those that give onto the indoor car park). The balconies massed with flowers are a nice touch.

Novotel Vieux-Port

36, bd Ch.-Livon (7th)
91 59 22 22, fax 91 31 15 48
Open year-round. 90 rms 450-560 F. Restaurant. Air cond. Conf. Pool. Garage pkg. V, AE, DC, MC.
Well situated in the Vieux-Port area, most of this chain hotel's rooms were remodeled not long ago. All are comfortable, functional, and especially spacious, with fine views.

12/20 L'Oursinade

Centre Bourse, 1, rue Neuve-St-Martin
(1st) - 91 39 20 14 (R), 91 39 20 00 (H), fax 91 56 24 57
Closed Sun. Open until 10:30pm. Priv rm: 250. Terrace dining. Air cond. Valet pkg. V, AE, DC, MC.
Enjoy the sweeping view of all Marseille from the panoramic dining room, and the top-flight brasserie fare is pleasing. Try the savory salad of quail confit with warm potatoes, perfectly cooked leg of lamb roasted with fresh thyme blossoms, and fine desserts. Prices are very reasonable, for both food and the well chosen wines. Smooth, smiling welcome and service. M 98 F, 133 F, 168 F, 188 F.

Mercure

(See restaurant above)
Open year-round. 1 ste 880 F. 199 rms 395-495 F. Rms for disabled. Air cond. Pkg. V, AE, DC, MC.
Ask for an upper-floor room with an enchanting view of the bay. All are comfortable and well equipped. First-class service, gargantuan breakfasts.

Passédat

Corniche Kennedy, Anse de Maldormé
(7th) - 91 59 25 92, fax 91 59 28 08
Closed Sat lunch, Sun, Nov-Apr. Open until 10pm. Garden dining. Air cond. Pool. Valet pkg. V, AE, MC.
Nestled in a fold of the corniche with a breathtaking view of the islands across the way, the setting seems like a sliver of the Côte d'Azur washed ashore in Marseille. Jean-Paul Passédat had some trouble convincing the Marseille mainstream, but now his son Gérald, who has taken over the kitchen, can profit from his father's persistent efforts to bring luxury dining to Marseille. Passédat remains the area's sole top-flight establishment with a truly ambitious menu. On our last visit we reveled in the compressé of bouille-abaisse; the sautéed gambas with carrots, turnips, and orange juice; the "cake" of frog's legs with pig's foot; and the admirable squab cooked in a jus enhanced with Oriental spices, mustard, and figs. We were less impressed by the gillons of veal sweetbreads au suc de champignons, but overall, a meal here is a celebration of sunny savors and colors. The desserts are all delicious, from the simplest to the most complex. The cellar is outstanding, although Provençal wines could be better represented. Don't miss the sun-drenched terrace and shady garden. Perfect welcome and service, and high prices (but no more so than in top restaurants along the Côte d'Azur). Chic international clientele. C 500-800 F. M 295 F (lunch), 580 F, 680 F.

Le Petit Nice

(See restaurant above)
Closed Sat & Sun (Nov-Apr). 3 stes 2,500-3,900 F. 13 rms 800-1,900 F. Half-board 1,150-2,560 F. Air cond. Conf. Pool. Golf. Valet pkg. V, AE, MC.
Set in a stunningly beautiful and peaceful spot overlooking the sea, Le Petit Nice has a handful of lovely, comfortable rooms and suites done in "designer" style (which you'll either love or hate), and superbly equipped bathrooms. Amenities include a salt-water swimming pool, sun room, water skiing, and sea fishing. A nearby villa houses two additional rooms and a sumptuous suite with a private terrace and sauna. Relais et Châteaux.

Patalain

49, rue Sainte (1st)
91 55 02 78, fax 91 54 15 29
Closed Sat lunch, Sun, Jul 14-Sep 1. Open until 11pm. Priv rm: 14. Air cond. Valet pkg. V, AE, DC.
Many a Marseillais considers this the best address in town, and Suzanne Quaglia's sincere, full-flavored cooking has convinced us that there's more than a little truth in what they say! She offers authentic dishes like fish soup with firey rouille, green ravioli stuffed with langoustines, daube provençal, and state-of-the-art pieds et paquets (a Marseille specialty). Fine choice of regional wines. C 300-800 F. M 150 F (weekday lunch, wine incl), 180 F, 210 F, 230 F, 270 F, 370 F.

Le Petit Nice

See restaurant Passédat

Pullman Beauvau
4, rue Beauvau (1st)
91 54 91 00, fax 91 54 15 76
*Open year-round. 1 ste 1,950 F. 71 rms 400-850 F.
Restaurant. Air cond. Conf. Valet pkg. V, AE, DC, MC.*
   Though remodeled in 1985, this grand hotel situated near the Old Port maintains the charm of bygone days, when George Sand and Chopin stayed here and pianist-composer Francis Poulenc tickled the ivories on the grand piano he had hoisted up to the fifth floor. The sunny, restful, soundproofed rooms are furnished with handsome antiques. Bar open until 1am. Room service.

Résidence Sainte-Anne
50, bd Verne (8th)
91 71 54 54, fax 91 22 63 43
Open year-round. 45 rms 310 F. Restaurant. Air cond. Pkg. V, AE, DC.
   Near the Prado beaches, this modern, comfortable hotel sits in a quiet garden.

Saint-Ferréol's Hotel
19, rue Pisançon (1st)
91 33 12 21, fax 91 54 29 97
Closed Aug 1-20. 19 rms 280-420 F. Air cond. V, AE, MC.
   You can't miss it: a glowing, revolving globe sits atop this cheerfully renovated old hotel. The mid-sized rooms sport personalized furnishings; all are efficiently soundproofed. Warm welcome; generous breakfasts.

12/20 Sauveur Rive Neuve
4 & 5, quai Rive-Neuve (1st)
91 33 33 32
Open daily until 11pm. Priv rm: 60. Terrace dining. Air cond. V, AE.
   An unpretentious menu of pizzas, Sicilian-style tomatoes, sweet peppers with anchovies, and meats grilled over a wood fire is served with good little French and Italian wines. Attractive portside location. C 170-230 F.

Sofitel
See restaurant Les Trois Forts

Les Trois Forts
36, bd Ch.-Livon (7th)
91 52 90 19, fax 91 31 46 52
Open daily until 10:15pm. Priv rm: 120. Air cond. Pool. Valet pkg. V, AE, DC, MC.
   You would come here for the superb view of the Old Port from the refined but cozy dining room, even if there were no other attraction. But the cooking is worth the visit, too. Dominique Frérard offers tasty Mediterranean dishes based on fine local products: red tuna tartare with ginger, panisse with chive cream, petits farcis de Provence in a basil-scented bouillon, and thigh of young rabbit stuffed en rognonnade. Fine selection of regional wines at reasonable prices. M 195 F.

Sofitel

(See restaurant above)
Open year-round. 3 stes 1,750-2,100 F. 130 rms 590-930 F. Rms for disabled. Air cond. Conf. Pool. Valet pkg. V, AE, DC, MC.
   The newly equipped bathrooms are an improvement, but the decor of the bedrooms is rather impersonal. On the other hand, the view of the town across the Old Port is superb. Excellent breakfast buffet, and a pleasant bar.

And also...
Our selection of places for inexpensive, quick, or late-night meals.
L'Atelier du Chocolat (91 33 55 00 - 18, pl. aux Huiles, 1st. Open until 10:30pm.): A master *pâtissier* makes fresh salads and *plats du jour*, as well as marvelous chocolates (120-160 F).
La Coupole (91 54 88 57 - 5, rue Haxo, 1st. Open until 10pm.): Brasserie fare and *plats du jour* in the heart of the shopping district (150-180 F).
La Gentiane (91 42 88 80 - 9, rue des Trois-Rois, 6th. Open until 11pm.): Light, steamed dishes full of the scents and savors of Provence (150-250 F).
New York (91 33 60 98 - 33, quai des Belges, 1st. Open until 11:30pm.): The favorite brasserie of the local chic set, with a great view of the Old Port and cooking that doesn't live up to the surroundings (200-350 F).
L'Oliveraie (91 33 34 41 - 10, pl. aux Huiles, 1st. Open until midnight.): An inexpensive, reliable brasserie near the Old Port (150-240 F).
Taverne de Maître Kanter (91 33 84 85 - 38, cours d'Estienne-d'Orves, 1st. Open until 12:30am, 1am w-e.): Oysters, choucroute, or good (but expensive) fish, and beer to go with them (139-235 F).

MARTIN-ÉGLISE 76 → **Dieppe**

MARTRE (LA)	∘	83840

Paris 830 - Castellane 18 - Draguignan 46 - La Bastide 6   *Var*

Château de Taulane
Le Logis du Pin, N 85
93 40 60 80, fax 93 60 37 48
Closed Nov-Mar. 4 stes 800-1,800 F. 39 rms 810-1,420 F. Rms for disabled. Restaurant. Conf. Heated pool. Golf. Valet pkg. Helipad. V, AE, DC, MC.
   A luxurious establishment where the focus is clearly on golf. Set in 340 hectares of verdant grounds, the eighteenth-century château houses quiet, charmingly personalized rooms. White-tile baths, terracotta floors, old-fashioned taps and fittings. Guests are greeted with hospitable warmth. Heliport.

MASSANA (LA)
→ **Andorra (Principality of)**

MAULÉVRIER 49 → **Cholet**

MAUSSANE-LES-ALPILLES	13520

Paris 717 - Marseille 85 - Arles 18 - Salon 28   *B./Rhône*

Les Magnanarelles
104, av. de la Vallée-des-Baux
90 54 30 25, fax 90 54 50 04
Closed Jan 3-Feb 15. 2 stes 380 F. 16 rms 220-280 F. Restaurant. Half-board 250-270 F. Conf. Golf. Pool. Valet pkg. V, AE, MC.
   This quiet little inn boasts a pleasant garden. The modest, recently renovated rooms are perfectly kept. Outdoor restaurant in season.

La Petite France

15, av. de la Vallée-des-Baux - 90 54 41 91
*Closed Thu lunch & Wed off-seas. Open until
9:30pm. Priv rm: 30. Air cond. Pkg. V, MC.*
Young, talented chef Thierry Maffre-Bogé offers classic Provençal cooking: ravioli stuffed with olives, sage, and ricotta; fillet of lamb with thyme sauce and garlic confit; nougat glacé with pistachio ice cream. Don't miss the lièvre (hare) à la royale in season. The cellar is magnificent, the decor features wine-oriented objects and posters, and wine-tasting evenings are organized. Friendly welcome **C** 250-400 F.
M 150 F, 220 F, 300 F.

Le Pré des Baux

Rue du Vieux-Moulin - 90 54 40 40
Closed Jan 10-Easter. 10 rms 480-640 F. Rms for disabled. Pool. Golf. Garage pkg. V, MC.
In a quiet setting, this new hotel has sunny, modern rooms with terraces that give onto a swimming pool. Attentive service.

Ou Ravi Provençau

34, av. de la Vallée-des-Baux
90 54 31 11, fax 90 54 41 03
Closed Tue. Open until 9:30pm (10:30pm in summer). Priv rm: 15. Terrace dining. No cards.
Jean-François Richard's cheerily decorated Provençal restaurant is warm and welcoming. So is his cuisine, which the locals flock to sample. Try his truffled pumpkin soup, ragoût of artichokes à la barigoule, veal sweetbreads with fava beans and tiny peas, rabbit sautéed with thyme, and pieds et paquets (a local veal specialty) that regular customer Jean-Pierre Dennery, president of Souleïado fabrics, says are the best in the region. (We agree.) And on the reasonably priced wine list you'll find a fine Trévallon 1990 for a bargain price of 160 F. **C** 280-350 F.
M 160 F, 230 F.

MAUZAC	24150

Paris 545 - Périgueux 62 - Bergerac 29 - Brive 95   *Dordogne*

La Métairie

Route du Cingle-de-Trémolat
53 22 50 47, fax 53 22 52 93
Closed Tue, Oct 15-Apr 1. Open until 9pm. Garden dining. Pool. Pkg. V, MC.
The spectacular, meandering Dordogne River snakes away before you from this lovely old Périgord dwelling. Some find the Louis XIII–style interior stuffy, but the terrace is a treat, with its lovely pool. You can expect generous, honest, regionally rooted cooking: fillet of red gurnard (an ocean fish) with vegetables, curried lamb with preserved lemons, farm-raised chicken with truffles, and a caramelized banana feuilleté. Hospitable reception; average cellar. For lovers, including ones who love nature. **C** 260-380 F.
M 120 F, 160 F, 250 F.

La Métairie

(See restaurant above)
Closed Jan 1-Mar 31, Oct 15-Dec 31. 1 ste 800 F. 9 rms 390-550 F. Half-board 410-500 F. Pool. Golf. Pkg. Helipad. V, MC.
This delightful old inn is lost in a leafy park that opens onto peaceful countryside. The air is sweet and clean. The uniformly neat, well-equipped rooms are pretty and comfortable

(some have modern, others rustic decor). Polite staff.

MAZAMET	81200

Paris 743 - Carcassonne 47 - Castres 18 - Toulouse 83   *Tarn*

Château de Montledier

5 km on D 54, route d'Anglès, Pont Arn
63 61 20 54, fax 63 98 22 51
Closed Jan. 9 rms 250-490 F. Restaurant. Half-board 350-410 F. Conf. Pool. Golf. Pkg. V, AE, DC, MC.
Big, beautiful rooms with sensational views, housed in a medieval château. Pretty wooded grounds.

MEAUX	77100

Paris 54 - Reims 98 - Soissons 65 - Melun 57   *Seine/Marne*

■ **In Poincy 77470**   6 km NE

Le Moulin de Poincy

Rue du Moulin
60 23 06 80, fax 60 23 12 56
Closed Tue dinner, Wed. Open until 9:15pm. Priv rm: 20. Garden dining. Pkg. V, AE, MC.
A lovely old mill with a cozy dining room and an idyllic terrace bounded by rose bushes and linden trees next to the water. Armel Abit's refined cuisine is dappled with nuanced flavors. Try his mushroom and delicate ratatouille tart, chicken breast coated with ground hazelnuts, and a light white chocolate mousse with berries.
C 300-450 F. **M** 195 F, 260 F, 340 F, 450 F.

■ **In Sancy-lès-**
   Meaux 77580   12 km S on N 36 and D 228

Demeure de la Catounière

1, rue de l'Église
60 25 71 74, fax 60 25 60 55
Closed 2 wks at Christmas & in Aug. 22 rms 356-402 F. Restaurant. Half-board 770 F. Conf. Heated pool. Tennis. Golf. Pkg. V, AE, DC, MC.
A venerable country estate transformed into a luxurious weekend hideaway. Commodious rooms with every amenity look out over manicured grounds. Equestrian club on the premises.

MEGÈVE	74120

Paris 613 - Annecy 60 - Chamonix 35 - Lyon 197   *H.-Savoie*

Chalet du Mont d'Arbois

Route du Mont-d'Arbois
50 21 25 03, fax 50 21 24 79
Closed end Mar-mid Jun, end Sep-mid Dec. Open until 9:45pm. Terrace dining. Air cond. Heated pool. Valet pkg. V, AE, DC, MC.
The split-level dining room with its baroque wood-paneled decor is reminiscent of a deluxe hunting lodge; beyond the window, patrons can admire a picture-postcard view of Megève in the distance. The fine cuisine of Jean-Pierre Minery has won a local following for the likes of a chartreuse of asparagus tips and green beans over a caviar cream, pickerel roasted in its skin with paysanne potatoes and roasting juices, and Bresse chicken roasted over the fireplace. Supremely elegant welcome and service. An

327

extra point this year. **C** 380-480 F. **M** 195 F, 280 F, 440 F.

Chalet du Mont d'Arbois
(See restaurant above)
See restaurant for closings. 1 ste 2,900-5,900 F. 20 rms 700-1,800 F. Half-board 725-1,220 F. Conf. Heated pool. Tennis. Golf. Valet pkg. V, AE, DC, MC.
A lovely mountain chalet, tastefully decorated in regional style by Nadine de Rothschild. Uncommonly pretty furnishings of dark wood. Heated pool. Relais et Châteaux (a very aristocratic one).

Le Fer à Cheval

36, route du Crêt-d'Arbois
50 21 30 39, fax 50 93 07 60
Closed Sep 15-Dec 20, Apr 10-Jun 30. Open until 9:30pm. Priv rm: 40. *Garden dining. Air cond. Heated pool. No pets. Valet pkg. V, AE, MC.*
A chalet with a pleasing blond wood dining room, where the chef prepares light dishes (lightly smoked sea bass, oyster coulis, millefeuille of veal sweetbreads and preserved tongue), as well as Savoyard specialties based on Aravis mountain cheeses (berthoud, pela, and fondue). Efficient welcome and service. **C** 260-380 F. **M** 280 F (dinner, wine incl).

Le Fer à Cheval
(See restaurant above)
See restaurant for closings. 8 stes 1,780-2,000 F. 41 rms 740-1,280 F. Rms for disabled. Half-board 675-890 F. Conf. Heated pool. Golf. Pkg. V, AE, MC.
Two connected mountain chalets share a fresh, comfortable decor as well as a swimming pool, sauna, Jacuzzi, and brand-new lounges. Huge, lovely guest rooms.

Ferme-Hôtel Duvillard
Plateau du Mont-d'Arbois
50 21 14 62, fax 50 21 42 82
Closed Apr 15-Jun 15, Sep 15-Dec 15. 19 rms 640-998 F. Restaurant. Half-board 560-690 F. Heated pool. Golf. Pkg. V, AE, DC, MC.
A rambling chalet just opposite the ski lifts. The decor is rudimentary, but the view of the valley is most scenic. Rooms at the back are particularly quiet. Sauna.

Les Fermes de Marie

Chemin de Riante-Colline
50 93 03 10, fax 50 93 09 84
Closed Apr 15-Jun 15, Sep 20-Dec 15. Open until 10pm. Priv rm: 100. *Garden dining. Heated pool. Valet pkg. V, AE, MC.*
This Savoyard farmhouse restaurant and hotel are worth the trip in themselves—a geranium-spangled dream hamlet and doubtless the most inviting spot in Megève. Hence chef Guillaume Sourrieu's laudable ambition—to make the cooking the establishment's main draw. He's well on his way, proposing precise, inventive fare that reflects the region's culinary riches: sautéed cèpes, grilled pork "amourettes" (spinal bone marrow) and ears, a court-bouillon of gambas with a ragoût of white beans, and foie gras perfectly paired with delightfully acidic rhubarb. Rhubarb appears again in a luscious bread pudding with ice cream. The wine list is much improved (try the Domaine de la Violette Gamay). Two well deserved toques this year. **C** 350-400 F (dinner). **M** 350 F (Sat dinner, Sun, wine incl), 280 F (weekday dinner, wine incl), 220 F (wine incl).

Les Fermes de Marie
(See restaurant above)
See restaurant for closings. 10 stes 2,520-2,980 F half-board in. 42 rms 1,490-2,320 F half-board inc. Conf. Heated pool. Golf. Valet pkg. V, AE, MC.
For a storybook winter holiday in Megève: a hamlet of ten rustic yet utterly refined farmhouses has been restored as a luxury resort. The interiors are all done up in floral fabrics, regional antiques, folk art, etc. Slimming and beauty facilities are on hand (enlarged and improved this year), as well as a magnificent swimming pool. Individual chalets for families. Superb welcome and service.

Michel Gaudin
Carrefour d'Arly - 50 21 02 18
Closed Tue off-seas. Open until 10pm. Terrace dining. V, AE, DC, MC.
Michel Gaudin's cooking is based on scrupulously selected ingredients handled with respect, all brimming with the earthy flavors of Savoie and the Mediterranean. In his comfy, rustic restaurant, sample dishes ranging from the refreshingly simple to the subtly refined, all perfectly prepared: brouillade of red mullet with tarragon cream, leg of lamb confit en navarin, and for dessert, a giboulée of warm cherries in Armagnac over ice cream. The prices are more than reasonable. Short wine list. **C** 200-350 F. **M** 98 F, 128 F, 155 F, 175 F, 195 F.

La Grange d'Arly
10, rue Allobroges
50 58 77 88, fax 50 93 07 13
Closed Apr 15-Jun 15, Nov 12-Dec 15. 3 stes 760-1,565 F. 19 rms 480-900 F. Restaurant. Conf. Golf. No pets. Pkg. V, AE, DC, MC.
A stone's throw from the center of Megève, this cozy chalet hotel proposes comfortable rooms furnished in typical Alpine style.

Les Loges du Mont-Blanc
Pl. de l'Église - 50 21 20 02, fax 50 21 45 28
Open year-round. 3 stes 900-1,400 F. 44 rms 500-1,200 F. Restaurant. Half-board 730-1,480 F. Conf. Heated pool. Golf. V, AE, DC, MC.
Luxurious, thoroughly renovated accommodation in the middle of town. This establishment is a traditional favorite for its large rooms with balconies, and the indoor terrace for sun-dappled lunches. Sauna; billiards.

Le Mont Joly
Rue du Crêt-du-Midi
50 21 26 14, fax 50 58 75 20
Closed Apr 15-Jun 15, Sep 15-Dec 20. Open until 9:30pm. Garden dining. **Hotel:** *22 rms 670-760 F. Half-board 625-710 F. No pets. Pkg. V, AE, DC, MC.*
It's hard not to notice that the decor has faded badly, especially in contrast to the elegant, stylish reception and service (renovation is ongoing). But the setting surely won't interfere with the delight you'll take in the solid, inventive cuisine, unfortunately described with a bit of preciousness on the menu: langoustine in aromatic salts bathed in peppery hazelnut butter; seafood ragoût with herbs, morels, and fresh peas; poached capaletti; and desserts that, the menu tells you, spring "From the insolence of a desire for the pleasures of gourmandise". We wouldn't mind a bit of simplification, although everything is good and well prepared. Charming welcome; capable service. **C** 400-500 F. **M** 290 F, 340 F.

Parc des Loges

100, rue d'Arly
50 93 05 03, fax 50 93 09 52
*Closed Apr 20-Jun 15, Oct-Dec 24. 13 stes 900-
3,000. 39 rms 450-2,000 F. Rms for disabled. Restaurant. Half-board 230-280 F. Conf. Heated pool.
Golf. Valet pkg. V, AE, DC, MC.*
A true "snow palace" from the 1930s,
sumptuously restored to its Art Deco glory, right
down to the authentic room furnishings. The
opulent amenities even include the rarest of all:
sun-lit bathrooms.

12/20 Le Prieuré
Pl. de l'Église - 50 21 01 79
*Closed Mon (exc school hols), Jun 10-Jul 1, Oct 20-
Dec 1. Open until 10:30pm. Terrace dining. V, AE.*
Here's pleasant cooking the likes of croustillan
of pleurote mushrooms with beurre nantais
sauce, bourride, tagliatelle with sea scallops and
langoustines, and quail roasted with spices, all
served in a bright and tidy little dining room with
a terrace beneath the church steeple. C 260-
400 F. M 110 F, 139 F, 179 F.

Princesse de Megève

Demi-Quartier
50 93 08 08, fax 50 21 45 65
*Closed Apr 10-Jul 1, Sep 10-Dec 18. 14 rms 590-
2,600 F. Rms for disabled. Restaurant. Half-board
675-1,550 F. Conf. Heated pool. Golf. Valet pkg. V,
AE, DC, MC.*
In a peaceful little hamlet outside town stands
this beautiful chalet with eleven sunny, spacious,
tastefully decorated rooms. All have either a
balcony or a patio overlooking the mountains.
Sumptuous breakfasts. Lots of amenities: Jacuzzi, beauty center, swimming pool.

Saint-Jean

97, boucle des Houilles
50 21 24 45, fax 50 58 78 50
*Closed Apr 10-Jul 1, Sep 15-Dec 20. 15 rms 290-
474 F. Restaurant. Half-board 320-385 F. Golf. No
pets. Pkg. V, MC.*
Near the center of town, yet blessedly quiet,
this big chalet provides lovely wood-panelled
rooms with views over the great outdoors.

Au Vieux Moulin

188, rue A.-Martin
50 21 22 29, fax 50 93 07 91
*Closed Oct 31-Nov 30. 3 stes. 34 rms 440-1,360 F.
Restaurant. Half-board 490-680 F. Conf. Heated
pool. Golf. Pkg. V, MC.*
A good old-fashioned mountain chalet with
pretty rooms and a big garden.

MÉJANNES-LÈS-ALÈS 30	→ Alès

MELUN	77000
Paris 55 - Meaux 57 - Sens 66 - Orléans 104	Seine/Marne

Bleu Marine
Grand Monarque
Melun-la-Rochette, av. de Fontainebleau
64 39 04 40, fax 64 39 94 10
*Open year-round. 5 stes 580 F. 45 rms 390-480 F.
Conf. Restaurant. Heated pool. Tennis. Sauna. V, AE,
DC, MC.*
The small but perfectly equipped rooms open
onto the verdant grounds that lead into the
forest. Excellent service.

Ibis
81, av. de Meaux
60 68 42 45, fax 64 09 62 00
See page 95.
A comfortable hotel with reasonably priced
rooms.

■ **In Moissy-Cramayel 77550**   8 km NW on N 6

La Mare au Diable
5 km N on N 6 - 64 10 20 90
*Closed Sun dinner & Mon (exc hols). Open until
10pm. Priv rm: 150. Garden dining. Heated pool.
Pkg. V, AE, DC, MC.*
The cooking is getting better all the time, so
we're awarding this charming manor house,
formerly owned by George Sand, an extra point
this year. The warm, rustic dining room overlooks romantic grounds where meals are served
in summer; in winter, meats are grilled in a huge
fireplace. Chef Philippe Noël offers tasty dishes
based on regional recipes. C 350-400 F.
M 200 F (lunch, wine inc)150 F, 235 F, 330 F.

MÉNAT	63560
Paris 363 - Riom 34 - Montluçon 40	Puy-de-Dôme

12/20 Vindrié Jean Marc
Gorges de Chouvigny
73 85 51 48, fax 73 85 55 24
*Closed Jan. Open until 9:30pm. Priv rm: 20. Terrace
dining. Valet pkg. V, AE, DC, MC.*
Jean-Marc Vindrié lures food lovers into his
comfortable country-style restaurant with an irresistible 109 F menu: calf's head with
vinaigrette, trout fillet grenobloise, coq au vin
d'Auvergne, cheeses, and dessert. The cellar
overflows with interesting discoveries at even
more interesting prices. Cordial reception and
service. C 140-260 F. M 109 F, 185 F, 250 F.

MÉNERBES	84560
Paris 713 - Cavaillon 16 - Apt 21 - Bonnieux 12	Vaucluse

Le Roy Soleil
Route des Beaumettes, Le Fort
90 72 25 61, fax 90 72 36 55
*Closed Nov 15-Mar 15. 2 stes 900-1,350 F. 18 rms
480-950 F. Restaurant. Half-board 565-800 F. Air
cond. Conf. Pool. Tennis. Golf. Pkg. V, AE, MC.*
A traditional Provençal homestead in the heart
of the Lubéron, set amidst fragrant garrigue at
the foot of a fortified village. It is tastefully
decorated in rustic style (white walls, antiques),
and offers quality service and delicious poolside
breakfasts.

MENTON	06500
Paris 961 - Nice 31 - San-Remo 34 - Cannes 63	Alpes-Mar.

L'Aiglon
7, av. de la Madone
93 57 55 55, fax 93 35 92 39
*Closed Nov 3-Dec 20. 3 stes 750-1,200 F. 28 rms
280-620 F. Restaurant. Half-board 380-500 F. Air
cond. Heated pool. Pkg. V, AE, DC, MC.*
A beautiful nineteenth-century mansion
situated not far from the center, and just 50
meters from the sea, presents big, well-outfitted
rooms and delightful gardens. Mismatched furniture, however.

329

Ambassadeurs
2, rue du Louvre
93 28 75 75, fax 93 35 62 32
Open year-round. 7 stes 1,400-1,900 F. 42 rms 470-1,000 F. Rms for disabled. Restaurant. Half-board 690-1,220 F. Air cond. Conf. Pkg. V, AE, DC, MC.
The prettily decorated, air-conditioned rooms and suites provide all the amenities one might require, including beautiful marble bathrooms. Breakfasts are inexplicably stingy. Piano bar; excellent welcome and service.

Chambord
6, av. Boyer
93 35 94 19, fax 93 41 30 55
Closed Nov-Jan 5. 40 rms 280-540 F. Air cond. Pkg. V, AE, DC, MC.
Close to the sea, this hotel features fairly spacious, sunny rooms next to the municipal gardens.

Méditerranée
5, rue de la République
93 28 25 25, fax 93 57 88 38
Open year-round. 90 rms 350-500 F. Rms for disabled. Restaurant. Half-board 220-350 F. Conf. Pkg. V, AE, DC, MC.
A fairly new hotel in the center of town, featuring a modern decor and good leisure and conference facilities. Terrace and sun-room on the top floor.

Napoléon
29, porte de France
93 35 89 50, fax 93 35 49 22
Closed Nov-Dec 18. 40 rms 350-640 F. Restaurant. Half-board 120-140 F. Air cond. Conf. Heated pool. Golf. Pkg. V, AE, DC, MC.
You will enjoy a view either of the mountains or the sea, depending on which of these well-outfitted rooms you occupy. Panoramic restaurant.

12/20 Piccolo Mondo
10, rue Trenca - 93 57 53 11
Closed Wed, for dinner exc Sat. Open until 9:30pm (10pm in summer). V.
Monica Cannavina's charming restaurant, located near the marketplace, has a summery decor and draws local Italians. The fresh home cooking features excellent herb-stuffed ravioli, delicious scaloppine alla milanese, and fine house ice creams and tarts. Enticing little cellar. C 150-180 F. M 80 F.

Viking
2, av. du Gal-de-Gaulle
93 57 95 85, fax 93 35 89 57
Open year-round. 2 stes 550-680 F. 32 rms 220-500 F. Restaurant. Half-board 280-400 F. Air cond. Conf. Pool. Pkg. V, AE, DC, MC.
This roomy, white hotel opposite the beach is built around a salt-water swimming pool. Bright, nicely appointed accommodation with views of the sea or the mountains.

■ **In Bordighera**   *12 km E, in Italy*

Antica Maddalena
Via Arziglia, 83 - (0184) 26 60 06
Closed Tue, 2 wks in Oct. Open until 10:30pm. Priv rm: 40. Terrace dining. Pkg. V, AE, DC, MC.
You'll love the classic Ligurian dishes (an appetizing array of starters, excellent homemade pasta, and crispy, light fried fish and vegetables) at this appealing restaurant on the seafront road beyond Bordighera heading towards San Remo. Also worth sampling are the seafood appetizers, cheese ravioli, oven-cooked fish, and a pear compote with walnut ice cream. Pleasant terrace. Owner Marc Ballo's welcome is warm indeed. Limited selection of wines. C 230-300 F.

Le Chaudron
Piazza Bengasi, 2 - (0184) 26 35 92
Closed Mon, Jan 8-31, Jul 1-15. Open until 10pm. Air cond. V, MC.
Set in an old warehouse built of brick, with a handsome vaulted ceiling, a veranda, and a rather ostentatious salon, this Franco-Italian establishment specializes in updated and lightened regional fare with an emphasis on seafood. An extra point this year for the calamari cassolette with tiny peas and artichokes, a delicious turbot served boned with excellent vegetables, and a choice of fine dessert classics (chocolate cake, frangipane tart) served in stingy portions. Excellent Italian wines at reasonable prices. Charming welcome and service. C 300 F.

La Via Romana
Via Romana, 57 - (0184) 26 66 81
Closings not available. Open until 10pm. Priv rm: 35. Air cond. V, AE, DC, MC.
Chef Giuseppe Graziano's light and savory Ligurian cooking is served in a magnificent turn-of-the-century dining room with bevelled-glass windows, gleaming parquet floors, and ornate mouldings. On offer is a mouthwatering roster of dishes that includes remarkable fresh gambas (rare along this stretch of coast) fished the night before, delicious and original Sicilian couscous (only 70 F), and excellent ravioli with light-as-air pasta sautéed with local artichokes. For dessert, try the wonderful, creamy *budino* (pudding) with raspberry sauce. Friendly, professional welcome; efficient service. Excellent wine list featuring Italy's best, as well as some good French and Californian bottlings. C 200-350 F. M 180 F (lunch exc Sun, wine incl), 580 F (weekday dinner, Sun, wine incl), 240 F (weekdays), 310 F.

■ **In Camporosso**   *15 km E, in Italy*

Gino
(0184) 29 14 93
Closed Mon dinner, Tue, Dec 11-21, Mar 6-17, Jun 19-Jul 7. Open until 9:15pm (9:30pm in summer). Priv rm: 40. Terrace dining. Pkg. V, AE, DC, MC.
The environs lack charm and the eponymous Gino is long gone, but today Giovanna Beglia cooks for a flock of regulars who swear by her traditional Ligurian repertoire served in a dining room overlooking a pretty interior garden. Passing travelers are also welcome to try her delicious stuffed vegetables with mesclun salad; a mixed grill of monkfish, sardines, gambas, and tiny squid; a fine fig tart; and a perfect tiramisu. Enticing wine list; genial though rather timid service. C 350-450 F.

The C (A la carte) restaurant prices given are for a complete three-course meal for one, including a half-bottle of modest wine and service. M (Menus) prices are for a complete fixed-price meal for one, excluding wine (unless otherwise noted).

■ In Grimaldi Inferiore   5 km E, in Italy

Baia Beniamin
Corso Europa, 63
(0184) 38 002, fax (0184) 38 027
Closed Sun dinner, Mon, 2 wks in spring, 10 days in autumn. Open until 9:30pm. Garden dining. No pets. Valet pkg. V, AE, DC, MC.
Even the sunsets seem to conspire to make this seaside terrace an oasis of understated luxury. No wonder it has earned a reputation as one of the most seductive restaurants on these golden shores. The dynamic Carlo Brunelli adds to the pleasure with his luminous, magical, voluptuous cooking: try his celestial fried tiny squid, or the marvelously simple and flavorful ravioli over lightly sautéed cèpes or langoustines. The meat dishes and desserts fail to reach these heights of culinary bliss; if you must end with something sweet, opt for the simple roast peaches. Stylish, witty service overseen by Oscar Falsiroli, and fabulous wines from northern Italy and France (try the fine Chardonnay from the Domaine Gaja in the Piedmont). **C** 300-450 F. **M** 144 F, 270 F.

Baia Beniamin
(See restaurant above)
Closed 2 wks in spring & in autumn. 6 rms 630-815 F. No pets. Valet pkg. Helipad. V, AE, DC, MC.
Half a dozen bright, inviting rooms open onto a veranda between the garden and the beach. The ambience is edenic. Tempting breakfasts. A bit of redecorating may be in the works, but in our view, why tamper with paradise?

■ In Ponte San Ludovico   1 km E, in Italy

Balzi Rossi
Piazzale de Gasperi
(0184) 38 132, fax (0184) 38 532
Closed Mar 1-15, Nov 15-30. Open until 10:30pm. Priv rm: 45. No pets. No cards.
It would be hard to find a border town more romantic than this one. The red rocky coast (*balzi rossi* in Italian) is on one side, the bay of Cap Martin on the other. Giuseppina Beglia's cuisine also straddles the border, inspired by Italian and Provençal muses, in a menu that highlights Liguria's freshest, most beautiful produce.
Come here to discover the radiantly authentic flavors of boiled octopus in a salad with famed Nervia valley white beans, ravioli stuffed with whiting in pistou sauce, fresh taglioni with San Remo shrimps, sea bass braised with apples and artichokes in a veal jus, fish cooked in a salt crust and anointed with herby olive oil, ravioli stuffed with basil-scented young rabbit and black Taggia olives, cheese with white truffles from Alba, and a luscious Muscat sabayon. The cellar offers treasures from Liguria, Piedmont, and Burgundy. **C** 300-420 F. **M** 320 F (wine incl), 550 F.

■ In San Remo   17 km E, in Italy

Bagatto
Via Matteotti, 145
(0184) 53 19 25
Closed Sun, Jun 15-Jul 15. Open until 11pm. Priv rm: 50. Air cond. Garage pkg. V, AE, DC, MC.
Behind the façade of a fifteenth-century *palazzo* you'll find a handsome, contemporary restaurant. Some 45 patrons (usually a mix of tourists and locals) can lunch or dine together on tasty tortelli with slices of potato and a delicate pesto, cuttlefish and artichoke soup in a crust, tender kid flavored with rosemary, and a gianduja bavarian cream with mint sauce. Alluring cheeses. Excellent cellar. **C** 250-300 F. **M** 170 F (wine incl), 250 F.

Osteria del Marinaio   ☺
Via Gaudio, 28 - (0184) 50 19 19
Closed Mon, Nov 15-Dec 15, Oct 20-30. Open until 10pm. Air cond. No cards.
This unpretentious trattoria tucked away in a tiny street in old San Remo, is the best address in town (and beyond!) for fresh seafood. Maria Locatelli shops at the fish market next door for her raw materials, and prepares them with superb simplicity: tiny boiled octopus or local shrimp served warm in olive oil, a wonderful mixed seafood platter, and the best spaghetti alla bottarga (with dried cod roe) on the coast, as well as a splendid frittura of mixed fish (squid, cuttlefish, octopus). If you have room for dessert, take our advice and opt for the fabulous vanilla or gianduia gelati. Fine little cellar with the best Italian white wines, including a Pigato (Anfossi) from the region. **C** 400-450 F.

MERCUÈS 46	→ Cahors

MERCUREY	71640

Paris 348 - Autun 40 - Chalon 13 - Chagny 12   Saône/Loire

Le Val d'Or
Grande-Rue - 85 45 13 70
Closed Tue lunch, Mon (exc hols lunch), Dec 17-Jan 19. Open until 9pm. Priv rm: 15. Air cond. No pets. Pkg. V, MC.
Jean-Claude Cogny's cooking is so reliable and professional that we could review his restaurant once or twice per century and feel confident that all would always be well. That said, Cogny certainly doesn't sleep on his saucepans. Witness this year's grilled langoustines with cumin and honey sauce, Limousin veal chops roasted in the oven and served with the roasting juices, and an aumônire of fresh fruit with raspberry sauce. The cellar celebrates wines of the Côte Chalonnaise. Pleasantly rustic decor that could use a bit of a facelift. Slow service. **C** 300-500 F. **M** 160 F, 240 F, 290 F, 410 F.

MÉRIBEL-LES-ALLUES	73550

Paris 637 - Chambéry 93 - Albertville 45 - Annecy 90   Savoie

Allodis
Le Belvédère
79 00 56 00, fax 79 00 59 28
Closed Apr 25-Jun, Sep 15-Dec 10. Open until 10pm. Priv rm: 30. Terrace dining. Heated pool. No pets. Pkg. V, DC, MC.
Slowly but surely, Alain Plouzane is working his way into the pack of Méribel's leading chefs with his well prepared dishes like semi-wild duck glazed with Alpilles honey, Pauillac lamb with Savoyard criques, and a nage of sole with black ravioli. Warm welcome and zealous service; large, flower-filled dining room. **C** 250-350 F. **M** 170 F (lunch), 240 F, 300 F, 350 F (dinner).

331

Allodis
(See restaurant above)
Closed May-beg Jul, mid Sep-mid Dec. 12 stes 1,100-1,380 F. 31 rms 850-1,660 F. Rms for disabled. Half-board 870-1,380 F. Conf. Heated pool. Golf. No pets. Pkg. V, DC, MC.

On the slopes above the resort area, these spacious wood-paneled rooms enjoy a great view of the Olympic runs. Wonderfully convivial atmosphere; gym and sauna.

Altiport Hôtel
BP 24 - 79 00 52 32, fax 79 08 57 54
Closed Apr 29-Jun 24, Sep 23-Dec 16. 8 stes 690-2,100 F. 34 rms 1,320 F. Restaurant. Half-board 490-960 F. Conf. Heated pool. Tennis. Pkg. V, AE.

This modern, attractively appointed chalet, close to the runs and the forest, provides beautiful rooms decorated in rustic style. There is a program of summer activities (tennis, golf) as well as winter sports. Jacuzzi; sauna. The welcome leaves a bit to be desired.

Aspen Park Hotel
Rond-Point des Pistes
79 00 51 77, fax 79 00 53 74
Closed Apr 15-Jun 15, Oct 15-Dec 15. 16 stes 2,400-5,800 F. 49 rms 1,000-2,600 F. Restaurants. Half-board 750-1,600 F. Conf. Heated pool. Pkg. V, AE, DC.

Of all the luxury hotels built to accommodate spectators of the 1990 Olympic Games, this is one of the handsomest. Its location, though, is not ideal (the view is blocked by a tall building). Beautiful, well-designed rooms; youthful, charming staff. Three restaurants: Japanese, Moroccan, and French. The future of the establishment may be in question, though, we hear.

Cassiopée
79 23 28 23, fax 79 23 28 18
Closed Apr 11-Dec 17. Open until 10pm. Terrace dining. Air cond. Heated pool. Pkg. V, AE, DC, MC.

The Antarès hotel is generally considered to be the star of the new crop of luxury establishments that sprang up for the Olympics. Chef Christian Farenasso has infused the menu with the flavors of his native Provence; the cuisine is remarkably well crafted and often original to boot. Offerings on a recent visit included a soupière of truffles and veal sweetbreads in puff pastry, langoustine gazpacho, red mullet fillet with olive caviar and potatoes with aïoli, and a delicate apple tart with caramel juice. Jocelyne Genty oversees the splendid cellar, which she is filling out with her personal discoveries. Excellent welcome and service. C 415-485 F. M 180 F (lunch), 280 F, 410 F.

L'Antarès
(See restaurant above)
Closed Apr 20-Dec 17. 16 stes 2,350-4,520 F. 60 rms 1,500-2,420 F. Rms for disabled. Half-board 1,900-4,750 F. Conf. Heated pool. Golf. V, AE, DC, MC.

The electronic equipment and bath fixtures found in these huge, beautiful rooms may take some getting used to! The fitness center and swimming pool are superb; the reception is excellent.

Le Chalet
Le Belvédère
79 23 28 23, fax 79 23 28 18
Closed Apr 20-June 30, Sep 1-Dec 15. 6 stes 2,440-3,780 F. 29 rms 1,370-2,460 F. Half-board 1,400-2,350 F. Conf. Heated pool. Golf. V, AE, DC, MC.

Michel and Dominique Bisac have built the ski chalet that they—and perhaps you—have always dreamed of. Above the resort, just opposite the runs, this all-pine structure is a stunning marriage of modern and traditional Savoyard architecture. Every one of the huge rooms boasts a fireplace, a balcony, thick carpet, beautiful fabrics, and a superb bathroom. Amenities include a heated swimming pool with Jacuzzi.

La Chaudanne
79 08 61 76, fax 79 08 57 75
Closed May 3-Jun, Sep 10-Dec 3. Open until 10:30pm. Heated pool. No pets. Garage pkg. V, AE, DC, MC.

Well-heeled patrons gather round the lordly fireplace of this rustic dining room to sample René Théveniot's interesting, accomplished cuisine: a turnover filled with langoustines and artichoke purée, casserole-roasted slices of veal kidney, and, for dessert, a basket of crisp cakes. C 300-430 F. M 150 F (dinner), 220 F, 280 F.

La Chaudanne
(See restaurant above)
Closed May-Jun, Oct-Nov. 5 stes 800-1,400 F. 65 rms 400-1,350 F. Half-board 450-890 F. Conf. Heated pool. Golf. Pkg. V, AE, DC, MC.

Set right at the resort's center, this imposing chalet offers commodious, cozy new rooms with impeccable appointments. The fitness center is fully equipped.

Le Grand Cœur
79 08 60 03, fax 79 08 58 38
Closed Apr 23-Dec 16. Open until 10pm. Terrace dining. Valet pkg. V, AE, DC, MC.

It's hard to predict what will happen to the restaurant this year, with all the changes of management and ownership. But if we judge only by current facts, chef Marc Dach's regional cuisine is well worth sampling: Mouraillons salad with Savoyard cheese cromesquis, croustillant of pig's foot with Chambéry mustard, and, for dessert, plump, chocolaty macaroni stuffed with praline and paired with Mascarpone sherbet. A point extra for this elegant cooking. C 350-400 F (dinner). M 300 F.

Le Grand Cœur
(See restaurant above)
Closed Apr 10-Dec 15. 2 stes 2,750-4,100 F half-board inc. 38 rms 1,400-2,950 F half-board inc. Conf. Valet pkg. V, AE, DC, MC.

Spacious, well-designed rooms with views of the Vanoise summits. Excellent fitness equipment is featured, along with a Jacuzzi, sauna, and Turkish bath. Relais et Châteaux.

■ In **Le Mottaret 73550**   6 km S

12/20 Mont Vallon
Méribel, at Le Mottaret
79 00 44 00, fax 79 00 46 93
Closed Apr 24-Dec 16. Open until 10:30pm. Priv rm: 25. Terrace dining. Heated pool. Valet pkg. V, AE, DC, MC.

Unremarkable pension-style cooking served in a luxury-version Alpine chalet. The Schuss brasserie does a roaring trade with decent pizzas, pasta, fondues, and raclette (melted cheese and potatoes). C 300-450 F. M 250 F (dinner).

Mont Vallon
(See restaurant above)
Closed Apr 15-Dec 15. 7 stes 1,600-2,800 F. 92 rms 1,400-2,200 F. Half-board 800-1,225 F. Conf. Heated pool. Golf. Helipad. V, AE, DC, MC.
An immense, sumptuous chalet with intimate, warmly elegant decor. Wonderfully comfortable rooms, superb facilities (fitness club, squash, solarium, etc.).

MÉRIGNAC 33 ➜ **Bordeaux**

MESNULS (LES) 78 ➜ **Montfort-l'Amaury**

METZ **57000**
Paris 313 - Nancy 59 - Strasbourg 157 - Luxembourg 60 *Moselle*

 Le Chambertin
22, pl. St-Simplice
87 37 32 81, fax 87 36 70 89
Closed Sun dinner, Mon, Mar 15-30, Sept 4-25. Open until 9:30pm. Terrace dining. Pkg. V, AE, DC, MC.
Classic setting, classic cuisine: Francis Loyon's cooking is ever careful, but some dishes we sampled this year were a bit disappointing: the raw Scottish salmon tartare lacked character, the fine aiguillette of beef with sweet peppers was marred by a dull sauce, but the generous fillet of oven-roasted sea bream was good and served generously in the pretty dining room with Louis XV furniture. A point less this year. Rich and pricey wine list. Friendly welcome, good service. **C** 250-300 F. **M** 165 F, 250 F.

 Le Crinouc
79-81, rue du Gal-Metman
87 74 12 46, fax 87 36 96 92
Closed Sat lunch, Sun dinner, Mon. Open until 9:30pm. Air cond. No pets. Pkg. V, AE, DC, MC.
Spacious and refined, the new pastel-toned interior is a welcome counterpoint to the crassly commercial suburban surroundings. The *patronne* welcomes you warmly, and talented chef Jean-Claude Lamaze regales you with classic cuisine given modern touches: veal sweetbreads paired with goose foie gras, John Dory with cèpes, and a kouglof glacé with honey cake and Corinthe raisins. **C** 300-450 F. **M** 260 F, 370 F (Sat dinner, Sun lunch), 190 F (weekdays).

 La Dinanderie
2, rue de Paris
87 30 14 40, fax 87 32 44 23
Closed Sun, Mon, 1 wk in Feb, 3 wks in Aug. Open until 9:30pm. Priv rm: 30. Air cond. Pkg. V, AE, MC.
Arguably the best chef in town, Claude Piergiorgi continues to polish his classic repertoire by using rigorous, precise cooking techniques and flawless ingredients. Depending on his mood and the time of year, you might encounter croustillant of sea scallops and shrimp with a pepper and olive piperade, scallops of veal sweetbreads flavored with summer savory and paired with little zucchini fritters, and a warm rhubarb tart with a creamy vanilla quenelle. Splendid cellar of Burgundies and Bordeaux. Attentive service and courteous welcome. **C** 320-420 F. **M** 160 F (exc Sat dinner), 240 F, 350 F.

12/20 Flo
2 bis, rue Gambetta
87 55 94 95, fax 87 38 09 26
Open daily until 12:30am. Terrace dining. Air cond. V, AE, DC, MC.
The former Café des Arts has gone with the Flo group, and now wears an attractive brasserie decor that suits the classic brasserie fare on the menu: seafood platters, curried seafood gratins, sole stuffed with tiny sea scallops. The cellar is short on half bottles. **C** 190-300 F. **M** 95 F (dinner, wine incl, after 10pm), 99 F, 141 F (wine incl).

12/20 La Gargouille
29, pl. de Chambre
87 36 65 77, fax 85 77 89 78
Open daily until 10pm. Pkg. V, MC.
This friendly little restaurant smiles back at the cathedral's grimacing gargoyles overhead, and serves tasty dishes like a mushroom and snail fricassée, tiny sea scallops in Noilly-Prat, pork filet mignon with mirabelle plums, soufflé glacé, and crème brûlée. Reasonable prices. **C** 210-260 F (wine incl). **M** 105 F (lunch exc Sun, wine incl), 148 F, 178 F, 200 F (exc Sun, wine incl).

 Mercure-Centre
29, pl. St-Thiébault
87 38 50 50, fax 87 75 48 18
Open year-round. 4 stes 650 F. 108 rms 390-450 F. Restaurant. Air cond. Conf. Garage pkg. V, AE, DC.
In the center of town between the railway station and the pedestrian district, this chain hotel offers modern, pleasant rooms that are very well kept and provided with all the usual amenities.

 Novotel-Centre
Centre St-Jacques, pl. des Paraiges
87 37 38 39, fax 87 36 10 00
Open year-round. 3 stes 650 F. 117 rms 450-490 F. Restaurant. Air cond. Pool. Golf. Pkg. V, AE, DC.
This recently renovated hotel in the center of Metz provides spacious, comfortable rooms. Youthful, attentive service.

 A la Ville de Lyon
7, rue des Piques
87 36 07 01, fax 87 74 47 17
Closed Sun dinner, Mon, Feb 17-21, Aug 1-27. Open until 10pm. Air cond. Pkg. V, AE, DC, MC.
An arm of the Moselle laps the ancient walls of Metz's cathedral quarter, where you'll find this old coaching inn, a jewel in the charming maze of narrow streets. The somewhat heavy-handed decor does not detract from the generous, attractively presented cuisine prepared by owner-chef Michel Vaur. We relished his fresh foie gras, grilled veal kidney, squab in Bordeaux wine sauce, and soufflé glacé of mirabelle plums. Majestic cellar. **C** 220-350 F. **M** 185 F (exc Sun), 105 F, 180 F, 310 F.

And also...
Our selection of places for inexpensive, quick, or late-night meals.
La Baraka (87 36 33 92 - 25, pl. de Chambre. Open until 10:30pm.): Metz's best for couscous, tajines, and squab pastilla (120 F).
Le Breg Much (87 74 39 79 - 22, pl. des Char-

rons. Open until 10pm.): French family-style cooking at good-value prices (150-200 F).

■ In **Plappeville 57050**   3 km W

La Grignotière
50, rue du Gal-de-Gaulle - 87 30 36 68
Closed Sun dinner, Mon, Feb school hols, Aug 21-Sep 1. Open until 10pm. Priv rm: 18. V, MC.
In a charming flower-bedecked building with low-ceilinged, white-walled dining rooms overlooking a garden terrace, you can sample classic cuisine marked by lightness and pure flavors: delicate buisson of lightly smoked sole, ultrafresh and perfectly prepared red mullet fillets with Mediterranean seasonings, and a light-as-air chocolate and orange feuilleté glacé. Splendid wine list. Attentive service. **C** 280-380 F. **M** 195 F (weekday lunch, wine incl), 120 F (weekday lunch), 290 F.

MEUDON 92	→ **PARIS Suburbs**

MEURSAULT	**21190**

Paris 320 - Beaune 8 - Chalon-sur-Saône 30   Côte-d'Or

Les Charmes
10, pl. Murger
80 21 63 53, fax 80 21 62 89
Closed Dec 11-Jan 20. 14 rms 390-550 F. Heated pool. No pets. Pkg. V, MC.
A pleasant stop along the wine route in this cozy hotel surrounded by a large park. Each of the pretty rooms is named for one of Burgundy's gread crus. Attentive welcome.

Les Magnolias
8, rue P.-Joigneaux
80 21 23 23, fax 80 21 29 10
Closed Dec-Mar. 1 ste 650-700 F. 11 rms 350-580 F. No pets. Garage pkg. V, AE, MC.
You'll revel in the authentic Burgundian atmosphere at this manor house, converted into a fine hotel by a transplanted Englishman. Attractive rooms, decorated with country antiques.

MEYLAN 38	→ **Grenoble**

MEYRUEIS	**48150**

Paris 630 - Millau 42 - Florac 35 - Mende 58   Lozère

Château d'Ayres
66 45 60 10, fax 66 45 62 26
Closed Nov 15-Mar. Open until 10:45pm. Priv rm: 18. Terrace dining. Pool. No pets. V, AE, DC, MC.
Set in the center of sequoia-dotted grounds, this mainly eighteenth-century château has plenty of character, and you'll find the cooking reliable and flavorful: crayfish ravioli, fillet of venison, chive-perfumed salmon millefeuille, and a warm raspberry soufflé. The wine list needs fleshing out. **C** 250-310 F. **M** 110 F (lunch), 149 F, 185 F, 265 F.

Château d'Ayres
(See restaurant above)
Closed Nov 15-Mar. 4 stes 730-840 F. 22 rms 355-840 F. Half-board 365-575 F. Tennis. No pets. Valet pkg. Helipad. V, AE, DC, MC.
The Montjou family lovingly care for this architecturally eclectic château; it is a delightful

place to stay, with its period furnishings, sequoia grove, and the calm beauty that reigns everywhere.

MILLAU	**12100**

Paris 640 - Béziers 125 - Albi 113 - Rodez 71   Aveyron

International
1, pl. de la Tine
65 59 29 00, fax 65 59 29 01
Closed Sun dinner & Mon off-seas, Jan. Open until 9:30pm. Air cond. Garage pkg. V, AE, DC, MC.
The vast, elegant dining room occupies the ground floor of a modern tower. Here, chefs Jean-François Pomarède and Maurice Daize employ unassailable technique to turn out tasty monkfish with pepper and caramelized spices, fillet of Causses lamb in puff pastry with rosemary, gigolette of duck with foie gras, and a honey crouquant with a light lytchee cream and a grapefruit sauce. Fine cellar. **C** 280-400 F. **M** 98 F, 138 F, 175 F, 325 F.

International
(See restaurant above)
Open year-round. 2 stes 505-541 F. 102 rms 258-438 F. Half-board 231-362 F. Air cond. Conf. Garage pkg. V, AE, DC, MC.
The salon and terrace on the top floor of this large, pleasantly modern building afford a splendid view, while the rooms are comfortable and spacious.

MIMIZAN	**40200**

Paris 676 - Bordeaux 108 - Dax 73 - Arcachon 65   Landes

Au Bon Coin du Lac
34, av. du Lac
58 09 01 55, fax 58 09 40 84
Closed Sun dinner, Mon, Feb. Open until 10pm. Priv rm: 35. Garden dining. Air cond. Pkg. V, AE.
A very peaceful sort of luxury reigns over this lakeside establishment. Either in the plush dining room with bay windows that frame views of the grounds and the lake, or on the terrace shaded by plane trees, the surroundings conspire to heighten one's enjoyment of Jean-Pierre Caule's impeccable classic cuisine. This year he provoked our admiration with deliciously tender tiny crabs stuffed with baby vegetables and shrimp, and a remarkably delicate lobster chartreuse. The desserts are very good, too. Madame Caule orchestrates the service in the spacious, sunny dining room with decor in autumn shades and a terrace overlooking the lake. Long and tempting wine list. **C** 400-450 F. **M** 300 F (Sat, Sun), 150 F, 250 F, 350 F.

Au Bon Coin du Lac
(See restaurant above)
Closed Sun, Mon, Feb. 4 stes 580-700 F. 4 rms 360-600 F. Half-board 550-630 F. Air cond. Pkg. V, AE.
This idyllic lakeside setting is complemented by perfectly comfortable rooms. Superb breakfasts (charcuterie, eggs, homemade jam...). Warm welcome.

MIONNAY 01	→ **Lyon**

MIRAMAR 06	→ **Théoule-sur-Mer**

MIRAMBEAU   17150
Paris 520 - Saintes 43 - Bordeaux 70 - Blaye 30   *Charente-M.*

Château de Mirambeau
46 70 71 77, fax 46 70 71 10
Closed Jan 2-Mar 31. Open until 10pm. Priv rm: 60. Terrace dining. Air cond. Heated pool. No pets. Valet pkg. V, MC.
Now magnificently restored, this 800-year-old château boasts a lovely dining room done up in subtle shades of grey. The refined decor harmonizes with chef Daniel Thomas's skillful cuisine, which blends the region's best with a pinch of Provence. Try the flavorful compressé of young rabbit with virgin olive oil, croustillant of sea bream with tomato-basil butter paired with cumin-spiced polenta croquettes, craquelin of spiced strawberries and sherbet spiked with Gewurtztraminer brandy. Well chosen wine list.
C 330-450 F. **M** 160 F (lunch exc Sun), 220 F, 350 F.

Château-Hôtel de Mirambeau
(See restaurant above)
Closed Jan 2-Mar 31. 6 stes 1,350-1,900 F. 42 rms 600-1,050 F. Rms for disabled. Half-board 910-1,360 F. Heated pool. Tennis. Golf. Pkg. V, DC, MC.
Every leisure pursuit is provided for: nine-hole golf course right on the grounds, tennis courts, swimming pool, satellite TV in any language you wish. Beautiful rooms equipped with the latest electronic gadgetry.

MIRANDE   32300
Paris 730 - Auch 25 - Tarbes 48   *Gers*

12/20 Les Pyrénées
5, av. d'Étigny
62 66 51 16, fax 62 66 79 96
Closed Mon. Open until 9:30pm. Priv rm: 40. Terrace dining. Valet pkg. V, AE.
Tourists favor this warm, family-run establishment full of get-up-and-go. The regional *terroir* cooking is tasty and well prepared: warm salad of foie gras and giblet confit, beef in a sea-salt crust, and nougat glacé with mint cream.
C 270-370 F. **M** 95 F, 135 F, 180 F, 220 F, 300 F.

Les Pyrénées
(See restaurant above)
Open year-round. 3 stes 350 F. 20 rms 200-350 F. Half-board 210-220 F. Air cond. Pool. Pkg. V, AE.
Ask for a spacious, well-equipped room in the annex facing the main building. Manicured garden and lawns. Fine breakfasts.

MOËLAN-SUR-MER   29116
Paris 514 - Concarneau 26 - Lorient 25 - Pont-Aven 16   *Finistère*

Manoir de Kertalg
D 24, route de Riec-sur-Belon
98 39 77 77, fax 98 39 72 07
Closed Nov 4-Apr 15. 1 ste 1,100 F. 9 rms 490-980 F. Conf. Golf. Pkg. Helipad. V, MC.
The stables of this old Breton manor set in an immense estate were converted into a hotel with spacious, comfortable rooms. There are many amenities (hairdresser, massage...), and the staff is most pleasant. Good breakfasts; tea room and bar, too.

Les Moulins du Duc
98 39 60 73, fax 98 39 75 56
Closed Jan 15-end Feb. Open until 10pm. Garden dining. Heated pool. Valet pkg. V, AE, DC, MC.
The chef of this delightful mill tucked away in the woods and lulled by the nearby Belon waterfall favors superbly fresh seafood, but sometimes stumbles in the execution: dryish smoked salmon, perfectly cooked fresh cod with a vegetable bohémienne, tasty and rustic Baye andouille, and a dull apple cake. Smiling welcome and service, but the wine list is short and pricey. **C** 280-400 F. **M** 90 F (weekday lunch), 140 F, 195 F, 310 F.

Les Moulins du Duc
(See restaurant above)
Closed Jan 15-Feb. 5 stes 1,010-1,300 F. 22 rms 440-805 F. Rms for disabled. Half-board 525-725 F. Conf. Heated pool. Golf. Pkg. V, AE, DC, MC.
A charming hideaway indeed, situated in a verdant hamlet, the Moulins are a group of cottages housing pleasantly peaceful rooms, some of them freshly decorated (others could stand brushing up). Good breakfasts. Sauna.

MOISSY-CRAMAYEL 77   → Melun

MOLINEUF 41   → Blois

MOLITG-LES-BAINS   66500
Paris 978 - Quillan 53 - Prades 7 - Perpignan 50   *Pyrénées-O.*

Château de Riell
On D 116 - 68 05 04 40, fax 68 05 04 37
Closed Jan 2-Apr 1. Open until 10pm. Heated pool. No pets. Valet pkg. V, AE, DC, MC.
Young Philippe Migot presides over the kitchens of this stunning medieval fortress, and offers superbly prepared dishes enlivened by a touch of fantasy: puff pastry filled with wild mushrooms and tiny squid, pig's foot tournedos in a simple jus, and a gooey chocolate and chicory cake. Courteous welcome; dogs are permitted in the dining room for an extra charge.
C 300-450 F. **M** 230 F (weekdays), 180 F, 270 F, 390 F.

Château de Riell
(See restaurant above)
Closed Nov 2-Mar 31. 3 stes 1,600 F. 19 rms 970-1,250 F. Half-board 835-1,620 F. Conf. Heated pool. Tennis. Valet pkg. V, AE, MC.
In a marvelous wooded setting that towers above the thermal spa, this fantastic nineteenth-century version of a medieval castle contains charming, romantic rooms that contrast markedly with the heavy-handed exterior. Exceptional facilities including spa facilities and two swimming pools. Relais et Châteaux.

MONACO (PRINCIPALITY OF)
Paris 955 - Nice 18 - Menton 9 - San-Remo 44

■ In Monte-Carlo

Abela Hôtel
Quartier Fontvieille, 23, av. des Papalins
92 05 90 00, fax 92 05 91 67

Open year-round. 18 stes 990-1,550 F. 176 rms 610-1,160 F. Rms for disabled. Restaurant. Air cond. Conf. Valet pkg. V, AE, DC, MC.

A recent addition to the Abela group, which also owns the Gray d'Albion in Cannes and the Beach Regency in Nice. The very attractive and comfortable rooms overlook the Princess Grace rose garden and the harbor. Excellent service and equipment; delicious breakfasts.

Balmoral

12, av. de la Costa
93 50 62 37, fax 93 15 08 69

Open year-round. 8 stes 1,200-1,500 F. 65 rms 400-850 F. Restaurant. Air cond. Conf. No pets. Garage pkg. V, AE, DC, MC.

The rooms of this vintage hotel near the port are gradually being renovated and a seventh floor was recently added. Small snack bar.

Beach Plaza

22, av. Princesse-Grace
93 30 98 80, fax 93 50 23 14

Open year-round. 9 stes 2,550-5,300 F. 304 rms 800-2,300 F. Rms for disabled. Restaurant. Half-board 2,805-5,705 F. Air cond. Conf. Heated pool. Golf. Valet pkg. V, AE, DC, MC.

This elegant hotel has a private beach, three swimming pools and a "sea club" offering a range of sporting activities. The rooms are spacious and prettily decorated. Private beach.

12/20 Café de la Mer

Hôtel Loews, av. de Spélugues
93 50 65 00, fax 93 30 01 57

Open daily until 10:30pm. Priv rm: 55. Terrace dining. Air cond. Heated pool. No pets. Valet pkg. V, AE, DC, MC.

Flooded with light from the sea and sky, this good-value (for Monaco) brasserie has a varied menu that includes superb charcuterie, salads geared to dieters, and fine grilled meat and fish. C 200-350 F.

12/20 Café de Paris

Pl. du Casino
92 16 20 20, fax 93 25 46 98

Open daily until 4am. Priv rm: 200. Garden dining. Air cond. Pkg. V, AE, DC, MC.

A wide, sun-washed terrace opens in front of this enormous brasserie decorated in Belle Époque style. Despite the crowds, the service is smiling and the cooking fresh and good. You can plump for salade gourmande with goose "ham", slices of saddle of rabbit with tapenade, délice glacé au nougat, or a three-chocolate dessert. C 310-460 F. M 200 F (wine incl), 220 F, 240 F, 260 F, 280 F.

La Coupole

1, av. Princesse-Grace
92 16 65 65, fax 93 50 84 85

Open daily until 10pm. Priv rm: 100. Terrace dining. Air cond. Heated pool. No pets. Valet pkg. V, AE, DC, MC.

Joël Garault's careful cooking, based on fine ingredients in sunny Southern dishes, is solemnly served (by waiters arrayed in formal attire) in an overblown decor. An extra toque this year for the likes of a delicious olivade of tiny artichokes with asparagus tips, harmonious small red mullet cooked quickly on one side only, and a delicate and perfectly spiced veal sweetbread caillette.

Fine desserts, like the gooey chocolate cake with bitter orange coulis. Well chosen wine list. C 450-650 F. M 280 F, 410 F.

Mirabeau

(See restaurant above)

Open year-round. 24 stes 3,000-4,000 F. 103 rms 900-2,000 F. Half-board 930-1,930 F. Air cond. Conf. Heated pool. Golf. No pets. Pkg. V, AE, DC, MC.

The well-equipped rooms have individual air conditioning and terraces overlooking the sea. Heated swimming pool. Free access to activities sponsored by the Société des Bains de Mer, reduced prices on tennis and golf fees. Note that the Coupole restaurant closes in July and August, but the Café Mirabeau is open for lunch, and the Terrasse de La Coupole is open at night.

Hermitage

Square Beaumarchais
92 16 40 00, fax 93 50 47 12

Open year-round. 25 stes 2,500 F. 216 rms 1,150-2,800 F. Rms for disabled. Air cond. Conf. Heated pool. Tennis. Golf. Valet pkg. V, AE, DC, MC.

This stunning Belle Époque hotel is perched on a cliff and offers huge rooms, a splendid swimming pool, and a fitness center.

Loews

Av. de Spélugues
93 50 65 00, fax 93 30 01 57

Open year-round. 69 stes 4,000-7,500 F. 650 rms 1,200-1,600 F. Restaurant. Half-board 1,700-2,000 F. Air cond. Conf. Heated pool. Golf. Valet pkg. V, AE, DC, MC.

As well as its luxurious suites and bright, welcoming rooms and broad terraces, this hotel offers a host of facilities: five restaurants, bars, cabaret, casino, boutiques, swimming pool, and a fitness club with unparalleled equipment.

Le Louis-XV

Alain Ducasse, pl. du Casino
92 16 30 01 (R), 92 16 30 00 (H),
fax 92 16 69 21

Closed Wed (exc dinner in seas), Tue, 2 wks in Feb, Nov 29-Dec 29. Open until 10:30pm. Priv rm: 60. Terrace dining. Air cond. No pets. Valet pkg. V, AE, DC.

Supremely refined, yet with its roots plunged deep into the Southern terroir, the sublime "country cooking" of Alain Ducasse is visibly at odds with this ostentatious dining room, a backdrop for a flashy, superficial clientele whose gastronomic savvy stretches all the way from caviar to lobster. Though these gilt-edged patrons may not have a clue about the true merits of a cuisine based on the finest produce of farm and field, they hide their perplexity under a torrent of superlatives—after all, Ducasse has been awarded more toques, stars, and kudos than any chef around! With ultimate artistry, he combines the sensual, keen flavors of Provence, Liguria, and Tuscany, with a pinch of Southwestern France, to create delicate dishes that clash almost comically with the heavy-handed extravagance of the setting. And now something that we have long wished for him seems to have come true: he has acquired a lovely seventeenth-century bastide in the idyllic Provençal countryside around Moustiers-Sainte-Marie, where, beginning in the spring of 1995, he plans to offer savory Provençal country cooking at low prices. He is so attached to this new "enfant" that we wonder why he doesn't just go live with him, but he plans to stay put. We can hardly blame him for taking advantage of the golden opportunity that the Louis-XV represents: security, unlimited means, a guaranteed full house, an active cash register... The wine list boasts treasures from every corner of France, not all of them unaffordable! **C** 900-1,500 F. **M** 730 F, 820 F.

Le Louis-XV
(See restaurant above)
Open year-round. 41 stes 5,700-16,000 F. 157 rms 1,500-2,900 F. Air cond. Conf. Heated pool. Tennis. Valet pkg. V, AE, DC.
The last of Europe's really grand hotels has been welcoming the rich and famous since it opened in 1865. Now completely modernized, it has divinely comfortable rooms, luxury shops, a chic bar, and a fine indoor pool.

10/20 Le Pinocchio
30, rue Comte-F.-Gastaldi
93 30 96 20, fax 93 50 77 96
Dinner only in seas. Closed Wed off-seas, Dec 20-Jan 21. Open until 11pm (midnight in summer). Priv rm: 30. Garden dining. Air cond. Pkg. V.
The tiny terrace, near a small square with a well, provides an attractive setting for supping on ravioli with sage or carpaccio with Parmesan. Two short-and-sweet set menus offer a starter and main course. **C** 200-250 F. **M** 110 F, 140 F.

11/20 Polpetta
2, rue Paradis - 93 50 67 84
Closings not available. Open until 11pm. Priv rm: 30. Air cond. V.
The Guasco brothers' simple, Italian-style cooking at reasonable prices is as popular as ever with Monaco's upper crust. **C** 250-350 F. **M** 150 F.

12/20 La Potinière
Av. Princesse-Grace - 93 28 66 43 (R), 93 28 66 66 (H), fax 93 78 14 18
Lunch only. Closed mid Sep-beg Jun. Terrace dining. Heated pool. No pets. Valet pkg. V, AE, DC, MC.
Reliable, professional cooking served in a splendid dining room with sea views. But don't let the splendid panorama make you overlook the sunny, carefully prepared cooking of François Fusero: a salad of sea scallops with strips of vegetables, langoustines with a tarragon sauce and Creole rice, and a gratiné of peaches and wild strawberries with a Muscat sabayon. Too bad the prices are less digestible than the cuisine. **C** 350-500 F.

Monte-Carlo Beach Hotel
(See restaurant above)
Closed Oct 9-beg Apr. 3 stes 3,600-5,500 F. 41 rms 1,650-2,550 F. Rms for disabled. Air cond. Conf. Heated pool. Tennis. Golf. Garage. Valet pkg. V, AE, DC, MC.
Billionaires lurk behind the splendid curved façade of this luxury hotel with its Olympic swimming pool and service reminiscent of a more leisurely age. The magnificently restored rooms all have loggias overlooking the sea. The luncheon buffet—one of the best in Monaco—is served on the "La Vigie" covered terrace which affords glorious sweeping views of the Côte d'Azur.

12/20 Le Saint-Benoît
10 ter, av. de la Costa
93 25 02 34, fax 93 30 52 64
Closed Mon, Dec 19-Jan 9. Open until 10:30pm (11pm in summer). Terrace dining. Air cond. Garage pkg. V, AE, DC, MC.
One of the principality's finest views, and the food is fresh and appealing, prepared with care: warm leek "biscuit", shellfish salad, roast sea bass in a salt crust, and a feuilleté of lobster and veal sweetbreads. **C** 280-450 F. **M** 200 F (lunch exc Sun, wine incl), 160 F, 225 F.

Sans Soucis
42, bd d'Italie - 93 50 14 24
Closed Sun (exc Jul-Aug). Open until 11pm. Terrace dining. V, AE, MC.
Join the many Italians who flock to this convivial bistrot for uncontrived dishes made with luminously fresh ingredients. Frisky Italian wines accompany assorted frittatas, risotto with cèpes, pasta with poutargue (dried roe) and tutti quanti. Jolly, swift service. **C** 250-400 F.

Paris 646 - Avignon 46 - Bollène 6 - Pont-St-Esprit 8 · Vaucluse

La Beaugravière
On N 7 - 90 40 82 54
Closed dinner Sun (& Mon off-seas), Sep 15-30. Open until 9:30pm. Priv rm: 40. Garden dining. Air cond. Pkg. V, AE, MC.
Guy Jullien is widely known for his dishes using Tricastin truffles, but this year his focus is more on Provençal fare: truffle "gâteau" in olive gelatin, eel matelot à l'avignonnaise, and a gooey biscuit au chocolat with mint jelly. Settle into the comfortable 1930s dining room and enjoy it all. The noise of the TGV and the nearby N7 highway won't, we trust, interfere with your pleasure. Happily, the vibrations seem to have no ill effect on the cellar, a treasure trove of rare and ancient Côtes-du-Rhône wines. **C** 290-500 F. **M** 390 F (wine incl), 130 F, 198 F.

→ **Serre-Chevalier**

Paris 613 - Montauban 54 - Agen 40 - Moissac 33 · Tarn/Gar.

■ **In Saint-Beauzeil 82150**   10 km W

12/20 Château de l'Hoste
63 95 25 61, fax 63 95 25 50
Closed Sun dinner & Mon off-seas, Feb 15-Mar 15. Open until 9:30pm (10pm in summer). Priv rm: 15. Terrace dining. V. Hotel: 32 rms 200-250 F. Half-board 270-300 F. Conf. Pool. Pkg.
Sample the 110 F menu served in this little manor house: foie gras, mixed seafood, cheese, dessert. Limited wine list. Friendly welcome and service in a rather austere dining room with stone walls and a high ceiling. **C** 200-310 F. **M** 265 F (summer only), 110 F, 160 F.

MONTARGIS · 45200
Paris 113 - Orléans 71 - Fontainebleau 50 · *Loiret*

La Gloire
74, av. du Gal-de-Gaulle
38 85 04 69, fax 38 98 52 32
*Closed Tue dinner, Wed, Feb school hols, Aug 15-27.
Open until 9:30pm. Air cond. No pets.* **Hotel***: 2 stes.
9 rms 250-700 F. Garage pkg. V, MC.*
Maybe it's not yet on the path to glory, but Jean-Louis Jolly's cooking is getting better and better, and we award him an extra point this year for his 240 F menu: delicious asparagus charlotte, perfectly cooked nage of sea scallops and monkfish seasoned with star anise, tender roast squab with mushrooms, fine cheeses, and an excellent nougat glacé mousse and orange cake for dessert. Friendly welcome and proficient service in a sunny, elegant dining room. C 320-450 F. M 160 F (weekdays, Sat lunch), 200 F, 240 F, 320 F.

■ **In Fontenay-sur-Loing 45210** · 13 km N on N 7

Domaine de Vaugouard
Chemin des Bois
38 95 71 85, fax 38 95 77 47
*Open year-round. 38 rms 360-595 F. Restaurant.
Half-board 385 F. Conf. Heated pool. Tennis. Golf.
No pets. Pkg. Helipad. V, AE, DC, MC.*
Spacious, motel-style rooms that are well equipped and prettily decorated. Facilities include an eighteen-hole golf course, stables, tennis courts, a fitness center, and a sauna.

MONTAUBAN · 82000
Paris 665 - Albi 72 - Cahors 60 - Toulouse 53 · *Tarn/Gar.*

Au Fil de l'Eau
14, quai du Dr-Lafforgue - 63 66 11 85
*Closed Sun dinner, Mon, Jan 17-26, Aug 15-Sep 3.
Open until 9pm. Pkg. V, AE.*
Jean-François Pech is always on his toes, turning out tasty dishes like those on the first set menu: saffrony fish soup, slices of duck breast with raspberries, cheeses, and house pastry. Friendly welcome in an old-fashioned dining room. C 240-330 F. M 110 F, 170 F, 220 F, 270 F.

Hostellerie Les Coulandrières
3 km W on D 958, route de Castelsarrasin,
82290 Montbeton
63 67 47 47, fax 63 67 46 45
*Open daily until 10pm. Priv rm: 300. Terrace dining.
Air cond. Pool. Pkg. V, MC.*
This modern, sunny dining room (renovated this year) offers generous and carefully prepared fare based on top-quality products: poached lobster with a cream sauce flavored with leeks and Sauternes, profiteroles of beef fillet with foie gras, and a chocolate soufflé glacé with just a hint of coffee. Fine cellar with a focus on regional wines; a simple grill operates in summer. C 220-320 F. M 95 F, 125 F, 180 F.

*The **prices** in this guide reflect what establishments were charging at press time.*

Hostellerie Les Coulandrières
(See restaurant above)
Open year-round. 22 rms 290-440 F. Half-board 320-470 F. Air cond. Conf. Pool. No pets. V, MC.
Set in lovely countryside, this hostelry offers pleasant, bright rooms that give onto the garden or a terrace. Bar and lounge.

12/20 Le Ventadour
23, quai Villebourbon - 63 63 34 58
Closed Mon dinner, Sun, Aug 1-16. Open until 10pm. Pkg. V, MC.
Built in the seventeenth century as a dye works, Le Ventadour offers a charming dining room, a friendly *patronne*, and generous regional cooking: egg cassoulet, lobster nage aux deux juliennes, duck breast with foie gras, and a chocolate and Grand Marnier délice for dessert. C 220-320 F. M 85 F, 110 F, 140 F, 180 F, 240 F.

■ **In Brial 82700** · 10 km S on N 20

Jacques Depeyre
RN 20 - 63 23 05 06, fax 63 02 18 18
Closed Sun dinner & Mon (exc hols), Jan 9-Feb 4, Jun 6-14. Open until 9:30pm. Priv rm: 50. Garden dining. Air cond. Garage pkg. V, AE, DC, MC.
The elegant, pale-grey-and-green dining room of Jacques Depeyre's little garden villa is a charming setting for his refined cuisine based on top-quality ingredients. The appealing repertoire is chock-a-block with clever dishes: a salad of pink scorpion fish with avocado, pickerel fillet studded with truffles and paired with a vegetable mirepoix and mushroom jus, half a young rabbit in mustard sauce, strawberry feuilleté en chaud-froid, and a strawberry charlotte. The chef trained with many of France's culinary stars, and it shows. Louisette Depeyre lavishes smiles and kind attentions on her guests, while keeping an eye on the stylish service. C 350-450 F. M 150 F (weekday dinner, Sat, Sun lunch), 135 F (lunch exc Sun), 195 F, 330 F.

MONTBAZON · 37250
Paris 247 - Chinon 41 - Tours 12 - Loches 32 · *Indre/Loire*

La Chancelière
1, pl. des Marronniers - 47 26 00 67
Closed Sun dinner & Mon (exc hols), Feb 13-Mar 6, 1st wk of Sep. Open until 9:30pm. Air cond. Pkg. V.
Three toques to the talented team of Jean-Luc Hatet, Jacques de Pous, and chef Michel Gangneux for top-flight, cooking with a discreet regional flavor served in a redecorated and ever more gorgeously baroque setting. This restaurant is doubtless the best thing going for miles around, and the good people of Touraine clearly know it. Savor Gangneux's succulent oyster ravioli with an intensely flavored jus, memorably luscious sweetbreads with linden-blossom butter sauce and fresh fava beans, and, new on the menu this year, the osso buco of turbot with morels, simply sautéed foie gras, and a saddle of rabbit with caramelized onions in a creamy, mustardy jus. The 330 F "menu-carte" offers a choice of à la carte dishes with only two at a supplementary charge (the lobster main cour-

ses). An intelligent selection of Burgundies and Loire Valley wines complements the food, and there's a special list of half bottles. Delightful, obliging service. The same winning team operates the Le Jeu de Cartes bistrot annex (see below). C 400-450 F. M 330 F.

Château d'Artigny

Route d'Azay-le-Rideau
47 26 24 24, fax 47 65 92 79
Closed Dec 26-Jan 6. Open until 9:30pm. Garden dining. Heated pool. Valet pkg. V, AE, DC, MC.
We may as well tell you: this "eighteenth-century" château seemingly steeped in history is in fact a bit of megalomania built in 1919 by perfumer René Coty. Revived at huge expense by the late René Traversac, the decor is a spectacular—if not always harmonious—jumble of antiques, tapestries, and all the other trappings of Château Life. As you might expect, the menu strikes rich, full chords but it avoids the heaviness that often marks this genre. This year chef Francis Maignaut has come up with elegant, pleasing dishes like the superb Loches lamb simply roasted and accompanied by its roasting juices and grilled leek confit, and, in a luscious marriage of rustic and noble, slices of ratte potatoes and Touraine truffles in shallot vinegar. For dessert, try the tasty coconut ice cream with sliced mango, bitter orange sauce, and little disks of chocolate. The château's stunning cellar is one of the finest in France (the wine list is seventy pages long!). Distinguished welcome and service. C 350-450 F. M 250 F (lunch exc Sun, wine incl), 280 F, 440 F.

Château d'Artigny 🌲🍴

(See restaurant above)
Closed Nov 26-Jan 6. 2 stes 2,520-3,150 F. 51 rms 600-1,575 F. Rms for disabled. Half-board 680-1,220 F. Air cond. Conf. Heated pool. Tennis. Golf. Valet pkg. Helipad. V, AE, DC, MC.
An immense terrace overlooking the River Indre, vast landscaped grounds, and formal French gardens unrolling to the horizon: such is the magnificent setting for the Château d'Artigny's luxuriously appointed, over-decorated rooms and suites. Exercise room; golf; musical weekends. Relais et Châteaux.

Domaine de la Tortinière

2 km N on N 10 & D 287, Les Gués de Veigné - 47 26 00 19, fax 47 65 95 70
Closed Dec 20-Feb. Heated pool. No pets. Pkg. V, MC.
It looks like a Renaissance château, but in fact this imposing structure dates only from the Second Empire. Édouard Wehrlin's proficient cuisine is of a classic cast but some dishes do draw inspiration from the region's *terroir*. We prefer his simple preparations like warm foie gras flavored with vanilla and balsamic vinegar, roast pickerel with bacon and meat jus, and a warm chocolate soufflé with coffee sauce. Fine selection of Loire wines. The dining rooms with classic decor are preferable to the aging Orangerie. C 300-400 F. M 195 F (lunch, wine incl), 265 F, 350 F.

Domaine de la Tortinière 🌲🍴

(See restaurant above)
Closed Dec 20-Feb. 6 stes 990-1,340 F. 15 rms 435-830 F. Rms for disabled. Half-board 540-875 F. Heated pool. Tennis. Golf. No pets. Pkg. Helipad. V, MC.

Set down in wooded grounds, here is a luxurious stopover with impeccably equipped and decorated rooms (the ones in the separate pavilions have been recently renovated), a heated pool, and tennis courts. Some rooms are equipped with Jacuzzis; all have good bathrooms.

Le Jeu de Cartes

1, pl. des Marronniers
47 26 00 67, fax 47 73 14 82
Closed Sun dinner & Mon (exc hols), Feb 13-Mar 6, 1st wk of Sep. Open until 10pm. Air cond. Pkg. V.
The bistrot operated by the owners and chef of La Chancelière (see above) adjoins the main restaurant and has a pleasing contemporary garden decor. The locals flock here to savor well prepared traditional dishes at welcoming prices: perfectly caramelized spiced chicken wings, red mullet en papillote with bacon paired with tender mashed potatoes, chocolate tart with a delicate crust, and vanilla-caramel ice cream. Well chosen little cellar. Stylish welcome and service. M 150 F, 200 F.

MONTCHENOT 51 → Reims

MONT-DE-MARSAN 40000

Paris 686 - Bordeaux 123 - Bayonne 97 - Tarbes 100   *Landes*

Le Renaissance

Route de Villeneuve
58 51 51 51, fax 58 75 29 07
Closed Sat lunch. Open until 10pm. Priv rm: 100. Garden dining. Pool. Pkg. V, AE, MC.
Here's a most romantic setting for a restaurant: a neoclassic manor surrounded by landscaped grounds, where animals and exotic birds roam free. The young chef's regional *terroir* cooking is deft indeed. Try the 145 F menu, with an amusing and tasty "millaci" (crêpe stuffed with Roquefort and ham), generous and perfectly cooked duck breast with tiny peas, and unctuous vanilla crème brûlée. The dining room's decor is pleasant and contemporary, the service efficient, and the wine list has some appealing Bordeaux. C 240-330 F. M 110 F (weekdays), 145 F, 190 F, 250 F.

Le Renaissance

(See restaurant above)
Open year-round. 1 ste 550 F. 28 rms 250-420 F. Rms for disabled. Half-board 300-350 F. Conf. Pool. Golf. Pkg. V, AE, MC.
Huge, pleasant rooms with modern appointments and good equipment. There's a pond in the huge garden.

See also: Eugénie-les-Bains

MONT-DORE (LE) 63240

Paris 436 - Clermont-Ferrand 47 - Aubusson 90   *Puy-de-Dôme*

Le Puy Ferrand 🌲🍴

4 km S on D 983, Pied puy de Sancy
73 65 18 99, fax 73 65 28 38
Closed Mar 27-Apr 7, Oct 9-Dec 22. 1 ste 350-470 F. 37 rms 200-350 F. Restaurant. Half-board 235-320 F. Conf. Pool. Golf. Pkg. V, AE, DC, MC.
This quiet hotel facing the mountains is popular among hikers and other sporting types.

It offers simple, sunny rooms, along with some boutiques and a sauna.

MONTE-CARLO → **Monaco (Principality of)**

MONTÉLIMAR **26200**

Paris 604 - Valence 46 - Marseille 182 - Lyon 145 *Drôme*

 ### Relais de l'Empereur
1, pl. M.-Dormoy
75 01 29 00, fax 75 01 32 21

Closed Nov 11-Dec 22. Open until 9:30pm. Priv rm: 40. Terrace dining. Garage pkg. V, AE, DC, MC.

The old-fashioned dining room—decorated with venerable engravings and knickknacks—seems stuck in a Napoleonic time warp, but the skillful cooking is up-to-date. Worth ordering are the brouillade à la truffe, lobster cassolette, squab vigneronne, parsleyed lamb, parfait glacé nougatine, and a fine choice of regional wines. **C** 370-450 F. **M** 160 F (weekdays, wine incl), 178 F, 210 F, 380 F.

Relais de l'Empereur
(See restaurant above)

Closed Nov 11-Dec 20. 2 stes 570-700 F. 38 rms 410-565 F. Half-board 268-298 F. Conf. Garage pkg. V, AE, DC, MC.

The Emperor Napoléon did indeed spend the night here, in the middle of Montélimar, on 24 April 1814. Rather spacious, well-kept rooms. Porter; bar.

MONTEUX 84 → **Carpentras**

MONTFAVET 84 → **Avignon**

MONTFORT-L'AMAURY **78490**

Paris 50 - Mantes 35 - Rambouillet 19 - Versailles 27 *Yvelines*

■ **In Les Mesnuls 78490** *4 km SE*

La Toque Blanche
12, Grande-Rue - 34 86 05 55

Closed Sun dinner, Mon, Dec 24-30, Aug 10-28. Open until 10pm. Priv rm: 40. Garden dining. Pkg. V, AE, DC, MC.

Jean-Pierre Philippe, a sturdy Breton, favors lighter versions of classic cuisine. He imports excellent seafood from his native province but doesn't neglect dishes to please landlubbers, and all his offerings are meticulously prepared: langoustine croustillant, fillet of John Dory with fried parsley, calf's head with six sauces. Attentive welcome and pricey wine list. **C** 380-480 F. **M** 360 F.

MONTGRÉSIN 60 → **Chantilly**

MONTHAIRONS (LES) 55 → **Verdun**

MONTIGNAC **24290**

Paris 496 - Brive 38 - Sarlat 25 - Limoges 102 *Dordogne*

Château de Puy-Robert
1.5 km S on D 65
53 51 92 13, fax 53 51 80 11

Closed Wed lunch, mid Oct-beg May. Open until 9:30pm. Valet pkg. V, AE, DC, MC.

Tourists who come to admire the caves at Lascaux can recover from their emotion in this Second Empire dining room. The new chef, Olivier Pons, offers dishes that are neither too refined nor ordinary, influenced by regional tradition but sparked with personality: croustillant of rabbit fillet with herbs, perch with potatoes and a cèpe fumet, coffee parfait, and toasted honey cake with chicory sauce. **C** 350-450 F. **M** 180 F (lunch), 280 F, 360 F.

Château de Puy-Robert
(See restaurant above)

Closed mid Oct-beg May. 5 stes 1,180-1,570 F. 33 rms 600-970 F. Half-board 700-980 F. Air cond. Conf. Pool. Valet pkg. V, AE, DC, MC.

A quiet, woodland setting only a few minutes from Lascaux and its renowned cave paintings. The comfortable rooms are divided between the château itself and an attractive annex.

MONTLOUIS-SUR-LOIRE 37 → **Tours**

MONTLUÇON **03100**

Paris 320 - Bourges 93 - Lyon 227 - Limoges 154 *Allier*

Château Saint-Jean
Domaine du Château, Parc St-Jean
70 05 04 65, fax 70 05 97 75

Open year-round. 5 stes 600-1,000 F. 15 rms 350-480 F. Restaurant. Half-board 500-600 F. Conf. Heated pool. Golf. Pkg. V, AE, DC, MC.

This former commandery of the Knights Hospitallers is set in grounds planted with century-old trees. Elegant decor.

12/20 ### Aux Ducs de Bourbon
Pl. de la Gare
70 05 22 79, fax 70 05 16 92

Closed Sun dinner, Mon. Open until 10pm. Priv rm: 40. Air cond. Pkg. V, AE, DC, MC.

The conservative but generously served repertoire is served in the cozy modern dining room: éventail of asparagus with three types of smoked fish, sea scallop millefeuille, perch fillet meunière, and duck breast tournedos. **C** 200-320 F. **M** 110 F, 146 F, 187 F.

Le Grenier à Sel
Pl. des Toiles, 8, rue Sainte-Anne
70 05 53 79, fax 70 05 87 91

Closed Mon (exc Jul-Aug), 10 days beg Jan. Open until 10pm. Priv rm: 20. Terrace dining. Pkg. V, AE, DC, MC.

A manor house with a lovely garden and courtyard, converted into an elegant restaurant with pretty old-fashioned table settings. Jacky Morlon's cooking is part of the appeal, and the first set menu is a real bargain: excellent cod rissoles, tender and savory mitonné of beef cheeks, a rather scanty serving of Chambérat (a local cheese) and a fine pot de chocolat. **C** 320-370 F. **M** 120 F, 160 F, 240 F, 340 F.

Le Grenier à Sel
(See restaurant above)

Open year-round. 4 rms 350-500 F. No pets. V, AE, DC, MC.

The pleasant rooms of this beautiful manor house have parquet floors, fireplaces, and large beds. The welcome is warm, and the breakfasts excellent.

MONTMEYRAN 26 → Valence

MONTMORENCY 95 → PARIS Suburbs

MONTPELLIER 34000
Paris 760 - Marseille 164 - Perpignan 161 - Nîmes 51   Hérault

 ### Le Chandelier
3, rue Leenhardt - 67 92 61 62
Closed Mon lunch, Sun. Open until 10pm. Air cond. V, AE, DC.
Gilbert Furlan's cooking is fueled by a constant quest for new taste sensations. Luckily, the experiments are backed up by a sound technique that ensures balance and harmony. His creative 250 F menu offers émincé of young rabbit in spicy oil, a reduced nage of plump shrimp in a black tea emulsion, saddle of lamb in an anise-scented crust, a cheese selection, and dessert. Very well chosen cellar. Neoclassic decor provides a serene atmosphere, punctuated by the splash of a tiny fountain, but Furlan is planning to move to new quarters in the autumn of 1995; the neighborhood here is not the most picturesque. **C** 320-450 F. **M** 140 F (lunch), 250 F, 290 F, 360 F.

La Closerie
3, rue du Clos-René
67 58 11 22, fax 67 92 13 02
Closed Sat, Sun. Open until 10pm. Priv rm: 80. Garden dining. Air cond. Valet pkg. V, AE, DC, MC.
Under the direction of chef Charles Semeria, this elegant villa with a dining room overlooking a garden became the city's best culinary deal. But he has left, and we will give the new chef time to settle in before rating his salmon marinated with fines herbes, millefeuille of veal in a crust with black-olive tapenade, and terrine of crêpes glacées à la réglisse. **C** 200-300 F. **M** 98 F, 145 F (weekdays).

Alliance Metropole
(See restaurant above)
Open year-round. 4 stes 740-940 F. 77 rms 430-580 F. Half-board 440 F. Air cond. Conf. Valet pkg. V, AE, DC, MC.
Thoroughly modernized, this hotel near the pedestrian precinct has retained a certain olde-worlde charm. Quiet, pleasant garden.

Demeure des Brousses 🌲🍴
Route de Vauguières
67 65 77 66, fax 67 22 22 17
Open year-round. 17 rms 380-580 F. Restaurant. Half-board 580-780 F. Golf. Pkg. V, AE, DC, MC.
You wouldn't expect to stumble upon this lovely eighteenth-century farmhouse, set in an oasis of exotic trees and vines, right on the edge of town. Handsomely furnished rooms. Rather haughty reception.

12/20 Isadora
6, rue du Petit-Scel
67 66 25 23, fax 67 66 25 23
Closed Sat lunch, Sun. Open until 10pm. Priv rm: 15. Terrace dining. Air cond. V, AE, DC, MC.
Enjoy honest, well-presented food in Isadora's cozy little vaulted dining room, or on the new terrace facing Sainte-Anne's church. On the menu you'll find fresh crab with grapefruit, sautéed red mullet and artichokes with a tomato

cream, and a delicate although rather bland chestnut charlotte. Warm welcome; rather awkward service. **C** 220-320 F. **M** 80 F (weekday lunch), 120 F, 250 F.

Le Jardin des Sens 🕄
11, av. St-Lazare
67 79 63 38, fax 67 72 13 05
Closed Sun, Jan 2-13, Jul 25-Aug 15. Open until 10pm. Priv rm: 45. Garden dining. Air cond. V, AE.
At first, the food lovers of Montpellier didn't quite know how to react to Jacques and Laurent Pourcel's cuisine, a style characterized by surprising combinations of tastes, contrasting textures, and highly evolved sauces. They found the restaurant's austere, stripped-down decor a bit off-putting too. But today, the Pourcel twins number among the foremost chefs of the Midi, and even if the contemporary dining room doesn't suit your tastes, you can always enjoy the view of a pretty garden crossed by a burbling brook. Trained in the kitchens of Michel Bras, Michel Trama, Marc Meneau, and Pierre Gagnaire, the Pourcels' technique is impeccably sharp and precise—but the spotlight is never trained on their "virtuosity". No, the Pourcels use their skill to show off the natural savors of Languedoc's finest foodstuffs, and if they ever slip, it's because they've tried something a bit too complex.
Recent examples of the twins' prowess were an extraordinary dried-fruit risotto served with sautéed sot-l'y-laisse and langoustines in a truffled poultry jus, and a sublime fillet of monkfish (cooked for a long time at a very low temperature) adorned with salmon marinière and oysters (the latter were unnecessary, we thought). Other tasty choices on the lengthy menu are foie gras in a Banyuls syrup, a fricassée of langoustines with crisp bacon and lamb sweetbreads, turbot sautéed with squid, and casserole-roasted squab with a fricassée of spelt, morels, and buttered pears. One disappointment was the bland Australian crayfish, but they were served with an exquisite fricassée of fava beans flavored with mint. The desserts are out of this world (ah, that warm gaufre with wild strawberries, apricot compote, and pumpkin seeds!) and it's a joy to let Olivier Chateau guide you through the wide choice of fine Languedoc wines from the cellar (like the superb Saint-Louis 1992 chardonnay, classified a vin de pays) and great Bordeaux that will make a dint in your budget. The prices are, overall, very reasonable, and the lunch menu is a gift. Guest rooms are in the works, we hear. **C** 360-500 F. **M** 165 F (weekday lunch), 270 F, 430 F.

 ### Le Mas
Demeure des Brousses, route de Vauguières - 67 65 52 27, fax 67 65 21 93
Closed Sun dinner, Mon, 2 wks in Jan. Open until 10pm. Priv rm: 30. Garden dining. Pkg. V, AE, DC.
An eighteenth-century farmhouse has been transformed to create a dining room that overlooks an attractive garden. Michel Loustau earns our approval for his skillful use of regional ingredients, in dishes like crab fondant and delicate slices of salmon with caviar, aiguillette of turbot with a concassé of shellfish and tomatoes, dark chocolate truffles, and Muscat sabayon. **C** 360-430 F. **M** 200 F, 260 F, 380 F.

New Hotel du Midi

22, bd Victor-Hugo
67 92 69 61, fax 67 92 73 63
Open year-round. 47 rms 340-350 F. Air cond. Conf. V, AE, DC, MC.
A pretty hotel in the center of town, housed in a remodeled nineteenth-century building. Stylish, spacious, well equipped rooms.

L'Olivier

14

12, rue A.-Ollivier - 67 92 86 28
Closed Sun, Mon, Dec 24-Jan 2, Aug 15-31. Open until 9:30pm. Air cond. No pets. V, AE, DC.
The pink-and-cream decor is a bit hard to digest. Not so chef Michel Breton's stunningly flavorful, personalized versions of classic bourgeois dishes: a "gâteau" of farm-raised rabbit with aromatic herbs, fillet of oven-baked turbot with Bouziges clams in a savarin, and nougatine glacée with a warm rissole of fresh figs. Well-chosen Burgundies and Corbières wines; pleasant welcome. **C** 300-400 F. **M** 145 F, 185 F.

Pullman Antigone

Rue Pertuisannes
67 65 62 63, fax 67 65 17 50
Open year-round. 1 ste 1,400 F. 88 rms 595-795 F. Rms for disabled. Air cond. Conf. Pool. Valet pkg. V, AE, DC, MC.
This hotel in the heart of Montpellier's business district offers a wide range of services. Attractive, well-equipped rooms. Zealous staff. The "Privilège" floor offers rooms with marble bathrooms. It's a fifteen-minute walk to the center of town.

Sofitel

Le Triangle, allée J.-Milhau
67 58 45 45, fax 67 58 77 50
Open year-round. 2 stes 750-950 F. 96 rms 400-500 F. Restaurant. Air cond. Pkg. V, AE, DC, MC.
Around one hundred comfortable, well equipped rooms are available in this modern building near the Place de la Comédie. One floor is reserved for non-smokers. Hearty breakfasts; meals served in the rooms.

And also...

Our selection of places for inexpensive, quick, or late-night meals.
L'Aromate (67 66 06 27 - 8, rue Puits-des-Esquilles. Open until 10:30pm.): Young, convivial atmosphere and Italian cooking in a recently renovated former stables. Try the excellent beef carpaccio, tortellini al pesto, or tiramisu (120-190 F).
Brasserie Saint-Germain (67 22 27 98 - Esplanade de l'Europe. Open until 11:30pm.): Paris-style brasserie (so say the locals) overlooking the water, where excellent plats du jour and meats grilled over an open fire are winning fare (100-150 F).
Fazenda do Brasil (67 92 90 91 - 5, rue École-de-Droit. Open until 11:30pm.): South American wines and dishes such as churrasco, comprising meat, bananas, red kidney beans, and fries. Salads available for smaller appetites (155 F).
Les Fines Gueules (67 64 67 67 - Centre Commercial Polygone, allée Jules-Mily. Lunch only.): In the Polygone shopping center, this bistrot offers nice traditional main courses as well as homemade desserts (150-180 F).

Chez Marceau (67 66 08 09 - 7, pl. Chapelle-Neuve. Open until 10:30pm, 11:30pm in summer.): You can enjoy sturdy cuisine (rumpsteak, smoked trout) and ultrafresh fish in the comfortable dining room or outside on the pleasant terrace (110-150 F).
Tire-Bouchon (67 66 26 50 - 2, pl. Jean-Jaurès. Open until 11:30pm.): A trendy bistrot with a friendly atmosphere on the town's liveliest square; a varied range of dishes at reasonable prices (120-150 F).
Les Vignes (67 66 01 39 - 2, rue Bonnier-d'Alco. Open until 11pm.): Sample generous traditional fare in a restaurant shaded by plane trees near the flower market (69 F, 200 F).

■ In Lattes 34970
5 km S

Mas de Couran

Route de Fréjorgues
67 65 57 57, fax 67 65 37 56
Open year-round. 2 stes 525 F. 16 rms 300-420 F. Restaurant. Half-board 515 F. Conf. Pool. Golf. Pkg. V, AE, DC, MC.
A nineteenth-century manor house, renovated in perfect taste. Extensive grounds, charming accommodation. The industrial park is close by, but you would never suspect it, although you will here the passing traffic. Remarkable welcome and service; there's a swimming pool.

Le Mazerand

13

CD 172, route de Fréjorgues
67 64 82 10, fax 67 20 10 73
Closed Sat lunch, Mon. Open until 9:30pm. Priv rm: 55. Garden dining. Air cond. Pkg. V, AE, DC.
Jacques Mazerand's cuisine features regional offerings that change with the seasons, served in a lovely dining room with a terrace overlooking a large garden. Sample the "all mushroom" menu: a mushroom terrine, intensely flavored fricassée of wild mushrooms, roast saddle of hare (a tad overcooked) with a minipâte of cèpes, a delicious wild mushroom galette, and a tasty chestnut tart with vanilla ice cream. Fine choice of regional wines; friendly welcome. **C** 270-400 F. **M** 165 F, 200 F, 230 F, 310 F.

Paris 531 - Bergerac 42 - Ste-Foy-la-Grande 23
Dordogne

Auberge de l'Éclade

14

2 km N on D 730 - 53 80 28 64
Closed Tue dinner, Wed, and Feb-beg Mar, Sep 27-Oct 15. Open until 9:30pm. Priv rm: 45. Terrace dining. Air cond. Pkg. V, MC.
In this simple, rustic setting between Bordeaux and Périgueux, you can enjoy a feast at a most delectable price. Christian Martin's skillful cooking draws inspiration from the regional repertoire. Try his first set menu: croustillant of scrambled eggs with smoked ham and cèpes, young rabbit in mustard sauce, cheese and salad with walnuts, and dessert. **C** 190-250 F. **M** 70 F (weekday lunch, Sat), 110 F, 150 F, 210 F.

Château des Grillauds

Route de Coutras
53 80 49 71, fax 53 81 32 63
Closings not available. 7 rms 270-305 F. Restaurant. Half-board 340-390 F. Conf. Tennis. Pkg. V.

The rooms are bright and spacious, furnished in a modern style. Well-equipped bathrooms; bucolic views.

MONTREUIL 28 → Dreux

MONTREUIL-SUR-MER 62170
Paris 204 - Le Touquet 23 - Boulogne 37 - Lille 114   P./Calais

Château de Montreuil ⚫
4, chaussée des Capucins
21 81 53 04, fax 21 81 36 43
Closed Mon off-seas & Thu lunch (exc hols), Dec 11-Feb 3. Open until 9:30pm. Priv rm: 20. Garden dining. Valet pkg. V, AE, DC.
"Château" is a big word to describe this handsome manor house attractively situated near the town ramparts. Call it what you may, the decor of white-painted beams and pillars setting off bright, old-fashioned blues and yellows, is appealing indeed. Chef Christian Germain produces refined yet lively cooking with intense flavor using top-quality local ingredients: warm duck foie gras with red cabbage and cherries; monkfish tournedos with bacon, beef marrow, and red butter sauce; and a coconut and banana crème brûlée. Fine choice of Burgundies; perfect welcome. C 450-550 F. M 270 F (lunch, wine incl), 200 F (lunch), 300 F (dinner), 400 F.

Château de Montreuil ▲●
(See restaurant above)
Closed Mon off-seas, Dec 13-Feb 4. 1 ste 950-1,200 F. 13 rms 730-880 F. Half-board 800-1,090 F. Conf. Valet pkg. V, AE, DC.
The spacious, comfortable rooms have well-equipped bathrooms and views of the English-style garden much appreciated by visitors from across the Channel. Courteous service. Relais et Châteaux.

MONTREVEL-EN-BRESSE 01340
Paris 402 - Mâcon 26 - Bourg 17 - Tournus 36   Ain

Léa ⚫
74 30 80 84, fax 74 30 85 66
Closed Sun dinner, Wed, Dec 23-Jan 2, Jul. Open until 9pm. V, MC.
Lyons' top chefs come to the area for the December capon market drop by to savor the delicious cooking—available all year round, needless to say. We heartily recommend the marvelous Bressane set menu featuring regional specialties (chicken-liver terrine, frog's legs, poulet à la crème) and à la carte offerings like lobster roasted with cabbage. For a less pricey alternative, try the Comptoir annex in the style of a Lyonnais "bouchon", where you can sample regional dishes and wines by the "pot" (carafe) for around 100 F. Everyone is very happy here. C 350-400 F. M 150 F, 250 F, 320 F.

MONTRICHARD 41400
Paris 204 - Tours 44 - Blois 32 - Loches 31   Loir/Cher

12/20 Château de la Menaudière
Route d'Amboise
54 32 02 44, fax 54 71 34 58
Closed Sun dinner & Mon off-seas, Dec-Feb. Open until 9:30pm. Terrace dining. Pkg. V, AE, DC, MC.
The understated charm of this fine Renaissance château, swaddled in a verdant setting, is the setting for traditional dishes like warm salad of sea scallops and mushrooms, fillet of turbot with truffle sabayon, casserole-roasted stuffed saddle of rabbit, and a gratin of citrus fruits spiked with Muscat. C 300-400 F. M 160 F (weekday lunch), 190 F, 285 F.

Château de la Menaudière ▲●
(See restaurant above)
Closed Dec-Feb. 25 rms 360-670 F. Half-board 540-750 F. Air cond. Tennis. Pkg. Helipad. V, AE, DC, MC.
This handsome sixteenth- and eighteenth-century château boasts classically decorated, comfortable if faded rooms with views of the surrounding countryside or a pretty inner courtyard with a fountain. Warm welcome.

■ In Chissay-en-Touraine 41400   4 km W on N 76

Château de Chissay
54 32 32 01, fax 54 32 43 80
Closed Nov 15-Mar 15. Open until 9:30pm. Priv rm: 40. Terrace dining. Pool. No pets. Pkg. V, AE, DC.
The vaulted Gothic dining room and handsome Renaissance furniture make an elegant setting for the carefully prepared dishes on the 160 F menu: fresh and generous salade périgourdine with beans and pine nuts, slightly oversalted seafood panaché with basil cream sauce, nice cheese selection, and a yummy amandine of spiced, honey-roasted pears. Courteous welcome; competent service. But how could they offer only shippers' wines here in the heart of Touraine wine country? C 350-450 F. M 160 F, 210 F, 295 F.

Château de Chissay ▲●
(See restaurant above)
Closed Nov 15-Mar 15. 8 stes 920-1,600 F. 23 rms 450-1,000 F. Half-board 560-995 F. Conf. Heated pool. Pkg. V, AE, DC, MC.
A château erected in the twelfth and fifteenth centuries, set among wooded grounds and gardens. The rooms, luxuriously decorated, have eighteenth-century furniture and mosaic tile bathrooms (but no televisions). The lounges and other public rooms are simply magnificent, and the welcome and service are very attentive.

MONTROND-LES-BAINS 42210
Paris 441 - St-Etienne 28 - Lyon 68 - Montbrison 14   Loire

Hostellerie La Poularde
2, rue de St-Étienne
77 54 40 06, fax 77 54 53 14
Closed Tue lunch & Mon (exc hols), Jan 2-15. Open until 10pm. Air cond. Pkg. V, AE, DC, MC.
As ever, the polished luxury of fine silverware and waxed woodwork permeates the atmosphere of this belle province institution, patronized assiduously by the region's gourmets. Gilles Etéocle's superbly crafted cooking, based on the very best ingredients available, has one flaw: it doesn't seem to evolve. So we've decided to drop the rating by a point this year, although the restaurant is still a model of the "two-toque" provincial establishment that keeps the spirit of fine cooking alive and well in this country. Sample the rich, classic dishes like foie gras in pot-au-feu gelatin, tender casserole-roasted Forez squab with lentils, mitonnée of

veal sweetbreads and amourettes, magnificent cheeses, and satisfying traditional desserts. The superb cellar is ruled by a young sommelier whose passion for his job is communicative. Excellent first set menu. The service could be swifter, but then you shouldn't come to a place like this if you're in a hurry. **C** 400-600 F. **M** 200 F (exc Sat dinner, Sun lunch), 270 F, 400 F, 470 F, 530 F.

Hostellerie La Poularde
(See restaurant above)
Closed Mon, Jan 2-15. 3 stes 600-800 F. 11 rms 310-500 F. Air cond. Conf. Valet pkg. V, AE, DC, MC.
The cozy, restful rooms (some are freshly redecorated) have good soundproofing and the suites overlook a revamped courtyard and hedges of lavender. Remarkable breakfasts, with wonderful brioches and jam. Relais et Châteaux.

MONT-SAINT-MICHEL (LE) 50116
Paris 323 - Rennes 66 - St-Malo 52 - Fougères 47   *Manche*

Mercure Mont-Saint-Michel
33 60 14 18, fax 33 60 39 28
Closed Nov-Dec, Jan-mid Feb. 100 rms 350-560 F. Rms for disabled. Restaurant. Half-board 310-470 F. Conf. No pets. Garage pkg. V, AE, MC.
Modern, functional hotel on the road to Mont-Saint-Michel. The bright, spacious, very well equipped rooms look out on to trees.

La Mère Poulard
14
33 60 14 01, fax 33 48 52 31
Open daily until 10pm. Garage pkg. V, AE, DC, MC.
Thierry Quilfen and his team preside over this world-renowned establishment, where the prices are getting more down to earth and the cooking is winning raves from the locals and visitors alike, and an extra point from us this year. Quilfen's creations include John Dory steamed over seaweed with truffle essence (savory but a trifle complicated), superbly simple lamb fillets, and a flaky pineapple pithiviers. Small, affordable cellar. Charming welcome, dedicated service. **C** 350-500 F. **M** 180 F, 275 F, 295 F, 350 F (tasting menu).

La Mère Poulard
(See restaurant above)
Open year-round. 1 ste 1,000-1,600 F. 26 rms 400-950 F. Half-board 570-790 F. Conf. Garage pkg. Helipad. V, AE, DC, MC.
The comfortable, contemporary rooms offer views over the bay and salt meadows.

11/20 Saint-Pierre
Grande-Rue - 33 60 14 03
Closed Dec 15-Feb 2. Open until 10pm. Garden dining. Hotel: 2 stes 790-970 F. 21 rms 490-880 F. Half-board 395-650 F. Conf. Golf. V, AE, MC.
A listed fifteenth-century building beneath the ramparts that offers good, fresh shellfish and fish, brasserie-style food, and appealing set menus. Folkloric entertainment. **C** 135-260 F. **M** 85 F, 105 F, 135 F, 245 F.

Les Terrasses Poulard
Rue Principale
33 60 14 09, fax 33 60 37 31
Open year-round. 29 rms 200-950 F. Restaurant. Half-board 325-490 F. Conf. Helipad. V, AE, DC, MC.

Of recent vintage, this hotel fits admirably into its historic setting, a fair step away from the restaurant. The elegant, cheerful rooms are on the small side, but afford views of the sea or the town. Excellent service.

MORIÈRES-LÈS-AVIGNON 84 → Avignon

MORIGNY 91 → Etampes

MORLAIX 29210
Paris 532 - Brest 60 - St-Brieuc 84 - Quimper 83   *Finistère*

L'Europe
15
1, rue d'Aiguillon
98 62 11 99, fax 98 88 83 38
Open until 9:30pm. Pkg. V, AE, DC, MC.
Olivier Brignou's cooking never fails to respect the quality of his fine products, and he succeeds in creating direct, uncontrived flavors in dishes like tiny stuffed scallops in anise butter, veal sweetbreads in a crust with mushrooms and foie gras, and for dessert, a grapefruit millefeuille with lime sherbet. Exceptional wine list; friendly service. Try to overlook the audacious halogene lighting in the high ceiling. **C** 310-410 F. **M** 115 F, 165 F, 225 F.

L'Europe
(See restaurant above)
Open year-round. 3 stes 500-655 F. 57 rms 210-365 F. Half-board 270-380 F. Pkg. V, AE, DC, MC.
Fairly spacious, well modernized rooms in this town-center hotel.

See also: **Plounérin**

MORNAC-SUR-SEUDRE 17113
Paris 504 - Royan 13 - Saintes 37 - Rochefort 36   *Charente-M.*

12/20 La Colombière
On the harbor - 46 22 62 22
Closed Mon dinner, Tue (exc Jul-Aug), Nov 14-Dec 13. Open until 9:30pm. Priv rm: 40. Pkg. V, MC.
With good reason, Mornac belongs to the charm-village association known as *les plus beaux villages de France.* This warm and welcoming inn is decorated with pretty watercolors painted by the owner-chef, whose fish dishes are palatable indeed, though the quality can be a bit uneven: bland morels stuffed with an overly powerful crab mousse, fresh and perfectly cooked cod with cabbage, and a very good lamb navarin with baby vegetables. Very attentive welcome and service. **C** 250-300 F. **M** 95 F, 140 F, 230 F.

La Gratienne
Route de Breuillet - 46 22 73 90
Closed Tue & Wed (exc Jul-Aug), Oct-Easter. Open until 10pm. Priv rm: 25. Terrace dining. Pkg. V, MC.
This charming former farmhouse in a garden setting is just about to change hands, so we'll reserve our rating until a new team settles in. **C** 230-300 F. **M** 110 F (lunch exc Sun, wine incl), 130 F, 190 F.

Restaurant names in red draw attention to restaurants that offer particularly good value.

Hôtel de Mornac
21, rue des Halles
46 22 63 20, fax 46 22 66 22
Closed Oct-Mar. 9 rms 250-340 F. Half-board 100-190 F. Conf. Golf. Pkg. Helipad. V, MC.
Opposite the town hall and a stone's throw from the harbor, this pleasantly bourgeois hotel's simple but rather spacious rooms are well kept and equipped with spotlessly clean bathrooms. Conservatory.

MORTAGNE-SUR-SÈVRE	85290
Paris 358 - Bressuire 40 - Nantes 56	Vendée

La Taverne
4, pl. du Dr-Pichat
51 65 03 37, fax 51 65 27 83
Closed Sat (exc Jul-Aug), Jul 27-Aug 12. Open until 9:30pm. Priv rm: 45. Terrace dining. Air cond. Heated pool. Pkg. V, AE, DC, MC.
This Vendée *auberge* overlooking a lovely garden has long been known for its soothing, old-fashioned atmosphere. It's the right setting for chef Guy Jagueneau, now seconded by Bertrand Chusseau, who favors generous traditional cooking with a few modern touches: ravioli stuffed with lobster and caviar in a cream sauce sparked with vanilla, steamed leg of baby milk-fed lamb with mogettes (a local variety of white beans), and a white-peach granité in a rosemary infusion. Attentive welcome. The wine list features some fine Bordeaux and Burgundies.
C 270-430 F. M 150 F, 230 F, 310 F.

Hôtel de France
(See restaurant above)
Open year-round. 1 ste 320-480 F. 24 rms 210-380 F. Half-board 350-480 F. Air cond. Conf. Heated pool. Pkg. V, AE, DC, MC.
Spacious, nicely furnished rooms, some with inadequate bathrooms. The most appealing and peaceful have balconies overlooking greenery. Videos; sauna; generous buffet breakfast.

MORZINE	74110
Paris 602 - Lyon 230 - Chamonix 71 - Evian 42	H.-Savoie

La Bergerie
50 79 13 69, fax 50 75 95 71
Closed Apr 15-Jun 25, Sep 10-Dec 20. 5 stes 650-1,100 F. 23 rms 350-700 F. Restaurant. Conf. Heated pool. Golf. Pkg. V, MC.
Most of the well-designed rooms and suites have a kitchenette and nearly all have a terrace or balcony. Pleasant reception and service in a restful, relaxed atmosphere. There's also a sauna, gym, and games room.

Le Carlina
Av. de Joux-Plane
50 79 01 03, fax 50 75 94 11
Closed Nov 3-Dec 10, May 10-Jun 15. 1 ste 550-700 F. 17 rms 250-480 F. Restaurant. Half-board 300-460 F. Conf. Pkg. V, MC.
This renovated chalet at the foot of the Pleney ski runs has spacious yet cozy rooms. Cocktail bar.

La Chamade
50 79 13 91
Closed Tue, Wed, Apr 15-Jun 30, Sep 15-Dec 15. Open until 9pm. Terrace dining. Air cond. Pkg. V, AE, DC, MC.

Thierry Thorens has to offer a wide choice if he's to survive in this seasonal resort. Hence the casual ground-floor dining room where you can sample pizzas, crêpes, and plats-du-jour; the bacon soup simmering in a bubbling cauldron in front of the restaurant to restore skiers at the end of a day on the slopes; and the "gastronomic" dining room upstairs. The decor is basically clean-lined and rustic, but with some touches that verge on the precious (ducks made out of sugar). But on your plate you'll find ample evidence of sure technique: a salad of boeuf mironton combined with sesame, coriander, beets, and langoustines; shellfish soup; casserole-roasted sea scallops and pickerel; and perfect apple, coconut, and raspberry sherbets. The "terroir" menu at 98 F (wine included) is a great deal. *C 280-350 F. M 98 F, 210 F, 360 F.*

Les Côtes
50 79 09 96, fax 50 75 97 38
Closed Apr 18-Jun 30, Sep 4-Dec 20. 19 stes 295-580 F. 6 rms 270-320 F. Restaurant. Half-board 280-365 F. Conf. Heated pool. Golf. Pkg. V, MC.
A splendid traditional chalet in a magnificent setting, welcoming and admirably run. It offers a well-designed health club with top-quality fitness equipment.

Le Dahu
Chemin du Mas Metout
50 75 92 92, fax 50 75 92 50
Closed Tue, Apr-Jun, Sep-Dec 18. Open until 9pm. Garden dining. Heated pool. No pets. Pkg. V, MC.
Here's a trim and tidy wood-paneled restaurant, with an unspoiled view of the village and mountains. Le Dahu is a popular place, where patrons return time and again for the owners' kind welcome, the attentive service, and Daniel Le Goff's satisfying food based on top-quality ingredients. This year his menu features a wonderfully rustic roasted Tomme de Savoie cheese with warm pears, buckwheat crêpes stuffed with morels and foie gras, red mullet braised in white wine with basil, and a croustillant of spiced caramelized apples. *C 230-270 F. M 160 F, 285 F.*

Le Dahu
(See restaurant above)
Closed Apr 14-Jun 19, Sep 11-Dec 18. 4 stes 900-1,200 F. 40 rms 325-810 F. Half-board 470-825 F. Conf. Heated pool. No pets. Pkg. V, MC.
Le Dahu, on its sunny slope a little distance from the town center, is now the resort's top hotel. It offers a sauna and a fully equipped fitness center with two pools, Jacuzzi, and body-building equipment. The well-tended rooms are decorated in period style. Guests benefit from a free shuttle service to the ski lifts and numerous leisure activities. Warm, friendly atmosphere.

■ **In Avoriaz 74110**   5 km NE, access by cable-car

12/20 La Grignotte
Pl. du Téléphérique - 50 74 02 66
Closed Apr 25-Dec 20. Open until 10pm. Terrace dining. V, MC.
Fresh, imaginative market cuisine is La Grignotte's specialty. Try the chiffonade of sauerkraut with giblets and chestnuts, croustillant of black and white blood sausages, and

almond cake for dessert. Attractive, chalet-style decor. C 200-310 F. M 180 F.

Les Hauts Forts
50 74 22 03, fax 40 50 78 76

Closed May-Jun. 35 rms 290-535 F. Restaurant. Half-board 415-640 F. Conf. Heated pool. Helipad. V, AE, DC, MC.
This spacious, modern hotel is well equipped for winter holidays with a sauna, bar, and boutiques.

MOSNAC 17	→ Pons

MOTTARET (LE) 73	→ Méribel-les-Allues

MOTTIER   38260
Paris 522 - Grenoble 42 - Vienne 43 - Bourgoin-Jallieu 21   *Isère*

Les Donnières
74 54 42 06

Closed Sun dinner, Wed, Thu, Jan, Jul 14-Aug 15. Open until 8:30pm. Pkg. AE.
If you complain to Jean-Luc and Line Boland that everything is going up, they're likely to smile. The only thing on the rise here is the number of guests (limited by the fact that there are only a few tables) who flock to this former barn overlooking a pocket-sized garden. They come to sample Jean-Luc's tasty, well-turned country cooking at more than reasonable prices: feuilleté of blood sausage with apple cream (31 F), veal kidney in mustard sauce (52 F), and prune and Armagnac ice cream (13 F). Don't forget to reserve ahead! C 140-170 F.

MOUANS-SARTOUX   06370
Paris 910 - Nice 35 - Cannes 13 - Grasse 7   *Alpes-Mar.*

12/20 Le Relais de la Pinède
Route de la Roquette - 93 75 28 29
Closed Wed, Feb 14-28. Open until 9:30pm. Priv rm: 70. Terrace dining. Pkg. V, AE, DC, MC.
A modest log cabin in a pine grove, with fine cooking at modest prices: veal sweetbreads in mushroom cream sauce, beef fillet with cèpes, and nougat glacé with peach coulis. Tiny wine list. **M** 99 F (exc Sun lunch), 149 F, 169 F, 220 F, 280 F.

12/20 Le Relais de Sartoux
400, route de Valbonne
93 60 10 57, fax 93 60 17 36
Closed Wed, Nov 1-Dec 1. Open until 9:30pm. Terrace dining. Pool. Pkg. V, AE, MC.
The rustic dining room of this cozy little inn boasts a fireplace that roars in winter. Tuck into palate-pleasers like fish soup, a blanquette of monkfish and tiny scallops, beef fillet, and dark chocolate cake. **C** 180-310 F. **M** 130 F, 160 F.

Le Relais de Sartoux
(See restaurant above)
Closed Wed, Nov 10-Dec 10. 12 rms 300-340 F. Half-board 295-380 F. Conf. Pool. Golf. No pets. Pkg. V, AE, MC.
Located near Cannes, this pleasant Provençal farmhouse boasts rooms that give onto a peaceful inner garden.

MOUGINS   06250
Paris 902 - Nice 32 - Grasse 11 - Cannes 8   *Alpes-Mar.*

12/20 Le Bistrot de Mougins
Pl. du Village
93 75 78 34, fax 93 75 25 52
Closed Wed, Nov 14-Dec 16. Open until 10pm. Air cond. V, MC.
In the heat of summer this fashionable restaurant's cellar-like interior is a cool retreat, and the cooking is pure bistrot fare: truffle with chard, seafood timbale with spinach, sardines spiked with mint, and pieds et paquets (a local veal specialty). But the cooking blows hot and cold. Local growths top the wine list. M 170 F (lunch exc Sun), 120 F.

La Ferme de Mougins
10, av. Saint-Basile
93 90 03 74, fax 92 92 21 48
Closed Sun dinner & Mon off-seas. Annual closings not available. Open until 9:30pm (10pm in summer). Priv rm: 100. Terrace dining. Pkg. V, AE, DC, MC.
Chef Thierry Thiercelin stumbled on our visit here last year, and we suspended the rating. But now he's regained his balance, and offers sunny, intensely flavored dishes like those on the 380 F menu: fresh and tasty turbot with leeks and squid-ink sauce, slightly dryish sea scallops in cream sauce, luscious honey-glazed roast squab, fine cheese selection, and excellent desserts. The lovely dining room with country-French decor opens onto a pretty garden. Too bad the welcome and service lack charm. C 550-700 F. M 195 F (weekday lunch, Sat), 250 F, 380 F.

Feu Follet
Pl. de la Mairie
93 90 15 78, fax 92 92 92 62
Closed Mon. Open until 10pm. Priv rm: 30. Terrace dining. Air cond. V, AE, MC.
It's no surprise that Feu Follet is a twinkling success. The decor is chic (despite the tryingly cramped dining room), the prices are mercilessly restrained, and the cooking—based on top-quality ingredients—is full of sun and simple flavors: scampi sautéed with basil, lemony sautéed sea scallops, rack of lamb, beef fillet with marrow, and an orange craquant. Small but well chosen wine list. C 240-300 F. M 148 F, 185 F.

Le Manoir de l'Étang
66, allée du Manoir, route d'Antibes
93 90 01 07, fax 92 92 20 70
Closed Nov-Dec 20, Feb-Mar 15. Open until 10pm. Garden dining. Pool. Pkg. V, AE, MC.
Picture this: a luxurious poolside terrace next to a splendid manor house. Makes you want to take a holiday? This is the place for it... And the food is good too, authentic and generous: perfectly prepared ravioli stuffed with lamb moistened with thyme jus, savory émincé of veal kidneys in tarragon butter sauce, and a luscious millefeuille of caramelized apples scented with rosemary. Fine choice of Provençal wines. Friendly welcome, good service, and an extra point from us this year! C 250-350 F. M 165 F (weekday lunch, Sat, wine incl), 145 F, 190 F.

A red hotel ranking denotes a place with charm.

Le Manoir de l'Étang

(See restaurant above)
See restaurant for closings. 1 ste 1,300-1,500 F. 15 rms 600-950 F. Conf. Pool. Golf. Pkg. Helipad. V, AE, MC.
This sumptuous Provençal dwelling dates from the nineteenth century; it is set in handsomely groomed grounds and offers lovely rooms (some are huge). Golf course nearby.

12/20 Le Mas Candille

Bd Rebuffel
93 90 00 85, fax 92 92 85 56
Closed Tue lunch & Wed off-seas. Open until 10pm. Priv rm: 20. Garden dining. Heated pool. No pets. Valet pkg. V, AE, DC.
In fine weather, one may dine on the magnificent terrace and savor the view of the mountains along with one's mushroom ravioli, langoustine fricassée, guinea fowl stuffed with fresh white cheese, or the "ruche au miel du berger" for dessert. Diverse but expensive wine list; charming welcome and stylish service.
C 280-400 F. M 185 F, 205 F, 250 F.

Le Mas Candille

(See restaurant above)
Closed Nov 1-Jan 3. 2 stes 1,800-2,100 F. 21 rms 680-980 F. Half-board 970-1,390 F. Air cond. Conf. Heated pool. Tennis. Golf. Pkg. V, AE, DC.
Bright, comfortable rooms with excellent facilities look out onto a delightful green landscape. Absolute, blessed quiet. Heated pool; tennis courts.

Le Moulin de Mougins

Quartier Notre-Dame-de-Vie
424, chemin du Moulin
93 75 78 24, fax 93 90 18 55
Closings not available. Priv rm: 40. Air cond. No pets. Valet pkg. V, AE, DC.
Roger Vergé is still one of the country's great chefs, an artist in the fullest sense of the term, and it was with great regret that we suspended his toques last year. But an anonymous visit this year unfortunately confirmed our disappointment, and we are suspending the rating this year. The menu itself is still as exciting as when we first praised Vergé, inventor of the "cuisine du soleil". But the kitchen falls short in execution and even, we fear, in the quality of certain ingredients. Apart from the very fine vegetable galette with girolle mushrooms and fresh herb sauce, nothing served to us in the lovely dining room lived up to Vergé's glorious past. Tasty baby artichokes were matched with strangely tasteless cuttlefish, oven-baked sole was overcooked and paired with an insipid sauce, and the veal kidney was mediocre, overcooked, and drowning in a heavy cream sauce. Vergé still receives his regulars and chic clientele with his habitual great charm, but he needs to take things in hand here. We would be the first to praise him if he managed it.
C 700-900 F.

Le Moulin de Mougins

(See restaurant above)
Open year-round. 2 stes 1,300 F. 3 rms 800-1,000 F. Air cond. No pets. Valet pkg. V, AE, DC.
The three rooms and two small suites are delightful and much cheaper than a grand hotel, but harder to obtain than a place in Paradise.

Les Muscadins

18, bd Courteline
93 90 00 43, fax 92 92 88 23
Closed Tue off-seas, Feb 6-Mar 2, Dec 6-20. Open until 10:30pm. Priv rm: 25. Terrace dining. Pkg. V, AE, DC, MC.
This attractive restaurant on the outskirts of Mougins, with a terrace overlooking the bay of Cannes, boasts a comfortable and elegant dining room done in tones of ochre and blue. Under the direction of chef Noël Mantel, it is one of the most pleasant restaurants along the Côte. Try the bargain-priced 165 F menu: fresh and tasty warm skate salad, delicious leg of milk-fed Sisteron lamb with an excellent cassoulette of tiny bacon-spiked peas, fresh goat cheese, and an appealing buffet of classic desserts. Well chosen wines. Professional welcome; young and friendly serving staff. C 250-350 F. M 115 F (lunch exc Sun), 165 F, 290 F.

Les Muscadins

(See restaurant above)
Open year-round. 1 ste 1,200 F. 7 rms 750-950 F. Half-board 900-1,350 F. Air cond. Conf. Tennis. Golf. Pkg. V, AE, DC, MC.
Eight delightful rooms, each one individually decorated and attractively furnished. Charming, intimate bar and lounge.

Le Relais à Mougins

Pl. de la Mairie
93 90 03 47, fax 93 75 72 83
Closed Tue lunch, Mon (exc hols), Nov. Open until 10:30pm. Terrace dining. V, AE, MC.
"La marmite du boeuf Henri IV on the menu? Oh, that's chicken in a pot," says André Surmain. But does everyone know the king promised his subjects a chicken in every pot? There's much more to confuse us here this year: warm oysters in a thin, overly spiced saffron sauce; sea bass with a strange chicken-liver vinaigrette; tiramisu stretched with egg white and encumbered with an unnecessary raspberry coulis. Prices have dropped, it's true, but then so has the quality of the cooking and service (which is very slow). We're suspending the rating until the establishment gets back on track. Note that the Le Zinc bistrot in the same premises offers plats-du-jour for less than 50 F. C 250-450 F. M 100 F, 155 F, 275 F.

Paris 292 - Vichy 57 - Nevers 54 - Bourges 98 - Mâcon 139 *Allier*

Hôtel de Paris

Jacquemart, 21, rue de Paris
70 44 00 58, fax 70 34 05 39
Closed Sun dinner, Mon, Aug 7-21. Open until 9:30pm. Priv rm: 80. Terrace dining. Air cond. Heated pool. Garage pkg. V, AE, DC, MC.
Renowned local restaurateurs, the Robertys, are making the elegant Hôtel de Paris an exemplary provincial hostelry, better all the time. The cuisine, based on superb products, is always carefully prepared and tempting. This year, we loved the vinaigrette of lobster with walnuts and basil, lemony veal sweetbread craquant, sliced turbot with anchovies, and a splendid selection of desserts. The welcome and service are just about perfect. To keep the bill manageable (and the prices are slowly but surely rising here),

choose a tasty Saint-Pourçain wine from the region. **C** 420-500 F. **M** 170 F, 260 F, 350 F, 440 F.

Hôtel de Paris
(See restaurant above)
Open year-round. 4 stes 850-1,000 F. 24 rms 310-780 F. Half-board 520-800 F. Conf. Heated pool. Golf. Garage pkg. V, AE, DC, MC.
Some of the attic rooms are tiny, but all have been tastefully renovated and attractively furnished, complete with minibars. There's an attractive garden.

MOUSTIERS-SAINTE-MARIE	04360
Paris 792 - Castellane 45 - Digne 48 - Aix 86	*Alpes-H.-P.*

La Bastide de Moustiers
Quartier Saint-Michel
92 74 62 40, fax 92 74 62 41
Information not available.
The latest establishment of great chef Alain Ducasse is nothing like his palatial surroundings in the Louis XV in Monte Carlo. Here, he has created a Provençal fantasy in a seventeenth-century "bastide" surrounded by fields of lavender in one of the most stunningly beautiful landscapes we know, near the Verdon gorges. Although the restaurant will not open its doors until April this year, we couldn't resist giving you a little something to whet your appetite. Here, a maximum of thirty lucky guests can savor sunny dishes based on the region's finest products, created by the master and prepared and served by a capable team, either in front of a roaring fireplace in winter or on a lovely outdoor terrace. Guest rooms (seven of them offered at between 450 F and 850 F), moderately priced menus, and, in the surrounding park, a heated pool, peacocks, ponies and horses, and even a chicken yard.

La Ferme Rose
92 74 69 47, fax 92 74 60 76
Closed Jan 15-Feb 28. 7 rms 320-350 F. Restaurant. Conf. Pkg. V, AE, DC, MC.
An ancient pink-stucco farm lost in the countryside, offering rooms with views of the surrounding landscape (some rooms have amazing 1950s furnishings), and a pleasant terrace. Warm welcome.

Les Santons
Pl. de l'Église
92 74 66 48, fax 92 74 63 67
Closed Mon dinner off-seas, Tue, Dec-Jan. Open until 9:30pm. Priv rm: 25. Terrace dining. V, DC, MC.
A pretty dining room filled with bouquets of fresh flowers, with a terrace overlooking a swift-flowing river, is the setting for André Albert's carefully prepared regional dishes based on top-quality ingredients: langoustine ravioli with baby fennel, roast milk-fed kid with tiny fava beans, and a dessert "triangle" flavored with chocolate, coconut, and banana. Impressive cheese assortment (around thirty types). It's too bad the prices are so high (even the set menus). Fine choice of Provençal wines; warm welcome. **C** 350-450 F. **M** 160 F, 230 F, 360 F.

*The **prices** in this guide reflect what establishments were charging at press time.*

MULHOUSE	68100
Paris 537 - Belfort 44 - Colmar 41 - Strasbourg 116	*Haut-Rhin*

Mercure-Gare Centrale
4, pl. Ch.-de-Gaulle
89 36 29 39, fax 89 36 29 49
Open year-round. 96 rms 330-420 F. Half-board 480 F. Air cond. Conf. Pkg. V, AE, DC, MC.
Comfortable, recently renovated rooms with thick carpets, modern furnishings, and fine white-tile bathrooms. Professional reception.

Restaurant du Parc
26, rue de la Sinne - 89 66 12 22
Open daily until 10pm. Priv rm: 250. Air cond. Valet pkg. V, AE, DC, MC.
Don't be put off by the austere façade. The light, comfortable Art Deco interior has charm to spare, and Jean-Bernard Hermann's cooking does too, featuring inventive and successful flavor combinations: sautéed artichokes and mushrooms, Scottish salmon roasted with garlic and bacon, and a croquant de fromage blanc for dessert. The wine list offers some bargain-priced bottles each week. Couteous welcome, stylish service. **C** 280-380 F. **M** 195 F, 250 F (lunch weekday & Sun), 280 F, 320 F (dinner exc Sun).

Hôtel du Parc
(See restaurant above)
Open year-round. 7 stes 1,200-2,950 F. 73 rms 490-950 F. Rms for disabled. Air cond. Conf. Golf. Valet pkg. V, AE, DC, MC.
Meticulously renovated, the hotel's interior has been restored to its full Art Deco glory. Superbly equipped; excellent service.

Au Quai de la Cloche
5, quai de la Cloche - 89 43 07 81
Closed Sat lunch, Sun dinner, Mon, Jul 26-Aug 15. Open until 9:30pm. Terrace dining. Pkg. V, AE.
A comfortable, though not wildly attractive restaurant in a drab part of town. But come anyway, for Jacques Michel's regionally rooted cooking. He transforms prime-quality ingredients into delicious macaroni gratin, salmon in brik (flaky pastry), beef in red wine sauce, duck breast with ham and walnuts, and excellent pastries. Adequate wine list, with some reasonably priced Bordeaux and some well chosen Burgundies. **C** 260-350 F. **M** 320 F (exc weekday lunch), 90 F, 120 F (weekdays), 240 F.

Wir
1, porte de Bâle - 89 46 08 78
Closed Sun dinner, Mon, Jul 15-Aug 9. Open until 10pm. Pkg. V, AE, DC, MC.
One of the city's culinary institutions, Wir's cozy, wood-paneled dining room (which could use a bit of a facelift) is a favorite with families and well-heeled businessmen. And Raymond Wir's cooking merits a toque this year for the likes of perfectly cooked and flavorful monkfish roasted in shellfish jus with couscous, veal kidney in Port sauce (very tasty in spite of an overly liquid sauce), and a luscious Grand Marnier mousse glacée. Fine cellar, and a huge serving staff. **C** 250-400 F. **M** 120 F, 160 F(exc Sun), 250 F.

And also...
Our selection of places for inexpensive, quick, or late-night meals.
Auberge du Vieux Mulhouse (89 45 84 18 -

Place de la Réunion.): Take a table on the terrace in the city's prettiest square and savor regional specialties (quenelles, schiefallas, tête de veau) while contemplating St-Étienne's church (150-270 F). **Aux Caves du Vieux Couvent** (89 46 28 79 - 23, rue du Couvent.): Regional food (winemaker's tart, coq au riesling, Munster feuilleté), local crowd (130-190 F). **Obernois** (89 59 03 75 - 1, rue du Siphon. Open until 10pm.): Cooking as local as you'll find, from the traditional baeckeoffe (pork, lamb, and beef stew) and the fillet of Charolais beef, to the flamed apple tart (150-230 F). **Wistuwa zum Mehlala** (89 59 41 32 - 7, rue d'Illzach. Open until 11pm.): Near the cinema district, one of Mulhouse's few *winstubs* (wine bars): try the liver quenelles, pork shanks, and flambéed tarts served in a friendly atmosphere (130-260 F).

■ **In Ensisheim 68190**   17 km N

La Couronne
47, av. de la Ire-Armée-Française
89 26 43 26, fax 89 26 40 05
Closed Sun dinner, Sat lunch, Mon. Open until 9pm. Terrace dining. Pkg. V, AE, DC, MC.
   Master chef Jean-Marc Kohler offers intelligent, balanced cooking in an elegantly decorated seventeenth-century dwelling. We urge you to sample his duck liver with onion confit, sea bass in an olive oil emulsion, and gooey chocolate cake. Judiciously chosen wines. Gabrielle Kohler's welcome is charming, and the service is refined. **C** 350-450 F. **M** 200 F, 275 F, 375 F.

■ **In Steinbrunn-le-Bas 68440**   8 km S on D 21

Moulin du Kaegy
89 81 30 34, fax 89 81 31 10
Closed Sun dinner, Mon, Jan. Open until 10:30pm. Priv rm: 45. Pkg. V, AE, DC, MC.
   Bernard Begas came to this delightful half-timbered mill some 30 years ago to pioneer *la nouvelle cuisine*. Today, he is still combining the best of old, new, and regional styles in his own highly personal repertoire. Sample his 370 F "Tradition" menu: sage-marinated duck tartare, grey mullet fillets in anise butter, civet de boeuf bourguignon, and duck with lemon. On the 500 F "La Fête" menu, you'll find corn blini stuffed with raw salmon and caviar, sea bass croustillant, veal sweetbreads and snails in a cassoulet, and spiced lamb fillet. Children are invited into the kitchen to learn about fine taste and choose their own meal, a splendid idea. After they eat they can breathe clean mountain air while playing in the park, and come back later for dessert. **C** 450-500 F. **M** 210 F (weekday lunch), 370 F (wine incl), 300 F, 500 F.

MURBACH	68530
Paris 480 - Gérardmer 65 - Guebwiller 6 - Colmar 31	*Haut-Rhin*

Hostellerie Saint-Barnabé
89 76 92 15, fax 89 76 67 80
Closed Sun dinner off-seas, Jan 15-Feb. Open until 9:30pm. Terrace dining. Pkg. V, AE, DC, MC.
   Éric Orban doesn't revise his *carte* very often, but it would be graceless to complain about his

intelligent, flavorful cuisine. Without reservation we can recommend his quick-cooked sea scallops and salad with caviar cream, sautéed veal sweetbreads with a touch of vanilla, and a pear craquelin with fromage blanc mousse for dessert. Well chosen wine list. **C** 300-400 F. **M** 125 F, 225 F, 315 F.

Hostellerie Saint-Barnabé
(See restaurant above)
See restaurant for closings. 3 stes 695-750 F. 24 rms 310-560 F. Half-board 458-661 F. Conf. Tennis. Pkg. V, AE, DC.
   A delightful, perfectly quiet setting. Nearly all of the well-equipped rooms have been recently renovated and are very comfortably furnished (satellite TV). Good service.

MUR-DE-BRETAGNE	22530
Paris 455 - Saint-Brieuc 45 - Pontivy 16	*Côtes/Armor*

Auberge Grand' Maison
1, rue L.-le-Cerf
96 28 51 10, fax 96 28 52 30
Closed Sun dinner, Mon, Feb 15-Mar 3, Oct. Open until 9pm. Priv rm: 16. V, AE, DC, MC.
   Jacques Guillo's dining room—handsome stone walls, red carpet and chairs, and white table cloths—is a lovely place to savor this skilled chef's imaginative, personal, and satisfying cuisine based on sublime local ingredients. Witness his extraordinarily flavorful spider-crab soup, a symphony of sapid counterpoints, flanked by crispy toast topped with sea-urchin coral; Saint Malo ormeaux (shellfish) in a civet with sea snails; turbot with bacon paired with a honey- and parsley-enhanced shallot confit; sweetbreads of milk-fed veal with baby onions and carrots; and warm mandarin orange crêpes. The 230 F menu is a real bargain. The service is very professional, and the wine list, one of the finest in Brittany, offers some real bargains, too. Madame Guillo provides a warm welcome. **C** 380-400 F. **M** 160 F (exc Sun), 200 F, 230 F, 360 F.

Auberge Grand' Maison
(See restaurant above)
See restaurant for closings. 12 rms 280-600 F. Half-board 400-600 F. Conf. V, AE, DC, MC.
   Each of the dozen rooms is charmingly decorated with antique furniture. Brigitte Guillo greets guests warmly.

MURS 84	→ Gordes

MUSSIDAN	24400
Paris 530 - Bergerac 25 - Angoulême 84	*Dordogne*

■ **In Beaupouyet 24400**   9 km W on N 89

Le Clos Joli
On N 89 - 53 81 10 01
Closed for dinner Sun & Mon. Open until 10:15pm. Priv rm: 30. Garden dining. Pkg. V, MC.
   In a painstakingly restored former presbytery, a stone's throw from the main Bordeaux-to-Périgueux road, new chef Frank Cuzuel offers regional specialties with a personal touch: flavorful duck liver sautéed in Muscat and duck breast

349

with pears, original and tasty veal "au blason du chef" (with ham and creamy mushroom sauce), generous and very tasty tiramisu. Friendly welcome and service in the spacious dining room. **C** 260-370 F. **M** 85 F (weekdays, Sat lunch), 140 F, 165 F, 185 F, 225 F.

NAJAC	12270

Paris 640 - Rodez 86 - Albi 50 - Villefranche-de-R. 24   *Aveyron*

Jean-Marie Miquel
65 29 74 32, fax 65 29 75 32
Closed Mon off-seas, Nov-Mar. Open until 9:30pm. Priv rm: 35. Terrace dining. Pkg. V, AE.
We were all set to praise Jean-Marie Miquel's fresh, flavorful cooking with a focus on garden herbs and vegetables, when we learned to our sadness that he was killed in an accident. It's too soon to say what will happen to this lovely establishment, and we send our sympathies to his wife, Caroline. **C** 330-400 F. **M** 98 F (lunch exc Sun, wine incl), 138 F, 210 F, 260 F, 320 F.

Oustal del Barry
(See restaurant above)
Closed Nov-Mar. 21 rms 245-450 F. Half-board 295-350 F. Conf. Pkg. V, AE.
The comfortable, well-equipped rooms are furnished in rustic style. Large garden, guaranteed peace and quiet. Wine cellar. Pool, tennis, and equestrian facilities nearby.

■ In **La Fouillade 12270**   *7 km NE on D 39*

Longcol
65 29 63 36, fax 65 29 64 28
Closed Tue lunch (exc Jun 15-Sep 15), Nov 15-Easter. Open until 9:30pm. Priv rm: 30. Terrace dining. Heated pool. Pkg. V, AE, MC.
Lovely Oriental fabrics give a bright touch to this pleasant dining room with a terrace overlooking wooded grounds. Chef Arnaud Daré offers inventive dishes like perfectly cooked foie gras terrine, farm-raised guinea fowl en deux cuissons seasoned with mace and paired with an excellent sweet-pepper chutney, and delicious basil and cinnamon ice cream with caramel sauce. Well chosen wine list; warm welcome. **C** 200-390 F. **M** 130 F (lunch), 185 F, 350 F.

Longcol
(See restaurant above)
Closed Nov 15-Easter. 1 ste 950 F. 17 rms 550-800 F. Restaurant. Half-board 520-645 F. Conf. Heated pool. Tennis. Golf. Pkg. Helipad. V, AE, MC.
Restored from the remains of a twelfth- and thirteenth-century farm, this delightful hotel on the Aveyron River is set in 25 hectares of wooded grounds surrounded by hills (fishing on the premises). The rooms are decorated in impeccable taste, with superb furniture and carpets.

NANCY	54000

Paris 307 - Metz 57 - Epinal 69 - Dijon 201   *Meurthe/M.*

12/20 Chez Bagot
Le Chardon Bleu, 45, Grande-Rue
83 37 42 43, fax 83 35 78 38
Closed Tue dinner, Sun, Aug 20-Sep 10. Open until 10:30pm. Priv rm: 25. Terrace dining. V, MC.

The vaulted dining room of this charming family-run establishment boasts a pleasant, crowd-pulling atmosphere. Patrick Bagot's well-honed cuisine draws inspiration from the deep blue sea (no wonder, he's from Brittany). But the 120 F menu left us feeling all wet and lost him a toque this year: mediocre mussel and cockle crème brûlée, adequate Belle Epoque turbot, and overly chilled, bland berry-wine soup. Efficient welcome and service in the blue and white dining room with nautical decor. **C** 200-300 F. **M** 70 F (lunch), 120 F, 190 F.

Le Capucin Gourmand
31, rue Gambetta
83 35 26 98, fax 83 35 75 32
Closed Aug. Open until 10pm. Air cond. V.
Gérard Veissière's cooking is inventive, especially in the dessert department, and his 130 F menu is a bargain: an original "gâteau" of melon and Parma ham, ethereal little tomatoes stuffed with chicken and gratinéed, excellent honey nougat glacé and candied ginger with caramelized almonds. Short but judiciously chosen wine list with lots of finds (fine Chardonnay from the Ardèche, for example). Professional yet warm welcome. **C** 400-500 F. **M** 130 F, 220 F, 450 F.

La Chine
31, rue des Ponts - 83 30 13 89
Closed Sun dinner, Mon, Aug 8-29. Open until 10:30pm. Air cond. V, AE, DC.
A stone dragon guards the entrance to this good-value Chinese restaurant. We're impressed by the fresh, precise cooking: fried sole with a pastry coating served with sweet-sour sauce, duck breast with cashew nuts, apple crêpes en chausson, and mandarin orange sherbet. Ordinary little wine list. **C** 170-270 F. **M** 145 F, 185 F.

12/20 Comptoir du Petit Gastrolâtre
1, pl. de Vaudémont
83 35 51 94, fax 83 32 96 79
Closed Mon lunch, Sun, May 1-10, Sep 1-15. Open until 10:45pm. Priv rm: 15. Terrace dining. Pkg. V.
In a jolly bistrot atmosphere you can enjoy baeckeoffe made with foie gras, bouillabaisse, pieds et paquets (a southern veal dish) à la marseillaise, and potée lorraine (stick-to-your-ribs soup), all served swiftly and with a smile. Pleasant little wines. **C** 200-330 F. **M** 90 F (exc Sat dinner), 150 F.

Le Goéland
27, rue des Ponts
83 35 17 25, fax 83 35 72 49
Closed Mon lunch, Sun. Open until 9:30pm. Priv rm: 15. Air cond. Garage pkg. V, AE, MC.
Jean-Luc Mengin's imaginative way with fish and seafood has few rivals in France or anywhere else! His focused, clean-lined style is reflected in the restaurant's elegantly modern decor, a setting as appetizing as the Gewurztraminer that Danièle Mengin, a confirmed *sommelière*, will surely suggest as an apéritif. A meal here is a voyage of discovery: langoustines and calf's head with Parmesan, roast sea bass with caviar cream and coriander-enhanced semolina, fresh cod studded with bits of country ham and paired with creamed lentils, and a pot-au-feu of monkfish and veal sweetbreads with horseradish

cream. Though the wines of Alsace have pride of place on the list, there is an impressive choice of bottles from the Rhône and the Loire, many half bottles, and some great eaux-de-vie that make a perfect match for the desserts. Fine service. **C** 370-450 F. **M** 165 F, 275 F.

Le Stanislas
2, pl. Stanislas
83 35 03 01, fax 83 32 86 04
Open daily until 10pm. Priv rm: 72. Terrace dining. Valet pkg. V, AE, DC, MC.
It was obviously impossible to impose a modern decor on this listed hotel on Nancy's sublime eighteenth-century Place Stanislas. Happily, the dining room's new look strikes a successful balance between simplicity and elegance. Michel Douville's classic, adroitly executed cooking suits the setting, as is amply demonstrated by his 240 F menu: eel compote in a fresh, perfectly prepared gelatin; chicken fricassée in bilberry vinegar, a selection of goat cheeses, and a limited choice of desserts. Excellent welcome and service. The cellar is fully stocked. **C** 250-470 F. **M** 240 F (weekday lunch, Sat, wine incl), 180 F (weekday lunch, Sat), 290 F.

Grand Hôtel de la Reine
(See restaurant above)
Open year-round. 8 stes 1,260-2,100 F. 40 rms 630-880 F. Conf. Valet pkg. V, AE, DC, MC.
This luxuriously equipped hotel occupies one of the historic buildings on the beautiful Place Stanislas and has a listed staircase and public rooms. The bedrooms are decorated in Louis XV style.

La Toison d'Or
11, rue R.-Poincaré
83 39 75 75, fax 83 32 78 17
Closed Jul 24-Aug 24. Open until 10pm. Air cond. V, AE, DC.
The dining room's contemporary look is both bright and intimate, conducive to a tête-à-tête over the chef's seasonal, deftly rendered dishes. Although prices are rising, the set menus offer good deals. For 220 F, you'll have a tartare of Scottish salmon with a caviar-horseradish cream (fresh but under-seasoned), perfectly cooked and generously served fricassée of veal kidneys with girolle mushrooms in Muscat wine sauce, and good caramelized-fruit sherbet. Efficient service. **C** 300-400 F. **M** 175 F, 220 F (wine incl).

Altea Thiers
(See restaurant above)
Open year-round. 7 stes 1,000 F. 178 rms 375-625 F. Half-board 415-540 F. Air cond. Conf. Garage pkg. V, AE, DC, MC.
Extensive renovation has added 80 new rooms, a luxury floor, new bar, and breakfast lounge to this functional hotel opposite the station. Sauna; mini-gym; room service.

La Toque Blanche
1, rue Mgr-Trouillet
83 30 17 20, fax 83 32 60 24
Closed Sun dinner, Wed, Feb 20-Mar 5. Open until 10:30pm. Terrace dining. Air cond. V, AE, DC.
Jean-Pierre Grandemange offers light, interesting cooking that the local family-lunch crowd loves. On the first set menu: tuna rillettes with fennel paired with a fresh and flavorful salad,

cleverly conceived and well prepared pork noisettes with rhubarb and white mustard, and a delicate pot-de-crème flavored with caramel and bergamot. Well chosen wine list. The *patronne*'s welcome is charming. The cozily decorated, flower-filled dining room gives onto a covered terrace. **C** 250-350 F. **M** 98 F, 172 F, 258 F.

12/20 Le Wagon
57, rue de Chaligny
83 32 32 16, fax 83 35 68 36
Closed Sat, Sun, hols, Jul 7-Aug 7. Open until 9:30pm. Air cond. Pkg. V, AE, MC.
A genuine 1927 railway carriage (with original brass fittings, banquettes, and marquetry) offering simple dishes like cassoulet, mixed fish, and crème brûlée. **C** 150-280 F. **M** 80 F, 130 F, 180 F.

And also...
Our selection of places for inexpensive, quick, or late-night meals.
Flo (83 35 24 57 - 50, rue H.-Poincaré. Open until 12:30am.): Open later than all the rest. Flo has succeeded in giving some personality to this exceptional setting (160-220 F).
Rôtisserie Au P'tit Cuny (83 32 85 94 - 97-99, Grande-Rue. Open until 11pm.): Good value and a warm atmosphere (120-200 F).

■ In Flavigny-
sur-Moselle 54630   16 km S on N 57

Le Prieuré
3, rue du Prieuré
83 26 70 45, fax 83 26 75 51
Closed Sun dinner, Wed, Feb school hols, Aug 26-Sep 8. Open until 10pm. Priv rm: 50. Garden dining. Pkg. V, AE, DC, MC.
Overlook the building's unprepossessing exterior. The salon's pastel-toned, blond-wood decor, and the dining room's fireplace and regional antiques, are counterpointed by the sober yet harmonious garden terrace with arcades that remind us of a cloister. We think the restrained, tasteful look and feel of this former priory resemble Joël Roy's cooking. His dishes are appealing indeed, with well balanced flavors, but they lack personality. He favors fish, often prepared with a Mediterranean touch: sea bass roasted with herbs, fried eggplant with a sweet-pepper cream, and a tasty bourride (garlicky fish soup). We much prefer his parsleyed frog's legs and potatoes en caquelon, the sumptuous regional crème brûlée with bergamot, and the "assiette lorraine" (a choice of desserts made with mirabelle plums). The wine list is evenly divided between Bordeaux and Burgundies. **C** 450-500 F. **M** 180 F (weekday lunch), 250 F (weekdays), 320 F, 400 F.

Le Prieuré
(See restaurant above)
See restaurant for closings. 4 rms 600 F. Rms for disabled. Conf. Pkg. V, AE, DC, MC.
Four huge, comfortable rooms overlook the new cloistered garden. Fine bathrooms, and breakfasts that will make you jump out of bed.

NANS-LES-PINS   83860
Paris 811 - Toulon 61 - Aix 43 - Marseille 41   *Var*

Domaine de Châteauneuf
N 560, Logis de Nans
94 78 90 06, fax 94 78 63 30
Closed Mon off-seas, Dec-Feb. Open until 10pm. Garden dining. Heated pool. Pkg. V, AE, DC, MC.

Owner Gilbert Duval came up a winner with chef Gilles Chirat, whose last posts were with Guérard and Trama. On second thought, it's the Domaine's patrons who win big. You'll share that view when you taste Chirat's exciting 380 F menu: creamy hure of lamb and garlic cloves in lavender milk; a fork-tender daube of beef cheeks, tongue, and neck of beef with mashed potatoes worthy of Joël Robuchon; pleasant thyme and rosemary granité; perfectly cooked boned young squab roasted with sweet spices; excellent Roquefort with walnut bread; and intensely flavored chocolate truffles iced with honey. A point extra this year. Fine, wide-ranging cellar; warm, attentive service. **C** 320-450 F. **M** 170 F (weekday lunch, Sat), 230 F, 380 F, 410 F.

Domaine de Châteauneuf 🔺🔹
(See restaurant above)
Closed Dec-Feb. 5 stes 1,200-2,250 F. 25 rms 560-1,160 F. Half-board 570-890 F. Conf. Heated pool. Tennis. Golf. Valet pkg. Helipad. V, AE, DC, MC.

Surrounded by wooded grounds and a superb eighteen-hole golf course, this seventeenth-century residence is decorated in infinite taste with clear, bright colors and fine antique furniture. Excellent breakfasts and perfect reception. Relais et Châteaux.

NANTES   44000
Paris 392 - Rennes 106 - Angers 87   *Loire-Atlantique*

Hôtel Amiral
26, rue Scribe
40 69 20 21, fax 40 73 98 13
Open year-round. 49 rms 269-319 F. Rms for disabled. Restaurant. Conf. Pkg. V, AE, DC, MC.

This recently built hotel is a fine address. Rooms are stylishly decorated and equipped with all the amenities (including minibar and double-glazed windows). Tasty breakfasts and light meals from room service.

Astoria
11, rue de Richebourg
40 74 39 90, fax 40 14 05 49
Closed Jul 29-Aug 28. 45 rms 290-350 F. Pkg. V, MC.

Set in a quiet street near the station and botanical gardens. The comfortable rooms are redecorated regularly.

L'Atlantide
Centre des Salorges, 16, quai E.-Renaud
40 73 23 23, fax 40 73 76 46
Closed Dec-Feb, Sun, Aug 6-28. Open until 10:30pm. Terrace dining. Air cond. Pkg. V.

High atop Nantes's Chamber of Commerce, L'Atlantide offers a splendid view of the city, a sleek, modern dining room designed by Jean-Pierre Wilmotte, and inspired cuisine by Pierre Lecoutre. His seductive repertoire accentuates exotic spices, used judiciously to point up the intrinsic flavors of magnificent, hand-picked ingredients. This year, he shows a passion for fortified wines; there's a whole menu devoted to

them. His 250 F "menu-carte" is still the best deal in the city: peppery oyster gratinée; a daring and successful sea bass cooked with ginger and Port wine perfectly paired with endives; cheeses; a fine little salad; and an exquisite five-spice chocolate effeuillé with chicory sauce. Impeccable service and rather complete wine list. **M** 220 F, 330 F (weekday dinner, Sat), 130 F, 250 F.

Auberge du Château
5, pl. de la Duchesse-Anne
40 74 31 85, fax 40 37 97 57
Closed Sun, Mon, Dec 24-Jan 3, Jul 30-Aug 21. Open until 9:30pm. Pkg. V, MC.

There is nothing château-like about the pale, wood-paneled Art Deco-style interior warmed by the charming *patronne*'s smiles. Chef Bernard Bourhis's traditional, well-crafted cooking is based on fine ingredients: tasty salad of spider crabs and langoustines, fillet of sea bass with a delicious Champagne sauce, and less successful desserts (runny crème brûlée). Interesting red Bordeaux at reasonable prices. Professional service. **C** 250-350 F. **M** 128 F, 170 F, 225 F.

12/20 La Cigale
Pl. Graslin - 40 69 76 41, fax 40 73 75 37
Open daily until 12:30am. Priv rm: 25. Terrace dining. V.

Come to admire the dining room's listed nineteenth-century decor, and stay on to sample fresh shellfish (sardine parmentier, langoustine cressonnette, gigolette of monkfish). Friendly reception; diligent service. **C** 130-280 F. **M** 130 F (wine incl), 69 F, 89 F, 100 F.

Le Gavroche
139, rue des Hauts-Pavés - 40 76 22 49
Closed Sun dinner, Aug 1-23. Open until 10:30pm. Priv rm: 35. Terrace dining. Air cond. Pkg. V, AE.

Hervé Hilaire's classic but seasonal repertoire has occasional ups and downs, but is marked by sure talent. Try the generous 135 F menu: oxtail salad in gelatin, cod fricassée à la provençale, gigolette of young rabbit in tarragon sauce, warm goat cheese crêpes, and dessert. The cellar is as enthralling as ever. **C** 250-350 F. **M** 195 F (weekday lunch, wine incl), 135 F, 185 F, 300 F.

Le Manoir de la Régate
9 km NE, 155, route de Gachet
40 18 02 97, fax 40 25 23 36
Closed Sun dinner, Mon, Feb 15-26, Aug 18-Sep 7. Open until 10pm. Garden dining. V, DC, MC.

This vine-covered dwelling on the banks of the Erdre houses a charming restaurant with beams, pastel decor, and soft lighting. Alain Hillenmeyer emphasizes quality ingredients in his classic cooking. Specialties include tuna in a marinade, grilled red mullet with fennel, pickerel with beurre blanc, and thyme-scented lamb. More than 100 fine wines to choose from. **C** 260-380 F. **M** 160 F (weekdays, Sat lunch, wine incl), 105 F (weekday lunch, Sat), 170 F, 210 F, 310 F.

Le Pressoir
11, allée Turenne
40 35 31 10, fax 51 84 06 45
Closed Sun, dinner Sat & Mon, Aug. Open until 10pm. V.

Michel Bachelet's restaurant is the kind of place you would rather share only with a few close friends. The appealing, traditional repertoire is served in a mellow wood-paneled dining room and includes traditional fare like a cassoulette of green asparagus and morels, roast squab with snow peas, and fig tart. Wash these delicacies down with wines from the deep cellar stocked with excellent finds (some served by the glass). Reasonable prices. **C** 190-250 F.

Le San Francisco
3, chemin des Bateliers
40 49 59 42, fax 40 68 99 16
Closed Sun dinner, Mon, Aug. Open until 9:45pm. Priv rm: 28. Terrace dining. Pkg. V, AE, DC, MC.
The Loire flows past the terrace, reflected in the dining room's strategically placed mirrors; and from the kitchen comes reliable cooking with lots of local flavors, at its best when it stays simple: sautéed eels, pike fillet with beurre blanc, and goat cheese blinis with salad, all on the 140 F menu. **C** 290-380 F. **M** 140 F, 195 F, 260 F, 320 F.

Torigaï
Ile de Versailles
40 37 06 37, fax 40 93 34 29
Closed Sun. Open until 10pm. Priv rm: 40. Garden dining. Pkg. V, AE, MC.
Little wonder Nantes has adopted Japanese chef Shigeo Torigaï with such alacrity. His split-level, glassed-in restaurant lapped by the Erdre River is a veritable jungle of lush green plants where, at comfortably spaced tables, guests savor his expert, beguilingly exotic cuisine. Torigaï, who married a Breton wife, trained under Michel Guérard and Alain Senderens, and has skillfully integrated French principles into his native gastronomy. The results are thrilling, as in his special menus like "Retour au Japon" (Return to Japan) featuring tempura-style beignets and raw fish, or "Balade en Muscadet" (Tour of the Muscadet Region), as well as a choice of classic dishes (red mullet with tapenade, milk-fed lamb in an eggplant-caviar crust) and inventive creations full of personality. Of these, we savored the sea scallops and truffle seasoned with coriander and saffron, cooked sealed in their shells; they fairly exploded with sublime flavor. Or the subtle and perfectly seasoned turbot with fava beans and caramelized asparagus. Torigaï proves his considerable talents as a pastry chef with delicate desserts like lime soufflé and fresh fruits in Malvoisie wine jelly. The cellar offers some delightful bottles from the Loire, especially Muscadets. **C** 350-500 F. **M** 180 F (lunch, wine incl), 250 F (dinner, wine incl), 420 F (wine incl), 295 F, 320 F.

Le Jules-Verne
3, rue du Couëdic
40 35 74 50, fax 40 20 09 35
Open year-round. 65 rms 300-389 F. Rms for disabled. Air cond. Garage pkg. V, AE, DC, MC.
Seven stories of well-equipped, soundproofed rooms in the town center. The staff are very friendly. Good breakfasts.

And also...
Our selection of places for inexpensive, quick, or late-night meals.
Les Enfants Terribles (40 47 00 38 - 4, rue Fénelon. Open until 10:30pm.): Traditional cooking, prepared honestly and at reasonable prices, near the Beaux Arts school (90 F, 260-420 F).
Chez Georges (40 74 25 43 - 87, rue du Mal-Joffre. Open until 8:30pm.): Good, cheap food and heady punches from the Indian Ocean island of La Réunion (50-120 F).
La Nouvelle Héloïse (40 73 62 99 - 15, rue J.-J.-Rousseau. Open until 7pm.): Sample the salads and warm starters, quiches and savory pies, and monumental desserts (80-100 F).

■ In Basse-Goulaine 44115 8 km E on D 119

Villa Mon Rêve
Route des Bords-de-Loire
40 03 55 50, fax 40 06 05 41
Closings not available. Open until 9:30pm. Priv rm: 40. Garden dining. Pkg. V, AE, DC.
Our own dream is that Gérard Ryngel will continue to choose his products with great care and offer well prepared classic dishes at amicable prices. A second toque this year for the likes of his harmonious lobster gazpacho, flavorful turbot in meat jus (but the onions with it had been overly caramelized), and a deliciously puckery apricot tart. Superb selection of Loire wines (especially Muscadets), some of them historic vintages. Warm welcome and attentive service in the pleasant dining room filled with fresh flowers or on the lovely garden terrace. **C** 250-350 F. **M** 168 F (exc Sun, wine incl), 98 F (exc Sun), 130 F, 185 F, 225 F.

■ In Champtoceaux 49270 30 km NE on N 23

Les Jardins de la Forge
1, pl. des Pilliers
40 83 56 23, fax 40 83 59 80
Closed Wed, dinner Sun & Tue, Feb 15-Mar 1, Oct 10-25. Open until 9:15pm. Priv rm: 20. Pkg. V, AE, DC, MC.
The restaurant faces a medieval château with two towers, which you can contemplate from the dining room or terrace as you savor Paul Pauvert's well prepared cooking based on sublime products. He has such talent for sauces and combining flavors that we would like him to be a bit more daring. In any case, we revel in his langoustine tails and mussels in saffron sauce, slices of John Dory with mango, and pickerel sautéed in a sesame seed vinaigrette. The desserts are luscious: warm pear feuilleté with almond-milk ice cream, featuring perfect fruits in perfectly prepared pastry. Fine wine list with high-priced Bordeaux and reasonably priced Loire wines (20 at less than 100 F). Friendly welcome by Madame Pauvert, and very professional service. **C** 350-400 F. **M** 155 F (weekdays), 225 F, 270 F, 385 F.

■ In Orvault 44700 7 km NW on N 137 and D 42

Le Domaine d'Orvault
Chemin des Marais-du-Cens
40 76 84 02, fax 40 76 04 21
Closed Mon lunch, Feb school hols. Open until 9:30pm. Garden dining. Air cond. Pkg. V, AE, MC.
The Domaine's refreshing bucolic setting—five acres of wooded grounds only ten minutes out-

side Nantes—clashes oddly with the dining room's stifling decor of red-patterned carpet and dark curtains. Jean-Yves Bernard won his toques back in 1986 for technically precise cuisine seasoned with a pinch of refinement. And indeed, his ingenious recipes are beautifully presented and generously served (the "carte" is long, and there are several menus, too). We could do with a bit more simplicity, but that's not Bernard's style. Savor his langoustines royales with chutney and curry cream, orange-scented asparagus and shellfish gratin, a less successful aumônière of veal sweetbreads with slices of lobster, and a fine sauté of caramelized pears with a Champagne sabayon. Charming welcome; attentive service. Encyclopaedic wine list. C 400-600 F. M 160 F, 200 F, 270 F, 330 F, 440 F.

Le Domaine d'Orvault
(See restaurant above)
Open year-round. 2 stes 750-1,050 F. 24 rms 330-690 F. Half-board 625-820 F. Conf. Tennis. Golf. Garage pkg. V, AE, DC, MC.
Set in wooded grounds in a residential area. The huge, comfortable rooms are richly decorated and newly renovated. New too: a gym complete with whirlpool bath. Cordial welcome and gorgeous breakfasts. Relais et Châteaux.

■ In **Les Sorinières 44840** 12 km S on N 137, D 178

Abbaye de Villeneuve
Route des Sables-d'Olonne
40 04 40 25, fax 40 31 28 45
Open daily until 9:30pm. Priv rm: 50. Garden dining. Pool. Pkg. V, AE, DC.
In the library where monks were wont to spend many a studious hour huddled round the fireplace, you can now dine on fresh and enticing cuisine: a salad of young squab with an infusion of Szechuan peppercorns, poached sole with a wild mushroom glaze, and a caramel bavarian cream with figs. The cellar is focused on fine Bordeaux. Hospitable welcome. C 270-350 F. M 245 F (wine incl), 160 F, 195 F, 225 F, 340 F.

Abbaye de Villeneuve
(See restaurant above)
Open year-round. 3 stes 1,150-1,310 F. 24 rms 390-940 F. Half-board 430-970 F. Conf. Heated pool. Pkg. Helipad. V, AE, DC, MC.
An atmosphere of harmony reigns in the spacious grounds and the luxurious, delightfully decorated rooms. Splendid swimming pool. Nutritious breakfasts; courteous, professional service.

■ In **Sucé-sur-Erdre 44240** 16 km N on D 69

Delphin
La Châtaigneraie, 156, route de Carquefou
40 77 90 95, fax 40 77 90 08
Closed Sun dinner, Mon (exc hols), Jan 2-23. Open until 9:30pm. Garden dining. Pkg. V, AE, DC, MC.
The 1930s–style interior in shades of beige and grey complements the peaceful, wooded setting near the River Erdre. Joseph Delphin's son Jean-Louis, who trained with Bocuse, Chapel, Robuchon, and the Troisgros brothers, turns out inventive dishes with a light touch: perfectly cooked foie gras sautéed with baby spinach, audacious but remarkable monkfish piccata flavored with vanilla, and a well made but rather ordinary raspberry puff pastry. The cellar boasts exquisite Loire Valley wines, and the waiters clad in long white aprons dispense smiling service. C 350-450 F. M 260 F, 340 F (weekday lunch, wine incl), 170 F (weekday lunch), 245 F, 310 F, 320 F, 420 F.

Ermitage du Riou
Av. H.-Clews
93 49 95 56, fax 92 97 69 05
Open year-round. 4 stes 1,600-2,700 F. 37 rms 650-1,600 F. Rms for disabled. Restaurant. Half-board 225 F. Air cond. Pool. Golf. Valet pkg. V, AE, DC, MC.
This Provençal-style hotel has a delightful setting and pretty garden. The rooms and suites, some with large terraces, overlook the sea, harbor, golf course, or pool.

L'Oasis
Rue Jean-Honoré-Carle
93 49 95 52, fax 93 49 64 13
Closings not available. Open until 9:30pm (10:30pm in summer). Priv rm: 30. Garden dining. Air cond. Valet pkg. V, AE, DC, MC.
Louis Outhier, once La Napoule's 19.5/20 chef, sold L'Oasis to a Japanese group, and promised to remain on the scene long enough to get the place going again, with the young, talented Stéphane Raimbault heading up the kitchens. Raimbault knows the Outhier repertoire by heart, having practiced it for nine years in Japan. But today he has gone beyond that "gospel" to create a cuisine that expresses his personality, and his own profoundly flavorful, perfectly rendered dishes have grabbed the spotlight. They often feature an astute mingling of Oriental and Mediterranean influences, and always reflect careful balances of flavors. Try his red mullet en escabèche paired with a watercress and shrimp salad; the marinière of langoustines in basil oil accompanying sot-l'y-laisse (poultry "oysters") with Siamese spices; admirable John Dory roasted in a tian of ratte potatoes, sun-dried tomatoes, fennel, olives, and garlic cloves; the langouste with Thai herbs that made Outhier a legend; the exquisite wing of young squab with lemons and tomato confit; and the unctuous bayildi of lamb fillet with peppery mint. Success from beginning to end, including the desserts prepared by the chef's younger brother, source of the great pastries on offer in the little boutique near the Oasis's entrance. The dining room still isn't exactly our idea of a Mediterranean oasis, so suggestively hinted at by the lovely garden court, but we're hoping Outhier can convince the Japanese owners to accept his idea of covering the whole garden courtyard with a sliding glass roof for a garden dining room open all year long. The cellar offers a superb choice of great bottles and more than 40 Provençal wines chosen by the knowledgeable young sommelier (try the

Château Simone white, the Marguerite "M", the Mas Négret, or the Domaine La Courtade). The à la carte prices are holding steady, and there's a fantastic 250 F Provençal lunch menu offering a choice of five first courses, five main dishes, a dessert cart, coffee, little cakes and even wine. C 500-700 F. M 250 F (lunch, wine incl), 350 F, 450 F, 550 F, 650 F.

Royal Hôtel Casino
605, av. du Gal-de-Gaulle
92 97 70 00, fax 93 49 51 50
Open year-round. 30 stes 2,200-4,100 F. 180 rms 580-1,850 F. Rms for disabled. Restaurant. Air cond. Conf. Heated pool. Tennis. Golf. Pkg. V, AE, DC.
The contemporary rooms with sea views sport fresh, attractive decor. The hotel provides an hourly shuttle service to Cannes and excellent facilities for business meetings, but the soundproofing is not up to par on the street side. Piano bar and many deluxe services.

See also: **Cannes, Mandelieu**

NARBONNE	11100

Paris 850 - Perpignan 62 - Béziers 27 - Carcassone 56   *Aude*

L'Alsace
2, av. P.-Sémard
68 65 10 24, fax 68 90 79 45
Closed Mon dinner, Tue. Open until 10pm. Priv rm: 30. Air cond. Pkg. V, AE, DC, MC.
Rodolphe Sinfreu turns first-rate fish and seafood into wholesome, forthright fare. Try the lobster and sweet pepper salad, sea bream in a salt crust, and a tasty strawberry feuillantine. In autumn, there's a selection of game dishes. The cellar offers a fine choice of Languedoc wines. Madame Sinfreu's welcome is warm, the service friendly and efficient, the decor quintessentially provincial. C 300-400 F. M 120 F, 170 F (wine incl), 98 F, 150 F, 260 F.

Novotel
Quartier Plaisance, 3 km S on N 9 or A 9
68 42 72 00, fax 68 42 72 10
Open year-round. 96 rms 400-450 F. Rms for disabled. Restaurant. Air cond. Pool. Pkg. V, AE, MC.
As long as your accommodation is not on the highway side, you'll spend a quiet night at this good chain hotel. Kind reception.

L'Olibo
51, rue Parerie - 68 41 74 47
Closed Wed dinner, Sun. Open until 10:30pm. Priv rm: 40. Pkg. V, AE, DC, MC.
Accomplished chef Claude Giraud is in fine form at this pleasant Old Town restaurant with 1920s–style decor, considered the city's best dining-out destination. His focus is on local products treated with care, as in the generous set menus. For 110 F, you can sample a terrine of oxtail and vegetables in paprika vinaigrette, squid-ink tagliatelle, and dessert. Fine regional cellar. Sabine Giraud's welcome is smiling, the service affable. C 250-380 F. M 110 F, 175 F, 250 F.

La Résidence
6, rue 1er-Mai
68 32 19 41, fax 68 65 51 82
Open year-round. 26 rms 290-460 F. Air cond. Conf. Valet pkg. V, AE, MC.

This attractive nineteenth-century hotel is set in a quiet street in the town center. Rooms are refurbished regularly. Charming reception.

■ **In Bages 11100**   4 km S on N 9 and D 105

Le Portanel
Passage du Portanel - 68 42 81 66
Closed Sun dinner, Dec 19-24. Open until 10:30pm. Priv rm: 48. Air cond. Pkg. V.
The dining room of this lovingly restored fisherman's cottage boasts a sweeping view of the Étang de Bages. Ultrafresh seafood is the natural focus here, fished by the "patron" himself. Try the stuffed sea bass, eels, tournedos with an oyster jus, and sumptuous homestyle desserts. Good selection of regional wines, priced more reasonably than the food. C 250-300 F. M 98 F, 120 F, 158 F, 195 F, 198 F.

■ **In Ornaisons 11200**   14 km W on N 113 and D 24

Relais du Val d'Orbieu
On D 24 - 68 27 10 27, fax 68 27 52 44
Closed Sun (Nov-Feb). 5 stes 750-1,440 F. 15 rms 390-740 F. Restaurant. Half-board 625 F. Conf. Pool. Tennis. Pkg. V, AE, DC.
Spacious, comfortable suites and rooms (some with balconies) overlook the kitchen garden and vines of this picturesque village. Numerous sporting activities on offer.

NEMOURS	77140

Paris 79 - Orléans 87 - Fontainebleau 17   *Seine/Marne*

Altea
On A 6, service area Darvault-Nemours
64 28 10 32, fax 64 28 60 59
Open year-round. 2 stes 485-540 F. 100 rms 330-455 F. Conf. Pkg. V, AE, DC.
Easily accessible from the highway, a modern hotel in a verdant setting with large, soberly decorated rooms.

12/20 Les Roches
1, av. L.-Pelletier - 64 28 01 43
Closings not available. Open until 9:45pm. Priv rm: 24. Terrace dining. Pkg. V, AE, DC, MC.
The dining room is cozy and cheerful, the chef's cooking tasty and reliable. Try the scrambled eggs with morels, pan-roasted red mullet in a saffron cream sauce, croustade of veal kidney and sweetbreads, and a strawberry-raspberry soufflé. Fine choice of desserts. Robust 145 F set menu. C 290-350 F. M 90 F (weekdays), 145 F, 210 F, 250 F.

NESMY 85	→ Roche-sur-Yon (La)

NESTIER	65150

Paris 840 - Lannemezan 14 - St-Gaudens 24   *H.-Pyrénées*

Relais du Castéra
62 39 77 37
Closed Sun dinner, Mon, Jan 6-26, Jun 10-17. Open until 9:30pm. Terrace dining. Hotel: 8 rms 220-280 F. Half-board 230-320 F. Pkg. V, AE, MC.
Serge Latour, a disciple of Gascony's André Daguin, has won us over with his lusty, full-bodied cooking, served in a convivial atmos-

phere, in spite of the less-than-appealing 1930s decor. Sample his generous 138 F menu: an authentic rib-sticking garbure soup, a savory cassoulet du pays tarbais, and a tasty vanilla vacherin with cherries. These rustic dishes are so tasty and satisfying that you'll want to ask for seconds! And indeed, at these prices one could easily eat twice and still not break the bank. Well chosen, reasonably priced wines. **C** 200-260 F. **M** 95 F (weekday lunch), 138 F, 168 F, 230 F.

NEUILLY-LÈS-DIJON 21 → Dijon

NEUILLY-SUR-SEINE 92 → PARIS Suburbs

NEVERS 58000
Paris 239 - Dijon 190 - Bourges 68 - Auxerre 112   *Nièvre*

Jean-Michel Couron
21, rue St-Étienne
86 61 19 28, fax 86 36 02 96
Closed Sun dinner, Mon. Annual closings not available. Open until 10pm. V, MC.
It takes time to win the locals over, and Jean-Michel Couron, formerly second-in-command to Michel Bras, only moved to Nevers in late 1992. Bold and inventive, he produces fresh, very personal dishes like a succulent oxtail terrine, state-of-the-art chicken with olives, a perfect roast chicken, a tasty squab ballottine, and sea bass in lavender leaves. This is a thoroughly original *cuisine d'auteur*. And the 100 F menu is nothing short of miraculous. If only he would simplify the descriptions on the "carte"! In spite of that one quibble, this is unquestionably the city's best restaurant. And the cellar is full of finds, with many wines offered by the glass. Friendly, competent service. This is a chef to watch. **C** 220-350 F. **M** 100 F, 155 F, 220 F.

Hôtel de Diane
38, rue du Midi
86 57 28 10, fax 86 59 45 08
Closed Dec 20-Jan 10. 30 rms 300-590 F. Restaurant. Half-board 395 F. Golf. Pkg. V, AE, DC, MC.
A well-kept hotel in a quiet but central street with a small garden at the back. The decor is rather outdated, but the fittings and comfort are adequate.

12/20 Jardins de la Porte du Croux
17, rue de la Porte-du-Croux
86 57 12 71, fax 86 36 08 80
Closed Sun dinner & Mon off-seas, 1 wk in Feb. Open until 10:30pm. Garden dining. Pkg. V, AE, MC.
The former "historic" dining room with a fine view of the ramparts, the fourteenth-century Croux gate, and the cathedral, has been redecorated to match the pleasant terrace massed with bright flowers. The accent on the cooking has shifted to less decorous dishes that reflect modern tastes: oxtail egg rolls, calf's head terrine, carp crépinette with lentils, fillet of salmon and pork au cocao, and médallions of beef shoulder with hazlenuts in a Morvan beer sauce. Very fine cellar of Loire wines. The prices are reasonable indeed. **C** 200-280 F. **M** 120 F, 160 F, 190 F.

See also: **Magny-Cours**

NICE 06000
Paris 943 - Lyon 475 - Marseille 188 - Turin 222   *Alpes-Mar.*

Abela Hôtel Nice
223, promenade des Anglais
93 37 17 17, fax 93 71 21 71
Open year-round. 12 stes 1,400-5,500 F. 320 rms 700-1,100 F. Restaurant. Air cond. Conf. Heated pool. V, AE, DC, MC. **A6-25**
The huge, extremely comfortable rooms of this seafront palace on the Baie des Anges boast loggias with superb views.

12/20 L'Allégro
4, pl. Guynemer
93 56 62 06, fax 93 56 38 28
Closed Sun. Open until 10:45pm. Priv rm: 50. Pkg. V, AE, MC. **E6-44**
Frescoes depicting the Commedia dell'Arte grace this eating house near the port. No pizzas here: L'Allegro specializes in "real" Italian food. Try the pan-roasted salmon with pistou, carpaccios, homemade pasta dishes, squid-ink black fettucini, risottos, and delicious cheeses. **C** 200-300 F. **M** 125 F (lunch).

L'Âne Rouge
7, quai des Deux-Emmanuel - 93 89 49 63
Closed Sat, Sun, Jul 20-Aug. Open until 10pm. Priv rm: 16. Terrace dining. Pkg. V, AE, DC, MC. **F5-47**
Quality ingredients, careful cooking, and prohibitive prices are still the rule in this restaurant overlooking the harbor. The specialties include oysters in Champagne, Breton lobster, and Provençal bourride, all accompanied by fine white wines and served with a smile. And those sunsets! **C** 390-600 F.

Asia
12, rue Cassini - 93 56 80 83
Open daily until 10:30pm. Air cond. V, MC. **E5-29**
Classic Vietnamese and Chinese dishes are skillfully prepared by chef Nam Vu Van, who merits a toque this year for the fried fish papillotes, beef émincé in Sake sauce with a judicious choice of condiments, and an ethereal apple beignet accompanied by vanilla ice cream. Small Provençal wine list; friendly welcome in a pleasant bistrot setting with a touch of the exotic East. **C** 160-250 F. **M** 120 F (weekdays, Sat).

Beau Rivage
See restaurant Le Relais

12/20 Le Bistrot du Florian
22, rue A.-Karr
93 16 08 49, fax 93 87 31 98
Closings not available. Open until 10:30pm (11pm Fri & Sat). Priv rm: 52. Air cond. V, MC. **C5-17**
This mirrored bistrot reminds us of the old Montparnasse, with its cosmopolitan but friendly atmosphere. But the kitchen would do well to choose its products with more care and to prepare them more precisely: characterless stuffed zucchini, generously served red mullet that looked good but tasted bland, and heavy tiramisu have lost this establishment its toque. **C** 200-300 F.

---

*The **prices** in this guide reflect what establishments were charging at press time.*

12/20 Boccaccio
7, rue Masséna - 93 87 71 76
Open daily until 11pm. Priv rm: 50. Terrace dining. Air cond. V, AE, DC, MC. **D5-36**
The pleasing nautical decor of this center-city restaurant mixes mahogany, sky-blue fabrics, and etched glass. The strong point is the welcome, the weak point is the chef's sauce-making, and the young Niçois crowd is much better looking than the tiramisu. **C** 300-350 F.

Bong-Laï

14, rue d'Alsace-Lorraine - 93 88 75 36
Closed Mon, Tue, Dec 6-26. Open until 10pm. Air cond. AE, DC. **C3-6**
Authentic Vietnamese cooking, with fresh cuisine by André Costa that merits a toque this year. Try the delicious soup of crab and asparagus tips, sixteen kinds of steamed dumplings (all original and delicious), and interesting chicken with almonds and mushrooms. Prices are high, but servings are so large you can share. Charming welcome by the *patronne*. **C** 250-350 F.

Hôtel Brice
44, rue du Mal-Joffre
93 88 14 44, fax 93 87 38 54
Open year-round. 58 rms 395-665 F. Restaurant. Half-board 449-596 F. Conf. Valet pkg. V, AE, DC, MC. **C5-4**
At nightfall, this centrally situated, fully redecorated hotel lights up like a Christmas tree. Guests may enjoy a verdant garden-terrace as well as spacious rooms (for the most part) with country-style furniture.

Campanile
459-461, promenade des Anglais
93 21 20 20, fax 93 83 83 96
See page 95. **A6-5**
Small, functional, perfectly well kept rooms with efficient air conditioning. The reception is cordial, and the breakfast buffet inviting.

Chantecler ₡₃

37, promenade des Anglais
93 88 39 51, fax 93 88 35 68
Closed mid Nov-mid Dec. Open until 10:30pm. Priv rm: 50. Air cond. Valet pkg. V, AE, DC, MC. **B5-24**
It's not easy to make a name for yourself in the shadow of such culinary luminaries as Maximin and Ducasse, but Dominique Le Stanc, supported by the Negresco's owners, has taken his time and has never been in finer form. It's no wonder the opulent dining room in this Niçois palace has never been quite as popular as it is today. Le Stanc's cooking is ever harmonious, featuring pure, perfectly balanced flavors and superb technique. Everything is so goo (and so much better than in the menu's descriptions) that it's hard to choose. You'll be tempted as we are by the open ravioli, a mosaic of langoustines, artichokes, and asparagus annointed with fine thyme-scented olive oil; fresh pasta with morels and ultratender tiny local peas; perfectly pan-roasted red mullet whose savory juices mingle with vegetable tartines; roast turbot with artichokes en barigoule; and anise-roasted sea bass with asparagus and chervil. And then there's the incomparable roast kid with thyme paired with gnocchi and vegetables in truffle butter, roast squab enlivened by cumin, and

sage-scented rack of lamb flanked by potatoes and smoked bacon. As for the desserts, the "chocolate tear" is better at Michel Trama's (who invented it), but the marbré of warm chocolate over almond cream paired with an iced chicory, coffee, and honey cake mousse is sublime. The sommelier has many fine surprises in store, especially among Provençal wines; the service is efficient but never stiff (as you might expect in these surroundings), and the set lunch menu is the best deal on the Promenade des Anglais. An extra point this year. **C** 450-750 F. **M** 250 F (lunch, wine incl), 390 F, 490 F, 550 F.

Negresco
(See restaurant above)
Open year-round. 21 stes 3,750-7,500 F. 122 rms 1,250-2,250 F. Half-board 1,400-2,520 F. Air cond. Conf. Valet pkg. V, AE, DC, MC.
Witness to turn-of-the-century wealth and extravagance, the Negresco still oozes luxury and style. The fine old paintings and period furniture would fill an auction room several times over, and there's even a huge chandelier that is listed as a historic monument (its twin hangs in the Kremlin). The 6,000 square meters of rooms and suites require constant maintenance, and the owners spare no efforts to keep them freshly decorated. The riot of color in the guest rooms may not be to everyone's taste but these opulent lodgings provide a glimpse of a more leisured era (as does the much-photographed car attendant in his jaunty plumed hat). It's worth noting that this is the last great palatial hotel along the Côte d'Azur to still remain in private (Niçois) hands.

11/20 Coco Beach
2, av. Jean-Lorrain - 93 89 39 26
Closed Sun, Mon, lunch in Jul-Aug, mid Nov-end Dec. Open until 9:30pm. Priv rm: 90. Terrace dining. V, AE, DC. **G7-1**
So what if the prices are so high they almost make you forget the spectacular view? So what if the kitchen takes ultrafresh seafood and treats it with less respect than it deserves (overchilled oysters, overcooked grilled John Dory)? You come to this place, after all, to see the stars—from Johnny Halliday to Robert De Niro, no less—not to mention the stars in the sky above the bay. **C** 400 F.

12/20 Le Comptoir
20, rue St-François-de-Paule - 93 92 08 80
Closed Sun. Open until 11pm. Priv rm: 80. Terrace dining. Air cond. Pkg. V, AE, DC, MC. **D5-15**
Local night owls and trendies gather in this big bistrot with 1930s decor and a terrace, to feast on simple but tasty salmon tartare, flank steak with beef marrow, persillade of sea scallops, and fresh fruit gratin. Fine little cellar; warm welcome; quick, competent service. **C** 230-350 F. **M** 120 F.

Côte d'Azur
57, bd Gambetta
93 96 10 10, fax 93 97 13 63
Open year-round. 35 rms 320-400 F. Pkg. V, AE, DC, MC. **B4-48**
Set between the station and the beach, this typically Niçois hotel boasts pleasant, well-equipped rooms. Smiles and efficient service.

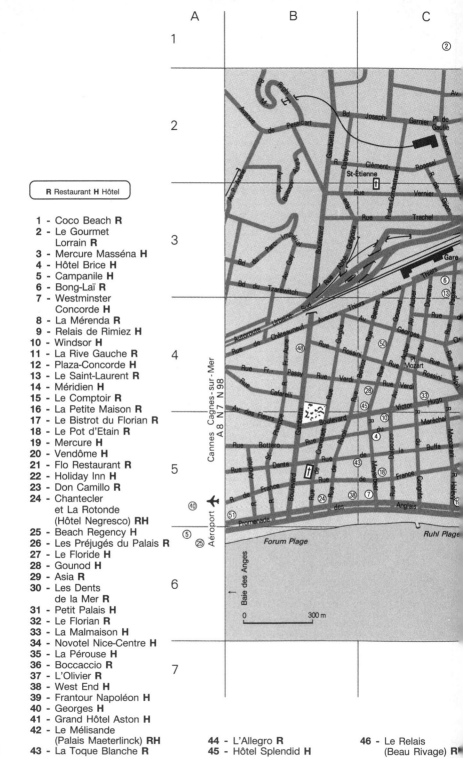

R Restaurant H Hôtel

1 - Coco Beach **R**
2 - Le Gourmet
    Lorrain **R**
3 - Mercure Masséna **H**
4 - Hôtel Brice **H**
5 - Campanile **H**
6 - Bong-Laï **R**
7 - Westminster
    Concorde **H**
8 - La Mérenda **R**
9 - Relais de Rimiez **H**
10 - Windsor **H**
11 - La Rive Gauche **R**
12 - Plaza-Concorde **H**
13 - Le Saint-Laurent **R**
14 - Méridien **H**
15 - Le Comptoir **R**
16 - La Petite Maison **R**
17 - Le Bistrot du Florian **R**
18 - Le Pot d'Etain **R**
19 - Mercure **H**
20 - Vendôme **H**
21 - Flo Restaurant **R**
22 - Holiday Inn **H**
23 - Don Camillo **R**
24 - Chantecler
    et La Rotonde
    (Hôtel Negresco) **RH**
25 - Beach Regency **H**
26 - Les Préjugés du Palais **R**
27 - Le Floride **H**
28 - Gounod **H**
29 - Asia **R**
30 - Les Dents
    de la Mer **R**
31 - Petit Palais **H**
32 - Le Florian **R**
33 - La Malmaison **H**
34 - Novotel Nice-Centre **H**
35 - La Pérouse **H**
36 - Boccaccio **R**
37 - L'Olivier **R**
38 - West End **H**
39 - Frantour Napoléon **H**
40 - Georges **H**
41 - Grand Hôtel Aston **H**
42 - Le Mélisande
    (Palais Maeterlinck) **RH**
43 - La Toque Blanche **R**

44 - L'Allegro **R**
45 - Hôtel Splendid **H**

46 - Le Relais
    (Beau Rivage) **RH**

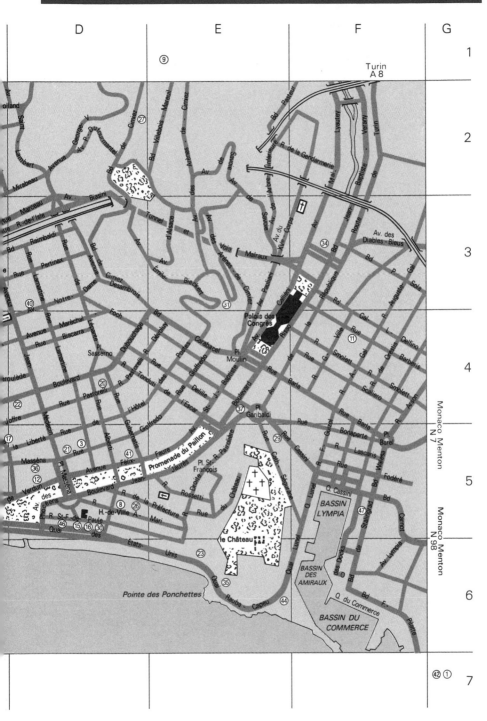

Les Dents de la Mer

2, rue St-François-de-Paule
93 80 99 16, fax 93 85 05 78
Open daily until 11pm. Terrace dining. Air cond. V, AE, DC, MC. **D5-30**
A fine terrace shaded by an awning, an up-turned boat, and tanks full of fish compose the decor of this chic, popular restaurant serving Michel Devillers' nicely prepared dishes like fish cannelloni scented with basil, monkfish ragoût with coco beans, and calf's liver in balsamic vinegar. Fine little wine list. C 270-360 F. M 145 F, 198 F.

Don Camillo ☺

5, rue des Ponchettes - 93 85 67 95
Closed Sun. Open until 9:30pm. Air cond. Heated pool. V. **E6-23**
Behind the discreet façade of a building in the chic Ponchettes district near the flower market, you'll discover a bright, unassuming restaurant that has become one of Nice's best. The chef makes use of top-quality market offerings reflecting the Provençal and Italo-Niçois tradition. Savor the pumpkin risotto with crisp bacon, and squab with Piedmont polenta and delicious winter vegetables annointed with olive oil. Or the interesting chard ravioli in veal jus, or the remarkable saddle and shoulder of fork-tender rabbit roasted in red wine and paired with ethereal gnocchi. For dessert, a crisp chestnut and walnut tart with "fior di latte" ice cream. Delicious house olive-oil bread and excellent Espuno bread. Short wine list with a good choice of regional bottles. The decor and the affected service are not this wonderful establishment's strong points. C 330-400 F. M 200 F, 320 F.

Élysée Palace

59, promenade des Anglais
93 86 06 06, fax 93 44 50 40
Open year-round. 22 stes 1,350-3,300 F. 121 rms 800-1,300 F. Rms for disabled. Restaurant. Half-board 750 F. Air cond. Conf. Heated pool. Valet pkg. V, AE, DC, MC. **B5-51**
The façade features a female giant, 26 meters tall and 15 across, fashioned in bronze by the sculptor Sosno. Inside there are deluxe rooms, a piano bar, gym, sauna, and conference rooms. And on the roof, a swimming pool.

L'Esquinade

5, quai des Deux-Emmanuel
93 89 59 36, fax 93 44 50 40
Closed Sat lunch, Sun, Jan 6-Feb 6. Open until 11pm. Terrace dining. Air cond. Pkg. V, AE, MC. **F5-47**
This Niçois institution features a cozy dining room and a new chef who prepares typical Niçois dishes like zucchini blossoms in olive oil, sea bream roasted with thyme and basil, and a berry gratin. Sumptuous cellar rich in Bordeaux and Burgundies. Liliane Béraud's welcome is smiling, the decor pleasantly rustic. C 350-500 F. M 180 F, 280 F.

12/20 Flo Restaurant

2-4, rue S.-Guitry
93 13 38 38, fax 93 62 37 79
Open daily until 12:30am. Air cond. V, AE. **D5-21**
A few concessions to the Provençal repertoire have been made, but otherwise the menu is pure Flo (raw seafood platters, foie gras au poivre mignonnette, monkfish marmite à la bretonne,

strawberry soup, and fromage blanc ice cream). In other words, satisfying brasserie fare, served here in a clever setting left behind by Jacques Maximin. C 170-300 F. M 95 F (after 10pm, wine incl), 99 F (lunch, wine incl), 141 F (wine incl).

Le Florian

22, rue A.-Karr
93 88 86 60, fax 93 87 31 98
Closed Sat lunch, Sun. Open until 10:30pm. Air cond. V, MC. **C4-32**
Claude Gillon's fine classic cooking has picked up a Midi accent. No complaints with the expertly prepared and harmoniously flavorful Niçois-style red mullet, milk-fed lamb à la provençale and, in a nod to the Southwest, pastis gascon (a flaky pastry). Well chosen wine list; friendly welcome and efficient service. The seductively elegant dining rooms are made cozy by woodwork, sculpted columns and etched-glass mirrors. C 330-500 F.

Le Floride

52, bd de Cimiez
93 53 11 02, fax 93 81 57 46
Open year-round. 20 rms 195-300 F. Pkg. V. **D2-27**
Located on the town's most fashionable boulevard, Le Floride's rooms are very well kept and modestly priced. Smiling welcome, homey atmosphere.

Frantour-Napoléon

6, rue Grimaldi
93 87 70 07, fax 93 16 17 80
Open year-round. 2 stes 600-800 F. 83 rms 420-700 F. Rms for disabled. Air cond. Golf. V, AE, DC, MC. **C5-39**
This imposing 1930s hotel a stone's throw from the Promenade des Anglais offers good-sized, fairly quiet renovated rooms and a wide array of services.

Georges

3, rue H.-Cordier
93 86 23 41, fax 93 44 02 30
Open year-round. 18 rms 310-450 F. Air cond. Pkg. V, AE, MC. **A5-40**
Just 200 meters from the sea, with a family atmosphere. You can have breakfast and admire the view from the third-floor terrace.

Gounod

3, rue Gounod
93 88 26 20, fax 93 88 23 84
Closed Nov 20-Dec 15. 5 stes 770 F. 44 rms 400-600 F. Air cond. Conf. Heated pool. Garage pkg. V, AE, DC, MC. **C4-28**
This stylish hotel of the Belle Époque has attractive decor and minibar in all the rooms. Excellent reception. Guests benefit from free access to the pool, sauna, restaurant, and other facilities of the nearby Hôtel Splendid.

12/20 Le Gourmet Lorrain

7, av. Santa-Fior
93 84 90 78, fax 92 09 11 25
Closed Sun dinner, Mon. Open until 9:30pm. Terrace dining. Air cond. V, AE, DC, MC. **C1-2**
In this restaurant's charmingly rustic dining room, new chef Cyrille Jacquemarin offers lemon-marinated gambas, an aumônière of tiny snails and shallots, gigolette of capon stuffed with morels, and a millefeuille especially

designed for chocolate freaks. The cheese and wine list are sensational, and the welcome is friendly. **C** 300-400 F. **M** 95 F (lunch), 150 F, 160 F, 170 F, 190 F.

Grand Hôtel Aston

12, av. F.-Faure
93 80 62 52, fax 93 80 40 02
Open year-round. 3 stes 1,200-1,400 F. 157 rms 500-1,000 F. Restaurant. Half-board 660-770 F. Air cond. Conf. V, AE, DC, MC. **D5-41**
Some of the rooms overlook a square with floodlit fountains. The superb garden-terrace on the roof affords a view of the Mediterranean.

Holiday Inn Nice
20, bd V.-Hugo
93 16 55 00, fax 93 16 55 55
Open year-round. 2 stes 1,200-1,600 F. 129 rms 570-1,000 F. Rms for disabled. Restaurant. Half-board 135-1,080 F. Air cond. Conf. Valet pkg. V, AE, DC, MC. **D4-22**
This hotel of recent vintage stands on a broad boulevard in the heart of Nice. It offers fine, thoughtfully equipped rooms (satellite television, minibar, air conditioning) furnished with wicker pieces.

La Malmaison
48, bd V.-Hugo
93 87 62 56, fax 93 16 17 99
Open year-round. 2 stes 600-800 F. 46 rms 350-550 F. Restaurant. Half-board 440-500 F. Air cond. Conf. Garage pkg. V, AE, DC, MC. **C4-33**
A late-nineteenth-century corner building with up-to-date facilities. The rooms are comfortable, with soundproofing and air conditioning, and are redecorated regularly. Satellite television.

Le Mélisande

Basse corniche, 30, bd M.-Maeterlinck
92 00 72 00, fax 93 26 39 91
Closings not available. Open until 10pm. Priv rm: 90. Terrace dining. Air cond. Pool. Pkg. V, AE, DC. **G7-42**
Chef Jean-Marc Thivet exercises his craft in a high-tone Riviera hostelry with painfully high prices, but he has skirted the trap of conventional luxury, making the most of Provençal flavors and native ingredients. His classic, accomplished repertoire features zucchini blossoms stuffed with a chicken and morel mousse, red mullet fillets and tapenade quenelles accompanied by a potato cake, and a gooey warm chocolate dessert with a strawberry jelly and vanilla ice cream. Impeccable welcome and service; elegant dining room decorated with nineteenth-century paintings and fine furniture; terrace with a splendid sea view; excellent but expensive wines. **C** 470-600 F. **M** 190 F, 260 F, 370 F.

Le Palais Maeterlinck

(See restaurant above)
Closings not available. 14 stes 2,200-8,000 F. 22 rms 1,350-2,600 F. Air cond. Conf. Pool. Valet pkg. Helipad. V, AE, DC, MC.
Designed by a Swiss financier for his friends and the occasional rich customer bored by the average luxury hotel. Here you can admire a profusion of murals and *trompe-l'œil* paintings by Serge Megter. Huge terraces, and a private beach, landing stage, and helipad. The superb swimming pool is surrounded by Ionic columns; the amenities include private safes, minibars, VCRs, and satellite TV.

Mercure

2, rue Halévy
93 82 30 88, fax 93 82 18 20
Open year-round. 124 rms 450-990 F. Air cond. Pkg. V, AE, DC. **C5-19**
Looking bright and new following a series of facelifts, this hotel provides cheerful, well-equipped rooms. Good buffet breakfasts.

Mercure Masséna
58, rue Gioffredo
93 85 49 25, fax 93 62 43 27
Open year-round. 116 rms 360-795 F. Rms for disabled. Air cond. Golf. Pkg. V, AE, DC, MC. **D5-3**
This fine traditional hotel 500 meters from the sea boasts newly renovated bathrooms. Modern facilities, plenty of amenities, and meals served in the rooms at all hours. Many deluxe services.

La Mérenda

4, rue de la Terrasse
(No phone)
Closed Sat, Sun, Mon, Feb, Aug. Open until 9:30pm. Air cond. No cards. **D5-8**
You can't book a table here because there's no telephone, the bar stool seating is uncomfortable, and there's only one type of wine (De Marchi, available in red, white, or rosé). Nonetheless, Jean Giusti's small restaurant is packed all year with customers eager to taste the best zucchini-blossom fritters in the world, the earthy Niçois blood sausage called trulle, pasta with basil-bright pistou, and a famous chocolate mousse. Authentic cooking at bargain prices. **C** 180-230 F.

Hôtel Méridien

1, promenade des Anglais
93 82 25 25, fax 93 16 08 90
Open year-round. 24 stes 2,500-3,300 F. 290 rms 1,020-1,880 F. Restaurant. Air cond. Conf. Heated pool. Valet pkg. V, AE, DC, MC. **C5-14**
The very modern, well-furnished rooms all overlook the sea. There's a piano bar, tea room, admirably appointed fitness center—and the service is perfect.

Hôtel Negresco
See restaurant Chantecler

Novotel Nice-Centre
8, esplanade du Parvis-de-l'Europe
93 13 30 93, fax 93 13 09 04
Open year-round. 2 stes 780-900 F. 173 rms 450-550 F. Restaurant. Half-board 155 F. Air cond. Conf. Pool. Pkg. V, AE, DC, MC. **F3-34**
Situated in the city's new shopping and cultural center. The rooms are clean and practical, with minimal decor. Pleasant reception, eager service, and a free shuttle service to the airport.

L'Oasis
23, rue Gounod
93 88 12 29, fax 93 16 14 40
Open year-round. 1 ste 450 F. 37 rms 320-480 F. Garage pkg. V, AE, DC, MC. **C4-50**
An oasis of greenery in the center of Nice. The rooms are simply decorated, well equipped, and most comfortable.

> *Some establishments change their **closing times** without warning. It is always wise to check in advance.*

12/20 L'Olivier
2, pl. Garibaldi - 93 26 89 09
Closed Sun, Wed dinner, Aug. Open until 9:30pm.
Terrace dining. Air cond. V, AE, MC. E4-37
The Musso brothers have changed their style
here in their cozy little bistrot; now the focus is
on generous home cooking accompanied by
good wines, at very reasonable prices. Try the
savory fish soup, well prepared roast andouillette with mustard sauce, and tasty orange marmelade crêpes. C 150-200 F.

Le Palais Maeterlinck
See restaurant Le Mélisande

La Pérouse

11, quai Rauba-Capeu
Open year-round. 3 stes 1,480-2,000 F. 62 rms 360-
1,210 F. Restaurant. Air cond. Conf. Pool. Valet pkg.
V, AE, DC, MC. E6-35
One of the most pleasant hotels in Nice, La
Pérouse has magnificent rooms with loggia or
terrace and sea views. Sun room with panoramic
views, sauna, and hydrotherapy pool. Grill in
summer.

Petit Palais
10, av. E.-Bieckert
93 62 19 11, fax 93 62 53 60
Open year-round. 25 rms 480-780 F. Restaurant.
Conf. Golf. Pkg. V, AE, DC, MC. E3-31
This Petit Palais sits majestically on a hilltop
overlooking Nice. The interior decor follows the
lead of the building's handsome Belle Époque
architecture: the attractive, well-equipped
rooms—with terrace or private garden—boast
fine paintings, comfortable armchairs, and superb bathrooms. Very attentive service.

12/20 La Petite Maison
11, rue St-François-de-Paule
93 92 59 59, fax 93 92 28 51
Open daily until midnight. Priv rm: 60. Terrace
dining. Air cond. Pool. Pkg. V, AE, MC. D5-16
This sunny, discreetly elegant establishment
has returned to our guide. The *patronne* still
rather too obviously favors her regulars, but the
cooking is back on track: flavorful Niçois stuffed
vegetables, fresh and savory Mediterranean sea
bass, and a fine berry salad served with vanilla
ice cream. Friendly service. C 250-400 F.
M 250 F, 300 F.

Plaza-Concorde
12, av. de Verdun
93 87 80 41, fax 93 82 50 70
Open year-round. 8 stes 1,600-2,600 F. 175 rms
650-1,500 F. Half-board 750-1,050 F. Air
cond. Conf. Pkg. V, AE, DC, MC. D5-12
Wonderful rooftop terrace and well-equipped,
air-conditioned conference rooms. The rooms
are modern and magnificently appointed. Bar,
grill, and various shops and services.

12/20 Le Pot d'Étain
12, rue Meyerbeer
93 88 25 95, fax 93 87 75 04
Open daily until 11pm. Priv rm: 28. Air cond. V, AE,
MC. C5-18
Éric Régnier offers traditional cooking in this
convivial restaurant decorated with warm wood
paneling and mirrors. Sample his 120 F menu:

harmonious médallion of liver sautéed with
reinette apples (stingy portion, though), excellent beef filet mignon with pink peppercorns and
an unctuous sweet-pepper ratatouille, and a
mandarin orange and lime bavarian cream with
rather muted flavors. All in all, this is a nice little
restaurant, and that's rare in the center of Nice.
C 260-400 F. M 120 F, 188 F.

Les Préjugés du Palais

1, pl. du Palais - 93 62 37 03
Closed Sun (exc hols), Oct 15-Nov 15. Open until
10pm (11pm in summer). Terrace dining. Air cond.
V, AE, MC. D5-26
Take a table under a parasol on the sunny
terrace facing the Palais de Justice, or nip into
the cool, mirrored dining room (sadly a bit empty
in the evenings) filled with bouquets of fresh
flowers. Henri Scoffier's delicious cooking—
traditional, yes, but with a light, inventive touch—
is as appealing as ever. Try his delicate warm
oysters with poached quail eggs, delicious
sautéed sea scallops with spices paired with a
creamy sauce, and a perfect marquise au
chocolat with vanilla sauce. The lowest-priced
set menu is a gift. Friendly welcome; competent
service. C 300-450 F. M 150 F, 280 F, 400 F.

Pullman
28, av. Notre-Dame
93 13 36 36, fax 93 62 61 69
Open year-round. 9 stes 990-1,500 F. 192 rms 495-
830 F. Air cond. Pool. Pkg. V, AE, DC, MC. D3-49
A remarkably soundproofed modern hotel in
the center of town. The comfortable rooms have
various amenities that can be conveniently
operated by remote control from the bed. The
rooftop terrace offers a bar, swimming pool, and
sauna, with a poolside grill from May to October.

12/20 Le Relais
24, rue St-François-de-Paule
93 80 80 70, fax 93 80 55 77
Open daily until 10:30pm. Priv rm: 20. Terrace
dining. Air cond. V, AE, DC, MC. D5-46
A restaurant for all seasons: in summer, you
can opt for a table on the Beau Rivage private
beach, and in the off season settle in to the
spacious, sunny, comfortable dining room. The
cooking is unpretentious and finely crafted:
mesclun salad with warm goat cheese, salmon
en croûte with a well made cream sauce, and
perfectly cooked calf's liver with grapes. Nice
little wine list. Friendly welcome; youthful, relaxed
service. M 160 F.

Beau Rivage
(See restaurant above)
Open year-round. 12 stes 1,500-1,800 F. 106 rms
850-1,050 F. Rms for disabled. Restaurant. Air cond.
Conf. Valet pkg. V, AE, DC, MC.
Near the opera and favored by prima donnas.
The rooms are charming, air-conditioned, and
soundproof, and have lovely marble bathrooms.
Very warm welcome.

Relais de Rimiez

128, av. de Rimiez
93 81 18 65, fax 93 53 51 23
Closed Jan 4-Feb 15. 24 rms 200-340 F. Rms for dis-
abled. Air cond. Conf. Pkg. V, AE. E1-9
Quiet, comfortable rooms with broad terraces
and views of the hills. A regular bus service runs
to the beach and central Nice.

12/20 La Rive Gauche

27, rue Ribotti - 93 89 16 82
Closed Sun & Mon (Jul-Aug). Open until 10pm. Air cond. V, AE, MC.   **F4-11**
Generous Provençal cooking in a cheerful, bistrot atmosphere. A generous set menu priced at 125 F brings an appetizing pistou soup, artichoke hearts, salmon in sorrel sauce, and nougatine glacé with raspberry coulis. The long dining room is decorated with dance photos. Affordable cellar; speedy service. C 200-280 F. M 125 F.

12/20 La Rotonde

Hôtel Negresco, 37, promenade des Anglais - 93 88 39 51, fax 93 88 35 68
Open daily until midnight. Priv rm: 120. Terrace dining. Air cond. Valet pkg. V, AE, DC, MC.   **B5-24**
A chic clientele has adopted this restaurant with the look of a merry-go-round, situated under the Belle Époque cupola of the Negresco hotel. Ingeniously modernized brasserie fare (overseen by Dominique Le Stanc) is the order of the day: popular offerings include grilled salmon fillet, lobster à la nage de légumes, and beef fillet au poivre. But the prices can make your head spin! C 230-380 F. M 150 F.

10/20 Le Saint-Laurent

12, rue Paganini - 93 87 18 94
Closed Tue, Fri dinner, Wed. Open until 9:45pm (10:15pm in summer). Air cond. V, AE, MC.   **C3-13**
A nice little family-style restaurant in the center of town, with an 80 F menu offering slightly watery fish soup, nice lamb's brain beignets, and a tasty warm apple tart. C 150-200 F. M 80 F, 120 F.

Hôtel Splendid

50, bd V.-Hugo
93 16 41 00, fax 93 87 02 46
Open year-round. 12 stes 1,200-1,650 F. 115 rms 690-990 F. Restaurant. Half-board 640-740 F. Air cond. Conf. Pool. Golf. Pkg. V, AE, DC, MC.   **C4-45**
The smallish rooms are air conditioned and well equipped, decorated in apricot tones, and with smallish bathrooms. Friendly service, mediocre breakfasts, and the high prices typical of the Côte.

La Toque Blanche

40, rue de la Buffa - 93 88 38 18
Closed Sun in Jul-Aug (exc lunch off-seas), Mon. Open until 9:30pm. Priv rm: 30. Air cond. Pkg. V, MC.   **B5-43**
Denise Sandelion welcomes guests warmly to this pretty pastel dining room, where they enjoy sparkling fresh fish (and other dishes) cooked with precision by her husband, Alain. He indeed deserves his toque, and the generous set menus have drawn crowds of satisfied customers. But don't overlook the fine à la carte offerings, like raw salmon marinated in olive oil, pan-roasted veal sweetbreads with langoustines, and nougat glacé, all fresh and carefully prepared. C 320-380 F. M 160 F (exc Sun dinner), 140 F (exc Sun), 290 F.

Vendôme

26, rue Pastorelli
93 62 00 77, fax 93 13 40 78
Open year-round. 56 rms 340-590 F. Half-board 405-685 F. Air cond. Pkg. V, AE, DC, MC.   **D4-20**

This former town house with its superb staircase has been restored in the best of taste. The pleasant rooms are decorated in attractive colors and have handsomely designed furniture. Room service (including meal trays); garden.

West End

31, promenade des Anglais
93 88 79 91, fax 93 88 85 07
Open year-round. 4 stes 1,150-1,600 F. 126 rms 550-1,300 F. Restaurant. Half-board 880-1,580 F. Air cond. Golf. Garage pkg. V, AE, DC, MC.   **B5-38**
Close to the sea, a traditional hotel with outstanding views. Services include laundry, a safe, and a sauna.

Westminster Concorde

27, promenade des Anglais
93 88 29 44, fax 93 82 45 35
Open year-round. 5 stes 1,000-1,200 F. 100 rms 500-1,200 F. Restaurant. Half-board 550-1,200 F. Air cond. Conf. No pets. V, AE, DC, MC.   **C5-7**
This 1880 hotel midway down the Promenade des Anglais was renovated in 1986 and was recently equipped with air conditioning. Yet with all the modern conveniences, the service has remained soothingly old-fashioned. Bar.

Windsor

11, rue Dalpozzo
93 88 59 35, fax 93 88 94 57
Open year-round. 60 rms 350-670 F. Restaurant. Half-board 435-695 F. Air cond. Conf. Pool. V, AE, DC, MC.   **C5-10**
A lovely garden and moderate prices. This elegant hotel with superb frescoes in the rooms also boasts modern facilities such as offices for business meetings and a fitness club.

And also...

Our selection of places for inexpensive, quick, or late-night meals.

L'Avion Bleu (93 87 77 47 - 10, rue A.-Karr. Open until 11:30pm, w-e midnight.): Airplanes abound, with posters and scale models everywhere in the trendy American-style decor. You'll enjoy the salads and grilled meats (68-250 F).

Lou Balico (93 85 93 71 - 20, av. St-Jean-Baptiste. Open until midnight.): The full Niçois repertoire can be found here, mostly well prepared. Relaxed atmosphere (153-308 F).

Brasserie de l'Union (93 84 65 27 - 1, rue Michelet. Open until 9:30pm.): Play *boules* with the locals, then grab a table under the arbor and tuck into the stuffed vegetables, "Tante Marietta" gnocchi, and stockfish (55-150 F).

Choupette (93 80 28 69 - 20, rue Barillerie. Open until 11pm.): An appealing little place in Old Nice with a fine fixed-price menu (served until 10pm) and house specialities like zucchini blossoms stuffed with girolles and saddle of lamb with garlic (120-250 F).

L'Escalinada (93 62 11 71 - 22, rue Pairolière. Open until 11pm.): This family restaurant is set in one of the old town's prettiest streets. Dishes include ravioli, gnocchi, and daube (the local beef stew) (65-150 F).

Fjord (93 26 20 20 - 21, rue F.-Grisol. Lunch only.): A corner with tables where you can sample the Scandinavian products sold in the shop: blini, marinated herring, and gravlax (pickled salmon with dill) (90-200 F).

Grand Café de Turin (93 62 29 52 - 5, pl. Garibaldi. Open until 10pm, 11pm in summer.): The freshest shellfish in town, served from 8:30am onwards.

Chez Nino (93 88 07 71 - 50, rue Trachel. Open until 10:30pm.): For beer lovers. The brew crops up in the duck, andouillette sausage, and even in a sorbet. Good draught lager (90-150 F).

La Petite Sirène (93 87 73 68 - 8, rue Maccarani. Open until 10pm, 11pm w-e.): Danish smorgasbord served in a handsome blue-toned setting. Charming service (130-160 F).

Chez Pipo (93 55 88 82 - 13, rue Bavastro. Dinner only. Open until 11pm.): A 70-year-old institution serving only socca (a kind of thin pizza made from chickpea flour), cooked in a wood-burning oven and washed down with a glass of red. Picturesque.

Le Vendôme (93 16 18 28 - 1, pl. Grimaldi. Open until 11pm.): An authentic *bistrot à apéritifs* serving tasty homestyle cooking like calf's head ravigote and navarin of lamb (100-150 F).

Ville de Siena (93 80 12 45 - 10, rue St-Vincent. Open until 11pm, w-e 11:30pm.): Lovely fresh pasta cooked to order and rabbit cooked over a wood fire, served in a lively, Italian-style setting (100-200 F).

■ In St-Martin-du-Var 06670   27 km N on N 202

Issautier $\Diamond$
3 km S on N 202
93 08 10 65, fax 93 29 19 73
Closed Sun dinner, Mon, mid Feb-mid Mar, Nov 1-9. Open until 9:30pm. Air cond. Pkg. V, AE, DC, MC.
Sun-gorged seasonal produce from the hilly Niçois hinterland is the keynote of Issautier's full-bodied cooking, which we have long enjoyed. But this year we were disappointed. The dishes we sampled were good, but ordinary, and not worth the 18 rating. Did we overrate the place last year? In any case, the petit salé and artichokes en barigoule showed complexity of flavors, but the pâté "like they make it down on the farm", the purple-tinged asperges violettes and the navarin of Sisteron lamb were real letdowns. They all featured excellent products cooked with precision, but there was nothing that made our heart sing. We feel the best course is to suspend the rating for now. We should add that the service was exemplary, as is the reasonably priced wine list, with a wide choice of Provençal wines. C 380-650 F. M 200 F, 300 F, 485 F.

Servotel
6 km S on N 202,
in Castagniers-les-Moulins
93 08 22 00, fax 93 29 03 66
Open year-round. 42 rms 250-340 F. Rms for disabled. Restaurant. Half-board 240-280 F. Conf. Pool. Golf. Tennis. Garage pkg. V, AE, MC.
Set on two hectares of grounds, this is just the place for a relaxing or sporting break. Pool; games room; hairdresser.

See also: Beaulieu-sur-Mer

---

*The **prices** in this guide reflect what establishments were charging at press time.*

Château de Nieuil $\Diamond$
Route de Fontafie
45 71 36 38, fax 45 71 46 45
Closed Nov 2-Apr 27. Open until 9:30pm. Garden dining. Air cond. Pkg. V, AE, DC, MC.
A hodgepodge restoration job in the last century grafted pseudo-medieval elements onto this Renaissance château. As a result, the dining room is handsome but rather austere. We prefer the sunny summer terrace, a fitting site in which to savor the intelligent, assertively flavored cooking of Luce Bodinaud and Pascal Pressac. Try their 185 F menu: generous Charente-style farci, slightly overspiced chicken fricassée in Jarnac vinegar, fine cheese assortment, and a choice of yummy desserts. Friendly host Jean-Michel Bodinaud has assembled a terrific collection of Cognacs to put diners in a mellow post-prandial mood, as well as offering some fine Bordeaux. C 350-460 F. M 185 F (lunch exc Sun), 240 F, 320 F.

Château de Nieuil
(See restaurant above)
Closed Nov 2-Apr 27. 3 stes 1,300-1,950 F. 11 rms 630-1,350 F. Half-board 735-950 F. Air cond. Conf. Pool. Tennis.
The Bodinauds' avocation is collecting antiques. It shows, in the regally elegant decor and sybaritic comforts of the immense guest rooms and grandiose bathrooms. Stroll around the vast grounds, fish in the private pond, and take rides in a horse-drawn carriage. Relais et Châteaux.

Atria Novotel
Esplanade Ch.-de-Gaulle
66 76 56 56, fax 66 76 26 36
Open year-round. 7 stes 800 F. 112 rms 470-520 F. Restaurant. Air cond. Conf. Golf. Garage pkg. V, AE, DC, MC.
Just 100 meters from the Roman arena, the rooms here are quite spacious, soundproofed, and sunny. Office and secretarial services available.

12/20 Le Caramel Mou
5, rue J.-Reboul - 66 21 27 08
Closed Mon, Tue, Aug. Open until 10:30pm. V, MC.
Lively, beaming Mady Grangier entertains a trendy crowd in this art poster–plastered dining room. Nothing stodgy about the bill of fare, either: try the tasty artichoke and fennel barigoule with a dandelion-greens salad, lamb with olives and green beans, and scorpion fish in pistou with red and green beans. C 170-220 F.

Cheval Blanc
Pl. des Arènes
66 76 32 32, fax 66 76 32 33
Closed Sat lunch, Sun, Aug. Open until 10pm (10:30pm in summer). Priv rm: 60. Air cond. Valet pkg. V, AE, DC.
A thorough overhaul directed by celebrity architect Jean-Michel Wilmotte left this Cheval Blanc looking fit and frisky. In the kitchen chef Thierry Marx, a Touraine native, has taken eagerly to sun-bright Mediterranean flavors. He uses

fine, classic products and treats them in imaginative ways, as in his 320 F menu: delicious and harmoniously flavored foie gras sautéed in Port with a nectarine confit, followed by an assortment of lamb dishes (steamed, grilled, panroasted), then an interesting cheese assortment, and a roast fig with bergamot ice cream and little glacé cream puffs flavored with verbena. Fine choice of wines. Stylish service. C 250-350 F. M 220 F, 320 F.

Cheval Blanc
(See restaurant above)
Open year-round. 1 ste 900 F. 25 rms 500-800 F. Air cond. Conf. Pkg.
Cocteau and Picasso used to stay at this magnificent hotel, newly remodeled by Jean-Michel Wilmotte. The results are visually superb, but some errors (small bathrooms, lack of storage space, etc.) dampen our enthusiasm.

L'Enclos de la Fontaine
Quai de la Fontaine
66 21 90 30, fax 66 67 70 25
Open daily until 9:45pm. Garden dining. Air cond. Valet pkg. V, AE, DC, MC.
This proud patrician establishment filled with fine antiques has a pleasant interior garden, an elegant setting for sampling Jean-Michel Nigon's carefully prepared cuisine based on the best possible products. Sample his house foie gras terrine served with chestnut bread, whole sea bass grilled with olive oil and served with a fennel gratin, and a strawberry nage flavored with star anise. Classic cellar; stylish service. C 350-480 F. M 150 F, 220 F, 280 F.

Impérator Concorde
(See restaurant above)
Open year-round. 2 stes 1,400-1,800 F. 60 rms 530-1,000 F. Half-board 550-1,200 F. Air cond. Conf. Golf. Pkg.
A major renovation has freshened up this handsome old hotel, set between the Maison Carrée and the Jardins de la Fontaine. Charming, Provençal-style rooms.

12/20 Le Jardin d'Hadrien
11, rue de l'Enclos-Rey - 66 21 86 65
Closed Sun dinner, 10 days in Feb & in Nov. Open until 10:30pm. Priv rm: 23. Terrace dining. V, MC.
The chef and maître d'hôtel of the Château d'Arpaillargues, near Uzès, are the duo behind this promising new spot. So far, so good, thanks to set meals that offer excellent value. Try the fine terrine of glazed tomatoes with fresh goat cheese and the rack of lamb roasted with sage. Simple, terrifically tasty food. C 230-310 F. M 90 F, 130 F.

Le Magister
5, rue Nationale
66 76 11 00, fax 66 67 21 05
Closed Sat lunch, Sun, Feb school hols, 2 wks in Aug. Open until 10:30pm. Air cond. V, AE, DC, MC.
Le Magister's bourgeois bistrot decor is a study in contrasts (raw wood paneling and Louis XVI-style chairs), but the cuisine holds no surprises: it's generous and solid. Try the tasty salmon tartare, tuna fricasséed with sweet red peppers, and chocolatine à la fine-champagne (Cognac). Interesting wine list with a focus on good little Bordeaux; motherly welcome and service by the

friendly owner. C 220-330 F. M 150 F (lunch, wine incl), 170 F (lunch), 240 F.

New Hotel La Baume
21, rue Nationale
66 76 28 42, fax 66 76 28 45
Open year-round. 33 rms 300-350 F. Half-board 350-450 F. Rms for disabled. Air cond. Conf. Golf. V, AE, DC, MC.
A charming hotel set in the heart of old Nîmes in a seventeenth-century dwelling (notice the monumental staircase). All the rooms, large or small, boast modern comforts. Very friendly welcome. There's a bar, and a parking garage 300 meters away.

Novotel Nîmes Ouest
499, rue de l'Hostellerie
66 84 60 20, fax 66 38 02 31
Open year-round. 2 stes 550-600 F. 96 rms 400-460 F. Restaurant. Air cond. Pool. Pkg. V, AE, MC.
This modern hotel near the highway has good facilities for conferences. Among the amenities: golf practice green, children's playground, body-building equipment, bar, restaurant (open 6am-midnight).

L'Orangerie
755, rue de la Tour-de-L'Évêque
66 84 50 57, fax 66 29 44 55
Open daily until 9:30pm. Terrace dining. Air cond. Hotel: 3 stes 500-950 F. 28 rms 330-500 F. Half-board 370-415 F. Rms for disabled. Air cond. Conf. Pool. Pkg. Helipad. V, AE, DC, MC.
Ancient plane trees dot the grounds of this estate, where Hervé and Perrine Pringalle converted a family dwelling into a modern restaurant. Opt for the poolside terrace rather than the slightly chilly decor of the dining room; you'll be served good cooking that has regional touches. Sample the fine 150 F menu: Nîmes-style brandade with gazpacho, fricassée of chicken with raspberries, and crème caramélisée à l'ancienne. Small wine list with a regional focus. Friendly welcome. C 250-320 F. M 110 F (weekday lunch), 150 F, 190 F, 250 F.

Le P'tit Bec
87 bis, rue de la République - 66 38 05 83
Closed Sun dinner, Mon, Feb school hols, 2 wks in Aug. Open until 9:30pm. Priv rm: 25. Garden dining. No pets. Pkg. V, AE, MC.
The two dining rooms are bright and cheerful, and the leafy walled garden is an oasis of charm. Against this pretty backdrop, Serge Beldio's menu highlights sun-kissed dishes based on top-quality products, at reasonable prices. Try the 150 F menu: salad of cod cheeks (the tastiest part) and tiny squid, salmon in sorrel sauce, well aged cheeses, and dessert. C 260-320 F. M 90 F (lunch exc Sun), 150 F, 220 F.

Plazza
10, rue Roussy
66 76 16 20, fax 66 67 65 99
Open year-round. 28 rms 255-410 F. Air cond. Pkg. Golf. No pets. V, AE, DC, MC.
A few streets away from the Roman arena and Maison Carrée, this hotel has been entirely rebuilt behind its nineteenth-century façade. The quiet rooms are furnished and decorated in 1930s style.

■ In **Garons 30128**   9 km S on D 42 and D 442

■ **Alexandre**
2, rue X.-Tronc
66 70 08 99, fax 66 70 01 75
Closed Sun dinner, Mon, Feb 21-Mar 8, end Aug-beg Sep. Open until 9:15pm. Priv rm: 24. Garden dining. Air cond. Pkg. V, AE, MC.
The lovely house in which owner-chef Michel Kayser is based now has a veranda and a pleasant terrace overlooking a flower-filled garden. Here the chic local set comes for subtle, perfectly prepared, classic cooking. The 250 F menu in itself merits an extra point this year: a light and delicious île flottante with Provençal truffles; fillet of fresh cod on a superb, delicately garlicky brandade; excellent aged cheeses; and a fine choice of desserts. The newly expanded wine list offers the region's best bottles. Charming welcome by the young *patronne*; friendly and efficient service. C 400-500 F. M 170 F, 250 F, 320 F, 450 F.

■ In **Marguerittes 30320**   8 km NE on N 86

L'Hacienda
Mas de Brignon
66 75 02 25, fax 66 75 45 58
Open daily until 9:30pm. Priv rm: 20. Terrace dining. Garage pkg. No pets. V, MC.
The "country" dining room is not necessarily cozy; it manages to be pompous and chilly despite its rustic fittings. Opt instead for the poolside terrace. Jean-Pierre Ragot's accomplished cooking is a trifle precious, but full of Midi charm: fresh anchovies with piperade, young rabbit roasted with summer savory and served with an eggplant cake, and a chocolate-cinnamon shell perched on a pool of verbena cream. The prices of the wines do not make your bill any easier to bear. C 300-430 F. M 95 F (weekday lunch), 140 F (lunch), 200 F, 260 F, 320 F.

L'Hacienda 🌲
(See restaurant above)
Open year-round. 12 rms 350-500 F. Half-board 425-550 F. Air cond. Pool. Golf. Pkg. Helipad. V, DC, MC.
This grand old country farmhouse, set around a swimming pool and patio, has elegantly decorated rooms with handsome furniture. Outstanding facilities and services. Charming welcome.

| NIORT | 79000 |

Paris 412 - Angers 149 - Nantes 144   *Deux-Sèvres*

La Belle Étoile 〇
115, quai M.-Métayer
49 73 31 29, fax 49 09 05 59
Closed Sun dinner, Mon, 1st 2 wks of Aug. Open until 9:30pm. Garden dining. Pkg. V, AE, DC, MC.
Anglers and *boules* players dot the banks of the Sèvre Niortaise next to the leafy garden of this regional restaurant. The tasty cooking served in the bright, plush dining rooms is quite well prepared: langoustines and foie gras, fricassée of lamb with green garlic, fresh goat cheese à la purée angélique de Niort, and "nègre en chemise" with cherries. Friendly welcome; well

chosen wine list. C 300-380 F. M 410 F (wine incl), 130 F, 195 F, 255 F.

Le Golden 〇
5 km, route de Paris, in Chavagné
49 25 50 38, fax 49 05 31 57
Closed Sat lunch off-seas, Feb school hols. Open until 9:30pm (10pm in summer). Priv rm: 50. Terrace dining. Air cond. Pkg. V, AE, DC, MC.
We won't miss our words: Bruno Ménard is one of the best chefs of his generation. He's only 32, but he has trained with some culinary greats, and, more important than that, he has real talent. Sample marvelous dishes like roast sea bass with basmati rice, rabbit thigh with eggplant, croustillant of monkfish seasoned with cumin, and langoustines in a jus fit for a king, and you'll see what we mean. This year, we reveled in his salad of potatoes with smoked eel paired with a paprika-seasoned watercress cream, Marennes oysters ribboned with salmon marinated in tart cream, roast turbot in pistou butter with a shellfish coulis, and milk-fed Poitou lamb with a vegetable croustillant. Alas, the breads and especially the wines are not up to the chef's standard. But if you look hard, you can find a few good bottles hidden among the many very ordinary shippers' wines. Service is efficient. As for the restaurant itself, it's housed in a series of low buildings complete with a swimming pool that has its own grill, and the decor is nothing to write home about. Ignore all this and concentrate on what's on your plate. C 380-500 F. M 120 F (wine incl), 150 F, 220 F, 350 F.

Hôtel des Rocs 🌲
(See restaurant above)
Open year-round. 50 rms 300-520 F. Half-board 355-630 F. Conf. Pool. Tennis. Pkg.
Extensive grounds surround this hotel complex. The decor is rather dull, but the rooms are spacious and well equipped. Many services and leisure activities are offered. Unremarkable breakfasts.

12/20 La Poêle d'Or
Terminus, 82, rue de la Gare
49 28 04 58, fax 49 24 00 38
Closed Sat off-seas, Dec 20-Jan 5. Open until 9:30pm. Priv rm: 30. Hotel: 32 rms 180-290 F. Half-board 210 F.
Fresh, nicely turned-out cuisine is served here in a nostalgic setting. Try chef Dominique Douaud's foie gras, kid with green garlic, beef fillet in mustard sauce, and a chocolate feuillantine with caramel sauce. Nice little cellar with a focus on regional wines. C 210-300 F. M 155 F (wine incl), 95 F, 180 F.

Le Relais Saint-Antoine
Pl. de la Brèche
49 24 02 76, fax 49 24 79 11
Closed Sat lunch, Sun, 1 wk at Feb, Easter school hols, Jul 10-25. Open until 9:30pm. Priv rm: 50. Garden dining. V, AE, DC, MC.
The dining room here sports trendy, neo–1930s decor, with halogen lamps and peach-colored walls. The setting suits Patrick Cardin's skillful, traditional cuisine: turbot with foie gras, chicken breast stuffed Vendée-style with a tasty creamed jus, and deliciously simple orange-butter crêpes. Large but uninteresting wine list with

too few half bottles. Warm welcome. **C** 280-420 F. **M** 95 F, 130 F, 175 F, 220 F, 360 F.

■ In **Granzay-Gript 79360**   13 km S on N 150

Domaine du Griffier   🏨🍽️
A 10 exit 23, on N 150, Le Griffier
49 32 62 62, fax 49 32 62 63
Closed end Dec-beg Jan. 29 rms 330-545 F. Restaurant. Half-board 340-705 F. Conf. Heated pool. Golf. Pkg. Helipad. V, AE, DC, MC.
This fortified farmhouse built of white stone is surrounded by lawns and trees. The comfortable, sunny, stylishly furnished rooms are slightly sterile. Large, well-equipped bathrooms. Golf course nearby.

NOGENT-LE-PHAYE 28   → Chartres

NOGENT-LE-ROTROU   **28400**

Paris 151 - Le Mans 65 - Châteaudun 53   *Eure/Loir*

🔲14 La Papotière
3, rue de Bourg-le-Comte
37 52 18 41, fax 37 52 94 71
Closed Sun dinner, Mon. Open until 9pm. Pkg. V, MC.
Another new chef for the kitchen of this pretty Renaissance dwelling with stained-glass windows and an elegant decor. His cooking is more classic than that of his predecessor (hence the white toque). On the generous 145 F menu, sample the calf's head salad with potatoes and an endive timbale, émincé of duck breast à l'orange (tender and perfectly cooked), good cheeses, and a pleasant assortment of desserts. Minute wine list. Friendly, efficient service by the *patronne.* **C** 300-400 F. **M** 95 F, 145 F, 250 F.

■ In **Condeau 61110**   10 km N on N 23, D 918, D 10

Moulin de Villeray   🏨🍽️
33 73 30 22, fax 33 73 38 28
Closed Jan 3-Feb 13. 2 stes 850-1,150 F. 16 rms 450-950 F. Restaurant. Half-board 710-860 F. Conf. Pkg. Golf. Helipad. V, AE, DC, MC.
It is well worth going out of one's way to spend the night here in a splendid old mill. The guest rooms are spacious, soundproofed and nicely equipped, although the bathrooms are spare. Friendly welcome. Excellent breakfasts. High prices.

NOIRMOUTIER (ILE DE)   **85000**
Vendée

■ In **Le Bois-de-la-Chaize 85330**

🏨 Saint-Paul
Quartier Milieu des Bois
51 39 05 63, fax 51 39 73 98
Closed Nov 3-Feb 15. 40 rms 290-590 F. Restaurant. Half-board 430-525 F. Pool. Tennis. Pkg. V, AE.
Set in green grounds, this comfortable, family-style hotel is just 150 meters from the beach. The rooms and bathrooms have been recently remodeled. Fitness classes.

> *Restaurant prices in red draw attention to restaurants that offer particularly good value.*

■ In **La Guérinière 85680**

🏨 Punta Lara
Bois des Éloux
51 39 11 58, fax 51 39 69 12
Open year-round. 11 stes 740-1,150 F. 51 rms 490-850 F. Restaurant. Half-board 460-640 F. Conf. Heated pool. Tennis. Pkg. V, AE, DC, MC.
Each of the seafront bungalows has a terrace or balcony, and direct access to the beach.

🏨 La Volière
D 948 - 51 39 82 77, fax 51 39 08 50
Open year-round. 36 rms 265 F. Restaurant. Half-board 260-390 F. Conf. Heated pool. Tennis. Pkg. V, AE, MC.
Of recent vintage, this pleasant holiday hotel is situated 200 meters from the sea, and has well-equipped, soundproofed rooms. Grill restaurant.

■ In **L'Herbaudière 85330**

🏨 Bord à Bord
6, rue de la Linière - 51 39 27 92
Open year-round. 2 stes 490-610 F. 20 rms 300-410 F. Rms for disabled. Pool. Pkg. V, AE, MC.
This pleasant, modern hotel faces the harbor. The rooms have kitchenettes and look out on the sea. Sixteen split-level rooms. Bar. Sauna.

■ In **Noirmoutier-en-l'Ile 85330**

11/20 Côté Jardin
1 bis, rue du Grand-Four
51 39 03 02, fax 51 39 24 46
Closed Thu & Sun dinner, Mon. Open until 9pm (10pm in summer). Garden dining. V, AE.
In this sweet little country-style dining room patrons fetch up for good seafood, prepared with care and a touch of wit: saffron-scented langoustine galette, turbot in truffle jus, and a goujonnette of sole. **C** 200-330 F. **M** 85 F, 125 F, 138 F, 158 F, 180 F.

Fleur de Sel
Rue des Saulniers, 500 meters behind the church - 51 39 21 59, fax 51 39 75 66
Closed Nov 2-beg Feb. Open until 9pm (10pm in seas). Priv rm: 30. Garden dining. Pool. Pkg. V, MC.
Set between the beaches and salt flats, and with a view of the Noirmoutier church, this appealing restaurant has been afflicted with revolving chefs. We'll give the newest arrival, Eric Pichou, time to settle in before sampling his menu, which includes skate terrine with a tomato-olive oil sauce, lamb sweetbreads in a chestnut crust with green asparagus, and prune fritters with almonds. The dining room offers a view of a pretty garden; there's also a poolside terrace. **C** 200-250 F. **M** 120 F (exc Sun), 160 F, 230 F.

🏨 Fleur de Sel   🏨🍽️
(See restaurant above)
Closed Nov-beg. Feb. 35 rms 325-595 F. Half-board 370-510 F. Conf. Heated pool. Tennis. Pkg. Helipad.
Ideal for stopovers or holidays, this hotel has modern, pleasant rooms with English furniture. Most give onto a lawn. Facilities include new tennis courts, a sauna, and a tanning machine.

367

Général d'Elbée
Pl. d'Armes
51 39 10 29, fax 51 39 08 23
Closed Oct-Easter. 1 ste 1,100-1,650 F. 26 rms 350-715 F. Conf. Pool. Pkg. V, AE, DC, MC.
This eighteenth-century town house near the port provides old-fashioned rooms decorated in good taste. Indoor garden; terrace.

NOIRMOUTIER-EN-L'ILE 85
→ **Noirmoutier (Ile de)**

NOIZAY   37210
Paris 230 - Tours 18 - Amboise 9 - Blois 43   *Indre/Loire*

 Château de Noizay
Route de Chançay
47 52 11 01, fax 47 52 04 64
Closed Nov 15-Mar 15. Open until 9:45pm. Priv rm: 20. Garden dining. Garage pkg. V, AE, MC.
"Be, rather than appear to be" is the motto engraved on a window in this elegant, understated dining room. It would seem that chef Didier Frébout has taken this homily very much to heart. His personalized yet disciplined cuisine displays subtle seasonings and interesting associations of flavors. Taste his fillet of Breton sardines à la brandade with a watercress jus, beef tournedos marinated in aged Vouvray, and apple egg rolls with a sauce of caramelized cider and Calvados. Superb selection of Loire wines. **C** 30-450 F. **M** 145 F (lunch), 250 F (wine incl), 240 F, 340 F.

 Château de Noizay   🌲
(See restaurant above)
Closed Nov 15-Mar 15. 14 rms 680-1,150 F. Half-board 710-945 F. Conf. Pool. Tennis. Golf. Pkg. Helipad. V, AE, MC.
This sixteenth-century château offers very comfortable, prettily decorated rooms (number five has a four-poster bed) that open onto a formal French garden. Professional reception, elegant ambience. Good breakfasts with homemade pastries. Relais et Châteaux.

NOVES   13550
Paris 700 - St-Rémy-de-Provence 16 - Avignon 14   *B./Rhône*

 Auberge de Noves   ✪
2.5 km NW on D 28
90 94 19 21, fax 90 94 47 76
Closed Jan. Open until 10pm. Garden dining. Air cond. Valet pkg. V, AE, DC, MC.
This Auberge is in fact a *bastide*, set high on a hilltop in a gorgeous Provençal landscape. On balmy days the garden beckons, while winter feasts take place around the fireplace in a dining room with huge bay windows. Chef Robert Lalleman, son of the chef who put this establishment on the Provençal culinary map, interprets the Provençal repertoire with remarkable brio. Sample his fresh-tasting dishes based on the finest products, like superbly simple farm-fresh eggs over a cèpe croustillant paired with a dandelion-greens salad or lamb shanks braised with rosemary and served with carrot confit, or more elaborate but still finely crafted dishes like a sea scallop brochette paired with black rice and lobster butter, a magnificent lobster ragoût with a velouté of lamb's lettuce and lettuce, or the

duck in an herb crust with acacia honey. The desserts are delicious (dark chocolate tart and fromage blanc ice cream, crème brûlée flavored with licorice), the house breads superb, and the wine list strong in the best Côtes du Rhône, ably presented by an enthusiastic and competent young sommelier. A well deserved third toque this year. **C** 430-500 F. **M** 200 F (weekdays), 250 F (wine incl), 435 F, 490 F.

 Auberge de Noves   🌲
(See restaurant above)
Closed Jan. 4 stes 1,150-1,800 F. 19 rms 1,150-1,500 F. Air cond. Conf. Heated pool. Tennis. Pkg.
The recent renovation has exposed the handsome timbers and stone façade of this dreamy inn lost among tall pines and cypresses. It is now less austere, and the lovely rooms are more comfortable and spacious than ever. Fabulous breakfasts. Helipad. Relais et Châteaux.

NOYAL-SUR-VILAINE 35   → Rennes

NUITS-SAINT-GEORGES   21700
Paris 330 - Beaune 16 - Dijon 22   *Côte-d'Or*

La Côte d'Or
37, rue Thurot
80 61 06 10, fax 80 61 36 24
Closed Thu lunch, Wed, Feb, 1st wk of Aug. Open until 9pm. Priv rm: 28. Pkg. V, AE, DC, MC.
Chef Jacky Vanroelen has now taken charge of the kitchen in this huge, rather sinister building, a Burgundy culinary landmark. All we can tell you is that the blood sausage we sampled here was good, the other dishes less so. Let's wait a year for a rating; we know this chef has talent. **C** 270-420 F. **M** 140 F (weekday lunch), 180 F, 250 F.

La Côte d'Or
(See restaurant above)
Closed Feb, 1st 2 wks of Aug. 1 ste 600 F. 6 rms 320-490 F. Pkg. V, AE, DC, MC.
Some of the rooms in this old hotel are very spacious. All have been nicely restored in various styles. Good soundproofing and amenities.

La Gentilhommière
13, vallée de la Serrée
80 61 12 06, fax 80 61 30 33
Closed Wed lunch, Tue, Dec 15-Jan 15. Open until 9pm. Garden dining. Pool. Pkg. V, AE, DC.
The son of the owners has now, after solid training, taken over the kitchens of this lovely establishment nestled in a country valley. The dishes we sampled show undeniable culinary talent and inventiveness, and we award him a toque of encouragement for his snail-stuffed egg rolls, beef fillet in a well reduced jus with polenta, and brill with mashed potatoes. The cellar is full of tempting Burgundies; the prices are a bit out of hand. **C** 320-380 F. **M** 140 F (weekdays), 180 F, 260 F.

La Gentilhommière   🌲
(See restaurant above)
Closed Dec 15-Jan 15. 20 rms 400 F. Air cond. Conf. Heated pool. Tennis. Pkg. Helipad. V, AE, DC, MC.
This modern, motel-style building blends into the greenery of the surrounding countryside.

The spacious rooms (all on the ground floor) give onto extensive, marvelously peaceful grounds graced with a trout stream.

■ In Gilly-
lès-Cîteaux 21640   6 km NE on N 74, D 25

Château de Gilly   🕄
Clos Prieur - 80 62 89 98, fax 80 62 82 34
Closed Jan 29-Mar 9. Open until 9:30pm. Pkg. V.
Set down among the vineyards between Dijon and Beaune, this former Cistercian monks' retreat has been respectfully restored; the château is handsome, and though the decor of the cellar restaurant is rather cold, the regional cooking is warming and admirably executed. Chef Louis Schwendenmann strikes a balance between earthy, traditional offerings and modern ideas with his eggs poached in Chardonnay and Pinot Noir wines, fricassée of Bresse chicken with baby fava beans and cébettes (a vegetable resembling leeks), and for dessert an opulent chocolate-and-cherry "half-moon" glacé embellished with coffee beans. Top-notch cellar of Burgundies; competent welcome and service.
C 300-500 F. **M** 190 F, 260 F, 390 F.

Château de Gilly   ⚲
(See restaurant above)
Closed Jan 29-Mar 10. 8 stes 1,560-2,500 F. 39 rms 650-1,390 F. Air cond. Conf. Tennis. Pkg. Helipad. V.
A blend of aristocratic grandeur and bourgeois comfort, this hotel offers large and extremely well equipped rooms with lovely furnishings, and opulent bathrooms. Sumptuous breakfasts. Several luxury suites are available (including a split-level one as big as an apartment), as are simpler rooms in the former stables. Relais et Châteaux.

NYONS   **26110**
Paris 660 - Montélimar 51 - Orange 42 - Carpentras 44   *Drôme*

Le Petit Caveau   🕄
9, rue V.-Hugo - 75 26 20 21
Closed Sun dinner, Mon (exc hols). Open until 9:30pm. Air cond. V, MC.
Under the vaulted ceiling of a small, whitewalled dining room decorated with Provençal fabrics, Christian Cormont offers interesting cooking featuring fresh flavor combinations (sometimes a bit off track) and unusual blends of ingredients. The two first menus are excellent; on the 140 F one you'll find duck carpaccio with shallot confit, sautéed rabbit and veal sweetbreads with a grilled bacon cream, well aged cheeses, and a dark chocolate fondant with pistachio cream. Good Provençal wines at reasonable prices, chosen and ably presented by the patronne-sommelier. **C** 230-330 F. **M** 95 F, 140 F, 170 F, 260 F, 320 F.

■ In **Aubres 26110**   4 km E on D 94

**Auberge du
Vieux Village d'Aubres**   ⚲
Route de Gap
75 26 12 89, fax 75 26 38 10
Closed Nov 15-Dec 15. 4 stes 1,100 F. 19 rms 300-780 F. Rms for disabled. Restaurant. Half-board 360-657 F. Conf. Pool. Golf. Pkg. V, AE, DC, MC.

Built on the ruins of an old château, this handsome group of buildings boasts a spectacular setting with views of the distant Alps. Each room has a character of its own, with a small balcony and rustic furniture. Terraced garden. Gym and sauna. The restaurant is not the hotel's best feature; best to eat elsewhere, unfortunately.

OBERNAI   **67210**
Paris 486 - Strasbourg 27 - Sélestat 23 - Erstein 16   *Bas-Rhin*

■ In **Ottrott-le-Haut 67530**   4 km W

Beau Site
Pl. de l'Église
88 95 80 61, fax 88 95 86 41
Closed Sun dinner, Mon. Open until 9:30pm. Priv rm: 40. Garden dining. Pkg. V, AE, DC, MC.
Owner Martin Schreiber is full of ideas. He's become an expert in the wines of the lower Rhine, available on the wine list, and has brought in talented chef Pascal Steffan who has turned this cozy Alsatian establishment with its marquetry paneling into a bastion of none other than Mediterranean cuisine. We were enchanted with the chef's velouté of coco beans accompanied by ravioli stuffed with ricotta and mascherpone, and a thick fillet of turbot roasted with garlic and flanked by mashed potatoes flavored with parsley and fruity olive oil, madarin oranges, and basil cream. The chef is also inspired by Alsatian specialties, witness his langoustines with bacon and sauerkraut. All in all, the Beau Site is an original but also reassuring restaurant. **C** 270-460 F. **M** 140 F, 200 F, 320 F.

Beau Site
(See restaurant above)
Open year-round. 8 stes 450-600 F. 7 rms 260-400 F. Half board 350-550 F. Conf. Pkg. V, AE, DC, MC.
The well equipped rooms with modern decor offer pretty views of the Mont Sainte-Odile or of the Alsatian plain. Very warm welcome.

Le Clos des Délices   ⚲
17, route de Klingenthal
88 95 81 00, fax 88 95 97 71
Open year-round. 1 ste 800-1,100 F. 22 rms 380-680 F. Half-board 430-520 F. Conf. Heated pool. Pkg. V, AE, DC, MC.
Wooded, manicured lawns protect this cluster of buildings from street and traffic noise. The guest rooms are perfectly quiet, tastefully appointed, and provide all the expected amenities. Facilities include a sauna and solarium; a courteous welcome is always offered.

12/20 Winstub Fritz   🕄
8, rue des Châteaux
88 95 80 81, fax 88 95 84 85
Closed Wed, Jan 4-18. Open until 9pm. Priv rm: 30. Terrace dining. Pkg. V, AE, DC, MC.
Nothing could be more delightfully Alsatian than this pretty little wood-paneled house chocka-block with *bibelots* and fresh flowers. The chef's deft and full-flavored cooking rouses the appetite: try the fillet of pickerel in beer butter, rack of boar with Ottrott red wine sauce, or a soufflé glacé flavored with plum brandy. Superb cellar ably presented by the friendly staff. **C** 200-300 F. **M** 105 F (weekday lunch), 125 F, 185 F, 275 F.

OLÉRON (ILE D') 17000
Paris 500 - Marennes 10   *Charente-M.*

■ In **Boyardville 17190**   17 km from Oléron bridge

La Perrotine

5, rue des Quais - 46 47 01 01
Closed Tue (exc school hols), Jan 3-31. Open until 9pm (10pm in summer). Terrace dining. Pkg. V, MC.
The fish are fabulously fresh and perfectly cooked by Alain Orillac, and there are dishes for landlubbers, too. Try to tear your eyes away from the view of passing fishing boats and concentrate on the sea scallops pan-roasted with Jerusalem artichokes, rack of lamb with artichoke purée, and an apple with honey cake and green-apple sherbet. Well chosen wine list; friendly welcome. The first set menu is a bargain. **C** 230-360 F. **M** 130 F, 170 F.

■ In **La Cotinière 17310**   16 km from Oléron bridge

12/20 L'Écailler
65, rue du Port
46 47 10 31, fax 46 47 10 23
Closed Mon (Mar 15-Apr 15 & Oct), Nov 11-Feb 6. Open until 11pm in seas. Garden dining. Hotel: 8 rms 300-400 F. Half-board 355-412 F. Golf. Pkg. V, AE, MC.
Enjoy seafood at reasonable prices on the terrace overlooking the port, or in the flower-filled garden. Try the generous 119 F menu: tasty fish soup, well seasoned snail cassoulette, and a panaché of sole, skate and black cod in a fine beurre blanc sauce. Tasty goat cheese with salad. Unfortunately the desserts are dull and the cellar limited. **C** 250-410 F. **M** 96 F, 119 F, 152 F, 187 F, 225 F.

Motel Ile de Lumière
46 47 10 80, fax 46 47 30 87
Closed Oct-Mar. 45 rms 350-570 F. Conf. Heated pool. Tennis. Golf. Pkg. V, AE, DC, MC.
The surf will rock you to sleep in this quiet motel with comfortable rooms on the island's west coast.

■ In **La Rémigeasse 17550**   10 km from Oléron bridge

Amiral
Hôtel Le Grand Large
46 75 37 89, fax 46 75 49 15
Closed Oct-Apr. Open until 9:15pm. Pkg. V, MC.
The Amiral has boldly set sail for new horizons, captained by Joël Lebeaupin. The dining room offers a view of dunes, the ocean and a garden, but the real interest here is the chef's elegant, versatile cuisine based on the region's best ingredients: an iced shellfish soup with a watercress "island," mignonettes of lamb breaded with ground hazelnuts, and a brochette of roasted fruit paired with licorice ice cream. Attentive welcome. Splendid, well-annotated wine list. **C** 350-400 F. **M** 160 F (exc dinner), 260 F, 360 F.

Le Grand Large
(See restaurant above)
Closed Oct-Apr. 5 stes 1,330-1,860 F. 21 rms 640-1,630 F. Half-board 690-1,195 F. Conf. Heated pool. Tennis. Golf. Pkg. Helipad. V, MC.

The hotel's modern, ivy-clad buildings are set in well-groomed grounds. Rooms are perfectly comfortable, and the nicest look out over the sea. A sailing school and an equestrian center are nearby. Relais et Châteaux.

■ In **Saint-Pierre-d'Oléron 17310**   14 km from Oléron bridge

Auberge de la Campagne

46 47 25 42
Closed Sun dinner, Mon, Jan-Feb. Open until 9pm. Priv rm: 25. Garden dining. No pets. Pkg. V, AE, DC, MC.
Bang in the center of the island you'll find this fine restaurant, housed in a converted stone barn. Rather timid chef Bernard Nicolas is on the right track with his personalized, seasonal menu, which might include ultrafresh seafood (superb oysters), a shellfish sauce, sea bass in a meat jus surrounded by sublime little vegetables, and a chocolate and pineapple délice. We feel he could easily earn a second toque if he continues like this, especially if he would make more use of the delicious vegetables and herbs in his wonderful garden. **C** 350-400 F. **M** 135 F, 185 F, 260 F.

Le Moulin du Coivre
D 734 - 46 47 44 23
Closed Sun dinner & Mon (exc school hols). Open until 9:30pm (10pm in summer). Priv rm: 12. Terrace dining. Pkg. V, MC.
Chef Patrice Gasse's market-fresh seafood cuisine is as pleasing as his more than generous prices. Try, for example, the 130 F menu: warm salad of cuttlefish with fresh coriander, a fresh cod parmentier with parsley, and a warm cherry clafoutis with a vanilla cream, all served in a cheery dining room with a terrace. Cordial welcome; charming service. **C** 230-350 F. **M** 130 F, 170 F, 250 F.

■ In **Saint-Trojan-les-Bains 17370**   8 km from Oléron bridge

Novotel
Plage Gatseau
46 76 02 46, fax 46 76 09 33
Closed Nov 27-Dec 17. 80 rms 440-780 F. Rms for disabled. Restaurant. Half-board 655-945 F. Heated pool. Tennis. Golf. Pkg. V, AE, DC, MC.
Situated at the island's southern tip, this modern beachfront hotel turns its back to a forest. For an invigorating or a restful holiday, it is an ideal address. Among the many facilities are a sauna, body-building and exercise equipment. Rooms are austere but pleasant; all have balconies.

OLMETO 20   → Corsica

ONET-LE-CHÂTEAU 12   → Rodez

Plan to travel? Look for Gault Millau's other Best of guides to Chicago, Florida, Hawaii, Hong Kong, Germany, Italy, London, Los Angeles, New England, New Orleans, New York, Paris, San Francisco, Thailand, Toronto, and Washington, D.C.

ONZAIN   41150
Paris 199 - Tours 45 - Blois 16 - Amboise 20   *Loir/Cher*

Domaine des Hauts de Loire
Route d'Herbault
54 20 72 57, fax 54 20 77 32
Closed Tue lunch & Mon off-seas, Dec-Jan. Open until 9:30pm. Garden dining. No pets. Pkg. V, AE, DC, MC.
Oak paneling, antique furniture, and subtly contrasting color schemes compose a setting of restrained elegance, and the menu follows suit with a choice of ambitious dishes that, this year, seemed to have their ups and downs. The beef fillet poached in Montlouis wine was original and tasty, but the interesting-sounding "pied de cheval" oysters with grapefruit and caramelized balsamic vinegar turned out to be not very exciting. As for the sea scallops marinated with coriander, the pan-roasted scallops were perfect but the marinade lacked flavor. Delicious prune ice cream, but the spiced wine over the "poire tapée" (dried pear) was too syrupy. The good-humored staff are supremely efficient, and there's a short but interesting wine list with many affordably priced half-bottles, although there should be more Loire wines in the cellar. C 350-400 F. M 280 F, 350 F, 480 F, 490 F.

Domaine des Hauts de Loire
(See restaurant above)
Closed Dec-Feb. 9 stes 1,600-2,200 F. 23 rms 650-1,400 F. Half-board 1,000-1,300 F. Air cond. Conf. Heated pool. Tennis. No pets. Pkg. Helipad.
The immense rooms, suites, and bathrooms of this enchanting domain have been decorated in impeccable taste. The best suites are in the Sologne-style annex. To relax, guests may fish in the lake, swim in the heated pool, or go for a ride in a hot-air balloon. Relais et Châteaux.

ORANGE   84100
Paris 660 - Avignon 31 - Nîmes 55 - Carpentras 23   *Vaucluse*

Altea Orange
80, route de Caderousse
90 34 24 10, fax 90 34 85 48
Open year-round. 99 rms 330-540 F. Restaurant. Half-board 290-340 F. Air cond. Conf. Pool. Golf. Pkg. V, AE, DC, MC.
A modern hotel located just outside town, the Altea offers well-designed, sunny, practical rooms, suited for business travelers. Bar; poolside restaurant.

Arène
Place Langes
90 34 10 95, fax 90 34 91 62
Closed Nov-Dec 15. 30 rms 320-420 F. Air cond. Golf. Pkg. V, AE, DC, MC.
Right in the historic city center, on a square shaded by plane trees. Rooms are well equipped. There's a nice lounge and terrace, but the parking lot is quite a distance away. Impeccable welcome and service.

12/20 Le Parvis
3, cours Pourtoules - 90 34 82 00
Closed Sun dinner, Mon, Nov 16-30. Open until 9:30pm. Terrace dining. Air cond. V, AE, DC, MC.
The dining room is slightly sombre (not to say cold and solemn), but the service cheers one, as

does the food: monkfish liver croustade, snail papillotes with a tomato sauce, and a gigotin of kid roasted with garlic. C 250-300 F. M 98 F (lunch exc Sun), 128 F, 152 F, 205 F.

■ **In Rochegude 26790** 14 km NW D 976, D 11 & 117

Château de Rochegude
75 04 81 88, fax 75 04 89 87
Closed Jan 15-mid Mar. 4 stes 1,800-2,500 F. 25 rms 500-1,500 F. Restaurant. Half-board 950-1,950 F. Air cond. Conf. Pool. Tennis. Golf. Pkg. V, AE, DC, MC.
Mount Ventoux and the Montmirail peaks stare back as you wander in the château's extensive grounds. This extremely elegant and charming hotel offers huge rooms furnished with rare antiques. Exemplary staff. Relais et Châteaux.

ORLÉANS   45000
Paris 116 - Chartres 72 - Tours 113 - Blois 56 - Bourges 105   *Loiret*

Les Antiquaires

2-4, rue au Lin
38 53 52 35, fax 38 62 06 95
Closed Sun, Mon, 1 wk at Christmas, Apr 16-24, Aug 1-22. Open until 9:30pm. Priv rm: 15. Air cond. V, AE, DC, MC.
You're sure to enjoy the classic cooking attuned to the seasons, served with flawless flair. Michel Pipet wins our wholehearted approval for his 190 F menu: salmon marinated in a citrus vinaigrette with sea salt, scorpion fish in a tart sorrel sauce, warm goat cheese with a salad, and a chocolate marquise with pistachio sauce. We doff our caps to the cellar, which includes many half-bottles and is reasonably priced. Warm welcome. C 250-350 F. M 110 F (weekday lunch), 190 F (wine incl), 290 F.

L'Archange
66, rue du Fbg-Madeleine - 38 88 64 20
Closed Mon, Sun dinner, Aug 1-22. Open until 10pm. Priv rm: 25. Terrace dining. Pkg. V.
There's a slightly morose feel to this outdated sea-green interior that seems to have infected Alain Schmitt's cooking. This year we sampled lime-spiked langoustine egg rolls that were interesting but too oily; the veal sweetbreads, kidney, and fillet with morels were drowning in a vermouth sauce. The cheese selection was adequate and the croquant of caramelized apples in cider butter was tasty. A point less this year. The wine list offers a diverse choice of shippers' wines. Efficient service. C 250-350 F. M 180 F (wine incl), 100 F, 135 F, 185 F.

12/20 Le Bigorneau
54, rue des Turcies - 38 68 01 10
Closed Sun, Mon, hols, Feb 13-20, Jul 4-19. Open until 10:30pm. Priv rm: 14. Air cond. V, AE, DC, MC.
The chef knows the tides and times like the Ancient Mariner. Seafood, absolutely fresh and simply prepared, is all you'll find here: sardine tart, tasty sea bream grilled without the fennel mentioned on the menu but paired with good vegetables, and a delicate apple tart. Tiny wine list. Friendly welcome; efficient service. C 280-420 F. M 150 F.

A red hotel ranking denotes a place with charm.

La Loire
6, rue J.-Hupeau - 38 62 76 48
Closed Sat lunch, Sun, Aug 1-15. Open until 9:30pm. V, AE, MC.
Godefroy Servais's primarily maritime cuisine sometimes takes the easy way out. The croustillants of langoustine tails with orange dust were tasty, as was the very good half-lobster roasted with sweet peppers, but the fresh cod with bacon and a garlic compote was just simple bistrot fare, and the goat cheese with honey was very ordinary. Even the fruit soup in Grand Marnier was bland, and served in a stingy portion. A point less this year. Warm welcome. **C** 250-300 F. **M** 105 F (weekdays), 150 F, 280 F.

Mercure Orléans Centre
44-46, quai Barentin
38 62 17 39, fax 38 53 95 34
Open year-round. 109 rms 435-495 F. Rms for disabled. Restaurant. Conf. Pool. Golf. Pkg. V, AE, DC, MC.
Spacious rooms with all the modern amenities (free parking garage, satellite TV, etc.) in this town-center hotel. There's a pleasant poolside terrace overlooking the Loire.

Novotel Orléans La Source
11 km S on N 20, 2, rue H.-de-Balzac
38 63 04 28, fax 38 69 24 04
Open year-round. 119 rms 395-450 F. Restaurant. Air cond. Conf. Pool. Tennis. Pkg. V, AE, DC, MC.
Modern, well-maintained, and comfortable, this chain hotel has sporting facilities and a children's playground. Set in wooded grounds, with a poolside bar.

Le Restaurant des Plantes
44, rue Tudelle - 38 56 65 55
Closed Sat lunch, Sun, Mon dinner, 1 wk at Christmas, 3 wks in Aug. Open until 9:15pm. V, MC.
This cozy dining room has the look of a family house, and the cooking is homestyle, too, with some bright touches. Try the tasty langoustine and mussel persillé with a fennel coulis, or the savory goujonnettes of cod and red mullet in balsamic vinegar sauce. The apple gratin with almond cream lacked finesse. Fine regional wines ably presented by the friendly, efficient owner. **C** 250-320 F. **M** 98 F (weekdays, Sat lunch), 130 F, 150 F, 210 F.

La Poutrière
8, rue de la Brèche
38 66 02 30, fax 38 51 19 38
Closed Mon dinner, Tue, Dec 20-Jan 4. Open until 10pm. Priv rm: 15. Garden dining. Heated pool. Pkg. V, AE.
Imposing beams, country furniture, and pretty *bibelots* make a charming setting for Simon Le Bras's good cooking. We award him an extra point this year for his generous and tasty Landes foie gras in Pineau de Charentes gelatin, goujonnettes of sole with anise and meat jus, delcious wild-mushroom duxelles, and a pleasant croquant of warm caramelized apples with apricot sherbet. Nice wine list with a good choice of Burgundies and Bordeaux; cheerful welcome and stylish service. **C** 300-400 F. **M** 160 F, 240 F, 350 F.

---

*Some establishments change their **closing times** without warning. It is always wise to check in advance.*

Saint-Aignan
Place Gambetta
38 53 15 35, fax 38 77 02 36
Open year-round. 29 rms 200-325 F. Conf. Golf. Pkg. V, AE, DC, MC.
Under new management, this hotel has been fully renovated. Pleasant and inexpensive. A warm welcome. Simple meals are served in the evening.

■ In **La Chapelle-St-Mesmin 45380** 3 km SW

Orléans Parc Hôtel
55, route d'Orléans
38 43 26 26, fax 38 72 00 99
Open year-round. 2 stes 580 F. 32 rms 300-450 F. Rms for disabled. Conf. Golf. Pkg. V, AE, MC.
The singular charm of this hotel (the centerpiece of a vast estate) lies in its location on the banks of the Loire, and in its elegant interior decoration. The personalized rooms, done up in royal blue and old rose, are designed to include a little *salon*. The equipment is flawless, the bathrooms large and handsome. Absolute quiet guaranteed.

Paris 251 - Caen 14 - Cabourg 19 - Bayeux 35   *Calvados*

11/20 Le Métropolitain
1, route de Lion - 31 97 18 61
Closed Mon dinner & Tue (May-Oct). Open until 9pm. Terrace dining. Pkg. V, AE, DC, MC.
Here you'll find a dining room with a "Paris métro" decor where a reliable 145 F menu offers a raw seafood platter, with a change for ham braised in apple juice; then your destination is cheese and nougat glacé with raspberry sauce. **C** 180-260 F. **M** 90 F, 145 F.

Le Phare
Pl. du Gal-de-Gaulle
31 97 13 13, fax 31 97 14 57
Open year-round. 18 rms 200-350 F. Restaurant. Pkg. V, MC.
Here's a big, comfortable hostelry opposite the lighthouse, with newly refurbished, well-designed rooms. Glass-enclosed bar and restaurant.

PACY-SUR-EURE   27120
Paris 84 - Rouen 62 - Evreux 18 - Vernon 13   *Eure*

■ **In Cocherel 27120**   6 km NW on D 836

La Ferme de Cocherel
Route de la Vallée d'Eure
32 36 68 27, fax 32 26 28 18
Closed Tue, Wed, Sep 5-14, Jan 2-25. Open until 9:15pm. Priv rm: 60. Pkg. V, AE, DC, MC.
A posh, polished farmhouse, where Pierre Delton proudly presents such classic dishes as snails simmered in pot-au-feu bouillon, sole with steamed vegetables, and a chocolate trio dessert. The wine list features Bordeaux. Children are not particularly welcome in the hotel. C 320-400 F. M 195 F (exc hols).

■ **In Douains 27120**   By D 181

Château de Brécourt
32 52 40 50, fax 32 52 69 65
Open daily until 9:30pm. Priv rm: 350. Terrace dining. Heated pool. Pkg. V, AE, DC, MC.
Refinement and elegance are watchwords at this Louis XIII château with an elegant dining room overlooking a splendid park. The smiling staff keep the atmosphere warm. And the cuisine is scrupulously fresh and skillfully prepared. Why not indulge in perfectly cooked fillet of fresh cod with tiny claims, savory and tender beef fillet, and an unctuous crème brûlée with an orange tuile. The cellars are well stocked with fabulous bottles. C 300-400 F. M 210 F (weekday lunch, wine incl), 180 F (weekday lunch), 350 F (Fri dinner), 225 F, 340 F.

Château de Brécourt 🌲
(See restaurant above)
Open year-round. 5 stes 1,100-1,600 F. 25 rms 390-990 F. Half-board 650-1,100 F. Conf. Heated pool. Tennis. Pkg. Helipad. V, AE, DC, MC.
The château provides mainly huge, comfortable, stylishly furnished rooms. Most have a splendid view over the grounds of this pretty Louis XIII château. Courteous reception.

PAIMPOL   22500
Paris 491 - St-Brieuc 45 - Guingamp 28   *Côtes/Armor*

Le Relais Brenner
Pont de Lézardrieux - 96 20 11 05
Closed Nov 2-Mar 20. Open until 9:45pm. Priv rm: 50. Garden dining. Pkg. V, AE, MC.
Gilbert Laurent invested his bottom *billet de 100 F* and worked late hours to make his Relais a splendid stopover. When it comes to cooking, Laurent's approach is interventionist: he chooses exceptional ingredients, handles them with a minimum of fuss, and lets their innate goodness shine through. You'll see what we mean when you taste his impeccable sea scallops and scrambled eggs with caviar, boned squab with tender tiny peas and a very pure jus, and a fine, generously served chocolate soufflé. There's a fine view of the sea and garden from the dining room. Friendly service, warm welcome, and better prices than last year on the wine list. C 400-600 F. M 150 F, 250 F, 350 F, 450 F.

Le Relais Brenner 🌲
(See restaurant above)
Closed Nov 2-Mar 20. 2 stes 1,500-1,800 F. 16 rms 350-1,300 F. Half-board 400-1,250 F. Conf. Heated pool. Golf. Pkg. V, AE, MC.
Admirably situated above the mouth of the Trieux, and surrounded by a flower-filled garden that sweeps down to the water's edge, the Relais has spacious, sunny, well-soundproofed rooms with luxurious bathrooms. Generous breakfasts too.

Repaire de Kerroc'h
29, quai Morand
96 20 50 13, fax 96 22 07 46
Closed Nov 16-Mar 14. Open until 9:30pm. Terrace dining. Pkg. V, MC.
The Directoire-style dining rooms overlooking the port and garden terrace offer no decorative high jinks, and the cooking has gained balance since last year. In fact, the toque turns red for the likes of a perfectly cooked and flavorful nage of langoustines and vegetables with a gingery jus, red mullet with potatoes and basil, chartreuse of veal sweetbreads with spider crabs in a slightly too rich sauce flavored with star anise, and an excellent banana tart. Good small set menu; friendly welcome and service. C 310-410 F. M 95 F, 135 F, 195 F, 350 F.

Repaire de Kerroc'h
(See restaurant above)
Closed Nov 16-Mar 14. 2 stes 580-990 F. 11 rms 250-450 F. Half-board 395 F. Conf. Golf. Pkg. V, MC.
All the rooms and suites here are spotlessly clean, with hessian wallcoverings. Ask for the third-floor attic room known as "l'île Tudy", which has a fine sea view through a bull's-eye window. Deep-sea fishing excursions can be arranged.

La Vieille Tour
13, rue de l'Église - 96 20 83 18
Closed Mon lunch (Jul-Aug), Sun dinner, Wed. Annual closings not available. Open until 9pm. Pkg. V, MC.
Alain Rosec's light, generously served seafood repertoire is based on excellent raw materials. Opt for the upstairs dining room to sample a fricassée of sea scallops with asparagus tips, John Dory with a sea-urchin cream, ham-raised squab spiced with Szechuan peppercorns and paired with warm foie gras, and a licorice bavarian cream. The cellar shows a penchant for Loire Valley wines. Sprightly service overseen by the energetic *patronne*. C 300-350 F. M 110 F (weekdays, Sat lunch), 135 F (Sat dinner, Sun), 195 F, 270 F.

PALAGACCIO 20   → CORSICA: Bastia

PAS-DE-L'ECHELLE 74   → Annemasse

☘

This symbol stands for "Les Lauriers du Terroir", an award given to chefs who prepare traditional or regional cuisine.

373

PAU   64000
Paris 759 - Bordeaux 195 - Toulouse 195   *Pyrénées-A.*

Auberge du Bois de Pau
366, bd Cami-Salié
59 02 84 94, fax 59 30 39 63
Closed Sun (exc Jul-Aug), 1 wk in Aug. Open until 10:30pm. Terrace dining. Pkg. V, AE.
On the edge of a wood, away from the road, stands an appealing, wood-paneled inn—the gathering place for faithful followers of Henri Philippe's clever, regionally rooted cuisine: émincé of sea scallops marinated in lemon and ginger, aumônière of lamb sweetbreads sautéed with cèpes and Madiran wine, and a licorice mousse glacé with a crème anglaise. The cellar is well stocked with interesting Bordeaux. The *patronne* offers a gracious welcome and service is perfect. C 210-280 F. M 90 F, 115 F, 170 F.

Colbert
1, rue Manescau
59 32 52 78, fax 59 32 68 38
Closed May 1-6, Sep. 21 rms 120-225 F. Restaurant. Half-board 215-235 F. Pkg. V, AE, MC.
Right in the city center, protected by the trees of a nearby park, this fine, vintage hotel provides spacious, soundproofed rooms. Bathrooms are well equipped. Generous breakfasts.

Continental
2, rue du Mal-Foch
59 27 69 31, fax 59 27 99 84
Open year-round. 2 stes 750-900 F. 80 rms 325-540 F. Rms for disabled. Restaurant. Half-board 340-550 F. Air cond. Conf. Golf. Pkg. V, AE, DC, MC.
The centrally located Continental is Pau's prestige hotel. Rooms are well equipped, stylishly decorated, and soundproofed. Attentive welcome and service.

Le Majestic
9, pl. Royale - 59 27 56 83
Closed Sun dinner, Mon lunch. Annual closings not available. Open until 10pm. Terrace dining. V.
How does Jean-Marie Larrère do it? The prices seem to be going down here, but the cooking is getting better and better. Try the generous chicken salad with black olives and morels (a subtle marriage), tasty thyme-scented rack of lamb with a fine ratatouille and black olive purée, and excellent vanilla profiteroles. The set menu is superb. Fine wine list, with many half bottles. Friendly welcome and efficient service in a pleasant dining room with a terrace. A point extra this year. C 220-350 F. M 118 F.

Paris
80, rue E.-Garet
59 82 58 00, fax 59 27 30 20
Open year-round. 41 rms 350-510 F. Conf. Garage pkg. V, AE, DC.
In the center of town near the Beaumont park, the rooms here are fairly quiet (all overlook the courtyard). Buffet breakfasts included in the cost of a room.

Pierre
16, rue L.-Barthou
59 27 76 86, fax 59 27 08 14
Closed Sat lunch, Sun. Open until 10pm. Air cond. V, AE, DC.
Raymond Casau's cooking is consistently refined and nicely presented. We urge you to try his red mullet fillets with a vegetable tartare, Béarn-style cassoulet with corn beans, and a delicate preserved-lemon feuilleté. In the cellar, there's a fine Bordeaux and other wines. Staff are absolutely on their toes. C 310-410 F.

La Table d'Hôte
19, rue des Cordeliers & 1, rue du Hédas
59 27 56 06
Closed Sat lunch, Sun, 1st 2 wks of Sep. Open until 10pm. Priv rm: 12. Terrace dining. Pkg. V, MC.
Pierre Bruneteau, the *patron* of this handsome establishment, is full of energy and bright ideas: fricassée of langoustines with foie gras lardons, sautéed lamb sweetbreads with cèpes and Espelette peppers, and a mint parfait with warm chocolate. The cellar is small but carefully chosen, and the welcome is warm. C 200-280 F. M 98 F.

Le Viking
33, bd Tourasse - 59 84 02 91
Closed Sat, Sun, Mon, 1 wk in Feb, Aug 1-15. Open until 9:15pm. Terrace dining. No pets. Pkg. V, AE, DC, MC.
Hubert David is definitely not into self-promotion. No menu is posted outside his restaurant, and barely a sign to tell you it's there. He obviously has faith in word-of-mouth—and in his cooking!—to attract patrons to this small dining room decorated with lovely, unostentatious furniture and objets d'art. The cuisine is similarly unpretentious. Try the magnificent assortment of smoked fish and smoked duck breast, lamb fillets "Laurette" with a tasty and unctuous sauce, and a tender, flavorful tarte normande. Madame David's welcome is bubbly and professional. Impeccable service; short but enticing list of wines. C 320-450 F. M 160 F.

■ **In Artiguelouve 64230**   10 km W on D 2, D 146

12/20 Alain Bayle
59 83 05 08
Closed Wed (exc Jul-Aug), Sun dinner. Open until 9:30pm. Garden dining. Pkg. V, AE, DC, MC.
Traditional fare, served in generous portions, draws in the locals: declicate stuffed piquillos, tasty guinea fowl sautéed with cèpes, and a fine berry gratin. Friendly, professional welcome and service. C 230-330 F. M 150 F, 220 F (Sat, Sun lunch), 85 F (weekdays, wine incl).

■ **In Jurançon 64110**   2 km SW on N 134

Castel du Pont d'Oly   ❂
2, av. Rausky
59 06 13 40, fax 59 06 10 53
Closed Sun dinner. Open until 10pm. Priv rm: 35. Garden dining. Pkg. V.
While the fire crackles in the fireplace of this elegant dining room (or while the sun shines on the terrace), hungry patrons treat their taste buds to the savory, skillful cuisine of Christian Marcoux. Try his fresh duck liver with grapes and Petit-Menseng juice, braised sole stuffed with cèpes, and a soufflé of caramelized orange crêpes. Fine cellar. C 300-400 F. M 165 F, 220 F, 310 F, 395 F.

Castel du Pont d'Oly
(See restaurant above)
Open year-round. 6 rms 350-400 F. Half-board 500 F. Conf. Pool. Pkg. V.
On the outskirts of Pau, this handsome hotel is on the ski resort route. Very comfortable, welcoming, and flawlessly maintained. Some rooms overlook the swimming pool and pretty garden.

PAUILLAC	33250

Paris 570 - Bordeaux 50 - Lesparre-Médoc 20   *Gironde*

Château Cordeillan-Bages ♻
Route des Châteaux
56 59 24 24, fax 56 59 01 89
Closed Sat lunch (exc in seas), Sun dinner, Mon lunch (& dinner in seas), Dec 15-Feb 1. Open until 9:30pm. Priv rm: 18. Garden dining. Valet pkg. V, AE, DC.
Waiting to see if a chef takes root is a bit like waiting to see how a new vine will do, particularly one that's been transplanted. We're terribly pleased then, to see that Pascal Charreyas (from the Flamiche in Roye) has taken admirably to Médoc's *terroir*. Trained by Trama and Loiseau, this young chef's cuisine is pure, focused, and precise. He handles ingredients with a contemporary touch, enhancing their essential flavors without interfering with them. In the luxurious dining rooms of this seventeeth-century wine château with a terrace overlooking the vines, sample the chef's pressed eels with girolle mushrooms, pickerel with golden potatoes, suckling pig or Pauillac lamb, boeuf mode au carottes, and a rhubarb tart. Pierre Paillardon, an award-winning sommelier, will tempt you with his monumental wine list. **C** 400-500 F. **M** 380 F (weekday dinner, Sat), 240 F (exc weekday lunch), 150 F, 220 F (weekday lunch), 180 F.

Château Cordeillan-Bages 🏆
(See restaurant above)
Closed Dec 1-Mar 1. 4 stes 790-1,100 F. 21 rms 690-890 F. Rms for disabled. Half-board 880-1,020 F. Conf. Valet pkg. V, AE, DC.
Latour's round tower is a stone's throw away. But why go farther? The rooms of this glorious château are elegant, airy, and comfortable, with views of a small vineyard where the owner grows the eight major varieties of Bordeaux grapes. Special amenities include computer jacks in the rooms, beds for children, and wine-tasting courses. Relais et Châteaux.

PEILLON	06440

Paris 953 - Nice 18 - L'Escarène 13 - Contes 13   *Alpes-Mar.*

Auberge de la Madone
93 79 91 17, fax 93 79 99 36
Closed Wed, Jan 8-24, Oct 20-Dec 20. Open until 9pm (by reserv only). Priv rm: 40. Terrace dining. Pkg. V, MC.
After an appetite-rousing trek among the *villages perchés* of the Niçois hill country, here is a delightful place to regather your strength. At their adorable *auberge* set in a blooming garden, the Millo family welcome walkers with open arms. You'll depart restored, having partaken of delicious traditional food based on top-notch raw materials. Sample the chicken liver terrine

with onion confit, red mullet fillet with new potatoes, sea bass with wild fennel and a vegetable fondue, and thyme-scented roast milk-fed lamb. Good cellar, too. **C** 280-330 F. **M** 130 F (lunch exc Sun), 160 F (dinner), 200 F (exc hols), 220 F (Sun, hols), 280 F.

 Auberge de la Madone 🏆
(See restaurant above)
See restaurant for closings. 3 stes 790-1,140 F. 17 rms 400-790 F. Half-board 440-680 F. Conf. Tennis. No pets. Pkg. V, MC.
Discover superb scenery at this comfortable country inn, where rooms are attractively decorated with Provençal fabrics. Perfect peace and quiet are assured.

PÉRIGNAT-LÈS-SARLIÈVE 63

→ **Clermont-Ferrand**

PÉRIGUEUX	24000

Paris 528 - Bordeaux 120 - Limoges 101   *Dordogne*

Les Berges de l'Isle
2, rue P.-Magne - 53 09 51 50
Closed Sat lunch, Sun, Nov 1-30. Open until 9:30pm. Terrace dining. V.
The hotel is not much to look at, but the pleasant, beige-toned dining room with a riverside terrace offers a good view of the old town. The sea inspires Claude Milhac's varying repertoire. Try the roast pickerel with wild mushrooms, a little foie gras soufflé with leeks and truffle jus, and a chocolate croustillant. Heartwarming welcome from the *patronne*. **C** 220-380 F. **M** 135 F, 170 F, 190 F.

L'Oison
31, rue St-Front
53 09 84 02, fax 53 03 27 94
Closed Sun dinner, Mon, Feb 15-Mar 2, Jul 1-15. Open until 9:30pm. Air cond. Pkg. V, AE, DC, MC.
Chef Régis Chiorozas has gone overboard for seafood. His menu offers delicious pairings of creatures from the deep with Périgord's finest, freshest vegetables. We recently relished his seafood mixed grill with tomato confit, fresh cod with black olive purée, and sole with a delicate ratatouille. Landlubbers can savor the foie gras, game dishes, duck breast, and superb cheeses served generously. For dessert, try the warm tourtière du Périgord with apples, luscious homemade ice creams, or the gooey chocolate tart. The cellar abounds in quality Bordeaux and fine regional wines (some are real bargains). Warm welcome. **C** 350-450 F. **M** 120 F (exc Sun, wine incl), 180 F, 250 F, 260 F, 350 F.

■ **In Antonne-et-Trigonant 24420**   10 km NE on N 21

12/20 Les Chandelles ♻
Le Parc - 53 06 05 10, fax 53 06 07 33
Closed Sun dinner & Mon off-seas, Jan. Open until 10:30pm. Priv rm: 30. Terrace dining. Pool. Pkg. V, AE, DC.
This converted fifteenth-century farmhouse offers a rustic dining room with a beamed ceiling, where you'll be warmly welcomed by the *patronne* and served tasty regional dishes prepared by the *patron*. Try his snail and cèpe

croustade, sole with artichokes en juillienne, duck breast with chestnut honey, and bergamot-scented crème brûlée. Well chosen cellar; competent service. **C** 280-380 F. **M** 95 F (lunch exc Sun), 145 F, 185 F, 395 F.

■ **In Chancelade 24650** 5 km NW on D 939

Château des Reynats

53 03 53 59, fax 53 03 44 84
Open daily until 10pm. Priv rm: 120. Terrace dining. Pkg. V, AE, DC, MC.
This lovely slate-roofed manor house contains a huge and splendid dining room with Empire decor, where you'll be served traditional regional specialties like duck carpaccio with truffle vinegar, a cassoulette of tiny sea scallops with mushrooms and parsley sauce, and duck confit with Sardalaise apples. **C** 270-370 F. **M** 140 F, 190 F, 280 F.

Château des Reynats ⚔♣

(See restaurant above)
Open year-round. 5 stes 700-1,500 F. 32 rms 450-850 F. Rms for disabled. Half-board 370-480 F. Conf. Pool. Tennis. Golf. Pkg. V, AE, DC, MC.
A lovely nineteenth-century château surrounded by a large park, with spacious, well equipped rooms.

PÉROUGES	01800

Paris 454 - Bourg 37 - Lyon 36 - Saint-André-de-Corcy 20   *Ain*

12/20 Ostellerie du Vieux Pérouges

Pl. du Tilleul
74 61 00 88, fax 74 34 77 90
Closed Thu lunch & Wed off-seas, Jan. Open until 9pm. Priv rm: 100. Pkg. V, MC.
Tourists flock to this medieval house right in the heart of the historic town. The *carte* proposes a liver "gâteau", fillet of stuffed carp à l'ancienne, crayfish pérougienne, and Bresse chicken with morels. All washed down with a frisky Seyssel wine, for preference. **C** 280-360 F. **M** 180 F, 220 F, 250 F, 340 F, 400 F.

Ostellerie du Vieux Pérouges ⚔♣

(See restaurant above)
Closed Wed off-seas, Jan. 3 stes 390-980 F. 25 rms 390-950 F. Half-board 650 F. Conf. Pkg. V, MC.
Embraced by massive fourteenth-century walls, the Ostellerie's huge, comfortable rooms are furnished with regional antiques and are breathtakingly beautiful. Family atmosphere. Breakfast is served on a covered terrace perched on top of the tower, with a spectacular view of the medieval city.

PERPIGNAN	66000

Paris 908 - Toulouse 208 - Béziers 93 - Foix 137   *Pyrénées-O.*

Le Chapon Fin

18, bd J.-Bourrat - 68 35 14 14
Closed Mon lunch, Sun, Jan 1-23, Aug 14-27. Open until 9:30pm. Priv rm: 100. Hotel: 67 rms 240-500 F. Half-board 350 F. Air cond. Conf. Garage pkg. V, AE, DC, MC.
The dining room of Le Chapon Fin, freshly decorated in tones of blue, is now one of

Perpignan's prettiest. Just the right sort of setting for Eric Lecerf's light, modern cooking that has made such progress we're awarding him a second toque this year. Try his roast sea scallops with a savory sea urchin velouté, succulent young Bresse chicken en vessie, and a delicious crème brûlée. The splendid wine list includes an affordable selection of regional bottles. High-class service. **C** 350-500 F. **M** 180 F, 350 F, 450 F.

⚔⚔ La Loge

1, rue des Fabriques Nabot
68 34 41 02, fax 68 34 25 13
Open year-round. 22 rms 200-350 F. Air cond. Conf. V, AE, DC, MC.
Part of this hotel is listed as an historic monument from the sixteenth century. Cozy rooms, bar.

⚔⚔ Mas des Arcades

840, av. d'Espagne
68 85 11 11, fax 68 85 21 41
Open year-round. 3 stes 750 F. 137 rms 280-460 F. Restaurant. Half-board 300-400 F. Air cond. Conf. Pool. Tennis. Golf. No pets. Pkg. V, MC.
On the road to Spain, the Arcades is a modern, comfortable hotel situated in a commercial district. The large, well-equipped rooms with full bathrooms are air conditioned. Good buffet breakfasts.

La Passerelle

1, cours Palmarole - 68 51 30 65
Closed Mon lunch, Sun, last 2 wks of Dec. Open until 9:45pm. Priv rm: 25. Air cond. V, AE.
Here you'll find the freshest fish, but why is it usually overcooked? Overly sautéed tiny red mullet, overly cooked sea bass, and an adequate but nothing special seafood salad all combined to bring down the rating by a point this year, in spite of the ultrafresh fish tartare. Tiny wine list. Friendly welcome in the two dining rooms, one with mahogany paneling and the other bigger and brighter. **C** 200-320 F.

12/20 La Serre

2 bis, rue Dagobert - 68 34 33 02
Closed Sat lunch. Open until 11pm. Priv rm: 35. Air cond. V, AE, DC, MC.
Pretty Belle Époque lamps set the little dining room aglow. The owner greets patrons with a smile, while in the kitchen, his wife and son produce an appealing array of dishes. Try the fresh anchovy gâteau, veal fillet with chive cream sauce, and a banana and chocolate tart. **C** 200-340 F. **M** 90 F, 130 F, 190 F.

12/20 Le Vauban

29, quai Vauban - 68 51 05 10
Closed Sun. Open until 10:30pm. Terrace dining. Air cond. V.
Come here for the elegant brasserie setting and dependable dishes like a fricasée of tiny clams with fennel, a warm snail and squid salad, and sliced beef fillet with beef marrow. Friendly service, and quality wines. **C** 200-240 F. **M** 100 F, 135 F.

12/20 Villa Duflot

109, av. Victor-d'Albiez
68 56 67 67, fax 68 56 54 05
Open daily until 11pm. Priv rm: 120. Terrace dining. Air cond. Pool. Garage pkg. V, AE, DC, MC.

In a lovely pink dining room within a villa surrounded by a huge park, you can sample a monkfish salad with crisp vegetables, chapon de mer (a local fish) roasted with saffroned apples and paired with tapenade, and a pig's foot croustillant with morels. C 200-280 F.

 Villa Duflot
(See restaurant above)
Open year-round. 1 ste 950 F. 24 rms 540-750 F. Rms for disabled. Restaurant. Half-board 500-600 F. Air cond. Conf. Pool. Golf. Pkg. V, AE, DC, MC.
The rooms are huge and well designed, with top-flight equipment and pretty furniture. Broad, green grounds keep the Villa hidden from the nearby superhighway and shopping centers.

PERREUX (LE) 94 → PARIS Suburbs

PERROS-GUIREC 22700
Paris 521 - St-Brieuc 76 - Lannion 12   Côtes/Armor

 Printania
Hauteur Trestraou, 12, rue des Bons-Enfants
96 49 01 10, fax 96 91 16 36
Closed Dec 15-Jan 15. 32 rms 310-650 F. Restaurant. Half-board 410-520 F. Air cond. Conf. Tennis. Golf. Pkg. V, AE, DC, MC.
This hotel offers smallish rooms with cozy British decor and great views of the sea and the Sept Iles nature reserve. There's a beach 250 meters away. Deep-sea fishing excursions can be arranged. The staff tends to be a bit slow-moving.

■ In **Ploumanach 22700**   6 km W on D 788

 Les Rochers
Chez Justin, port de Ploumanach
96 91 44 49, fax 96 91 43 64
Closed end Sep-beg Apr. 14 rms 300-500 F. Restaurant. Half-board 380-650 F. Golf. Pkg. V, MC.
The seafront rooms are fairly spacious and pleasant. The owner and staff bend over backwards to serve and inform guests.

PERTUIS 84120
Paris 747 - Manosque 20 - Aix-en-Provence 20   Vaucluse

12/20 L'Olivier
Av. de Verdun - 90 79 08 19
Closed Sun dinner & Mon off-seas,, Jan 2-31. Open until 10pm. Garden dining. Pool. Pkg. V, AE.
In an airy dining room coiffed with white beams, enjoy meticulously prepared cuisine with a local accent: red mullet gâteau with eggplant confit and pistou, breast of squab, casserole-roasted veal sweedbreads, and a warm chocolate biscuit with pistachio ice cream. C 240-350 F. M 115 F, 170 F.

 Sévan
Route de Monosque
90 79 19 30, fax 90 79 35 77
Closed Jan 2-Feb 15. 4 stes 612-793 F. 32 rms 397-582 F. Restaurant. Half-board 417-474 F. Air cond. Conf. Pool. Tennis. Garage pkg. V, AE, DC.
The Sévan's façade may be unattractive, but the garden is utterly charming and the rooms are comfortable and bright. Standard decor.

PESSAC 33 → Bordeaux

PETIT-PRESSIGNY (LE) 37
→ Grand-Pressigny (Le)

PEYRELEAU 12720
Paris 655 - Mende 80 - Rodez 85 - Millau 14   Aveyron

 Grand Hôtel Muse et Rozier
65 62 60 01, fax 65 62 63 88
Closed Nov 15-Mar 6. 3 stes 695-785 F. 35 rms 345-595 F. Restaurant. Half-board 418-498 F. Conf. Heated pool. Tennis. Pkg. V, AE, DC, MC.
One of the most spectacular hotels on the banks of the Tarn, the Muse et Rozier is modern yet blends well into the surrounding greenery. From the sunny, soberly decorated rooms you'll enjoy a sweeping view of the leafy landscape and rushing river.

PHALSBOURG 57370
Paris 430 - Sarrebourg 16 - Saverne 11 - Strasbourg 57   Moselle

 Au Soldat de l'An II
1, route de Saverne - 87 24 16 16
Closed Sun dinner, Mon, Jan 10-26, Nov 21-30. Open until 9pm (9:30pm in summer). Priv rm: 16. Terrace dining. Pkg. V, MC.
Former decorator Georges-Victor Schmitt converted this nineteenth-century farm into a luxurious eating house. The rustic stone walls and exposed beams harmonise with the charming, muted decor of Alsatian country antiques. An entirely self-taught cook, Schmitt has learned his craft well and chooses his ingredients with care. His cuisine this year features a new sunny touch in dishes like savory crème brûlant with snails and gnocchi, Italian-style scorpion fish (perfectly cooked) with a black-olive tapenade and Mediterranean seasonings, and a disappointing truffier with gold leaf and too little chocolate. But you'll also find classic Alsatian specialties like baeckeoffe of monkfish, popular among the restaurant's many German patrons. The wine list is sumptuous and a few fine vintages are available by the glass. Friendly welcome and proficient service. C 400-500 F. M 175 F, 270 F (weekdays, Sat lunch, wine incl), 310 F, 325 F, 420 F.

PIGNA 20 → CORSICA: Ile-Rousse (L')

PILA-CANALE 20 → CORSICA

PIOGGIOLA 20 → CORSICA

PLAGNE (LA) 73210
Paris 653 - Moûtiers 34 - Val-d'Isère 24 - Chambéry 109   Savoie

12/20 La Boule de Neige
In Montchavin - 79 07 83 30
Closed Apr 23-mid Jun, mid Sep-mid Dec. Open until 10:30pm. Terrace dining. Hotel: 4 stes 290-490 F. 22 rms 190-390 F. Half-board 140-428 F. Conf. Pkg. V, AE, DC, MC.
The mezzanine dining room is light and gay, with bright fabrics and windows that offer a clear view over the mountain. The cooking is simple

and not expensive: an artichoke gratin with blue cheese and bacon, perch fillets with lime, pork filet mignon with mussels and curry, and nougat glacé. **C** 150-200 F. **M** 68 F, 94 F, 134 F.

Graciosa

Plagne centre
79 09 00 18, fax 79 09 04 08
Closed Sep-Dec, May-Jul. 4 stes 650-850 F. 14 rms 410-480 F. Restaurant. Half-board 450-560 F. Pkg. V, AE, DC, MC.
A good little hotel overlooking the resort opposite the Biolley run. The rooms and suites have mountain views.

11/20 Piano-Bar

In Plagne-Bellecôte - 79 09 03 07
Closed mid May-Jun 1, beg Sep-mid Dec. Open until 11pm. Terrace dining. No pets. V, AE, DC, MC.
This place is a great success with the *après-ski* bunch. Every evening the owner leads the musicians and singers to entertain the resort's in-crowd. The food is a harmless diversion (salad of warm goat cheese, snails sautéed with Chartreuse, kidneys à l'ancienne, salmon with anchovies, and a damier au chocolat for dessert). **C** 210-320 F. **M** 123 F, 134 F, 164 F.

PLAINPALAIS (COL DE) (LE) 73

→ Chambéry

PLAISANCE-DU-GERS   32160

Paris 740 - Condom 64 - Auch 54 - Tarbes 44 - Pau 64   *Gers*

⑬ Ripa-Alta   ✪

3, pl. de l'Église - 62 69 30 43
Closed Mon off-seas. Open until 9:30pm. Priv rm: 30. Terrace dining. Pkg. V, AE, DC, MC.
The stained-glass windows and rustic charm evoke Alsace, an impression that dissipates immediately one enters the flowered-filled dining room and hears the *patron's* rich Southwestern accent. But we have to report, sadly, that an indifferent welcome and uninspired cooking lost the restaurant a toque this year: bland snail timbale with sorrel, respectable duck confit, and a tasty but miniscule cherry charlotte.You may count on an admirable selection of Bordeaux and local wines (the house Gers wine is tasty). Competent service. **C** 220-320 F. **M** 300 F (we), 78 F, 148 F (wine incl), 198 F.

PLAISIR   78370

Paris 35 - Versailles 9 - Pontchartrain 4   *Yvelines*

⑮ La Maison des Bois

30 54 23 17
Closed dinner Thu & Sun, Aug. Open until 10pm. Garden dining. No pets. Pkg. V, AE.
Here's a half-timbered country inn set amid trees and flowers: a perfect spot for a Sunday tuck-in. Roger Lavergne is a dyed-in-the-wool classicist, a dedicated (and highly talented) follower of the great Escoffier. If you shun neither butter nor cream, come and sample from a menu that features warm asparagus with morels, sea scallops with oyster jus, and fillet of venison sauce grand veneur. Friendly welcome and efficient service. A balanced wine list provides affordable options as well as grandiose bottles for celebrating. **C** 350-500 F.

PLANCOËT   22130

Paris 385 - Dinard 14 - Dinan 17 - St-Brieuc 47   *Côtes/Armor*

⑯ Chez Crouzil   ✪

Les Quais - 96 84 10 24, fax 96 84 01 93
Closed Sun dinner (exc Jul-Aug), Mon, Jan 10-Feb 18. Open until 9:30pm. Priv rm: 40. Garden dining. Valet pkg. V, AE, MC.
In a peach-toned dining room in the heart of Plancoët, Jean-Pierre Crouzil offers fabulously fresh, fine ingredients, an inventive way with seafood, and technique honed to acute precision. These features all come together in Crouzil's delicate slices of raw sea scallops intwined with bits of caviar, a superb taste of the sea; his scrambled eggs with spider crab perfectly paired with a zesty tomato sauce; and harmonious lobster and sea urchins on a bed of julienned endives. We also reveled in his duck liver ragoût with asparagus and truffles, rare-cooked liver with tasty asparagus and truffles, and the best warm apple tart you'll find in Brittany. Presentation is superb (oursinade in sea urchin shells, for example), the welcome is warm, and the service efficient. Wonderful, wisely priced wine list. **C** 300-400 F. **M** 120 F (lunch exc Sun), 235 F, 285 F, 400 F, 480 F.

⚏ L'Écrin

(See restaurant above)
Closed Jan 10-Feb 18. 7 rms 350-700 F. Half-board 450-550 F. Conf. Golf. No pets. Valet pkg. V, AE, MC.
The large rooms are prettily decorated with English furniture and have wide beds and huge, comfortable bathrooms with antique taps. The welcome is faultless, the service excellent, and the breakfasts are not to be believed (oysters, charcuterie, boiled eggs, fresh fruit juice, etc.). Unquestionably one of the best hotels in the region. And prices are reasonable given the high quality.

PLAN-DU-VAR   06670

Paris 867 - Nice 31 - Antibes 39 - Vence 27   *Alpes-Mar.*

⑭ Cassini

202, route Nationale - 93 08 91 03
Closed Sun dinner & Mon (exc Jul-Aug), 2 wks Jan-Feb, Jun 5-20. Open until 10pm (11pm in summer). Priv rm: 40. Terrace dining. Pkg. V, AE, MC.
Philippe Martin uses prime regional produce to turn out such tasty dishes as those on the 120 F menu: fish persillé with fresh herbs, chicken breast with chard and pine nuts, tiramisu, and a chocolate croustillant with currant sauce. Opt for the wonderful terrace rather than the rather ordinary dining room. Friendly welcome. Small, diverse wine list. **C** 220-330 F. **M** 80 F, 120 F (exc Sun), 140 F (Sun), 180 F.

PLAPPEVILLE 57   → Metz

PLÉNEUF-VAL-ANDRÉ   22370

Paris 417 - St-Brieuc 30 - Dinan 43 - Erquy 9   *Côtes/Armor*

⑮ La Cotriade

1 km, port Piégu - 96 72 20 26
Closed Mon dinner, Tue, Jan 9-Feb 11. Open until 9pm (10pm in summer). Pkg. V, MC.
Pléneuf Bay, framed in all its glorious beauty by the restaurant's picture windows, is the source for the fabulous seafood on the menu.

Lobsters—grilled or steamed over seaweed—get top billing here; co-starring with them are ultrafresh scallops and John Dory with island spices, among other capably prepared dishes. The few desserts on offer are quite good, and the cellar is gratifyingly diverse. **C** 410-610 F. **M** 130 F, 200 F, 270 F.

Grand Hôtel
80, rue de l'Amiral-Charner
96 72 20 56, fax 96 63 00 24
Closings not available. 39 rms 298-393 F. Rms for disabled. Restaurant. Half-board 400-440 F. Conf. Golf. Pkg. V, MC.
A commodious hotel with direct access to the beach. Some of the impeccably kept rooms offer sea views as well.

PLÉRIN-SOUS-LA-TOUR 22
→ Saint-Brieuc

PLEUGUENEUC   35720
Paris 380 - Dinan 14 - Rennes 37 - Combourg 13   *Ille/Vil.*

Château de la Motte-Beaumanoir
2 km N on N 137, exit Plesder
99 69 46 01, fax 99 69 42 49
Closed Tue, Dec-Mar. Open until 10:30pm. Priv rm: 35. Garden dining. Heated pool. Pkg. V, AE, MC.
The cuisine offered in this magnificent edifice is supremely classical: turbot fillet with red butter sauce, leg of lamb with basil, and fillet of sea bream en papillote. The setting—a blue-toned, Directoire-period dining room in a handsome eighteenth-century château—is as lovely as ever. Judicious cellar; attentive welcome. **C** 260-360 F. **M** 140 F.

Château de la Motte-Beaumanoir 🏶
(See restaurant above)
Open year-round. 2 stes 1,000-1,300 F. 6 rms 700-900 F. Half-board 550-650 F. Conf. Heated pool. Tennis. Golf. Pkg. Helipad. V, AE, MC.
Stop over at this lovely château (complete with a moat) to sleep in large, beautiful rooms that look out over the meadows, woods, and ponds of the surrounding estate.

PLEURTUIT 35 → Dinard
PLOEMEUR 56 → Lorient
PLOUMANACH 22 → Perros-Guirec
PLOUNÉRIN   22780
Paris 510 - Morlaix 23 - St-Brieuc 60   *Côtes/Armor*

Patrick Jeffroy
11, rue du Bon Voyage
96 38 61 80, fax 96 38 66 29
Closed Sun & Mon off-seas. Open until 10pm. Priv rm: 45. Pkg. V.
Patrick Jeffroy continues to strive away in the kitchens of his three-toque restaurant, a quiet, peaceful haven by the sea. Jeffroy's timid, taciturn nature conceals a chef full of culinary derring-do and panache, who passionately loves

Brittany. Who else would combine strips of pig's ear confit with green asparagus and langoustines, anise with warm oysters, sweet-sour mango with red mullet, and coconut milk with turbot? And he dares to serve you apple fries, and a fillet of fresh salmon sizzling on a hot stone that you annoint, as in bygone days, with garum sauce. As it happens, all these iconoclastic couplings work brilliantly. The pastry chef, William Moysan, is an ace, too. Don't miss the Roquefort bread-crumb terrine flavored with pure chocolate, or the praliné chocolate cake, buttery sablé with fresh fruit, or the dried-fruit crème brûlée. As for the service, you need patience, but just remember you're in Brittany, not Paris. **C** 450-570 F. **M** 100 F (weekday lunch, wine incl), 180 F, 285 F, 360 F.

POËT-LAVAL (LE) 26 → Dieulefit
POINCY 77 → Meaux
POITIERS   86000
Paris 338 - Tours 104 - Angoulême 109 - Angers 133   *Vienne*

Hôtel Continental
2, bd Solférino
49 37 93 93, fax 49 53 01 16
Open year-round. 39 rms 255-295 F. Conf. V, AE, DC, MC.
A classic construction in the town center; pleasant, soundproofed rooms with every comfort (number 27 has a minibar).

Maxime
4, rue Saint-Nicolas - 49 41 09 55
Closed Sat, Sun, Jan 16-27, Jul 10-20, Aug 10-20. Open until 10pm. Priv rm: 22. Pkg. V, AE, MC.
This is Poitiers's top restaurant, where hostess Jacqueline Rougier pampers a clientele made up mostly of regulars. In the kitchen, chef Christian Rougier keeps coming up with enticing new additions to his repertoire. Recent developments include creamed green lentils with warm foie gras, turbot with veal jus and fresh pasta, and the "jeu de pomme" dessert with thyme-scented applesauce, apple millefeuille with sherbet, and a roast apple. Magnificent cellar; fine selection of whiskies. **C** 280-320 F. **M** 155 F (lunch, wine & coffee incl), 99 F, 185 F, 240 F.

12/20 Le Saint-Hilaire
65, rue Th.-Renaudot - 49 41 15 45
Closed Sat (Jul-Aug), Sun, Dec 24-Jan 11. Open until 9:45pm. V, MC.
The basement of a nondescript modern building conceals this twelfth-century still room complete with ogival vaulting. Nowadays one comes here to enjoy traditional Poitevin cooking, such as that on the 150 F menu: fine squab salad with cabbage, veal fillet with star anise (a bit drowning in sauce), and a fresh fruit salad spiked with ginger. Friendly, efficient welcome and service; nice little local wines. **C** 270-350 F. **M** 120 F, 135 F, 150 F, 260 F.

*We're always happy to hear about **your discoveries** and receive your comments on ours. Please feel free to write to us stating clearly what you liked or disliked. Be concise but convincing, and take the time to argue your point.*

■ In Chasseneuil-
du-Poitou 86360   8 km N on N 10

Château Le
Clos de la Ribaudière   ▲🌳
10, rue du Champ-de-Foire
49 52 86 66, fax 49 52 86 32
*Open year-round. 19 rms 300-620 F. Restaurant.
Half-board 655-955 F. Golf. Pkg. V, AE, DC, MC.*
It took several months (and probably several million francs) to restore its former luster to this nineteenth-century residence, superbly situated in a delightful park. There are eleven spacious, fresh, comfortable rooms (as well as eight others in the caretaker's lodge next door), all with marble bathrooms.

■ In Croutelle 86240   6 km S on N 10

Pierre Benoist
RN 10 - A 10, Poitiers Sud exit
49 57 11 52
Open daily until 9:45pm. Garden dining. Pkg. V, MC.
It was no simple matter to step into Pierre Benoist's shoes, but André Chenu has brought it off nicely. A sure sign: the same loyal customers continue to fill this cozy, classic inn. Chenu's cooking is finely honed, precise, and generous, and very reasonably priced. Try the 165 F menu, with a soft-cooked egg over creamed tiny peas with a bacon gelatin, pickerel roasted in its skin with veal jus, farm-produced cheese, and a chocolate palet with chocolate-honey ice cream. The cellar is strong on Bordeaux and Loire wines. Friendly welcome.
C 280-400 F. **M** 125 F, 165 F, 220 F.

POLIGNY   39800
Paris 404 - Besançon 58 - Lons-le-Saunier 28 - Dole 37   *Jura*

12/20 Hostellerie
des Monts de Vaux
5 km E on N 5
84 37 12 50, fax 84 37 09 07
Closed Tue (exc dinner in seas), Wed lunch off-seas, end Oct-end Dec. Open until 8:45pm. Terrace dining. Valet pkg. V, AE, DC, MC.
The cuisine is reliably consistent at this likeable coaching inn set deep in the forest, and the antique furniture and dining room seem not likely to change either. Still, this is a stylish stop in the Jura. **C** 350-450 F. **M** 170 F (lunch), 350 F.

Hostellerie
des Monts de Vaux   ▲🌳
(See restaurant above)
Closed Tue (exc Jul-Aug), end Oct-end Dec. 3 stes 1,000 F. 7 rms 550-850 F. Half-board 650-900 F. Tennis. Golf. Valet pkg. Helipad. V, AE, DC, MC.
Perched at 600 meters of altitude, this peaceful, slightly old-fashioned inn reigns over a quiet forest. Delicious breakfasts. Relais et Châteaux.

> **Gault Millau's ratings** *are based solely on the restaurants' cuisine. We do not take into account the atmosphere, décor, service, and so on; these are commented upon within the review.*

PONS   17800
Paris 495 - Bordeaux 96 - Cognac 23 - Saintes 22   *Charente-M.*

■ In Mosnac 17240   11 km S on N 137 and D 134

 ### Le Moulin de Marcouze   🔾
46 70 46 16, fax 46 70 48 14
Closed Wed lunch & Tue off-seas (exc hols), Nov-mid Mar. Open until 9:30pm. Air cond. Pkg. V, AE.
Built around an old mill, this hotel-restaurant is a boon for those who like to relax in a leafy setting and watch the river flow—the Seugne runs right past the dining room. Dominique Bouchet's accomplished cooking shows to advantage here. If you manage to reserve in advance, order (a day ahead) the fabulous farm-raised chicken roasted with meltingly tender potatoes. Other sure bets in the regional repertoire are leg of lamb cooked seven hours, casserole-roasted veal kidney with morel cream, beef cheeks with carrot confit, and a pig's foot galette. Sumptuous wine list lacking half bottles but with some reasonably priced choices like an Entre-Deux-Mers Château Grand Monteil at 120 F. **C** 420-520 F. **M** 140 F, 250 F, 420 F.

Le Moulin de Marcouze
(See restaurant above)
Closed Nov-mid Mar. 10 rms 530-700 F. Half-board 710-760 F. Air cond. Conf. Pool. Golf. Pkg. Helipad. V, AE, MC.
Choice large rooms with red tile floors looking over the river or the lawn.

PONTARLIER   25300
Paris 452 - Belfort 125 - Besançon 58 - Geneva 120   *Doubs*

■ In Oye-et-Pallet 25160   7 km SW on N 5, D 437

Hôtel Parnet   ▲🌳
Riant Séjour
81 89 42 03, fax 81 89 41 47
Closed Sun & Mon (exc school hols), Dec 20-Jan. 17 rms 250-340 F. Restaurant. Half-board 360-395 F. Conf. Heated pool. Tennis. No pets. Pkg. V, MC.
This trim, tidy little hostelry is decked out with beflowered wallpaper and carpeting. The garden grounds are delightfully quiet, and there is a sauna and Turkish bath for complete relaxation.

PONT-AUDEMER   27500
Paris 168 - Rouen 52 - Honfleur 24 - Lisieux 36 - Evreux 68   *Eure*

12/20 Auberge du Vieux Puits   🔾
 6, rue Notre-Dame-du-Pré
32 41 01 48
Closed Mon dinner & Tue off-seas, Dec 20-Jan 28. Open until 9pm. Priv rm: 18. Pkg. V, MC.
Tourists adore this mellow country inn. While the young owners greet guests with a smile, the cooking disappointed us this year: bland langoustines with Sherry vinegar sauce, dull beef tournedos with a mustard sabayon, and an adequate chocolate and walnut tart with a paltry crème anglaise. The toque has to go. **C** 260-360 F. **M** 190 F (weekday lunch, Sat), 300 F.

Auberge du Vieux Puits
(See restaurant above)
Closed Dec 20-Jan 28. 12 rms 180-440 F. No pets.
Pkg.
A superb collection of seventeenth-century half-timbered buildings around a vast courtyard houses some simple, rustic, but charming rooms and a few larger, well equipped ones with antique furnishings. Friendly welcome; good breakfasts.

 Belle Isle-sur-Risle
1.5 km on N 175, 112, route de Rouen
32 56 96 22, fax 32 42 88 96
Open year-round. 3 stes 1,000-1,350 F. 16 rms 590-1,250 F. Restaurant. Half-board 690-1,150 F. Air cond. Conf. Heated pool. Tennis. Garage pkg. Helipad. V, AE, DC, MC.
This aristocratic house on wooded grounds has undeniable charm, shown to advantage in the spacious and elegant rooms (the ones on the third floor have better views of the park), as well as by the perfectly polished service.

PONTAULT-COMBAULT 77
→ PARIS Suburbs

PONT-AVEN 29930
Paris 522 - Lorient 36 - Concarneau 15 - Quimper 38   Finistère

 Moulin de Rosmadec
98 06 00 22, fax 98 06 18 00
Closed Sun dinner (Sep 6-Jun 14), Wed, Feb, last 2 wks of Oct. Open until 9:30pm. Garden dining. Pkg. V, MC.
The welcome at this fifteenth-century mill on the Aven is perfectly charming. The capable chef, Frédéric Sébilleau, pays close attention to defining the flavors of his excellent ingredients. Try his crab and langoustine pannequets, John Dory grilled with artichokes, and crêpes flambées. Well chosen wine list; warm welcome.
C 360-460 F. M 160 F, 295 F, 395 F.

 Moulin de Rosmadec
(See restaurant above)
See restaurant for closings. 4 rms 400-470 F. Conf. Golf. V, MC.
There are only four bedrooms, but they are charmingly decorated in fresh, simple tones, and perfectly comfortable. Tempting breakfasts.

 Rozaven
11, quai Th.-Botrel
98 06 13 06, fax 98 06 03 89
Closed Mon, Nov 15-Feb. 3 stes 500-900 F. 23 rms 340-600 F. Restaurant. Half-board 760 F. Pkg. V.
Here's an authentic eighteenth-century thatched-roof house (with five guestrooms) and a modern extension (twelve rooms) overlooking the river. All rooms are soundproof, and you can savor fine breakfasts featuring buckwheat crêpes. Billiard room.

 La Taupinière
Route de Concarneau, croissant Saint-André - 98 06 03 12, fax 98 06 16 46
Closed Tue (exc Jul-Aug), Mon dinner, Sep 25-Oct 19. Open until 9:30pm. Air cond. No pets. Pkg. V, AE.
Brittany's exceptional seafood is featured in the cozy dining room with exposed-beam ceiling within an authentic thatched-roof house. You'll

share our enthusiasm for this inn when you sample the chef's terrine of oysters and skate en gelée, croustillant of Breton lobster with wild mushrooms, and shelled crab with coral sauce and spinach leaves. The products are ultrafresh, the technique precise, and even the sauces and side dishes are perfectly prepared. The cellar is rich, with some surprising Bordeaux. From the peach-colored dining room guests can see and hear the busy kitchen brigade at work. Charming welcome, efficient service. C 310-420 F. M 260 F, 360 F, 460 F.

PONTCHARTRAIN 78760
Paris 40 - Rambouillet 21 - Versailles 17 - Montfort 10   Yvelines

 Le Bistro Gourmand
7, route du Pontel - 34 89 25 36
Closed Sun dinner, Mon, Dec 24-Jan 3, Aug 2-24. Open until 9:30pm. Priv rm: 20. Terrace dining. Air cond. Pkg. V, AE.
A peaceful stopover in a spacious, bright dining room away from the noise of the main road. Louis Peutin produces appealing dishes: hure of salmon and sea scallops, puff pastry stuffed with lamb sweetbreads and foie gras, chicken breast à la normande, and a pear croustillant with pistachio-chocolate sauce. The 85 F bistrot menu features one main course and a salad with Roquefort and walnuts. C 250-350 F. M 125 F, 185 F.

PONT-DE-BRIQUES 62
→ Boulogne-sur-Mer

PONT-DE-L'ISÈRE 26 → Valence

PONT-DU-GARD 30210
Paris 690 - Avignon 25 - Nîmes 23 - Alès 47   Gard

La Bégude Saint-Pierre
D 981, Les Coudoulières
66 22 96 96, fax 66 22 73 73
Open daily until 9:30pm (10:30pm in summer). Priv rm: 20. Garden dining. Air cond. Pool. Garage pkg. V, AE, DC, MC.
Bruno Griffoul fell under the spell of this former wine estate the moment he saw it. So he transferred all his pots, pans, and other kitchen impedimenta from the Auberge Saint-Maximin to this spot, right next to the famous Roman bridge. A classic repertoire, inspired by the fruits of local forests and fields, is represented on the 235 F menu: excellent feuilleté with scrambled eggs and asparagus tips, tasty Du Barry velouté, and a less successful dish of veal kidney and sweetbreads sautéed with crosnes and Jerusalem artichoke, followed by cheeses, and a delicate maduraò (a kind of Indian-style semifreddo). Friendly welcome and service. C 300-400 F. M 200 F (lunch exc Sun, wine incl), 115 F (lunch exc Sun), 235 F, 300 F, 360 F.

La Bégude Saint-Pierre
(See restaurant above)
Open year-round. 30 rms 415-785 F. Half-board 438-860 F. Air cond. Conf. Pool. Garage pkg. Helipad. V, AE, DC, MC.
A splendid dwelling set around an enclosed courtyard. The rooms are pleasing and nicely arranged.

381

PONTE SAN LUDOVICO (Italy) → Menton

PONTET (LE) 84 → Avignon

PONT-L'ÉVÊQUE 14130
Paris 190 - Deauville 11 - Lisieux 17 - Rouen 79 *Calvados*

■ In **Saint-André-d'Hébertot 14130** 9 km E on N 175

Auberge du Prieuré
31 64 03 03, fax 31 64 16 66
Closings not available. Open until 9:30pm. Garden dining. Hotel: 3 stes 800-950 F. 12 rms 310-950 F. Rms for disabled. Half-board 490-1,130 F. Conf. Heated pool. Golf. Garage pkg. V, AE, MC.
This romantic hideaway was once a priory. In a quaint, rustic setting you can partake of any number of robust dishes: duck neck with caramelized apples, sea scallops sautéed in balsamic vinegar, and a fish marmite. The cellar is expensive, so quaff the excellent local cider instead. The *patron's* friendly welcome is a lot more engaging than the bill. **C** 300-400 F. **M** 145 F, 180 F (lunch).

PONTONX-SUR-L'ADOUR 40 → Dax

PONTORSON 50170
Paris 326 - Dinan 45 - Rennes 57 - Avranches 22 *Manche*

Le Bretagne
59, rue Couesnon
33 60 10 55, fax 33 58 63 17
Closed Sun dinner & Mon off-seas, end Jan-mid Feb. Open until 9:30pm. Priv rm: 40. Terrace dining. Garage pkg. V, AE, MC.
In this comfortably elegant mansion lined with dark wainscotting, it's the son who prepares such clever dishes as crab parmentier with poached oysters in a truffle jus or lamb sweetbreads and kidneys simmered in Bordeaux. The 140 F set meal brings a salad of giblets and warm cabbage, salmon sauce verte, and chocolate mousse. **C** 240-330 F. **M** 70 F, 100 F, 140 F, 180 F, 240 F.

PORNICHET 44380
Paris 457 - St-Nazaire 11 - La Baule 6 - Nantes 72 *Loire-Atl.*

La Piscine
42, bd de la République
40 11 65 00, fax 40 61 73 70
Closed Sun dinner & Mon off-seas, Nov-Jan. Open until 10pm. Terrace dining. Pool. V, AE, DC, MC.
Arlette Bardouil's generous cooking takes its inspiration from the sea, as well as from spices (Brittany was once a center of the spice trade). Try her grilled langoustines in herb vinaigrette, monkfish with apples in curry sauce, and oven-roasted pork filet mignon. Diverse wine list. Friendly welcome in the opulent dining room with a view of an indoor pool. **C** 300-500 F. **M** 150 F, 190 F, 270 F.

Hôtel Sud Bretagne
(See restaurant above)
Closed Nov-Jan. 4 stes 1,000-1,500 F. 26 rms 350-800 F. Restaurant. Half-board 450-850 F. Conf. Tennis. Golf. Valet pkg. V, AE, DC, MC.

A large, amusing, and eccentric establishment about 200 meters from the beach. Very pleasant rooms and bathrooms. Boat trips can be arranged and there is a private club on the beach.

12/20 Sunset Beach
Bd des Océanides
40 61 29 29, fax 40 61 23 21
Closed Sun dinner & Thu off-seas, beg Jan-mid Feb. Open until 10pm (11:30pm in summer). Priv rm: 120. Terrace dining. Pkg. V, MC.
The Sunset is a very jolly beach restaurant that provides decent food as well as crowds and a good-humored ambience. We like the langoustines, shark steak, stuffed crab, and fresh cod cooked in its skin. Small, affordable cellar; stylish service. **C** 200-350 F. **M** 130 F (weekdays, Sat lunch, Sun dinner, wine incl), 75 F (weekday lunch, Sat).

PORQUEROLLES (ILE DE) 83400
Var

Auberge des Glycines
Place des Armes
94 58 30 36, fax 94 58 35 22
Closed Oct-Mar. Open until 11pm. Terrace dining. Air cond. Hotel: 13 rms 650-1,800 F. Half-board 450-900 F. Air cond. No pets. V, AE, MC.
Inside this picturesque pink house, Provence pops out all over in a profusion of pretty prints, while the food is laced with lashings of sun-sweet olive oil. Take a seat on the patio under the ancient fig tree, and feast on pistou soup, sardines au gros sel, grilled tuna with basil, sea bass with fennel, or leg of lamb. The local wine is overpriced, but the young owners are making a fine job of it on the whole. Undoubtedly the best spot on this side of the island. **C** 200-350 F. **M** 140 F.

Mas du Langoustier

94 58 30 09, fax 94 58 36 02
Closed Oct 15-Apr 30. Open until 9:45pm. Priv rm: 60. Garden dining. Valet pkg. V, AE, DC, MC.
Day trippers seldom venture here, for the Mas du Langoustier is well hidden behind cool umbrella pines and scented eucalyptus trees. This magical corner of paradise is the exclusive preserve of the hotel's residents and moneyed mariners whose yachts weigh anchor in the turquoise-tinted creek below. If, someday, you find yourself among this lucky crew, choose a table on the lovely terrace or in the big, bright dining room, and prepare for a gastronomic idyll. The kitchen is captained by chef Joël Guillet, who achieved three toques at his last post. But we'll give him a bit of time to settle in before assigning a definitive rating. We have high hopes; he has shown he can produce fine cuisine with a Provençal flare. Among his offerings this year are a red mullet and artichoke salad, warm foie gras with coco beans and chopped truffles, John Dory roasted with bacon served with a delicious velouté of tiny peas and baby onions, sea bass with meltingly tender potatoes enlivened with fennel seed, casserole-roasted tender kid with dried tomatoes, and squab glazed with lavender honey. We would say the moments of perfect felicity one spends here, with such marvelous

food and wines, are well worth a few 100 F bills—wouldn't you? **C** 320-550 F. **M** 300 F (wine incl), 400 F, 450 F, 500 F.

Mas du Langoustier
(See restaurant above)
Closed Oct-Apr. 3 stes 1,512-1,595 F. 47 rms 1,040-1,347 F. Half-board 791-1,027 F. Conf. Tennis. Garage pkg. Helipad. V, AE, DC, MC.
For all you lovers of the Mas, a terrible thing has happened: there is now color television in nearly all the rooms. Close your eyes, stop up your ears, and concentrate instead on the paradisaical tranquility of the island, pierced only by the murmur of the wind in the pines or the cicadas' creaking song. The sixty-odd rooms and suites have been further refurbished; the ones on the ground floor have private terraces overlooking the water. Air conditioning is provided by the sea breezes, and there's a sandy beach instead of a pool. Two tennis courts; and a heliport, of course.

Sainte-Anne
94 58 30 04, fax 94 58 32 26
Closed Nov 15-Dec 15, Jan 8-Feb 8. 11 rms 390-575 F. Restaurant. Half-board 340-450 F. Conf. V, AE, DC, MC.
Tidy, if a little drab, the rooms of this hotel are favored by folks who love the island, but can't (or won't!) pay the tariffs charged at Le Mas du Langoustier. And it's open even in the off-season. Two of the rooms have just been renovated.

PORT-CAMARGUE 30 → Grau-du-Roi (Le)

PORT-CROS (ILE DE) 83145
Var

12/20 Le Manoir
94 05 90 52, fax 94 05 90 89
Closings not available. Open until 9pm. Priv rm: 20. Terrace dining. No pets. V, MC.
Gérard Ré offers sunny specialties like a fricot of langoustines, simple grilled meats and fish, and chocolate profiteroles. The garden facing the bay is a lovely sight, with its huge white parasols, eucalyptus trees, and dancing butterflies. **M** 250 F, 300 F.

Le Manoir
(See restaurant above)
Closed Oct 2-beg May. 23 rms. Half-board 750-1,050 F. Conf. No pets. V, MC.
A charming white colonial-style hotel with large, quiet rooms (cars are banned on the island). Some rooms have private terraces.

PORT-DE-LANNE 40300
Paris 733 - Bayonne 30 - Dax 20 - Orthez 37   *Landes*

La Vieille Auberge ۞
Place de l'Église
58 89 16 29, fax 58 89 12 89
Closed Mon lunch, beg Oct-end May. Open until 9:30pm. Priv rm: 15. Terrace dining. Hotel: 2 stes 350-500 F. 6 rms 200-400 F. Half-board 320-400 F. Heated pool. Pkg. No cards.
Mireille Lataillade and her husband have breathed new life into this ravishing eighteenth-century inn. Here regional dishes reign supreme, with a smoked salmon tart, eel matelote, bar-

becued duck breast, and a semolina cake with fresh fruits. **M** 120 F, 185 F.

PORT-EN-BESSIN 14520
Paris 280 - Bayeux 9 - Caen 37 - Cherbourg 91   *Calvados*

■ In **Escures 14520**   2 km S on D 6

La Chenevière
Commune de Commes
31 21 47 96, fax 31 21 47 98
Closed Mon, Jan. 4 stes 900-1,400 F. 11 rms 700-1,100 F. Restaurant. Half-board 850-1,850 F. Conf. Golf. Pkg. Helipad. V, AE, DC, MC.
A sumptuous house with a slate roof not far from the beaches. The rooms are huge with superb bathrooms, tastefully decorated and opening onto a lovely park filled with flower beds and ancient trees. Tennis court, helipad, and golf course nearby. Good breakfasts.

PORTES-EN-RÉ (LES) 17 → Ré (Ile de)

PORT-GRIMAUD 83310
Paris 871 - Ste-Maxime 13 - St-Tropez 10 - Grimaud 6   *Var*

L'Amphitrite

Grand-Rue - 94 56 31 33, fax 94 56 33 77
Closed Oct-Easter. Open until 10pm. Priv rm: 50. Terrace dining. Air cond. Heated pool. Valet pkg. V, AE, DC, MC.
Chef Christophe Chabredier offers sunny, well prepared dishes based on fine ingredients: salmon with zucchini blossoms (not really a marriage made in heaven), sea scallops deliciously paired with orange butter, and fine caramelized squab with spices, in addition to ultrafresh fish served simply grilled or roasted. Musical evenings in summer. Outside, there's a lovely white-sand beach on the Bay of Saint-Tropez. **C** 300-400 F. **M** 160 F, 260 F, 295 F.

Giraglia
(See restaurant above)
Closed beg Oct-Easter. 1 ste 1,715-2,065 F. 47 rms 655-1,845 F. Air cond. Conf. Heated pool. Valet pkg. V, AE, DC, MC.
A very attractive set of Provençal-style buildings which blend in well with the village. Rooms are spacious, comfortable, and remarkably well-appointed. A fine sandy beach, water sports, and excursions into the hills are additional attractions. Magnificent swimming pool and terrace.

See also: **Grimaud**

PORTICCIO 20 → CORSICA

PORTICCIOLO 20 → CORSICA

PORT-MARLY (LE) 78 → PARIS Suburbs

PORTO 20 → CORSICA

PORTO-POLLO 20 → CORSICA

PORTO-VECCHIO 20 → CORSICA

PORT-VENDRES   66600
Paris 940 - Perpignan 30 - Collioure 4 - Banyuls 8   *Pyrénées-O.*

11/20 Le Chalut
8, quai F.-Joly - 68 82 00 91
*Closed Sun dinner & Mon off-seas, Dec-Jan. Open
until 9:30pm. Terrace dining. V, AE, DC, MC.*
Take a table on this adorable terrace overlooking the port and wait for the day's catch to find its way onto your plate. The best bets here are the shellfish assortment, sea scallops spiced with cinnamon, fresh lobster gratin, and bouillabaisse, washed down with the lipsmacking house white wine. **C** 200-350 F. **M** 70 F (weekdays, Sat), 125 F, 155 F, 190 F, 240 F.

La Résidence
29, route de Banyuls
68 82 01 05, fax 68 82 22 13
*Closings not available. 21 rms 280 F. Restaurant.
Half-board 160 F. Air cond. Conf. Heated pool. Golf.
Pkg. V, MC.*
Shaded by hundred-year-old palm trees in meticulously kept grounds, this hotel provides rooms with splendid sea or mountain views. Bar. Charming welcome.

PORT-VILLEZ 78   → Vernon

POUDENAS   47170
Paris 659 - Nérac 17 - Barbotan 23   *Lot/Garonne*

Moulin
de la Belle Gasconne
53 65 71 58, fax 53 65 87 39
*Closed Jan 2-Feb 28. Open until 9:30pm (exc by
reserv). Garden dining. Pkg. V, AE, DC, MC.*
This ancient (fourteenth-century) mill is a lovely backdrop for Marie-Claude Gracia, who digs deep into regional roots for inspiration and ingredients. As she listens to Verdi in her kitchen, she fashions superb dishes like foie gras sautéed with prune vinegar that she has made herself, a combination of noble and rustic that characterizes her cooking. Try her market-fresh dishes like snail tarts with chopped tomatoes and parsleyed mushroom jus, roast squab with a cabbage compote and poached garlic, pickerel soufflé enhanced with orange, and a classic duck confit with cruchade (Gascony polenta).The wine list highlights local growths. You can count on a hospitable welcome. **C** 320-380 F. **M** 175 F, 280 F.

A la Belle Gasconne
(See restaurant above)
Closed Jan 5-Feb. 1 ste 630 F. 6 rms 380-550 F. Half-board 570-715 F. Heated pool. Pkg. V, AE, DC, MC.
This age-old mill on the banks of a romantic river houses six rooms and one suite. There's a fine terrace on the river, cooking demonstrations, visits to wine growers, tennis in the village, and a golf course fifteen kilometers away.

> *Some establishments change their **closing times**
> without warning. It is always wise to check in advance.*

POUILLY-EN-AUXOIS   21320
Paris 270 - Beaune 47 - Saulieu 31 - Dijon 42   *Côte-d'Or*

L'Armançon
6 km W on D 977 bis, in Chailly-sur-Armançon - 80 90 30 30, fax 80 90 30 00
*Closed Dec 23-Jan. Open until 10pm. Priv rm: 25.
Heated pool. Valet pkg. V, AE, DC, MC.*
Come to this lovely château hidden away in the countryside to sample classic but never boring dishes like those on the attractive 180 F menu: luscious parfait with a fine Ratafia gelatin, lobster in a tasty but not rich jus, and a perfect roast chicken, always the mark of a careful kitchen. Good cellar; and it's only ten minutes from the autoroute, after all. **C** 300-450 F. **M** 180 F, 240 F (exc Tue & Sun dinner).

Château de Chailly
(See restaurant above)
*Closed Dec 23-Jan. 8 stes 1,800-3,000 F. 37 rms
600-1,400 F. Rms for disabled. Conf. Heated pool.
Tennis. Golf. Valet pkg. Helipad. V, AE, DC, MC.*
The suites under the eaves are sumptuous, but bogus luxury mars the other rooms. All the accommodation, however, offers top-notch facilities. And there's a Zen room in one tower.

■ In Sainte-
Sabine 21320   8 km SE on D 977 bis & D970

Château
de Sainte-Sabine
80 49 22 01, fax 80 49 20 01
*Closed Jan. 2 stes 890 F. 14 rms 300-560 F. Restaurant. Half-board 340-461 F. Conf. Pool. Golf. No
pets. Pkg. Helipad. V, MC.*
The ideal hotel for a romantic weekend offers spacious, sunny, tastefully decorated rooms with impeccable bathrooms and soundproofing. You'll have a fine view of the pretty countryside, and a good breakfast. Friendly welcome, and salons furnished with fine antiques.

POULIGNY-NOTRE-DAME 36
→ Châtre (La)

PRA-LOUP 04   → Barcelonnette

PROPRIANO 20   → CORSICA

PROVINS   77160
Paris 85 - Sens 47 - Fontainebleau 53 - Melun 48   *Seine/Marne*

Aux Vieux Remparts
3, rue Couverte
64 08 94 00, fax 60 67 77 22
*Open daily until 9:30pm. Priv rm: 25. Terrace dining.
Pkg. V, AE, DC, MC.*
An oasis of quiet in the center of the old town, with a charming garden to boot. Try Xavier Lanier's inventive dishes like foie gras with Szechuan peppercorns, generous civet of hare in a fine wine sauce served with tagliatelle, and a perfect fresh fruit gratin in Champagne sauce. Splendid wine list. **C** 330-400 F. **M** 175 F (weekdays), 230 F (exc weekdays), 340 F, 460 F.

Aux Vieux Remparts ♠♣

(See restaurant above)
Open year-round. 25 rms 250-650 F. Half-board 490-570 F. Conf. Pkg. V, AE, DC, MC.
The fittings are impeccable and some of the rooms have magnificent views of Caesar's tower and the rooftops of old Provins. Two rooms especially adapted for the disabled.

PUJOLS 47	→ Villeneuve-sur-Lot

PULIGNY-MONTRACHET	21190
Paris 327 - Autun 43 - Beaune 12 - Chagny 5	Côte-d'Or

Le Montrachet

Pl. des Marronniers
80 21 30 06, fax 80 21 39 06
Closed Wed lunch, Dec-Jan 10. Open until 9:30pm. Priv rm: 50. Terrace dining. Hotel: 2 stes 675-975 F. 30 rms 395-490 F. Half-board 450-550 F. Conf. Pkg. V, AE, DC, MC.
This large stone house sits on a leafy square and tempts one to try the tasty, Burgundian-based cuisine: snails in their shells, breast of Bresse chicken with foie gras, and warm apple tart with cider sherbet. The wine list is sumptuous and the sommelier's advice well worth heeding. Cheerful welcome. **C** 360-460 F. **M** 185 F, 295 F, 395 F.

PURPAN 31	→ Toulouse

PUTEAUX 92	→ PARIS Suburbs

PUYMIROL 47	→ Agen

QUARRÉ-LES-TOMBES	89630
Paris 246 - Saulieu 27 - Avallon 19 - Auxerre 72	Yonne

Auberge de l'Atre

Les Lavaults
86 32 20 79, fax 86 32 28 25
Closed Tue dinner & Wed off-seas, Nov 28-Dec 10, end Jan-Mar 10. Open until 9:30pm. Priv rm: 30. Terrace dining. Pkg. V, AE, DC, MC.
Francis Salamolard harbors a passion for fresh herbs (which he grows himself), local products, and mushrooms. Depending on the season, his menu might feature a pickerel terrine with bacon and Tannay wine, salad of Morvan truffles with petals of flowers, monkfish in an olive sauce spiked with hydromel (mead), and a surprising dandelion sherbet. It all works, and the prices are absolutely philanthropic. The enticing cellar, chock-a-block with half-bottles, is administered by an expert sommelier. Friendly service. **C** 300-350 F. **M** 135 F (weekday lunch), 210 F, 285 F.

QUEMIGNY-POISOT 21
→ Gevrey-Chambertin

QUENZA 20	→ CORSICA

QUESTEMBERT	56230
Paris 423 - Redon 33 - Vannes 26 - Rennes 88	Morbihan

Georges Paineau ✪✪

13, rue St-Michel
97 26 11 12, fax 97 26 12 37
Closed Sun dinner & Mon (exc hols), Jan 3-31. Open until 10:30pm. Priv rm: 45. Garden dining. Pkg. V, AE.
Georges Paineau, the godfather of Brittany's gastronomic revival, refuses to rest on his innumerable laurels. Seconded by son-in-law Claude Corlouer (who gets credit for the menu's most modern creations; he trained with Joël Robuchon), Georges proves anew, every blessed day, that he is still one of the region's top chefs. Each time we enter this oak-lined dining room, we tingle with anticipation. And each time we are rewarded with a procession of intelligent, inventive dishes, in which sauces, condiments, garnishes all underscore the deep, full flavors of perfectly paired ingredients. We award the two talents in the kitchen with four toques this year. The restaurant, lost in a village, is hard to find, but once there you will revel in the elegant dining room (adorned with Paineau's own paintings) opening onto a garden. In your pretty glass plate will appear succulent dishes based on fine regional foodstuffs: a sublime cauliflower cream with crab gelatin is almost too beautiful to eat (but we didn't leave a crumb), the oysters in a tarragon vapeur are a suberb union of land and sea, and the langoustines royales in spice butter are the best you'll have anywhere. Revel also in the foie gras and artichokes with sea salt in chicken jus, the grandiose lobster-stuffed cabbage, and the formidable turbot steamed over seaweed in a mussel infusion accompanied by chopped artichokes in beef marrow, a dish whose flavors explode in the mouth. In fact, everything on the menu is captivating: sole and snails with tomatoes and thyme confit, glacé of sea scallops with ginger, veal sweetbreads with nettle sauce, oxtail with anchovies, pig's foot crépinette with truffles and paprika-spiced pork jus, and breast of squab roasted with spices. Desserts are out of this world, like the dark chocolate croquant-fondant with a caramel-lemon coulis. Praise is also due to Georges's wife Michèle, who creates a wonderfully happy atmosphere and will help you choose a perfect wine to make your meal complete. **C** 360-550 F. **M** 150 F (weekday lunch), 270 F, 335 F, 480 F.

Georges Paineau

(See restaurant above)
Closed Jan 5-31. 3 stes 1,200-1,400 F. 11 rms 480-980 F. Rms for disabled. Half-board 580-1,100 F. Conf. Golf. Pkg. Helipad. V, AE.
Georges Paineau enlarged his ivy-clad hotel to make it more commodious and comfortable. Nine new rooms and deluxe suites now open out onto the garden. The breakfasts served here are among the best in the West. Relais et Châteaux. Boutique offering gifts, edible and otherwise.

Gault Millau's ratings *are based solely on the restaurants' cuisine. We do not take into account the atmosphere, décor, service, and so on; these are commented upon within the review.*

385

Paris 498 - Lorient 52 - Vannes 46 - Auray 28   *Morbihan*

Bellevue

Rue de Tiviec
97 50 16 28, fax 97 30 44 34
Closed Nov 2-Apr 1. 2 stes 535-660 F. 39 rms 355-
565 F. Rms for disabled. Restaurant. Half-board 310-
500 F. Heated pool. Golf. Pkg. V, AE, MC.
Bright, pleasant rooms extend out onto splendid terraces with views of the sea. The sea-water
spa is just steps away. Excellent reception.

Le Thalassa

Pointe de Goulvars
97 50 20 00, fax 97 30 47 63
Closed Jan 2-31. Open until 9:45pm. Priv rm: 200.
Terrace dining. Heated pool. No pets. Valet pkg. V,
AE, DC, MC.
Spa treatments and slimming are the principal
preoccupations of Le Thalassa's patrons. But we
had such a bad experience here this year that
we are suspending the rating in hopes of better
things next year: tired staff in a hurry to go home,
fine Quiberon oysters but disappointing fish in
insipid sauce that reminded us why hotel food
is often maligned. C 300-400 F. M 215 F, 250 F,
350 F.

Le Thalassa

(See restaurant above)
Closed Jan. 17 stes 1,955-3,715 F. 116 rms 620-
1,535 F. Half-board 885-1,300 F. Conf. Heated pool.
Tennis. Pkg. V, AE, DC, MC.
The hotel is right at the end of the Quiberon
headland, linked to the sea-water spa by a gallery. Facilities are luxurious, the rooms have all
been renovated (some have terraces or private
patios), sea views are magnificent, but the prices
have gotten way out of hand.

Paris 552 - Rennes 207 - Brest 79 - Lorient 68   *Finistère*

Les Acacias

88, bd Créac'h-Guen - 98 52 15 20
Closed Sat lunch, Sun dinner. Open until 9:30pm.
Priv rm: 15. Terrace dining. Air cond. Pkg. V, AE.
Philippe Hatté offers well prepared cuisine that
shows great respect for fine local ingredients:
cabbage stuffed with spider crab in an edible
seaweed fumet, croustillant of veal sweetbreads
with shitake mushrooms, and a warm chocolate
tart for dessert. The cellar has been assembled
with obvious discernment. Warm welcome.
C 250-350 F. M 95 F, 135 F, 168 F, 220 F,
230 F.

L'Ambroisie

49, rue E.-Fréron - 98 95 00 02
Closed Mon dinner, Jun 23-Jul 4. Open until
9:45pm. Priv rm: 32. V, AE, DC, MC.
Tucked away in a little street that slopes up
towards the town's ramparts, a modern, flower-
decked dining room (recently redecroated and
enlarged) is the setting for Gilbert Guyon's updated classic cuisine. Agreeably light and elegant
dishes like ballotin of fresh salmon with crab
meat, casserole-roasted veal with mushrooms,
and a craquant of white and dark chocolate.
C 290-320 F. M 99 F, 143 F, 199 F, 290 F.

Le Gradlon

30, rue de Brest
98 95 04 39, fax 98 95 61 25
Closed Dec 20-Jan 3. 1 ste 650-700 F. 23 rms 330-
450 F. Conf. No pets. Pkg. V, AE, DC, MC.
A centrally located hotel built around a court-
yard-cum-garden where guests can have breakfast. The rooms are quiet and comfortable.

Novotel

Route de Bénodet
98 90 46 26, fax 98 53 01 96
Open year-round. 92 rms 395-445 F. Rms for dis-
abled. Restaurant. Half-board 300 F. Conf. Heated
pool. Pkg. V, AE, DC, MC.
A good hotel, part of the chain, on the outskirts
of Quimper. The rooms are spacious and breakfasts average.

Paris 513 - Concarneau 32 - Lorient 20 - Quimper 48   *Finistère*

Le Bistro de la Tour

2, rue Dom-Morice
98 39 29 58, fax 98 39 21 77
Closed Sat lunch, Sun dinner. Open until 9:30pm.
Priv rm: 12. Pkg. V, AE, MC.
In these financially uncertain times, Bernard
Cariou, the owner/chef/antique dealer who runs
this charming 1930 style bistrot, is a cheering
fixture with his substantial country cooking. Try
the delicate sea scallop tart, fresh cod cooked in
its skin, oxtail compote, and honey cake ice
cream. The superb wine list holds a few notable
bargains. C 200-300 F. M 80 F (weekday lunch,
wine incl), 350 F (wine incl), 98 F, 140 F, 195 F.

Novalis

98 39 24 00, fax 98 39 12 10
Open year-round. 25 rms 220-240 F. Rms for dis-
abled. Restaurant. Half-board 298-325 F. Conf. Golf.
Pkg. Helipad. V, AE, MC.
The functional new hotel near the highway but
surrounded by a large lawn offers sunny, adequately equipped rooms. A practical choice.

Paris 892 - Hyères 54 - St-Tropez 10 - Draguignan 53   *Var*

Les Bergerettes

Route des Plages, quartier des Marres
94 97 40 22, fax 94 97 37 55
Closed at Easter. 29 rms 680-970 F. Restaurant. Air
cond. Conf. Pool. Golf. Valet pkg. V, AE.
This charming hotel, which looks rather like a
Provençal *bastide*, is set in a pine wood, facing
the beach. The rooms are very appealing, and
some have terraces.

Les Bouis

Route des Plages-Pampelonne
94 79 87 61, fax 94 79 85 20
Closed Oct 20-Mar 15. 4 stes 1,100-1,350 F. 14 rms
650-1,000 F. Restaurant. Air cond. Conf. Pool. Pkg.
V, MC.
A group of luxurious buildings in a pine grove
dotted around the swimming pool. The attractive rooms have cane furniture, tiled floors, and
private terraces with a sea view. Poolside snacks
available.

12/20 Chez Camille
Quartier de Bonne-Terrasse - 94 79 80 38
Closed Tue (exc dinner in summer), Oct-Mar. Open until 9:30pm. Terrace dining. Pkg. V, MC.
A standard bouillabaisse and perfectly good grilled fish are sufficient reason to stop for a meal and a view of the Bonne-Terrasse Bay. It's not great gastronomy, but the holiday hordes keep coming, so reserve your table ahead; it helps to be a regular. **C** 230-450 F.

La Ferme d'Augustin
Plage de Tahiti
94 97 23 83, fax 94 97 40 30
Closings not available. 1 ste 1,800 F. 46 rms 620-1,800 F. Air cond. Conf. Heated pool. Golf. Garage pkg. Helipad. V, AE, MC.
In the 1960s, this spot was the favorite of *Le Tout-Saint-Tropez.* Now it is a comfortable, wonderfully quiet hotel. Meal trays are available. Golf practice green on the premises.

La Ferme d'Hermès
Route de l'Escalet
94 79 27 80, fax 94 79 26 86
Closed Nov-Mar. 1 ste 950-1,000 F. 9 rms 600-850 F. Heated pool. Golf. Pkg. V, MC.
A charming little "mas" surrounded by vineyards, offering rooms with kitchenettes and a swimming pool among the vines.

La Figuière
Le Pinet, route de Tahiti
94 97 18 21, fax 94 97 68 48
Closed Oct 8-Easter. 45 rms 450-900 F. Restaurant. Air cond. Pool. Tennis. Pkg. V, MC.
An old farmhouse set among vineyards, 300 meters from the sea. Peace, comfort, and an elegant clientele of regulars.

12/20 Au Fil à la Pâte
7, rue Victor-Léon - 94 79 27 81
Closed Wed, Nov 15-Dec 15. Open until 11pm. Priv rm: 30. Terrace dining. Garage pkg. V, AE, MC.
Always jam-packed in summer, this tiny eating house specializes in delicious fresh pasta and simple Provençal fare. **C** 120-160 F.

La Garbine
Route de Tahiti
94 97 11 84, fax 94 97 34 18
Closed end Oct-Mar. 20 rms 450-950 F. Air cond. Conf. Pool. Tennis. Valet pkg. Helipad. V, AE.
A Provençal-style hotel surrounded by vineyards and not far from Tahiti beach. The decor is spare, bright, and attractive; the rooms are well equipped (minibars), and all have private terraces giving onto the pool.

L'Hacienda
Quartier des Marres
94 56 61 20, fax 94 97 05 24
Open year-round. 9 rms 550-1,000 F. Restaurant. Air cond. Conf. Pool. Golf. Pkg. V, AE, DC, MC.
An attractive Provençal house and veritable oasis of luxury and calm, right near Saint-Tropez and the beaches. The rooms are very comfortable and tastefully furnished. Meals are served only upon request (they're good) in the lovely poolside garden. Very warm welcome and service.

Chez Madeleine
Route de Tahiti - 94 97 15 74
Closed Oct 15-beg Apr. Open until 10:30pm. Garden dining. Pkg. V, AE, DC, MC.
Madeleine Serra's children somehow manage to grab the best of the catch from their fishermen friends, even at the height of summer. Wonderful bouillabaisse (order in advance), and the freshest fish. **C** 250-380 F. **M** 160 F.

Dei Marres
Route des Plages
94 97 26 68, fax 94 97 62 76
Closed Nov-Mar 15. 2 stes 550-1,100 F. 22 rms 300-1,100 F. Pool. Tennis. No pets. Pkg. V, AE, DC, MC.
This Provençal château in its flower-filled grounds at the foot of the Ramatuelle hills offers charmingly decorated rooms at reasonable prices.

La Vigne de Ramatuelle
Quartier Audrac, route des Plages
94 79 12 50, fax 94 79 13 20
Closed Nov 14-Dec 15, Jan 15-Feb 15. 13 stes 950-1,650 F. Air cond. Conf. Pool. Pkg. V, AE, MC.
This hotel perched on a hill (and not near the beaches) offers luxurious although smallish rooms with spectacular bathrooms; each room has a private balcony overlooking the lawn and pool.

12/20 Le Cheval Rouge
78, rue du Général-de-Gaulle
30 88 80 61, fax 34 83 91 60
Closed Sun dinner, Jul 21-Aug 17. Open until 9:30pm. Garden dining. Air cond. V, AE, DC, MC.
The flower-filled garden of this pleasant inn (renovated this year) is just the place to enjoy traditional dishes prepared from the freshest ingredients: lobster crêpes, duck breast with raspberry-vinegar sauce, poached fruit with warm caramel sauce. **C** 250-360 F. **M** 125 F (exc Sun dinner & hols), 185 F (exc Sun dinner).

Resthôtel Primevère
ZA du Bel-Air, rue J.-Jacquard
34 85 51 02, fax 30 59 25 66
Open year-round. 42 rms 260 F. Restaurant. Half-board 315-330 F. Conf. Pkg. V, AE, DC, MC.
Set back from the main road, this brand-new hotel offers bright, pleasant rooms and buffet breakfasts. The forest is nearby.

Karlina Club Hôtel
Chemin du Plageron
94 05 61 65, fax 94 05 62 53
Closed Oct 15-Apr 1. 10 rms 250-480 F. Restaurant. Half-board 495-625 F. Pool. Pkg. V, DC, MC.
Holm oaks and palm trees surround this hotel, whose rooms overlook the bay. Sporting equipment, a private landing, and a launch for boating excursions make one's stay even more pleasurable.

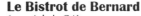
■ **In Ars-en-Ré 17590**

Le Bistrot de Bernard

1, quai de la Criée
46 29 40 26, fax 46 29 28 99
*Closed Sun dinnr, Mon, Dec 6-22, Jan 2-Feb 15.
Open until 11pm. Terrace dining. V, AE, MC.*
Bernard Frigière, now installed in a pleasant
white house near the port, offers fine dishes like
asparagus feuilleté, cod fillet à la provençale,
salmon with sea salt, and veal kidney in Calvados
sauce, followed by well seasoned fresh goat
cheese. **C** 220-300 F. **M** 120 F, 165 F.

■ **In Le Bois-Plage-en-Ré 17580**

Les Gollandières

46 09 23 99, fax 46 09 09 84
*Closed Nov 4-Mar. 32 rms 295-400 F. Rms for dis-
abled. Restaurant. Half-board 325-490 F. Conf.
Heated pool. Pkg. V, AE, DC, MC.*
Simple and agreeably rustic rooms in a hotel-
motel on the beach. Poolside grill.

■ **In La Couarde-sur-Mer 17670**

La Salicorne

16, rue de l'Olivette
46 29 82 37, fax 46 29 82 37
*Closed Thu lunch (in seas), Nov-Easter. Open until
11pm (in seas). Terrace dining. V.*
Giant morning glories cascade over the tiny
terrace where Luc Dumond serves his simple,
spirited cooking. Try his scallops with Roquefort,
mignon de veau flavored with coffee and ginger,
and crème brûlée flavored with jasmine. Interesting list of Loire wines. **C** 200-300 F. **M** 90 F
(weekday lunch), 130 F.

■ **In La Flotte-en-Ré 17630**

L'Écailler

3, quai de Sénac - 46 09 56 40
*Closed Mon (exc Jul-Aug), Nov-Easter. Garden
dining. V, MC.*
Marie-Josée Lagord, who has a degree in
oyster-farming, works away in the kitchen
preparing glossy shellfish and sparkling seafood.
Her repertoire also includes langoustines with
pasta, cod brandade, and fine raw seafood platters. Attentive service. **C** 220-300 F.

Le Lavardin

5, rue H.-Lainé
46 09 68 32, fax 46 09 54 03
*Closed Mon dinner & Tue (exc Jul-Aug), Jan 10-
Feb 10, Nov 14-Dec 15. Open until 9:30pm
(10:30pm in summer). Air cond. Pkg. V, MC.*
William Donny's lively seafood dishes include
feuillantine of warm smoked oysters, grilled salmon with fleur de sel, and a honey spice cream
for dessert, all served in a charming dining room
in an eighteenth-century house. Prices are not
bad for the island and the restaurant is near the
scenic harbor. **C** 260-420 F. **M** 95 F (weekday
lunch, Sat), 155 F, 195 F, 230 F, 330 F.

Le Richelieu

44, av. de la Plage
46 09 60 70, fax 46 09 50 59
*Closed Jan 5-Feb 12. Open until 10pm. Priv rm: 100.
Garden dining. Air cond. Pkg. V, MC.*
High prices keep the riff-raff away from this
luxurious terrace overlooking the harbor. Those
who can afford to pay for it can be sure of peace
and tranquility in which to feast on Dominique
Bourgeois' classic cooking based primarily on
fresh seafood: fine raw seafood platters, grilled
langoustines in a spice glaze, monkfish with
sliced confit tomatoes, and a pear émincé with
chicory ice cream for dessert. There's an imposing cellar, and the service is first-rate. **C** 400-
600 F. **M** 220 F, 310 F, 400 F.

Le Richelieu

(See restaurant above)
*Closed Jan 5-Feb 12. 5 stes 1,000-2,500 F. 35 rms
400-1,500 F. Half-board 450-2,200 F. Air cond. Conf.
Heated pool. Tennis. Pkg. V.*
All the rooms have been renovated in this, the
island's most luxurious hotel, and redecorated
with period furniture. The bathrooms have been
enlarged and there's now a magnificent terrace
overlooking the sea. Good breakfasts. All-new
fitness center and sea-water spa.

■ **In Les Portes-en-Ré 17880**

Auberge de la Rivière

D 101, La Rivière, 27, av. des Salines
46 29 54 55, fax 46 29 40 32
*Closed Tue dinner & Wed (exc school hols), Nov 15-
Dec 15, Jan. Open until 9:30pm (10pm in summer).
Priv rm: 30. Garden dining. Pkg. V, AE, MC.*
Choose the terrace rather than the less appealing dining room to sample Rémi Massé's skillful
cooking: we're partial to his langoustine tail
salad, fillet of turbot with saffrony shellfish, and
an apple gratin with cider butter. **C** 300-400 F.
M 120 F (weekdays, Sat lunch, Sun dinner),
185 F, 245 F, 350 F.

■ **In Rivedoux-Plage 17940**

12/20 Auberge de la Marée

46 09 80 02, fax 46 09 88 25
*Closed Mon & Tue lunch off-seas, Oct-May. Open
until 9pm. Priv rm: 20. Hotel: 6 stes 300-800 F.
28 rms 300-800 F. Half-board 320-550 F. Air cond.
Conf. Heated pool. Pkg. V, MC.*
Painted wrought-iron decoration in nautical
themes overlook a pleasant dining room with a
terrace near the market. The chef's cooking
doesn't make waves: marinated sardine fillets,
mixed fish in an herb infusion, beef fillet with
oysters, and an orange ice cream dessert. Small
choice of local wines. **C** 250-380 F. **M** 120 F
(lunch), 200 F, 300 F.

■ **In Saint-Clément-des-Baleines 17590**

Le Chat Botté

2, rue de la Mairie
46 29 42 09, fax 46 29 29 77
*Closed Wed, Jan 5-Mar 1. Open until 9:30pm. Priv
rm: 25. Garden dining. Pkg. V, MC.*

Daniel Massé chooses his seafood with discernment and prepares it with skill. Join the happy holiday-makers who love his generous sautéed langoustines with tarragon, roast turbot with fresh fava beans, and John Dory fillet with truffle mousseline. Good classic desserts. Charming welcome. C 280-380 F. M 110 F (weekdays, Sat lunch, Sun dinner), 170 F, 250 F, 350 F.

■ In Saint-Martin-de-Ré 17410

La Baleine Bleue

Quai Launay-Razilly
46 09 03 30, fax 46 09 30 86
Closed Mon (exc Feb school hols), Jan 15-Feb 15. Open until 10:30pm. Terrace dining. Pkg. V.
With its picture-postcard view of the pleasure boats in the marina, this winsome establishment with pretty contemporary decor has lots of appeal. New chef Didier Marchand favors seafood: a delicate oyster ragoût in a coriander-flavored infusion, sole and turbot with artichokes en barigoule, and a pear craquant with mint and ginger. There's a bargain-priced bistrot menu. Slightly scattered service; charming terrace.
C 300-400 F. M 190 F, 350 F.

11/20 Brasserie de la Paix
11, quai Poithevinière
46 09 20 55, fax 46 09 41 06
Closed Jan. Open until 12:30am (Mar-Sep). Priv rm: 20. Terrace dining. V, AE, DC, MC.
Fans of sparkling-fresh shellfish will be happy as (ahem) clams on this pleasant terrace with a view of the port. C 200-300 F. M 75 F, 90 F, 110 F, 130 F.

Le Galion
Allée de la Guyane
46 09 03 19, fax 46 09 13 26
Closed Nov 21-Dec 10. 31 rms 330-560 F. Rms for disabled. Restaurant. Conf. Golf. Pkg. V, AE, DC, MC.
Set on a quiet square near the little harbor, this hotel provides small but airy and well-equipped rooms. Sea views.

La Jetée
Quai G.-Clemenceau
46 09 36 36, fax 46 09 36 06
Open year-round. 2 stes 650-790 F. 29 rms 350-590 F. Rms for disabled. Conf. Golf. Pkg. V, MC.
An elegantly decorated, new establishment right on the port, with simple but tasteful rooms opening onto a curve of columns.

■ In Sainte-Marie-de-Ré 17740

12/20 Auberge de la Chauvetière
1, rue Beurelière - 46 30 21 56
Closed Wed, Feb 25-Mar 13, Oct 14-22. Open until 9:30pm. Air cond. V, AE, DC, MC.
Tasty seafood specialities are the focus in this pleasant, rustic village inn. Try the first set menu: mussels in white wine or six oysters, salmon trout with sorrel sauce, and sherbets. Good wines from the island and from Bordeaux. C 180-320 F. M 98 F, 170 F, 230 F.

> The **prices** in this guide reflect what establishments were charging at press time.

REDON — 35600
Paris 400 - La Baule 63 - Vannes 57 - Rennes 65 — Ille/Vil.

Jean-Marc Chandouineau

1, rue Thiers
99 71 02 04, fax 99 71 08 81
Closed Sun dinner & Sat (exc Jul-Aug & hols), Mar 25-Apr 2, Jul 31-Aug 10. Open until 9:30pm. Priv rm: 20. Pkg. V, AE, DC, MC.
There's always a smiling welcome from Marie-Françoise and Jean-Marc Chandouineau. Regular customers like to gather in the large, comfortable dining room to partake of generous, inventive cooking based on top-quality ingredients: tiny local snails with julienned vegetables, roast turbot with wild mushrooms, and a creamy chocolate dessert with mint sauce. C 300-420 F. M 120 F, 175 F, 210 F, 260 F, 290 F.

Jean-Marc Chandouineau
(See restaurant above)
See restaurant for closings. 7 rms 330-480 F. Half-board 500-680 F. Pkg. V, AE, DC, MC.
A nice hotel near the station. The rooms are all spacious, comfortable, and bright with fine fittings and fixtures. Totally soundproofed. Excellent breakfasts.

REIMS — 51100
Paris 145 - Lille 212 - Metz 187 - Verdun 118 — Marne

L'Assiette Champenoise
40, av. P.-V.-Couturier, 51430 Tinqueux
26 04 15 56, fax 26 04 15 69
Closings not available. Open until 10pm. Priv rm: 110. Pkg. V, AE, DC, MC.
Lots of luxury in this elegant château on the outskirts of Reims. Everything here is done on a grand scale (not excluding the prices). Jean-Pierre Lallement offers seductive cuisine marked by freshness and precision: savory sea scallop tartare and marinated salmon with a delicious saffrony sauce, crisp-skinned turbot with a finely chopped vegetable confit that wasn't really confit and served with an overly creamy sauce, and a delicate three-chocolate bavarian cream with pure flavors. Superb wine list. An extra point this year. C 450-550 F. M 480 F (wine incl), 250 F, 320 F, 460 F.

Château de la Muire
(See restaurant above)
Open year-round. 2 stes 1,100 F. 60 rms 505-1,100 F. Rms for disabled. Half-board 715-1,125 F. Conf. Heated pool. Golf. Pkg. V, AE, DC, MC.
Comfortable, well-appointed rooms in a château just outside Reims. Covered swimming pool and terrace; sauna.

Boyer

Les Crayères, 64, bd H.-Vasnier
26 82 80 80, fax 26 82 65 52
19.5 Closed Tue lunch, Mon, Dec 23-Jan 13. Open until 10:30pm. Priv rm: 24. Air cond. Valet pkg. V, AE, DC, MC.
So you think the end of the grand restaurant is at hand? You're persuaded, like many, that the future belongs to casual bistrots? Before you come to any hasty conclusions, you should consider the case—admittedly, the very special case—of Gérard Boyer. Like everyone else in the

business, Boyer has felt the impact of the recession. Nonetheless, for him the damage has been minimal. Maybe the Smiling Angel of Reims cathedral is looking after him... What is sure is that he, his wife Élyane, and their team are succeeding where others fail. Why? Because a glittering cosmopolitan clientele—people who spend money no matter how deep the crise—knows that Les Crayères provides all the charms, all the pleasures they require. And yet in spite of the undeniable luxury, you feel relaxed and at home here, proof of the Boyers' charm. A quintessentially French ideal of gracious living is embodied, in the decoration, the service, the serene atmosphere.

And then, of course, there is the food. Grounded in the classics, distinguished by remarkable sauces, Gérard Boyer's cuisine possesses a singular grace, a particular personality. There is a touch of the country boy in this sophisticated chef; it shows up in dishes like a truffle in a crust, or his unforgettable stewed pig's head served forth with a croustillant of pig's ear and toast points spread with brains. Boyer has a way of drawing all manner of novel nuances from his ingredients, here and there infusing a bit of southern sunshine: saffrony mussel soup with a delicious hint of orange, tiny snails with artichokes en barigoule, plump langoustines roasted in jus flavored with their coral, John Dory with white pepper served with chopped radishes and vegetable chips, red mullet spiked with tumeric, lamb fillet with a vegetable couscous, braised veal sweetbreads with a potato and Saint Nectaire cheese galette, and a splendid veal kidney cooked in its fat and garnished with cèpe and foie gras gaufrettes. For dessert, sample luscious rhubarb bonbons feuilleté, chocolate soup with honey cake ice cream, and caramelized mangoes with bread pudding.

Champagnes from major firms and smaller growers are available and temptingly priced. But wonderful Werner, the sommelier, will be happy to guide you around a cellar that also holds the cream of fine Burgundies and Bordeaux. C 570-900 F.

Boyer ⚔️🌳

(See restaurant above)

Closed Dec 23-Jan 13. 3 stes 1,780-1,880 F. 16 rms 990-1,880 F. Rms for disabled. Air cond. Tennis. Valet pkg. Helipad. V, AE, DC, MC.

Gérard and Elyane Boyer turned a formerly dilapidated pavilion in the grounds of their hotel into an island of charm and comfort with one suite and two duplexes. As for the château itself, we've said it all above. The rooms are elegantly decorated in period style (classic French, English, romantic, or exotic), and you'll find incomparable comfort and service for about what you would pay in a luxury chain hotel. On the edge of the grounds is a tennis court and on the other side of the wall, an herb garden. There's an English bar and you may request a hairdresser or masseur in your room. Relais et Châteaux.

Le Chardonnay

184, av. d'Épernay
26 06 08 60, fax 26 05 81 56
Closed Sat lunch, Sun dinner, Dec 26-31. Open until 10pm. Pkg. V, AE, DC, MC.

The Boyer's former cottage is more comfortable than attractive, but Jean-Jacques Lange's welcome is genuinely warm and his very traditional cooking usually skillful. But our last visit was a disappointment, so we're suspending the rating this year in hopes of better things to come. C 250-320 F. M 150 F (weekdays, wine incl), 140 F, 190 F, 420 F.

12/20 Le Continental

95, pl. Drouet-d'Erlon
26 47 01 47, fax 26 40 95 60
Open daily until 11:30pm. Priv rm: 80. Terrace dining. Air cond. V, AE, DC, MC.

At lunchtime, the place is packed but a jovial atmosphere reigns as people tuck hungrily into fresh frog's legs in a cassoulet, a generous steak of Charolais beef au poivre vert flambéed in Armagnac, and a classic but well prepared fruit cup. Efficient service; attractively priced Champagnes. C 220-320 F. M 94 F, 175 F, 180 F, 190 F, 260 F.

🍴 Le Florence

43, bd Foch
26 47 12 70, fax 26 40 07 09
Closed Sun (exc hols), Aug 1-20. Open until 9:30pm. Priv rm: 30. Garden dining. V, AE, DC, MC.

Colorful paintings and armloads of flowers add a splash of gaiety to the dining room, where patrons enjoy the cooking of chef Laurent Helleu. He favors fish although prepares meats with precision, too, and all his dishes show a real talent for flavor combinations. This year we savored his lobster and langoustines with turnips in a sweet-sour vinaigrette, grilled turbot curry with leeks, saddle of lamb in an herb crust with a celery root gratin, and a fricassée of veal sweetbreads and snails in truffle jus. Refined desserts. All the best Champagnes, of course, as well as many half bottles, a good choice of Burgundies and wines from other regions, and finds like a Domaine Damiens Madiran at 98 F. Efficient, smiling service. C 380-500 F. M 150 F (weekdays), 210 F, 290 F, 440 F.

🏨 Grand Hôtel des Templiers ⚔️🌳

22, rue des Templiers
26 88 55 08, fax 26 47 80 60
Open year-round. 2 stes 1,800 F. 17 rms 950-1,400 F. Heated pool. Valet pkg. V, AE, DC, MC.

The nineteenth-century building has superb lounges, a polished wood staircase, and huge rooms, each decorated in a different style and remarkably well equipped—hairdryer, bathrobe, slippers, magnifying make-up mirror. Marble bathrooms. The hotel also has a swimming pool, Turkish bath, sauna, and Jacuzzi. The reception and service are pleasant and solicitous. Meals on trays upon request.

Orphée

37, bd P.-Doumer
26 40 01 08, fax 26 40 34 13
Closed Sat lunch, Sun. Open until 10pm. Priv rm: 80. Terrace dining. Pkg. V, AE, DC, MC.

The restaurant is named for Orpheus, and features a rotunda dining room with a distant view of the canal; the back of the room tends to be dark, and the tourist groups flock here. But never mind. Yves Méjean's sun-kissed cooking makes you overlook all this. Frank, forthright flavors shine through in his dishes, which have earned him an extra point this year. Products are always top quality, flavors well balanced. Try his turbot salad (a perfect summer dish), lighty roasted ultrafresh fish nicely paired with savory baby onions and a tasty vinaigrette, and perfectly cooked saddle of lamb with a crisp and richly flavored crust, paired with girolle mushrooms. Two quibbles: the desserts don't quite match the level of the rest, and the wine list is short, with too few half bottles. Charming welcome; efficient service. **C** 280-340 F. **M** 150 F, 195 F, 390 F.

Quality Hôtel 🛦🛡
(See restaurant above)
Open year-round. 80 rms 340-430 F. Rms for disabled. Half-board 345-460 F. Air cond. Conf. Golf. Pkg. V, AE, DC, MC.
Although the hotel's name changed this year, it still offers modern, well equipped, soundproof rooms. Ask for one with a view of the canal and the barges. Enterprising service.

La Paix
9, rue Buirette
26 40 04 08, fax 26 47 75 04
Open year-round. 1 ste 520-700 F. 104 rms 370-700 F. Restaurant. Conf. Pool. Golf. Valet pkg. V, AE, DC, MC.
In a perfect setting near the imposing Sube fountain, this hotel is also convenient to the railway station and cathedral. Bar overlooking a tiny garden.

12/20 Le Paysan 🕄
16, rue de Fismes
26 40 25 51, fax 26 86 49 25
Closed Sat lunch. Open until 10:30pm. Priv rm: 20. V, MC.
A convivial restaurant in a quiet district, where Jean-Michel Champenois prepares hearty country cooking (his salade au lard figures in the *Guinness Book of Records*). Other good choices are the fricassée of chicken with langoustines and the poached haddock with lentils. **C** 160-290 F. **M** 78 F (weekday lunch), 98 F, 160 F, 200 F, 250 F.

Au Petit Comptoir
17, rue de Mars - 26 40 58 58
Closed Sat lunch, Sun, Aug 5-21, Jan 1-11. Open until 10:30pm. Terrace dining. Air cond. V, AE, MC.
This is Gérard Boyer's bistrot, complete with green banquettes and a jostling crowd enjoying great cuisine bourgeoise cooked by Fabrice Maillot: salmon rillettes, roast fresh cod, andouillette galette en persillade, and a warm soufflé of caramelized pears. Lovers of bubbly take note: the prices for Champagne (and other wines) are unbeatable! **C** 230-300 F.

Vonelly Gambetta
9-13, rue Gambetta
26 47 22 00, fax 26 47 22 43
Closed Sun dinner, Mon, Aug 8-28. Open until 9:45pm. No pets. V.
The many set menus and the "menu-carte" fail to reveal Éric Petit's considerable talent, but we understand that these are hard times for restaurants. Nevertheless, a point less this year. Our last meal included an "Assiette du Sud-ouest" with more salad than foie gras, tender duck breast with quail's eggs served in a stingy por-

tion, and fillets of lamb and beef served with a very ordinary sauce, followed by cheeses and excellent white-chocolate truffettes. The cellar is well stocked and now contains some less expensive bottles and half bottles. Friendly welcome and service. **M** 120 F, 190 F, 230 F.

And also...
Our selection of places for inexpensive, quick, or late-night meals.
Le Boulingrin (26 40 96 22 - 48, rue de Mars. Open until 11pm, w-e midnight.): The only true brasserie near the old food market, this Art Deco spot offers hearty traditional specialties (150 F).
La Grappa (26 08 66 78 - 49, rue du Col.-Fabien. Open until 11pm.): Good choice of pizzas, trattoria-style (100 F).
La Grille (26 88 65 70 - 46, rue Jard. Open until 10pm.): In a tiny dining room, sample bistrot classics; skip the first courses (150-200 F).
Au Petit Bacchus (26 47 10 05 - 11, rue de l'Université. Open until 10pm.): Inexpensive, traditional cooking (130-150 F).

◾ **In Champigny 51370** 6 km NW on N 31, D 275

La Garenne
Route de Suissons
26 08 26 62, fax 26 84 24 13
Closed Sun dinner, Mon, Aug 1-21. Open until 10pm. Priv rm: 16. Air cond. Pkg. V, AE, DC, MC.
Laurent Laplaige, who used to work with Gérard Boyer, is a rigorous professional whose cooking displays forthright flavors, and is always based on current market offerings. You can count on pleasure with dishes like foie gras with onion confit and beets, roast turbot with wheat germ, and a berry croquant. The welcome and service are also excellent and the cellar is filled with Champagne (lots of half-bottles), all well chosen and moderately priced. **C** 350-450 F. **M** 150 F, 220 F, 380 F.

◾ **In Montchenot 51500** 11 km S on N 51

Auberge du Grand Cerf
N 51 - 26 97 60 07, fax 26 97 64 24
Closed Sun dinner, Wed, Jan 2-15, Aug 8-20. Open until 9:30pm. Garden dining. Pkg. V, AE, MC.
On balmy days, the delicious, shady garden is a welcome extension to the pretty pink-and-green dining room where Dominique Giraudeau serves up classic, remarkably polished cuisine: we especially like his terrine of salmon and oysters en gelée, pig's foot stuffed with veal sweetbreads and mushrooms, and a gooey chocolate and almond milk dessert. Let sommelier Hervé Launois guide you around a seductive cellar chock-a-block with Champagnes. Competent service. **C** 320-480 F. **M** 160 F, 175 F, 250 F, 350 F, 420 F.

RÉMIGEASSE (LA) 17 → **Oléron (Ile d')**

*Some establishments change their **closing times** without warning. It is always wise to check in advance.*

RENNES **35000**

Paris 348 - Brest 245 - Nantes 106 - Le Mans 153   *Ille-et-Vilaine*

 Anne de Bretagne

12, rue Tronjolly
99 31 49 49, fax 99 30 53 48
Open year-round. 42 rms 399-499 F. Conf. Golf. Pkg. V, AE, DC, MC.

In the center of town, but quiet. The modern rooms are bright and well appointed.

L'Escu de Runfao

11, rue du Chapitre - 99 79 13 10
Closed Sat lunch, Sun, 1st wk of Jan, Aug 6-20. Open until 10pm (10:30pm in summer). Priv rm: 30. Terrace dining. V, AE.

In summer, rush to reserve one of the three outside tables of this lovely establishment in old Rennes where you can feast on dishes made with absolutely prime ingredients. (The seductive red dining room within this lovely sixteenth-century building is charming, too.) Alain Duhoux is a debonair and daring chef: delicious red mullet vinaigrette with veal sweetbreads, perfectly cooked and tasty roast turbot with girolles, and an excellent tarte Tatin. Attractive set menus. Interesting selection of Soutwest wines, friendly welcome, and competent service. **C** 350-500 F. **M** 125 F (weekdays exc Fri dinner), 195 F (Sat dinner, Sun lunch), 255 F, 400 F (Sun lunch).

Le Florian

12, rue de l'Arsenal - 99 67 25 35
Closed Sun (exc lunch in winter), Sat lunch off-seas, Jan 1-9, 10 days in May, Aug 1-15. Open until 9:30pm. V.

Rennes's gastronomes are talking about this discreet, unpretentious little eating house, run by a boyish owner-chef, Laurent Delimèle. His cooking is engagingly innovative, even in the first set menu served on weekdays: cauliflower cream with oysters and smoked fish, mitonnée of young rabbit aux fruits du mendiant, and a dark chocolate and caramel ganaché. The wine list is short but to the point, with some fine, accessibly priced offerings from the Loire. The young hostess greets guests with a charming smile. **C** 300-350 F. **M** 165 F, 215 F, 280 F (weekdays, Sat dinner, Sun lunch), 102 F (weekdays).

Le Four à Ban

4, rue St-Mélaine - 99 38 72 85
Closed Sun dinner, Mon, 1st wk of Jan & May, 2 wks in Aug. Open until 10pm. Pkg. V, AE, DC, MC.

Seasonal inspiration guides Francis Marx to turn out fresh, lively dishes like crab and buckwheat spiked with coriander, croustillant of beef cheeks, roast veal kidney with new potatoes, and a chaud-froid of orange peel in puff pastry, all served in a warm and cozy atmosphere. **C** 210-340 F. **M** 98 F (weekdays, Sat lunch), 148 F, 188 F, 228 F.

Garden Hotel

3, rue Duhamel (corner av. Janvier)
99 65 45 06, fax 99 65 02 62
Open year-round. 24 rms 145-280 F. Golf. Pkg. V, AE, MC.

Between the quays and the Maison de la Culture. The rooms are simple and quiet, and there are some family-sized duplexes. Indoor garden.

12/20 **Le Gourmandin**

4, pl. de Bretagne - 99 30 42 01
Closed Sat lunch, Sun, 2nd wk of Mar school hols, 1st 3 wks of Aug. Open until 10pm. Air cond. V, AE.

The salmon-pink dining room is extended by a pleasant glass-enclosed veranda, where obliging staff serve fresh, unpretentious food: chicken ballottine with cabbage and foie gras, seafood pot-au-feu, and a feuillantine stuffed with banana confit. The cellar offers nice little Loire wines at low prices. Attentive welcome. **C** 200-280 F. **M** 76 F (weekday lunch), 98 F, 150 F.

L'Ouvrée

18, pl. des Lices - 99 30 16 38
Closed Sat lunch & Mon (exc for groups). Open until 10:30pm. Priv rm: 100. Pkg. V, AE, DC, MC.

Only market-fresh produce goes into Gérard Jehannin's vibrant, good-humored cooking. In a jovial atmosphere, you can sit down to a generous, reasonably priced meal, such as the 125 F menu: a monkfish and raw salmon ballottine with fresh terragon, slices of duck breast with caramelized apples, a salad with Brie de Meaux, and nougat glacé. The dining room in this seventeenth-century hostelry is cozy. Intelligent cellar. **C** 270-350 F. **M** 80 F, 125 F, 170 F.

Le Palais

7, pl. du Parlement-de-Bretagne
99 79 45 01, fax 99 79 12 41
Closed Sun dinner, Mon. Annual closings not available. Open until 10pm. Priv rm: 26. Air cond. Garage pkg. V, AE, DC, MC.

Marc Tizon tirelessly seeks out Brittany's best suppliers, rarest ingredients, and ancient, near-forgotten culinary lore—his efforts give the menu a fascinating regional slant. This restaurant on the city's prettiest square is without a doubt the best place to dine. You shouldn't pass up a chance to try his perfectly cooked turbot with "broken" potatoes in chive juice, or veal sweetbreads (described on the menu as "studded" with bits of ham but not studded at all) paired with delicious baby vegetables. Nothing is astonishing, but everything tastes just the way it should. The cellar neds more half bottles. Service is competent and never stiff; prices are high, but this is an expensive city. The set menus are reasonably priced. **C** 450-600 F. **M** 98 F (lunch exc Sun), 170 F (wine incl), 130 F, 220 F.

Le Piano Blanc

Route de Ste-Foix - 99 31 20 21
Closed Sun, Aug 10-28. Open until 10pm. Priv rm: 18. Garden dining. Pkg. V, AE.

Pascal Piette's cooking is geared to market offerings, which govern whether he opts for the classic or the more personal. In any case, we savor his predominantly maritime dishes like langouste tails in a jus flavored with their coral, boned young squab in jus with girolles, and an authentic kouing-aman (buttery Breton cake). Attractive cellar; equally appealing neo-Art Deco decor. Charming welcome by Madame Piette. **C** 250-380 F. **M** 120 F (weekday lunch), 178 F, 225 F, 280 F.

Le Sévigné

47, av. Janvier
99 67 27 55, fax 99 30 66 10
Open year-round. 46 rms 165-310 F. Pkg. V, AE, DC.

These comfortable, well-soundproofed, and recently redecorated rooms are convenient to the TGV station. Perfectly equipped bathrooms. Friendly reception.

And also...

Our selection of places for inexpensive, quick, or late-night meals.
La Chope (99 79 34 54 - 3, rue de La Chalotais.): Fine brasserie-style meals served in a picturesque decor. Speedy service (100-150 F).
Le Galopin (99 31 55 96 - 21, av. Janvier. Open until 11pm, Sat midnight.): A popular, lively brasserie with dishes prepared from fine products (79-150 F).
Le Serment de Vin (99 30 99 30 - 20, bd de La Tour-d'Auvergne. Open until 10:30pm.): Good brasserie-style dishes and an interesting choice of wines (75-250 F).
Le Tire-Bouchon (99 79 43 43 - 15, pl. Sainte-Anne. Open until midnight.): Bistrot cooking and an interesting wine list; a former sommelier is the "patron" (60-120 F).

■ In **Châteaugiron 35410**   16 km SE on D 463

L'Aubergade
2, rue Gourdel - 99 37 41 35
Closings not available. Open until 9:30pm. Priv rm: 30. Pkg. V, AE.
Jean-Claude Barré is a confirmed Breton chef whose cuisine is resolutely regional. His menu offers lots of character and bright ideas: a gratinéed seafood crêpe, langoustine feuillantine, farm-raised chicken in brik (flaky pastry), John Dory flavored with coriander, chocolate cake with a touch of coffee, and an almond cream soufflé. The wine list is appealing but too costly. Nice welcome and competent service in two pretty, rustic dining rooms. C 230-370 F. M 115 F, 146 F, 150 F.

■ In **Noyal-sur-Vilaine 35530**   12 km E on N 157

Hostellerie Les Forges
22, av. du Gal.-de-Gaulle
99 00 54 08, fax 99 00 62 02
Closed dinner Sun & hols, last 2 wks of Feb. Open until 9:30pm. Priv rm: 80. Pkg. V, AE, DC, MC.
This opulent yet rustic restaurant outside Rennes celebrates tradition with André Pilard's generous cuisine based on top-quality products. Try the 138 F menu: gâtelet of shellfish with asparagus, médallions of monkfish with wild mushrooms, a trio of cheeses served with a salad, and a fruit gratin spiked with Grand Marnier. Tempting wine list, and a warm welcome by the patronne. C 290-360 F. M 138 F (weekdays, Sat lunch), 120 F (weekday lunch), 140 F (Sat dinner), 190 F (exc Sun), 250 F

■ In **Pacé 35740**   10 km NW on N 12 and D 287

La Griotte
In Pont-de-Pacé, 42, rue du Dr-Léon
99 60 62 48, fax 99 60 26 84
Closed Wed, dinner Sun & Tue, Feb 15-28, Aug 1-24. Open until 10pm. Priv rm: 35. Pkg. V, AE, DC, MC.

The robust country menu contrasts markedly with the dainty decor of this elegantly converted farmhouse. Noteworthy dishes include hearty buckwheat crêpes with andouille sausage, rabbit daube with pearl onions, and baked Camembert set atop mixed greens. Superb cellar; relaxed service. The prix-fixe meals are excellent value. C 180-280 F. M 90 F (weekdays, Sat lunch), 115 F, 160 F, 190 F, 240 F.

REPLONGES 01	→ Màcon

RETHONDES 60	→ Compiègne

REUILLY-SAUVIGNY	02850

Paris 110 - Château-Thierry 17 - Reims 47 - Epernay 33   Aisne

Auberge Le Relais

23 70 35 36, fax 23 70 27 76
Closed Tue dinner, Wed, Feb 20-Mar 15, Aug 21-Sep 6. Priv rm: 30. Pkg. V, AE, DC.
This cozy inn overlooking the Marne Valley is run by cordial staff who make you feel right at home. Line Berthuit smilingly ushers you into the dining room to enjoy her husband Martial's expert, full-flavored cuisine. Few frills interfere with the forthright tastes of his lobster lasagne with truffles, fillet of duck breast spiced with Szechuan peppercorns and paired with a spelt croustillant, and a luscious brik (flaky pastry) stuffed with caramelized bananas in piña colada sauce and accompanied by pineapple sherbet. Splendid cellar, with many bottles at reasonable prices. C 400-500 F. M 153 F (exc Sat dinner & Sun lunch), 215 F, 255 F, 405 F.

RIANS	83560

Paris 770 - Avignon 98 - Draguignan 69 - Aix-en-P. 39   Var

Le Bois Saint-Hubert
4 km, route de St-Maximin (D3)
94 80 31 00, fax 94 80 55 71
Closed Mon dinner, Tue, Jan 5-Mar 25. Open until 10pm. Priv rm: 150. Garden dining. Pkg. V, AE, MC.
Old-fashioned and modern elements are adroitly combined in this meticulously restored sheepfold, where Russian icons and Italian design pieces cohabit decoratively. Chef Gérard Gravier follows contemporary trends, but is unswerving in his devotion to local ingredients; he does best when he remembers to stay simple. The Provençal note is struck emphatically in dishes like sea bass tartare with chives, rack of Sisteron lamb persillé, and a fresh fruit gratin. Warm welcome. C 300-400 F. M 120 F, 160 F, 310 F.

Le Bois Saint-Hubert
(See restaurant above)
Closed Mon, Tue, Jan 5-Mar 1. 9 rms 450-900 F. Half-board 700 F. Conf. Heated pool. Valet pkg. Helipad. V, AE, MC.
Once a hunting lodge, this hotel on a wild, wind-swept plateau offers rooms (some on the small side) decorated with great attention to detail. The surroundings are absolutely quiet and peaceful; splendid pool; fine breakfasts.

RIBAUTE-LES-TAVERNES 30	→ Alès

RIBEAUVILLÉ   68150
Paris 434 - Colmar 15 - Sélestat 15 - Mulhouse 57   *Haut-Rhin*

 Clos Saint-Vincent   
Route de Bergheim
89 73 67 65, fax 89 73 32 20
Closed Nov 15-Mar 15. 3 stes 990-1,077 F. 12 rms 600-935 F. Rms for disabled. Restaurant. Half-board 830-900 F. Heated pool. Golf. Pkg. V, MC.
The quiet, spacious, and individually decorated rooms, all with balconies or terraces, offer views of surrounding vineyards and the distant Black Forest. Lovely bathrooms; TV on request. Friendly welcome.

Haut Ribeaupierre
1, route de Bergheim
89 73 62 64, fax 89 73 36 61
Closed Wed. Open until 10pm. Priv rm: 25. Terrace dining. Air cond. Pkg. V, AE, MC.
A trio of trim, tidy dining rooms: one is done up as a *winstub*, another in turn-of-the-century style, and the third as a winter garden. The menu, predictably, is eclectic. Olivier Reibel offers daring flavor combinations: poached oysters with bacon and parsley, langoustines pan roasted with ginger, fillet of lamb with a honey-lime sauce, and classic desserts. Good regional wines. Nice welcome and service. C 300-400 F. M 130 F, 150 F, 250 F, 330 F.

Les Vosges
2, Grand'Rue
89 73 61 39, fax 89 73 34 21
Closed Sun dinner, Mon, Feb. Open until 9:30pm. Pkg. V, AE, DC, MC.
The pink-toned decor may be resolutely bourgeois, but chef Jean-Philippe Le Roy's cooking is imaginative and market by finesse. Try his fresh and savory oxtail salad with macaroni, perfectly roasted cod croustillant with a sweet-pepper cream, and a delicious orange cake with saffron salad. Two toques for all this. Warm welcome; competent service. The fine wine list concentrates on Alsatian wines. C 290-400 F. M 160 F, 245 F, 380 F.

Les Vosges
(See restaurant above)
Closed Mon, Feb. 2 stes 500-550 F. 18 rms 370-385 F. Air cond. No pets. V, AE, MC.
A huge turn-of-the-century edifice offering very spacious although unexciting rooms and a warm welcome.

RIBÉRAC   24600
Paris 500 - Périgueux 37 - Angoulême 58   *Dordogne*

11/20 Mas de Montet
Petit Bersac
53 90 08 71, fax 53 90 55 87
Closed Jan 3-31, Feb (by reserv). Open until 9pm. Terrace dining. Pkg. V, AE, MC.
In a pleasant white dining room furnished with lovely antiques, savor traditional dishes like a tasty foie gras terrine flavored with Cognac, pleasant sole with cèpes, and an original Kirsch cake. Small and badly presented wine list; warm welcome. C 300-350 F. M 140 F (dinner exc Sat), 160 F, 180 F, 290 F.

Mas de Montet
(See restaurant above)
Closed Jan. 13 rms 475-650 F. Restaurant. Conf. Pkg. V, AE, MC.
Here's an authentic Renaissance château set in peaceful, luxuriant grounds. Commodious, recently renovated rooms provide perfect appointments and furnishings. Splendid bathrooms; charming welcome.

RIEC-SUR-BELON   29340
Paris 518 - Quimper 42 - Concarneau 19   *Finistère*

Le Kerland
3 km S on D 24, route de Moëlan-sur-Mer
98 06 42 98, fax 98 06 45 38
Closed Sun dinner (in winter). Open until 10pm. Priv rm: 80. Terrace dining. Hotel: 1 ste 600 F. 17 rms 360-650 F. Half-board 390-535 F. Air cond. Conf. No pets. Pkg. V, AE, MC.
Chef Christian Chatelain continues to cherish sauces spiced with curry, ginger, and cinnamon, but he now uses much less cream in them. And his desserts are still remarkable, particularly the strawberry soup spiked with Champagne. Respectable cellar, with some reasonably priced Loire wines. C 280-380 F. M 165 F, 198 F, 298 F.

RIGNAC 46   → Gramat

RILLIEUX-LA-PAPE 69   → Lyon

RIOM   63200
Paris 374 - Clermont-Ferrand 15 - Vichy 35   *Puy-de-Dôme*

Moulin de Villeroze
144, route de Marsat - 73 38 58 23
Open daily until 9:30pm. Priv rm: 60. Garden dining. Pkg. V, AE, DC, MC.
Each year brings its crop of improvements to the Moulin, already one of the finest tables in the region. Dominique Juvigny has plenty of fresh ideas, which he executes with commendable skill. His modern menu features interesting combinations of flavors: try the tuna feuillantine with a tomato compote, duck steamed over seaweed, and a lightly smoked coeur de filet. Warm welcome; diversified wine list. C 210-360 F. M 140 F (weekday lunch), 150 F, 170 F, 250 F, 320 F.

RIQUEWIHR   68340
Paris 437 - Colmar 13 - Sélestat 19 - St-Dié 46   *Haut-Rhin*

Auberge du Schœnenbourg
2, rue de la Piscine
89 47 92 28, fax 89 47 89 84
Closed Thu lunch, Wed, Jan 10-Feb 10. Open until 9:30pm. Terrace dining. Air cond. Pkg. V, MC.
The dining room now boasts a glass-enclosed veranda that offers views of the medieval ramparts and the Schœnenbourg vineyards (FYI: they yield the world's best Riesling). Prices remain moderate for François Kiener's forthright, appealing cuisine. We recommend you try his delicious duck foie gras carpaccio with aromatic herbs, squab with spices, and warm chocolate cake with sweet almond milk. The excellent local wines include one made by the Kiener family. Several wines by the glass, and fine eaux-de-vie. C 320-420 F. M 180 F (weekdays, Sat lunch), 230 F, 305 F, 365 F.

Le Schœnenbourg

Rue du Schœnenbourg
89 49 01 11, fax 89 47 95 88
Open year-round. 2 stes 670 F. 43 rms 300-530 F. Rms for disabled. Restaurant. Half-board 450-522 F. Conf. Golf. Pkg. V, MC.
At the foot of the village, with a delightful terraced garden surrounded by vines, this modern hotel features quiet, neat and functional rooms. Restaurant (see above).

RIVE-DE-GIER	42800
Paris 495 - Lyon 37 - St-Etienne 22 - Vienne 27	*Loire*

La Renaissance

41, rue A.-Marrel
77 75 04 31, fax 77 83 68 58
Closed Sun dinner, Mon, Jan 2-3. Open until 9:30pm. Garden dining. Pkg. V, AE, DC, MC.
La Renaissance injects a welcome dose of charm into the rather drear industrial surroundings, thanks largely to a well-tended rock garden. Chef Jean-Paul Mounier's frank, solid, generous bill of fare is the main attraction, however. He scores high in our book with a 168 F menu: snail cassoulette with wild mushrooms, gigot of rabbit cooked en chemise with garlic and rosemary and paired with a vegetable cake, cheese, and dessert. Warm welcome by the owners. The dazzling cellar is pricey. C 350-480 F. M 125 F, 168 F (weekdays, Sat lunch), 230 F, 280 F, 355 F.

La Renaissance

(See restaurant above)
Closed Mon, Sun, Jan 2-3. 2 stes 350-400 F. 6 rms 220-300 F. Pkg. V, AE, DC, MC.
Six rooms and two suites, all comfortable, are on offer in this hotel near the Pilat park and not far from Saint-Etienne.

RIVEDOUX-PLAGE 17	→ Ré (Ile de)

ROANNE	42300
Paris 390 - Lyon 88 - St-Etienne 77 - Mâcon 97	*Loire*

L'Astrée

17 bis, cours de la République
77 72 74 22, fax 77 72 72 23
Closed Sat, Sun, Dec 24-Jan 4, Aug 1-24. Open until 9:30pm. Priv rm: 30. Pkg. V, DC.
Setting up shop next to Troisgros (see below) demands a lot of nerve and verve. Simon Falcoz has what it takes. He's won over a loyal clientele with his creamed eggs and asparagus, Parmesan, and sea scallops; mixed fish with pistachios and an olive flan; and a yummy pear tarte Tatin with walnut ice cream and a saffrony crème anglaise. Rest assured there will be nothing but pleasant surprises here; Martine Falcoz's cordial welcome makes this prettily done-up establishment even more attractive. Good cellar; try the Robert Plasse Côte Rouannaise. C 250-350 F. M 175 F (weekday lunch, wine incl), 130 F, 190 F, 280 F, 350 F.

Troisgros

Pl. de la Gare
77 71 66 97, fax 77 70 39 77
19.5 *Closed Tue dinner, Wed, Feb school hols, 1st 2 wks of Aug. Open until 9:30pm. Priv rm: 25. Air cond. Valet pkg. V, AE, DC, MC.*

As other great restaurateurs expanded their establishments with lush grounds and swimming pools, the Troisgros were forced to decide whether to move out of Roanne or make the most of what they had. They elected to stay put and, judging by the steady flow of customers, the latest investments (most recently the purchase of two hectares of vineyard) have been right on target. And now, under Papa Pierre's approving eye, Michel Troisgros has taken complete control of the kitchen. We are happy to report that he fully deserves his 19.5—our highest rating.
Our sampling of new additions to his menu left us dazzled and delighted. No fault—far from it!—could be found in Michel's oysters flanked by turnips grilled in peanut oil, his toothsome confit of tomatoes with a peppery dill stuffing, his luscious Vienna-style frogs' legs with horseradish, his sea urchin "gâteau" (marred by a tad too much egg white), sea scallops with gingery endives, peerless turbot braised with bay leaves and sage, veal chop simmered with Moroccan herbs, and a marvelous croustillante (crispness is a favorite Troisgros touch) of veal sweetbreads with a lively vinegar jus that perfectly matches the raw spinach and tomato garnish. Michel never seems to fall short, offering not only adventurous dishes but also the Troisgros classics that regulars (and ourselves) adore: the celebrated salmon in sorrel sauce, or the chateaubriand steak in Fleurie wine sauce with beef marrow and a Forézien gratin. The cheeses are sublime, especially the fresh Chevenet goat cheese, and the dozen or so desserts are all lip-smacking: buttery coffee and chestnut sablé with caramel sauce, or a chocolate craquant flavored with a touch of tea, for example. The wine list is literally a weighty tome, but the sommelier ably guides guests through its pages: there are many wonderful discoveries to be made. Needless to say, the welcome, service, and comfort are absolutely tip-top—for that is the Troisgros way. C 600-800 F. M 300 F (weekday lunch), 540 F, 660 F, 760 F.

Troisgros

(See restaurant above)
Closed Feb school hols, 1st 2 wks of Aug. 6 stes 1,400-1,900 F. 14 rms 750-1,250 F. Air cond. Conf. Golf. Valet pkg. V, AE, DC, MC.
The hotel has two wings: the older one, completely transformed, offers ultramodern rooms with remote-controlled everything, overlooking either the garden or the station square. The new wing features five suites and three rooms, luxuriously decorated with contemporary furnishings, with views on a lush indoor garden and the breakfast room (exquisite breakfasts, of course). Relais et Châteaux.

■ In **Le Coteau 42120**   3 km E on N 7

Auberge Costelloise

2, av. de la Libération - 77 68 12 71
Closed Sun, Mon, Dec 26-Jan 5, May 1-8, Aug 1-24. Open until 9:15pm. Air cond. Pkg. V.
A colorful, modern establishment run by Solange Alex for those who can't eat every day chez Troisgros! Daniel Alex is in the kitchen thinking up delicious, clever recipes made with excellent ingredients but which won't break the

bank: snail soup with garden herbs, squab and foie gras tourte, fricassée of farm-raised chicken in cream sauce with wild-mushroom-stuffed morels, and honey and apple bread pudding. The pleasant dining room has been enlarged this year. The two first set menus and the "lunch club" are genuine bargains. **C** 250-350 F. **M** 185 F (weekday lunch, wine incl), 115 F (weekday lunch), 185 F, 250 F, 330 F.

ROCAMADOUR	46500
Paris 522 - Figeac 46 - Brive 54 - Gramat 9 - Cahors 61	*Lot*

Domaine de la Rhue

N 140 - 65 33 71 50, fax 65 33 72 48
Closed Oct 15-Apr 15. 12 rms 370-570 F. Pool. Golf. Pkg. V, MC.
In a wild setting near Rocamadour, this beautifully fitted hotel offers spacious, handsome rooms that feature wood beams and exposed-stone walls. Comfort and quiet are assured. Good breakfasts.

11/20 Sainte-Marie

Pl. des Senhals - 65 33 63 07
Closings not available. Open until 9pm (9:15pm in summer). Terrace dining. Hotel: 22 rms 175-275 F. Half-board 245-260 F. No pets. Pkg. V, MC.
A cliff-top restaurant with a magnificent terrace (to be covered soon during extensive renovations) where you can feast on a salad of lamb sweetbreads and chive-enhanced salmon, duck breast with juniper berries, and a walnut cake. There are 22 moderately priced guestrooms with delightful views. **C** 220-400 F. **M** 70 F, 90 F, 120 F, 220 F.

Jehan de Valon

Cité Médiévale
65 33 63 08, fax 65 33 65 23
Closed Nov 12-Dec 29, Jan 3-Feb 11. Open until 9pm (10pm in summer). Priv rm: 15. Terrace dining. No pets. Valet pkg. V, AE, DC, MC.
Christophe Besse has taken over at the stove with a new regional repertoire prepared with care. Sample his excellent potée quercinoise (rib-sticking soup), fine foie gras, slightly over-cooked grouper studded with salmon, and slighly overcooked lamb croustillant. There's a spectacular valley view from the dining room. Good cellar; flawless welcome and service. **C** 220-380 F. **M** 99 F, 145 F, 195 F, 250 F.

Le Beau Site

(See restaurant above)
See restaurant for closings. 2 stes 550-650 F. 42 rms 270-480 F. Half-board 250-480 F. Air cond. Conf. Valet pkg. V, AE, DC, MC.
This fine, family-owned hotel offers a variety of well-kept rooms housed in two buildings: one dates from the fifteenth century, the other from the turn of this one. Excellent breakfasts, warm welcome. Splendid valley views.

ROCHE-BERNARD (LA)	56130
Paris 441 - La Baule 31 - St-Nazaire 35 - Nantes 70	*Morbihan*

Auberge Bretonne

2, pl. Du Guesclin
99 90 60 28, fax 99 90 85 00
Closed Fri lunch, Thu, Nov 13-Dec 3, Jan 9-26. Open until 9pm. Priv rm: 20. Garage pkg. V, AE, MC.

What do a dray horse and a clarinet have in common? Jacques Thorel is the answer, for this stocky, mustachioed chef has a passion for both of the above. He raises pigs and fowl as well as horses on his farm, so don't be surprised to find a tender spit-roasted pork chop, old-fashioned bacon, or parmentier of andouille sausage on his menu. Nor should you wonder that the garden surrounded by the cloister-like dining room blooms with vegetables rather than flowers!
In Thorel's kitchen, harmony reigns. Inspired by the familiar refrains of cuisine bourgeoise, he improvizes some rather startling solos, often on the rustic side: a spicy salad of chervil and civelles de Camoël, superb roast sole with a bacon-spiked potato tourte, a thick slice of spit-roasted turbot with an almost caramelized crust, superb spit-roasted pork whose juices mingle with the accompanying potatoes, truffles, and leeks, and delectable, fork-tender veal shanks with a fennel cream. For dessert, don't miss the very unmonastic "Jesuite" of apricot confit with almond-milk ice cream. Choosing a wine here is no minor affair, for the cellar holds some 35,000 bottles. It's no wonder the locals flock to this stone house overlooking the port. One quibble: the set menus are rather expensive (except for the first one) and have to be ordered by everyone at the table. **C** 450-700 F. **M** 150 F (weekdays), 210 F, 350 F, 400 F, 450 F.

Auberge Bretonne

(See restaurant above)
Closed Thu, Nov 13-Dec 3, Jan 9-26. 11 rms 450-850 F. Conf. Golf. Pkg. V, AE, MC.
The cheerful rooms are a delight to the eye and perfectly appointed. Delicious breakfasts, with all manner of sweet treats.

ROCHECORBON 37	→ Tours

ROCHEGUDE 26	→ Orange

ROCHE-L'ABEILLE (LA)	87800
Paris 412 - Limoges 31 - St-Yrieix 10 - Brive 72	*H.-Vienne*

Au Moulin de la Gorce

2 km S on D 17
55 00 70 66, fax 55 00 76 57
Closed Sun dinner & Mon off-seas, Jan 2-Feb 8. Open until 9pm. Priv rm: 40. Pkg. V, AE, DC, MC.
This bucolic Renaissance mill compound (complete with a romantic pond) has a formal Louis XVI–style dining room and another, more rustic one, with stone walls and a fireplace. Here you can settle down and partake of Jean Bertranet's rich, well-wrought, resolutely classic cuisine. Sample his eggs (soft-boiled or scrambled) with truffles, a delicate foie gras terrine, sole paupiettes with risotto, and sautéed veal sweetbreads with cèpes. When the cheese board is presented (more than fifteen varieties, all perfectly matured), you may regret having dined so well! But even if you have to let your belt out a notch, don't miss Bertranet's sinfully delicious chocolate beignets: warm and liquid inside, crisp and biscuity on the outside, and served with saffrony crème anglaise; the delicate apple tart with nougatine ice cream is another good choice. Fine wine list with many dis-

coveries. C 350-500 F. M 180 F, 250 F, 380 F, 480 F.

 Moulin de la Gorce ⚜🍴
(See restaurant above)
See restaurant for closings. 1 ste 1,300-1,600 F. 9 rms 480-700 F. Half-board 750-1,100 F. Conf. Pkg. V, AE, DC, MC.
Nestled between a trout stream and a pond, this small, deftly restored pavilion offers ten perfectly quiet rooms, each named after a flower, seven of which were completely restored this year following a flood. In addition to impeccable, friendly service and reception, guests can anticipate delectable breakfasts, fishing on the five-hectare wooded grounds, tennis, a swimming pool just ten minutes away, and stables within easy reach. Relais et Châteaux.

ROCHELLE (LA)	17000
Paris 475 - Bordeaux 188 - Angoulême 128	Charente-M.

Bistrot de l'Entracte
22, rue St-Jean-du-Pérot - 46 50 62 60
Closed Sun. Open until 9:45pm. Air cond. V.
Didier Cadio is paddling along nicely with his tasty repertoire of clever seafood dishes, all offered at very reasonable prices: marinière of cockles and mussels seasoned with thyme, a cassoulet of fish and mojette beans with fresh herbs, and a Very British tapioca pudding soufflé with apricot sauce. The raw fish platters and "formule rapide" menus are also worthy of attention. The turn-of-the-century decor is soon to be changed to contemporary. M 145 F.

Le Bistrot du Belvédère
Le Belvédère, pont de Ré - 46 42 62 62
Closed Sun dinner off-seas, Mon, & Tue & Wed dinner Nov-Mar. Priv rm: 50. Terrace dining. Pkg. V, DC, MC.
Standing a few yards shy of the bridge for L'Ile de Ré (and with a view of said bridge and said island), this bistrot provides focused, full-flavored food (mainly seafood) based on fine ingredients and offered at reasonable prices. Sample the mushroom and langoustine croustillant, roast grouper with oysters, and turbot with two types of caviar. The à la carte prices are very reasonable, and the set menus are real bargains. C 190-250 F. M 65 F (lunch), 98 F, 145 F, 185 F, 220 F.

 Les Brises ⚜🍴
17, chemin de la Digue-Richelieu
46 43 89 37, fax 46 43 27 97
Open year-round. 48 rms 250-620 F. Conf. Golf. Garage pkg. V, AE, MC.
In a quiet location away from the center, this stolid, utterly charmless residence has a vast terrace looking out on the water, and large, attractively decorated rooms with balconies. Superb breakfasts.

Le Champlain
France et Angleterre, 20, rue Rambaud
46 41 23 99, fax 46 41 15 19
Open year-round. 4 stes 635-655 F. 36 rms 300-535 F. Air cond. Conf. Pkg. V, AE, DC.
Ranked among the city's finest, this beautiful former town house has comfortable, stylishly furnished rooms. Those on the Rue Rambaud are quiet at night, but not in the morning. Lovely flower garden; bar.

Richard Coutanceau
Plage de la Concurrence
46 41 48 19, fax 46 41 99 45
Closed Sun, Mon (exc Jun 1-Sep 30). Open until 9:30pm. Priv rm: 150. Air cond. Pkg. V, AE, DC.
Richard Coutanceau focuses squarely on seafood, befitting the dining room's splendid sea view. The very choicest seafood, which this demanding chef selects himself. Prepared with consummate skill and presented with flair, this is classic cuisine of a very high standard indeed. Coutanceau excels with dishes that shine with simple clarity, and even offers some fine choices for landlubbers (tiny petit gris snails, or roast lamb, for example). Savor his salad of oysters and roast langoustines, or his delicious marinated fillets of red mullet paired with celery rémoulade, and you'll have ample evidence of his art; his seasonings and flavor combinations are absolutely perfect. Other favorites this year are his flavorful matelote of eels with baby leeks; we were less enthralled by the slices of sea bass and onions cooked in vermouth and paired with a too-salty couscous. For dessert, opt for the fruit gratin. The 210 F menu, with some of the best dishes on the "carte", is a good deal. The fine wine list offers a wide choice, from a simple Haut-Poitou at 80 F to a fabulous Richebourg. C 350-500 F. M 210 F, 400 F.

La Marmite
14, rue St-Jean-du-Pérot
46 41 17 03, fax 46 41 43 15
Closed Wed off-seas. Open until 10pm. Priv rm: 45. Air cond. V, AE, DC, MC.
In a street chock-a-block with restaurants, local worthies and the business-lunch crowd home in on Louis Marzin's quiet establishment. The paneled dining room has a delightfully old-fashioned feel and one can sit back and tuck into good seafood (and a few meat dishes) prepared with a skillful hand. Sample the magnificent roast langoustines, the delectable sea scallops with truffled mashed potatoes, or the turbot with shellfish. Follow these with a fine raspberry feuilleté and excellent coffee. Madame Marzin, who helps you choose from the superb wine list, looks after her guests with maternal warmth. C 400-500 F. M 180 F, 300 F, 380 F.

La Monnaie ⚜🍴
3, rue de la Monnaie
46 50 65 65, fax 46 50 63 19
Open year-round. 4 stes 800-950 F. 32 rms 430-460 F. Rms for disabled. Restaurant. Air cond. Conf. Golf. Garage pkg. V, AE, DC, MC.
Opposite the old harbor, this distinguished seventeenth-century dwelling houses pleasant rooms with all the usual equipment. Uncommonly good service; light meals.

Yachtman
23, quai Valin - 46 21 20 68
Closed Sun dinner & Mon off-seas, Dec 24-30. Open until 10:30pm. Priv rm: 100. Garden dining. Pool. Pkg. V, AE, DC, MC.
In comfortable surroundings diners enjoy the fresh, light cooking of Frédéric Layec, who takes top products and prepares them with admirable simplicity. Savor his fresh foie gras, curried monkfish blanquette, or the desserts, all served generously. The 145 F set menu is a great deal. The service manages to be both relaxed and

efficient. **C** 250-400 F. **M** 145 F (wine incl), 98 F, 160 F.

 Hôtel Mercure
(See restaurant above)
Open year-round. 3 stes 650-850 F. 43 rms 360-540 F. Half-board 330-430 F. Pool. Pkg. V, AE, DC, MC.
A very comfortable hotel ideally located on the picturesque old harbor.

ROCHE-SUR-YON (LA)	85000

Paris 414 - Nantes 65 - Cholet 65 - Niort 90   *Vendée*

 Logis de la Couperie
51 37 21 19
Open year-round. 1 ste 380-470 F. 7 rms 270-390 F. No pets. Pkg. V, AE, MC.
A fourteenth-century manor house lost in the countryside, this hotel offers spacious rooms tastefully decorated with rustic furniture and offering lovely views of the countryside. Friendly welcome.

■ In **Nesmy 85310**   9 km S on D 746 and D 85

 Golf de la Domangère
51 07 60 15, fax 51 07 64 09
Closings not available. 1 ste 550 F. 18 rms 290-550 F. Restaurant. Half-board 295-425 F. Conf. Tennis. Golf. Garage pkg. Helipad. V, MC.
Set on the velvety lawns of a golf course, this hotel offers largish rooms with all the usual equipment. Good bathrooms; decent breakfasts. The service is pleasant and attentive.

RODEZ	12000

Paris 608 - Brive-la-Gaillarde 156 - Albi 78 - Aurillac 96   *Aveyron*

Goûts et Couleurs   ✿
38, rue de Bonald - 65 42 75 10
Closed Jan 15-Feb 8, Sep 7-13. Open until 9:30pm. Terrace dining. V, AE, MC.
The locals have already developed a taste for this new restaurant with a cozy pink-toned dining room decorated with the owner-chef's paintings and photographs; there's even a pleasant garden terrace. Jean-Luc Fau, a self-trained cook, offers creative, fresh-flavored dishes like those on the generous 120 F menu: fricassée of cod with fresh hot peppers and poached eggs, tasty chicken breast in a yoghurt sauce with Indian spices, a delicious trouffade (fresh cheese gratin), and an excellent cône craquant of coconut and pineapple cream. Tiny regional wine list. Friendly welcome and service; hurry up before the very reasonable prices start to climb. **C** 200-300 F. **M** 90 F (lunch exc Sun), 120 F, 170 F, 200 F, 250 F.

■ In **Onet-le-Château 12850**   7 km NW on D 901, D 568

 Hostellerie de Fontanges
3 km N, route de Conque
65 42 20 28, fax 65 42 82 29
Open daily until 10pm. Priv rm: 50. Garden dining. Pkg. V, AE, DC, MC.
Take a seat in the newly refurbished "medieval" dining room or on the terrace with its fine view of Rodez and the countryside: either one provides a pleasant backdrop for the chef's

modern, appealingly presented cuisine that is sometimes on the heavy side: pickerel fillet in watercress sauce, flambéed saddle of rabbit, and a three-chocolate millefeuille. **C** 290-360 F. **M** 98 F (weekdays, Sat lunch), 155 F, 200 F, 360 F.

 Hostellerie de Fontanges
(See restaurant above)
Open year-round. 4 stes 490-700 F. 41 rms 320-400 F. Half-board 370-430 F. Conf. Heated pool. Tennis. Golf. Pkg. Helipad. V, AE, DC, MC.
The surrounding countryside is still in fact the country—not suburbs. This neo-Gothic hotel boasts manicured grounds, a pool, and a sauna; it would all be perfect if only the breakfasts were better, the rooms given a bit of a facelift, and the service improved.

See also: **Belcastel, Laguiole**

ROISSY-EN-FRANCE 95	→ PARIS Suburbs

ROMAINVILLE 93	→ PARIS Suburbs

ROMANS-SUR-ISÈRE	26100

Paris 558 - Grenoble 83 - Valence 18 - Vienne 71   *Drôme*

■ In **Granges-lès-Beaumont 26600**   6 km W on D 532

 Les Cèdres
75 71 50 67, fax 75 71 64 39
Closed Thu dinner, Mon, Feb school hols, 3 wks in Sep. Open until 9:30pm. Priv rm: 12. Garden dining. Pool. Garage pkg. V.
A 250-year-old cedar stands majestically in the garden of this likeable establishment complete with swimming pool. As ever, Jacques Bertrand handles ingredients of exceptional quality with elegant simplicity and a pleasing personal touch. Savor his salad of warm red mullet with Nyons olives, lamb carpaccio marinated in truffle juice, and an apricot confit seasoned with lemon thyme and paired with sage-pineapple ice cream. Warm welcome and efficient, stylish service. The wine list offers an impressive choice of fine vintages, as well as more modest (and affordable) bottles. **M** 170 F (weekdays), 250 F, 310 F, 330 F, 420 F.

ROMORANTIN	41200

Paris 183 - Tours 92 - Bourges 65 - Blois 41   *Loir/Cher*

 Grand Hôtel du Lion d'Or
69, rue G.-Clemenceau
54 76 00 28, fax 54 88 24 87
Closed Feb 15-Mar 24. Open until 9pm. Priv rm: 30. Garden dining. Air cond. Valet pkg. V, AE, DC, MC.
The life of a "celebrity chef" is not for Didier Clément. He and his wife, Marie-Christine (author of works on George Sand and Colette, including "Colette Gourmande"), prefer to live far from media hoopla, amid the forests and streams of Sologne. The Cléments' roots in the region go deep. They spend their free hours exploring the countryside, coming up with new sources for rare vegetables, herbs, and authentic wild game (now so rarely found in restaurants).

Both are experts on exotic spices, and Marie-Christine seeks out forgotten recipes in her library of antique cookery books. The cuisine that evolves from this passionate quest is unlike any other. Complex and cerebral, it requires the diner's full attention. Didier blends herbs, calculates seasonings and spices, uses uncommon vegetables and unusual recipes to create dishes that are his alone.

So take a seat in the serene, elegant dining room of this ancient coaching inn, and let Colette Barrat, Marie-Christine's mother, ply you with an apéritif from her eye-popping collection of Loire Valley wines. And prepare to be bowled over by Didier's exquisite dishes, which this year include frogs' legs à la rocambole, zucchini blossoms stuffed with crab meat in a fragrant olive-oil-and-tomato coulis, sublime foie gras pan-roasted in a licorice-scented jus, asparagus feuilleté with a sabayon of tiny peas, sea scallops grilled with blood oranges, turbot with croustillant vegetables seasoned with celery salt, unforgettable langoustines with sweet spices, Pauillac lamb "au tabac de cuisine", or an incredibly tender fillet of Limousin beef from animals fed on beer like Japan's Kobe beef. Exquisite goat cheeses, and voluptuous desserts like caramelized brioche with angelica sherbet, strawberries in red wine with ice milk, and brochettes of cherries with a vanilla flan. Perfection? Very nearly. In fact, the only shadow over our happiness is the alarming size of the bill. And the set menus are not worth the diversion from the à la carte menu. C 550-800 F. M 400 F, 600 F.

Grand Hôtel du Lion d'Or
(See restaurant above)
Closed Feb 20-Mar 30. 3 stes 2,100 F. 13 rms 600-1,800 F. Air cond. Golf. Valet pkg. Helipad. V, AE, DC, MC.
What was formerly a dilapidated post house is now an inn with luxurious rooms and suites overlooking a Renaissance fountain. Elegant public rooms (a pianist plays on Friday evenings in the delightful lounge by the garden). Relais et Châteaux.

ROQUEBRUNE-CAP-MARTIN   06190
Paris 953 - Nice 26 - Menton 5 - Monte-Carlo 7   Alpes-Mar.

12/20 Le Grand Inquisiteur
18, rue du Château - 93 35 05 37
Closed Mon, Mar 21-31, Nov 2-Dec 26. Open until 10pm. Air cond. No pets. V, MC.
It's wise to book in advance for a table at this curious (but comfortable) former sheepfold. Try the ragoût of baby vegetables, veal kidney with sage, and a croustillant of wild strawberries with a rhubarb coulis. C 240-360 F. M 145 F, 215 F.

Le Roquebrune
100, Corniche-Inférieure
93 35 00 16, fax 93 28 98 36
Closed lunch in seas (exc w-e), Tue lunch & Mon off-seas, Nov 6-Dec 5. Open until 11:45pm. Terrace dining. Valet pkg. V, AE, DC.
From the terrace or the spacious dining room, well-heeled patrons ooh and aah over the view of Roquebrune Bay. The chef rightly handles his magnificent foodstuffs with respect, producing fine bouillabaisse, chicken-liver terrine, leg of milk-fed lamb, and vanilla soufflé. Warm wel-

come and excellent service. The cellar is judicious; prices are crippling. C 500-800 F. M 230 F, 360 F.

Le Vistaero
Grande-Corniche - 92 10 40 20 (R),
92 10 40 00 (H), fax 93 35 18 94
Open daily until 10:15pm. Priv rm: 90. Terrace dining. Air cond. Valet pkg. V, AE, DC, MC.
The gorgeous sea vista will make your heart leap—as will the prices! Jean-Pierre Pestre's sunny dishes are prepared with skill and flair: plump roast shrimp and a croquante of baby Provençal vegetables, roast fillet of veal with artichokes, asparagus with fresh pasta, and for dessert, a hazlenut piémontaise with chicory ice cream. Tempting wine list with nary a bargain. In summer, opt for the "panorama" room with its terrace. C 500-700 F. M 200 F (weekday lunch, Sat), 230 F (Sun lunch), 300 F (dinner), 560 F.

Vista Palace
(See restaurant above)
Open year-round. 26 stes 1,200-5,000 F. 42 rms 1,000-2,400 F. Rms for disabled. Half-board 2,220 F. Air cond. Conf. Heated pool. Golf. Valet pkg. Helipad. V, AE, DC, MC.
This very comfortable and luxuriously decorated hotel provides large, bright rooms and suites with awe-inspiring views; some have private swimming pools and Jacuzzis. Charming, experienced staff; fitness center. The Mont Agel golf course is within easy reach.

ROQUEFORT-LES-PINS   06330
Paris 935 - Nice 25 - Grasse 15 - Cannes 18   Alpes-Mar.

Auberge du Colombier
93 77 10 27, fax 93 77 07 03
Closed Tue off-seas, Jan 10. Open until 10pm. Garden dining. Pkg. V, AE, DC, MC.
A real charmer, this restaurant provides wonderfully attentive service and a fabulous terrace that overlooks the Bastidon Valley and a garden of rare trees. What's more, Pierre Pons' traditional cooking is a delight: sample the sea scallops à la provençale, John Dory with hollandaise, and veal kidneys and sweetbreads in mustard sauce. Good choice of classic desserts. Pleasant choice of Provençal wines. Courteous welcome. C 300-380 F. M 155 F, 195 F.

Auberge du Colombier
(See restaurant above)
Closed Jan 15-Feb 15, Nov 15-Dec 15. 2 stes 600-850 F. 18 rms 160-680 F. Half-board 380-870 F. Air cond. Conf. Pool. Tennis. Golf. Pkg. V, AE, DC, MC.
Some of the rooms are on the small side, but they are uniformly lovely and nicely equipped in the midst of a luxuriant garden. The two suites have a terrace-solarium, and are downright luxurious. Poolside snack bar; private club with dancing.

🌀

This symbol stands for "Les Lauriers du Terroir", an award given to chefs who prepare traditional or regional cuisine.

ROQUE-GAGEAC (LA) 24250
Paris 550 - Périgueux 69 - Sarlat 13 - Souillac 29   *Dordogne*

La Plume d'Oie
D 703 - 53 29 57 05, fax 53 31 04 81
Closed Sat & Mon lunch (Jul-Aug), Sun dinner & Mon (off-seas), end Jan-beg Mar. Open until 9:30pm. Priv rm: 35. **Hotel:** *4 rms 275-380 F. Half-board 420-450 F. Golf. V, MC.*
This lovely village in the Dordogne is also the home to one of the region's most interesting tables. The British chef handles his ingredients with a light touch, concentrating their savors and aromas. Sample his 175 F menu: terrine of veal tongue and sweetbreads with chives, fricassée of pleurote mushrooms with basil, duck thigh roasted with soy sauce and Modena vinegar, fine cheeses, and dessert. Good cellar, with lots of regional wines; friendly, relaxed service. The owners (half-English, half-Dutch) treat local traditions with more respect than many home-grown chefs! C 300-400 F. M 175 F, 255 F, 395 F.

ROSBRUCK 57 → Forbach

ROSCOFF 29680
Paris 561 - Brest 63 - Morlaix 28 - Landivisiau 27   *Finistère*

Le Temps de Vivre ⌘
Pl. Lacaze-Duthiers - 98 61 27 28
Closed Sun dinner, Mon. Annual closings not available. Open until 9:15pm. V, AE, MC.
English furniture graces this large, cream-colored dining room that opens out onto a splendid sea view. Chef Jean-Yves Crenn, whose credentials include stints with Senderens, Robuchon, and Loiseau, is fond of pairing seafood with fine ingredients from field and farm. Sample his super langoustines pan-roasted with asparagus, artichokes, and the house ham; excellent wild salmon casserole-roasted with potatoes; and tasty squab with a foie gras galette. Perfect gâteau Breton with stawberries and rhubarb. The wide-ranging cellar was assembled by a true connoisseur; try the Ostertag Sylvaner vielles Vignes for 100 F, and Domaine Pierre Bise Anjou for 75 F. Elegant reception; efficient service. C 300-400 F. M 110 F (weekdays), 160 F, 240 F, 340 F.

Thalasstonic
Rockroum - 98 29 20 20, fax 98 61 22 73
Closed Jan 3-Feb 14. 50 rms 395-505 F. Rms for disabled. Restaurant. Half-board 595 F. Pkg. V, AE, MC.
A recently built, functional, comfortable hotel facing Batz Island. Well-appointed rooms with wonderful views. Direct access to the sea-water spa.

Le Yachtman
Bd Ste-Barbe
98 69 70 78, fax 98 61 13 29
Closed Mon lunch, Oct 15-Mar 20. Open until 9:30pm. Priv rm: 30. No pets. Pkg. V, AE.
In this ancient manor house beside the sea, very elaborate dishes are offered at lower prices than last year, but we feel the quality of the products has slipped a bit. Excellent lobster with dauphine potatoes, but the veal was problematic. It's too bad, because the chef once had a solid 14 rating. Interesting Bordeaux. Courteous, stylish service in a grand dining room

(note the fine Gothic fireplace) that opens out to the sea. C 300-500 F. M 100 F, 150 F, 280 F.

Le Brittany ♠♣
(See restaurant above)
Closed Oct 15-Mar 20. 2 stes 620-780 F. 23 rms 370-590 F. Half-board 380-540 F. Conf. Heated pool. Pkg. V, AE.
This beautiful yet austere seventeenth-century mansion provides comfortable, nicely fitted rooms that overlook a beach; opt for one on an upper floor. Luxurious amenities include an indoor heated swimming pool, a fitness center, Jacuzzi, and sauna.

ROSIERS-SUR-LOIRE (LES) 49350
Paris 290 - Angers 30 - Bressuire 64 - Saumur 16   *Maine/Loire*

Auberge Jeanne-de-Laval
54, rue Nationale
41 51 80 17, fax 41 38 04 18
Closed Mon off-seas, Nov 22-Dec 7, Jan 23-Feb 5. Open until 9:45pm. Priv rm: 40. Terrace dining. Air cond. No pets. Pkg. V, AE, DC, MC.
Michel Augereau's sauce au beurre blanc is truly one of a kind, a culinary secret handed down from his father; Michel also picked up a few tips from Joël Robuchon, and these old and new influences combine, along with his own savoir-faire, to produce appetizing, classic cuisine. We urge you to taste his fresh foie gras cooked in a cloth and napped with Bordeaux-wine gelatin, Loire pickerel in the famous beurre blanc, and a hazlenut délice for dessert. Game in sason. The cellar is a treasure house of venerable Loire vintages. Charming welcome. C 330-450 F. M 180 F, 300 F, 400 F.

Ducs d'Anjou ♠♣
(See restaurant above)
See restaurant for closings. 10 rms 300-580 F. Rms for disabled. Half-board 540-620 F. Golf. Pkg. V, AE, DC, MC.
This hotel provides large, freshly renovated, thoughtfully appointed rooms that look onto a garden and the village church. Marvelous breakfasts; good soundproofing; excellent service.

ROUBAIX 59100
Paris 231 - Lille 12 - Tourcoing 14 - Tournai 19   *Nord*

Altea Grand Hôtel
22, av. J.-Lebas
20 73 40 00, fax 20 73 22 42
Open year-round. 92 rms 370-490 F. Restaurant. Half-board 260-380 F. Golf. Pkg. V, AE, DC, MC.
A splendid turn-of-the-century hotel, renovated with care. Rooms are functional, the decoration absolutely mundane. Good conference facilities; bar.

Le Caribou
8, rue Mimerel - 20 70 87 08
Closed dinner (exc Fri & Sat), Jul 15-end Aug. Open until 9:30pm. Priv rm: 60. Pkg. V.
The restaurant's opulent façade, the dining room's stained glass and high coffered ceilings all evoke Roubaix's prosperous heyday as a textile center. Classic cooking is the thing here, ably wrought by Christian Siesse, but it displays an occasional (discreet) modern touch, and is nicely attuned to the seasons. Try the salad of langoustine tails seasoned with vanilla salt, sea

bass in beurre blanc, rack of lamb with Provençal seasonings. Friendly welcome. Attractive cellar. **C** 300-420 F. **M** 180 F, 296 F.

ROUEN	**76000**

Paris 139 - Caen 124 - Amiens 116 - Le Havre 40   *Seine-Mar.*

Le Beffroy

15, rue Beffroy - 35 71 55 27
Closed Sun dinner. Open until 9pm. V, AE, DC.
This charming restaurant is the picture of Normandy: half-timbering, a vast fireplace, and bouquets of fresh flowers. Odile Engel offers dishes based on the best possible products: "earth and sea" salad, John Dory in tomato butter sauce, croustillant of sea bass flavored with lemon, canard rouennaise, and young chicken with morels. Remarkable choice of Alsatian wines. But the prices are high. **C** 300-400 F. **M** 150 F (weekdays, wine incl), 200 F, 275 F.

Colin's Hotel

33, rue du Vieux Palais
35 71 00 88, fax 35 70 75 94
Open year-round. 3 stes 445-650 F. 45 rms 445-650 F. Rms for disabled. Restaurant. Air cond. Conf. Valet pkg. V, AE, DC, MC.
This functional, charmless hotel is well located in a little courtyard near the Vieux-Marché square. The welcome and service are what they should be, and the breakfasts are copious.

La Couronne

31, pl. du Vieux-Marché
35 71 40 90, fax 35 71 05 78
Open daily until 10:30pm. V, AE, DC, MC.
Reputedly the oldest *auberge* in France, this majestic half-timbered dwelling is done up ye best olde style. Who could resist its charm? Well, we could, unless the kitchen shapes up: croustillant of langoustines and apples seasoned with too much curry powder, bland and badly presented sole with cèpes, adequate berry assortment. The toque is wobbly this year. Rather precious welcome, service with brio, and fine Bordeaux-dominated cellar. High prices. **C** 400-550 F. **M** 195 F (wine incl), 150 F, 240 F.

L'Écaille

26, rampe Cauchoise
35 70 95 52, fax 35 70 83 49
Closed Sun dinner. Open until 10pm. Priv rm: 30. Terrace dining. Air cond. V, AE, DC, MC.
L'Écaille's green-and-blue dining room hung with dainty watercolors somehow suggests the sea. Appropriately, as it happens, since Marc Tellier is happiest when he's working with fish and crustaceans. His style is more streamlined nowadays, the better to bring out seafood's delicate natural flavors. Sample his slices of sea bass marinated in lobster oil; monkfish with tomatoes, rosemary, and zucchini; and a roast fig seasoned with vanilla and paired with berries. Attentive welcome; diverse and well presented wine list. **C** 370-500 F. **M** 175 F (Sat dinner, Sun lunch), 145 F (exc Sat lunch), 245 F, 330 F, 445 F.

L'Épisode

37, rue aux Ours - 35 89 01 91
Closed Wed, Sun. Open until 9:30pm. V, MC.
Patrick Picard respects his clients as much as he does his top-flight ingredients, and tempts us to come here again and again to savor his intensely flavored, perfectly prepared dishes.

Trained at Gill, Rouen's grandest restaurant, Picard lets his culinary fancy wander where it will, now that he's his own master. We're particularly partial to his limpid cassolette of lobster, sea scallops, and langoustines; John Dory with julienned tomatoes and a sweet-sour sauce, perfectly fresh; an unctuous mousse flavored with hibiscus and paired with leaves caramelized in an orange sauce, a dessert that in itself merits the extra point this year. The first set menu is attractive, the cellar is improving, and Nadia Picard's welcome is warm in the long and pleasant pastel dining room. **C** 300-370 F. **M** 105 F (lunch), 165 F, 230 F.

Gill

9, quai de la Bourse
35 71 16 14, fax 35 71 96 91
Closed Sun (exc lunch Oct-May), Mon. Open until 10pm. Priv rm: 20. Air cond. V, AE, DC, MC.
This exemplary waterfront establishment is weathering the recession without lowering standards: Gill is still the best restaurant in Rouen. The bright 1930s-style dining room with comfortably spaced, white-clothed tables is overseen by Sylvie Tournadre, a graceful, welcoming hostess. In the kitchen, Gilles Tournadre turns out his beautifully balanced, modern cuisine with an occasional superficially chilly touch (which the decor also has, we feel). The 195 F set meal is a triumph, and the locals are lucky to be offered dishes of such high caliber on this menu: exquisite fish tartare seasoned with ginger; a crisp and delicious vegetable brunoise and red mullet in a marinade that's the essence of the sea; fine ragoût of calf's head; and fabulous prune soufflé. Other delicious choices are the monkfish roasted in veal jus, veal sweetbreads à l'andouille, and duck tourte. What to drink? There's a larger choice this year. **C** 350-480 F. **M** 195 F (weekdays, Sat lunch), 280 F, 370 F.

12/20 Le Marnaz

102, rue du Renard - 35 71 44 93
Dinner only. Closed Sun, Mon. Open until 11pm. V.
The jolly *patron*, a pot-bellied, chain-smoking chap called Nanar, has regaled Rouen for years with the marvelous mushrooms he gathers in the neighboring woods. His dishes all share a wonderfully rustic aroma, a quintessentially rural heartiness: just taste his confits, veal sweetbreads, sea scallops, and chateaubriand steak with snails and you'll see what we mean. Decor is not part of this place's appeal, though. **C** 180-330 F.

Mercure-Centre

Rue de la Croix-de-Fer
35 52 69 52, fax 35 89 41 46
Open year-round. 4 stes 800 F. 121 rms 430-510 F. Air cond. Conf. Golf. Pkg. V, AE, DC, MC.
An ideal base for a walking tour of town. Underground garage, very well equipped rooms; some have views of the cathedral's gables. Breakfasts are nothing special.

12/20 Les Nymphéas

7-9, rue de la Pie - 35 89 26 69
Closed Sun dinner, Mon. Open until 10pm. Priv rm: 25. Terrace dining. V, AE.

Though the food is occasionally muddled, the ingredients are reliably fresh and fine. Among the traditional offerings you'll find warm duck foie gras deglazed with cider vinegar, skate in tomato butter sauce, and an apple soufflé spiked with Calvados. Attractive dining room; repellent prices. C 350-480 F. M 250 F (wine incl), 160 F, 180 F, 240 F.

Les P'tits Parapluies
46, rue du Bourg-l'Abbé
35 88 55 26, fax 35 70 24 31
Closed Feb school hols, 1st 2 wks of Aug. Open until 10pm. V, AE, MC.
The low-ceilinged dining room of this handsome old house overflows with charm. The appeal of the setting, complete with a menu chalked up on a blackboard, and the quality of the food will make you eager to linger over dishes that are at their best when they stay closest to the natural and simple: uncertain salad of breaded oysters, but the sea bass with asparagus is at the two-toque level. The cellar is catholic; the hostess smiling and attentive. But it's very popular, and so you sometimes have to wait awhile for your meal. C 350-450 F. M 140 F (lunch exc weekdays), 180 F, 240 F.

Le Réverbère
5, pl. de la République - 35 07 03 14
Closed Sun dinner (lunch May-Aug), Aug 7-20. Open until 10pm. Priv rm: 20. V, AE.
A fine provincial restaurant, done up "Parisian-style" in dusty pink with smoked mirrors. The solidly middle-class customers adore José Rato's accomplished cuisine, and we understand why. Prices are eminently reasonable (meals include wine; the price is pegged to the main course you choose), so go ahead and treat yourself. To the 165 F menu, for example (wine included): sea scallops and celery émincé, warm sausage in lemon butter, and a strawberry millefeuille. C 220-300 F. M 165 F & 295 F (wine incl).

And also...
Our selection of places for inexpensive, quick, or late-night meals.
Brasserie de la Grande Poste (35 70 08 70 - 43, rue J.-d'Arc.): Opposite the flamboyant Gothic façade of the law courts, this Art Deco institution is open every day of the year (100-120 F).
La Taverne Saint-Amand (35 88 51 34 - 11, rue St-Amand.): Authentic cooking and good beers served in a picturesque part of old Rouen (160 F).
Le Veau d'Or (35 72 76 60 - 3, rue Desseaux.): Once the meeting-place for butchers and abattoir workers, now a good bet for excellent meats and traditional fare (130-200 F).

■ **In Bonsecours 76240**   3 km E on N 14

Auberge de la Butte
69, route de Paris - 35 80 43 11
Closed Sun, Mon, Christmas hols, Aug 1-24. Priv rm: 40. Terrace dining. V, AE, DC.
Pierre Hervé built this lovely inn with his own two hands, and this dedication shows in his cooking; it's marked by care, technique, and the influence of Escoffier. We just wish he could be a bit freer, use less ornamentation, achieve a bit

more of what we'll call grace. The millefeuille is superbly delicate. The spiced langoustines, squab with foie gras, and the service could use a bit of inspiration. Rather impressive wine list. C 350-500 F. M 200 F, 320 F.

■ **In Déville-lès-Rouen 76250**   6 km N

La Voûte Saint-Yves
9, av. du Gal-Leclerc - 35 75 03 17
Closed Sun dinner, Mon, Aug 9-22. Open until 9:30pm. Priv rm: 32. Terrace dining. Pkg. V, AE, MC.
Built to house the 1896 Colonial Exhibition in Rouen, this eccentric half-timbered structure is a curious sight indeed (just look at that roof!) The dining room is delightful, with polished parquet floors, fireplaces, and carved oak wainscoting. Traditional cuisine is quite naturally the thing here, and it's turned out with skill and a certain flair by Jean-Marc Toutain. Try the 105 F menu: brioché of salmon with currants, grilled sirloin steak au poivre, chiffonnade de brie, and île flottante. The varied wine list is priced fairly, and the welcome is warm. C 240-450 F. M 80 F (weekday lunch), 105 F, 160 F, 298 F.

■ **In Tourville-la-Rivière 76410**   11 km S on D 7

Le Tourville
A 13, exit 21,
12, rue D.-Casanova - 35 77 58 79
Closed Mon, 10 days at Easter, Aug. Open until 10pm. Priv rm: 40. Garage pkg. V.
The Florins alighted here in May 1968, with a repertoire that is resolutely counter-revolutionary. But what a treat to indulge in such subversively satisfying dishes as Michel Florin's chicken-liver terrine, skate in creamy mustard sauce, and three-chocolate cake. Excellent house breads. At 73, Michel Florin can out-cook many a younger chef. And Madame Florin is an energetic, charming hostess who offers good advice about the excellent wine list. C 300-500 F.

Paris 458 - Mulhouse 28 - Colmar 15 - Guebwiller 10   *Haut-Rhin*

Les Tommeries
89 49 63 53, fax 89 78 53 70
Closed Jan 15-Mar 15. Open until 10:15pm. Priv rm: 150. Garden dining. Valet pkg. V, AE, MC.
You would come here just for the view of the Alsatian plain all the way to the Black Forest, seen from the terrace or the elegant dining room. But the cuisine of Didier Lefeuvre, who has learned to make the most of the region's fine ingredients, is worth your attention. An extra point this year for his clean-flavored mackerel in Riesling sauce with sauerkraut, lamb croustillant seasoned with basil and paired with thyme lasagne, and a tender kouglof bread pudding. Superb choice of wines, ably presented. Perfect service. C 350-500 F. M 700 F (tasting menu, wine incl), 260 F, 360 F.

Château d'Isenbourg
(See restaurant above)
Closed Jan 15-Mar 15. 3 stes 1,570-1,770 F. 38 rms 850-1,400 F. Rms for disabled. Half-board 850-

1,110 F. Air cond. Conf. Heated pool. Tennis. Valet pkg. Helipad. V, AE, MC.

The Château d'Isenbourg stands perched amid vineyards, on the site of the Merovingian castle of Dagobert II. Today it is the Dalibert family who reign over the plush lounges and rooms (not all equally spacious and comfortable). A golf course is set to open nearby in the near future. Relais et Châteaux.

ROUSSES (LES)   39220
Paris 474 - Lons-le-Saunier 69 - Nyons 25 - Gex 29   Jura

Hôtel de France
323, rue Pasteur
84 60 01 45, fax 84 60 04 63
Closings not available. Open until 10:30pm. Priv rm: 20. Terrace dining. Pkg. V, AE, DC, MC.

Roger Petit, a disciple of legendary chef Fernand Point (with whom he worked many years ago), held sway here for decades, and now his former second-in-command, Jean-Pierre Ducrot, is making sure that his high standards are still maintained. Savor the foie gras poached in a black radish bouillon, roulade of sole au lait fumé, filet de mostelle au comté, or a grapefruit feuillantine. These are enlightened classics, not at all outdated. Service is relaxed but swift. Classic cellar, with a wide choice of half-bottles. High prices à la carte. C 400-500 F. M 135 F, 240 F, 320 F, 400 F.

Hôtel de France
(See restaurant above)
Closings not available. 33 rms 240-470 F. Half-board 310-415 F. Conf. Golf. Pkg. V, AE, DC, MC.

This is a perfect après-ski, family hotel. A bit basic but well maintained, with an attractive atmosphere. Sturdy mountain breakfasts.

ROUSSILLON   84220
Paris 727 - Apt 11 - Avignon 45 - Bonnieux 12   Vaucluse

Mas de Garrigon
Route de St-Saturnin-d'Apt, D 2
90 05 63 22, fax 90 05 70 01
Closed Sun dinner, Mon, Nov 15-Dec 27. Open until 9:30pm. Priv rm: 10. Terrace dining. Pool. No pets. Pkg. V, AE, DC, MC.

Roussillon's beautiful ochre cliffs stand in full view of this delightful Provençal mas surrounded by pine groves. The kitchen's raw materials are first-rate and prepared with considerable skill. We have nothing but praise for Philippe Anzallo's warm oyster salad with sweet potatoes, lamb with glazed turnips, and profiteroles filled with lavender ice cream. Charming reception. C 350-450 F. M 175 F, 265 F, 320 F.

Mas de Garrigon
(See restaurant above)
Open year-round. 2 stes 900-1,050 F. 7 rms 650-750 F. Rms for disabled. Half-board 590-730 F. Conf. Pool. Golf. Pkg. V, AE, DC, MC.

This hotel features delightful, Provençal-style rooms with splendid views of Roussillon and the Lubéron. Pleasant fireside lounge; sheltered swimming pool; horseback riding.

ROYAN   17200
Paris 490 - Bordeaux 124 - Saintes 37   Charente-M.

12/20 Le Chalet
6, rue Grandière - 46 05 04 90
Closed Wed (exc Jul-Aug), Jan 15-Feb 15. Open until 10pm (10:30pm in summer). Pkg. V, AE, MC.

Friendly and bright with its rough-cast walls and rustic beams, this little restaurant also boasts a glassed-in terrace that encroaches on the pavement (and lets passers-by peer into your plate!). The chef's 140 F menu gives you a generous and tasty salad of giblet confit and smoked duck breast, fresh cod with julienned leeks and mushrooms, cheeses, and sherbet with fruit. Attentive service and welcome. C 250-350 F. M 100 F (Sun lunch), 140 F, 190 F, 280 F.

Family Golf Hotel
Grande-Conche, 28, bd Garnier
46 05 14 66, fax 46 06 52 56
Closed Oct-Easter. 33 rms 330-500 F. Golf. Pkg. V, MC.

Located opposite Royan's main beach, this small, recently updated holiday hotel enjoys a fine view of the port and the Gironde estuary.

La Jabotière
In Pontaillac - 46 39 91 29
Closed Sun dinner & Mon off-seas, Christmas wk, Jan 2-Feb 2. Open until 10pm. Priv rm: 50. Terrace dining. Pkg. V, AE, DC.

Jean Auger is happy to receive customers to his beachfront restaurant, where he presents chef Patrick Bachelard's delectable seafood dishes. Savor the 220 F menu: tender crab and vegetable ravioli, succulent monkfish steaks, classic cheeses, crème brûlée with marinated raisins, and tiny cakes. Friendly welcome; competent and friendly service. C 310-390 F. M 120 F (weekday lunch), 155 F, 180 F, 220 F, 320 F.

Résidence de Rohan
3 km, in Vaux-sur-Mer
Parc des Fées, route de St-Palais
46 39 00 75, fax 46 38 29 99
Closed Nov 15-Mar 25. 41 rms 300-670 F. Tennis. Golf. Garage pkg. V, AE, MC.

An elegant hotel, surrounded by wooded grounds near the beach. Rooms are furnished charmingly with English, Empire, or rustic pieces. Twenty additional rooms in an annex.

In Breuillet 17920   14 km NW on D 733, D 14

La Grange
Le Grallet - 46 22 72 64, fax 46 22 79 55
Closed Sep 15-Jun. Open until 11pm. Priv rm: 20. Garden dining. Pool. Pkg. V.

This attractive holiday complex offers tennis, golf, and dance clubs as well as a fine restaurant. The elegant, understated dining room is extended by a pretty poolside terrace, where guests may take the measure of Pierre Dunand's high-precision cooking. The quality of his raw materials shines through in parsley-scented langoustine ravioli, duck breast with peppery pears, and a gooey chocolate galette with vanilla-orange sauce. Well chosen wine list. Friendly welcome. C 280-350 F. M 100 F (lunch), 150 F, 190 F, 220 F (dinner).

ROYAT 63 → Clermont-Ferrand

ROYE 80700
Paris 105 - Amiens 41 - Compiègne 38 - Péronne 29   *Somme*

La Flamiche
20, pl. de l'Hôtel-de-Ville
22 87 00 56, fax 22 78 46 77
Closed Sun dinner, Mon, Dec 20-Jan 10. Open until 9:30pm. Priv rm: 30. Air cond. Pkg. V, AE, DC, MC.
Owner Marie-Christine Klopp, weary of watching chefs come and go in her kitchens, decided one day to take matters culinary into her own capable hands. Abetted by a solid brigade, she won a third toque for La Flamiche, with her savory, visually delightful, daring cuisine mostly inspired by Picardy's terroir, but her scope extends well beyond the boundaries of her home province. This was the best restaurant between Paris and Calais; now, with the opening of the Channel Tunnel, it's the best one between Paris and London! Savor her audacious combo of raw foie gras, pink radishes, and toast; aïoli with langoustines; or kid flavored with cumin. Or her more homegrown specialties like breaded Somme eels in a garlic, shallot, and thyme jus; red mullet en papillote with slivers of tiny artichokes flavored with horseradish; or veal kidney in a potato crust stuffed with carrot purée. Klopp's desserts are ineffably delicate, like the Picardy rose ice cream strewn with candied rose petals. Everything is served as obligingly as can be, in a country-style dining room as bright and polished as a new penny, and decorated with a collection of all kinds of ducks. Top-notch cellar. C 400-600 F. M 125 F (weekdays, Sat lunch), 350 F (Sun lunch), 190 F, 250 F (exc Sun), 450 F.

RUMILLY 74150
Paris 535 - Annecy 17 - Geneva 51 - Aix-les-Bains 20   *H.-Savoie*

L'Améthyste
27, rue du Pont-Neuf - 50 01 02 52
Closed Mon dinner, 2 wks in Aug. Open until 10pm. Priv rm: 15. Air cond. V.
We've known chef Julien Valéro since the days when he was cooking at the Villa Saint-Elme in Issambres. Now he's in his own place, a shopfront restaurant in a new part of town that the mayor wisely embellished with new flower beds. Spices are Valéro's strong suit: he uses them with a mastery that surprises and delights. Try the fricassée of langoustines, sot-l'y-laisse (poultry "oysters") and smoked salmon flavored with anise, saffrony boned squab, and saddle of rabbit with almond milk. For dessert, don't miss the deliciously light chocolate croquant and the clever crème brûlée flavored with gentian. C 300-350 F. M 175 F (weekday lunch, wine incl), 88 F, 120 F, 220 F, 280 F, 350 F.

RUNGIS 94 → PARIS Suburbs

RUY 38 → Bourgoin-Jallieu

Red toques signify creative cuisine; white toques signify traditional cuisine.

SABLES-D'OLONNE (LES) 85100
Paris 450 - Nantes 90 - La Roche-sur-Yon 35   *Vendée*

Atlantic' Hotel
5, promenade Godet
51 95 37 71, fax 51 95 37 30
Open year-round. 30 rms 438-730 F. Restaurant. Half-board 515-595 F. Heated pool. Golf. V, AE, DC.
A beachfront hotel, quiet and clean, with rooms that are a trifle small for the price; all have loggias (some with a view of the sea). Gorgeous covered pool with sliding roof, and many amenities: laundry service, photo shop, hair salon, bar.

Beau Rivage
40, promenade G.-Clemenceau
51 32 03 01, fax 51 32 46 48
Closed Sun dinner & Mon off-seas (exc hols), Jan, Oct 2-12. Open until 9:30pm. Priv rm: 10. Hotel: 4 stes 500 F. 8 rms 270-390 F. Half-board 485-590 F. V, AE, DC, MC.
The restaurant's terrace gives onto the beach, but don't dream of drifting in here in a bathing costume. Understated elegance is the Beau Rivage style. The dining room looks out to sea, and so does Joseph Drapeau's classic, accomplished repertoire, although he has a talented hand for meats as well. We were impressed this year by his aiguillette of beef with beef marrow in Saint-Emilion jus, farm-raised Challans duck, farm-raised Limousin veal with baby vegetables, and feuilleté of veal sweetbreads with foie gras and truffles. But his full talents shine through in seafood dishes like parmentier of shellfish with olive oil and basil, carpaccio of sea bass with green asparagus and grilled almond oil, feuilleté of lobster with morels, sea bass in veal jus with morels, John Dory with fava beans and bacon, and sole meunière. Everything is of the highest quality, and the prices reflect that. Luckily the prices of the wines in the excellent cellar are very reasonable. C 390-550 F. M 180 F (weekdays, Sat lunch), 250 F (wine incl), 330 F, 400 F, 450 F.

Le Navarin
18, pl. Navarin - 51 21 11 61
Closed Sun dinner & Mon (exc Jul-Aug), 2 wks in Feb, 1 wk in Oct. Open until 9:30pm. Priv rm: 60. Terrace dining. Air cond. V, AE.
The waves that break just opposite this venerable brasserie do much to inspire Yves Privat's hearty 195 F menu which includes cassolette of shellfish, panaché of fish, émincé of beef in Médoc sauce, warm goat cheese salad, and fresh fruit gratin. Theme dinners (wine, jazz) are often organized. C 320-380 F. M 110 F (weekdays, Sat lunch), 85 F (lunch exc Sun), 195 F (wine incl), 155 F, 210 F, 290 F.

Les Roches Noires
12, promenade Clemenceau
51 32 01 71, fax 51 21 61 00
Open year-round. 37 rms 420-650 F. Rms for disabled. V, AE, DC.
The sunny, pleasant rooms look out to sea. Well-equipped bathrooms and friendly service

SAGONE 20 → CORSICA

SAINT-AGRÈVE 07320
Paris 580 - St-Etienne 69 - Aubenas 66 - Lamastre 20   *Ardèche*

Domaine de Rilhac
75 30 20 20, fax 75 30 20 00
*Closed Mon dinner & Tue off-seas. Open until
9:45pm. Priv rm: 25. Pkg. V, MC.*
Saint-Agrève is quite a climb from sea level, but
Ludovic and Florence Sinz have made it their
home. They bought and renovated an old
farmhouse, and opened a restaurant there, putting to good use lessons learned *chez* Chibois,
Ducasse, Robuchon, and Loiseau. We award
them a second toque this year for Ludovic's
inventive cuisine with intense yet natural flavors.
Try the fine 195 F menu: quail confit with grapes
and green Du Puy lentils, grilled salmon with a
green pea velouté, Ardèche cheeses, and fruits
sautéed in cream. Charming and competent
service. Fine cellar. **M** 100 F (weekday lunch),
135 F, 170 F, 195 F, 250 F.

Domaine de Rilhac
(See restaurant above)
*Closed Mon & Tue off-seas. 1 ste 590 F. 6 rms 295-
395 F. Half-board 315-365 F. Golf. Pkg. V, MC.*
This lovely hotel with its spacious, well-
equipped rooms stands deep in the Ardèche,
facing Mount Gerbier-de-Jonc where the Loire
has its source.

SAINT-ANDRÉ-D'HÉBERTOT 14
➡ Pont-l'Evêque

SAINT-ARNOULT 14   ➡ Deauville

ST-BEAUZEIL 82   ➡ Montaigu-de-Quercy

SAINT-BONNET-LE-FROID 43290
Paris 558 - St-Etienne 59 - Tournon 53   *Haute-Loire*

Auberge des Cimes
71 59 93 72, fax 71 59 93 40
*Closed Sun dinner, Wed, Nov 15-Easter. Open until
9:15pm. Priv rm: 20. Pkg. V.*
Régis Marcon transformed the village bistrot
of a tiny mountain hamlet into a mecca for
holiday-makers in search of pure air, country
walks, and fabulous food. Ensconced at a win-
dowside table with a view of blossom-dotted
meadows and the forest beyond, give yourself
over to the rich pleasures of Marcon's earthy,
regionally rooted yet adventurous cuisine.
Inspired by the bounty of these mountain fields
and streams, Marcon revels in finding new ways
to use his pure, authentic ingredients. A meal
here starts with bread: rye bread, lentil bread,
even fish-flavored bread—there's one to go with
every dish. Then taste Marcon's red mullet
marvelously paired with chestnuts, olives, and
saffron; breaded cabbage in a blue-cheese-
enlivened jus felicitously accompanying omble
chevalier (a lake fish); succulent rabbit with
hazelnuts and leeks. The arrival of a fabulous
cheese board loaded with prime local
specimens drives all other thoughts from one's
mind. Save room too for the exquisite desserts.
Michèle Marcon proceeds from table to table
dispensing smiles and sound counsel on wines
(the cellar holds some unusual Ardèche offer-

ings, as well as many fine Côtes-du-Rhônes).
Classes in cooking, drawing, or local plant life,
as well as guestrooms, are offered in the new
Clos des Cimes annex. **C** 400 F. **M** 135 F (weekdays), 200 F, 295 F, 350 F, 500 F.

Auberge des Cimes
(See restaurant above)
*See restaurant for closings. 16 rms 380-700 F. Half-
board 450-800 F. Conf. Golf. Pkg. V.*
The simple yet cozy village inn on the slopes
just above the new Clos des Cimes annex (see
above) offers large, bright rooms in keeping with
the rustic surroundings.

SAINT-BRIEUC 22000
Paris 445 - Brest 146 - Rennes 99 - Dinan 59   *Côtes/Armor*

L'Amadeus
22, rue du Gouet - 96 33 92 44
Closed Mon lunch, Sun. Open until 9:30pm. V.
The sea and the seasons dictate Thierry
Malotaux's deft, lively cuisine. We can vouch for
the goodness of his oyster and Breton lobster
ravioli, Niçoise lamb tian, and a delicate apple
tart seasoned with cinnamon. Friendly welcome.
C 250-350 F. **M** 100 F (lunch exc Sun, wine
incl), 85 F (dinner), 145 F, 230 F, 240 F.

Hôtel de Clisson
36, rue du Gouet
96 62 19 29, fax 96 61 06 95
*Open year-round. 24 rms 260-435 F. Rms for dis-
abled. No pets. Pkg. V, AE, MC.*
A classy hotel near the old town, with good-
sized rooms and fine equipment. Good breakfasts, too.

Le Quatre Saisons
61, chemin des Courses
96 33 20 38, fax 96 33 77 38
*Closed Sat dinner, Mon, 2 wks at Feb school &
beg Oct. Open until 9:30pm. Priv rm: 120. Terrace
dining. Pkg. V.*
Patrick Faucon has recovered all his energy
and verve: we can tell from the spicy, original
turn his cooking has taken. The à la carte prices
are on the high side, but the 150 F menu is a
good deal: tartare of sea scallops in a rice-vinegar
vinaigrette with edible seaweed, sage-scented
crépinette of farm-raised chicken with andouille
sausage, well aged cheeses, and dessert. Tempting cellar at reasonable prices. Enjoy all this
(weather permitting) beneath the fronds of the
weeping willow just outside. Smiling welcome.
C 320-450 F. **M** 135 F (wine incl), 99 F, 150 F,
195 F, 235 F, 295 F.

■ **In Plérin-sous-
la-Tour 22190**   3 km NE on D 24

La Vieille Tour
Port de St-Brieuc, Le Légué
75, rue de la Tour - 96 33 10 30
*Closed at Feb school hols, Sep 1-10. Open until
9:30pm. Priv rm: 35. Air cond. Pkg. V, MC.*
Nestled at the mouth of a river, this little Breton
port has always harbored a mariner's bistrot,
even before the advent of Marlène and Michel
Hellio. Michel's precise cuisine is a model of
rigor and discipline. For the diner, that translates
into the focused flavors of an expertly handled

main ingredient, a superbly concentrated sauce, and a perfectly cooked vegetable accompaniment. Elementary? Not at all: such apparent simplicity is the pay-off for years of paring down, streamlining, and getting to the essentials of flavor. Witness the fricassée of sole and langoustines with fava beans, sautéed sea scallops and foie gras, John Dory paired with baby onions and cabbage cooked in duck fat, veal sweetbreads with zesty lemon peel and honeyed carrots, and the delicious rye breads flavored with edible sea weed, rasins, bacon, and dried apricots. For dessert, don't miss the millefeuille with acacia honey, stawberries, and rhubarb. Attractive first set menus. Reliable cellar. Joyous, animated service. C 340-440 F. M 125 F (weekdays), 185 F, 260 F, 360 F.

<table><tr><td>SAINT-CÉRÉ</td><td>46400</td></tr></table>

Paris 521 - Cahors 76 - Tulle 58 - Figeac 45 - Brive 54   *Lot*

Les Trois Soleils de Montal

Les Prés-de-Montal
65 38 20 61, fax 65 38 30 66
Closed Jan 2-15. Open until 9:30pm. Priv rm: 14. Terrace dining. No pets. Valet pkg. V, MC.
Frederik Bizat is a real pro, and now offers a bargain 120 F menu: carpaccio of salmon with herbs, risotto of farm-raised chicken, cheeses, and dessert. On the à la carte menu, sample the sumptuous whole foie gras in a casserole with pears and spices, or delectably crisp yet meltingly tender veal shanks braised in cèpe jus. Well chosen wine list. A point extra this year. Guests are made to feel genuinely welcome in the warm and attractive modern dining room. There's a terrace too. C 260-360 F. M 120 F, 180 F, 275 F.

Les Trois Soleils de Montal

(See restaurant above)
Open year-round. 2 stes 500-650 F. 26 rms 300-450 F. Rms for disabled. Half-board 345-420 F. Air cond. Conf. Heated pool. Tennis. Golf. Pkg. V, MC.
A top-quality modern hotel in a magnificent setting. Attractive rooms open out onto views of green meadows; there is a sauna and an exercise room. The poolside grill is a popular spot in summer.

<table><tr><td>SAINT-CIRQ-LAPOPIE</td><td>46330</td></tr></table>

Paris 628 - Cahors 33 - Villefranche-de-Rouergue 36   *Lot*

Auberge du Sombral

65 30 26 37, fax 65 30 26 37
Closed Tue, Wed, Nov 11-Mar. 8 rms 300-420 F. Restaurant. V, AE.
The renovated, rustic rooms (some are quite small) look onto the handsome Place du Sombral.

<table><tr><td>SAINT-CLÉMENT-DES-BALEINES 17</td></tr></table>

→ Ré (Ile de)

<table><tr><td>SAINT-CLOUD 92</td><td>→ PARIS Suburbs</td></tr></table>

Plan to travel? *Look for Gault Millau's other Best of guides to Chicago, Florida, Hawaii, Hong Kong, Germany, Italy, London, Los Angeles, New England, New Orleans, New York, Paris, San Francisco, Thailand, Toronto, and Washington, D.C.*

<table><tr><td>SAINT-CYPRIEN</td><td>66750</td></tr></table>

Paris 920 - Perpignan 15 - Port-Vendres 20   *Pyrénées-O.*

L'Almandin

Les Capellans, bd de l'Almandin
68 21 01 02, fax 68 21 06 28
Closed Sun dinner & Mon (exc Jun 15-Sep 15), Jan 2-Feb 25. Open until 9:30pm. Priv rm: 14. Garden dining. Air cond. Pkg. V, AE, MC.
The bay windows of the comfortable dining room frame a lovely view over the lagoon, even better when seen from the terrace. Jean-Paul Hartmann, transplanted from his native Alsace to Catalonia, tacks back and forth between classic and regional cuisine. Try his fillets of Collioure anchovies with tapenade, sliced duck breast with olives, and a croustillant of apricots and wild strawberries with passion-fruit sherbet. Diverse and well chosen wine list. Competent welcome. C 320-400 F. M 160 F, 220 F, 340 F.

L'Ile de la Lagune

(See restaurant above)
See restaurant for closings. 4 stes 780-1,200 F. 18 rms 500-900 F. Rms for disabled. Half-board 490-830 F. Air cond. Conf. Pool. Tennis. Golf. Valet pkg. V, AE, MC.
This beautifully designed hotel has large terraces overlooking the lagoon. The comfortable rooms have fresh, pretty decor (and satellite TV) and small but pretty bathrooms. Private beach.

<table><tr><td>SAINT-DENIS 93</td><td>→ PARIS Suburbs</td></tr></table>

<table><tr><td>SAINT-ÉMILION</td><td>33330</td></tr></table>

Paris 549 - Bordeaux 38 - Libourne 7 - Langon 49   *Gironde*

Francis Goullée

27, rue Guadet
57 24 70 49, fax 57 74 47 96
Closed Sun dinner. Open until 9:30pm. Priv rm: 30. Air cond. V, MC.
This is no tourist trap! Francis Goullée and his adorable wife, Annie, greet guests as if they were long-lost friends, with genuine smiles and warmth. You'll discover some enticing, manageably priced meals featuring the likes of terrine de haricot grain au foie gras de canard, omble chevalier (lake fish) with apples and bacon, and delicious lamb sweetbreads cooked in a casserole with Parma ham. Luscious chocolate-oriented desserts, and a good choice of Saint-Émilions. A comfortable and engaging spot. C 250-300 F. M 120 F, 135 F (weekdays, Sat), 170 F, 220 F.

Hostellerie de Plaisance

Pl. du Clocher
57 24 72 32, fax 57 74 41 11
Closed Jan. Open until 9:15pm. Priv rm: 70. Air cond. Pkg. V, AE, DC, MC.
A plush provincial interior with tall windows offering a fine view of the roofs of the old city. Louis Quilain's cooking is organized around excellent ingredients and careful technique, and just needs a tiny touch of fantasy. Still, we enjoyed the tender sturgeon with fresh herbs, savory sliced breast of young squab, and classic desserts like white-chocolate cake with cinnamon and orange sherbet. The wine list is impressive, and not just in Saint-Émilions. M 136 F, 156 F (exc Sun), 215 F, 270 F.

Hostellerie de Plaisance

(See restaurant above)
Closed Jan. 2 stes 950-1,300 F. 10 rms 495-790 F. Air cond. Conf. Pkg. V, AE, DC, MC.
These beautifully appointed rooms range from spacious down to tiny; some have terraces, others tiny private gardens.

SAINT-ÉTIENNE	42000

Paris 520 - Lyon 59 - Le Puy 78 - Clermont-F. 150   *Loire*

Astoria

Le Rond-Point, rue H.-Déchaud
77 25 09 56, fax 77 25 58 28
Open year-round. 33 rms 280-350 F. Conf. Golf. Pkg. V, AE, DC, MC.
This small modern hotel with a garden is easy to find, just off the superhighway.

Les Colonnes

17, pl. J.-Jaurès
77 32 66 76, fax 77 33 56 47
Closed Sun, hols. Open until midnight. Priv rm: 36. Terrace dining. Air cond. V, AE, DC, MC.
A chic, even luxurious version of a brasserie, with an enclosed, flower-decked terrace. Join the night-owl locals and tuck into generous portions of reliably well-crafted cooking: salmon and red mullet mousse with tomato coulis, duck confit with cèpes, morel omelet, and scrambled eggs with foie gras. Attractive wines, some served by the glass; efficient service. **C** 200-300 F. **M** 80 F (lunch), 150 F (wine incl), 110 F, 165 F, 215 F.

Pierre Gagnaire

19.5
7, rue de la Richelandière
77 42 30 90, fax 77 42 30 95
Closed Sun dinner, 1 wk at Feb hols, Aug 1-15. Open until 10:30pm. Priv rm: 10. Terrace dining. Air cond. Valet pkg. V, AE, DC.
Pierre Gagnaire is now cooking in his dream restaurant, a vast 1930s town house with tall windows, terraces, and splendid wrought-iron work. The interior has been redesigned by award-winning architect Marcelo Joulia (who restored the villa Mallet-Stevens in Paris) in collaboration with the proud new owner and a host of brilliant craftsmen. In this superb environment filled with art and light, the flame of Gagnaire's inspiration burns brighter and clearer than ever. Just as a painter seized by a sudden vision might fling colors at his canvas, Gagnaire improvizes unprecedented—yet trenchant—conjunctions of flavors and textures. Experience has taught him to control his impulses; with time his hand has grown surer, and the risk of failure has diminished. But never forget that Gagnaire is not a chef who strives to please the majority of customers; what he does, he does to please himself. This chef, a tiny bit crazy, is, you see, an artist. His menu holds so many choices that it's hard to believe that every dish is cooked to order, and arrives without too much delay (or last-minute changes made to suit artistic whim in the kitchen), but in fact you finish your meal happy with just about everything. This year, if you like bacon, you'll be especially happy, because Gagnaire seems to be in his "bacon" period, and the meaty morsels have inspired at least two works of art: a velouté of tiny green peas in pistachioed pork jus, and a sensational chunk of smoked bacon in a casserole with pan-roasted rabbit kidneys and sea snails, and a bean purée with Chinese peppercorns! A radiant mingling of crisp, tender, and soft. Less impressed by the croûte of morels, turnips, and trompettes de mort mushrooms in Corsican Muscat wine, we were brought to our knees by the splendid noisette of veal with spiced orange dust flanked by a lovely foie gras and basil flan. And the desserts are ones you won't find anywhere else. But we'll let you discover them for yourself in this unknown world where duck sweetbreads are paired with wild dove, milk-fed veal is flavored with melissa, and lightly smoked duck breast audaciously hangs out with pineapple tart and quinquina butter. Picasso stretched the limits of painting; Gagnaire does it with cooking. **C** 700-850 F. **M** 300 F (weekday lunch), 590 F, 730 F, 780 F.

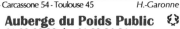

Midi

19, bd Pasteur
77 57 32 55, fax 77 59 11 43
Closed Aug 1-28. 33 rms 275-380 F. Air cond. Conf. Pkg. V, AE, DC, MC.
A modern and functional hotel on the southern outskirts of town.

Le Parc Fauriel

106, cours Fauriel
77 41 13 94, fax 77 21 47 40
Closed Sun dinner, Mon, Aug. Open until 9:30pm. Priv rm: 60. Garden dining. V, AE.
Serious, solid, and reliable: that pretty much sums up Jean-Paul Cartal's cuisine. Elegant technique and accurate cooking times produce such tasty offerings on the bargain "menu-cartes" as fish soufflé with curry sauce, sea bass in a salt crust, and beef fillet with truffle sauce. The flower-filled dining room with its pretty tables is well located in front of the convention center and planetarium. **C** 300-380 F. **M** 70 F, 125 F, 165 F, 190 F, 250 F.

SAINT-FÉLIX-LAURAGAIS	31540

Paris 755 - Carcassone 54 - Toulouse 45   *H.-Garonne*

Auberge du Poids Public

61 83 00 20, fax 61 83 86 21
Closed Sun dinner off-seas, Jan. Open until 9:30pm. Priv rm: 25. Terrace dining. Hotel: 13 rms 250-290 F. Half-board 270-310 F. Conf. Pkg. V, AE, MC.
Claude Taffarello is a chef in tune with his roots. He has an innate feel for the finest foodstuffs of his native region, and he handles them with intelligence and respect. The superb cassoulet "Saint-Félicien", a traditional family recipe, is alone worth the trip to this sleepy country town, and his versions of foie gras, squab, and Pyrénées lamb are other regional triumphs. And he also offers a splendid all-vegetable menu. This year, sample his standing rump of Lauragais veal, roast duck with olives, leg of milk-fed Pyrénées lamb with a stuffed zucchini blossom, or a feuilleté of green asparagus. But whatever you choose, don't miss the millas, a "porridge" of white corn, cooled, sliced, and fried, to be savored with warm foie gras or as a dessert with orange butter. Neighboring growers are well represented in the fine, decently priced cellar. Patrons receive a cordial welcome from Madame Taffarello, who escorts them into the rustic, flower-filled dining room with a roaring fireplace or (in summer) the

enchanting garden. **C** 290-430 F. **M** 135 F, 205 F, 300 F, 160 F.

SAINT-FLORENT 20 → CORSICA

SAINT-FLOUR 15100
Paris 490 - Le Puy 93 - Mende 83 - Aurillac 74 - Issoire 71 *Cantal*

Grand Hôtel des Voyageurs ○○
25, rue du Collège
71 60 34 44, fax 71 60 00 21
Closed Nov-Easter. Open until 9:30pm. Priv rm: 15. No pets. Hotel: 33 rms 150-340 F. Half-board 190-290 F. Conf. Pkg. V, AE, DC, MC.
In this quintessential French country restaurant, savor Diego Quinonero's fine regional dishes, such as those on the 130 F menu: cochonailles (pork dishes), farm-raised chicken with sweet garlic cream, green lentils with fresh herbs, cheeses, and a flaugnarde of caramelized sour cherries for dessert. **C** 180-250 F. **M** 88 F (exc Sun), 130 F, 160 F, 175 F, 220 F.

Grand Hôtel L'Étape
18, av. de la République
71 60 13 03, fax 71 60 48 05
Open year-round. 23 rms 300-415 F. Rms for disabled. Half-board 260-280 F. Pkg. V, AE, DC, MC.
A modern building offering comfortable rooms with period furniture. Half of them have mountain views. Bar.

SAINT-GENIS-POUILLY 01630
Paris 525 - Geneva 11 - Gex 11 - Bellegarde 28 *Ain*

■ In Thoiry 01630 3 km SW on D 89

Les Cépages
50 20 83 85, fax 50 41 24 58
Closed Sun dinner, Mon, Feb school hols. Open until 9pm. Priv rm: 14. Terrace dining. Pkg. V, MC.
A pretty garden sets off this elegant establishment where Jean-Pierre Delesderrier greets guests himself, talks with them about his great store of regional wines, and concocts dishes brimming over with bright ideas and clear flavor. Our only criticism is that perhaps he should stay in the kitchen more to eliminate the long wait you sometimes have for your meal. The classic young chicken with morels in Jura wine is perfection, the féra (lake fish) niçoise is sublime, and the simple chicken-liver mousse explodes with flavor. The desserts are not quite up to the rest. Nevertheless, this is a restaurant well worth discovering. **C** 340-450 F. **M** 120 F (weekday lunch), 180 F, 220 F, 310 F, 350 F.

ST-GERMAIN-EN-LAYE 78 → PARIS Suburbs

SAINT-GERVAIS-EN-VALLIÈRE 71350
Paris 328 - Beaune 13 - Chagny 18 *Saône/Loire*

Moulin de Hauterive
Hameau de Chaublanc
85 91 55 56, fax 85 91 89 65
Closed Sun dinner, Mon (exc Jul-Aug), Dec-Feb (exc w-e by reserv in Dec). Open until 9pm. Priv rm: 60. Garden dining. No pets. Pkg. V, AE, DC, MC.

This ancient stone mill, tucked away in the fertile plains of Burgundy, allows you to get away from it all without leaving earthly pleasures behind. The relaxed, friendly *patron* will put you at ease in the dining room full of cozy nooks and crannies, while Christiane Moille prepares her generous, personal cooking. Perhaps she should concentrate a bit more on technique, reduce her juices a bit more and lighten her sauces a tad. That said, we reveled in her duck with turnips and the celestial pear croustade this year. The costly wine list features many excellent growers' Burgundies. **C** 350-450 F. **M** 160 F (lunch), 240 F, 270 F, 300 F, 400 F.

Moulin de Hauterive ▲♣
(See restaurant above)
See restaurant for closings. 11 stes 650-850 F. 11 rms 350-650 F. Half-board 580-730 F. Conf. Heated pool. Tennis. Golf. Pkg. Helipad. V, AE, DC, MC.
Every room has a different version of chintz and country charm, every night is peaceful, and every breakfast delicious. Sauna, Jacuzzi, heliport.

SAINT-JEAN-CAP-FERRAT 06230
Paris 945 - Nice 14 - Monte-Carlo 11 - Menton 23 *Alpes-Mar.*

Brise Marine
58, av. J.-Mermoz
93 76 04 36, fax 93 76 11 49
Open year-round. 17 rms 565-685 F. Air cond. No pets. V, MC.
This hotel, 100 meters from the sea, has large rooms, a garden, and terraces for summer breakfasts.

Grand Hôtel du Cap Ferrat
Bd du Gal-de-Gaulle
93 76 50 50, fax 93 76 04 52
Closings not available. Open until 10pm. Priv rm: 30. Terrace dining. Air cond. No pets. Pkg. V, AE, DC.
This beautiful establishment is one of the last remaining palaces from the great days of the Côte d'Azur, with its veranda overlooking a park and its marvelous terrace. Chef Jean-Claude Guillon regales guests with fresh, light dishes that are the very antithesis of "hotel cuisine": pan-roasted fresh scampi and a warm vegetable salad, savory John Dory roasted with liver artichokes and girolle mushrooms, and noisettes of Sisteron lamb with Niçois-style stuffed vegetables. Excellent desserts by Jean-Paul Vanroy, such as an amazing candied fennel tart. Splendid, ably presented wine list. Perfect service. **C** 500-700 F. **M** 400 F, 450 F.

Grand Hôtel du Cap Ferrat ▲♣
(See restaurant above)
Closed Jan 1-Feb 18. 11 stes 2,700-8,200 F. 48 rms 950-4,700 F. Rms for disabled. Half-board 490 F. Air cond. Conf. Heated pool. Tennis. Golf. Valet pkg. V, AE, DC, MC.
This grand hotel from the Belle Époque is hidden away in six hectares of lawns, copses, and flower beds, but overlooks the sea. The Sazale group, a Japanese concern, invested plenty of yen to turn this into one of the Riviera's top luxury hotels, complete with an Olympic-sized swimming pool. The British decorators who embellished the lounges and rooms have done a bang-up job, creating an atmosphere that is elegant yet relaxed. The clientele is younger and

less flashy than one might expect. The Le Dauphin restaurant offers poolside dining. Piano bar.

Jean-Jacques Jouteux
Le Provençal, 2, av. D.-Semeria
93 76 03 97, fax 93 76 05 39
Closed Oct 15-Mar 15. Open until 11pm. Priv rm: 30. Garden dining. Air cond. V.
Like many artists, Jean-Jacques Jouteux has his moody moments which, according to our readers, sometimes affect his performance in the kitchen. Part of the problem this year seems to have been management and personnel difficulties, but beyond that, one of our anonymous researchers was served a totally unsuccessful meal, and he is not the only diner to have complained. In these circumstances, we can't let the 18 rating stand. Yet when this gifted chef is at the top of his form, he can stun you with his imaginative, accomplished cooking. In addition, the dining room is lovely, with a flower-filled terrace overlooking the port and a panoramic view of the bay. The menu is mouth-watering: sauté of squid with artichokes, sea bream with wild fennel, John Dory roasted in vine leaves, or duck in blood sauce with spices. But when things aren't going well, the flesh of the langoustines crumbles, the desserts are served in such tiny portions you need a magnifying glass to see them, the wine you order is replaced by another without explanation, and the bill is as high as a kite. The rating is suspended in hopes of better things later. C 600-800 F. M 200 F (weekday lunch), 350 F, 550 F.

Panorama
3, av. J.-Monnet
93 01 20 20, fax 93 01 23 07
Closed Nov-Dec 26. Open until 10pm (10:30pm in summer). Priv rm: 120. Garden dining. Air cond. No pets. Valet pkg. V, AE, DC, MC.
The views of the bay and the Greek villa Kerylos are so spectacular, especially at night, that it is easy to be distracted from your food. Which would be a pity, because Yves Merville's cooking is more inspired than ever! This year try cannelloni stuffed with cigales de mer (a crustacean) and coco beans, croustillants of langoustines with five spices, local fish with tomato confit, and boulangère of lamb with artichoke barigoule, with a raspberry soufflé to finish. Charming service, and a few excellent regional wines on offer. C 400-600 F. M 265 F, 285 F, 300 F.

Royal Riviera
(See restaurant above)
Closed Nov 10-Dec 23. 5 stes 3,300-4,350 F. 72 rms 850-2,600 F. Half-board 2,600 F. Air cond. Conf. Heated pool. Golf. Valet pkg. V, AE, DC, MC.
This superb Belle Époque hotel has been totally renovated and is now one of the area's most choice. The best of these luxuriously appointed rooms overlook the garden and the magnificent pool. Private beach.

Le Sloop
Port de Plaisance - 93 01 48 63
Open daily until 11pm. Terrace dining. Pkg. V, AE, DC, MC.
The cooking isn't the world's most creative, but it's very good and based on top-quality products:

fillet of sea bass cooked in its skin, tender and tasty veal fillet mignon, and a peach roasted in currant juice, all of which merit a toque this year. Friendly welcome in a pretty blue-and-white dining room with a terrace overlooking the port. Nice choice of regional wines. C 300-450 F. M 155 F.

La Voile d'Or
Port de plaisance
93 01 13 13, fax 93 76 11 17
Closed end Oct-Mar 15. Open until 10:30pm. Priv rm: 30. Garden dining. Air cond. Valet pkg. No cards.
This bastion of tradition has decided, against all expectations, to accept credit cards, but that's the only concession to modern times you'll find here. The geraniums have been cascading over the terrace for decades, and Jean Crépin's classic cooking is reminiscent of another age, with an occasional touch of exoticsm: langoustines with a julienne of coriander and ginger, turbot with smoked bacon, John Dory roasted with fennel paired with excellent ratatouille, bourride, or saddle of lamb with tiny Niçois-style stuffed vegetables, accompanied by superb wines selected by an award-winning sommelier. C 500-750 F. M 250 F, 350 F, 550 F.

La Voile d'Or
(See restaurant above)
Closed end Oct-Mar 15. 4 stes 2,100-3,760 F. 41 rms 600-3,160 F. Air cond. Conf. Heated pool. Valet pkg. No cards.
An Italian villa and its luxuriant gardens overlooking the harbor. The interior is highly decorative, with trompe-l'œil paintings, fine fabrics, and marble everywhere you look. Countless services and amenities.

See also: Beaulieu

SAINT-JEAN-DE-LUZ	64500

Paris 760 - Biarritz 15 - Hendaye 13 - Pau 128   Pyrénées-A.

12/20 L'Atlantique
Pl. Maurice-Ravel
59 51 51 51, fax 59 51 51 54
Open daily until 10pm. Terrace dining. Air cond. No pets. Pkg. V, AE, DC.
The new chef here has opted for a classic repertoire with no surprises: marinated fish carpaccio flavored with pistou, mignon of veal breaded with ground almonds (perfectly cooked and seasoned but in a rather stingy portion), and a delicious fruit tart flambéed with Calvados. Superb wine list. Relatively slow service in the elegant white dining room with its stunning view of the bay. C 300-400 F. M 130 F (weekday lunch, Sat), 190 F.

Hélianthal
(See restaurant above)
Open year-round. 6 stes 820-1,300 F. 94 rms 395-1,000 F. Half-board 650-1,250 F. Air cond. Conf. Pkg. V, AE, DC.
The rooms of this modern hotel set back from the beach glory in an attractive Art Deco style, right down to the mahogany trim, bow windows, and lithographs. All rooms have balconies or loggias. The breakfast buffet includes low-calorie options; imperfect air conditioning. Sea-water treatment spa.

409

Chantaco

Chantaco Golf Course
59 26 14 76, fax 59 26 35 97
*Closed Nov-Apr. Open until 10:30pm. Priv rm: 10.
Garden dining. No pets. Valet pkg. V, AE, DC, MC.*
The young chef's cuisine is certainly less spectacular than the majestic tapestries and paintings which adorn the walls of the Chantaco's dining room. Still, the food has plenty of personality: just taste the duck consommé with cèpes and a hint of truffles, or sea bream with piquillos and Szechuan peppercorns. For dessert, try the Izarra parfait glacé with a tart coulis. Well balanced wine list; courteous service. **C** 260-340 F. **M** 130 F (weekday lunch), 170 F (lunch exc weekdays), 240 F (weekday dinner), 290 F (dinner exc weekdays).

Chantaco

(See restaurant above)
Closed Nov-Apr. 4 stes 1,350-1,950 F. 20 rms 800-1,600 F. Rms for disabled. Half-board 850-1,250 F. Conf. Pool. Tennis. Golf. Valet pkg. Helipad. V, AE, DC, MC.
A beautiful Basque dwelling swaddled in leafy grounds. Superb rooms, mostly modernized, overlook a garden and the famous golf course. Excellent breakfasts; good service.

La Coupole

43, bd Thiers
59 26 35 36, fax 59 51 19 91
Closings not available. Open until 10pm. Terrace dining. Air cond. No pets. Pkg. V, AE, DC, MC.
Each table in this vast, panoramic rotunda decorated with frescoes, columns, and draped fabrics, boasts a breathtaking view of the bay. If you can tear yourself away from that mesmerizing sight, savor the carefully prepared, inventive cuisine based on a regional repertoire: pan-roasted red mullet fillet and stuffed chiperons (squid), casserole-roasted Pyrenées lamb, a "boléro" of berries à la Ravel, and sheep's milk sherbet. Long and well chosen wine list. Perfect welcome. **C** 400-550 F. **M** 170 F, 220 F.

Le Grand Hôtel

(See restaurant above)
Closings not available. 6 stes 1,000-2,400 F. 44 rms 700-1,400 F. Half-board 900-1,850 F. Air cond. Conf. Heated pool. Golf. Garage pkg. V, AE, DC, MC.
The former nightclub of this small luxury hotel is now, tellingly, a fitness center. Other signs of renewal include fresh decor. Excursions are organized on land or sea.

La Devinière

5, rue Loquin
59 26 05 51, fax 59 51 26 38
Open year-round. 8 rms 500-650 F. Golf. Pkg. Helipad. V, MC.
This hotel has eight delightfully decorated and furnished rooms in the heart of town. Pleasant welcome and quiet garden.

Parc Victoria

5, rue Cépé
59 26 78 78, fax 59 26 78 08
Closed Nov 15-Mar 15. 3 stes 1,200-1,500 F. 9 rms 800-1,250 F. Restaurant. Half-board 950-1,350 F. Air cond. Heated pool. Golf. Garage pkg. V, AE, DC.
A nineteenth-century town house set amid broad lawns and wooded grounds, the Victoria

is meticulously decorated in 1930s style. Elegant rooms, perfect bathrooms.

12/20 Petit Grill Basque

4, rue St-Jacques - 59 26 80 76
Closed Wed, Dec 20-Jan 20. Open until 9:30pm. Air cond. V, AE, DC.
Come here for a taste of fresh, unpretentious Basque fare: ttoro, squid stewed in their ink, chicken croquettes, monkfish à la luzienne, and crème caramel renversé. **C** 160-230 F. **M** 90 F.

Le Tourasse

25, rue Tourasse - 59 51 14 25
Open daily until 10pm (10:30pm in summer). Priv rm: 30. V, AE, MC.
Véronique Basset provides the warm welcome, and her husband Pascal the very fresh, interesting, seafood-oriented cooking on hand in this pleasant dining room. Sample the warm salad of shrimp with potatoes and cèpes, tacos of cod meunière, and veal sweetbreads studded with bacon. Fine homestyle desserts. **C** 270-390 F. **M** 110 F (weekdays, Sat lunch).

12/20 Txalupa

Harbor - 59 26 99 82, fax 59 51 23 97
Open daily until 1am. Priv rm: 25. Terrace dining. Air cond. Pkg. V, AE, DC, MC.
This attractive spot opposite the port has been relaunched by Georges Mailharro. Done up in nautical blue and white, it boasts warm paneling and a cozy little terrace. Txalupa is sailing along nicely now, offering fine dishes prepared with top-notch ingredients: savory sautéed cèpes, sea bream with Bayonne ham in a succulent vinegar and garlic sauce (but served in a small portion), and excellent regional cheeses. Prices are on the rise. **C** 240-350 F. **M** 140 F.

■ **In Ciboure 64500**   1 km SW

Chez Dominique   ۞

Quai M.-Ravel - 59 47 29 16
Closed Sun dinner, Mon (exc Jul-Aug), Feb. Open until 9:30pm (10:30pm in summer). Terrace dining. V, AE, MC.
No doubt about it, Georges Piron is one of those fine cooks with an eye for quality ingredients, spot-on cooking times, and ravishing presentation. Our most recent meal, taken on the terrace of this breezy establishment, included langoustine ravioli perfumed with tarragon, brill pan-roasted in its skin with a piperade pressée, and a pistachio sabayon. The short wine list has character, and the *patronne's* welcome is charming. The staff keep their cool despite the crush of eager diners. Hurry over then, before the prices heat up! **C** 250-350 F. **M** 130 F (weekday lunch).

Lehen-Tokia

1, chemin Achotaretta
59 47 18 16, fax 59 47 38 04
Open year-round. 1 ste 1,200 F. 5 rms 550-800 F. Conf. Pool. Golf. Valet pkg. V, MC.
This cozy hotel decorated in authentic Art Deco style has been classified an historic monument by Le Figaro newspaper. Family-style welcome, copious breakfasts, and a splendid view of the bay.

SAINT-JEAN-DE-MOIRANS 38 → Voiron

SAINT-JEAN-PIED-DE-PORT 64220
Paris 793 - Pau 102 - Bayonne 54 - Dax 86 Pyrénées-A.

Les Pyrénées
19, pl. du Gal-de-Gaulle
59 37 01 01, fax 59 37 18 97
Closed Mon dinner (Nov-Mar, exc hols), Tue (exc Jul-Aug & hols), Jan 6-28, Nov 20-Dec 22. Open until 9pm. Priv rm: 40. Terrace dining. Air cond. No pets. Garage pkg. V, AE, MC.
More and more Spaniards are taking to the Compostela pilgrimage route—but they're walking away from Santiago, towards Firmin Arrambide's Les Pyrénées. The salmon-hued dining room with its convivial atmosphere also draws crowds of holiday-makers from the Côte Basque, who are eager to sample Arrambide's famously full-flavored cooking. We've been fans of Firmin's for many years now, and on our latest visit found the chef in top form: an astonishing lamb's head with crisp-cooked brains, tongue en ravigote, and spiced cheeks, paired with a little curly endive salad perfumed with truffles, a rustic dish transformed into an elegant one. Then, a voluptuously rich and harmonious lasagne of foie gras and truffles, followed by inventive, ultrafresh grilled red mullet fillets and chiperons (squid) posed on an exquisite squid-ink sauce. The desserts are also fine, like the croustillante of white peaches, verbena ice cream, and prunes poached in Jurançon wine and paired with pistachio ice cream. The cellar is awash in superb (costly) Bordeaux, fine Spanish vintages, and tasty Irouléguys and eaux-de-vie made by the Brana family, Arrambide's neighbors, who have brought this long-neglected appellation back to life. C 400-600 F. M 220 F (exc Sun lunch), 300 F, 400 F, 500 F.

Les Pyrénées
(See restaurant above)
See restaurant for closings. 2 stes 950-1,050 F. 18 rms 540-900 F. Half-board 720-750 F. Air cond. Conf. Heated pool. No pets. Garage pkg. V, AE, MC.
Behind the façade is a long gallery which leads to well-equipped, pleasantly decorated rooms (the double beds are a bit small). In the enclosed courtyard with garden and grounds that go down to the river, there is a swimming pool and a terrace where one may sip an apéritif. Relais et Châteaux.

ST-LAMBERT-DES-BOIS 78 → Chevreuse

SAINT-LAURENT-DU-VAR 06700
Paris 925 - Nice 10 - Cannes 27 - Antibes 16 Alpes-Mar.

Hôtel Galaxie
Av. du Mal-Juin
93 07 73 72, fax 93 14 32 14
Open year-round. 28 rms 410-560 F. Air cond. Conf. Golf. Pkg. V, AE, DC, MC.
Just a stone's throw from the sea is a hotel offering well designed rooms, each with a private balcony; bathrooms are well equipped and there's a hairdresser on the premises.

Novotel
Nice Cap 3000, 80, av. de Verdun
93 31 61 15, fax 93 07 62 25
Open year-round. 103 rms 450-560 F. Rms for disabled. Restaurant. Half-board 425 F. Air cond. Conf. Pool. Golf. Pkg. V, AE, DC, MC.
Functional rooms near the sea and Nice's airport (free shuttle bus), with a grill restaurant open from 6am to midnight.

SAINT-LAURENT-SUR-SAÔNE 01 → Mâcon

SAINT-LOUBÈS 33 → Bordeaux

SAINT-LOUIS 68300
Paris 556 - Mulhouse 29 - Basel 5 - Altkirch 128 H.-Rhin

■ In Hagenthal 68220 12 km SE on D 469, D 12B

L'Ancienne Forge
Hagenthal-le-Haut,
52, rue Principale - 89 68 56 10
Closed Sun, Mon, Dec 24-Jan 2, Jul 17-31. Open until 9pm. Terrace dining. Pkg. V, MC.
This half-timbered house with a pretty pink-and-white dining room has all the charm of rural Alsace. Chef Hervé Paulus offers a dual menu: some specialties are pure Alsatian, while others come straight from sunny Provence. All dishes are imaginative, with well balanced flavors: a terrine of raw salmon with goat cheese, a strudel stuffed with pig's foot and pork shanks in truffle jus, and a tender chocolate cake with an orange coulis. Superb wine list. You'll find a warm welcome. C 300-400 F. M 190 F, 270 F, 340 F.

Jenny
2.5 km N on D 12b, 84, rue Hegenheim
89 68 50 09, fax 89 68 58 64
Open year-round. 26 rms 280-490 F. Rms for disabled. Restaurant. Half-board 320-420 F. Conf. Pool. Golf. Garage pkg. V, AE, DC, MC.
Here's a sizeable hotel of recent vintage, set in the green hills of the Sundgau. The contemporary rooms are most attractive; those on the street are smaller and less expensive than the garden rooms. All the usual comforts on tap; a good address.

SAINT-LYPHARD 44410
Paris 436 - La Baule 17 - St-Nazaire 21 - Nantes 71 Loire-Atl.

Auberge de Kerbourg
Route de Guérande - 40 61 95 15
Closed Mon, Sun dinner off-seas, Tue lunch, Feb 1-15. Open until 9:30pm. Priv rm: 50. Terrace dining. Pkg. V.
Who would guess that this pretty little farmhouse surrounded by a flower-filled garden offers some of the most irrepressibly creative cooking for miles around? Even when Bernard Jeanson works in a classic register, he brings flavors together in a bold, exciting way: an iced oyster tian with warm oysters; langoustines with garden herbs, pears, and tabac de cuisine; and squab in a cacao jus with sweet potatoes and hazelnuts. Charming welcome. Well-planned cellar. The prices are reasonable. C 200-250 F. M 125 F, 185 F, 250 F.

SAINT-MALO   35400
Paris 366 - Rennes 69 - Dinan 34 - St-Brieuc 76   *Ille/Vil.*

Le Cap Horn

Grand Hôtel des Thermes, 100, bd Hébert
99 40 75 75, fax 99 40 76 00
Open daily until 9:30pm. Priv rm: 16. Air cond. No pets. Valet pkg. V, AE, DC, MC.
This comfortable setting opposite the dike and sea resembles the hotel dining rooms of yesteryear, and offers a lovely maritime view. Henry Reverdy's classic, occasionally fussy menu proposes a clam bouillon with vegetable jus, fillet of Charolais beef sautéed in a buckwheat crêpe, and orange croquantes in a light cream sauce. Diverse and well stocked cellar; refined service. **C** 320-400 F. **M** 125 F (exc Sat dinner & Sun lunch), 145 F (Sun lunch), 185 F, 255 F.

Grand Hôtel des Thermes
(See restaurant above)
Open year-round. 3 stes 1,700-2,400 F. 186 rms 250-1,270 F. Half-board 515-1,640 F. Conf. Heated pool. Valet pkg. V, AE, DC, MC.
This hotel caters for guests taking health cures at the spa. It has been remodeled in a tasteful, pseudo-1920s-style.

Le Chalut
8, rue de la Corne-du-Cerf - 99 56 71 58
Closed Sun dinner & Mon (all-seas), Jan 1-15. Open until 10pm. Air cond. V, AE, MC.
In a typical seaside brasserie decor, sample Jean-Philippe Foucat's seafood cuisine based on the best ingredients: feuillantine of langoustine tails with a chive crème fumée, turbot roasted in semi-salted butter and shellfish jus, and a tender chocolate and pistachio soufflé. Interesting choice of white Burgundies. Friendly welcome. **C** 250-350 F. **M** 95 F (exc Sat dinner), 175 F, 250 F.

Hôtel de la Cité
26, rue Ste-Barbe
99 40 55 40, fax 99 40 10 04
Open year-round. 2 stes 735-940 F. 39 rms 360-510 F. Rms for disabled. Conf. Golf. Valet pkg. V, AE, DC, MC.
In the old town, behind the ramparts, this comfortably renovated hotel has cozy, bright rooms which are inefficiently soundproofed (and some are quite small). Pretty view of the sea. Decent breakfasts.

Delaunay
6, rue Ste-Barbe
99 40 92 46, fax 99 56 88 91
Closed Sun (Mon off-seas), Mar, Nov 15-Dec 15. Open until 9:30pm (10pm in summer). Pkg. V, AE, MC.
Set your course for this restaurant near the Place Chateaubriant to sample fine seafood prepared with brio and full of flavor. The delicate dishes (some a bit overcomplicated) include superb grilled sea bass, excellent tarte renversée with a rather ordinary tournedos, and a cod and vegetable quiche. Fine choice of Loire and Chablis wines. This is the city-center's best restaurant. **C** 300-400 F. **M** 98 F (lunch), 195 F, 295 F.

La Korrigane

39, rue Le Pomellec
99 81 65 85, fax 99 82 23 89
Closed Jan 17-31. 12 rms 400-800 F. Pkg. V, AE, DC.
A lovely bourgeois house near the center of town, offering well soundproofed rooms and pretty traditional furnishings. You can have breakfast in the garden.

Manoir de la Grassinais
12, rue de la Grassinais
99 81 33 00, fax 99 81 60 90
Closed Mon off-seas, Sun dinner, Feb. Open until 9:30pm. Priv rm: 45. Terrace dining. Hotel: 29 rms 220-320 F. Rms for disabled. Half-board 235-280 F. Air cond. Conf. Pkg. V, MC.
We applaud Christophe Bouvier's current repertoire, which features a gelée of tiny crabs with foie gras and bay scallops, pré salé lamb cooked for seven hours and paired with green cabbage couscous, and moka feuilles au pure malt for dessert. Small wine list with a choice of good Loire and Bordeaux wines. Friendly welcome. **C** 220-260 F. **M** 85 F (weekdays, wine incl), 98 F (weekdays), 140 F, 170 F, 220 F.

■ **In Saint-Servan 35400**   SE on N 137

Saint-Placide
6, pl. Poncel
99 81 70 73, fax 99 81 89 49
Closed Tue & Sat lunch (Jul 14-Aug 30); Wed & Tue dinner off-seas. Open until 9pm (9:30pm in summer). Priv rm: 14. Garden dining. No pets. Pkg. V.
The menu is succinct but it displays some bright ideas. For example: guinea fowl terrine forestière with dried tomatoes, salmon fillet seasoned with saffron, and beef fillet with beef marrow and violet mustard. You can choose the dining room filled with bouquets of fresh flowers, or the pleasant terrace. **C** 180-250 F. **M** 79 F (weekday lunch, Sat), 108 F (weekdays, Sat lunch), 174 F, 198 F.

Le Valmarin
7, rue Jean-XXIII
99 81 94 76, fax 99 81 30 03
Closed Nov 15-Feb 15 (exc Christmas school by reserv). 12 rms 500-700 F. Pkg. V, AE, MC.
Outside the town walls, this handsome eighteenth-century residence (built with the proceeds of piracy) rises before a pretty park. Good-sized, pleasing rooms with outdated decor. Cordial reception.

SAINT-MARTIN-AUX-CHARTRAINS 14
→ **Deauville**

SAINT-MARTIN-D'ARMAGNAC   32110
Paris 740 - Agen 90 - Auch 80 - Tarbes 59   *Gers*

Auberge du Bergerayre
62 09 08 72, fax 62 09 09 74
Closed Wed. Open until 8pm (9pm in summer). Priv rm: 30. Terrace dining. Hotel: 12 rms 390-425 F. Half-board 255-310 F. Conf. Pool. Pkg. V, MC.
Owner-chef Pierrette Sarran ushers one cordially into her Gascon inn where, by the fire in winter or under the garden arbor in summer, you'll surely enjoy her local specialties like cassolette of sea scallops with cèpes and potatoes, veal sweetbreads with foie gras and a Port jus,

and a pastis gascon (flaky apple pie) flambéed with Armagnac for dessert. Good choice of regional wines. **C** 200-300 F. **M** 80 F, 115 F, 170 F, 200 F.

SAINT-MARTIN-DE-LONDRES   34380
Paris 785 - Le Vigan 38 - Montpellier 25 - Nîmes 62   *Hérault*

 Les Muscardins
19, route des Cévennes
67 55 75 90, fax 67 55 70 28
Closed Tue lunch, Mon, Feb. Open until 9:30pm (10pm in summer). Pkg. V, AE, DC, MC.
Georges Rousset handed over his toques to his son Thierry, and now devotes himself to welcoming patrons with warm hospitality. We dare you not to drool when he describes in mouthwatering detail the dishes featured on the value-packed single-price menus! Rousset *fils* is living proof that youth is no impediment to valor. He continues in his father's tradition, but adds an original touch of his own. Taste his warm calf's liver with baby spinach and girolle mushrooms in walnut oil, Scottish salmon roasted in its skin with cardamom, and crayfish ravioli with friandises de cochonailles. Or the squab in a pistou pot-au-feu, Quercy lamb in star anise jus, and a blancmange with almonds and a fresh fruit croustillant for dessert. The prices are incredibly low for such quality. The wine list offers a wide range of fine choices. Special services include high chairs and coloring books for smaller gourmets. **M** 160 F, 230 F, 300 F, 380 F.

SAINT-MARTIN-DE-MIEUX 14   → Falaise

SAINT-MARTIN-DE-RÉ 17   → Ré (Ile de)

SAINT-MARTIN-DU-FAULT 87   → Limoges

SAINT-MARTIN-DU-VAR 06   → Nice

SAINT-MARTIN-LE-VINOUX 38   → Grenoble

SAINT-MÉLOIR-DES-ONDES 35   → Cancale

SAINT-NAZAIRE   44600
Paris 434 - Nantes 60 - La Baule 17 - Vannes 76   *Loire-Atl.*

 L'An II
L'Isle Thimée, 2, rue Villebois-Mareuil
40 00 95 33, fax 40 53 44 20
Open daily until 9:30pm (later by reserv). Priv rm: 30. V, AE, MC.
A pretty view of the Loire estuary lends additional charm to the large dining room; in the kitchen, Patrice Deschamps fine-tunes a repertoire designed to please the local clientele: sardines marinated in olive oil, calf's head in Guérande sea salt, cod brandade, and a crépinette of monkfish with smoked bacon. There's a tasty and delicate warm apple tart for dessert. The cellar is stocked by the *patron*, Jean-Luc Guéné, who offers sound advice on his collection of vintages. Youthful, friendly staff. **C** 250-400 F. **M** 150 F (wine incl), 105 F, 145 F, 195 F.

12/20   Le Moderne
46, rue d'Anjou - 40 22 55 88
Closed Sun dinner, Mon. Open until 9:30pm (10pm in summer). Priv rm: 20. Air cond. V.
Though the dull "modern" decor leaves much to be desired, the smiling welcome and engaging set meals offer quick relief. Sample the halibut fillet with sorrel butter, tasty and perfectly cooked chicken breast with cèpe sauce, and a classic île flottante. Timid but friendly welcome. **C** 220-310 F. **M** 78 F, 98 F, 118 F, 195 F.

SAINT-OMER   62500
Paris 254 - Amiens 110 - Lille 65 - Calais 40 - Arras 81   *P./Calais*

■ **In Tilques 62500**   6 km W on N 43 and VO

Château Tilques
21 93 28 99, fax 21 38 34 23
Open year-round. 1 ste 850 F. 51 rms 410-750 F. Rms for disabled. Restaurant. Conf. Tennis. Golf. No pets. Pkg. Helipad. V, AE, DC.
An English hotel group now owns this late-nineteenth-century manor nestled in a vast estate. The rooms are carefully appointed without being actually luxurious, and the rates are within reason. The service and reception, however, could stand improvement. Fine services for business meetings.

SAINT-OUEN 93   → PARIS Suburbs

SAINT-OUEN-LES-VIGNES 37   → Amboise

SAINT-PATRICE 37   → Langeais

SAINT-PAUL-DE-VARCES 38   → Grenoble

SAINT-PAUL-DE-VENCE   06570
Paris 925 - Cannes 27 - Nice 20 - Antibes 16   *Alpes-Mar.*

La Brouette
830, route de Cagnes - 93 58 67 16
Closed Mon off-seas, Feb. Open until 11pm. Priv rm: 12. Garden dining. Air cond. Pkg. V, MC.
Ole and Brigitte Bornemann serve authentic Danish specialties in a lively, pleasant atmosphere to only 20 guests at a time. Opt for a seat near the fireplace in winter, or in the garden with its great view of the village and a barbecue where fish are smoking. Sample the tasty liver terrine with cucumber confit, trout smoked with dill, and a leg of Greenland reindeer. Expansive welcome. **C** 180-250 F. **M** 95 F, 148 F.

12/20   La Colombe d'Or
Pl. du Gal-de-Gaulle
93 32 80 02, fax 93 32 77 78
Closed Nov 5-Dec 19. Open until 10pm. Priv rm: 35. Terrace dining. Valet pkg. V, AE, DC, MC.
Picture a paradise for art lovers, with works by Picasso, Rouault, Léger, Miró and others adorning the walls. Come here to enjoy the leafy terrace and garden; we just wish there were some set menus and that the à la carte prices weren't so high, because the cooking is simple indeed: turbot maraîchère, rack of lamb, chicken fricassée with morels, and an almond tart with Beaumes-de-Venise. **C** 360-460 F.

La Colombe d'Or
(See restaurant above)
Closed beg Nov-mid Dec. 10 stes 1,260-1,450 F.
16 rms 1,000-1,150 F. Half-board 775-875 F. Air
cond. Conf. Heated pool. Valet pkg. V, AE, DC, MC.
This warmly welcoming Provençal hotel is very
tastefully decorated. The rooms are delightful.
Superb swimming pool.

Mas d'Artigny
Route de La Colle
93 32 84 54, fax 93 32 95 36
Open daily until 10pm. Priv rm: 180. Garden dining.
Valet pkg. V, AE, MC.
The dining room with a dull decor but pleasant
views of the garden has been enlarged this year,
the better to help you savor the sun-kissed
flavors of Arthur Dorschner's terrine of young
rabbit with foie gras "Grand Maman", fillet of sea
bass with persillade and anise jus, and a caramelized fruit millefeuille. The fine cellar will not keep
your bill down. C 440-600 F. M 300 F, 410 F.

Mas d'Artigny
(See restaurant above)
Open year-round. 29 stes 1,470-2,680 F. 53 rms
460-1,830 F. Rms for disabled. Half-board 688-
1,740 F. Air cond. Conf. Heated pool. Tennis. Valet
pkg. Helipad. V, AE, MC.
The rooms and poolside suites have all it takes
to make you feel like a millionaire. There are
several marvelous multi-room villas scattered
among the eight hectares of pines. Relais et
Châteaux.

Les Orangers
Chemin Les Fumerates
93 32 80 95, fax 93 32 00 32
Open year-round. 2 stes 725-805 F. 7 rms 380-580 F.
Half-board 400-610 F. Pkg. V, MC.
Set in a handsome park planted with olive and
orange trees, the rooms here are stylishly furnished. Some have terraces with fine views of
the old village.

Le Saint-Paul
86, rue Grande
93 32 65 25, fax 93 32 52 94
Closed Thu lunch, Wed, Jan 10-Feb 25. Open until
10pm. Priv rm: 40. Terrace dining. Air cond. Valet
pkg. V, AE, DC, MC.
The old stones and frescoes of this charming
Provençal house look even better after a full-
dress renovation and the addition of a terrace.
All the more reason to linger over new chef
Frédéric Buzet's fine 290 F menu: pressed lamb
and eggplant with tapenade, savory salmon with
anchovies and capers, tender and tasty lamb
fillets coated with green and black olives, and a
delicious rosemary crème brûlée. Fine local
wines. Cheerful welcome; courteous service.
C 350-480 F. M 170 F (lunch), 290 F, 380 F.

Le Saint-Paul
(See restaurant above)
Closed Jan 10-Feb 25. 2 stes 1,150-1,700 F. 16 rms
750-1,250 F. Half-board 385 F. Air cond. Conf. Valet
pkg. V, AE, DC, MC.
This charming hotel dates from the Renaissance. The freshly refurbished rooms are most
attractive and comfortable (those with a view of
the countryside are the best), and the service is
very good indeed. Library; bar. Relais et
Châteaux.

■ In La Colle-sur-Loup 06480   3 km SW on D 7

Le Diamant Rose
Route de St-Paul
93 32 82 20, fax 93 32 69 98
Open daily until 10:30pm (11pm in summer). Priv
rm: 30. Terrace dining. Air cond. Valet pkg. V, AE.
Antoine Versini transformed a sumptuous villa
at the foot of Saint-Paul-de-Vence into a restaurant with a princely dining room with ceramic
floors and old-fashioned stucco, and a luxurious
terrace with a panoramic view. Chef Daniel
Ettlinger had the bright idea to devise two "cartes" here, one (expensive) featuring noble ingredients; the other, bourgeois cooking at
friendly prices. Dishes on both are remarkably
well prepared and satisfying, whether you opt
for the fresh cod brandade with peppers and
shellfish (60 F), or the magnificent lobster gazpacho, or the vegetable millefeuille with fennel
jus, or the whole langouste grilled over a wood
fire and napped with a lush butter sauce (740 F).
The veal chops roasted with olive oil and paired
with thyme-seasoned vegetables are a model of
pure tastes. The desserts can't help but please:
feuilleté of apples with frangipane, and a gooey
chocolate fondant, for example. The "carte de
saison" at 235 F to 300 F, Provençal wine included, has brought in flocks of fans. C 450-
750 F.

La Strega
1260, route de Cagnes
93 22 62 37
Closed Mon, Sun dinner (Jul-Aug), Tue lunch, Jan 3-
Feb. Open until 9:30pm (10pm in summer). Garden
dining. Pkg. V.
Summer is the best time to savor Gilbert
Stella's cooking, served on a lovely garden terrace. He gives a contemporary touch to the
traditional dishes on his 150 F menu: appetizers,
médaillons of veal pan-roasted with potato
crêpes, Brie-de-Meaux, and a vanilla crème
brûlée with brown sugar. Well chosen wine list.
Warm welcome; flawless service. M 125 F
(weekday lunch, Sat, wine incl), 150 F (exc Sun
dinner).

SAINT-PÈRE-SOUS-VÉZELAY 89 → Vézelay

ST-PIERRE-D'OLÉRON 17→ Oléron (Ile d')

SAINT-PONS-DE-THOMIÈRES   34220
Paris 877 - Béziers 51 - Castres 51 - Carcassonne 65   Hérault

Château de Pondérach
Route de Narbonne
67 97 02 57, fax 67 97 29 75
Closed Oct 15-Mar. 12 rms 295-470 F. Restaurant.
Half-board 550-775 F. Conf. Garage pkg. Helipad. V,
AE, DC, MC.
Here's an impressive eighteenth-century dwelling in landscaped grounds, with rooms that
could be better maintained. The place has undeniable charm, however, attentive service, and
wonderful breakfasts. Relais et Châteaux.

---

*Some establishments change their **closing times**
without warning. It is always wise to check in advance.*

SAINT-POURÇAIN-SUR-SIOULE   03500
Paris 325 - Montluçon 61 - Moulins 31 - Riom 50   *Allier*

Le Chêne Vert
35, bd Ledru-Rollin - 70 45 40 65
Closed Sun dinner off-seas, Mon, Jan 2-25. Open until 9pm. Terrace dining. Pkg. V, AE, DC, MC.
Tucked away in an unprepossessing old hotel, the Chêne Vert's dining room is regularly renovated: the current decor is a cheerful, modern mix of pastels. Jean-Guy Siret's scrupulous, strictly classic cuisine features a full complement of rich, traditional sauces. Sample his terrine of veal sweetbreads with an onion compote, sea scallops in Noilly-Prat vermouth sauce, Charolais beef, and red mullet à la niçoise with taboulé. Manageably priced cellar (lots of good Saint-Pourçains); most courteous welcome. **C** 200-300 F. **M** 90 F, 100 F (exc Sun lunch), 135 F, 180 F.

SAINT-PREST 28   → Chartres

SAINT-QUENTIN   02100
Paris 155 - Amiens 73 - Lille 116 - Reims 96   *Aisne*

Le Président
6-8, rue Dachery
23 62 69 77, fax 23 62 53 52
Closed Sat lunch & Sun (exc hols), Dec 19-27, Jul 31-Aug 28. Open until 10pm. Priv rm: 60. Valet pkg. V, AE, DC, MC.
Chef Jean-Marc Le Guennec has lived up to his culinary potential, bringing a welcome sea breeze into the heart of Picardy. Consider his marinière of langoustines with cucumber, red mullet pan-roasted with pistou, and pickerel sautéed with shrimp butter. We also reveled in his baluchon of smoked salmon, a great summer dish, paired with a flavorful ratatouille. The duck with foie gras, though, was not as tender as it should have been. A fine nougat glacé with seasonal fruits makes for a happy ending. Very professional service; the wine list is good but pricey, as is the à la carte menu. **C** 380-450 F. **M** 160 F (weekdays), 250 F (Sat), 195 F, 330 F.

Grand Hôtel
(See restaurant above)
Open year-round. 6 stes 500-600 F. 18 rms 420-550 F. Conf. Golf. Valet pkg. V, AE, DC, MC.
The Grand Hôtel's 24 newly remodeled, well-designed, and tastefully decorated rooms are set around a glassed-in patio with a panoramic glass-walled elevator.

SAINT-RAPHAËL   83700
Paris 892 - Cannes 44 - Toulon 96 - Aix 119   *Var*

L'Arbousier
6, av. de Valescure
94 95 25 00, fax 94 83 81 04
Closed for lunch Tue-Thu (in seas), Dec 12-Jan 3, Jun 6-14. Open until 10pm. Priv rm: 10. Terrace dining. Air cond. V, AE.
Happily ensconced in a dainty green-and-white restaurant, Philippe Troncy, who trained with Guérard, is simply the best, most inventive chef in Saint-Raphaël. Keen flavors combined with flair: his is Provençal cuisine at its most expressive. Well worth ordering are the fork-tender squab with a sausage made of foie gras

and squab giblets, served with an eggplant confit and an astonishing "pain de figues", a delicious spiral of bread holding fruit. We also savored the lobster ravioli in a navarin of baby vegetables. Choice cellar; heartwarming welcome from Christine Troncy. New this year: a flower-filled garden with a terrace and an area where children can play. **C** 320-380 F. **M** 140 F (weekday lunch, Sat), 160 F, 280 F.

11/20 La Bouillabaisse
Pl. V.-Hugo - 94 95 03 57
Closed Mon, Nov 15-Dec 20. Open until 10pm (11pm in summer). Terrace dining. Air cond. MC.
As the name suggests, fish soup is the speciality at this friendly portside bistrot. You'll also find langoustines à la rouille and some simple, sunny Provençal dishes to wash down with the tasty house wine. **C** 250-300 F.

Excelsior
Promenade du Pdt-R.-Coty
94 95 02 42, fax 94 95 33 82
Open year round. 36 rms 355-720 F. Restaurant. Half-board 355-830 F. Air cond. Pkg. V, AE, DC, MC.
Charming, air-conditioned rooms that afford views of the sea. The restaurant boasts a pretty terrace shaded by plane trees. The cooking is not the strong point here, though.

Golf-Hôtel de Valescure
Valescure Golf course, av. P.-Lhermite
94 82 40 31, fax 94 82 41 88
Closed Jan 7-31, Nov 15-Dec 22. 40 rms 470-810 F. Rms for disabled. Restaurant. Half-board 465-790 F. Air cond. Pool. Tennis. Golf. Pkg. V, AE, DC, MC.
Comfortable, sunny rooms (some facing the golf course) are available here. Golf and tennis lessons.

Pastorel
54, rue de la Liberté
94 95 02 36, fax 94 95 64 07
Closed Sun dinner, Mon (in Aug open daily for dinner). Open until 9:30pm. Priv rm: 40. Terrace dining. V, AE, DC, MC.
Take a terrace table if you can. There you'll enjoy even more Charles Floccia's updated traditional dishes from the Provençal repertoire. Try the first set menu: ravioli stuffed with goat cheese seasoned with garlic and sage, rabbit sautéed with tomatoes and artichokes, salad of blue cheese with walnuts, and dessert. **C** 250-350 F. **M** 155 F, 190 F.

La Potinière
5 km E on N 98, in Boulouris
94 95 21 43, fax 94 95 29 10
Open year-round. 4 stes 540-870 F. 24 rms 280-740 F. Restaurant. Half-board 285-522 F. Conf. Heated pool. Tennis. Golf. Pkg. V, AE, DC, MC.
The view from the well-equipped rooms with terraces, across grounds dotted with pines, eucalyptus, and mimosa trees, helps one forget the rather dog-eared decor of some of the other rooms. Charming but absent-minded staff.

Le San Pedro
Av. du Colonel-Brooke
94 83 65 69, fax 94 40 57 20
Open year-round. 28 rms 350-750 F. Restaurant. Half-board 460-510 F. Air cond. Conf. Pool. Pkg. V, AE, DC, MC.

415

Near the Valescure golf course and tennis club, an imposing hotel built in period style. The garden and pine-wood setting are pleasant. Good, recently remodeled rooms. Many amenities.

SAINT-RÉMY-DE-PROVENCE 13210
Paris 710 - Marseille 91 - Arles 24 - Avignon 21   B./Rhône

Alain Assaud
Le Marceau,
13, bd Marceau - 90 92 37 11
Closed Thu lunch, Wed. Open until 9:30pm (10pm in summer). Air cond. V, AE, DC, MC.
The dining room has just been redecorated at this restaurant run by a former Oustau de Baumanière pasty chef, all the more reason to sample his tasty, carefully prepared dishes: a feuilleté of asparagus in warm vinaigrette with truffle jus, lamb with an anchovy jus, and a coffee parfait glacé with licorice and caramel. Fine choice of regional wines. **C** 280-420 F. **M** 170 F, 280 F.

12/20 Le Bistrot des Alpilles
15, bd Mirabeau - 90 92 09 17
Closed Sun. Open until 10pm. Terrace dining. Air cond. V, AE.
This charming little bistrot has it all together: a jolly atmosphere, fresh, simple food (artichoke barigoule, sardines à l'escabèche, tartare, and lemon tart), and unbeatable prices. **C** 250-300 F. **M** 70 F (weekday lunch, Sat), 150 F.

Château de Roussan
2 km on N 99, route de Tarascon
90 92 11 63, fax 90 92 37 32
Closed Nov-Mar. 1 ste. 21 rms 360-750 F. Restaurant. Half-board 170 F. Air cond. Conf. Tennis. Golf. Garage pkg. V, AE, DC, MC.
A delightful eighteenth-century residence surrounded by a huge park dotted with rare trees, flower beds, and ponds. Large, attractively furnished guest rooms; bare-bones bathrooms. Excellent breakfasts.

Château des Alpilles
D 31 - 90 92 03 33, fax 90 92 45 17
Closed Jan 8-Mar 25, Nov 12-Dec 20. 4 stes 1,340-1,610 F. 15 rms 690-1,030 F. Restaurant. Air cond. Conf. Pool. Tennis. Golf. Valet pkg. Helipad. V, AE, DC, MC.
Serene and lovely, this early nineteenth-century château is surrounded by majestic trees. The rooms are huge and have been redecorated with impeccable taste. One of the most refined hotels in Provence. Sauna. Poolside grill in summer.

Domaine de Valmouriane
5 km on N 99 & D 27,
Petite route des Baux
90 92 44 62, fax 90 92 37 32
Open daily until 10pm. Priv rm: 12. Terrace dining. Air cond. Garage pkg. V, AE, DC, MC.
The new chef, Jean-Luc Robin, and an award-winning pastry chef offer classic cooking in a sunny dining room with a lovely terrace. Try the 260 F menu: fresh-tasting haddock and smoked salmon marinated with coriander and lemon, overcooked rack of Alpilles lamb, delicious apple and caramel tart. Fine wine from the estate. **C** 300-450 F. **M** 220 F (dinner), 105 F, 260 F, 330 F.

Domaine de Valmouriane
(See restaurant above)
Open year-round. 2 stes 1,160-1,550 F. 12 rms 490-1,310 F. Half-board 750-1,570 F. Air Cond. Heated pool. Tennis. Golf. Pkg. Helipad. V, AE, DC, MC.
This luxurious little hotel has spacious rooms (some with sun rooms and terraces), equipped with all modern amenities and decorated with rare attention to detail. Guests may enjoy billiards, tennis, archery, or practice their putting. Helipad.

Vallon de Valrugues
Chemin de Canto Cigalo
90 92 04 40, fax 90 92 44 01
Open daily until 9:30pm. Priv rm: 60. Garden dining. Air cond. No pets. Valet pkg. V, AE, DC, MC.
First discovered by our Guide last year, Joël Guillet won his third toque in record time. But he has now moved on to another enchanted southern setting (the Mas du Langoustier on the Ile de Porquerolles), and we cannot yet say whether his replacement, the young Gilles Blandin (who has impeccable credentials) will match his predecessor's three-toque level. In any case, this restaurant offers one of Provence's most beautiful terraces, shaded by parasol pines and overlooking a splendid valley. **C** 400-600 F. **M** 220 F (lunch), 290 F, 380 F, 460 F.

Vallon de Valrugues
(See restaurant above)
Open year-round. 18 stes 1,380-3,600 F. 35 rms 690-1,180 F. Half-board 840-1,210 F. Air cond. Conf. Heated pool. Tennis. Golf. Valet pkg. Helipad. V, AE, DC, MC.
Quiet, handsomely appointed, and graced with terraces overlooking olive groves or the Alpilles, the rooms here were recently enlarged and renovated (marble baths). One suite is like a country house, perched on the roof with a spectacular view and complete with a private pool and a kitchen. Leisure facilities include satellite TV, billiards, a sauna, Jacuzzi, and body-building equipment. Excellent breakfasts; irreproachable service.

And also...
Our selection of places for inexpensive, quick, or late-night meals, and smaller hotels.
L'Assiette de Marie (90 92 32 14 - 1, rue Jaune-Roux. Open until 10:30pm.): In the ancient heart of town, a friendly place with rustic decor offering simple regional specialties including great Corsican charcuterie (125-160 F).
Le Café du Lézard (90 92 59 66. Open until 10pm, 11pm in summer.): A chic hangout for small meals made from fine products, near the Nostradamus fountain (110-160 F).
Sette et Mezzo (90 92 59 27 - 34, bd Mirabeau. Open until 10pm.): The city's best pizzas, named in honor of Fellini films, attract a young and chic clientele (120-150 F).
Xa (90 92 41 23 - 24, bd Mirabeau.): Italian cooking in a friendly atmosphere (135-200 F).

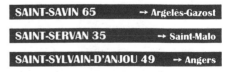

SAINT-SAVIN 65	→ Argelès-Gazost
SAINT-SERVAN 35	→ Saint-Malo
SAINT-SYLVAIN-D'ANJOU 49	→ Angers

Nice, the home port for visitors from the world over

Nice, cosmopolitan Nice. The second most-visited city in France offers visitors from the world over a wide range of irresistible attractions.

Nice can meet all your needs:
• **International airport**, just 7 minutes away from the city center.
• **10 000 hotel rooms**
• **2000 restaurants**
• **19 museums**
• and right in the heart of the city, there is the superbly equipped **Convention and Art Center**; not only a multi purpose complex for meetings and conventions, but a crossroad of culture.

But what really makes Nice so much more than any other tourist capital is its unique charm: nearly 8 km of beaches, a heavenly climate, a whole string of architectural gems, the famous flower market and a top-rated music scene: opera, philharmonic orchestra, festivals etc.

Nice has enchanted the world, now we're waiting to see you!

N I C E

Office du Tourisme et des Congrès
BP 79 06302 NICE - Cedex 04 - FRANCE
Tél. (33) 93 87 07 07 / Fax (33) 93 16 85 16

A real Mediterranean village

In the heart of Saint-Tropez, the Hotel Byblos offers the best of a Mediterranean Village, a Provencal way of life.

SAINT-TROPEZ

HOTEL BYBLOS

S^T TROPEZ

Membre des Palaces de la Côte d'Azur

The luxurious rooms and suites are individually decorated. The Lebanese lounge, the bars and the pool will become your favourite areas for relaxing. The restaurant "Les Arcades" will welcome you with the true flavour of the sunny Provencal cooking, before you enjoy Saint-Tropez by night at "Les Caves du Roy". The matchless quality of services will make your stay unforgettable.
For inquiry and reservations :
Tel. : 33/94 56 68 00 - Fax. : 33/94 56 68 01

A real palace in the French Alps

COURCHEVEL

At the foot of the largest expanse of ski slopes in the world, set in the very heart of the Alpin Garden of Courchevel, the Byblos des Neiges offers you a chance to rediscover the tradition of the great chalets of the past.

With an appetite whetted by the mountain air, enjoy the many culinary pleasures of the "L'Ecailler" restaurant with its sea-food platters and fish specialities, and a more traditional cuisine at "La Clairière" with its renowned buffets. After skiing, enjoy the swimming-pool and relax in the sauna, Turkish bath or hairstyling and beauty parlour. In the evening, enjoying your cocktail in front of a large wood fire, you will agree that such moments of exception bear the unique Byblos stamp. For inquiry and reservations :
Tel. : 33/ 79 00 98 00 - Fax. : 33/79 00 98 01

LE BYBLOS
DES NEIGES
COURCHEVEL
1850

Two of The Leading Hotels of the World

SAINT-SYLVESTRE-SUR-LOT 47
→ Villeneuve-sur-Lot

SAINT-SYMPHORIEN-LE-CHÂTEAU 28700
Paris 69 - Rambouillet 23 - Chartres 26   Eure-et-Loir

Château d'Esclimont
37 31 15 15, fax 37 31 57 91
Open daily until 9:30pm. Priv rm: 200. No pets. Valet pkg. V, AE.
"It is my pleasure" is the motto that La Rochefoucauld had sculpted above the entrance to this radiant sixteenth-century jewel. Our pleasure, under the high ceilings of the four comfortable dining rooms, is Didier Macouin's harmonious (but sometimes overly complicated) cuisine: canneloni of duck sweetbreads and foie gras, sea bream roasted with ginger and lemongrass, perfect gentian parfait. Superb wine list that will not be easy on your wallet. C 350-500 F. M 260 F (lunch exc Sun, wine incl), 320 F, 495 F.

Château d'Esclimont
(See restaurant above)
Open year-round. 6 stes 2,800 F. 47 rms 600-1,850 F. Conf. Heated pool. Tennis. Golf. Valet pkg. Helipad. V, AE.
The 47 rooms and 6 suites of this château are classic, comfortable, and handsomely situated amid 60 hectares of completely walled-in grounds. The site is at the bottom of a valley traversed by a river, near the road that connects Rambouillet and Chartres. Guests can play tennis, swim in the heated pool, and attend wintertime musical evenings. Perfect for a luxurious, romantic weekend, and only 45 minutes from Paris by car. There's even a helipad. Relais et Châteaux, of course.

SAINT-TROJAN-LES-BAINS 17
→ Oléron (Ile d')

SAINT-TROPEZ 83990
Paris 890 - Cannes 75 - Toulon 69 - Aix 120   Var

The Beaches
Generally open from Easter to October. Price: around 300 F.
Bora-Bora (94 97 19 75 - Plage de Pampelonne. Lunch only.): Same management and cooking as at La Mandarine hotel (a sure guarantee of quality) (200-250 F).
Club 55 (94 79 80 14 - Plage de Pampelonne. Lunch only.): Bring your tan for a warm welcome from Patrice de Colmont and some fresh-caught fish (200-350 F).
L'Épi-Plage (94 79 80 35 - Open until 10pm.): Two swimming pools, tennis courts, and a smart clientele for the good fish and meat grilled over a wood fire (95-260 F).
Liberty Plage (94 79 84 17 - Lunch only.): Admirably grilled fresh fish at this beach near the nudist colony.
Le Migon (94 79 83 68 - Bonne Terrasse, rte de Ramatuelle. Open until 11pm.): The trendiest beach, for wild nights of fun and frolic and good Provençal dishes cooked over a wood fire. Orchestra in the evenings (198-305 F).
Mooréa (94 97 18 17 - Route de Tahiti. Lunch

only.): A youthful atmosphere and good cooking, especially the seafood dishes.
Nioulargo (94 79 82 14 - Bd Patch. Dinner only.): Lovely beach, adequate cooking. Its sister restaurant, the Kai Largo, offers good Asian dishes (280-350 F).
Plage des Jumeaux (94 79 84 21 - Route de l'Épi. Lunch only, & dinner Jul-Aug.): The famous palm trees were a bit battered in a storm this year, but you can still enjoy the simple, pleasing food served on a terrace or in a wooden bungalow (150-220 F).
Tahiti Plage (94 97 18 02 - Le Pinet. Open until 10pm.): Once a showbiz hot-spot, the Tahiti still has good meat and local fish dishes (220-260 F).
Tropicana (94 79 83 96 - Plage de Pampelonne. Lunch only.): Right at the edge of Pampelonne near Camarat. Friendly atmosphere and tasty Provençal cooking.
La Voile Rouge (94 79 84 34 - Plage de Ramatuelle. Lunch only.): Very fashionable. Mamma Tomaselli prepares Italian-Provençal food at high prices (250 F and up).

12/20 L'Astragale
RN 98 - 94 97 48 98, fax 94 97 16 01
Closed Oct 15-May 15. Open until 10:30pm. Terrace dining. Air cond. Valet pkg. V, AE, DC, MC.
A clutch of rather overly decorated chalets (half Savoie, half Louisiana) surround a glorious pool. The Italian-Provençal cooking is served either in a wooden pavilion or around the pool. Sample pleasant dishes like beef carpaccio with basil and shavings of Parmesan, a risotto of tiny squid and baby morels, duck breast with sweet spices and a tomato tatin, and a tutti frutti gratin with almond-milk ice cream and almond jus. C 250-350 F. M 290 F (dinner).

L'Astragale
(See restaurant above)
Closed Oct 15-May 15. 34 rms 1,300-2,400 F. Rms for disabled. Half-board 380 F. Conf. Pool. Tennis. Valet pkg. V, AE, DC, MC.
Thirty luxurious rooms and suites set in beautiful grounds around the pool; the ones not on the ground floor have balconies. There's a private beach, with a restaurant.

La Bastide des Salins

Route des Salins
94 97 24 57, fax 94 54 89 03
Open year-round. 1 ste 1,700 F. 14 rms 590-970 F. Conf. Pool. Garage pkg. Helipad. V, AE, MC.
This is one of the most pleasant hotels in town. A fortified farmhouse built during the last century, it has huge, handsome rooms and superb grounds.

Bistrot des Lices

3, pl. des Lices
94 97 29 00, fax 94 97 76 39
Closed Jan-Feb. Open until 10:30pm. Priv rm: 35. Garden dining. Air cond. V, AE, MC.
Less crowded than the neighboring establishments, but equally lively: from the terrace, one may follow the action of hotly contested boules matches. Inside, the charming dining room with a view of walled garden is decorated with pretty turn-of-the-century knick-knacks and pictures, and populated with dressy, well-behaved patrons. The "Bistrot" title is a

417

misnomer; this is an elegant, high-class restaurant. Chef Laurent Tarridec offers sunny, inventive cooking with intense flavors: spelt risotto with tiny snails, spider-crab soup with tomatoes, grilled red tuna with raw vegetable anchoïade, lamb's foot barigoule, John Dory with aïoli (a delight), roast turbot with ratatouille, succulent shoulder of young rabbit in a tasty thyme jus, deliciously flavorful rack of Pyrenées lamb with an étouffée of vegetables, pork fillet and pig's foot in a casserole, or pressed farm-raised squab. For dessert, choose the dried-fruit galette with sabayon or the cherry gratin rather than the bland vanilla-licorice ice cream. Provençal's best wines are featured. In the adjoining "Boeuf sur la Place" bistrot, the chef offers meats and plats-du-jour at very reasonable prices. C 450-600 F. M 175 F (lunch), 255 F, 300 F, 360 F, 480 F.

10/20 Brasserie de la Renaissance
Pl. des Lices - 94 97 02 00
Closed Nov 20-Dec 10. Open until 10:30pm (1am in summer). Terrace dining. V, AE, DC, MC.
Jean de Colmont now owns this brasserie, which had fallen on hard times. Suddenly the terrace and dining room are filled with a who's who of locals and well heeled visitors, but the cooking is far less interesting than the clientele. C 220-350 F.

Byblos
Av. P.-Signac
94 56 68 00, fax 94 56 68 01
Closed mid Oct-mid Mar. Open until 11pm (11:30pm in seas). Priv rm: 130. Terrace dining. Air cond. Valet pkg. V, AE, DC, MC.
Philippe Audibert, formerly the assistant of the great Le Stanc at the Negresco in Nice, has taken over the kitchens of this establishment, which has long needed the services of a talented chef. His savory dishes redolent of Provençal sunshine are refreshingly down to earth: lamb's foot and fennel salad; ravioli stuffed with tomatoes, tiny fava beans, and Parmesan; asparagus risotto; royal sea bream with a leek coulis; grilled sea bass with an herby salad dressed with balsamic vinegar; duck in olive jus; croustillant de caramelized pears; and nougat glacé all reflect a sure talent. There's a lovely garden-terrace overlooking the pool. C 350-600 F. M 170 F (weekday lunch exc Jul-Aug), 280 F, 380 F (dinner).

Byblos
(See restaurant above)
Closed mid Oct-mid Mar. 49 stes 2,040-4,800 F. 58 rms 700-2,380 F. Restaurant. Air cond. Conf. Heated pool. Golf. Valet pkg. V, AE, DC, MC.
Each year, some of the hotel's occasionally cramped rooms and more spacious suites are redecorated. The layout is so skillful that customers are not bothered by the bustling attendance of Saint-Tropez's gilded set. Extremely luxurious appointments, magnificent pool.

Les Capucines
Domaine du Treizain
94 97 70 05, fax 94 97 55 85
Closed Oct 15-Mar 31. 24 rms 400-990 F. Air cond. Heated pool. Golf. Garage pkg. V, AE, DC, MC.
This group of pretty Provençal buildings is two kilometers from town, lost among pine trees near the sea (100 meters away). Jacuzzi. Snack bar and modest meals.

Château de la Messardière
Route de Tahiti
94 56 76 00, fax 94 56 76 01
Closed Oct 20-Mar. Open until 10:30pm. Terrace dining. Air cond. Valet pkg. V, AE, DC, MC.
Shipwrecked on the shoals of ambition, this curious, enormous turn-of-the-century villa has now been salvaged and made seaworthy again. If the food served in the chintz-decked dining room (or on the terrace with a splendid view of the Bay of Pampelonne) is any indication, the Château will be lovelier the second time around. Jean-Louis Vosgien, late of Mougins, proposes an interesting, eclectic menu showing the influences of Provence, Italy, and Southeast Asia (where the chef roams each winter). Try his saffrony shellfish risotto, shrimp soup seasoned with lemongrass, beef rouleaux with spices, sea bream with bouillabaisse sauce, red mullet with artichokes, squab with gingery sweet-sour sauce, and spiced orange soup. Fine choice of Provençal wines at a wide range of prices. Chic clientele. C 350-600 F. M 210 F, 240 F, 310 F, 420 F.

Château de la Messardière
(See restaurant above)
Closed Oct 20-Mar. 22 stes 2,500-4,000 F. 69 rms 1,000-2,500 F. Half-board 350 F. Air cond. Conf. Heated pool. Golf. Helipad. V, AE, DC, MC.
Despite vast sums already spent on the place, more buckets of money were needed to bring guest rooms and terraces up to par. Irreprochable comfort now reigns in this hotel set in eight hectares of grounds, with awe-inspiring views of the bays of Saint-Tropez and Pampelonne. The suites are vast; the rooms less so, but they're much cheaper. Magnificent pool. Prices have been lowered; and the conference facilities are just waiting to be filled.

Ermitage
Av. P.-Signac
94 97 52 33, fax 94 97 10 43
Open year-round. 28 rms 290-990 F. Valet pkg. V, AE, DC, MC.
Annie Bolloré has refurbished the decor, renovated several rooms, and restored the garden of this white 1930s villa on the Place de Lices at the foot of the citadel, with a sweeping view of old Saint-Tropez. The smallish rooms are filled with faithful return guests.

12/20 Chez Fuchs
7, rue des Commerçants
94 97 01 25, fax 94 97 81 82
Closed Tue, Nov 15-Dec 15. Open until 11:30pm. Air cond. V, AE, MC.
The cigar cellar gives this restaurant a chic atmosphere that the locals like a lot. The simple regional dishes include ravioli, beef stew, fresh fish, and generous cuts of meat. C 200-300 F.

12/20 Joseph
Rue Cepoun-San-Martin
94 97 03 90, fax 94 97 77 50
Open daily until midnight. Priv rm: 75. Terrace dining. Air cond. V, AE, MC.
The legendary Fifine has gone, leaving young Joseph to take her place. The once-modest bistrot is now a pretty, fashionable eatery filled until late at night with gilded youths and lasses. The food?

Eclectic, from mozzarella à l'osso bucco to bouil-labaisse tartare. C 250-400 F. M 168 F, 198 F, 255 F.

 Le Levant
Route des Salins
94 97 33 33, fax 94 97 76 13
Closed Oct 15-Mar 15. 28 rms 395-850 F. Restaurant. Air cond. Pool. Golf. Pkg. V, AE, DC, MC.
Scattered around the garden are a few small bungalows with charming, quiet, thoroughly remodeled rooms. Direct access to the sea.

La Maison Blanche
Pl. des Lices
94 97 52 66, fax 94 97 89 23
Open year-round. 1 ste 1,200-1,800 F. 7 rms 500-1,800 F. Restaurant. Air cond. Golf. Valet pkg. V, AE, DC, MC.
This turn-of-the-century residence in the center of town is flanked by a tiny garden. Pleasant, posh decor and atmosphere, antique furniture. Very attentive service. And now, there's a lovely summer bar set up in the garden.

La Mandarine
Route de Tahiti - 94 79 06 66
Closed mid Oct-end Mar. Open until 10:30pm. Terrace dining. Air cond. Heated pool. Valet pkg. V, AE, DC, MC.
Chirping birds and a peaceful country setting are part of the attraction of this modern, Provençal hotel-restaurant just three minutes from central Saint-Tropez. Of an evening, the terrace fills with a quiet clientele who appreciate the refined, authentic cooking: John Dory cooked in olive oil and lemon, pork sautéed with fennel, and rack of lamb in mustard sauce. C 250-350 F. M 180 F, 240 F.

La Mandarine
(See restaurant above)
Closed mid Oct-end Mar. 4 stes 2,000-2,800 F. 38 rms 850-1,800 F. Half-board 695-1,150 F. Air cond. Heated pool. Golf. Valet pkg. V, AE, DC, MC.
The accommodation consists of several pink neo-Provençal bungalows scattered around five acres of idyllic grounds. Luxurious rooms, impeccably tended, with views of vineyards and mountains. Pool on the premises; the hotel's private beach is Bora-Bora, at nearby Pampelonne.

L'Olivier ✪
Route des Carles, 1 km
94 97 58 16, fax 94 97 21 71
Closed Tue lunch & Mon off-seas, Jan 2-Feb 10. Open until 10:30pm. Garden dining. Valet pkg. V, AE, DC, MC.
Just minutes away from the Place des Lices you find yourself among verdant fields and vineyards, in a lush garden with a swimming pool surrounded by palm, olive, and fig trees. This is the realm of Francis Cardaillac, a Gascon by birth, whose sun-dappled, robustly flavored cooking often has a touch of the Southwest. Sample his fresh cod with aromatic herbs and spices, langoustines with spices and orange-scented chestnut-flour panisses, marinated fresh anchovies with artichoke barigoule and herb-filled fresh goat cheese, croustillant of squab in a vegetable coating, and a rice blancmange with Mascerpone and caramelized puff pastry. Some flavor combinations seem a bit confused, but everything is generally very appetizing. The cel-

lar is most appealing; the stylish service is excellent. C 280-600 F. M 210 F, 240 F, 270 F, 300 F, 340 F.

Bastide de Saint-Tropez
(See restaurant above)
Closed Jan 2-Feb 3. 12 stes 1,550-3,300 F. 14 rms 900-1,900 F. Rms for disabled. Half-board 1,220-2,220 F. Heated pool. Golf. Valet pkg. V, AE, DC, MC.
The rooms—some are on the small side— are housed in three charming buildings in a garden around the lovely pool. The decor is eclectic, but comfort is guaranteed.

11/20 La Ponche
Port des Pêcheurs, 3, rue des Remparts
94 97 02 53, fax 94 97 78 61
Closed Oct 20-end Mar. Open until midnight. Terrace dining. Air cond. Valet pkg. V, AE, DC, MC.
A cosmopolitan crowd haunts La Ponche's terrace overlooking the old fishing port, to sample simple Provençal cuisine prepared with care. C 240-380 F. M 115 F (lunch), 195 F, 240 F.

La Ponche
(See restaurant above)
Closed end Oct-Apr 1. 1 ste 1,600-2,100 F. 17 rms 750 1,350 F. Half-board 60 F. Air cond. Conf. Valet pkg. V, AE, MC.
Charming, remodeled, well equipped rooms with sea views. You'll find elegant decor and excellent comfort.

La Ramade
Rue du Temple - 94 97 00 15
Closed Wed (exc Jul-Aug), Nov-beg Apr. Open until 11pm. Garden dining. V, MC.
You can't fool Pierrot Aurelly, a former fisherman, about the freshness of the day's catch. And he loves to show you his fish—glistening with olive oil and stuffed with herbs and pine-nuts— before he grills them over vine-cuttings. Don't miss the fabulous bouillabaisse (on Thursdays and Sundays, and preferably if you order ahead) and superb pistou. Minimal wine list; few desserts. C 280-380 F.

Résidence de la Pinède
Plage de la Bouillabaisse
94 97 04 21, fax 94 97 73 64
Closed Oct 15-Mar 31. Open until 10:30pm. Terrace dining. Air cond. Valet pkg. V, AE, DC, MC.
The recession seems to have passed over the Résidence de la Pinède. Indeed, it's not hard to see why. The Riviera setting is out of this world, but even more vital to the hotel's success are the unflagging efforts of owner Jean-Claude Delion, who has turned a once somnolent *fin-de-siècle* villa into a divinely luxurious establishment. His latest crop of improvements includes renovated guest rooms, enlarged kitchens, a redecorated dining room, and a fabulous new swimming pool just above the beach.
In Hervé Quesnel, late of the Hôtel Crillon in Paris, Delion has found a thoughtful, expert chef. He is singularly equipped to run a restaurant that caters mainly for hotel guests, as well as a growing number of Tropéziens drawn by the Pinède's quiet, discreet luxury. Quesnel's cuisine brims over with vibrant local color. Discover it in his sauté of Tuscan scampi with creamed beans, langoustine minestrone with basil, red mullet

419

with fennel purée, pickerel with cuttlefish, extremely tasty veal chops with a parsley jus, and a choice of fabulous desserts. Welcome, service, and wines are all classy indeed, as are the chic clientele and spectacular sunsets from the terrace of this costly oasis. C 350-750 F. M 250 F, 350 F, 400 F, 480 F.

 Résidence de la Pinède
(See restaurant above)
Closed Oct 15-Mar. 5 stes 2,150-6,810 F. 37 rms 525-3,300 F. Rms for disabled. Half-board 260-405 F. Air cond. Conf. Heated pool. Golf. Valet pkg. Helipad. V, AE, DC, MC.

A screen of greenery keeps road noise out, and the Bay of Saint-Tropez spreads seductively below (direct access to the beach). Umbrella pines shade the huge, extremely comfortable rooms, all of which were recently remodeled and redecorated. Kidney-shaped swimming pool, private beach, and spectacular views from the balconies of each room and suite overlooking the sea. Relais et Châteaux.

Résidence des Lices
Av. A.-Grangeon
94 97 28 28, fax 94 97 59 52
Closed Jan 2-Apr 1, Nov 1-Dec 25. 41 rms 500-1,500 F. Air cond. Heated pool. Pkg. V, AE, MC.

Just steps away from the Place des Lices, an impeccably kept hotel with quiet rooms overlooking the pool and the garden.

 La Salle à Manger
38, rue Clemenceau
94 97 85 20, fax 94 97 85 60
Dinner only. Closed Oct 15-Mar 25. Open until 12:30am. Air cond. Pkg. V, AE.

Christophe Leroy has opened an intimate dining room—there's room for just fifteen guests—one floor up from his highly successful Table du Marché (see below). La Salle à Manger is a place for friends to feast by candlelight on the costly, elaborate dishes Leroy does so well, but which he cannot prepare for the numbers served in his larger establishment below.
Each night brings a new 540 F set menu, which Leroy himself describes in detail, as well as several à la carte dishes. Among them you'll find his renowned iced potato and truffle soup, gambas with "petals" of garlic, spit-roasted John Dory, or an assiette of milk-fed lamb. Pull the cork on a grand or modest bottle from the discriminating cellar, and you've got yourself a rare treat—one we reckon is well worth three toques! C 650-800 F. M 540 F.

Hôtel Sube
On the harbor
94 97 30 04, fax 94 54 89 08
Open year-round. 31 rms 390-1,500 F. Air cond. Conf. Golf. Valet pkg. V, AE, DC, MC.

Behind the recently renovated rust-colored façade are some expensive, though pleasant little rooms with views of Saint-Tropez's quays, yachts, and crowds.

La Table du Marché
38, rue Clemenceau - 94 97 85 20
Open daily until 12:30am. Priv rm: 25. Air cond. Pkg. V, AE, DC, MC.

Christophe Leroy knows what it takes to create a convivial, relaxed ambience (shelves lined with bottles and jars give this simple, winsome dining room the look of a gourmet grocery), and there's a view of the kitchen brigade in action, as well as of diners whose faces you may have seen before on the screen. On offer are tasty, substantial dishes made with splendid ingredients, but at prices that won't break the bank. Celebrities and unknowns alike tuck cheerfully into the satisfying fresh tagliatelle with gambas, tomato tart, parmentier de canard et foie gras, spit-roasted Bresse chicken, or lamb sauté with ratatouille, followed by superb chocolate cake. There's a pleasant lunch set menu, too. C 220-300 F. M 115 F.

 La Tartane
Route de la plage des Salins
94 97 21 23, fax 94 97 09 16
Closed Oct 25-Mar 25 (exc at Christmas & New-Year's day). 12 rms 350-890 F. Air cond. Heated pool. Garage pkg. V, AE, MC.

La Tartane's fourteen handsome bungalows, nestled in a verdant setting form a sort of hamlet, with superb, well-equipped rooms and comfortable terraces. The beach is 800 meters away.

 Lou Troupelen
Chemin des Vendanges
94 97 44 88, fax 94 97 41 76
Closed Nov-Apr 6. 45 rms 320-490 F. No pets. Pkg. V, AE, DC, MC.

These two roomy neo-Provençal buildings are located between the shore and the town center. Lodgings are comfortable and pleasantly decorated, with attractive views. Breakfast is served in the garden.

 Le Yaca
1, bd d'Aumale
94 97 11 79, fax 94 97 58 50
Closed Oct 12-Apr 15. 1 ste 2,500-3,300 F. 22 rms 900-2,285 F. Restaurant. Air cond. Heated pool. Golf. Valet pkg. V, AE, DC, MC.

In the heart of Saint-Tropez, Le Yaca is an elegant, expensive hotel with a score or so of rooms. The nicest are on the upper floors. There's also a lovely enclosed garden.

And also...
Our selection of places for inexpensive, quick, or late-night meals, and smaller hotels.
Bar à Vins (94 97 46 10 - 13, rue des Féniers.): Wine by the glass, and a convivial atmosphere in the *salle de billard*. Tanned guests sample pleasant dishes at marble tables (180-250 F).
La Barlière (94 97 41 24 - Route du Pinet. 14 rms 450-700 F.): A quiet hotel surrounded by greenery, with well cared for rooms.
Café des Arts (94 97 02 25 - Pl. des Lices. Open until 11pm.): If you don't mind the crush, you can enjoy robust dishes while the trendy habitués watch the world go by (195 F wine incl).
Le Girelier (94 97 03 87 - On the harbor. Open until 11pm.): The fish is fresh and perfectly grilled in this simple place with a view of the yachts of visiting millionaires (300-450 F).
Lou Revelen (94 97 06 34 - 4, rue des Remparts.): Perfectly low set meals at particularly good (for Saint-Tropez) prices (150-200 F).

See also: Cogolin, Gassin, Grimaud, Port-Grimaud, Ramatuelle

SAINT-VAAST-LA-HOUGUE 50550
Paris 350 - Cherbourg 31 - Barfleur 13 - Valognes 17　　*Manche*

Fuchsias ❊
13
18, rue du Mal-Foch
33 54 42 26, fax 33 43 46 79
Closed Mon (Oct-mid May), Tue lunch (Nov-Mar), Jan 8-Feb 23. Open until 9:15pm (9:45pm in summer). Terrace dining. Hotel: 1 ste 550 F. 32 rms 140-395 F. Half-board 220-335 F. V, AE, DC, MC.
The fishing port is a stone's throw away from this pleasant establishment with a thatched-roof porch and a courtyard dripping with fuschias. Enjoy the fish soup with croûtons, country terrine with hazlenuts, fillet of cod with celery cream, and homemade sherbets and ice creams. Good cellar; warm welcome. **C** 220-300 F. **M** 72 F (weekdays), 115 F, 155 F, 185 F, 235 F.

SAINT-VALERY-EN-CAUX 76460
Paris 198 - Rouen 59 - Dieppe 32 - Fécamp 32　　*Seine-Mar.*

■ In Ingouville 76460　　*3 km SW*

Les Hêtres
16
Le Bourg, rue des Fleurs
35 57 09 30, fax 35 57 09 31
Closed Mon dinner, Tue, Jan 22-Feb 3, Sep 5-13. Open until 10pm. Priv rm: 20. Terrace dining. Garage pkg. V, MC.
We knew and liked the Warin-Liberge duo when they worked in Rouen. Now here they are, deep in the Normandy countryside, still as professional as can be, but far happier and more relaxed. Éric Liberge captains the stylish, elegant staff, while in the kitchen Bernard Warin polishes his classically grounded yet imaginative repertoire. His sauces and gelatins have perfect consistency and exquisite flavor, his meats and fish are perfectly cooked, and his tiny vegetables tasty and crisp. We savored his asparagus feuilleté with chervil cream, sea bream with tomato butter served with an eggplant caviar whipped up with olive oil, turbot with foie gras and fried onions, and veal sweetbreads with sea scallops. For dessert, there's a lovely berry soup flavored with orange-flower water. Splendid cellar with plenty of top vintages, but a goodly stock of reasonable bottles too. **C** 300-370 F. **M** 160 F, 230 F, 330 F.

SAINT-VALLIER 26240
Paris 531 - Annonay 21 - St-Etienne 61 - Tournon 15　　*Drôme*

Albert Lecomte
15
116, av. J.-Jaurès
75 23 01 12, fax 75 23 38 82
Closed Sun lunch, Mon, Feb school hols, Aug 9-23. Open until 9:30pm. Priv rm: 24. Air cond. Hotel: 10 rms 270-380 F. Conf. Golf. Pkg. V, AE, DC.
Chef Albert Lecomte is a whiz at sniffing out the best ingredients and inventing ways to vary their intrinsic flavors. He won our admiration this year with his croustillant of veal sweetbreads with gambas, and "burned" tuna with asparagus. Truffles often appear on the menu in season. Efficient yet relaxed staff; enticing cellar with many regional offerings. **C** 350-450 F. **M** 150 F, 220 F, 270 F, 320 F, 390 F.

ST-VINCENT-STERLANGES 85110
Paris 408 - La Roche-sur-Yon 31 - Nantes 66　　*Vendée*

Lionel Guilbaud ❊
16
51 40 23 17, fax 51 40 26 46
Closed Sun dinner (off-seas), Mon (exc lunch in seas). Open until 9:30pm. Priv rm: 14. Terrace dining. Pool. Pkg. V, AE, DC, MC.
Every dish is lovely to look at, every ingredient is seasonal, local, and fresh as can be: that, in a nutshell, is why we're so fond of Lionel Guilbaud's cuisine, and the plus is that it's served in a lovely Vendée house that just celebrated its bicentennial. Guilbaud is a culinary patriot. His potatoes come from Noirmoutier, his mussels from Aiguillon Bay, his sardines from Les Sables d'Olonne, his poultry (such as the ducks for his canard au sang) from Challans. Settle down in the warm, rustic dining room to sample his tasty dishes on a menu that changes with the seasons: printanière of vegetables, cabbage "gâteau", wild mushrooms, and Jerusalem artichokes are among the garnishes you'll find, depending on the time of year. In winter, calf's head, poule au pot, braise ham, roast duck, and other homey dishes make an appearance. The discerningly stocked cellar holds home-grown vintages (Mareuil, Pissotte) and some elegant bottles from the Loire. And you can count on the services of an affable maître d', who oversees the diligent staff. Special dishes can be ordered 72 hours in advance for a minimum of four people. **C** 330-420 F. **M** 380 F (exc weekdays), 115 F (weekdays, wine incl), 295 F (wine incl), 170 F.

SAINTE-ADRESSE 76　　→ Havre (Le)

SAINTE-ANNE-D'AURAY 56　　→ Auray

SAINTE-ANNE-LA-PALUD 29127
Paris 569 - Quimper 25 - Douamenez 16　　*Finistère*

La Plage ❊
16
98 92 50 12, fax 98 92 56 54
Closed Oct 15-Mar. Open until 9pm. Priv rm: 40. Air cond. Heated pool. No pets. Pkg. V, AE, DC, MC.
Follow the gorse bushes past the last chapel, all the way down to where the land ends and the Atlantic crashes against the cliffs of Finistère. There you'll discover Jean-Pierre Gloanec's spirited regional cooking, a marvelous marriage of Armor (sea, in Breton) and Argoat (land) that, this year, seemed to show even more inventiveness. Sample his squab with langoustines, or the salamandre of mackerel en cotriade with pig's foot crépinette, a rustic dish with real style. Or the spider-crab tarama seasoned with coriander, and superbly flavorful and delicate red mullet in an olive oil bouillon. All the ingredients are superb and treated with care and finesse. Splendid, accessibly priced cellar with many half bottles at lower prices this year; bravo! Warm hospitality and efficient, dedicated service. **C** 340-380 F. **M** 430 F (Sun lunch), 190 F, 330 F.

La Plage

(See restaurant above)
Closed Oct 15-Mar. 4 stes 980-1,200 F. 26 rms 450-980 F. Half-board 580-800 F. Conf. Heated pool. Tennis. Pkg. Helipad. V, AE, DC, MC.

All the rooms of this Relais et Châteaux hotel are sunny and spacious. The delicious breakfasts include fresh fruit and wonderful pain au chocolat. Excellent service; charming welcome. Fine collection of paintings by Mathurin Méheust and the Pont Aven school.

SAINTE-LIVRADE 31	→ Toulouse

SAINTE-MARIE-DE-RÉ 17	→ Ré (Ile de)

SAINTE-MARINE 29	→ Benodet

SAINTE-MAXIME	83120

Paris 880 - Toulon 63 - St-Raphaël 23 - Cannes 61 - Aix 122   Var

Amiral

On the harbor - 94 43 99 36
Closed nov 15-30. Open until 10pm (11pm in summer). Priv rm: 30. Terrace dining. V, AE, MC.
At this pleasant restaurant overlooking the yacht basin, you can choose the dishes on the set menus (cod tian with leeks, steamed sea bass, casserole-roasted veal shanks, lamb blanquette, craquelin au pralin or chocolate desserts) or go à la carte: bourride, bouillabaisse, and a fine choice of grilled fish. But the artichoke barigoule isn't really barigoule. C 300-350 F. M 100 F (weekday lunch, Sat), 160 F, 250 F.

Calidianus
Bd J.-Moulin
94 96 23 21, fax 94 49 12 10
Open year-round. 33 rms 290-930 F. Restaurant. Air cond. Conf. Pool. Tennis. Golf. Pkg. V, AE, MC.
Nestled in leafy grounds near the sea, the Calidianus comprises a group of small buildings in the local style. The rooms are spacious and well furnished; most have balconies or terraces giving onto the swimming pool. All have minibars.

La Gruppi
Av. du Gal-de-Gaulle - 94 96 03 61
Closed Mon. Open until 9:30pm (11:30pm in summer). Terrace dining. Air cond. V, AE, MC.
Skip the more complicated dishes and go straight for those made with fish fresh from the morning's catch. They're delicious and cooked with care. C 250-450 F. M 128 F, 188 F, 240 F.

Hostellerie de la Belle Aurore
4, bd J.-Moulin
94 96 02 45, fax 94 96 63 87
Closed end Sep-Mar 25. Terrace dining. Air cond. Garage pkg. V, AE, DC, MC.
Beyond the dining room spreads a magnificent view of the bay, with the village of Saint-Tropez in the distance. After a charming welcome, you can sit down to a memorable meal of Lionel Maucler's Provençal-inspired cuisine. Sample his mashed potatoes with truffles and watercress, langoustines with a croquant of celery and cucumber, turbot with cabbage and cumin sauce, a fish matelote paired with polenta, lamb fillet with garlic purée, vanilla crème brûlée, or a brousse à l'ancienne au chocolat noir. C 300-450 F. M 180 F (weekday lunch), 235 F, 380 F.

Hostellerie de la Belle Aurore
(See restaurant above)
Closed Nov 10-Dec 20, Jan 5-Feb. 1 ste 1,300-2,000 F. 16 rms 600-1,800 F. Half-board 700-1,300 F. Air cond. Pool. Golf. Pkg. V, AE, DC, MC.
Dawn's rosy fingers reach across the bay into the rooms of this Riviera inn perched above the sea. Provençal-style furniture, handsome fabrics, cane chairs. Swimming pool with diving board.

Hostellerie La Croisette

2, bd des Romarins - 94 96 17 75
Dinner only (exc hols). Closed Nov-Feb. Open until 11pm. Garden dining. Hotel: 17 rms 400-650 F. Half-board 450-600 F. Conf. Pkg. V, AE, MC.
Walk a few steps from the beach to find this likeable little spot, a pink villa with blue shutters: smiles and warm greetings abound and the food is forthright and fresh as can be. We like the 150 F menu: duck tourte with olives, lemony gambas fricassée, and a tarte grande-mère, all prepared by capable chef Bruno Bluntzer. C 200-300 F. M 150 F, 195 F, 250 F (Sun, weekday & Sat dinner), 120 F (weekday dinner).

Hôtel de la Poste
7, bd F.-Mistral
94 96 18 33, fax 94 96 41 68
Closed Oct 25-May 15. 24 rms 300-620 F. Pool. V, AE, DC, MC.
Just 100 meters from the harbor, in the center of town, this outstanding modern hotel is elegant and bright, with handsome rooms (some connecting, for families). Breakfast is served on the poolside terrace.

Le Relais de Provence
Golfe de Sainte-Maxime
94 56 66 66, fax 94 56 66 00
Closings not available. Open until 10pm. No pets. V, AE, DC, MC.
Luckily you can't see the grandiose façade of the Golf Plaza hotel from the dining room here, but you do note that the coast is mostly covered with buildings these days. There's a nice view of the sea to compensate, and Provençal dishes by a chef who should try to simplify a bit more. C 350 F. M 195 F (dinner).

Golf Plaza
(See restaurant above)
Open year-round. 13 stes 1,350-2,000 F. 98 rms 625-1,200 F. Rms for disabled. Half-board 723-1,395 F. Air cond. Conf. Heated pool. Tennis. Golf. Valet pkg. Helipad. V, AE, DC.
Opened in December 1992, the hotel with its garish façade, a developer's dream, dominates the Sainte-Maxime golf course. The attractive rooms are nicely equipped, with south-facing terraces that look out onto the Bay of Saint-Tropez. Lots of sporting facilities: eight tennis courts, fitness club, private beach. Panoramic restaurant.

12/20 Le Sarrazin
7, pl. Colbert - 94 96 10 84
Closed dinner in Jul-Aug, Wed lunch, Tue, Jan 4-Feb 4. Open until 10pm. Terrace dining. V, MC.
Foie gras in raspberry vinegar, pan-roasted gambas, and tournedos with cèpes are on offer in a rustic dining room. C 180-280 F. M 110 F, 220 F.

SAINTE-SABINE 21 → **Pouilly-en-Auxois**

SAINTES 17100

Paris 465 - Bordeaux 118 - Royan 37 Charente-M.

 Relais du Bois Saint-Georges
1.5 km W on D 137,
rue de Royan-Cours Genêt
46 93 50 99, fax 46 93 34 93
Open daily until 9:30pm. Priv rm: 160. Garden dining. Valet pkg. V, MC.
Philippe Gault's cuisine is laudably modest: he respects his raw materials and works hard on his sauces (so many chefs hereabouts rely on butter as a smokescreen). Sample his gelée of langoustines and foie gras with baby vegetables, Limousin beef with beef marrow confit, chartreuse of tiny snails, and a caprice à l'angelique with caramel sauce for dessert. Classic cellar; professional welcome. C 180-400 F. M 250 F, 480 F (wine incl), 170 F.

 Relais du Bois Saint-Georges ▲♣
(See restaurant above)
Open year-round. 3 stes 950-1,500 F. 30 rms 360-980 F. Rms for disabled. Air cond. Conf. Heated pool. Tennis. Golf. Valet pkg. Helipad. V, MC.
Tucked away in a vast estate on the edge of Saintes, the Relais is scented by the sweet smell of century-old magnolia trees. The setting is peaceful, the hotel elegantly decorated, and the spacious rooms fetchingly finished with modern touches. Guests enjoy a heated, covered pool and gracious hospitality. Generous breakfasts (don't forget to keep any leftover bread to feed the ducks!).

STES-MARIES-DE-LA-MER (LES) 13460

Paris 777 - Marseille 129 - Nîmes 53 - Arles 38 B./Rhône

L'Estelle
4 km on D 38, route du Petit-Rhône
90 97 89 01, fax 90 97 96 84
Closed Nov 5-Dec 20, Jan 6-Mar 25. 17 rms 420-580 F. Restaurant. Pool. Tennis. Pkg. V, AE, DC, MC.
Set on the edge of the Camargue marshes on the site of an old farmhouse, these pretty bungalows done up in regional style boast private terraces and fine appointments. Splendid pool with a waterfall. Horseback riding.

L'Étrier Camarguais ▲♣
2 km N on N 570,
chemin bas des Launes
90 97 81 14, fax 90 97 88 11
Closings not available. 27 rms 540 F. Restaurant. Half-board 660 F. Conf. Tennis. Pkg. V, AE, DC, MC.
A group of small houses in a verdant setting outside Saintes-Maries. The nicely furnished rooms are spacious and decorated in bold colors. All have fine terraces opening onto a garden.

Mas de la Fouque ▲♣
Route d'Aigues-Mortes, 4 km
90 97 81 02, fax 90 97 96 84
Closed Nov 5-Dec 20. 2 stes 2,150 F. 13 rms 1,340-2,000 F. Restaurant. Half-board 965-1,295 F. Heated pool. Tennis. Golf. Pkg. Helipad. V, AE, DC, MC.
Enjoy your breakfast on a sheltered poolside patio or a terrace facing the Étang des Launes.

The rooms have original, elegant decor and dreamy bathrooms. Smiling service and welcome. Leisure pursuits include golf (on a practice green), shooting, and riding on the large estate.

Lou Mas du Juge ♦♥
D 85, quartier Pin-Fourcat
66 73 51 45, fax 66 73 51 42
Open by reserv only. Open until 9pm. Priv rm: 200. Air cond. Hotel: 7 rms 750-800 F. Conf. No pets. Pkg. No cards.
Renée Granier's set menus attract hearty eaters, with such robust offerings as tourtes stuffed with meat or cheese, fish grilled over a wood fire, and game dishes. You'll like the charming welcome and the convivial atmosphere and picturesque decor of this old Camargue farmhouse. M 300 F, 350 F (wine incl).

Mas du Tadorne
3 km N on N 570, Chemin Bas
90 97 93 11, fax 90 97 71 04
Closed Jan 7-Mar 15. 4 stes 1,100-1,300 F. 11 rms 650-1,000 F. Rms for disabled. Restaurant. Half-board 800-900 F. Air cond. Conf. Pool. Garage pkg. Helipad. V, AE, DC.
The rooms are on the small side, but are refined and charming, with balconies overlooking the garden and pool. Contemporary amenities, including VCRs.

SALLANCHES 74700

Paris 590 - Megève 13 - Chamonix 28 - Annecy 75 H.-Savoie

 Michel Perrin
50 58 06 15, fax 50 58 48 70
Closed Sun dinner. Open until 9:15pm. Priv rm: 25. Terrace dining. No pets. Hotel: 18 rms 320-480 F. Half-board 380-440 F. Conf. Pkg. V, AE, DC.
Michel Perrin offers traditional yet amazingly light cooking in the dining room of a large chalet, where his charming daughter provides a warm welcome and supervises the excellent service. Try the cassoulette of snails with fresh herbs and a garlic cream, slices of foie gras in a simple jus and "breaded" with honey cake, and Bresse chicken with Champagne butter. The large, bright dining room is out of bounds to smokers, who can repair to a small fumoir for a fix. C 290-350 F. M 290 F (wine incl), 185 F, 285 F.

SALON-DE-PROVENCE 13300

Paris 730 - Marseille 55 - Avignon 46 - Nîmes 71 B./Rhône

 Abbaye de Sainte-Croix ♦♥
3 km NE on D 16, route du Val-de-Cuech
90 56 24 55, fax 90 56 31 12
Closed Mon lunch (exc hols), Nov-Mar 10. Open until 9:30pm. Priv rm: 150. Terrace dining. Pool. No pets. Pkg. V, AE, DC.
An ancient abbey in a spectacular setting, with a lovely terrace shaded by mulberry trees. Pascal Morel, who trained under Roger Vergé and Georges Blanc, heads the Abbaye's kitchen, and his dishes display more charm and imagination all the time. This year he earned our admiration with his original saffron-scented flan of green asparagus, fava beans, and sea snails; a gâteau of zucchini and salmon with virgin olive oil and grated truffles (superb ingredients and a tasty marinade); and a pleasingly simple chicken breast with barigoule artichokes, mushrooms, and crisp-cooked baby vegetables. Delicious

423

warm apple tart. Our only quibble: the bread was stale. Attentive, professional service; fine wine list at reasonable prices. **C** 300-500 F. **M** 190 F (lunch exc Sun), 250 F (Sun lunch), 375 F, 400 F.

L'Abbaye de Sainte-Croix

(See restaurant above)

Closed Nov-Mar 10 (exc Nov-Dec 15 & Mar 1-10 for groups). 5 stes 1,290-2,030 F. 19 rms 585-1,145 F. Half-board 1,055-1,615 F. Conf. Pool. Tennis. Golf. Pkg. Helipad. V, AE, DC.

The modern additions to this ancient abbey are remarkably faithful to the original. The rooms are furnished with fine antiques, and offer eye-popping views. Leisure pursuits include riding and swimming. Relais et Châteaux.

11/20 Domaine Roquerousse

RN 538 - 90 59 50 11, fax 90 59 53 75

Closed Dec 24-25. Open until 9pm (10pm in summer). Priv rm: 90. Terrace dining. **Hotel:** 30 rms 235-400 F. Half-board 280-375 F. Air cond. Conf. Pool. Tennis. Pkg. V, AE, DC, MC.

Meat, meat, and more meat—all of it tender and tasty—makes this old bastide a carnivore's paradise (although fish also appears on the menu). At weekends, tourists turn up to hunt on the 550-hectare estate, then retire here for a relaxed meal. **C** 200-300 F. **M** 75 F (weekdays), 115 F, 165 F.

Francis Robin

Le Mas du Soleil
Le Pilon-Blanc, 38, chemin St-Côme
90 56 06 53, fax 90 56 21 52

Closed Sun dinner, Mon. Open until 9:30pm. Priv rm: 35. Garden dining. Air cond. Pkg. V, AE, MC.

Hard times have brought out Francis Robin's fighting spirit! He's doing his utmost to make his charming, elegant restaurant a mecca for gourmets. And he's succeeding, note his 160 F menu: scorpion fish mousse with grelette sauce, lamb navarin with green cabbage and sweet red peppers, a selection of cheeses, and a choice of fine desserts. Tempting selection of regional wines. Professional welcome. **C** 350-480 F. **M** 160 F, 190 F, 250 F, 380 F.

Le Mas du Soleil

(See restaurant above)

Open year-round. 1 ste 850-1,000 F. 9 rms 480-850 F. Half-board 600-850 F. Air cond. Conf. Pool. Golf. Pkg. V, AE, MC.

Though not far from the town center, these new, very comfortable and charming rooms have a distinctly rural feel, owing to the large, shady garden. Guests may expect a kindly welcome.

■ **In Cornillon-Confoux 13250**   5 km S on D 19

Le Devem de Mirapier

5 km N on D 19 on D 70
90 55 99 22, fax 90 55 86 14

Closings not available. 16 rms 400-700 F. Restaurant. Half-board 480-600 F. Air cond. Conf. Pool. Tennis. Pkg. V, AE, DC.

The surrounding garrigue and pine wood make a lovely backdrop for this farmhouse-style hotel. Rooms are comfortable and very bright, though a trifle small.

SANCERRE   **18300**

Paris 201 - Bourges 46 - Cosne 16 - Nevers 50   Cher

Hôtel Panoramic

Remparts des Augustins
48 54 22 44, fax 48 54 39 55

Open year-round. 2 stes 750-780 F. 55 rms 270-350 F. Rms for disabled. Restaurant. Half-board 280-330 F. Heated pool. Golf. Pkg. Helipad. V, AE, MC.

More than half the rooms live up to the hotel's name, with their splendid views of Sancerre's vineyards.

La Tour

31, pl. de la Halle
48 54 00 81, fax 48 78 01 54

Open daily until 10pm. Priv rm: 26. Terrace dining. Air cond. Pkg. V, AE, MC.

Here's a perfectly charming spot: La Tour is a fourteenth-century dwelling perched atop a rocky peak. The decor is deliciously rustic and the dining room on the upper floor affords a wonderful view of the vineyards. Chef Daniel Fournier's mainly maritime menu is deft and stylish, and his 145 F menu is a good deal: potato fondant and pig's foot with fresh goat cheese, duck thigh confit in red Sancerre wine sauce, local crottin-de-chavignol goat cheese, and dessert. The cellar, as one might expect, is afloat in premium Sancerres. **C** 240-320 F. **M** 75 F, 98 F (exc Sat dinner & Sun lunch), 145 F, 180 F, 220 F.

SANCY-LÈS-MEAUX 77   → **Meaux**

SAN SEBASTIAN

Paris 796 - Bilbao 90 - Biarritz 47 - Hendaye 19   Spain

Akelare

Barrio de Igueldo
Paseo del Padre Orcolaga, 56
(43) 21 20 52, fax (43) 21 92 68

Closed Sun dinner, Mon, Jan 21-Feb, 1st 2 wks of Oct. Open until 11pm. Priv rm: 35. Air cond. No pets. Pkg. V, AE, DC, MC.

Don't let the fabulous view of the sea distract you from the fine cuisine of Pedro Subijana, which is modern and sophisticated (although sometimes over-complicated). Try his ethereal carpaccio of sea scallops and shrimp with lentils; lasagne of crab, cockles, and baby vegetables; louvine (local striped bass) in a carrot jus with a chive-scented oil; and perfectly cooked sole in its skin with artichokes. And to round it all off, sample the special menus of coffees, Ports, Sherries, Aguardientes, and cigars. **C** 400-600 F. **M** 314 F.

Arzak

21, alto de Miracruz
(43) 27 84 65, fax (43) 27 27 53

Closed Sun dinner, Mon, Jun 13-30, Nov 7-30. Open until 11pm. Priv rm: 40. No pets. Valet pkg. V, AE, DC.

Delicious tiny shrimp stuffed within morels and posed on a little purée of almonds and cauliflower with a ribbon of peanut oil and carrot jus; tender cod brandade on a corn galette paired with a crème of sweet garlic and walnuts, tomato confit, beets, and sweet red pepper jus. Pierre Gagnaire? No, Jean Mari Arzak. Piqued by the loss of a point last year, the chef made every effort to prove he's still very much in charge, still creative, and even more the master of a classical repertoire that serves as a point of departure for more unusual dishes. And he has succeeded. Savor his grouper in sorrel sauce, or grouper grilled in its skin and accompanied by winkles, a touch of grapeseed oil, a bit of squid ink, a cabbage leaf, and a delicate turnip and celery root purée. The same quest for quality and elegance is seen in his fabulous desserts: feuilleté stuffed with blackberries and fromage blanc, or bread pudding with mango, orange, zucchini jam, and rosemary syrup, among others. We also savored his rare-cooked, tender gingered squab, and the divine little ortalan (but note that this bird is protected on the French side of the border and can't be served there). Jean Mari has won back his points. The superb service is still performed by waiters dressed all in elegant black. **C** 500-600 F (weekdays, wine incl). **M** 350 F.

Maria Christina-Cigahotels

Paseo República Argentina, 4
(43) 42 49 00
Open year-round. 27 stes 2,050-4,100 F. 109 rms 738-902 F. Restaurant. Air cond. Conf. No pets. Valet pkg. V, AE, DC, MC.
A palatial hotel that oozes luxury, from the decor to the huge, perfectly equipped rooms. Piano bar; magnificent salons with marble columns.

■ **In Oyarzun**   10 km SW, in Spain

Zuberoa

Barrio de Iturriotz
(43) 49 12 28, fax (43) 47 16 08
Closed Sun dinner, Mon, Jan 1-15, Jun 1-15, Oct 15-31. Open until 11pm. Terrace dining. Air cond. No pets. Pkg. V, AE, DC, MC.
This venerable auberge operated by the Arbelaitz brothers is not far from the San Sebastian highway exit, but seems lost in the verdant countryside. We were completely seduced this year by the charming old-fashioned dining room, the warm welcome, and the superb cuisine. Savor the delicate just-cooked sea scallops interspersed with slices of turnips, posed on a cauliflower cream, and accompanied by clams in parsley jus. Or the plump, flavorful langoustines cooked in their shells with caramelized orange sauce and a jus of tiny peas; or tender foie gras invigorated by its match with a rustic chickpea soup with tiny croutons; or the veal muzzle in a compote with baby vegetables paired with a fabulous potato purée; and finally the fantastic dessert labeled "tout à la pomme" with its marvelous brioche. Excellent cellar; this is one of the best tables on the other side of the Pyrenées. Two added points this year. **C** 240-400 F.

SANSSAT 03   → Varennes-sur-Allier

SAPPEY-EN-CHARTREUSE (LE) 38
→ Grenoble

SARLAT-LA-CANÉDA   **24200**
Paris 535 - Périgueux 67 - Brive 50 - Cahors 62   Dordogne

12/20 La Madeleine

1, pl. de la Petite-Rigaudie
53 59 10 41, fax 53 31 03 62
Closed Mon lunch (exc Aug), mid Nov-mid Mar. Open until 9:30pm. Priv rm: 15. Terrace dining. Garage pkg. V, AE, DC, MC.
This is a serious regional restaurant, housed in an imposing stone building. The formal atmosphere is enlivened by groups feasting on Philippe Melot's goose foie gras, médallion of monkfish, tournedos périgourdine, duck breast, and Poire William. No surprises. Very fine cellar. **C** 240-320 F. **M** 175 F (wine incl), 135 F, 240 F, 305 F.

La Madeleine

(See restaurant above)
Closed mid Nov-mid Mar. 3 stes 365-455 F. 19 rms 295-380 F. Half-board 360-410 F. Air cond. Conf. Golf. Garage pkg. V, AE, DC, MC.
La Madeleine exudes the slightly threadbare rusticity of old-fashioned touring hotels catering for holiday-makers. Friendly welcome.

SARPOIL   **63490**
Paris 430 - Issoire 11 - Clermont-Ferrand 46   P./Dôme

La Bergerie

St-Jean-en-Val - 73 71 02 54
Closed Sun dinner, Mon, Jan 2-31. Open until 9:30pm. Priv rm: 8. Garden dining. Pkg. V, AE, DC.
Local gourmets have turned in their verdict: Laurent Jury is the best cuisinier for miles around! Set in splendid isolation on a wooded hillside, La Bergerie is known for its generous set meals, and for the chef's creative use of prime local produce. Not yet 30, Jury is only at the start of what could be a stellar career. Need convincing? Sample his dishes with regional roots, like lamb stuffed with herbs and mountain thyme, confit of young rabbit, stuffed cabbage, and sheep's milk crème brûlée. But he can also expertly prepare dishes like John Dory roasted in its skin with an asparagus mousseline enlivened by langoustine jus, or red mullet with sweet pepper confit and sushi in Nori seaweed. The reasonably priced wine list offers finds from many regions, including Boues and Saint-Pourçain. We'd be happy to come here all year long. **C** 250-300 F. **M** 110 F, 160 F, 200 F, 240 F, 300 F.

SARREGUEMINES   **57200**
Paris 383 - Saverne 61 - Metz 69   Moselle

Hôtel d'Alsace

10, rue Poincaré
87 98 44 32, fax 87 98 39 85
Closed Dec 24, Good Fri. 2 stes 630 F. 26 rms 315-390 F. Restaurant. Conf. No pets. Pkg. V, AE, DC, MC.
Comfortable, convenient, discreet, and centrally located, the Alsace offers very simple, very clean, and very dull rooms. Minimal service. There are two restaurants on the premises.

Gault Millau's ratings are based solely on the restaurants' cuisine. We do not take into account the atmosphere, décor, service, and so on; these are commented upon within the review.

■ **In Wœlfling-lès-Sarreguemines 57200** 11 km E

Pascal Dimofski
113, route de Bitche - 87 02 38 21
Closed Mon dinner, Tue, Feb school hols, Aug 23-Sep 8. Open until 9:30pm. Priv rm: 30. Garden dining. Pkg. V, AE, DC, MC.

The Dimofski family's roomy, comfortable restaurant, set just beyond the village, wears a plain, unremarkable exterior and a dining room with a rather austere decor in autumnal tints. But chef Pascal Dimofski provides plenty of fireworks, visual and gustatory, with his exquisite, complex cuisine. Sample his bouillon of artichokes, langoustines caramelized with coriander, and ravioli stuffed with veal kidney and sweetbreads. For dessert, try the excellent barbotin of minted fruits. The cellar is admirably composed, and Madame Dimofski's welcome is as gracious as ever. By the way, don't go into the village, but keep on the Nationale 62 which runs by the restaurant. **C** 330-420 F. **M** 140 F (weekday lunch), 160 F, 200 F, 350 F.

SAULIEU	21210
Paris 255 - Dijon 73 - Autun 41 - Avallon 39	Côte-d'Or

La Côte d'Or
Bernard Loiseau, 2, rue d'Argentine
80 64 07 66, fax 80 64 08 92
19.5 Open daily until 10pm. Priv rm: 50. Valet pkg. V, AE, DC, MC.

Bernard Loiseau has been known as a celebrity chef, the media's darling. But, perhaps realizing that the proof is always in the pudding, he has turned his focus back to his cooking and is first and foremost a cuisinier of rare professionalism. Not only did he undertake crippling financial burdens to renovate his restaurant and hotel, but he continues to practice his craft with genuine energy and zest. While other chefs have damped down their creative fires, Loiseau adds fuel to his, always seeking and experimenting with novel flavor harmonies.

La Côte d'Or is now a must on the itineraries of dedicated gastronomes. A glance round the elegant salon-bar at lunch or dinnertime reveals an international cohort of food lovers studying the menu over an apéritif. After that agreeable prelude, guests are placed in the capable hands of Hubert, the urbane maître d'hôtel, and seated in one of the intimate dining rooms with a view of the garden. From that moment on, one has no other care than to sit back and succumb to the exquisite and varied pleasures of Loiseau's intelligent, graceful cuisine. Sample his superbly simple potato salad with egg yolk vinaigrette, poached eggs perched on truffled onion purée, and red mullet stuffed with its liver and baby vegetables in a light oil sauce. Or more elaborate creations like snails in a parsley velouté with garlic chips, sea scallops with endive in an astonishing green apple jus, John Dory with an oyster jus whipped up with olive oil (this dish will make you go down on your knees in gratitude), roast rabbit à la moutarde, and succulent veal sweetbreads with warm foie gras and truffled mashed potatoes, a dish that makes you want to hug everyone in sight. The wonderfully pure jus are a lesson for cream addicts; they are full of flavor but never overwhelm. Many diners come expressly to taste the famous poularde truffée à la vapeur: when the steamed chicken with truffled basmati rice arrives at the table, its indescribable aroma turns every head in the room. Naturally, all the best Burgundies are on hand for the asking—provided you have the means! But when it comes to trading pennies for pleasure, we can hardly imagine a better return on investment than a feast chez Loiseau! **C** 650-1,000 F. **M** 350 F (weekday lunch), 295 F, 580 F, 780 F.

La Côte d'Or
(See restaurant above)
Open year-round. 8 stes 1,600-2,200 F. 19 rms 310-1,600 F. Conf. Valet pkg. V, AE, DC, MC.

The garden has grown fuller and greener; now it's lovely to open a window onto the grounds at breakfast time. This year, the ten suites in the Résidence de la Côte d'Or (Relais et Châteaux) have been joined by five new suites (including one huge one on the top floor), all opening onto the lovely garden to which Loiseau plans to add a swimming pool. In 1996, five more rooms, and then he plans to work on the wing that now contains small, comfortable, but simple rooms that have not won the Relais et Châteaux rating.

La Poste
1, rue Grillot
80 64 05 67, fax 80 64 10 82
Open year-round. 45 rms 170-485 F. Rms for disabled. Restaurant. Half-board 350-480 F. Air cond. Conf. Garage pkg. V, AE, DC, MC.

This former post house dating from the seventeenth century has been renovated and all the rooms were redecorated in 1992. They are well equipped and soundproofed.

SAULZET-LE-CHAUD 63
→ **Clermont-Ferrand**

SAUMUR	49400
Paris 300 - Angers 53 - Tours 65 - Nantes 127	Maine/Loire

Anne d'Anjou
32-33, quai Mayaud
41 67 30 30, fax 41 67 51 00
Closed Dec 21-31. 50 rms 280-540 F. Restaurant. Rms for disabled. Conf. Pkg. V, AE, DC, MC.

At the foot of the château and overlooking the Loire, this wonderful eighteenth-century hotel is in part a listed monument (the façade and grand staircase). Recently remodeled, the rooms are pleasant and well equipped (the spectacular number 102 was designed by Napoleon's architects). Restaurant: see Les Ménestrels, below.

12/20 Les Chandelles
71, rue St-Nicolas - 41 67 20 40
Closed Wed, Mar. Open until 9:30pm. Priv rm: 22. Terrace dining. Pkg. V, AE, DC, MC.

The decor of this former boutique is rather coy, but never mind. Find a place under the silver chandeliers to sample the snails in Saumur red wine sauce with cervelas julienne, lamb with a sweet pepper cream and tomato concassé, cheese assortment, and dessert, all on the 134 F menu. **C** 260-360 F. **M** 90 F (lunch), 110 F, 134 F, 194 F.

Le Clos des Bénédictins ♨♟
2 km SW on D 751, in St-Hilaire-St-Florent
41 67 28 48, fax 41 67 13 71
Closed Dec 15-Jan 15. 1 ste 500-600 F. 23 rms 260-420 F. Restaurant. Half-board 345-460 F. Rms for disabled. Golf. Conf. Pool. Helipad. Pkg. V, AE, MC.
This quiet hotel looks down on the town and the Loire. The welcoming rooms are modern, well-equipped, spacious, and considerably more comfortable than in the past. The young chef offers tasty, simple dishes in the restaurant.

Les Délices du Château
Les Feuquières - 41 67 65 60
Closed Sun dinner & Mon off-seas, Dec. Open until 10pm. Garden dining. Pkg. V, AE, DC.
Foremost among the *délices* of this particular château are appetizing, light, and lively dishes like lobster salad with a hint of orange, slightly overcooked monkfish in a shrimp cream sauce, and a rather bland saumurois au crémant dessert saved by a fine fruit coulis. But the "carte" didn't always match what was on the menu outside the establishment. Fine cellar and attentive service. **C** 280-380 F. **M** 130 F (weekday lunch & Sat), 170 F, 270 F (lunch).

Les Ménestrels
11, rue Raspail - 41 67 71 10
Closed Sun (Nov-Apr), Sun lunch & Mon (May-Oct, exc Jul-Aug). Open until 9:30pm. Terrace dining. V, AE, DC, MC.
Two of the tables in this charming dining room with big bay windows have a view of a pretty garden courtyard. Christophe Hosselet offers an harmonious tuban of pink shrimp and crab with avocado (the portion was a bit stingy), milk-fed lamb unfortunately roasted with a garlicky bread-crumb crust but paired with a good zucchini tian, miniscule sablé too sparingly garnished with rhubarb, and an adequate mango ice cream. Fine selection of local wines. Charming welcome and service. See hotel Anne d'-Anjou, above. **C** 230-380 F. **M** 120 F (weekdays) 195 F, 250 F, 320 F.

■ **In Chênehutte-**
   les-Tuffeaux 49350   8 km NW

Le Prieuré
D 751 - 41 67 90 14, fax 41 67 92 24
Closed Jan 3-Mar 5. Open until 9:15pm. Priv rm: 50. Terrace dining. Pool. Garage pkg. V, AE.
A charming tone pervades Le Prieuré; one feels it the moment one steps into the pretty bar-salon. The splendid view over the Loire can be admired there, or from the airy dining room and summer terrace. Chef Jean-Noël Lumineau turns out splendid, classic dishes in perfect tune with the setting, and the top-quality ingredients are always market-fresh. Enjoy his langoustine salad with asparagus tips, pan-roasted red mullet fillets with a craquant of basil-scented cabbage, salmon cooked in its skin with Montpellier butter sauce, veal sweetbreads braised with smoked ham, and fillet of lamb roasted with green coffee beans. For dessert, a strawberry millefeuille. Sumptuous wine list offering local wines at reasonable prices, and Bordeaux and Burgundies at much higher prices. The reception and service are stylish yet unstuffy. **C** 320-450 F. **M** 220 F, 400 F, 525 F (wine incl).

Le Prieuré
(See restaurant above)
Closed Jan 3-Mar 5. 35 rms 420-1,350 F. Half-board 650-1,055 F. Conf. Heated pool. Tennis. Golf. Pkg. V, AE, MC.
A basket of fresh fruit awaits guests in each room of this former priory nestled in verdant grounds above the Loire. Wine-tasting courses available. Good pastries for breakfast. Relais et Châteaux.

SAUTERNES	33210
Paris 613 - Langon 11 - Villandrau 11 - Bazas 21	Gironde

Le Saprien ۞
Le Bourg - 56 76 60 87
Closed Sun dinner, Mon, Dec 1-15, Feb 15-28. Open until 9:30pm. Terrace dining. Pkg. V, AE.
Word of mouth is drawing flocks of customers to this address, where Jean-Claude Garrigues prepares market-fresh dishes full of bright, charming touches. In the fresh, simple dining room or on the terrace overlooking the vineyards of Sauternes, sample his lemony tartare of salmon and oysters with shallots, pork fillet roasted with ginger, and an ailette caramélisée aux poires for dessert. Some delicious Sauternes are thoughtfully served by the glass. **C** 230-350 F. **M** 107 F, 157 F, 197 F.

SAUVETERRE-DE-COMMINGES	31510
Paris 776 - Luchon 36 - St-Gaudens 10	H.-Garonne

Hostellerie
   des Sept Molles ۞
3 km S on D 9, in Gesset
61 88 30 87, fax 61 88 36 42
Closed Oct-Apr. Open until 9pm. Priv rm: 30. Pkg. V, AE, DC, MC.
Up here at 450 meters above sea level, the Pyrenees are not far away. This cozy inn provides a dining room warmed by a fire in winter, and a pretty flowered terrace for sunny days. The chef's specialty is farm-reared meat: try his blood sausage with apples, roast Pyrenees lamb with a lusty garnish of beans à la languedocienne, or veal steamed over summer savory with broad beans. To round things off, taste the praline mousseline drizzled with chocolate sauce, or apple tart with a dollop of Armagnac-laced whipped cream. Fine cellar. **C** 320-430 F. **M** 185 F, 290 F.

Hostellerie
   des Sept Molles ♨♟
(See restaurant above)
Closed Oct-Apr. Open until 9pm. 16 rms 550-750 F. Half-board 530-675 F. Air cond. Conf. Heated pool. Tennis. Golf. Pkg. V, AE, DC, MC.
The seven ancient millstones for which the inn is named dot the garden. Rooms are large and bright, breakfasts are generous. Relais et Châteaux.

۞

This symbol stands for "Les Lauriers du Terroir", an award given to chefs who prepare traditional or regional cuisine.

427

SAUVETERRE-DE-ROUERGUE 12800
Paris 644 - Albi 54 - Rodez 40 - Millau 95 *Aveyron*

Le Sénéchal
65 71 29 00, fax 65 71 29 10
Closed Sun dinner & Mon (exc Jul-Aug & hols), Jan 15-Mar 15. Open until 9:30pm. Terrace dining. Air cond. No pets. Pool. Pkg. V, AE, DC.
Out here amid the rye fields of the Rouergue, where generosity, not refinement, is the standard by which cooking is judged, the food served at this country *auberge* is remarkable for its elegance, its professionalism—and the prices it commands! This year the establishment moved to a new, modern building built of local materials near the thirteenth-century fortifications. The sunny new dining room is decorated with reproductions of medieval tapestries and has a lovely terrace. Michel Truchon is extraordinarily attentive to the quality of his ingredients. You're sure to appreciate his tiny petit gris snails in a delicate bouillon scented with wild anise, farm-raised duck with a truffle jus and baby vegetables, and a craquelin of strawberries and sheep's milk cheese with tea sauce. **C** 350-450 F. **M** 130 F, 260 F, 400 F.

Le Sénéchal
(See restaurant above)
See restaurant for closings. 3 stes 650-950 F. 8 rms 450-550 F. Half-board 420-570 F. Air cond. Heated pool. Pkg. V, AE, DC.
The Truchon's new hotel, opened last year, offers plenty of comfort and charm, as well as a patio, a covered swimming pool, fine furniture, and well-appointed rooms (some with balconies). Superb breakfasts.

SAUZE 04 → Barcelonnette

SCIEZ 74 → Thonon-les-Bains

SEDAN 08200
Paris 237 - Metz 139 - Reims 96 *Ardennes*

■ In Bazeilles 08140
4 km SW on N 43, D 764

L'Orangerie
24 27 52 11, fax 24 27 64 20
Closed Sun dinner, Mon, Aug 1-15. Open until 9:30pm. Pkg. V, MC.
The charm of this former orangery—it boasts a soaring roof and elegant decor—may distract your attention from the subtle, accomplished cooking of Maxence Belloir, which is showing more and more focus on fine regional products. Sample the tasty boned and breaded pig's feet with eggs in red wine sauce, perfectly cooked and flavorful monkfish roasted with Vire andouille and paired with a crème parmentier, and a bitter-almond clafoutis with tart cherry sauce. Well chosen cellar; obliging service. **C** 330-400 F. **M** 220 F (weekdays, wine incl), 280 F, 320 F.

Château de Bazeilles
(See restaurant above)
Open year-round. 20 rms 390-577 F. Conf. Golf. Pkg. Helipad. V, MC.
Far from noisy roads, the Bazeilles is a luxurious hotel set on the edge of a magnificent wooded estate. Friendly welcome.

SÉGOS 32 → Aire-sur-l'Adour

SÉGURET 84 → Vaison-la-Romaine

SÉLESTAT 67600
Paris 434 - Strasbourg 47 - Colmar 22 - St-Dié 46 *B.-Rhin*

Abbaye La Pommeraie
8, av. Foch - 88 92 07 84, fax 88 92 08 71
Closed Sun, Jul 17-Aug 7. Open until 9:30pm. Terrace dining. Air cond. Valet pkg. V, AE, DC, MC.
The garden-terrace gives guests an opportunity to bask in the beauty of this seventeenth-century Cistercian abbey, but the luxurious dining room has plenty of charm and character too. Chef Daniel Stein cultivates a classic technique, but his interesting menu never fails to deliver some agreeable surprises: we greatly enjoyed his fresh salmon tartare, squab in a bread crust with coriander-spiked green cabbage, and brik (flaky pastry) stuffed with an apple, almonds, and honey. The new "Apfelstubel" annex brings relief from the high prices of the main restaurant. Fine cellar. **C** 340-450 F. **M** 230 F, 280 F, 420 F.

Abbaye La Pommeraie
(See restaurant above)
Open year-round. 2 stes 1,800 F. 12 rms 850-1,500 F. Half-board 1,100-1,750 F. Air cond. Pkg. V, AE, DC, MC.
The former abbey has been tastefully transformed into a charming hotel, with spacious, elegant guest rooms on the first floor, and mansard-roofed rooms on the floors above. A country style was adopted for the decor, but the appointments are all up to date. Lovely views of the garden and the old town. Perfect welcome. Relais et Châteaux.

SENLIS 60300
Paris 50 - Compiègne 35 - Soissons 60 - Lille 172 *Oise*

■ In Fleurines 60700
6.5 km N on N 17

Le Vieux Logis
105, rue de Paris - 44 54 10 13
Closed Sat lunch (Nov-Easter), Sun dinner, Mon, Aug 1-15. Open until 9:30pm. Priv rm: 40. Terrace dining. Pkg. V, AE, DC, MC.
The Vieux Logis's pretty terrace complements a comfortable dining room brightened by floral bouquets and smiling staff. Yann Nivet's classic cuisine shows polish and a dash of personality. Sample the herbed red mullet croutons, veal sweetbreads en cocotte, and warm stawberries with gingerbread ice cream. For around 200 F, you can have a very nice meal, in spite of the high-priced wine list. **C** 280-480 F. **M** 200 F and up.

SENS 89100
Paris 118 - Troyes 65 - Fontainebleau 53 - Reims 151 *Yonne*

La Madeleine
1, rue d'Alsace-Lorraine - 86 65 09 31
Closed Sun dinner. Open until 9:30pm. Priv rm: 15. Air cond. Pkg. V, AE, DC, MC.
The young chef, who worked for a long time at Lamazère, has a taste for luxury; the dining room decor is opulent (a bit too much so) and

the cuisine is based on rich products treated with care. Try the turbot with potatoes, the chicken, and the little madeleines, all really two-toque dishes, but we just couldn't accept the grey truffles marinated in alcohol, a true heresy. A very competent sommelier is in charge of the magnificent wine list; stylish service. **C** 350-550 F. **M** 170-360 F.

12/20 Paris et Poste
97, rue de la République
86 65 17 43, fax 86 64 48 45
Closings not available. Open until 10pm. Priv rm: 20. Terrace dining. Air cond. Valet pkg. V, AE, DC, MC.
A quintessential provincial hostelry. The cuisine has been rejuvenated by the new young chef, son of the owners; he offers red mullet fillet and veal sweetbreads served over potatoes, fricassée of langoustines and asparagus, and standing rump of veal with morels and baby fava beans, all prepared with care. The welcome is not the world's warmest, though. **C** 300-350 F. **M** 160 F, 200 F (weekdays, Sat lunch), 250 F (Sat dinner, Sun), 350 F

Paris et Poste
(See restaurant above)
Open year-round. 7 stes 540-600 F. 18 rms 400-510 F. Half-board 500 F. Air cond. Conf. Valet pkg.
A comfortable hotel with well-equipped, thoroughly refurbished facilities. Let's hear it for life in the provinces.

SÉREILHAC 87 → Limoges

SERRE-CHEVALIER 05240
Paris 674 - Grenoble 110 - Col du Lautaret 22   *H.-Alpes*

■ In Chantemerle 05330

12/20 Auberge La Fourchette
92 24 06 66
Dinner only. Closed mid Apr-Dec 15. Open until 10:30pm. Priv rm: 15. No pets. V, MC.
The food, like the setting, is utterly unpretentious, yet the rugged Alpine atmosphere has undeniable charm. The Savoyard specialties are all equally successful, so choose whatever strikes your fancy: raclette, fondues, charcuterie, duck breast with honey and ginger, and walnut cake with mountain honey. Bring a bit appetite! **C** 150-250 F. **M** 90 F (dinner).

Hôtel Plein Sud
92 24 17 01, fax 92 24 10 21
Closed Apr 17-Jun 17, Sep 17-Dec 16. 42 rms 290-510 F. Conf. Heated pool. Golf. No pets. Pkg. V, MC.
Bright, spacious rooms with small terraces overlooking the ski slopes. Amenities include a Jacuzzi, gym, and heated indoor pool. Wake up to a terrific buffet breakfast.

■ In Le Monêtier-les-Bains 05220

Auberge du Choucas
17, rue de la Fruitière
92 24 42 73, fax 92 24 51 60
Closed Nov 2-Dec 15. 4 stes 1,050-1,250 F. 8 rms 500-700 F. Restaurant. Half-board 440-880 F. Golf. Valet pkg. V, MC.

Set right in the heart of the village, these pretty chalet-style rooms are tastefully decorated and well-appointed. Each has a very comfortable little sitting area. Bathrooms are a mite small. Nice welcome; cozy atmosphere.

10/20 Le Castel Pèlerin
4 km N on N 91, Lauzet - 92 24 42 09
Closed Apr-Jun 20, Sep-Dec 20. Open until 8:30pm. Pkg. V, AE, MC.
This restaurant was a stable once upon a time. Nowadays, it's a local favorite owing to the simple, robust menu: meats grilled in the huge fireplace, bacon omelet, roast lamb shoulder, and beef au poivre, washed down with tasty little Savoie wines. **M** 90 F (weekdays, Sat lunch), 130 F, 150 F.

SERRIERA 20 → CORSICA: Porto

SERRIÈRES 07340
Paris 520 - St-Etienne 54 - Privas 90 - Annonay 15   *Ardèche*

Schaeffer
Quai J.-Roche
75 34 00 07, fax 75 34 08 79
Closed Sun dinner & Mon (exc Jul-Aug). Open until 9:30pm. Priv rm: 15. Terrace dining. Air cond. Valet pkg. V, AE, MC.
Chef Bernard Mathé, late of Léon de Lyon, is happy as can be at Schaeffer. The dining room, now elegantly refurbished (mirrors, pink wall hangings, comfortable seating) shows Mathé's cuisine to even better advantage. If you can come here in game season, sample his velouté of wood pigeon with green lentils, casserole-roasted grouse with green-tomato chutney, and tasty fillets of venison cooked rare and accompanied by chard sautéed with orange and a jus flavored with cacao beans. All the desserts are luscious, as are the fine Côtes du Rhône. This is a cozy yet elegant establishment with an up-to-date sensibility. **C** 300-400 F. **M** 120 F (Sat lunch), 168 F, 225 F, 320 F.

Schaeffer
(See restaurant above)
Open year-round. 13 rms 165-285 F. No pets. Valet pkg. V, AE, MC.
A great stopover. The tastefully decorated rooms have excellent beds, and the breakfast is prepared by the chef.

SÈTE 34200
Paris 790 - Béziers 53 - Montpellier 35 - Lodève 72   *Hérault*

Le Grand Hôtel
17, quai de Lattre-de-Tassigny
67 74 71 77, fax 67 74 29 27
Closed Dec 24-Jan 2. 4 stes 499-1,150 F. 43 rms 195-480 F. Restaurant. Half-board 263-525 F. Air cond. Conf. Garage pkg. V, AE, DC, MC.
This turn-of-the-century hotel has a breathtaking view of Sète and the Mont Saint-Clair from the upper floors. Very comfortable rooms, with elegant decor and outstanding amenities, at reasonable rates.

*The **prices** in this guide reflect what establishments were charging at press time.*

La Palangrotte
Quai de la Marine - 67 74 80 35
Closed Sun dinner, Mon, Nov 21-30, Jan 23-30. Open until 10:30pm (11pm in summer). Terrace dining. Air cond. Pkg. V, AE.
Alain Gémignani prepares subtly modernized dishes from Languedoc's Mediterranean repertoire. Good choices are his rémoulade of marinated fresh salmon with shrimp, grouper fillet with a confit of baby vegetables and ratatouille jus spiked with saffron, and a strawberry terrine with Muscat jelly. Splendid wines; remarkable service in a pleasant dining room with a terrace overlooking the port. **C** 250-400 F. **M** 140 F, 180 F, 280 F.

12/20 La Rascasse
27, quai du Gal-Durand - 67 74 38 46
Open daily until 10:30pm (11pm in summer). Terrace dining. Air cond. V, AE, DC, MC.
All the local favorites are to be found here: sea scallops paired with marinated salmon, sole and turbot in Chablis sauce, and duck breast with pears. **C** 250-350 F. **M** 80 F, 130 F, 175 F.

 **Les Terrasses du Lido**
Rond-point de l'Europe
67 51 39 60, fax 67 53 28 90
Closed Sun dinner & Mon off-seas, Feb. Open until 10pm. Priv rm: 20. Terrace dining. Air cond. Hotel: 1 ste 550-700 F. 9 rms 240-450 F. Half-board 280-380 F. Air cond. Conf. Pool. Pkg. V, AE, DC, MC.
It's not quite the Lido, but the terrace of this peaceful, recently renovated establishment is most agreeable. As is the cuisine of Colette Guironnet based on fresh seafood: sample her poached oysters with a zucchini purée, lemony mussels, anise-flavored sea bass, and monkfish pan-roasted with herbs. The first set menu is a good deal, offering eggs in red wine sauce with pleurote mushrooms, mignon of veal in mustard sauce, and homemade pastries. Smiling welcome and service. **C** 230-400 F. **M** 130 F, 200 F, 300 F.

SÉZANNE 51120
Paris 110 - Meaux 75 - Troyes 60 - Châlons-sur-Marne 57 *Marne*

12/20 La Croix d'Or
53, rue Notre-Dame
26 80 61 10, fax 26 80 65 20
Closed Jan 2-17. Open until 9:30pm. Priv rm: 22. Terrace dining. Pkg. V, AE, DC, MC.
This typically provincial hotel-restaurant offers classic, seasonal cooking at attractive prices. An assiette of warm lobster and foie gras (served in a rather stingy portion), savory squab cooked in three different ways, and huge dessert cart featuring well prepared goodies. The set menus are excellent bargains, as is the fine wine list. **C** 180-300 F. **M** 90 F (wine incl), 65 F, 100 F, 160 F, 220 F.

 Hôtel de France
25, rue L.-Jolly - 26 81 41 48
Closed Sun, Jan 15-Feb 15. 24 rms 220-320 F. Restaurant. Half-board 350 F. Conf. Pkg. V, AE, DC, MC.

In the center of town, this hotel provides pleasant rooms with period furniture. Horse-back-riding weekends arranged.

SIGEAN 11130
Paris 830 - Narbonne 21 - Perpignan 41 - Port-la-Nouvelle 9 *Aude*

 Château de Villefalse
Route de Narbonne
68 48 54 29, fax 68 48 34 37
Closings not available. 15 stes 850-1,800 F. 10 rms 650-910 F. Restaurant. Half-board 690-1,165 F. Air cond. Conf. Pool. Pkg. Helipad. V, AE, MC.
This manor house surrounded by vineyards offers luxurious rooms and suites with fine furniture, embroidered linen, and, from the upper floor, lovely views of the vines. Fitness center and a huge swimming pool (to work off the sumptuous breakfasts).

SIORAC-EN-PÉRIGORD 24170
Paris 533 - Bergerac 45 - Sarlat 29 - Périgueux 57 *Dordogne*

■ In **Le Buisson-de-Cadouin 24480** 7 km NW on D 25

Manoir de Bellerive
53 27 16 19, fax 53 22 09 05
Closed Nov 15-Mar. 16 rms 400-730 F. Restaurant. Half-board 475-550 F. Air cond. Conf. Pool. Tennis. Golf. Pkg. Helipad. V, MC.
Surrounded by lovely grounds on the banks of the Dordogne, this handsome little Second Empire château is decorated with fine period furniture and pretty fabrics; the rooms on the top floor have modern decor, however. Windows open onto the park or the river. Satisfying breakfasts are served on a glorious terrace overlooking the Dordogne Valley. There's a bar; expect a very warm welcome.

SOISSONS 02200
Paris 100 - Amiens 114 - Lille 185 - Reims 56 *Aisne*

■ In **Courcelles-sur-Vesle 02220** 21 km E on N 31

Château de Courcelles
23 74 13 53, fax 23 74 06 41
Closed Jan 15-Feb 15. Open until 9:30pm. Priv rm: 20. Terrace dining. Heated pool. Pkg. V, AE, MC.
This beautifully restored baroque château is set in a wooded estate. In record time, it has won over a loyal clientele of business travelers and tourists. Everyone loves to linger around the sculpted stone fireplace, enjoying the remarkably polished classic cuisine: lobster fricassée with baby vegetables, thyme-scented duck breast with turnip confit, and a warm chocolate fondant with almond-milk sauce. The costly cellar of well-chosen wines boasts a splendid selection of Champagnes and Bordeaux. Courteous welcome; impeccable service. **C** 400-500 F. **M** 220 F, 350 F.

Château de Courcelles
(See restaurant above)
Closed Jan 15-Feb 15. 1 ste 1,100-1,200 F. 12 rms 550-1,200 F. Half-board 800-1,450 F. Conf. Pool. Tennis. Golf. Pkg. Helipad. V, AE, MC.

Tastefully decorated to provide superb comfort, this charming château-hotel is ideal for conferences or a relaxing holiday.

SOPHIA-ANTIPOLIS 06	→ Valbonne

SORINIÈRES (LES) 44	→ Nantes

SOUILLAC	46200

Paris 525 - Cahors 67 - Brive 35 - Sarlat 29 - Figeac 74   *Lot*

Le Quercy

1, rue Récège
65 37 83 56, fax 65 37 07 22
Closed Dec-Mar 15. 25 rms 200-280 F. Restaurant. Heated pool. Golf. Garage pkg. V, MC.
A totally renovated hotel in a quiet district. Rooms are bright, well equipped, and some have private balcony-terraces. Garden; light meals served in the evening.

Le Redouillé

28, av. de Toulouse
65 37 87 25, fax 65 37 09 09
Closed Tue off-seas. Open until 10pm. Priv rm: 20. Terrace dining. Air cond. Garage pkg. V, AE, DC, MC.
A pleasant, attractive spot on the south side of town; unfortunately, traffic noise plagues you when you're sitting on the terrace. Try the first set menu: croquembouches, terrine of young rabbit with black mushrooms, cassoulet with three kinds of confit, and a coconut cream dessert. Simple dishes are the best choice here. Exhaustive selection of regional wines, as well as a choice of fine cigars, and a selection of teas and coffees. C 250-370 F. M 95 F, 125 F, 160 F, 200 F, 350 F.

STEINBRUNN-LE-BAS 68	→ Mulhouse

STRASBOURG	67000

Paris 488 - Colmar 69 - Basel 137 - Lyon 489   *Bas-Rhin*

12/20 L'Arsenal

11, rue de l'Abreuvoir
88 35 03 69, fax 88 35 03 69
Closed Sat lunch, Sun, Jul 30-Aug 20. Open until 11pm. Priv rm: 25. Air cond. V, AE, DC, MC.
A charming atmosphere envelops L'Arsenal's cozy dining room; professors, Euro MPs, and tourists gather peaceably around the inventive house repertoire, which is cheerfully and competently served. Try the snail kouglof, frog's legs cassoulette, a salmon and pickerel duo with sauerkraut, and pineapple roasted with pepper and caramel. Efficient service. C 230-300 F. M 130 F (weekday lunch), 120 F, 185 F.

Hôtel Baumann

See restaurant Maison Kammerzell

Beaucour

5, rue des Bouchers
88 76 72 00, fax 88 76 72 60
Open year-round. 5 stes 900 F. 40 rms 550-750 F. Air cond. Conf. Valet pkg. V, AE, DC, MC.
The eighteenth-century half-timbered buildings that make up this hotel have retained their period charm, though they've been renovated to the most modern standards. Clustered around a beautiful enclosed courtyard, they offer cozy rooms, each decorated in a bright, distinctive style. Magnificent bathrooms (Jacuzzi); exemplary reception.

12/20 Au Bœuf Mode

2, pl. St-Thomas
88 32 39 03, fax 88 21 90 80
Closed Sun, Dec 24-Jan 3. Open until 10:30pm. Priv rm: 25. Terrace dining. V, AE, DC, MC.
To make room for more customers, this popular establishment has added a bistrot annex with a pretty terrace (serving typical Alsatian dishes). The main dining room features more elaborate fare like a salad of young rabbit and mushrooms, pickerel and sauerkraut à l'alsacienne, and a crème brûlée spiked with Cointreau. C 250-350 F. M 100 F (lunch), 160 F, 210 F.

Buerehiesel

4, parc de l'Orangerie
88 61 62 24, fax 88 61 32 00
Closed Tue, Wed, Dec 22 Jan 4, Mar 2-14, Aug 10-24. Open until 9:30pm. Priv rm: 60. Air cond. Pkg. V, AE, DC, MC.
The half timbered house transported piece by piece from Molsheim and rebuilt here is a mecca for inventive, surprising, full-flavored cuisine. Antoine Westermann displays a rare talent for reinterpreting half-forgotten traditional recipes (schniederspœttle, dampfnudeln, knepfles and the like...) with a light, contemporary touch. He updates these hearty classics with sunny herbs, creating unexpected and most appetizing alliances of very pure flavors. Parliamentarians from the nearby European Union building flock to this converted farmhouse surrounded by a park to savor jambonnette of frog's legs in an excellent herb jus, fresh cod accented by an olive purée and an ultrafresh tomato sauce, and delicious John Dory cooked with spices and paired with creamed leeks, a superb example of a union between tradition and imagination. We also reveled in the veal tongue, brains, and fritot (organs) in a delicious vinaigrette, and guinea fowl pan-roasted with mousseron mushrooms in a succulent jus. Fine wine list. The staff, though, seems to have let success go to their heads; someone should make sure that the welcome and service match the quality of the cooking. C 450-600 F. M 320 F (exc weekday lunch), 290 F (weekday lunch), 600 F, 630 F.

La Cambuse

1, rue des Dentelles - 88 22 10 22
Closed Sun, Mon, Dec 24-Jan 9, Apr 30-May 15, Aug 6-21. Open until 10pm. No pets. V, MC.
Shellfish and fish, full stop. But that summary repertoire is more than adequate in the capable hands of chef Élisabeth Lefebvre, who loves to experiment with Oriental touches. Try her shrimp breaded with spices, red mullet with lemongrass, and turbot cooked with sesame and coriander. Limited choice of desserts; excellent wine list. C 280-320 F.

Cathédrale

12, pl. de la Cathédrale
88 22 12 12, fax 88 23 28 00
Open year-round. 3 stes 700-850 F. 29 rms 340-750 F. Conf. No pets. Valet pkg. V, AE, DC, MC.

431

Superbly situated opposite the cathedral (the booming bells wake one up on Sundays) this comfortable hotel's soberly decorated, well-equipped rooms have fine views. Fitness club.

12/20 D'Choucrouterie
20, rue St-Louis
88 36 52 87, fax 88 24 16 49
Closed Jan 1-10. Open until midnight. Priv rm: 55. Terrace dining. V.
This converted choucroute (sauerkraut) factory continues to serve the Strasbourg specialty prepared with salmon, smoked beef, and garlic sausages. Also on offer: smoked trout, duck breast au poivre vert, fresh farm cheese and sautéed potatoes, and a cinnamon ice cream tart with white chocolate sauce. Actors, musicians, and theatregoers enjoy the convivial atmosphere, lubricated with tasty, low-priced Alsatian wines. Bohemian decor (musical instruments, caricatures, and original paintings). **C** 180-280 F. **M** 110 F, 150 F.

Le Crocodile ❆
10, rue de l'Outre
88 32 13 02, fax 88 75 72 01
Closed Sun, Mon, Dec 25-Jan 1, Jul 10-31. Open until 10pm. Priv rm: 90. Air cond. Pkg. V, AE, DC.
Émile Jung is now as popular as the Nile crocodile (brought back by a soldier from Napoléon's Egyptian campaign) for whom the restaurant is named. Jung aims to please, and indeed, he rarely disappoints. We were slightly disappointed in the past by the lack of creativity in his cooking, which lost the establishment a point in 1992. But this year all seems to have been taken in hand; Jung's dishes show concentrated, well balanced flavors, and the 18 rating returns. Sample the gelée of young rabbit with exquisite tiny girolles and fresh tomatoes, a model of fresh flavors; the thick and juicy sole fillet with a complex jus; oysters in a cardamom gelatin with a fennel cream; turbot with green asparagus; farm-raised guinea fowl with "gypsy" sauerkraut; chartreuse of quail with goose liver; and pickerel with poultry livers. The desserts are sublime, as is the wine list, the best we know in Alsace. **C** 580-700 F. **M** 290 F, 390 F (exc Sat), 600 F.

Hôtel du Dragon
2, rue de l'Écarlate
88 35 79 80, fax 88 25 78 95
Closed Dec 24-27. 32 rms 440-620 F. Rms for disabled. Conf. No pets. Pkg. V, MC.
In 1987 this hotel was created within the walls of a seventeenth-century town house in a quiet cul-de-sac in the historic center. The rooms are very neat and comfortable, with resolutely modern decor in shades of grey. Friendly service by a refined, multilingual staff.

Estaminet Schlœgel
19, rue de la Krutenau - 88 36 21 98
Closed Sun, Mon. Open until 10pm. Priv rm: 40. Air cond. V, AE, MC.
Behind the blue façade is a contemporary dining room with a lovely old zinc bar. Gérard Deprez prepares classic food with a personal spin. Try his potato galettes stuffed with goose liver, veal sweetbreads braised in shrimp fumet, and for dessert, palets au chocolat amer, and a

vanilla-fresh raspberry mousseline. Friendly welcome and service. **C** 280-350 F. **M** 110 F, 160 F (weekday lunch), 200 F, 240 F, 290 F.

11/20 Le Fuji
39, av. des Vosges - 88 35 54 75
Closed Sun, lunch Sat & Mon, Dec 24-26. Open until 10pm. Priv rm: 25. V, AE, DC, MC.
Lots of grilled fish and meat dishes (teppanyaki) but also sushis and sahsimis, tempuras and sukiyakis galore served in two new dining rooms. Pair it with a good Tokay d'Alsace. **C** 250-330 F. **M** 125 F, 150 F, 175 F.

Au Gourmet sans Chiqué
15, rue Ste-Barbe
88 32 04 07, fax 88 22 42 40
Closed Mon lunch, Sun, 2nd wk of Feb school hols, Aug 1-18. Open until 10pm. Priv rm: 45. Air cond. V, AE, DC, MC.
Sans chiqué (unpretentious) but elegant all the same, this little restaurant in downtown Strasbourg surprises diners with a varying bill of light, inventive fare prepared by Daniel Klein. Sample his leek and caviar gelatin with a langoustine compotée, saddle of rabbit cooked in hazelnut oil with onion purée and fried celery, and a delicate warm apple tart with caramel sauce. Seductive choice of Alsatian wines. **C** 300-430 F. **M** 160 F (weekday lunch), 240 F, 285 F, 350 F.

Hilton ♠♣
Av. Herrenschmidt
88 37 10 10, fax 88 36 83 27
Open year-round. 6 stes 3,200-6,200 F. 241 rms 1,000-1,100 F. Half-board 775-1,200 F. Air cond. Pkg. V, AE, DC.
Set in leafy surroundings off a busy avenue, the Hilton offers functional, well-soundproofed, large, and perfectly furnished (though charmless) rooms. Some have a fine view of the town and cathedral, and all have individual air conditioning. Excellent welcome. Amenities include a sauna, solarium, piano bar, shops, and round-the-clock room service.

Holiday Inn
20, pl. de Bordeaux
88 37 80 00, fax 88 37 07 04
Open year-round. 170 rms 630-990 F. Restaurant. Half-board 98 F. Air cond. Conf. Heated pool. Golf. Pkg. V, AE, DC, MC.
This modern, functional hotel features a solarium, sauna, Turkish bath, and gym. Other facilities include a discothèque, bank, and travel agency.

Maison Kammerzell
16, pl. de la Cathédrale
88 32 42 14, fax 88 23 03 92
Closed for Chrisstmas eve. Open until 10:30pm. Priv rm: 160. Terrace dining. Air cond. Pkg. V, AE, DC, MC.
This culinary institution is a must for tourists, but also attracts the local citizenry, thanks to its warm brasserie-style atmosphere. Nestling at the foot of the cathedral, this fairytale fifteenth-century building features frescoes, wood paneling, stained-glass windows, and polished furniture. Guy-Pierre Baumann regales customers with his famous fish choucroute, hearty Alsatian specialties, and other more inventive dishes such as sea bream with curried apples. **C** 240-340 F. **M** 190 F, 260 F.

Hôtel Baumann
(See restaurant above)
Open year-round. 9 rms 420-630 F. Air cond. Conf. Golf. Pkg. V, AE, DC, MC.
A handful of posh, contemporary guest rooms fitted out under the eaves of the Maison Kammerzell.

Maison Rouge
4, rue des Francs-Bourgeois
88 32 08 60, fax 88 22 43 73
Open year-round. 2 stes 1,200-1,500 F. 140 rms 430-590 F. Rms for disabled. Air cond. Conf. No pets. Pkg. V, AE, DC, MC.
The Place Kléber is just down the road from this hotel, built between the wars and recently renovated. The modern decor is mellowed by period furniture and stained-glass windows, luxurious fabrics, handsome paintings, splendid marble bathrooms, and comfortable lounges. Buffet breakfasts, and meals served in the rooms.

Mercure
25, rue Thomann
88 75 77 88, fax 88 32 08 66
Open year-round. 98 rms 420-650 F. Rms for disabled. Air cond. Pkg. V, AE, DC, MC.
Conveniently situated, brand-new, sporting a futuristic design, this chain hotel offers rooms done in blue with pretty bow windows, and a private garden. Generous buffet breakfasts; cheerful staff.

Mercure-Pont de l'Europe
Parc du Rhin
88 61 03 23, fax 88 60 43 05
Open year-round. 4 stes 550-650 F. 89 rms 380-480 F. Restaurant. Air cond. Conf. Pool. Pkg. V, AE, DC, MC.
An imposing group of modern, rather charmless buildings surrounded by a large park on the banks of the Rhine. The functional rooms are well equipped. Pleasant reception; many amenities (swimming pool, sauna, Turkish bath, fitness room). Bar.

Novotel
Quai Kléber
88 21 50 50, fax 88 21 50 51
Open year-round. 97 rms 530-580 F. Rms for disabled. Restaurant. Air cond. Conf. Pkg. V, AE, DC, MC.
Perched above a large shopping center within walking distance of the Place Kléber, this is a modern hotel with functional rooms. Bar.

12/20 Au Pont des Vosges
15, quai Koch - 88 36 47 75
Closed Sat lunch, Sun, hols. Open until midnight. Terrace dining. V, AE.
A genuinely warm and cozy brasserie much beloved by the Strasbourgeois for its fresh regional cooking (presskopf and raw vegetables, pickerel in Pinot Noir sauce, veal kidney with vegetables and mashed potatoes, and crème brûlée), good house wines, and friendly service. C 180-300 F.

Le Pont Tournant
5, rue des Moulins
88 76 43 43, fax 88 76 43 76
Closed Sun, Dec 23-Jan 3. Open until 10:30pm. Terrace dining. Air cond. Valet pkg. V, AE, DC, MC.
There's a pretty view of the most picturesque part of town from the elegant dining room done

in a pleasant, contemporary style (a few bouquets of fresh flowers wouldn't hurt). Chef Laurent Lergenmuller serves forth an interesting menu with a few regional accents: a rather overly rustic salad containing marinated mackerel and salmon roe in a saffrony horseradish vinaigrette, involtini of veal (little veal rolls) with langoustines and mushrooms (very tasty, but the potato chips served with it were superfluous), and a luscious dark chocolate dessert. Game dishes in season. The cellar is wide-ranging but pricey. Professional, friendly service. C 220-340 F. M 185 F.

Régent-Petite France
(See restaurant above)
Closed Dec 23-Jan 3. 5 stes 1,680-1,900 F. 72 rms 850-1,300 F. Rms for disabled. Air cond. Golf. Pkg.
In the heart of Strasbourg's most scenic district, this hotel is composed of three parts, which form an "H" that touches both banks of the River Ill. Rooms and suites are decorated in contemporary style, with the most up-to-date equipment and excellent bathrooms. Bar with live music. You can have breakfast on a rooftop terrace overlooking the locks. Finnish sauna.

Régent-Contades
8, av. de la Liberté
88 36 26 26, fax 88 37 13 70
Open year-round. 9 stes 1,200-1,400 F. 36 rms 750-1,050 F. Restaurant. Air cond. Conf. Golf. Valet pkg. V, AE, DC, MC.
Reigning princes (in the guise of Euro MPs) like to stay at this imposing, handsome hotel built during the Prussian era and set on the green banks of the Ill. The reception is exceptionally friendly. The rooms are huge, and tastefully decorated in a restrained modern manner that blends in well with the Bismarck-style mouldings. Round-the-clock room service. Brand-new luxury suites were created this year. Bar, sauna, solarium.

Hôtel des Rohan
17-19, rue du Maroquin
88 32 85 11, fax 88 75 65 37
Open year-round. 36 rms 360-625 F. Air cond. Pkg. V, AE, MC.
Located 50 meters from the cathedral in the pedestrian precinct, this is one of Strasbourg's finest hotels. The rooms are elegant and quiet, and the equipment and facilities are regularly refurbished.

12/20 Saint-Sépulcre
15, rue des Orfèvres - 88 32 39 97
Closed Sun, Mon, Jun. Open until 9:45pm. Air cond. V, MC.
A jolly, ever-crowded *winstub* run by a colorful owner (an erstwhile actor). In its vein, the food is excellent: try the pork-tongue confit, wonderful jambon en croûte, homemade quiches, and hazelnut ice cream; the wine list is excellent, offering some fine little regional wines. C 120-160 F.

Sofitel
Pl. St-Pierre-le-Jeune
88 32 99 30, fax 88 32 60 67
Open year-round. 24 stes 1,150 F. 134 rms 995 F. Restaurant. Air cond. Conf. Valet pkg. V, AE, DC, MC.
This hotel is ideally situated on a quiet, leafy square in the center of town. The rooms are

rather small but well equipped. Remarkable welcome and service.

La Vieille Enseigne
9, rue des Tonneliers
88 32 58 50, fax 88 75 63 80
Closed Sat lunch, Sun, last 2 wks of Jul. Open until 10pm. Priv rm: 20. Terrace dining. Air cond. V, AE, DC, MC.
A father-son duo, Franz and Jean-Christophe Langs, offer delicious cooking that combines tradition (papa) and innovation (son) in this ancient winstub. An extra point this year for the likes of an harmonious terrine of sea scallops and leeks in a green-cabbage and truffle-oil vinaigrette, red tuna steak roasted with honey cake in a luscious wine sauce accompanied by shallot confit, and a yummy millefeuille of banana crêpes with brown sugar ice cream. Nicely composed cellar; warm welcome; competent service. C 350-450 F. M 160 F (weekday lunch), 225 F, 295 F.

12/20 Winstub Le Clou ۞
3, rue du Chaudron
88 32 11 67, fax 88 75 72 83
Closed Wed lunch, Sun, hols. Open until 12:30am. Air cond. V, AE, MC.
Marie and Roger Sengel have made a success of this lovely *winstub* decorated with gorgeous marquetry. Show-biz celebrities rub elbows with the locals to feast on choucroute salad with grilled cervelas sausages, calf's head vinaigrette, pickerel on a bed of choucroute, and kouglof glacé for dessert. Tasty house wines. C 220-320 F. M 145 F (weekday lunch, Sat, wine incl).

Chez Wong
13, quai des Bateliers
88 36 36 64, fax 88 36 23 73
Open daily until 11pm. Air cond. Valet pkg. V, AE, DC, MC.
This discreet address on the banks of the Ill marries Alsatian comfort with Chinese hospitality. The cuisine, based on top-notch ingredients, is only moderately spicy, to suit local tastes: light-as-air meat and shrimp ravioli, shrimp sautéed in spicy sauce (that wasn't spicy enough for our taste), tender and savory Canton-style roast duck, and crisp soybean crêpes. Friendly service. Small but diverse wine list. C 220-350 F. M 125 F, 250 F (weekday lunch), 372 F, 412 F, 474 F (for 2 pers).

Zeyssolff
8, pl. d'Austerlitz
88 35 55 75, fax 88 25 11 42
Closed Sun dinner, Mon, 1 wk in Jan, 2 wks in Aug. Open until 9:30pm. Priv rm: 14. Terrace dining. Air cond. V, AE, DC, MC.
The cozy pink dining room features Ionic columns, curios, and antiques. Chef Gilbert Zeyssolff's cuisine is similarly eclectic and appealing: we like his salmon carpaccio with aromatic herbs, squab salmis, whole pickerel with fennel seeds, and a parfait glacé of cherries with Kirsch. Good cellar; smiling, efficient staff. C 260-400 F. M 120 F, 185 F, 220 F, 270 F.

And also...
Our selection of places for inexpensive, quick, or late-night meals.
L'Ami Schutz (88 32 76 98 - 1, rue des Ponts-Couverts. Open until 11pm.): Bang in the middle

of the adorable Petite France district, a delicious Alsatian inn offering regional treats at fairly reasonable prices (180-300 F).
s'Klostertuewel (88 23 59 84 - 16 bis, rue du Sanglier.): A winstub offering classics like melted Munster with cumin-sautéed potatoes, smoked sausage with lentils, and an apple-rhubarb tart (75-260 F).
Aux Mille Pâtes (88 35 55 23 - 8, pl. St-Étienne. Open until 11pm.): Popular with the locals, who come for the *patron*'s marvelous pasta and other authentic Italian fare (150-280 F).
Restaurant Lutz (88 61 65 41 - 17, rue Geiler. Open until 10pm.): Oxtail presskopf, ostrich brochette, wild boar, and other hearty treats (120-230 F).
S'Thomas Stuebel (88 22 34 82 - 5, rue du Bouclier. Open until 11pm.): Discover this secret *winstub* where you can sample onion tart, horse-meat fillet seasoned with garlic, and chocolate fondue (140-230 F).

■ In Ostwald 67400   4 km SW

Château de l'Ill
88 66 85 00, fax 88 66 85 49
Open daily until 10pm. Priv rm: 250. Terrace dining. Valet pkg. V, AE, MC.
This ancient château at the edge of town, surrounded by a verdant park, has been converted into an elegant (sometimes too elegant) establishment where a chef with savoir-faire is trying to bring a new spirit to the rich, classic repertoire. He does lovely things with duck, and the caramelized milk ice cream is delightful. But the atmosphere is chillingly formal, as is the service. Superb, wide-ranging wine list. There's a winstub annex. C 300-400 F.

Château de l'Ill
(See restaurant above)
Open year-round. 7 stes 1,560-3,200 F. Rms for disabled. Half-board 1,030-1,960 F. Air cond. Conf. Tennis. Golf. Valet pkg. Helipad. V, AE, MC.
An elegant new hostelry at the edge of town, with all sorts of luxury amenities, fine bathrooms, and opulent fabrics. Very good breakfasts, served in rather stingy portions given the prices.

■ In La Wantzenau 67610   13 km NE on D 468

A la Barrière
3, route de Strasbourg
88 96 20 23, fax 88 96 25 59
Closed Tue dinner, Wed, Feb school hols, Aug 18-Sep 7. Open until 10pm. Priv rm: 14. Terrace dining. Pkg. V, AE, DC, MC.
Claude Sutter wins a second toque this year for his intelligent, savory dishes like bouillon of baby vegetables with truffles, plump turbot roasted with fennel in a vinegar-tart jus, and a rhubarb-wild stawberry tart. Suberb choice of Alsatian wines. The pleasantly rustic dining room is brightened by springtime colors. Friendly welcome. C 280-460 F. M 150 F (weekday lunch, Sat), 250 F.

---

*Some establishments change their **closing times** without warning. It is always wise to check in advance.*

Relais de la Poste
21, rue du Gal-de-Gaulle
88 96 20 64, fax 88 96 36 84
Closed Sun dinner, lunch Sat & Mon, Dec 24-Jan 15,
Jul 26-Aug 6. Open until 10pm. Priv rm: 25. Garden
dining. Air cond. Pkg. V, AE, DC, MC.
An atmosphere of quiet luxury pervades the
handsomely paneled dining room and lovely
winter garden of this venerable coaching inn.
Chef-owner Jérôme Daull's robust, rather old-
fashioned repertoire satisfies the soul as well as
the stomach, with red mullet served with a
fondue of just-cooked vegetables, tender and
savory pan-roasted lamb with persillade and
tomato confit, and an ethereal citrus-fruit
bavarian cream. Fine wine list; friendly welcome
and efficient service. **C** 300-400 F. **M** 250 F
(weekday lunch, wine incl), 165 F (weekday
lunch), 215 F, 265 F, 380 F.

 **Relais de la Poste**
(See restaurant above)
Closed Dec 24-Jan 15. 2 stes 500 F. 17 rms 250-
500 F. Half-board 700 F. Air cond. Conf. Pkg. V, AE,
DC, MC.
This old coaching inn's rooms are comfortable
and elegantly decorated, with perfect appointments. Those at the back are quieter. Exemplary
reception and service. Stables, golf, and fitness
facilities nearby.

See also: **Marlenheim**

 Hostellerie du Grand Sully
10, bd du Champ-de-Foire
38 36 27 56, fax 38 36 44 54
Closed Dec 20-Jan 3. 10 rms 200-250 F. Restaurant.
Half-board 270-370 F. Pkg. V, AE, DC, MC.
A good family hotel, decorated in pastel tones,
with wall-to-wall carpeting, and cane furniture.
Its spacious rooms on the street side are
soundproofed. Good breakfasts.

 Reynaud
82, av. du Pdt-Roosevelt
75 07 22 10, fax 75 08 03 53
Closed Sun dinner, Mon, 1st 3 wks of Jan, Aug 16-24.
Open until 9:30pm. Priv rm: 25. Garden dining.
Garage pkg. V, AE, DC, MC.
Elegant, well-wrought cuisine devoid of
gimmicks and tricks: chef Jean-Marc Reynaud
is a master craftsman, and his restaurant is
surely one of the region's best, offering a
splendid view of the Rhône as a plus. What's
more, his 160 F set menu is very generous.
But this year we noted a few inconsistencies

in the cooking: underseasoned vegetables and
overcooked sea bass resulted in the loss of a
point this year. We hope to bring it back again
when generosity is matched by precision. **C** 320-
400 F. **M** 160 F, 200 F, 250 F, 350 F.

 Reynaud
(See restaurant above)
Closed Jan, Aug 16-24. 10 rms 350-500 F. Air cond.
Conf. Heated pool. Golf. Pkg. V, AE, DC, MC.
Comfortable, inexpensive rooms looking onto
a swimming pool. Ideal for short stays.

 **Jean Brouilly**
3 ter, rue de Paris
74 63 24 56, fax 74 05 05 48
Closed Sun (exc hols lunch), Mon, Feb school hols,
Aug 7-22. Open until 9:30pm. Priv rm: 16. Terrace
dining. Air cond. Pkg. V, AE, DC, MC.
Don't be misled by the staid, substantial look
of this solid manse set in green grounds just
outside Tarare. Inside, the dining room has an
elegant, resolutely contemporary look. And Jean
Brouilly's cooking is as creative and modern as
ever, based on superb ingredients that he roams
the region to find. Sample the famous all-truffle
menu: perfectly seasoned hare parmentier, lovely salad of sea scallops with lamb's lettuce and
chopped violette potatoes, wild omble (a lake
fish) with perfectly balanced truffle jus, and rabbit thigh with pasta. Everything is absolutely
top-flight, including the wonderful Auvergne
cheeses and the gooey chocolate fondant with
almond milk. The wine list offers the best of
Burgundy and Beaujolais. The elegant dining
room offers a veranda, an Italian fountain, and
lovely grey porcelain plates. Flawless service
ably overseen by Josette Brouilly. A well-earned
third toque this year. **C** 350-400 F. **M** 160 F,
230 F, 300 F, 370 F.

Les Mazets des Roches
Route de Fontvieille
90 91 34 89, fax 90 43 53 29
Closed Nov-Easter. 1 ste 850 F. 38 rms 290-650 F.
Restaurant. Half-board 265-465 F. Air cond. Pool.
Tennis. Golf. Pkg. Helipad. V, AE, DC, MC.
Set in a thirteen-hectare park at the foot of Les
Baux, this agreeable hostelry features comfort-
able, perfectly equipped, air-conditioned rooms
with beautiful bathrooms.

L'Ambroisie
38, rue Larrey - 62 93 09 34
Closed Sun, Mon. Annual closings not available.
Open until 9pm. No pets. V, DC.
Opposite the covered market stands this
bright, pretty restaurant, where chef-owner
Daniel Labarrère will warmly welcome you and
offer savory dishes with a personal touch: quail

poached with foie gras and served with a sherry-vinegar salad, milk-fed lamb paired with a salpicon of garlicky cèpes, and a Valrhona chocolate biscuit. The cellar is a wine buff's delight. **C** 300-350 F. **M** 95-270 F.

Le Petit Gourmand
62, av. B.-Barrère - 62 34 26 86
Closed Sat lunch, Mon. Open until 9:30pm. Terrace dining. V, AE, DC.
Guy Espagnacq's clever *carte* has taken on an earthy regional accent (quail salad, truffled loin of Pyrenees lamb with its kidneys), while the 70 F set menu honors tradition: green salad with goat cheese and walnuts, beef steak in a robust mustard-seed sauce, and delicious Damson plum clafoutis. Charming welcome in a cozy, flowerfilled bistro setting. **C** 250-300 F. **M** 70 F (weekday lunch), 98 F, 160 F.

■ **In Juillan 65290**   6 km SW on N 21

La Caravelle
Tarbes-Ossun-Lourdes airport
62 32 99 96, fax 62 32 05 25
Closed Sun dinner, Mon, Jan 2-23, Jul 17-Aug 2. Open until 10pm. Air cond. Pkg. V, AE, DC, MC.
An airport restaurant with two bright, comfortable dining rooms and an indoor garden, where diners can observe takeoffs and landings against the dramatic background of the Pyrenees. The cuisine takes flight, particularly on the first set menu: fine piperade with grilled ham, perfectly roasted grouper with béarnaise sauce and tasty saffron rice, and an impeccable chocolate fondant. An extra point this year. Excellent cellar with a focus on regional wines. **C** 250-400 F. **M** 155 F (exc Sun), 250 F.

TAVERS 45	→ Beaugency

TESTE (LA) 33	→ Arcachon

TETEGHEM 59	→ Dunkerque

THÉOULE-SUR-MER	06590
Paris 895 - Saint-Raphaël 36 - Cannes 10 - Nice 41   *Alpes-Mar.*

■ **In Miramar 06590**   6 km S on N 98

Miramar Beach Hotel
On La Corniche d'Or, 47, av. de Miramar
93 75 41 36, fax 93 75 44 83
Open year-round. 9 stes 780-1,380 F. 51 rms 450-1,080 F. Rms for disabled. Restaurant. Half-board 460-775 F. Air cond. Conf. Heated pool. Tennis. Golf. Pkg. V, AE, DC, MC.
Conveniently located, with direct access to a private beach, this modern hotel offers pretty, functional rooms with terraces and loggias. Special amenities include babysitting and a health center.

Père Pascal
16, av. du Trayas
93 75 40 11, fax 93 75 03 28
Closed Thu (exc hols & Jul-Aug). Open until 10:30pm. Garden dining. Pkg. V, AE, DC, MC.
George Cozzolino takes the best possible local catch and turns it into pleasing dishes like a

mousseline of sea bass with a crayfish coulis, lobster roasted with ginger, and a berry millefeuille, all served on a terrace overlooking the sea. The prices are a bit much, though. **C** 350-500 F. **M** 135 F (exc Sun), 198 F, 260 F.

THIONVILLE	57100
Paris 342 - Luxembourg 32 - Metz 29 - Nancy 83   *Moselle*

Le Concorde
6, pl. du Luxembourg - 82 53 83 18
Closed Sun dinner, 1st wk of Jan, 1st wk of Aug. Open until 10pm. Priv rm: 20. Pkg. V, AE, DC, MC.
This dining room offers a panoramic view from the top of a tower, and chef Daniel Nachon's undeniable skill accounts for the success of his classic repertoire. But this year we noticed a few ups and downs: a generous serving of perfectly prepared Landes foie gras in gelatin, a delicate feuilleté of lobster cooked in Vin Jaune but drowning in sauce, and dry pizzette of lamb with Aosta ham. A point less this year, especially since the prices of the set menus have gone up and they don't even include a cheese course. Competent service. **C** 350-460 F. **M** 150 F (exc Sat dinner), 220 F (wine incl), 180 F, 320 F, 390 F.

L'Horizon
50, route du Crève-Cœur
82 88 53 65, fax 82 34 55 84
Closed Sat lunch, Jan. Open until 9pm. Priv rm: 30. Terrace dining. Garage pkg. V, AE, DC, MC.
Nothing but nice surprises in this sunny, stylishly decorated dining room where Jean-Pascal Speck offers regional cooking enlivened by original personal touches: delicious ravigote of suckling pig with warm herbs, intensely flavored squab roll with baby vegetables, and strawberry soup in orange-scented wine sauce. Our only quibble: the high prices of the good wine list. Attentive, competent welcome and service. **C** 310-380 F. **M** 195-295 F.

L'Horizon
(See restaurant above)
Closed Jan. 10 rms 440-740 F. Restaurant. Half-board 720-1,100 F. Pkg. Helipad. V, AE, DC, MC.
All the rooms in this hotel have been provided with plush carpets and curtains and lovely period furniture typical of the region. Sweeping valley views. Relais et Châteaux.

THIVARS 28	→ Chartres

THOIRY 01	→ Saint-Genis-Pouilly

THOISSEY	01140
Paris 411 - Mâcon 16 - Lyon 56 - Villefranche-sur-S. 29   *Ain*

Restaurant Paul-Blanc
Rue P.-Blanc
74 04 04 74, fax 74 04 94 51
Closed Tue (exc lunch Oct 1-Mar). Open until 9:30pm (10pm in summer). Priv rm: 50. Terrace dining. Hotel: 20 rms 250-680 F. Conf. Pkg. V, AE, DC, MC.
Bruno Maringue unswervingly follows in the footsteps of his famous grandfather, Paul Blanc. Enshrined on the menu is the dish that made Au Chapon Fin a byword in gastronomic circles: fricassée de volaille de Bresse à la crème with parmentier crêpes, frog's legs with salmon fillet,

roast lobster seasoned with coriander, and Challans duck. The 160 F lunch menu is worthy of attention for the snails and Bresse chicken in vinegar sauce. These dishes have their charm, of course, but we wish Bruno would now see fit to renew a repertoire that is holding his talent hostage. Splendid cellar. C 350-450 F. M 160 F (lunch), 250 F, 330 F, 420 F, 520 F.

THOLONET 13	→ Aix-en-Provence

THOMERY 77	→ Fontainebleau

THONON-LES-BAINS	74200
Paris 575 - Geneva 33 - Evian 9 - Annecy 72	*H.-Savoie*

Le Prieuré
68, Grande-Rue - 50 71 31 89
Closed Sun dinner & Mon (exc dinner off-seas). Open until 10:30pm. Priv rm: 40. V, AE, DC, MC.
Comfortably ensconced at Le Prieuré's elegant tables, you'll be impressed by the imaginative dishes (expensive, but well worth the money) dreamed up by Charles Plumex. We admire his daube de carottes en cappuccino, roast langoustines with coriander, beef fillet, tarte au vin flavored with cinnamon, and a marjoram gunduja with licorice ice cream. There's a touch of preciousness in all this (as in the service). Fine wine list at high prices. C 370-500 F. M 200 F (weekday lunch, wine incl), 280 F, 350 F.

■ **In Sciez 74140**   10 km SW

Château de Coudrée
50 72 62 33, fax 50 72 57 28
Closed Nov-Apr. 19 rms 600-1,600 F. Restaurant. Half-board 650-950 F. Conf. Heated pool. Tennis. Golf. Pkg. V, AE, DC.
The quiet of the well-groomed grounds, a fine view of Lake Geneva, and sumptuously decorated rooms are some of the reasons why this hotel is one of the most pleasant Relais et Châteaux. Sauna; disco; private beach.

THOUARS	79100
Paris 327 - Bressuire 29 - Niort 81 - Parthenay 39	*Deux-Sèvres*

Le Clos Saint-Médard
14, pl. St-Médard
49 66 66 00, fax 49 96 15 01
Closed Sun dinner, Mon, Feb school hols, 1st wk of Aug. Open until 9:30pm. Priv rm: 20. Terrace dining. Pkg. V, AE, MC.
In the heart of historic Thouars is a lovely twelfth-century house where old and new come together in a warm, attractive atmosphere; this is one of the region's best restaurants. It's a real pleasure to take a seat in the elegant dining room or garden, and feast on Pierre Aracil's lively, colorful cuisine. Try the 138 F menu: a gâteau of melon, tomato, and quail with a bacon-laced mesclun salad; steamed grouper with two sauces (beurre blanc and a reduced red-wine sauce), blue cheese à la crème, and a peach with bread pudding and wine jelly. On the à la carte menu, you'll find a tasty salad of langoustines and green beans in a slightly overpowering vinaigrette seasoned with cardamom, and a savory émincé of beef en papillote with beef

marrow and herbs. The wine list offers fine Loire wines at reasonable prices; friendly welcome and excellent service overseen by Yanelle Aracil. An extra point this year. This is truly the kind of place it's a pleasure to visit. C 230-330 F. M 98 F, 150 F (weekdays, wine incl), 138 F, 198 F, 310 F.

Le Clos Saint-Médard
(See restaurant above)
See restaurant for closings. 4 rms 230-280 F. Half-board 320-360 F. Conf. Golf. Pkg. V, AE, MC.
The light-colored rooms with rattan furniture are well equipped. Wine-tasting courses are offered and in summer you can take carriage rides.

TIGNES	73320
Paris 690 - Bourg-St-Maurice 30 - Val-d'Isère 13	*Savoie*

10/20 Clin d'Œil
Quartier du Rosset - 79 06 59 10
Closed May 1-Jun 30, Aug 30-Oct 23. Open until 10:30pm. Terrace dining. Pkg. V, MC.
A lively, family-style atmosphere warms this intimate restaurant opposite the Grande Motte glacier. Don't expect *grande cuisine*, but the leek terrine, cèpes and foie gras, pot-au-feu au confit, lentil sabodet and lamb en croûte are sure to satisfy. C 150-200 F. M 85 F.

Curling
In Le Val-Claret
79 06 34 34, fax 79 06 46 14
Closed May 8-Jul 8, Aug 29-Oct 28. 35 rms 450-850 F. Half-board 400-535 F. Conf. Golf. Pkg. V, AE, DC, MC.
A hotel near the lifts, with attractively decorated, perfectly comfortable rooms, and a bar famed for its cocktails.

Le Ski d'Or
In Le Val-Claret
79 06 51 60, fax 79 06 45 49
Closed May 1-Dec 1. Open until 9:30pm. Pkg. V, AE, MC.
With assets like a handsome dining room and splendid view, it's a shame that the Ski d'Or closes in summer. Particularly since chef Christophe Moyon has revived the reputation of Tignes's best restaurant. He experiments with Savoyard dishes in his Beaufort cheese soufflé and filet of féra (lake fish) with polenta, but also offers treats from his native Southwest, like foie gras and a rib-sticking garbure soup. Warm welcome; competent service. C 300-350 F. M 125 F (lunch), 250 F, 295 F.

Le Ski d'Or
(See restaurant above)
Closed May-Nov. 23 rms 980-1,100 F. Half-board 980 F. Conf. Helipad. V, AE, MC.
Renovation of this lovely Val Claret residence has been completed, and all the rooms are now spacious and flawlessly equipped. Relais et Châteaux.

Le Terril Blanc
Lac de Tignes
79 06 32 87, fax 79 06 58 17
Closed May 10-Jul 3, Aug 29-Dec 24. 26 rms 500-600 F. Restaurant. Half-board 490-520 F. Golf. Pkg. Helipad. V.

A small lakeside hotel near the lifts with recently renovated, well-kept rooms that afford lovely views.

TILQUES 62   → Saint-Omer

TONNERRE   89700

Paris 196 - Troyes 57 - Avallon 52 - Sens 73 - Auxerre 35   *Yonne*

L'Abbaye Saint-Michel

Montée de St-Michel
86 55 05 99, fax 86 55 00 10
Closed Mon & Tue lunch off-seas, Jan 2-Feb 9. Open until 9:30pm. Priv rm: 100. Garden dining. Valet pkg. V, AE, DC, MC.

The high-perched abbey where Joan of Arc once stopped in 1429 has recovered a considerable portion of its former glory, thanks to the Cussac family's intelligent, painstaking restoration. Part of the cloister has been rebuilt, and the chapter room is now an elegant place to sip apéritifs (a locally grown Chablis Premier Cru would not be amiss). Christophe Cussac's cuisine is simply dazzling: light, full-flavored, impertinently inventive. He excels in both "city" dishes (that the locals tend to order) and "country" dishes (ordered, of course, by city people). Savor his calf's head with garden herbs, chicken wings with Epoisse cheese ravioli, and pot-au-feu de foie gras à la paysanne (some peasant mama knows her bouillons...). We also reveled in the very traditional quasi de veau (standing rump of veal) with tiny onions and tomato confit, and the innovative gelée of salmon en civet with shrimp. And this year the abbey's own wine, Montée Saint Michel, is added to the sumptuous list of great Burgundies in the cellar. C 400-600 F. M 270 F (wine incl), 300 F, 480 F, 590 F.

L'Abbaye Saint-Michel

(See restaurant above)
Closed Mon off-seas, Jan 2-Feb 9. 5 stes 1,600-1,900 F. 9 rms 580-1,500 F. Air cond. Conf. Tennis. Golf. Valet pkg. Helipad. V, AE, DC, MC.

The accommodation is composed of two distinct parts: the old rooms (note the medieval frescoes in the "Chartier" room), and the sumptuous new suites, where contemporary design blends beautifully with the noble original stones and beams. Panoramic views of the pretty town of Tonnerre. The surrounding park contains a medieval garden, an orchard, and an herb and vegetable garden. Minigolf; helipad. Relais et Châteaux.

TOUL   54200

Paris 283 - Bar-le-Duc 61 - Metz 74 - Nancy 23   *Meurthe/M.*

Le Dauphin

Route de Villey-St-Etienne
83 43 13 46, fax 83 64 37 01
Closed Sun dinner. Open until 10:30pm (11pm in summer). Garden dining. Pkg. V, AE, DC, MC.

This former American officers' mess surrounded by an industrial district is now a spacious dining room overlooking a flowered garden. You'll have a smiling welcome, and then can savor the magical cooking of Christophe Vohmann, three-toques level from start to finish.

He offers inventive, astutely balanced, expertly prepared dishes using the best possible ingredients that he seeks out from local producers. We urge you to sample the vinaigrette of sea bass and red mullet with sea snails paired with a delicate little tomato feuilleté, a perfect foie gras cooked whole with artichokes and potatoes, tender chops of milk-fed veal with truffled pasta, and sublime desserts like a peach roasted with rosemary paired with caramel ice cream, or a goat cheese cheesecake with currants and a mirabelle-plum jam. The only drawback here? The prices. There's no set menu for less than 190 F, and even if you opt for the reasonably priced local Pinot Noir at 120 F on the well chosen wine list, you'll still pay a tidy sum. In times like these, the owners need to pay attention to this. Véronique Vohmann and her maître d'hôtel provide the amiable service. C 450-520 F. M 190 F (weekdays, Sat lunch), 250 F (exc Sun dinner).

TOULON   83000

Paris 833 - Nice 152 - Aix 81 - Marseille 66 - St-Raphaël 96   *Var*

La Chamade

25, rue Denfert-Rochereau - 94 92 28 58
Closed Sat lunch, Sun, Aug 1-20. Open until 9:30pm. Priv rm: 20. Air cond. V, AE, MC.

Véronique Bonneau's warm welcome adds to the charm of La Chamade's brand-new decor. Her husband Francis, an alumnus of Taillevent and the Château de Locguénolé (where he wore two toques), has composed a very up-to-date menu based on top-quality products: pig's ear with petits violets (sea figs, a local shellfish), sea bass grilled in its skin with wild mushrooms, and a craqueline of dates flavored with gentian. Charming service. C 320-420 F. M 125 F, 175 F, 280 F, 350 F.

12/20 La Corniche

17, littoral F.-Mistral
94 41 35 12, fax 94 41 24 58
Open daily until 10:30pm. Priv rm: 12. Garden dining. Pkg. V, AE, DC, MC.

Three venerable pines grow right through (yes!) the attractive dining room that opens out onto the bay, stretching their branches up into the Southern sun. The cuisine still has a Midi accent, but it lacked personality this year: savory zucchini-blossom fritters and warm oysters, roast cod served with a runny sauce and bland artichoke purée, very ordinary veal piccata, and a pleasant although not authentic tiramisu. The toque disappears. Well chosen though short wine list. C 240-300 F. M 99 F, 140 F.

La Corniche

(See restaurant above)
Open year-round. 3 stes 380-580 F. 19 rms 320-490 F. Air cond. Conf. Pkg. V, AE, DC, MC.

This hotel provides well-equipped, distinctive, comfortable rooms, half of which have balconies or terraces overlooking the sea.

Le Dauphin

21 bis, rue J.-Jaurès - 94 93 12 07
Closed Sat lunch, Sun, hols. Open until 9:30pm. Air cond. V, AE, MC.

This is not the nicest part of Toulon, but Le Dauphin's pretty garden-terrace and dining room draw diners nonetheless, thanks to chef Alain Biles's pleasing Provençal dishes. Try his 135 F menu: eggplant papetons au coulis de pommes d'amour, fillet of scorpion fish with tapenade, a selection of cheeses, and prunes in spiced red wine. Well chosen wine list. Cheerful, highly competent service. **C** 250-350 F. **M** 90 F, 135 F, 195 F.

Le Gros Ventre
Corniche du Mourillon, in front of Fort St-Louis - 94 42 15 42, fax 94 31 40 32
Closed Thu lunch, Wed, Dec 24-28. Open until 11pm. Terrace dining. Pkg. V, AE, DC, MC.
Alain Audibert's attractive repertoire is based on seafood, noble products, and dishes served en croûte (such as sea bass fillet); desserts are the house sherbets. **C** 250-380 F. **M** 94 F (lunch), 138 F, 220 F.

Les Terrasses
Bd de l'Amiral-Vence
94 24 41 57, fax 94 22 42 25
Open daily until 10:30pm. Priv rm: 300. Terrace dining. Air cond. Pool. Pkg. V, AE, DC, MC.
Come to this comfortable modern dining room with a panoramic view of the sea to sample carefully prepared cooking with a Midi accent: avocado île flottante with smoked salmon, roast sea bass with aïoli, and grilled lamb chops with basil butter. Fine choice of Provençal and Bordeaux wines. Competent welcome. **C** 200-260 F. **M** 90 F (wine incl).

New Hotel Tour Blanche 🔼🔼
(See restaurant above)
Open year-round. 3 stes 495 F. 89 rms 395 F. Half-board 420 F. Air cond. Conf. Pool. Golf. Pkg. V, AE, DC, MC.
Bright, very nicely equipped, air-conditioned rooms and comfortable bathrooms (some with a balcony overlooking the sea). Fully renovated.

■ **In Cuers 83390**   20 km NE on N 97

Le Lingousto
Route de Pierrefeu - 94 28 69 10
Closed Sun dinner, Mon, Feb. Open until 9:30pm. Priv rm: 25. Terrace dining. Pkg. V, AE, DC.
Local gourmets gather at this *bastide* set under the plane trees to savor the peace and quiet, the view of the surrounding vineyards, and Alain Ryon's sensitive, imaginative cooking. This year, you can enjoy his star attraction, a rich and savory squab rouelle stuffed with foie gras. Other good choices are the warm salade du Lingousto, sar (similar to sea bream) in potato "scales", and a tourte stuffed with truffled pig's foot. The fine wine list is rich in regional offerings, and offers a good choice of half bottles. Perfect welcome and service. Special amenities include a children's play ground in the garden. **M** 160 F (weekdays), 230 F, 320 F, 400 F.

TOULOUSE	31000
Paris 681 - Marseille 400 - Bordeaux 249	H.-Garonne

🔼🔼 Hôtel des Beaux-Arts
1, pl. du Pont-Neuf
61 23 40 50, fax 61 22 02 27
Open year-round. 20 rms 340-575 F. Air cond. V, AE, DC, MC.

A friendly hotel, with well-equipped, soundproofed rooms that are attractively decorated. Fine views of the Garonne; meals served on trays. Restaurant (see Brasserie des Beaux-Arts, below).

🔲 Benjamin
7, rue des Gestes - 61 22 92 66
Open daily until 11pm. Air cond. V.
The city's late-night crowd loves this bistrot in the pedestrian precinct of old Toulouse, for its trompe-l'œil decor, attractive prices, and generous cooking. Try the generous 125 F menu: hors-d'oeuvres (tapas, chorizo sausage, etc.), a good feuilleté stuffed with basil-scented squid and served with an unctuous sauce, fine slice of leg of lamb cooked with five kinds of peppers and served with delicious garnishes, and a copious rice pudding with crème anglaise sauce. Nice little house wine by the carafe. Friendly welcome. A toque this year. **M** 59 F, 78 F (lunch), 89 F, 125 F.

🔲 Le Bistrot du Vanel
22, rue Maurice-Fonvieille
61 21 51 82, fax 61 23 69 04
Closed Aug 1-15. Open until 11pm. V, AE, MC.
In a 1930s decor, you'll find a restaurant, bar and bistrot all in the same space. Sample the 120 F menu: foie gras in a tasty Jurançon gelatin (the slices are cut too thin, though), generous and tender duck breast with caramelized pears, and a fine prune parfait spiked with Armagnac. The first set menu is good, too. Nice little wines; friendly welcome and service. **C** 150-200 F. **M** 98 F, 120 F (exc Sun).

12/20 Brasserie des Beaux-Arts
1, quai de la Daurade
61 21 12 12, fax 61 21 14 80
Closed Christmas eve. Open until 1am. Terrace dining. Air cond. V, AE, DC, MC.
The Art Nouveau decor (walnut paneling, mirrors), brisk and efficient line of staff, reliable cooking, and the ever-present line of customers waiting to be seated remind us of the Brasserie Flo in Paris. A most successful cloning. Sample the raw seafood platters, salmon fillet with sorrel sauce, chicken fricassée with morels, and delicate warm apple tart. Reasonably priced, eclectic wine list. **C** 170-230 F. **M** 99 F (lunch, wine incl), 95 F (dinner, wine incl), 141 F (wine incl).

🔼🔼 Hôtel de Brienne
20, bd de Mal-Leclerc
61 23 60 60, fax 61 23 18 94
Open year-round. 3 stes 550-825 F. 68 rms 330-460 F. Restaurant. Air cond. Pkg. V, AE, DC, MC.
Contemporary (not to say futuristic) architecture for this city-center hotel with functional, well-equipped rooms, most of which look onto a patio. Meals on trays available.

12/20 Le Capoul
13, pl. du Pdt-Wilson
61 21 08 27, fax 61 21 96 70
Open daily until 11:30pm. Terrace dining. Air cond. V, AE, DC, MC.
This elegantly mirrored and paneled brasserie is open late, seven days a week. The new chef offers a well composed traditional menu including pot-au-feu salad, steak with blue cheese and sautéed potatoes (a bit bland), and a tasty pastis

439

gascon pastry that needed a bit more Armagnac. Boring wine list. Dynamic service. **C** 150-250 F.

 ### Le Capoul
(See restaurant above)

Open year-round. 7 stes 1,000-1,500 F. 133 rms 550-700 F. Air cond. Conf. V, AE, DC, MC.

A fine hotel in the center of Toulouse with perfectly comfortable, though rather impersonal accommodation. For guests' leisure moments, there is a lovely winter garden and a Jacuzzi.

Le Clocher de Rodez
14-15, pl. Jeanne-d'Arc
61 62 42 92, fax 61 62 68 99

Open year-round. 46 rms 240-285 F. Restaurant. Half-board 350-395 F. Air cond. Golf. Pkg. V, AE, DC.

Among the city's oldest, this well-maintained hotel in the center of town features pleasantly decorated, comfortable rooms. Bar.

12/20 La Côte de Bœuf
12, rue des Gestes - 61 21 19 61

Closed Mon lunch, Sun, Aug 1-24. Open until 10:30pm. Terrace dining. V, MC.

Huge ribs of beef seem to dominate all other items on this friendly restaurant's menu. If you're in the mood for something else, try the simple homestyle plats-du-jour at reasonable prices. **C** 180-250 F. **M** 115 F.

Hôtel de Diane
See restaurant Le Saint-Simon

 ### Chez Émile
13, pl. St-Georges
61 21 05 56, fax 61 21 42 26

Closed Sun, Mon, end Dec. Open until 10:30pm. Priv rm: 30. Terrace dining. Air cond. V, AE, DC, MC.

Chef Philippe Puel offers cuisine that takes its inspiration from the sea and the Southwest region. On the 220 F menu: a generous serving of salmon marinated in lime with ginger, a parillade canarienne (grilled seafood, that could use a bit more seasoning), and a fine and delicate apple tart. Professional welcome and service in the paneled ground-floor dining room. The superb cellar is full of exciting finds. **C** 250-350 F. **M** 99 F (lunch, wine incl), 115 F, 150 F (lunch in summer), 210 F, 230 F (summer), 195 F, 220 F.

12/20 Grand Café de l'Opéra
1, pl. du Capitole
61 21 37 03, fax 61 23 41 04

Closed 3 wks in Aug. Open until 12:30am. Priv rm: 11. Terrace dining. Air cond. V, AE, DC, MC.

Local bigwigs like to congregate on the terrace for fine brasserie-style cooking served in a convivial atmosphere: artichoke bottoms with Parma ham, pot-au-feu salad, lemony chicken with terragon, and cod à la portugaise. **C** 200-360 F. **M** 95 F, 129 F, 160 F (weekdays).

Grand Hôtel de l'Opéra
See restaurant Les Jardins de l'Opéra

 ### Le Grande-Bretagne
298-300, av. de Grande-Bretagne
61 31 84 85, fax 61 31 87 12

Open year-round. 2 stes 700-900 F. 41 rms 320-440 F. Rms for disabled. Restaurant. Half-board 350-460 F. Air cond. Conf. Golf. Pkg. V, AE, DC.

A modern hotel on the left (i.e. Gascon) bank of the Garonne, with tastefully decorated, efficiently soundproofed rooms. Numerous services.

 ### Holiday Inn Crowne Plaza
7, pl. du Capitole
61 61 19 19, fax 61 23 79 96

Open year-round. 2 stes 1,000-1,400 F. 160 rms 780-920 F. Rms for disabled. Restaurant. Air cond. Conf. Valet pkg. V, AE, DC, MC.

This beautiful building on the Place du Capitole offers spacious, sophisticated rooms. Some are reserved for non-smokers and some are designed for the disabled. Excellent reception, New Orleans–style bar, many lounges. The health club includes a sauna and Jacuzzi.

Les Jardins de l'Opéra
1, pl. du Capitole - 61 23 07 76 (R),
61 21 82 66 (H), fax 61 23 41 04

Closed Sun, hols, Aug 8-31. Priv rm: 80. Garden dining. Air cond. V, AE, DC.

The dining room with its calculated theatricality—glass ceilings, opulent fabrics, sensuous lighting, elegant tables, sumptuous flowers—is more "Opéra" than "Jardin". Staged in a Tuscan-style courtyard, the setting is both larger and more convincing than life. One forgets that the Place du Capitole, with its traffic and noise, is but a few yards away. Here the only sounds are of quiet conversation and the splash of the fountain under the veranda.

Dominique Toulousy is showing the full range and depth of his repertoire in the Jardins' kitchens these days. The first act of our opera begins with a love duo between oysters and salmon joined in the most suave of tartares paired with a tart chive cream sauce, a marvelous harmony; the warm terrine of cèpes and eggplant with tiny petit gris snails sings a song of the garden and woods. Next comes a little air of the Mediterranean from the sea bream grilled over a wood fire, a diva accompanied by potatoes with black olives and tomatoes; and from the red mullet fillets with fennel paired with a mirepoix of baby vegetables and shellfish annointed with olive oil. You can almost hear the clatter of "grande-mère's" polished copper pots with an old-fashioned song in the background as you sample "peasant" dishes raised to new heights, like the gigotin of Pyrenées chicken stuffed with pigs's foot and truffled potatoes, the Lauraguais squab, or the farm-raised veal chops in a cèpe croûte with casserole-roasted "grande-mère" potatoes. The cassoulet toulousain has fans and detractors; some feel the powerful aria of the sausages overwhelms the delicate song of the tiny fresh fava beans in their jus. But everyone wants to cry "encore" for the roast lamb shanks with pink Lautrec garlic croquettes and the accompanying zucchini gâteau à l'anchoïade. An allegro vivace finale with the plump figs in Banyuls stuffed with vanilla ice cream, and the warm chocolate tart, and we hereby lower the curtain. The discreet chef doesn't come out to take a well deserved bow; we would also like to applaud his wife Maryse for the attentive direction of the service and for the superb wine score composed with the help of the sommelier. **C** 600 F. **M** 200 F, 480 F.

Grand Hôtel de l'Opéra

(See restaurant above)
Open year-round. 7 stes 1,350-1,500 F. 42 rms 700-1,300 F. Air cond. Conf. Heated pool. V, AE, DC.
Entering here from the turbulent Place du Capitole is like traversing a time warp. Back to another age of grace and beauty: this former convent has been remodeled with a sure hand, in elegant taste. In addition to charm, there is modern comfort (saunas, Jacuzzis, air-conditioning...). Guest rooms are extremely restful and comfortable. Some are sparkling new and have balconies overlooking the city's red-tiled roofs. Excellent reception.

La Marmite en Folie

28, rue P.-Painlevé
61 42 77 86, fax 61 59 57 36
Open daily until 10:15pm. Priv rm: 15. Garden dining. Air cond. V.
In a refined, understated setting Marc Brandolin presents a bill of fare based on top-flight foodstuffs handled with respect and skill. Try the oxtail terrine, saffrony shellfish fricassée, and squab with foie gras and seasonal vegetables. Lots of interesting surprises on the wine list.
C 250-350 F. M 100 F, 150 F.

Mercure

Rue St-Jérôme, pl. Occitane
61 23 11 77, fax 61 23 19 38
Open year-round. 170 rms 350-480 F. Rms for disabled. Restaurant. Half-board 400-500 F. Air cond. Conf. V, AE, DC, MC.
Set above a shopping center, this modern and centrally located hotel offers recently renovated, well-equipped rooms (though those opposite the Place Occitane are poorly soundproofed). Excellent breakfasts that include scrambled eggs and pastries.

Mercure Les Capitouls

29, allées J.-Jaurès
61 62 63 33, fax 61 63 15 17
Open year-round. 2 stes 550-750 F. 50 rms 390-515 F. Rms for disabled. Restaurant. Half-board 550-650 F. Air cond. Conf. Golf. Pkg. V, AE, DC, MC.
Centrally placed on the Allées Jean-Jaurès (the "Champs-Élysées" of Toulouse), this recently built hotel offers stylish rooms, but those on the street are noisy, while those at the back are stuffy. The young, efficient staff provide a pleasant welcome.

Mercure Wilson

7, rue Labéda (corner pl. Wilson)
61 21 21 75, fax 61 22 77 64
Open year-round. 4 stes 700 F. 91 rms 350-495 F. Air cond. Conf. Pkg. V, AE, DC, MC.
An excellent, centrally located hotel with many amenities and small, pastel-hued rooms. Piano bar; room service until 10pm.

Mermoz

50, rue Matabiau
61 63 04 04, fax 61 63 15 64
Open year-round. 1 ste 490-690 F. 52 rms 450 F. Restaurant. Air cond. Garage pkg. V, AE, DC, MC.
Near the station and built round a peaceful enclosed courtyard, this modern hotel has 1930s-style rooms that have personality and good equipment. Wonderful breakfasts. Meals served on trays round the clock.

Novotel Toulouse Centre

5, pl. A.-Jourdain
61 21 74 74, fax 61 22 81 22
Open year-round. 6 stes 800 F. 125 rms 450-510 F. Rms for disabled. Restaurant. Air cond. Conf. Pool. Golf. Pkg. V, AE, DC, MC.
Recently built, this well-designed hotel with its own garden next to the Japanese gardens offers numerous amenities, such as non-smoking rooms and free access to tennis courts. Superb breakfasts.

Orsi

Le Bouchon Lyonnais, 13, rue de l'Industrie - 61 62 97 43, fax 61 63 00 71
Closed Sun (exc hols). Open until 11pm. Priv rm: 20. Air cond. V, AE, DC, MC.
The 1930s brasserie decor is fashioned after that of the restaurant Pierre Orsi in Lyon, and the menu features the same andouillette sausages and saucisson chaud, though there's a hearty cassoulet for local culinary chauvinists to fall back on. But Laurent Orsi also cooks seafood and Mediterranean dishes with notable success: try his galettes of red mullet fillets à la niçoise. Wine buffs will love the cellar, and everyone will love the charming, hard-working service. C 300-420 F. M 120 F, 200 F (wine incl) 135 F, 168 F, 180 F.

Palladia

271, av. de Grande-Bretagne
62 12 01 20, fax 62 12 01 21
Open year-round. 4 stes 750-1,200 F. 82 rms 690 F. Rms for disabled. Restaurant. Air cond. Conf. Pool. Pkg. V, AE, DC, MC.
In an ultra-contemporary metal and smoked glass building, you'll find brand-new, spacious, elegantly decorated rooms, soundproofed an air-conditioned, with fine bathrooms. Bar, fitness center, and excellent conference facilities. Friendly, competent welcome.

Le Pastel

237, route de St-Simon - 61 40 59 01
Closed 1 wk in Dec, 3 wks in Aug. Open until 10pm. Priv rm: 20. Terrace dining. No pets. Pkg. V, AE.
It's not easy to find this restaurant in a converted mansion, but you'll be glad you did when you settle into one of the two yellow-tinted dining rooms to sample chef Gérard Garrigues' cooking. He has excellent credentials (he spent ten years with Alain Dutournier), his cuisine is well crafted, and his prices offer the city's best quality-price ratio. Sample the succulent terrine of duck foie gras accompanied by lamb's lettuce scattered with pine nuts, particularly flavorful Jerusalem artichokes with foie gras and truffles, veal shanks à l'etouffée, or veal kidney sautéed with truffled purple artichokes, excellent sheep's milk cheese from Péraille, and a delicate apple tart seasoned with cinnamon. Choose the Serre-Mazard Corbières wine, and you'll have a meal for which you will pay a more than reasonable 300 F à la carte; and there's a 160 F lunch menu served in the generous portions demanded in Toulouse, a city of trenchermen. C 280-350 F. M 120 F, 160 F (lunch).

12/20 Le Pavillon d'Argent

43, rue du Taur - 61 23 36 48
Closed Sun, Aug 1-15. Open until 10pm. Air cond. V, AE, DC, MC.

Pleasant Vietnamese specialties prepared from high-quality products: crisp and tender egg rolls, beef in a slighly spicy sauce, brochettes, soups, and stews. **C** 120-200 F. **M** 65 F, 89 F.

12/20 Le Saint-Simon
3, route de St-Simon
61 07 59 52, fax 61 86 38 94
Closed Sat lunch, Sun. Open until 10pm. Priv rm: 30. Garden dining. Air cond. Pkg. V, AE, DC.
Between sets of tennis or squash, sporty types jog into the bright, spacious modern veranda or the Louis XV-style dining room for dishes based on fine products but sometimes plagued by lapses in culinary technique. On the 180 F menu: monkfish and salmon ravioli, curiously black and underseasoned; perfectly grilled grouper; cheeses; and an apple crisp that wasn't crisp. Fine choice of Bordeaux. Very friendly welcome and service. **C** 220-300 F. **M** 95 F, 105 F, 135 F, 180 F.

▲▲ Hôtel de Diane
(See restaurant above)
Open year-round. 1 ste 580-620 F. 34 rms 390-505 F. Rms for disabled. Half-board 370-700 F. Conf. Pool. Tennis. Golf. Pkg. V, AE, DC.
This nineteenth-century manor house sits in five acres of grounds especially suited for sports-minded guests (tennis, squash, swimming pool, minigolf). Two modern annexes house additional well-equipped, comfortable rooms.

▲▲ Sofitel-Centre
84, allées Jean-Jaurès
61 10 23 40, fax 61 10 23 20
Open year-round. 16 stes 1,100-1,250 F. 103 rms 790-850 F. Rms for disabled. Restaurant. Half-board 625 F. Air cond. Conf. Golf. Valet pkg. V, AE, DC, MC.
This town-center hotel not far from the train station and convention center offers all the comforts and services for which the chain is known.

Ubu Club
16, rue St-Rome
61 23 97 80, fax 61 23 14 56
Closed Sun. Open until 2am. Air cond. No pets. Garage pkg. V, AE, DC.
Under the vaulted ceilings of this comfortable, English-style dining room (you have to cross the club's dance floor to get here), the city's late-night set feed on fresh dishes prepared by Honoré Guillem, who wins an extra point this year for the generously served and harmonious langouste salad, roast kid in a tasty jus, and delcious pastis gascon (flaky apple pastry). On the wine list, sample the excellent Côtes du Frontennais Château Montauriol 1990 for 90 F. **C** 250-450 F. **M** 150 F (dinner, wine incl).

Vanel
22, rue M.-Fonvielle
61 21 51 82, fax 61 23 69 04
Closed Sun, Aug 1-15. Air cond. V, AE, MC.
As Lucien Vanel enjoys his retirement, his former assistant Fructuoso Polo has brought new life to this landmark restaurant that went through a difficult period for awhile. The cozy 1930s dining room is divided into a bistrot and a retaurant, separated by a bar. In the restaurant, decorated with lovely modern paintings, you'll

be served flavorful, carefully prepared dishes like those on the excellent 250 F menu: croustillant of red mullet in an herb salad, delicious milk-fed lamb in a jus with baby vegetables, and a magnificent feuilleté of caramelized apples with vanilla ice cream, all served by a friendly and efficient staff. Fine choice of Southwest wines at reasonable prices. **C** 360-500 F. **M** 200 F (lunch, wine & coffee incl), 250 F, 500 F.

And also...
Our selection of places for inexpensive, quick, or late-night meals.
Attila (61 29 83 59 - Marché V.-Hugo.): A rare jewel among the many ordinary bistrots in the city's center, offering market-fresh ingredients prepared with care: game, parillada, bouillabaisse. Mixed crowd (55-150 F).
La Bascule (61 52 09 51 - 14, av. M.-Hauriou. Open until 10:30pm.): Regulars know that this is a reliable spot for fine regional fare. Excellent cellar (150 F).
Bistrot des Vins (61 25 20 41 - 5, rue Riguepels.): Wines are available by the glass (50 featured each day from a cellar boasting 400). A variety of cheeses, charcuteries, and bistrot dishes provide solid sustenance (150 F).
Le Bon-Vivre (61 23 07 17 - 15 bis, pl. Wilson. Open until 12:30am.): Gascony cooking by a true mère gasconne, Huguette Meliet, offered in a dining room festooned with braids of garlic. Low prices. Fine collection of Armagnacs (65-150 F.
La Tantina de Burgos (61 55 59 29 - 27, rue de la Garonnette. Open until midnight.): Join the happy crowd at the large tables to savor tapas, paella, zarzuela, and nice little wines in a bodega atmosphere (50-170 F).

■ In Blagnac 31700   7 km W

Pujol
21, av. du Gal-Compans
61 71 13 58, fax 61 71 69 32
Closings not available. Open until 9:45pm. Priv rm: 36. Garden dining. Pkg. V, AE, DC, MC.
A terrace and veranda overlook the scenic wooded grounds which surround this nineteenth-century manse. Genial Michel Pujol prepares a traditional repertoire enlivened by a few flights of fantasy this year: sea scallop terrine à la grecque, and young squab with a caramelized honey and spice glaze now appear on the menu along with the fricassée of sole with chanterelle mushrooms and cassoulet au confit de canard. Competent service. **C** 330-430 F. **M** 190 F (wine incl), 175 F, 225 F.

▲▲ Sofitel
At the airport
61 71 11 25, fax 61 30 02 43
Open year-round. 100 rms 690-720 F. Restaurant. Air cond. Conf. Heated pool. Tennis. Golf. Valet pkg. V, AE, DC, MC.
This hotel provides spacious, well-equipped rooms, and a number of amenities. Sauna; covered pool.

Red toques signify creative cuisine; white toques signify traditional cuisine.

■ In **Garidech 31380**   *17 km NE on N 88*

 Le Club
61 84 20 23, fax 61 84 43 21
Closed Tue dinner, Wed, Aug 16-beg Sep. Open until 9:30pm (10:30pm in summer). Terrace dining. Pkg. V.
Jean-Pierre Delsol is a solid craftsman who knows how to choose fine ingredients and give them a delicate, personal spin. We go for very generous first set menu: asparagus cream with morels, scorpion fish fillet with tomatoes and basil, and dessert. Well chosen wines and a fine collection of Bas-Armagnacs. Competent service in the pleasant pastel-toned dining room with views of the flower-filled garden and the countryside. Friendly welcome. **C** 220-320 F. **M** 90 F (weekday lunch), 130 F, 180 F, 220 F.

■ In **Purpan 31300**   *3 km W*

Novotel
23, impasse Maubec
61 15 00 00, fax 61 15 88 44
Open year-round. 123 rms 400-410 F. Rms for disabled. Restaurant. Air cond. Conf. Pool. Tennis. Golf. Pkg. V, AE, DC, MC.
The modern, well-fitted rooms (two equipped for the disabled) look onto pleasant grounds. There's a children's play area and tennis court. The rooms have recently been more completely soundproofed.

■ In **Ramonville-**
Saint-Agne 31520   *8 km SE on N 113*

12/20 La Chaumière
102, av. Tolosane (N 113)
61 73 02 02, fax 61 75 17 02
Open daily until 10pm. Priv rm: 200. Garden dining. Pool. Pkg. V, AE, DC.
This large suburban restaurant with a big fireplace has a cozy, rustic decor and offers traditional dishes like the salad of crisp peas and slices of dried duck, as well as more modern creations like a tasty rack of lamb with aromatic herbs and spices. Rather chilly welcome and rather muddled service. **C** 250-320 F. **M** 70 F, 150 F.

La Chaumière
(See restaurant above)
Open year-round. 43 rms 270-350 F. Half-board 480 F. Air cond. Conf. Pool. Pkg. V, AE, DC.
Set in verdant grounds, this large, modern building offers pleasant, comfortable, air-conditioned rooms that have recently been refurbished.

■ In **Sainte-**
Livrade 31530   *28 km NW on N 124, D 24, D 17*

Restaurant d'Azimont
61 85 61 13, fax 61 85 46 16
Closed Sun dinner, Mon, Jan 2-22. Open until 9:45pm. Terrace dining. Pkg. V, AE, DC, MC.
The lovely nineteenth-century manor house contains an elegant, sunny dining room with views of greenery, where you will be served the generous and carefully crafted cuisine of Bruno Heintschel. Sample his iced salmon with brousse (fresh cheese), fricassée of squab with acacia honey, foie gras with pears in an infusion, and pineapple soufflé with currants. Excellent wine list. **C** 320-400 F. **M** 135 F, 175 F, 230 F, 330 F.

Restaurant d'Azimont
(See restaurant above)
Closed Jan 2-22. 2 stes 1,200 F. 15 rms 500-1,000 F. Half-board 450-600 F. Air cond. Conf. Pool. Tennis. Pkg. V, AE, DC.
In the heart of a wooded park, a charming manor house containing spacious rooms with refined decor. Superb salons. Bar, smoking room, billards, and croquet.

■ In **Tournefeuille 31170**   *8.5 km W on D 632*

Les Chanterelles
277, chemin Ramelet-Moundi
61 86 21 86
Open year-round. 7 stes 260-350 F. Golf. No pets. Pkg. No cards.
Well-equipped chalets (living room, covered terrace, garage) in pleasant and restful grounds.

TOUQUES 14   → Deauville

TOUQUET (LE)   **62520**
Paris 222 - Abbeville 61 - Boulogne 32 - Lille 132   P./Calais

Le Café des Arts
80, rue de Paris - 21 05 21 55
Closed Tue (exc school hols), Mon, 3 wks in Jan. Open until 10pm. Priv rm: 14. V, AE, DC, MC.
Jérôme Panni enlarged and refurbished his city-center establishment, giving patrons an even better reason to come and try his clever cooking. On offer this year on the generous first set menu: appetizers, creamed frog's legs and snail ravioli with sweet garlic, a hochepot of oxtail and beef cheeks, well aged cheeses, and dessert, all served in a dining room decorated profusely with paintings. Warm welcome by the *patronne*. **C** 350-430 F. **M** 150 F (exc dinner Sat & hols), 140 F, 300 F.

Flavio-Club de la Forêt
1, av. du Verger - 21 05 10 22
Closed Mon, Jan 4-Feb 10. Open until 10pm. Priv rm: 25. Terrace dining. V, AE, DC, MC.
If you don't own a Bentley or a Porsche, aim at least for a suitably yuppie look (blazer and cravat for gents, Hermès scarf and lots of gold bracelets for ladies). Otherwise, you'll feel out of place when tasting the lobster, langoustine, foie gras and other fine ingredients in the perfectly prepared dishes on the menu. We especially liked the foie gras au sauternes, navarin of sole fillets and asparagus, and mellow fricassée with charlotte potatoes. Just in case you forget your Gold card, opt for the upstairs restaurant where you can sample a 200 F, wine included, menu. The cellar is vast, noble, and—you guessed it!—expensive. **C** 550-650 F. **M** 200 F, 380 F, 720 F.

Grand Hôtel
4, bd de la Canche
21 06 88 88, fax 21 06 87 87
Open year-round. 10 stes 950-3,000 F. 125 rms 500-860 F. Rms for disabled. Restaurant. Half-board 750-960 F. Pool. Golf. Valet pkg. V, AE, DC, MC.

Here's a new and blessedly quiet luxury hotel, swaddled in groomed green grounds with a view of Canche Bay. There has been no skimping on the decoration: marble, Persian rugs, and crystal chandeliers meet the eye at every turn. The commodious guest rooms are furnished à l'anglaise, and are remarkably well equipped. Fine breakfasts; but the service could (and should) be better.

Manoir Hôtel
Av. du Golf
21 05 20 22, fax 21 05 31 26
Closed Jan 3-Feb 2. Open until 9:30pm. Terrace dining. No pets. Pkg. V, AE, MC.
The Manoir has a British accent, provided notably by the English rugby club emblems that adorn the high ceiling. Yet chef Bruno Andrieux's cuisine is resolutely Southern French, judging by his carpaccio of langoustines royales in watercress-enhanced balsamic vinegar, rack of lamb roasted with picholine olives, and strawberries marinated with thyme. Well chosen, eclectic cellar, ably presented by the staff. Professional welcome. C 260-430 F. M 140 F (lunch), 150 F, 195 F.

Manoir Hôtel
(See restaurant above)
Closed Jan 3-Feb 2. 1 ste 1,210-1,510 F. 41 rms 580-1,000 F. Half-board 535-1,005 F. Heated pool. Tennis. Golf. Pkg. V, AE, MC.
An inviting, Normandy-style residence with beautiful, comfortable rooms, some of which have been renovated. Golf course (reduced rates for guests), billards.

Novotel-Thalassa
Beach front
21 09 85 00, fax 21 09 85 10
Closed Jan 3-23. 3 stes 880-1,340 F. 146 rms 415-650 F. Rms for disabled. Restaurant. Half-board 640-840 F. Air cond. Conf. Golf. Pkg. V, AE.
This large, contemporary seafront hotel provides bright, functional rooms with superb views. Direct access to the spa facilities. Sauna.

Le Pavillon
Av. du Verger
21 05 48 48, fax 21 05 45 45
Closed Tue off-seas, Jan 10-Feb 15. Open until 9:30pm. Priv rm: 90. Garden dining. Air cond. Valet pkg. V, AE, DC, MC.
A fresh, bright dining room in a majestic "avant-guerre" luxury hotel. The cuisine is resolutely modern: fricassée of green asparagus and morels, pot-au-feu of farm-raised squab with aromatic herbs and spices, slices of John Dory fillet braised in a light pumpkin cream, and a macaronade of strawberries seasoned with star anise dust. The prices are a bit too high. C 300-500 F. M 210 F, 360 F.

Le Pavillon
(See restaurant above)
Closed Tue, Jan 22-Feb 10. 2 stes 1,500-1,900 F. 113 rms 400-1,080 F. Rms for disabled. Half-board 625-685 F. Conf. Heated pool. Golf. Valet pkg. V, AE, DC, MC.
Within easy reach of the casino and forest, this survivor of Le Touquet's grand hotels features entirely refurbished, perfectly comfortable rooms, as well as numerous amenities (covered swimming pool, fitness center, sauna, solarium, squash courts).

■ **In Étaples 62630**   5 km E on N 39

11/20 Les Pêcheurs d'Étaples
Quai de la Canche - 21 94 06 90
Closed Jan. Open until 9:30pm. Air cond. Pkg. V.
The main attraction here is luminously fresh seafood. Opt for uncomplicated offerings, like the briny shellfish platters, sea bream roasted with thyme, and fresh cod in mustard sauce. C 180-280 F. M 69 F (weekdays), 100 F, 130 F.

TOUR-DE-SALVAGNY (LA) 69   → Lyon

TOURCOING   59200
Paris 234 - Lille 14 - Roubaix 4 - Ghent 61 - Ostende 66   Nord

La Baratte
395, rue du Clinquet - 20 94 45 63
Closed Sat, Sun, Feb school hols, Aug 1-20. Open until 9:30pm. Priv rm: 50. Air cond. V, AE, MC.
This restaurant in an out-of-the-way district is well worth seeking, particularly for Didier Bajeux's clever, capable preparations. Bravo for the 136 F menu: salmon marinated in lime juice, fillets of limande sole with herbs, cheeses, and a grape cake. Competent welcome, discreet and swift service. C 240-340 F. M 98 F (weekdays), 136 F, 180 F.

Ibis
Centre du Gal-de-Gaulle
20 24 84 58, fax 20 26 29 58
See page 95.
Opposite a municipal park, this hotel provides recently refurbished rooms in the heart of town.

Au P'tit Bedon
5, bd de l'Égalité - 20 25 00 51
Closed Mon, last 2 wks of Jul, 1st 3 wks of Sep. Open until 11pm. Air cond. Pkg. V, AE, DC, MC.
Sample Philippe Fermier's flavorful, carefully prepared dishes with a few fanciful touches: salad of young rabbit seasoned with vanilla, turbot in cuttlefish ink, and crème brûlée with apples. The sunny yellow interior with chintz tablecloths makes you forget the grey factories nearby, and the service is most attentive (the young wine steward obviously loves his job, and has put together a fine wine list). C 230-380 F. M 160 F (weekday lunch, wine incl), 250 F (wine incl), 300 F (exc weekday lunch).

TOURNEFEUILLE 31   → Toulouse

TOURNUS   71700
Paris 360 - Mâcon 30 - Chalon 27 - Bourg-en-B. 53   Saône/Loire

Greuze

1, rue A.-Thibaudet
85 51 13 52, fax 85 51 75 42
Open daily until 9:45pm. Priv rm: 25. Air cond. Pkg. V, AE, MC.
Jean Ducloux is a living monument to all that is best about fine traditional French cuisine, and as he celebrates, at the age of 75, his fifty-first year in the kitchen, he still manages to hone his magnificent technique, ever more closely approaching perfection. He single-handedly keeps alive a style of dining that the world has nearly forgotten. Even if there were the tiniest hope of

convincing him that the gastronomic scene had changed, would we want to? For his is virtuous cooking, based on absolute respect for products and culinary integrity. Those who will put just about anything on a plate these days should spend some time in Ducloux's kitchen. He would show them how to make a true pâté en croûte, a perfect quenelle de brochet, an authentic gratin of langoustine tails, an ideal lobster timbale, quintessential rognons de veau dijonnaises, or perfectly cooked entrecôte à la charolaise. He is passing the flame to his assistants, Laurent Para and Christophe Cannet, but remains the soul of his kitchen and of this lovely provincial establishment next to Tournus abbey. The able service and superb wine list are overseen by Claude Bouillet. Come here for a taste of the good life of another era. **C** 450-650 F. **M** 260 F, 490 F.

🏰 Hôtel de Greuze
5-6, pl. de l'Abbaye
85 51 77 77, fax 85 51 77 23
Open year-round. 2 stes 1,870 F. 21 rms 560-1,230 F. Restaurant. Air cond. Pkg. V, AE, DC, MC.
A former town house opposite the abbey, this luxury hotel contains twenty-odd magnificently upholstered, curtained, and carpeted guest rooms with fine ultramodern amenities. Marvelous breakfasts.

🍴 Le Rempart
2-4, av. Gambetta - 85 51 10 56
Open daily until 9:30pm. Priv rm: 40. Air cond. Valet pkg. V, AE, DC, MC.
Once a guardhouse, now a hotel-restaurant, this sixteenth-century structure has seen a lot of traffic flow by since the Renaissance. It offers pleasing classical cooking, a fine wine list, and a cozily elegant decor; the prices (high) are the only drawback. We have no quibbles with the turbot coated with almonds, young Bresse squab (Bresse poultry is a house specialty), and perfectly prepared desserts. Very fine wine list with a glorious Mâcon Clessé made from *botrytis cinera* ("noble rot", in the style of Sauternes) grapes by Jean Thévenet, a rarity in this region of dry whites. We just wish the cooking showed a bit more soul. **C** 400-450 F. **M** 159 F, 275 F, 399 F.

🏰 Le Rempart
(See restaurant above)
Open year-round. 6 stes 750-1,100 F. 31 rms 340-795 F. Rms for disabled. Half-board 430-700 F. Air cond. Conf. Golf. Valet pkg. V, AE, DC, MC.
Young staff provide traditional French service in this updated provincial institution overlooking Saint Philibert abbey (of which some rooms have a view). The decor is not particularly charming, but the rooms are comfortable and well equipped.

TOURS	37000
Paris 234 - Angers 105 - Orléans 113	Indre/Loire

🍴 Jean Bardet 😊
57, rue Groison
47 41 41 11, fax 47 51 68 72
19.5 *Closed dinner Sun & Mon (Nov-Mar), Mon lunch (Apr-Oct). Open until 9:30pm. Priv rm: 100. Garden dining. Valet pkg. V, AE, DC, MC.*

The good life the Loire Valley is known for doesn't get much better than here in Jean and Sophie Bardet's romantic white villa. We look forward to each visit as an opportunity to delight in—and share—this couple's generosity, their gourmandise, and their insatiable appetite for life.
With one foot in his garden of rare vegetables, and the other in his cellar of fabulous Loire Valley wines, Jean Bardet is a happy man. And a uniquely gifted chef. Bardet puts the diner in direct contact with authentic, essential flavors, and with all the emotion he expresses through his spontaneous, creative cuisine. What's his secret? A maximum of restraint, a minimum of fat, and a supreme artistry in orchestrating flavors.
In the butter-hued dining room which opens onto verdant grounds, guests linger over their food, savoring every delectable nuance. Here all is perfection: a simple salad, sautéed wild mushrooms with sot-l'y-laisse (poultry "oysters") and livèche, a bean and foie gras terrine, sea bass with bacon and cives de vigne, a fabulous civet of lobster and shellfish in aged Vouvray with a piquant touch of ginger, squab with caramelized spices, or veal sweetbreads with Parma ham and marjoram. The desserts are a taste of paradise: dôme au guanaja, ethereal coffee ice cream, rhubarb crumble, or the irresistible "fascination" in four different services. The "terroir" menu (assiette of garden vegetables, carp and rabbit in Chinon white wine sauce seasoned with summer savory, farm-produced cheeses, and a cherry giboulée en chaud-froid pistaché) has miraculously been reduced in price by 30 F this year, to 270 F, an admirable gesture. Partnered with a young Touraine or venerable Vouvray, these dishes and all the new ones Bardet will have invented by the time you read this, leave indelible memories. And Sophie is always brimming over with ideas to please her guests: theme dinners, or tours of nearby châteaux and vineyards, for example. **C** 550-900 F. **M** 270 F (weekdays, Sat lunch), 300 F (weekdays, Sat lunch, wine incl), 420 F (Sun, wine incl), 590 F, 720 F.

🏰 Jean Bardet 🌲🌸
(See restaurant above)
Open year-round. 5 stes 1,400-1,800 F. 16 rms 500-1,300 F. Air cond. Conf. Heated pool. Golf. Valet pkg. V, AE, DC, MC.
A high wall encloses the wide, romantic, stream-fed grounds that surround this grand villa. The supremely comfortable rooms and suites are furnished in an attractive mix of period and contemporary charm. Fabulous marble bathrooms; breakfasts that must be tasted to be believed. Gift shop; pool. The Bardets will send their Rolls to fetch you at the station if you wish. Relais et Châteaux.

🍴 Le Canotier
6, rue des Fusillés - 47 61 85 81
Closed Mon lunch, Sun, hols, last wk of Dec, 1 wk in Feb. Terrace dining. Air cond. Pkg. V, AE.
Valérie Bardet's charming bistrot is a cheerful spot indeed—especially when mom and dad (Sophie and Jean) drop by between services. Like the other happy patrons, they love their daughter's beef marrow on toast, hachis parmentier of guinea fowl, grilled lobster, and little orange-and-chocolate pots de crème. Accom-

pany all this with nice little Vouvrays and Saumur-Champignys that won't hurt your wallet. Convivial atmosphere. **C** 160-230 F. **M** 90 F (weekday lunch, wine incl), 150 F.

Le Francillon
9, rue des Bons-Enfants
47 66 44 66, fax 47 66 17 18
Open year-round. 1 ste 600 F. 10 rms 360-420 F. Restaurant. Half-board 520-720 F. Conf. V.
A seductive half-timbered town house in a pedestrian street, equipped with pleasant, nicely decorated rooms of varying size.

Hôtel Harmonie
15, rue Fr.-Joliot-Curie
47 66 01 48, fax 47 61 66 38
Closed mid Dec-mid Jan. 6 stes 550-885 F. 48 rms 450-500 F. Restaurant. Half-board 375 F. Conf. Golf. Pkg. V, AE, DC, MC.
Located on a quiet street not far from the railway station, these modern rooms are beautifully appointed in a bright, Art Deco spirit. English bar.

Le Lys
63, rue Bl.-Pascal - 47 05 27 92
Closed Sun dinner, Mon, Dec 20-Jan 3, Aug 1-20. Open until 9:30pm. Priv rm: 12. V.
The decor needs some serious attention, but otherwise Le Lys is a model of its kind: a modest restaurant serving clean-lined cuisine that is complex without being finicky. Try the 150 F menu, a real bargain: langoustines with snow pea cream, saddle of young rabbit with tangy roquette (rocket greens) and terragon butter, cheeses, and a prune cake served with a tea cream sauce and walnut ice cream. Pleasant Loire wines. Friendly welcome. **C** 300-350 F. **M** 100 F (weekdays), 150 F, 250 F, 290 F.

Mercure Tours Centre
4, pl. Thiers
47 05 50 05, fax 47 20 22 07
Open year-round. 8 stes 550 F. 112 rms 380-450 F. Restaurant. Half-board 410 F. Air cond. Conf. Golf. Garage pkg. V, AE, DC, MC.
On the city's main drag, a new hotel built of stone and glass, offering sunny, soundproofed, well equipped rooms with good bathrooms. Very professional staff.

La Roche Le Roy
55, route de St-Avertin
47 27 22 00, fax 47 28 08 39
Closed Sun, Aug 1-22. Open until 9:45pm. Priv rm: 24. Garden dining. Pkg. V, AE.
The lovely Renaissance manor surrounded by a garden has been refurbished this year, all the more reason to join the local foodies flocking here to sample the cuisine of Alain Couturier, one of the most exciting up-and-coming chefs in the formerly sleepy Val de Loire. You are bound to love such savory, seasonal dishes as marbré of young rabbit braised in Sauternes and served with a piquant onion confit, matelote of eels with prunes in aged Chinon wine, and a pear gratin with cinnamon sauce. Game dishes in season. The cellar will please wine buffs, and the service, directed by Marilyn Couturier, would please anyone. **C** 300-400 F. **M** 150 F (weekday lunch), 200 F, 330 F.

Le Royal
65, av. de Grammont
47 64 71 78, fax 47 05 84 62
Open year-round. 50 rms 335-398 F. Rms for disabled. Conf. Golf. Pkg. V, AE, DC, MC.
A hideous modern building conceals beautiful, well-equipped rooms, most with period furnishings. Private garage. Professional reception.

La Touraine
5, bd Heurteloup
47 05 37 12, fax 47 61 51 80
Open daily until 10:30pm. Priv rm: 140. Air cond. Pkg. V, AE, DC, MC.
A stylish maître d' who knows what he's about seats guests in this comfortable, newly refurbished dining room. On the menu are fairly conservative dishes, well crafted with an occasional bright touch: salmon marinated in dill, pickerel fillet with cabbage, veal grenadin, and a dark chocolate truffé for dessert. Rather ordinary small wine list; professional service. **C** 220-350 F. **M** 110 F, 140 F, 180 F.

L'Univers
(See restaurant above)
Open year-round. 10 stes 850-1,500 F. 80 rms 680-780 F. Rms for disabled. Air cond. Conf. Golf. Pkg. V, AE, DC, MC.
Almost all the rooms of this centrally situated hotel give onto the courtyard, assuring guests of a quiet stay. The fine, large, freshly renovated rooms are attractively decorated in a partly Art Deco, partly contemporary style. All are perfectly equipped, and there are facilities for conferences and banquets. Bar.

Les Tuffeaux
19, rue Lavoisier - 47 47 19 89
Closed Mon lunch, Sun, Jan 16-30. Open until 9:30pm. Air cond. V, MC.
It must be a record: Gildas Marsollier's wonderful 110 F menu hasn't gone up a centime in five years! That modest sum buys (for example) smoked-salmon pannequets with avocado and salad, turkey paupiettes stuffed with lamb sweetbreads, a fine Saint-Maure cheese, and a chocolate "hérisson" (porcupine) for dessert. Tempting selection of Loire wines. This delicious meal is served in an exquisite, typically Touraine setting of beams, limestone walls, and bright tiles. **C** 230-280 F. **M** 110 F (weekdays, Sat lunch), 150 F, 200 F.

■ In **Montlouis-sur-Loire 37270**   12 km E on D 751

Château de la Bourdaisière
25, rue de la Bourdaisière
47 45 16 31, fax 45 45 09 11
Open year-round. 2 stes 750-1,050 F. 10 rms 550-1,100 F. Conf. Heated pool. Tennis Golf. No pets. Garage pkg. V, MC.
Philippe-Maurice and Louis-Albert de Broglie give château buffs a princely welcome to this Renaissance castle in the Cher Valley. Rooms are large and bright with lots of charm. Swimming pool and tennis court in the grounds.

A red hotel ranking denotes a place with charm.

■ **In Rochecorbon 37210** 5 km E on N 152

Les Hautes Roches
86, quai de la Loire
47 52 88 88, fax 47 52 81 30
Closed Sun dinner & Mon off-seas, end Jan-mid Mar.
Open until 9:30pm. Priv rm: 30. Garden dining. Pkg.
V, AE, MC.
This lovely mansion built partly into the cliffs and with splendid terraces above the Loire features the cooking of a feverishly inventive young chef. He has plenty of talent, but does best when he avoids complication: tasty hure of salmon and veal sweetbreads, squab with candied citrus peel, and a tarte sablée au chocolat pur caraïbe. Superb wine list. Service is straightforward and smiling. **C** 350-500 F. **M** 145 F (weekday lunch), 250 F, 350 F.

Les Hautes Roches
(See restaurant above)
Closed end Jan-mid Mar. 3 stes 1,300 F. 8 rms 600-1,300 F. Half-board 635-995 F. Air cond. Conf. Golf. Pkg. V, AE, MC.
The stupendous size of these eight rooms and three suites accepts with ease the opulent yet elegant decor: refined appointments provide an exquisite contrast to the walls of barc, pale stone. Visions of the broad, sandy banks of the Loire flood the rooms, while the spire of Tours cathedral keeps watch from a distance. Relais et Châteaux.

TOURTOUR 83690
Paris 860 - Draguignan 20 - Aups 10 - Salernes 11 *Var*

Bastide de Tourtour
94 70 57 30, fax 94 70 54 90
Closed Nov-Mar. 25 rms 400-1,365 F. Rms for disabled. Restaurant. Half-board 600-1,050 F. Conf. Heated pool. Tennis. Pkg. Helipad. V, AE, DC, MC.
You can take in a hundred kilometers of Var scenery from this luxurious mountain fastness among the pines. Jacuzzi, exercise room. Relais et Châteaux.

Les Chênes Verts
2 km on route de Villecroze
94 70 55 06, fax 94 70 59 35
Closed Tue dinner, Wed, Jan-Feb 15. Open until 9pm. Priv rm: 15. Garage pkg. No cards.
Can a chef follow the same path for twenty years, yet continue to improve? Paul Bajade shows that it is indeed possible: he refines his solidly classic repertoire year by year, just as he slowly embellishes his dining room. Regional dishes are well represented on his menu—lamb, duck, pigeon, crayfish—but Bajade's chief claim to culinary fame is his roster of truffle specialties, and the feuilleté de foie gras which in itself is worth a visit. Come during the truffle season, from January to March, and taste the fabulous truffle menu; other worthwhile choices are golden veal sweetbreads with cèpe jus, émincé of lamb fillet with summer savory, and other perfectly prepared regional specialties. Savor a fine wild strawberry feuilleté with vanilla ice cream for dessert. Courteous welcome; gorgeous regional wine list (we recommend the excellent Villecroze cabernet-sauvignon at 130 F). Take note: the house does not accept credit cards. **C** 380-600 F. **M** 200 F, 390 F.

TOURVILLE-LA-RIVIÈRE 76 → Rouen

TRÉBEURDEN 22560
Paris 519 - Perros-Guirec 13 - St-Brieuc 72 *Côtes/Armor*

12/20 Ker an Nod
2, rue Port-Termen
96 23 50 21, fax 96 23 63 30
Closed Tue lunch, Jan 1-Feb 15. Open until 9:30pm (10pm in summer). Priv rm: 15. V, AE, MC.
One of those rare and wonderful seashore establishments where happy holiday-makers are served good, honest, family-style cooking at reasonable prices: chicken livers with tiny onions, warm sea-scallop terrine, beef cheeks long-simmered in Burgundy wine, and a fondant aux trois chocolats for dessert. The cellar needs work. Smiling staff. **C** 200-300 F. **M** 78 F, 98 F, 145 F, 195 F.

Manoir de Lan Kerellec
Allée Centrale
96 23 50 09, fax 96 23 66 88
Closed Mon off-seas, Nov 15-Mar 15. Open until 10pm. Priv rm: 30. Valet pkg. V, AE, DC, MC.
This quiet, luxurious manor faces the rocky shore and distant islands. The menu zeroes in on local specialties such as oysters, fish, and salt-meadow lamb, all carefully selected and very well prepared; we especially enjoyed the oxtail terrine with foie gras and the ultrafresh fish this year. The cozily elegant dining room offers a lovely maritime panorama, and the prices are very reasonable for a Relais et Châteaux establishment. **C** 300-400 F. **M** 140 F (lunch), 175 F, 260 F, 350 F.

Manoir de Lan Kerellec
(See restaurant above)
Closed Nov 15-Mar 15. 2 stes 1,530-2,000 F. 16 rms 500-1,500 F. Half-board 620-900 F. Conf. Tennis. Valet pkg. V.
Thanks to the polished taste of the lady of the house, this beautiful seafront establishment has become luxurious while preserving its family ambience. There are mahogany bathrooms, water-massage bathtubs, and private terraces looking out to sea, where guests may enjoy delicious breakfasts. Perfect service. Relais et Châteaux.

TREMBLAY-SUR-MAULDRE (LE) 78490
Paris (Pte de St-Cloud) 42 - Versailles 20 *Yvelines*

L'Astrée
Pl. de l'Église
34 87 92 92, fax 34 87 86 27
Closed 1 wk at Christmas, Aug. Open until 9:30pm (10pm in summer). Garden dining. V, AE, DC, MC.
The chance to spend a weekend emptying your wallet here in this impressive, forest-bound Louis XIII château will seem all the more attractive when you make the acquaintance of the excellent cuisine. Sumptuous chandeliers and mirrors light up a clever and well-prepared classic menu conceived by Jean-Pierre Bouchereau, featuring, for example, ravioli stuffed with guinea fowl in a truffle fumet, monkfish with fresh artichokes, and a delicate berry tart. The wine list is diversified and offers a good choice of Champagnes, but it's pricey. **M** 190 F, 290 F (exc Sun dinner).

Château-Hôtel ♠♥
(See restaurant above)

See restaurant for closings. 30 rms 550-1,150 F. Half-board 555-860 F. Golf. Pkg. Helipad. V, AE, DC, MC.

You will be courteously welcomed to this superb seventeenth-century château set in 40 hectares of wooded grounds. Mostly huge, luxurious rooms; splendid breakfasts; peace and quiet guaranteed. Magnificent conference rooms. Helipad; golf course; gardens.

TRÉMOLAT	24510
Paris 530 - Périgueux 54 - Sarlat 46 - Bergerac 34	*Dordogne*

Le Vieux Logis
53 22 80 06, fax 53 22 84 89
Open daily until 9:30pm. Priv rm: 20. Garden dining. Valet pkg. V, AE, DC, MC.

Rarely in this world does it happen that a setting, service, and food conspire to create such a heavenly impression of well-being. Here one sits among glowing antiques or on the lovely terrace next to a burbling brook to feed upon Pierre-Jean Duribreux's vibrant, light yet earthy repertoire. Pinch yourself as you pull up to a feast: a splendid potato stuffed with sweetbreads and truffles (the house specialty), redolent of rich, subtly intermingled flavors, duck in every possible guise, and various dishes using fine crayfish, lamprey eel, and eels. By special order (24 hours in advance) you can savor roast farm-raised chicken, lièvre (hare) à la royale, or oven-baked duck. For dessert, try the millas, sautéed corn, a regional specialty. A stunning wine list rich in superb regional bottlings and rare vintages does nothing to restore one's sense of reality! You'll find a warm welcome, and friendly yet very professional service. C 380-400 F. M 180 F (wine incl), 230 F, 370 F.

Le Vieux Logis ♠♥
(See restaurant above)

Open year-round. 5 stes 1,500 F. 19 rms 720-1,240 F. Half-board 742-1,002 F. Conf. Pool. Golf. Valet pkg. Helipad. V, AE, DC, MC.

These remarkably comfortable rooms, so tastefully decorated, are surrounded by an exuberant garden. Blessedly quiet. Wonderful breakfasts; picnic baskets packed upon request. Relais et Châteaux.

TRIGANCE	83840
Paris 818 - Draguignan 44 - Grasse 72 - Castellane 20	*Var*

12/20 Château de Trigance
94 76 91 18, fax 94 85 68 99
Closed Wed lunch (Oct-Nov), Nov 8-Mar 19. Open until 9:30pm. Pkg. V, AE, DC, MC.

Unless you have X-ray vision, you'll miss the breathtaking panorama of the Verdon Valley on the other side of these stout, windowless eleventh-century walls. Concentrate instead on the fresh cuisine based on excellent products: a marinade of sea trout en homardine, young squab à la provençale, grilled sea bream fillet with red cabbage, and a dark-chocolate "shell" for dessert. C 250-400 F. M 140-350 F.

Château de Trigance ♠♥
(See restaurant above)

Closed Nov 8-Mar 19. 2 stes 850 F. 8 rms 520-900 F. Half-board 530-700 F. Tennis. Golf. Pkg. Helipad. V, AE, DC, MC.

These beautiful rooms are handsomely furnished (canopied beds), and equipped with excellent bathrooms. Relais et Châteaux.

TRINITÉ-DE-PORTO-VECCHIO (LA) 20
→ CORSICA: Porto-Vecchio

TRINITÉ-SUR-MER (LA)	56470
Paris 482 - Auray 12 - Vannes 30 - Quiberon 22	*Morbihan*

L'Azimut
1, rue du Men-Dû - 97 55 71 88
Open daily until 10:30pm. Priv rm: 20. Terrace dining. Pkg. V, MC.

A rustic fireplace is the centerpiece of this roomy restaurant: that is where chef Hervé Le Calvez grills pristinely fresh fish and lobsters. There's also a terrace with a great view of the port. Sample fine dishes like a printanière of shellfish with green asparagus and oyster beignets, fillets of sole and plaice with a gingery shallot compote, and a fine dark-chocolate croquant flavored with wild mint. Generous set menus. Friendly welcome; attentive service. C 270-370 F. M 95 F (exc dinner in Aug), 125 F, 148 F, 165 F, 195 F.

TROIS-ÉPIS (LES)	68410
Paris 450 - Munster 17 - Colmar 12 - Orbey 12	*Haut-Rhin*

Le Jardin d'Hiver
Pl. de l'Église
89 49 80 65, fax 89 49 89 00
Closed Jan. Open until 9:30pm. Priv rm: 180. Terrace dining. Pkg. V, AE, DC.

Chef Beekes, despite his Dutch name, is a native of Tours, recently transplanted to Alsace. He's adapted splendidly to the local *terroir*, using fresh, seasonal ingredients to compose a first-class menu. Balanced sauces, split-second timing, and bold (though never outrageous) combinations of flavors are Beekes's trademarks. We urge you to sample his intensely flavored consommé of game birds with marrow, tasty and delicate cabbage stuffed with juniper-seasoned hare, and a refreshing sliced reinette apple with melted Munster and bacon. For dessert, don't miss the yummy mirabelle-plum crème brûlée. Excellent choice of Alsatian wines. C 250-400 F. M 250 F.

Le Grand Hôtel ♠♥
(See restaurant above)

Closed Jan. 4 stes 860-1,900 F. 44 rms 420-850 F. Rms for disabled. Half-board 390-1,200 F. Conf. Heated pool. Golf. Pkg. V, AE, DC.

A sophisticated mountain theme runs through these thoroughly modern rooms. Among the amenities are a covered pool, solarium, sauna, and verandas that afford a stunning view of the Vosges. Excellent conference facilities.

The **C** *(A la carte) restaurant prices given are for a complete three-course meal for one, including a half-bottle of modest wine and service.* **M** *(Menus) prices are for a complete fixed-price meal for one, excluding wine (unless otherwise noted).*

Deep in the Southern Rockies lie two hundred and fifty spectacular square miles known as Forbes Trinchera. Its tallest peak reaches 14,345 feet into the Colorado sky, and its mountains sweep down into valleys as green and fertile as a Kentucky meadow.

This historic tract of land was bought by publisher Malcolm S. Forbes in 1969 as a natural escape to a place far from Wall Street and corporate stress. And now, for the first time it is being offered to Incentive Planners looking for something unique.

The buildings of Forbes Trinchera have been remodeled to provide superb accommodation, but it is still, essentially, a ranch.

Whilst there, guests can ride the land on horseback, or on trail-bike. They can fly-fish on its miles of streams, or hike its thousands of trails. They will have special rights at a nearby golf club, or they can shoot skeet until every clay looks as big as a house. And, as you can imagine, the cross-country skiing and snowmobile rides are nothing short of breathtaking. When there's work to be done, the main conference room can seat up to sixty.

However they choose to use it, Forbes Trinchera will provide a lookout point from which to view the world. Two hundred and fifty square miles. Fifty staff. Mountains. Valleys. Lakes. Streams.

Call 1-800-FORBES-5, and allow us to tell you more.

FORBES TRINCHERA RANCH
A Forbes Executive Retreat

FT

TROUVILLE

14360

Paris 206 - Le Havre 76 - Caen 43 - Lisieux 29   *Calvados*

🔼🔼 Beach Hotel

Quai Albert-I[er]
31 98 12 00, fax 31 87 30 29
*Closed mid Nov-mid Dec. 8 stes 880-1,360 F.
102 rms 320-590 F. Rms for disabled. Restaurant.
Half-board 425-515 F. Pool. Pkg. V, AE, DC, MC.*
Guests may go directly from their big, well-equipped rooms to the casino and the spa facilities. Or they can stay put and enjoy the harbor view. Good breakfasts. Solarium; bar. Interesting weekend packages for two (1,150 F with meal and breakfast).

11/20 La Petite Auberge

7, rue Carnot - 31 88 11 07
Closings not available. Open until 10pm. V, AE.
In a pleasantly rustic decor, sample fresh cod fillet with a tomato fondue, duck breast in a spicy crust, fresh fruit soup and a ginger madeleine, and a Baked Alaska with apples and Calvados. To drink? A good farm-produced cider. **C** 240-350 F. **M** 115 F, 190 F, 250 F.

14 Les Roches Noires

16, bd L.-Breguet - 31 88 12 19
*Closings not available. Open until 10pm. Priv rm: 14.
Terrace dining. Pkg. V, AE, MC.*
The lady chef loves aromatic dishes, and serves them in one of the town's rare restaurant terraces overlooking the sea: thyme-scented cockles without the slightest bit of sand (and that means lots of care in the kitchen), fresh cod with sautéed apples, farm-raised chicken in cider vinegar, and apple tart that doesn't quite match the level of the rest. The *patron* offers many wines that won't inflate your bill (Quincy, Epineuil). **C** 250-300 F. **M** 170 F.

13 Les Vapeurs

160, bd F.-Moureaux - 31 88 15 24
Open daily until 1am. Priv rm: 35. Terrace dining. Air cond. V, AE.
As many as 800 hearts and tummies each day are warmed by the tasty Normandy oysters, mussels in cream, hot shrimps, tartares of salmon or bass, and delicately unctuous crème brûlée. Choose the spacious, bustling dining room or the huge terrace. Rivers of cool white wine serve as irrigation at this seaside brasserie. **C** 180-400 F.

TROYES

10000

Paris 158 - Amiens 276 - Dijon 151 - Reims 121   *Aube*

🔼🔼 Le Relais Saint-Jean

Rue Paillot-de-Montabert
25 73 89 90, fax 25 73 88 60
Open year-round. 22 rms 430-650 F. Rms for disabled. Air cond. Conf. Valet pkg. V, AE, DC, MC.
This stately hotel that has completely redone in modern style is located in the center of the town's historic district. Tasteful contemporary rooms, excellently equipped.

14 La Table Gourmande

1-3, rue R.-Poincaré - 25 73 05 05
Closed Sun dinner, Mon. Open until 10:30pm (11pm on Sat). Priv rm: 20. Air cond. Pkg. V, AE.
There's nothing very new under the Art Deco chandeliers of this comfortable establishment.

Patrick Jolain is a classically trained chef who keeps abreast of culinary fashions. Sample his monkfish studded with bacon, caramelized veal shanks paired with cèpe-stuffed macaroni, and an andouillette sausage made from foie gras and veal sweetbreads. The wine list is studded with very high quality Bordeaux and Burgundies at altruistic prices—not to be missed! **C** 230-290 F. **M** 150 F, 240 F.

🔼🔼 La Poste

(See restaurant above)
Open year-round. 2 stes 650-900 F. 26 rms 370-520 F. Air cond. Conf. Garage pkg. V, AE.
Everything about this renovated hotel is right: the tasteful luxury, the elaborate bathrooms, the attractive furnishings, and the fine breakfasts. Do note, however, that the rooms are not overly large.

16 Le Valentino

11, cour de la Rencontre
25 73 14 14, fax 25 73 74 04
Closed Sun dinner, Mon, Aug 16-Sep 7. Open until 9:45pm. Priv rm: 20. Garden dining. V, AE, DC, MC.
A turn-of-the-century bistrot with a veranda and adorable courtyard for summer dining, Le Valentino is Troyes's top table, in spite of the numerous changes in the kitchen. The current chef (who arrived last year) wisely simplified the menu and given the cuisine a real personality; he has real talent for sauces, too. Sample the red cabbage jus with fish and the delicately smoky sauce with the veal sweetbreads and you'll see what we mean. Opt for the pleasant terrace in summer. The wine list is well chosen, with finds like a Pinot de Saint-Bris at just 130 F. The 165 F menu in itself is worth the extra point we award this restaurant this year. **C** 400-450 F. **M** 165 F, 360 F.

TULLE

19000

Paris 480 - Limoges 87 - Clermont-Ferrand 145   *Corrèze*

🔺 Limouzi

16, quai de la République
55 26 42 00, fax 55 20 31 17
Open year-round. 3 stes 650-900 F. 44 rms 250-400 F. Restaurant. Conf. Golf. Pkg. V, AE, DC, MC.
Thoroughly equipped rooms fill this big hotel in the town center. Prompt, smiling service.

12/20 Restaurant de la Gare

25, av. W.-Churchill
55 20 04 04, fax 55 20 15 87
Closed Feb 1-7, Sep 1-15. Open until 9pm. V.
Opposite the eponymous railway station, this cozy restaurant features a neo-rustic decor (lace curtains, wrought-iron decorative objects) and two set menus that will help you escape the high à la carte prices. For 85 F: foie gras terrine, leg of lamb, cheeses, and a dessert cart. **M** 85 F, 96 F (exc Sun lunch), 140 F (Sun lunch).

13 La Toque Blanche

29, rue J.-Jaurès
55 26 75 41, fax 55 20 93 95
Closed Sun dinner & Mon off-seas, Jan 15-Feb 8. Open until 9pm. Priv rm: 12. Air cond. V, AE.
The culinary honor of this inviting establishment is being defended, nowadays, by Bruno Estival—the owners' son. He prepares the house repertoire with straightforward skill, evident in

the lentil terrine, effiloché of oxtail, or pickerel with sauerkraut. There's a "autour d'un plat" menu that offers one main course, dessert, and wine for 100 F. Charming welcome. **C** 235-300 F. **M** 100 F (weekdays, Sat lunch), 140 F, 190 F.

URCUIT 64	→ Bayonne

URIAGE 38	→ Grenoble

URT 64	→ Bayonne

USTARITZ 64	→ Bayonne

UZÈS	30700
Paris 706 - Avignon 38 - Alès 33 - Nîmes 25 - Arles 54	*Gard*

12/20 Les Jardins de Castille
8, rue de la Calade
66 22 32 68, fax 66 22 57 01
Open daily until 9pm (10pm in summer). Priv rm: 25. Terrace dining. Air cond. Pkg. V, AE, DC, MC.
This covered, flower-filled patio affords a marvelous view of Uzès cathedral. But Bruno Guillout's cooking was less inspiring than the surroundings, on our last visit. Very ordinary rack of veal with truffles and too old-fashioned salmon millefeuille and cream quenelle reflect a kitchen that has lost enthusiasm. The fine poached peach with Champagne sabayon couldn't save the toque. Pleasant welcome; efficient service. **C** 250-380 F. **M** 100 F (weekdays, Sat dinner, Sun lunch off-seas; lunch exc Sun in Jul-Aug), 190 F.

 Entraigues
(See restaurant above)
Open year-round. 18 rms 185-475 F. Half-board 225 F. Air cond. Heated pool. Pkg. V, AE, DC, MC.
Charming old hotel facing the restaurant with rustic furniture and nicely tended interiors; some rooms were refurbished this year, and their bathrooms updated. Lovely view over the Eute Valley.

■ **In Collias 30210**   8 km SE on D 981 and D 3

Le Castellas
Grand-Rue - 66 22 88 88, fax 66 22 84 28
Closed beg Jan-beg Mar. Open until 9:30pm. Priv rm: 20. Garden dining. Pkg. V, AE, DC, MC.
The charming dining room opens onto a fragrant garden, a lovely spot indeed for sampling young chef Frédéric Fournier's personalized cooking that attracts a chic young crowd: tasty vinaigrette of fruits and vegetables, tender and perfectly cooked squab stuffed with pearl barley, and an interesting salad of strawberries with basil and fresh mint (we could have done with less mint, however). Fine cellar. Excellent welcome; competent service. **C** 300-400 F. **M** 100 F (lunch exc Sun), 160 F, 225 F, 350 F.

 Le Castellas
(See restaurant above)
Closed beg Jan-beg Mar. 1 ste 600-800 F. 17 rms 395-580 F. Half-board 490-575 F. Air cond. Conf. Pool. Golf. Pkg. V, AE, DC, MC.
A lovely late seventeenth-century domain converted into a hotel offers very well equipped,

attractive rooms with pretty bathrooms tiled with galets (small round stones). Charming welcome; small swimming pool, horseback riding available.

VAISON-LA-ROMAINE	84110
Paris 670 - Avignon 46 - Carpentras 28	*Vaucluse*

12/20 Le Bateleur
1, pl. Th.-Aubanel - 90 36 28 04
Closed Sun dinner, Mon, Oct. Open until 9pm (9:30pm in summer). V, MC.
Pretty bouquets add a colorful touch to the restful dining room, where the lady of the house serves guests the generous 122 F menu: scorpion fish soufflé with langoustine butter, rabbit thigh with cèpes, dauphinois potato gratin, and a puckery lemon tart topped with meringue. Small cellar of Côtes du Rhône and Loire wines. **C** 170-230 F. **M** 160 F (Sun exc hols), 122 F.

La Fête en Provence
Pl. du Vieux-Marché
90 36 36 43, fax 90 36 21 49
Closed Wed (exc Jul-Aug), Nov 11-Dec 15, Jan 2-Feb. Open until 10pm. Priv rm: 30. Terrace dining. V, AE, DC, MC.
A self-taught Scandinavian chef, Niels Christensen, has created a lovely, tranquil restaurant serving unpretentious regional fare. Try his soft-boiled eggs with morel purée, omble chevalier (a lake fish) with beurre blanc, and a quail thigh with sautéed foie gras. Carefully chosen wine list ably presented by the friendly *patronne*. **C** 260-420 F. **M** 90 F, 150 F.

Hostellerie Le Beffroi
Rue de l'Évêché
90 36 04 71, fax 90 36 24 78
Closed Feb 15-Mar 15, Nov 15-Dec 15. 22 rms 320-640 F. Restaurant. Half-board 740 F. Conf. Golf. Pkg. V, AE, DC, MC.
Here's a beautiful Renaissance dwelling, in the heart of old Vaison. Rooms are huge, furnished with antiques; there are terraced gardens and lovely views. Half the rooms are housed in an equally handsome seventeenth-century annex.

■ **In Entrechaux 84340**   7 km SE on D 938, D 54

La Manescale
Route de Faucon, D 205
90 46 03 80, fax 90 46 03 89
Closed Nov-Easter. 2 stes 460-800 F. 4 rms 350-560 F. Restaurant. Half-board 400-610 F. Pool. Garage pkg. V, AE, DC, MC.
Pretty, cheerful, and well-maintained rooms are provided in this charmingly converted sheepfold. Efficient service in a family atmosphere. Ideal for a restful holiday, but reserve well in advance!

■ **In Séguret 84110**   10 km SW on D 88

Auberge de Cabasse
90 46 91 12, fax 90 46 94 01
Closed Jan 7-Apr 4. 13 rms 250-650 F. Restaurant. Half-board 280-500 F. Conf. Pool. No pets. Pkg. V, AE, MC.
This establishment is an agreeable stopover in the wine country, at the foot of the Montmirail

peaks, with pleasant rooms overlooking a terrace and swimming pool.

La Table du Comtat

Le Village - 90 46 91 49, fax 90 46 94 27
Closed Tue dinner (Oct 25-Mar 30), Wed, Feb, Nov 27-Dec 8. Open until 9pm. Air cond. Hotel: 8 rms 430-600 F. Half-board 600-680 F. Conf. Pool. Golf. Garage pkg. V, AE, DC, MC.

The sweeping view framed by this fifteenth-century hospice is typically Provençal, and Franck Gomez used Provençal foodstuffs with flair in carefully prepared dishes like cold lobster soup with asparagus tips, fricassée of young rabbit with tiny peas and purple artichokes, and a pear and apple millefeuille. Interesting selection of Côtes du Rhône. Friendly welcome in a vaguely rustic, slightly overdecorated dining room (but what a view!). C 380-450 F. M 150 F (lunch exc hols), 240 F, 310 F, 420 F.

VALBONNE   06560
Paris 913 - Cannes 13 - Grasse 9 - Nice 30   Alpes-Mar.

L'Auberge Fleurie
1016, route de Cannes
93 12 02 80, fax 93 12 22 27
Closed Wed, Dec 15-Jan 30. Open until 9:30pm. Terrace dining. Pkg. V, MC.

Jean-Pierre Bataglia offers dishes with fresh tastes and well balanced flavors, served in the dining room or on a pleasant tree-shaded terrace. This year, he adds an à la carte menu to his set menus. We enjoyed the duck pâté with eggplant confit, black cod in red wine sauce, and a fromage blanc cake with a raspberry coulis. Fine regional wines; friendly welcome. C 200-260 F. M 110 F, 150 F, 180 F.

11/20 Le Bistro de Valbonne
11, rue de la Fontaine
93 12 05 59, fax 93 12 09 59
Closed Sun, Mon, Nov. Open until 9:30pm. Terrace dining. Air cond. V, AE, DC, MC.

Lively service, the patronne's radiant smile, and two appealing prix-fixe offerings attract crowds to this little restaurant and its even smaller terrace. We like the 165 F menu: mussels à la provençale, fine noisettes of lamb, and a pear bavarian cream with crème anglaise and raspberry sauce. Competent welcome and service. C 220-300 F. M 105 F (lunch), 165 F, 250 F.

12/20 Cave Saint-Bernardin
8, rue des Arcades - 93 12 03 88
Closed Sun (exc hols lunch), Mon, Jan 15-Feb 15. Open until 9:30pm. Priv rm: 35. Pkg. V, AE, MC.

The 140 F set menu is a model of generosity: it brings turbot and spinach salad, mixed grill with a potato gratin and vegetables, cheese, and prunes steeped in Armagnac. The cellar holds some appealing regional wines. C 200-300 F. M 120 F, 140 F.

12/20 Relais de la Vignette
Route de Cannes - 93 12 05 82
Closed Sat lunch, Tue. Open until 10pm. Terrace dining. Pkg. V, AE, MC.

Pewter, stained glass, chandeliers, and a huge fieldstone fireplace create a distinctly medieval atmosphere that doesn't match the light, sunny

cuisine. On the generous first set menu, you'll savor the salmon tartare, lamb poupetons, cheese aged au "peirouos", and dessert. Good cellar. C 270-400 F. M 135 F, 175 F.

■ In Sophia-Antipolis 06560   7 km SE on D 3 and D 103

L'Arlequin
Country club, 3550, route des Dolines
92 96 68 78, fax 92 96 68 96
Closed Fri dinner-Sun (exc Jul-Aug). Open until 10:30pm. Priv rm: 300. Terrace dining. Air cond. Pkg. V, AE, DC, MC.

Thierry Maynier has taken over from Olivier Boizet at this attractive establishment. From your seat in the dining room or on the broad terrace, you can enjoy a view of the hotel's pool and grounds, while sampling Maynier's partly classic, partly informal repertoire. Savor his foie gras ravioli with Corinthe raisins, tartine of red mullet roasted with fennel, and honey-pecan ice cream adorned with none other than a chocolate cookie. Well chosen wine list. C 200-260 F. M 150 F.

Pullman
(See restaurant above)
Open year-round. 3 stes 800-1,350 F. 104 rms 560-690 F. Rms for disabled. Half-board 150-180 F. Air cond. Conf. Pool. Tennis. Golf. Pkg. V, AE, DC, MC.

An immense sporting complex set in extensive grounds just a few minutes from the sea (free shuttle bus to the beach). Guest rooms are well appointed, soundproofed, and have private balconies. Among the many services on tap are a masseur, exercise classes, a beauty salon, gift shop, and car-rental agency. Piano bar.

Mercure
Rue A.-Caquot (Les Lucioles 2)
92 96 04 04, fax 92 96 05 05
Open year-round. 104 rms 480-600 F. Rms for disabled. Restaurant. Half-board 470 F. Air cond. Conf. Pool. Golf. Garage pkg. V, AE, DC, MC.

In the heart of the complex, a pretty modern building built in local style, offering well equipped rooms with a modern, pastel decor. Good quality-price ratio, in spite of the uneven breakfasts.

Novotel
Rue Dostoïevski
93 65 40 00, fax 93 95 80 12
Open year-round. 97 rms 395-580 F. Rms for disabled. Restaurant. Half-board 368-433 F. Air cond. Conf. Pool. Tennis. Golf. Pkg. V, AE, DC, MC.

In front of the big Sophia-Antipolis park, this is an excellent hotel for conferences.

VAL-D'ISÈRE   73150
Paris 690 - Chambéry 133 - Albertville 85 - Briançon 158   Savoie

Altitude
Route de la Balme
79 06 12 55, fax 79 41 11 09
Closed May 10-Jun 25, Sep-Nov. 40 rms 530-810 F. Restaurant. Half-board 570-600 F. Conf. Heated pool. No pets. Pkg. V, AE, MC.

A modern chalet at the foot of the ski trails. The rooms face south, and are perfectly comfortable. Amenities include a fireside lounge, sauna, solarium, and a bar.

L'Ancolie

(See restaurant above)

Closed May 6-Nov. 14 stes 940-1,180 F. 94 rms 800-1,820 F. Half-board 690-1,000 F. Conf. Valet pkg. V, AE, DC, MC.

This sprawling hotel in the heart of the old village offers comfortable, well-designed rooms. Skiers will appreciate the sauna, Jacuzzi, and sporting-goods shop on the premises.

Le Blizzard

79 06 02 07, fax 79 06 04 94

Closed May 3-Jun 30, Aug 30-Nov. 10 stes 800-1,700 F. 70 rms 470-1,210 F Restaurant. Half-board 355-705 F. Conf. Heated pool. V, AE, DC, MC.

This is one of the resort's most reputable hotels, complete with refurbished rooms (with newly redone bathrooms) that are cozy and bright, a fitness center, and a disco.

Christiana

BP 48 - 79 06 08 25, fax 79 41 11 10

Closed Apr 25-Nov 27. 11 stes 1,986-4,004 F. 57 rms 826-1,712 F. Rms for disabled. Restaurant. Half-board 842-1,872 F. Pool. Valet pkg. V, AE, MC.

Here is Val-d'Isère's most concentrated glitter. Lovely rooms, with fine appointments; the whole place has just been totally renovated. The runs are just outside the door. Sauna; hydrotherapy center.

Grand Paradis

79 06 11 73, fax 79 41 11 13

Closed May 10-Jul 1, Aug 23-Dec 1. 4 stes 854-1,070 F. 40 rms 450-1,200 F. Restaurant. Half-board 536-900 F. Conf. Valet pkg. V, AE, DC, MC.

The trail-side location is truly exceptional. Some of the huge rooms are cozy and charming, with balconies overlooking the mountains, and some smaller ones are emphatically not. Sketchy breakfasts.

Mercure

79 06 12 93, fax 79 41 11 12

Closed May 8-Jun 12. 4 stes 960-1,680 F. 41 rms 580-980 F. Restaurant. Half-board 640-730 F. Conf. Pkg. V, AE, DC, MC.

Regular clients of the Mercure chain are going to be really taken by this one; its huge, functional rooms are right on the slopes. Fitness center; bar.

11/20 Le Pré d'Aval

Immeuble Le Solaise, rue Principale
79 41 14 05, fax 79 41 17 87

Closed Thu off-seas, May 10-Jun 15, Sep 30-Oct 30. Open until 10:30pm. V, MC.

A rustic, wood-paneled eating house that serves generous, simple food: raclette, fondue, tartiflette and other polentas, washed down with pleasant local wines served by the carafe. C 180-280 F.

Savoyarde

79 06 01 55, fax 79 41 11 29

Closed May 4-Aug 8, Aug 24-Nov. 3 stes 1,420-2,000 F. 44 rms 440-880 F. Rms for disabled. Restaurant. Half-board 520-780 F. Conf. Pkg. V, AE, DC.

Here's a traditional mountain chalet, just 100 meters from the lifts, with attractive rooms, pine furnishings, and wood-panelled bathrooms. Sauna; Jacuzzi; massage service.

> **Prices for rooms and suites** are per room, not per person. Half-board prices, however, are per person.

Sofitel Le Val d'Isère

79 06 08 30, fax 79 06 04 41

Closed May 2-Jul 7, Aug 21-Dec 2. 4 stes 1,700-2,500 F. 48 rms 900-1,450 F. Restaurant. Half-board 800-950 F. Heated pool. Golf. Pkg. V, AE, DC, MC.

These fine modern rooms located in the heart of the resort boast wide bay windows. Hydrotherapy center with up-to-date equipment.

Le Solaise

Immeuble Solaise Plein Sud
79 06 08 10, fax 79 06 06 05

Closed Tue, beg May-Dec 20. Open until 11pm. V, AE, MC.

Light floods the posh dining room while even posher patrons study the interesting wine list and the appetizing menu composed by chef Laurent Caffot. Savor his fresh langoustine and mussel consommé, fillet of scorpion fish and tiny ravioli with star-anise-scented tomatoes, and rack of lamb in a spice jus. Fine but pricey wine list. C 380-500 F. M 230 F, 480 F.

Paris 230 - Châteauroux 41 - Issoudun 44 - Vierzon 49   *Indre*

Hôtel d'Espagne

9, rue du Château
54 00 00 02, fax 54 00 12 63

Closed Jan-Feb. 6 stes 900-1,100 F. 10 rms 450-650 F. Restaurant. Half-board 950-1,400 F. Conf. Garage pkg. V, AE, DC, MC.

We wish the management would take a critical look at the wallpaper and the upholstery of the rooms and lounges, for the grand old decor is getting out of date. Comfort is assured, however, and the service is wonderfully attentive. Relais et Châteaux.

Paris 560 - Lyon 100 - Grenoble 99 - Marseille 215   *Drôme*

La Licorne

13, rue H.-Chalamet - 75 43 76 83

Closed Sat lunch, Sun, Aug 1-Sep 1. Open until 10:30pm. Priv rm: 18. Air cond. V, AE, DC, MC.

The nondescript façade conceals an enormous split-level dining room that is always jam-packed with happy diners. So it's best to reserve if you want a taste of Bernard Hegy's fresh, attractively priced cooking. Full marks for the 135 F set menu, which brings médaillon of foie gras, grilled turkey leg with morel cream sauce, cheese assortment, and dessert (apéritif, wine and coffee included). The *patronne* is charming, the service cheerful and efficient. C 200-280 F. M 680 F (for 2 pers, wine incl), 135 F (wine incl), 78 F, 100 F, 160 F.

Pic

285, av. V.-Hugo
75 44 15 32, fax 75 40 96 03

Closed Sun dinner, Wed, 2 wks in Aug. Open until 10pm. Priv rm: 100. Garden dining. Air cond. Valet pkg. V, AE, DC, MC.

Up in paradise, where he is probably sharing a fine Hermitage with Saint Peter, our good friend Jacques Pic can rest in peace. The establishment he left behind in the summer of 1992 is going great guns under the direction of his son, Alain Pic, aided by his family and faithful staff. Jacques

Pic was not one to spend much time meeting and greeting in the dining room, but his son is practically invisible, seen only in brief glimpses in his rare moments of venturing out of the kitchen. For this is a chef who loves to work, and it shows in his astonishing technique and attention to detail. His cuisine is purely classical; wild experimentation is definitely not his style, and when he does try something new, you can be sure he is in complete control of it. This year we savored his "strate" of beef and duck liver in Cornas wine that says what it intends to say, even if the expression doesn't bowl you over. Truffles appear often, in a galette with celery and foie gras, pan-roasted with langoustines, scattered in slices over red mullet, en chausson, or in a marmite with potatoes. Grand old classics include noisettes of lamb with a courgette tian, veal with morels, kidney au poivre, or breast of guinea fowl paired with mushroom ravioli. This is not innovative cooking, but what of it? Better to have such a reliable sanctuary devoted to the classics than to force the chef to go against his personality and experiment. The wine list is a treasure trove of Côtes du Rhône, among other wines. The dark cloud? The bill. But there's a glimmer of light in the form of the set menu offered at lunch (sea bream à la provençale, émincé of veal kidney, cheeses, and dessert). **C** 600-800 F. **M** 280 F (weekday lunch), 520 F, 620 F.

🏠🏠 Pic
(See restaurant above)
Closed Wed, Sun, 2 wks in Aug. 2 stes 850-1,000 F. 3 rms 700-850 F. Air cond. Conf. Golf. Valet pkg. V, AE, DC, MC.
The house offers a grand total of two suites and three guest rooms (a new wing of rooms is in the works, though). Expect to spend a very comfortable night and to waken to birdsong and a sumptuous breakfast. Relais et Châteaux.

■ In Charmes-sur-Rhône 07800   11 km S on N 86

🍴 La Vieille Auberge
Autour d'une Fontaine
75 60 80 10, fax 75 60 87 47
Closed Sun dinner, Mon. Annual closings not available. Open until 9:30pm. Garden dining. Air cond. Garage pkg. V, AE, DC, MC.
Here's a pretty place to pull up a chair and tuck into Jean-Maurice Gaudry's traditional repertoire, produced with good intentions although the execution can be a bit paltry at times. Still, we enjoyed the fillets of galinette (tub gurnard, a fish) with dried tomatoes, émincés of kidney in Saint Joseph wine, veal sweetbreads à la mignonette of noisettes, and farm-raised squab in Banyuls jus. Interesting Ardéchois menu at 100 F. **C** 250-400 F. **M** 100 F, 140 F, 160 F, 200 F, 240 F, 300 F.

🏠🏠 La Vieille Auberge
(See restaurant above)
Closed Sun, Mon. 15 rms 220-600 F. Half-board 350-450 F. Air cond. Conf. Pkg. V, AE, DC, MC.
Spanking new rooms in a charming old inn. The windows frame views of trees and flowers.

Looking for a city in a département? Refer to the index.

■ In Montmeyran 26120   14 km SE on N 538a

🍴 La Vieille Ferme   ❄
D 125, Les Dorelons - 75 59 31 64
Closed Tue, Sun dinner, Mon, Aug. Open until 9pm. Priv rm: 40. Terrace dining. Pkg. V, MC.
If you blink, you'll miss the sign that indicates La Vieille Ferme. That would be a shame, since everything you order here is savory and carefully prepared. This year we especially liked the house terrines and a compote of young rabbit en gelée, deffarde de Crest (lamb tripe), and the partridge, hare, and mallard duck that, in winter, replace the rappit with summer savory on the menu. Tasty homemade desserts. Sample a good Côtes du Rhône from the cellar. **C** 180-280 F. **M** 170 F, 198 F (weekday dinner, Sat, Sun lunch), 110 F, 160 F (weekday lunch, Sat).

■ In Pont-de-l'Isère 26600   9 km N on N 7

🍴 Chabran
Av. 45ᵉ Parallèle (N 7)
75 84 60 09, fax 75 84 59 65
Open daily until 10:30pm. Priv rm: 40. Garden dining. Air cond. Pkg. V, AE, DC, MC.
The arrival of a new dining-room director has immeasurably improved the service chez Chabran. Pampered patrons are now in a perfect frame of mind to savor dishes composed of startlingly fresh foodstuffs supplied by local farmers (the lamb, the asparagus, the fruit all hail from the Rhône Valley), and given the inimitable Chabran treatment. He's not only one of the region's best chefs; he's also a real character who lives his cooking intensely, searches everywhere to find the best possible products, and takes risks (which means that he sometimes falls on his face, but you don't care because there's always another wonderful thing on the menu to make you forget). Some of his dishes are remarkably simple, like a salad of ratte potatoes and Drôme truffles that is an inspired combination. We also reveled in his langoustine risotto with truffles, in which the firm langoustines are impregnated with the heady truffle taste; and a masterpiece of refined rusticity, the fork-tender roast kid paired with roast potatoes, a garlic flan, and olive-oil-infused giblets. The sublime Saint Marcellin cheese from La Mère Roland is unforgettable. Desserts include a luscious assiette de chocolat with caramel sherbet. The young *sommelier* guides guests expertly through the admirable wine list: he'll steer you to the vintage Hermitage of your dreams, or to a simple Côtes-du-Rhône that is the equal in finesse of many a more prestigious label. **C** 500-750 F. **M** 200 F (lunch), 255 F, 355 F, 425 F, 545 F, 745 F.

🏠🏠 Chabran
(See restaurant above)
Open year-round. 12 rms 350-700 F. Air cond. Conf. Golf. Pkg. V, AE, DC, MC.
All the modern rooms are luxuriously comfortable, but some are considerably more charming than others. The breakfasts are delicious (orchard-fresh fruit, homemade jam, just-baked rolls...). Chabran has just acquired two houses adjoining the restaurant, where he plans to open

453

more guest rooms and a bistrot. Relais et Châteaux.

 La Campagnette   ❍
Route de Cahors - 63 39 65 97
Closed Sun dinner, Mon. Open until 9:30pm. Priv rm: 12. Garden dining. Pkg. V.
A beacon for local food lovers, this charming little country restaurant is home to Gérard Lerchundi's sparkling, inventive cuisine that nevertheless has its ups and downs. He can produce a superb foie gras perfectly paired with asparagus tips (a clear 17 rating), or chocolate desserts that are so good you feel ecstatic, and then turn around and offer a tronçon of brill en crépine stuffed with sausage that is too salty and in which the sausage overwhelms the taste of the fish (scarcely worth a 12 rating). Charming welcome and friendly service in a charming, luminous dining room. **C** 250-380 F. **M** 95 F (weekdays), 155 F, 240 F, 320 F.

L'Albéroi
Buffet de la Gare, Pl. de la Gare
27 46 86 30, fax 27 29 80 26
Closed Sun dinner, hols. Open until 10pm. Priv rm: 100. Pkg. V, AE, DC, MC.
Watch the trains whiz (silently) along the tracks outside, while you relish the chef's salad of tiny snails, steak with shallots, and crème à la cassonade. Well-stocked cellar; very good service, friendly welcome. **C** 280-400 F. **M** 300 F (Sun lunch), 120 F, 160 F, 220 F.

Grand Hôtel de Valenciennes
8, pl. de la Gare
27 46 32 01, fax 27 29 65 57
Open daily until 10:30pm. Priv rm: 200. Air cond. No pets. V, AE, DC.
The façade, the dining room's columns, the old-fashioned service all put one in mind of a luxury liner from the 1930s. Traditional *cuisine bourgeoise* displays all its lush and saucy charms in such dishes as calf's head vinaigrette, fricassée of monkfish with leek fondue, and filets mignons in Jenlain beer sauce. Jovial welcome; excellent service. The cellar highlights the wines of Alsace. **C** 240-360 F. **M** 162 F (exc Sun, wine incl), 95 F, 155 F, 203 F (exc Sun), 170 F, 210 F (Sun).

 Grand Hôtel de Valenciennes
(See restaurant above)
Open year-round. 5 stes 540-650 F. 93 rms 350-590 F. Conf. Golf. V, AE, DC.
You will be welcomed warmly into this huge, classic hotel opposite the railway station, and to its modernized, well-equipped rooms. The bathrooms boast hydrotherapy equipment. Continental breakfasts.

12/20 Le Grand Hôtel
28, av. du Gal-de-Gaulle
90 35 00 26, fax 90 35 60 93
Closed Sat dinner & Sun off-seas, Dec 25-Jan 30. Open until 8:45pm. Priv rm: 25. Garden dining. Garage pkg. V, MC.
An exemplary traditional hotel, with an old-fashioned dining room that is beginning to show its age, as is, unfortunately, the cuisine: fine ravioli in an herby cream sauce, but overcooked rack of lamb with overcooked baby vegetables, and a runny berry gratin. The toque disappears. Friendly welcome and service. **C** 250-330 F. **M** 98 F, 150 F, 250 F.

 Le Grand Hôtel
(See restaurant above)
Closed Sat & Sun off-seas, Dec 25-Jan 30. 15 rms 260-390 F. Half-board 280-380 F. Conf. Pkg. V, MC.
These large, inviting, country-style rooms were recently refreshed and soundproofed. Good bathrooms; charming staff.

Le Vivarais   ❍
5, rue Cl.-Expilly
75 94 65 85, fax 75 37 65 47
Closed Feb-Mar 15. Open until 9:30pm. Priv rm: 25. Garden dining. Valet pkg. V, AE, DC.
An engaging menu served forth by smiling staff, a flower-decked terrace, and a bright dining room: no wonder the ambience at Le Vivarais is always so jolly! Christiane Giuliani's repertoire runs to fresh, earthy dishes like snail soup with chives and crique d'Ardèche, cassolette de cousinat (chestnut soup), and a tender kid blanquette à la Tante Louise. Satisfied readers have written thanking us for sending them all the way here! Enticing selection of wines from the Côtes-du-Rhône. **C** 250-450 F. **M** 130 F, 145 F, 190 F, 250 F.

Le Vivarais
(See restaurant above)
Open year-round. 3 stes 600 F. 44 rms 300-550 F. Half-board 400-550 F. Conf. Pool. Golf. Valet pkg. V, AE, DC.
Charming spa hotel surrounded by trees next to a park. Rooms are stylish and comfortable (some are on the small side), and decorated with their original 1930s furniture. Attentive welcome.

11/20 La Chaumière
Centre de Caron - 79 00 01 13
Closed May 8-Jun, Sep-Dec 15. Open until 11pm. Priv rm: 30. Terrace dining. Pkg. V, MC.
Cooking here is simple with a rustic flavor: foie gras, veal sweetbreads à la provençale, tartiflette savoyarde, and a fresh-fruit feuilleté with vanilla cream sauce, as well as salads, pâtés, and fon-

dues, all served in a snug paneled dining room. C 200-280 F.

Le Sherpa
79 00 00 70, fax 79 00 08 03
Closed May-Dec 10. 42 rms. Restaurant. Half-board 380-600 F. MC.
A modern building in a quiet setting on the ski slopes. Lovely rooms with balconies. Good amenities, including a sauna, Jacuzzi, solarium, and lounge-bar.

⑭ La Table du Roy
79 00 04 78, fax 79 00 06 11
Closed May 10-Nov. Open until 10:30pm. Terrace dining. Air cond. Valet pkg. V, AE, DC, MC.
François Prudent is a self-taught chef, one who never stops learning if we're to judge by his refined, balanced cuisine. This year we tasted and approved a cèpe soup with warm foie gras and chestnut-flour-bread toasts, chops of milk-fed veal flavored with audépine, and pear tatin with génépi-flavored whipped cream. In summer the whole team here moves to Saint-Florent, in Corsica. C 400-500 F. M 280 F, 380 F, 500 F.

Fitz Roy
(See restaurant above)
Closed May 5-Nov. 4 stes 1,000-1,500 F. 33 rms 900-1,300 F. Rms for disabled. Half-board 1,000-1,500 F. Conf. Heated pool. Valet pkg. Helipad. V, AE, DC, MC.
A huge, modern, deluxe chalet with spacious, cozily paneled rooms. Panoramic lift. For fitness worshippers, there's a swimming pool and superb exercise and slimming equipment. Some readers complained that this year the welcome wasn't up to snuff. Relais et Châteaux.

12/20 Le Val Thorens
79 00 04 33, fax 79 00 09 40
Closed May 2-Dec 4. Open until 10:30pm. Terrace dining. No pets. Hotel: 80 rms 410-1,205 F. Rms for disabled. Conf. Valet pkg. V, AE, DC, MC.
In a pleasant wood-paneled dining room near the pistes, savor carefully prepared dishes like a salad of smoked duck breast with morels, flambéed veal kidneys, and crêpes Suzette. C 280-360 F. M 95 F (lunch), 180 F (dinner).

VANNES	56000

Paris 454 - Lorient 56 - Nantes 109 - Rennes 106   Morbihan

Aquarium' Hôtel
Le Parc du Golfe
97 40 44 52, fax 97 63 03 20
Open year-round. 48 rms 370-460 F. Rms for disabled. Restaurant. Half-board 358-393 F. Conf. Pkg. V, AE, DC, MC.
A futuristic construction in a verdant setting near the Gulf of Morbihan. Functional rooms, all with sea views.

⑱ Régis Mahé
Le Richemont
Pl. de la Gare - 97 42 61 41
Closed Sun dinner, Mon, last 2 wks of Feb, Nov. Open until 9:30pm. Pkg. V, AE, MC.
It's not easy to capture a conservative clientele with a cooking style that goes against the regional grain. But Régis Mahé has won over the good citizens of Vannes with a vivacious repertoire that combines the best of Brittany's seafood and produce with a sunny touch of Provence. And this year the Gothic decor of the dining room has been painted white, a more pure look in keeping with the chef's concentration on producing dishes in which natural flavors shine through. This year we savored his wonderful "Retour des Halles" (Back from the Market) menu at 250 F: catalane of red mullet and coco beans; fresh cod en daube with capers and mussels; a meunière of sole, tiny scallops, and clams; a salad of rocket leaves with potatoes and Gorgonzola annointed with olive oil; and a strawberry soup in Sherry with spice ice cream. Divine! And his 160 F menu is not to be missed, either: tripe soup à l'andalouse, or rabbit osso bucco à l'orange with saffron risotto. Regis Mahé offers talent and modesty, a combination that's so rare it's one of the reasons we regard him as one of our most deserving three-toque chefs. Warm welcome and excellent service. We just wish the TGV went all the way to the station facing the restaurant.... C 400-580 F. M 160 F (weekday lunch, Sat, wine incl), 200 F, 250 F, 280 F, 350 F.

Manche-Océan
31, rue du Lt-Col.-Maury
97 47 26 46, fax 97 47 30 86
Open year-round. 42 rms 240-360 F. Pkg. V, AE, DC, MC.
Not far from the railway station and the town hall. Rooms are well soundproofed, constantly updated, with good bathrooms. Excellent breakfasts.

⑯ Le Pressoir
5 km N on D 757, 7, rue de l'Hôpital, 56890 Saint-Avé
97 60 87 63, fax 97 44 59 15
Closed Sun dinner, Mon, Mar 6-16, Jun 26-Jul 4, Oct 3-20. Open until 9:30pm. Priv rm: 20. Air cond. Pkg. V, AE, DC, MC.
The locals crowd into this bright dining room, made even sunnier by the dazzling smile of Christiane Rambaud. She'll also advise you on the wine list composed by her husband, Bernard, a chef who knows where to get the best ingredients, and how to coax out all their flavor. Sample his morels and sliced sea scallops in a succulent rabbit jus, plump langoustines with ultrafresh and tasty cabbage, and unctuous lobster cooked absolutely perfectly. Luscious desserts created by pastry chef Mickaël Vallée, like a pineapple millefeuille craquant and coconut mousse. A well earned extra point this year. Superb wine list, and professional service in the elegant dining room. C 300-400 F. M 120 F (weekday lunch), 175 F (weekdays, Sat lunch), 230 F, 285 F, 360 F.

12/20 La Varende
22, rue de la Fontaine
97 47 57 52, fax 97 42 47 22
Closed Sun lunch, Mon. Open until 9:30pm (10pm in summer). Priv rm: 30. V, AE, MC.
In the blond-wood dining room with a big granite fireplace, sample seasonal specialties like mackerel rillettes, potato galette with andouille sausage, chartreuse of squab with sage, and blancmange with a rhubarb compote. Wash them down with a carafe of wine or tasty farm-produced cider. C 180-260 F. M 79 F (week-days), 98 F, 122 F, 149 F.

■ In **Arradon 56610**   7 km SW on N 165

L'Arlequin
Parc de Botquelen
97 40 41 41, fax 97 40 52 93
Closed Sun dinner. Open until 9:30pm. Priv rm: 20. Pkg. V, AE, DC.
Manuel Caradec's light and elegant cuisine is progressing nicely. Why not sample the 138 F menu: a bavaroise of smoked salmon and avocado with parsley cream, sirloin steak with an onion and celery fondue, gaufrette glacée flavored with a vanilla bean, and a bilberry compote. Fine cellar. Charming welcome and efficient service in a warm, garnet-hued dining room that offers a panoramic view of the grounds. C 240-280 F. M 150 F (weekdays, wine incl), 88 F (weekdays), 138 F, 168 F, 228 F.

See also: Billiers, Questembert

VANVES 92   → **PARIS Suburbs**

VARENNE-SAINT-HILAIRE (LA) 94
→ **PARIS Suburbs**

VARENNES-SUR-ALLIER   **03150**
Paris 324 - Digoin 58 - Moulins 30 - Vichy 27   *Allier*

■ In **Sanssat 03150**   10 km SE on N 209 and D 125

Château de Theillat   ⚜🌲
70 99 86 70, fax 70 99 86 33
Open year-round. 18 rms 650-1,230 F. Restaurant. Half-board 650 F. Conf. Heated pool. Tennis. Golf. Garage pkg. V, AE, DC, MC.
This luxuriously restored eighteenth-century château houses eighteen spacious, well-equipped rooms decorated in classic style. Perfect bathrooms; superb views. The welcome is friendly, and so are the staff.

VARETZ 19   → **Brive-la-Gaillarde**

VARS   **05560**
Paris 737 - Gap 72 - Briançon 47 - Barcelonnette 37   *H.-Alpes*

Caribou
92 46 50 43, fax 92 46 59 92
Closed Apr 20-Jun 10, Sep 10-Dec 10. 37 rms 280-700 F. Restaurant. Half-board 332-650 F. Conf. Heated pool. Pkg. V, MC.
A large chalet with terrace, solarium, and indoor games. Rooms are pleasant and well equipped. You can ski right up to the hotel's doorstep.

Chez Plumot
Vars-Les Claux - 92 46 52 12
Closed Apr 25-Jun, Sep 1-Dec 8. Open until 10:30pm. Terrace dining. Air cond. Pkg. V, MC.
The reputation of this restaurant has much to do with Dominique Lallez's consistent, classic cuisine. He lends clever, personal touches to dishes like taboulé with red mullet, parmentier of duck with foie gras, and iced chocolate truffles. The *patronne*'s cordial welcome and the polished service in this split-level dining room add to the charm. C 260-390 F. M 100 F (lunch), 130 F, 190 F.

VAUCHOUX   **70170**
Paris 354 - Epinal 88 - Gray 55 - Vesoul 15   *Haute-Saône*

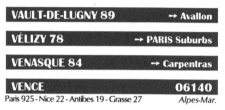
Château de Vauchoux
Route de la Vallée-de-la-Saône
84 91 53 55, fax 84 91 65 38
Closed Tue lunch, Mon, Jan 15-Feb 15. Open until 10pm. Priv rm: 20. Garden dining. Pool. Tennis. No pets. Pkg. V.
Jean-Michel Turin has an eye for prime ingredients and a well-honed classic technique. Highlights of a recent meal here were a panaché of fish and shellfish, saddle of rabbit stuffed with veal kidney, roast squab "Edwige Feuillère", and profiteroles amandines glacées au chocolat. Long list of prestigious wines, with a remarkable choice of Bordeaux and Burgundies. It's not surprising that this pretty eighteenth-century château attracts the region's chic set, as well as visitors boating down the Saône. C 400-550 F. M 280 F, 340 F, 380 F, 420 F (exc Sun).

VAULT-DE-LUGNY 89   → **Avallon**

VÉLIZY 78   → **PARIS Suburbs**

VENASQUE 84   → **Carpentras**

VENCE   **06140**
Paris 925 - Nice 22 - Antibes 19 - Grasse 27   *Alpes-Mar.*

12/20 **Auberge des Templiers**
39, av. Joffre - 93 58 06 05
Closed Sun dinner & Mon off-seas, Jan. Open until 9:30pm. Garden dining. V, AE, MC.
Sit back in the quiet, shady garden and sample dishes based mostly on noble ingredients from the region: zucchini blossoms stuffed à la forestière, Mediterranean potée, fillet of Sisteron lamb roasted in a crust, and sea bass in red Bandol wine with a garlic purée. C 300-380 F. M 145 F, 200 F, 320 F.

Château Saint-Martin
Av. des Templiers
93 58 02 02, fax 93 24 08 91
Closed Wed off-seas (exc for residents), end Oct-beg Apr. Open until 9:30pm. Priv rm: 20. Garden dining. Valet pkg. V, AE, DC, MC.
The Knights Templar, who founded this castle, rode two to a horse as a sign of poverty. Saint Martin is said to have cut his mantle in two to share with a beggar here. The patrons of Château Saint-Martin have plenty of horsepower under the hoods of their fancy cars, and they are also willing to sacrifice half the price of a mink coat to spend a weekend admiring the stupendous view and gorging on well-made, classic dishes: Milan-style risotto with duck liver, veal filet mignon casserole-roasted with carrots, and a pear craquant with caramel sauce. Service worthy of a palace. C 500-700 F. M 300 F (weekday lunch), 430 F, 490 F.

Château Saint-Martin   ⚜🌲
(See restaurant above)
Closed end Oct-beg Apr. 10 stes 2,680-3,200 F. 14 rms 1,560-2,280 F. Air cond. Conf. Heated pool. Tennis. Golf. Valet pkg. Helipad. V, AE, DC, MC.
Guests are housed in little villas whose richly decorated rooms have an uninterrupted view

over the hills. Lovely swimming pool; beautiful grounds. Relais et Châteaux.

Hôtel Floréal
440, av. Rhin-et-Danube
93 58 64 40, fax 93 58 79 69
Closed Nov-Feb. 43 rms 460-570 F. Conf. Pool. Valet pkg. V, MC.
A modern building set in pretty grounds. The rooms are bright and cozy, with tasteful decoration and a view over the countryside. Snacks are served round the swimming pool.

Miramar
Plateau St-Michel
93 58 01 32, fax 93 58 20 22
Closed Jan 5-Feb 1, Nov-Dec 1. 17 rms 340-420 F. Golf. Pkg. V.
Situated just 300 meters from the town center, surrounded by exotic trees and plants, this elegantly simple hotel affords views of the sea and the Alps. Pleasant rooms, regularly refurbished. Bar.

Le Vieux Couvent
68, av. du Gal-Leclerc, 37, av. A.-Torcille
93 58 78 58
Closed Wed, 3 wks at Feb school hols, 2 wks beg Nov. Open until 9:30pm (10:30pm in summer). Priv rm: 20. V, MC.
Jean-Jacques Bissière marries traditional cooking with today's tastes in dishes that show real virtuosity: fava-bean salad with a langoustine ragoût, Tarn duck roasted with cherries, and a layered strawberry croustillant. The cellar is still a trifle thin, but there are some good finds at reasonable prices. Excellent welcome; convivial atmosphere; the dining room is the former chapel of a seventeenth-century convent. C 300-400 F. M 150 F (weekday lunch, wine incl), 200 F, 270 F, 370 F.

VENOY 89 → Auxerre

VERDUN **55100**
Paris 265 - Metz 78 - Nancy 120 - Châlons-sur-Marne 88   *Meuse*

Le Coq Hardi
8, av. de la Victoire
29 86 36 36, fax 29 86 09 21
Closed Fri. Open until 9:45pm. Priv rm: 60. Terrace dining. Pkg. V, AE, DC, MC.
High prices rule the roost at this venerable restaurant on the banks of the River Meuse. Still, foreign tourists and local gourmands continue to fill the plush dining room, and rave about the chef's infinitely classic cooking. We, too, admire the duck liver with zucchini blossoms, turbot with tomatoes and eggplant confit, duck in raspberry vinegar sauce, and a peach stuffed with apricots. Friendly welcome; sumptuous wine list. C 400-500 F. M 135 F (weekdays, wine incl), 250 F, 290 F, 450 F.

Le Coq Hardi
(See restaurant above)
Open year-round. 3 stes 620-850 F. 37 rms 330-380 F. Rms for disabled. Air cond. Conf. Pkg. V, AE, DC, MC.
The refurbished rooms of this large half-timbered establishment are decorated in regional style, and boast impeccable new bathrooms.

■ In **Les Monthairons 55320**   13 km S on D 334

Château des Monthairons
29 87 78 55, fax 29 87 73 49
Closed Mon (exc hols), Jan 2-Feb 11. Open until 10pm. Priv rm: 40. Garden dining. Garage pkg. V, AE, DC, MC.
Set in the quiet of a huge park on the banks of the Meuse, this faux Renaissance château has been tastefully and lavishly restored. The Thouvenin family courteously greets visitors while son Benoît presides over the kitchen. His cooking is good, although his technique is still a bit imprecise: boar carpaccio with sweet-sour salads and vegetables, langoustine tails with terragon and black rice, and a warm currant-jelly soufflé.Service is attentive and there's a well-composed wine list. C 340-390 F. M 130 F (weekday lunch, wine incl), 165 F (exc Sun lunch), 280 F, 380 F.

Château des Monthairons
(See restaurant above)
Closed Jan 2-Feb 12. 3 stes 900-1,200 F. 18 rms 390-750 F. Half-board 450-650 F. Conf. Garage pkg. Helipad. V, AE, DC, MC.
The rooms and bathrooms are huge, with austere decor, very high ceilings, and a marvelous view over the park. Guests wake up to delicious breakfasts. Canoeing and kayaking on the Meuse; horseback riding nearby.

VERNON **27200**
Paris 82 - Evreux 31 - Rouen 63 - Mantes-la-Jolie 25   *Eure*

12/20 Les Fleurs
71, rue Carnot
32 51 16 80, fax 32 21 30 51
Closed Sun dinner, Mon, Feb school hols, Jul 30-Aug 20. Open until 9:30pm. Priv rm: 12. No pets. V.
Flowers brighten up the walls, the chair covers, and fill vases too in the pretty and cheerful dining room. The owner-chef offers an interesting menu of well prepared dishes like escargots à la normande, lamb fillet with truffles, snail-stuffed crêpes, and parfait au chocolat. Warm welcome. C 210-340 F. M 100 F, 140 F, 190 F, 220 F.

Normandy
1, av. P.-Mendès-France
32 51 97 97, fax 32 21 01 66
Open year-round. 45 rms 295-350 F. Half-board 430 F. Air cond. Conf. Golf. Pkg. V, AE, MC.
This modern, convenient hotel has just opened in the town center. The rooms at the back are the quietest; all are comfortable, though somewhat lacking in originality. Breakfasts are generous and the welcome courteous.

12/20 Le Relais Normand
11, pl. d'Évreux
32 21 16 12, fax 32 21 32 73
Closed Sun (exc hols). Open until 9:30pm. Priv rm: 16. Garden dining. Pkg. V, AE, DC, MC.
The cooking isn't going to set the world on fire: foie gras sautéed with apples, cauchoise omelet, pig's foot sausage in truffle jus, and a delicate hot apple tart. C 270-350 F. M 115 F, 165 F, 220 F.

■ In **Giverny 27620** 6 km E on D 5

12/20 Les Jardins de Giverny

Chemin du Roy - 32 21 60 80
Closed Sun dinner, Mon, Feb, Nov 2-16. Open until 9pm. Terrace dining. Pkg. V, AE.
A stone's throw from Claude Monet's house, this fine Norman residence is surrounded by roses and rare trees. This year, owner-chef Serge Pirault's cuisine seemed less concerned with product quality and less generously served than in the past. Confusing lobster salad with walnut vinaigrette and bland grilled red mullet with ratatouille lost the establishment its toque, in spite of the luscious chocolate and cherry ganache. Ups and downs in the cellar, too, but there's a great choice of Loire Valley whites. It's too bad, because the place itself is lovely. **C** 240-350 F. **M** 130 F (exc Sun), 190 F, 250 F.

■ In **Port-Villez 78270** 5 km SE on N 15

La Gueulardière

At Le Village - 34 76 22 12
Closed Sun dinner & Mon (exc hols). Annual closings not available. Open until 9:30pm. Priv rm: 20. Garden dining. Air cond. Pkg. V, MC.
This picturesque site on the Seine, just across from Monet's house and gardens at Giverny, provides a perfect setting for Claude Marguerite's attractive dishes: chunks of lobster and artichokes with basil, duck fricassée, John Dory with creamed morels, and game in season. Excellent wines; wonderful welcome. **C** 350-400 F. **M** 150 F (exc Sun).

VERSAILLES 78 → PARIS Suburbs

VERTUS **51130**

Paris 140 - Châlons-sur-Marne 30 - Fère-Champenoise 17 *Marne*

■ In **Bergères-les-Vertus 51130** 4 km S on D 9, on N 33

Hostellerie du Mont Aimé

4-6, rue de Vertus
26 52 21 31, fax 26 52 21 39
Open daily until 9:30pm. Priv rm: 80. Garden dining. Hotel: 1 ste 500 F. 29 rms 230-380 F. Rms for disabled. Conf. Pool. Pkg. V, AE, DC, MC.
An enlarged veranda gives an even better view of the garden, and chef Jean Sciancalepore wins a toque this year for fresh-tasting dishes prepared with brio: veal sweetbreads in a salad, perfectly cooked lamb in a mushroom croûte, and a pretty but dull crème au chocolat. Interesting choice of Champagnes and Bordeaux. Friendly welcome; good service. **C** 320-400 F. **M** 100 F (weekdays), 150 F, 220 F, 350 F.

VEULES-LES-ROSES **76980**

Paris 200 - Dieppe 24 - Rouen 57 *Seine-Mar.*

Les Galets

3, rue V.-Hugo - 35 97 61 33
Closed Tue dinner & Wed (exc Jul-Aug), Jan 5-Feb 3. Open until 9:30pm. Priv rm: 60. Air cond. Pkg. V, AE, DC, MC.

The dining room's modern decor is already outdated, but Gilbert Plaisance does his best to distract patrons with ultrafresh seafood prepared with admirable simplicity: fricassée of lobster with orange butter and a seafood risotto, roast monkfish in curry sauce with fresh pasta laced with slivers of green pepper, and gaufrettes of turbot with white truffles and oysters. Fine classic desserts. The prices of the wines on the admirable wine list will drive up your bill. **C** 360-500 F. **M** 160 F, 230 F, 380 F.

VEYRIER-DU-LAC 74 → Annecy

VÉZELAY **89450**

Paris 221 - Clamecy 23 - Avallon 13 - Auxerre 52 *Yonne*

Résidence-Hôtel Le Pontot

Pl. de la Mairie - 86 33 24 40
Closed Nov-Easter. 3 stes 800-1,050 F. 7 rms 600-950 F. Conf. Valet pkg. Helipad. V, DC, MC.
A listed, fortified residence built in the fifteenth and eighteenth centuries with luxuriously appointed rooms and suites in period style. Lovely flower-filled garden where you can have breakfast.

■ In **St-Père-sous-Vézelay 89450** 3 km SE

Marc Meneau

86 33 39 10 (R), 86 33 20 45 (H), fax 86 33 26 15
Closed Wed lunch & Tue off-seas, Feb 1-beg Mar. Open until 10pm. Priv rm: 40. Air cond. Valet pkg. V, AE, DC, MC.
Marc Meneau's cooking comes straight from the soul; it reflects the sensitive nature of a man close to his roots. Over the years, Meneau has learned that less is more—his brilliant, pared-down technique has attained a limpid purity that is the hallmark of a great artist. His talent never fails him: even when the house is full to bursting, he remains unruffled, master of his craft. He and his wife, Françoise, give diners who visit their conservatory-style dining rooms an unforgettable gastronomic experience.
Françoise Meneau, a wonderfully attentive hostess, seems to divine your wishes even before you do. And Meneau's cuisine this year was, as always, marked by miraculous purity: crème de chair de homard en chaud-froid, vegetable tart, celery with truffles and Parmesan in a turkey jus, eel with bay leaves, and a lemon-scented fricassée d'avants de poularde-de-bresse. And few other chefs can master as many different styles of dishes as well as he can. The poached young chicken à la Lucien Tendret shows just how good bourgeois cooking can be, and as for inventiveness, savor his oysters in seawater gelatin (now copied by other chefs, but Meneau created it!), chicken consommé with macaroons, salad of white coco beans with caviar, or monkfish breaded with rice. And as for rusticity: ah, that spit-roasted pig's head with a potato galette seasoned with blood sausage! From such seemingly disparate elements Meneau has created a unique, very personal style unlike any other. Even his desserts are extraordinary, like the crème chiboust made with almond milk and stuffed prunes, a semolina tart with walnuts, or

pineapple with truffles. And the wine list contains a collection of the best wines available in Burgundy. **C** 650-1,000 F. **M** 550 F (Sun lunch, wine incl), 350 F (lunch exc Sun), 630 F, 850 F.

L'Espérance
(See restaurant above)
Open year-round. 6 stes 2,200-2,800 F. 34 rms 300-1,500 F. Half-board 850-1,600 F. Air cond. Conf. Heated pool. Valet pkg. Helipad. V, AE, DC, MC.

There are charming little rooms done in soft, fresh colors above the restaurant, with a view on the garden. A charming mill, at the bottom of a quiet field, houses eight lovely suites (number 31, which has a private stair, a living room, bedroom, and superb bathroom, is the most sought-after). Relais et Châteaux.

Le Pré des Marguerites
86 33 20 45, fax 86 33 26 15
Closings not available. 2 stes 2,000-4,000 F. 14 rms 1,400 F. Restaurant. Air cond. Conf. Pool. No pets. Pkg. V, AE, DC, MC.

Opposite L'Espérance, on the other side of the road, Marc Meneau has opened a functional, well-equipped hotel which is ideal for seminars and conferences. The rooms are on the small side but have charm, and a large swimming pool gives the place a holiday feel. In a large, rather noisy dining room one of Meneau's assistants serves up good country cooking (count on spending around 150 F to 250 F).

VIALAS   **48220**
Paris 650 - Mende 77 - Florac 40 - Génolhac 9   *Lozère*

Chantoiseau
Route-du-Haut
66 41 00 02, fax 66 41 04 34
Closed Tue dinner, Wed, Nov 15-Mar. Open until 8:30pm. Priv rm: 12. Air cond. No pets. Pkg. V, AE, DC, MC.

This centuries-old wood-and-stone post house clinging to a slope of Mont Lozère offers no luxurious trappings, just the natural beauty of the Cévennes Mountains where wolves still howled not so long ago. This is the realm of Patrick Pagès, poet and chef, who draws incomparable notes and nuances from the bounty of this rugged land. How strange and surprising to find a *carte* so diverse in this remote corner of France. Pagès proposes a repertoire that is as modern and inventive as it is true to its regional roots. We urge you to savor his bradade of fresh green asparagus with a trout tartare in a black jus, Bouzigues mussels in mousseron mushroom butter, morel soup with tender oxtail, breast of guinea fowl in a green parsley jus, saddle of kid paired with cèpes and chestnuts, Roquefort annointed with walnut oil, and wine-marinated fruit, among many other luscious treats possible on a menu offering ten dishes, each paired with a glass of Languedoc-Roussillon wine, best enjoyed with a group of gourmand friends. Or sample the chef's equally delicious croquant of pig's foot with tart reinette apples in a veal jus, lamb sweetbreads and cèpes flavored with linden blossoms, calf's head in gelatin with hot chochonnailles (pork dishes) made from pigs raised on the region's high plateau—an extravaganza of flavors in dishes much lighter than you would expect, since the chef takes such care

to reduce and de-grease his sauces. Pagès is in fact a modern chef, one who loves the traditional specialties of his region but who knows when to wring tradition's neck when it goes too far. And as a suitable finale to this gastronomic adventure, take a tour of the cellar, where over 1,000 wines have been put at your disposal. **C** 350-450 F. **M** 140 F, 260 F, 300 F, 310 F, 380 F, 420 F, 730 F.

Chantoiseau
(See restaurant above)
Closed Nov 20-Mar. 15 rms 400-520 F. Half-board 420-450 F. Conf. Pool. No pets. Pkg. V, AE, DC, MC.

Overlooking the village, the rooms have been redecorated and are very comfortable. Nice little pool. Wonderful breakfasts and attentive service. This is a refuge for nature-lovers and those who appreciate simplicity but are, nevertheless, epicurians.

VICHY   **03200**
Paris 348 - Clermont-Ferrand 59 - Lyon 160 - Roanne 74   *Allier*

L'Alambic
8, rue N.-Larbaud - 70 59 12 71
Closed Tue (exc hols), Mon (exc hols), 2 wks end Feb-beg Mar, 3 wks end Aug-mid Sep. Open until 10pm. V, MC.

Jean-Jacques Barbot's is the best cuisine in Vichy, an assertion we're sure you'll second when you try his masterly smoked-skate ravioli with green cabbage and cumin-spiked cream sauce, veal sweetbreads with apples and Pommeau (a drink made of cider and Calvados), and a licorice soufflé glacé served with minty crème anglaise. Prices won't hurt your pocketbook. Balanced cellar, with bottles for every budget, such as a nice little Châteaugay red for next to nothing. **C** 250-400 F. **M** 160 F, 280 F.

12/20 Brasserie du Casino
4, rue du Casino
70 98 23 06, fax 70 98 53 17
Closed Tue dinner, Wed, 1st wk of Mar, Nov. Open until 10pm. Terrace dining. Pkg. V, AE, MC.

Vichy's best and prettiest brasserie adorned with genuine 1920s wood paneling and copperware. The empereur aux girolles, rabbit in basil sauce, pot-au-feu of duck with vegetables, and chocolate fondant are sure to please. Pianist in the evenings. **C** 200-300 F. **M** 98 F (weekday lunch, Sat), 145 F.

Grignan
7, pl. Sévigné
70 32 08 11, fax 70 32 47 07
Closed Oct 15-Nov 15. 121 rms 200-345 F. Rms for disabled. Restaurant. Half-board 275-300 F. Conf. Golf. No pets. Pkg. V, AE.

One of the biggest hotels in Vichy with very well-equipped rooms.

Pavillon Sévigné
50, bd J.-F.-Kennedy
70 32 16 22, fax 70 59 97 37
Closed Jan 15-Feb. Open until 9:15pm (10pm in summer). Priv rm: 100. Garden dining. Valet pkg. V, AE, DC, MC.

Having long abandoned it to spa-goers, Vichyites are now rediscovering the vast baroque dining room of the Pavillon Sévigné. Perhaps the grandiose decor has cowed chef

Bernard Bordaries, however, because his cooking seemed timid this year: a pleasant lisette (tiny mackerel) salad, bland slice of lamb with vegetables, and tart crêpes Suzette. A point less this year. The prices of the wine won't keep your bill down. Very professional welcome and service. **C** 350-450 F. **M** 160 F (wine incl), 220 F, 260 F.

 Pavillon Sévigné

(See restaurant above)
Closed Jan 15-Feb. 4 stes 960-1,390 F. 47 rms 530-1,300 F. Half-board 630-985 F. Air cond. Conf. Golf. Valet pkg. V, AE, DC, MC.
A brilliant facelift has left the Pavillon Sévigné fitter than ever to welcome guests and spa-goers to the Marquise de Sévigné's seventeenth-century dwelling. Rooms have been remarkably well renovated. Lovely lounges and public rooms. Breakfasts are a treat.

 Hôtel du Portugal

121, bd des États-Unis
70 31 90 66, fax 70 31 04 38
Closed Oct 4-Apr 26. 50 rms 350-545 F. Restaurant. Half-board 480-620 F. Conf. Golf. Valet pkg. V, MC.
Pleasant, well kept, and conveniently situated near the Allier River and the spa.

 Régina

4, av. Thermale
70 98 20 95, fax 70 98 60 05
Closed Oct 15-Apr 15. 80 rms 350-600 F. Restaurant. Half-board 400-680 F. Golf. Valet pkg. V, AE.
This charming, old-fashioned hotel has superb modern amenities and a garden.

11/20 Le Temps des Cerises

13, rue Th.-de-Banville - 70 97 72 00
Closed Fri lunch, Thu, mid Jan-mid Feb. Open until 10pm. Terrace dining. Pkg. V, MC.
A winsome little eatery just a stone's throw from the casino. We like the salad of chicken giblets confit and red beans, fillets of red mullet and salmon, and pickerel with Bordelaise sauce paired with tagliatelle. **C** 200-300 F. **M** 110 F.

Thermalia

1, av. Thermale
70 31 04 39, fax 70 31 08 67
Open year-round. 128 rms 420-540 F. Restaurant. Half-board 603-673 F. Air cond. Conf. Heated pool. Golf. Pkg. V, AE, DC, MC.
A modern building in the town center, with spacious, comfortable rooms and direct access to the spa. Bar and restaurant.

La Véranda

3, pl. J.-Aletti
70 31 78 77, fax 70 98 13 82
Closed Jan 1-Mar 3. Open until 10pm. Priv rm: 250. Terrace dining. Air cond. Valet pkg. V, AE.
Majestically situated opposite the casino and lake, this venerable pile now boasts an enormous, luxurious restaurant. The cuisine of Michel Brelière, who came here in January 1994, is carefully prepared but occasionally too complicated; the products are all top-quality. Verdurette of foie gras and gambas, good grilled squab with fresh-tasting, lightly caramelized grated carrots, and a berry croquant. Fairly well stocked cellar, but there's no sommelier. **C** 300-470 F. **M** 160 F, 200 F, 280 F.

Aletti Palace Hotel

(See restaurant above)
Closed Nov-Mar. 7 stes 790-1,100 F. 126 rms 580-850 F. Rms for disabled. Half-board 810-960 F. Air cond. Heated pool. Tennis. Golf. Valet pkg. V, AE.
This imposing turn-of-the-century hotel looms over the casino in fully renovated splendor. Note the grandiose entrance, Belle Époque–style rooms, and elegant bathrooms. Attentive welcome.

■ **In Abrest 03200**   4 km S on D 906

La Colombière

1 km SE on D 906, route de Thiers
70 98 69 15, fax 70 31 50 89
Closed Sun dinner off-seas, Mon, mid Jan-mid Feb, 1 wk in Oct. Open until 9pm. Priv rm: 40. Air cond. Pkg. V, AE, DC, MC.
Sit and look out on the green banks of the Allier from this charming converted dovecote, and enjoy Michel Sabot's proficient cuisine. Choose the fricassée of tiny snails in a peanut cream sauce, fillet of roast lamb with garlic cream, and a pistachio nougat glacé. Very pleasant welcome. **C** 250-320 F. **M** 95 F (exc Sun), 115 F (Sun), 170 F, 200 F, 270 F.

VIDAUBAN   83550
Paris 846 - Cannes 65 - Fréjus 29 - Toulon 64   *Var*

Château Les Lonnes

3 km NW on D 84,
chemin des Moulins-d'Entraigues
94 73 65 76, fax 94 73 14 97
Open year-round. 2 stes 1,800-3,600 F. 12 rms 650-1,650 F. Rms for disabled. Restaurant. Conf. Pool. Tennis. Golf. Valet pkg. Helipad. V, AE, DC, MC.
Set in 22 hectares of woodland, this luxury hotel is admirably appointed. There are leather armchairs and solid wood furniture in the rooms; marble in the bathrooms. Facilities include a library with reading room, sauna, massage room, and beauty salon.

12/20 Le Concorde

9, pl. G.-Clemenceau
94 73 01 19
Closed Nov 20-Dec 5. Open until 9:30pm (11pm in summer). Priv rm: 15. Terrace dining. Pkg. V, MC.
An irresistible perfume of Provence wafts through this inviting little inn, that has won an extra point this year for the generous 130 F menu: stuffed cabbage with fresh-tasting tomato sauce, unctuous daube provençale simmered with calf's foot, and a tasty tarte Tatin. Good choice of regional wines. Charming welcome and competent service in the rustic dining room or on a pleasant terrace. **C** 230-360 F. **M** 130 F, 230 F, 270 F.

VIENNE   38200
Paris 488 - Grenoble 86 - Lyon 31 - St-Etienne 50   *Isère*

La Pyramide

Fernand Point, 14, bd F.-Point
74 53 01 96, fax 74 85 69 73
Closed Thu lunch, Wed, Sep 16-Jun 14. Open until 9:30pm. Priv rm: 30. Garden dining. Air cond. Valet pkg. V, AE, DC, MC.

Patrick Henriroux, unquestionably one of the Rhône valley's best chefs, manages to combine the spirit and flavors of three "countries": Mediterranean south (he has even sought out the rare and luscious Corsian oil from the Saint-Joseph convent), the Rhône-Alpes region where the restaurant is based, and a discreet touch of his native Fougerolles (Kirsch country). What a brilliant feast he prepared for us a few months back! A mountain lad from the Jura, Henriroux is obviously bewitched by the perfumes of Provençal olive oil and aromatic herbs: "rich peasants" soup with bacon and pistou paired with garlic and olive oil croûtons, plump langoustines pan-roasted with sea salt and accompanied by simple spring vegetables in an avocado vinaigrette, pearl-barley risotto with Dombes frog's legs and green asparagus in a celery jus, roast lobster with ground and roasted hazlenuts, and superb cheeses. Desserts were equally stunning: cinnamony pear beignets, and a parfait des moines de la Chartreuse (nougatine cream with walnuts). One also comes to La Pyramide for the opulent cellar and the good-humored, professional service. If he could see how it is thriving, the late Fernand Point would be ever so proud! **C** 500-800 F. **M** 270 F (exc Sun), 400 F, 510 F, 620 F.

 La Pyramide
(See restaurant above)
Closed Feb. 4 stes 1,300 F. 21 rms 750-880 F. Air cond. Conf. Valet pkg. V, AE, DC, MC.
The 22 rooms and 4 suites overlooking the garden provide the perfect place to stop halfway between Paris and the Riviera. The decor is bright and modern, redone this year in Provençal style, although the bathrooms are on the small side. Breakfast, coffee, and the wonderful collection of old Port and liqueurs are served in the pleasant conservatory.

■ **In Chonas-l'Amballan 38121** 9 km S on N 7

Le Marais Saint-Jean
74 58 83 28, fax 74 58 81 96
Closed Thu lunch, Wed, Feb-Mar. Open until 9pm. Priv rm: 15. Garden dining. Pkg. V, AE, DC, MC.
The view over the grounds is as restful as the soft, pale-pink dining room. In the kitchen, Hervé Girardon juggles very good ingredients with mastery and delicacy to produce a langoustine navarin with a shellfish cream sauce, beef fillet en aumônière sauce Périgueux, and a timbale croquante of pears with a berry coulis. Well stocked and diversified cellar; friendly welcome. **C** 300-350 F. **M** 165 F, 225 F, 300 F.

**Hostellerie
Le Marais Saint-Jean**
(See restaurant above)
Closed Feb-Mar. 10 rms 550 F. Half-board 450-850 F. Conf. Pkg. Helipad. V, AE, DC, MC.
Quiet, comfortable, very well kept rooms in a small Provençal-style hotel.

Some establishments change their **closing times** without warning. It is always wise to check in advance.

VIEUX-MAREUIL   **24340**
Paris 500 - Périgueux 45 - Angoulême 45   Dordogne

 Château de Vieux-Mareuil
Mareuil-sur-Belle
53 60 77 15, fax 53 56 49 33
Closed Sun dinner & Mon off-seas, Jan 10-Feb 26. Open until 9:45pm. Priv rm: 30. Garden dining. Valet pkg. V, AE, DC, MC.
Set on a hillside among the wooded valleys of Périgord, this five-century-old château is more like a private residence turned into a hotel-restaurant. Here, Patrick Fremondière skillfully reinterprets a classic repertoire (aumônière of langoustines with sea-urchin coral, truffled veal sweetbreads, Monbazillac crème glacé, and crème brûlée) and an inexpensive set menu which we find most appealing (sea trout marinated with dill, pork fillet mignon with pink peppercorns, cheese, and sherbets). Judiciously composed cellar. Good service. **C** 370-470 F. **M** 130 F, 230 F, 330 F.

Château de Vieux-Mareuil
(See restaurant above)
Closed Nov-beg Apr. 2 stes 1,000-1,800 F. 12 rms 500-1,100 F. Half-board 550-850 F. Air cond. Conf. Heated pool. No pets. Pkg. V, AE, DC, MC.
The rooms of the château and the fifteenth-century tower have been tastefully decorated. They afford views of field and forest, as well as minibars, television, and excellent breakfasts with homemade pastries. The hosts will organize sightseeing excursions for their guests.

VIGERIE (LA) 16   → Angoulême

VILLARD-DE-LANS   **38250**
Paris 590 - Lyon 125 - Valence 70 - Grenoble 35 - Die 68   Isère

Grand Hôtel de Paris
76 95 10 06, fax 76 95 10 02
Closed Apr 18-Jun 5, Sep 18-Dec 18. 9 stes 515-750 F. 54 rms 336-470 F. Restaurant. Half-board 395-442 F. Conf. Tennis. Golf. Pkg. V, AE, DC, MC.
Well equipped for conferences and skiing holidays, the spacious rooms overlook the three hectares of grounds and the mountains beyond.

Le Tétras
Av. du Pr-Nobécourt
76 95 12 51, fax 76 95 00 75
Closed Sun dinner, Mon (exc school hols), Apr 15-May 15, Sep 30-Dec 15. Open until 9pm. Priv rm: 26. Terrace dining. Pkg. V, AE, DC, MC.
André Buisson, trained by Blanc and Lameloise, offers a feuillantine of lamb tongue paired with a salad, roast saddle of rabbit à la forestière, and honey profiteroles with apricot sauce, while the rest of the Buisson family makes sure guests receive a warm welcome in their huge chalet facing the mountains. **C** 260-350 F. **M** 158 F, 185 F, 230 F.

Le Christiania
(See restaurant above)
Closed Apr 15-May 15, Sep 30-Dec 15. 24 rms 380-590 F. Half-board 400-498 F. Conf. Heated pool. Golf. Pkg. V, AE, DC, MC.
Here's an appealing mountain hotel opposite the municipal tennis courts. Almost all the comfortable rooms have a south-facing balcony, but the quality of the soundproofing on the street

side is not as good as it should be. Covered pool; hydrotherapy equipment.

VILLARS-LES-DOMBES   01330
Paris 451 - Villefranche 27 - Lyon 33 - Mâcon 41 - Bourg 28   *Ain*

Jean-Claude Bouvier   ۞
83, route de Lyon - 74 98 11 91 (R),
74 98 08 03 (H), fax 74 98 29 55
*Closed Sun dinner, Mon, Dec 27-31. Open until
9:30pm (10pm in summer). Priv rm: 65. Terrace
dining. Pkg. V, AE, DC, MC.*
Jean-Claude Bouvier likes to clomp around in
clogs—he owns quite a collection— while cooking up hearty country fare: try his frogs' legs and
langoustines in a gratin, saddle of rabbit with
polenta made with milk, and an apple and pear
crique with caramelized milk. Christiane, the
patronne, welcomes guests winsomely to the
rustic dining room and flower-banked terrace,
and helps you make a choice from the fine wine
list. C 280-450 F. M 130 F (weekdays), 140 F,
175 F, 220 F, 295 F.

Ribotel
(See restaurant above)
*Open year-round. 4 stes 460 F. 43 rms 240-280 F.
Rms for disabled. Half-board 280 F. Conf. Golf. Pkg.
V, AE, DC, MC.*
These modern buildings with pretty, well-kept
rooms are just a quick crow's flight from the
ornithological park. Leisure pursuits include
mini-golf, trail biking, horseback riding, and golf
lessons for beginners.

VILLE-BLANCHE (LA) 22   ➜ Lannion

VILLEFORT   48800
Paris 607 - Mende 59 - Le Puy 91 - Aubenas 60 - Alès 55   *Lozère*

Balme
Pl. du Portalet
66 46 80 14, fax 66 46 85 26
*Closed Sun dinner & Mon off-seas, Nov 15-Jan,
Oct 8-14. Open until 9:30pm. Priv rm: 20. Terrace
dining. Hotel: 20 rms 150-300 F. No pets. Pkg. V, AE,
DC, MC.*
The façade has been renovated and, by the
time you read this, the dining room will have
been refurbished, to provide a better background for Michel Gomy's intelligent, flavorful
cuisine that has won a second toque this year.
Sample his fine 175 F menu: delicious and
original foie gras flan with a smoked-chestnut
coulis, fresh and harmonious monkfish seasoned
with five-spice powder (the chef is often inspired
by his frequent visits to the Far East), superb
choice of cheeses, and a delicately subtle tea-
and jasmine-flavored cream for dessert. The cellar has been expanded this year, especially in
Médocs and Burgundies. Adorable welcome by
Micheline Gomy. M 115 F, 175 F, 250 F.

VILLEFRANCHE-DE-ROUERGUE 12200
Paris 620 - Albi 72 - Cahors 61 - Montauban 73   *Aveyron*

Le Relais de Farrou
3 km, route de Figeac
65 45 18 11, fax 65 45 32 59
*Closed Sun dinner & Mon off-seas, Oct 22-Nov 6,
Feb 19-Mar 6. Open until 9:30pm (10pm in summer). Priv rm: 20. Terrace dining. Pkg. V, MC.*

This roadside restaurant may not look promising, but the spruce, spacious dining room frames
a view of a pretty garden where you can partake
of Joël Ricco's good 112 F regional men: pig's
foot ravigote, trout with bits of bacon, a choice
of cheeses, and a chocolate marquise cake with
vanilla sauce. Fine wine list. C 250-350 F.
M 112 F, 153 F, 206 F, 350 F.

Le Relais de Farrou
(See restaurant above)
*Open year-round. 1 ste 490-545 F. 25 rms 270-
420 F. Rms for disabled. Half-board 295-350 F.
Air cond. Pool. Tennis. Garage pkg. Helipad. V,
MC.*
The more pleasant rooms overlook the garden
and swimming pool; others are on the main
road. Among the many services and facilities:
hot tub, Turkish baths, heliport.

12/20 L'Univers
2, pl. de la République
65 45 15 63, fax 65 45 02 21
*Closed Fri dinner & Sat (exc Jul-Sep & hols), Nov 18-
26, Jan 7-22. Open until 9pm. Priv rm: 30. Terrace
dining. Garage pkg. V, AE, DC, MC.*
There's space on the terrace for a few tables
overlooking the Aveyron River in this welcoming, very traditional auberge where the 150 F
menu offers bisque rochelaise, trout with almonds, noisette of lamb en chevreuil, cheeses,
and classic desserts. C 190-360 F. M 75 F, 85 F,
98 F, 150 F, 245 F, 295 F.

L'Univers
(See restaurant above)
*Open year-round. 30 rms 185-350 F. Half-board
290 F. Conf. Pkg. V, AE, DC, MC.*
The owners have brought the decor and
amenities of the small rooms attractively up to
date. Views over the old town and the hills
across the river. Pleasant reception and service;
very nice breakfasts.

VILLEFRANCHE-DU-PÉRIGORD 24550
Paris 570 - Cahors 40 - Périgueux 85 - Sarlat 45   *Dordogne*

10/20 La Clé des Champs
8 km NW on D 660, in Mazeyrolles
53 29 95 94, fax 53 28 42 96
*Closed Dec-Mar (exc reserv). Open until 9pm.
Terrace dining. Hotel: 13 rms 255-315 F. Half-
board 230-280 F. Pool. Tennis. Golf. Pkg. V, AE, DC,
MC.*
The *patronne* is a self-taught cook who serves
plentiful, homey dishes in the rustic, beamed
dining room: ballotin of fresh foie gras, beef fillet
in morel sauce, or red mullet fillets in lemon
butter sauce. C 210-280 F. M 80 F, 135 F,
180 F, 275 F.

VILLEFRANCHE-SUR-MER   06230
Paris 935 - Monte-Carlo 15 - Nice 6 - Cannes 39   *Alpes-Mar.*

Le Saint-Pierre
1, quai de l'Amiral-Courbet
93 76 76 93, fax 93 01 88 81
*Closed Nov 10-Dec 23. Open until 10:30pm (mid-
night in summer). Priv rm: 25. Terrace dining. Air
cond. No pets. V, AE, DC, MC.*
The semi-covered terrace in the heart of the
port is the main attraction in this sunny restaurant, but the seafood-oriented cooking is also
worthy of attention. Try the 220 F menu: fine

crab terrine, too-liquid but tasty fish soup, very good red mullet fillets, dryish although flavorful sea bream fillet with zucchini, and a delicious apple tart. The small wine list offers a good choice of regional wines. Very professional welcome and service. **C** 500 F. **M** 150 F, 220 F, 380 F.

 ### Welcome
(See restaurant above)
Closed Nov 20-Dec 20. 32 rms 490-890 F. Rms for disabled. Restaurant. Half-board 435-635 F. Air cond. Conf. Golf. Pkg. V, AE, DC, MC.
This former convent where writer Jean Cocteau liked to stay, was recently modernized. The rooms are comfortable and air conditioned, with some spectacular ones on the fifth floor overlooking the sea.

VILLEFRANCHE-SUR-SAÔNE   69400
Paris 436 - Lyon 31 - Mâcon 41 - Bourg-en-Bresse 51   *Rhône*

Faisan Doré
Pont de Beauregard
74 65 01 66, fax 74 09 00 81
Closed Sun dinner, Mon. Open until 9:30pm (10pm in summer). Priv rm: 50. Garden dining. Pkg. V, AE, DC, MC.
Typical of the kind of plush *auberge* where the French like to enjoy a relaxed Sunday lunch. The duck terrine with pistachios, veal sweetbreads in Port sauce, farm-raised chicken in vinegar sauce, and crêpes Suzette are expensive, but the regulars remain faithful. Delightful riverside terrace shaded by chestnut trees. **C** 280-360 F. **M** 150 F, 195 F, 240 F, 330 F.

12/20 La Fontaine Bleue
18, rue Jean-Moulin
74 68 10 37, fax 74 68 70 38
Closed Sun (in Aug), Dec 22-Jan 12. Open until 9:30pm. Priv rm: 60. Terrace dining. Air cond. No pets. Pkg. V, AE, DC, MC.
Honest cooking is on hand in this restaurant facing an historic fountain. On the 130 F menu: cassoulet of snails and veal sweetbreads, féra (lake fish) meunière or a fricassée of rabbit and pleurote mushrooms. Fine choice of Beaujolais. **C** 220-320 F. **M** 98 F (weekdays), 130 F, 175 F, 220 F.

Plaisance
96, av. de la Libération
74 65 33 52, fax 74 62 02 89
Closings not available. 68 rms 300-400 F. Air cond. Conf. Golf. Garage pkg. V, AE, DC, MC.
A pleasant address in the center of town facing a tree-shaded square with a fountain. Well equipped rooms; bar.

■ **In Anse 69480**   6 km S on N 6

12/20 Hôtel Saint-Romain
Route de Graves
74 60 24 46, fax 74 67 12 85
Closed Sun dinner, Nov 28-Dec 4. Open until 9:30pm. Priv rm: 10. Garden dining. Pkg. V, AE, DC, MC.
This quiet, traditional hotel-restaurant is set down in a sizeable garden. The creditable *carte* features the likes of duck carpaccio, breast of guinea fowl in lobster butter, escargot de daurade, and veal sweetbreads in Noilly-Prat

sauce. Fine cellar of Beaujolais. **C** 220-330 F. **M** 99 F (exc Sun lunch), 139 F, 179 F, 250 F, 300 F.

VILLEMAGNE   11310
Paris 740 - Carcassonne 40 - Castelnaudary 16 - Saissac 6   *Aude*

 ### Castel de Villemagne
68 94 22 95
Closed Nov 1-Mar 15. 7 rms 255-430 F. Restaurant. Half-board 293-355 F. Pkg. V.
Four hundred meters up, this delightful fifteenth-century manor restored in the eighteenth century has quiet rooms with fine country antiques.

VILLEMUR-SUR-TARN   31340
Paris 671 - Albi 62 - Toulouse 33 - Montauban 26   *H.-Garonne*

La Ferme de Bernadou
Av. du Gal-Leclerc
61 09 02 38, fax 61 35 94 87
Closed Sun dinner, Mon, Jan 1-15, Feb school hols. Open until 9:30pm. Priv rm: 40. Garden dining. Pkg. V, AE.
Discreetly set back from the road, this engaging farm-restaurant stands swaddled in a verdant garden and has a pretty terrace. Jean-Claude Voisin takes infinite pains with his flavorful dishes based on the finest local products: gratin of tiny snails and hazelnuts, a pig's ear stuffed with veal sweetbreads in Voile wine sauce, and a millefeuille stuffed with roasted apricots and paired with a vanilla and almond milk ice cream. Very complete and ably presented wine list. Élisabeth Voisin is an exquisite hostess, and the service is high class. **C** 300-450 F. **M** 130 F, 165 F, 230 F, 320 F.

VILLENEUVE-DE-MARSAN   40190
Paris 690 - Mont-de-Marsan 17 - Aire-sur-l'Adour 21   *Landes*

 ### Francis Darroze
Grand-Rue
58 45 20 07, fax 58 45 82 67
Closed Jan 1-23. Open until 9:30pm. Priv rm: 30. Garden dining. Garage pkg. V, AE, DC, MC.
The comfortable dining room of this famous restaurant where chef Francis Darroze once held sway looks out over a garden planted with pines and lime trees, and its decor is elegant (staw-colored walls, white drapes, Flemish paintings), but the welcome is stiff, and, worst of all, the kitchen seems to be sleeping on its laurels: the feuilleté of Landes asparagus was a success, it's true, with flaky pastry and perfectly cooked asparagus, but the roast squab lacked flavor and the "tiny" peas that came with it were big and hard. The blancmange was tasty and well presented. But the kitchen and welcome need to be attended to if the 16 rating is to stay much longer; it looks pretty wobbly. Good game in season, and a fantastic cellar. **C** 310-440 F. **M** 180 F, 290 F, 380 F.

 ### Francis Darroze
(See restaurant above)
Closed Jan 1-23. 3 stes 950 F. 16 rms 450-750 F. Half-board 650-750 F. Conf. Pool. Golf. Garage pkg. Helipad. V, AE, DC, MC.
A very pleasant hotel with a well-tended garden, swimming pool, and bright, modern rooms furnished with antiques. Relais et Châteaux.

L'Europe
Pl. de la Boiterie
58 45 20 08, fax 58 45 34 14
Open daily until 9:30pm (10pm in summer). Priv rm: 200. Terrace dining. Valet pkg. V, AE, DC, MC.
Franck Augé's strong suit is creative country cooking, and his original, flavorful dishes won him an extra toque this year: zucchini blossoms stuffed with sautéed foie gras (an unexpected but very savory combination), scorpion fish fillets with saffrony potatoes and a delicious langoustine sauce, and an excellent dark-and-white-chocolate parfait flavored with mint. Sunny welcome and service, and a well stocked cellar that now holds many half bottles. C 280-380 F. M 130 F, 210 F, 300 F.

L'Europe
(See restaurant above)
Open year-round. 2 stes 450 F. 13 rms 260-360 F. Half-board 310-550 F. Conf. Pool. Golf. Valet pkg. V, AE, DC, MC.
Cozy, well-kept rooms on a pleasant square. Pretty little swimming pool.

VILLENEUVE-LÈS-AVIGNON 30 → Avignon		
VILLENEUVE-SUR-LOT		**47300**
Paris 614 - Bergerac 60 - Agen 29 - Cahors 76		Lot/Garonne

12/20 Aux Berges du Lot
3, rue de l'Hôtel-de-Ville
53 70 84 41, fax 53 70 43 15
Closed Sun dinner & Mon off-seas, 2 wks in Nov. Open until 9:30pm. Priv rm: 30. Terrace dining. V, AE.
On balmy days we walk right past the rather chill dining room and ask instead for a table on the wisteria-shaded terrace. Along with a beguiling view of the River Lot, we enjoy the chef's fresh and harmonious raw salmon with cucumbers and the pleasant prunes and fresh fruit dessert, but we were disappointed this year by the bland brochettes of monkfish and salmon with sabayon. Friendly and professional welcome and service. C 180-300 F. M 69 F (weekday lunch), 98 F, 125 F, 160 F, 195 F.

12/20 Hostellerie du Rooy
Chemin de Labourdette
53 70 48 48, fax 53 49 17 84
Closed Sun dinner, Mon, 1st wk of Jan & Jul. Open until 9:30pm. Garden dining. Pkg. V, AE, DC.
A sun-dappled terrace under an arbor is a charming spot in which to savor a salad of raw marinated salmon, a little ragoût of sea scallops in whisky sauce, tournedos Rossini, quail roasted with prune chutney, and cabécou (a goat cheese) roasted with acacia honey. Heartwarming welcome. C 230-350 F.

Hôtel des Remparts
1, rue E.-Marcel - 53 70 71 63
Open year-round. 9 rms 100-155 F. Golf. Pkg. V.
A good-value hotel with unpretentious rooms; there's an additional charge for the garage. Good breakfasts.

> *Red toques signify creative cuisine; white toques signify traditional cuisine.*

■ **In Pujols 47300** 4 km SW on D 118 and CC 207

La Toque Blanche
53 49 00 30, fax 53 70 49 79
Closed Mon (lunch in Aug), Sun dinner (exc hols), Feb school hols, Jun 26-Jul 10. Open until 9:45pm. Priv rm: 25. Garden dining. Air cond. Pkg. V, AE, DC, MC.
Bernard Lebrun has a splendid showcase in this low-slung dwelling blessed with a glorious view. His superb cuisine is going great guns, with pleasure exploding on the palate at the first mouthful. He has just created with eight other chefs in the region a "Saveurs et Traditions" association to promote local products, and was initiating a new "savors and traditions" menu just as we were going to press that should be well worth your attention. On our last visit we savored the chef's foie gras with green asparagus and apples, monkfish braised in Buzet wine lees, and veal sweetbreads in truffle sauce. In season, morels and game dishes make an appearance. The desserts are as good as they look; that is to say, delicious. The impressive cellar is awash in fine Bordeaux and regional wines, ably presented by a competent sommelier. Service is attentive and professional. Books and games are kept on hand for children, a nice touch. C 330-520 F. M 145 F (weekdays), 195 F, 285 F, 320 F, 450 F.

■ **In Saint-Sylvestre-sur-Lot 47140** 8 km E on D 911

Château Lalande
53 36 15 15, fax 53 36 15 16
Open daily until 10pm. Priv rm: 50. Air cond. No pets. Valet pkg. V, AE, DC, MC.
Beaudelaire's "luxe, calme, et volupté" are combined in the elegant dining room with widely spaced tables overlooking the gardens. But the real interest is on your plate, as Jean-Luc Rabanel offers inventive, carefully prepared dishes that have quickly won him two toques. One first course was overly sophisticated (tiny ravioli stuffed with a confit of baby vegetables and foie gras, in an herb and truffle bouillon, with Parmesan "tuiles"). But the sea bass with shallot shoots marvelously paired with chopped green olives and baby fava beans with basil was a lesson in freshness and precision. And the warm tart with a passion-fruit infusion was a joy. The cellar needs fleshing out. Exemplary welcome; perfect service. C 320-450 F. M 200 F (lunch exc Sun, wine incl), 190 F, 250 F, 320 F.

Château Lalande
(See restaurant above)
Open year-round. 4 stes 1,300-1,600 F. 18 rms 850-1,200 F. Rms for disabled. Half-board 690-1,865 F. Conf. Heated pool. Tennis. Golf. No pets. Valet pkg. Helipad. V, AE, DC, MC.
Parts of this magnificent château date back to medieval times, other portions were built in the eighteenth century. The entire structure has been thoroughly renovated, soundproofed, and handsomely decorated. The rooms offer every comfort. Extensive grounds, with extraordinary "waterfall" pools. Excellent welcome.

VILLERÉAL 47210

Paris 590 - Bergerac 35 - Agen 59 - Marmande 57   *Lot/Garonne*

Le Lac
Route de Bergerac - 53 36 01 39
Closed Sep-May. 1 ste 420 F. 24 rms 220-240 F. Rms for disabled. Restaurant. Half-board 230 F. Conf. Pool. Golf. Garage pkg. V, MC.
For fishermen and bathers staying at this unpretentious hotel with a pretty garden and honest cooking, the lake is 300 meters away through the trees.

VILLERS-BOCAGE 14310

Paris 266 - Caen 26 - Vire 34 - Bayeux 25 - St-Lô 35   *Calvados*

Le Relais Normand
9 km NE on N 175, 14210 Noyers-Bocage
31 77 97 37, fax 31 77 94 41
Closed Wed, Nov 15-30, Jan 24-Feb 12. 8 rms 160-250 F. Restaurant. Half-board 270-300 F. Conf. Pkg. V, MC.
Well-modernized, comfortable, quiet rooms for an overnight stop on the way to Mont-Saint-Michel.

12/20 Les Trois Rois
2, pl. Jeanne-d'Arc
31 77 00 32, fax 31 77 93 25
Closed Sun dinner & Mon (exc hols), Jan, last wk of Jun. Open until 9:15pm. Priv rm: 25. Pkg. V, AE, DC, MC.
The chef keeps customers of this pleasant inn happy with his inventive, full-flavored repertoire. We're partial to the suckling pig cooked three different ways, tripes à la mode de Caen, fresh-fruit ravioli, and hot soufflés. The somber dining room is considerably brightened by the smiles of the staff. C 250-380 F. M 125 F, 180 F, 300 F.

Les Trois Rois
(See review above)
Closed Jan. 14 rms 220-380 F. Pkg. V, AE, DC, MC.
The simple, comfortable, and well-soundproofed rooms have pretty little bathrooms. Manned parking lot. Attentive service.

VILLERS-COTTERÊTS 02600

Paris 75 - Soissons 23 - Château-Thierry 48 - Compiègne 29   *Aisne*

12/20 Le Commerce
17, rue du Gal-Mangin
23 96 19 97, fax 23 96 43 72
Closed Sun dinner, Mon, Jan 20-Feb 13, Aug 14-28. Open until 9pm. Garden dining. Pkg. V, MC.
Though the dining room is comfortable enough, we much prefer to sit on the broad, leafy terrace, and enjoy the chef's 130 F set menu: calf's head ravigote, duck fillet in Banyuls sauce, cheeses, andd a tart of seasonal fruits. The selection of Bordeaux is quite impressive. C 200-290 F. M 80 F, 130 F.

Le Régent
26, rue du Gal-Mangin
23 96 01 46, fax 23 96 37 57
Open year-round. 1 ste 580-630 F. 17 rms 155-385 F. Restaurant. Conf. Pkg. V, AE, DC, MC.
Perfectly equipped period-style rooms grace this well-kept hotel in a magnificent Renaissance post house. Laundry service and bicycle rentals.

VILLERS-LE-LAC 25130

Paris 459 - Besançon 72 - Salin-les-Bains 79 - Morteau 6   *Doubs*

Hôtel de France ❊
8, pl. M.-Cupillard
81 68 00 06, fax 81 68 09 22
Closed Sun dinner, Mon, Dec 20-Feb 1. Open until 9pm. Priv rm: 60. Hotel: 14 rms 270-330 F. Half-board 290-300 F. Conf. Pkg. V, AE, DC, MC.
The quiet harmony of this family hotel is based on cooperation: Madame Droz welcomes patrons with inimitable warmth, while Hugues Droz, her son, prepares an honest, heartwarming regional menu, and Monsieur Droz looks after the cellar. Uncork a fine bottle of Jura wine to accompany the tiny snails in an absinthe-flavored infusion, trout with fennel and maniguette, pork cheeks with fava beans and Szechuan peppercorns. He needs to work on lightening up his reduced sauces, but the extra point this year is well deserved. Ask to see the little watch museum upstairs. C 350-450 F. M 155 F (exc hols), 190 F, 235 F, 265 F, 450 F.

VILLEURBANNE 69 → Lyon

VINAY 51 → Épernay

VINON-SUR-VERDON 83560

Paris 777 - Aix-en-Provence 43 - Manosque 16   *Var*

12/20 Olivier
Route de Manosque
92 78 86 99, fax 92 78 89 65
Closed Dec-Feb. Open until 11pm. Priv rm: 30. Garden dining. Air cond. Hotel: 5 stes 550-700 F. 20 rms 340-420 F. Half-board 395 F. Conf. Pool. Tennis. Golf. Pkg. V, AE, DC, MC.
In the sunny dining room or on the terrace by the pool, you can enjoy cooking that is fresh and well balanced: smoked salmon, veal kidney roasted in its fat, seafood platter, and a strawberry gratin. C 220-330 F. M 98 F, 138 F, 178 F.

VIOLÈS 84150

Paris 670 - Avignon 31 - Orange 13 - Carpentras 17   *Vaucluse*

Le Mas de Bouvau
Route de Cairanne
90 70 94 08, fax 90 70 95 99
Closed Sun dinner, Mon, Feb school hols, Aug 22-Sep 7, Dec 20-30. Open until 8:45pm. Priv rm: 15. Garden dining. Pkg. V.
A family atmosphere, fine food, and good local wines are the strong points of this country restaurant, which this year boasts a new dining room with Provençal decor. Come here to savor the fresh and generous cooking: potée of snails and mushrooms, duck breast with honey and mustard sauce, and an orange-flavored chocolate mousse. C 200-300 F. M 130 F (exc Sun), 190 F, 260 F.

Plan to travel? *Look for Gault Millau's other Best of guides to Chicago, Florida, Hawaii, Hong Kong, Germany, Italy, London, Los Angeles, New England, New Orleans, New York, Paris, San Francisco, Thailand, Toronto, and Washington, D.C.*

VIRE 14500
Paris 272 - Caen 59 - Fougères 67 - St-Lô 39   *Calvados*

Hôtel de France
4, rue d'Aignaux
31 68 00 35, fax 31 68 22 65
Closed Dec 18-Jan 10. 20 rms 170-320 F. Rms for disabled. Restaurant. Half-board 250-300 F. Air cond. Conf. Golf. Pkg. V, AE, MC.
Centrally situated by a busy crossroads, this hotel nonetheless has quiet rooms.

12/20 Manoir de la Pommeraie
2 km SE (from Paris road), in Roullours
31 68 07 71, fax 31 67 54 21
Closed Sun dinner, Mon, Feb 13-27. Open until 9:30pm. Priv rm: 60. Garden dining. Pkg. V, AE, DC.
This lovely manor set in wooded grounds has a flower-filled dining room where you can enjoy fairly elaborate, traditional dishes like warm langoustine salad, local andouillette sausage en chartreuse, brill with ratatouille, and veal sweetbreads in cider vinegar. **C** 280-370 F. **M** 115 F (weekday lunch), 140 F, 168 F, 235 F, 300 F.

VIVÈS 66400
Paris 939 - Amélie-les-Bains 15 - Céret 8   *Pyrénées-O.*

11/20 Hostalet de Vivès   ✪
Rue de la Mairie - 68 83 05 52
Closed Tue & Wed off-seas, Jan 15-Mar 5. Open until 9pm. Air cond. Pkg. V, MC.
A typically Catalan establishment, from the furniture to the serving staff, wines, and food. Order the robust local ham and charcuterie, fresh Collioure anchovies, grilled meats, and cargolade (grilled snails served with a garlic sauce), and flambéed walnuts, all washed down with tasty local vintages. **C** 155-240 F. **M** 85 F (lunch exc Sun).

VIVEY 52160
Paris 328 - Langres 31 - Auberive 8 - Dijon 57   *Haute-Marne*

12/20 Relais du Lys
25 84 81 01, fax 25 84 22 39
Closed Jan 5-31. Priv rm: 45. Garden dining. No pets. Pkg. V, AE, MC.
A new dining room has helped to enlarge this pretty little Baroque château, where foreign tourists flock to savor homemade soup under a golden pastry lid, turnovers filled with smoked salmon and langoustines, and stuffed rabbit à la rouergaise. Note, however, that portions are a bit stingy and prices are high. **C** 500 F. **M** 150 F (weekday lunch), 200 F, 280 F.

Relais du Lys   🌲
(See restaurant above)
Closed Nov 5-Dec 24, Jan 2-Feb 15. 2 stes 665-820 F. 6 rms 480-580 F. Half-board 500-550 F. Air cond. Conf. Garage pkg. Helipad. V, AE, MC.
Wonderfully quiet, in an isolated setting. The huge, comfortable rooms are furnished in old-fashioned style and overlook the verdant countryside. Horseback riding nearby.

A red hotel ranking denotes a place with charm.

VOIRON 38500
Paris 520 - Bourg 108 - Grenoble 27 - Valence 80   *Isère*

Philippe Serratrice
50 m from the railway station,
3, av. des Frères-Tardy
76 05 29 88, fax 76 05 45 62
Closed Sun dinner, Mon, Jun 20-Sep 10. Open until 9:30pm. Priv rm: 30. Pkg. V, AE, DC, MC.
You might need a compass to find Philippe Serratrice's ship-shape seafood establishment—just remember that it is 50 meters from the railway station. Serratrice is a sailor who takes off every summer on his catamaran, to return from the sea refreshed and brimming with bright ideas. The à la carte offerings are expensive (such as the raw seafood platter), but the set menus give you a bit of sea breeze without breaking the bank: pink Glénans clams à la provençale, scorpion fish tian, and Boulogne sole, for example. **C** 250-600 F. **M** 100 F, 150 F (lunch exc Sun, wine incl), 140 F, 195 F, 280 F.

■ **In Saint-Jean-de-Moirans 38430**   5 km S

Le Beauséjour
Route de Grenoble
76 35 30 38, fax 76 35 59 80
Closed Jan 2-16, Aug 16-30. Open until 9:15pm. Priv rm: 30. Terrace dining. Pkg. V, AE, DC.
Though we'd like his cooking even better if the flavors were more assertive, Jacques Meunier-Carus displays plenty of solid know-how (although the prices have gotten out of hand). Ragoût d'empereur flavored with saffron and paired with snow peas, kid with creamed morels, and a cappuccino of lobster and pike quenelles spiked with paprika. **C** 300-400 F. **M** 150 F (wine incl), 205 F, 350 F, 495 F.

VONNAS 01540
Paris 419 - Mâcon 19 - Lyon 66 - Villefranche 39   *Ain*

Georges Blanc
74 50 00 10, fax 74 50 08 80
Closed Thu (exc dinner in summer), Wed (exc hols), Jan 2-Feb 10. Open until 9:30pm. Priv rm: 60. Air cond. Valet pkg. V, AE, DC, MC.
How did Georges Blanc celebrate the 120th anniversary of his family inn? With a special menu, perhaps, or a festive reception? No, he merely restructured his hotel, created new suites, redecorated the restaurant's dining rooms, and completed renovations on the nearby Château d'Epeyssoles! Oh yes, and he revised his menu as well, adding a dozen new dishes to the house repertoire! Blanc devises his recipes with infinite care, yet no food on earth seems more fresh and spontaneous. The vivid flavors, the couplings of concentrated savors and brilliant colors that distinguish his cuisine indicate a rare temperament, and a truly authentic personal style.
Welcomed by Jacqueline Blanc into the bright, serene dining rooms that overlook the river, we succumbed to Georges Blanc's most recent inventions this year, seduced as ever by the savory juxtaposition of Bressane traditions, Mediterranean touches, and a bit of exoticism. You

begin with luscious appetizers that you sample as Marcel Périnet or one of the sommeliers pours a little something (perhaps a Mâcon) in your glass. Then you move on to succulent parmentier de sot-l'y-laisse (poultry "oysters") and pig's foot cooked for a long time at a very low temperature that we could have even enjoyed as a main course if we hadn't had a look at the other temptations on the menu: lobster with endives and basil (an extraordinary union of flavors), a blanquette of frogs' legs that seemed to have been reinvented by the exquisite spices and garlic powder that flavored it, Bresse chicken prepared like a hare à la royale sausage, followed by cheeses and admirable desserts (from the vanilla, coffee, and chocolate biscuit with hazelnut sauce, to the nage of citrus fruits and banana with honey and the plate of little danties to be gobbled up with the coffee). On another visit, we reveled in the pomme d'amour and delicious gnocchi seasoned with summer savory, and a tourte of veal sweetbreads in Noilly-Prat vermouth sauce. The superlative cellar is overseen by Marcel Périnet, who will guide you to such rare finds as a Montrachet from the Comtes Lafon, or the Musigny Vieilles Vignes of the Comte de Vogüé. Anyone who can manage to be unhappy in Vonnas with all the sensual pleasures it provides, is, we're sad to say, a desperate case! C 650-950 F. M 780 F (all-truffle), 450 F, 580 F, 680 F.

Georges Blanc
(See restaurant above)
Closed Jan 2-Feb 10. 6 stes 1,750-3,000 F. 32 rms 850-1,800 F. Air cond. Conf. Heated pool. Tennis. Golf. Valet pkg. Helipad. V, AE, DC, MC.
On the banks of the romantic River Veyle, the supremely comfortable Mère Blanc now has 32 rooms and 6 suites, all made even more lovely this year. The breakfasts are exquisite, there's a helipad in the grounds, and within ten kilometers you'll find three eighteen-hole golf courses. A covered bridge across the road provides access to La Cour aux Fleurs, built in traditional Bressane style. A boutique offers wines and Georges Blanc charcuterie, and there's even a pasty shop and gift shop. Relais et Châteaux.

Résidence des Saules
74 50 00 10, fax 74 50 08 80
Closed Jan 2-Feb 10. 4 stes 700 F. 6 rms 500 F. Restaurant. Conf. Heated pool. Tennis. Golf. Valet pkg. Helipad. V, AE, DC, MC.
Georges Blanc recently opened this extremely comfortable, moderately priced three-star hotel on the village square, just upstairs from his gourmet food and wine shop.

VOREPPE 38	→ Grenoble

VOUILLÉ	86190
Paris 343 - Parthenay 32 - Poitiers 19 - Thouars 52	Vienne

12/20 Château de Périgny
49 51 80 43, fax 49 51 90 09
Closed Dec 26-Jan 31. Open until 10pm. Priv rm: 100. Garden dining. Pkg. V, AE, DC, MC.
Périgny has the potential to become a truly fine address: superb grounds, an elegant medieval castle, and vast outbuildings which house the

tastefully decorated restaurant. At our last meal here, we enjoyed the langoustine ravioli with pleurote mushrooms, warm oxtail salad, fillet of brill with hazlenuts, and veal sweetbreads with pink peppercorns and vanilla. For dessert, try the pear croustillant with sherbet. The cellar holds some good Bordeaux, and there's a magnificent terrace in an enclosed courtyard. C 280-330 F. M 140 F, 165 F, 230 F, 320 F.

Château de Périgny
(See restaurant above)
Closed Dec 26-Jan 31. 3 stes 975-1,200 F. 39 rms 450-975 F. Conf. Pool. Tennis. Golf. Pkg. Helipad. V, AE, DC, MC.
Set in a vast swathe of open green countryside, the eponymous Renaissance château is not used as a hotel. Rather, the comfortable guest rooms decorated in mock-medieval style are housed in the (even older) outbuildings. Excellent sporting facilities, stables, and helipad, as well as accommodation for pets.

VOULTE-SUR-RHÔNE (LA)	07800
Paris 590 - Valence 19 - Privas 20 - Crest 33	Ardèche

Le Musée
Pl. 4-Septembre
75 62 40 19, fax 75 85 35 79
Closed Sat off-seas, Feb. 15 rms 130-300 F. Restaurant. Half-board 260-300 F. Pkg. V, MC.
Good small hotel with simple, pretty rooms and an attractive terrace for relaxing.

VOUVRAY	37210
Paris 233 - Blois 49 - Tours 10 - Amboise 16	Indre/Loire

10/20 La Cave Martin
66, la Vallée Coquette
47 52 62 18, fax 47 52 79 34
Closed Sun dinner, Mon, 3 wks in Dec, 1 wk in Nov. Open until 9:30pm. Terrace dining. Pkg. V, AE.
A picturesque restaurant carved into the rock. In the rustic dining room or on the tiny terrace you can nibble on duck fillet with berries, saddle of lamb with garlic cream, and a fromage blanc bavarian cream with raspberries. Good little cellar; friendly welcome. C 150-200 F. M 60 F (lunch exc Sun, wine incl), 95 F, 130 F.

VOVES	28150
Paris 97 - Ablis 34 - Chartres 24 - Orléans 58	Eure-et-Loir

Le Quai Fleuri
15, rue Texier-Gallas
37 99 15 15, fax 37 99 11 20
Closed Fri off-seas, Sun, Dec 20-Jan 6. 17 rms 245-390 F. Restaurant. Half-board 270 F. Conf. Pkg. V, AE, MC.
Cheery, well-equipped bungalows set deep in wooded grounds. Amenities include games room, gym, and rides in a horse-drawn carriage.

WANGENBOURG	67710
Paris 465 - Strasbourg 41 - Saverne 20 - Molsheim 29	Bas-Rhin

Parc Hôtel
88 87 31 72, fax 88 87 38 00
Closed Jan 3-Mar 22, Nov 3-Dec 22. 34 rms 246-390 F. Restaurant. Half-board 310-359 F. Conf. Heated pool. Tennis. Valet pkg. V, MC.
Fine, spacious rooms, and some studios with kitchenettes. Various leisure activities are or-

ganized; there is, for example, a giant outdoor chessboard.

WANTZENAU (LA) 67 → Strasbourg

WIMILLE 62 → Boulogne-sur-Mer

WISSEMBOURG 67160
Paris 510 - Strasbourg 54 - Haguenau 32 *B.-Rhin*

A l'Ange
2, rue de la République - 88 94 12 11
*Closed Tue dinner, Wed, Feb 22-Mar 10, Aug 1-5.
Open until 9pm. Terrace dining. Pkg. V, AE, MC.*
German gourmets often cross the border to visit this lovely half-timbered establishment. Pierre Ludwig's crowd-pleasing bill of fare fills both of his dining rooms, one a rustic winstub and the other more elegant. He gives regional recipes an innovative dash of elegance and creativity (hence the red toque). Try his oxtail presskopf with foie gras, a happy marriage of a noble product with an humble one; matelote of fresh-water fish paired with tasty fromage blanc quenelles; and excellent dampfneudel (fritter) of cheese and poppy seeds, a recipe from out of the past. Modest little cellar. C 310-390 F. **M** 200 F (weekday lunch, wine incl), 165 F (weekday lunch), 310 F (dinner), 230 F.

WŒLFLING-LÈS-SARREGUEMINES 57
→ **Sarreguemines**

YVETOT 76190
Paris 175 - Fécamp 34 - Le Havre 51 - Rouen 36 *Seine-Mar.*

12/20 Auberge du Val-au-Cesne
4 km SE on D 5, Val-au-Cesne
35 56 63 06, fax 35 56 92 78
Open daily until 9pm. Priv rm: 30. Terrace dining. Pkg. V, MC.
One half expects to run into Guy de Maupassant in this nostalgic manor with its many intimate rooms. In keeping with the old-fashioned ambience, the menu harks back to cream-rich Norman specialties: calf's head and "fraise" ravigote, sole stuffed with langoustine mousse, turkey fillet, roast young squab, and a meringue glacée with sweetened whipped cream. Modest cellar. Courteous welcome and valiant service. C 260-350 F. **M** 150 F.

Auberge du Val-au-Cesne ♣♥
(See restaurant above)
Open year-round. 5 rms 350 F. Half-board 350-550 F. Conf. Golf. Pkg. V, MC.
Set in a charming valley, a Norman cottage with outbuildings that house a few prettily decorated rooms.

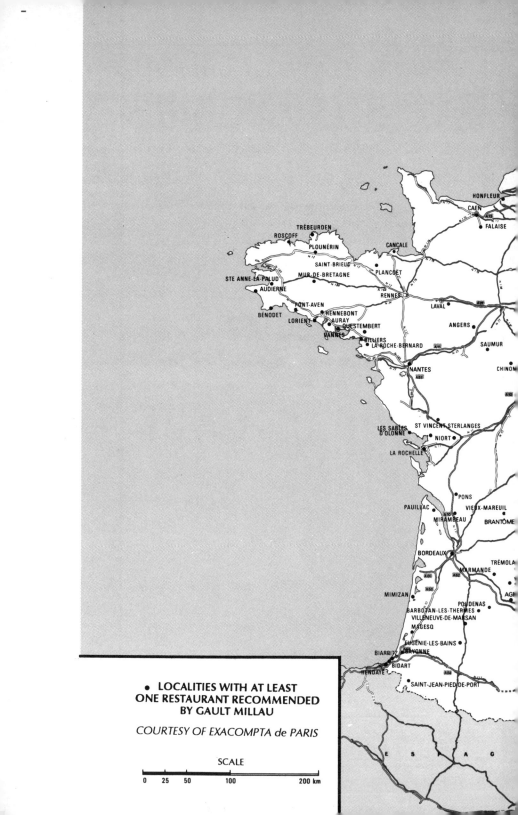

HONFLEUR
CAEN
FALAISE

TRÉBEURDEN
ROSCOFF
CANCALE
PLOUNÉRIN
SAINT-BRIEUC
STE ANNE-LA-PALUD   MUR-DE-BRETAGNE   PLANCOËT
AUDIERNE
RENNES
PONT-AVEN   LAVAL
BÉNODET   HENNEBONT
LORIENT   AURAY
QUESTEMBERT   ANGERS
VANNES
BILLIERS   SAUMUR
LA ROCHE-BERNARD

NANTES   CHINON

LES SABLES   ST VINCENT-STERLANGES
D'OLONNE   NIORT
LA ROCHELLE

PONS
PAUILLAC   VIEUX-MAREUIL
MIRAMBEAU   BRANTÔME

BORDEAUX
TRÉMOLA
MARMANDE
MIMIZAN   AGI
POUDENAS
BARBOTAN-LES-THERMES
VILLENEUVE-DE-MARSAN
MAGESQ
EUGÉNIE-LES-BAINS
BIARRITZ   BAYONNE
BIDART
HENDAYE   SAINT-JEAN-PIED-DE-PORT

E   S   A   G

- **LOCALITIES WITH AT LEAST
ONE RESTAURANT RECOMMENDED
BY GAULT MILLAU**

COURTESY OF EXACOMPTA de PARIS

SCALE

0   25   50   100   200 km

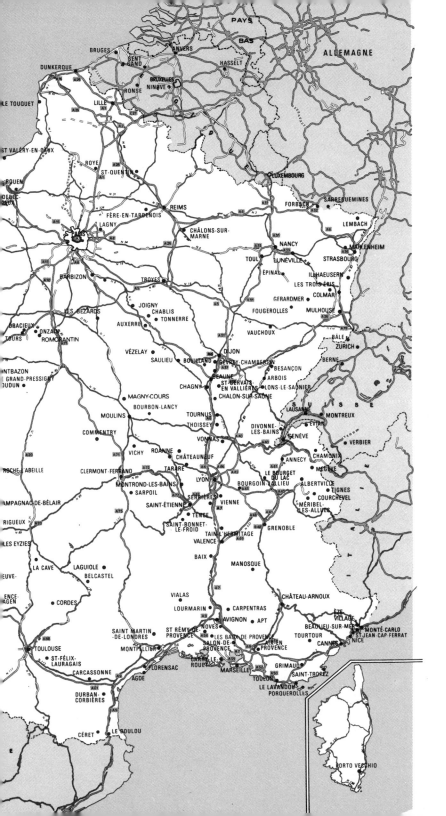

CITIES INDEX
CLASSIFIED BY DEPARTEMENTS

R : restaurants with or without toques - H : hotels